Fundamentals of Operations Management

McGraw-Hill/Irwin Series
Operations and Decision Sciences

OPERATIONS MANAGEMENT

Bowersox, Closs, and Cooper
Supply Chain Logistics Management
First Edition

Chase, Aquilano, and Jacobs
Operations Management for Competitive Advantage
Ninth Edition

Cohen and Apte
Manufacturing Automation
First Edition

Davis, Aquilano, and Chase
Fundamentals of Operations Management
Fourth Edition

Dobler and Burt
Purchasing and Supply Management
Sixth Edition

Fitzsimmons and Fitzsimmons
Service Management
Third Edition

Flaherty
Global Operations Management
First Edition

Gray and Larson
Project Management
First Edition

Harrison and Samson
Technology Management
First Edition

Hill
Manufacturing Strategy: Text & Cases
Third Edition

Hopp and Spearman
Factory Physics
Second Edition

Knod and Schonberger
Operations Management: Customer-Focused Principles
Seventh Edition

Lambert and Stock
Strategic Logistics Management
Third Edition

Leenders and Fearon
Purchasing and Supply Chain Management
Twelfth Edition

Melnyk and Swink
Value-Driven Operations Management
First Edition

Moses, Seshadri, and Yakir
HOM Operations Management Software
First Edition

Nahmias
Production and Operations Analysis
Fourth Edition

Nicholas
Competitive Manufacturing Management
First Edition

Olson
Introduction to Information Systems Project Management
First Edition

Pinedo and Chao
Operations Scheduling
First Edition

Sanderson and Uzumeri
Managing Product Families
First Edition

Schroeder
Operations Management: Meeting Customers' Demands
First Edition

Simchi and Levi
Designing and Managing the Supply Chain
First Edition

Stevenson
Operations Management
Seventh Edition

Vollmann, Berry, and Whybark
Manufacturing Planning & Control Systems
Fourth Edition

Zipkin
Foundations of Inventory Management
First Edition

QUANTITATIVE METHODS AND MANAGEMENT SCIENCE

Bodily, Carraway, Frey, and Pfeifer
Quantitative Business Analysis
First Edition

Bonini, Hausman, and Bierman
Quantitative Analysis for Business Decisions
Ninth Edition

Hillier, Hillier, and Lieberman
Introduction to Management Science
First Edition

Sterman
Business Dynamics
First Edition

Fundamentals of Operations Management

Fourth Edition

Mark M. Davis
Bentley College

Nicholas J. Aquilano
The University of Arizona

Richard B. Chase
University of Southern California

Boston Burr Ridge, IL Dubuque, IA Madison, WI New York San Francisco St. Louis
Bangkok Bogotá Caracas Kuala Lumpur Lisbon London Madrid Mexico City
Milan Montreal New Delhi Santiago Seoul Singapore Sydney Taipei Toronto

McGraw-Hill Higher Education

A Division of The ***McGraw-Hill*** *Companies*

Fundamentals of Operations Management

Published by McGraw-Hill/Irwin, a business unit of The McGraw-Hill Companies, Inc., 1221 Avenue of the Americas, New York, NY, 10020.

This book is printed on acid-free paper.

Domestic 3 4 5 6 7 8 9 0 DOW/DOW 0 9 8 7 6 5 4

International 3 4 5 6 7 8 9 0 DOW/DOW 0 9 8 7 6 5 4

ISBN 0-07-240285-7

Publisher: *Brent Gordon*
Executive editor: *Scott Isenberg*
Senior developmental editor: *Wanda J. Zeman*
Senior marketing manager: *Zina Craft*
Senior project manager: *Christine A. Vaughan*
Production supervisor: *Gina Hangos*
Senior designer: *Pam Verros*
Producer, media technology: *Todd Labak*
Lead supplement producer: *Becky Szura*
Senior digital content specialist: *Brian Nacik*
Photo research coordinator: *Jeremy Cheshareck*
Photo researcher: *Amy Bethea*
Cover design: *JoAnne Schopler*
Interior design: *Pam Verros*
Cover image: ©*Digital Vision*
Typeface: *10/12 Times Roman*
Compositor: *Interactive Composition Corporation*
Printer: *R. R. Donnelley & Sons Company*

Library of Congress Cataloging-in-Publication Data

Davis, Mark M., 1944-
Fundamentals of operations management/Mark M. Davis, Nicholas J. Aquilano, Richard B. Chase.—4th ed.
p. cm.
ISBN 0-07-240285-7 (alk.paper)—ISBN 0-07-119469-X (international: alk. paper)
1. Production management. I. Aquilano, Nicholas J. II. Chase, Richard B. III. Title.
TS155 .D248 2003
658.5—dc21 2002023523

International Edition ISBN 0-07-119469-X

www.mhhe.com

To our wives
Cookie, Nina, and Harriet

And to our children
Andy and Alex
Don, Kara, and Mark
Laurie, Andy, Glenn, and Rob

About the Authors

Mark M. Davis Dr. Davis is professor of Operations Management at Bentley College in Waltham, MA. He received his BS degree in Electrical Engineering from Tufts University and his MBA and DBA degrees from Boston University's School of Management. He worked as a manufacturing engineer for the General Electric Company and is a graduate of its Manufacturing Management Program. He was also a programs manager for the U.S. Army Natick Research Laboratories.

Dr. Davis's primary research interest is service operations management with a focus on customer waiting time issues. He has published articles in this area in several journals, including *The Journal of Operations Management, Decision Sciences, The Journal of Services Marketing, The Journal of Business Forecasting, OM Review, The International Journal of Production and Operations and Production Management,* and *The International Journal of Service Industry Management.*

Dr. Davis is currently secretary of the Decision Sciences Institute and is a past president of the Northeast Decision Sciences Institute. In 2000, he was named a Fellow in the Decision Sciences Institute. In 1998, Dr. Davis received Bentley College's Scholar of the Year Award. He was appointed to the 1996 Board of Examiners for the Malcolm Baldrige National Quality Award. Dr. Davis currently serves the editorial review board of *The International Journal of Service Industry Management.*

Richard B. Chase Dr. Chase is professor of Operations Management and director of the doctoral program at the Marshall School of Business, University of Southern California. He received his Ph.D. in Operations Management, as well as an MBA and BS from UCLA. He has taught at the Harvard Business School, IMD (Switzerland), and the University of Arizona. He has written and lectured extensively on the subject of service. His other books include *Service Management Effectiveness, Fail-Safe Service* and *Operations Management for Competitive Advantage.* Two of his *Harvard Business Review* articles, "Where Does the Customer Fit in a Service Operation?" and "The Service Factory" (with D. Garvin), have been cited as classics.

Recent articles include "Want to Perfect Your Company's Service? Use Behavioral Science" (with S. Dasu), forthcoming in the *Harvard Business Review;* "Constructing an Empirically Derived Measure for Customer Contact" (with D. Kellogg) in *Management Science;* "Beefing Up Operations in Service Firms" (with R. Hayes) and "Make Your Service Failsafe" (with D. Stewart), both in the *Sloan Management Review;* "The Mall Is My Factory: Reflections of a Service Junkie" in *Production and Operations Management;* and "The Strategic Levers of Yield Management" (with S. Kimes) in *The Journal of Service Research.*

In 1995, the *Journal of Retailing* identified him as one of the leading scholars in services marketing. His work has been quoted in Tom Peters' *Liberation Management* and Davidow and Malone's *The Virtual Organization,* and most recently in Heskett et al., *The Service Profit Chain.* He is a Fellow of the Academy of Management and the Decision Sciences Institute, and served as an examiner for the Malcolm Baldrige National Quality Award. His money-back service guarantee for his MBA course on Service Management has received international attention in the business press.

Nicholas J. Aquilano Dr. Aquilano, now in well-deserved retirement, was professor of Management at the University of Arizona in Tucson, where he has been writing books and teaching undergraduate and graduate-level courses in Operations Management and Project Management for over 25 years. He received his Ph.D. from UCLA and has taught at Northeastern University.

Preface

Operations management continues to be an evolving discipline. Just as the economies of the major countries of the world were once largely dependent on manufacturing for growth, operations management initially focused almost exclusively on manufacturing-related issues. In the last 20 years, however, the field of operations management has changed dramatically. The reasons are many, including: (a) the emergence of a truly global economy, (b) significant advances in technology, specifically information economy, and (c) the continued growth of services in all of the world's economies, to the point where services now represent a major portion of the economies in the more highly developed countries.

For these same reasons, the fundamentals of managing a business, in general, have also changed. No longer are the functional areas within a firm seen as being independent from each other; instead they are viewed as being interrelated. As a consequence, operations management cannot be studied in isolation from marketing and finance. Equally important, the study of operations management is no longer confined to manufacturing. Today, operations management also includes services. In addition to the growing importance of services in today's economies, manufacturers are also recognizing the need to provide their customers with high-quality service, which can provide them with a significant advantage in today's highly competitive environment.

A major goal of this edition of *Fundamentals of Operations Management* is to reflect these changes that have taken place in business. The inclusion of services has always been a hallmark of *Fundamentals of Operations Management*. This fourth edition continues to set the standard by placing even greater emphasis on services, and the need for manufacturing and services to become more fully integrated in order to better meet customer requirements. To reinforce this emphasis on services, examples from a wide variety of service organizations have been liberally included throughout the text to provide students with both a link between theory and practice, as well as a contemporary view of operations management.

Another goal of this fourth edition has been to acknowledge the significant impact of technology on the study of operations management. As we embark on the twenty-first century, technology, and especially information technology, continues to change the ways in which companies do business. And we are seeing only the tip of the iceberg. Technology will continue to advance in the form of faster and more accurate transmission lines, more powerful computers, and larger electronic data storage equipment that is capable of storing *petabytes* of data (1 petabyte = 1,125,899,906,842,624 bytes). At the same time, unit costs in all of these areas will continue to decrease.

In addition, barriers to trade across national borders continue to be lowered with the creation of regional free trade zones such as the European Union, the North American Free Trade Agreement (NAFTA), and Mercursor (a free trade agreement among several South American countries).

The combination of advances in technology and lower trade barriers has facilitated the world's economies to continue their trend toward a single *global village* or *global landscape*. Both customers and suppliers now exist in every corner of the world, with no company being immune to international competition. In such a hypercompetitive environment, it is imperative that managers continue to develop innovative applications for these new technologies as they become available. This ever-changing environment has a significant impact on the operations management function in terms of how goods and services are produced and delivered.

To address these changes, as well as to link theory with practice, this fourth edition provides

- New coverage and emphasis on several topics in operations management that are currently high-priority issues with both business and operations managers. Two new chapters are devoted to this coverage: new product and service development (Chapter 3) and the role of technology in operations management (Chapter 4).
- A pedagogical feature, entitled "Managerial Issues," begins the text in each chapter to provide students with not only a managerial framework for the topic, but also an understanding of how the topic contributes to the success of the organization.
- The continued development of relevant concepts in operations management that are now recognized as critical success factors in business. These include yield management (Chapters 15 and 16), which focuses on maximizing capacity utilization and profits in service operations, and supply chain management (Chapter 13), which addresses both the changing role of the supplier and the fact that supply chains are becoming longer as firms now look to the four corners of the world for suppliers.
- Recognition that the operations function in every organization involves individuals and that their role is changing as are the organizations themselves. As part of these changes, there is an increasing emphasis on teamwork (Chapters S3 and 10).
- Demonstration of how operations management needs to be fully integrated with the other functional areas within an organization, and that many of the operations management tools are being applied in these other functional areas, such as marketing, engineering, and finance. For example, business process analysis can show engineering managers how to accelerate the development and introduction of new products (Chapters 3 and 4), and just-in-time (JIT) concepts (Chapter 14) are used to market mass-customized products that can be delivered to customers with minimal delays. These tools and techniques from operations management are also now used in a wide variety of new applications that go far beyond the walls of the traditional factory. As an illustration, quality management tools (Chapter S6) such as statistical process control (SPC) are now used to predict impending medical problems for patients with asthma or congestive heart failure.

We tried to do this in a brief and interesting way, focusing on core concepts and utilizing quantitative techniques only where necessary while making the mathematics intuitive and less formal.

Specific Objectives of This Book

Most students do not major in operations management. In fact, many schools and colleges do not even offer a major in operations management. Nevertheless, it is important for you to understand how the operations management function contributes to the overall success of an organization. The reasons are twofold. First, understanding how the different elements within the OM function fit into the overall organizational structure will provide you with a broader perspective that, in turn, will allow you to do your own job better. In addition, as we stated above, the concepts developed initially within the OM function have application in all of the other functional areas within an organization. Understanding and applying these tools and concepts can improve your ability to be both effective and efficient in the way you do your work.

Many students don't appreciate the importance of operations management until after they graduate and begin work. For example, consider the "hot" employment area of information technology (IT). Specialists in IT really should have a working knowledge of the best practices in process management, forecasting, quality control, and project planning to correctly apply many of the software tools that they will encounter on the job.

For these reasons, the specific objectives of this book are to

1. Introduce the various elements that comprise the field of operations management, and some of the new and evolving concepts within OM.
2. Identify some of the OM tools and concepts that can be applied to a wide variety of situations, including non-OM-related areas.

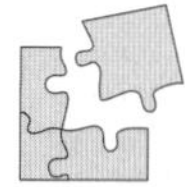

3. Develop an appreciation of the need for interaction between operations management and the other management functions within an organization.
4. Explain the role of technology in operations management and its impact on the different OM elements.

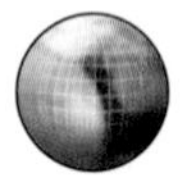

5. Describe the growing trend toward globalization among firms and how it affects operations management.
6. Demonstrate that manufacturing and services are becoming more integrated within companies.
7. Provide an integrated framework for understanding the field of OM as a whole and its role in an organization.

With respect to the last objective, our goal is to demonstrate that operations management is not just a loosely knit aggregation of tools but rather a *synthesis* of concepts and techniques that relate directly to operating systems and enhance their management. This point is important because OM is frequently confused with operations research (OR), management science (MS), and industrial engineering (IE). The critical difference between OM and these fields is this: OM is a field of management, whereas OR and MS are branches of applied mathematics and IE is an engineering discipline. Thus, while operations managers use the tools of OR and MS in decision making, and are concerned with many of the same issues as IE, OM has a distinct business management role that differentiates it from OR, MS, and IE.

Special Features of the Book

In an attempt to facilitate the learning process, we have incorporated several pedagogical features, including

- *Chapter objectives.* At the beginning of each chapter, a list of objectives is presented to highlight the important concepts on which the chapter focuses.
- *Vignettes.* Each chapter begins with a short vignette that shows how the chapter topic is actually applied in a real-world setting, to create student interest for the chapter material.
- *Application of OM concepts.* Examples of how many of the OM concepts presented in this text are applied in actual business situations are provided throughout the text. The use of real-world examples reinforces the critical role of operations management, showing how it contributes to the overall success of an organization. These applications take several forms, including the opening vignette to each chapter and Operations Management in Practice boxes, as well as in the numerous examples that are included throughout the text itself.

- *Internet exercises.* The Internet continues to be a powerful tool for obtaining and disseminating information, and this information is constantly changing. Where appropriate, an Internet exercise is provided at the end of a chapter to encourage students to obtain the latest information on a particular topic.
- *The application of Excel® spreadsheets.* Again, where appropriate, examples are provided using Excel® spreadsheets that encourage the student to explore alternative solutions.
- *Highlighting links with other functional areas.* Ideas and processes flow seamlessly across traditional functional boundaries in successful organizations, often to the point where it is practically impossible to determine where one function leaves off and another begins. To emphasize this integration within organizations, icons are used throughout the text to highlight examples of how OM is linked to other functional areas.

- *Global perspective.* Another feature of the book is its emphasis on the global impact of operations today; where appropriate, we show how the concepts apply in a global context. Special icons are used in the book to highlight this area.

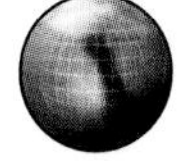

- *Margin definitions.* Key terms are in boldface when first defined and definitions added in the margin. At the end of the chapter these key terms are listed with page numbers for quick student reference.
- *Full-color art.* This fourth edition includes photos and exhibits to enhance the visual appeal and interest of students, to clarify and extend the text discussions, and to help students see operations in action.
- *Examples with solutions.* Examples follow quantitative topics and demonstrate specific procedures and techniques. These are clearly set off from the text and help students understand the computations.
- *Formula review.* Key formulas and equations are numbered within each of the more quantitative chapters and are repeated in summary form at the end of those chapters for easy student review.
- *Solved problems.* Representative example problems are included at the end of appropriate chapters. Each includes a detailed, worked-out solution and provides another level of support for students before they try homework problems on their own.
- *Review and discussion questions.* These questions allow students to review the chapter concepts before attempting the problems and provide a basis for classroom discussion. Suggested responses are included in the Instructor's Manual.
- *Problems.* A wide range of problem material follows each chapter, asking students to solve realistic, interesting problems.
- *Cases.* Located at the end of most chapters, short cases allow students to think critically about issues discussed in the chapter. These also can provide good classroom discussions or provide a capstone problem for the chapter. We've included both long and short cases such as Kristen's Cookie Company from Harvard.

Ancillary Materials

- *Student CD-ROM,* packaged with each copy of the text, contains chapter quizzes, Excel® spreadsheets, PowerPoint® slides, and short video clips illustrating key operations topics.

- *Instructor's Resource CD-ROM* is an all-in-one resource offered to adopters of the text. It contains the Instructor's Manual, Test Bank, and PowerPoint slides (described below), as well as video clips, all text exhibits, and Excel templates.
    - *Instructor's Manual,* prepared by Ross Fink of Bradley University, includes answers to discussion and review questions and solutions to text problems. There is a useful reference grid showing which problems correspond to specific topics in the chapters for ease in assignment.
    - *Test Bank,* prepared by Daniel Tracy of University of Tennessee at Martin, provides true/false, multiple/choice, and narrative problems for each chapter. Along with the manual, a separate computerized testing package is available allowing instructors to generate, add, and edit questions; save and reload tests; and select questions based on type or level of difficulty.
    - *PowerPoint Presentation Slides,* prepared by Charlie Cook of University of West Alabama, provides lecture outlines plus graphic material from the text to complement and customize lectures.
- *Videos.* **The Irwin Operations Management Video Series** consists of 29 segments on eight volumes covering quality, inventory, lean production, computer-integrated manufacturing, production processes and services, and global supply chains. They show students chapter concepts at work and how critical operations management is to organizations such as Motorola, Toyota, Hewlett-Packard, United Airlines, and others.
- *Operations Management Center Website (http://www.mhhe.com/pom/).* This site supports students and faculty in search of resources related to all aspects of operations management. There are sites with company tours, organizations, on-line publications, resources by topic, and textbook support.

We also have tried to practice what we preach. In applying the quality concept of continuous improvement, we have attempted to incorporate many of the suggestions made by our reviewers.

There is an old Chinese proverb that states, "May you live in interesting times." Like it or not, from an operations management perspective, those "times" are now and we should take full advantage of the opportunity—and enjoy it while doing so!

Acknowledgments

Although only three names appear on the cover of this book, a project of this magnitude could not be successfully completed without the assistance and cooperation of many individuals. Specifically, we would like to thank the reviewers for their evaluation of the second edition text and for their manuscript reviews. We thank them for their suggestions and comments. They include

Sal Agnihothri, State University of New York

Gary Alcorn, University of Pittsburgh

Kwasi Amoako-Gyampah, University of North Carolina–Greensboro

Fred P. Anderson, Indiana University of Pennsylvania

Bonnie F. Daily, New Mexico State University

Harry Ekholm, Texas Christian University

Michael R. Godfrey, University of Wisconsin–Oshkosh

Robert D. Klassen, University of Western Ontario

Ajay K. Mishra, State University of New York

Philip Musa, University of Alabama

Leonard Presby, William Paterson University

Robert M. Saltzman, San Francisco State University

Stephen Starling, California State University–Hayward

Constantin A. Vaitsos, University of Southern California

Samuel Wathen, Coastal Carolina University

Joel Wisner, University of Nevada

Several chapters were either written or rewritten with the assistance of colleagues. Specifically we would like to acknowledge the following individuals for their contributions to this fourth edition:

Richard Franza, *Bentley College* (Chapter 3 on New Product and Service Development and Process Selection)

James Salsbury, *Bentley College* (Chapter 13 on Supply Chain Management)

We once again thank those individuals whose contributions to past editions have helped the book evolve to its present form: Timothy Bergquist, *University of Oregon;* Dave Carhart, *Bentley College;* Gayla Delong, *Northwestern Oklahoma State University;* Lissa Galbraith, *Florida State University;* John Haehl, *Lewis-Clark State College;* Janelle Heineke, *Boston University;* Marilyn Jones, *Winthrop College;* Birsen Karpak, *Youngstown State University;* Dennis Krumwiede, *Kansas State University;* Vicki LaFarge, *Bentley College;* Rich Luebbe, *Miami University (Ohio);* Mary Jo Maffei, *Miami University (Ohio);* Robert Mefford, *University of San Francisco;* Rao Tatikonda, *University of Wisconsin–Oshkosh;* and Hans Thamhain, *Bentley College.*

Special thanks to Constantin A. Vaitsos who solved all of the examples and problems and checked our answers for accuracy. Ross Fink of Bradley University prepared the Instructor's Manual, Charlie Cook of University of West Alabama prepared the PowertPoint slides, and Daniel Tracy of University of Tennessee at Martin prepared the Test Bank. These supplements take a great deal of time and effort to write and we appreciate their efforts.

Finally, we wish to thank the staff at Irwin/McGraw-Hill for their support, encouragement, and assistance: Scott Isenberg, Executive Editor; Wanda Zeman, Senior Developmental Editor; Zina Craft, Senior Marketing Manager; Christine Vaughan, Senior Project Manager; Gina Hangos, Production Supervisor; and Pam Verros, Designer.

Mark M. Davis
Nicholas J. Aquilano
Richard B. Chase

Brief Contents

Contents

Chapter 1
Introduction to Operations Management 2

Chapter 2
Operations Strategy: Defining How Firms Compete 26

Chapter 3
New Product and Service Development, and Process Selection 50

AVIS
Car Return

Supplement 6
Quality Control Tools for Improving Processes 248

Chapter 7
Facility Decisions: Location and Capacity 288

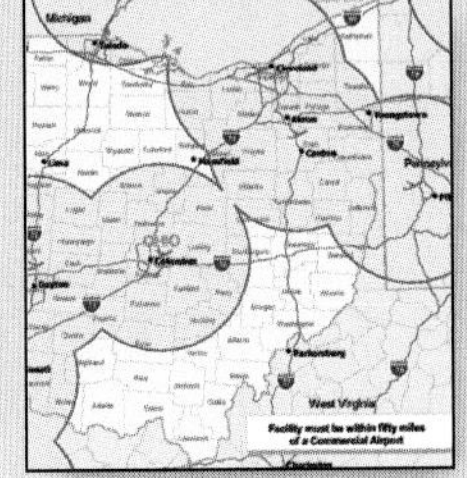

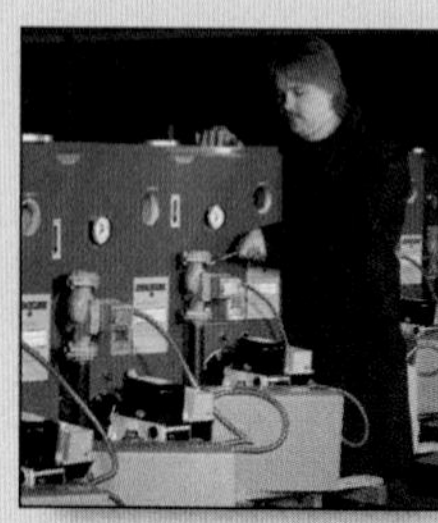

Chapter 11
Waiting Line Management 444

Supplement S11
Waiting Line Theory 462

Chapter 12
Scheduling 482

Chapter 13
Supply Chain Management 514

Chapter 14
Just-in-Time Systems 536

Chapter 15
Aggregate Planning 568

Fundamentals of Operations Management

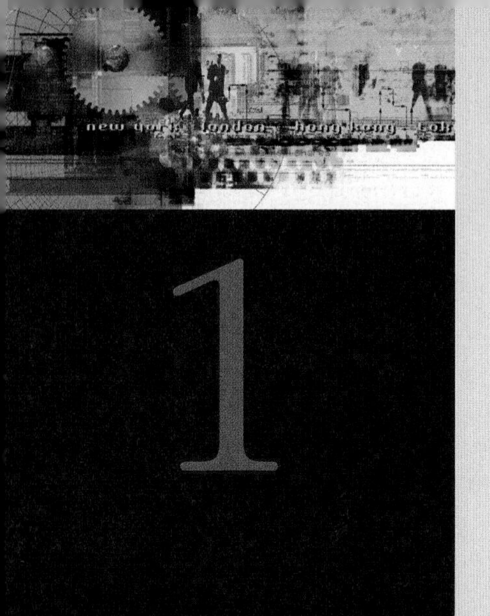

Introduction to Operations Management

Chapter Objectives

- Introduce and define operations management (OM) in terms of its contribution to an organization and the activities it involves.
- Describe how operations management contributes to the overall betterment of society.
- Present operations management as a function that addresses issues in both manufacturing and services.
- Show how operations management is gaining more recognition both internally and externally to an organization.
- Demonstrate how the operations management function interacts with the other functional areas within an organization.
- Present a brief history of operations management as a field and its evolution to its current role in an organization.

DAILY PERFORMANCE REVIEW MEETING PROVIDES FORUM FOR ESTABLISHING PRIORITIES AT AVID TECHNOLOGY, INC.

At 8:30 A.M. sharp, the gavel comes down on the conference room table calling the daily operational performance review meeting to order at Avid Technology's main manufacturing plant and headquarters in Tewksbury, Massachusetts. Avid designs and manufactures software and hardware that enable professionals in the video, film, audio, animation, special effects, and streaming media industries to digitally manipulate media content. Avid is an industry leader, in terms of both sales and quality, and has even won an Oscar® award for the special effects its equipment produced, which is proudly displayed at its Tewksbury headquarters.

The purpose of the meeting is to provide a daily forum or clearinghouse for each of the different manufacturing operations to report on their individual performances, to establish priorities, and to identify both current and potential problems that may prevent them from meeting their objectives. When problems do arise, they are quickly resolved and/or courses of action identified, because all of the involved individuals are present. This meeting provides everyone with the same information at the same time, eliminating potential miscommunications and delays. Performance measures that are reported at the meeting include products that have been completed and shipped, as well as the completion dates for products that are scheduled for shipment during the coming week. Quality performance measures also are reported along with inventory levels and product manufacturing costs.

On any given day, there can be 15 to 20 people attending the meeting. This meeting is clearly an operations management meeting conducted under the auspices of Paul Senechal, Avid's vice president of manufacturing. However, marketing and finance managers frequently attend. The marketing managers typically focus on the completion of products to meet customer delivery requirements; the finance managers focus on manufacturing costs and meeting shipping targets from an overall revenue perspective. The attendance of marketing and finance personnel emphasizes the importance of a cross-functional, integrated approach that is mandatory in today's highly competitive environment. Today's meeting also includes managers from Avid's plant in Ireland who participate through the use of teleconferencing technology.

At 8:40 A.M., after all of the reports have been made and the current issues addressed and the priorities for the day established, the gavel once more comes down on the table to adjourn the meeting, and the members return to their respective areas to focus on the work for that day.

Source: Special thanks to Paul Senechal, vice president of manufacturing, Avid Technology.

Managerial Issues

Today's operations managers, those responsible for producing and delivering the goods and services that we use every day, face a wide variety of challenges as we enter the twenty-first century. The highly competitive business environment that currently exists, caused in large part by the globalization of the world's economies in conjunction with the growth in e-commerce, has shifted the balance of power from the producers to the consumers. In so doing, consumers are now demanding increased value for their money. To put it simply, they want more for less.

From an operations management perspective this means providing continuously higher-quality products with shorter delivery times and better customer service while simultaneously reducing labor and material costs, and increasing the utilization of existing facilities—all of which translates into higher productivity.

To accomplish all of this, operations managers are turning to a wide variety of technologies. These include the use of robotics on assembly lines and automation, which can take the form of ATMs and vending machine purchases with cell phones. In the forefront is the increasing use of information technology, driven by an improved telecommunications infrastructure, which also is providing faster service at lower costs. Examples here include the Internet and customer support centers, which now can be located in any corner of the world.

Those firms that ignore the important role of operations management within an organization pay a price: failure, as evidenced by the many dot-com bankruptcies that have occurred in recent years. Many of these firms were virtual in every sense, in that all they had were websites with no operational infrastructure to support them. (This can be compared to putting up wallpaper without having a wall behind it!) Stories abound of Christmas shoppers who could not get deliveries on time (and couldn't even speak to someone about the problem) and virtual banks that were incapable of providing customers with something as simple as deposit slips. In every case, these customers took their business elsewhere as a result of their bad experiences, never to return.

What Is Operations Management?

An Organizational Perspective

operations management

Management of the conversion process that transforms inputs such as raw material and labor into outputs in the form of finished goods and services.

Operations management, as is the case with every functional area within an organization, can be defined from several perspectives: one being with respect to its overall role and contribution within an organization; the other focusing more on the day-to-day activities that fall within its area of responsibility. From an organizational perspective, **operations management** may be defined as the management of the direct resources that are required to produce and deliver an organization's goods and services.

The marketplace—the firm's customers for its goods and services—determines the corporate strategy of the firm. This strategy is based on the corporate mission, and in essence reflects how the firm plans to use all of its resources and functions (marketing, finance, and operations) to gain an advantage over its competition. The operations strategy specifies how the firm will employ its production capabilities to support its corporate strategy. (Similarly, the marketing strategy addresses how the firm will sell and distribute its goods and services, and the finance strategy identifies how best to utilize the financial resources of the firm, as shown in Exhibit 1.1.)

Within the operations function, management decisions can be divided into three broad areas:

- Strategic (long-range) decisions.
- Tactical (medium-range) decisions.
- Operational planning and control (short-range) decisions.

Operations Management in Practice

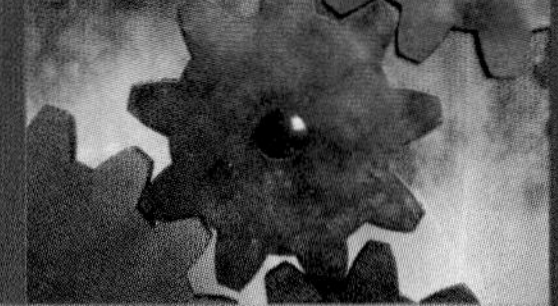

OPERATIONS MANAGEMENT PLAYS AN IMPORTANT ROLE AS AMAZON.COM GENERATES ITS FIRST PROFITS

Amazon.com, which announced its first profits in January 2002, provides a good example of a firm that has applied many of the operations management concepts that are presented in this book:

- In 2001, Amazon increased worker productivity, which resulted in 35% more units being shipped with the same number of workers, reducing its order fulfillment costs by $22 million even though sales increased 15%. As a result, between 2000 and 2001, its fulfillment costs dropped from 13.5% of sales to only 9.8%.
- Using new software, Amazon increased the forecasting accuracy of customer purchases, which resulted in a $31 million reduction in inventory in the fourth quarter of 2001. Inventory turns for 2001 were 15, which translates into a little more than an average of three weeks of inventory, significantly below the retail industry average.
- Shipping costs were reduced by millions of dollars by consolidating 40% of its shipments into full truckloads (as compared to zero consolidations in the previous year).
- Continued development of its supply chain with retailers like Toys 'R' Us and Target generated revenues of $225 million and profit margins that were double Amazon's overall 25% margin.

Sources:

Saul Hansell, "A Profitable Amazon Looks to Do an Encore," *The New York Times,* New York, January 26, 2002, p. 2.

Robert D. Hof and Heather Green, "How Amazon Cleared That Hurdle," *Business Week,* February 4, 2002, pp. 60–61.

Andy Kessler, "The New New Economy: The Web Grows Up," *The Asian Wall Street Journal,* New York, January 28, 2002, p. 11.

Operations Management in Practice

EXCERPTS FROM TWO LETTERS FROM FORMER STUDENTS

". . . part of an audit for a CPA firm includes learning about the systems of a client. A by-product of the audit is a management letter which suggests how the client might improve their systems. By systems I am referring to the accounting information systems, the inventory control systems, as well as the production process.

In evaluating these systems, one must first understand the generalities underlying all systems. OM explains these generalities as they apply to production processes. The better one understands how processes work, the easier it is to apply this understanding to different systems and provide your client with good suggestions for improving the efficiency of their operations . . .

The course you teach in Operations Management is invaluable, and any student of accounting would be a fool to blow it off and try to just get by without learning anything. . . ."

Gary S. Fortier
B.S.B.A., C.P.A.
Atlanta, GA

". . . if I were to call you on the phone and tell you what I do for work, I think I would hear some of the following from you:

'I told you so.'

'You should have paid more attention in class.'

'Maybe if you even went to class . . .'

Well, I have been busy working for the Gillette Company as a production analyst. Basically, it's OM all over again, making sure that the production is running smoothly and keeping management pleased. It's unreal how much of your class takes place in my everyday work.

Scrap rates, net average hours of production, efficiency, sample sizes, shifts, the number of hours a machine can run with a certain product. Putting in 60–70 hours a week and learning OM all over again just kills me, because if I had given some effort in your class, . . . who knows?

I am sure that you are giggling to yourself and saying ha ha, that ought to teach him not to have missed any of my classes. I thought that maybe some of your students that are like me could benefit from this e-mail. . . ."

Erik Geagan
B.S.B.A.
Boston, MA

Exhibit 1.1
Role of OM within an Organization

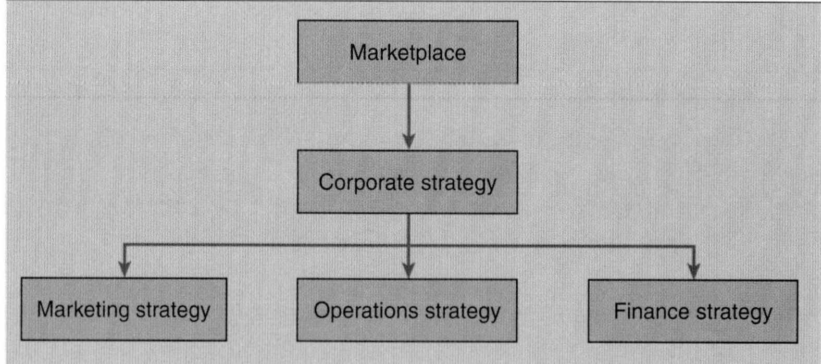

These three areas can be viewed as a top-down approach to operations management, with the decisions made at the higher level(s) acting as constraints on the lower level(s).

The strategic issues are usually very broad in nature, addressing such questions as

- How will we make the product?
- Where do we locate the facility or facilities?

- How much capacity do we need?
- When should we add more capacity?

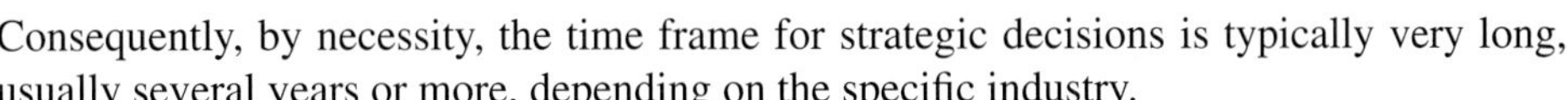

Consequently, by necessity, the time frame for strategic decisions is typically very long, usually several years or more, depending on the specific industry.

Operations management decisions at the strategic level impact the long-range effectiveness of the company in terms of how well it can address the needs of its customers. Thus, for the firm to succeed, these decisions must be closely aligned with the corporate strategy. Decisions made at the strategic level then define the fixed conditions or constraints under which the firm must operate in both the intermediate and short term. For example, a decision made at the strategic level to increase capacity by building a new plant becomes a capacity constraint with respect to tactical and operational decisions.

Looking at the next level in the decision-making process, tactical planning primarily addresses the issue of how to efficiently schedule material and labor over a specific time horizon and within the constraints of the strategic decisions that were previously made. Thus, some of the OM issues at this level are

- How many workers do we need?
- When do we need them?
- Should we work overtime or put on a second shift?
- When should we have material delivered?
- Should we have a finished goods inventory?

These tactical decisions, in turn, define the operating constraints under which the operational planning and control decisions are made.

The management decisions with respect to operational planning and control are very narrow and short term, by comparison. For example, issues at this level include

- What jobs do we work on today or this week?
- To whom do we assign what tasks?
- What jobs have priority?

An Operational Perspective

The day-to-day activities within the operations management function focus on adding value for the organization through its **transformation process** (as illustrated in Exhibit 1.2), which is sometimes referred to as the *technical core,* especially in manufacturing organizations. Some examples of the different types of transformations are

transformation process

Actual conversion of inputs into outputs.

- Physical, as in manufacturing.
- Locational, as in transportation.
- Exchange, as in retailing.
- Storage, as in warehousing.
- Physiological, as in health care.
- Informational, as in telecommunications.

The inputs are customers and/or materials which undergo the transformation. Also part of the transformation process are a variety of components supplied by the organization, such as labor, equipment, and facilities, which convert the inputs into outputs. Every transformation process is affected by external factors, which are outside the control of management. External factors include random, unexpected events such as natural disasters, economic cycles, changes in government policies and laws, as well as changes in consumer preferences and tastes. These external factors can also include anticipated changes, such as seasonality, over which management has little or no control.

Another important role of the operations management function is the measurement and control of the transformation process. This consists of monitoring the outputs in various ways, including quality and quantity, and then using this information as feedback to make the necessary adjustments that will improve the process.

These various transformations that take place, of course, are not mutually exclusive. For example, a department store can (*a*) allow shoppers to compare prices and quality (informational), (*b*) hold items in inventory until needed (storage), and (*c*) sell goods (exchange). Exhibit 1.3 presents sample input–transformation–output relationships for a

Exhibit 1.2

The Transformation Process within OM

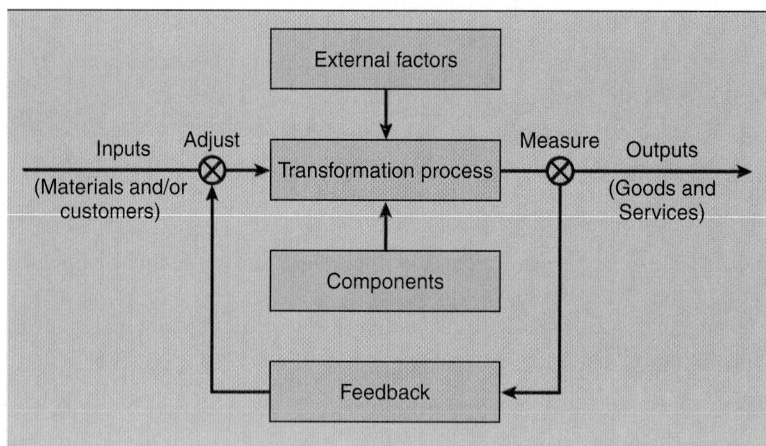

Exhibit 1.3

Input–Transformation–Output Relationships for Typical Systems

System	Inputs	Components	Primary Transformation Function(s)	Typical Desired Output
Hospital	Patients, medical supplies	MDs, nurses, equipment	Health care (physiological)	Healthy individuals
Restaurant	Hungry customers, food	Chef, waitstaff, environment	Well-prepared food, well served; agreeable environment (physical and exchange)	Satisfied customers
Automobile factory	Sheet steel, engine parts	Tools, equipment, workers	Fabrication and assembly of cars (physical)	High-quality cars
College or university	High school graduates, books	Teachers, classrooms	Imparting knowledge and skills (informational)	Educated individuals
Department store	Shoppers, stock of goods	Displays, salesclerks	Attract shoppers, promote products, fill orders (exchange)	Sales to satisfied customers
Distribution center	Stockkeeping units (SKU)	Storage bins, stockpickers	Storage and redistribution	Fast delivery, availability of SKUs

wide variety of processes. Note that only the direct components are listed; a more complete system description, of course, also would include managerial and support functions.

Operations Management's Contributions to Society

Operations management plays an important, although not always obvious, role in the societies in which we live. It is responsible for the food we eat and even the table on which we eat it; it provides us with the clothing we wear and with transportation, whether in the form of an automobile, train, or airplane, as well as being responsible for making these vehicles themselves. In other words, operations management affects nearly all aspects of our day-to-day activities.

Higher Standard of Living

A major factor in raising the standard of living in a society is the ability to increase its productivity. (Productivity, which can be broadly defined as how efficiently inputs are converted into outputs, is discussed in greater detail in Chapter 5.) Higher productivity is the result of increased efficiency in operations, which in turn translates into lower-cost goods and services. Thus, higher productivity provides consumers with more discretionary income, which contributes to their higher standard of living. As seen in Exhibit 1.4, the United States had significant increases annually in productivity during the 1990s, which was a major factor in the economic prosperity we experienced during that decade.

Better Quality Goods and Services

One of the many consumer benefits of increased competition is the higher-quality products that are available today. Quality standards are continually increasing. Many companies today, as we will learn in Chapter 6, have established six-sigma quality standards (pioneered by Motorola in the late 1980s), which means no more than 3.4 defects per million opportunities. Such high-quality standards were once considered not only prohibitively expensive but also virtually impossible to achieve even if cost wasn't a consideration. Today

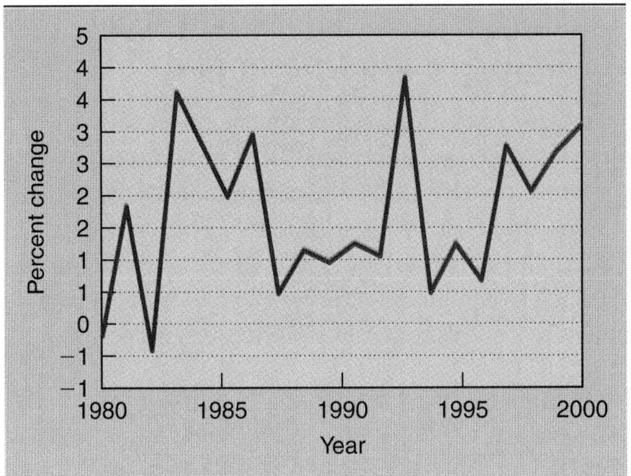

Source: *Economic Report of the President* (Washington, DC: United States Government Printing Office, January 2001).

Exhibit 1.4

Annual Change in Productivity in the United States (1980–2000)

we know that such high-quality standards are not only very possible, but they also result in lower costs, as firms no longer have large amounts of waste and rework to deal with.

Concern for the Environment

Many companies today are taking up the challenge to produce environmentally friendly products with environmentally friendly processes, all of which falls under the purview of operations management. The Veryfine Corporation, which is located in Westford, Massachusetts, and produces a wide variety of beverage drinks, is a good example of such firms. All of its packaging is made from 100% recyclable materials and it also recycles 94% of all solid waste materials that are generated throughout the production process.[1] Ford's new River Rouge manufacturing plant in Detroit provides another good example. No longer will raw waste be dumped into the waterways or the air polluted with smoke from its operations. Vegetation will be used to clean up contaminated land, and the River Rouge will be restored so fish will have access to the upper part of the river.[2]

Improved Working Conditions

Managers recognize the benefits of providing workers with better working conditions. This includes not only the work environment but also the design of the jobs themselves. Workers are now encouraged to participate in improving operations through suggestions. After all, who would know better how to do a particular operation than that person who does it every day. Managers also have learned that there is a very clear relationship between satisfied workers and satisfied customers, especially in service operations.

The Emergence of Operations Management

Operations management has been gaining increased recognition in recent years for several reasons, including (*a*) the application of OM concepts in service operations, (*b*) an expanded definition of quality, (*c*) the introduction of OM concepts to other functional areas such as marketing and human resources, and (*d*) the realization that the OM function can add value to the end product.

Application of OM to Service Operations

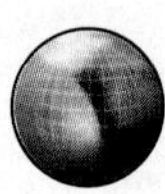

Initially, the application of operations management concepts was much more narrowly focused, concentrating almost entirely on manufacturing. However, as shown in Exhibit 1.5, as countries become more developed, services continue to represent a larger percentage of their respective Gross Domestic Products (GDPs). This growth in services over time, as presented for the United States in Exhibit 1.6, combined with the increased recognition that services could learn much from manufacturing and vice versa, expanded the application of operations management to also address related issues in services.

---

[1] www.veryfine.com/environment

[2] John Holusha, "Ford Thinks Green for Historic River Rouge Plant," *The New York Times,* November 26, 2000, p. 11.7.

Exhibit 1.5

Services as a Percent of Gross Domestic Product (GDP) for Different Countries

Country	Services as a Percent of GDP
Industrialized Countries:	
United States	80%
United Kingdom	73%
France	70%
Canada	66%
Japan	63%
Lesser Developed Countries:	
Brazil	50%
Thailand	49%
Peru	45%
India	45%
Ghana	30%

Source: The World Factbook 2000, Central Intelligence Agency, Washington, DC.

Exhibit 1.6

Growth in Services in the United States

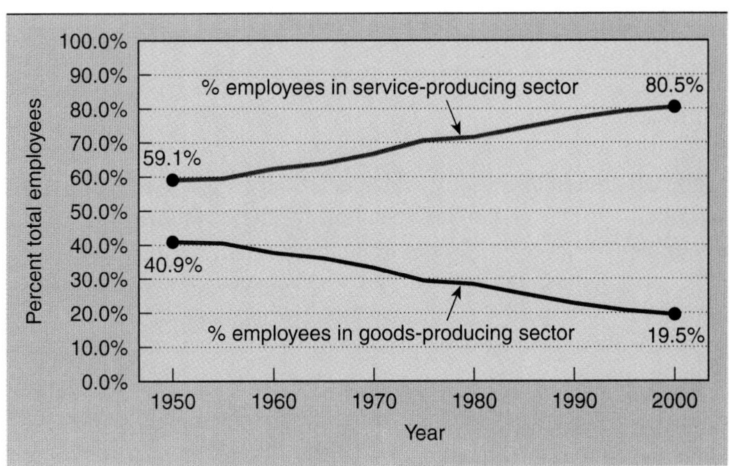

Source: Handbook of U.S. Labor Statistics, edited by Eva E. Jacobs, Fifth Edition, Bernan Press, 2001, Table 2-1, pp. 161–164.

As an example, Theodore Levitt of Harvard Business School, in his article entitled "Production-Line Approach to Service,"[3] was one of the first to recognize that many of the concepts that had been previously developed for manufacturing can actually be applied to service operations. He observed that operations concepts can be seen readily at McDonald's fast-food outlets (where hamburgers are cooked in batches of 12 at a time) or at Benihana's of Tokyo restaurants (where customers are batched into groups of eight to increase efficiency). More recently, an article entitled "JIT in Services: A Review of Current Practices and Future Directions for Research," by Duclos, Siha, and Lummus, showed that just-in-time (JIT) concepts also are being applied to a wide variety of service operations such as the Customer Service Center at Northern Telecom, Inc., and the automatic replenishment

[3]Theodore Levitt, "Production-Line Approach to Service," *Harvard Business Review* 50, no. 5 (September–October 1972), pp. 41–52.

Exhibit 1.7

Differences between Goods and Services

Goods	Services
Tangible	Intangible
Can be inventoried	Cannot be inventoried
No interaction between customer and process	Direct interaction between customer and process

Exhibit 1.8

Most Products Are a "Bundle" of Goods and Services

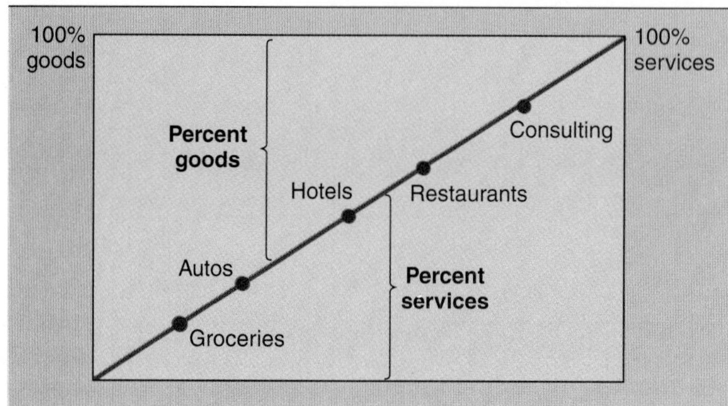

system at Wal-Mart's retail operations, which is actually a pull-type system.[4] (JIT is often described as a pull system for moving material. In this example, the selling of an item "pulls" a replacement order from stock or a supplier.)

Exhibit 1.7, lists some of the major differences between goods and services. Goods are tangible, something "you can drop on your foot," while services, being acts rather than objects, are considered to be intangible. Another difference between goods and services is that goods can be inventoried, whereas services cannot. For example, you can buy a good, such as a book, or even food, and use it sometime in the future. This is not possible with services, because they are acts associated with a specific point in time. The revenue from a hotel room that remains vacant for a given night, or an airline seat that is not sold on a scheduled flight, or a rental car that is not leased on a given day is lost forever. (Wouldn't it be great if the airlines could save in inventory all the empty seats they have during the year to use at peak holiday periods?) The third distinguishing characteristic between goods and services is that the customer does not have to be present when the good is actually produced, but must be present for the performance of a service. For example, you do not have to go to an automobile assembly plant to buy a car, but it would be difficult to have your hair cut without you actually being at the barbershop or beauty salon, or to undergo a series of tests in a hospital without being physically present.

However, it is becoming more difficult to differentiate between services and manufacturing. Consequently, instead of looking at operations from two perspectives (that is, manufacturing and services), today's approach suggests that the vast majority of products consist of both a goods component and a service component, as suggested in Exhibit 1.8, p. 12, and that both elements need to be addressed as a whole in order for a firm to be successful. (Note: Throughout this book, *product* will refer to the combination or "bundle" of

[4]L. Duclos, S. Siha, and R. Lummus, "JIT in Services: A Review of Current Practices and Future Directions," *International Journal of Service Industry Management* 6, no. 5 (1995), pp. 36–52.

goods and services being provided, whereas *goods* will refer to the tangible output and *services* will refer to the intangible output.)

An Expanded Definition of Quality

Another key component in operations management is quality. Successful firms now acknowledge that quality is no longer limited to the operations management function, but is important in all the functional areas throughout an organization. Within marketing, for example, the customer's order must be accurate in terms of (*a*) the correct product and quantity ordered, (*b*) the specified price, and (*c*) the proper location for delivery. Quality is also important in accounting: The bill for the items purchased must be properly prepared to reflect any special terms of payment and appropriate discounts, and then sent to the customer at the correct address.

The integration of manufacturing and services also has expanded the definition of quality. Quality is no longer limited to the technical requirements of the goods being produced on the manufacturing floor. Service quality (that is, how we deal with our customers on a wide variety of issues) is equally important. How companies integrate all of these aspects of quality to properly meet the needs of their customers is a major challenge to today's managers. The customer service department of a car dealership, for example, must know how to resolve customer complaints so that they will continue to do business with the dealership in the future. For these reasons, today's managers are recognizing that improving quality in all areas of their businesses improves customer satisfaction and increases customer loyalty.

Expansion of OM Concepts into Other Functions

Successful companies also are recognizing that, in addition to quality, many of the tools and concepts that are now widely used within the operations function also have application in the other functional areas of an organization such as marketing, finance, and accounting. For example (as we shall see in Chapter 5), process analysis is a major tool that provides insight into understanding how inputs are converted into outputs, and can be applied to every type of process regardless of where they exist in an organization. As an illustration, the hiring of personnel in human resources is a process, as is the design of a new product in engineering and the rolling out of a new product by marketing. In accounts receivable, the preparing and mailing of an invoice to a customer is also a process.

A New Paradigm for OM

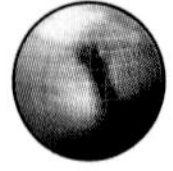

For many years following World War II, the United States was the obvious world leader in manufacturing. U.S. dominance was the result of several factors, including (*a*) available capacity built to support the war effort, (*b*) pent-up demand for consumer goods during the war, and (*c*) the virtually total destruction of most of the production capabilities of the other leading industrialized nations of the world. As Tom Peters said, "You couldn't screw up an American Fortune 500 company between 1946 and 1973 if you tried."[5] With demand significantly exceeding capacity during this period of time, emphasis was placed on output, and the operations function typically reacted to situations only when they occurred. Corporate managers during this period usually told operations managers to focus only on controlling production costs.

[5]Tom Peters and KQED Golden Gate Productions, *The Power of Excellence: The Forgotten Customer* (Jack Hilton Productions, Video Publishing House, Inc., 1987).

Founded in 1866, the Coca-Cola Company is the clear leader in its industry with more than 50% of the global soft drink market. Although its principal brand is Coca-Cola, it distributes more than 230 brands in nearly 200 countries worldwide. With its focus on global growth, more than 70% of the company's income comes from sales outside the United States.

As we shall see in Chapter 2, in the early 1970s, Wickam Skinner at Harvard Business School introduced the notion of operations strategy. He proposed that the operations function, rather than being only reactive, could take a proactive role in developing the overall strategy for an organization. In other words, Skinner suggested that the operations function could actually add value to the products a company manufactured (that is, adding value in terms of what a customer is willing to pay for the products). In developing this concept of operations strategy, he suggested that a firm could compete on dimensions other than cost to increase profit margins. These dimensions included *quality, speed of delivery,* and *process flexibility*. Each of these dimensions, in their own way, adds value to the end product. Skinner's notion of an operations strategy resulted in a new paradigm for the operations function.

The Ever-Changing World of Operations Management

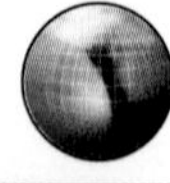

Operations management is continuously changing to meet the new and exciting challenges of today's business world. This ever-changing world is characterized by increasing global competition and advances in technology. Emphasis is also shifting within the operations function to link it more closely with both customers and suppliers.

global economy, global village, global landscape

Terms used to describe how the world is becoming smaller and countries are becoming more dependent on each other.

Increased Global Competition

The world is rapidly transforming itself into a single **global economy,** which is also referred to as a **global village** or **global landscape.** Markets once dominated by local or national companies are now vulnerable to competition from literally all corners of the world. For example, in the 1960s, only 7 percent of the firms in the United States were exposed to foreign competition; by the late 1980s, this figure exceeded 70 percent and that

Exhibit 1.9

Ford's Global Network to Support the Manufacturing of the Escort

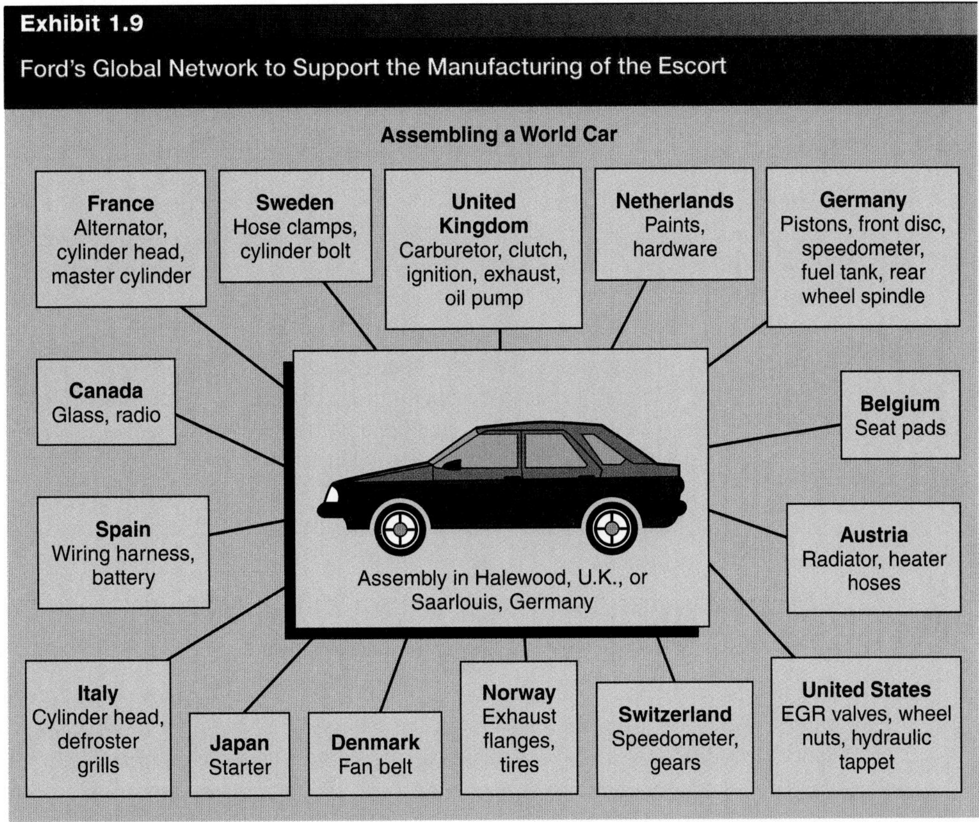

Source: From Joseph E. Stiglitz, *Principles of Micro-economics*, 2nd ed. (New York: W. W. Norton and Company, 1997), p. 58. Reprinted with permission.

percentage has continued to grow.[6] Consequently, as companies expand their businesses to include foreign markets, so too must the operations management function take a broader, more global perspective in order for companies to remain competitive. To survive and prosper in such a global marketplace companies must excel in more than one competitive dimension, which previously was the norm. With the rise of the global economy, companies are no longer limited as to where they can make or buy their products and components. As seen in Exhibit 1.9, Ford's Escort in Europe is assembled in two locations, England and Germany, using components that are produced in no less than 15 countries from all over the world. This trend toward globalization has placed increased emphasis on the logistics of where to locate facilities and the issues associated with moving material long distances, both of which are addressed in Chapter 13.

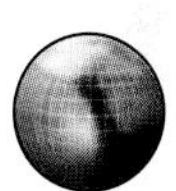

Advances in Technology

Advances in technology in recent years also have had a significant impact on the operations management function. Information technology (IT) now allows us to collect detailed customer data so that we can "mass customize" products to meet the needs of individual customers. The increased use of automation and robotics also has permitted us to

[6]S. C. Gwynne, "The Long Haul," *Time,* September 25, 1992, pp. 34–38.

improve the quality of the goods that are being manufactured. Automated teller machines (ATMs), which can provide customers with 24-hour service, are a good example of technology being applied in service operations, particularly in those countries with high labor costs.

The explosive growth of the Internet in recent years also has had an impact on operations. Electronic marketplaces, a major factor in the emergence of B2B (business-to-business) transactions, quickly identify the lowest-priced suppliers. The wide use of e-mail now allows companies to communicate rapidly with suppliers, customers, and other operations within their respective organizations. Customer contact centers, be they for making hotel or airline reservations, receiving customer orders, or handling customer complaints (or any combination of these), can now be located anywhere in the world.

However, advances in technology place new requirements on the workforce and even on customers, especially in service operations. (For example, customers now must have computer skills to access companies that are advertising on the Internet or the World Wide Web.) Consequently, skilled workers are replacing unskilled workers in all types of operations. As we shall see in Chapter 10, an organization's workforce should be considered its most valuable asset, only increasing in value as it becomes more educated.

Linking Operations Management to Customers and Suppliers

In the past, most manufacturing organizations viewed operations strictly as an internal function that had to be buffered from the external environment by other organizational functions. Orders were generated by the marketing function; supplies and raw materials were obtained through the purchasing function; capital for equipment purchases came from the finance function; the labor force was obtained through the human resources function; and the product was delivered by the distribution function.

Buffering the transformation process from the external environment was traditionally desirable for several reasons:

- Interaction with environmental elements (e.g., customers and salespeople on the production floor) could have a disturbing influence on the transformation process.
- The transformation process was often more efficient than the processes required for obtaining inputs and distributing finished goods.
- With certain processes (e.g., auto assembly lines and continuous-flow processes such as petroleum refining), maximum productivity was achieved only by operating at a continuous rate that assumed the market could absorb all of the product being manufactured. This meant that the production process had to shift at least some of the input and output activities to other parts of the firm.
- The managerial skills required for the successful operation of the transformation process were often different from those required for the successful operation of boundary functions such as marketing and human resources, for example.

However, there were some inherent disadvantages when the transformation process was totally isolated. One was that information lagged between the process and the boundary functions, which inevitably led to inflexibility. Another was that for high-tech products in particular, communications between the shop floor and the customer could be extremely valuable in solving technical problems during production. As shown in the OM in Practice box, Foxboro Company's Customer Friend Program provides a good example of how manufacturing is now directly interacting with customers.

A Ford Mondeo being built on a conveyor-based production system at the Genk Ford Motor plant in the Netherlands.

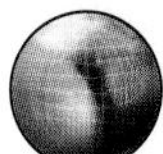

More and more firms are recognizing the competitive advantage achieved when the transformation process is not isolated, as when customers are invited to view their operating facilities firsthand. For example, Green Giant believes that the tours of their production facilities that they provided to Japanese distributors were a major factor in their ability to penetrate that market with their Green Giant food products.[7] Similarly, National R_X Services, which offers a mail-order prescription service, encourages insurance companies and HMOs to visit their facilities to assure themselves of the high quality of its prescription-filling process.

In a like manner, companies are working more closely with suppliers. Firms like Toyota, for example, have suppliers deliver product directly to the factory floor, eliminating any need for a stockroom. Texas Instruments encourages many of its vendors to automatically replenish items on the factory floor without individual purchase orders or incoming reports every time a delivery is made.

value chain

Steps an organization requires to produce a good or a service regardless of where they are performed.

This trend toward having the transformation process work more closely with both suppliers and customers alike is often referred to as a product's **value chain.** We can define a value chain as consisting of all those steps that actually add value to the product without distinguishing where they are added. This concept attempts to eliminate all nonvalue-added steps (such as inspections and inventory), and consequently results in a higher

[7]J. Ammeson, "When in Rome," *Northwest Airlines World Traveler,* March 1993.

Operations Management in Practice

THE CUSTOMER FRIEND PROGRAM AT FOXBORO'S SYSTEMS MANUFACTURING OPERATION

The Foxboro Company's systems manufacturing operation, which produces control systems for process industries such as refineries, chemical plants, and breweries, has a Customer Friend Program that directly links its customers to manufacturing. This program is offered free of charge and provides each customer with a contact person or "friend" in manufacturing who is responsible for helping the customer resolve any and all product- and service-related problems. Since its inception in 1992, more than 40 individuals from manufacturing have taken part in the Customer Friend Program involving more than 300 customer systems, both large and small.

The benefits of this program to manufacturing are to (*a*) identify more closely with the customer's needs, (*b*) feel the customer's pain when a problem does occur, (*c*) gain a better understanding of how manufacturing can improve its support to its customers, and (*d*) obtain direct feedback from "where the rubber meets the road" in terms of how manufacturing can improve its processes and products.

The program benefits the customer by (*a*) identifying more closely the customer's needs, (*b*) passing the pain directly to the source when a problem does occur, (*c*) having a dedicated individual within manufacturing who has a personal commitment to customer satisfaction, (*d*) having direct contact with manufacturing to analyze product failures, and (*e*) acting as a conduit for new and improved ideas.

Foxboro's Customer Friend Program is proactive rather than reactive. Depending on the needs and desires of the customer, the Foxboro friend will call his assigned customer every one to four weeks just to make sure everything is running smoothly. Many of these customer–friend relationships are long standing. Ray Webb, the employee involvement manager at Foxboro's Systems Manufacturing Operation, for example, has had a five-year association with Ergon Refining of Mississippi.

Source: Special thanks to Ray Webb, Systems Manufacturing Operation, The Foxboro Company.

Exhibit 1.10

The Value Chain and Its Support Functions

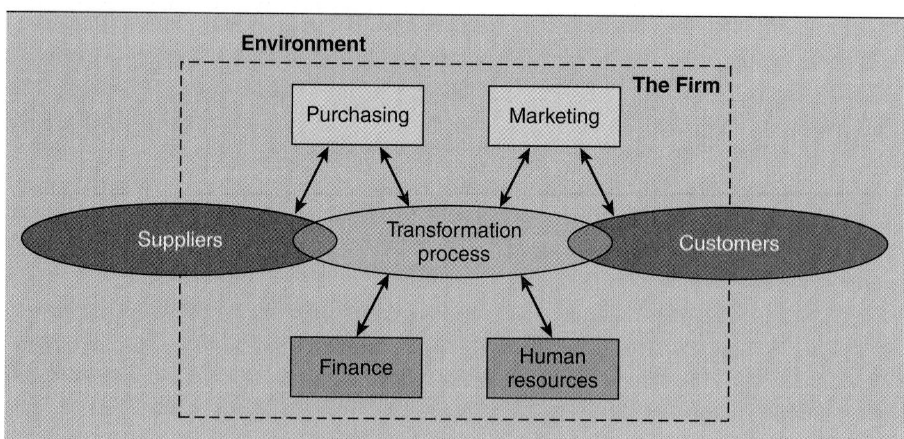

virtual enterprise

Company whose boundaries are not clearly defined due to the integration of customers and suppliers.

degree of dependence among the value-added functions within the chain. The relationship between the transformation process, its support functions, and the other value-added functions is shown in Exhibit 1.10.

This integration of both suppliers and customers into the transformation process begins to blur the boundaries between what were previously totally independent organizations. What appears to be emerging now is a concept known as the **virtual enterprise,** which is a fully integrated and interlocked network of *inter*dependent organizations. With this new approach, it is often difficult to determine where one organization leaves off and the next one begins. As one example, FedEx has several employees who work full time at the L.L. Bean Mail Order Distribution Center in Freeport, Maine.

Job Opportunities in Operations Management: Relating OM to Other Business Functions

Exhibit 1.11 lists some of the line and staff jobs that usually fall within the operations function. There are more staff specializations in manufacturing than in services because of the focus on materials management and control.

Operations Management is a required course in many business schools, not only because it deals with the basic question of how goods and services are created, but also because many of the concepts developed in OM have direct applications in every other functional area within an organization. As seen in Exhibit 1.12, processes exist within every function. These processes can be continuously improved by applying OM tools and

Exhibit 1.11
Line and Staff Jobs in Operations Management

Organizational Level	Manufacturing Industries	Service Industries
Upper	Vice president of manufacturing Regional manager of manufacturing	Vice president of operations (airline) Chief administrator (hospital)
Middle	Plant manager Program manager	Store manager (department store) Facilities manager (wholesale distributor)
Lower	Department supervisor Foreman Crew chief	Branch manager (bank) Department supervisor (insurance company) Assistant manager (hotel)
Staff	Production controller Materials manager Quality manager Purchasing agent Work methods analyst Process engineer	Systems and procedures analyst Purchasing agent Inspector Dietician (hospital) Customer service representative

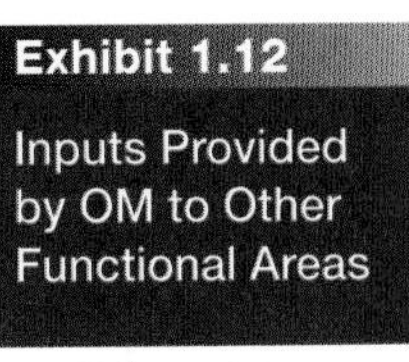
Exhibit 1.12
Inputs Provided by OM to Other Functional Areas

Functional Area	Processes Performed by That Area	Input Provided by OM
Accounting	Asset valuation Financial statements	On-hand inventory Labor and material costs
Finance	Capital investment analysis Cash flow management	Capacity utilization Make-or-buy decisions
Marketing	New product introduction Customer orders	New process requirements Delivery dates
Human resources	Hiring Training	Job descriptions Worker skills requirements
MIS	Software evaluation Hardware requirements analysis	Data requirements Terminal requirements

techniques. In addition, as also seen in Exhibit 1.12, each of these functional areas interacts with the OM function. Therefore, in order to do their jobs correctly, it is important for individuals working in these areas to understand the fundamental concepts of operations management.

Historical Development of OM

Prior to 1900

Up through the end of the eighteenth century, agriculture was the predominant industry in every country. Manufacturing, as we know it today, did not exist. Items were usually custom made by skilled artisans who spent many years in apprenticeship learning every facet of how to make a good or provide a service. No two products were ever the same. For many products, trades or guilds were established to provide a common basis of knowledge for these apprenticeship programs.

This cottage industry approach to manufacturing began to change at the beginning of the nineteenth century. Watt invented the steam engine in England in 1765, which provided a source of power for manufacturing. In 1801, Eli Whitney introduced the concept of standardized parts to President Thomas Jefferson with a demonstration in which he selected parts at random to assemble and then fire a musket. (Prior to this, every musket was hand crafted with customized parts.) The middle of the nineteenth century saw the onrush of the Industrial Revolution with its large manufacturing facilities that were powered by either steam or water. However, even with the advent of these large facilities, manufacturing, to a large degree, still remained an art rather than a science.

Scientific Management

scientific management

Systematic approach to increasing worker productivity introduced by Frederick W. Taylor.

This all changed with the introduction of **scientific management** at the beginning of the twentieth century. Although we could claim that operations management has existed since the dawn of civilization, scientific management was probably the first historical landmark in the field in that it represented for the first time a systematic approach to manufacturing. This concept was developed by Frederick W. Taylor, an imaginative engineer and insightful observer of organizational activities.

The essence of Taylor's philosophy was that scientific laws govern how much a worker can produce per day and that it is the function of management to discover and use these laws in its production systems (and that it is the function of the worker to carry out management's wishes without question). Taylor's philosophy was not greeted with approval by all his contemporaries. On the contrary, some unions resented or feared scientific management—and with some justification. In too many instances, managers of the day were quick to embrace the mechanisms of Taylor's philosophy—time study, incentive plans, and so forth—but ignored their responsibility to organize and standardize the work to be done. For many firms, workers often were viewed as just another interchangeable asset, like plant and equipment.

Taylor's ideas were widely accepted in contemporary Japan, and a Japanese translation of Taylor's book, *Principles of Scientific Management* (which was titled in Japan as *The Secret of Saving Lost Motion*), sold more than two million copies. To this day, there is a strong legacy of Taylorism in Japanese approaches to manufacturing management.[8]

[8]C. J. McMillan, "Production Planning in Japan," *Journal of General Management* 8, no. 4 (1984), pp. 44–71.

Notable co-workers of Taylor were Frank and Lillian Gilbreth (motion study, industrial psychology) and Henry L. Gantt (scheduling, wage payment plans). However, it is probably not well known that Taylor, a devout Quaker, requested "cussing lessons" from an earthy foreman to help him communicate with workers; that Frank Gilbreth defeated younger champion bricklayers in bricklaying contests by using his own principles of motion economy; or that Gantt won a presidential citation for his application of the Gantt chart to shipbuilding during World War I.

Moving Assembly Line

The year 1913 saw the introduction of one of the machine age's greatest technological innovations: the moving assembly line for the manufacture of Ford automobiles. (Ford is said to have gotten the idea for an assembly line from observing a Swiss watch manufacturer's use of the technology. Incidentally, all Model-T Fords were painted black. Why? Because black paint dried the fastest.) Before the assembly line was introduced in August of that year, each auto chassis was assembled by one worker in about 12½ hours. Eight months later, when the line was in its final form, with each worker performing a small unit of work and the chassis being moved along the line mechanically, the average labor time per chassis was reduced to 93 minutes. This technological breakthrough, coupled with the concepts of scientific management, represents the classic application of labor specialization and still exists today in both manufacturing and service operations.

Hawthorne Studies

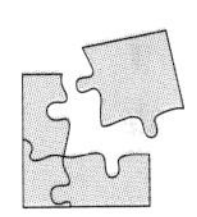

Mathematical and statistical developments dominated the evolution of operations management from Taylor's time up to around the 1940s. One exception was the Hawthorne studies, conducted during the late 1920s and early 1930s by a research team from Harvard Business School and supervised by the sociologist Elton Mayo. These experiments were designed to study the effects of certain environmental changes on the output of assembly workers at Western Electric's Hawthorne plant in Chicago, Illinois. The unexpected findings, reported in *Management and the Worker* by F. J. Roethlisberger and W. J. Dickson,[9] intrigued sociologists and students of "traditional" scientific management alike. To the surprise of the researchers, changing the level of illumination, for example, had much less effect on the output than the way in which the changes were introduced to the workers. That is, reductions in illumination in some instances led to increased output because workers felt an obligation to their group to keep output high. Discoveries such as these had tremendous implications for work design and worker motivation, and ultimately led to the establishment of personnel management and the human resources departments in most organizations.

Operations Research

World War II, with its complex problems of logistics control and weapons-systems design, provided the impetus for the development of the interdisciplinary, mathematically

[9]F. J. Rothlisberger and W. J. Dickson, *Management and the Worker* (Cambridge, MA: Harvard University Press, 1939).

oriented field of operations research. Operations research (OR) brings together practitioners in such diverse fields as mathematics, psychology, and economics. Specialists in these disciplines customarily form a team to structure and analyze a problem in quantitative terms so that a mathematically optimal solution can be obtained. Operations research, or its approximate synonym *management science,* now provides many of the sophisticated quantitative tools that are used today in operations management as well as in other business disciplines.

OM Emerges as a Field

In the late 1950s and early 1960s, scholars began to write texts dealing specifically with operations management as opposed to industrial engineering or operations research. Writers such as Edward Bowman and Robert Fetter (*Analysis for Production and Operations Management* [1957]) and Elwood S. Buffa (*Modern Production Management* [1961]) clearly noted the commonality of problems faced by all manufacturing organizations and emphasized the importance of viewing a production operation as a system.

Today, operations management is acknowledged as a legitimate functional area within many organizations, be they for-profit or not-for-profit, public or private, manufacturing or service.

The Marriage of OM and Information Technology

Today, as we noted earlier, information technology (IT) plays a critical role in the design and management of production processes. Business process reengineering, supply chain management, and sophisticated tools for systems integration such as SAP (all defined later in the book) require "integrated solutions" that marry OM and IT. To illustrate, a survey of consulting practice areas showed that 31 percent of the services offered by the 40 largest consulting firms were in the process/operations management area, which implies the blending of OM and IT.[10] Thus, while information technology has always been a key factor in the management of factory operations, its application throughout the firm to other functional areas such as marketing and finance suggests a major evolutionary step in the development of the field.

OM in Services

As stated earlier, Theodore Levitt was probably one of the first to demonstrate how many of the concepts and tools that had been developed for manufacturing operations could also be applied to service operations. By using these tools, services also could realize many of the efficiencies of operation that had previously been limited to manufacturing. McDonald's provided several good examples of these applications, from the efficient cooking and assembly of hamburgers in a batch operation to the use of specially designed scoops that quickly package french fries in consistent portion sizes.

Integration of Manufacturing and Services

More recently, managers have recognized the importance of both manufacturing and services, and the need to integrate the two. A primary objective of this text is to emphasize

[10]"Consultant News," cited in *The Economist,* March 22, 1997, p. 40.

this integration. Companies that want to succeed as world-class operations therefore must devote resources to both areas. In addition, production and service must be compatible with each other and strategically aligned with the firm's overall goals.

Conclusion

Operations management is recognized today as a critical functional area within every organization. No longer is operations management considered to be subservient to the finance and marketing areas; instead, it is now treated as an equal. Firms that fail to recognize the significant contribution of the operations management function will lose profits and market share to those firms that do. The once-reactive role of operations management, which concentrated solely on minimizing costs, has been replaced by a more proactive position of maximizing the value added to the goods and services that the organization provides.

Some of the major issues facing operations management executives today in this constantly changing business environment include

1. Reducing the development and manufacturing time for new goods and services.
2. Achieving and sustaining high quality while controlling costs.
3. Integrating new technologies and control systems into existing processes.
4. Obtaining, training, and keeping qualified workers and managers.
5. Working effectively with other functions of the business (marketing, engineering, finance, and human resources) to accomplish the goals of the firm.
6. Integrating production and service activities at multiple sites in decentralized organizations.
7. Working effectively with suppliers and being user-friendly for customers.
8. Working effectively with new partners formed by strategic alliances (for example, IBM and Apple Computers).

All of these issues are interrelated. The key to success is for operations management to do all of these at a level that is competitive in both global and domestic markets.

Key Terms

global economy p. 14
global landscape p. 14
global village p. 14
operations management p. 4
scientific management p. 20
transformation process p. 7
value chain p. 17
virtual enterprise p. 18

Review and Discussion Questions

1. What is operations management and how is it different from operations research?
2. What were the underlying reasons for the lack of emphasis on operations management in the post–World War II years?
3. What are the advantages of bringing customers into the transformation process or technical core?
4. Take a look at the want ads in *The Wall Street Journal* and evaluate the opportunities for an OM major with several years of experience.

5. What are the major factors leading to the resurgence of interest in OM today?
6. Explain the difference, from an operations management perspective, between cost minimization and value maximization.
7. Using Exhibit 1.3 as a model, describe the input–transformation–output relationships found in the following systems.
   a. An airline.
   b. A state penitentiary.
   c. A branch bank.
   d. A bakery.
   e. A clothing manufacturer.
   f. A dry cleaner.
   g. An automobile assembly line.
   h. An accounting firm.
8. What do we mean by the expression *value chain,* as it applies to the transformation process of a good or service?
9. Identify a product that is 100 percent goods without any service component. Identify a product that is 100 percent service without any goods component.
10. Speculate on the future role of the OM function within an organization and the future role of the operations manager.

Internet Exercise

Go to the McGraw-Hill/Irwin website at www.mhhe.com/pom and visit the website of one of the companies that provides a virtual plant tour of their operations. Identify the company and describe the various operations presented in the tour. What do you think distinguishes this firm from its competition?

Bibliography

Ammeson, Jane. "When in Rome." *Northwest Airlines World Traveler,* March 1993.

Chase, Richard B., and David A. Garvin. "The Service Factory." *Harvard Business Review* 67, no. 4 (July–August 1989), pp. 61–69.

Chase, Richard B., and Eric L. Prentis. "Operations Management: A Field Rediscovered." *Journal of Management* 13, no. 2 (October 1987), pp. 351–66.

"Consultant News," cited in *The Economist,* March 22, 1997, p. 40.

Duclos, Leslie K., Samia M. Siha, and Rhonda R. Lummus. "JIT in Services: A Review of Current Practices and Future Directions for Research." *International Journal of Service Industry Management* 6, no. 5 (1995), pp. 36–52.

Flaherty, M. Therese. *Global Operations Management*. New York: McGraw-Hill, 1996.

Greene, Constance. *Eli Whitney and the Birth of American Technology*. Boston: Little, Brown and Company, 1956.

Gwynne, S. C. "The Long Haul." *Time,* September 25, 1992, pp. 34–38.

Hammonds, K. H., and M. Roman. "Itching to Get onto the Factory Floor." *Business Week,* October 14, 1991.

Hansell, Saul, "A Profitable Amazon Looks to Do an Encore," *The New York Times,* New York, January 26, 2002, p. 2.

Hof, Robert D., and Heather Green, "How Amazon Cleared That Hurdle," *Business Week,* February 4, 2002, pp. 60–61.

Holusha, John, "Ford Thinks Green for Historic River Rouge Plant," *The New York Times,* November 26, 2000, p. 11.7.

Kessler, Andy, "The New New Economy: The Web Grows Up," *The Asian Wall Street Journal,* New York, January 28, 2002, p. 11.

Levitt, Theodore. "Production-Line Approach to Service." *Harvard Business Review* 50, no. 5, (September–October 1972), pp. 41–52.

———. "The Industrialization of Service." *Harvard Business Review* 54, no. 5 (September–October 1976), pp. 63–74.

McMillan, Charles J. "Production Planning in Japan." *Journal of General Management* 8, no. 4 (1984), pp. 44–71.

Narayandas, Das and V. Kasturi Rangan, "Dell Computer Corporation," Harvard Business School case No. 9-596-058, revised September, 1996.

Peters, Tom, and KQED Golden Gate Productions. *The Power of Excellence: The Forgotten Customer*. Jack Hilton Productions, Video Publishing House, Inc., 1987.

Rothlisberger, F. J., and W. J. Dickson. *Management and the Worker*. Cambridge, MA: Harvard University Press, 1939.

Serwer, Andy, "Dell Does Domination," *Fortune,* January 21, 2002. pp. 71–75.

Shah, Jennifer Baljko, "Dell Writes The Book On Efficiency—Processes Focus On Understanding Where Supply, Demand Diverge," *Ebn,* December 17, 2001, p. 32.

Skinner, Wickham. "Manufacturing—Missing Link in Corporate Strategy." *Harvard Business Review,* May–June 1969, pp. 136–45.

———. "The Focused Factory." *Harvard Business Review,* May–June 1974, pp. 113–21.

www.veryfine.com/environment

2

Operations Strategy

Defining how firms compete

Chapter Objectives

- Introduce the concept of operations strategy and its various components, and show how it relates to the overall business strategy of the firm.
- Illustrate how operations strategy pertains to adding value for the customer.
- Identify the different ways in which operations strategy can provide an organization with a competitive advantage.
- Introduce the concept of trade-offs between different strategies and the need for a firm to align its operations strategy to meet the needs of the particular markets it is serving.
- Explain the difference between order-qualifiers and order-winners as they pertain to operations strategy.
- Describe how firms are integrating manufacturing and services to provide an overall "bundle of benefits" to their customers.

DELL COMPUTER UNDERSTANDS OPERATIONS STRATEGY!

No one will argue that the market for personal computers (PCs) is highly competitive. Consequently, PCs are typically viewed as a commodity in which there is little or no difference among the major competitors. Nevertheless, Dell Computer continues to gain market share while simultaneously generating significant profits, and is now the leader in both categories. (Between 1994 and 2001 Dell's share of the PC market grew from 4.2% to 24.9%, with Compaq a distant second with 13.3% market share, and Hewlett-Packard in third place with 9.7%.) How has Dell been able to accomplish this?

First, its Dell Direct Model links the firm directly to its customers, eliminating costly distributors and retailers. Originally a mail order firm, Dell now also uses the Internet to take customer orders. In addition, by applying information age technology, it can build individually customized computers, most of which are shipped within 3–5 days after the order has been received. (Because each computer is built to order, Dell does not have any finished goods inventory.) And it does all this at a reasonable price.

Dell Computer provides a good example of a firm that understands the concept of operations strategy and has designed and installed processes which allow it to do an excellent job of executing that strategy. In addition to competing on speed, customization, quality, and price, Dell also provides various services to its customers. (Services, which are very profitable, represent about $3 billion of Dell's $7.5 total annual revenues.)

Sources:

Andy Serwer, "Dell Does Domination," *Fortune,* January 21, 2002. pp. 71–75.

Das Narayandas and V. Kasturi Rangan, "Dell Computer Corporation," Harvard Business School case No. 9-596-058, revised September, 1996.

Jennifer Baljko Shah, "Dell Writes The Book On Efficiency—Processes Focus On Understanding Where Supply, Demand Diverge," *Ebn,* December 17, 2001, p. 32.

Managerial Issues

An organization's operations strategy provides an overarching framework for determining how it prioritizes and utilizes its resources to gain a competitive advantage in the marketplace. Today's operations managers face many new challenges with respect to strategy issues, from developing effective strategies to properly implementing them throughout the organization.

As we shall see, there are several external factors that affect operations strategy decisions, including an increase in competition that has resulted from the globalization of business and advances in technology. Consequently, operations managers, in many instances, are now being asked to do more with less: more, in terms of faster delivery times, more variety and higher quality; less, in terms of lower material costs, lower labor costs, and less available time.

At the same time, managers know all too well that competitors can copy successful strategies and can usually implement them quickly, thereby neutralizing, to some degree, their advantage. As a result, these same managers, from a strategic perspective, must keep a watchful eye to the future, constantly looking for the next strategy that will separate their firms from those of competitors.

corporate strategy

Overall strategy adopted by the parent corporation.

strategic business unit (SBU)

Stand-alone business within a conglomerate that operates like an independent company.

business strategy

How a strategic business unit (SBU) addresses the specific markets it serves and products it provides.

types of business strategies:

low-cost

Producing the lowest-cost products.

market segmentation

Satisfying the needs of a particular market niche.

Operations Strategy—An Overview

Definitions

There often develops within an industry or company a unique set of terms that are familiar only to those associated with that industry or company. This is also true for the functional areas within an organization. Since operations strategy is a relatively new and evolving concept, several of the terms more commonly used are defined here.

Today, many corporations, especially the larger conglomerates such as General Electric and Hewlett-Packard, consist of several stand-alone businesses that focus on different industries. Within this context, **corporate strategy** defines the specific businesses in which the firm will compete and the way in which resources are acquired and allocated among these various businesses. For example, one of GE's corporate strategies under Jack Welch was to shift from being a traditional manufacturing company and expand into services such as broadcasting and financial services.

These stand-alone businesses within these conglomerates often are referred to as **strategic business units (SBUs)**. The individual strategy adopted by each SBU, which is referred to as **business strategy,** defines the scope and boundaries of the SBU, in terms of how it addresses the specific markets that it serves and the products that it provides.

In order to not only survive but also prosper in today's fiercely competitive marketplace, an SBU needs to differentiate itself from its competition. In such a highly competitive environment, customers will buy solely on the basis of price, thereby driving prices down and shrinking profit margins. In this type of situation, only the low-cost producer in an industry can be successful and Michael Porter, a professor at the Harvard Business School and perhaps today's leading authority on competitive strategy, has suggested that even this isn't guaranteed.[1]

Porter recommends, therefore, that beyond a **low-cost strategy,** there are two other business strategies that a firm can adopt: **market segmentation** and **product differentiation.**

[1]M. Porter, *Competitive Strategy: Techniques for Analyzing Industries and Competitors* (New York: The Free Press, 1980).

Functional strategies (for example, operations, marketing, human resources) are developed to support or align with the established business strategy.

A company or SBU's **competitiveness** refers to its relative position in the marketplace in terms of how it competes with the other firms in its industry. **Operations strategy** refers to how the operations management function contributes to a firm's ability to achieve its competitive advantage in that marketplace.

Operations strategy can be divided into two major categories: *structural elements* consisting of facility location, capacity, vertical integration, and choice of process (all of which are considered to be long term or "strategic" in nature) and *infrastructural elements* consisting of the workforce (in terms of size and skills), quality issues, planning and control, and organizational structure (all of which are often viewed as "tactical" because they can be changed in a relatively short time).

Operations strategies are developed from the **competitive priorities** of an organization, which include (*a*) **low cost,** (*b*) **high quality,** (*c*) **fast delivery,** (*d*) **flexibility,** and (*e*) **service.**

Core capabilities are the means by which competitive priorities are achieved. Consequently, core capabilities must align directly with competitive priorities.

product differentiation

Offering products that differ significantly from the competition.

functional strategy

Strategy developed by a function within an organization to support the business strategy.

competitiveness

Company's position in the marketplace relative to its competition.

operations strategy

How the operations function contributes to competitive advantage.

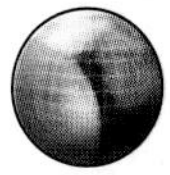

competitive priorities

How the operations function provides a firm with a specific competitive advantage.

A Short History of Operations Strategy

In the period following World War II, corporate strategy in the United States was usually developed by the marketing and finance functions within a company. With the high demand for consumer products that had built up during the war years, U.S. companies could sell virtually everything they made at comparatively high prices. In addition, there was very little international competition. The main industrial competitors of the United States today, Germany and Japan, lay in ruins from massive bombings. They could not even satisfy their own markets, let alone export globally.

Within the business environment that existed at that time, the manufacturing or operations function was assigned the responsibility to produce large quantities of standard products at minimum costs, regardless of the overall goals of the firm. To accomplish this, the operations function focused on obtaining low-cost, unskilled labor and installing highly automated assembly-line-type facilities.

With no global competition and continued high demand, the role of operations management (that is, to minimize costs) remained virtually unchanged throughout the 1950s and early 1960s. By the late 1960s, however, Wick Skinner of the Harvard Business School, who is often referred to as the grandfather of operations strategy, recognized this weakness among U.S. manufacturers. He suggested that companies develop an operations strategy that would complement the existing marketing and finance strategies. In one of his early articles on the subject, Skinner referred to manufacturing as the missing link in corporate strategy.[2]

Subsequent work in this area by researchers at the Harvard Business School, including Abernathy, Clark, Hayes, and Wheelwright, continued to emphasize the importance of using the strengths of a firm's manufacturing facilities and people as a competitive weapon in the marketplace, as well as taking a longer-term view of how to deploy them.

[2]C. W. Skinner, "Manufacturing—The Missing Link in Corporate Strategy," *Harvard Business Review* 47, no. 3 (May–June 1969), pp. 136–45.

What Is Operations Strategy?

Operations strategy is concerned with the development of a long-term plan for determining how to best utilize the major resources of the firm so that there is a high degree of compatibility between these resources and the firm's long-term corporate strategy. Operations strategy addresses very broad questions about how these major resources should be configured in order to achieve the desired corporate objectives. As stated earlier, some of the major long-term structural issues addressed in operations strategy include

strategic planning

Long-range planning such as plant size, location, and type of process to be used.

How big do we make the facilities?

Where do we locate them?

When do we build them?

What type of process(es) do we install to make the products?

tactical planning

Focuses on producing goods and services as efficiently as possible within the strategic plan.

planning and control

Scheduling of daily tasks to determine which operator is assigned to work on which job and machine.

Each of these issues is addressed in greater detail in subsequent chapters. In this chapter we want to take a more macroscopic perspective to better understand how these issues are interrelated.

In developing an operations strategy, management also needs to take other factors into consideration. These include (*a*) the level of technology that is or will be available, (*b*) the required skill levels of the workers, and (*c*) the degree of vertical integration, in terms of the extent to which outside suppliers are used.

As shown in Exhibit 2.1, operations strategy supports the long-range strategy developed at the SBU level. One might say that decisions at the SBU level focus on being effective, that is, "on doing the right things." These decisions are sometimes referred to as **strategic planning.** Strategic decisions impact intermediate-range decisions, often referred to as **tactical planning,** which focus on being efficient, that is, "doing things right." Here the emphasis is on when material should be delivered, when products should be made to best meet demand, and what size the workforce should be. Finally, we have **planning and control,** which deals with the day-to-day procedures for doing work, including scheduling, inventory management, and process management.

Operations Strategy Means Adding Value for the Customer

How often have we heard the expression "customers want their money's worth"? Unfortunately, from a manager's point of view, it's not that easy. Customers want more than their money's worth, and the more they receive for their money, the more value they see in the goods and services they are purchasing.

In determining the value of a product, be it a good or a service, customers take into consideration all of the benefits derived from the product and compare it with all of the costs of that product. If, in the opinion of the customer, the benefits exceed the costs, then

Exhibit 2.1

Hierarchy of Operational Decision-Making

Type of Planning	Time Frame	Typical Issues
Strategic	Long range	Plant size, location, type of process
Tactical	Intermediate range	Workforce size, material requirements
Planning and control	Short range	Daily scheduling of workers, jobs, and equipment; process management; inventory management

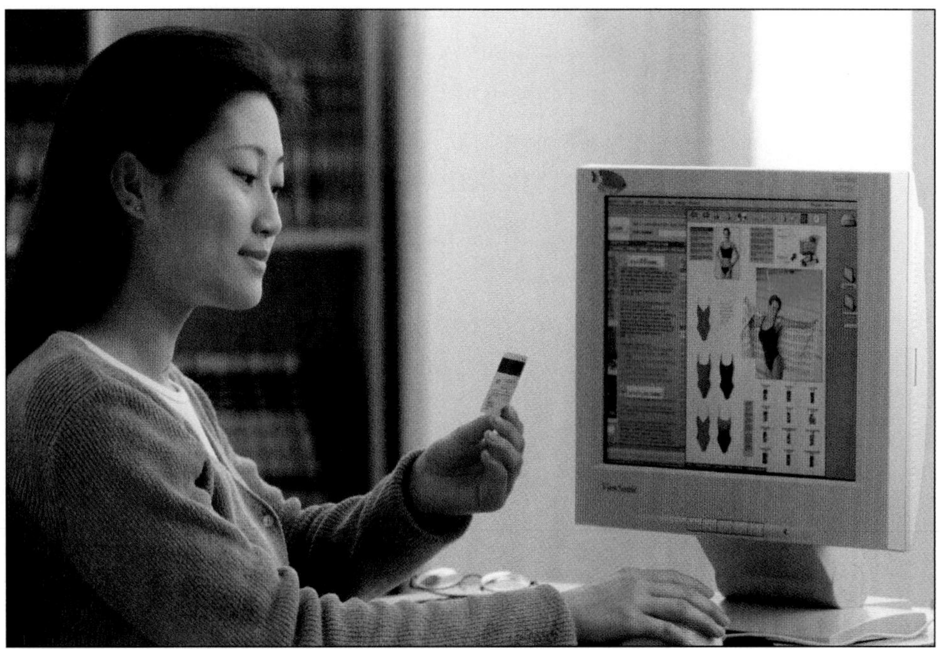

Shopping online has gained in popularity due to both the increasing number of sites offering products and services and the convenience of shopping any time, any place.

customers perceive value in the product. The more the benefits exceed the costs, the more value the product provides.

In other words,

$$\text{Perceived customer value} = \frac{\text{Total benefits}}{\text{Total costs}} \tag{2.1}$$

When this ratio is >1, customers perceive value; the greater the number, the more value. When this ratio is <1, customers feel they have overpaid for the product, that they have been "ripped off," and are highly unlikely to buy that product again in the future. Another way of looking at this is

$$\text{Perceived customer value} = \text{Total benefits} - \text{Total costs} \tag{2.2}$$

When the difference between the benefits and costs is positive, customers perceive value; when it is negative, they believe they have overpaid for the product.

One of the goals in the development of an operations strategy, therefore, should be to maximize the value added to the goods and services that are provided by the firm, as suggested in Exhibit 2.2.

Adding customer value during the transformation process can take many forms and translate into different things to different customers. As seen in Equations 2.1 and 2.2, one way to add value is to reduce the cost of the product, as when you buy books at Amazon.com. Added value to the customer also can mean that the product is more readily available, such as when you order groceries online or buy a camera through the Internet. Added value can be seen as receiving faster service, as when you use the fast lane on the highway to pay a toll automatically, or it may take the form of information, as when Amazon.com tells you what other books have been purchased by buyers who have purchased the same book you bought, or when Expedia.com provides you with a list of different airlines going to a particular city and a comparison of their air fares. Added value also can take the form of a more customized product, be it personal computer from Dell or more personalized service, as when you check into a hotel and they know that you have stayed there before and have certain preferences.

Exhibit 2.2
Maximizing Value Added in Operations

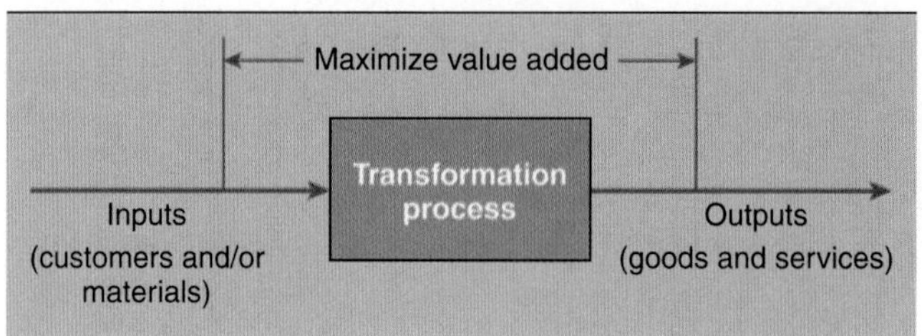

The key element in developing a successful operations strategy is for a firm to provide its customers with additional benefits at an increase in cost that is perceived to be less than those benefits.

Trends Affecting Operations Strategy Decisions

Two major trends that have significantly impacted the role of operations strategy within an organization are an increasing trend towards the globalization of business and advances in technology, especially information technology.

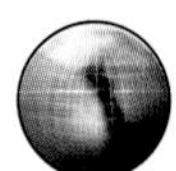

Globalization

As we saw in the first chapter, the world is quickly becoming a global village, caused in large part by technology. As a result, competition in most industries has intensified significantly in recent years, and this trend towards *hyper-competition* is expected to continue. At the same time, globalization provides new opportunities for companies in the form of new, previously untapped markets, for their products as well as new sources for raw materials and components at significantly lower costs.

This movement towards a single world economy has occurred for several reasons, including (*a*) continued advances in information technology that facilitate the rapid transfer of data across vast distances, (*b*) the growing trend to lower trade barriers as evidenced by NAFTA and the formation of the European Union, (*c*) the trend toward lower transportation costs, and (*d*) the emergence of high-growth markets with associated high-profit margins in **newly industrialized countries (NIC).**[3] These new markets can be compared to the saturated markets and shrinking profit margins that are being experienced in the more highly developed countries. For example, McDonald's growth in the United States between 1984 and 1994 was 6.4 percent annually while its international sales grew 19.0 percent annually during this same time period.[4]

newly industrialized countries (NIC)

Emerging countries that compete in global markets with their goods and have populations with a high standard of living.

As a result of this globalization of business, managers must extend their visions beyond their own national borders when developing operations strategies. This includes the location of manufacturing plants in Southeast Asia because of low labor rates, or the establishment of call centers in Ireland because of a combination of inexpensive labor, an educated workforce, and the necessary technology infrastructure that exists.

In addition to structural strategy decisions, such as where to locate a new plant, infrastructural issues also must be evaluated when looking to expand a company's operations

[3]Naisbitt and P. Aburdene, *Megatrends 2000* (New York: William Morrow and Co., 1990).

[4]G. Loveman, "The Globalization of Services: Four Strategies That Drive Growth across Borders," *Proceedings of the 4th International Research Seminar in Service Management,* Agelonde-LaLonde les Maures, France, June 4–7, 1996.

strategy globally. Here the education level of the workforce, the language, and the impact of local laws and customs must be taken into consideration. For example, a major attraction for locating in Ireland is its highly educated workforce. As an another illustration, employees in Germany can work up to 70 hours in some weeks without being paid overtime, and then work as little as 30 hours or less in other weeks, as long as the total hours worked over a given time period (such as 6 or 12 months) meets an agreed-upon amount.

Technology

Stan Davis and Chris Meyer, in their book entitled *Blur,* identify three factors that are significantly affecting the way in which business is being conducted: (*a*) connectivity, (*b*) speed, and (*c*) intangibility. They suggest that the combination of all three is causing changes to occur in business at such a rate that managers can only view business today as a blur, hence the title of the book.[5]

All three factors are directly related to advances in technology. Connectivity refers to the fact that virtually everyone is connected now electronically, be it through e-mail, the Internet, the telephone, or the fax. At the same time, firms with these connected networks, in many cases, provide services that are now available 24/7 (24 hours a day, seven days a week) in place of the more traditional hours of nine to five, Monday through Friday. Examples here include banking services, stock exchange transactions, and airline and hotel reservations. As a result of this connectivity, information is transmitted in a matter of seconds or minutes, instead of hours or days (or even weeks), which was the previous norm. The combination of connectivity and speed suggests that firms are now focusing on the intangible aspects of their business in order to gain a competitive advantage in the marketplace, which translates into providing better and more innovative services.

As we shall see shortly, technology also has dramatically affected one of the basic concepts in operations strategy: that of making trade-offs between priorities. With advances in technology, managers no longer have to make pure trade-offs between competitive priorities as they once did. Instead, today's technology allows firms to compete on several priorities simultaneously, resulting in shifts to superior performance curves (which are described later in the chapter).

competitive priorities

cost

Providing low-cost products.

quality

Providing high-quality products.

delivery

Providing products quickly.

flexibility

Providing a wide variety of products.

service

How products are delivered and supported.

Competitive Priorities

The key to developing an effective operations strategy lies in understanding how to create or add value for customers. Specifically, value is added through the competitive priority or priorities that are selected to support a given strategy.

Skinner and others initially identified *four basic competitive priorities.* These were **cost, quality, delivery,** and **flexibility.** These four priorities translate directly into characteristics that are used to describe various processes by which a company can add value to the products it provides. There now exists a fifth competitive priority—**service**—and it was the primary way in which companies began to differentiate themselves in the 1990s.

Cost

Within every industry, there is usually a segment of the market that buys strictly on the basis of low cost. To successfully compete in this niche, a firm must necessarily, therefore,

[5]Stan Davis and Christopher Meyer, *Blur: The Speed of Change in the Connected Economy* (New York: Ernst & Young Center for Business Innovation, Warner Books, 1998).

be the low-cost producer. But, as noted earlier, even doing this doesn't always guarantee profitability and success.

Products sold strictly on the basis of cost are typically commodity-like. (Examples of commodities include flour, petroleum, and sugar.) In other words, customers cannot easily distinguish the products made by one firm from those of another. As a result, customers use cost as the primary determinant in making a purchase.

However, this segment of the market is frequently very large and many companies are lured by the potential for significant profits, which are associated with large unit volumes of product. As a consequence, the competition in this segment is exceedingly fierce—and so is the failure rate. After all, there can only be one low-cost producer, and that firm usually establishes the selling price in the market. As an example, Kmart declared bankruptcy in January, 2002 due primarily to its inability to compete head to head with Wal-Mart based on low prices. Wal-Mart is clearly the low-cost producer in this segment of the retail industry because of its tremendous size, which allows it to keep its operating costs down through economies of scale. If Kmart is to survive, it will have to find another market niche, other than cost, on which to compete.[6]

Quality

Quality can be divided into two categories: product quality and process quality. The level of quality in a product's design will vary as to the particular market that it is aimed to serve. Obviously, a child's first two-wheel bicycle is of significantly different quality than the bicycle of a world-class cyclist. The use of thicker sheetmetal and the application of extra coats of paint are some of the product quality characteristics that differentiate a Mercedes-Benz from a Hyundai. One advantage of offering higher-quality products is that they command higher prices in the marketplace.

The goal in establishing the "proper level" of product quality is to focus on the requirements of the customer. Overdesigned products with too much quality will be viewed as being prohibitively expensive. Underdesigned products, on the other hand, will lose customers to products that cost a little more but are perceived by the customers as offering much greater benefits.

Process quality is critical in every market segment. Regardless of whether the product is a child's first two-wheeler or a bicycle for an international cyclist, or whether it is a Mercedes-Benz or a Hyundai, customers want products without defects. Thus, the goal of process quality is to produce error-free products.

Delivery

Another market niche considers speed of delivery to be an important determinant in its purchasing decision. Here, the ability of a firm to provide consistent and fast delivery allows it to charge a premium price for its products. George Stalk Jr., of the Boston Consulting Group, has demonstrated that both profits and market share are directly linked to the speed with which a company can deliver its products relative to its competition.[7] In addition to fast delivery, the reliability of the delivery is also important. In other words, products should be delivered to customers with minimum variance in delivery times.

---

[6]Joann Muller, "Attention Kmart: Find a Niche," *Business Week,* February 4, 2002, p. 72.

[7]George Stalk Jr., "Time—The Next Source of Competitive Advantage," *Harvard Business Review* 66, no. 4 (July–August 1988), pp. 41–51.

Operations Management in Practice

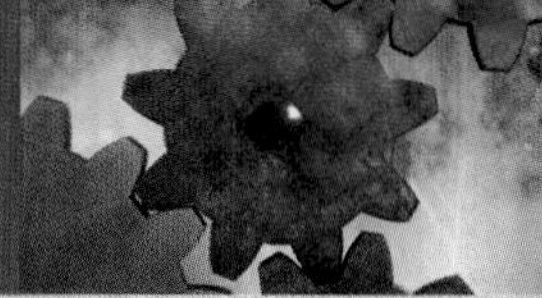

ZARA EXCELS ON PRICE, SPEED, AND FLEXIBILITY

Zara, a retail chain of high-fashion boutique clothing stores, has grown rapidly since Amancio Ortega opened his first store in Spain in 1975. Headquartered in northern Spain, Zara, with more than 400 retail stores in 25 countries, now generates sales of more than US$2 billion annually, primarily in Europe, but is now beginning to penetrate the US market. The reasons for its success are attributed to several factors including low prices, speed of delivery, and flexibility. Merchandise is delivered to each Zara retail location twice a week. (Merchandise is air-freighted to its stores in the United States.) This fast and almost continuous replenishment concept reduces the need for significant in-store inventories and the possibility of clothes going out of fashion.

A major factor in Zara's ability to react quickly to changes in the customer buying behavior is its use of information and technology. Salespeople in each retail location use handheld computers to record buyer preferences and trends. This information along with actual sales data are transmitted daily through the Internet to Zara's headquarters in Spain.

In addition, unlike its major competitors, which outsource manufacturing, Zara produces most of its merchandise in its state-of-the-art factory in Spain. Products are designed, produced and delivered to its stores in as little as two weeks after they have appeared for the first time in a fashion show. (In contrast, competitors like the GAP and H&M require between five weeks and five months lead time to fill orders from its retail operations.)

Sources:

William Echikson, "The Mark of Zara," *Business Week,* May 29, 2000, pp. 98–100.

Jane M. Folpe, "Zara has a Made-to-Order Plan for Success," *Fortune,* September 4, 2000, p. 80.

Stryker McGuire, "Fast Fashion; How a secretive Spanish tycoon has defied the postwar tide of globalization, bringing factory jobs from Latin America and Asia back to Europe," *Newsweek,* International Edition, September 17, 2001, p. 36.

Richard Heller, "Galician Beauty," *Forbes,* May 28, 2001, p. 98.

Flexibility

From a strategic perspective, in terms of how a company competes, flexibility consists of two dimensions, both of which relate directly to how the firm's processes are designed. One element of flexibility is the firm's ability to offer its customers a wide variety of products. The greatest flexibility along this dimension is achieved when every product is customized to meet the specific requirements of each individual customer. This is often referred to as **mass customization.** Examples of firms that have achieved this level of flexibility include Dell Computers and the National Bicycle Industrial Company in Japan. (See OM in Practice box.)

mass customization

Providing high volume products that are individually customized to meet the specific needs of each customer.

The other dimension of flexibility is how fast a company can change over its production facilities to produce a new line of products. This dimension is growing in importance, as product life cycles become shorter and shorter. Sony provides a good example here with its ability to quickly produce new models of its Walkman. Because it has this high degree of changeover flexibility, Sony is able to easily substitute new Walkman models for those models that do not sell well.

Service

With product life cycles becoming shorter and shorter, the actual products themselves tend to quickly resemble those of other companies. As a consequence, these products are often viewed as commodities in which price is the primary determinant in deciding which one to buy. A good example of this is the personal computer (PC) industry. Today, the differences in the products offered among the different PC manufacturers are relatively insignificant, so price is the prime selection criterion.

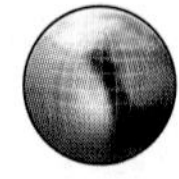

To obtain an advantage in such a competitive environment, firms are now providing "value-added" service. This is true for firms that provide goods and services. The reason is simple. As Sandra Vandermerwe puts it, "The market power is in the services, because the value is in the results." (Specific examples of how manufacturers are using services as a competitive advantage are presented later in this chapter.)

Within the service sector, Putnam Investments in Boston offers a wide range of mutual funds through independent brokers. To obtain a competitive advantage over other mutual fund companies, Putnam now provides brochures and prospectuses of their mutual funds to brokers within 24 hours of request.

The Next Sources of Competitive Advantage?

Managers are always looking for new ways in which to distinguish their firms from the competition. Currently, two new trends in business appear to be offering firms such an advantage: (*a*) the use of environmentally friendly processes and environmentally friendly products and (*b*) the use of information.

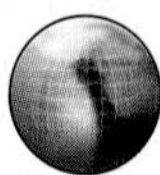

Environmentally Friendly Processes and Products As consumers become more aware of the fragility of the environment, they are increasingly turning towards products that are safe for the environment. Ford now advertises an environmentally friendly automobile. The Body Shop, an international retail chain headquartered in England, sells various cosmetics and skin lotions that are made without harming the environment. Veryfine Products of Westford, Massachusetts, which produces a line of fruit drinks, promotes its concern for the environment by noting that it uses a very high percentage of recycled products in its containers and packaging.

The Use of Information Although the term "Information Age" was initially used when the first mass-produced computers were introduced, it wasn't until recently that we actually did enter the information age. This is due in large part to advances in information technology that now allow large quantities of data to be transmitted and stored accurately, and, equally important, inexpensively. As a result, companies are looking to use information in different ways to obtain a competitive advantage in the marketplace. For example, GE Medical Systems and EMC Corporation both sell high-performance products with built-in systems that automatically "call home" when failures occur, or even potential failures are anticipated. Many times these problems or anticipated problems are repaired remotely, with little or no interruption in product performance. Feedback on existing products can also take the form of the "voice of the customer," as explained in the next chapter. In some instances this information is collected automatically, or through *service guarantees,* which are explained in detail in Chapter 7.

Developing an Operations Strategy from Competitive Priorities

Factory Focus and Trade-Offs

The notion of factory focus and trade-offs was central to the concept of operations strategy during the late 1960s and early 1970s. The underlying logic was that a factory could not excel simultaneously on all four competitive priorities. Consequently, management had to decide which priorities were critical to the firm's success, and then concentrate or focus the resources of the firm on those particular characteristics. For firms with very large manufacturing facilities, Skinner suggested the creation of a plant-within-a-plant (PWP) concept, in which different locations within the facility would be allocated to different product lines, each with their own competitive priority. Even the workers, under the PWP concept, would be separated in order to minimize the confusion associated with shifting from one type of priority to another.[8]

For example, if a company wanted to focus on speed of delivery, then it could not be very flexible in terms of its ability to offer a wide range of products. As an example, McDonald's provides very fast service but offers a very limited menu of highly standardized products; in contrast, Wendy's makes your request to order but takes longer to deliver. Similarly, a low-cost priority was not seen to be compatible with either speed of delivery or flexibility. High quality also was viewed as a trade-off to low cost.

The need for focus has been recognized in other service operations as well. Hotel chains such as Marriott and Holiday Inn have segmented the hotel industry and now offer a wide variety of products, each focused on a different market segment. For example, within the Marriott group there is Fairfield Inns for economy-minded customers; Marriott Hotels and Resorts for conferences and for customers wanting full-service hotels; Residence Inns for customers wanting more than just a hotel room; and Marriott Courtyards for those wanting certain hotel conveniences such as meals, but who are still concerned about price. Skinner's PWP concept is now also being applied to the health care industry where "hospitals-within-hospitals" allow specialized firms to focus only on specific ailments. For example, Intensiva accepts only long-term acute patients and operates independently within the facilities of St. Francis Hospital in Beech Grove, Indiana. Because it specializes in only one area (intensive care), Intensiva's operating costs are 50 percent lower than those of a typical intensive care ward.[9]

Other examples of focused operations in the service sector include BankBoston's Private Bank Division, which focuses on providing a full line of banking services to wealthy customers ("A bank within a bank," which is again not unlike Skinner's plant-within-a-plant concept), and Shouldice Hospital in Toronto, Canada, which performs only one type of hernia operation. The benefits of a focused operation can be readily demonstrated at Shouldice Hospital, whose very unusual product is a "hernia vacation." Patients are admitted to a mansionlike hospital in a beautiful setting outside Toronto. Every detail of the hospital's operations is focused on providing high-quality hernia care and a congenial, restful atmosphere. Patients mingle, mix, and generally relax, enjoying the experience so much that the annual reunion dinner is oversubscribed. This highly focused care permits Shouldice to keep operating costs low while maintaining high quality, both in terms of medical care and patient service. However, by becoming a specialist facility, Shouldice does not have the capabilities to perform other types of medical treatments.

Questioning the Trade-Offs

With the world becoming a single global village, there has emerged a group of companies that have adopted an international perspective toward both manufacturing and marketing.

[8]C. W. Skinner, "The Focused Factory," *Harvard Business Review* 52, no. 3 (May–June 1974), pp. 113–22.

[9]Keith Hammonds and Nicole Harris, "Medical Lessons from the Big Mac," *Business Week,* February 10, 1997, pp. 94–98.

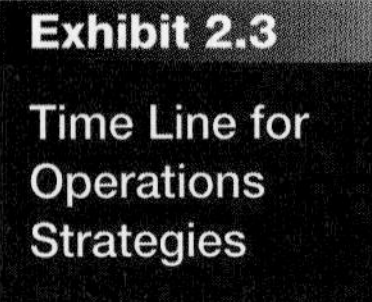
Exhibit 2.3
Time Line for Operations Strategies

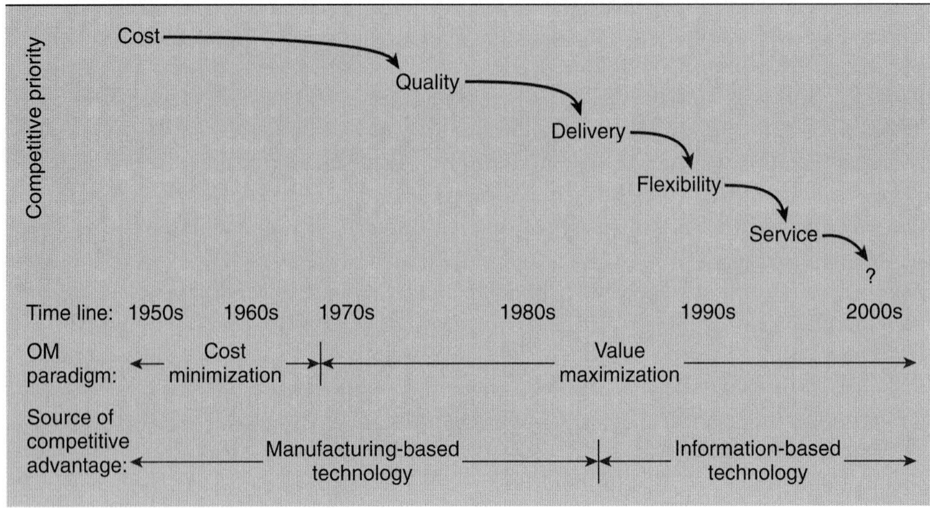

Within this global arena, competition is significantly more intense, due to both the greater number of "players" and the tremendous profit opportunities that exist.

Those companies that have excelled on this global level often have been referred to as *world-class operations.* Events in the world marketplace during the 1970s and 1980s, in terms of the growing intensity in competition, forced these companies to reexamine the concept of operations strategy, especially in terms of the so-called necessary trade-offs. Managers began to realize that they didn't have to make trade-offs to the same extent that they had previously thought. What emerged instead was a realization of the need to establish a hierarchy among the different priorities, as dictated by the marketplace. Exhibit 2.3 presents the sequence in which these priorities were introduced over time.

Specifically, in the late 1960s and early 1970s, cost was the primary concern, a holdover from the philosophy of the 1950s that manufacturing's only objective was to minimize production costs. However, as more and more companies began to produce low-cost products, the need became apparent to develop other ways to differentiate themselves from their competitors. The priority thus shifted to quality. Companies at this time obtained a competitive advantage by producing high-quality products, which allowed them to charge more—although price still was a factor in the consumer's buying decision. However, competition again soon caught up, and everyone was offering high-quality products that were reasonably priced.

Companies, in looking to obtain another competitive advantage in the marketplace, turned to speed and reliability of delivery as a means of differentiating themselves from the rest of the pack. Now the ante into the "game" was high-quality products that were reasonably priced and that could be delivered quickly and reliably to the customer.

In the 1980s, George Stalk Jr., a leading management "guru," as previously noted, identified speed of delivery as a major factor in determining the success of a company.[10] Companies therefore concentrated their resources on reducing product lead times with very dramatic results. Products that once took weeks or months to deliver were now being shipped within hours or days of the receipt of an order.

[10]George Stalk Jr., "Time—The Next Source of Competitive Advantage," *Harvard Business Review,* July–August 1988, pp. 41–51.

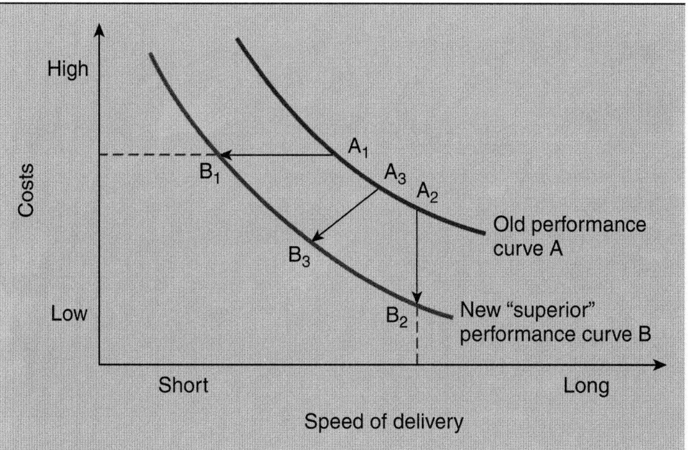

Exhibit 2.4
Example of Trade-Offs on Superior Performance Curves

Eventually, the competition again caught up and the more aggressive firms looked for still another means to obtain a competitive advantage. This time flexibility was selected, as measured in terms of the firm's ability to produce customized products. Now the marketplace dictated that for firms to be successful, they had to produce reasonably priced, customized products of high quality that could be quickly delivered to the customer.

A good example of a firm that has accomplished this is the National Bicycle Industrial Company in Japan.[11] (See the OM in Practice box on Japan's Personalized Bike Production.)

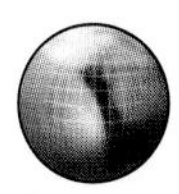

As the "rules" for operations strategy shifted from that of primarily reducing costs to that of including quality, speed of delivery, flexibility, and service, the strategy for the operations management function also has shifted. The strategy of minimizing production costs has been replaced with that of maximizing the value added.

This emphasis on being competitive on more than one dimension might lead to the conclusion that there are no longer any trade-offs. This is not the case. As Wickham Skinner said at a breakfast meeting of the Boston P/OM Pancake Society in April 1995, "There will always be trade-offs." Today, however, those trade-offs occur on what can be described as a superior performance curve, as shown in Exhibit 2.4.

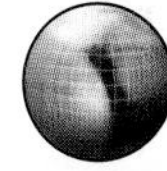

In moving to a higher performance curve, managers are no longer only concerned with trade-offs, which take place when one moves along an established curve such as going from point A_1 to point A_2 on curve A in Exhibit 2.4. Instead, the same speed of delivery can be provided, but at a lower cost, as shown in going from point A_2 to point B_2. Another approach is to improve the speed of delivery while maintaining the same cost, as seen in going from point A_1 to point B_1. A third alternative is to both improve the speed of delivery and reduce cost, as seen in going from point A_3 to point B_3. The important issue here is that in all three examples, the value to the customer is increased significantly, which is the primary purpose for moving to the superior performance curve.

order-qualifiers

Minimum characteristics of a firm or its products to be considered as a source of purchase.

order-winners

Characteristics of a firm that distinguish it from its competition so that it is selected as the source of purchase.

Order-Qualifiers and Order-Winners

Terry Hill of the London Business School has developed the strategic concept of **order-qualifiers** and **order-winners.**[12] Order-qualifiers can be defined as the minimum elements

[11]Susan Moffat, "Japan's New Personalized Production," *Fortune,* October 22, 1990, pp. 132–35.

[12]T. Hill, *Manufacturing Strategy: Text and Cases,* 3rd ed. (Burr Ridge, IL: Irwin/McGraw-Hill, 2000).

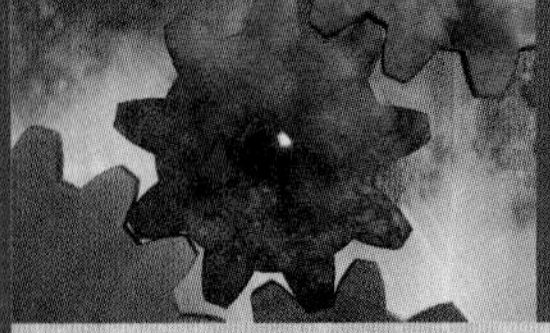

Operations Management in Practice

JAPAN'S PERSONALIZED BIKE PRODUCTION

Customers are custom-fitted in the retail store with options for 11,231,862 possible variations.

Does your bike fit you to a "t"? Would you like one that does? If you are willing to pay 20 to 30 percent more than you would pay for a mass-produced bike, you can get a Panasonic bike manufactured to exactly match your size, weight, and color preference. You can even get your bike within three weeks of your order (only two weeks if you visit Japan). This is accomplished via a process called the Panasonic Individual Customer System (PICS), which skillfully employs computers, robots, and a small factory workforce to make one-of-a-kind models at the National Bicycle Industrial Company factory in Kokubu, Japan.

The National Bicycle Industrial Company (NBIC), a subsidiary of electronics giant Matsushita, began making the bikes under the Panasonic brand in 1987. With the introduction of its personalized order system (POS) for the Japanese market (PICS was developed for overseas sales), the firm gained international attention as a classic example of mass customization—producing products to order in lot sizes of one.

The factory itself has 21 employees and a computer-aided design (CAD) system, and is capable of producing any of 8 million variations on 18 models of racing, road, and mountain bikes in 199 color patterns for virtually any size person.

The PIC system works in the following way. A customer visits a local Panasonic bicycle store and is measured

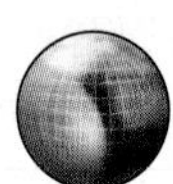

or characteristics that a firm or its products must have in order to even be considered as a potential supplier or source. In Europe, for example, the vast majority of companies today require that their vendors be ISO-9000 certified. (This certification ensures that a firm has documented all of its processes.) Thus, ISO-9000 certification is an order-qualifier in Europe. In contrast, most companies in the United States at this time are not ISO-9000 certified (those firms that are certified in the United States have done so primarily to do business in Europe). As a consequence, ISO-9000-certified companies in the United States use their certification as an order-winner (that is, ISO-9000 certification distinguishes them as being better than their competition).

Basically, when very few firms offer a specific characteristic, such as high quality, customization, or outstanding service, that characteristic can be defined as an order-winner. However, over time, as more and more firms begin to offer that same enhancement, the order-winner becomes an order-qualifier. In other words, it becomes the minimum acceptable level for all competitors. As a result, the customer uses some other new enhancement or characteristic to make the final purchase. The shift of a product characteristic from being an order-winner to an order-qualifier is shown in Exhibit 2.5. We have arbitrarily selected 50 percent to represent the point at which an order-winner becomes an order-qualifier, as that is when the majority of firms provide a particular enhancement.

on a special frame. The storeowner then faxes the specifications to the master control room at the factory. There an operator punches the specs into a minicomputer, which automatically creates a unique blueprint and produces a bar code. (The CAD blueprint takes about three minutes as opposed to three hours required by company draftspeople prior to computerization.) The bar code is then attached to metal tubes and gears that ultimately become the customer's personal bike. At various stages in the process, line workers access the customer's requirement using the bar code label and a scanner. This information, displayed on a CRT terminal at each station, is fed directly to the computer-controlled machines that are part of a local area computer network. At each step of production, a computer reading the code knows that each part belongs to a specific bike, and tells a robot where to weld or tells a painter which pattern to follow.

Despite the use of computers and robots, the process is not highly automated. Gears are hand-wired, assembly is manual, and the customer's name is silk-screened by hand with the touch of an artisan. The entire manufacturing and assembly time required to complete a single bike is 150 minutes, and the factory can make about 60 a day. NBIC's mass-production factory (which makes 90 percent of its annual production) can make a standard model in 90 minutes. One might ask why a customer must wait two to three weeks given that it takes less than three hours to make a custom model. According to the general manager of sales, "We could have made the time shorter, but we want people to feel excited about waiting for something special."

To provide a more personal touch to mass customization, the factory is given the responsibility to communicate directly with the customer. Immediately after the factory receives the customer's order, a personalized computer-generated drawing of the bicycle is mailed with a note thanking the customer for choosing the bike. This is followed up with a second personal note, three months later, inquiring about the customer's satisfaction with the bicycle. Finally, a "bicycle birthday card" is sent to commemorate the first anniversary of the bicycle.

NBIC is now contemplating extending the Panasonic system to all of its bicycle production, while Matsushita is considering applying the concept to industrial machinery.

Source: Surech Kotha, "The National Bicycle Industrial Company: Implementing a Strategy of Mass-Customization," case study from the International University of Japan, 1993; and Susan Moffat. "Japan's New Personalized Production," *Fortune,* October 22, 1990, pp. 132–35.

Exhibit 2.5

Distinguishing between Order-Qualifiers and Order-Winners

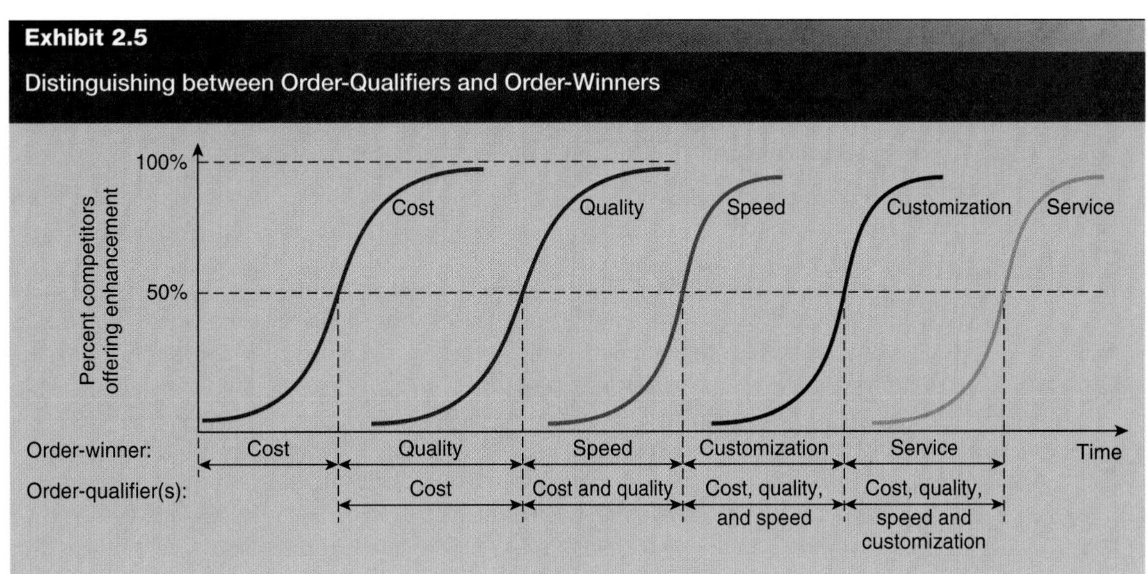

Focusing on Core Capabilities

core capabilities

Specific strengths that allow a company to achieve its competitive priorities.

In order to successfully implement an operations strategy, be it within a manufacturing firm or within a service, certain **core capabilities** must be identified. These core capabilities allow the firm to establish its competitive priorities in the marketplace. Core capabilities can thus be defined as that skill or set of skills that the operations management function has developed that allows the firm to differentiate itself from its competitors. Similar core capabilities need to be identified in the other functional areas too, and each of these functional capabilities should be aligned to meet the overall goals of the firm. For example, in the opening vignette to this chapter, Dell Computer has developed a core capability for producing these new products both quickly and in a wide variety to meet the specific needs of individual customers.

In order to focus on these core capabilities, firms, both in manufacturing and services, have begun to divest themselves of those activities that are not considered to be critical to their success. In manufacturing, more and more components and subassemblies that were previously built in-house are now being subcontracted or outsourced to suppliers. As a result, the material cost in most manufacturing companies, as a percentage of total manufacturing costs, has substantially increased in recent years. On the other hand, the labor cost, as a percentage, has been drastically reduced, often to less than 5 percent of total costs.

This focus on core capabilities also has impacted services. More and more service operations are now subcontracting out ancillary support services that were previously provided in-house. Again, this strategy has allowed these services to concentrate on improving their core capabilities. For example, many colleges and universities now subcontract their food service operations to firms such as Sodexho and their bookstore operations to retailers such as Barnes and Noble. As another example, ServiceMaster has built a very successful business providing housekeeping services to hospitals and office buildings at substantial savings to these businesses. In many instances, the companies that have subcontracted these support services have discovered that the subcontractors can perform them better and at a lower cost than when they were done internally. This focus on core capabilities further supports the concept of a *value chain*. Here each company focuses on its core capabilities, thereby allowing it to maximize its value contribution to the end product that is provided to the customer. (A word of caution, however. Casually subcontracting a function that is not viewed as a core competency may result in losing knowledgeable people who know how the broader system operates and who can deal with unexpected emergencies that might shut down a core activity.)

Integration of Manufacturing and Services

Many firms are now looking to integrated and user-friendly service as a means of obtaining a competitive advantage in the marketplace. In so doing they are recognizing the need to align and integrate the products that are being offered. This is true for both manufacturing and service operations.

For example, Ritz-Carlton, a hotel chain that focuses on the top 5 percent of the hotel market, has operators answering its 800 reservation number instead of having a more efficient menu-driven system. Although the menu-driven system is more cost efficient, management at the Ritz knows that its high-income customers will not waste their time with such a system. Similarly, CTI-Cryogenics in Mansfield, Massachusetts, a leading producer of vacuum pumps that are critical items in the manufacture of computer chips, now has a "GUTS" program (Guaranteed Up-Time Service). When a pump fails, it impacts the

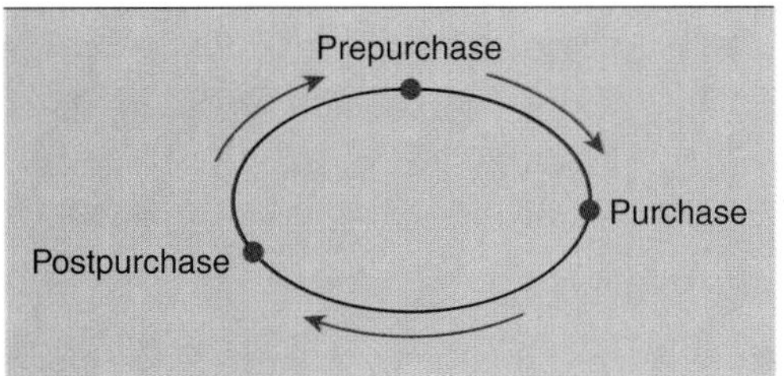

Exhibit 2.6
The Customer's Activity Cycle

production of a computer chip fabrication facility that typically costs more than a billion dollars. A call to the 800 number, therefore, puts the customer in contact with an engineer who diagnoses the problem and ships out the required parts within 24 hours. This high level of service allows the computer fabrication plant to resume operations as quickly as possible, thereby minimizing downtime.

By integrating goods and services into a total package, companies are better able to address the overall needs of their customers.

The Customer's Activity Cycle (CAC)

To provide a framework for properly aligning the goods and services that a firm offers, Sandra Vandermerwe introduced the concept of the customer's activity cycle (CAC). As seen in Exhibit 2.6, there are three major components of the CAC: (*a*) the prepurchase activities, (*b*) the purchase activities, and (*c*) the postpurchase activities.[13]

The prepurchase activities focus on being responsive to customer inquiries and the ability to demonstrate technical expertise. The purchase activities center around the actual sale and delivery of the product and collecting payment. The postpurchase activities include after-sales support services and product warranties.

The better a firm can identify and understand each of the elements that take place within these three components, the greater the competitive advantage it has in the marketplace. In other words, the larger the portion of the customer's activity cycle that a company is involved with, the stronger its position in the marketplace. As part of the CAC concept, Vandermerwe suggests that firms should shift their emphasis from selling only products to their customers (that is, goods) to assisting their customers in solving their problems (that is, services).

For example, Hendrix Voeders is no longer in the business of providing only livestock feed to pig farmers in Holland. Today it also provides a wide range of services to these farmers, including consulting on pig breeding, nutrition management, delivery to the slaughterhouse, and distribution of pork products to retail outlets. As another illustration, SKF in Sweden no longer produces only ball bearings for its after-market or replacement business. It also provides advice to its customers on spare parts management, training, and installation, and suggests good preventive maintenance practices that will extend the life of the bearings.

These two companies exemplify an emerging trend among world-class businesses in that they demonstrate how manufacturing companies today are turning to service in order to obtain a competitive advantage in the marketplace. Where once manufacturing was considered to be totally separate from services, this is no longer the case. Both are essential and

[13]Sandra Vandermerwe, *From Tin Soldiers to Russian Dolls: Creating Added Value Through Services* (Oxford, England: Butterworth-Heinemann, 1993).

must be properly integrated and in alignment for a firm to succeed in today's highly competitive markets, especially at the international level.

Looking Toward Downstream Services

Richard Wise and Peter Baumgartner have identified four service strategies for manufacturing firms, each of which looks downstream from the production process.[14] The rationale here is that the market for product-related services is significantly much larger than it is for the products themselves. For example, in both the automobile and personal computer markets, the sales of product-related services are five times greater than the sales of the actual products themselves. In addition, the profit margins for these services are significantly larger than they are for their respective products.

The four ways Wise and Baumgartner have identified in which services can be used downstream are (*a*) embedded services, (*b*) comprehensive services, (*c*) integrated solutions, and (*d*) distribution control. Embedded services consist of specific functions that are part of the product itself. For example, Honeywell has developed an airplane information management system (AIMS) that provides a series of self-diagnostic tests on the airplane equipment. Previously, these tests were performed manually by airline mechanics. With comprehensive services, the manufactured product "is married" to additional services, which often facilitates the purchase itself. As an example, GE Capital provides many of the aspects of ownership and financing for the customers of GE's locomotive manufacturing operation.

Integrated solutions focus on combining product and services into a seamless offering that addresses a specific customer requirement. For example, Nokia, the Finnish manufacturer of cell phones, has used this approach with telephone carriers. With distribution control, the manufacturing firm goes downstream to assume responsibility for product distribution, which was previously performed by an independent firm. As an illustration, Coca Cola has taken over the bottling and distribution of Coke products, activities that were previously done by independent bottlers.

Additional Approaches for Integrating Manufacturing and Services

Demonstration of Knowledge and Expertise Dick Chase and Dave Garvin point out that firms can achieve a competitive advantage by demonstrating their technical knowledge and expertise in the production process.[15] By showing customers all of the various steps involved in the production process and how quality is ensured at each of these steps, customers obtain a certain level of comfort, especially when the specific details of the inner workings of the product itself are difficult to comprehend, as is often the case with sophisticated high-technology products.

In addition, as customers tour the manufacturing facility, they can be introduced to new products and options for existing ones. EMC Corp in Hopkinton, Massachusetts, a leading manufacturer of electronic storage equipment, understands these benefits of providing plant tours to potential as well as existing customers. As a result, they conduct more than 1,000 tours a year at their manufacturing facilities in Massachusetts. Visitors cannot help but be impressed by the great lengths EMC tests their products at each stage of the

[14]Richard Wise and Peter Baumgartner, "Go Downstream: The New Profit Imperative in Manufacturing," *Harvard Business Review* 77, no. 5 (September–October 1999), pp. 133–41.

[15]R. B. Chase and D. A. Garvin, "The Service Factory," *Harvard Business Review* 67, no. 4 (July–August 1989), pp. 61–69.

process, ensuring that a highly reliable product is shipped to its customers. Employees are also readily available throughout the plant to answer any questions. According to Gordon Nichols, a senior manager at EMC, the plant tours are very successful with more than 90 percent of the potential customers buying EMC products, and, often, they buy more than they had initially planned.

For similar reasons, the Foxboro Company, a leading producer of process control equipment, also encourages both customers and potential customers alike to visit their manufacturing facilities in Foxboro, Massachusetts. As visitors enter the manufacturing facility, they are greeted with a display showing the various awards that Foxboro has won through the years, including the Shingo Prize, the Massachusetts' Quality Award, and *Industry Week*'s Plant of the Year Award. During the tours of the manufacturing processes, employees will often take time from their work to talk to visitors about specific projects they have worked on to improve the quality of the product and/or to make the processes more efficient. These employee presentations again reinforce knowledge and skill about the processes and products.

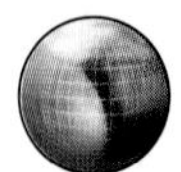

The benefits of demonstrating knowledge and expertise are not limited to only high-technology products. Green Giant of Minneapolis, Minnesota, which produces a wide variety of high-quality canned and frozen-food products, had difficulty penetrating the Japanese markets with their products. Only after they invited Japanese food distributors to visit their production facilities in Minnesota, where they were able to show the quality of both their processes and the resulting products, were they able to succeed in doing business in Japan.[16]

Customer Training Some manufacturers have recognized the benefits of providing extensive customer training in the use of their products. By providing such training, their customers quickly become familiar with how the products are used. Such training can be viewed as a competitive advantage in that it acts as a barrier to entry for similar products that are offered by competitors. For example, why would a firm invest time and money to train workers in how to use another product if they are currently satisfied with the product they are currently using, and have already been trained on that product? FedEx provides a good example of a service firm that does an outstanding job of this. Even if a customer ships only a few packages a day, FedEx will provide that customer with a dedicated computer that is directly linked into the FedEx system and also will teach the customer how to use it. This is one of the major reasons FedEx's competitors have significant difficulty in convincing FedEx's customers to switch.

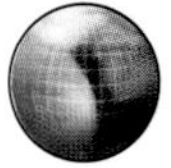

As another illustration, Le Grand, which is located in Limoges, France, produces electrical components such as outlets, switches, and junction boxes, all of which are considered to be commodity-type products. To provide itself with a competitive advantage, Le Grand has constructed a large training facility in Limoges where architects and electrical contractors are invited to view its wide variety of products and also to learn how to install them in various settings. To accomplish this, the training facility has set up different rooms to demonstrate how the various components should be installed. These rooms include a kitchen, a bathroom, and a bedroom in a private residence, as well as a patient's room in a hospital.

The Foxboro Company, which was mentioned previously, also uses training to distance itself from its competition. Before its process control products are delivered, customers are invited to Foxboro's manufacturing facility, where their equipment is set up and they learn how to use it under the guidance of Foxboro instructors. This is one of the reasons Foxboro experiences a very high percentage of repeat business from existing customers.

---

[16] J. Ameson, "When in Rome," *Northwestern Airlines World Traveler,* March 1993.

Conclusion

The concept of operations strategy plays an important role in determining the overall long-term success of an organization. Developing an operations strategy means looking to new ways to add value for the customer in the goods and services that the firm produces and delivers. Value can have many meanings. Managers must therefore align the operations strategy of their firm with the strategies of other functional areas and with the firm's overall business strategy.

The combination of the globalization of business coupled with advances in technology have created a hyper-competitive environment in which managers must constantly be looking for new and innovative strategies to stay ahead of the competition. In order to properly implement these strategies, managers need to clearly understand the core capabilities of their firm and focus their resources on maintaining and improving these capabilities.

Successful firms today are looking to develop strategies that integrate goods and services into a single product offering or "bundle of benefits," which attempts to solve problems for customers rather than just selling them products.

Key Terms

- business strategies p. 28
  - low-cost p. 28
  - market segmentation p. 28
  - product differentiation p. 29
- competitive priorities p. 29
  - cost p. 33
  - delivery p. 33
  - flexibility p. 33
  - quality p. 33
  - service p. 33
- competitiveness p. 29
- core capabilities p. 42
- corporate strategy p. 28
- functional strategy p. 29
- mass customization p. 35
- newly industrialized countries (NIC) p. 32
- operations strategy p. 29
- order-qualifiers p. 39
- order-winners p. 39
- planning and control p. 30
- strategic business unit (SBU) p. 28
- strategic planning p. 30
- tactical planning p. 30

Review and Discussion Questions

1. What is meant by competitiveness?
2. Identify the different types of competitive priorities. How has their relationship to each other changed over the years?
3. For each of the different competitive priorities, describe the unique characteristics of the market niche with which it is most compatible.
4. Describe the difference between order-qualifiers and order-winners. What is the relationship between the two over time?
5. Explain the concept of the core capabilities within an organization.
6. How does understanding a customer's activity cycle allow a firm to achieve a competitive advantage in the marketplace?
7. In your opinion, do business schools have competitive priorities?
8. Why does the "proper" operations strategy keep changing for companies that are world-class competitors?
9. What is meant by the expression "manufacturing is entering the information age"?
10. Describe the customer's activity cycle involved in taking a transcontinental flight. What could be done to facilitate the process for the customer?

11. What kind of information do you think would add value to the following goods and services?
    a. Used car.
    b. Hotel in a foreign city.
    c. Cruise ship.
    d. College.
12. Describe the type of service that would make the following items more attractive to purchase.
    a. Suit of clothes.
    b. Used car.
    c. Personal computer.
    d. Fruits and vegetables.
13. For each of the following, what, in your opinion are the order-qualifiers and order-winners?
    a. Selecting an airline to fly on.
    b. Deciding which supermarket to buy groceries.
    c. Buying an automobile.
    d. Picking a restaurant for Saturday night.

Internet Exercise

Go to the McGraw-Hill homepage at www.mhhe.com/pom and take several company tours for the purpose of describing some of their competitive priorities. For each tour identify the company, the product it makes, and its competitive priorities.

Bibliography

Ameson, J. "When in Rome." *Northwestern Airlines World Traveler,* March 1993.

Chase, R. B., and D. A. Garvin. (1989). "The Service Factory." *Harvard Business Review,* 67, no. 4 (July–August 1989), pp. 61–69.

Davidow, W. H., and B. Uttal. "Service Companies: Focus or Falter." *Harvard Business Review* 67, no. 4 (July–August 1989), pp. 77–85.

Davis, Stan, and Christopher Meyer. *Blur: The Speed of Change in the Connected Economy.* New York: Ernst & Young Center for Business Innovation, Warner Books, 1998.

Garvin, D. A. *Operations Strategy: Text and Cases.* Englewood Cliffs, NJ: Prentice Hall, 1992.

Hammonds, Keith, and Nicole Harris. "Medical Lessons from the Big Mac." *Business Week,* February 10, 1997, pp. 94–98.

Hart, C. W. L. "The Power of the Unconditional Service Guarantees." *Harvard Business Review* 66, no. 4 (July–August 1988), pp. 56–62.

Hayes, Robert, and Gary Pisano. "Beyond World Class: The New Manufacturing Strategy." *Harvard Business Review* 72, no. 1 (January–February 1994), pp. 77–86.

Henkoff, Ronald. "Keeping Motorola on a Roll." *Fortune,* April 18, 1994, pp. 67–78.

Hill, T. *Manufacturing Strategy: Text and Cases,* 3rd ed. Burr Ridge, IL: Irwin/McGraw-Hill, 2000, pp. 49–85.

Loveman, G. "The Globalization of Services: Four Strategies That Drive Growth Across Borders." *Proceedings of the 4th International Research Seminar in Service Management.* Agelonde-LaLonde les Maures, France, June 4–7, 1996.

Martin, Justin. "Give 'Em Exactly What They Want." *Fortune,* November 10, 1997, pp. 238–85.

Moffat, Susan. "Japan's New Personalized Production." *Fortune,* October 22, 1990, pp. 132–35.

Muller, Joann, "Attention Kmart: Find a Niche," *Business Week,* February 4, 2002, p. 72.

Naisbitt, J., and P. Aburdene. *Megatrends 2000.* New York: William Morrow Co., 1990.

Narayandas, Das and V. Kasturi Rangan, "Dell Computer Corporation," Harvard Business School case No. 9-596-058, revised September 1996.

Normann, Richard, and Rafael Ramirez. "From Value Chain to Value Constellation: Designing Interactive Strategy." *Harvard Business Review* 71, no. 3 (July–August 1993), pp. 65–77.

Porter, M. *Competitive Strategy: Techniques for Analyzing Industries and Competitors*. New York: The Free Press, 1980.

Porter, Michael E., and Claas van der Linde. "Green and Competitive: Ending the Stalemate." *Harvard Business Review* 73, no. 5 (September–October 1995), pp. 120–34.

Serwer, Andy, "Dell Does Domination," *Fortune,* January 21, 2002, pp. 71–75.

Shah, Jennifer Baljko, "Dell Writes The Book On Efficiency—Processes Focus On Understanding Where Supply, Demand Diverge," *Ebn,* December 17, 2001, p. 32.

Skinner, C. Wickham. "Manufacturing—The Missing Link in Corporate Strategy." *Harvard Business Review* 47, no. 3 (May–June 1969), pp. 136–45.

———. "The Focused Factory." *Harvard Business Review* 52, no. 3 (May–June 1974), pp. 113–22.

Stalk, George, Jr. "Time—The Next Source of Competitive Advantage." *Harvard Business Review* 66, no. 4 (July–August 1988), pp. 41–51.

Vandermerwe, S. *From Tin Soldiers to Russian Dolls: Creating Added Value Through Services*. Oxford, England: Butterworth-Heinemann, 1993.

Wise, Richard, and Peter Baumgartner. (1999). "Go Downstream: The New Profit Imperative in Manufacturing." *Harvard Business Review* 77, no. 5 (September–October 1999), pp. 133–41.

Case

Motorola's Plantation, Florida, Factory

Motorola strives to measure every task performed by every one of its 120,000 employees, and calculates that it saved $1.5 billion by reducing defects and simplifying processes last year. While that figure is hard to verify, here's one that isn't: Since 1986, productivity (sales per employee) has increased 126 percent, even though Motorola has expanded its workforce.

What does the company do with all the money it saves? Some goes into R&D, some goes to workers as bonuses keyed to return on net assets, and some goes straight to the bottom line. But mostly, says corporate quality director Richard Buetow, "we've been giving it away at the marketplace." Motorola cut the price of cellular telephones 25 percent last year yet still raised its net profit margins.

At some Motorola factories quality is so high that they've stopped counting defects per million and started working on defects per *billion.* Overall, the company aims to reduce its error rate tenfold every two years and to increase the speed of its processes—cut its cycle time—tenfold every five years. At those levels, says Buetow, "you are hitting the limits of the capabilities of many of your machines." And those of your people as well.

Jerry Mysliwiec, manufacturing director at the Land Mobile Products factory in Plantation, Florida, begins each morning meeting of his factory supervisors with a singular request: "Okay, guys, tell me what records you broke, because if you didn't break records, you didn't improve."

Four years ago the Plantation factory wasn't breaking much of anying except the patience of its managers. It took Motorola as long as 10 days to turn out a finished radio. To decide which models to make, analysts crunched out elaborate forecasts of consumer demand, which were rarely on target. The company began building the radios at a "feeder plant" in Malaysia, where labor costs were low, then shipped them to Plantation for final assembly.

These days Plantation's Jedi line (named after the good guys in *Star Wars*) can make a specific radio—any one of more than 500 variations—for a specific customer in just two hours. They no longer rely on a forecast or a feeder plant. As the radios zip around the U-shaped assembly line, pallets marked with binary codes tell the robots, and the casually clad workers who monitor them, what to do. Plantation's most useful innovation: inventing a computer-controlled soldering process that eliminates the need for costly and time-consuming tool changes. Motorola is now converting the two-way radio plant in Malaysia, along with its other major operation in Ireland, into clones of Plantation's "focused flexible factory."

As part of its quality drive, Motorola has given new meaning to the phrase "team spirit." At the cellular equipment plant in Arlington Heights. Illinois, self-directed teams hire and fire their coworkers, help select their supervisors, and schedule their own work (in consultation with other teams). Last year, the factory's 1,003 workers also mustered into no fewer than 168 special teams dedicated to improving quality, cutting costs, and reducing cycle time.

Question What operations capabilities is Motorola using to compete?

Source: Ronald Henkoff, *Fortune,* April 18, 1994.

3

New Product and Service Development, and Process Selection

Chapter Objectives

- Illustrate the importance of the development of new products and services to a firm's competitiveness.
- Identify the various types of new products that are developed by companies.
- Introduce the new product design process and the concept of a product's life cycle.
- Demonstrate the necessity of concurrent product and process design as a new product or service is developed.
- Present a framework for understanding how new services are developed and introduced into the marketplace.

GILLETTE'S NEW WOMEN'S RAZOR IS A HIT!

Venus, Gillette's new women's wet shaving razor, was introduced into the marketplace in March 2001, and within six months, it had captured more than 45 percent of the women's wet razor market. The new Venus "shaving system" features many innovative characteristics that Gillette hopes will redefine women's shaving. Venus's development took advantage of more than 50 separate Gillette patents, including previous research efforts in developing men's razors, notably MACH3 and Sensor. In addition, there were new characteristics that were unique to Venus. Venus's design, which consists of three progressively aligned blades, provides a much closer and smoother shave than does the conventional twin blade razor. Other special features of the Venus include (*a*) soft cushions that help smooth the skin prior to the razor cutting the hair, (*b*) indicator strips that show the user when the lubricant is used up, (*c*) a long sleek handle that allows for an easier grip, and (*d*) a razor storage system that is designed to hang in the shower or bathtub.

Although Gillette used some of its existing processes to manufacture Venus, it also invested more than $300 million additional in research and development, as well as manufacturing. Another key factor that contributed to Venus's success was the ability of Gillette to team up with several of its suppliers to design and produce an exceptional package for displaying the Venus in retail outlets.

Over the years, Gillette has consistently demonstrated an ability to bring new products to market, thereby capturing and/or maintaining a significant market share within its industry. It accomplishes this by carefully coordinating and integrating product and process research and development, manufacturing, and its suppliers. The end result is the continuous successful introduction of new products in a timely and cost efficient manner. Gillette projects that its sales of female shaving products, in total, will reach $1 billion, driven in large part by Venus.

Sources:

http://www.cama.net/New/ad_budgets.html and http://www.packworld.com and then doing a search on the word "Gillette;"

Maremont, Mark, "Gillette's Venus Razor for Women to be Born Amid a Big Ad Drive," Wall Street Journal, Nov. 11, 2000.

Managerial Issues

A fact of life for most companies and their managers in today's highly competitive environment is that product life cycles are becoming shorter and shorter. In order to remain competitive and retain overall market share within their respective industries, managers therefore need to focus their resources on developing new products and bringing them to market more quickly and efficiently—and doing it on a continuous basis. From golf shoes to computers, new products often represent the majority of a company's sales. Thus, a failure to introduce new products will ultimately erode a firm's market share and its associated profits.

Why the Emphasis on New Goods and Services

Firms today are under more pressure than ever before to develop new goods and services and the processes necessary to produce and deliver them. Two of the major causes for this increased emphasis on developing new products are (*a*) increased competition and (*b*) advances in technology.

Increased Competition

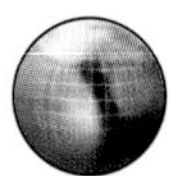

As the world becomes a single global economy, most firms have seen a significant increase in foreign competition in their respective markets. The reasons for this increase in foreign competition are many, including

- Advances in telecommunication technology (such as the Internet, which now provides connections to literally every corner of the world).
- A trend to lower trade barriers such as import duties and tariffs on foreign goods, and the creation of trade organizations such as NAFTA and the European Union.
- The faster speed at which goods can be transported.

The combination of increased competition and the greater availability of information has also resulted in more educated consumers who now expect new products to be introduced more frequently.

In such a highly competitive environment, the markets for these goods and services tend to reach their maturity much sooner than was previously the case. As a result, these products become commodities much sooner, and their profit margins therefore tend to erode more quickly.

Advances in Technology

Rapid advances in technology are causing many products to become obsolete more quickly. For example, microcomputer chip technology has significantly reduced the size of cellular phones while at the same time expanding their capabilities. Cell phones in Finland, for example, are now equipped with *smart cards,* which actually allow purchases to be transacted through the phone, the cost of the purchase being charged to the individual's credit card. If you want a drink from a vending machine, you just aim your phone at it and an infrared signal translates the necessary transaction information to the machine, and your drink is dispensed.

Computers are another good example of products that have been significantly impacted by advances in technology. The speeds and storage capacities of today's computers

The multi-information display panel on the Toyota Prius, Toyota's fuel-efficient gas/electric car, features a computerized display that includes real-time information on fuel consumption at various speeds.

far exceed anything imaginable 15 years ago, and this trend will most likely continue into the foreseeable future.

Technology also has impacted the processes by which goods and services are produced and delivered. Computer-aided design (CAD) and computer-aided manufacturing (CAM) systems now provide firms with the ability to significantly reduce the time between product development and production. As another example of how technology has affected the production process, the increased use of robotics on the factory floor not only reduces labor costs but also significantly increases product quality.

The Benefits of Introducing New Products Faster

Greater Market Share

Those firms with the ability to bring new products to market quickly have several advantages over their slower competitors. First, as illustrated in Exhibit 3.1A, early market entrants take market share, which is easier to accomplish when there is no competition, as compared to trying to take market share away from an entrenched competitor. This is especially true for revolutionary products (which are discussed shortly) for which there are no alternatives. For example, in the semiconductor industry, history has shown that the first two firms to enter a market with a new product tend to capture the vast majority of the market share for those products. Similarly, the rapid introduction of new automobiles is associated with gains in market share in that industry. Further evidence of the need to quickly bring new products to market is seen in the personal computer industry, where one manufacturer estimated a 50 to 75 percent loss in sales due to a six- to eight-month delay in bringing a new product to market.

Price Premiums

Second, when a firm is the first to bring a new product to market, it has little or no competition, and can therefore charge premium prices, as shown in Exhibit 3.1B, while the competition struggles to catch up. This combination of market share and price premiums translates into significant profits, as seen in Exhibit 3.1C (which, in turn, provide the necessary funding to develop and introduce the next round of new products). Thus, the faster a product is

Exhibit 3.1

The Impact of Speed to Market on Market Share, Profit Margins, and Profits

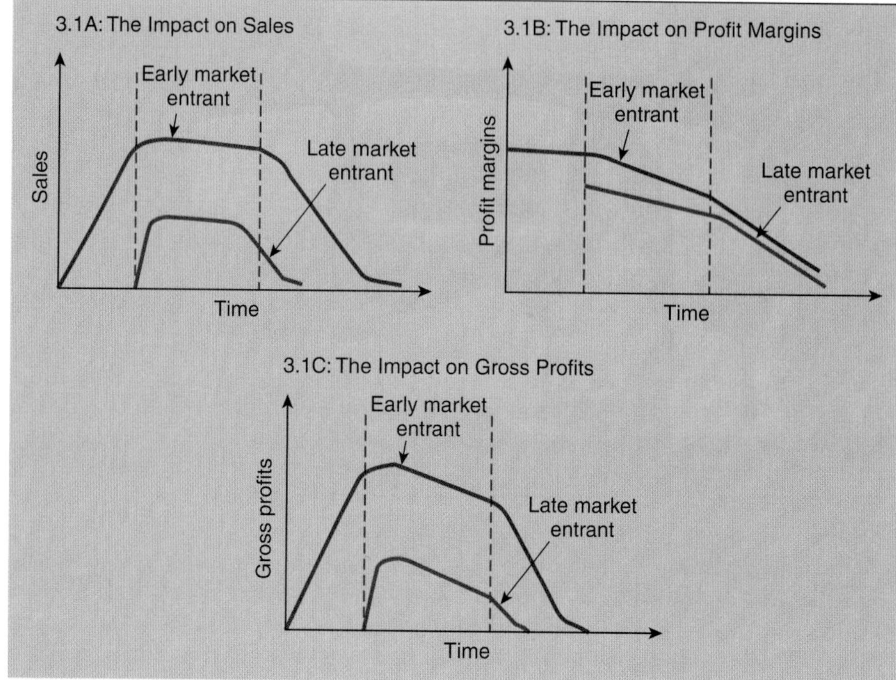

introduced into the market ahead of the competition, the more profitable that product is over its entire life cycle. In fact, products that are late to market have a much more negative impact on profitability than do cost overruns in either the product development phase or production.[1]

Quick Reaction to Competition

A company that has the resource capability to bring new products to market quickly is also in a much better position to respond quickly to a competitor's surprise announcement of the introduction of a new product. With such resources in hand, the firm can significantly limit the competitive disadvantage that is usually associated with being a market latecomer.

Set Industry Standards

For revolutionary products, the first firm into the market often has the luxury of setting the standards for that industry. This, in many cases, acts as a barrier to entry, further delaying competitors. Microsoft, first with DOS and then with Windows, provides good examples of this.

Categories of New Products

New products can be grouped according to the degree of innovation associated with them in comparison to existing products. Within this framework, we define three broad categories of new products: (*a*) incremental or derivative products, (*b*) next generation or platform

[1]S. Hamilton, "New-Product Development and Manufacturing Competitiveness: A Hewlett-Packard Perspective," in *Time-Based Competition: The Next Battleground in American Manufacturing,* ed. J. D. Blackburn, (Homewood, IL: Business One Irwin, 1991), chap. 8.

products, and (*c*) breakthrough or radical products. Each of these types of products places specific requirements upon the firm, with those that are the most innovative usually requiring the greatest commitment of resources. Equally important is the fact that each plays an important role in the long-term success of the firm.

Incremental or Derivative Products

On one end of the spectrum are those products that have the least amount of innovation. These are often referred to as *incremental* or *derivative products* and are typically hybrids or enhancements of existing products. These products are often cost-reduced versions of existing products or simply similar products with added features or functions. For example, the minor model-year changes made in the automobile industry can be seen as derivative or incremental products. Such new products require minimal changes in both product design and the manufacturing process. The resource requirements to develop these products are significantly less than those for products that break entirely new ground, because they tend to leverage off of existing products by extending their applicability. Products in this category are crucial to the firm in that they ensure continuing near-term cash flows. They also allow a firm to maintain market share in the short term by continually improving and refining existing product lines. As mentioned earlier, the yearly model changes in automobiles (when there are minor changes) provide a good example of this type of product.

Companies usually can bring incremental or derivative products to market quickly. However, this does not occur automatically. A minor design change in a product sometimes can significantly impact a firm's production process. Decisions on proceeding with such changes in a product therefore must be made with careful considerations. (This issue will be presented later in the chapter when we consider the interaction between product and process design.)

Next Generation or Platform Products

The middle of these three categories is referred to as *next generation* or *platform products,* which often represent new "system" solutions for the customer. They provide a broad base for a product family that can be leveraged over several years and, therefore, require significantly more resources than do derivative or incremental products. Intel's 286, 386, 486, Pentium, Pentium II, Pentium III, and Pentium 4 microprocessors provide an excellent example of products that fall into this category. Major model changeovers in the automobile industry, like the new Mustang from Ford, are also examples of next generation and platform products. Products in this category are the key to a company's continued growth in revenue in that they provide the necessary foundation for a series of evolutionary products, to which the firm's customers can then migrate over several years.

Breakthrough or Radical Products

At the other end of the new products spectrum are those products that are defined as *breakthrough* or *radical products.* The development of these products typically requires substantial product design and process change. When successfully introduced, this type of product often creates an entirely new product category, which becomes a new core business for the firm. In so doing, it creates an opportunity for it to be the first to enter an entirely new market. The first personal computer, the first laptop, and the first cellular phone are all good examples of breakthrough or radical products. In the development of these breakthrough products, management also must recognize that significant process development is required.

Products in this category are necessary for the long-term success of the firm. A combination of competitive, environmental, and technological forces often render existing products obsolete in the long term. Breakthrough products therefore enable the firm to succeed in its current markets, as well as in new markets, that will be created in the more distant future.

The New Product Development (NPD) Process

With the trend toward shorter product life cycles, the successful company must be able to (*a*) continuously generate new product ideas, (*b*) convert these ideas into reliable functional designs that are user-friendly, (*c*) ensure that these designs are readily producible, and (*d*) select the proper processes that are most compatible with the needs of the customer. In addition, as seen in Exhibit 3.2, all this must be accomplished within an increasingly shorter time frame.

new product development (NPD) process

The method by which new products evolve from conceptualization through engineering to manufacturing and marketing.

Designing new products and delivering them to the market quickly are the challenges facing manufacturers in every industry, from computer chips to potato chips. (See OM in Practice box on successful product design.) As a result, the more successful firms are focusing their resources on reducing the **new product development (NPD) process** to a fraction of what it once was.

The NPD process includes most of the functions within an organization. Marketing (which identifies the target market and forecasts demand for the product), research and development (which develops the technology and subsequently designs the product), and operations (which involves supplier selection and designing the manufacturing process) play the most prominent roles. However, finance, accounting, and information systems also provide important inputs into the process. As seen in Exhibit 3.3, the three major functions (that is, marketing, research and development, and operations) were traditionally conducted in sequence, with the next function usually not beginning its activities until after the previous function was completed. This was the major reason why the NPD process took so long.

concurrent engineering

The simultaneous and coordinated efforts of all functional areas which accelerates the time to market for new products.

In order to shorten the NPD process, many of these activities are now done in parallel or concurrently, as seen in the comparison in Exhibit 3.4. This coordinated effort from all of the functional areas is known as **concurrent engineering** (also referred to sometimes as concurrent design or simultaneous engineering).

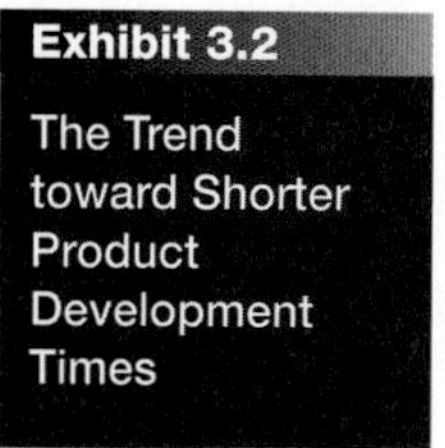

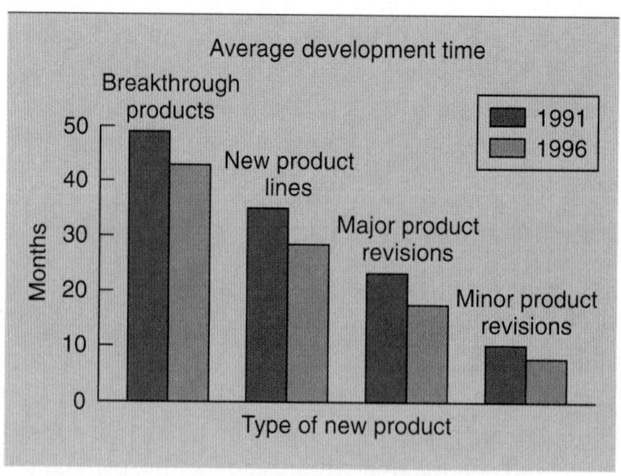

Note: From a survey of 200 U.S. companies.
Source: Data: Product Development & Management Association, *Business Week,* January 27, 1997, p. 6.

Exhibit 3.3

Sequential Flow of Activities in Product Design and Process Selection

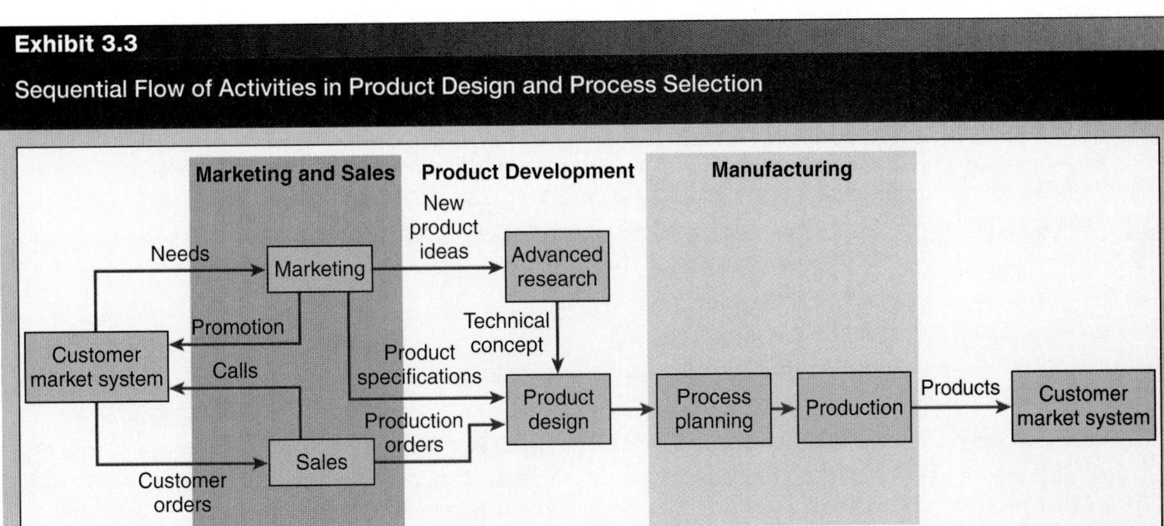

Source: Reprinted with the permission of The Free Press, an imprint of Simon & Schuster, from *Fast Cycle Time: How to Align Purpose, Strategy, and Structure for Speed* by Christopher Meyer. Copyright © 1993 by Christopher Meyer.

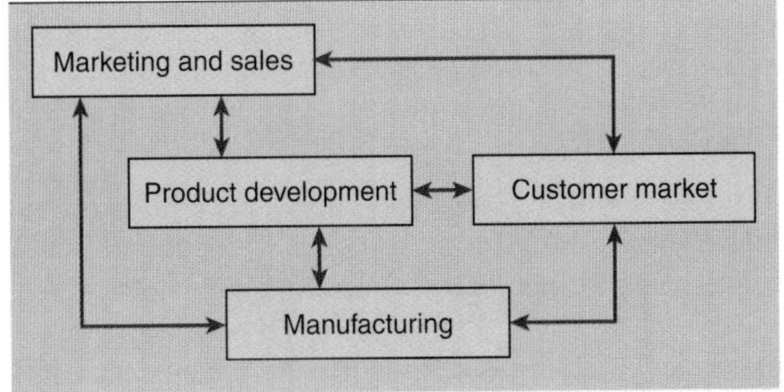

Exhibit 3.4

Concurrent Engineering Approach to NPD

Idea Generation

The NPD process begins with an idea for a new product, which can come from one of several sources. Most often it comes from marketing, which developed the idea through its interaction with customers and is often referred to as the **voice of the customer.** When a new product is identified in this manner, it is often called *market pull,* which refers to the primary force driving its development. In other words, the customer's identified need for the product in the market is "pulling" it from the firm. The other major method for generating new products is called *technology push.* In this case, the customers are not even aware of the need for the product; rather, it is developed by the company's R&D function and "pushed" through the company to the marketplace. Polaroid cameras, PCs, and 3M's Post-it notes provide good examples of new products that were the result of technology push.

voice of the customer

Customer feedback used in quality functional deployment process to determine product specifications.

It is important to note that products resulting from technology push also must have a market need in order for them to be successful. (Polaroid's instant movie system provides a good example of a technology push product for which there was no demand.) At the same time, while technology push products tend to be less common than market pull products, most breakthrough and radical products are the result of technology push.

Operations Management in Practice

FACTORS THAT CONTRIBUTE TO SUCCESSFUL PRODUCT DESIGNS

A recent review of successful product designs, ranging from razors and laptop computers to power tools and outdoor grills, identified several factors that these products and their manufacturers shared, including

- *Design from the outside in.* Make the customer's use of the product the focus of all product development.
- *Partner deeply.* Involve all of the relevant functional areas (e.g., marketing, engineering, purchasing, and manufacturing) early in the design process to assist in defining the new product. (This is often referred to as concurrent engineering.)
- *Partner widely.* With the emergence of the virtual enterprise, organizational boundaries are becoming unclear. Designers, therefore, must partner with all stakeholders—both internal and external.
- *Design the product upfront.* Match the right product to the right market niche. Upfront design analysis will eliminate faulty concepts early.
- *Get physical fast.* Use prototypes to visualize a concept and to obtain quick feedback from both users and managers.
- *Design for manufacturability.* Always design a product that will meet established quality, cost, and delivery parameters. Manufacturing issues are as important to success as ergonomics, aesthetics, and function.
- *Surprise the user.* Always build something extra into the product that will unexpectedly delight the customer. This creates customer loyalty and increases the chances of having a truly "hot" product.

Concept Development

Once a new product idea has been generated, it needs to be further developed and tested. This includes an initial design of the product (which is conducted by R&D) along with a detailed analysis of the market and the customers' requirements (which is conducted by marketing).

Businesses today recognize the need to involve their customers in all aspects of the design, production, and delivery of the goods and services that they offer. In the past, this was often not the case. However, with the trend toward increased competition, companies who do not listen to their customers on a continuous basis will find them taking their business to firms who will listen. While there are many approaches for obtaining information from customers, such as surveys and focus groups, we present one that links directly to the processes that produce these goods and services.

Quality Function Deployment

quality function deployment (QFD)

Process for translating customer requirements into a product's design.

A fairly rigorous method for translating the needs of the customer into the design specifications of a product is **quality function deployment (QFD).** This approach, which uses interfunctional teams from marketing, design engineering, and manufacturing, has been credited by Toyota Motor Corporation for reducing the costs on its cars by more than 60 percent by significantly shortening design times.

The QFD process begins with studying and listening to customers to determine the characteristics of a superior product. This customer feedback is often referred to as the *voice of the customer.* Through market research, the consumers' product needs and preferences are defined and broken down into categories called *customer attributes.* For example, an automobile manufacturer would like to improve the design of a car door. Through

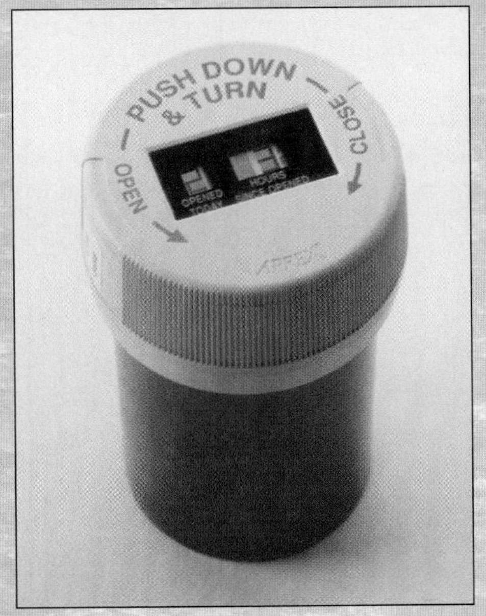

One example of a successful product design is the "smart" bottle cap. Forgetful and/or reluctant patients who don't take their medicine accumulate an estimated $25 billion in avoidable hospital bills annually and billions more in unnecessary nursing home admissions. To reduce these costs, Aprex Corp, located in Fremont, California, now offers a smart bottle cap. Built with a computer chip, alarm clock, and small display panel, the smart cap maintains a record of how frequently the bottle is opened, and is also equipped with a beeper to remind those patients who forget to take their medications. The addition of a modem reads the cap's memory and automatically transmits it to Aprex. If the number of times the bottle has been open is incorrect, the patient receives a "reminder call."

Source: B. Nussbaum, "Hot Products: Smart Design Is the Common Thread," *Business Week,* June 7, 1993; and Otis Port, "These Bottles Nag You to Take Your Medicine," *Business Week,* February 13, 1995.

customer surveys and interviews, it determines that two important customer attributes desired in a car door are that it "stays open on a hill" and is "easy to close from the outside." After the customer attributes are defined, they are weighted based on their relative importance to the customer. Next, the consumer is asked to compare and rate the company's products with those of its competitors. This process helps the company to determine those product characteristics that are important to the consumer and to evaluate its product in relation to others. The end result is a better understanding and focus on the product characteristics that require improvement.

Customer attribute information forms the basis for a matrix called the **house of quality** (see Exhibit 3.5). By building a house of quality matrix, the cross-functional QFD team can use customer feedback to make engineering, marketing, and design decisions. The matrix helps the team to translate customer attribute information into concrete operating or engineering goals. The important product characteristics and goals for improvement are jointly agreed on and detailed in the house. This process encourages the different departments to work closely together and results in a better understanding of one another's goals and issues. However, the most important benefit of the house of quality is that it helps the team to focus on building a product that satisfies customers.

house of quality

Part of the quality function deployment process that uses customer feedback for product design criteria.

Another important part of this phase of the NPD process includes building models of the new product (both physical models as well as computer-generated models), small-scale testing of the various elements and components of the new product, and conducting detailed investment and financial analyses over the product's anticipated life cycle. In addition, manufacturing and process development personnel should be involved in this phase as early as possible, in order to ensure optimal compatibility between the new product and the process by which it will be made. The first major hurdle in the NPD process (often referred to as program approval) takes place at the conclusion of this phase, when management has sufficient information to decide whether or not the project should go forward.

Exhibit 3.5

Completed House of Quality Matrix for a Car Door

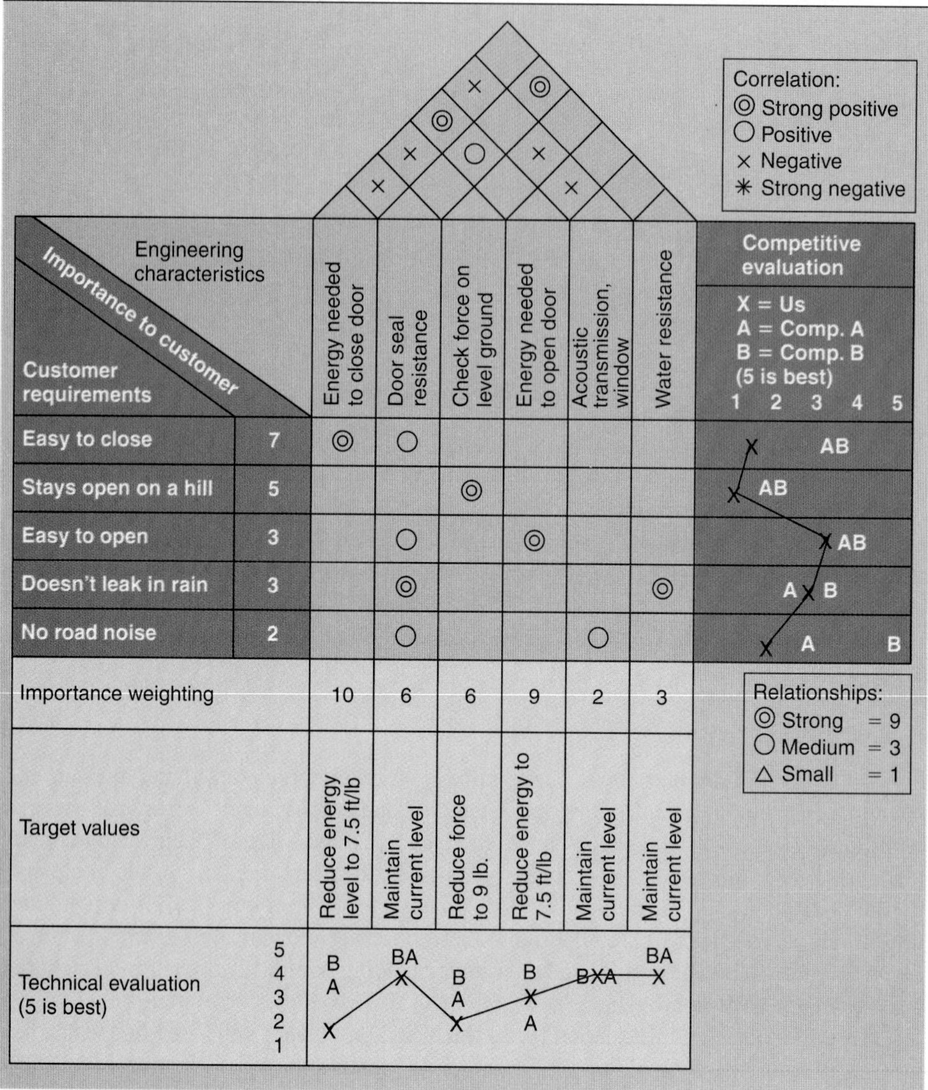

Design for Manufacturability (DFM)

In translating the functional product design into a manufacturable product, designers must consider many aspects. They can use a variety of methods and alternative materials to make a product. Material choices can be ferrous (iron and steel), aluminum, copper, brass, magnesium, zinc, tin, nickel, titanium, or several other metals. The nonmetals include plastic, wood, leather, rubber, carbon, ceramics, glass, gypsum, concrete, as well as several others. Further, all of these materials can be formed, cut, and shaped in many ways. There are extrusions, stampings, rolling, powder-metal, forgings, castings, injection molding, along with a very large selection of machining processes.

In designing for manufacturability, it is also desirable to keep the number of individual parts to a minimum. In electronics, manufacturers accomplish this by combining circuits that have been in different components into larger and larger integrated circuits. Not only does this increase the speed within the circuits, because electrons don't have to travel

Exhibit 3.6

Design Change to Reduce the Number of Parts in a Bracket

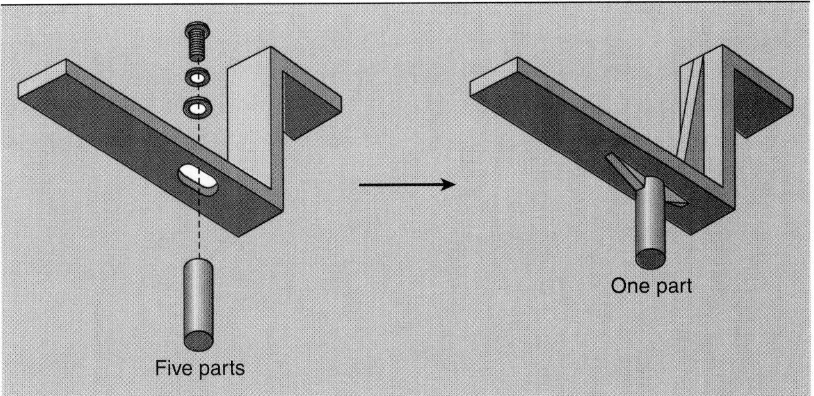

Source: Bart Huthwaite. "Managing at the Starting Line: How to Design Competitive Products," Workshop at the University of Southern California–Los Angeles, January 14, 1991, p. 7.

as far, but it also reduces the physical size and increases reliability. Reliability is increased by eliminating the many connections necessary when the circuits were in separate parts. Exhibit 3.6 shows how to reduce a simple bracket from five parts to one by focusing on the purpose of the part, the fabrication, and the assembly procedure used for its manufacture.

product's specifications

Output from the design activity that states all criteria for building a product.

The output of the product design activity is the **product's specifications.** These specifications provide the basis for production-related decisions such as the purchase of materials, selection of equipment, assignment of workers, and the size and layout of the production facility. Product specifications, while commonly thought of as blueprints or engineering drawings, often take other forms ranging from precise quantitative and qualitative statements to rather fluid guidelines. Physical products tend to have traditional blueprint specifications, while a service firm's design specifications tend to be more general.

While designing for manufacturability, we must still remember to design for the consumer. A basic rule in design is to

Be obvious. Design a product so that a user can look at it, understand it, and figure out how to use it—quickly, and without an instruction manual.

Process Selection in Manufacturing

Types of Processes

Manufacturing operations, as shown in Exhibit 3.7, are categorized into three broad types of process structures, each category depending to a large extent on the volume of item(s) to be produced. These three categories are often referred to as **project processes, intermittent processes,** and **line-flow processes.** While we identify three discrete categories, we should emphasize that the different types of manufacturing processes that exist should be viewed as a continuum, and that any one company may incorporate a combination of these processes in the manufacture of its products.

project process

Process that focuses on making one-of-a-kind products.

Project Process A project-oriented process usually involves the manufacture of a single, one-of-a-kind product. Examples here include the production of a movie and the erection of a skyscraper. Building a customized car to compete in the Indianapolis 500

Using project-management tools and techniques, Taco Bell was able to construct and open this restaurant in Compton, California in just two days compared to the usual 60 days that is typically required.

Exhibit 3.7
Types of Processes

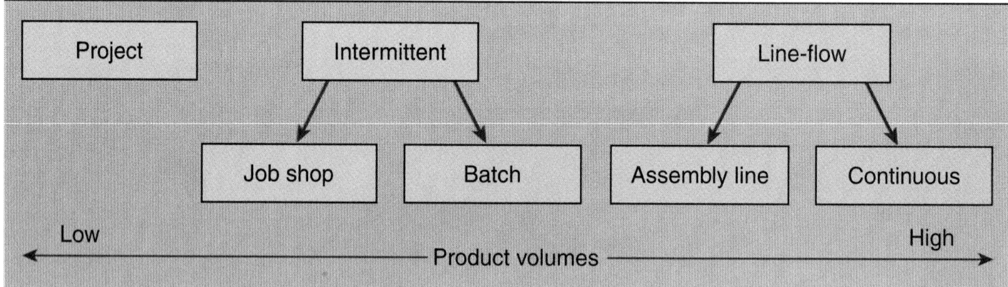

race is another good example. The major strength of a project-type process is that it is totally flexible to meet the individual needs of the customer. Projects are usually analyzed using network-solving techniques like those presented in the supplement to this chapter.

Variable costs in this category are comparatively very high. On the other hand, fixed costs are negligible or even nonexistent. (In the extreme case, when there is truly only one product to build, all costs are expensed and consequently there are no fixed costs.)

Highly skilled personnel are usually required for this type of process, as they often must work independently, with minimal guidance and supervision. In addition, workers here need to be well trained in a variety of tasks.

intermittent process

Process that produces products in small lot sizes.

Intermittent Process As shown in Exhibit 3.7, intermittent-type processes can be further subdivided into job shop and batch processes. We define a *job shop* as a process where a specific quantity of a product is produced only once. Numbered prints from a painting, programs for concerts, and T-shirts commemorating specific events are good examples of products made in a job shop process.

A batch process produces the same item again and again, usually in specified lot sizes. McDonald's is a good example of a batch process where hamburgers are cooked throughout the day in lot sizes of 12. The manufacture of shoes provides another example of a batch process. Here a batch consists of one size and style of shoe. (Some facilities, such as machine shops, are a combination of job shop and batch processes.)

Line-flow processes perform a variety of operations, ranging from filling and capping bottled beer at the Miller Brewing Company to assembling motorcycles at Kawasaki Motors Manufacturing Company.

Variable costs are still relatively high with intermittent processes, although they are usually lower than those of a project-type process. However, higher fixed costs are incurred with these processes. Similarly, worker skills remain high, though somewhat less than those required for projects.

line-flow process

Continuous process that produces high-volume, highly standardized products.

Line-Flow Process As with intermittent processes, line-flow processes also are frequently subdivided into two processes: assembly line and continuous. Assembly-line processes manufacture individual, discrete products. Examples here include electronic products such as VCRs and CD players, as well as automobiles and kitchen appliances. Continuous processes are exactly what their name implies—continuous, producing products that are not discrete. Petroleum refineries and chemical plants provide good examples of continuous processes.

Line-flows are characterized by high fixed costs and low variable costs, and are often viewed as the most efficient of the three types of processes. Labor skill, especially in assembly-line operations, is typically very low, as workers are required to learn only a very few simple operations. Line-flows are used for only the highest volumes of products, are very focused, and consequently are the most inflexible of the three processes.

The Product-Process Matrix

The relationship between the different types of processes and their respective volume requirements is often depicted on a product-process matrix, shown in Exhibit 3.8, which is adapted from the widely cited Hayes and Wheelwright product-process matrix. In this matrix, as volume increases and the product line narrows (the horizontal dimension), specialized equipment and standardized material flows (the vertical dimension) become economically feasible. This evolution in process structure is frequently related to the different stages of a product's life cycle (introduction, growth, maturity, and finally decline).

The industries listed within the matrix are presented as ideal types that have found their process niche. It certainly is possible for an industry member to choose another

Exhibit 3.8

Matching Major Stages of Product and Process Life Cycles

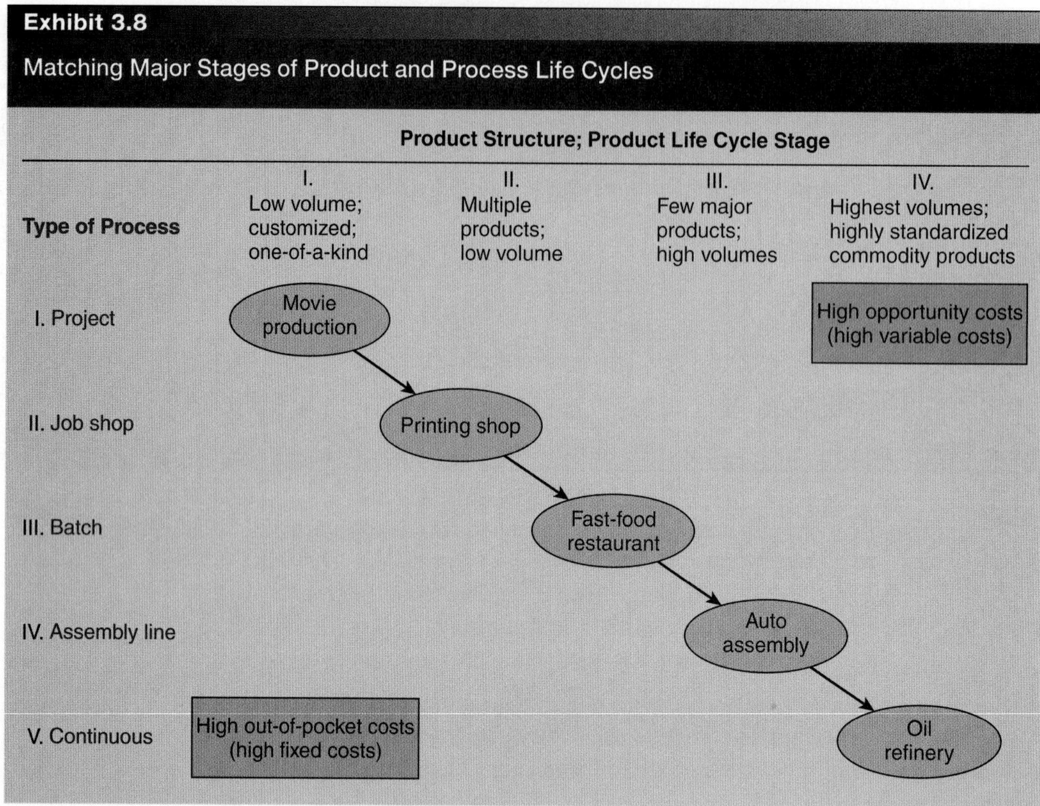

Source: Adapted from Robert Hayes and Steven Wheelwright, *Restoring Our Competitive Edge: Competing through Manufacturing* (New York: John Wiley & Sons, 1984). Copyright © 1984, John Wiley & Sons, Inc. This material is used by permission of John Wiley & Sons, Inc.

position on the matrix, however. For example, Volvo makes cars on movable pallets rather than on an assembly line. Thus, on the matrix it would be at the intersection of process stage II and product stage III. Volvo's production rate is lower than that of its competitors because it is giving up the speed and efficiency of the line. On the other hand, the Volvo system has more flexibility and better quality control than the classic automobile production line. Similar kinds of analysis can be carried out for other types of process-product options through the matrix.

In looking at Exhibit 3.8, it is interesting to note that companies that try to operate in either of the corners opposite the diagonal are doomed to failure. Companies in the upper right-hand corner reflect those firms that are too slow to react to changes in the marketplace. As a result, they try to compete in a market that requires high-volume, low-cost products with a project-type process that not only has very high variable costs, but also has very limited capacity. As a consequence, these firms incur very high opportunity costs from lost sales because high prices encourage customers to take their business elsewhere.

In the lower left-hand corner are companies that anticipated selling greater volumes of product than actually materialized. As a result, these firms have incurred very high out-of-pocket costs in the form of very high fixed costs, which are associated with the capital-intensive processes that were installed.

It may be a little easier to understand the logic of a product-process matrix if we divide it into its component parts. Part A of Exhibit 3.9 shows a traditional product life cycle from product conception through product termination. Part B relates the frequency of changes

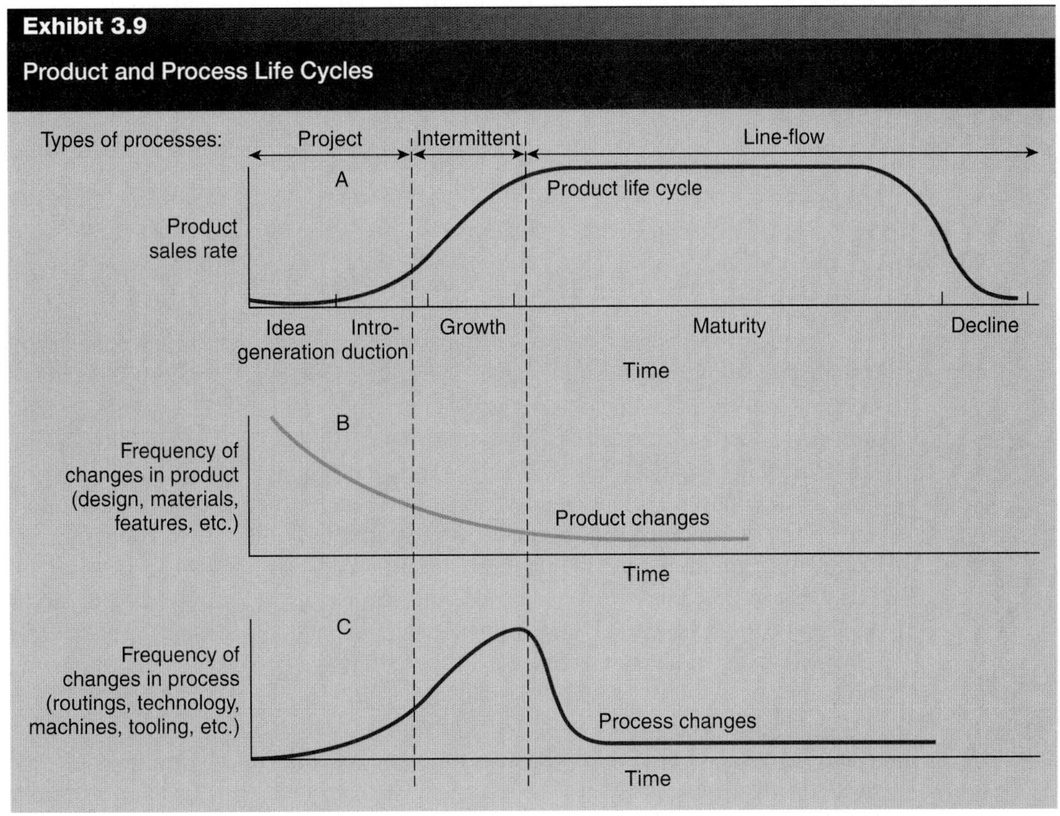

made in the product design to the stages of the product life cycle. Logically, most of the product changes occur during the initial stages of the life cycle, before major production starts. This suggests that a project-type process is appropriate for this stage. The product then tends to go through many changes: simplification, adding features, newer materials, and so forth. The motivation here is for more performance and perhaps greater appeal to a broader market. The flexibility of an intermittent-type process allows for these changes. During the maturity stage of the product, very few additional changes are made and the focus is on low costs, which can be provided by a line-flow process.

Changes in the production process, as shown in Part C of Exhibit 3.9, occur most rapidly during the early stages of production design and startup. This is where choices are made in the production layout, equipment, tooling, and so on. The goal here is to reduce production costs. Also, both product and process engineers work together to reduce costs and increase product performance. When full production occurs during the maturity phase, few additional changes are made and volumes remain relatively constant. During the decline phase of the product, however, some additional process changes occur; these are due in part to switching the smaller production volumes to different equipment and facilities.

During the early stages in a product's life cycle when production quantities are small (certainly during the product research and development stages), intermittent processes are typically used. Here, all similar machines and processes are grouped together in one location and are used for many different products. As production volumes increase, machines and processes may be grouped in a line-flow process to simplify the product's flow through the factory.

Exhibit 3.10

Types of Incremental and Radical Services

Incremental Services	Radical Services
Service line extensions	Major innovations
Service improvements	Start-up services
Style changes	New services for current markets

Categories of New Services

As discussed in Chapter 1, services differ from goods in many ways. In comparison to the study and classification of the various types of new products, which began several years ago, the study and classification of the different types of new services is more recent. In addition, services are viewed as being more complex, in that they not only involve the delivery of an end "product," but also include the process by which that product is delivered.

Susan Johnson et al. divide new service innovations into two major categories: *incremental* services and *radical* services, as presented in Exhibit 3.10. Each of these major categories, in turn, is divided into three subcategories.[2]

Under incremental services, *service line extensions* are viewed as new services that augment current services. Examples here would include new items on a restaurant menu, new airline routes, and new courses at a college or university. *Service improvements* are defined as new services in which the features have changed relative to existing services. E-ticketing for railroads and airlines provides good examples in this category. *Style changes,* which are the most common form of new service, are viewed as those that are seen to have modest forms of visible change with respect to how they impact customer perceptions, emotions, and attitudes. These changes do not fundamentally change the service, only its appearance. An example in this category would be the renovation of an existing restaurant or the exterior painting of an airplane with a new logo.

Radical services are defined as new service offerings that were not previously available or new delivery systems for existing services. This category also is divided into three subcategories. *Major innovations* consist of new services that address markets that are not fully defined and are often driven by information and computer-based technologies. Internet banking provides a good example in this category. *Start-up services* provide new services to established markets that are already served by existing services. The development of the smart card for retail transactions is an example of such a service. *New services for current markets* are defined as new service offerings that are provided to existing customers of an organization, for example, a bank kiosk in a supermarket.

As stated earlier, services are more complex than goods in that they include not only the "end product" but also the method by which that product is delivered. A classification scheme for new services, therefore, should recognize that services involve both. In other words, when attempting to classify the various types of new services, we should categorize them not only by how the end product is changed (that is, what is actually being delivered), but also by how the delivery process of the service has changed. Within this dual framework, which is illustrated in Exhibit 3.11, we define the following four categories of new services: (*a*) "window dressing," (*b*) breadth of offerings, (*c*) revolutionary, and (*d*) channel development.

[2]Susan Johnson, Larry Menor, Aleta Roth, and Richard Chase, "Critical Evaluation of the New Service Development Process: Integrating Service Innovation and Service Design," in *New Service Development: Creating Memorable Experiences* (Sage Publications, 2000), Thousands Oaks, CA, chap. 1.

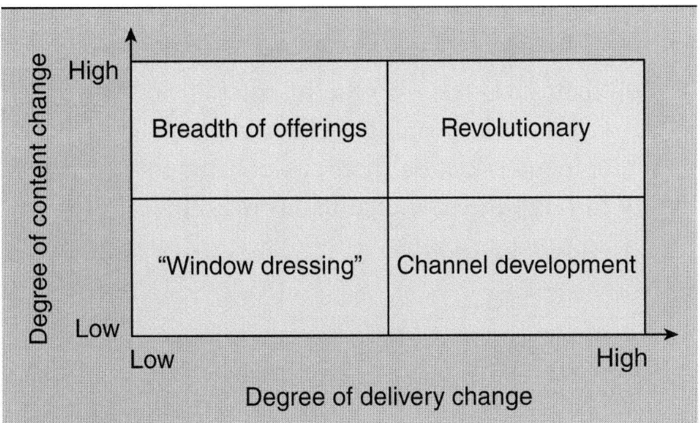

Exhibit 3.11

A Framework for Categorizing New Services

"Window Dressing" Services

The lower-left quadrant of Exhibit 3.11 defines those services that have a relatively small increment of change along both dimensions. In other words, the product that is delivered as part of the service does not differ significantly from the company's current offerings, and it is delivered in a very similar fashion. Examples of services that we would call "window dressing" include new items on restaurant menus, new routes and destinations for airlines, and new courses at colleges and universities. Services that fall into this category usually have a very small impact on the firm's existing service operations and consequently can be brought to market in a relatively short period of time.

Breadth-of-Offering Services

The upper-left quadrant of Exhibit 3.11 represents a significant design change in the content of the service, but it is delivered to the customer in much the same manner as existing services. Marriott, which began with a single hotel concept catering to a particular market segment, now has a wide variety of "products" such as Fairfield Inns, Residence Inns, Marriott Courtyards, and Marriott Suites, each of which focuses on a different market segment. While the specific "content" of each type of hotel is different, in terms of room size, amenities, and ancillary services that are provided (for example, on-site restaurants, health spas, business support services, etc.), the basic method of delivering the service remains the same. For firms developing new products in this category, the challenge is how to deliver all of the different types of content to each of the corresponding different market segments in an effective and efficient manner.

Revolutionary Services

The upper-right quadrant of Exhibit 3.11 represents new services that provide both very new content and a very new method of delivery. These services typically take much longer to bring to market and require significantly more of the firm's resources than do any of the other categories. For example, FedEx created the overnight delivery service, using the delivery component of airplanes rather than the more traditional ground transportation. Priceline.com provides another good example in this category with its on-line bidding for hotel rooms and airline tickets through the Internet.

Channel Development Services

New services that fall in the lower-right quadrant of Exhibit 3.11 are those in which the service that is provided is the same as that currently offered by the firm, but it is delivered differently through another channel, which is often entirely new. The automated teller machine (ATM) provides a good example of services in this category. Traditional brick-and-mortar retailers that sell their products over the Internet through a website provide another example in this category. When developing these new channels, managers need to recognize that process development is critical here, as consumers expect to receive the same level of service quality through the new channel as they have been accustomed to receiving in the older, more traditional channels.

The New Service Development (NSD) Process

new service development (NSD) process

The method by which new services evolve from conceptualization through to marketing and delivery to the customer.

The **new service development (NSD) process** is very similar to the NPD process with one major difference. When developing a service, you are inherently designing both the product and the process at the same time, because the product is typically inherent in the process. Since services are intangible, rather than something "you can drop on your foot," it is nearly impossible to separate the product from the process. The NSD process typically begins in the same fashion as the NPD process. An idea will come forth either from marketing/customer (market pull or voice of the customer) or from operations (service operations push). In services, there currently is not the same type and level of R&D as there is for products. The R&D in services occurs primarily in the operations process with respect to how the service is delivered.

The NSD process also consists of four stages that are similar to the stages of the NPD process. The first step, *design,* consists of the formulation of the objectives and strategy of the new service, followed by concept development and testing of the concept. Concurrently, the *analysis* phase considers the financial implications of the new service and examines the supply chain issues relevant to its delivery. Upon successful completion of these two phases, the new service project is approved for continuation. The third and most resource-intensive phase of NSD is the *development* phase. In this phase, the service design is completed and tested, all the processes that ensure service delivery are fully designed and tested, personnel are trained, and a pilot run of the service is conducted. Once the new service passes the pilot test, *full launch,* the fourth stage in the NSD process, begins when the service is released to the marketplace.

The study of the NSD process is significantly less mature than that of the NPD process. While much work has been done in the development of new service design, particularly with respect to the degree of customer contact (which is presented shortly), overall there has been limited research on the total NSD process. To address this need, Susan Johnson et al. have developed a series of propositions that provide some direction for the future of NSD research.[3] These propositions include

- The NSD process is more likely to be nonlinear for new services that are less standardized or are delivered through more industrialized service channels.
- Competence in the planning phase activities of the NSD process drives successful radical innovations, whereas competence in the execution phase activities of the NSD process drives successful incremental innovations.
- Service failures and subsequent recovery efforts are often the result of using an ad hoc NSD process or the lack of NSD competence, rather than from poor service execution.

---

[3]Ibid.

- Effective portfolio management of individual NSD efforts will decrease the total risk of a firm's NSD program and increase the probability of high NSD returns (similar to the portfolio management approvals that mutual funds use).
- Portfolio-like management of NSD efforts will increase the fulfillment of heterogeneous customer needs.

The Customer Contact Approach to Designing Service Processes

Service systems are generally classified along industry lines (financial services, health services, transportation services, and so on). These groupings, though useful in presenting aggregate economic data, are not particularly appropriate for OM purposes because they tell us little about the process. In manufacturing, by contrast, there are, as we have seen, fairly well-defined terms for classifying production activities that transcend industry lines (such as *intermittent* and *continuous production*); when applied to a manufacturing setting, they readily convey the essence of the process. While it is possible to describe services in these same terms, we need another item of information to reflect the level of customer involvement in the process. That item, which we believe operationally distinguishes one type of service from another in its production function, is the extent of customer contact in the creation of service.

Customer contact refers to the presence of the customer in the system, and *creation of the service* refers to the work process that is involved in providing the service itself. *Extent of contact* here may be roughly defined as the percentage of time the customer must be involved in the system relative to the total time it takes to perform the customer service. Generally speaking, the greater the percentage of contact time between the service system and the customer, the greater the degree of interaction between the two during the production process.

high degree of customer contact

Service operations that require a high percentage of customer contact time.

From this concept of customer contact, it follows that service systems with a **high degree of customer contact** are usually more difficult to manage and consequently harder to justify than those with a **low degree of customer contact.** In high-contact systems, the customer can affect the time of demand, the exact nature of the service, and the quality of the service since the customer is involved in the process.

low degree of customer contact

Service operations that require a low percentage of customer contact time.

Exhibit 3.12 illustrates the differences between high- and low-contact service systems in a bank. Here we see that each design decision is impacted by whether or not the customer is present during the service delivery. We also see that when work is done behind the scenes (in this case, a bank's processing center), it is performed on substitutes for the customer, that is, customer reports, databases, and invoices. We, therefore, can design these behind-the-scenes operations according to the same principles we would use in designing a factory—that is, to maximize the amount of items processed during the production day.

Obviously, there can be tremendous diversity of customer influence and hence system variability within high-contact service systems. For example, a bank branch offers both simple services such as cash withdrawals that take just a minute or so, as well as complicated services such as loan application preparation that can take in excess of an hour. Moreover, these activities may range from being self-service through an ATM, to coproduction where bank personnel and the customer work together as a team to develop the loan application.

In another attempt to better understand services in general, Roger Schmenner proposes a method for classifying services along two dimensions.[4] The first dimension, degree of customer interaction and customization, closely parallels the degree of customer contact

---

[4]Roger W. Schmenner, "How Can Service Businesses Survive and Prosper?" *Sloan Management Review* 27, no. 3 (Spring 1986), pp. 21–32, by permission of publisher. Copyright © 1986 by Sloan Management Review Association. All rights reserved.

Exhibit 3.12

Major Differences between High- and Low-Contact Systems in a Bank

Design Decision	High-Contact System (a branch office)	Low-Contact System (a check processing center)
Facility location	Operations must be near the customer.	Operations may be placed near supply, transport, or labor.
Facility layout	Facility should accommodate the customer's physical and psychological needs and expectations.	Facility should focus on production efficiency.
Product design	Environment as well as the physical product define the nature of the service.	Customer is not in the service environment, so the product can be defined by fewer attributes.
Process design	Stages of production process have a direct, immediate effect on the customer.	Customer is not involved in majority of processing steps.
Scheduling	Customer is in the production schedule and must be accommodated.	Customer is concerned mainly with completion dates.
Production planning	Orders cannot be stored, so smoothing production flow will result in loss of business.	Both backlogging and production smoothing are possible.
Worker skills	Direct workforce constitutes a major part of the service product and so must be able to interact well with the public.	Direct workforce need only have technical skills.
Quality control	Quality standards are often in the eye of the beholder and hence variable.	Quality standards are generally measurable and hence fixed.
Time standards	Service time depends on customer needs, and therefore time standards are inherently loose.	Work is performed on customer surrogates (e.g., forms), thus time standards can be tight.
Wage payment	Variable output requires time-based wage systems.	"Fixable" output permits output-based wage systems.
Capacity planning	To avoid lost sales, capacity must be set to match peak demand.	Storable output permits capacity at some average demand level.

we discuss above. In addition, Schmenner also includes the degree of labor intensity required to deliver the service. From these two factors he develops a service process matrix, as shown in Exhibit 3.13.

Within this matrix, Schmenner defines four broad categories of services:

1. *Service factory* is characterized by a low degree of labor intensity and a low degree of customer interaction and customization.
2. *Service shop* has the same low degree of labor intensity, but has a higher degree of customer interaction and customization.
3. *Mass service* is defined by a high degree of labor intensity, but has a relatively low degree of customer interaction.
4. *Professional service* requires both a high degree of labor intensity as well as a high degree of customer interaction and customization.

Exhibit 3.13

The Service Process Matrix

		Degree of Interaction and Customization	
		Low	**High**
Degree of Labor Intensity	**Low**	Service factory: Airlines Trucking Hotels Resorts and recreation	Service shop: Hospitals Auto repair Other repair services
	High	Mass service: Retailing Wholesaling Schools Retail aspects of commercial banking	Professional service: Doctors Lawyers Accountants Architects

Source: Roger W. Schmenner, "How Can Service Businesses Survive and Prosper?" *Sloan Management Review* 27, no. 3 (Spring 1986), pp. 21–32, by permission of publisher.

This type of classification scheme provides service managers with some insights in developing strategies for their respective organizations. For example, those services that exhibit a low degree of labor intensity are usually capital intense with high fixed costs. These firms cannot easily adjust capacity to meet changes in demand and, therefore, must attempt to smooth out the demand during peak periods by shifting it to off-peak times.

The issues confronting service managers with high labor intensity operations require a different focus. Here, workforce management is paramount, with emphasis being placed on hiring, training, and scheduling.

More important, this approach to classifying services cuts across industry lines, providing service managers with a better understanding of the strengths and weaknesses within their own operations. Through this perspective, managers can look to similar operations in other service industries to seek ways for improving their respective operations.

Designing a New Service Organization

Designing a service organization entails the execution of four elements of what James Heskett refers to as the "Service Vision."[5] The first element is identification of the target market (Who is our customer?); the second is the service concept (How do we differentiate our service in the market?); the third is the service strategy (What is our service package and the operating focus of our service?); and the fourth is the service delivery system (What are the actual processes, staff requirements, and facilities by which the service is created?).

Choosing a target market and developing the service package are top management decisions which then set the stage for the direct operating decisions of service strategy and delivery system design.

Several major factors distinguish service design and development from typical manufactured product development. First, the process and the product must be developed simultaneously; indeed, in services the process is the product. (We make this statement with the general recognition that many manufacturers are using such concepts as concurrent engineering and DFM [design for manufacture] as approaches to more closely link product design and process design.)

[5]James L. Heskett, "Lessons from the Service Sector." *Harvard Business Review,* March–April 1987. pp. 118–26.

Second, although equipment and software that support a service can be protected by patents and copyrights, a service operation itself lacks the legal protection commonly available to goods production. Third, the service package, rather than a definable good, constitutes the major output of the development process. Fourth, many parts of the service package often are defined by the training individuals receive before they become part of the service organization. In particular, in many professional service organizations such as law firms and hospitals, prior certification is necessary for hiring. Fifth, many service organizations can change their service offerings virtually overnight. Routine service organizations such as barbershops, retail stores, and restaurants have this flexibility.

Designing the Customer Service Encounter

Karl Albrecht and Ron Zemke's *Service America!* gets to the heart of the issue of managing service operations when they state "every time a customer comes into contact with any aspect of the company it is a 'moment of truth,' and it can create either a positive or a negative impression about the company."[6] How well these moments of truth or encounters are managed depends on a carefully designed service delivery process. Service encounters can be structured in a number of different ways. The **service-system design matrix** in Exhibit 3.14 identifies six common alternatives.

service-system design matrix

Framework for relating sales opportunities with ways a service can interact with a customer.

The top of the matrix shows the degree of customer/server contact: the *buffered core,* which is physically separated from the customer; the *permeable system,* which the customer can penetrate via phone or face-to-face contact; and the *reactive system,* which is both penetrable and reactive to the customer's requirements. The left side of the matrix shows what we believe to be a logical marketing proposition, namely, that the greater the amount of contact, the greater the opportunity to generate additional sales; the right side shows the impact on production efficiency as the customer exerts more influence on the operation.

As one would anticipate, production efficiency decreases as the customer contact time increases, thereby giving the customer more influence on the system. To offset this, however, the face-to-face contact provides greater opportunity to sell additional products. Conversely, low contact, such as mail, allows the system to work more efficiently because the customer is unable to significantly affect (or disrupt) the system. However, there is relatively little, if any, sales opportunity for additional product sales at this end of the spectrum.

There can be some shifting in the positioning of each entry. Consider the "face-to-face tight specs" entry in Exhibit 3.14. This refers to those situations where there is little variation in the service process—neither customer nor server has much discretion in creating the service. Fast-food restaurants and Disneyland come to mind. "Face-to-face loose specs" refers to situations where the service process is generally understood, but there are options in the way it will be performed or the physical goods that are a part of it. A full-service restaurant and a car sales agency are examples. "Face-to-face total customization" refers to service encounters whose specifications must be developed through some interaction between the customer and server. Legal and medical services are of this type, and the degree to which the resources of the system are mustered for the service determines whether the system is reactive or merely permeable. Examples would be the mobilization of an advertising firm's resources in preparation for an office visit by a major client, or an operating team scrambling to prepare for emergency surgery.

[6]Jan Carlzon, president, Scandinavian Airlines System, quoted in Karl Albrecht and Ron Zemke, *Service America! Doing Business in the New Economy* (Homewood, IL: Dow Jones-Irwin, 1985), p. 19.

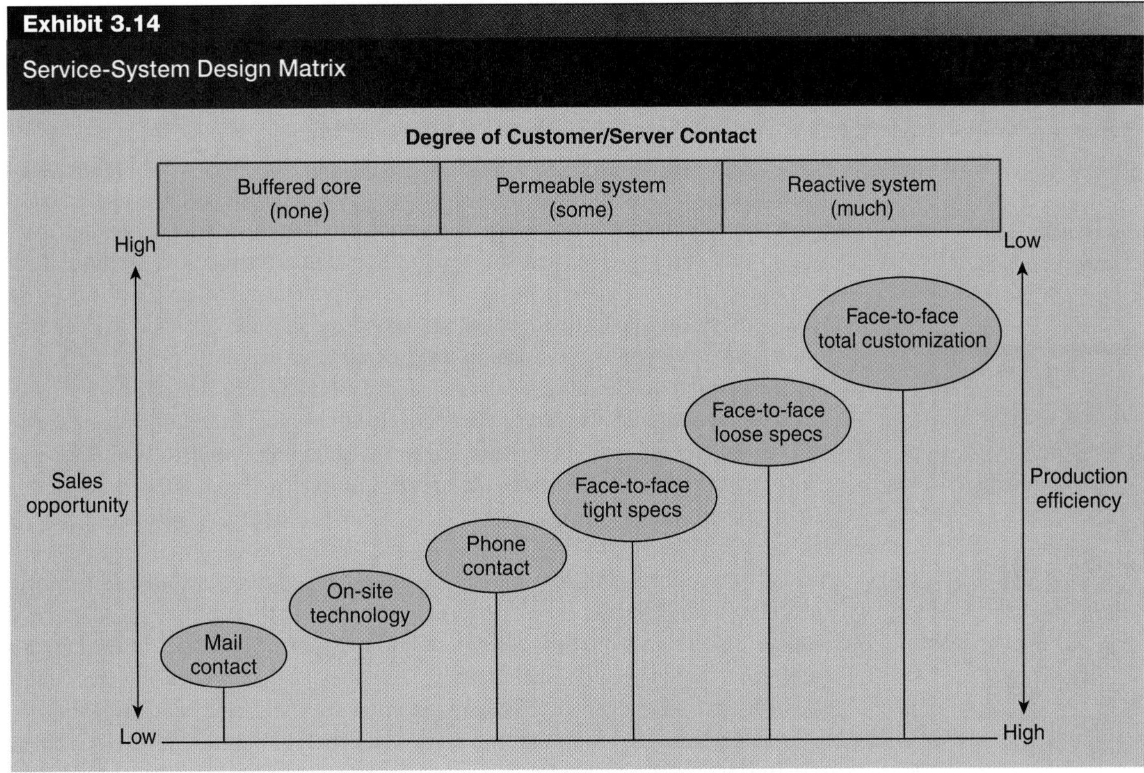

Strategic Uses of the Matrix The service-system design matrix has both operational and strategic uses. Its operational uses are reflected in its identification of worker requirements, focus of operations, and innovations previously discussed. Some of its strategic uses are

1. *Enabling systematic integration of operations and marketing strategy.* Trade-offs become more clear-cut, and, more important, at least some of the major design variables are crystalized for analysis purposes. For example, the matrix indicates that it would make little sense relative to sales for a service firm to invest in high-skilled workers if it plans to operate using tight specs.
2. *Clarifying exactly which combination of service delivery the firm is actually providing.* As the company incorporates the delivery options listed on the diagonal, it is becoming diversified in its production process.
3. *Permitting comparison with other firms in the way specific services are delivered.* This helps to pinpoint a firm's competitive advantage.
4. *Indicating evolutionary or life cycle changes that might be in order as the firm grows.* Unlike the product-process matrix for manufacturing, where natural growth moves in one direction (from intermittent to line-flow as a volume increases), the evolution of service delivery can move in either direction along the diagonal as a function of the trade-off between efficiency and the potential to generate additional sales.
5. *Providing flexibility.* The user of the matrix can go into depth, placing particular service products of a small firm or individual department on it, or cover a large service organization at a more aggregated level.

Process Selection in Services

Types of Service Organizations

facilities-based services

Services that require the customer to go to the service facility.

field-based services

Services that can be performed at the customer's location.

Service management issues exist in three broad organizational contexts:

1. *Service businesses* are organizations whose primary business requires interaction with the customer to produce the service. Familiar examples of service businesses include banks, airlines, hospitals, law firms, retail stores, restaurants, and so on. Within this category, we can make a further major distinction: **facilities-based services,** where the customer must go to the service facility, and **field-based services,** where production and consumption of the service take place in the customer's environment (e.g., cleaning and home repair services).

   Technology has allowed for the transfer of many facility-based services to field-based services. Dental vans bring the dentist to your home. Some auto repair services have repair-mobiles. Telemarketing brings the shopping center to your TV screen.
2. *Customer support services* provide support to external customers who have already purchased the goods and/or services of the company. Included here are 800-numbers for registering complaints and obtaining additional information on the firm's products. Product maintenance and repair services also fall into this category.

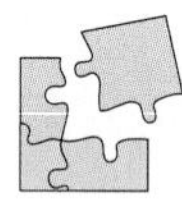

3. *Internal services* are the services required to support the activities of the larger organization. These services include such functions as data processing, accounting, engineering, and maintenance. Their customers are the various departments within the organization that require such services. (It is not uncommon for an internal service to start marketing its services outside the parent organization and become a service business itself.)

The three general approaches to delivering on-site services are the production line approach made famous by McDonald's Corporation, the customer involvement approach made famous by ATMs and gas stations, and the personal attention approach made famous by Nordstrom department stores.

The Production Line Approach

The production line approach pioneered by McDonald's refers to more than just the steps required to assemble a Big Mac. Rather, as Theodore Levitt notes, it is treating the delivery of fast food as a manufacturing process rather than a service process.[7] The value of this philosophy is that it overcomes many of the problems inherent in the concept of service itself. That is, service implies subordination or subjugation of the server to the served; manufacturing, on the other hand, avoids this connotation because it focuses on things rather than people. Thus, in manufacturing and at McDonald's, "the orientation is toward the efficient production of results, not on the attendance on others." Levitt notes that besides McDonald's marketing and financial skills, the company carefully controls "the execution of each outlet's central function—the rapid delivery of a consistently uniform, high-quality mix of prepared foods in an environment of obvious cleanliness, order, and cheerful courtesy. The systematic substitution of equipment for people, combined with the carefully planned use and positioning of technology, enables McDonald's

[7]Theodore Levitt, "Production-Line Approach to Service," *Harvard Business Review* 50, no. 5 (September–October 1972), pp. 41–52.

to attract and hold patronage in proportions no predecessor or imitator has managed to duplicate."

Levitt cites several aspects of McDonald's operations to illustrate the concepts:

- The McDonald's french fryer allows cooking of the optimum number of french fries at one time.
- A wide-mouthed scoop is used to pick up the precise amount of french fries for each order size. (The employee never touches the product.)
- Storage space is expressly designed for a predetermined mix of prepackaged and premeasured products.
- Cleanliness is pursued by providing ample trash cans in and outside each facility (and the larger outlets have motorized sweepers for the parking area).
- Hamburgers are wrapped in color-coded paper.
- Through painstaking attention to total design and facilities planning, everything is built integrally into the (McDonald's) machine itself—into the technology of the system. The only choice available to the attendant is to operate it exactly as the designers intended.

The Customer Involvement Approach

In contrast to the production line approach, C. H. Lovelock and R. F. Young propose that the service process can be enhanced by having the customer take a greater participatory role in the production of the service.[8] Automatic teller machines (ATMs), self-service gas stations, salad bars, and in-room coffee-making equipment in hotels are good examples of where the burden of providing service is shifted to the consumer. Obviously, this philosophy requires some selling on the part of the service organization to convince customers that this is beneficial to them. To this end, Lovelock and Young propose a number of steps, including developing customer trust, promoting the benefits of cost, speed, and convenience, and following up to make sure that the procedures are being effectively used. In essence, this turns customers into "partial employees" who must be trained in what to do and be compensated primarily through lower prices that are charged for the service.

The Personal Attention Approach

The personal attention approach is basically the concept of mass-customization applied to services. With this approach, each customer is treated as an individual, with the service firm often maintaining a database of each customer's likes and dislikes. This data can be collected manually in "personal books," as noted below at Nordstrom's, or more formally by electronic means, as the Ritz-Carlton does with all of its guests. In the latter case, this information is then available throughout the entire organization. The following example by Tom Peters describes how Nordstrom's operationalizes its personal attention philosophy.[9]

> After several visits to a store's men's clothing department, a customer's suit still did not fit. He wrote the company president, who sent a tailor to the customer's office with a new suit for fitting. When the alterations were completed, the suit was delivered to the customer—free of charge.

---

[8] C. H. Lovelock and R. F. Young, "Look to Customers to Increase Productivity," *Harvard Business Review* 57, no. 2 (May–June 1979), pp. 168–78.

[9] Tom Peters, *Quality!* Palo Alto, CA: TPG Communications, 1986, pp. 10–12.

This incident involved the $1.3 billion, Seattle-based Nordstrom, a specialty clothing retailer. Its sales per square foot are about five times that of a typical department store. Who received the customer's letter and urged the extreme (by others' standards) response? Co-chairman John Nordstrom.

The frontline providers of this good service are well paid. Nordstrom's salespersons earn a couple of bucks an hour more than competitors, plus a 6.75 percent commission. Its top salesperson moves over $1 million a year in merchandise. Nordstrom lives for its customers and salespeople. Its only official organization chart puts the customer at the top, followed by sales and sales support people. Next come department managers, then store managers, and the board of directors at the very bottom.

Salespersons religiously carry a "personal book," where they record voluminous information about each of their customers; senior, successful salespeople often have three or four bulging books, which they carry everywhere, according to Betsy Sanders, the vice president who orchestrated the firm's wildly successful penetration of the tough southern California market. "My objective is to get one new personal customer a day," says a budding Nordstrom star. The system helps him do just that. He has a virtually unlimited budget to send cards, flowers, and thank-you notes to customers. He also is encouraged to shepherd his customer to any department in the store to assist in a successful shopping trip.

He also is abetted by what may be the most liberal returns policy in this or any other business: Return *anything,* no questions asked. Sanders says that "trusting customers," or "our bosses" as she repeatedly calls them, is vital to the Nordstrom philosophy. President Jim Nordstrom told the *Los Angeles Times,* "I don't care if they roll a Goodyear tire into the store. If they say they paid $200, give them $200 (in cash) for it." Sanders acknowledges that a few customers rip the store off—"rent hose from us," to use a common insider's line. But this is more than offset by goodwill from the 99 percent-plus who benefit from the "No Problem at Nordstrom" logo that the company lives up to with unmatched zeal.

No bureaucracy gets in the way of serving the customer. Policy? Sanders explains to a dumbfounded group of Silicon Valley executives, "I know this drives the lawyers nuts, but our whole 'policy manual' is just one sentence, 'Use your own best judgment at all times.'" One store manager offers a translation, "Don't chew gum. Don't steal from us."

No matter what approach is taken, seven common characteristics of well-designed service systems have been identified:

1. *Each element of the service system is consistent with the operating focus of the firm.* For example, when the focus is on speed of delivery, each step in the process should help to foster speed.
2. *It is user-friendly.* This means that the customer can interact with it easily—that is, it has good signage, understandable forms, logical steps in the process, and courteous service workers that are available to answer questions and it is easily accessible.
3. *It is robust.* That is, it can cope effectively with variations in demand and resource availability. For example, if the computer goes down, effective backup systems are in place to permit service to continue.
4. *It is structured so that consistent performance by its people and systems is easily maintained.* This means that the tasks required of the workers can be performed repeatedly with a high level of consistency, and the supporting technologies are truly supportive and reliable.
5. *It provides effective links between the back office and the front office so that nothing falls between the cracks.* In other words, the barriers between the different functional areas are reduced or eliminated.
6. *It manages the evidence of service quality in such a way that customers see the value of the service provided.* Many services do a great job behind the scenes but fail

to make this visible to the customer. This is particularly true where a service improvement is made. Unless customers are made aware of the improvement through explicit communication about it, the improved performance is unlikely to gain maximum impact.

7. *It is cost-effective.* There is minimum waste of time and resources in delivering the service.

Conclusion

Product life cycles are becoming shorter and shorter, as a result of both increased global competition and advances in technology. As a result, businesses need to be able to design, develop and introduce new goods and services on a continuous and consistent basis. The more quickly a company can introduce a new product ahead of its competition, the more substantial the profits. These profits are attributable to both the premium prices that new products can command while the competition catches up and the large percentage of the market that is typically captured by the firm that is first to market with its products. To accomplish this, today's companies need to be well-integrated, well-disciplined organizations.

New goods and services fall into one of several categories, the differences between them being dependent on the relative amount of innovation. A company needs to have a portfolio of new offerings from all categories in order to obtain a balance in both the short term and the long term.

The processes for developing new goods and services are no longer as haphazard as they once were, although new service development still lags new product development in this respect. Those firms that have invested the necessary resources in these processes have a significant advantage, in terms of both staying ahead of their competition, as well as having the ability to react quickly to unexpected competitive surprises.

The choice of which process to adopt is also a critical success factor. Goods and services can be produced by any of several different types of processes, each of which has a distinctive set of characteristics. It is therefore important for management to identify these process characteristics when selecting a process in order to ensure that the goods and services being produced and delivered meet the needs of the firm's customers. In other words, a company's processes should be compatible with the customer requirements of the specific market niche that it is trying to serve.

Key Terms

concurrent engineering p. 56
facilities-based services p. 74
field-based services p. 74
house of quality p. 59
high degree of customer contact p. 69
low degree of customer contact p. 69
new product development (NPD) process p. 56
new service development (NSD) process p. 68
product's specifications p. 61
quality function deployment (QFD) p. 58
service-system design matrix p. 72
types of processes p. 61
  intermittent p. 62
  line-flow p. 63
  project p. 61
voice of the customer p. 57

Review and Discussion Questions

1. Why it is important for a firm to have an effective new product (or service) development process?
2. What are the benefits to the firm that can develop new products faster than its competition?
3. Describe the three different categories of new products. Discuss how each category differs from the others in terms of resources expended and the impact on the firm's manufacturing processes.
4. Discuss the four different types of new services that are categorized by the amount of change in content and delivery method with respect to a firm's existing services.
5. What is the difference between incremental and radical service innovations?
6. Describe what is meant by the "voice of the customer."
7. Identify the two methods used by firms to generate new product ideas.
8. Identify and describe the four major phases of the new product development process.
9. What is concurrent engineering and why is it critical for a successful new product development effort? Describe the concept of design for manufacturability and indicate why it is closely connected to concurrent engineering.
10. Identify and describe the four stages of the new service development (NSD) process.
11. What are the three major categories of manufacturing processes and how do they differ in terms of operational characteristics?
12. Why is it important for managers to understand the relationship between the various stages of a product's life cycle and the different types of processes that are available to manufacture that product?
13. Identify the high-contact and low-contact operations that exist in each of the following services:
    a. A dental office.
    b. An airline.
    c. An accounting office.
    d. An automobile dealership.
14. Where would you place a drive-in church, a campus food vending machine, and a bar's automatic mixed-drink dispensing machine on the service-system design matrix?
15. *a.* List specific products that you especially like. What do you like most about them?
    b. Create a list of products that you dislike or are unhappy with. What don't you like about them?
    c. Are there some common reasons for your lists? For example, is it more important for products that you don't see or see very little to be functional rather than attractive (e.g., the furnace or air conditioning in the house, the transmission or engine in the car)? Is it more important for things to be well designed that other people see and relate to you such as your car, your clothes, or your apartment or home furnishings?

    Can you formulate some general design guidelines based on your answers?
16. Pick a product and make a list of issues that need to be considered in its design and manufacture. The product can be something such as a stereo, a telephone, a desk, a kitchen appliance, and so on. Consider the functional and aesthetic aspects of design as well as the important concerns for manufacturing.
17. Place the following functions of a department store on the service-system design matrix: Mail order (i.e., catalog), phone order, hardware, stationery, apparel, cosmetics, customer service (i.e., complaints).
18. Place the following functions of a hospital on the service-system design matrix: Physician/patient, nurse/patient, billing, medical records, lab tests, admissions, diagnostic tests (e.g., X-rays).

19. The first step in studying a production process is to develop a description of that process. Once the process is described, we are better able to determine why it works well or poorly and to recommend production-related improvements. Since we are all familiar with fast-food restaurants, try your hand at describing the production process employed at, say, a McDonald's. In doing so, answer the following questions:
    a. What are the important aspects of the service package?
    b. Which skills and attitudes are needed by the service personnel?
    c. How can customer demand be altered?
    d. Can the customer/provider interface be changed to include more technology? More self-serve?
    e. How does it measure up on the seven characteristics of a well-designed service?

Internet Exercise

Go to the McGraw-Hill/Irwin website (www.mhhe.com/pom) and look at the various companies that offer virtual tours of their operations. These firms often highlight their new products on their sites and also have press releases about their new products available on their sites. Companies known for their strong ability to introduce new products quickly, such as Gillette, 3M, and Hewlett-Packard, are also good sources. For at least two of these firms, describe the new products that they are currently offering. What type of new product would you categorize them as?

Bibliography

Adler, Paul S., A. Mandelbaum, V. Nguyen, and E. Schwerer. "Getting the Most Out of Your Product Development Process." *Harvard Business Review* 74 (1996).

Albrecht, Karl, and Ron Zemke. *Service America! Doing Business in the New Economy*. Homewood, IL: Dow-Jones Irwin, 1985.

Blackburn, J. D. *Time-Based Competition: The Next Battleground in American Manufacturing*. Homewood, IL: Business One Irwin, 1991.

Chase, Richard B. "The Customer Contact Approach to Services: Theoretical Bases and Practical Extensions." *Operations Research* 21, no. 4 (1981), pp. 698–705.

Clark, Kim B. "Project Scope and Project Performance: The Effect of Parts Strategy and Supplier Involvement on Product Development." *Management Science* 35 (1989), pp. 1247–63.

Clark, Kim B., and Steven C. Wheelwright. *Managing New Product and Process Development: Text and Cases*. New York: The Free Press, 1993.

Cohen, Morris A., J. Eliashberg, and T. Ho. "New Product Development: The Performance and Time-to-Market Tradeoff." *Management Science* 42 (1996), pp. 173–86.

Davis, D. B. "Beating the Clock." *Electronic Business,* May 29, 1989, pp. 21–29.

Ettlie, John E. "Integrated Design and New Product Success." *Journal of Operations Management* 15 (1997), pp. 33–55.

Fitzsimmons, James A., P. Kouvelis, and D. N. Mallick. "Design Strategy and Its Interface with Manufacturing and Marketing: A Conceptual Framework." *Journal of Operations Management* 10 (1991), pp. 398–415.

Griffin, A. "Metrics for Measuring Product Development Cycle Time." *Journal of Product Innovation Management* 10 (1993), pp. 112–25.

Gupta, A. K., and D. L. Wilemon. "Accelerating the Development of Technology-Based New Products." *California Management Review* 32 (1990), pp. 24–44.

Hamilton, S. "New-Product Development and Manufacturing Competitiveness: A Hewlett-Packard Perspective." In *Time-Based Competition: The Next Battleground in American Manufacturing,* ed. J. D. Blackburn, chap. 8. Homewood, IL: Business One Irwin, 1991.

Heskett, James L. *Managing in the Service Economy*. Cambridge, MA: Harvard University Press, 1986.

Johnson, Susan, Larry Menor, Aleta Roth, and Richard Chase. "Critical Evaluation of the New Service Development Process: Integrating Service Innovation and Service Design." In *New Service Development: Creating Memorable Experiences,* chap. 1. Sage Publications, Thousand Oaks, CA 2000.

Krishnan, V., S. D. Eppinger, and D. E. Whitnewy. "A Model-Based Framework to Overlap Product Development Activities." *Management Science* 43, no. 4 (1997), pp. 437–51.

Kurawarwala, A. A., and H. Matsuo. "Cost of Delay in Time to Market and Capacity Restriction." Working Paper 93-01-02, University of Texas at Austin, April 15, 1993.

———. "Forecasting and Inventory Management of Short Life-Cycle Products." *Operations Research* 44 (1996), pp. 131–50.

Schmenner, Roger W. "How Can Service Businesses Survive and Prosper?" *Sloan Management Review* 27, no. 3 (Spring 1986), pp. 21–32.

Stalk, G., Jr., and T. M. Hout. *Competing Against Time: How Time-Based Competition Is Reshaping Global Markets*. New York: The Free Press, 1990.

Swink, M., J. Sandvig, and V. A. Mabert. "Customizing Concurrent Engineering Processes: Five Case Studies." *Journal of Product Innovation Management* 13 (1996), pp. 229–44.

Terwiesch, C., and C. H. Loch. "Measuring the Effectiveness of Overlapping Development Activities." *Management Science* 45 (1999), pp. 455–65.

Urban, G. L., T. Carter, S. Gaskin, and Z. Mucha. "Market Share Rewards to Pioneering Brands: An Empirical Analysis and Strategic Implications." *Management Science* 32 (1986), pp. 645–59.

Wheelwright, S. C., and K. B. Clark. "Creating Project Plans to Focus Product Development." *Harvard Business Review* 70 (1992).

———. *Revolutionizing Product Development: Quantum Leaps in Speed, Efficiency and Quality*. New York: The Free Press, 1992.

The Best Engineered Part Is No Part

Case

Putting together NCR Corp.'s new 2760 electronic cash register is a snap. In fact, William R. Sprague can do it in less than two minutes—blindfolded. To get that kind of easy assembly, Sprague, a senior manufacturing engineer at NCR, insisted that the point-of-sale terminal be designed so that its parts fit together with no screws or bolts.

The entire terminal consists of just 15 vendor-produced components. That's 85 percent fewer parts, from 65 percent fewer suppliers, than in the company's previous low-end model, the 2160. And the terminal takes only 25 percent as much time to assemble. Installation and maintenance are also a breeze, says Sprague. "The simplicity flows through to all of the downstream activities, including field service."

The new NCR product is one of the best examples to date of the payoffs possible from a new engineering approach called "design for manufacturability," mercifully shortened to DFM. Other DFM enthusiasts include Ford, General Motors, IBM, Motorola, Perkin-Elmer, and Whirlpool. Since 1981, General Electric Co. has used DFM in more than 100 development programs, from major appliances to gearboxes for jet engines. GE figures that the concept has netted $200 million in benefits, either from cost savings or from increased market shares.

Nuts to Screws

One U.S. champion of DFM is Geoffrey Boothroyd, a professor of industrial and manufacturing engineering at the University of Rhode Island and the co-founder of Boothroyd Dewhurst Inc. This tiny Wakefield (R.I.) company has developed several computer programs that analyze designs for ease of manufacturing.

The biggest gains, notes Boothroyd, come from eliminating screws and other fasteners. On a supplier's invoice, screws and bolts may run mere pennies apiece, and collectively they account for only about 5 percent of a typical product's bill of materials. But tack on all of the associated costs, such as the time needed to align components while screws are inserted and tightened, and the price of using those mundane parts can pile up to 75 percent of total assembly costs. "Fasteners should be the first thing to design out of a product," he says.

Had screws been included in the design of NCR's 2760, calculates Sprague, the total cost over the lifetime of the model would have been $12,500—per screw. "The huge impact of little things like screws, primarily on overhead costs, just gets lost," he says. That's understandable, he admits, because for new-product development projects "the overriding factor is hitting the market window. It's better to be on time and over budget than on budget but late."

But NCR got its simplified terminal to market in record time without overlooking the little details. The product was formally introduced last January, just 24 months after development began. Design was a paperless, interdepartmental effort from the very start. The product remained a computer model until all members of the team—from design engineering, manufacturing, purchasing, customer service, and key suppliers—were satisfied.

That way, the printed-circuit boards, the molds for its plastic housing, and other elements could all be developed simultaneously. This eliminated the usual lag after designers throw a new product "over the wall" to manufacturing, which then must figure out how to make it. "Breaking down the walls between design and manufacturing to facilitate simultaneous engineering," Sprague declares, "was the real breakthrough."

Case

The design process began with a mechanical computer-aided engineering program that allowed the team to fashion three-dimensional models of each part on a computer screen. The software also analyzed the overall product and its various elements for performance and durability. Then the simulated components were assembled on a computer workstation's screen to assure that they would fit together properly. As the design evolved, it was checked periodically with Boothroyd Dewhurst's DFM software. This prompted several changes that trimmed the parts count from an initial 28 to the final 15.

No Mock-Up

After everyone on the team gave their thumbs-up, the data for the parts were electronically transferred directly into computer-aided manufacturing systems at the various suppliers. The NCR designers were so confident everything would work as intended that they didn't bother making a mock-up.

DFM can be a powerful weapon against foreign competition. Several years ago, IBM used Boothroyd Dewhurst's software to analyze dot-matrix printers it was sourcing from Japan—and found it could do substantially better. Its Proprinter had 65 percent fewer parts and slashed assembly time by 90 percent. "Almost anything made in Japan," insists Professor Boothroyd, "can be improved upon with DFM—often impressively."

Question What development problems has the NCR approach overcome?

Source: Otis Port, "The Best-Engineered Part Is No Part at All," *Business Week,* May 8, 1989, p. 150.

Case

Kinko's Copier Stores

"We're not your average printer," says Annie Odell, Kinko's regional manager for Louisiana. She's right. She may have the only printshops in town where customers come as much for the company as for the copies. It's a free-wheeling, high-tech operation that marches to the beat of a different drum machine. It looks chaotic; it is chaotic. Yet it produces profit as well as fun.

Kinko's keeps its sales figures a secret, but Odell estimates that her five New Orleans stores make about 40 million copies a year. At the firm's advertised $4\frac{1}{2}$-cents-per-copy price, that would mean around \$1.8 million a year in sales, or an average of over \$300,000 per shop.

Printers Sneer

Kinko's is unique. For one thing, it doesn't do a lick of offset printing. It makes copies, copies, and almost nothing but copies. On the side it binds, folds, staples, collates, makes pads, and takes passport photos.

Kinko's is also unique among quick printing chains in that it doesn't franchise. All 300 or so Kinko's stores are divided among a few closely held corporations, and founder Paul Orfalea holds a piece of virtually all of them. Odell explains that the company avoids franchising to ensure tight control over quality at its outlets.

For the record, Orfalea, who plugged in his first photocopier when he was in college, was nicknamed by classmates as "Kinko" for his curly head of hair.

Broadway and Benihana

Kinko's management style draws on both the restaurant business and the stage. Fast copies are like fast food, say the managers. It's not just that every Big Mac is a copy of every other one. Images of eating come up again and again as they try to explain what keeps their customers coming back.

"Making copies is addictive," says Windsor, and points to her clientele of "regulars," who "have made this their office. They will spend four or five hours here although they don't spend more than \$5 or \$6. People have suggested we open a bar in here."

"Instant gratification is what Kinko's is offering," says another manager.

The last time managers from around the country huddled in Santa Barbara for the company "picnic," they studied looseleaf binders crammed full of floor plans for McDonald's and Benihana of Tokyo—a variation on the acclaimed art of Japanese management.

"You'd find it hard to believe," says Odell, "but Benihana is a lot like Kinko's. They're masters of efficiency. We'll try to set up the floor to get one person operating two copiers, just like Benihana puts one cook between two tables. Our paper is centrally located, just as they have all the chopping prepared ahead of time. Then there's the floater, who floats around and pops in wherever he's needed."

Both Kinko's and Benihana's use theater to attract clients, charging their employees with putting on a good show as well as putting out good service. At the Japanese restaurant, the show is the cook, who sizzles a sukiyaki right in front of your table. At Kinko's, it's the clatter of copy machines and the Charlie Chaplinlike spectacle of operators running back and forth between them.

"They do it right in front of you and you get instant quality control," says Odell, "There's no way you're going to drop that document with the customer watching you."

She deliberately displays all her machines and personnel in one big room. "We work out with the public. That's why it's fun," says Odell, "The other guys are behind closed doors."

Windsor enjoys working in a fishbowl. "My personality changes," she says. "I'll be a little more dramatic and louder than I would be in a closed group. I walk quickly. I'll wad up and throw papers a lot."

She believes customers unconsciously get into the act. "Some of the mildest-mannered people get aggressive in here. I've seen a little old lady elbow her way in ahead of people, where if she were in a bank she'd stand in line neatly."

Kinko's does no broadcast and little print advertising, counting on price and word-of-mouth to draw customers, and ambience doesn't hurt. Each Kinko's has its "regulars," who get friendly with particular operators and who favor particular machines. The area in front of the counter is strewn with typewriters, lettering machines, and light tables, all the better to hook people into making themselves comfortable and coming back.

A recent addition to that melange is the customer comment form. The customer mails the postage-paid form straight to headquarters in Santa Barbara, where senior management review it and send a thank-you note to the author before routing it back to the shop manager for action. Odell has several inches of forms on file, along with notes on the follow-up calls she made to the customers.

"We don't choose our market so much as our market chooses us," she says. Each shop keeps a different mix of machines, depending on the needs of its patrons. An operator learns quickly that the Xerox 1000 series picks up blue but not yellow, while the 9000 series picks up yellow and black but not blue. Thus, the store adjoining the Tulane campus does not have a 9000 because students tend to bring in notes and books highlighted with yellow markers.

Another adaptation to the market is "Professor Publishing," a service that lets professors excerpt chapters from several books and print them up together as a single textbook. During the first two weeks of every semester, the Broadway office works virtually around-the-clock on this specialty.

Odell maintains that her managers clear all material with publishers before printing a professor's anthology. Indeed, Kinko's says it is one of the most scrupulous of the copy chains about observing copyright laws.

Printing in a Fishbowl

If working at the Kinko's shops in New Orleans is like working in a fishbowl, it's a two-way fishbowl where the fish are always peering back at their audience. The crazy-quilt mix of customers provides endless entertainment and a fund of oddball stories to exchange over beers. A sampling:

- One woman insisted that the manager throw away the ribbon on the self-service typewriter she'd just used, fearing that someone might try to use it to recreate her document. Another customer wanted several confidential pages typed, and asked, "Can you get me a typist who won't read them?"
- Some artists enjoy using the photocopiers for the oddest things. One woman brings in stuffed dead birds for reproduction. Another brought in a box of pecans purported to be from the backyard of a house where Tennessee Williams once lived.

Case

Questions

1. Can general operational standards be developed and implemented in all or a majority of Kinko's shops?
2. Discuss the idea of grouping copiers in machine centers so that certain copiers are available for specific tasks.
3. How do the different services offered (private copying versus copying services provided) present separate types of problems for management?
4. Kinko's Professor Publishing apparently did not pan out. What might have been the cause?

Source: Mark Ballard, "Working in a Fishbowl," *Quick Printing,* May 1987, pp. 30–32. Reprinted by permission.

S3 Project Management

Supplement Objectives

- Recognize that project management involves both people skills to coordinate and motivate individuals from a range of disciplines and technical skills to properly plan and schedule a project.
- Explain the role of the project manager in organizing and coordinating all activities performed in a project.
- Introduce critical path scheduling as a tool for identifying activities that require immediate attention.
- Identify the time–cost trade-offs involved in expediting the completion of a project.
- Discuss some of the criticisms often associated with project management techniques.

One strategy that many firms adopt to maintain a competitive advantage, especially those in high-tech industries, is to have the ability to constantly introduce new products that incorporate the latest, state-of-the-art technologies. Intel, which introduces next-generation computer chips while there is still strong demand for current-generation chips, is a good example of these types of firms. The speed with which these firms can introduce these new products, is often a critical element in their success.

The ability to react quickly to changing customer demands is also applicable to services. The design and rollout of an advertising campaign for a new product or service, the development of a new financial services instrument, and the planning of the Olympics are all examples of services that fall under the heading of projects. Another example of a service that would benefit by using project management concepts is one that designs and develops websites for companies.

The design, development, and introduction of a new product or service is viewed as a one-of-kind type activity that is often referred to as a project. The speed with which firms can introduce and provide new goods and services is dependent, in large degree, on management's ability to understand and apply the concepts of project management to all of the required and, very often, dependent activities.

Project management techniques are also very appropriate for exactly the opposite type of environment: one where a product's lead time may be long. The key factor in this case is that where frequency of production is low, each item produced tends to be viewed as a separate project. Examples include construction, shipbuilding, airplane manufacture, and the production of satellites. (See OM in Practice box on Hughes Electronics.)

There are two main components in project management: one heavily emphasizes the organization and the behavior of *people;* the other focuses on the technology of the *method* (computing start and completion times, critical paths, etc.). In this supplement we address both elements, although we lean more toward describing the technical aspects of project management and leave the people issues to a course on management and organizational behavior.

Consequently, project managers focus their efforts on three major elements:

- *Time:* How long will the project take from start to finish and will it be completed on schedule.
- *Performance:* Does the project meet or exceed the quality required by the customer.
- *Cost:* What are all of the costs, both direct and indirect, associated with the project, and will it be completed on schedule.

Definition of Project Management

A project is basically an organized undertaking to accomplish a specific goal. In a technical sense, a **project** is defined as a series of related jobs or tasks that are usually directed toward some major output and require a significant period of time to perform. *Project management* can be defined as planning, directing, and controlling resources (i.e., people, equipment, material) to meet the technical, cost, and time constraints of the project.

project

Series of related jobs or tasks focused on the completion of an overall objective.

While projects are often associated with single, one-of-a-kind type products, the fact is that many projects can be repeated or transferred to other settings or products. The result will be another project output. A contractor building houses or a firm producing customized, low-volume products such as supercomputers, locomotives, or linear accelerators can effectively consider such products as individual projects.

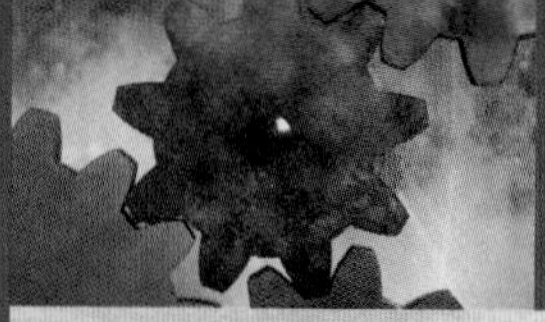

Operations Management in Practice

HUGHES ELECTRONICS LAUNCHES COMMUNICATION SATELLITES WITH PROJECT MANAGEMENT TECHNIQUES

Hughes Electronics markets direct broadcast satellite (DBS) services through PanAmSat Corporation, offering 150 channels of movies, cable TV programs, and sporting events directly to anyone in the United States, Canada, and parts of South America. It currently has three million subscribers with annual revenues of over $6 million. The factory where it produces the satellites for this venture is located in El Segundo, California, but it is unusual in that it is not a "traditional" manufacturing plant. There are no assembly lines, no conveyor belts, and no grinding tools. Instead, teams of workers gather around a half-dozen shiny objects doing the final assembly on satellites before they are launched. To successfully undertake the enormous challenges in this high-technology growth industry, Hughes has adopted many project management concepts and applied them through a complex cross-functional team that reaches across company lines and international boundaries. During the implementation of this project, several technological breakthroughs occurred that ultimately resulted in the successful launching of Hughes into the DBS business. For example, in the world's first application of video compression technology, Hughes will at least quadruple the capacity of satellite transponders that are needed to receive radio signals from earth and then to rebroadcast them on designated frequencies.

Source: Special thanks to Hans Thamhain, Bentley College.

There are some distinct differences between managing ongoing processes and managing projects. One difference relates to organizational structure. Repetitive processes are very likely to be managed within the formal organization structure while the group of people working together on a project are often brought together specifically to accomplish the single project and may stop working together when the project is completed. Because project teams are often newly formed groups, it can take time for these groups to be effective, requiring the conscious effort of all those involved as well as a major emphasis on communication.

Another major difference between the management of ongoing processes and project management relates to the tasks themselves. Since projects are by definition not repetitive, flexibility is an important element in successful project management. Unique, first-time tasks cannot always be totally defined or understood until they actually are begun, so project plans must continually evolve over the life of the project. Effective project management requires continuous monitoring, updating, and replanning throughout the life of the project.

A project starts out as a *statement of work (SOW).* The SOW may be a written description of the objectives to be achieved, with a brief statement of the work to be done and a proposed schedule specifying start and completion dates. It also could contain performance measures in terms of budget and completion steps (milestones) and the written reports to be supplied.

program

Synonym for a project, although it also can consist of several interrelated projects.

If the proposed work is a very large endeavor, it is frequently referred to as a **program,** although the terms *project* and *program* are often used interchangeably. A program, which is the highest order of organizational complexity, may take several years to complete, and may consist of interrelated projects completed by many organizations. The development of a new outer-space missile system and the introduction of a new national medical health care system would be good examples of programs.

A *task* or *activity* is a subdivision of a project. It is usually not longer than several months in duration and is performed by one group or organization.

A *subtask* may be used if needed to further subdivide the project into more meaningful pieces.

A *work package* is a group of activities combined to be assignable to a single organizational unit. It still falls within the format of project management in that the package provides a description of what is to be done, when it is to be started and completed, the budget, measures of performance, and specific events to be reached at points in time, which are called **milestones.** Typical milestones in the introduction of a new product might be the completion of the design phase, the production of a prototype, the completed testing of the prototype, and the approval of a pilot run.

milestones

Specific major events to be completed at certain times in the project.

Work Breakdown Structure

The **work breakdown structure (WBS)** is the heart of project management. This subdivision of the objective into smaller and smaller pieces more clearly defines the system in detail and contributes to its understanding and success. Conventional use shows the work breakdown structure decreasing in size from top to bottom and shows this level by indentation to the right in the following format:

work breakdown structure (WBS)

Method by which a project is divided into tasks and subtasks.

Level	
1	Program
2	Project
3	Task
4	Subtask
5	Work package

Exhibit S3.1 shows part of the work breakdown structure for a project to open a restaurant. Note the ease in identifying activities through the level numbers. For example, determine

Exhibit S3.1

Part of a Work Breakdown Structure for Opening a New Restaurant.

Level 1	2	3	4	5		
X					1.0	Open new restaurant
	X				1.1	Recruit workers
		X			1.1.1	Determine worker requirements
		X			1.1.2	Recruit workers
			X		1.1.2.1	Place advertisements
			X		1.1.2.2	Screen applicants
				X	1.1.2.2.1	Conduct interviews
				X	1.1.2.2.2	Check references
		X			1.1.3	Hire and train workers
	X				1.2	Purchase and install kitchen equipment
		X			1.2.1	Design menu
			X		1.2.1.1	Develop recipes
			X		1.2.1.2	Determine equip. requirements
		X			1.2.2	Purchase equipment
			X		1.2.2.1	Obtain quotes
			X		1.2.2.2	Select vendor
		X			1.2.3	Install equipment
			X		1.2.3.1	Connect electrical
			X		1.2.3.2	Connect plumbing

worker requirements (the third item down) is identified as 1.1.1 (the first item in level 1, the first item in level 2, and the first item in level 3). Similarly, install equipment (the 17th item down) is 1.2.3.

The key factors in having a good work breakdown structure are to

- Allow the activities to be worked on independently.
- Make them manageable in size.
- Give authority to carry out the program.
- Monitor and measure the program.
- Provide the required resources.

Organizational Considerations in Project Management

As stated previously, the timely completion of successful projects requires an understanding of both the technical and human resource components of project management. The technical component is required to identify the critical activities that affect the overall length of time a project takes to complete. The human resource elements address the issues of leadership and worker motivation within a group or team environment. While Chapter 10 addresses many of these human resource issues as they pertain to working in teams, our goal here is to present a brief overview on those aspects that appear to exist in most projects.

Role of the Project Manager

Project managers typically have a unique role within the traditional organization structure. Most project management teams are multidisciplinary in nature, involving a wide variety of skills and organizational units. Often these teams include people from engineering, operations, and marketing, and from support services that include risk management, systems operations, auditing, and legal groups. Consequently, today's project managers must often cross traditional functional lines in order to obtain the support necessary for the completion of a project. In most instances, this support is requested without formal authority. Thus the project manager must create a collaborative culture that relies heavily on social skills as well as technical expertise.

Without the authority of a traditional functional manager and the associated system of rewards and punishments, project managers must earn their authority by building trust, respect, and credibility among project members, as well as by demonstrating sound decision making—all within a stimulating work environment.

High-Performance Project Teams

In today's complex and technologically sophisticated environment, the group has re-emerged in importance in the form of project teams. The characteristics of a project team and its ultimate performance depend on many factors that involve both people and structural issues. Although each organization has its own measures of performance, there is general agreement among project managers on which factors are necessary for the creation of a successful project team. These factors are divided into the following four categories:[1]

1. *Task-related variables* are direct measures of task performance, such as the ability to produce quality results on time and within budget, innovative performance, and the ability to change.
2. *People-related variables* affect the inner workings of the team and include good communications, high involvement, the capacity to resolve conflict, and mutual trust and commitment to project objectives.
3. *Leadership variables* are associated with the various leadership positions within the project team. These positions can be created formally, such as the appointment of project managers and task leaders, or emerge dynamically within the work process as a result of individually developed power bases such as expertise, trust, respect, credibility, friendship, and empathy. Typical leadership characteristics include the ability to organize and direct tasks, facilitate group decision making, motivate, assist in conflict and problem resolutions, and foster a work environment that satisfies the professional and personal needs of the individual team members.
4. *Organizational variables* include the overall organizational climate, command-control-authority structure, policies, procedures, regulations, and regional cultures, values, and economic conditions.

It is interesting to note that managers, in describing the characteristics of an effective, high-performing project team, not only focus on task-related skills for producing technical results on time and within budget, but also focus on team members and leadership qualities.

Barriers to High Team Performance As a functioning group, the project team is subject to group dynamics. In addition, because it is usually a highly visible and focused work group, the project team often takes on special significance and is accorded high status with commensurate expectations of performance. Although a project team brings significant energy to a task, the possibility of the group malfunctioning is significant. This occurs because there are several barriers to high performance that can exist in a project team. These include (*a*) different points of view, (*b*) role conflicts, and (*c*) power struggles. Each of these barriers must be overcome if the team is to successfully complete its assigned project. Hewlett-Packard's successful introduction of its Deskjet printer demonstrates that those firms that can overcome these barriers experience significant growth and profitability. (See OM in Practice box.)

Project Control

The Department of Defense was one of the earliest large users of project management and has published a variety of useful standard forms. Many are used directly or have been modified by firms engaged in project management. Since those early days, however, graphics

[1]Hans J. Thamhain, "Managing Technologically Innovative Team Efforts Towards New Product Success," *Journal of Production Innovation Management* 7, no. 1 (March 1990); and Hans J. Thamhain, "Effective Leadership Style for Managing Project Teams," in *Handbook of Program and Project Management*, ed. P. C. Dinsmore (New York: AMACOM, 1992).

Operations Management in Practice

THE INTRODUCTION OF HEWLETT-PACKARD'S DESKJET PRINTER

The design and development of the DeskJet printer was one of Hewlett-Packard's (HP) first attempts to integrate its major functional areas such as manufacturing, marketing, and R&D. Its successful introduction was due, in large part, to HP's ability to apply many of the concepts in project management. The overall DeskJet printer project was subdivided into three project teams—firmware, electronics, and mechanical—with a project manager leading each team. The team members represented all of the functional areas of HP's Vancouver Division, including R&D, manufacturing, marketing, and quality assurance, with special assistance from personnel and finance. With all these functional groups in constant communication with each other, HP was able to identify specific project activities that could be performed concurrently, which significantly reduced both development time and manufacturing costs. As a result, the DeskJet printer provided HP with an unprecedented competitive advantage in the marketplace in both cost and speed of introduction.

Source: John D. Rhodes, "Managing the Development of the Deskjet Printer," *Hewlett-Packard Journal,* October 1988.

software has been written for most computers, so management, the customer, and the project manager have a wide choice of how data are presented. Exhibit S3.2 shows a sample of available presentations.

Gantt chart

Graphical technique that shows the amount of time required for each activity and the sequence in which activities are to be performed.

Exhibit S3.2A is a sample **Gantt chart** showing both the amount of time involved and the sequence in which activities can be performed. For example, "long lead procurement" and "manufacturing schedules" are independent activities and can occur simultaneously. All of the other activities must be done in sequence from top to bottom. Exhibit S3.2B graphically shows the proportion of money spent on labor, material, and overhead. Its value is its clarity in identifying sources and amounts of cost.

Exhibit S3.2C shows the percentage of the project's labor hours that come from the various areas of manufacturing, finance, and so on. These labor hours are related to the proportion of the project's total labor cost. For example, manufacturing is responsible for 50 percent of the project's labor hours, but this 50 percent represents just 40 percent of the total labor dollars charged.

The top half of Exhibit S3.2D shows the degree of completion of these projects. The dotted vertical line signifies today. Project 1, therefore, is already late since it still has work to be done. Project 2, although on schedule, is not being worked on temporarily, which is why there is a space before the projected work. Project 3, also on schedule, continues to be worked on without interruption. The bottom of Exhibit S3.2D shows actual total costs compared to projected costs. The exhibit shows that two cost overruns occurred.

Exhibit S3.2E is a milestone chart. The three milestones mark specific points in the project where checks can be made to see if the project is on time and where it should be. The best place

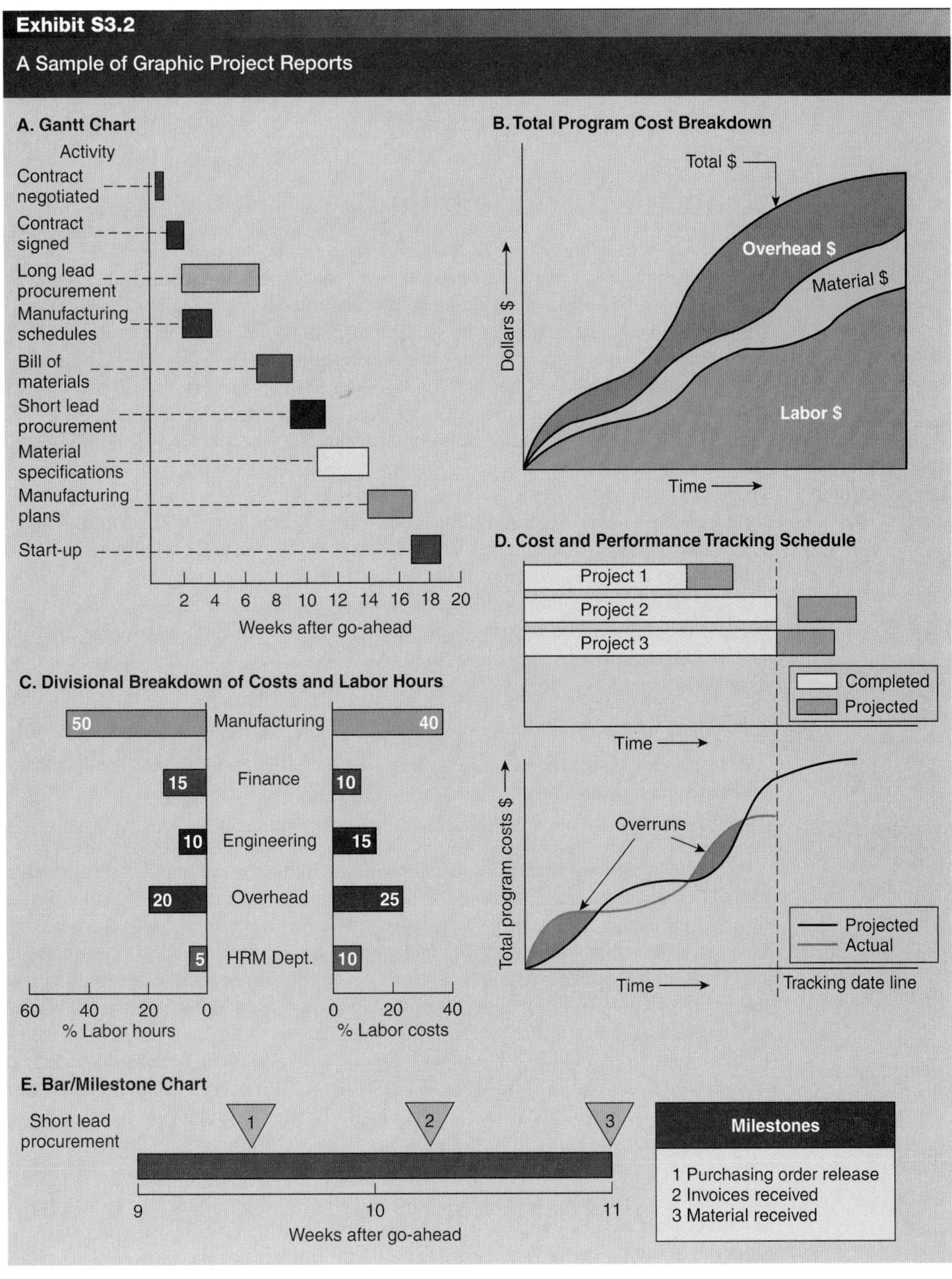
Exhibit S3.2
A Sample of Graphic Project Reports
A. Gantt Chart
Activity
Contract negotiated
Contract signed
Long lead procurement
Manufacturing schedules
Bill of materials
Short lead procurement
Material specifications
Manufacturing plans
Start-up
2 4 6 8 10 12 14 16 18 20
Weeks after go-ahead
B. Total Program Cost Breakdown
Total $
Overhead $
Material $
Labor $
Dollars $
Time
C. Divisional Breakdown of Costs and Labor Hours
50 Manufacturing 40
15 Finance 10
10 Engineering 15
20 Overhead 25
5 HRM Dept. 10
60 40 20 0
% Labor hours
0 20 40
% Labor costs
D. Cost and Performance Tracking Schedule
Project 1
Project 2
Project 3
Completed
Projected
Time
Total program costs $
Overruns
Projected
Actual
Time
Tracking date line
E. Bar/Milestone Chart
Short lead procurement
1
2
3
9
10
11
Weeks after go-ahead
Milestones
1 Purchasing order release
2 Invoices received
3 Material received

to locate milestones is at the completion of a major activity. In this exhibit, the major activities completed were "purchasing order release," "invoices received," and "material received."

Other standard reports can be used for a more detailed presentation comparing cost to progress (such as a cost schedule status report—CSSR) or reports providing the basis for partial payment (such as an "earned value" report).

Critical Path Scheduling

Critical path scheduling refers to a set of graphic techniques used in planning and controlling projects. In any given project, the three factors of concern are time, costs, and resource availability. Here, time refers to the total elapsed time from the beginning of the project until its completion; costs are defined as all of those expenses directly related to the project, including material and labor; resources include the labor available to work on the project, as well as equipment and facilities that can be assigned to the project. Critical path techniques have been developed to deal with each of these, individually and in combination.

PERT (program evaluation and review technique)

Technique developed by the U.S. Navy for planning the Polaris missile project.

CPM (critical path method)

Technique developed to schedule preventive maintenance shutdowns of chemical processing plants.

PERT (program evaluation and review technique) and **CPM (critical path method),** the two best-known techniques, were both developed in the late 1950s. PERT was developed under the sponsorship of the U.S. Navy Special Projects Office in 1958 as a management tool for scheduling and controlling the Polaris missile project. CPM was developed in 1957 by J. E. Kelly of Remington-Rand and M. R. Walker of Du Pont to aid in scheduling maintenance shutdowns of chemical processing plants.

Critical path scheduling techniques display a project in graphic form and relate its individual tasks in a way that focuses attention on those tasks that are critical to the project's completion. For critical path scheduling techniques to be most applicable, a project must have the following characteristics:

1. It must have well-defined jobs or tasks whose completion marks the end of the project.
2. The jobs or tasks are independent; they may be started, stopped, and conducted separately within a given sequence.
3. The jobs or tasks are ordered; certain ones must follow others in a given sequence.

The construction, aerospace, and shipbuilding industries commonly meet these criteria, and critical path techniques find wide application within them. We previously noted also that the applications of project management and critical path techniques are becoming much more common within firms in rapidly changing industries.

Project management techniques also are becoming more common in health care, with the objective of reducing a patient's overall stay in a hospital. Here, each patient is viewed as a project and the various procedures he or she undergoes are considered to be the tasks in that project. (It should be noted that there is a growing trend toward defining "care paths," which provide standard steps that all patients follow. For example, Massachusetts General Hospital has established a paper checklist of what should happen with a patient on each day of a five-day stay for coronary artery bypass graft surgery.)

Time-Oriented Techniques

The basic forms of PERT and CPM focus on identifying the longest time-consuming path through a network of tasks as a basis for planning and controlling a project. Both PERT and CPM use nodes and arrows for display. Originally, the basic differences between PERT and

CPM were that PERT used the arrow to represent an activity and CPM used the node. The other original difference between these two techniques was that PERT used three estimates—optimistic, pessimistic, and most likely—of an activity's required time, whereas CPM used just a single, best-time estimate. This distinction reflects PERT's origin in scheduling advanced scientific projects (like the lunar missions) that are characterized by uncertainty and CPM's origin in the scheduling of the fairly routine activity of plant maintenance. Thus, PERT was often used when the primary variable of interest was time, whereas CPM was used when the primary variable of interest was cost. As years passed, these two features no longer distinguished PERT from CPM. This is because CPM users started to use three time estimates and PERT users often placed activities on the nodes.

We believe the activity on the node is much easier to follow logically than the activity on the arrow. However, the three time estimates are often very valuable in obtaining a measure of the probability of completion times. Therefore, in this supplement we use the activity on the node and either a single estimate for activity time or three time estimates, depending on our objective. We use the terms *CPM* and *PERT* interchangeably and mean the same thing, although we tend to use the term *CPM* more frequently.

In a sense, both techniques owe their development to their widely used predecessor, the Gantt chart. While the Gantt chart is able to relate activities to time in a visually usable fashion for very small projects, the interrelationship of activities, when displayed in this format, becomes extremely difficult to visualize and to work with for projects with more than 25 or 30 activities. Moreover, the Gantt chart provides no direct procedure for determining the critical path, which, despite its theoretical shortcomings, is of great practical value.

CPM with a Single Time Estimate

With the following as an example, we will develop the typical approach taken in project scheduling. The times for each activity have been given as a most likely estimate (rather than three estimates, which will be discussed in a later example).

Example

Many firms that have tried to enter the portable computer market have failed. Suppose your firm believes that there is a big demand in this market because existing products have not been designed correctly. They are either too heavy, too large, or too small to accommodate a standard-size keyboard. Your intended computer will be small enough to carry inside a jacket pocket if need be. The ideal size will be no larger than 4 inches × 9½ inches × 1 inch with a standard typewriter keyboard. It should weigh no more than 15 ounces, have a 4- to 8-line × 80-character back-lit display, and have a micro disk drive and a micro printer. It should be aimed primarily toward word processing use but have plug-in ROMs to accommodate an assortment of computer languages and programs. These characteristics should appeal to traveling businesspeople, but then could also have a much wider market. If it can be priced to sell retail in the $175–$200 range, the computer should appeal to a wide market.

The project, then, is to design, develop, and produce a prototype of this portable computer. In the rapidly changing computer industry, it is crucial to hit the market with a product of this type in less than a year. Therefore, the project team has been allowed approximately nine months, or 39 weeks, to produce the prototype.

The first assignment of the project team is to develop a project network chart to determine whether or not the prototype computer can be completed within the 39 weeks. Let's follow the steps in the development of this network.

Solution

Step 1: Activity Identification
The project team decides that the following activities constitute the major components of the project: (A) designing the computer, (B) constructing the prototype, (C) evaluating automatic assembly equipment, (D) testing the prototype, (E) preparing an assembly equipment study report, (F) writing methods specifications (to be summarized in a report), and (G) preparing a final report summarizing all aspects of the design, equipment, and methods.

Step 2: Activity Sequencing and Network Construction
On the basis of discussion with her staff, the project manager develops the precedence table and sequence network shown in Exhibit S3.3. Activities are indicated as nodes while arrows show the sequence in which the individual activities must be completed.

Using the precedence table, we can construct a network diagram, taking care to ensure that the activities are in the proper order and that the logic of their relationships is maintained. For example, it would be illogical to have a situation where Activity A precedes Activity B, B precedes C, and then C precedes A.

critical path

Longest sequence of activities that determines the overall length of the project.

Step 3: Determine the Critical Path
A path is defined as any sequence of connected activities through the network.

The **critical path** is defined as the longest sequence of connected activities through the network. In other words, the shortest time in which the project can be completed is

Exhibit S3.3

CPM Network for Computer Design Project

CPM Activity/Designations and Time Estimates

Activity	Designation	Immediate Predecessors	Time in Weeks
Design	A	—	21
Build prototype	B	A	4
Evaluate equipment	C	A	7
Test prototype	D	B	2
Write equipment report	E	C, D	5
Write methods report	F	C, D	8
Write final report	G	E, F	2

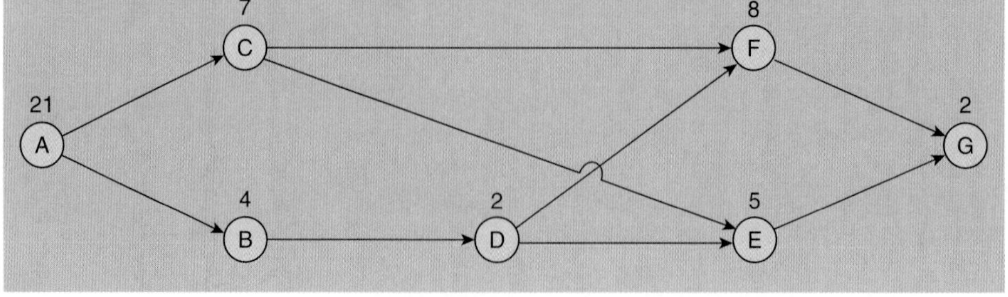

determined by the length of the critical path. To find the critical path, we simply identify all of the paths through the network, from beginning to end, and calculate their respective completion times. That path with the longest completion time is, by definition, the critical path. For our example, the different paths and their respective completion times are as follows:

Path	Completion Time (in weeks)
A–C–F–G	21 + 7 + 8 + 2 = 38
A–C–E–G	21 + 7 + 5 + 2 = 35
A–B–D–F–G	21 + 4 + 2 + 8 + 2 = 37
A–B–D–E–G	21 + 4 + 2 + 5 + 2 = 34

Path A–C–F–G takes the longest amount of time to complete, which is 38 weeks, and is therefore the critical path for this project. Consequently, this project as it now exists cannot be completed in fewer than 38 weeks. Inasmuch as the project has been allowed 39 weeks in which to be completed, there appears to be no problem. If the project were required to be completed in fewer than 38 weeks, then one or more of the activities on the critical path would have to be "crashed" or accelerated in order to meet the required project completion date.

Step 4: Determine Slack Times

The total **slack time** for an activity is defined as that amount of time that an activity can be delayed without affecting the overall completion time of the project. In order to calculate the slack time for each activity, the following terms are defined:

slack time

Amount of time an activity can be delayed without affecting the completion date of the overall project.

- *Early start time* (ES), the earliest possible time that the activity can begin.
- *Early finish time* (EF), the early start time plus the time needed to complete the activity.
- *Late finish time* (LF), the latest possible time that an activity can end without delaying the project.
- *Late start time* (LS), the late finish time minus the time needed to complete the activity.

To determine the slack time for an activity requires the calculation of either the early start (ES) time and the late start (LS) time or the early finish (EF) time and the late finish (LF) time for that activity.

The difference between the early start time and the late start time (or between the early finish time and the late finish time) is the slack time. The difference between the ES and EF times, and the LS and LF times, is the same, being the amount of time required to complete that specific activity; hence EF − ES = LF − LS = activity completion time.

These values and the resulting total slack time for each of the activities in our example will now be calculated with the following procedure.

Step 4.1: Find the ES and EF for Each Activity

The early start time for each activity is determined with a "forward pass" through the network, beginning with the first activity A, for which we set the ES = 0, representing the start of the project. To find the ES for the activities that follow A (i.e., B and C), we simply add the time it takes to complete activity A, which in this case is 21 weeks, to the

ES for A, which is zero. Therefore, the earliest we could start either activity B or C is 21 weeks after we begin the project, which is when activity A is completed. (In other words, ES_B or $ES_C = 0 + 21 = 21$.) Likewise, the ES for activity D is the ES for activity B (21 weeks) plus the time to complete B (4 weeks) making ES = 25 weeks for activity D (i.e., $ES_D = 21 + 4 = 25$).

This procedure is repeated for each activity in the network. When more than one activity precedes the activity being evaluated, then the ES for each path leading to that activity is calculated, and the latest ES is selected, as that becomes the constraining factor as to when that activity can begin. For example:

$$ES_F = \text{MAX}\ (ES_C + C, ES_D + D)$$
$$ES_F = \text{MAX}\ (21 + 7, 25 + 2)$$
$$ES_F = \text{MAX}\ (28, 27) = 28 \text{ weeks}$$

where

C = Completion time for activity C
D = Completion time for activity D

Therefore, the earliest we could start activity F is 28 weeks after we begin the project. Likewise, through similar calculations, $ES_E = 28$ weeks and $ES_G = 36$ weeks. (The EF for an activity is simply the ES plus the completion time for the activity.)

Step 4.2: Find the LS and LF for Each Activity

To obtain the LS for each activity, we simply reverse the procedure for calculating the ES, beginning at the end of the project. The LS for an activity is defined as the latest time that an activity can be started without delaying the completion of the overall project. Since we start at the end of the network and work our way back to the beginning, this is called a "backwards pass" through the network.

We begin with the last activity, G. As we determined earlier, the critical path for the project is 38 weeks. Therefore, the latest that we could start activity G and still complete the project in 38 weeks is 36 weeks, as it takes two weeks to do activity G. Similarly, $LS_F = LS_G - F = 36 - 8 = 28$ weeks, and $LS_E = LS_G - E = 36 - 5 = 31$ weeks. The other LS times for the remaining activities are likewise calculated.

When more than one activity follows the activity being evaluated, then the LS for all paths leading out of the activity must be calculated and that path with the earliest LS time is used, as that time becomes the constraining factor as to the latest time that activity can begin. For example:

$$LS_C = \text{MIN}\ (LS_F - C, LS_E - C)$$
$$LS_C = \text{MIN}\ (28 - 7, 31 - 7)$$
$$LS_C = \text{MIN}\ (21, 24) = 21 \text{ weeks}$$

Thus, the latest we can start activity C is 21 weeks after we begin the project. Similarly, $LS_D = 25$ weeks and $LS_A = 0$ weeks. The earliest start and the latest start times for all of the activities in the computer design project are shown in Exhibit S3.4. As stated earlier, the difference between the EF time and the ES time for an activity is simply the time it takes to complete that activity. This is also the difference between the LF and the LS times for the activity. The EF and LF times, thus, also are shown in Exhibit S3.4.

Exhibit S3.4

CPM Network for Computer Design Project

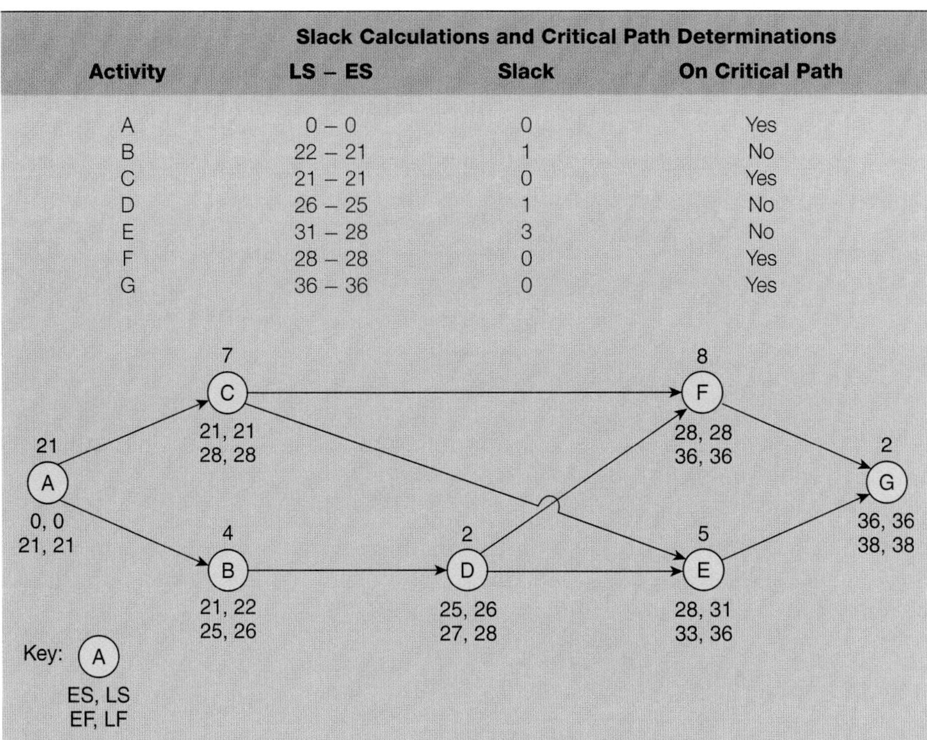

Slack Calculations and Critical Path Determinations

Activity	LS – ES	Slack	On Critical Path
A	0 – 0	0	Yes
B	22 – 21	1	No
C	21 – 21	0	Yes
D	26 – 25	1	No
E	31 – 28	3	No
F	28 – 28	0	Yes
G	36 – 36	0	Yes

Step 4.3: Determine the Total Slack Time for Each Activity

As stated previously, the total slack time for each activity is defined as either LS – ES or LF – EF. In the computer design project, the slack time for activity E is three weeks, and for activities B and D, one week each. Notice that the activities on the critical path (i.e., A, C, F, and G) do not have any slack times, because, in fact, they are all on the critical path and any delay in these activities will therefore affect the overall project's completion time. Typically, the project completion time is calculated using network analysis and then compared with the desired deadline. Thus, while there is no slack in any of the activities on the critical path with respect to the calculated project completion time, there can be slack in the critical path when the desired deadline is longer. In this example, with the desired deadline at 39 weeks and the calculated project completion time at 38 weeks, there is a one-week slack time in the critical path.

Early Start and Late Start Schedules

An **early start schedule** is one that lists all of the activities by their early start times. For activities not on the critical path, there is slack time between the activity completion and the start of the next activity that succeeds it. These slack times represent flexibility and should be used wisely by the project manager. The early start schedule completes the project and all of its activities as soon as possible.

A **late start schedule** lists the activities to start as late as possible without delaying the completion date of the project. One of the motivations for using a late start schedule is that savings are realized by postponing purchases of materials, the use of labor, and other costs until necessary.

early start schedule

Earliest time that each activity in the project can be started.

late start schedule

Latest start time that each activity can be started without affecting the overall completion time.

CPM with Three Activity Time Estimates

If a single estimate of the time required to complete an activity is not reliable, the alternative is to use three time estimates. By incorporating three estimates for each activity, we have the opportunity to obtain a probability for the completion time for the entire project. Briefly, the procedure using this approach is as follows: The estimated activity time is a weighted average, with more weight given to the best estimate and less to the maximum and minimum times. The estimated completion time of the network is then computed using basic statistics.

We continue with the computer design project, only now each of the activities has three time estimates associated with it, and the seven-step procedure for solving this problem is as follows:

Step 1: Identify Each Activity to be Done in the Project (which is identical to the CPM method with a single time estimate)

Step 2: Determine the Sequence of Activities and Construct a Network Reflecting the Precedence Relationships (again, this is identical to the CPM method with a single time estimate)

Step 3: Define the Three Time Estimates for Each Activity The three time estimates for each activity are defined as

a = *Optimistic time:* the minimum reasonable period of time in which the activity can be completed. (There is only a small probability, typically assumed to be about 1 percent, that the activity can be completed in a shorter period of time.)

m = *Most likely time:* the best guess of the time required. Since m would be the time thought most likely to appear, it is also the mode of the beta distribution (which is discussed in the next step).

b = *Pessimistic time:* the maximum reasonable period of time the activity would take to be completed. (There is only a small probability, typically assumed to be about 1 percent, that it would take longer.)

Typically, the information about the three estimates is obtained from those people who are to perform the activity or others with expertise about the activity.

Step 4: Calculate the Expected Time (ET) for Each Activity The formula to calculate the expected activity completion time is:

$$\text{ET} = \frac{a + 4m + b}{6}$$

This formula is developed from the beta probability distribution and weights the most likely time (m) four times more than either the optimistic time (a) or the pessimistic time (b). The beta distribution is an extremely flexible distribution. It can take on a variety of forms that typically arise in project management activities, and it has finite end points, which limit the possible activity times to the area between a and b and, in the simplified version, permits a straightforward computation of the activity mean and standard deviation. Four typical beta curves are illustrated in Exhibit S3.5.

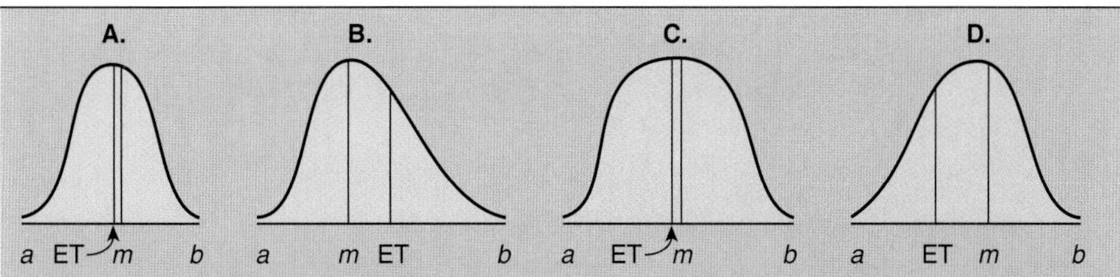

Curve A indicates very little uncertainty about the activity time, and since it is symmetrical, the expected time (ET) and the most likely or modal time (*m*) fall along the same point.

Curve B indicates a high probability of finishing the activity early, but if something goes wrong, the activity time could be greatly extended.

Curve C is almost a rectangular distribution, which suggests that the estimator sees the probability of finishing the activity early or late as equally likely, and $m \cong$ ET.

Curve D indicates that there is a small chance of finishing the activity early, but it is more probable that it will take an extended period of time.

Exhibit S3.5

Typical Beta Curves

Step 5: Calculate the Variance (σ^2) for Each Activity The variance, σ^2, associated with each ET is computed using the following formula:

$$\sigma^2 = \left(\frac{b-a}{6}\right)^2$$

As you can see, the variance is the square of one-sixth the difference between the two extreme time estimates, and, of course, the greater this difference, the larger the variance. A summary of the expected time and variance for each activity involved in making the portable computer discussed previously is presented in Exhibit S3.6.

Step 6: Identify All of the Paths in the Network and Their Estimated Completion Times and Variances Using the data in Exhibit S3.6, the expected completion time for each path is simply the sum of the expected completion times for the activities that are on that path. Likewise, to calculate the variance for each path, we simply add together the variances of the activities on the path. Again using the data in Exhibit S3.6, the path variances are calculated, and summarized in Exhibit S3.7, along with the path expected completion times.

Exhibit S3.6

Activity Expected Times and Variances

Activity	Activity Designation	Time Estimates a	m	b	Expected Times (ET) $\frac{a+4m+b}{6}$	Activity Variances (σ^2) $\left(\frac{b-a}{6}\right)^2$
Design	A	10	22	28	21	9.00
Build prototype	B	1	4	7	4	1.00
Evaluate equipment	C	4	6	14	7	2.78
Test prototype	D	1	2	3	2	0.11
Write report	E	1	5	9	5	1.78
Write methods report	F	7	8	9	8	0.11
Write final report	G	2	2	2	2	0.00

Exhibit S3.7

Path Estimated Completion Times and Variances

Path	Expected Completion Time (in weeks)	Variance (σ_p^2)
A–C–E–G	35	13.56
A–B–D–F–G	37	10.22
A–B–D–E–G	34	11.89
A–C–F–G	38	11.89

Step 7: Determine the Probability of Completing the Project by a Given Date

The probability of completing the project by a given date is dependent on the probability of each path in the network being completed by that date. In our example, the desired completion time for the project is 39 weeks. In other words, we want to calculate the probability of completing the project in 39 weeks or less. To do this we need to calculate the probability of each of the paths in the network being completed in 39 weeks or less. All of the paths need to be completed in 39 weeks or less for the project to be completed within that same time period. Thus, the probability of the project being completed within a given time is equal to the minimum of the probabilities of the different paths.

Using the data in Exhibit S3.7, we can now construct the probability distribution for each path and calculate the probability of each path being completed in 39 weeks or less. This is shown graphically in Exhibit S3.8. Note that in order to calculate the probability of completing each path in 39 days or less, we use σ_p, which is the square root of the variance, σ_p^2.

In Exhibit S3.8, the shaded area to the left of the line representing 39 weeks is the probability of that path being completed within the 39-week period. To obtain the value of that probability, we use the normal table in Appendix B or C. In order to be able to use this table we need to calculate a Z-value associated with each path, indicating how many standard deviations the 39 weeks is from the expected completion time for that path. The formula for this is:

$$Z = \frac{\mathrm{D} - \mathrm{ET}_p}{\sigma_p}$$

where

D = Desired completion date for the project

ET_p = Expected completion time for the path

σ_p = Standard deviation for the path

In this manner, the Z-value for each path is calculated and presented in Exhibit S3.9, along with the corresponding probability that we obtain from the normal table in Appendix B or C. As an approximation, one can determine the probability of completing the project within 39 weeks or less as the minimum of the individual path probabilities, or

$$\text{Prob (Proj} < 39) = \text{MIN } [(0.8621), (0.7357), (0.9265), (0.6141)] = 0.6141$$

Thus, the probability of completing this project within 39 weeks is 61.41 percent, even though its expected completion time, as determined by the average activity times on the critical path, is 38 weeks.

Maintaining Ongoing Project Schedules

It is important to keep a project schedule accurate and current. The schedule tracks the progress of the project and identifies problems as they occur while time to correct the

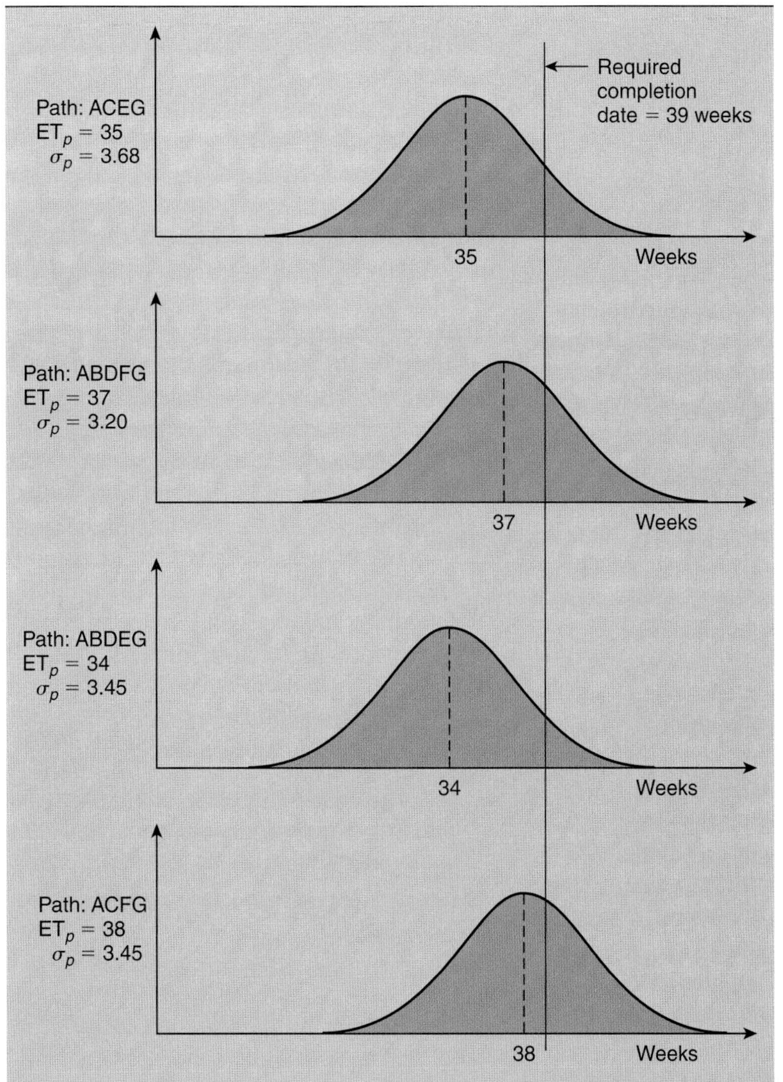

Exhibit S3.8 Probability of Each Path Being Completed in 39 Weeks or Less

Path	*Z*-Value	Completion Probability
A–C–E–G	1.09	0.8621
A–B–D–F–G	0.63	0.7357
A–B–D–E–G	1.45	0.9265
A–C–F–G	0.29	0.6141

Exhibit S3.9 Path *Z*-Values and Probabilities of Completing Each Path in 39 Weeks or Less

situation may still be available. In some situations, for example, it may be necessary to shift limited resources, be it labor, equipment, or facilities, from noncritical activities that are not on the critical path, and therefore have some slack time, to critical activities without slack times that are on the critical path. The schedule also monitors the progress of the costs and is often the basis for partial payments. In practice, however, schedules are often sloppily kept, or even totally abandoned.

Operations Management in Practice

THE E.SCHWAB PROJECT: DEVELOPING AN ONLINE SERVICE AT CHARLES SCHWAB

The Charles Schwab Corporation, which was founded in 1974 as one of the country's first discount brokerages, provides a broad array of financial services to individual investors, independent investment managers, retirement plans, and institutions through a network of over 398 branches, offices, telephone service centers, automated phone services, and the Internet.

In 1995, however, Schwab had no Internet presence at all. But by 1998, Schwab had 2.2 million online accounts and traded $4 billion of securities each week on its website—more than half its total trading volume. However, Schwab's Internet success didn't just happen. Co-CEOs Charles Schwab and David Pottruck believed that while lowering prices to compete on the Web could cost them millions in forgone revenues, they also believed that an Internet service was the key to the firm's future success.

The project began in 1995, when chief information officer Dawn Lepore received a message from one of her staff about some software that would link Schwab's different computer systems. The technical challenge could be solved in a number of ways, but the engineers chose a simple Web-based stock trade that enabled a Schwab server to take a web order, execute it, and send a confirmation back to the customer's PC. While this sounds straightforward today, it was groundbreaking at the time, since most existing Web trading systems required that each order be printed and then re-entered into another system.

Lepore and Schwab immediately recognized the project's implications with respect to the long-term success of the firm. Within weeks a Web trading project team was formed. The team grew to 30 people and evolved into an electronic brokerage unit called e.Schwab that reported directly to Pottruck.

At the same time, brokerages such as E*Trade and Ameritrade were working on their own Web trading products, so competition was fierce and pressure was high. In 1996, e.Schwab went live. To open an account, investors sent a check (or wire transfer) but after that first transaction they could trade any security just by logging on to e.Schwab's website. For this service, investors paid a flat fee of $39 (which was later reduced to $29.95) for stock trades of up to 1,000 shares (versus the usual sliding scale of higher commissions for larger trades).

To encourage the use of its website, e.Schwab provides a free online learning center, which has an interactive, "Tell me. Show me. Let me do it," approach.

The announcement of e.Schwab was made at an annual shareholders' meeting, but without any further publicity, the new service was an immediate success, reaching 25,000 Web accounts in the first two weeks—their goal for the entire first year. By the end of 1997, e.Schwab had grown to 1.2 million online accounts with assets of $81 billion. There were several key factors that contributed to the success of this project, including:

- e.Schwab was developed internally by personnel familiar with Schwab's financial services.
- E.Schwab was not really a new product, but rather an extension of Schwab's core business.
- The project was completed quickly and in a cost-efficient manner.

Sources:

Erick Schonfield, "Schwab Puts It All Online," *Fortune,* December 7, 1998, pp. 94–100.

Andrew Rafalaf, "Schwab Takes on New Role as Educator," *Wall Street and Technology,* April, 2000, p. 21.

John Donohue, Joe Spinelli, and Phil Schefter, "Look—at Amex and Schwab Models—Before Leaping into Corporate Ventures," *American Banker,* June 29, 2001, pp. 26–27.

Perhaps the most important reason for this happening is that managers are not committed enough to the technique to insist that the schedules be kept up to date. The resulting poor schedules consequently give project scheduling a bad name. Experience in project scheduling techniques is important and this job should not be carelessly relegated to the closest warm body. The project manager must support the schedule and see to it that it is maintained.

Time–Cost Trade-Off Models

In practice, project managers are as much concerned with the cost to complete a project as they are with the time to complete the project. For this reason, **time–cost trade-off models** have been devised. These models, which are extensions of PERT and CPM, attempt to develop a minimum-cost schedule for the entire project and to control budgetary expenditures during the project.

time–cost trade-off models

Models that develop the relationship between direct project costs, indirect costs, and time to complete the project.

Minimum-Cost Scheduling (Time–Cost Trade-Off)

The basic assumption in minimum-cost scheduling is that there is a relationship between activity completion time and the cost of a project. On one hand, it costs money to expedite an activity; on the other, it costs money to sustain (or lengthen) the project. The costs associated with expediting activities in order to shorten their completion times are termed *activity direct costs* and add to the project's direct costs. These additional costs that are included when an activity is accelerated also are referred to as **crash costs.** Worker-related crash costs include overtime pay to reduce the overall completion time. Another example of crash costs would be the additional expenses incurred in shipping items by airfreight to expedite their delivery, instead of through slower, more normal distribution channels such as the mail or on trucks.

crash costs

Additional costs of an activity when time to complete it is shortened.

The costs associated with sustaining the project are termed *project indirect costs;* overhead, facilities, and resource opportunity costs, and, under certain contractual situations, penalty costs or lost incentive payments. Since *activity direct costs* and *project indirect costs* are opposing costs dependent on time, the scheduling problem is essentially one of finding that project duration that minimizes their sum or, in other words, finding the optimum point in a time–cost trade-off.

The procedure for finding this point consists of the following five steps and is illustrated using the simple four-activity network that is shown in Exhibit S3.10. Assume in this example that the indirect costs remain constant for eight days and then increase at the rate of $5 per day.

Step 1: Prepare a CPM-Type Network Diagram For each activity this diagram should list

a. Normal cost (NC): The lowest expected activity cost (these are the lesser of the cost figures shown under each node in Exhibit S3.10).

b. Normal time (NT): The time associated with each normal cost.

c. Crash time (CT): The shortest possible activity time.

d. Crash cost (CC): The cost associated with each crash time.

Step 2: Determine the Cost per Unit of Time (assume days) to Expedite (or crash) Each Activity The relationship between activity time and cost may be shown graphically by plotting CC and CT coordinates and connecting them to the NC and NT coordinates by a concave, convex, or straight line—or some other form, depending on the actual cost structure of the activity's performance, as shown in Exhibit S3.10. For Activity A, we assume a linear relationship between time and cost. This assumption is common in practice and facilitates the derivation of the cost per day to expedite since this value may be found directly by taking the slope of the line using the formula: Slope = (CC − NC) ÷ (NT − CT). (When the assumption of linearity cannot be made, the cost of expediting must be determined graphically for each of the days the activity may be shortened.)

Exhibit S3.10

Example of Time–Cost Trade-Off Procedure

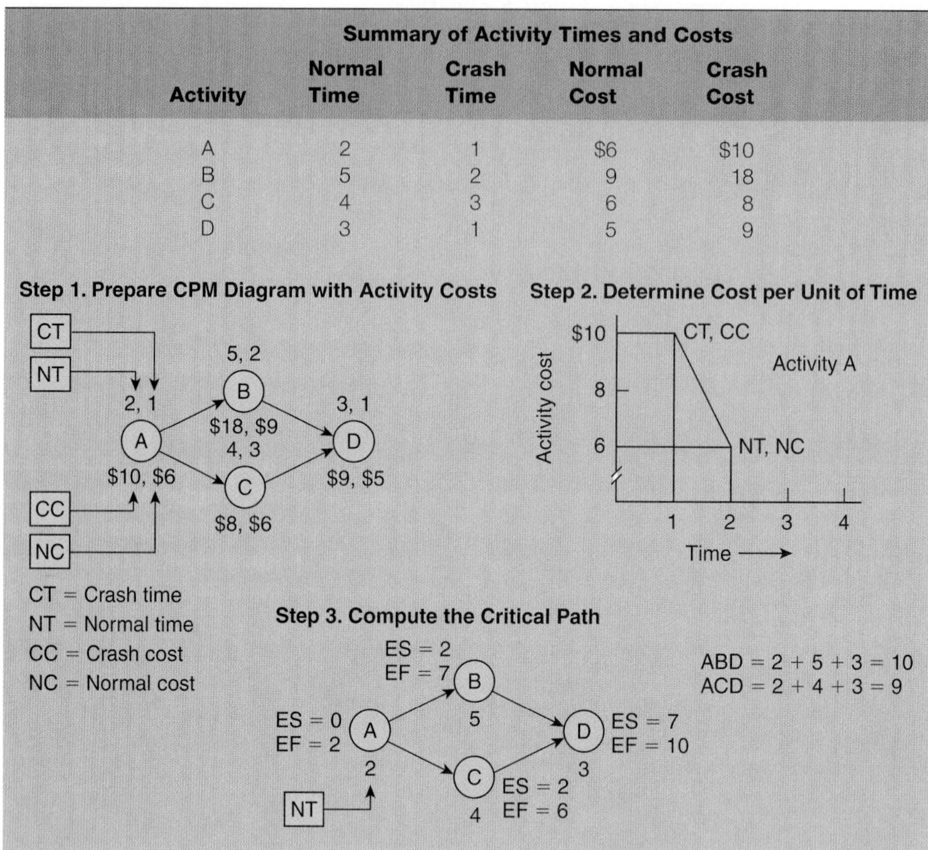

Summary of Activity Times and Costs

Activity	Normal Time	Crash Time	Normal Cost	Crash Cost
A	2	1	$6	$10
B	5	2	9	18
C	4	3	6	8
D	3	1	5	9

Exhibit S3.11

Calculation of Cost per Day to Expedite Each Activity

Activity	CC – NC	NT – CT	$\frac{CC - NC}{NT - CT}$	Cost per Day to Expedite	Number of Days Activity May Be Shortened
A	$10 – $6	2 – 1	$\frac{\$10 - 6}{2 - 1}$	$4	1
B	$18 – $9	5 – 2	$\frac{\$18 - \$9}{5 - 2}$	$3	3
C	$8 – $6	4 – 3	$\frac{\$8 - \$6}{4 - 3}$	$2	1
D	$9 – $5	3 – 1	$\frac{\$9 - \$5}{3 - 1}$	$2	2

The calculations needed to obtain the cost of expediting the remaining activities are shown in Exhibit S3.11.

Step 3: Compute the Critical Path For the simple network we have been using, this schedule would take 10 days. The critical path is A–B–D.

Step 4: Shorten the Critical Path at the Least Cost The easiest way to proceed is to start with the normal schedule, find the critical path, and reduce the path time by one day using the lowest-cost activity. Then recompute and find the new critical path and reduce it by one day also. Repeat this procedure until the time of completion is satisfactory, or until there can be no further reduction in the project completion time. Exhibit S3.12 shows the reduction of the network one day at a time.

Step 5: Plot Project Direct, Indirect, and Total-Cost Curves and Find Minimum-Cost Schedule Exhibit S3.13 shows the indirect cost plotted as a constant $10 for the first eight days and increasing $5 per day thereafter. The direct costs are plotted from Exhibit S3.12 and the total project cost is shown as the total of the two costs.

Summing the values for direct and indirect costs for each day yields the project total cost curve. As you can see, this curve is at its minimum for an eight-day schedule, which costs $40 ($30 direct + $10 indirect).

Criticisms of PERT and CPM

There are several assumptions that need to be made when applying CPM or PERT analysis to project networks. This section summarizes some of the more significant assumptions and their criticisms. One point of particular difficulty for the operating personnel is understanding

Exhibit S3.12

Reducing the Project Completion Time One Day at a Time

Current Critical Path(s)	Remaining Number of Days Activity May Be Shortened	Cost per Day to Expedite Each Activity	Least-Cost Activity to Expedite	Total Cost of All Activities in Network	Project Completion Time
A–B–D	All activity times and costs are normal			$26	10
A–B–D	A–1, B–3, D–2	A–4, B–3, D–2	D	28	9
A–B–D	A–1, B–3, D–1	A–4, B–3, D–2	D	30	8
A–B–D	A–1, B–3	A–4, B–3	B	33	7
A–B–D, A–C–D	A–1, B–2, C–1	A–4, B–3, C–2	A*	37	6
A–B–D, A–C–D	B–2, C–1	B–3, C–2	B & C†	42	5
A–B–D, A–C–D	B–1	B–3	B	45	5

*To reduce both critical paths by one day, reduce either A alone, or B and C together at the same time (since either B or C by itself modifies the critical path without shortening it).
†B & C must be crashed together to reduce both critical paths by one day.

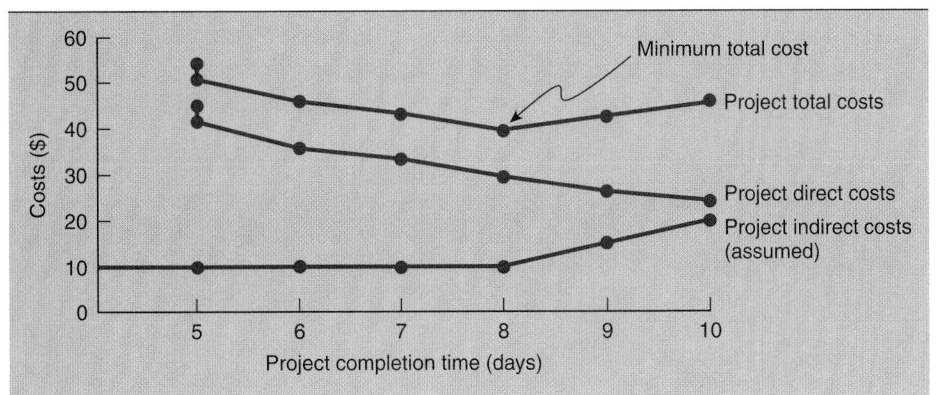

Exhibit S3.13

Plot of Costs and Minimum Cost Schedule

the statistics when three time estimates are used. The beta distribution of activity times, the three time estimates, the activity variances, and the use of the normal distribution to arrive at project completion probabilities are all potential sources of misunderstandings, and with misunderstanding comes distrust and obstruction. Thus, management must be sure that the people charged with monitoring and controlling activity performance have a general understanding of the statistics.

1. *Assumption:* Project activities can be identified as entities (that is, there is a clear beginning and ending point for each activity).
   Criticism: Projects, especially complex ones, change in content over time, and therefore a network made at the beginning may be highly inaccurate later on. Also, the very fact that activities are specified and a network formalized tends to limit the flexibility that is required to handle changing situations as the project progresses.
2. *Assumption:* Project activity sequence relationships can be specified and networked.
   Criticism: Sequence relationships cannot always be specified beforehand. In some projects, in fact, ordering certain activities is conditional on previous activities. (PERT and CPM, in their basic form, have no provision for treating this problem, although some other techniques have been proposed that present the project manager with several contingency paths, given different outcomes from each activity.)
3. *Assumption:* Project control should focus on the critical path.
   Criticism: It is not necessarily true that the longest time-consuming path (or the path in which each of the activities has zero slack) obtained from summing activity expected time values ultimately determines project completion time. What often happens as the project progresses is that some activity not on the critical path becomes delayed to such a degree (which exceeds the slack time for that activity) that it extends the entire project. For this reason it has been suggested that a "critical activity" concept replace the critical path concept as a focus of managerial control. Under this approach, attention would center on those activities that have a high potential variation and lie on a "near-critical path." A near-critical path is one that does not share any activities with the critical path and, though it has slack, could become critical if one or a few activities along it become delayed. Obviously, the more parallelism in a network, the more likely that one or more near-critical paths exist. Conversely, the more a network approximates a single series of activities, the less likely it is to have near-critical paths.
4. *Assumption:* The activity times in PERT follow the beta distribution, with the variance of the project assumed to be equal to the sum of the variances along the critical path.
   Criticism: Although originally the beta distribution was selected for a variety of good reasons, each component of the statistical treatment has been brought into question. First, the formulas are in reality a modification of the beta distribution mean and variance, which, when compared to the basic formulas, could lead to absolute errors on the order of 10 percent for expected time (ET) and 5 percent for the individual variances. Second, given that the activity-time distributions have the properties of unimodality, continuity, and finite positive end points, other distributions with the same properties would yield different means and variances. Third, obtaining three "valid" time estimates to put into the formulas presents operational problems—it is often difficult to arrive at one activity time estimate, let alone three, and the subjective definitions of a and b do not help the matter. (How optimistic and pessimistic should one be?)

Another problem that sometimes arises, especially when CPM or PERT is used by subcontractors working with the government, is the attempt to "beat" the network to get on or off the critical path. Many government contracts provide cost incentives for finishing a project early or on a "cost-plus-fixed-fee" basis. Contractors on the critical path generally have more leverage in obtaining additional funds since they have a major influence on the project duration. On the other hand—for political reasons that we will not go into here—some contractors deem it desirable to be less visible and therefore adjust their time estimates and activity descriptions to ensure they *won't* be on the critical path.

Finally, the cost of applying critical path methods to a project is sometimes used as a basis for criticism. However, the cost of applying PERT or CPM rarely exceeds 2 percent of the total project cost. When used with added features of a work breakdown structure and various reports, it is more expensive but rarely exceeds 5 percent of total project costs. Thus, this added cost is generally justified by the additional savings resulting from improved scheduling and the resulting reduced project time.

The critical path techniques of PERT and CPM have proved themselves for more than four decades and promise to be of continued value in the future. With the rapidly changing business environment and the high costs associated with these changes, management needs to be able to both quickly and efficiently plan and control the activities of the firm. The inherent value of a tool that allows management to structure complex projects in an understandable way, to pick out possible sources of delay before they occur, to isolate areas of responsibility, and, of course, to save time in costly projects virtually ensures that the use of project management will expand.

Project Management Software

Project management software is a necessity for today's project managers. No longer do project managers have to be dependent on manually drawn networks that are arduously updated at great time and expense to reflect the latest project changes and status. Instead there are now a large number of project management software packages available, which can readily incorporate changes in the project, thereby providing the manager with fast updates on a frequent basis.

Project management software can be divided into two major categories: (*a*) desktop products such as Microsoft Project and Primavera Project and (*b*) Web-enabled products such as that provided by PlanView.

One of the key factors to consider when purchasing a project management software package is price. Dick Billows[2] of the Hampton Group in Denver, Colorado, has divided today's project management software into three price categories. In the low end of the market at prices under $100, there are products such as TurboProject, Milestone Simplicity, and Project Vision. With these products, project managers can automate the network drawing process, prepare occasional status reports, and produce some simple Gantt and PERT charts.

Larger, cross-functional projects place additional requirements on both the project manager and software. Products that fall in this intermediate price level can simulate the project and have the ability to reschedule activities to optimize results, based on the latest developments. With these larger-sized projects, budgets are an important consideration, and project management therefore needs to include estimates of the labor required to complete them. Software in this category have this ability to schedule and track labor hours and

---

[2]Richard Billows, "A Buyer's Guide to Selecting Project Management Software" (Denver, CO: The Hampton Group, 2001), www.4pm.com/articles/selpmsw.html.

costs. The cost of software in this category can range from $300 to $500, with Microsoft Project and Primavera products being the market leaders.

The high end of the software market ranges from $400 to $20,000 and, as one might expect, differs considerably in terms of what they provide. These software packages are typically for project managers who are managing more than one project simultaneously. Products that are available in this category include Microsoft Project 2000 (with Project Central), Primavera Project Planner, Open Plan, Cobra, and Enterprise PM.

Conclusion

Product life cycles are becoming shorter as more new products are continuously being introduced into the marketplace. A key factor in the ability of a company to introduce these products quickly, add new facilities, or make major operational changes of any kind is an understanding of project management concepts and techniques.

Successful projects require both technical skills and people skills. Technical skills identify the critical activities on which the project team should focus its efforts. People skills provide the motivation and team efforts that are necessary for the project to be completed in a timely manner.

Although much of this chapter has dealt with network solving techniques used in project management, effective project management involves much more than simply setting up a CPM or PERT schedule. It requires, in addition, clearly identified project responsibilities, a simple and timely progress reporting system, and good people-management practices.

Projects fail for a number of reasons. The most significant reason is that those involved do not take project scheduling seriously. Often, personnel who have been newly exposed and those who have had unsatisfactory experiences do not comply with the procedure. They may neither spend the time to properly develop their parts of the network, nor even submit good time and cost estimates. This attitude usually continues throughout the project with a reluctance to revise schedules.

Key Terms

CPM (critical path method) p. 94
crash costs p. 105
critical path p. 96
early start schedule p. 99
Gantt chart p. 92
late start schedule p. 99
milestones p. 89
PERT (program evaluation and review technique) p. 94
program p. 88
project p. 87
slack time p. 97
time–cost trade-off models p. 105
work breakdown structure (WBS) p. 89

Review and Discussion Questions

1. Define project management.
2. Describe or define work breakdown structure, program, project, task, subtask, and work package.
3. How does the role of a project manager differ from that of a traditional functional manager?
4. What are some of the key characteristics of high performance work teams?
5. What are some of the reasons project scheduling is not done well?

6. Discuss the graphic presentations in Exhibit S3.2. Are there any other graphic outputs you would like to see if you were the project manager?
7. Which characteristics must a project have for critical path scheduling to be applicable? What types of projects have been subjected to critical path analysis?
8. What are the underlying assumptions of minimum-cost scheduling? Are they equally realistic?
9. "Project control should always focus on the critical path." Comment.
10. Why would subcontractors for a government project want their activities on the critical path? Under which conditions would they try to avoid being on the critical path?
11. What is meant by "Crashing a project," and when do you do this?

Internet Exercise

The increasing application of project management techniques has resulted in the development of a large number of project management software packages. Your boss has asked you to conduct a search on the Internet to identify six different project management software packages that are currently available. She has requested that you prepare a one-page memo (plus any additional pages for exhibits, if necessary) that evaluates these different packages. You should include in your software evaluation the following information:

- Name of software.
- Name and location of company offering the software.
- Price.
- Computer requirements.
- Description.
- Unique features.
- Unique applications.

Suggested key words to help you in your search are PROJECT, MANAGEMENT, and SOFTWARE.

Solved Problems

Problem 1

A project has been defined to contain the following list of activities, along with their required times for completion:

Activity	Immediate Predecessors	Time (days)	Activity	Immediate Predecessors	Time (days)
A	—	1	F	C, D	2
B	A	4	G	E, F	7
C	A	3	H	D	9
D	A	7	I	G, H	4
E	B	6			

a. Draw the critical path diagram.
b. Show the early start and early finish times.
c. Show the critical path.
d. What would happen if Activity F were revised to take four days instead of two?

Solution

The answers to *a*, *b*, and *c* are shown in the following diagram.

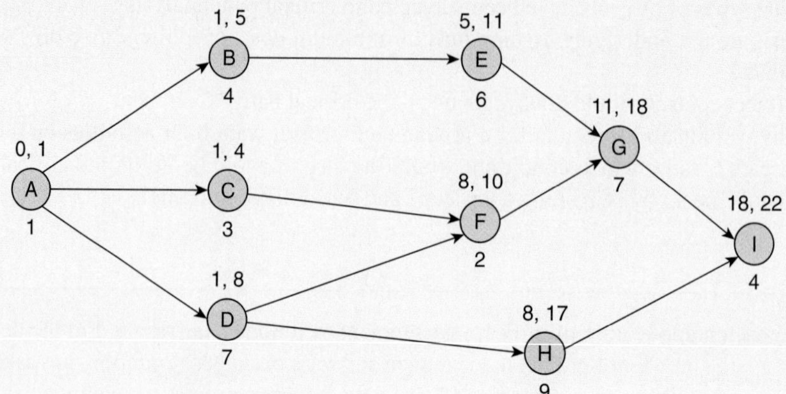

d. New critical path: A–D–F–G–I. Time of completion = 23 days.

Problem 2

Following are the precedence requirements, normal and crash activity times, and normal and crash costs for a construction project.

Activity	Preceding Activities	Required Time (weeks) Normal	Crash	Cost Normal	Crash
A	—	4	2	$10,000	$11,000
B	A	3	2	6,000	9,000
C	A	2	1	4,000	6,000
D	B	5	3	14,000	18,000
E	B, C	1	1	9,000	9,000
F	C	3	2	7,000	8,000
G	E, F	4	2	13,000	25,000
H	D, E	4	1	11,000	18,000
I	H, G	6	5	20,000	29,000

a. What are the critical path and the estimated completion time?

b. To shorten the project by three weeks, which tasks would be shortened and what would the final total project cost be?

Solution

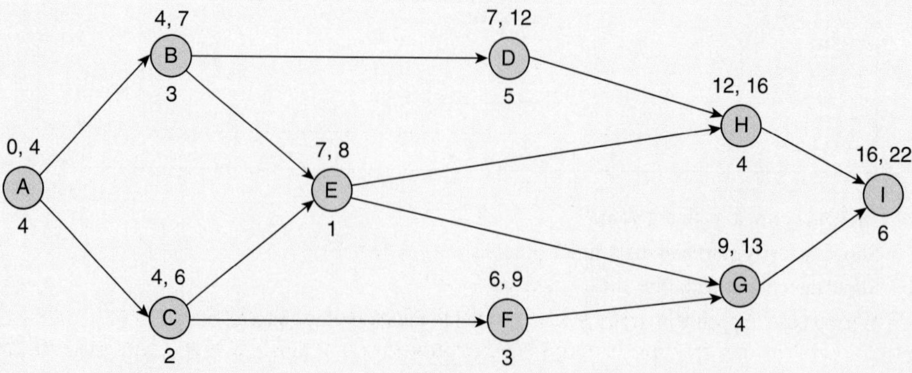

a. Critical path A–B–D–H–I.
Normal completion time = 22 weeks.

b.

Activity	Crash Cost	Normal Cost	Normal Time	Crash Time	Cost per Week	Possible Number of Weeks to Decrease
A	$11,000	$10,000	4	2	$ 500	2
B	9,000	6,000	3	2	3,000	1
C	6,000	4,000	2	1	2,000	1
D	18,000	14,000	5	3	2,000	2
E	9,000	9,000	1	1		0
F	8,000	7,000	3	2	1,000	1
G	25,000	13,000	4	2	6,000	2
H	18,000	11,000	4	1	2,333	3
I	29,000	20,000	6	5	9,000	1

1. 1st week: CP = A–B–D–H–I. Cheapest activity is A at $500. Critical path stays the same.
2. 2nd week: A is still the cheapest at $500. Critical path stays the same.
3. 3rd week: Since A is no longer available, the choices are B (at $3,000), D (at $2,000), H (at $2,333), or I (at $9,000).

Therefore, choose D at $2,000.
Total cost for the project shortened three weeks is:

A	$11,000
B	6,000
C	4,000
D	16,000
E	9,000
F	7,000
G	13,000
H	11,000
I	20,000
	$ 97,000

Problems

1. The following activities are part of a project to be scheduled using CPM:

Activity	Immediate Predecessors	Time (weeks)
A	—	6
B	A	3
C	A	7
D	C	2
E	B, D	4
F	D	3
G	E, F	7

a. Draw the network.
b. What is the critical path?
c. How many weeks will it take to complete the project?
d. How much slack time does Activity B have?

2. American Steam Turbine and Generator Company manufactures electric power–generating systems for the major electric power companies. Turbine/generator sets are

made to specific order and generally require a three- to five-year lead time. Costs range from $8 to $15 million per set.

Management has been planning their production using traditional planning techniques such as planning charts, Gantt charts, and other shop floor control methods. However, management would now like to introduce CPM project planning and control methods where each turbine/generator set is considered a separate project.

Following is a segment of the total activities involved in the turbine/generator production:

Activity	Immediate Predecessors	Time (weeks)
a	—	8
b	a	16
c	a	12
d	a	7
e	b, c	22
f	c, d	40
g	e, f	15
h	—	14
i	h	9
j	i	13
k	i	7
l	j	36
m	k	40
n	l, m	9
o	g, n	10

a. Draw the network.

b. Find the critical path.

c. Which activities would you decrease to cut the project time by two weeks?

d. Which activities would you decrease to cut the project time by 10 weeks?

3. The R&D department is planning to bid on a large project for the development of a new communication system for commercial planes. The table below shows the activities, times, and sequences required.

Activity	Immediate Predecessors	Time (weeks)
A	—	3
B	A	2
C	A	4
D	A	4
E	B	6
F	C, D	6
G	D, F	2
H	D	3
I	E, G, H	3

a. Draw the network diagram.

b. What is the critical path?

c. Supposing you wanted to shorten the completion time as much as possible, and had the option of shortening any or all of B, C, D, and G each two weeks (in effect, activity G takes zero time to complete). Which would you shorten?

d. What are the new path and earliest completion time?

4. A construction project is broken down into the 10 activities listed below.

Activity	Preceding Activity	Time (weeks)
1	—	4
2	1	2
3	1	4
4	1	3
5	2, 3	5
6	3	6
7	4	2
8	5	3
9	6, 7	5
10	8, 9	7

a. Draw the precedence diagram.

b. Find the critical path.

c. If activities 1 and 10 cannot be shortened, but activities 2 through 9 can be shortened to a minimum of 1 week each at a cost of $10,000 per week per activity, which activities would you shorten in order to shorten the project by four weeks?

5. A manufacturing concern has received a special order for a number of units of a special product that consists of two component parts, X and Y. The product is a nonstandard item that the firm has never produced before, and scheduling personnel have decided that the application of CPM is warranted. A team of manufacturing engineers has prepared the following table:

Activity	Description	Immediate Predecessors	Expected Time (days)
A	Plan production	—	5
B	Procure materials for Part X	A	14
C	Manufacture Part X	B	9
D	Procure materials for Part Y	A	15
E	Manufacture Part Y	D	10
F	Assemble Parts X and Y	C, E	4
G	Inspect assemblies	F	2
H	Completed	G	0

a. Construct a graphic representation of the CPM network.

b. Identify the critical path.

c. What is the length of time to complete the project?

d. Which activities have slack time and how much?

6. The following is a CPM network with activity times in weeks:

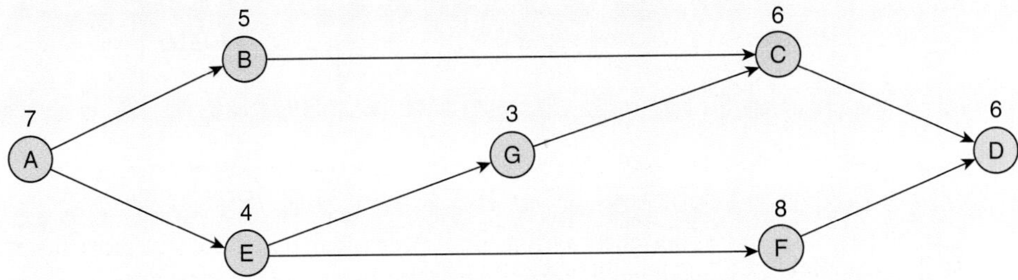

a. Determine the critical path.

b. How many weeks will the project take to complete?

c. Supposing F could be shortened by one week and B by two weeks. What effect would this have on the completion date?

7. The following represents a plan for a project:

Job No.	Predecessor Job(s)	*a*	*m*	*b*
1	—	2	3	4
2	1	1	2	3
3	1	4	5	12
4	1	3	4	11
5	2	1	3	5
6	3	1	2	3
7	4	1	8	9
8	5, 6	2	4	6
9	8	2	4	12
10	7	3	4	5
11	9, 10	5	7	8

a. Construct the appropriate network diagram.

b. Identify the critical path.

c. What is the expected completion time for the project?

d. What is the probability that the project will be completed in 30 days or less?

8. Following is a network with the activity times shown above the nodes in days:

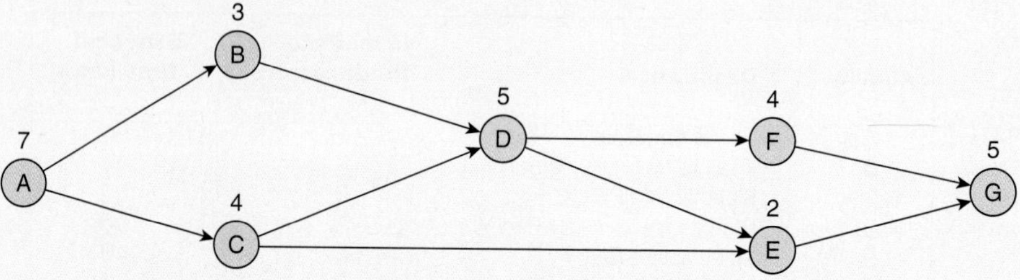

a. Find the critical path.

b. The following table shows the normal times and the crash times, along with the associated costs for each of the activities.

Activity	Normal Time	Crash Time	Normal Cost	Crash Cost
A	7	6	$7,000	$ 8,000
B	3	2	5,000	7,000
C	4	3	9,000	10,200
D	5	4	3,000	4,500
E	2	1	2,000	3,000
F	4	2	4,000	7,000
G	5	4	5,000	8,000

If the project is to be shortened by four days, show which activities in order of reduction would be shortened and the resulting total project costs.

9. The home office billing department of a chain of department stores prepares monthly inventory reports for use by the stores' purchasing agents. Given the following information, use the critical path method to determine
   a. How long the total process will take.
   b. Which jobs can be delayed without delaying the early start of any subsequent activity.

	Job and Description	Immediate Predecessors	Time (hours)
a	Start	—	0
b	Get computer printouts of customer purchases	a	10
c	Get stock records for the month	a	20
d	Reconcile purchase printouts and stock records	b, c	30
e	Total stock records by department	b, c	20
f	Determine reorder quantities for coming period	e	40
g	Prepare stock reports for purchasing agents	d, f	20
h	Finish	g	0

10. For the network and the data shown:

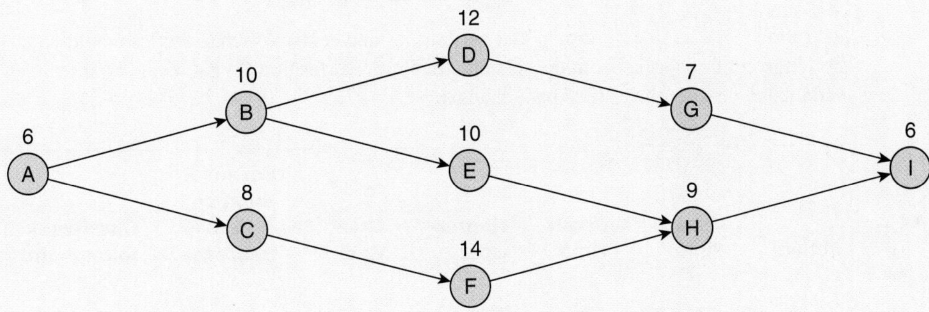

   a. Determine the critical path and the early completion time for the project.

Activity*	Normal Time (weeks)	Normal Cost	Crash Time (weeks)	Crash Cost
A	6	$ 6,000	4	$12,000
B	10	10,000	9	11,000
C	8	8,000	7	10,000
D	12	12,000	10	14,000
E	10	10,000	7	12,000
F	14	14,000	12	19,000
G	7	7,000	5	10,000
H	9	9,000	6	15,000
I	6	6,000	5	8,000

*An activity cannot be shortened to less than its crash time.

   b. Reduce the project completion time by four weeks. Assume a linear cost per day shortened and show, step by step, how you arrived at your schedule. Also indicate the critical path.

11. The following CPM network has estimates of the *normal time* listed for the activities:

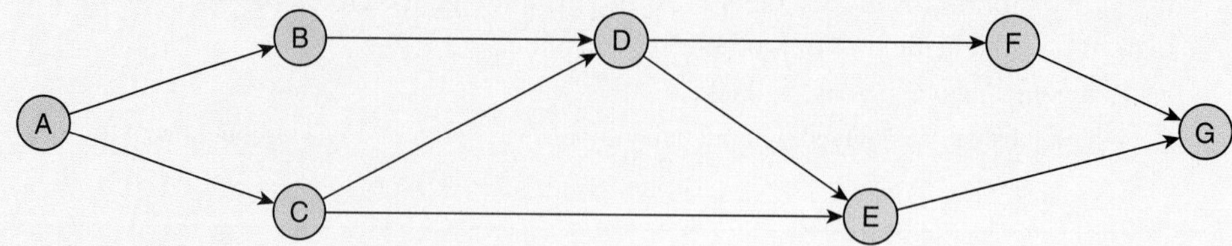

a. Identify the critical path.

b. What is the length of time to complete the project?

c. Which activities have slack, and how much?

Activity	Time (weeks)
A	7
B	2
C	4
D	5
E	2
F	4
G	5

d. The following is a table of normal and crash times and costs. Which activities would you shorten to cut two weeks from the schedule in a rational fashion? What would be the incremental cost? Is the critical path changed?

Activity	Normal Time	Crash Time	Normal Cost	Crash Cost	Possible Number of Weeks Decrease	Cost/Week to Expedite
A	7	6	$7,000	$ 8,000		
B	2	1	5,000	7,000		
C	4	3	9,000	10,200		
D	5	4	3,000	4,500		
E	2	1	2,000	3,000		
F	4	2	4,000	7,000		
G	5	4	5,000	8,000		

Bibliography

Billows, Richard. "A Buyer's Guide to Selecting Project Management Software." Denver, CO: The Hampton Group, 2001. www.4pm.com/articles/selpmsw.html.

Carrillo, Karen M. "Is It All a Project?" *InformationWeek,* February 23, 1998, pp. 100–104.

Cleland, David (ed.). *Field Guide to Project Management.* New York: John Wiley & Sons, 1997.

Devaux, Stephen A. *Total Project Control: A Manager's Guide to Integrated Project Planning, Measuring, and Tracking.* New York: John Wiley & Sons, 1999.

Fox, Terry L., and J. Wayne Spence. "Tools of the Trade: A Survey of Project Management Tools." *Project Management Journal,* September 1998, pp. 20–29.

Gay, Clifford F., and Erik W. Larson, *Project Management*, Burr Ridge, IL, Irwin/McGraw-Hill, 2000.

Hughes, Michael William. "Why Projects Fail: The Effects of Ignoring the Obvious." *Industrial Engineering* 18, no. 4 (April 1986), pp. 14–18.

Kerzner, Harold. *Applied Project Management: Best Practices on Implementation.* New York: John Wiley & Sons, 1999.

Meredith, Jack, and Samuel J. Mantel. *Project Management: A Managerial Approach.* New York: John Wiley & Sons, 1999.

Martin, Paula, and Karen Tate. *Getting Started in Project Management.* New York: John Wiley & Sons, 2001.

Shtub, A., J. F. Bard, and S. Globerson. *Project Management: Engineering, Technology and Implementation.* Englewood Cliffs, NJ: Prentice Hall, 1994.

Thamhain, Hans J. "Effective Leadership Style for Managing Project Teams." In *Handbook of Program and Project Management,* ed. P. C. Dinsmore. New York: AMACOM, 1992.

———. "Managing Technologically Innovative Team Efforts Towards New Product Success." *Journal of Production Innovation Management* 7, no. 1 (March 1990).

Wheelwright, S., and J. Weber. "Massachusetts General Hospital: CABG Surgery (A)." Boston, MA: Harvard Business School Publishing, 1997.

Case

The Addition to Harvey Hall at Berkshire School of Business

In an effort to improve the level of quality of its classroom instruction, the Berkshire School of Business recently decided to reduce the average size of its undergraduate classes. As a result of this decision, Lydia Keene, the undergraduate dean, calculated that she would have to hire an additional 35 faculty members, which meant that more offices were needed. An initial analysis determined that the most cost-effective way to add these new offices was to put an addition onto Harvey Hall, the existing faculty office building.

To complete the building addition in time for the faculty to be in their new offices before the start of the fall semester, John Yates, the school's VP for finance and who had overall responsibility for the project's completion, decided to apply some project management techniques he learned in his undergraduate operations management course. This required that he identify all the various activities that were required as part of this project and understand how they were related.

John knew that the first step in this project was to obtain approval from the school's Board of Trustees. Once this was done, building permits could be obtained at the same time that bids for furniture were requested and the faculty recruitment process was initiated. With the necessary permits in hand, the actual construction of the addition could begin. Upon completion of the building exterior, the landscaping could be started and the interior work on the offices could be done simultaneously. Once the interiors were completed, a certificate of occupancy could be issued upon a final building inspection by the town fire marshal. A final cleanup of both the interior and the exterior of the building would then be done (landscaping had to be completed by this time). Following the cleanup, the office furniture would then be installed and the faculty allowed to move into their new offices.

Activity	Normal Time*	Normal Costs†	Crash Time‡	Crash Costs¶
A. Board Trustees approval	4	$ 10	2	$ 16
B. Obtain building permits	2	5	2	5
C. Construct building	21	1,500	17	1,700
D. Request bids for furniture	4	3	4	3
E. Recruit faculty	30	150	27	165
F. Order furniture	16	200	12	240
G. Complete interiors	6	110	3	131
H. Landscape site	4	68	2	80
I. Obtain certificate of occupancy	1	2	1	2
J. Final cleanup	2	20	1	26
K. Install furniture	1	12	1	12
L. Building occupied	—	—	—	—
	Totals:	2,080		2,380

*Times listed are in weeks.
†Costs listed are in thousands of dollars.
‡Crash time is the minimum time in which an activity can be completed.
¶Crash costs are the total costs associated with the acceleration of an activity. The weekly increase in costs for a given activity is assumed to be constant.

John, in preparation for the upcoming board meeting, developed an initial budget for the project based on the normal costs associated with each of the project's individual activities. John's estimated cost for each activity is shown in the table below, along with the activity's estimated completion time. Also listed are crash costs and crash times, in the event it would be necessary to accelerate a specific activity so that the project would be completed on schedule before the start of the fall semester.

Case

Questions

1. What are the minimum time and overall cost in which the addition to Harvey Hall can be occupied by faculty under normal times and costs?
2. If you were operating under a very limited budget, how could you reduce the overall length of the project by one week at the least cost? By two weeks?
3. If John decides to complete this project in the shortest time possible, what are the minimum time and associated costs for which the project can be completed (without incurring any unnecessary costs)?
4. After receiving approval from the school's board in the normal time of four weeks, John ran into a problem obtaining the necessary building permits. The original 125 acres on which the current campus is located was initially subdivided into one-acre housing lots. As a result, permits are required for each of the building lots on which the addition was to be built, along with any immediately adjacent lots. These additional permits required an additional two weeks to obtain and increased the cost of obtaining the permits by $4,000. If John wants to complete the project in the original time that was determined in question 1, what specific actions must he now take to minimize costs while still completing the building as scheduled?

Source: © Mark M. Davis.

4

The Role of Technology in Operations

Chapter Objectives

- Introduce the different ways in which technology can add value to the operations function within an organization.
- Identify the various ways in which technology can be used in a manufacturing company.
- Describe enterprise resource planning (ERP) systems and how they impact an organization.
- Demonstrate the different ways in which technology can be integrated into service operations.
- Present a framework for defining the different types of e-services that are currently being offered.

TECHNOLOGY IS ONLY A TOOL!

After completing some business in the LA area, I returned my rental car to the Avis parking lot at Los Angeles International Airport (LAX). As I started to get out of the car and unload my bags, an Avis attendant greeted me with a handheld computer and asked me for a copy of my rental agreement.

I said to him, "Don't bother. I need to go to the check-in desk anyway, as I forgot to give Avis my frequent flyer number when I rented the car last week."

"No problem," he replied, "I can handle that here too, so you don't have to go to the desk."

Impressed by his ability to handle this non-routine activity with his handheld computer, I commented, "Today's technology is truly amazing!" To which he curtly answered, "It's only a tool!"

Caught off guard by his statement, I asked him to explain what he meant. He continued, "It's only a tool. Just like a wrench is only as good as the mechanic who has been trained to use it, so technology is only as good as the people who have been properly trained to use it in their everyday work."

To which I could only respond, "You're 100 percent right!"

Source: Mark M. Davis.

The hand-held computer is just one of many technology tools that Avis uses to improve its operations in terms of both increased efficiency and better customer service. For example, customers now have a choice of making a reservation either online at the Avis website or by speaking with a customer representative at a call center. Technology in the form of software allows Avis to (*a*) use yield management techniques (which are discussed in a later chapter) to maximize revenues, (*b*) schedule workers, and (*c*) forecast demand for both cars and customer calls.

Managerial Issues

Advances in technology are affecting every aspect of business, and operations management is no exception. From robotics and automation on the factory floor to information technology in the form of enterprise resource planning (ERP) systems and the Internet, technology, and especially information technology, is dramatically changing the way in which both manufacturing and service operations are being designed and managed.

However, as the Avis attendant correctly pointed out in the opening vignette, technology is only a tool, not an end in itself. In other words, technology should not be installed if it doesn't properly satisfy the needs of the firm with respect to being aligned with its overall goals. Having said that, managers also need to realize that there are times when only technology will provide the necessary means to meet their customers' needs in today's highly competitive environment. Equally important, managers also must recognize the need for these new technology-driven infrastructures to be compatible with all of the organization's functional elements so that information can be quickly and efficiently transmitted and shared with a minimum of errors.

To properly integrate technology into their organizations, operations managers first need to understand what technology can and cannot do. In addition, managers must recognize the need for workers at all levels to be properly trained in the use of the technology, and that this training is not just a one-shot deal, but rather a continuous, ongoing process.

How Technology Affects Operations

Operations strategy defines the way in which a firm competes in the marketplace. Examples of these strategies include (*a*) low cost, (*b*) quality, (*c*) speed of delivery, and (*d*) customization. As we learned in Chapter 2, managers in the past had to decide which of these strategies was most applicable to the particular market segment they were serving. In so doing, they recognized that there were trade-offs involved. For example, you couldn't have both low cost and a high degree of customization, or that there was a choice to be made between providing fast product delivery and providing a highly customized product.

These traditional trade-offs are no longer valid for most businesses because technology has "raised the performance bar" by allowing firms to compete on several of these dimensions simultaneously. For example, firms using technology, such as Dell Computer, can now produce and quickly deliver individually customized products, and at a very competitive price. Technology now provides firms with the opportunity to move to a "superior" performance curve, as previously presented in Chapter 2, and shown again in Exhibit 4.1.

Exhibit 4.1

How Technology Impacts Operational Performance

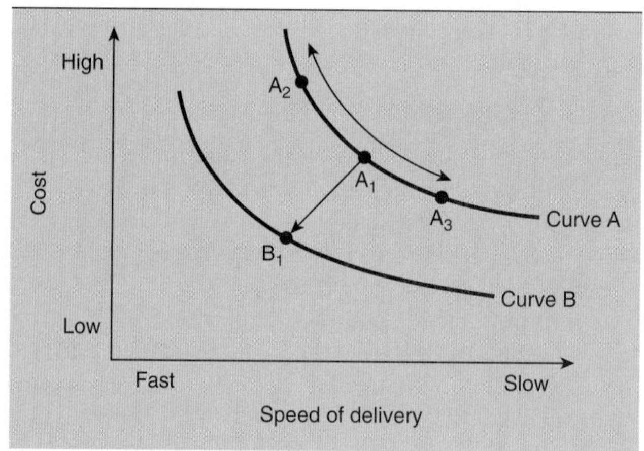

In moving from A_1 to B_1, a firm, for example, can achieve superior performance in terms of both lower cost and also faster service. In comparison, a firm that doesn't use technology must remain on Curve A and consequently must revert to the traditional trade-off where improvement in one dimension is accomplished only at the sacrifice of another dimension (for example, in going from A_2 to A_3 along Curve A, where lower cost is achieved only by providing slower service).

Technology in Manufacturing

Automation

The term *automation* is familiar to all, but a commonly agreed-upon definition still eludes us. Some authorities view automation as a totally new set of concepts that relate to the automatic operation of a production process; others view it simply as an evolutionary development in technology in which machinery performs some or all of the process-control function. Automation is a set of concepts, but it is also evolutionary in the sense that it is a logical and predictable step in the development of equipment and processes.

Some major developments in manufacturing automation include machining centers, numerically controlled machines, industrial robots, computer-aided design and manufacturing systems, flexible manufacturing systems, computer-integrated manufacturing, and islands of automation.

machining centers

Operations where machine tools are changed automatically as part of the process.

Machining centers not only provide automatic control of a machine but carry out automatic tooling changes as well. For example, a single machine may be equipped with a shuttle system of two worktables that can be rolled into and out of the machine. While work is being done at one table, the next part is mounted on the second table. When machining on the first table is complete, it is moved out of the way and the second part is moved into position.

numerically controlled (NC) machines

Manufacturing equipment that is directly controlled by a computer.

Numerically controlled (NC) machines are under the control of a digital computer. Feedback control loops determine the position of the machine tooling during the work, constantly compare the actual location with the programmed location, and correct as needed. This eliminates time lost during setups, and applies to both high-volume, standardized types of products as well as low-volume, customized products.

industrial robots

Programmable machines that can perform multiple functions.

Industrial robots are substitutes for human manipulation and other highly repetitive functions. A robot is a reprogrammable machine with multiple functions that can move devices through specialized motions to perform any number of tasks. It is essentially a mechanized arm that can be fitted with a variety of handlike fingers or grippers, vacuum cups, or a tool such as a wrench. Robots are capable of performing many factory operations ranging from machining processes to simple assembly.

computer-aided (or -assisted) design (CAD)

Designing a product using a specially equipped computer.

One of the major contemporary approaches to the product design process is **computer-aided (or -assisted) design (CAD).** *CAD* may be defined as carrying out all structural or mechanical design processes of a product or component at a specially equipped computer terminal. Engineers design through a combination of console controls and a light pen that draws on the computer screen or electronic pad. Different perspectives of the product can be visualized by rotating the product on the screen, and individual components can be enlarged to examine particular characteristics. Depending on the sophistication in software, on-screen testing may replace the early phases of prototype testing and modification.

CAD has been used to design everything from computer chips to potato chips. Frito-Lay, for example, used CAD to design its O'Grady's double-density, ruffled potato chip. CAD is also now being used to custom design swimsuits. Measurements of the wearer are fed into the CAD program, along with the style of suit desired. Working with the customer, the designer modifies the suit design as it appears on a humanform drawing on the computer screen. Once the design is decided upon, the computer prints out a pattern, and the suit is cut and sewn on the spot.

computer-aided design and manufacturing system (CAD/CAM)

Integration of design and production of a product through use of a computer.

Computer-aided design and manufacturing (CAD/CAM) uses a computer to integrate component design and processing instructions. In current CAD/CAM systems, when the design is finalized, the link to CAM is made by producing the manufacturing instructions. Because of the efficiency of CAD/CAM systems, design and manufacture of small lots can be both fast and low in cost.

Even though CAD/CAM systems are usually limited to larger companies because of the high initial cost, they do increase productivity and quality dramatically. More alternative designs can be produced, and the specifications can be more exact. Updates can be more readily made, and cost estimates more easily drawn. In addition, computer-aided process planning (CAPP) can shorten and, in some cases, even eliminate traditional process planning.

flexible manufacturing system (FMS)

Manufacturing facility that is automated to some extent and produces a wide variety of products.

A **flexible manufacturing system (FMS)** actually refers to a number of systems that differ in the degree of mechanization, automated transfer, and computer control and are sufficiently flexible to produce a wide variety of products.

A flexible manufacturing module is a numerically controlled (NC) machine supported with a parts inventory, a tool changer, and a pallet changer. A flexible manufacturing cell consists of several flexible manufacturing modules organized according to the particular product's requirements. A flexible manufacturing group is a combination of flexible manufacturing modules and cells located in the same manufacturing area and joined by a materials handling system, such as an automated guided vehicle (AGV).

A flexible production system consists of flexible manufacturing groups that connect different manufacturing areas, such as fabrication, machining, and assembly. A flexible manufacturing line is a series of dedicated machines connected by AGVs, robots, conveyors, or some other type of automated transfer device.

computer-integrated manufacturing (CIM)

Integration of all aspects of manufacturing through computer.

Computer-integrated manufacturing (CIM) integrates all aspects of production into one automated system. Design, testing, fabrication, assembly, inspection, and materials handling may all have automated functions within the area. However, in most companies, communication between departments still flows by means of paperwork. In CIM, these islands of automation are integrated, thus eliminating the need for the paperwork. A computer links all sectors together, resulting in more efficiency, less paperwork, and less personnel expense.

islands of automation

Automated factories or portions that include NC equipment, automated storage/retrieval systems, robots, and machining centers.

Islands of automation refer to the transition from conventional manufacturing to the automated factory. Typical islands of automation include numerically controlled machine tools, robots, automated storage/retrieval systems, and machining centers.

Information Technology

As illustrated in Exhibit 4.2, the use of information technology in manufacturing operations can be divided into four major groups of software systems: (*a*) enterprise resource planning (ERP), (*b*) supply chain management (SCM), (*c*) new product development (NPD), and (*d*) customer relationship management (CRM). These software packages, as the exhibit suggests, have significant overlap in terms of their capabilities and what they provide.

Enterprise Resource Planning (ERP) An ERP system provides a firm with a common software infrastructure and database. These systems are discussed in detail in the next section of this chapter.

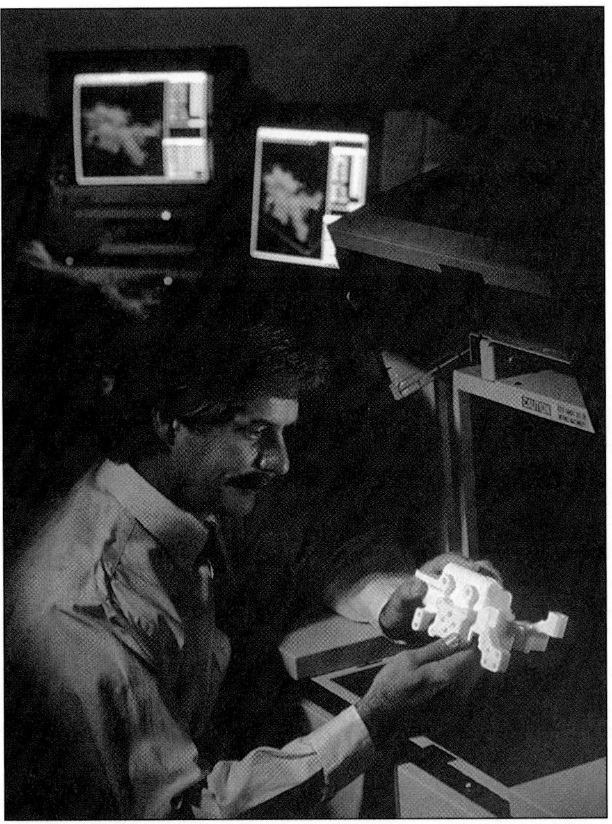

The speed with which a company can design and develop new products is critical to its ability to introduce them quickly into the marketplace. Rapid prototyping machines are a new generation of CAD equipment that can produce three-dimensional prototypes quickly in the initial stages of the product design cycle. These rough draft models result in both higher-quality products and lower development costs.

Exhibit 4.2

Major Categories of Software Systems in Manufacturing

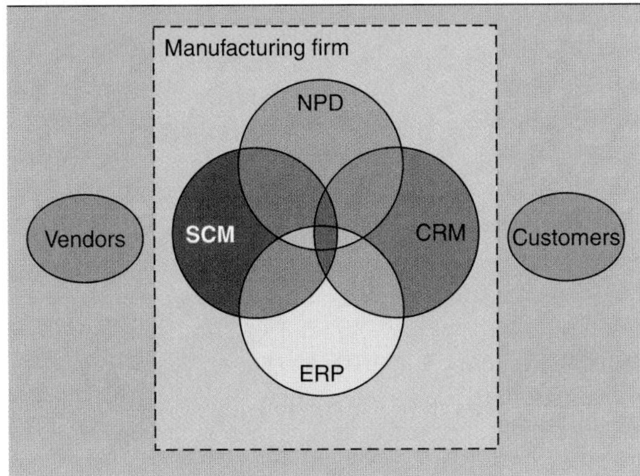

Supply Chain Management (SCM) These software systems primarily focus on how firms interact with the suppliers that are part of their overall supply chain. Depending on where the firm is in its supply chain, this also can involve customers. The topic of supply chain management is presented in detail in Chapter 13.

New Product Development (NPD) New product development software focuses on linking the engineering function with the operations function within a firm to facilitate the transfer of new product drawings and models into manufactured products. These software systems include CAD/CAM, which was discussed earlier in this chapter. Some software packages, such as that offered by Parametric Technology, also provide similar links with vendors who are directly involved in a firm's new product development process. The topic of new product development is addressed in detail in Chapter 3.

Customer Relationship Management (CRM) Customer relationship management software, such as that provided by Siebel Systems, focuses on the interface between the firm and its customer. In addition to having order entry capability, these systems collect customer-specific data, which allow the firm to provide customer-specific solutions. These software systems are typically addressed in marketing.

Enterprise Resource Planning (ERP) Systems

In the last decade, there has emerged a new generation of software systems that link all of the various functional areas within an organization. The goal of these systems, which are known as **enterprise resource planning (ERP) systems,** is to provide a company with a single, uniform software platform and database that will facilitate transactions among the different functional areas within a firm, and, in some cases, between firms and their customers and vendors.

enterprise resource planning (ERP) systems

A fully integrated software system that links all of the major functional areas within an organization.

Defining ERP Systems

Prior to the introduction of ERP systems, each functional area within an organization typically had its own software and database. These software packages often were incompatible with each other, which prevented transactions from taking place directly between systems. In addition, with more than one database, there often were multiple records for the same piece of data, which, in turn, caused delays and unnecessary errors throughout the firm. For example, an employee might be listed as John Smith in the Human Resources database, John S. Smith in the Accounting Department, and Dr. John Smith in the Engineering Department. From the computer systems' perspective, these would be viewed as three different people. In such an environment, transactions between functions often were done manually, which was tedious, slow, and a source of additional errors. As a result, each of the functional areas within an organization was viewed as an independent operation, as illustrated in Exhibit 4.3a.

To address this issue of incompatibility and multiple databases, ERP systems were developed to provide an infrastructure with a common information technology platform that would not only electronically link all of the functional areas with a single database, but also address their individual needs, as shown in Exhibit 4.3b.

Exhibit 4.4 illustrates how SAP, the leading ERP software firm, specifically provides this integration.

Evolution of ERP Systems

ERP Systems didn't just happen overnight. Rather, they are an outgrowth, or the next generation, of materials requirements planning (MRP) systems and manufacturing resources planning (MRP II), which were developed and introduced within the manufacturing function in the late 1960s and 1970s, and which are discussed in detail in Chapter 18.

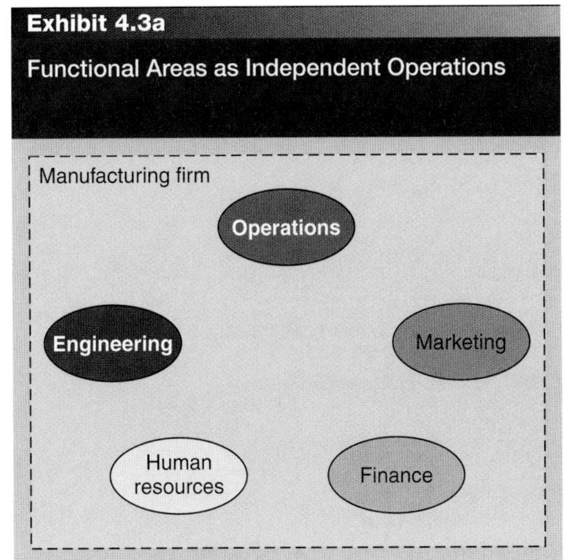

Exhibit 4.3a

Functional Areas as Independent Operations

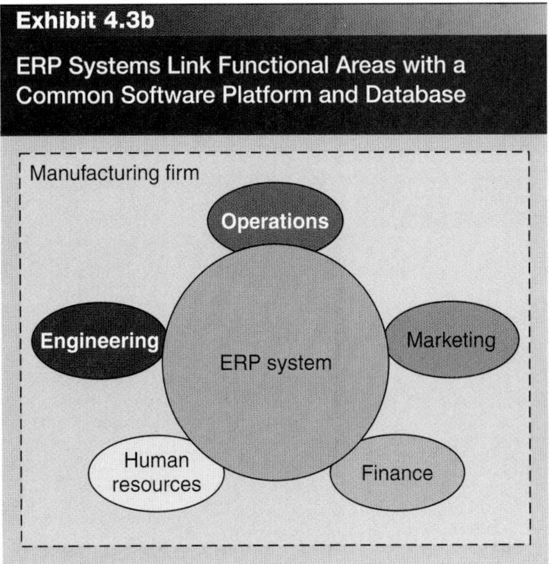

Exhibit 4.3b

ERP Systems Link Functional Areas with a Common Software Platform and Database

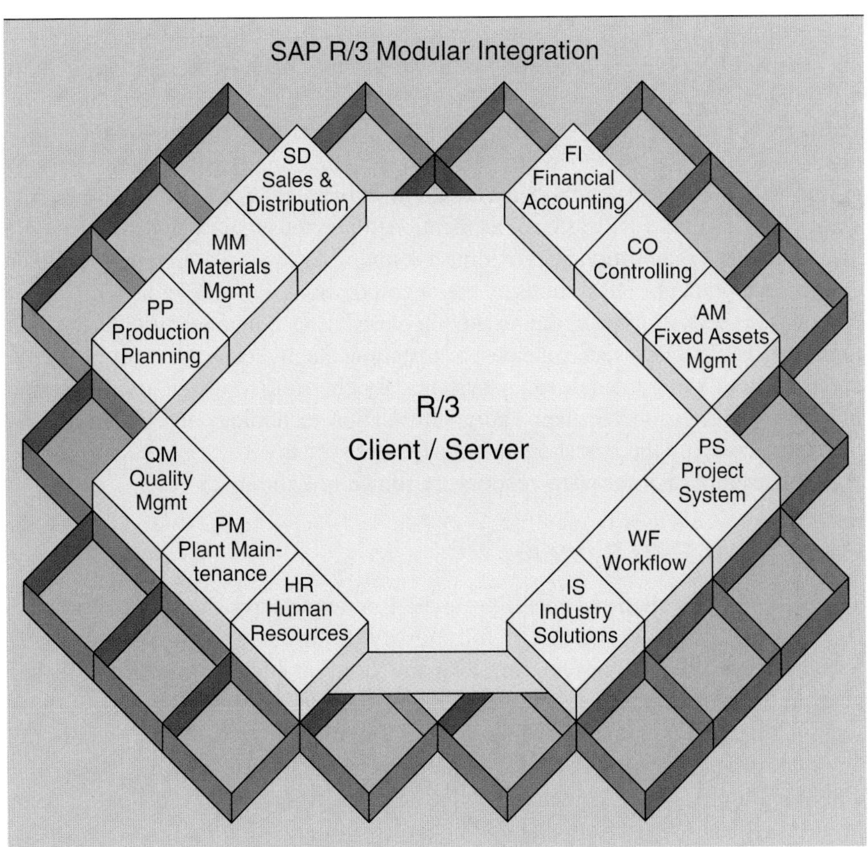

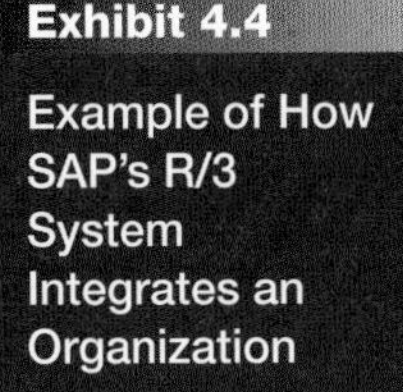

Exhibit 4.4

Example of How SAP's R/3 System Integrates an Organization

Exhibit 4.5

Leading ERP Software Companies and Respective Market Shares

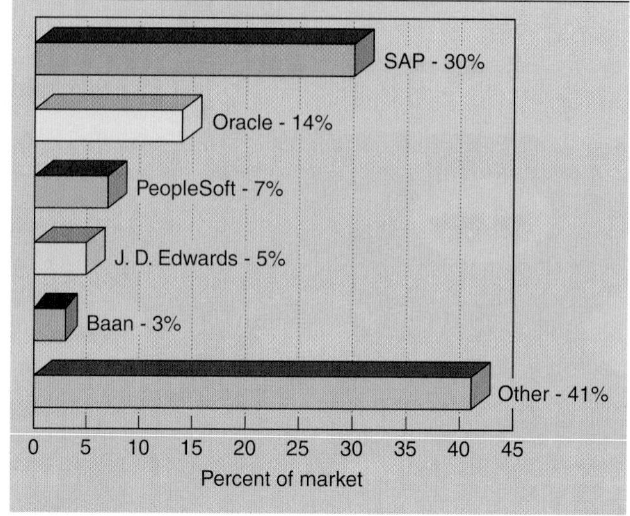

(Total 1999 ERP Software and Services Revenue = $18.2 billion)
Source: AMR Research

MRP systems provided the manufacturing function with a common database and software platform to link all of its areas, which included purchasing, planning, materials, and operations. Prior to the introduction of MRP systems, each of these individual areas was managed more or less as an independent operation, which often resulted in excessive inventories of materials and slow, inefficient, and often erroneous transactions. MRP II systems were a first attempt to integrate operations, marketing, finance, and engineering.

Just as MRP systems provided a common software platform and database for the manufacturing function, ERP systems, as mentioned previously, now link all of the functional areas within an organization by providing a common software platform and shared database.

The adoption of ERP systems by major corporations was accelerated in 1998 and 1999 by possible "Y2K problems" that existed in older legacy computer systems that dated back to the 1970s. For many firms, the cost of installing a new, state-of-the-art ERP system was comparable to fixing the old legacy systems. By choosing to install an ERP system, these firms were able to update their entire information technology infrastructure, instead of merely patching up their existing and much older systems.

The leading ERP software vendors are shown in Exhibit 4.5.

Benefits of ERP Systems

When properly installed and operating, an ERP system can provide a firm with a significant competitive advantage, which can fully justify the investment of time and money. The benefits of using an ERP system can take many forms, including (*a*) reduction in the number of errors through the use of a common database, (*b*) faster customer response times, (*c*) faster order fulfillment times, and (*d*) better overall communication within the organization.

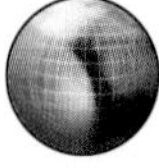

For example, Hewlett-Packard's computer system's manufacturing and distribution facility for Europe, which is located in Geulstein, Germany, achieved significant improvements in operational performance after implementing SAP's ERP system, including on time delivery exceeding 95 percent, cycle time reduced by 80 percent, inventories reduced by 30 percent, operating costs reduced by 30 percent, and distribution costs reduced by 70 percent.

Why ERP Systems Fail

The business landscape is littered with failed attempts at installing ERP systems. Hershey Foods, for example, incurred significant product distribution problems after it implemented SAP's R/3 system, resulting in its candy not being on retail shelves during its peak season between Halloween and Christmas. Whirlpool, a major appliance manufacturer, also attributed shipping delays to its difficulties in implementing SAP's R/3 system. (These difficulties in implementing ERP systems are not unique to SAP but exist with all ERP systems.) Some of the more common reasons for these difficulties and failures are presented here. It is interesting to note that many of these causes are the same as those that were identified as the reasons for MRP implementation failures 25 years ago.

Lack of Top Management Commitment By its very definition, the installation of an ERP system is an organizationwide undertaking, involving all of the functions within a firm. Therefore, the implementation of an ERP system requires a major commitment from top management in order for it to be successful. This means not only the commitment of resources, but also the commitment of top management's time to ensure the proper coordination among the various functions.

Lack of Adequate Resources Many firms underestimate the resources that are required to properly install an ERP system. In addition to the actual cost of the software, which often represents only about a third of the total implementation costs, there are also the costs of outside consultants and the costs of labor for company personnel that are assigned to the project.

Lack of Proper Training In a desire to convert to the new system quickly, there is often a shortfall in the training of personnel at all levels. Proper training is required from the technical perspective as well as from the users' perspective. The IT department within an organization needs to fully understand all of the technical characteristics of the system in order to provide the proper support to the business functions that use it. At the same time, the business functions need to understand the different procedures for entering data and generating reports. Because an ERP system is fully integrated across all functions, system users also need to know how their particular segment of the system affects other segments, so when mistakes do occur, the impact of those mistakes throughout the organization is known.

Lack of Communication Because the installation of an ERP system is an organizationwide undertaking, there is need for continuous communication within and across all functional areas with respect to the status of the implementation. All too often, as the implementation proceeds, some parts of the organization are unaware of what is occurring, and consequently fail to take the appropriate actions that are necessary. Effectively communicating the progress of the ERP implementation should be one of the primary responsibilities of top management.

Criticisms of ERP Systems

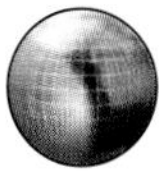

As HP's facility in Germany clearly demonstrates, there are significant advantages to installing an ERP system. However, these systems have been criticized in many respects for their failure to provide the desired infrastructure support that management expected. Two of these concerns are presented below.

A Single ERP System versus Best of Breed Each of the different ERP software packages has its particular strengths and weaknesses. One may be very strong in the financial module, while another is strong in the human resources area. Still a third may be strong in the production or marketing area. By adopting a single system, a company must accept all of the strengths and weaknesses of the system it selected. In contrast, a firm using a *best of breed* approach selects that software that has the best attributes for each functional area and then builds an interface that links all of the various software packages together. (Obviously, this approach also has its drawbacks.)

Inflexibility Each software package is designed around a specific business model with its own inherent business processes. These are usually based upon best business practices, which are determined by the software vendor. Consequently, in adopting a particular ERP system, a company also must adopt the built-in business model and its associated business processes. While this represents an improvement for many firms, especially those that never had well-designed processes, those firms that already have good businesses in place still need to reconfigure them to be compatible with those in the ERP system.

Similarly, certain ERP systems are designed to work best in process-oriented industries such as petroleum or chemicals, and consequently are not as readily applicable to discrete parts manufacturing such as automobiles or appliances.

Technology in Services

Technology Trends in Services

Advances in technology, including improved automated equipment, voice recognition systems, high-speed data transmission lines (like broadband), and faster and more powerful computers, also have had a significant impact on services. Contributing to the growing trends in services is the fact that large amounts of data are readily accessible today and can be transmitted inexpensively over long distances. We identify several major trends in the delivery of services that are a direct result of technology. It is important to note that these trends are not mutually independent; rather, the exact opposite is true: they are highly dependent on one another.

Increase in Self-Service Many service industries have seen an increase in self-service operations. Examples include self-service gas stations, ATMs at banks, and automated toll collections on highways. Self-service also is used extensively in e-businesses, ranging from the purchasing of sweaters from L.L. Bean and airline tickets from American Airlines to the purchase of stocks and bonds through Fidelity and conducting online checkbook transactions with your bank.

As another example of how technology increases opportunities for self-service, many supermarket and drug store chains have installed self-service checkout lanes. (See Operations Management in Practice box.) With this new equipment, customers scan their own purchases, bag them, and then pay by either cash or credit card. In this case, labor isn't completely eliminated, as an individual must be assigned to every three or four automated lanes to assist shoppers as the situation requires.[1]

The primary reason for the increase in self-service is that it reduces labor costs. With automated self-service equipment, gas station attendants are no longer needed to pump gas,

[1]Dinah W. Brin, "Check it Out!" *The Middlesex News* (Framingham, MA), August 11, 1996.

Operations Management in Practice

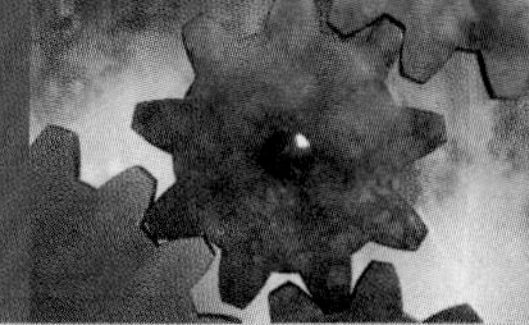

SELF-SERVE CHECKOUT COUNTERS INCREASE PRODUCTIVITY AND REDUCE WAITING TIMES

Kroger, one of the nation's largest supermarket chains, is introducing self-service checkout counters. The U-Scan self-service checkout system, which is manufactured by Optimal Robotics, has been installed in approximately one-third of Kroger's 2,380 stores. The U-Scan system accepts all forms of payments, including cash, credit cards, and ATMs.

One of the most common complaints about shopping at supermarkets, according to Gary Rhodes of Kroger, is the time it takes to check out. No one likes waiting in long checkout lines. The self-service units provide customers with a faster checkout alternative where they can control how long the checkout process takes. As a result, the U-Scan systems have proved to be enormously popular with Kroger's customers. In addition, the U-Scan systems are much more economical to operate than the traditional checkout counter with a cashier ringing in the items.

Source: Special thanks to Gary Rhodes of Kroger and Robin Yaffe of Optimal Robotics.

Exhibit 4.6 Methods of Pricing to Encourage Self-Service

Type of Service	Incentive to Use Self-Service
Gas station	Higher price for full-service gas
Investment firm	Higher commission for using a broker
Airline	Reduced fares available only on the Internet
Bank	Additional fee for using a teller

bank tellers are no longer needed to process customer deposits and withdrawals, and customer service representatives are no longer needed to answer telephone calls.

However, service managers need to recognize that by going entirely to a self-service delivery system, they will exclude certain market segments. For example, some customers do not want to pump their own gas at a gas station; similarly, other individuals prefer to obtain professional advice on investing in the stock market rather than doing their own analysis. Consequently, many service firms offer self-service as only one of several distribution channels for marketing their products.

Inasmuch as it is usually the least costly channel, many service firms will offer customers incentives, often in the form of discounts, to use this channel, or, conversely, charge more when the interaction with an individual is required. Exhibit 4.6 provides some examples of how firms encourage customers to use self-service delivery systems.

Decrease in the Importance of Location The combination of inexpensive data storage, transmission, and retrieval costs coupled with electronic access to virtually every corner of the world has decreased the importance of location for many services. Online banking services reduce the need for a customer to go to the bank. Home delivery services for groceries, dry cleaning, and so forth eliminate the need for customers to visit these retail locations. Similarly, any purchase made on the Internet, whether it is a book from Amazon.com or airline tickets from Expedia.com, eliminates the need for the customer to visit a specific retail location that offers these goods and services. When such services can be conducted remotely, it doesn't matter where they are located as far as the customer is concerned.

The continued development of a worldwide communication network has facilitated the location of back-office service operations to areas where labor costs are relatively inexpensive. As a result, customer call centers can be located anywhere. For example, a U.S. airline has one of its reservation call centers located in the Caribbean, while the customer call center for a major bank in the middle Atlantic states is located in Maine. For the same reasons, many firms have their call centers located in Ireland. It is important to note, however, that in addition to providing low-cost labor, these locations also must have the necessary communication infrastructure in place to provide the level of service required by these firms.

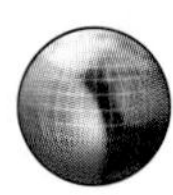

Shift from Time-Dependent to Non-Time-Dependent Transactions There is a growing trend away from time-dependent service transactions toward non-time-dependent transactions. Time-dependent transactions are those transactions that require a service worker to be available at that exact time when the customer requests the service. Examples of time-dependent service transactions can include the waitress at a restaurant who is there to serve you when you are hungry, the reservations clerk at an airline call center who answers the telephone when you call to reserve a flight, the front-desk personnel who is on duty at the hotel when you check in, and your stockbroker who is available when you want to conduct a stock transaction. Non-time-dependent transactions do not require the presence of the service worker at the exact moment when the customer requests service. Examples of non-time-dependent transactions include e-mail, faxes, and voice messages. Time-dependent transactions often are referred to as **synchronous transactions** or communications while non-time-dependent transactions are referred to as **asynchronous transactions** or communications.

synchronous transactions

Transactions that take place in real time without any time delays, usually between individuals.

asynchronous transactions

Transactions in which there is a delay in time with respect to the communication between the parties involved.

There are several reasons for the shift towards non-time-dependent transactions. First, it is more economical from the firm's perspective. As stated above, with time-dependent transactions, service workers must always be available to conduct a customer transaction. To allow for uncertainty in customer demand as well as to minimize customer waiting time, extra workers must be on duty, which adds to the expense. With non-time-dependent activities, a company has greater flexibility in scheduling workers in a more efficient manner, as well as the ability to prioritize the transactions.

Asynchronous transactions are usually more efficient from the customer's perspective too. For example, rather than trying to speak to someone in person, and playing endless rounds of "phone tag," it is much more efficient to send a single e-mail. However, an important point with asynchronous transactions is the need to have a service recovery process in place that assures personal contact when problems do occur.

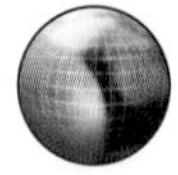

In addition, with the world quickly becoming a *global village* or single world economy that is linked together electronically, a significant number of transactions do not take place during "regular business hours" (whatever that means these days!). Thus, a customer in Australia who orders something through the Internet from a firm in England can place the order at any time, regardless of what time it is in England, and that order will be processed at the beginning of the next business day. Non-time-dependent transactions permit firms to receive transactions on a *24 × 7 basis* (24 hours a day, seven days a week), and then to respond to these transactions efficiently during normal business hours.

disintermediation

The elimination of intermediate steps or organizations.

Increase in Disintermediation Stan Davis introduced the term **disintermediation** to mean the elimination of intermediate steps or organizations.[2] Technology allows buyers

[2]Stan Davis, *Future Perfect* (Reading, MA: Addison-Wesley, 1987).

and sellers to come closer together, often dealing directly with each other without having to go through any intermediate organizations. For example, when travelers purchase airline tickets directly from the airlines through the Internet, they eliminate the need for a travel agent. Likewise, trading stocks and bonds on the Internet eliminates the need for a stockbroker. Similarly, many manufacturers now sell their products directly to consumers, eliminating the need for distributors and/or retailers. eBay, the online auction firm, is doing exactly this by providing a network that directly links buyers and sellers.

Integrating Technology into Services

Technology needs to be properly integrated into an organization in order to provide a competitive advantage, in terms of both increasing the efficiency of the operations as well as increasing effectiveness with respect to better serving its customers. We identify three areas where technology can significantly contribute to the success of an organization.

Strategic Planning Strategic planning, from an operations perspective, is typically concerned with the long-range view of how an organization conducts business. As we have seen, strategic planning within the operations function of a manufacturing company is concerned with addressing such issues as (*a*) where do we locate our facilities? (*b*) how big do we make them? (*c*) when do we build them? and (*d*) what processes do we adopt to make our products?

However, a service organization, because it deals directly with its customers, also must strategically evaluate how it will interact with them. Service managers also must recognize that technology can significantly alter the way in which a company does business. For example, most of the major airlines now have home pages on the Internet that provide information about special airfare promotions. As discussed earlier, these special fares that are available only on the Web encourage customers to buy through the website, which is more cost efficient from an operations perspective. By adopting the proper strategy and associated technology, a firm can substantially increase its revenues and market share. Failure to do so can result in losing customers to competitors.

Improved Performance Service managers also must recognize that the decision to adopt technology is often driven by the need to not only to increase productivity but also to improve the existing performance of their operations. (Improved performance, as defined earlier, includes faster speed of delivery, more product variety, and improved customer responsiveness, to name a few.) Often, however, with the proper technology, both performance and productivity can be improved, creating a win–win situation for the firm.

Faster service. Technology has allowed service operations to significantly reduce and, in some cases, totally eliminate the need for customers to wait in line for service. In addition to providing faster service, technology can simultaneously reduce labor costs by entirely eliminating the customer–worker encounter.

For example, many hotels now provide an in-room checkout option. Guests who want to take advantage of this option simply follow the menu-driven instructions on the television in their room, leave their hotel keys in the room, and never have to wait in line at the front desk to check out. In this case, customer waiting time is totally eliminated and the requirement for front desk personnel is also reduced when guests take advantage of this option.

Car rental agencies have similar processes. As we saw in the opening vignette, customers are no longer required to go into the office to finalize their bills when returning their rental cars at an airport. A worker greets them at the car when they drive up and quickly prints out a statement from a handheld computer and printer, thereby allowing the customers to go directly to the shuttle bus and the terminal.

As another example, the use of bar code readers at the checkout counters in supermarkets has significantly reduced the amount of time a customer may expect to stand in line while also reducing labor costs and errors in keying in the proper item prices. Barcoding also reduces the need to consistently check inventories, which provides managers with better control.

Improved knowledge about customers. In many services, databases now provide managers with detailed information on their customers' purchasing characteristics and their firm's past relationships with these customers. As part of their focus on attention to personal detail, for example, the Ritz-Carlton hotel chain, through its management information system, tracks individual guest preferences, including the type of bed they like to sleep in (such as a queen or king-size bed) and the type of wine they prefer. In addition, any previous incidents involving the customer, particularly complaints, also are recorded in the database to ensure that similar incidents do not occur again. (This same database also keeps tracks of habitual complainers who are eventually asked to take their business elsewhere.)

Another method of using technology for obtaining data on individual customers is through membership cards. Many retail operations now require membership cards or provide discount incentives to encourage the use of these cards. Such cards allow the retailer to track the buying patterns of individual customers, thereby providing management with in-depth information about their customers that can be used for future planning purposes. For example, BJ's Wholesale Club, Costco, and Sam's Club all require their customers to have membership cards. Shaw's, Stop & Shop, and PriceChopper are examples of supermarket chains that also have introduced a similar type of card, the use of which entitles customers to significant discounts on products.

The proper use of technology thus can provide a service company with a competitive advantage through its ability to better understand the individual behavior patterns and past experiences of each of its customers.

Increased product customization. Technology also allows service managers to provide their customers with a wider variety of options than they could previously offer. The terms "microniching" and "mass customization" have evolved, in part, as a direct result of advances in technology that now permit firms to identify and provide customized goods and services to meet the needs of individual customers.

As an illustration, Levi Strauss now provides customers in its retail stores with the option of buying jeans that are made to the customer's exact size. The customer's specific measurements are entered into the computer and a few weeks later the jeans are delivered to the customer's home. Additional pairs can be ordered with only a telephone call, thereby eliminating the need to visit the store.

Another example is L.L. Bean, the mail-order company in Freeport, Maine, which will sew a customer's name or monogram on many of its products. Computerized sewing machines allow operators to select the style, size, and letter(s) in a matter of seconds. A monitor screen located above the sewing machine shows the operator how the name will appear on the product before it is actually stitched on the article.

Increased Efficiency As stated earlier, the initial thrust by services to adopt technology was driven primarily by the need to reduce operating costs. This is still a major reason for purchasing new technology. Just as capital equipment often is used to reduce costs in a manufacturing company, technology can be similarly applied in a service environment. The two

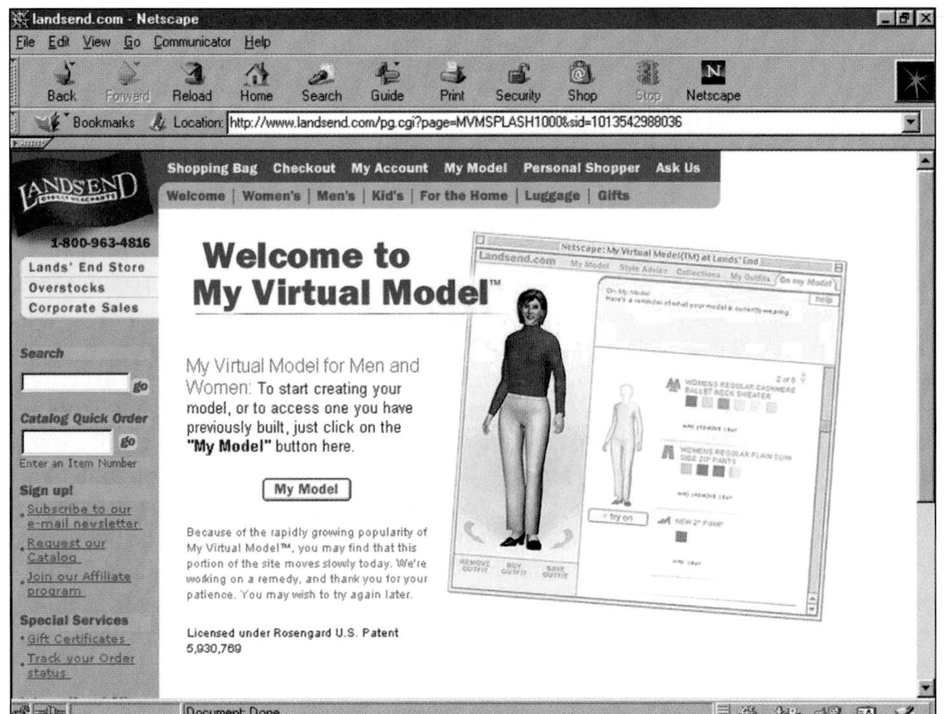

The Landsend's website allows the customer to create a likeness of him or herself and "try on" clothing for a custom fit.

primary ways in which the efficiency or productivity of the operation can be increased are (*a*) economies of scale and (*b*) reduced labor costs, recognizing that there is some degree of overlap between the two.

Economies of scale. Advances in communication technology have allowed service companies to reduce the number of locations for many types of activities. As an illustration, reservation operations for hotels, airlines, and car rental agencies have been consolidated to a few central locations. Economies of scale with these larger operations occur, in part, as a result of the ability to schedule a larger number of operators. For example, if the demand in a given hour (that is, the number of calls received) doubles, the number of operators necessary to provide the same level of service is less than double. Economies of scale also are reflected in the reduced overhead costs (as measured on a per-unit basis) that are typically associated with larger facilities. As stated earlier, an additional savings that frequently occurs as a result of the firm's ability to locate its operation anywhere is the reduced cost associated with locating in a low-cost-of-living area. Citibank, as an example, has located its credit card operations in South Dakota for this very reason. Similarly, many hotel central reservation call centers are located in Nebraska, rather than on either the West Coast or the East Coast of the United States, where the cost of living is more expensive.

Reduced labor costs. Technology can reduce labor costs in services in two ways. First, it can be used as a total replacement for labor. In addition, technology can provide support to existing labor, thereby increasing labor productivity.

As an example, automatic teller machines (ATMs) in banks are a total substitute for the traditional bank teller for many routine operations, but cost only a fraction of what a teller costs. Therefore, bank customers should be encouraged to use ATMs when conducting certain types of transactions.

Organizations also can use the Internet to reduce labor costs. The Massachusetts Registry of Motor Vehicles is now online, which allows motorists with speeding tickets to pay their fines over the Internet without having to appear in person, which was the previous norm. Increased use of the Internet in this manner also will reduce long lines at Registry locations and hopefully reduce its annual operating expenses.[3]

A note of caution is necessary, however, when contemplating the introduction of totally automated services. First, as we have noted already, there are some segments of the market that are not totally comfortable with using automation. In addition, while automation can usually do a good job performing routine transactions, there are often complex and highly customized transactions that can be resolved only with the customer interacting directly with a knowledgeable employee.

Technology in the form of automation also can be used in service operations to perform repetitive, time-consuming tasks. The use of technology in this manner cannot only increase worker productivity, but also reduce or eliminate errors. At the same time, it ensures the delivery of a more consistent product to the customer. In some instances, technology also can increase performance in the form of faster service.

For example, in many fast-food restaurants, the timed drink dispensers do not require servers to stand by the beverage machine holding the button. Instead, a quick push of the button begins the flow of a specific amount of beverage, permitting the server to assemble the rest of the order while the drink is being poured. Other examples of technology being used in fast-food operations include a conveyor belt broiler at Burger King restaurants that ensures a consistently cooked hamburger, again without the worker being continuously present during the cooking operation, and deep fat fryers with timers that automatically lift the french fries out of the oil when they have finished cooking.

Technology in the form of computerized order-entry devices allows waiters and waitresses to place orders in the kitchen without having to walk across the restaurant. Instead of having to make two trips to the kitchen—one to place the order and another to pick it up when it has been cooked—waitstaff are now only required to make a single trip to pick up the food when it is ready.

E-Services

Communication Network Environment

With the rapid growth in e-services, a new set of terms has emerged to describe the different types of networks through which information can flow. Each of these networks is defined by the type of users who have access to it. There are currently three major categories for e-services: (*a*) Internet, (*b*) intranet, and (*c*) extranet. A fourth type of network that is also currently being used is called electronic data interchange, or EDI, which is really a different form of the extranet. Exhibit 4.7 illustrates how these various networks link an organization with its customers, suppliers, and the general public.

Internet

A worldwide electronic network of more than 70 million computers.

Internet An **Internet** network has the fewest, if any, restrictions in terms of who has access to it. Firms use the Internet primarily when dealing with the general public. For those firms that sell directly to consumers such as Amazon.com (books, etc.) and Expedia.com (discounted airline tickets, hotel rooms, etc.), the Internet is the communication network that connects customers to these firms' websites to purchase goods and services. The Internet also provides access to websites that provide general information about a firm. This

[3]Mark Maremont, "No Waiting at This DMV," *Business Week,* August 19, 1996.

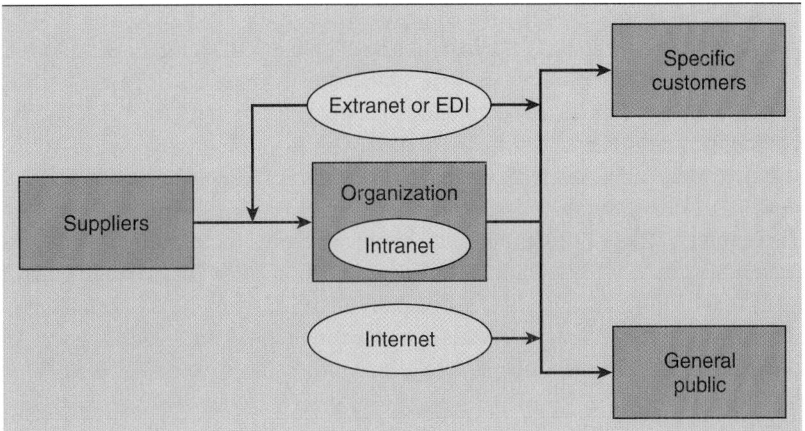

Exhibit 4.7

The Role of the Internet, Intranet, Extranet, and EDI in an Organization

type of website also can be used to disseminate news releases, provide contacts within the firm, and issue directions about how to obtain additional information about the firm. In addition, the Internet also allows firms to offer customers richer information and after-sales support with the goal of building customer loyalty.

Intranet An **intranet** is a network that operates only internally within an organization. As such, only those individuals who work within the organization have access to its intranet. Quite often the intranet is used to communicate among employees and as means for management to disseminate information quickly. For example, both Wal-Mart and FedEx have intranets that provide employees at all locations with up-to-date information on new procedures, changes in company policies, performance measurements, and recognition of outstanding employees. The FedEx intranet even includes its own television station that broadcasts company-related news 24 hours a day.

intranet

A network that operates only internally within an organization.

Extranet An **extranet** is defined as a network that allows specific external sources, be they individuals or organizations, to have limited access to a firm. As an example, an extranet will link a company with an approved group of suppliers. Electronic data interchange (to be discussed shortly) is a good example of an extranet. Organizations use an extranet to share classified or highly sensitive data with their business partners. For example, through an extranet, Procter & Gamble has access to Wal-Mart's sales and inventory data. By sharing such data, these two firms both benefit through lower costs of production and distribution as well as improved levels of customer service to the consumer.

extranet

A network that allows specific external sources to have limited access to a firm.

Electronic Data Interchange (EDI) **Electronic data interchange (EDI)** can be defined as the electronic exchange of data in highly specified formats that takes place typically between organizations. Some of the different types of transactions that can be done through EDI include (*a*) requests for quotations, (*b*) purchase orders, (*c*) acknowledgments and confirmations, (*d*) invoicing, and (*e*) payments.

electronic data interchange (EDI)

The electronic exchange of data in highly specified formats that takes place between organizations.

While the use of EDI is very fast and efficient, it does have several shortcomings. First, companies must painstakingly link their operations to a specific EDI software and then synchronize protocols (such as which version of the software they use) with the firms with which they want to conduct business. The format for EDI is very inflexible and often does not adapt well to new applications. In addition, EDI moves data in batch mode and, consequently, there is a time delay from when the data are sent to when they are actually received (although it is still much faster than nonelectronic methods). For example, at Boston Scientific's Customer Fulfillment Center in Quincy, Massachusetts, incoming EDI orders from customers are accumulated in batches and downloaded for processing every 30 minutes.

In addition, EDI transmissions typically take place through a third party such as General Electric Information Systems that is referred to as a **value-added network (VAN).** The cost of using a VAN can be quite expensive, often into the $10,000s per month for medium to large companies.

value-added network (VAN)

A third party service that is used in conjunction with EDI to provide the link between customers and suppliers.

Because of the many shortcomings and high costs of EDI, the extranet will most likely replace EDI in the future as a medium of communication. This is already happening with many firms that are now connected electronically with their suppliers through an extranet. These suppliers now need only an extranet connection and a web browser in place of the dedicated EDI software and connections to a VAN.

Types of E-Services

E-services can be divided into several broad categories that are defined by the types of individuals and/or organizations that provide and use these services. Three of these major categories are referred to as (*a*) business-to-consumer (B2C), (*b*) consumer-to-consumer (C2C), and (*c*) business-to-business (B2B). In addition, there are also e-services that can involve a government agency, which are referred to as either government-to-business (G2B) or government-to-consumer (G2C).

Within these broad categories, there are several different types of services that can be provided. We present five of these services within the e-service framework: (*a*) e-tailers, (*b*) customer support, (*c*) network providers, (*d*) information providers, and (*e*) application service providers. Some firms provide only one type of service, while others may provide several. For example, an e-tailer will often also provide customer support.

E-tailers (Goods and Services) E-tailers are firms that provide goods and services through the Internet. Pure e-tailers are those firms that conduct business exclusively through the Internet, such as Amazon.com or e-trade. These services typically have their counterparts in brick-and-mortar establishments. In many cases, however, e-tail operations are part of a larger organization that also has brick-and-mortar locations, such as Barnes and Noble or Wal-Mart. Some of these firms (often referred to as *bricks and clicks* or *clicks and mortar*) such as The Gap also provide access to their websites at their brick-and-mortar locations, thereby making the difference between the two even fuzzier.

The major challenge for pure e-tailers that sell goods is to have the necessary infrastructure in place that can efficiently and quickly deliver the goods to its customers. The lack of such infrastructures was clearly evident during the 1999 holiday season when many irate customers who had made purchases through the Internet didn't receive delivery until well into January 2000. Some e-tailers such as Amazon have elected to build their own infrastructures in terms of distribution centers, while others have elected to partner with established brick-and-mortar retail operations.

E-tailers that offer services typically do not need the supply chain infrastructure required of those e-tailers that provide goods. This allows for faster entry into the market, significantly less investment costs, and consequently a quicker return on investment. For example, the online travel industry is one of the first e-service industries that is generating profits.

A major challenge for pure e-tailers is the lack of tangibility. With a brick-and-mortar operation, the customer has a place to go for customer service or to voice a complaint. There is nothing more frustrating for a customer than to wait endlessly on the phone for customer service, and to have no other recourse, as is the case when dealing with pure e-tailers.

Equally important for e-tailers is how they can differentiate themselves in the marketplace. Without differentiation, these services offer only commodities, and therefore must compete solely on price. This translates into very small profit margins, which cannot sustain growth.

Customer Support This type of e-service provides customer support services in a wide variety of forms. At FedEx, for example, customers are able to track the location of their packages through the Internet. Customer support also can take the form of chat rooms, which provide a forum for customers, or a web page that addresses frequently asked questions (FAQs). Many firms combine their e-service customer support activities with their call center activities. With proper design, such operations can provide fast service and be highly efficient at the same time.

As with e-tailers, there are some firms that focus solely on providing customer support, often under contract to other firms, while other customer support activities can be part of the overall organization.

A major challenge for these types of services is to persuade customers, in a positive manner, to switch from requesting customer support through call centers, which are time-dependent and involve interacting with an actual person, to Internet activities, which are non-time-dependent and are therefore more efficient.

Network Providers Network providers are e-services that provide a connected network for buyers and sellers to exchange goods and services. Electronic marketplaces are one form of network provider. These marketplaces, which are usually B2B, will typically focus on a particular commodity such as chemicals, plastic, or steel. By using these marketplaces, buyers can place their order requirements on one website and receive several quotations within a matter of hours.

Such marketplaces are very efficient in terms of their ability to link buyers and sellers, and have advantages for both parties. From the buyer's perspective, less time is required to obtain quotes from a number of vendors and the efficiency of the marketplace translates into significant savings. From the seller's perspective, the marketplace eliminates the need for a distributor or salesperson (an example of disintermediation), thereby reducing costs. These savings can either be passed on to the customer or go directly to the bottom line as additional profits.

Firms that conduct auctions are another example of network providers. Auctions can be between businesses and consumers (B2C), such as priceline.com, which auctions off airline tickets and hotel rooms, or between consumers, such as eBay, which will auction off just about anything. Again, these firms provide networks that link a large number of buyers with a large number of sellers, thereby creating a very efficient marketplace and eliminating intermediaries (except for the firm providing the network, which charges a percentage of the price for which the item was sold).

Information Providers We are clearly in the information age, and it should therefore not come as a surprise that there are some e-service businesses, often referred to as **infomediaries,** that primarily focus on providing information. Some firms focus exclusively on providing information, while others provide information as part of the value added to their core business.

infomediaries

E-service businesses that primarily focus on providing information.

These firms often provide information on several levels. Hoover's Online, as an illustration, provides information on three levels. The first level, which is free to users, is general information on companies' financial information. The second level adds value by segmenting or sorting the information to fit the needs of individual users, who pay a fee for this service. The third level involves custom searches that are designed specifically to meet the needs of an individual customer.

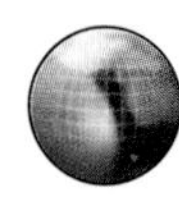

Companies that provide information as part of their total offering often also provide chat rooms where customers can discuss issues relevant to the focus of the firm. For example, Magicmaman.com, an e-service firm in Paris, France, that focuses on parents with young children, provides a chat room where parents can discuss problems they are having with their children and how some parents have dealt with them (either successfully or unsuccessfully).

application service providers (ASPs)

Firms that provide remote services to customers.

Application Service Providers (ASPs) **Application service providers (ASPs)** are firms that provide remote services to customers. For example, an ASP accounting firm will have on its own server the most current accounting software package that reflects the latest changes in the tax laws. A customer then logs into the accounting firm's website and uses that accounting package to prepare its financial statements. With an accounting ASP, customers no longer need to buy a new software package every time the tax law changes.

A major challenge for ASPs is to convince customers that they are not fly-by-night operations and will be in business for the long term. Along with demonstrating financial strength to survive in the long term, ASPs also must convince customers that they provide highly reliable services and that they are very trustworthy with sensitive customer data that are given to them. Finally, customers must have confidence in the reliability of the network over which they will connect to their ASPs.

Technology-Related Issues

The integration of new technologies into an organization requires a significant amount of training and support in order for both workers and customers to reap the full benefits. The lack of proper training and support, in many instances, will not only fail to yield the expected improvements in performance and/or productivity, but could also prove disastrous financially as frustrated workers quit and unhappy customers take their business elsewhere.

Overcoming Barriers to Entry

As new technologies become available, there are often barriers that prevent customers from using them, and managers need to be aware of this. Such barriers can significantly hinder the growth of the organization. One barrier is the "fear of the unknown" that is often associated with new technologies, a good example being the first time one purchases goods and services over the Internet. Here, because there are no tangibles associated with the firm, customers are concerned about misuse of their credit cards and whether or not they will actually get delivery of the goods or services they have purchased.

Another barrier is lack of knowledge of the consumer in using the service. This is especially true for self-service operations as well as for those services that use new technologies. Self-service gas stations provide a good example here, as there are many individuals who do not know how to operate a gas pump.

ATMs provide a good example of a service involving a new technology where customers must not only overcome their fear of the unknown, but also must learn how to properly use the technology.

Training and Support

Significant amounts of up-front training must be built into the overall new technology process. This training is often required of both workers and customers. Failure to provide proper training will lead to inefficient operations and frustration. In addition, both workers and customers must have the necessary technical support when questions arise and/or equipment malfunctions occur.

Worker Training Workers often are required to develop additional skills when a new technology is introduced into the operation. These new skills can be developed through training classes that not only describe the use of the technology but also simulate its use. This allows workers to become familiar with the new equipment and to "debug the process" prior to actually using it online in the presence of a customer. It is important for managers to recognize that worker training is an ongoing process. Many leading-edge firms, like FedEx, in fact, require their workers to spend a specific number of days each year in training.

Customer Training Customers also frequently are required to undergo some degree of training when a new technology interacts directly with them. Depending on the type of technology and the level of sophistication required to use it, customer training can vary from a simple pamphlet describing how to use the new technology to attending classes that carefully document the proper use of the technology.

Conclusion

Technology plays a significant role in the successful operation of every organization. With the constant introduction of new state-of-the-art technologies, this trend will most likely continue into the foreseeable future. However, operations managers must realize that the adoption of technology is not a simple undertaking and therefore must be carefully planned.

In the past, many firms looked to technology primarily to help them increase productivity. However, there are several additional reasons companies elect to incorporate new technologies into their processes, such as building a stronger relationship with their customers and improving their overall performance by providing better customer service.

Finally, the installation of new technology must be accompanied with the proper technical support. In addition, sufficient time must be allocated in the initial start-up phase to provide proper training to both workers and, where necessary, also customers. When deciding to purchase new technology, the service manager must ensure that there is compatibility between the desired technology and the overall long-term goals of the firm.

Key Terms

application service provider (ASP) p. 142
asynchronous transactions p. 134
computer-aided (or -assisted) design (CAD) p. 125
computer-aided design and manufacturing (CAD/CAM) p. 126
computer-integrated manufacturing (CIM) p. 126
disintermediation p. 134
electronic data interchange (EDI) p. 139
enterprise resource planning (ERP) systems p. 128
extranet p. 139
flexible manufacturing system (FMS) p. 126
industrial robots p. 125
infomediary p. 141
Internet p. 138
intranet p. 139
islands of automation p. 126
machining centers p. 125
numerically controlled (NC) machines p. 125
synchronous transactions p. 134
value-added network (VAN) p. 140

Review and Discussion Questions

1. What are the different ways in which technology can impact an operation? Use examples in both manufacturing and service operations.
2. Identify and compare the perceived benefits and costs for each of the following pairs of services:

Traditional Service	Technology-Driven Service
a. Traditional grocery store	Home delivery grocery service (Peapod)
b. Neighborhood travel agent	Internet travel agent (Expedia)
c. Local bank branch office	Internet bank (Wingspan)
d. Traditional bookstore	Virtual bookstore (Amazon)

3. Describe how technology is adding value for each of the technology-driven services identified in Question 2.
4. What are the benefits of automation in a manufacturing company?
5. What are the different ways in which infomediaries add value?
6. Visit any of the following services and identify the various ways in which technology is changing the way in which these services are being delivered.
   a. Retail store.
   b. Restaurant.
   c. Bank office.
   d. Supermarket.

Internet Exercise

Visit the website of a major airline such as American, Northwestern, or Delta and compare the different ways to obtain information on a flight between two major cities of your choosing. Then visit the website of an online travel agency such as Expedia.com, Orbitz.com, or Travelocity.com and do a similar comparison. What are the advantages and disadvantages of using an airline's website? What are the advantages of using an online travel agency's website? What are the advantages of ordering airline tickets online versus buying them through your local travel agent, who is located in a nearby shopping mall?

Bibliography

Brin, Dinah W. "Check it Out!" *The Middlesex News* (Framingham, MA), August 11, 1996.

Collier, David A. *Service Management: The Automation of Services.* Reston, VA: Reston Publishing, 1986.

Davenport, Thomas. "Putting the Enterprise into Enterprise Systems." *Harvard Business Review* 76, no. 4 (July–August 1998), pp. 121–31.

Hackett, Gregory P. "Investing in Technology: The Service Sector Sinkhole?" *Sloan Management Review,* Winter 1990, pp. 97–103.

Judge, Paul C. "Customer Service: EMC Corp." *Fast Company,* June, 2001, pp. 138–45.

Laughlin, Stephen. "An ERP Game Plan." *Journal of Business Strategy* 20, no. 1 (January–February 1999), pp. 32–37.

Maremont, Mark. "No Waiting at This DMV." *Business Week,* August 19, 1996.

Quinn, J. B. "Technology in Services: Past Myths and Future Challenges." In *Technology in Services: Policies for Growth, Trade and Employment.* Washington, DC: National Academy Press, 1988.

Quinn, J. B., and M. N. Bailey. "Information Technology: Increasing Productivity in Services." *Academy of Management Executive* 8, no. 3 (1994).

Roach, S. S. "Services Under Siege—The Restructuring Imperative." *Harvard Business Review,* September–October 1991.

Scott, Karyl, "EMC Shores Up Its Offense." *InformationWeek,* October 2, 2000, pp. 72–82.

Stein, Tom. "The Great ERP Debate." *InformationWeek,* February 8, 1999, pp. 132–40.

Wheatley, Malcolm. "ERP Training Stinks." *CIO Magazine,* June 1, 2000, pp. 86–96.

Zellner, Wendy. "Where the Net Delivers: Travel." *Business Week,* June 11, 2001, pp. 142–44.

Case

EMC Uses Technology to Enhance Its Customer Service

The best kind of problem is no problem, or one that is anticipated and fixed before it even occurs. And no one is better at doing this than EMC Corporation, a manufacturer of data storage systems. Using state-of-the-art technology, a wide variety of sensors are installed in its storage systems. These sensors measure almost everything, from the operating environment, like temperature and vibration, to technical performance, like faulty sectors on a storage disk or abnormal power surges. In total, there are more than a 1,000 diagnostics that are done routinely. Whenever any of these parameters falls outside of its accepted tolerances, the storage system automatically "calls home" to EMC's call center in Hopkinton, MA to report the problem. In fact, more than 80 percent of the 4,000 calls received at the call center each day are not from EMC's customers themselves, but rather from EMC's storage systems. Customer support engineers then either fix the problem remotely from the call center, or if that is not possible, dispatch a technician to the site. With this ability to anticipate problems before they occur, the first time a customer is even aware of a potential problem is when the technician arrives to replace a potentially faulty component before it actually fails.

One of the key factors in EMC's significant growth over the past decade has been its fanatical devotion to customer service. Providing great customer service, however, requires more than the ability to perform remote diagnostics, it requires commitment from the entire company. For starters, the customer service call center is located right in the middle of the engineering department, easily accessible to both hardware and software engineers. If the engineer receiving the call can't resolve the problem in 15 minutes, the responsible design engineer is called in. If it still isn't resolved in another 15 minutes, the vice president for

engineering is called in. An unresolved problem will continue to escalate through EMC's organization, to the point where if it isn't solved within eight hours, Mike Ruettgers, EMC's executive chairman and Joe Tucci, EMC's president and CEO are both notified.

As further evidence of its commitment to service excellence, EMC doesn't treat its customer service organization as a profit center, as many firms do. By including the service in the cost of the product, customer service is treated as an expense item, without a need to generate profits. This allows the customer service to focus entirely on doing whatever is necessary to satisfy the customer.

Does EMC charge more for its products? Absolutely. But its customers believe that EMC products are worth the additional cost. When Forrester Research surveyed 50 big companies about their various technology suppliers, "EMC came out looking like God," says Carl Howe, a director of research at Forrester. "It has the best customer service reviews we have ever seen, in any industry."[4]

In an *InformationWeek* study conducted on enterprise storage vendors, EMC received a satisfaction score of 8.53 (on a scale of 1 to 10, where 1 is not at all satisfied and 10 is extremely satisfied), compared to scores of 7.21 for Compaq, 7.16 for IBM, and 7.05 for Dell. As further evidence of customer satisfaction, the same study asked customers to rank their enterprise storage vendors in terms of "Service-Level Guarantees" and After-Sales Service" with the following results:[5]

Customer Rankings of the Enterprise Storage Vendors

Service-Level Guarantees	After-Sales Service
1. EMC	1. EMC
2. Dell	2. Dell
3. IBM	3. IBM
4. Sun Microsystems	4. Sun Microsystems
5. Compaq	5. Compaq

Questions

1. How does technology provide EMC with a competitive advantage in the marketplace?
2. What are some of the concerns that EMC might have when potential problems are fixed remotely without the customer ever knowing about them?
3. What is the role of technology in building customer loyalty at EMC?

[4]Paul C. Judge, "Customer Service: EMC Corp.," *Fast Company,* June, 2001, pp. 138–45.

[5]Karyl Scott, "EMC Shores Up Its Offense," *InformationWeek,* October 2, 2000, pp. 72–82.

5

Process Measurement and Analysis

Chapter Objectives

- Illustrate how all activities within an organization are actually processes that need to be managed.
- Present the various measures of performance that can be used to evaluate a process.
- Show how process analysis can provide managers with an in-depth understanding of how a process is performing, while at the same time identifying areas for improvement.
- Present the concept of service blueprinting and illustrate how it is used to evaluate processes within a service environment.
- Introduce the concept of business processes and show how they are providing managers with a broader perspective for managing their organizations.
- Present the concepts of benchmarking and reengineering, and show their roles in creating world-class operations.

EVEN HAMBURGER CHAINS LINK PROCESSES TO STRATEGY

Prior to the fast-food era, hamburgers, like any other sandwich in a restaurant, were made to order. The process began when the cook, upon receipt of the order, reached into the refrigerator for a raw hamburger patty and placed it on the grill. The customer could specify the degree of doneness (e.g., rare, medium, or well done) and request certain condiments. The roll could be toasted or not. However, the quality of the hamburger produced in this fashion was highly dependent on the skill of the cook, and consequently the quality could vary significantly between cooks, even within the same restaurant. In addition, hamburgers prepared using this method took a relatively long time to deliver, as they were cooked only after the order was received (see Exhibit 5.1A).

The arrival of Burger King and McDonald's in the 1950s, and later Wendy's, totally changed the way in which hamburgers were cooked and delivered to the customer. Unlike most restaurants at that time, which offered a wide variety of food items, Burger King and McDonald's were highly focused operations with very limited menus. In addition, both firms offered low-cost products that were delivered quickly. However, each has taken a different approach in the type of process they have adopted to cook and deliver hamburgers and the particular markets that they serve.

Managerial Issues

The primary role of managers, in essence, is to manage processes, including the individuals involved in those processes. And what managers are now recognizing is that every set of activities represents a process. Examples include *processing* a payroll, *processing* an application for employment, *processing* a purchase order, *processing* a customer complaint, and *processing* a product design change. In addition, managers also are acknowledging that these individual processes do not operate in a vacuum, but rather are linked to other processes in other functional areas, thereby creating larger, more complex business processes, which by definition span these functional areas within an organization.

As we learned earlier in the book, the choice of what type of process to adopt is part of operations strategy. Once this decision has been made and the process has been installed, it must then be managed. Management means identifying the critical performance measures of the process and monitoring them on a regular basis to ensure that established standards or goals are being achieved. Management here also includes taking the necessary corrective actions when these measures indicate that there is a problem. Process performance measures are divided into two major categories: those that pertain to all processes and those that are specific to individual processes. Both are necessary.

Standards of performance are constantly being raised. New products are being designed and introduced faster. They also are being delivered faster to customers and are of higher quality than was the previous norm. As a result, processes must constantly be improved. To assist managers in doing this, benchmarking (defined in detail later in the chapter) often is used to identify how a firm's process performance compares to that of other firms. Such comparisons provide managers with the information that is necessary in creating world-class operations. When significant differences are identified, the process often is reengineered with the goal of improving its overall performance.

Defining a Process

An analysis of the methods used by various food service operations to prepare and deliver hamburgers provides us with some insight into the trade-offs that managers face when selecting one particular process over another. This type of analysis also allows us to identify the strengths and weaknesses of each process, which then can be related to the specific market segments on which each firm is focusing.

To continue the chapter opener, McDonald's cooks its hamburgers on grills in batches, with 12 hamburgers per batch. The rolls are similarly toasted or caramelized in batches of 12. After cooking, the hamburgers are assembled (that is, placed on rolls with condiments, etc.) and wrapped, also in batch sizes of 12. The finished products are then stored in holding bins for immediate delivery to the customer. This low-cost, highly efficient, make-to-stock process produces highly standardized products that can be delivered quickly to the customer (see Exhibit 5.1B). As a result, a major market for McDonald's is families with small children for whom speed of delivery is important. Thus, fast service is emphasized in many of McDonald's advertisements.

Burger King, on the other hand, cooks its hamburgers with a conveyor-broiler, which is a highly specialized piece of equipment. Using this method, a worker places raw hamburgers on one end of a moving conveyor which proceeds under a broiler where the burgers are cooked from both the top and bottom. Ninety seconds later the hamburgers emerge from the other end of the conveyor, cooked to the desired degree. The rolls also are toasted in the conveyor-broiler. The use of this highly focused process ensures consistency of product quality with minimum dependence on worker skill; however, the process is very limited in terms of flexibility. Because all hamburgers are cooked in 90 seconds, the thickness of the patty cannot vary. Consequently, when Burger King came out with the Whopper, the only way it could make the bigger burger was to make it wider because the thickness had to remain the same as that of the regular-sized patties.

Exhibit 5.1
Process Flowcharts for Making Hamburgers

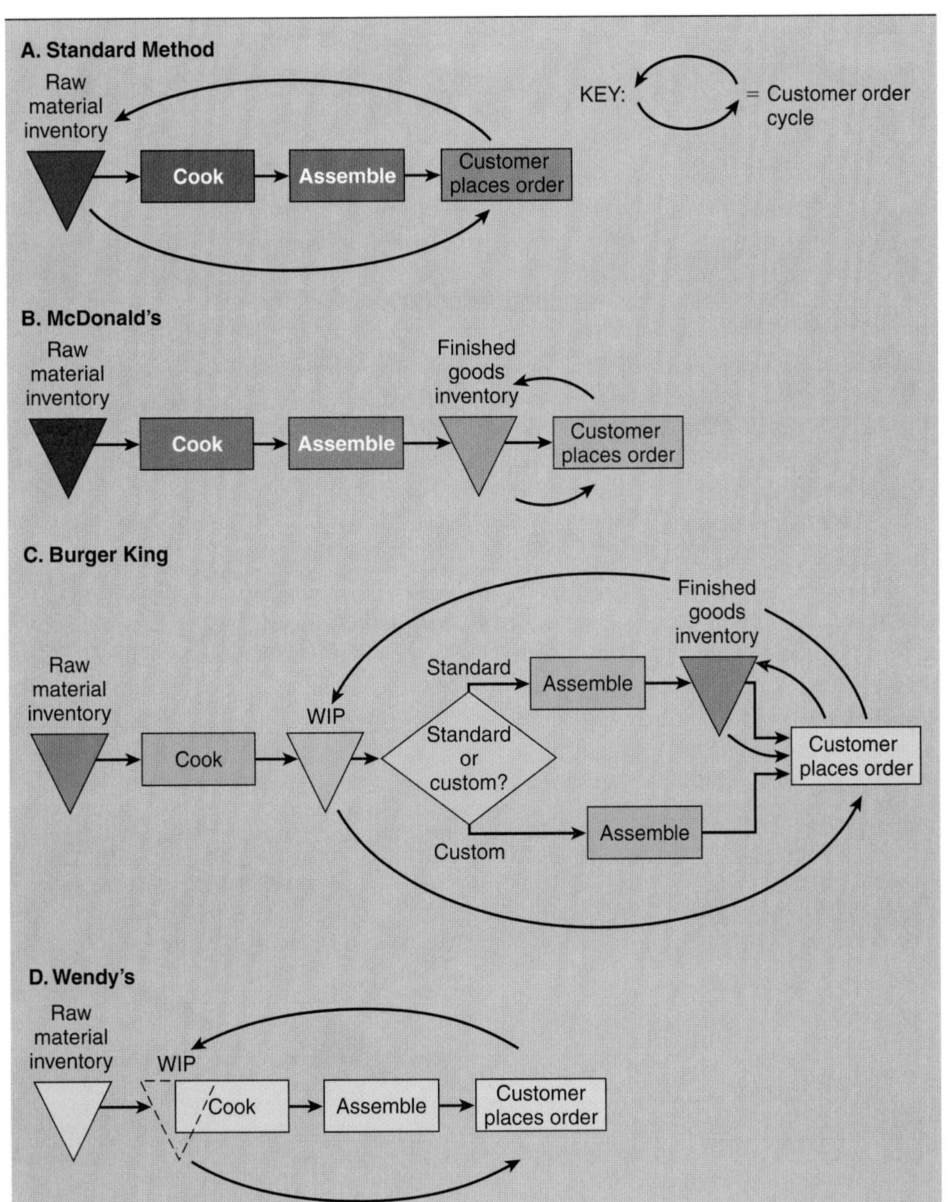

Once cooked, the hamburgers at Burger King are placed on rolls and stored in a steam cabinet. This work-in-process (WIP) inventory is then used to replenish standard items in the holding bins (or finished goods inventory). It is also used as the starting point for assembling hamburgers to meet individual customer requests. The WIP inventory of cooked hamburgers allows Burger King to custom assemble hamburgers in a relatively short time (as compared to cooking them from the raw state) while simultaneously reducing the level of finished goods inventory in holding bins (as compared to McDonald's) because replenishment time is shorter (see Exhibit 5.1C). The strength of Burger King's process lies in its ability to quickly deliver assembled-to-order products; therefore, it tries to attract individuals who "want it their way."

Exhibit 5.2

Relative Comparison of Hamburger Preparation Processes

Company	Cost	Flexibility	Speed	Quality
Standard method	High	Very high	Very slow	Very high/variable
McDonald's	Low	Low	Fast	Low/consistent
Burger King	Medium	Medium	Medium	Medium/consistent
Wendy's	Medium	High	Slow	High/consistent

Wendy's has adopted still a different approach. Here hamburgers are cooked on a grill, awaiting individual customer orders. Upon receipt of the order, the hamburger is taken off the grill and placed on a bun with the specific condiments requested, all within view of the customer. Customers perceive this assemble-to-order process as higher quality in comparison to that at McDonald's or Burger King, due, in part, to the fact that everything is done in front of the customer. The trade-off here is that an average hamburger takes longer to prepare than a special request at Burger King because the order begins farther upstream in the process (see Exhibit 5.1D).

As we have noted, each of these operations has its strengths and weaknesses, which are summarized in Exhibit 5.2. All three fast-food chains are successful because they recognize their respective strengths and focus advertising and promotional efforts on attracting those segments of the market that value their particular process characteristics.

Process Measurement

A key factor in the success of every organization is its ability to measure performance. Such feedback on a continuous basis provides management with the data necessary to determine if established goals or standards are being met. As Peter Drucker, a well-known management guru, has said, "If you can't measure it, you can't manage it." Without proper measures of performance, managers cannot assess how well their organizations are doing or compare their performance with that of their competitors. Without these performance measures, managers would be like ships' captains, adrift on the ocean with no land in sight and no compass or other navigational instruments to guide them.

However, with a growing number of performance measures available, managers today must be selective in choosing only those measures that are critical to their firm's success. Depending on the specific industry and market niche within that industry, some measures of performance are more important to management than others. For example, in a fast-food outlet, a key performance indicator is the speed with which food is delivered to the customer. In an upscale restaurant, on the other hand, key performance measures may be the variety of items offered on the menu and the quality of food served.

In today's information-intense environment, managers, like everyone else, are deluged with reams of reports containing data on all aspects of a company's performance. It is, therefore, essential for management to identify those key indicators that measure those parameters that are critical to the success of their firms.

Types of Performance Measures

productivity

Efficiency of a process.

Productivity The efficiency with which inputs are transformed into outputs is a measure of the process's **productivity.** In other words, productivity measures how well we convert inputs into outputs. In its broadest sense, productivity is defined as

$$\text{Productivity} = \frac{\text{Outputs}}{\text{Inputs}}$$

Ideally, we would like to measure the total productivity of a process, which would be the total outputs divided by the total inputs. Unfortunately, the inputs come in various forms. For example, labor is measured in hours, a building is measured in square feet, raw material is measured in pounds, units, and so forth. It therefore would be impossible to obtain a measure for the total inputs into a process unless we converted all of the inputs to a common denominator like money. However, in doing so, the operations manager loses an understanding of how the process is performing. Consequently, management will adopt one or more partial measures of productivity, which is the output of the process (in either revenues or units) divided by a single input. Some commonly used partial measures of productivity are presented in Exhibit 5.3. Such measures give managers the necessary information in familiar units, thereby allowing the manager to more easily relate to the actual performance of the operation. As noted in the exhibit, productivity can be measured for many factors, including labor, facilities, and equipment.

Productivity is what we call a *relative measure.* In other words, to be meaningful it needs to be compared with something else. For example, what can we learn from the fact that we operate a restaurant, and that its productivity last week was 8.4 customers/labor hour? (Nothing!)

Productivity comparisons can be made in two ways. First, a company can compare itself with similar operations within its industry, or can use industry data when they are available (e.g., comparing productivity among the different stores in a franchise).

Another approach is to measure productivity over time within the same operation. Here we would compare productivity in one time period with that of the next.

Capacity The output capability of a process is referred to as the **capacity** of the process. This performance measure is typically presented in units of output per unit of time, although, as we shall see later in the section, this is not always practical. Examples of measures of capacity are shown in Exhibit 5.4.

capacity

Output of a process in a given time period.

As noted by these examples, measures of capacity exist for both manufacturing and services. The major difference between manufacturing and services, in terms of measuring capacity, is that with service operations the measures of capacity usually include the customer, since the customer is typically an integral part of the process. (Because customers very often participate in the service delivery process, they can be viewed as both an input and an output.)

Design capacity is defined as the ideal output rate at which a firm would like to produce under normal circumstances and for which the system was designed. Depending on

Exhibit 5.3

Partial Measures of Productivity

Type of Business	Productivity Measure (Output/Input)
Restaurant	Customers (meals)/labor hour
Retail store	Sales/square foot
Chicken farm	Pounds of meat/pound of feed
Utility plant	Kilowatts/ton of coal
Paper mill	Tons of paper/cord of wood

Exhibit 5.4
Measures of Capacity

Type of Operation	Measure of Capacity
Fast-food restaurant	Customers per hour
Brewery	Barrels of beer per year
Hotel reservation call center	Telephone calls per hour
Automobile assembly plant	Cars per hour
Paper mill	Tons of paper per year
College	Students per class period

the product or process and goals of the company, design capacity could even be established using a five-day-a-week, single-shift operation. *Maximum capacity* is used to define the maximum potential output rate that could be achieved when productive resources are used to their maximum. Typically, most firms can operate effectively at maximum capacity for only short periods of time. Operating at maximum capacity, for example, results in higher energy costs, the need for overtime wage premiums, and increased machine breakdowns due to the lack of time to conduct scheduled preventive maintenance. Worker fatigue resulting from extended hours on the job also can cause an increase in defective products as well as a decrease in labor productivity.

capacity utilization

Percentage of available capacity that is actually used.

The degree to which a firm utilizes its productive capacity is referred to as **capacity utilization,** which is defined as follows:

$$\text{Capacity utilization} = \frac{\text{Actual output}}{\text{Design capacity}}$$

For example, if an automobile assembly plant had a design capacity of 3,600 cars per week, and actually produced only 2,700 cars in one week, then its capacity utilization for that week would be

$$\text{Capacity utilization} = \frac{2{,}700}{3{,}600} = 75\%$$

With this definition of capacity utilization, it is possible to have utilization rates that are in excess of 100 percent, which should be a warning to management that excessive production costs are being incurred.

So far, we have measured capacity in terms of units of output per unit of time, which is appropriate as long as the output is relatively homogeneous (e.g., cars, stereos, etc.). However, when the output units are highly variable, especially in terms of process requirements, a more meaningful measure of capacity is often expressed in terms of one of the inputs. Consider, for example, a flexible machining center that can make parts that take anywhere from five minutes to two hours to produce. The capacity of the center, in terms of units produced per week, could vary significantly depending on which particular units were being produced. In this case, a better measure of capacity utilization would be:

$$\text{Capacity utilization} = \frac{\text{Actual machine hours used}}{\text{Total machine hours available}}$$

Such measures of capacity utilization will become more popular as the flexibility of processes increases to permit wider varieties of products to be made. This approach to measuring capacity utilization is also more applicable to many service operations that have a very high labor content and also require that labor to perform a wide variety of tasks.

Examples here include medical doctors, whose tasks can vary from performing surgical operations to having office visits and attending required meetings. College professors provide another good example. In addition to teaching students, they also are required to conduct research and be of service to the college and the community. In both these instances, capacity as measured in terms of available hours per week is clearly the appropriate measure.

Quality The quality of a process usually is measured by the defect rate of the products produced. Defects include those products that are identified as nonconforming, both internally (prior to shipping the product to the customer) as well as externally (i.e., products whose defects are found by the customer). The topic of process quality measurement and control is presented in greater detail in Chapter 6 and its supplement.

There are additional measures of a process's overall quality. With increasing awareness and concern for the environment, for example, the amount of toxic waste generated is also a measure of a process's quality. Similarly, the amount of scrap and waste material produced is another process quality indicator.

Speed of Delivery Many companies are experiencing increased pressure with respect to speed of delivery. Firms that once took weeks and months to deliver a product are now delivering those products in hours and days. FedEx provides a good example of a firm that adds value by providing fast overnight delivery of packages.

Speed of delivery has two dimensions to measure. The first is the amount of time from when the product is ordered to when it is shipped to the customer, which is known as a product's *lead time*. Companies that produce standard products significantly reduce lead times by producing products for finished goods inventory. For such situations, orders are immediately filled from existing inventories. Companies that produce customized products, however, do not have the luxury of a finished goods inventory. Firms producing such products typically require a significant lead time before the finished product can be shipped.

The other dimension in measuring speed of delivery is the variability in delivery time. In many cases, this dimension is more critical than the estimated lead time itself. In other words, customers, whether they be other companies or end users, do not like uncertainty. Uncertainty affects work scheduling, capacity utilization, and so forth, which negatively affects the overall efficiency of the process. Thus, the less variability in delivery times, the better.

Flexibility Currently, the competitive advantage for many companies lies in their ability to produce customized products to meet individual customer needs. The capability of a company to provide such customized products in a timely manner is often referred to as **agile manufacturing.** Flexibility is the measure of how readily the company's transformation process can adjust to meet the ever-changing demands of its customers.

agile manufacturing

Ability of a manufacturing process to respond quickly to the demands of the customer.

There are three dimensions of flexibility. The first type of flexibility indicates how quickly a process can convert from producing one product or family of product(s) to another. For example, many U.S. automobile assembly plants still require a minimum of several weeks' shutdown annually in order to convert from one model year to the next, indicating a degree of inflexibility in this area.

Another measure of a process's flexibility is its ability to react to changes in volume. Those processes that can accommodate large fluctuations in volume are said to be more flexible than those that cannot. Most service operations need to be very flexible in this dimension because of their inability to inventory demand. (For example, customers wanting to eat at a restaurant on Saturday night will not wait until Monday morning.) Thus, service operations such as retail stores, restaurants, and health clinics must have the ability to adjust to meet the demand from a few customers per hour to several hundred customers per hour. The typical assembly-line operation in a manufacturing facility cannot similarly adjust. The volume of output from an assembly line is fixed, and consequently companies with this type of process must resort to other means of balancing supply and demand. For example, appliance makers and automobile companies offer discounts and low-cost financing to encourage consumer buying during slow periods of demand, due in part to their inability to adjust the outputs of their manufacturing facilities without shutting them down entirely.

The third dimension of flexibility is the ability of the process to produce more than one product simultaneously. Thus, the more products that a process can produce at a time, the more flexible it is said to be. The dimension of flexibility is especially important in producing customized products. For example, the flexibility of Dell's computer assembly processes allows it to custom build computers that meet the individual requirements of each customer.

process velocity

Ratio of total throughput time for a product to the value-added time.

Process Velocity A relatively new measure of performance is **process velocity.** Also referred to as *manufacturing velocity,* process velocity is the ratio of the actual throughput time that it takes for a product to go through the process divided by the value-added time required to complete the product or service. (Value-added time is defined as that time when work is actually being done to complete the product or deliver the service.)

For example, if the throughput time for a product is six weeks, and the actual value-added time to complete the product is four hours, then the process velocity of this product is

$$\text{Process velocity} = \frac{\text{Total throughput time}}{\text{Value-added time}}$$

$$\text{Process velocity} = \frac{6 \text{ weeks} \times 5 \text{ days per week} \times 8 \text{ hours per day}}{4 \text{ hours}} = 60$$

A process velocity of 60, in this case, means that it takes 60 times as long to complete the product as it does to do the actual work on the product itself. In other words, process velocity is like a golf score—the lower it is, the better.

Process velocities in excess of 100 are not uncommon. For example, University Microfilms, Inc. (UMI), the largest publisher of dissertations in the United States, took 150 days to process a manuscript, although only two hours were actually spent adding value to the manuscript. For UMI, the process velocity for a manuscript was therefore:

$$\text{Process velocity} = \frac{150 \text{ days per manuscript} \times 8 \text{ hours per day}}{2 \text{ hours}} = 600$$

UMI was able to reduce the throughput time to 60 days, thereby lowering its process velocity to 240.[1]

James Womack and Daniel Jones provide another good example of measuring process velocity. In their book *Lean Thinking,* they analyze the value stream of a carton of cola.[2] In their analysis, they identify only three hours where value is actually being added to the product, although the overall process takes 319 days. In this case, the process velocity for a carton of cola is

$$\text{Process velocity} = \frac{319 \text{ days} \times 8 \text{ hours per day}}{3 \text{ hours}} = 851$$

[1] A. Bernstein, "Quality Is Becoming Job One in the Office, Too,"*Business Week,* April 29, 1991.

[2] James P. Womack and Daniel T. Jones, *Lean Thinking: Banish Waste and Create Wealth in Your Corporation* (New York: Simon and Shuster, 1996), p. 43.

As noted by the above examples, the concept of process velocity is equally applicable to manufacturing and services. Process velocity also can be applied to any particular segment of the process, or to the overall process. For example, a firm may want to focus only on its manufacturing velocity, in which case it would look at the throughput time from when the product is first begun to when it is completed and ready to ship. A broader perspective may measure process velocity from the time when the customer first places the order for the product to when payment is finally received and the check has cleared.

In the past, especially in the United States, companies have focused primarily on increasing the efficiency of the value-added time, which often constitutes only a very small portion of a product's overall time in the process.

Process Analysis

Definitions

As a first step in understanding the important characteristics of processes, we define here some of the more commonly used terms.

Hybrid Process Most of the processes that we encounter consist of more than one stage or step to produce the required goods or services. These are often referred to as **multistage processes.** Within a multistage process, a different type of process can exist at each stage. When this occurs, these multistage processes are frequently referred to as **hybrid processes.** For example, in making potato chips at Cape Cod Potato Chips in Hyannis, Massachusetts, the potatoes are first washed in a continuous process, cooked in a batch process, and then packaged in an assembly-line type of operation. Within a given industry, different firms may adopt different types of processes to produce the same or similar products. As an example, some potato chip manufacturers cook their potatoes with a continuous process instead of a batch process. To further illustrate, at McDonald's, the hamburgers are both cooked and assembled in batches. This approach produces a highly standardized product. Burger King, on the other hand, cooks its hamburgers on a continuous flow broiler but assembles them individually to meet specific customer requests.

multistage process

Process that consists of more than one step.

hybrid process

Multistage process that consists of more than one type of process.

Make-to-Stock versus Make-to-Order Which type of process is chosen for each stage is dependent on the firm's operations strategy and the type of product being manufactured. A **make-to-stock system** is compatible with producing a highly standardized product that can be stored in a finished goods inventory for quick delivery to the customer. As a result, these products are usually forecasted in anticipation of future customer orders. In contrast, a **make-to-order system** focuses on producing customized items that have already been ordered by the customer. It is important to note here that a make-to-order system requires more flexibility than a make-to-stock system, and as a result tends to be slower and more inefficient and, therefore, more expensive.

However, a make-to-stock system tends to limit the number of product variations to a few highly standardized items. In order to achieve maximum process efficiency while at the same time increase product variety, firms will delay the customization step until the last possible moment. A good example of this application is the mixing of custom colored paints at home improvement centers while the customers wait.

make-to-stock system

Process for making highly standardized products for finished goods inventory.

make-to-order system

Process for making customized products to meet individual customer requirements.

Modularization Another approach that attempts to combine process efficiency with some degree of customization is called **modularization.** With this approach, the end product is designed so it can be assembled from several individual components that are considered to

modularization

Use of standard components and subassemblies to produce customized products.

be standard items. The concept of modularization is used extensively throughout the computer industry. As an illustration, suppose a computer firm produces four different types of central processors, three different kinds of input/output devices, and two varieties of printers. From a customer's perspective, this firm offers a choice of 24 different computer configurations ($4 \times 3 \times 2$), although manufacturing has to produce only nine standard products ($4 + 3 + 2$). The final assembly of automobiles provides another good example. Here standard components are delivered to the automobile assembly plant and the selection of a particular combination of these components produces a "custom-made" car. Modularization also has application in services. For example, an Italian restaurant can offer its customers a choice of 60 different dishes by combining four types of pasta, three types of sauces, and five varieties of meat ($4 \times 3 \times 5$).

Exhibit 5.5 shows a comparison of the process flow charts for make-to-stock, make-to-order, and modularized production processes.

Exhibit 5.5

A Comparison of Make-to-Stock, Make-to-Order, and Modularized Processes

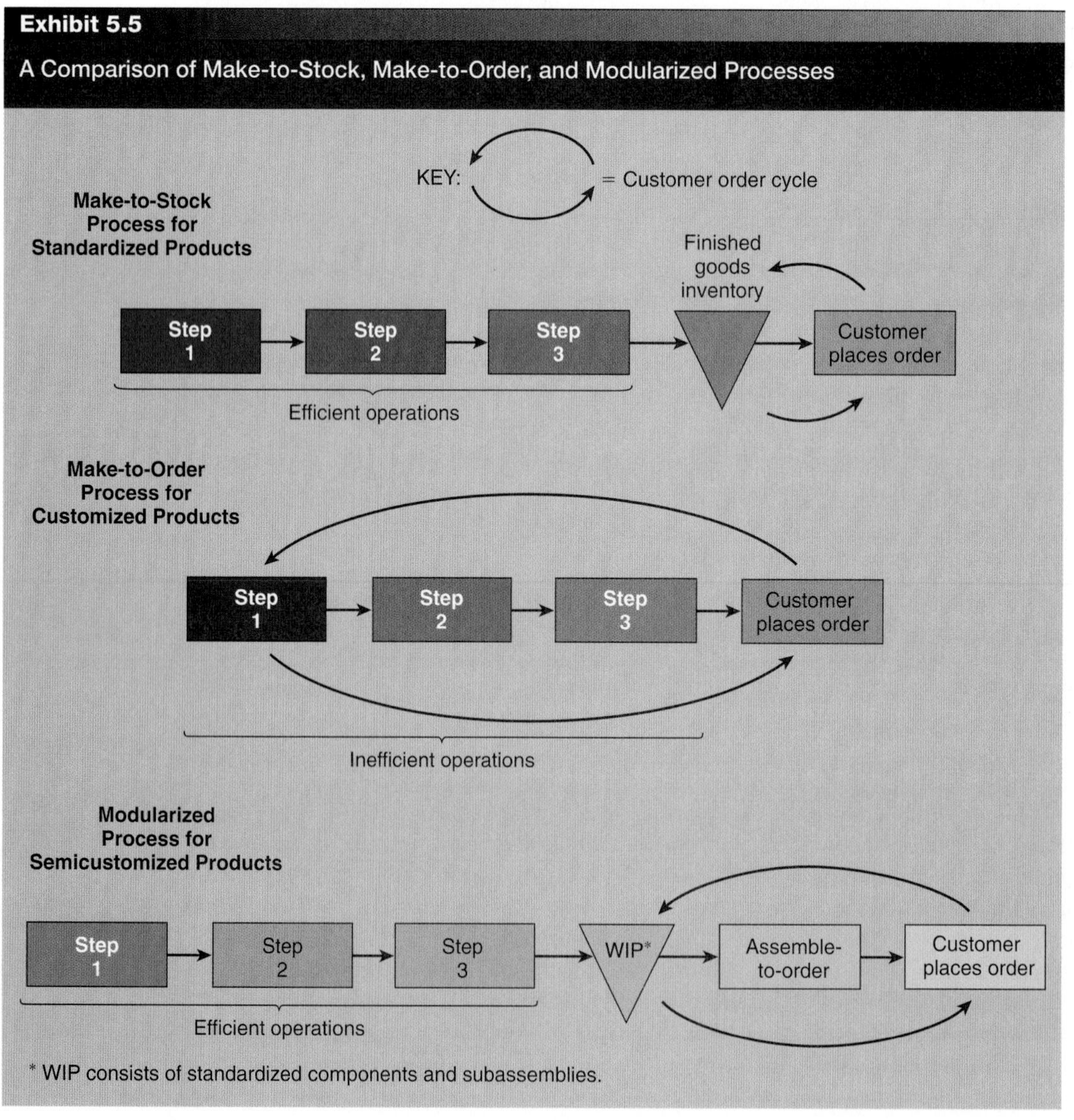

* WIP consists of standardized components and subassemblies.

Tightness and Dependence The relationship between the various stages in a process is frequently referred to as the degree of *tightness* in the process. Processes that are considered very tight, like assembly lines, have a great deal of *dependence* between stages. In other words, if production stops due to a machine breakdown at an early stage in the process, work ceases almost immediately at all of the subsequent operations. This high degree of dependence among the stages is caused by a lack of buffer inventories between adjacent stages. The greater the buffer inventories, the greater the independence between stages and the "looser" the process. Batch processes typically exhibit a high degree of independence between stages as shown by the large amounts of buffer inventories in the form of work-in-process (WIP). With these types of processes, a failure at one stage in the process does not impact any other stages until the WIP between them is depleted.

Bottlenecks The capacity of each stage in a multistage process often varies for several reasons, including dissimilar output rates of the different pieces of equipment that comprise the overall process. In these situations, the stage of the process with the lowest capacity is referred to as the **bottleneck** in the process. Adding additional capacity to alleviate the bottleneck at one stage in the process often will shift the bottleneck to another stage. When this occurs, the full capacity potential of the additional equipment may not be realized.

bottleneck

Stage or stages that limit the total output of a process.

Example

A commercial bread bakery wants to evaluate its capacity, in terms of how many pounds of bread it can produce per hour. A simplified version of the process is shown below:

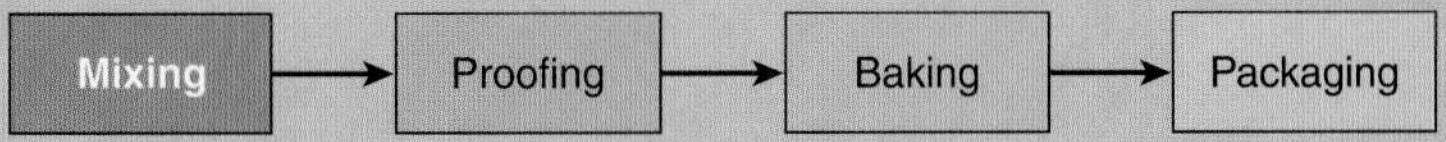

In the mixing stage, all of the ingredients are combined to form the dough. The dough must then rise in a controlled environment called a proofing box or proofing oven, which monitors humidity and temperature. Following the proofing, the bread is then formed into loaves and baked. In the final stage, the bread is packaged prior to distribution to retail outlets. The bakery currently has the following equipment:

Stage	Capacity (Lb/Hr/Machine)	Number of Machines
Mixing	60	3
Proofing	25	6
Baking	40	4
Packaging	75	3

a. What is the current capacity of the bakery in pounds of bread per hour?

b. Where is the bottleneck in the process?

c. If an additional piece of equipment is purchased to increase the capacity of the bottleneck, what is the new capacity of the bakery?

Solution

a. The total capacity of the bakery is determined by calculating the total capacity at each stage of the process as follows:

Stage	Equipment Capacity (Lb/Hr/Machine)	Number of Machines	Total Capacity (Lb/Hr)
Mixing	60	3	180
Proofing	25	6	150
Baking	40	4	160
Packaging	75	3	225

The overall capacity of the bakery is 150 pounds per hour, as determined by the proofing operation, which is that stage with the smallest capacity.

b. Currently, the bottleneck is at the proofing stage because that has the smallest hourly capacity.

c. If another proofing oven is purchased, the capacity of the proofing stage is now 175 pounds per hour. However, with the addition of the new proofing oven, the bottleneck in the process now shifts to the baking stage because that has the lowest capacity of 160 pounds per hour. Thus the new overall capacity of the bakery with the addition of another proofing oven is only 160 pounds per hour.

Capacity versus Demand

In the above example, we have focused entirely on the available capacity of the process without considering the demand for the bread. It is important when analyzing the capacity requirements for a process that we do not confuse the capacity of the process with the demand for the firm's products. For example, if the demand for a product is less than the capacity of the smallest stage, then no bottleneck really exists (in the bakery example, if demand was less than 150 pounds per hour, there would not be any bottleneck). As a result, no additional equipment is needed. Only when demand exceeds the capacity at one or more stages do we have to address the problem of a bottleneck and consider installing additional equipment.

Process Flowcharts

process flowchart

Schematic diagram for describing a process.

A **process flowchart** provides management with an opportunity to view the entire process step by step. The traditional symbols used in drawing a process flowchart are presented in Exhibit 5.6.

Example

A potato chip manufacturer in Hawaii produces "Maui-style, kettle-cooked" potato chips for distribution throughout the Hawaiian Islands to retail outlets as well as to hotels and resort areas. The process of making potato chips is relatively simple. Raw potatoes, which are delivered once a week to the factory, are first washed and peeled. After a visual inspection to ensure all of the peel and eyes are removed, the potatoes are then sliced and immediately fried in a large kettle. (The peeling and frying operations

Exhibit 5.6

Elements in a Process Flowchart

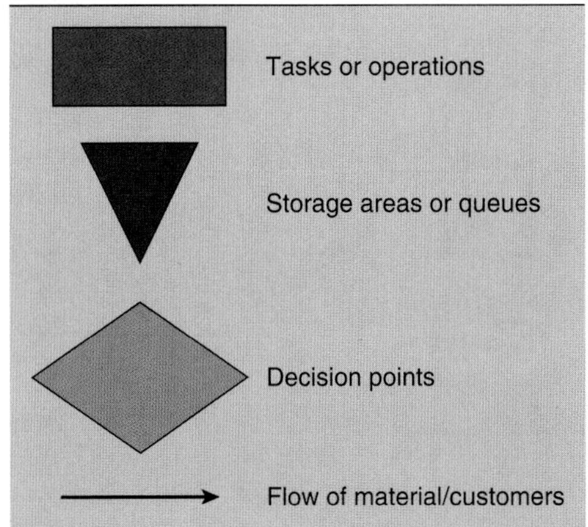

are done in batches while the slicing is a continuous operation.) After frying, the cooked chips are inspected and any burnt ones are removed. The chips are then salted and stored in large cartons. This first phase of the process is done on two shifts of eight hours each. In contrast, the packaging operation is run only eight hours a day because of the large capacity of the equipment. The cooked chips are packaged in either one-ounce or eight-ounce packages. The last step in the process places the packages in cartons for delivery. (There are 24 one-ounce packages to a carton and 12 eight-ounce packages to a carton.

Draw the process flowchart for this operation.

Solution

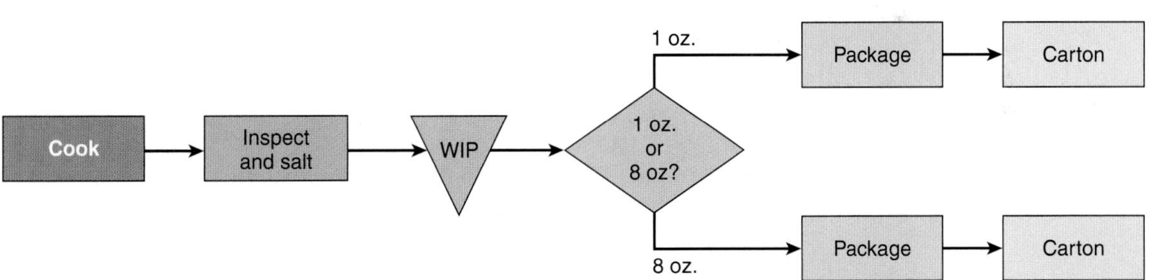

Example

To continue with a more in-depth analysis of the potato chip company, the following information is given about the capacities of the different stages in the operation.

Stage	Capacity per Machine	Number of Machines
Peeling	600 lb./hr.	2
Slicing	1,500 lb./hr.	1
Cooking	250 lb./hr.	2
Packaging (1 oz.)	160 pkgs./min.	2
Packaging (8 oz.)	30 pkgs./min.	1
Cartoning (1 oz.)	5 cartons/min.	2
Cartoning (8 oz.)	4 cartons/min.	1

The weekly demand is 30,000 cartons of 1 ounce chips and 5,000 cartons of 8 ounce chips.

a. Using Excel, set up a worksheet that shows all of the stages involved in producing potato chips and determine the capacity of each stage in pounds per week.

b. Identify the bottleneck(s) in the process.

c. Make recommendations for eliminating the bottleneck(s).

Solution

a. See spreadsheet.

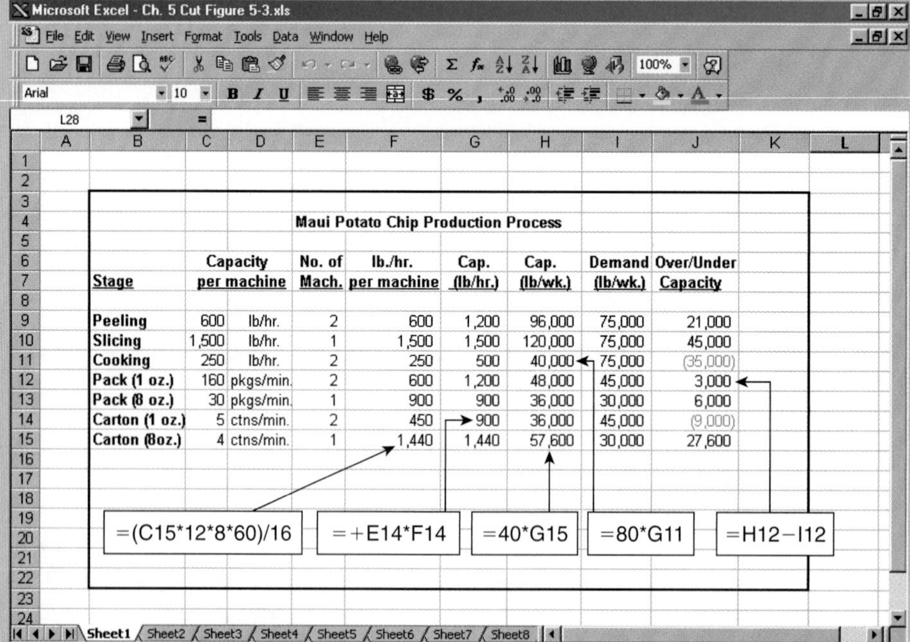

Maui Potato Chip Production Process

Stage	Capacity per machine		No. of Mach.	lb./hr. per machine	Cap. (lb/hr.)	Cap. (lb/wk.)	Demand (lb/wk.)	Over/Under Capacity
Peeling	600	lb/hr.	2	600	1,200	96,000	75,000	21,000
Slicing	1,500	lb/hr.	1	1,500	1,500	120,000	75,000	45,000
Cooking	250	lb/hr.	2	250	500	40,000	75,000	(35,000)
Pack (1 oz.)	160	pkgs/min.	2	600	1,200	48,000	45,000	3,000
Pack (8 oz.)	30	pkgs/min.	1	900	900	36,000	30,000	6,000
Carton (1 oz.)	5	ctns/min.	2	450	900	36,000	45,000	(9,000)
Carton (8oz.)	4	ctns/min.	1	1,440	1,440	57,600	30,000	27,600

b. The bottlenecks are the cooking stage, and the cartoning of the 1-ounce packages, because the demand in each case exceeds the available capacity.

c. Add two additional fryers for cooking the potatoes, and one additional operation for putting the 1-ounce packages into cartons.

The use of process flowcharts in conjunction with a capacity analysis of each stage in the process provides management with a thorough understanding of the major process issues that need to be addressed. In addition, as part of the process analysis, it is often necessary to draw three different flowcharts. These three flowcharts define (*a*) what the official or documented method is, (*b*) how the work is actually being performed, and (*c*) what the proper procedures should be.

Service Blueprinting

As with manufacturing process analysis, the standard tool for service process analysis is the flowchart. In 1978, Lynn Shostack added to the standard process flowchart the concept of the *line of visibility* and emphasized the identification of potential fail points in her version of the flowchart, calling it a **service blueprint.**[3] She also has made a compelling argument for having blueprints on every aspect of a service, and for having the "keeper of the blueprint" as a specific job function in any large service organization. Current practice in some companies is to have blueprints available on computers so when problems arise, senior managers can zero in on any portion of a service process, thereby making more informed decisions about how to resolve them. One example is the service blueprint for a cash account at a discount brokerage, as shown in Exhibit 5.7.

service blueprint

Process flowchart for services that includes the customer.

A key element in developing the service blueprint is the *line of visibility.* All activities above the line take place in direct contact with the customer. Those activities below the line are considered to be "backroom" operations, taking place without the customer's presence. Activities above the line of visibility, therefore, need to focus on providing good service; backroom operations, on the other hand, should focus on process efficiency.

As an example, the steps involved in developing a blueprint for a simple shoeshine process, including a profitability analysis, are as follows:

1. *Identify processes.* The first step in creating such a blueprint is mapping the processes that constitute the service. Exhibit 5.8 maps out the various steps in providing a shoeshine. As the service is simple and clear-cut, the map is straightforward. It might be useful to specify how the proprietor will perform the step called *buff.*
2. *Isolate fail points.* Having diagrammed the processes involved, the designer now can see where the system might go awry. For example, the shoeshiner may pick up and apply the wrong color wax, so the process designer must build in a subprocess to correct this possible error. The identification of fail points and the design of fail-safe processes are critical. The consequences of service failures can be greatly reduced by analyzing fail points at the design stage.
3. *Establish a time frame.* Since all services depend on time, which is usually the major cost determinant, the process designer should establish a standard execution time.
4. *Analyze profitability.* The customer can spend the three minutes between standard and acceptable execution time at the shoeshine parlor waiting in line or during service, if an error occurs or if the shoeshiner does certain things too slowly. Whatever its source, a delay can affect profits dramatically. Exhibit 5.9 quantifies the cost of delay; at four minutes the proprietor loses money. A service designer must establish a time-of-service-execution standard to ensure a profitable business.

Fail-safing

Services processes typically involve the customer. Consequently, any errors that occur during the process take place in front of the customer, thereby providing management with little or no opportunity to correct the situation before the customer is affected by it. In many of these situations, especially where self-service is involved, a concept of **fail-safing** or foolproofing has been developed, which is similar to *poka-yoke* in manufacturing.

fail-safing

Designing a service process so as to make it error free or foolproof.

One example of fail-safing is the bathroom in an airplane. To avoid possible embarrassment resulting from an unlocked door, the light will not go on until the bathroom door is actually locked. Another example of fail-safing is provided in some hotels that require that the room card be placed in a specific slot in order for the electricity in the room to be turned on. In this way, the guest always knows where the room card is while in the room,

[3]G. Lynn Shostack, "Designing Services That Deliver," *Harvard Business Review* 62, no. 1 (January–February 1984), p. 135.

Exhibit 5.7

Service Blueprint for a Cash Account at a Discount Brokerage

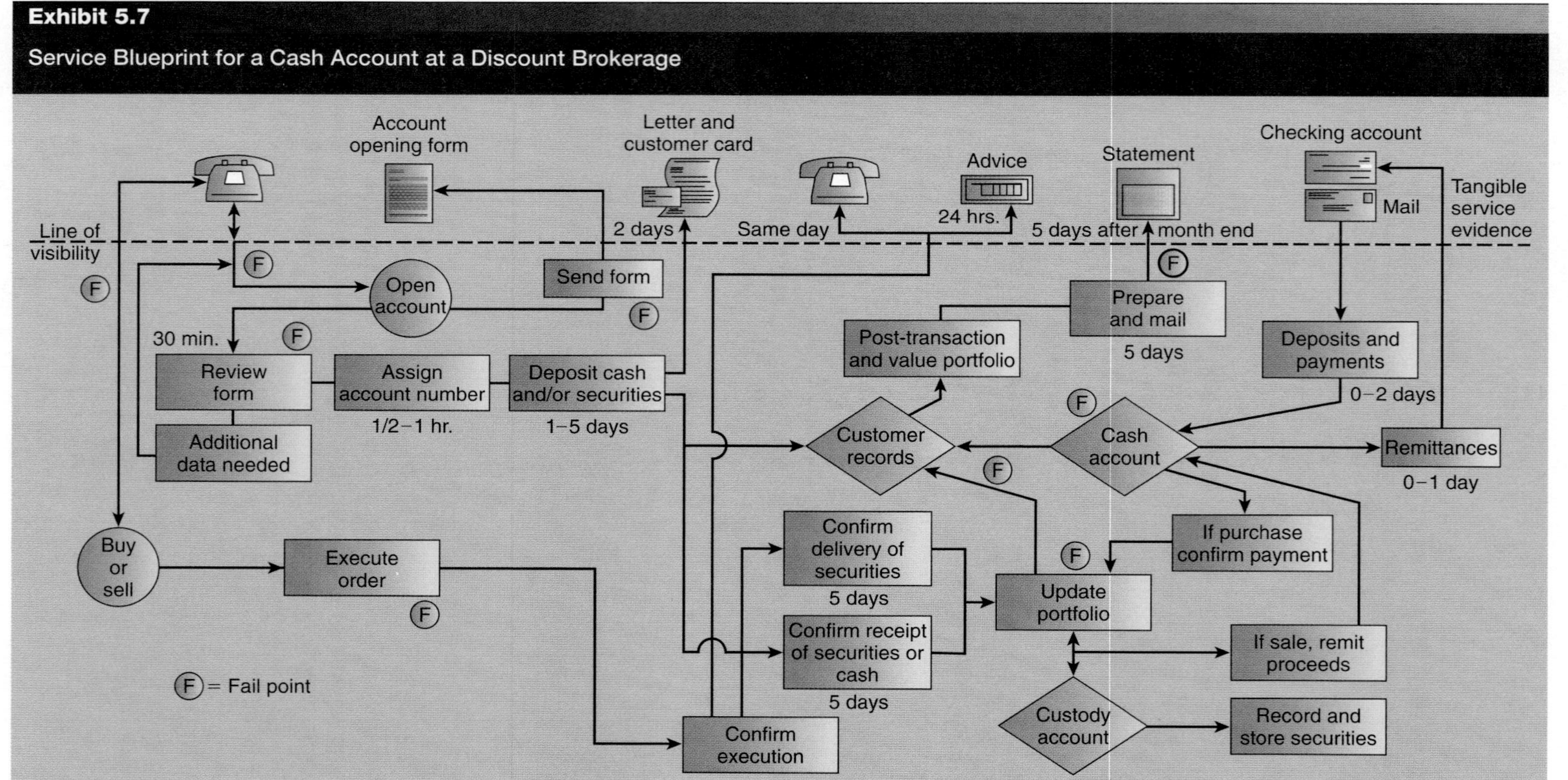

Source: Reprinted by permission of *Harvard Business Review.* From G. Lynn Shostack, "Designing Services That Deliver," *Harvard Business Review* 62, no. 1 (January–February 1984), p. 138.

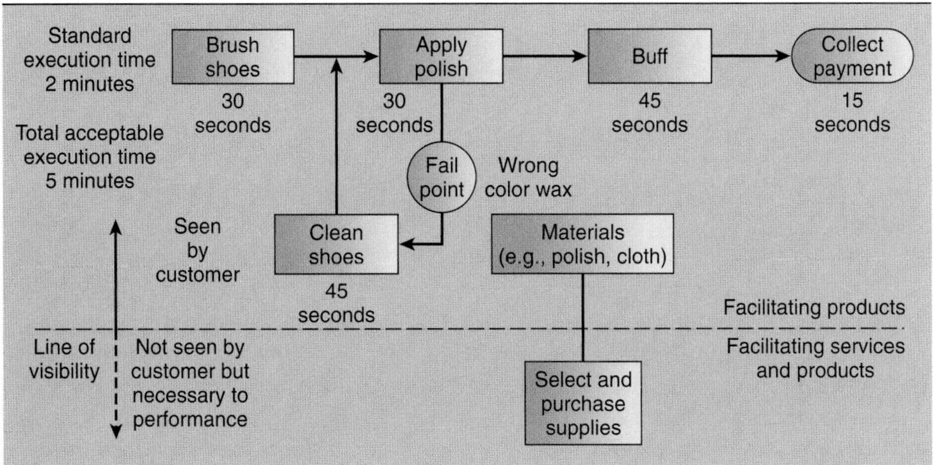

Exhibit 5.8

Blueprint for a Corner Shoeshine

Source: Reprinted by permission of *Harvard Business Review.* From G. Lynn Shostack, "Designing Services That Deliver." *Harvard Business Review* 62, No. 1, January–February 1984, p. 134.

Exhibit 5.9

Shoeshine Profitability Analysis

	Execution Time		
	2 Minutes	**3 Minutes**	**4 Minutes**
Price	$.50	$.50	$.50
Costs			
Time @ $.10 per minute	.20	.30	.40
Wax	.03	.03	.03
Other operating expenses	.09	.09	.09
Total costs	$.32	$.42	4.52
Pretax profit	$.18	$.08	($.02)

Source: Reprinted by permission of *Harvard Business Review.* From G. Lynn Shostack, "Designing Services That Deliver." January–February 1984, p. 134.

and at the same time, the electricity is shut off when the guest is not in the room, thereby saving the hotel money in terms of reduced energy costs.

Business Processes

We define a **business process** as "a logical set of tasks or activities that *crosses functional boundaries* and recognizes its *interdependence* with other processes or business processes." In other words, business processes cut across "the white spaces" in an organizational chart, linking the various functional areas to accomplish a common task or goal. Exhibit 5.10 identifies some of the more common business processes and the respective functional areas that they link.

business process

A set of sequential tasks or activities that cross functional boundaries and recognize their interdependence with other processes or business processes.

Business Process Analysis

The analysis of business processes uses basically the same methodology that is described earlier in this chapter with respect to process analysis. In addition, however, as noted above, business process analysis recognizes that the business process being analyzed is dependent on the outputs of other business processes (or processes) and similarly, other

Exhibit 5.10

Examples of Business Processes

Business Process	Functional Areas That Are Linked
New product development	Operations, marketing, finance, engineering
Order fulfillment	Marketing, operations, accounting
Supply chain management	Purchasing, operations, accounting
Asset management	Operations, accounting, finance
Recruitment	Human resources, operations, accounting

business processes (or processes) are dependent on the output of the business process under evaluation. The analysis of a business process involves benchmarking and reengineering, both of which are explained in detail in the following sections.

Likewise, the performance measures for business processes are similar to those used to evaluate processes. In addition to the operational-oriented measures described earlier in this chapter, there are often additional measures of performance that are specific to each business process. Examples of these business process–specific measures are presented in Exhibit 5.11.

The first step in analyzing a business process is to define the process boundaries. It is extremely important to clearly establish (*a*) where the process begins and ends, (*b*) the inputs and outputs of the process, and (*c*) the other processes in the organization that either impact on or are impacted by the process under evaluation. In determining the process boundaries, the scope of the process is defined, which is critical. Process analyses that have too wide a scope are often too complex to analyze properly, and therefore become unmanageable. The resulting analysis, in these cases, is very often difficult to understand, measure, and ultimately change. On the other hand, processes that are too narrow in scope only have the potential for limited improvement.

granularity

A term used to describe the level of detail that is used in analyzing a process.

Business process analysis can take place at various levels within an organization. The degree of detail that is used in the analysis is often referred to as **granularity.** Business process analysis that is conducted at a high level but does not get into a great amount of detail is said to be of large granularity, whereas an analysis that is done in greater detail is referred to as being of small granularity.

Once the boundaries of the business process being analyzed are established, the firm must then link its overall corporate strategies to the process. In other words, the firm must clearly understand how the process under evaluation contributes to its competitive advantage. For example, if a company competes by being low cost and providing fast delivery, the process must be analyzed with respect to how the process contributes to low cost and

Exhibit 5.11

Measures of Performance for Specific Business Processes

Business Process	Specific Measures of Performance
Order fulfillment	Service level (percent orders filled from stock) Lead time (time between receipt of customer order and delivery)
Supply chain management	Percent on-time deliveries Lead time (time between placement of vendor order and delivery)
New product development	Time to market (time from product conception to availability) Market share (percent of market captured by new product)
Human resource management	Employee turnover rate Employee satisfaction

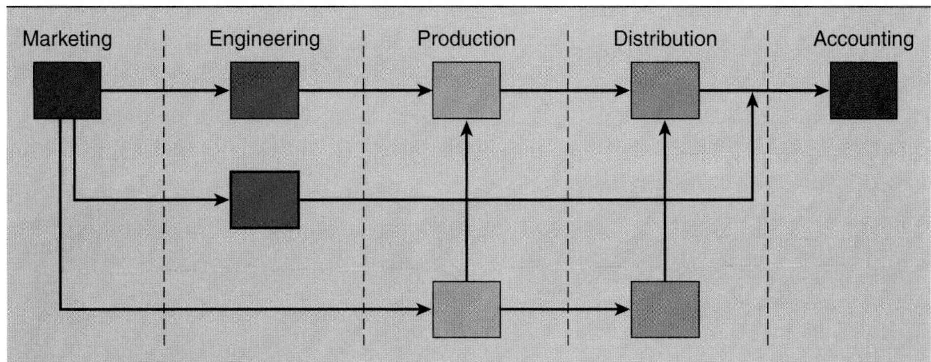

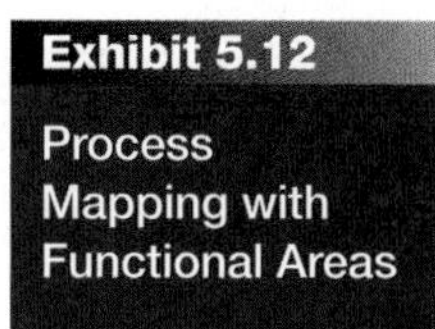

fast delivery. By linking strategy to the business process, the firm can more easily identify the key measures that it will use to evaluate the process.

The third step is mapping the process. Here a process flow chart is developed, providing a visual context for analyzing the process. This chart provides both the analyst and the process owner with a clear understanding of the boundaries of the process and the various steps that are involved. When mapping the process, it is important to understand the specific order in which the steps are performed, how long each step takes, and the resources that are required. As part of the mapping process, the various steps that are required are often grouped by functional area to more clearly illustrate the cross functionality of the process, as shown in Exhibit 5.12.

As stated above, the firm's strategies provide a basis for determining which key measures are to be used to evaluate the process. After the process is evaluated, it is *benchmarked* to determine how it compares with similar processes both internally within the firm and externally with those of other firms. The combination of performance measures and benchmarking provides management with some clear insights for identifying the major problems with the process that need to be corrected.

In the last step, the process is improved through *reengineering,* which identifies and addresses the root causes of the problem. However, determining how the process is to be reengineered is not sufficient. The successful implementation of the necessary process changes is just as important as the changes themselves. As a final note, these process evaluations should be conducted on a periodic basis to ensure that the process continues to perform in the desired manner.

Benchmarking[4]

Benchmarking is simply a comparison of a company's performance in certain areas with that of other firms in its industry and/or with those firms that are identified as world-class competitors in specific functions and operations. Benchmarking can cut across traditional industry lines, providing opportunities for new and innovative ways to increase performance. For example, Xerox, in its desire to deliver products quickly, studied how L.L. Bean of Freeport, Maine, a mail-order company well-known for fast and accurate service, accomplished this.

benchmarking

Comparison of a company's measures of performance with those of firms that are considered to be world class.

[4]This section has drawn heavily on the following two books: Robert C. Camp, *Benchmarking: The Search for Industry Best Practices That Lead to Superior Performance* (Milwaukee, WI: ASQC Quality Press, 1989), and Robert C. Camp, *Business Process Benchmarking: Finding and Implementing Best Practices* (Milwaukee, WI: ASQC Quality Press, 1995).

Operations Management in Practice

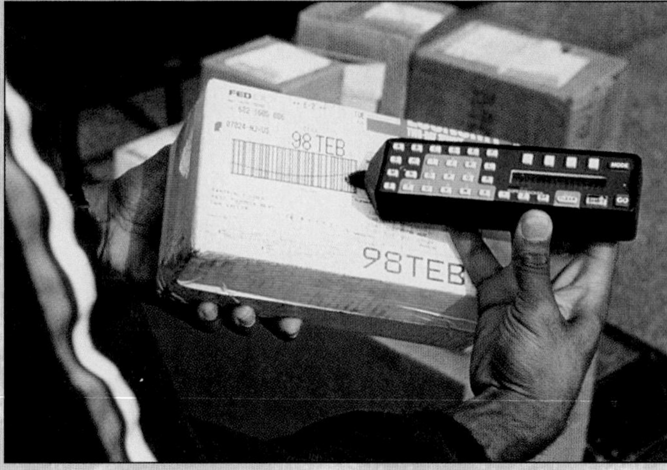

Process management at FedEx is viewed as a systematic examination of how the actual work of operating a business gets done. This approach, which cuts across divisional, functional, and departmental lines, entails collaborative investigation, analysis, and then refinement of the basic processes, activities, and tasks by which a business operates.

The five core business processes defined at FedEx are (*a*) providing direction; (*b*) acquiring and retaining customers; (*c*) servicing customers; (*d*) moving, tracking, and delivering the product; and (*e*) invoicing and collecting payment. Process management at FedEx is customer-driven. It focuses first on customer requirements to assure that the process is designed to meet the expectations of the customer. It utilizes analytical techniques to identify high-leverage opportunities for standardizing work processes, as well as for creating opportunities for continuous improvement.

Measurement is also important at FedEx. The old business maxim, "You cannot manage what you cannot measure," has been an inspiration for measuring both customer satisfaction and service quality. Measurement is accomplished through the use of process quality indicators (PQIs), which measure the outputs of processes, as well as other process indicators, which measure such factors as the quality of the process results, the cycle time of each operation within a process, and the cost of the process. An example of a PQI within the moving, tracking, and delivering the product core process is "the total number of conveyances (trucks and aircraft) arriving late at Hubs, destination ramps, and destination stations, which is measured on a daily basis at the corporate level."

FedEx recognizes that its future success depends on many factors, including its ability to improve its business processes. It believes that only if it can adopt and fully utilize analytical business tools, such as process management, to improve operations will it be able to compete against other companies in the marketplace. However, the full utilization of the techniques of process management depends on the motivation and competencies of its frontline management. Its managers must have analytical, communication, and decision-making skills, and Fed-Ex provides training to ensure that these managers obtain these required skills.

Source: Adapted from a letter from Fred Smith, CEO, FedEx, to FedEx management, October 7, 1996.

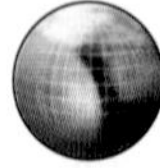

Firms that want to compete as world-class organizations in the highly competitive global arena must attain *best of breed* status in those performance parameters that are critical for success in their respective industries and market segments. This can be accomplished only through measuring and comparing their performance with that of others, and then instituting the necessary actions for improvement. Companies such as AT&T, Du Pont, Ford Motor, IBM, Eastman Kodak, Milliken, Motorola, Xerox, and other industry leaders, in an attempt to increase both quality and productivity, now use benchmarking as a standard management tool.

David T. Kearns, CEO of Xerox Corporation, defines benchmarking as follows:

> Benchmarking is the continuous process of measuring products, services, and practices against the toughest competitors or those companies recognized as industry leaders.[5]

[5]Camp, *Benchmarking,* p. 10.

Several key elements in this definition should be emphasized. Continuous measuring implies that benchmarking is an iterative process with no end. With competition constantly "raising the bar," accepted levels of performance today will not be tolerated by the customer tomorrow. Only through constant monitoring of our performance and that of our competitors will we be able to know where we stand at any point in time. (One of the requirements of the Malcolm Baldrige National Quality Award (MBNQA) is that a firm's performance be benchmarked against other companies.)

Benchmarking means measurement. This can be accomplished internally within the organization as well as externally with competitors and world-class firms. It is important for management to be cognizant that benchmarking is not limited only to manufacturing, but can also be applied to the other functional areas in an organization.

Benchmarking should not be limited only to direct competitors. Rather it should focus on those firms or business functions or operations within firms that have achieved recognition as world-class operations. In other words, as Robert Camp states in the title of his book, "benchmarking is the search for best practices that leads to superior performance."[6]

What Should We Benchmark?

Benchmarking can be applied to many areas within an organization. Robert Camp identifies three of these: (*a*) goods and services, (*b*) business processes, and (*c*) performance measures.

Goods and Services Benchmarking identifies the features and functions of the goods and services that are desired by the firm's customers. This information is incorporated into product planning, design, and development in the form of product goals and technology design practices.

Business Processes Benchmarking in this area provides the basis for business process improvement and reengineering. These changes should be an integral part of the continuous quality improvement initiative.

Performance Measures The end result of benchmarking goods, services, and processes is to establish and validate objectives for the key performance measures that have been identified as critical to the success of the organization.

Key Steps in Benchmarking

Robert Camp, based on his experience with Xerox Corporation, has identified five phases that are necessary to successfully implement benchmarking within an organization: planning, analysis, integration, action, and maturity.

Planning This phase of benchmarking identifies the areas that we should benchmark, the specific organizations against which we should be benchmarking, the types of data we should collect, and the ways we should collect those data.

Analysis The analysis phase focuses on obtaining an in-depth understanding of our firm's existing practices and processes as well as those of the organizations against which we will be benchmarking.

[6]Ibid.

John Deere, the farm equipment manufacturer, uses technology to be more responsive to their customers. This technology allows dealers and farmers to communicate directly with John Deere warehouses, providing them with ready access to parts and equipment.

Integration Here we use the findings from the first two phases to define those target areas that we want to change. As part of this phase, we need to ensure that benchmarking concepts are implemented in the corporate planning process, and that benchmarking is accepted by all levels of management.

Action The benchmarking findings and associated goals must be translated into action. Those individuals who actually perform the tasks should determine how the findings can best be incorporated into the existing process.

Maturity An organization reaches maturity when the best business practices that have been identified have been incorporated into all of the relevant business processes, thereby ensuring superior performance for the organization as a whole.

Types of Benchmarking

There are four general categories of benchmarking: (*a*) internal, (*b*) competitive, (*c*) functional, and (*d*) generic.

Internal Benchmarking This type of benchmarking provides for a comparison among similar operations or processes within a firm's own organization. It is often the starting point for identifying best practices that currently exist within the company. Internal benchmarking also provides the first step to documenting processes, which is necessary for identifying future areas for improvement. Internal benchmarking is especially appropriate for organizations (both manufacturing and services) with multiple locations.

Competitive Benchmarking This provides a comparison between an organization's performance and that of its best direct competitors. The relative information obtained here will show how the company compares to other firms in its industry. Benchmarking within an industry is often difficult because of the natural unwillingness of competitors to share critical information.

Functional Benchmarking This type of benchmarking addresses performance comparisons with the best functional areas, regardless of the industry in which they are located.

The benefits to this are several. First, a firm may have less difficulty in obtaining benchmarking partners in other industries where there are not direct competitors. In addition, it is often easy to identify those firms that are considered to be the "best of breed" in performing a specific function. The L.L. Bean example presented at the beginning of this section provides a good example of functional benchmarking. Other examples of leaders in specific functional areas include General Electric (information systems), John Deere (service parts logistics, see photo), and Ford (assembly automation).

Generic Benchmarking Here performance measures are concerned with specific work processes that are virtually the same for all industries that use these processes. Generic benchmarking can easily identify those firms that have adopted innovative processes, thereby providing targets that can be more readily acceptable by members of the organization. Examples of leaders in generic benchmarking include the Federal Reserve Bank (bill scanning) and Citicorp (document processing).

Business Process Reengineering[7]

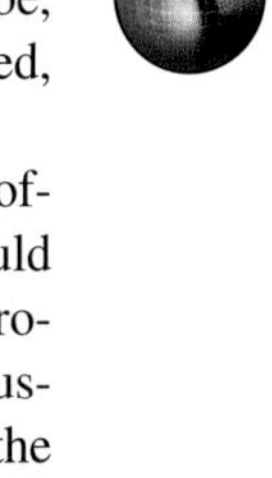

For many years, dating well back into the 19th century, companies were organized and structured both to maximize efficiency and also to control growth. However, with the emergence of a single world economy and increased competition from all corners of the globe, today's competitive priorities for success have shifted from efficiency to innovation, speed, service, and quality.

To increase efficiency in the factory, job design was dominated by the division-of-labor concept in which the work to be done was subdivided into a series of tasks that could be performed by less-skilled individuals. However, this approach, while increasing productivity among lower-skilled workers, had its disadvantages. With each individual focusing primarily on his or her assigned task, no one assumed overall responsibility for the process itself. The result was that these conventional process structures were fragmented and piecemeal, and consequently lacked the integration necessary to support the current competitive priorities, for example, quality and service. This shift in priorities has forced managers to rethink how their firms operate, and to focus on redesigning their core business processes. This is the goal of reengineering. To accomplish this, we need to "get back to the basics," by applying some of the concepts presented in this chapter that allow us to better understand these processes.

Reengineering Defined

reengineering

Process of rethinking and restructuring an organization.

This process of rethinking and restructuring an organization is often referred to as **reengineering.** Reengineering means literally starting from the beginning with a clean sheet of paper in terms of how we design our organizations to better serve our customers. It focuses on processes, not individuals performing individual tasks. A key element of reengineering is the notion of "discontinuous thinking"—identifying and discarding antiquated rules and assumptions that are often the foundation for current business operations, and that continue to exist when only small, incremental changes are made.

A cornerstone of reengineering is the use of computer technology. With advances in database management, speed of processing, and networking capabilities, today's computers

[7]Adapted from Michael Hammer and James Champy, *Reengineering the Corporation: A Manifesto for Business Revolution* (New York: HarperCollins, 1993).

should be used to formulate new approaches that are based on the computer's strengths. Instead, many companies simply transfer existing manual systems onto the computers and wonder why their problems still exist even though they have "automated" their systems.

An example of reengineering is shown with Ford's desire to reduce its accounts payable department in the early 1980s. Initially, through traditional methods, management determined that the 500-person department should be reduced by 100 people (a 20 percent reduction in that workforce). However, investigation revealed that Mazda's accounts payable department consisted of only five people. Even though Mazda was smaller than Ford, this didn't explain the tremendous difference in department sizes. Subsequently, Ford decided to completely rethink its accounts payable department.

Under the old system, the 500 workers in accounts payable were constantly shuffling paper—matching vendor invoices to purchase orders and receiving documents, for example. Most of their time was spent trying to reconcile the paperwork when it didn't match up. This was the biggest cause of delayed payments. Under the new system, all of the paperwork has been virtually eliminated, thanks to the computer. When goods are received, a clerk on the dock uses the computer to instantly reconcile each delivery with its purchase order. The clerk now has the authority to accept the goods and to issue an order to the computer to pay the vendor. As a result, the bill is paid when the goods are received, not when the invoice is received. With the significant reduction in paperwork, the accounts payable department has been reduced to 125 people (a 75-percent reduction), who can now accomplish the same work previously done by 500 people, and do it faster.

Citicorp provides another good example of how effective reengineering can be. Over a two-year period, Citicorp slashed its workforce by 15 percent (14,000 employees), and trimmed its operating expenses by 12 percent. The number of data processing centers has been reduced from 240 to 60, with the goal of eventually consolidating them down to 20. Although much of these savings were attributed to traditional expense reduction, a substantial portion was the result of reengineering.[8]

Characteristics of a Reengineered Process

Based on their many years of experience with companies that have successfully reengineered their processes to better meet the needs of the marketplace, Michael Hammer and James Champy have identified several characteristics of reengineered processes, which are described below, that they have observed on a recurring basis.

Several Jobs Are Combined into One Assembly lines are no longer used because of their inherent fragmentation of work. Specialists are replaced with "case workers," who have the responsibility for overseeing the entire process. This is referred to as horizontal work compression. By combining tasks and jobs under one person, errors that occur in transferring information from one individual to another are eliminated. In addition, the cycle time is significantly reduced because only one person has responsibility.

Workers Make Decisions Decision making becomes a part of every person's job, eliminating the need for the traditional and costly hierarchical organizational structure with its many layers of management. This is referred to as vertical work compression. The benefits include faster customer response, lower overhead costs, and increased worker empowerment.

[8]Steven Lipin, "A New Vision," *The Wall Street Journal,* June 25, 1993.

Exhibit 5.13
Comparison between Strategic and Tactical Deployment Techniques for Reengineering

	Tactical	Strategic
Scope	Function	Strategic business unit (SBU)
Focus	Single process	All critical core processes
Targets	Process workflow	Holistic: workflow, systems, structure, incentives, culture
Role	Isolated improvement initiative	Focused vision for all improvement initiatives
Results	Decrease in expense, headcount, space	Increase in profit, return, market share

Source: Gateway Management Consulting.

The Steps in the Process Are Performed in a Natural Order With reengineering, processes no longer have to be forced into a sequential order. Instead, a natural sequence of events is permitted, based on what needs to be done next. This allows many jobs to be performed simultaneously, thereby reducing the throughput time.

Processes Have Multiple Versions Unlike assembly lines, which are totally inflexible and therefore can produce only standardized products, reengineered processes have several versions to meet the unique requirements of different market niches as well as individual customers. An advantage of the multiple-version approach is that these processes tend to be relatively clean and simple in comparison to the traditional assembly processes, which are usually quite complex.

Work Is Performed Where It Makes the Most Sense This involves shifting work across traditional functional boundaries. No longer, for example, are all purchases made by the purchasing department. For small purchases, such as office supplies, it may be more efficient to have each department do its own purchasing.

Issues with Reengineering

In recent years, both manufacturing and service companies have adopted business process reengineering in an attempt to be more responsive to the marketplace as well as to increase the overall efficiency of their operations. However, very few of these reengineering efforts have been successful. One reason for this is the inability of management to link the reengineering effort to the overall corporate strategy. The result is often a piecemeal approach where the reengineering program has to compete for scarce resources along with other management initiatives such as total quality management, self-directed work teams, and outsourcing.

A successful reengineering program must be linked to the corporate strategy of the firm. In other words, reengineering is a strategic issue that must be addressed by the entire organization, at least at the strategic business unit (SBU) level, rather than being viewed as a tactical program. The differences in these two approaches to implementing reengineering are shown in Exhibit 5.13.[9]

As with all major projects that require significant organizational changes, the successful implementation of a reengineering effort is highly dependent upon the commitment and participation of top management.

[9]Raymond L. Manganelli and Steven R. Raspa, "Why Reengineering Has Failed," *Management Review,* July 1995.

Conclusion

Processes exist in every type of business environment, be it manufacturing or service, and the type of processes that are used and how well they perform are directly related to the success of every organization. Managers, therefore, need to understand how these processes work and measure their performance on a continuous basis. An integral part of managing processes is process analysis, which is used to identify weaknesses in the process or areas for improvement.

For every process there are a multitude of performance measures. It is therefore essential for managers to identify those key performance measures that best provide them with the proper information that will allow intelligent and effective decision making.

To be most meaningful, performance measures should be compared with something. Traditionally these comparisons have been made within an organization, looking at trends over a period of time. Other comparisons were made with industry data that were readily available.

More recently, however, companies have begun looking outside their industries in order to find those firms that have the best practices in a particular functional area or in a specific type of process. This policy of seeking out the best of the best is referred to as benchmarking.

Proper performance measurement and benchmarking are critical elements for those firms that want to compete successfully in the global marketplace. In such a fiercely competitive environment, where rules are constantly changing and standards are constantly being raised, only those firms that are cognizant of both their capabilities and those of their competitors will survive.

Managers now recognize that there are many processes that cross functional lines. Process flowcharts and analysis, which were once used solely within the manufacturing function, also can be applied to these business processes.

The lessons learned in manufacturing also can be applied in a service environment. Here, however, the customer's direct interaction with the service process must be taken into consideration. This type of analysis of service operations is often referred to as service blueprinting.

In an effort to improve processes, in terms of both effectiveness and efficiency, business process reengineering often starts from ground zero in redesigning a process. This approach provides an opportunity for new and innovative ideas to be introduced while at the same time taking advantage of the latest state-of-the-art technology that is available.

Key Terms

agile manufacturing p. 155
benchmarking p. 167
bottleneck p. 159
business process p. 165
capacity p. 153
capacity utilization p. 154
fail-safing p. 163
granularity p. 166
hybrid process p. 157
make-to-order system p. 157
make-to-stock system p. 157
modularization p. 157
multistage process p. 157
process flowchart p. 160
process velocity p. 156
productivity p. 152
reengineering p. 171
service blueprint p. 163

Review and Discussion Questions

1. Why are performance measures important?
2. What do we mean when we say productivity is a "relative" measure?
3. What are the typical performance measures for quality, speed of delivery, and flexibility?
4. What should the criteria be for management to adopt a particular performance measure?

5. What is benchmarking? Why is it important for firms that want to compete globally to adopt benchmarking?
6. What are the different types of benchmarking?
7. What is the difference between a make-to-stock and a make-to-order process?
8. How does modularization allow a company to increase efficiency while at the same time provide its customers with a wide variety of products?
9. What is the definition of *bottleneck?* How does a bottleneck impact the output of a process?
10. Identify the major elements in a process flowchart.
11. How does service blueprinting differ from process flow analysis?
12. How does a business process differ from a process?
13. Describe the order fulfillment business process for purchasing a book from Amazon .com, and map the process in a flowchart.
14. What is meant by *business process reengineering?* Why have so many of these types of projects failed in recent years?

Internet Exercise

Go to the Irwin/McGraw-Hill Operations Management homepage at http://www.mhhe.com/pom and take a plant tour. Describe the firm's process in detail and draw a process flowchart for the operation.

Problems

1. Your parents are visiting you, and you decide to take them out to dinner at a fancy restaurant. As you drive up to the restaurant, a parking attendant greets you and takes your car to the parking lot. Upon entering the restaurant, you give your name to the hostess, who tells you there will be a short wait. You go into the lounge where you order drinks. Your name is called shortly thereafter, and you are seated in the main dining room where all of you enjoy your meal.
   a. Draw a service blueprint for your visit to this restaurant. Be sure to include the line of visibility and identify all of the processes associated with your visit.
   b. Identify what you think are the strengths and weaknesses of this process.
2. You have just dropped your car off at the local gas station for an oil change and tune-up. When you pick up your car, you drive up to a gas pump and fill up. You then pay for the gas and the work that you had done. Draw a service blueprint for your visit to this gas station, including the line-of-visibility.
3. As the regional manager of a small chain of pizza stores, you have just received the following data from two of your locations:

	Store A	**Store B**
Sales (week)	$8,500	$12,500
Number of customers (week)	2,150	4,175
Total labor hours worked (week)	440	535
Total square feet of operation	1,275	1,650

   a. Define at least three measures of productivity for these two operations and calculate the productivity for each of these measures for the two stores.

b. Based on these productivity measures, briefly analyze and compare these two operations.

c. What might be some of the reasons for the differences in productivity?

4. The Top Hat Popcorn Company produces high-quality gourmet popcorn that is delivered to independently owned specialty food shops. Currently, the weekly demand is 6,000 cartons of 2-ounce bags and 5,000 cartons of 8-ounce packages. (There are 24 2-ounce packages and 12 8-ounce packages per carton.) The facility where the popcorn is made is operating on a five-day-a-week, eight-hour-a-day schedule. Currently, this facility has the following equipment and respective capacities:

Equipment	Capacity	Batch Time	Number
Corn popper	50 lb/batch	6 min.	3
Packaging (2 oz.)	40 pkgs/min.		2
Packaging (8 oz.)	20 pkgs/min.		1
Carton operation (2 oz.)	1 min./carton		2
Carton operation (8 oz.)	1 min./carton		1

a. Draw a process flowchart for producing and packaging the popcorn.

b. Determine the capacity utilization of each stage in the process when the daily demand is produced, and identify any bottlenecks that exist.

c. If bottleneck(s) do exist, what are your recommendations for meeting the daily demand?

5. Speedy Tax Service offers low-cost tax preparation services in many locations throughout New England. In order to efficiently expedite a client's tax return, Speedy's operations manager has established the following process: Upon entering a tax preparation location, each client is greeted by a receptionist who, through a series of short questions, can determine which type of tax service the client needs. This takes about five minutes. Clients are then referred to either a professional tax specialist, if their tax return is complicated, or a tax preparation associate, if the return is relatively simple. The average time for a tax specialist to complete a return is one hour, while the average time for an associate to complete a return is 30 minutes. Typically during the peak of tax season, an office is staffed with six specialists and three associates, and it is open for 10 hours a day. After the tax returns have been completed, the clients are then directed to see a cashier (there are two at a location) to pay for having their tax return prepared. This takes about six minutes per client to complete. During the peak of tax season, an average of 100 clients per day come into a location, of which 70 percent require the services of a tax specialist.

a. Draw a flowchart for the above process.

b. Identify any bottleneck(s) that exist during tax season.

c. Calculate the average client throughput times (assuming there is no waiting) for a client seeing a specialist and for a client seeing an associate.

6. The Dainty Donuts Store has both a take-out section and an eat-in area. The take-out section consists of four stations, and there are 10 seats in the eating area. The average take-out order takes about three minutes to fill. The average eat-in customer consumes his or her coffee and donut(s) in an average time of 12 minutes, although the server is only required to spend two minutes to complete these orders. The peak hour of the day is from 7:00 A.M.–8:00 A.M., during which approximately 100 customers will typically arrive. Of these, 60 percent are take-out orders.

a. In order to prevent worker burn-out, management believes that worker utilization should not exceed 80 percent. Using this criterion, how many workers should be scheduled during the peak hour of 7:00 A.M.–8:00 A.M.?

b. Determine the capacity utilization for both the take-out counters and the seats during this peak period.

7. The walk-in clinic at a local hospital has received a grant from the federal government to analyze how well it is treating its patients. In order to conduct this analysis, a business student has been hired to identify and define the various steps required to process a patient through the clinic. Her report contains the following information:

Upon entering the clinic, each patient is given a form to complete, which takes about five minutes, and then has to wait an additional three minutes before being seen by a triage nurse, who assesses the severity of the patient's illness. This step in the process takes about two minutes per patient. Based on the nurse's evaluation, the patient is assigned to see either a doctor or a nurse practitioner or is sent immediately to the hospital's emergency room.

Patients assigned to see a doctor wait an average of about 12 minutes before actually seeing the doctor. The average treatment time with a doctor is 15 minutes. Patients directed to nurse practitioners wait an average of 18 minutes. With nurse practitioners, the average treatment time is 17 minutes.

Following treatment by either the doctor or nurse practitioner, each patient then must check out with a cashier to settle how they are going to pay for their visit. The wait to see a cashier is five minutes, and the time spent with the cashier is approximately six minutes.

a. What is the average throughput time in the walk-in clinic for a patient seeing a doctor? For a patient seeing a nurse practitioner? For a patient who is transferred to the emergency room?

b. Determine the process velocity for a patient seeing a doctor and for a patient seeing a nurse practitioner.

Bibliography

Albrecht, Karl, and Ron Zemke. *Service America! Doing Business in the New Economy.* Homewood, IL: Dow Jones-Irwin, 1985.

Anupindi, Ravi; Sunil Chopra; Sudhakar D. Deshmukh; Jan A. Van Mieghem; and Eitan Zemel. *Managing Business Process Flows.* Upper Saddle River, NJ: Prentice Hall, 1999.

Bernstein, A. "Quality Is Becoming Job One in the Office, Too." *Business Week,* April 29, 1991.

Bitran, Gabriel R., and Johannes Hoech. "The Humanization of Service: Respect at the Moment of Truth." *Sloan Management Review,* Winter 1990, pp. 89–96.

Camp, Robert C. *Benchmarking: The Search for Industry Best Practices That Lead to Superior Performance.* Milwaukee, WI: American Society for Quality Control, Quality Press, 1989.

———. *Business Process Benchmarking: Findings and Implementing Best Practices.* Milwaukee, WI: ASQC Quality Press, 1995.

Chase, R. B. "The Customer Contact Approach to Services: Theoretical Bases and Practical Extensions." *Operations Research* 21, no. 4 (1981), pp. 698–705.

Davenport, Thomas H. "Reengineering a Business Process." Harvard Business School Note 9-396-054. Harvard Business School Publishing, November 13, 1995.

Fitzsimmons, James A., and Mona J. Fitzsimmons. *Service Management: Operations, Strategy, and Information Technology.* 3rd ed. New York: McGraw-Hill/Irwin, 2000.

Hall, Gene; Jim Rosenthal; and Judy Wade. "How to Make Reengineering Really Work." *Harvard Business Review,* November–December 1993.

Hammer, Michael. "Reengineering Work: Don't Automate, Obliterate." *Harvard Business Review,* July–August 1990, pp. 104–12.

Hammer, Michael, and James Champy. *Reengineering the Corporation.* New York: HarperCollins Books, 1993.

Harrington, H. James; Erik K. C. Esseling; and Harm Van Nimwegen. *Business Process Improvement Workbook.* New York: McGraw-Hill, 1997.

Levitt, Theodore. "Production-Line Approach to Service." *Harvard Business Review* 50, no. 5 (September–October 1972), pp. 41–52.

Lipin, Steven. "A New Vision." *The Wall Street Journal,* June 25, 1993.

Main, Jeremy. "How to Steal the Best Ideas Around." *Fortune,* October 19, 1992.

Manganelli, Raymond L., and Steven P. Raspa. "Why Reengineering Has Failed." *Management Review,* July 1995, pp. 39–43.

Port, Otis, and Geoffrey Smith. "Beg, Borrow and Benchmark." *Business Week,* November 30, 1992.

Roehm, Harper A.; Donald Klein; and Joseph F. Castellano. "Springing to World-Class Manufacturing." *Management Accounting,* March 1991, pp. 40–44.

Shostack, G. Lynn. "Designing Services That Deliver." *Harvard Business Review* 62, no. 1 (January–February 1984), pp. 133–39.

Stoddard, Donna; B. Sirkka; L. Jarvenpaa; and Michael Littlejohn. "The Reality of Business Reengineering: Pacific Bell's Centrex Provisioning Process." *California Management Review* 38, no. 3 (Spring 1996), pp. 57–76.

Rikert, David C. *Burger King.* Harvard Business School Case No. 681–045. Boston: Harvard Business School, 1980.

———. *McDonald's Corporation.* Harvard Business School Case No. 681–044. Boston: Harvard Business School, 1980.

Womack, James P., and Daniel T. Jones. *Lean Thinking: Banish Waste and Create Wealth in Your Corporation.* New York: Simon and Shuster, 1996, p. 43.

Kristen's Cookie Company (A)

Case

You and your roommate are preparing to start Kristen's Cookie Company in your on-campus apartment. The company will provide fresh cookies to starving students late at night. You need to evaluate the preliminary design for the company's production process to figure out many variables, including what prices to charge, whether you will be able to make a profit, and how many orders to accept.

Business Concept

Your idea is to bake fresh cookies to order, using any combination of ingredients that the buyer wants. The cookies will be ready for pickup at your apartment within an hour.

Several factors will set you apart from competing products such as store-bought cookies. First, your cookies will be completely fresh. You will not bake any cookies before receiving the order; therefore, the buyer will be getting cookies that are literally hot out of the oven.

Second, like Steve's Ice Cream,[10] you will have a variety of ingredients available to add to the basic dough, including chocolate chips, M&M's, chopped Heath bars, coconut, walnuts, and raisins. Buyers will telephone in their orders and specify which of these ingredients they want in their cookies. You guarantee completely fresh cookies. In short, you will have the freshest, most exotic cookies anywhere, available right on campus.

The Production Process

Baking cookies is simple: mix all the ingredients in a food processor; spoon out the cookie dough onto a tray; put the cookies into the oven; bake them; take the tray of cookies out of the oven; let the cookies cool; and, finally, take the cookies off the tray and carefully pack them in a box. You and your roommate already own all the necessary capital equipment: one food processor, cookie trays, and spoons. Your apartment has a small oven that will hold one tray at a time. Your landlord pays for all the electricity. The variable costs, therefore, are merely the cost of the ingredients (estimated to be $.60/dozen), the cost of the box in which the cookies are packed ($.10 per box; each box holds a dozen cookies), and your time (what value do you place on your time?).

A detailed examination of the production process, which specifies how long each of the steps will take, follows. The first step is to take an order, which your roommate has figured out how to do quickly and with 100 percent accuracy. (Actually, you and your roommate devised a method using the campus electronic mail system to accept orders and to inform customers when their orders will be ready for pickup. Because this runs automatically on your personal computer, it does not take any of your time.) Therefore, this step will be ignored in further analysis.

You and your roommate have timed the necessary physical operations. The first physical production step is to wash out the mixing bowl from the previous batch, add all of the ingredients, and mix them in your food processor. The mixing bowls hold ingredients for

[10]Steve's Ice Cream was started in the Boston area by a young entrepreneur to provide make-to-order ice cream, using mix-ins.

Case

up to three dozen cookies. You then dish up the cookies, one dozen at a time, onto a cookie tray. These activities take six minutes for the washing and mixing steps, regardless of how many cookies are being made in the batch. That is, to mix enough dough and ingredients for two dozen cookies takes the same six minutes as one dozen cookies. However, dishing up the cookies onto the tray takes two minutes per tray.

The next step, performed by your roommate, is to put the cookies in the oven and set the thermostat and timer, which takes about one minute. The cookies bake for the next nine minutes. So total baking time is 10 minutes, during the first minute of which your roommate is busy setting the oven. Because the oven only holds one tray, a second dozen takes an additional 10 minutes to bake.

Your roommate also performs the last steps of the process by first removing the cookies from the oven and putting them aside to cool for five minutes, then carefully packing them in a box and accepting payment. Removing the cookies from the oven takes only a negligible amount of time, but it must be done promptly. It takes two minutes to pack each dozen and about one minute to accept payment for the order.

That is the process for producing cookies by the dozen in Kristen's Cookie Company. As experienced bakers know, a few simplifications were made in the actual cookie production process. For example, the first batch of cookies for the night requires preheating the oven. However, such complexities will be put aside for now. Begin your analysis by developing a process flow diagram of the cookie-making process.

Key Questions to Answer before You Launch the Business To launch the business, you need to set prices and rules for accepting orders. Some issues will be resolved only after you get started and try out different ways of producing the cookies. Before you start, however, you at least want a preliminary plan, with as much as possible specified, so that you can do a careful calculation of how much time you will have to devote to this business each night, and how much money you can expect to make. For example, when you conduct a market survey to determine the likely demand, you will want to specify exactly what your order policies will be. Therefore, answering the following operational questions should help you:

1. How long will it take you to fill a rush order?
2. How many orders can you fill in a night, assuming you are open four hours each night?
3. How much of your own and your roommate's valuable time will it take to fill each order?
4. Because your baking trays can hold exactly one dozen cookies, you will produce and sell cookies by the dozen. Should you give any discount for people who order two dozen cookies, three dozen cookies, or more? If so, how much? Will it take you any longer to fill a two-dozen cookie order than a one-dozen cookie order?
5. How many food processors and baking trays will you need?
6. Are there any changes you can make in your production plans that will allow you to make better cookies or more cookies in less time or at lower cost? For example, is there a bottleneck operation in your production process that you can expand cheaply? What is the effect of adding another oven? How much would you be willing to pay to rent an additional oven?

Problems for Further Thought

1. What happens if you are trying to do this by yourself without a roommate?
2. Should you offer special rates for rush orders? Suppose you have just put a tray of cookies into the oven and someone calls up with a "crash priority" order for a dozen cookies of a different flavor. Can you fill the priority order while still fulfilling the order for the cookies that are already in the oven? If not, how much of a premium should you charge for filling the rush order?
3. When should you promise delivery? How can you look quickly at your order board (list of pending orders) and tell a caller when his or her order will be ready? How much of a safety margin for timing should you allow?
4. What other factors should you consider at this stage of planning your business?
5. Your product must be made to order because each order is potentially unique. If you decide to sell standard cookies instead, how should you change the production system? The order-taking process?

S5 Financial Analysis in Operations Management

Supplement Objectives

- Introduce various cost definitions and demonstrate how they are applied in operations management.
- Demonstrate how break-even analysis is used within an operations management context.
- Demonstrate how the concepts of obsolescence, depreciation, and taxes impact the decision-making process within an operations management context.
- Introduce and demonstrate how the time value of money can be used as a financial tool in the decision-making process with respect to various types of operations management issues.
- Demonstrate the use of various financial functions that are available on Excel.

The focus of operations management is to add value during the transformation process. However, this value added, which is ultimately determined by the customer, cannot exceed the actual cost of the transformation. Therefore, an integral part of the operations manager's job requires a thorough understanding of various methods and concepts of financial analysis. With these financial tools, the operations manager can properly assess the consequences of various courses of action relative to the transformation process, specifically with respect to capital investment decisions. The goal of this supplement, therefore, is to provide a basic understanding of these various financial tools and concepts as they pertain to operations management.

Cost Definitions

As a starting point, we begin with some basic definitions of standard financial terms.

Fixed Costs

A **fixed cost** is any expense that remains constant regardless of the level of output. Although no cost is truly fixed, there are many types of expenses that remain virtually fixed over a wide range of outputs. Typical examples of fixed costs include rent, property taxes, most types of depreciation, insurance payments, and salaries of top management, all of which remain the same whether the firm is producing one unit or 10,000 units.

fixed costs

Expenses such as rent that remain constant over a wide range of output volumes.

Variable Costs

Variable costs are expenses that fluctuate directly with changes in the level of output. For example, to clean a hotel room requires a specific amount of material (soap, shampoo, clean towels, etc.) and labor. The incremental cost of this material and labor can be isolated and assigned to each hotel room that is cleaned. Typically, these costs are directly proportional to the output, that is, to clean two hotel rooms costs exactly twice as much as to clean one room.

Exhibit S5.1 illustrates the fixed and variable cost components of total cost. Note that total costs increase at the same rate as variable costs because fixed costs remain constant.

variable costs

Expenses such as material and direct labor that vary proportionately with changes in output volume.

Sunk Costs

Sunk costs are expenses that have previously been incurred or investments that have no salvage value; therefore, they should not be taken into account when considering investment

sunk costs

Expenses already incurred that have no salvage value.

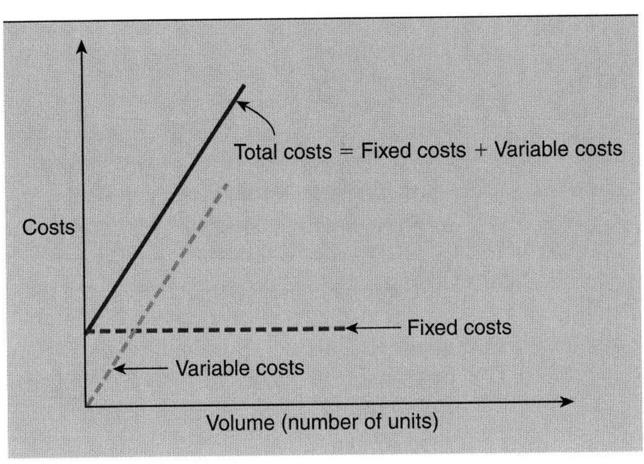

Exhibit S5.1

Fixed and Variable Cost Components of Total Costs

alternatives. Sunk costs also could be current costs that are essentially fixed, such as rent on a building with a long-term lease. For example, suppose an ice cream manufacturing firm occupies a rented building and is considering making sherbet in the same building. If the company decides to enter sherbet production, its cost accountant will assign some of the rental expense to the sherbet operation. However, the building rent remains unchanged and therefore is not a relevant expense to be considered in making the decision. The rent is *sunk;* that is, it continues to exist and does not change in amount regardless of the decision.

Opportunity Costs

opportunity costs

Profits lost when one alternative is chosen over another that would have provided greater financial benefits.

Opportunity costs represent the benefits *forgone,* or the advantage *lost,* as a result of choosing one alternative over another that could have provided a greater financial return. For example, suppose a firm has $100,000 to invest, and two alternatives of comparable risk present themselves, each requiring a $100,000 investment. Investment A will net $25,000; Investment B will net $23,000. Investment A is clearly the better choice, with a $25,000 net return. If the decision is made to invest in B instead of A, the opportunity costs associated with B are $2,000.

Avoidable Costs

avoidable costs

Expenses such as higher labor costs resulting from poor productivity incurred if an investment is not made.

Avoidable costs include any expense that is *not* incurred if an investment is made but that *must* be incurred if the investment is *not* made. Suppose a company owns a metal lathe that is not in working condition, but the firm needs a working lathe. Since the lathe must be repaired or replaced, the repair costs are avoidable if a new lathe is purchased. Avoidable costs reduce the cost of a new investment because they are not incurred if the investment is made. Avoidable costs are an example of how it is possible to "save" money by spending money.

Out-of-Pocket Costs

out-of-pocket costs

Actual cash outflows associated with a particular alternative.

Out-of-pocket costs are actual expenses that are incurred by the firm and are typically related to the selection of a particular alternative. For example, if a company is considering the conversion of an empty warehouse into office space, then the out-of-pocket costs with respect to the cost of this space (that is, the rent if the building was leased or the amortization if the building was purchased) would be zero. There would be, however, out-of-pocket expenses with respect to renovations, equipment purchases, and other items that would have to be bought in order to convert this space into working offices. Thus, out-of-pocket costs represent actual cash that leaves the firm.

Cost of Capital

cost of capital

Usually expressed as an annual percentage rate, it reflects the cost of the money that is invested in a project.

The **cost of capital** is usually expressed as a percentage cost on an annual basis. The determination of the actual percentage to use is dependent on the financial condition of the company. We present here three different scenarios for determining the cost of capital.

If a company has to go out and borrow the money required to pay for the project under consideration, then the cost of capital is the cost of borrowing that money. On the other hand, if a company is cash rich, then the cost of capital is the interest lost on short-term notes such as certificates of deposit where the money could otherwise be invested. Finally, if the firm has a limited amount of cash and has a choice on investing it in one of several projects, then the cost of capital is the opportunity cost of forgoing one of the other projects. Larger corporations usually calculate a weighted average of the three approaches while at the same time taking into consideration the expected return on investment of the owners of the firm.

Activity-Based Costing

In order to determine the total costs involved with making a certain product or delivering a service, some method of allocating overhead costs must be applied. The traditional approach has been to allocate overhead costs to products on the basis of direct labor dollars or hours. The overhead rate can be established by dividing the total estimated overhead costs by total budgeted direct labor hours. The problem with this approach is that direct labor as a percentage of total costs has fallen dramatically over the past decade, especially in manufacturing companies. For example, the introduction of advanced manufacturing technology and other productivity improvements has driven direct labor to less than 10 percent of total manufacturing costs in many industries. As a result, overhead rates of 600 percent or even 1,000 percent are found in some highly automated plants.[1]

This traditional accounting practice of allocating overhead to direct labor can lead to questionable investment decisions; for example, automated processes may be chosen over labor-intensive processes based on a comparison of projected costs. Unfortunately, overhead does not disappear when the equipment is installed and overall costs may actually be lower with the labor-intensive process. It also can lead to wasted effort since an inordinate amount of time is spent tracking direct labor hours. For example, one plant spent 65 percent of its computer costs tracking information about direct labor transactions even though direct labor accounted for only 4 percent of total production costs.[2]

activity-based costing

Accounting technique that allocates overhead costs in actual proportion to the overhead consumed by the production activity.

Activity-based costing techniques have been developed to alleviate these problems by refining the overhead allocation process to more directly reflect actual proportions of overhead consumed by the production activity. Causal factors, known as cost drivers, are identified and used as the means for allocating overhead. These factors might include machine hours, beds occupied, computer time, flight hours, or miles driven. The accuracy of overhead allocation, of course, depends on the selection of the appropriate cost drivers.

Activity-based costing involves a two-stage allocation process with the first stage assigning overhead costs to cost activity pools. These pools represent activities such as performing machine setups, issuing purchase orders, and inspecting parts. In the second stage, costs are assigned from these pools to activities based on the number or amount of pool-related activity required in their completion. Exhibit S5.2 shows a comparison of traditional cost accounting and activity-based costing.

Consider the example of activity-based costing in Exhibit S5.3. Two products, A and B, are produced using the same number of labor hours. Applying traditional cost accounting methods, identical overhead costs (usually expressed as a percentage of direct labor costs) would be charged to each product. For example, in Exhibit S5.3, the $875,000 would be divided by the total labor costs required to make products A and B in order to obtain an overhead rate. By applying activity-based costing, traceable costs are assigned to specific activities. Because each product requires a different amount of transactions, different overhead amounts, expressed here as $s per transaction, are allocated to these products from the pools.

As stated earlier, activity-based costing overcomes the problem of cost distortion by creating a cost pool for each activity or transaction that can be identified as a cost driver, and by assigning overhead costs to products or jobs on the basis of the number of separate activities required for their completion. Thus, in the previous situation, the low-volume

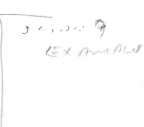

[1]Matthew J. Libertore, *Selection and Evaluation of Advanced Manufacturing Technologies* (New York: Springer-Verlag, 1990), pp. 231–56.

[2]Thomas Johnson and Robert Kaplan, *Relevance Lost: The Rise and Fall of Management Accounting* (Boston: Harvard Business School Press, 1987), p. 188.

Exhibit S5.2

Traditional and Activity-Based Costing

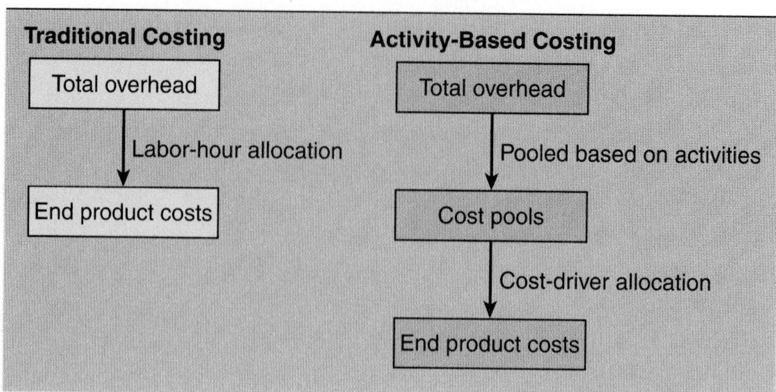

Exhibit S5.3

Overhead Allocations by an Activity Approach

Basic Data

Activity	Traceable Costs	Events or Transactions Total	Product A	Product B
Machine setups	$230,000	5,000	3,000	2,000
Quality inspections	160,000	8,000	5,000	3,000
Production orders	81,000	600	200	400
Machine-hours worked	314,000	40,000	12,000	28,000
Material receipts	90,000	750	150	600
	$875,000			

Overhead Rates by Activity

	(*a*) Traceable Costs	(*b*) Total Events or Transactions	(*a*) ÷ (*b*) Rate per Event or Transaction
Machine setups	$230,000	5,000	$46/setup
Quality inspections	160,000	8,000	$20/inspection
Production orders	81,000	600	$135/order
Machine-hours worked	314,000	40,000	$7.85/hour
Material receipts	90,000	750	$120/receipt

Overhead Cost per Unit of Product

	Product A		Product B	
	Events or Transactions	Amount	Events or Transactions	Amount
Machine setups, at $46/setup	3,000	$138,000	2,000	$ 92,000
Quality inspections, at $20/inspection	5,000	100,000	3,000	60,000
Production orders, at $135/order	200	27,000	400	54,000
Machine-hours worked, at $7.85/hour	12,000	94,200	28,000	219,800
Material receipts, at $120/receipt	150	18,000	600	72,000
Total overhead cost assigned (*a*)		$377,200		$497,800
Number of units produced (*b*)		5,000		20,000
Overhead cost per unit, (*a*) ÷ (*b*)		$75.44		$24.89

Source: Ray Garrison, *Managerial Accounting,* 6th ed. (Homewood, IL: Richard D. Irwin, 1991), p. 94.

product would be assigned the bulk of the costs for machine setup, purchase orders, and quality inspections, thereby showing it to have high unit costs compared to the other product.

Finally, activity-based costing is sometimes referred to as *transactions costing.* This transactions focus gives rise to another major advantage over other costing methods; that is, it improves the traceability of overhead costs and thus results in more accurate *unit* cost data for management.

Break-Even Analysis

Break-even analysis, as we define it here, can be viewed from two perspectives. From the overall view of the company, break-even analysis usually refers to determining how much volume of business the company must do in order to break-even, that is, to have neither profits nor losses. The *break-even point,* in this case is where total revenues equal total costs. Break-even analysis from a purely operational perspective usually focuses on the choice of processes. Here, break-even implies that the two processes have equal costs for a specific level of volume, which is again referred to as the break-even point. We will address both of these types of break-even analysis. In each case we apply a simple linear model that uses only fixed costs and variable costs.

break-even analysis

Determination of product volume where revenues equal total costs or costs associated with two alternative processes are the same.

Revenues versus Costs

As stated above, the objective here is to determine how much volume of business a company has to do to break even. The volume can be stated in either monetary units or product units, although the latter is usually easier to conceptualize from an operational perspective.

The underlying assumptions in this linear model are:

- *The selling price per unit is constant.* In other words, there is one selling price for a unit, with no allowances for quantity discounts or special terms for major customers.
- *Variable costs per unit remain constant.* Here, the cost to produce each unit remains the same over the range of volume with which we are concerned. (Consequently, there are no allowances for economies of scale.) Since variable costs refer to the material and direct labor that go into making each unit, additional unit costs such as overtime, second shift premiums, or subcontracting, therefore, are excluded from consideration.
- *Fixed costs remain constant.* Over the range of volume with which we are concerned, the fixed costs of the operation do not change regardless of the volume produced. As defined earlier, these fixed costs usually include rent, insurance, and taxes on the facility; senior management salaries; and other overhead expenses.

Example

The West Pacific Toy Company, a small manufacturing firm located in Manila, Philippines, produces cloth dolls for export to the United States. The company sells these dolls to major retail chains for US$3.00 each, which does not include shipping costs of US$0.50 per doll. (These dolls are then marked up to a retail selling price in the United States of US$14.95 per doll.) The workers in the factory are paid, on the average, the equivalent of US$8.00 per day, and it is estimated that the average daily output per worker is 50 dolls. The cost of the material is estimated at US$1.25 per doll. Fixed costs for this operation are estimated to be US$160,000 per year.

a. What is the break-even point for this company, in terms of the number of dolls per year?

b. If the company sold 135,000 dolls last year, how much profit (loss) did it have for the year?

Solution

a. As seen in Exhibit S5.4, the break-even point is that point on the graph where the total sales line intersects with the total cost line. This point can be calculated as follows:

$$\text{Selling price} = SP = \text{US\$3.00 per doll}$$

$$\text{Variable cost} = VC = \text{Material cost} + \text{Labor cost}$$

$$= 1.25 + 8.00/50$$

$$= \text{US\$1.41 per doll}$$

$$\text{Fixed costs} = FC = \text{US\$160,000 per year}$$

$$X = \text{Number of dolls sold per year}$$

As seen in Exhibit S5.4, total annual sales

$$= TS = (SP)(X)$$

Total annual costs equals fixed costs plus variable costs

$$= TC = FC + (VC)(X)$$

The point at which the total sales line and the total costs line intersect is the break-even point, which is where they are equal to each other.

Thus

$$TS = TC$$

$$(SP)(X) = FC + (VC)(X)$$

Solving for X we have

$$X = \frac{FC}{(SP - VC)}$$

(continued)

Exhibit S5.4

Break-Even Analysis for Revenues versus Costs

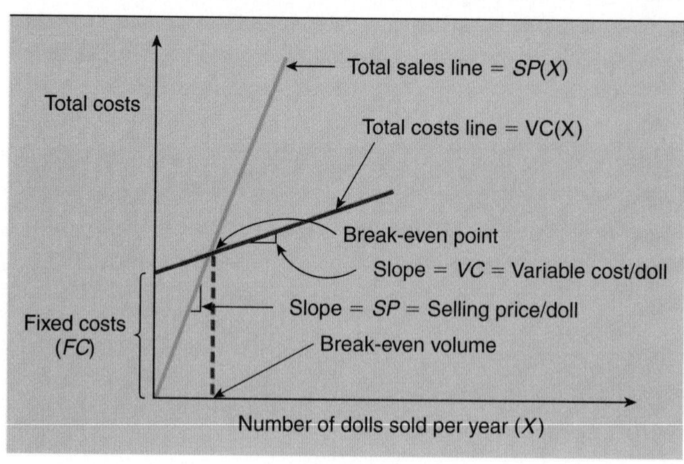

(concluded)

Substituting the values for *SP*, *VC*, and *FC* we have

$$X = \frac{160{,}000}{(3.00 - 1.41)}$$

$$X = 100{,}629 \text{ dolls per year}$$

b. Profits = *P* = Total sales − Total costs

$$P = TS - TC$$

$$P = (SP)(X) - [FC + (VC)(X)]$$

$$P = (3.00)(135{,}000) - [160{,}000 + (1.41)(135{,}000)]$$

$$P = 405{,}000 - [160{,}000 + 190{,}350]$$

$$P = 405{,}000 - 350{,}350$$

Profits for the year = US$54,650

Choice of Processes

Break-even analysis also can be used to choose from among alternative processes a company can use. Again, we assume that both the variable costs per unit and the fixed costs over the range of volumes being evaluated remain constant. Sales are not considered in this analysis, in terms of identifying the break-even points. (Although the forecasted level of sales is definitely a factor in selecting the process to be used.) Here, we define the break-even point as that volume where we are indifferent with respect to the costs of the two alternative processes.

Example

Allison and Jon, to earn extra money while they are in high school, have a small catering business. They provide a variety of freshly made sandwiches in the evenings to college students. Currently, they prepare the sandwiches at their home, which is about 15 miles away. The average cost per sandwich, including the transportation, material, and direct labor, is approximately $2.55. The school has recently offered to lease them a small kitchen on campus. The rent for this kitchen is $360.00 per month for each of the nine months that the school is open full time. (The building in which the kitchen is located is closed for the other three months, so the kitchen is also closed.) Allison and Jon estimate that they will be able to produce the sandwiches at this new location at an average cost of $1.80 per sandwich. (The savings are attributed to working more efficiently in a professional kitchen.)

a. How many sandwiches a month do Allison and Jon have to sell in order to be indifferent to the costs of working at home versus working in the kitchen on campus?

b. The parents of Allison and Jon have decided that they are going to charge them $120.00 per month because of the additional out-of-pocket costs involved with preparing the sandwiches at home (electricity, cleaning supplies, etc.). What is the new break-even point under these circumstances between working at home and working on campus?

Solution

a. Alternative 1: Working at Home

$$\text{Total costs} = TC_1 = VC_1X$$

where

VC_1 = Variable costs per sandwich of \$2.55

X = Number of sandwiches sold

or

$$TC_1 = 2.55X$$

Alternative 2: Working on Campus

$$\text{Total costs} = TC_2 = FC_2 + VC_2X$$

where

FC_2 = Fixed costs of \$360.00 per month

VC_2 = Variable cost per sandwich of \$1.80

As seen in Exhibit S5.5A, the break-even point between these two alternatives is where the two total costs lines intersect.

The break-even point is calculated as follows:

$$TC_1 = TC_2$$

Substituting for TC_1 and TC_2 from above, we have

$$VC_1X = FC_2 + VC_2X$$

$$2.55X = 360 + 1.80X$$

$$0.75X = 360$$

$$X = 480 \text{ Sandwiches a month}$$

Note that when we analyze process alternatives, we do not need to know the selling price per unit. The decision here is based upon the forecasted volume to be sold, with the goal being to select that process that has the lowest total costs at the forecasted volume.

(continued)

Exhibit S5.5A

Break-Even Analysis for Alternative Types of Processes

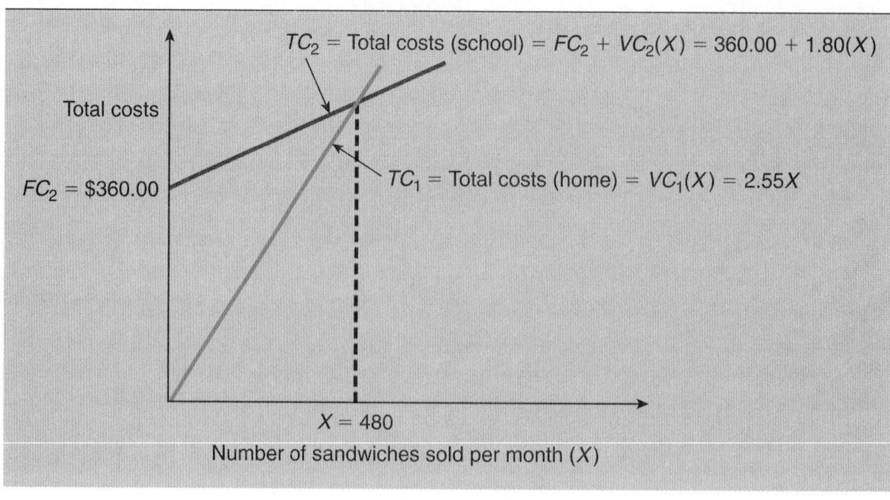

(concluded)

In this example, if the forecast per month is greater than 480 sandwiches, then they should rent the kitchen on campus; otherwise they should continue working at home.

b. Alternative 1: Working at Home

$$\text{Total costs} = TC_1 = FC_1 + VC_1X$$

where

FC_1 = Fixed costs of \$120.00 per month

VC_1 = Variable cost per sandwich of \$2.55

X = Number of sandwiches sold

or

$$TC_1 = 120 + 2.55X$$

Alternative 2: Working on Campus

$$\text{Total costs} = TC_2 = FC_2 + VC_2X$$

where

FC_2 = Fixed costs of \$360.00 per month

VC_2 = Variable cost per sandwich of \$1.80

As seen in Exhibit S5.5B, the new break-even point between these two alternatives is again where the two total costs lines intersect. Under these conditions, the break-even point is calculated as follows:

$$TC_1 = TC_2$$
$$FC_1 + VC_1X = FC_2 + VC_2X$$
$$120 + 2.55X = 360 + 1.80X$$
$$.75X = 240$$
$$X = 320 \text{ Sandwiches a month}$$

Here, if the forecast is more than 320 sandwiches a month, they should use the kitchen at school; if it is less, they should continue working at home.

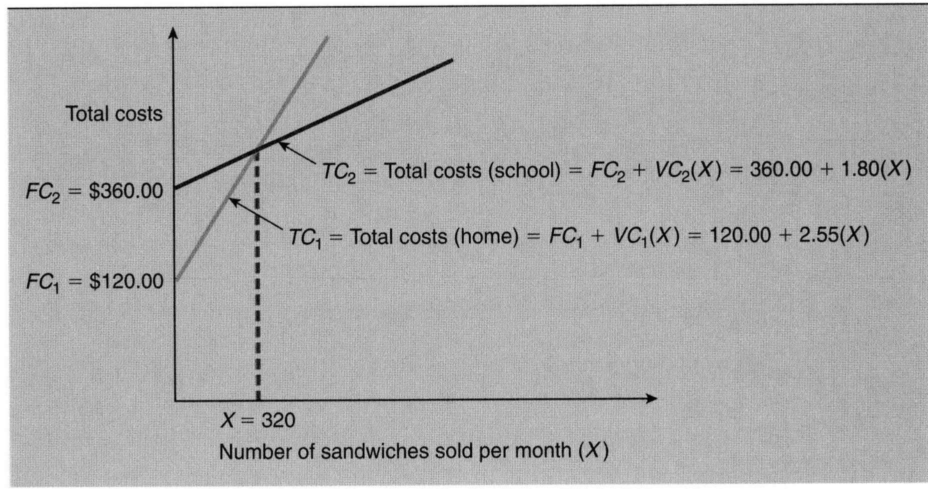

Exhibit S5.5B

Break-Even Analysis for Alternative Types of Processes

Obsolescence, Depreciation, and Taxes

Economic Life and Obsolescence

obsolete

Status of an asset when it has worn out or been surpassed by a superior performing asset.

economic life

Useful life of an asset over which it provides the best method of operation to an organization.

When a firm invests in an income-producing asset, the economic life of the asset is estimated. For accounting purposes, the asset is depreciated over this period. It is assumed that the asset will perform its function during this time and then be considered **obsolete** or worn out, and replacement will be required. However, this view of asset life rarely coincides with reality.

To illustrate this, assume that a machine with an expected productive life of 10 years is purchased. If at any time during the ensuing 10 years a new machine is developed that can perform the same task more efficiently or economically, the old machine is considered to be obsolete. Whether it is "worn out" or not is irrelevant.

The **economic life** of a piece of equipment is the period over which it provides the best method for performing its task. When a new, superior method is developed, the actual value of the existing equipment is usually significantly less than the stated *book value* of a machine (that is, the "official" remaining value).

Types of Depreciation

depreciation

Method for allocating capital equipment costs over more than one time period.

Depreciation is a method for allocating the costs of capital equipment over more than one time period (for discussion here, we will use years). The value of any capital asset—buildings, machinery, and so forth—decreases as its useful life is expended. *Amortization* and *depreciation* are often used interchangeably. Through convention, however, *depreciation* refers to the allocation of costs due to the physical or functional deterioration of *tangible* (physical) assets, such as buildings or equipment, while *amortization* refers to the allocation of costs over the useful life of *intangible* assets, such as patents, leases, franchises, or goodwill.

Depreciation procedures may not reflect an asset's true value at any point in its life because obsolescence at any time may result in a large difference between the true value and the book value of the asset. Also, since depreciation rates significantly affect taxes, a firm may choose a particular depreciation method from the several alternatives that are available, giving more consideration to its effect on taxes than its ability to make the book value of an asset reflect the true resale value.

We describe five commonly used methods of depreciation:

1. *Straight-line method.* With this method, an asset's value is reduced in uniform annual amounts over its estimated useful life. The general straight-line depreciation formula is

$$\text{Annual amount to be depreciated} = \frac{\text{Cost} - \text{Salvage value}}{\text{Estimated useful life}}$$

For example, a machine costing \$10,000, with an estimated salvage value of \$0 and an estimated life of 10 years, would be depreciated at the rate of \$1,000 per year for each of the 10 years. If its estimated salvage value at the end of the 10 years is \$1,000, the annual depreciation then becomes:

$$\frac{\$10{,}000 - \$1{,}000}{10} = \$900 \text{ per year}$$

2. *Sum-of-the-years'-digits (SYD) method.* The purpose of the SYD method is to reduce the book value of an asset rapidly in the early years of its life and at a lower

rate in its later years. This is done both for tax purposes and to more accurately reflect the true value of an asset.

To illustrate this, suppose that the estimated useful life of a piece of equipment is five years. Here, the sum of the years' digits is $1 + 2 + 3 + 4 + 5 = 15$. Therefore, the asset is depreciated by $5 \div 15$ (or 33 percent) after the first year, $4 \div 15$ (or 26.7 percent) after the second year, and so on, down to $1 \div 15$ (or 6.7 percent) in the last year. (We are assuming here that the salvage value at the end of the fifth year is zero.)

3. *Declining-balance method.* This method also provides for an accelerated depreciation. The asset's value is decreased each year by reducing its book value by a constant percentage each year. The percentage rate selected is often the one that just reduces book value to salvage value at the end of the asset's estimated life. In any case, the asset should never be reduced below its estimated salvage value. Use of the declining-balance method and allowable rates are controlled in the U.S. by Internal Revenue Service regulations. As a simplified illustration, the example in the next table uses an arbitrarily selected rate of 40 percent. (Salvage value after five years is estimated at $2,000.) Depreciation with this method is based on full cost, *not* cost minus salvage value.

Year	Depreciation Rate	Beginning Book Value	Depreciation Charge	Accumulated Depreciation	Ending Book Value
1	0.40	$17,000	$6,800	$ 6,800	$10,200
2	0.40	10,200	4,080	10,880	6,120
3	0.40	6,120	2,448	13,328	3,672
4	0.40	3,672	1,469	14,797	2,203
5		2,203	203	15,000	2,000

Note that in the fifth year, reducing book value by 40 percent would have caused it to drop below salvage value. Consequently, the asset was depreciated by only $203, which decreased book value to salvage value.

4. *Double-declining-balance method.* Again, for tax advantages, the double-declining-balance method offers higher depreciation early in the economic life of the asset. The double-declining-balance method uses a percentage that is equal to twice the straight line rate over the life of the item but applies this rate to the undepreciated original cost. The method is the same as the declining-balance method, but the term *double-declining balance* means double the straight-line rate. Thus, equipment with a 10-year lifespan would have a straight-line depreciation rate of 10 percent per year and a double-declining-balance rate (applied to the undepreciated amount) of 20 percent per year. (At some point, usually near the end of the equipment's life span, one switches to straight-line depreciation.)
5. *Depreciation-by-use method.* The purpose of this method is to depreciate a capital investment in proportion to its use. It is applicable, for example, to a machine that performs the same operation many times. The life of the machine is not estimated in years but rather it is estimated in the total number of operations it may reasonably be expected to perform before wearing out. Suppose that a metal-stamping press has an estimated life of 1 million stampings and costs $100,000. The charge for depreciation per stamping is then $\$100{,}000 \div 1{,}000{,}000$, or $0.10.

Assuming a $0 salvage value, the depreciation charges are as shown:

Year	Total Yearly Stampings	Cost per Stamping	Yearly Depreciation Charge	Accumulated Depreciation	Ending Book Value
1	150,000	0.10	$15,000	$15,000	$85,000
2	300,000	0.10	30,000	45,000	55,000
3	200,000	0.10	20,000	65,000	35,000
4	200,000	0.10	20,000	85,000	15,000
5	100,000	0.10	10,000	95,000	5,000
6	50,000	0.10	5,000	100,000	0

The depreciation-by-use method is an attempt to allocate depreciation charges in proportion to actual use and thereby coordinate expense charges with productive output more accurately. Also, since a machine's resale value is related to its remaining productive life, it is expected that with this method the book value will more closely approximate the resale value.

The Effects of Taxes

Tax rates and the methods of applying them occasionally change. When analysts evaluate investment proposals, tax considerations often prove to be the deciding factor since depreciation expenses directly affect taxable income and, therefore, profit. The ability to write off depreciation in early years provides an added source of funds for investment.

Types of Economic Decisions

The capital investment decision has become highly rationalized, as evidenced by the variety of techniques that are now available. In contrast to pricing or marketing decisions, the capital investment decision usually can be made with a higher degree of confidence because the variables affecting the decision are relatively well known and can be quantified with a relatively high degree of accuracy.

Investment decisions may be grouped into six general categories:

1. *Purchase of new equipment of facilities.* When a company experiences continued growth, capital investment decisions need to be made with respect to the purchase of new equipment and/or the addition of facilities. These decisions related directly to the operations strategy of the firm, in terms of how much capacity should be added, when it should be added, where it should be added, and what type of process(es) should be installed. The primary basis for decision making here is to determine if the additional profits that will be generated as a result of this new equipment and facilities justifies the cost of this added capacity.
2. *Replacement of existing equipment or facilities.* Often, the operations manager must decide as to the best time to replace or update existing equipment and/or facilities. This replacement can occur because of new process technologies and/or equipment obsolescence that results in increased maintenance costs and machine downtime. Here the decision typically focuses on the incremental increase in productivity that can be realized by the installation of new equipment and/or facilities in comparison to the cost of the new equipment and/or facilities.

3. *Make-or-buy decisions.* While cost is a major factor in the decision to make a part or component internally or to purchase it from a supplier, other factors also need to be considered, including (*a*) the competitive priorities or core competencies of the firm, (*b*) the need to maintain control, and (*c*) the need for flexibility to react quickly to changes in the marketplace. For these reasons, many companies continue the trend to purchase larger percentages of their products' components and subassemblies from suppliers instead of making them in-house.
4. *Lease-or-buy decisions.* In many industries, the technology is changing so rapidly that firms need to replace equipment on a more frequent basis. For example, Solectron, a major contract manufacturer of electronic components and products, replaces its process equipment approximately every 18 months. In such an environment, it is often more beneficial to lease the equipment rather than to purchase it outright. The benefits of leasing include no need for an initial outlay of capital and the salvage value of the equipment being known at the time of purchase (usually expressed in terms of the lease). This improves cash flow and eliminates uncertainty. The financial decision here focuses on the cost of the monthly fee for leasing the equipment as compared to the initial capital outlay if the equipment were to be purchased.
5. *Temporary shutdown or plant-closing decisions.* With cyclical and/or seasonal products in particular, the operations manager is often confronted with the decision as to whether or not to temporarily shut down part or all of a facility. Here the decision needs to address the incremental costs associated with the shutdown (and start-up, if it is temporary) in comparison to the costs of carrying excess inventories of finished goods.
6. *Addition or elimination of a product or product line.* While a firm may have some products or product lines that lose money when total costs are considered, some of these products nevertheless still contribute a significant portion to overhead expenses. Therefore the elimination of these products and/or product lines increases the overhead rate for the remaining products, resulting in some of them becoming nonprofitable. Consequently, it is necessary to look at the incremental contribution of these products to the overhead expenses before deciding to eliminate them.

Investment decisions are usually made with regard to the *lowest acceptable rate of return* on investment. This is often referred to as the "threshold" rate of return. As a starting point, the threshold rate of return may be considered to be the cost of investment capital needed to underwrite the expenditure. Certainly an investment will not be made if it does not return at least the cost of capital.

Investments are generally ranked according to the return they yield in excess of their cost of capital. In this way, a business with only limited investment funds can select investment alternatives that yield the highest *net returns.* (*Net return* is the earnings an investment yields after gross earnings have been reduced by the cost of the funds used to finance the investment.) In general, investments should not be made unless the return in funds exceeds the *marginal* cost of investment capital (*marginal cost* is the incremental cost of each new acquisition of funds from outside sources).

Financial Definitions

There are two basic methods to account for the effects of interest accumulation. One is to compute the total amount accumulated over the time period into the future as the *compound value.* The other is to remove the interest rate effect over time by reducing all future sums to present-day dollars, or the *present value.*

Compound Value of a Single Amount

Albert Einstein was once quoted as saying that compound interest is the eighth wonder of the world. After reviewing this section, with its dramatic growth effects during a longer term of years, you might wish to propose a new government regulation: on the birth of a child, the parents must put, say, \$1,000 into a retirement fund for that child at age 65. This might be one way to reduce the pressure on Social Security and other state and federal pension plans. While inflation will decrease the value significantly, there is still a lot left over. At 14 percent interest, our \$1,000 increased to \$500,000 after subtracting the \$4.5 million for inflation (assuming that inflation erodes 90 percent of the gain!). That's still 500 times larger than the original \$1,000.

Most calculators make such computation easy. However, many people still refer to tables for compound values. Using Appendix A, Table 1 (compound sum of \$1), for example, we see that the value of \$1 at 10 percent interest after three years is \$1.331. (Note: Tables 1 through 4 are in Appendix A.)

Compound Value of an Annuity

An *annuity* is the receipt of a constant sum each year for a specified number of years. Usually an annuity is received at the end of a period and does not earn interest during that period. Therefore, an annuity of \$10 a year for three years would bring in \$10 at the end of the first year, \$10 at the end of the second year, and \$10 at the end of the third year. If the annuity receipts were placed in a bank savings account at 5 percent interest, the total or compound value of the \$10 at 5 percent for the three years would be:

Year	Receipt at End of Year	Compound Interest Factor $(1 + i)^n$	Value at End of Third Year
1	\$10.00 ×	$(1 + 0.05)^2 =$	\$11.02
2	10.00 ×	$(1 + 0.05)^1 =$	10.50
3	10.00 ×	$(1 + 0.05)^0 =$	10.00
			\$31.52

The general formula for finding the compound value of any annuity is

$$S_n = R[(1+i)^{n-1} + (1+i)^{n-2} + \cdots + (1+i)^1 + 1] \tag{S5.1}$$

where

S_n = Compound value of an annuity
R = Periodic receipts in dollars
n = Length of the annuity in years

Applying this formula to the above example, we get

$$\begin{aligned} S_n &= R[(1+i)^2 + (1+i) + 1] \\ &= \$10[(1+0.05)^2 + (1+0.05) + 1] \\ &= \$31.52 \end{aligned}$$

Appendix A, Table 2 lists the compound value factor of \$1 for 5 percent after three years as 3.152. Multiplying this factor by \$10 yields \$31.52.

As an alternative, we can use Excel, or other spreadsheet equivalent, to arrive at the same result. For example, to find the compound or future value of an annuity, we use the following Excel function:

= FV (%, nper, pmt)

where

FV = Future value function

% = Interest rate per period

nper = Number of periods

pmt = Amount of each payment per period

Using the data from the above example, we have

= FV (.05, 3, −10) = $31.52

Consider the beneficial effects of investing $2,000 each year, starting at the age of 21. Assume investments in AAA-rated bonds are available today yielding 9 percent. From Table 2 in Appendix A, after 30 years (age 51), the investment is worth 136.3 times $2,000, or $272,600. Fourteen years later (age 65), this would be worth $962,993 (using a hand calculator, since the table only goes up to 30 years, and assuming the $2,000 is deposited at the end of each year)! But what 21-year-old thinks about retirement?

Present Value of a Future Single Payment

Compound values are used to determine the future value of a stream of cash flows after a specified period has elapsed; present-value (PV) procedures accomplish just the reverse. They are used to determine the current value of a sum or stream of receipts expected to be received in the future. Most investment decision techniques use present-value concepts rather than compound values. Since decisions affecting the future are made in the present, it makes more sense to convert future returns into their present value at the time the decision is being made. In this way, investment alternatives are viewed from a better perspective in terms of current dollars.

Example

If a rich uncle offers to make you a gift of $100 today or $250 after 10 years, which should you choose? You must determine whether $250 in 10 years will be worth more than the $100 now. Suppose that you base your decision on the rate of inflation in the economy and believe that inflation will be 10 percent per year. By deflating the $250, you can compare its relative purchasing power with $100 received today. Procedurally, this is accomplished by solving the compound formula for the present sum, P, where V is the future amount of $250 in 10 years at 10 percent.

Solution

The general formula for compound value is

$$V_n = P(1+i)^n \tag{S5.2}$$

where

V_n = Value of principal at the end of year n

n = Length of the compounding period in years

P = Present value of principal
i = Interest rate

Dividing both sides by $(1 + i)^n$ gives

$$P = \frac{V_n}{(1+i)^n}$$

$$= \frac{250}{(1+0.10)^{10}}$$

$$= \$96.39$$

This shows that, at a 10 percent inflation rate, \$250 in 10 years will be worth \$93.39 today. The rational choice is to take the \$100 now based on a belief that inflation will remain constant at 10 percent per year for the next 10 years.

The use of tables is also standard practice in solving present-value problems. With reference to Appendix A, Table 3, the present-value factor for \$1 received 10 years hence is 0.386. Multiplying this factor by \$250 yields \$96.50.

Present Value of an Annuity

The present value of an annuity is the value of an annual amount to be received over a future period expressed in terms of the present. To find the value of an annuity of \$100 for three years at 10 percent, find the factor in the present-value table that applies to 10 percent in *each* of the three years in which the amount is received and multiply each receipt by this factor. Then sum the resulting figures. Remember that annuities are usually received at the end of each period.

Year	Amount Received at End of Year		Present-Value Factor at 10%		Present Value
1	\$100	×	0.909	=	\$ 90.90
2	100	×	0.826	=	82.60
3	100	×	0.751	=	75.10
Total receipt	\$300		Total present value	=	\$248.60

The general formula used to derive the present value of an annuity is

$$A_n = R\left[\frac{1}{(1+i)} + \frac{1}{(1+i)^2} + \cdots + \frac{1}{(1+i)^n}\right] \tag{S5.3}$$

where

A_n = Present value of annuity of n years
R = Periodic receipts
n = Length of the annuity in years

Applying the formula to the above example gives

$$A_n = \$100\left[\frac{1}{(1+0.10)} + \frac{1}{(1+0.10)^2} + \frac{1}{(1+0.10)^3}\right]$$

$$= \$100(2.488)$$

$$= \$248.80$$

Appendix A, Table 4 contains present values of an annuity for varying maturities. The present-value factor for an annuity of $1 for three years at 10 percent (from Appendix A, Table 4) is 2.487. Since our sum is $100 rather than $1, we multiply this factor by $100 to arrive at $248.70. The slight variance from the previous answers results from rounded figures in the table.

Again, we can use a similar Excel spreadsheet function to obtain the same results:

= PV (%, nper, pmt)

where

PV = Present value function
% = Interest rate
nper = Number of payments
pmt = Amount of each payment

Using the data from the above example, we have

= PV (0.1, 3, −100) = $248.69

Note that the difference in answers ($248.80 versus $248.69) is the result of the table values being rounded off.

When the stream of future receipts varies for each period, the present value of each annual receipt must be calculated individually. The present values for each of the years are then summed up to determine the total present value. This is a very tedious process if done manually. Fortunately, we can again use Excel, applying its net present value (NPV) function, which is explained in the next section.

Discounted Cash Flow

The term *discounted cash flow,* or DCF, refers to the total stream of payments that an asset will generate in the future discounted to the present time. This is simply present value analysis that includes all flows: single payments, annuities, and all others.

Methods for Evaluating Investment Alternatives

Net Present Value

The **net present value** method is commonly used in business. With this method, decisions are based on the amount by which the present value of a projected income stream exceeds the cost of an investment.

net present value

Present cash value of a stream of future cash flows.

Example

A firm is considering two alternative investments: the first, Alternative A, costs $30,000 and the second, Alternative B, costs $50,000. The expected yearly cash income streams for each of the two alternatives are shown in the following table.

	Cash Inflow	
Year	Alternative A	Alternative B
1	$10,000	$15,000
2	10,000	15,000
3	10,000	15,000
4	10,000	15,000
5	10,000	15,000

To decide which of the two alternatives is better, we need to determine which has the higher net present value. (For this calculation, we need the cost of capital; let's assume it is 8 percent.)

Solution

Alternative A

3.993 (PV factor) × $10,000 = $39,930
Less cost of investment = 30,000
Net present value = $ 9,930

Alternative B

3.993 (PV factor) × $15,000 = $59,895
Less cost of investment = 50,000
Net present value = $ 9,895

Based purely on economic criteria, management would prefer Alternative A because its net present value exceeds that of Alternative B by $35 ($9,930 − $9,895 = $35).

Here we apply Excel's net present value (NPV) function:

= NPV (%, value1, value2, . . .) − Initial investment

where

NPV = Net present value function
% = Interest rate
value1 = Annual cash flow at the end of year 1, etc.

Using the data from the above example, we have for Alternative A

= NPV (0.08, 10000, 10000, 10000, 10000, 10000) − 30000 = $9,927.10

For Alternative B we have

= NPV (0.08, 15000, 15000, 15000, 15000, 15000) − 50000 = $9,890.65

The differences in the Excel answers from those obtained using the table values are again due to rounding.

Payback Period

payback period

Time necessary for the firm to recover its initial investment.

The **payback period** method ranks investments according to the time required for each investment to return earnings equal to the cost of the investment. The rationale is that the sooner the investment capital can be recovered, the sooner it can be reinvested in new revenue-producing projects. Thus, supposedly, a firm will be able to get the most benefit from its available investment funds.

Consider two alternatives, each requiring a \$1,000 investment. The first will earn \$200 per year for six years; the second will earn \$300 per year for the first three years and \$100 per year for the next three years.

If the first alternative is selected, the initial investment of \$1,000 will be recovered at the end of the fifth year. The income produced by the second alternative will total \$1,000 after only four years. The second alternative will permit reinvestment of the full \$1,000 in new revenue-producing projects one year sooner than the first.

Although the payback period method is declining in popularity as the sole measure for evaluating investments, it is still frequently used in conjunction with other methods to give an indication of the time commitment of funds. The major problems with the payback period method are that it does not consider income beyond the payback period and it ignores the time value of money. Any method that ignores the time value of money must be considered questionable.

Internal Rate of Return

internal rate of return

Interest rate that equates present value of future cash flows with cost of an investment.

The **internal rate of return** (IRR) can be defined as the interest rate that equates the present value of an income stream with the cost of an investment. There is no procedure or formula that may be used directly to compute the internal rate of return—it must be found by interpolation or iterative calculation (in other words, trial and error, which can be performed quite easily with a computer).

Example

Suppose we wish to find the internal rate of return for an investment costing \$12,000 that will yield a cash inflow of \$4,000 per year for four years.

Solution

We see that the present value factor sought is

$$\text{PV factor} = \frac{\$12{,}000}{\$4{,}000} = 3.000$$

and we seek the interest rate that will provide this factor over a four-year period. The interest rate must lie between 12 percent and 14 percent because 3.000 lies between 3.037 and 2.914 (in the fourth row of Appendix A, Table 4). Linear interpolation between these two values, according to the following equation

$$i = 12 + (14 - 12)\frac{(3.037 - 3.000)}{(3.037 - 2.914)}$$

$$= 12 + 0.602 = 12.602\%$$

provides us with a good approximation to the actual internal rate of return.

With Excel, we use the internal rate of return (IRR) function, which is defined as follows:

IRR = (values, est.%)

where

values = The annual cash flows in chronological order
(at least one of which must be negative to represent the investment)

est. % = Estimated rate of return

Using the above example, we calculate the internal rate of return using Excel as follows:

= IRR (A11:A15, 0.1) = 12.6%

Here, the values in cells A11 to A15 represent the initial investment (A11 = −$12,000) and the annual cash flows (A12 to A15 = $4,000).

When the income stream is discounted at 12.6 percent, the resulting present value closely approximates the cost of the investment. Thus, the internal rate of return for this investment is 12.6 percent. The cost of capital can be compared with the internal rate of return to determine the net rate of return on the investment. If, in this example, the cost of capital were 8 percent, the net rate of return on the investment would be 4.6 percent.

The net present value and internal rate of return methods involve procedures that are essentially the same. They differ in that the net present value method enables investment alternatives to be compared in terms of the dollar value in excess of cost, whereas the internal rate of return method permits a comparison of rates of return on alternative investments. Moreover, the internal rate of return method occasionally encounters problems in calculation, as multiple rates frequently appear in the computation.

Ranking Investments with Uneven Lives

When proposed investments have the same life expectancy, comparison among them using the preceding methods will give a reasonable picture of their relative value. When the lives of the investments are unequal, however, several questions arise as to how to relate the two different time periods, including: Should replacements be considered the same as the original? Should productivity for the shorter-term unit that will be replaced earlier be considered to have higher productivity? How should the cost of future units be estimated?

No estimate dealing with investments unforeseen at the time of decision can be expected to reflect a high degree of accuracy. Still, the problem must be dealt with, and some assumptions must be made in order to determine a ranking. The following section presents several different examples of how different methods can be applied to OM-related investment decisions.

Sample Problems on Investment Decisions

An Expansion Decision

Example

William J. Wilson Ceramic Products, Inc., leases plant facilities in which firebrick is manufactured. Because of rising demand, Wilson could increase sales by investing in new equipment to expand output. The selling price of $2.50 per brick will remain unchanged if output and sales increase. Based on engineering and cost estimates, the accounting department provides management with the following cost estimates based on an annual increased output of 400,000 bricks:

Cost of new equipment having an expected life of five years	$500,000
Equipment installation cost	20,000
Expected salvage value	0
New operation's share of annual lease expense	40,000
Annual increase in utility expenses	40,000
Annual increase in labor costs	160,000
Annual additional cost for raw materials	400,000

The sum-of-the-years'-digits method of depreciation will be used, and taxes are paid at a rate of 40 percent. Wilson's policy is not to invest capital in projects earning less than a 20 percent rate of return. Should the proposed expansion be undertaken?

Solution

Compute cost of investment:

Acquisition cost of equipment	$500,000
Equipment installation costs	20,000
Total cost of investment	$520,000

Determine yearly cash flows throughout the life of the investment.

The lease expense is a sunk cost. It will be incurred whether or not the investment is made and is therefore irrelevant to the decision and should be disregarded. Annual production expenses to be considered are utility, labor, and raw materials. These total $600,000 per year.

Annual sales revenues are $2.50 × 400,000 units of output, or $1,000,000. Yearly income before depreciation and taxes is thus $1,000,000 gross revenues less $600,000 expenses, or $400,000.

Next, determine the depreciation charges to be deducted from the $400,000 income each year using the SYD method (sum-of-years'-digits = 1 + 2 + 3 + 4 + 5 = 15):

Year	Proportion of $500,000 to Be Depreciated		Depreciation Charge
1	5/15 × $500,000	=	$166,667
2	4/15 × 500,000	=	133,333
3	3/15 × 500,000	=	100,000
4	2/15 × 500,000	=	66,667
5	1/15 × 500,000	=	33,333
Accumulated depreciation			$500,000

Find each year's cash flow when taxes are 40 percent. Cash flow for only the first year is illustrated:

Earnings before depreciation and taxes	$400,000
Less depreciation	– $167,667
Earnings before taxes	$233,333
Less federal taxes (40%)	– 93,333
Net earnings	$140,000
Net cash flow = Net earnings + Depreciation (first year)	$306,667

Determine the present value of the cash flow. Since Wilson demands at least a 20 percent rate of return on investments, multiply the cash flows by the 20 percent present-value factor for each year. The factor for each respective year must be used because the cash flows are not an annuity.

Year	Present Value Factor (20%)		Cash Flow		Present Value
1	0.833	×	$306,667	=	$255,454
2	0.694	×	293,333	=	203,573
3	0.579	×	280,000	=	162,120
4	0.482	×	266,667	=	128,533
5	0.402	×	253,334	=	101,840
Total present value of cash flows (discounted at 20%)				=	$851,520

Now find whether net present value is positive or negative:

Total present value of cash flows	$851,520
Total cost of investment	520,000
Net present value	$331,520

The net present value is positive when returns are discounted at 20 percent. Wilson will earn an amount in excess of 20 percent on the investment and the proposed expansion should be undertaken.

A Replacement Decision

Example

For five years Bennie's Brewery has been using a machine that attaches labels to bottles. The machine was purchased for $4,000 and is being depreciated over 10 years to a $0 salvage value using straight-line depreciation. The machine can be sold now for $2,000. Bennie can buy a new labeling machine for $6,000 that will have a useful life of five years and cut labor costs by $1,200 annually. The old machine will require a major overhaul in the next few months at an estimated cost of $300. If purchased, the new machine will be depreciated over five years to a $500 salvage value using the straight-line method. The company will invest in any project earning more than the 12 percent cost of capital. The tax rate is 40 percent. Should Bennie's Brewery invest in the new machine?

Solution

Determine the cost of investment:

Price of new machine		$6,000
Less: Sale of old machine	$2,000	
Avoidable overhaul costs	300	2,300
Effective net cost of investment		$3,700

Determine the increase in cash flow resulting from investment in the new machine:

Yearly cost savings = \$1,200

Differential depreciation:

Annual depreciation on old machines: $\frac{\text{Cost} - \text{Salvage}}{\text{Expected life}} = \frac{\$4{,}000 - \$0}{10} = \$400$

Annual depreciation on new machines: $\frac{\text{Cost} - \text{Salvage}}{\text{Expected life}} = \frac{\$6{,}000 - \$500}{5} = \$1{,}100$

Differential depreciation = \$1,100 − \$400 = \$700

Yearly net increase in cash flow into the firm:

Cost savings		\$1,200
Deduct: Taxes at 40%	\$480	
Add: Advantage of increase in depreciation (0.4 × 700)	280	200
Yearly increase in cash flow		\$1,000

Determine the total present value of the investment:

The five-year cash flow of \$1,000 per year is an annuity.
Discounted at 12 percent, the cost of capital, the present value is 3.605 × \$1,000 = \$3,605
The present value of the new machine, if sold at its salvage value of \$500 at the end of the fifth year, is 0.567 × \$500 = \$284
Total present value of the expected cash flows: \$3,605 + \$284 = \$3,889

Determine whether the net present value is positive:

Total present value	\$3,889
Cost of investment	3,700
Net present value	\$ 189

Bennie's Brewery should make the purchase because the investment will return slightly more than the cost of capital.

Note: The importance of depreciation has been shown in this example. The present value of the yearly cash flow resulting from operations is only

$$\begin{matrix}(\text{Cost savings} - \text{Taxes}) \times (\text{Present value factor}) \\ (\$1{,}200 - \$480) \quad \times \quad (3.605)\end{matrix} = \$2{,}596$$

This figure is \$1,104 less than the \$3,700 cost of the investment. Only a very large depreciation advantage makes this investment worthwhile. The total present value of the advantage is \$1,009:

$$\begin{matrix}(\text{Tax rate} \times \text{Differential depreciation}) \times (\text{PV factor}) \\ (0.4 \times \$700) \quad \times \quad 3.605\end{matrix} = \$1{,}009$$

A Make-or-Buy Decision

Example

The Triple X Company manufactures and sells refrigerators. It makes some of the parts for the refrigerators and purchases others. The engineering department believes it might be possible to cut costs by manufacturing one of the parts currently being purchased for $8.25 each. (It is assumed that there is an unlimited supply of these parts at this price.) The firm uses 100,000 of these parts each year, and the accounting department compiles the following list of costs based on engineering estimates.

Fixed costs will increase by $50,000.

Labor costs will increase by $125,000.

Factory overhead, currently running $500,000 per year, may be expected to increase 12 percent if the part is made in house.

Raw materials used to make the part will cost $600,000.

Given these estimates, should Triple X make the part or continue to buy it?

Solution

Find total cost incurred if the part were manufactured:

Additional fixed costs	$ 50,000
Additional labor costs	125,000
Raw materials cost	600,000
Additional overhead costs = 0.12 × $500,000	60,000
Total cost to manufacture	$835,000

Find cost per unit to manufacture:

$$\frac{\$835{,}000}{100{,}000} = \$8.35 \text{ per unit}$$

Triple X should continue to buy the part. Manufacturing costs exceed the present cost to purchase by $0.10 per unit.

An Example Using Excel

Example

It is July 1, 1990, and you are currently operating a re-export business in Hong Kong. Your warehouse where you store the products you receive from Ghuangzhou in the People's Republic of China is old and very poorly laid out. Consequently, your operating expenses are very high.

You have just been approached by a developer who has an empty warehouse that he built for a client that went bankrupt. He offers to sell you the warehouse for HK$8,250,000. However, the warehouse is located on land that is leased from the government, and the lease expires on June 30, 1997, when Hong Kong becomes part of the People's Republic of China. As a result, you do not anticipate that you will be able to renew this lease.

Your current annual operating expenses are HK$3,200,000. You hire a consultant to conduct an analysis of the new warehouse. The consultant estimates that because of its efficiencies, your annual operating expenses in the new warehouse will be HK$1,750,000. In addition, the developer has told you that he can sell your current warehouse for HK$2,600,000.

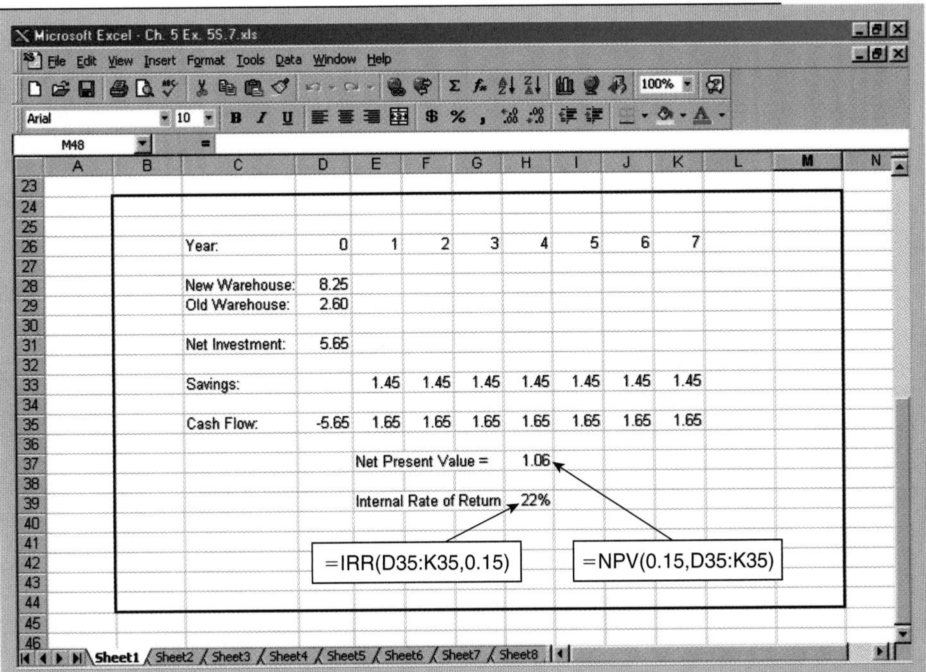

Exhibit S5.6

Application of Excel to Determine Net Present Value and Internal Rate of Return

a. If your current cost of capital is 15 percent, what is the net present value of purchasing this new warehouse?

b. What is the internal rate of return for this investment?

c. Should you buy this new warehouse?

Solution

a. Using Excel, set up a worksheet showing the net cost of the warehouse and the projected savings for the next seven years, as shown in Exhibit S5.6. Using the net present value (NPV) function, as shown in Exhibit S5.6, determine the net present value of the project, which is HK$1,060,000. Since the NPV is positive, this means that the overall return on this investment exceeds your cost of capital of 15 percent.

b. Again using the same Excel worksheet, use the internal rate of return (IRR) function, as shown in Exhibit S5.6, to determine the internal rate of return for this investment, which is 22 percent. (*Note:* The .15 in the IRR function is an estimate that is needed to start the IRR calculation.)

c. Inasmuch as the project has a 22 percent return on the investment, which exceeds your minimum requirement of 15 percent, you should buy the new warehouse, even though the lease expires in seven years.

Key Formulas

Compound Value of an Annuity

$$S_n = R[(1+i)^{n-1} + (1+i)^{n-2} + \cdots + (1+i)^1 + 1] \quad \text{(S5.1)}$$

where

S_n = Compound value of an annuity

R = Periodic receipts in dollars

n = Length of the annuity in years

Present Value of a Future Single Payment

$$V_n = P(1+i)^n \tag{S5.2}$$

where

V_n = Value of principal at the end of year n
n = Length of the compounding period in years
P = Present value of principal
i = Interest rate

Present Value of an Annuity

$$A_n = R\left[\frac{1}{(1+i)} + \frac{1}{(1+i)^2} + \cdots + \frac{1}{(1+i)^n}\right] \tag{S5.3}$$

where

A_n = Present value of annuity of n years
R = Periodic receipts
n = Length of the annuity in years

Key Terms

activity-based costing p. 185
avoidable costs p. 184
break-even analysis p. 187
cost of capital p. 184
depreciation p. 192
economic life p. 192
fixed costs p. 183
internal rate of return p. 201
net present value p. 199
obsolete p. 192
opportunity costs p. 184
out-of-pocket costs p. 184
payback period p. 201
sunk costs p. 183
variable costs p. 183

Review and Discussion Questions

1. List three examples of capital investments in operations management.
2. Define the following terms: *fixed, variable, opportunity, and avoidable costs; obsolescence,* and *depreciation.*
3. What are the goals of the two types of break-even analysis?
4. What are the main advantages of activity-based costing techniques?
5. How do taxes affect profits? Why?
6. How does depreciation affect capital investment? Why?
7. If a firm is short of capital, what action might it take to conserve the capital it has and to obtain more?
8. What are the reasons for using present-value analysis rather than "future-value" analysis?
9. Why might a decision maker like to use the payback period method as well as the rate of return and the net present value?
10. Discuss why the comparison of alternative investment decisions is especially difficult when the investment choices have different life lengths.
11. Compare the advantages and disadvantages of the following depreciation methods: straight-line, sum-of-the years' digits, double-declining balance.

Problems

1. Jana and Marla, two recent business school graduates, have decided to open their own copy-service business on a part-time basis. They estimate that their annual fixed costs are $32,000 and their average variable cost for each copy sold is $.03. They expect their selling price to average $.07 per copy.

a. Draw the break-even chart for their business, and indicate all of the relevant costs.

b. What is their break-even point in dollars? In number of copies?

c. After their first year of operations, in which they generated $84,000 in revenues, Jana and Marla decide to pay themselves each $5,000 per year in salaries. What do their annual sales have to be in the second year if they want to make the same amount of profit as they did in their first year?

2. Peter McWalters is president of Transformonics, a firm that produces power transformers for personal computer manufacturers. Peter's analysis of the various methods by which a new model of transformer can be built has been narrowed down to one of three alternatives. Because of the rapidly changing technology in the industry, Peter estimates the product life of the transformer to be one year. Marketing has estimated that it can sell 5,000 of these new transformers within that time period. The three alternative processes are

   - Use existing equipment and fixtures, and hire high-skilled machinists and technicians at $16.00 per hour (including benefits). With this method, each transformer will require two (2) labor-hours to assemble.
   - Use existing equipment, but invest $30,000 in new fixtures and instruction manuals to simplify some of the more complicated operations. Semiskilled workers could be employed at $12.00 per hour (including benefits), with each transformer requiring one (1) labor-hour to complete.
   - Invest $75,000 in new equipment, fixtures, and instruction manuals. This approach would eliminate all of the complicated procedures, thereby requiring only unskilled labor, which could be hired at $6.00 per hour (including benefits). With this method, each transformer would require only 20 labor-minutes to complete.

   a. Draw a break-even chart using total cost versus volume for the above processes.

   b. Calculate the two break-even volumes (i.e., those volumes at which you shift from one process to another).

   c. Which alternative would you recommend, and why?

3. Marisa Strauss, a financial analyst for Green Garden Salads, Inc., is currently evaluating three different sites for locating its plant in the greater San Francisco area. This plant will produce prepackaged tossed salads in five- and ten-pound bags. The three locations are (*a*) Oakland, (*b*) Petaluma, and (*c*) San Jose. Marisa estimates that the fixed costs and the variable unit costs associated with each site are as follows:

Location	Fixed Costs per Year	Variable Costs per Unit
Oakland	$250,000	$10.00/100 lb.
Petaluma	$100,000	$30.00/100 lb.
San Jose	$150,000	$20.00/100 lb.

   a. Plot the total costs curves for each of these locations on a single graph and identify the range of outputs for which each alternative site is the most economical.

   b. If the vice president of marketing has estimated the demand for prepackaged salads to be 500,000 lb. per year, which location would you pick and why?

4. What is the depreciation expense for the third year, using the sum-of-the-years'-digits method, for the following cost of a new machine?

Cost of machine	$35,000
Estimated life	6 years
Estimated salvage value	$5,000

5. Disregarding tax considerations, is it cheaper to buy or to lease a piece of equipment with the following costs for a five-year term? (Assume the cost of capital is 10 percent.)

	To Buy	To Lease
Purchase (or lease) cost	$50,000	$10,000/yr.
Annual operating cost	4,000/yr.	4,000/yr.
Maintenance cost	2,000/yr.	0
Salvage value at end of 5 years	$20,000	0

6. A new piece of office equipment must be purchased, and the choice has been narrowed down to two styles, each capable of meeting the intended needs. With a 10-year horizon and an interest rate of 8 percent, which piece of equipment should be purchased?

	Equipment A	Equipment B
Initial cost	$10,000	$7,000
Salvage value (10 years hence)	4,000	2,000
Estimated annual operation and maintenance cost	1,000	1,500

7. The local university is accepting bids for the hot dog and cold drink concession at the new stadium. The contract is for a five-year period, and it is your feeling that a bid of $40,000 will win the contract. A preliminary analysis indicates that annual operating costs will be $35,000 and average annual sales will be $50,000. The contract can be written off during the five years. Taxes are at the 40 percent rate, and your goal is to make a 20 percent return on your investment.
   a. Will you meet your goal if you use straight-line depreciation?
   b. Would you meet your goal using sum-of-the-years'-digits depreciation?
8. In adding a new product line, a firm needs a new piece of machinery. An investigation of suitable equipment for the production process has narrowed the choice to the two machines listed.

	Machine A	Machine B
Type of equipment	General purpose	Special purpose
Installed cost	$8,000	$13,000
Salvage value	800	3,000
Annual labor cost	6,000	3,600
Estimated life (years)	10	5

   Assume that at the end of five years, a comparable replacement for Machine B will be available. Using present-value analysis with a 10 percent interest rate, which machine would you choose?
9. Pete's Cabinets, Inc. (PCI), a manufacturer of kitchen cabinets, has been growing rapidly due to its high-quality products and fast delivery. Pete D'Amato, the president of PCI, therefore is evaluating another method for producing the cabinets that requires the purchase of some semiautomatic equipment. (Currently, the cabinets are being produced primarily by hand with highly skilled workers.) The cost of this equipment is $45,000, and Pete projects that this new equipment will result in an annual savings,

after taxes, of $15,000 per year for the next four years. The cost of borrowing money is 12 percent.

a. What is the net present value for this equipment?

b. What is the payback period?

c. What is your recommendation to Pete?

10. Matt Koslow, having just graduated from business school, has decided to open his own brewery, which he named JoJo Brewery in honor of his grandparents, Joe and Joan. He purchases the necessary brewing and fermenting equipment to get started for $60,000, and locates his brewery in an old brick building that was previously a textile mill. His annual fixed costs are estimated to be $45,000. In addition, the variable costs are estimated to be $14.00 per barrel of beer. Initially, to save money, he will produce only kegs of beer, which he will sell to local bars and restaurants. Based on a market survey that he had conducted, Matt forecasts his sales for the first five years to be as follows:

Year:	1	2	3	4	5
Barrels:	3,000	4,400	6,200	7,000	7,800

Currently, the cost of money is 15 percent and the tax rate is 35 percent. The average selling price per barrel is estimated to be $35.00.

Using a spreadsheet software program, answer the following questions:

a. If Matt uses straight-line depreciation and a five-year life on the equipment with no salvage value, what is the net present value (NPV) of his investment? If he uses sum-of-the-years' digits method of depreciation, what is his NPV?

b. What is the internal rate of return (IRR) on this investment with the current tax rate of 35 percent? If the tax rate was increased to 42 percent?

c. What is the NPV at the current cost of money (15 percent) and tax rate (35 percent) if sales each year are 20 percent lower than his original forecast?

Bibliography

Bodie, Zvi; and Robert C. Merton. *Finance.* Upper Saddle River, NJ: Prentice Hall, 2000.

Brigham, Eugene F. *Fundamentals of Financial Management.* 7th ed. Fort Worth, TX: The Dryden Press, 1995.

Garrison, Ray. *Managerial Accounting.* 6th ed. Homewood, IL: Richard D. Irwin, 1991.

Gitman, Lawrence. *Principles of Managerial Finance.* 7th ed. New York: HarperCollins, 1994.

Helfert, E. *Techniques of Financial Analysis: A Modern Approach.* 9th ed. Burr Ridge, IL: Irwin/McGraw-Hill, 1997.

Hodder, James E., and Henry E. Riggs. "Pitfalls in Evaluating Risky Projects." *Harvard Business Review,* January–February 1985, pp. 128–35.

Johnson, Thomas, and Robert Kaplan. *Relevance Lost: The Rise and Fall of Management Accounting.* Boston: Harvard Business School Press, 1987, p. 188.

Libertore, Matthew J. *Selection and Evaluation of Advanced Manufacturing Technologies.* New York: Springer-Verlag, 1990, pp. 231–56.

Ross, Stephen A.; Randolph W. Westerfield; and Bradford D. Jordan. *Essentials of Corporate Finance.* 2nd ed. Burr Ridge, IL: McGraw-Hill, 1999.

Shapiro, Alan C., and Shelden D. Balbirer. *Modern Corporate Finance: A Multidisciplinary Approach to Value Creation.* Upper Saddle River, NJ: Prentice Hall, 2000.

Van Horne, James C. *Financial Management and Policy.* 9th ed. Englewood Cliffs, NJ: Prentice Hall, 1992.

6 Quality Management

Chapter Objectives

- Introduce those individuals, often referred to as quality gurus, who have played a significant role in the evolution of quality management, and describe their specific contributions.
- Identify the different dimensions of quality as they relate to both goods and services.
- Define the various elements that comprise the cost of quality.
- Describe the more successful management quality initiatives such as total quality management (TQM) and six sigma.
- Present the various quality awards and recognition that promote and encourage firms to provide high-quality goods and services.

CUSTOMER SATISFACTION IS KEY TO SUCCESS AT SUNNY FRESH FOODS

(From NIST website)

Sunny Fresh Foods (SFF) manufactures and distributes more than 160 different egg-based food products to more than 1,200 foodservice operations across the United States: Its customers include quick-serve restaurants, schools, hospitals, and convenience stores. Competing with about 40 other companies, SFF is ranked second in its industry (up from 14th in 1988) with more than a 19 percent market share in the United States.

The 1999 recipient of the Malcolm Baldrige National Quality Award in the small business category attributes much of its success to its high levels of customer satisfaction. One hundred percent of its customers are "satisfied" or "very satisfied" with SFF in three of its five key categories—on-time delivery, technical support, and customer service access—and more than 90 percent are "satisfied" or "very satisfied" in the remaining two categories: product performance and product freshness. Not coincidentally, claims filed by its customers have decreased dramatically from initially low levels to what is now better than six sigma levels of quality.

Its combination of innovative new products, a near-perfect record for on-time delivery, and resulting high level of customer satisfaction has been a major factor in SFF becoming the sole supplier for several major national restaurant chains. In addition, many of its customers have recognized SFF's superior performance with supplier awards.

As proof that providing high quality products and services pays, SFF's return on gross investment tripled between 1994 and 1999, and it experienced an average increase in operating profits of 25 percent per year over the same five-year period.

Source: National Institute of Science and Technology (NIST) website, www.quality.nist.gov.

Managerial Issues

Quality will always matter to customers—so it should be a high priority for every manager. This is true for both manufacturing operations as well as services. Defining quality from the customer's perspective, however, is very difficult as it can mean different things to different people. This is one of the major challenges facing managers today. At the same time, the level of quality being provided in the goods and services being sold today continues to increase, due in part to a combination of increased global competition and an increased knowledge of customers. Service quality is especially difficult to manage, for a variety of reasons. Unlike product quality, service quality is often highly subjective, varying from customer to customer even under identical circumstances. As a result, good service quality to one customer may be viewed as poor service quality by another.

The reason that quality is difficult to define is that it is a very broad concept that encompasses many dimensions, which vary for both goods and services. Good managers will identify those quality dimensions that are most important to their customers.

Another reason managers should be concerned with quality is that quality and cost are closely related. There are significant costs associated with producing bad products. Similarly there are costs related to providing poor service to customers. Bad quality results in dissatisfied customers who eventually take their business elsewhere. Thus, high quality in goods and services is essential to maintain customer loyalty and long-term customer relationships, which has been shown to significantly increase profits.

With the growth in global competition, the markets for goods and services has shifted from being a producers' market, where customers are at the mercy of the firms that are providing the goods and services, to being a consumers' market, where customers have a wide variety of sources from which to buy the goods and services they desire. This trend is expected to only increase as more and more consumers purchase goods and services on the Internet from literally any corner of the world. In such a highly competitive environment, managers are acknowledging the importance of customer loyalty, and recognize

The Quality Gurus

quality gurus

Individuals who have been identified as making a significant contribution to improving the quality of goods and services.

Over the years there have been many individuals involved in the quality revolution. Several have been recognized as **quality gurus** for their valuable contributions and forward thinking. Walter A. Shewhart, W. Edwards Deming, Joseph M. Juran, Armand Feigenbaum, Philip Crosby, and Genichi Taguchi. While they share much in common in terms of how they view quality, each has left his own unique stamp on the quality movement. Consequently, their philosophical approaches to quality are significantly different. A comparison of the philosophies of three of the more prominent quality gurus is presented in Exhibit 6.1.

Walter A. Shewhart

Walter A. Shewhart, as mentioned earlier, was a statistician at Bell Laboratories who studied randomness in industrial processes. He developed a system that permitted workers to determine whether the variability of a process was truly random or due to assignable causes. If a process exhibited only random variation, it was considered to be "in control." If a process exhibited nonrandom variation, the cause for the variation had to be identified and addressed in order for the process to be brought back into control. In addition to developing the foundations for modern statistical process control, Shewhart also developed the "plan–do–check–act" (PDCA) cycle shown in Exhibit 6.2. Prior to the PDCA cycle, organizations typically managed activities as though they had identifiable beginning and end points. The PDCA cycle uses a circular model to emphasize the need for continuous improvement. Shewhart's pioneering work in statistical process control had a strong influence on both Deming and Juran.

that a key element in maintaining customer loyalty is the ability to provide only the highest quality goods and services. It is no longer acceptable to only satisfy customers; now customer loyalty depends on the ability of a firm to "delight" its customers. However, as we shall see, quality can have many meanings, and each firm therefore needs to identify those specific elements of quality that are most important to the particular market on which it is focusing.

From a historical perspective, the quality movement can trace its roots back to the 1920s when Walter Shewhart developed the concept of statistical process control for measuring and monitoring the quality of a process. However, Shewhart's concepts were not widely accepted by industry until World War II, when, by necessity, firms began to apply his ideas because of both the vast quantities of material being produced to support the war effort and also a critical shortage of labor.

Following World War II, consumer demand, which had been building during the war years, was unleashed, creating an unprecedented demand for products in the United States. In such an environment, companies focused their efforts on turning out high volumes of goods to meet this demand, often sacrificing quality. During this same time period, W. Edwards Deming and Joseph Juran, two of the quality gurus presented in this chapter, were teaching managers in Japan to lower costs and to improve quality by "doing it right the first time." As a result of their efforts, the quality of Japanese goods increased significantly, to the point where by the 1970s they were considered to be among the best in the world.

The beginnings of the quality movement in the United States can be traced to an NBC documentary televised in 1980 entitled "If Japan Can, Why Can't We?" which included Deming's significant contributions to improving the quality of Japanese products. The morning after this documentary was aired, Deming's telephone was ringing off the hook with calls from U.S. managers asking him for assistance in improving the quality of their firms' products.

Today, providing high-quality goods and services is a mandatory requirement for the long-term success of every organization.

W. Edwards Deming

A thorough understanding of **statistical process control (SPC)** is the basic cornerstone of Deming's approach to quality. In fact, the Japanese were so impressed with his knowledge of SPC that they invited him back to teach the subject to Japanese managers and workers. Deming emphasized the importance of having an overall organizational approach for quality management. He therefore insisted that top managers attend his lectures, knowing that the QC staff by itself could not support and sustain an ongoing organizationwide quality effort. The Japanese have recognized Deming's tremendous contribution to the success of their companies by naming their highest award for industrial excellence after him—the Deming Prize. (Another indicator that U.S. companies have made significant progress toward improving quality is that Florida Power & Light, a non-Japanese company, was awarded the Deming Prize.)

statistical process control (SPC)

Methods, such as control charts, that signal shifts in a process that will likely lead to products and/or services not meeting customer requirements.

One of Deming's major contributions focused on disproving the fallacy that it costs more to make better-quality products. He demonstrated that just the opposite is true: a high-quality process is, in fact, less costly than a low-quality one. When products are made properly the first time, substantial savings accrue from the elimination of unnecessary labor for rework and repairs and the cost to scrap nonconforming material.

Deming also introduced the plan–do–check–act (PDCA) cycle to the Japanese.

According to Deming, 85 percent of the quality problems generated by a company can be attributed to management, because they have the power to make the decisions that impact on the current systems and practices. His extensive consulting experiences with such companies as Ford, Nashua Corp., and Florida Power & Light have supported this claim. Over the years, Deming identified 14 points that he believed to be critical for improving quality. These 14 points are presented in Exhibit 6.3.

Exhibit 6.1
Three of the Quality Gurus Compared

	Crosby	Deming	Juran
Definition of quality	Conformance to requirements	A predictable degree of uniformity and dependability at low cost and suited to the market	Fitness for use
Degree of senior management responsibility	Responsible for quality	Responsible for 85% of quality problems	Less than 20% of quality problems are due to workers
Performance standard/ motivation	Zero defects	Quality has many "scales": use statistics to measure performance in all areas; critical of zero defects	Avoid campaigns to do perfect work
General approach	Prevention, not inspection	Reduce variability by continuous improvement; cease mass inspection	General management approach to quality, especially human elements
Structure	14 steps to quality improvement	14 points for management	10 steps to quality improvement
Statistical process control (SPC)	Rejects statistically acceptable levels of quality	Statistical methods of quality control must be used	Recommends SPC but warns that it can lead to tool-driven approach
Improvement basis	A process, not a program; improvement goals	Continuous to reduce variation; eliminate goals without methods	Project-by-project team approach; set goals
Teamwork	Quality improvement teams; quality councils	Employee participation in decision making; break down barriers between departments	Team and quality circle approach
Costs of quality	Cost of nonconformance; quality is free	No optimum; continuous improvement	Quality is not free; there is an optimum
Purchasing and goods received	State requirements; supplier is extension of business; most faults due to purchasers themselves	Inspection too late; allows defects to enter system through AQLs; statistical evidence and control charts required	Problems are complex; carry out formal surveys
Vendor rating	Yes and buyers' quality audits useless	No, critical of most systems	Yes, but help supplier improve
Single sourcing of supply		Yes	No, can neglect to sharpen competitive edge

Source: Modified from John S. Oakland, *Total Quality Management* (London: Heinemann Professional Publishing Ltd., 1989), pp. 291–92.

Joseph M. Juran

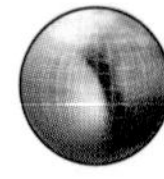

Like Deming, Juran also visited Japan shortly after the end of World War II to assist in rebuilding its industrial base. Also like Deming, Juran emphasized the importance of producing quality products, and thus directed his efforts while in Japan toward teaching quality

Exhibit 6.2

Shewhart's Plan-Do-Check-Act (PDCA) Cycle

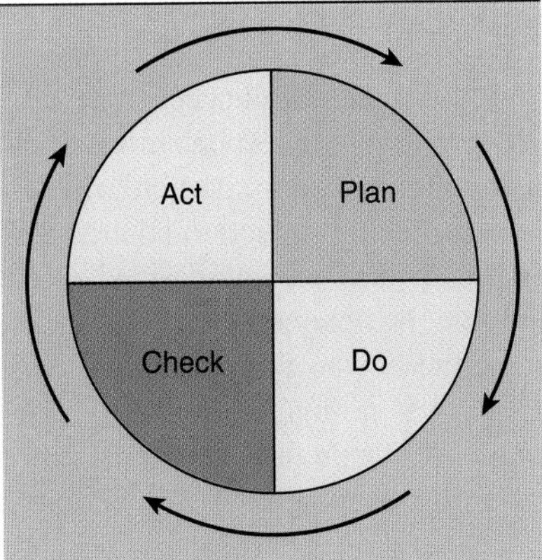

Source: "The PDCA Cycle" from *Deming Management at Work* by Mary Walton, copyright © 1990 by Mary Walton. Used by permission of G. P. Putnam's Sons, a division of Penguin Putnam, Inc.

Exhibit 6.3

Deming's 14-Point Program for Improving Quality

1. Create constancy of purpose for improvement of product and service.
2. Adopt the new philosophy.
3. Cease dependence on mass inspection.
4. End the practice of awarding business on the price tag alone.
5. Improve constantly and forever the system of production and training.
6. Institute training.
7. Institute leadership.
8. Drive out fear.
9. Break down barriers between staff areas.
10. Eliminate slogans, exhortations, and targets for the workforce.
11. Eliminate numerical quotas.
12. Remove barriers to pride in workmanship.
13. Institute a vigorous program of education and retraining.
14. Take action to accomplish the program.

Source: "14 Point System" from *Deming Management at Work* by Mary Walton, copyright © 1990 by Mary Walton. Used by permission of G. P. Putnam's Sons, a division of Penguin Putnam, Inc.

concepts and their application to the factory floor. Based on his experiences with Japanese companies, Juran developed an approach to quality that focuses primarily on three areas: (*a*) quality planning, (*b*) quality control, and (*c*) quality improvement.

According to Juran, the quality of a product is defined as fitness for use, as viewed by the customer. Juran further defines fitness for use as consisting of five components: (*a*) quality of design, (*b*) quality of conformance, (*c*) availability, (*d*) safety, and (*e*) field use. In evaluating a product's fitness for use, Juran takes into account the total life cycle of the product.

Juran uses the cost of quality as his framework for introducing his approach to quality. In doing so, he divides the cost of quality into three major categories: (*a*) cost of prevention, (*b*) cost of detection/appraisal, and (*c*) cost of failure, all of which are presented in greater detail later in this chapter.

Armand Feigenbaum

In 1956, Armand Feigenbaum proposed the concept of "total quality control," which begins with the recognition that quality is the responsibility of everyone in the organization. He stressed interdepartmental communication, particularly with respect to product design control, incoming material control, and production control. Like Juran, he believed in the power of the cost-of-quality framework, and emphasized careful measurement and reporting of these costs. Also like Juran, he believed that a new type of quality professional was needed, the quality control engineer, who would oversee cross-functional elements. The application of statistics by itself was no longer enough. The Japanese embraced this concept and expanded it to "companywide quality control." In recognition of his contribution to improving quality, The Massachusetts Quality Award is named in honor of Armand Feigenbaum.

Philip Crosby

Unlike Deming and Juran, both of whom were trained initially as statisticians, Crosby was educated as an engineer and began his career in manufacturing. After working for several large companies, primarily in quality-related positions, he founded his own "Quality College" in Florida in 1979.

Crosby's philosophy, which is similar in some respects to Deming's, states that any organization can reduce its total overall costs by improving the quality of its processes. In one of his first books, Crosby preached that "quality is free." According to Crosby, the cost of providing poor-quality goods and services is significant. He estimated that the cost of producing poor quality can run as high as 25 percent of revenues for manufacturing companies and 40 percent of operating expenses in service operations. Crosby also claims that companies that have successfully implemented quality programs can expect to reduce their costs of quality to less than 2.5 percent of sales.[1]

Genichi Taguchi

Genichi Taguchi has contributed importantly to both the refinement of quality management philosophy and the development of quality tools. Taguchi takes an engineering approach to design quality, focusing on the design of experiments to improve both the yield and performance quality of products. He emphasizes the minimization of variation, which is also the cornerstone of his philosophical approach. While Juran emphasized the cost of quality to the firm, Taguchi is also concerned with the cost of quality to society as a whole. He takes Juran's concept of external failure much further, including not only the cost to the firm that ships the defective product, but also the cost to the firm that accepts it, the customer that buys and uses it, and so on. His dual engineering-philosophical perspective shows how much is lost when products fail to meet specifications, which "ups the stakes" for managers concerned with the quality of their products and services.

Defining Quality

For many years following World War II, quality was viewed primarily as a defensive function rather than as a competitive weapon for use in developing new markets and increasing

[1]Philip B. Crosby, *Quality Is Free* (New York: New America Library, 1979), p. 15.

market share. In this role, the quality emphasis was on quality control (QC): reducing the number of customer complaints that were received. As a result, there was a heavy reliance on inspection (sorting the good from the bad) rather than on prevention. Identifying defective output and either fixing it (rework) or disposing of it (scrap) incurred costs. It was therefore believed that higher quality must be more costly. Quality control managers often reported to manufacturing managers, who were measured primarily on output; consequently they had little or no power to either halt production or delay the shipment of faulty products.

Today, however, more and more companies are recognizing that quality can be defined in many ways. With the realization that quality has many dimensions, firms are now able to not only identify new market niches, but also increase their market share in existing ones.

Quality in Goods

David Garvin has identified eight different **quality dimensions,** with respect to goods, on which a company can compete: (*a*) performance, (*b*) features, (*c*) reliability, (*d*) durability, (*e*) conformance, (*f*) serviceability, (*g*) aesthetics, and (*h*) perceived quality.[2]

quality dimensions

Recognition that quality can be defined in many ways and that companies can use quality as a competitive advantage.

Performance Performance is a measure of a product's primary operating characteristics. Since performance usually can be measured in specific quantitative terms, a product's performance characteristics are often compared and ranked with those of the competition. With an automobile, for example, performance characteristics would include how fast it can accelerate from 0 to 60 mph and its fuel efficiency in terms of miles per gallon. For a personal computer, performance characteristics would include operating speed and random access memory (RAM) capacity.

Features Features are the "bells and whistles" that are offered with a product. While features are not the primary operating characteristics of a product, they may, nonetheless, be very important to the customer. For example, a moon roof and stereo system may be the deciding factors for a new car buyer while a specific type of refrigerator may appeal to a customer because it offers an icemaker and water dispenser.

Reliability The reliability of a product relates to the probability that the product will fail within a specified time. Reliability is often measured as the mean time between failures (MTBF) or the failure rate per unit of time or other measure of usage. High product reliability is important in such products as airplanes, computers, and copying machines. Stratus Computers, for example, has successfully carved out a niche for itself in the highly competitive computer industry by offering "fault-free" computer systems. The bored Maytag repairman with no service calls and Sears' Die Hard battery offer additional examples of product reliability.

Durability The durability dimension of quality relates to the expected operational life of a product. In some instances, as with a light bulb, the filament eventually burns out and the entire product must be replaced. In other cases, such as with an automobile, the consumer

[2]David Garvin, "Competing on the Eight Dimensions of Quality," *Harvard Business Review*, November–December 1987, pp. 101–10.

must evaluate the trade-off between replacing the product entirely versus spending money on repairs for the existing one.

Conformance A product's conformance to design specifications is primarily process oriented, in that it reflects how well the product and its individual components meet the established standards.

Serviceability Serviceability is concerned with how readily a product can be repaired and the speed, competence, and courtesy associated with that repair. This dimension of quality is sometimes overlooked in the design stage. For example, Chevrolet in the 1970s designed a car in which one of the spark plugs could not be removed without pulling out the entire engine. The speed of the repair is also important, in that it affects the overall number of products needed for those businesses that require constant coverage. Using a city's paramedic service as an example, the frequency and the amount of time a paramedic vehicle requires repair and maintenance impact directly on the total number of vehicles the city needs to provide the proper level of coverage.

Aesthetics Aesthetics is obviously a dimension of quality for which there is a high degree of individual judgment and that is also highly subjective. In fact, in terms of aesthetics, good quality to one group of customers might even be perceived as poor quality to another group. Companies, therefore, have an opportunity with this quality dimension to seek out a very specific market niche.

Perceived Quality According to David Garvin, perceived quality is directly related to the reputation of the firm that manufactures the product. Often, total information about the various quality aspects of a product is not available, especially when it is a new product that is being introduced for the first time. Consequently, customers rely heavily on the past performance and reputation of the firm making the product, attaching a perceived value based on the previous performance of the company's other products.

Quality in Services

Parasuraman, Zeithaml, and Berry (1986, 1990)[3,4] identified the following 10 "generic" factors or dimensions that contribute to the level of service quality a firm provides to its customers.

Tangibles Tangibles are the physical evidence of the service. The boxy brown UPS truck or the clean, white FedEx truck is an easily recognized tangible. The type of uniform a restaurant's waitstaff wears and the cleanliness of the uniforms are some of the tangibles that you observe when you go out to eat. The food served at the music festival and the t-shirts that celebrate that festival are also examples of tangibles.

Reliability As previously described, reliability relates to the consistency of performance and dependability of the service. FedEx provides a good example of a firm that provides highly reliable service.

---

[3]A. Parasuraman, V. A. Zeithaml, and L. L. Berry, "SERVQUAL: A Multiple-Item Scale for Measuring Consumer Perceptions of Service Quality," *Marketing Science Institute,* Cambridge, MA, 1986.

[4]L. L. Berry, V. A. Zeithaml, and A. Parasuraman, "Five Imperatives for Improving Service Quality," *Sloan Management Review* 29 (Summer 1990), pp. 29–38.

Responsiveness This refers to the willingness and/or readiness of employees to provide service. How easily you can get the attention of the clerk at Bloomingdale's Department Store is a measure of responsiveness. The length of time it takes to receive a return call on a complaint or a solution to a problem is also a measure of a firm's responsiveness.

Competence Competence relates to workers having the required skills and knowledge to properly perform the service. How qualified are the tellers at your bank? Are they able to correctly handle your transaction, or do they often seem uncertain or seek assistance from others? When you call your computer's technical support hotline, does the person on the other end appear to be knowledgeable in terms of understanding your problem?

Courtesy This refers to the politeness, respect, consideration, and friendliness of contact personnel. Once you've gotten the attention of the clerk at Macy's, is she pleasant, or does she continue her discussion of her parents with her co-worker while you wait awkwardly for her to ring up your purchases and accept your payment?

Credibility Credibility refers to the characteristics of trustworthiness, believability, and honesty of the service worker. Do you feel more or less comfortable with paying for a major repair after you discuss it with your auto mechanic? How much trust do you place in the sales clerk that is trying to sell you a computer?

Security Security refers to freedom from any danger, risk, or doubt. This is a particularly important dimension of professional service quality. Most consumers of health care or legal services, for example, are unable to assess the appropriateness of the recommendations of their physicians or attorneys, but their services are often sought when there are significant risks involved.

Access Access relates to approachability and ease of contact. How difficult is it to find a repair service for your computer? How many times are you transferred when you call your credit card company to resolve a billing problem?

Communication This is a very important dimension of quality in some services. When you are in an emergency room with a sick child, how well are you kept informed of the process of your child's care? How well do the nurses, doctors, and clerks listen to you?

Understanding the Customer This dimension refers to how well the service worker makes the effort to understand the specific needs of each customer.

Parasuraman, Berry, and Zeithaml used these definitions and key elements as a basis for identifying five principal service quality gaps. These gaps address the *customer's perception* of service performance rather than the managerial decisions around changing *actual* service performance.

Additional Views of Quality

Technical Quality versus Functional Quality In service operations, as in manufacturing operations, it is important to note the distinction between *technical quality,* which relates to the core element of the good or service, and *functional quality,* which relates to the customers' perception of how the good functions or the service is delivered. For example, the appropriateness of the medical treatment ordered by a physician for a patient's ailment

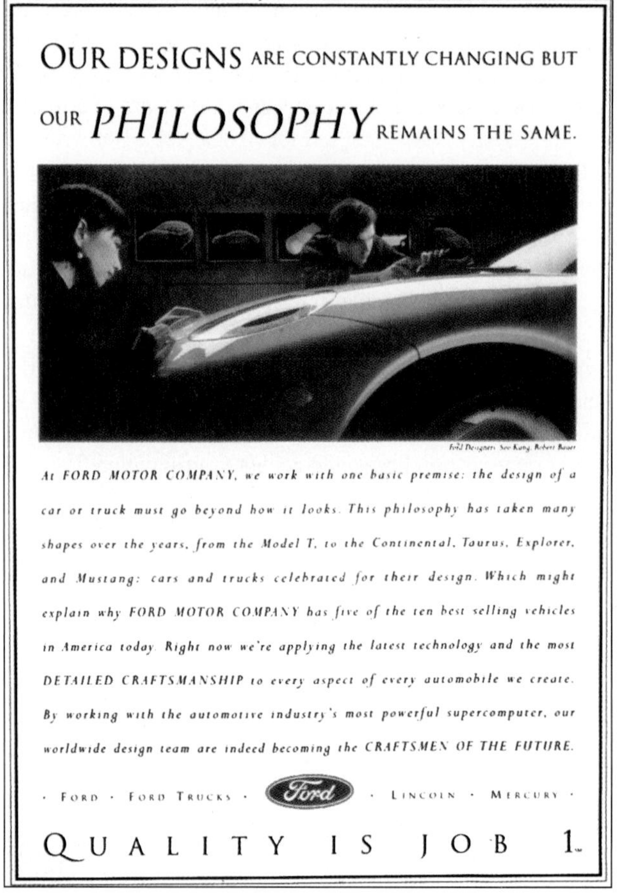

OUR DESIGNS ARE CONSTANTLY CHANGING BUT
OUR PHILOSOPHY REMAINS THE SAME.
Ford Designers: Soo Kang, Robert Bauer
At FORD MOTOR COMPANY, we work with one basic premise: the design of a car or truck must go beyond how it looks. This philosophy has taken many shapes over the years, from the Model T, to the Continental, Taurus, Explorer, and Mustang: cars and trucks celebrated for their design. Which might explain why FORD MOTOR COMPANY has five of the ten best selling vehicles in America today. Right now we're applying the latest technology and the most DETAILED CRAFTSMANSHIP to every aspect of every automobile we create. By working with the automotive industry's most powerful supercomputer, our worldwide design team are indeed becoming the CRAFTSMEN OF THE FUTURE.
· FORD · FORD TRUCKS · Ford · LINCOLN · MERCURY ·
QUALITY IS JOB 1.

A Ford quality ad with a focus on the application of the most current technology when building cars.

is a measure of the technical quality of the care. The physician's "bedside manner"—how empathetic he or she is, how well he or she listens and explains, how much care he or she takes to make the patient comfortable both physically and psychologically—is a measure of the functional quality of the care.

Customers can readily assess functional quality because it relates primarily to the interaction between the firm providing the good or service and its customers. Technical quality, however, may not be something that customers are able to assess because they do not have the technical knowledge required to do so. For example, unless they know a great deal about automobiles, customers may be uncertain about what the technical specifications of a new car mean or whether a mechanic has appropriately identified and solved their car problems. Similarly, most of us who are not trained in dentistry are unable to tell whether our dentists know a cavity in a tooth from a hole in the wall! To compensate for not having the knowledge required to assess technical quality, customers often will use some measures that they hope are objective to help them make those assessments. For example, when we evaluate the quality of physicians, we may consider where they trained, how much experience they have, and whether they are certified by a specialty board. When we evaluate an MBA program, we may look to see if the school is accredited and at the percentage of faculty with doctoral degrees as measures of technical quality. The inability of most customers to properly assess technical quality makes functional quality all the more important. Good managers care about both aspects of quality.

Expectations and Perceptions Another approach that is used to define quality in services is to measure how satisfied the customer is with the service received. Customers' satisfaction with service is related to both their prior expectations about the service and their perception of how well the service was provided. Customers develop a certain set of expectations based on a variety of inputs. They consider their previous experiences with services in general and with each specific kind of service they have encountered. For example, customers might have specific expectations about service in a retail clothing store that provides a basis for what they should expect when they speak with an employee on the phone—as well as when they are served in another retail clothing store. Customers also develop expectations when they hear about services from others. If you hear that your friend was delighted with her stay at a particular hotel, you're more likely to expect a similar level of service if you stay there. Customers also form expectations based on a service provider's advertisements and promotions. Promises of positive service bring in customers—but a promise isn't enough. Customers will be satisfied only if the service meets or exceeds their expectations. And the service performance is colored by the customer's perceptions of the quality of service, so that the relationship between expectations, service performance, and the perception of that performance can be described in the following equation:

$$\text{Satisfaction} = (\text{Perception of performance}) - (\text{Expectation})$$

The equation shows that there are two ways to increase satisfaction: improve the customers' perception of performance or decrease their expectations. But what happens to expectations for the next service encounter when satisfaction is high? It is likely that the customer will expect that high level of service again, thereby raising the stakes for the service provider.

The service satisfaction equation is therefore a dynamic one: each encounter affects customer expectations for the next encounter, so managing both performance and expectations is important for achieving high levels of customer satisfaction. Before managers can think about managing service performance, however, they must understand what service quality is. What is it that customers want? How can their needs be consistently met?

The Cost of Quality

Following Juran's model, we divide the **cost of quality** into three major categories: (*a*) cost of prevention, (*b*) cost of detection/appraisal, and (*c*) cost of failure. The third category, the cost of failure, is further subdivided into internal failure costs and external failure costs.

The total cost of quality is the sum of the costs in all three categories. The typical percentages of total quality costs that are estimated for each of the three categories are shown in Exhibit 6.4.

The cost of poor quality includes detection/appraisal costs and both internal and external failure costs, and can range from 15 to 25 percent of the total cost of a product. These costs of poor quality include the more traditional, visible items such as waste, rework, inspections and recalls, as well as the often-overlooked "invisible" categories such as customer allowances, complaint handling, lost or wasted capacity and excessive overtime.[5]

cost of quality

Framework for identifying quality components that are related to producing both high-quality products and low-quality products, with the goal of minimizing the total cost of quality.

Cost of Prevention

cost of prevention

Costs associated with the development of programs to prevent defectives from occurring in the first place.

Costs of prevention, by definition, are those costs incurred by an organization in its effort to prevent defective goods and services from being produced. Included in this category are

[5]Joseph A. DeFeo, "The Tip of the Iceberg," *Quality Progress,* May 2001, pp. 29–37.

Exhibit 6.4

Typical Quality Cost Ratios

Category	Feigenbaum	Juran and Gryna
Prevention costs	5%–10%	0.5%–5%
Detection/appraisal costs	20%–25%	10%–50%
Failure costs	65%–70%	Internal: 25%–40%
		External: 20%–40%
Total cost of quality	100%	100%

Source: A. V. Feigenbaum, *Total Quality Control,* 3rd ed. (New York: McGraw-Hill, 1983), p. 112; and Joseph M. Juran and F. M. Gryna, *Quality Planning and Analysis* (New York: McGraw-Hill, 1970), p. 60.

investments in machinery, technology, as well as education and training programs, which are designed to reduce the number of defects that the process produces. Also included in this category are the costs to administer the firm's quality program, data collection and analysis, and vendor certification. All of the quality gurus strongly support investments in this category because the returns are so high, including the benefits gained from increasing customer satisfaction and reducing scrap losses and rework expenses.

cost of detection/ appraisal

Costs associated with the test and inspection of subassemblies and products after they have been made.

Cost of Detection/Appraisal

Costs of detection or **appraisal** are those costs associated with evaluating the quality of the product. Costs included in this category are incoming material inspection, tests and inspection throughout the transformation process, test equipment maintenance, and products destroyed during destructive testing.

Cost of Failure

cost of failure

Costs associated with the failure of a defective product.

Costs of failure pertain to nonconforming and nonperforming products. Also included in this category are the costs associated with the evaluation and disposition of customer complaints. As stated earlier, we further subdivide failure costs into internal and external failure costs.

internal failure costs

Costs associated with producing defective products that are identified prior to shipment.

Internal failure costs are identified as those costs that are incurred when defects are produced within the system. They include only those costs attributed to defects that are found before the products are delivered to the customer. Examples of internal failure costs include scrap, rework/repair, retesting of reworked/repaired products, downtime, yield losses due to process variability, and the disposition of the defective items.

external failure costs

Costs associated with producing defective products that are delivered to the customer.

External failure costs are those costs that are incurred after the product has been delivered to the customer. Included in this category are the cost of returned material, warranty charges, field survey costs, legal expenses from lawsuits, customer dissatisfaction, loss of revenues due to downgrading products as seconds, and costs of allowances/concessions made to customers.

It is generally now recognized that increased spending on prevention provides significant returns in the form of reductions in detection/appraisal and failure costs—and in the overall cost of quality. Thus the old adage, "An ounce of prevention is worth a pound of cure" is also most appropriate for quality.

At the same time, Deming suggested that total quality costs can be decreased by improving the process itself. An improved process reduces both the number of defects produced and the costs of prevention and appraisal. A comparison of Deming's model with the previously traditional view toward quality is presented in Exhibit 6.5.

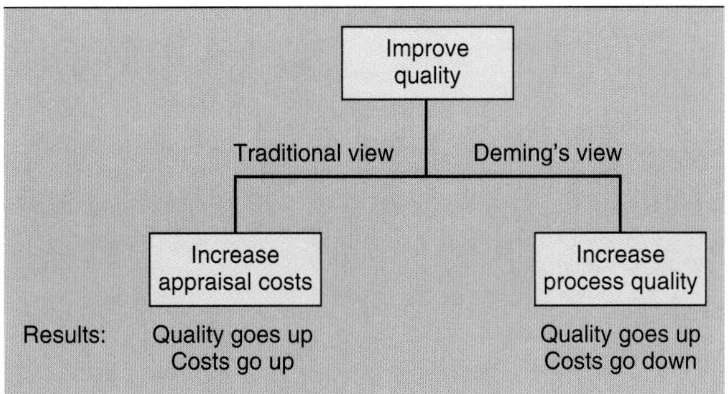

Exhibit 6.5
Two Views of the Cost of Improved Quality

When defective products or services are eliminated, there are two direct effects. First, there are more good units produced (and capacity is therefore increased) and second, each unit produced costs less because the cost of the failures is both reduced and also spread over a larger number of nondefective goods or services. For example, if a plastic injection molding process scraps 15 defective pen barrels out of every 100 that are produced, the cost to produce the 15 scrapped units must be spread over the remaining 85 units—and there are only 85 units available to sell. If the quality of the process is improved and only five units are scrapped per 100 produced, then there are 95 units that are available for sale, and the cost of only the five scrapped units is now spread over the 95 good units rather than 85 as was previously the case.

A bank, for example, that set out to improve quality and reduce its costs found that it also had boosted productivity. The bank developed this productivity measure for the loan processing area: the number of loans processed divided by the resources required (labor cost, computer time, loan forms). Before the quality improvement program, the productivity index was 0.2660 [2,080/($11.23 × 640 hours + $0.05 × 2,600 forms + $500 for systems costs)]. After the quality improvement project was completed, labor time fell to 546 hours and the number of forms processed increased to 2,100 for a change in the index to 0.3088, or an increase in productivity of 16 percent.

Service Guarantees

Warrantees are common for products such as automobiles, washing machines, and televisions. Such warrantees guarantee that these products will work throughout a stated period of time or else they will be either repaired or replaced free of charge. Less common are guarantees for services. Nevertheless, Christopher Hart has suggested that the service guarantee can be a powerful tool for obtaining feedback from customers on how service operations are performing.

In order for a service guarantee to be effective, it must contain the following elements: It must be (*a*) unconditional, (*b*) easy to understand and communicate, (*c*) meaningful, (*d*) easy and painless to invoke, and (*e*) easy and quick to collect on. For example, at FedEx, the service guarantee is simple: if your package is not delivered on time, then there is no charge. At L. L. Bean, a leading mail-order firm located in Freeport, Maine, the guarantee is "100 percent satisfaction in every way." If you buy an L. L. Bean product and are not satisfied with it, you can return it for an exchange or a refund, regardless of how long you have owned it.

From a quality standpoint, the unconditional service guarantee provides management with continuous customer feedback. If it is easy to invoke and collect on, then customers

Operations Management in Practice

A GUARANTEE OF SERVICE EXCELLENCE (GOSE) PLAYS A MAJOR ROLE IN THE SUCCESS OF NORTHEAST DELTA DENTAL

Northeast Delta Dental, a nonprofit dental insurance company located in Concord, New Hampshire, attributes much of its growth and success in recent years to its Guarantee of Service Excellence (GOSE).

According to Tom Raffio, president of Northeast Delta Dental, having a service guarantee is ". . . like putting water through a hose. You turn on the pressure and you find out where all the holes are. An unconditional service guarantee like GOSE, when properly designed and implemented, quickly identifies all of the flaws that exist in the current system."

The Guarantee of Service Excellence Program at Northeast Delta Dental consists of the following seven elements:

1. Smooth implementation to Northeast Delta Dental.
2. Exceptional customer service.
3. Quick processing of claims.
4. No inappropriate billing by participating dentists.
5. Accurate and quick turnaround of identification cards.
6. Timely employee booklets.
7. Marketing service contacts.

With each element, the guarantee is clearly explained and the customer is refunded a stated amount when the service in that element is not provided—no hassles, no questions asked!

Source: Special thanks to Tom Raffio, president and CEO of Northeast Delta Dental.

will use the service guarantee to voice their complaints rather than just taking their business elsewhere. (See OM in Practice box.)

Organizationwide Quality Initiatives

As the quality movement gained momentum, managers looked to develop initiatives that would allow them to integrate quality throughout their entire organizations. The purpose of these initiatives is to provide a common framework for identifying quality issues with the goal of improving the overall quality of the firm's goods and services. Two of the more successful quality initiatives that been adopted by many firms are total quality management and six sigma.

total quality management (TQM)

Approach for integrating quality at all levels of an organization.

Total Quality Management

Total quality management (TQM) can be viewed as an organizationwide approach that focuses on producing high-quality goods and services. TQM, when properly used, is an integral part of an organization, not a separate, stand-alone program, and it encompasses all of the functional areas and levels within the organization, including suppliers.

Elements of TQM There are four primary elements that are integral to every successful TQM program: (*a*) leadership, (*b*) employee involvement, (*c*) product/process excellence, and (*d*) customer focus.

Leadership. The leadership provided by an organization's management is a major cornerstone in the development and implementation of a successful TQM program. When properly executed, a TQM program is companywide, transcends the traditional functional areas, and involves all of the firm's employees. It therefore requires vision, planning, and communication, all of which are the responsibility of top management. Studies have indicated that total commitment from management is considered to be a critical element in successfully implementing such programs.

Top management can demonstrate its commitment to a TQM program in several ways. These include incorporating TQM into the firm's overall strategy and demonstrating by actions as well as by words that quality is the number one operating priority of the organization.

Employee involvement. Employee involvement is another critical element in successfully implementing a TQM program. By involving all employees in the decision-making process, management is able to receive inputs from those nearest the problems and in the best position to recommend viable solutions. Employee involvement, which appears to be prevalent in most world-class operations, also takes advantage of the skills and knowledge of all employees.

A key element in employee involvement is that each worker assumes the responsibility for inspecting the quality of his or her own work. This is referred to as quality at the source and extends beyond the worker to include the work group, all departments, and the suppliers of parts and services to the organization. This view changes the often-adversarial practice of having a QC inspector, typically from the QC department, making decisions about good or bad quality.

Product/process excellence. Product/process excellence involves the quality of the product's design and analysis of field failures. It also includes statistical process control (SPC) and other analytical tools (which are discussed later in this chapter and in Supplement 6).

Process control is concerned with monitoring quality *while the product is being produced or the service is being performed.* Typical objectives of process control plans are to provide timely information on whether currently produced items are meeting design specifications and to detect shifts in the process that signal that future products may not meet the customer's requirements. The actual control phase of process control occurs when corrective action is taken, such as when a worn part is replaced, a machine is overhauled, or a new supplier is found. Process control concepts, especially statistically based control charts, are used in services as well as in manufacturing.

continuous improvement

Concept that recognizes that quality improvement is a journey with no end and that there is a need for continually looking for new approaches for improving quality.

An underlying philosophy in achieving product/process excellence is the concept of **continuous improvement.** This has a general meaning as well as a specific TQM meaning. Its general meaning is an ongoing effort to improve in every part of the organization and all of its outputs. Its more specific meaning focuses on continual improvement in the processes by which work is accomplished.

In Japanese companies, the concept of continuous improvement is referred to as *kaizen.* It can be interpreted to mean a systematic approach to eliminating errors and improving the quality of the product that is delivered to the customer. One of the ways kaizen is achieved is through the use of **poka-yoke** or foolproofing in the methods that are used to make the products. United Electric Controls in Watertown, Massachusetts, a winner of the Shingo Prize in Manufacturing, attributes much of its quality improvements to introducing poka-yoke into its manufacturing processes. In manufacturing, poka-yoke often requires that a part be redesigned so that it can fit only one way. As stated earlier, a good example of poka-yoke in services is the bathroom onboard an airplane. Here the light will not go on until the door is locked, ensuring privacy. Also, height bars at amusement parks ensure proper height for the rides.

poka-yoke

Simple devices, such as automatic shutoff valves or fixtures to orient parts, that prevent defects from being produced.

Customer focus. The customer's perception of quality must be taken into account in setting acceptable quality levels. In other words, a product isn't reliable unless the customer says it's reliable and a service isn't fast unless the customer says it's fast. Translating customer quality demands into specifications requires marketing (or product development) to accurately determine what the customer wants and product designers to develop a product (or service) that can be produced to consistently achieve that desired level of quality. This, in turn, requires that we have an operational definition of quality, an understanding of its various dimensions, and a process for including the voice of the customer in those specifications. The quality of a product or service may be defined by the quality of its design (product quality) and the quality of its conformance to that design (process quality). **Design quality** refers to the inherent value of the product in the marketplace and is thus a strategic decision for the firm, as discussed earlier.

design quality

Specific characteristics of the product that determine its value in the marketplace.

Conformance quality refers to the degree to which the product or service meets design specifications. It, too, has strategic implications, but the execution of the activities involved in achieving conformance are of a tactical day-to-day nature. It should be evident that a product or service can have high design quality but low conformance quality, and vice versa.

conformance quality

Defines how well the product is made with respect to its design specifications.

The operations function and the quality organization within the firm are primarily concerned with quality of conformance. Achieving all the quality specifications is typically the responsibility of manufacturing management (for products) and branch operations management (for services).

Both design quality and conformance quality should provide products that meet the customer's objectives for those products. This is often termed the product's *fitness for use,* and it entails identifying those dimensions of the product (or service) that the customer wants and developing a quality control program to ensure that these dimensions are met.

Implementing TQM As seen in Exhibit 6.6, companies have adopted several approaches to implementing TQM. However, only when quality is totally integrated into the day-to-day operations of the firm can a TQM program be truly successful.

The implementation of a successful quality program throughout an organization is not a simple undertaking. As a result, there have been many failed attempts. Edward Fuchs identifies two major causes for the inability of firms to successfully adopt an organization-wide quality program: "lack of focus on strategic planning and core competencies, and obsolete, outdated cultures."[6]

In addition to these two underlying causes, companies have identified the following obstacles that need to be addressed if a quality program is to be truly successful within an organization:[7]

- Lack of a companywide definition of quality.
- Lack of a formalized strategic plan for change.
- Lack of a customer focus.
- Poor interorganizational communication.
- Lack of real employee empowerment.
- Lack of employee trust in senior management.

[6]Edward Fuchs, "Total Quality Management from the Future," *Quality Management Journal,* October 1993, pp. 26–34.

[7]Gary Salegna and Farzaneh Fazel, "Obstacles to Implementing Quality," *Quality Progress,* July 2000, pp. 53–57.

Exhibit 6.6

Three Schools of Total Quality Management Programs

	Total Quality Harangue	Total Quality Tools	Total Quality Integration
Noticeable characteristics	Exhortation, lots of talk about quality; generally a marketing campaign intended to create buying signals without incurring the expense of fundamental changes	Introduction of specific tools; viz., statistical process control, employee involvement programs, and/or quality circles	Serious review of all elements of the organization; efforts to involve suppliers and customers
Rationale	Management may believe that quality is better than generally known or may be creating a smoke screen; viz., "everybody's doing it," "it's the thing to do these days"	Valued customers insist on implementation of a team program; or competitors have introduced successful programs creating a "bandwagon" effect	Systematic effort to improve earnings through differentiation based on quality
Responsibility for quality	Unchanged; specific function within organization assigned responsibility for quality	Lower-level members of organization regardless of function	Shared responsibility; senior management accepts responsibility to create an environment encouraging quality
Structural changes	None; the organization remains unchanged	Incremental changes within functional areas or processes	Dramatic changes integrating functions within the organization and involving customers and suppliers in the total production process
Representative employee attitudes and behaviors	Total quality is just a fad, "this too shall pass"; smart employees learn to keep their heads down—they talk about quality when expected to but know that business continues as usual	"It's a nice idea, too bad management isn't really serious about quality"; clever employees participate in seminars and use appropriate tools to fix obvious flaws in their areas of responsibility, but are careful not to rock the boat	"At last, we've got a chance to do it right"; committed employees study the total quality vision, actively search for opportunities to improve performance across the organization, challenge conventional assumptions, and seek to involve customers and suppliers
Role of the quality professional	Police officer, watchdog	Resident expert, advisor	Strategic leaders, change agent

Source: Eric W. Skopec, Strategic Visions Inc. (used by permission).

- View of quality program as a quick fix.
- Drive for short-term financial results.
- Politics and turf issues.

Six Sigma

Motorola, in large part to respond to the very-high-quality products that were being manufactured in Japan, introduced a quality improvement program during the 1980s known as

Exhibit 6.7
Quality Performance Levels for Various Processes

Process Description	Quality Performance Level
IRS phone-in tax advice	2.2σ
Restaurant bills, doctors' prescription writing, payroll processing	2.9σ
Average company	3.0σ
Airline baggage handling	3.2σ
Best-in-class companies	5.7σ
U.S. Navy aircraft accidents	5.7σ
Watch off by 2 seconds in 31 years	6.0σ
Airline industry fatality rate	6.2σ

Source: Dave Harrold, "Designing for Six Sigma Capability," *Control Engineering,* January 1999.

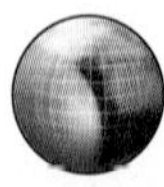

six sigma

A statistically-based, structured methodology for identifying and eliminating causes of errors in a process.

six sigma. The goal of a six sigma program is to reduce process variation to the point where there are only 3.4 defects per million opportunities. (The quantitative analysis associated with six sigma is presented in the supplement to this chapter.) Six sigma is especially im portant for those businesses such as services and high-volume manufacturing firms that involve a very large number of operations or transactions on a continuous basis. For example, if the following processes were only 99 percent reliable (which corresponds to 4σ quality), they would have the respective number of defects:

- 20,000 pieces of mail lost every hour.
- Unsafe drinking water almost 15 minutes every day.
- 5,000 incorrect surgery operations every week.
- Two short or long landings at most major airports each day.
- 200,000 incorrect drug prescriptions filled every year.
- No electricity for almost seven hours every month.[8]

For comparison purposes, Exhibit 6.7 provides some benchmarks of the quality of various processes in terms of their relative levels of performance.

Over the years, six sigma has evolved into a management tool to reduce all forms of waste within an organization. The methodologies of a six-sigma program provide a common language and set of goals that can be used throughout an organization.

In order to ensure that customers' requirements are being met on a consistent basis, organizations need to develop processes that are capable of meeting these requirements. The managerial thrust of a six-sigma program is to effectively provide a framework and associated methodologies to analyze and evaluate business processes with the overall goal of reducing the waste. The six-sigma improvement process typically begins with identifying a problem to be solved and then defining a project to solve that problem. The process used by the project team is often referred to as DMAIC, which stands for **d**efine, **m**easure, **a**nalyze, **i**mprove, and **c**ontrol.

Six sigma, as with any organizational quality initiative, requires the commitment of top management and the alignment of incentives in order for it to succeed. At organizations like General Electric, many of its top executives have their incentive bonuses tied to six-sigma performance.

[8] *Source:* Motorola.

Operations Management in Practice

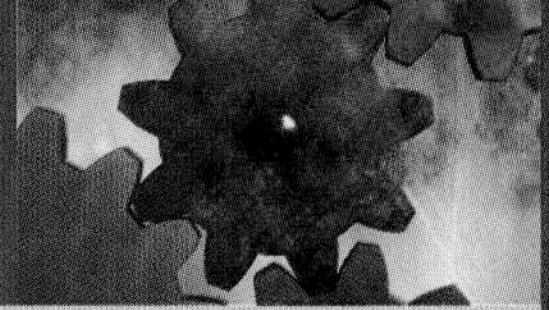

SIX SIGMA IS A KEY FACTOR TO SUCCESS AT GENERAL ELECTRIC

Nowhere has the impact of six sigma on an organization been more clearly evident than at General Electric, where it has been embraced, since 1995, first by Jack Welch, and now by Jeff Immelt , GE's current CEO. Welch attributed GE's sustained increase in sales and profit margins in large part to its six-sigma program. In recent years, GE has saved more than $2 billion annually as a direct result of its six-sigma program through the elimination of defects. Today, six sigma is considered to be an integral part of GE's corporate culture, embedding quality thinking at every level and in every operation around the world.

At GE, six sigma is a highly disciplined process that provides a common language throughout the company for identifying and then systematically eliminating errors, with the goal of providing its customers with near-perfect products and services. All of its employees are trained in the strategy, statistical tools, and techniques of six-sigma quality.

GE has identified three key elements in its six-sigma quality program: the customer, the process, and the employee. GE recognizes the need to delight its customers in every facet of its business, including on-time delivery, product performance, service, and reliability. GE looks at its processes from the customer's perspective, what is often referred to as "outside-in thinking." By understanding the customer's view, GE can add significant value to the goods and services it currently provides. Involving all employees is an essential ingredient to GE's approach to quality, and therefore GE provides its employees with opportunities and incentives to focus their efforts on satisfying customers.

Source: GE's six-sigma website, www.ge.com/sixsigma.

A key element in the successful implementation of a six-sigma program involves the selection and training of the workforce throughout the organization so that the philosophy of reducing variation and waste and improving output is a part of everyone's everyday work. To accomplish this, key employees, referred to as "Black Belts" are chosen to lead the major improvement projects. These six-sigma project leaders receive intensive training in quantitative improvement tools using statistical software and also are trained on teamwork and communication.

Another key ingredient in the success of six-sigma programs is the impressive cost savings that have been achieved as a direct result of their implementation. At Honeywell, the cost savings are more than $2 billion since it first implemented six sigma in 1994. At GE, six sigma generated more than $2 billion in savings in 1999 alone, and Black and Decker's six-sigma productivity savings increased to $75 million in 2000.[9]

Recognizing and Rewarding Quality

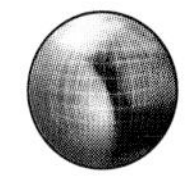

To encourage and promote high-quality goods and services, government and quasi-government organizations have begun recognizing those firms that provide outstanding levels of quality in the goods and services that they provide. Most countries, in fact, have some sort of quality award to recognize outstanding companies. In Japan for example, it is the Deming Prize, while in the European Union it is the European Quality Award. Some of these national awards, such as the Malcolm Baldrige National Quality Award (MBNQA) in the U.S., recognize outstanding firms in several categories. Other forms of recognition, such as ISO 9000, which is international, take the form of certification.

[9]Joseph A. DeFeo, "The Tip of the Iceberg," *Quality Progress,* May 2001, pp. 29–37.

Malcolm Baldrige National Quality Award (MBNQA)

Background The Malcolm Baldrige National Quality Improvement Act was passed in 1987 to recognize total quality management in American industry. The Malcolm Baldrige National Quality Award (MBNQA), named after Malcolm Baldrige, who served as secretary of commerce from 1981 until his death in 1987, represents the United States government's endorsement of quality as an essential part of successful business strategy.

Without question, the MBNQA and its comprehensive criteria for evaluating total quality in an organization have had considerable impact. As seen in Exhibit 6.8, the MBNQA, until recently, has been awarded in three categories: manufacturing, services, and small business. Beginning in 1999, two additional categories were added: healthcare and education. The MBNQA in education were presented for the first time in 2001 to three educational organizations. There were (*a*) the Chugach School District in Anchorage, Alaska, (*b*) the Pearl River School District in New York, and (*c*) the University of Wisconsin–Stout.

Baldrige criteria

Process for assessing the overall quality of an organization and for determining the winner(s) of the Malcolm Baldrige National Quality Award.

The Baldrige Criteria To evaluate and recognize effective quality systems, Baldrige administrators created a comprehensive process and set of quality criteria based on the comments and observations of experts from throughout the country. The **Baldrige criteria** consequently reflects the combined experience and wisdom of many people. As a set of principles, it is nondenominational in the sense that it does not favor any one system. Instead, the Baldrige criteria are designed to be flexible, evaluating quality on three broad dimensions: (*a*) the soundness of the approach or systems, (*b*) the deployment or integration of those systems throughout the entire organization, and (*c*) the results generated by those systems.

The Baldrige quality criteria focus on seven broad topical areas that are dynamically related, as seen in Exhibit 6.9, which provides an integrated framework for the Baldrige criteria.

In short, the Baldrige criteria create an integrated set of indicators of excellence and continuity that describe total quality. In the Baldrige view, total quality is a value system. It is a way of life, an approach to doing business that affects every corporate decision and permeates the entire organization.

When a company applies for the Baldrige Award or uses the Baldrige criteria internally to evaluate its quality program, its organization must address 20 subcategories that fall under the seven broad topical areas. Each topical area and subcategory are weighted according to general importance (see Exhibit 6.10).

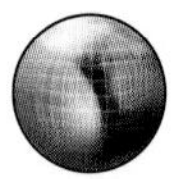

For evaluation purposes, a maximum of 1,000 points are allocated for the seven Baldrige quality categories. Just as the Japanese stress the importance of both the means and ends when considering quality, the Baldrige criteria tie approximately half their points to the quality process (methods and means) and half to the results (ends and trends). The means or process is a leading indicator of the ends that will be attained. In turn, the results verify that the appropriate process is in place and being used effectively.

Exhibit 6.8

Malcolm Baldrige National Quality Award Winners

Year	Manufacturing	Service	Small Business
2001	Clark American Checks, Inc.		Pal's Sudden Service
2000	Dana Corp.—Spicer Driveshaft Division KARLEE Company, Inc.	Operations Management International, Inc.	Los Alamos National Bank
1999	STMicroelectronics, Inc.—Region Americas	BI The Ritz-Carlton Hotel Company, L.L.C.	Sunny Fresh Foods
1998	Boeing Aircraft and Tanker Programs Solar Turbines, Inc.		Texas Nameplate Company, Inc.
1997	3M Dental Products Division Solectron Corporation	Merrill Lynch Credit Corporation Xerox Business Services	
1996	ADAC Laboratories	Dana Commercial Credit	Custom Research, Inc. Trident Precision Manufacturing, Inc.
1995	Armstrong World Industries, Inc., Building Products Operations Corning Inc., Telecommunications Products Division		
1994		AT&T Consumer Communications Services GTE Directories Corporation	Wainwright Industries, Inc.
1993	Eastman Chemical Company		Ames Rubber Corporation
1992	AT&T Network Systems Group, Transmission Systems Business Unit Texas Instruments, Inc.—Defense Systems & Electronics Group	AT&T Universal Card Services The Ritz-Carlton Hotel Company	Granite Rock Company
1991	Solectron Corporation Zytec Corporation		Marlow Industries, Inc.
1990	Cadillac Motor Car Company IBM Rochester	Federal Express Corporation	Wallace Company, Inc.
1989	Milliken & Company Xerox Corp., Business Products & Systems		
1988	Motorola, Inc. Westinghouse Electric Corp.—Commercial Nuclear Fuel Division		Globe Metallurgical, Inc.

Source: National Institute of Science and Technology (NIST) website, www.quality.nist.gov.

Benefits of the Baldrige Quality Criteria For companies using them, the Baldrige criteria serve many purposes. Indeed, part of the Baldrige criteria's power lies in the fact that they can be applied in many different ways to organizations whose quality improvement programs are of different maturities.

As a practical tool for assessing operations, the Baldrige guidelines can be used to

1. Help define and design a total quality system.
2. Evaluate ongoing internal relationships among departments, divisions, and functional units within an organization.

Exhibit 6.9

The Integrated Framework of the Baldrige Award Criteria

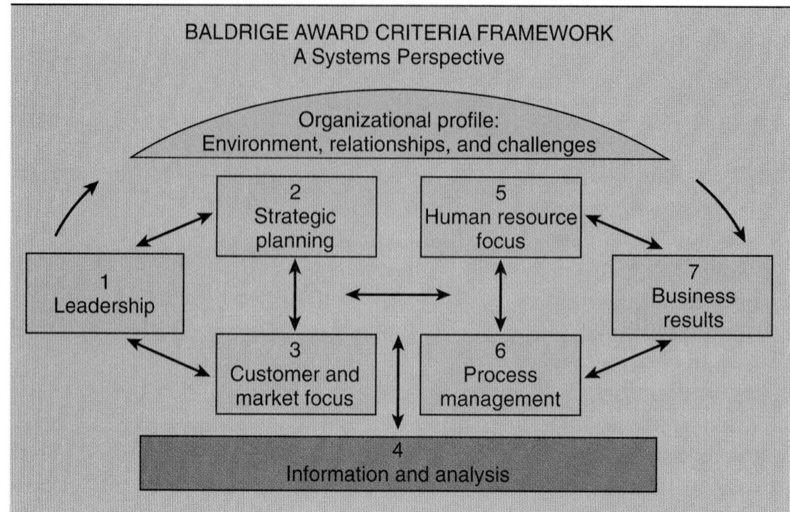

Source: 2002 Criteria for Performance Excellence, U.S. Dept. of Commerce, Baldrige National Quality Program, National Institute of Standards and Technology, Gaithersburg, MD 20899. (www.quality.nist.gov)

Exhibit 6.10

2001 Award Criteria—Item Listing

Categories/Items	Points Values
1.0 Leadership	120
2.0 Strategic planning	85
3.0 Customer and market focus	85
4.0 Information and analysis	90
5.0 Human resource focus	85
6.0 Process management	85
7.0 Business results	450
Total Points	1,000

Source: 2002 Criteria for Performance Excellence, U.S. Dept. of Commerce, Baldrige National Quality Program, National Institute of Standards and Technology, Gaithersburg, MD 20899. (www.quality.nist.gov)

3. Assess and assist outside suppliers of goods and services to a company.
4. Assess customer satisfaction.

Early-stage companies can literally use the Baldrige guidelines as a checklist or blueprint to help them design their overall quality programs. Middle-stage companies can use them as a road map to guide them down the road to continued quality improvement. Finally, advanced-stage companies can use them as an evaluative tool to help fine-tune their quality programs and benchmark them against other industry and world leaders.

The Baldrige guidelines also provide a common language for discussing quality across companies, functional areas, industries, and disciplines. By providing a broad, flexible approach to assessing total quality, the Baldrige system fosters improved information sharing and overall communications. These activities, in turn, lead employees and management to develop a shared meaning of total quality that can be built into the organization's goals and policies. From such shared meaning develops an organizational value system that is customer-focused, quality-driven, and central to the culture of the company. So deeply does

Operations Management in Practice

QUALITY PAYS

Since 1995, The National Institute for Standards and Technology (NIST) has compared its "Baldrige Index" with the Standard & Poor's (S&P) 500 Index. The Baldrige Index is a fictitious stock fund consisting of publicly held US companies that received the Malcolm Baldrige National Quality Award between 1990 and 2000. In 1995, the Baldrige Index outperformed the S&P 500 Index by 6.5 to 1, and it has beaten the S&P 500 Index every year since.

NIST also tracked a group made up of whole company winners and the parent companies of 18 subsidiary winners. This group outperformed the S&P 500 by 4.2 to 1, achieving a 685 percent return on investment, compared to a 163 percent return on investment for the S&P 500.

Further evidence that quality pays was demonstrated in a study conducted by Professors Kevin Hendricks and Vinod Singhal, which showed that the stock price of companies which had effectively instituted TQM programs outperformed the S&P 500 Index by 34 percent over a five year period.

These gains can be directly attributed to the application of the Baldrige criteria within these companies. For example:

- GTE Directories Corporation (1994 winner) reduced publishing errors by 9 percent between 1991 and 1993 and lowered billing and collection errors by 71 percent.
- Ames Rubber Corporation (1993) reports that by sharing their quality techniques, their suppliers have achieved a 99.9 percent quality and on-time delivery status.
- AT&T Network Transmission Group, Transmission Systems Business Unit (1992) improved customer satisfaction in part by a 15 percent improvement in product reliability.
- The Ritz-Carlton Hotel Company (1992 and 1998) has eliminated $75 million in costs through the initiation of improvement projects.

Sources:

National Institute for Standards and Technology.

Vinod R. Singhal, "Boosting the Bottom Line Over Time: Study Shows That TQM Pays Off in Higher Stock Prices and Profitability," *Competitive,* vol. 8, no. 2, summer 1999, American Society for Quality (ASQ), pp. 1,4.

Motorola believe in the value of total quality control that the company has required all 3,500 of its suppliers to apply for the Baldrige Award, as tangible evidence of their commitment to total quality management, or lose Motorola's business.

Most important, as seen in the OM in Practice box, those firms that have won the MBNQA have increased the value of their stock significantly.

Award Process Baldrige applications are scored by quality experts from business, consulting, and academia. Of the 1,000 points that can possibly be awarded on the overall application, none of the applicants received more than 751 points in 1994. A good company usually falls in the 500 range on the Baldrige scoring.

Only about 10 percent of the applicants become Baldrige finalists and receive site visits from a team of examiners. From this group of finalists, the Baldrige winners are chosen. All companies applying for the award receive from the examiners written feedback reports summarizing the examiners' findings of the company's organizational strengths and weaknesses.

The Baldrige guidelines have proven to be useful and inspirational to scores of companies at all different stages of developing and deploying total quality systems. Moreover, the award itself has brought international attention and prestige to those American companies that have clearly demonstrated their preeminent leadership in total quality management.

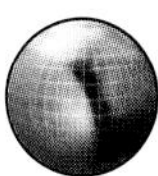

The experience of the award's winners suggests that companies throughout the country—indeed, around the world—are deeply interested and concerned about quality. In fact, many of the leading companies in the United States that plan to do business in the European Union (EU) are adopting the Baldrige Award criteria as their vision to be followed beyond the basic requirements of the ISO 9000 standards.

ISO 9000

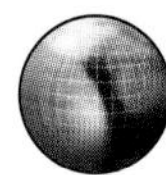

During the 1980s and into the 1990s, organizations around the world became more concerned about efficiently and effectively meeting the needs of their customers. Though national quality awards like the Deming Prize in Japan and the Malcolm Baldrige National Quality Award in the United States had been bestowed on companies that had achieved high quality in their goods and services, increasing international trade made universal standards for quality more important. However, until 1987, there was no standardized way for supplier organizations around the world to demonstrate their quality practices or to improve the quality of their manufacturing or service processes. In that year, the International Organization for Standardization (ISO) published its first standards for quality management.

The International Organization for Standardization ISO, headquartered in Geneva, Switzerland, is made up of representatives from each of the national standards bodies from over 90 countries. ISO and the International Electrotechnical Commission (IEC), both nongovernmental organizations, work together to develop and publish voluntary standards, introducing as many as 800 new and revised standards each year. In 1986, after several years of development, ISO Technical Committee 176 completed the **ISO 9000 series quality standards.** It immediately became apparent that the ISO 9000 standards were different from the usual engineering standards, which often related to units of measure, standardization of terminology, and methods of testing. Instead, these new standards incorporated the belief that management practice can be standardized to the benefit of both the producers of goods and services and their customers.

ISO 9000 series quality standards

International set of standards for documenting the processes that an organization uses to produce its goods and services.

The ISO 9000 Series of Standards The purpose of the ISO 9000 standards is to satisfy the customer organizations' quality assurance requirements and to increase the level of confidence of the customer organizations in their suppliers. The first major revisions to the ISO 9000 standards were completed in December 2000 with the issuance of the following three new standards that replaced the previously existing standards:[10]

- *ISO 9001:2000—Quality Management Systems—Requirements.* This standard is used to demonstrate the conformity of a quality management system to meet the requirements of customers and third parties. This standard is used for the certification of a firm's quality management systems.
- *ISO 9004:2000—Quality Management Systems—Guidelines for Performance Improvement.* This standard provides organizations with guidelines that can be used to establish a quality management system that is focused not only on meeting customer requirements but also on improving performance.
- *ISO 9000:2000—Quality Management Systems—Fundamentals and Standards.* This standard provides the terminology and definitions used in the first two standards.

[10]John E. West, "Implementing ISO 9001:2000," *Quality Progress,* May 2001, pp. 65–70.

ISO 9000 standards played a particularly important role in the formation of the European Union because they promoted a single worldwide quality standard that would foster international trade and cooperation. Before long, organizations recognized that service management also could be improved through the application of the fundamentals of management practice that were set forth in the ISO 9000 standards.

ISO 9000 Certification In the United States, there are three ways an organization can become ISO 9000 certified. A company can audit itself against the appropriate standards and issue a conformance statement to achieve *first-party* certification. Customers can audit their suppliers for *second-party* certification, which can mean considerable duplication of effort because most customers will have similar requirements for their suppliers. Companies also can be assessed by *third-party* registrars for ISO 9000 certification.

The role of the registrars. The quality processes that are used by firms seeking third-party ISO 9000 are assessed by an external organization called a registrar; the individuals from the registrar who conduct the assessment are called auditors. To govern the process in the United States, ASQ has established a separate corporation called the Registration Accreditation Board (RAB).

Registrars apply to the RAB, which reviews their application information in order to determine if there is a conflict of interest (for example, a consultant organization who has been advising a company on ISO certification cannot be a registrar for that company).

The ISO 9000 registration process. Supplier companies follow a fairly straightforward process to obtain ISO 9000 registration. First, the firm submits an application to a registrar. Generally this involves providing information about the size and locations of the company, its products, what products will be included in the scope of the registration, who the firm's ISO contact people will be, and how the 20 elements of the standard are documented and supported by procedures. The registrar reviews the Quality Manual prior to the on-site audit.

The next step in the audit is a preliminary assessment, which can be either an on-site document review or a mock audit lasting several days. The preliminary assessment determines the current state of operations at the supplier firm. The registrar provides feedback to the supplier firm and suggestions for corrective action. When the issues of concern have been addressed, a full audit is performed.

The full audit typically takes two or three auditors two to four days to complete. Auditors review the supplier's facility and determine how processes have been documented. The auditor's final report is submitted to the registrar's Review Board, which makes a final determination about registration. If a supplier is not approved for registration, it has the right to appeal, first to the registrar, then to the RAB. Once a supplier firm has been registered, it has the right to use its registrar's mark on stationary and advertising, along with the mark of the RAB. However, it may not use these marks on its products because ISO 9000 registration certifies processes rather than products.

Registration audits cost between $10,000 and $30,000. Companies will typically take 18 to 24 months to prepare for and undergo the registration process. Some companies undertake the registration process on their own; others engage outside consultants. The usual registration period is three years, although this can vary by registrar. During the registration period, surveillance audits are conducted every six months.

Exhibit 6.11

Overview of the EFQM Excellence Model

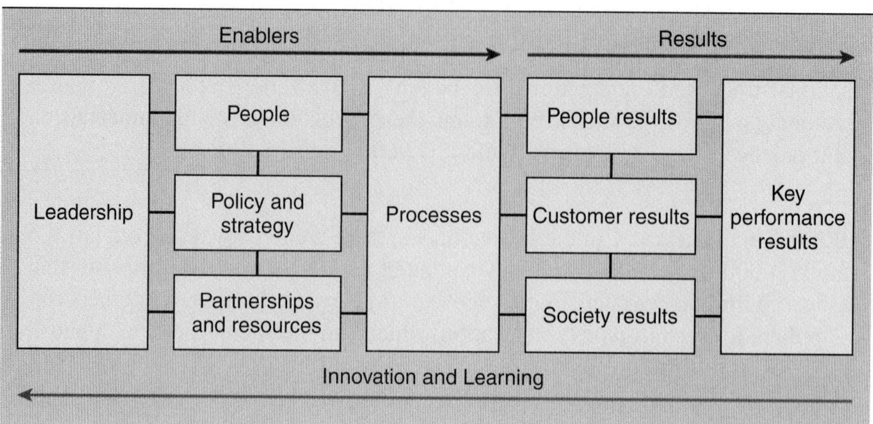

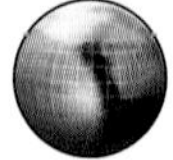

Toward a Global Market Today, over 40,000 companies are ISO certified, with the vast majority of them located within the 12 nations that currently comprise the European Union. When customer organizations have an objective way to evaluate the quality of a supplier's processes, the risk of doing business with that supplier is significantly reduced. When quality standards are truly standardized around the world, customer firms can be more confident that supplier firms will produce the goods and services that will satisfy their needs.

European Quality Award[11]

The European Quality Award (EQA) is sponsored by the European Foundation for Quality Management (EFQM), which was founded in 1988 by the presidents of 14 European companies, and with the endorsement of the European Commission. EFQM's present membership exceeds 600 organizations.

EFQM's mission is twofold:

- To stimulate and assist organizations throughout Europe to participate in improvement activities leading ultimately to excellence in customer satisfaction, employee satisfaction, impact on society, and business results.
- To support the managers of European organizations in accelerating the process of making total quality management a decisive factor for achieving global competitive advantage.

EFQM Excellence Model The EFQM has developed a framework in the form of an "Excellence Model" that can be used as a practical tool for assisting organizations to establish an appropriate management system. The EFQM is a nonprescriptive framework based on nine criteria that recognizes that there are many approaches to achieving sustainable excellence. As seen in Exhibit 6.11, five of these criteria are "enablers" and four are "results." The enabler criteria cover what an organization does, while the results criteria address what the organization achieves.

[11]EFQM website, www.efqm.org.

Exhibit 6.12 Recent Winners of the European Quality Award

Year	Category	Company
2000	Large businesses	Nokia Mobile Phones (Finland)
	Public sector	Inland Revenue, Accounting Office (United Kingdom, Scotland)
	SMEs—subsidiaries	Burton-Apta Refractory Manufacturing Ltd. (Hungary)
1999	Large businesses	Yellow Pages (United Kingdom)
	Operational units	Volvo Cars Gent (Belgium)
	Independent SMEs	DIEU, Danish International Continuing Education (Denmark)
	SMEs—subsidiaries	Servitique Network Services (France)
1998	Large businesses	TNT United Kingdom (United Kingdom)
	Independent SMEs	Schlinderhof (Germany)
	SME—subsidiaries	Beko Ticaret (Turkey)

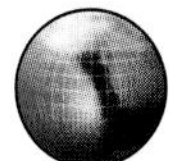

Recent EQA Winners The EQA is presented to outstanding companies in several categories. The recent winners of the EQA and the respective categories are presented in Exhibit 6.12.

The Deming Prize

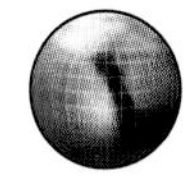

Japan initiated the Deming Prize in 1951 to recognize the importance of producing high-quality products. This award was named after W. Edwards Deming, the American statistician, after his visit to Japan in 1950 during which he gave several presentations. The Deming Prize is administered by the Union of Japanese Scientists and Engineers (JUSE).

In 1984, the Deming Prize Committee allowed foreign companies to apply for and receive the Deming Prize. Florida Power & Light was the first US company to apply for and receive the Deming Prize in 1989. As noted below, the Deming Prize is awarded to both individuals and organizations.

There are three categories of the Deming Prize:[12]

The Deming Prize for Individuals This is awarded to individuals who have made an outstanding contribution to the study of TQM or statistical methods used for TQM, or who have made an outstanding contribution in the dissemination of TQM.

The Deming Application Prize Awarded to companies or divisions within companies that have achieved distinctive performance improvement through the application of TQM in a specific year.

The Quality Control Award for Operations/Business Units Presented to business units of companies that have achieved distinctive performance improvement through the application of quality control/management in the pursuit of TQM in a specific year.

[12] *The Deming Prize Guide,* Union of Japanese Scientists and Engineers (JUSE), Tokyo, Japan, 1999.

Conclusion

The production and delivery of high-quality goods and services are critical elements in determining the long-term success of an organization. No longer is quality looked upon only from the narrow perspective of defects. Rather, managers are now recognizing that quality has many dimensions and that they need to identify those dimensions that are most important to the specific market segments that they serve.

The quality of the goods and services that are now being provided has increased significantly over the last several decades, due in large part to increased global competition. With competition expected to continue in the near future, we can likewise expect the quality of goods and services to increase.

Thus, quality management as a strategic issue should not be approached with an off-the-shelf program devised by others. Quality must be integrated internally and externally (see Exhibit 6.6). Managers are paid to use new quality concepts, but more important, to lead customization and integration of these concepts into their organizations.

Key Terms

Baldrige criteria p. 232
conformance quality p. 228
continuous improvement p. 227
cost of detection/appraisal p. 224
cost of failure p. 224
 external failure costs p. 224
 internal failure costs p. 224
cost of prevention p. 223
cost of quality p. 223
design quality p. 228
ISO 9000 series quality standards p. 236
poka-yoke p. 227
quality dimensions p. 219
quality gurus p. 214
six sigma p. 230
statistical process control (SPC) p. 215
total quality management (TQM) p. 226

Review and Discussion Questions

1. Is quality free? Debate!
2. Identify the quality dimensions for each of the following:
   a. IBM personal computer
   b. School registration process
   c. Steakhouse
   d. University
   e. Travel agency
   f. Television
3. An agreement is made between a supplier and a customer such that the supplier must ensure that all parts are within tolerance before shipment to the customer. What is the effect on the cost of quality to the customer?
4. In the situation described in Question 3, what would be the effect on the cost of quality to the supplier?
5. If line employees are required to assume the quality control function, their productivity will decrease. Discuss this.
6. "You don't inspect quality into a product; you have to build it in." Discuss the implications of this statement.
7. How could you apply the Baldrige Award criteria to your college or university?
8. How is the Baldrige award process beneficial to companies who do not win?
9. What is the major contribution of the ISO 9000 standards?
10. Compare the ISO certification process with the Malcolm Baldrige National Quality Award criteria. What are the main differences?

11. What are some of the reasons that quality initiatives fail in organizations? How can these be overcome?
12. What are some of the major reasons for the success of six sigma?
13. Find out if your home state has a quality award, and if it does, describe it.

Internet Exercise

Go to the home page of the Malcolm Baldrige National Quality Award (MBNQA), www.quality.nist.gov, and read the profile and application summary of one of the award winners since 1999. Describe the company and how its focus on continuous quality improvement has impacted its business.

Bibliography

Berry, L. L.; V. A. Zeithaml; and A. Parasuraman. "Five Imperatives for Improving Service Quality." *Sloan Management Review,* no. 29 (Summer 1990), pp. 29–38.

Bounds, Greg; Lyle Yorks; Mel Adams; and Gipsie Rannet. *Total Quality Management: Towards the Emerging Paradigm.* New York: McGraw-Hill, 1994.

Crosby, Philip B. *Quality without Tears.* New York: McGraw-Hill, 1984.

DeFeo, Joseph A. "The Tip of the Iceberg." *Quality Progress,* May 2001, pp. 29–37.

Deming, W. Edwards. *Quality, Productivity and Competitive Position.* Cambridge, MA: MIT Center for Advanced Engineering Study, 1982.

Feigenbaum, A. V. *Total Quality Control.* 3rd ed. New York: McGraw-Hill, 1983.

Fuchs, Edward. "Total Quality Management from the Future." *Quality Management Journal,* October 1993, pp. 26–34.

Garvin, David. "Competing on the Eight Dimensions of Quality." *Harvard Business Review,* November–December 1987, pp. 101–109.

Gitlow, Howard; Allan Oppenheim; and Rosa Oppenheim. *Quality Management: Tools and Methods for Improvement.* 2nd ed. Burr Ridge, IL: Irwin/McGraw-Hill, 1995.

Goetsch, David L., and Stanley B. Davis. *Introduction to Total Quality: Quality Management for Production, Processes and Services.* 2nd ed. Upper Saddle River, NJ: Prentice Hall, 1997.

Harrold, Dave. "Designing for Six Sigma Capability." *Control Engineering,* January 1999.

Harry, Mikel J. "Abatement of Business Risk Is Key to Six Sigma: A Closer Link to Executive Thinking." *Quality Progress,* July 2000, pp. 72–76.

Hart, Christopher W. L. "The Power of Unconditional Service Guarantees." *Harvard Business Review,* July–August 1988, pp. 54–62.

Hoyer, R.W., and Brooke B. Y. Hoyer. "What Is Quality?" *Quality Progress,* July 2001, pp. 53–62.

Huyink, David S., and Craig Westover. *ISO 9000: Motivating the People; Mastering the Process; Achieving Registration!* Burr Ridge, IL: Irwin Professional Publishing, 1994.

Ishikawa, Kaoru. Translated by David J. Lu. *What Is Total Quality Control?—The Japanese Way.* Englewood Cliffs, NJ: Prentice Hall, 1985.

Juran, Joseph M. *Juran on Quality by Design: The New Steps for Planning Quality in Goods and Services.* New York: The Free Press, 1992.

Lucas, James M. "The Essential Six Sigma," *Quality Progress,* January, 2002, pp. 27–30.

March, A. "A Note on Quality: The Views of Deming, Juran and Crosby." Note No. 9-687-011. ICCH, Harvard Business School, Cambridge, MA, 1986.

Parasuraman, A.; L. L. Berry; and V. A. Zeithaml. "SERVQUAL: A Multiple-Item Scale for Measuring Consumer Perceptions of Service Quality." Marketing Science Institute, Cambridge, MA, 1986.

———. "Understanding, Measuring, and Improving Service Quality: Findings from a Multiphase Research Program." *Service Breakthroughs: Changing the Rules of the Game.* New York: The Free Press, 1989.

Peters, Tom. *Thriving on Chaos.* New York: Knopf, 1987.

Peters, Tom, and Robert H. Waterman Jr. *In Search of Excellence.* New York: Harper and Row, 1982.

Rabbitt, John T., and Peter A. Bergh. *The ISO 9000 Book: A Global Competitor's Guide to Compliance and Certification.* 2nd ed. White Plains, NY: Quality Resources, a Division of The Kraus Organization Limited, 1994.

Rao, Ashok; L. P. Carr et al. *Total Quality Management: A Cross Functional Perspective.* New York: John Wiley & Sons, 1996.

Reichhold, F. F., and W. E. Sasser. "Zero Defections: Quality Comes to Services." *Harvard Business Review* 68, no. 5 (September–October 1990), pp. 105–11.

Ross, Joel E. *Total Quality Management: Text, Cases and Readings.* Delray Beach, FL: St. Lucie Press, 1993.

Salegna, Gary, and Farzaneh Fazel. "Obstacles to Implementing Quality." *Quality Progress,* July 2000, pp. 53–57.

Taguchi, G. *On-Line Quality Control During Production.* Tokyo: Japanese Standards Association, 1987.

Tenner, A. R., and I. J. DeToro. *Total Quality Management.* Reading, MA: Addison-Wesley, 1992.

Turner, Joseph. "Is an Out-of-Spec Product Really Out of Spec?" *Quality Progress,* December 1990, pp. 57–59.

Walton, Mary. *Deming Management at Work.* New York: Perigree Books, 1991.

West, John E. "Implementing ISO 9001:2000." *Quality Progress,* May 2001, pp. 65–70.

Zeithaml, V. A.; L. L. Berry; and A. Parasuraman. "Communication and Control Processes in the Delivery of Service Quality." *Journal of Marketing* 52 (April 1988), pp. 35–48.

Death on the Highway: Quality Problems at Ford and Firestone

Case

On August 9, 2000, Bridgestone/Firestone, Inc., officially announced that it was voluntarily recalling 6.5 million of its Wilderness AT tires, a large portion of which had been installed on Ford's very popular sports utility vehicle (SUV), the Explorer. In the ensuing months, it was revealed that Ford Explorers that were equipped with Firestone's Wilderness AT tires had been involved in a significant number of rollover accidents resulting in more than 170 deaths and over 700 injuries on U.S. highways, and more than 40 deaths elsewhere in the world.[1]

Both Ford and Firestone began firing off verbal salvos to the media and public, each blaming the other for the accidents. Congressional investigations also were initiated to determine the causes of these accidents, with the heads of both firms called to testify. In the period following Bridgestone/Firestone's initial recall, it was revealed that multiple product-liability lawsuits had been filed against both companies.

In May 2001, 10 months after the initial recall announcement, Bridgestone/Firestone announced that it would no longer supply tires to Ford, citing "significant concerns" relating to the safety of the Explorer. A day later, Ford's then CEO Jacques Nasser announced the recall of 13 million Firestone Wilderness AT tires that had been installed on Ford Explorers and pickup trucks, noting a lack of confidence in "the future performance of these (Firestone) tires in keeping our customers safe."[2]

Without warning, when an Explorer is traveling at relatively high speeds, the tread on the Wilderness AT tires can separate from the tire, resulting in a noisy blowout. The Explorer, a heavy vehicle like many SUVs, has a high center of gravity and much of its weight is over its axles. Consequently, when a blowout occurs, the Explorer has a tendency to roll over, often causing death or serious injury to one or more of the vehicle's occupants.

In designing the Explorer to combine ruggedness, room, comfort, and a smooth ride, Ford mounted the cabin, which has all of the luxury of a relatively expensive car, on a narrow truck frame. To accomplish this, Ford needed to set both higher load limits and also lower tire pressure requirements for the Explorer. Unfortunately, while this combination may have met consumer preferences pertaining to size and aesthetics, it ignored the reality of American driving habits: Americans tend to drive fast, with little attention to tire maintenance, and to rely heavily on built-in safety features such as seatbelts, airbags, and roll-bar construction to keep them from harm in the event of an accident. While there is little or no margin of safety from vehicle rollover with underinflated tires on a vehicle such as the Explorer, Ford recommended tire pressure of 26 psi (pounds per square inch), which was lower than Firestone's recommendation of 30 psi.[3] In addition, little effort was made by either Ford or Firestone to emphasize to Explorer owners (or owners of any vehicle for that matter) the importance of maintaining adequate tire pressure. In cool weather, tires can lose 1 to 2 pounds of air pressure per month, and more in warmer weather. To compound this problem, car owners seldom check tire pressure. In fact, it was reported that 8 percent of the tires replaced during Firestone's 2000 recall had tire pressure below 23 psi.[4]

Financial Impact

Since voluntarily recalling 6.5 million tires in August 2000, Bridgestone/Firestone, Inc., Bridgestone's U.S. subsidiary and builder of the recalled tires, has posted a $510 million

Case

loss for fiscal year (FY) 2000, resulting from special charges of $750 million associated with the recall and anticipated liability damage claims. Bridgestone officials also anticipated a $200 million loss for its U.S. subsidiary in FY 2001. Shares of Japan's Bridgestone stock have lost more than half their value since the August 2000 tire recall, and Bridgestone's consolidated net profit for FY 2000 was 80 percent lower than for the previous fiscal year and its lowest profit in the past 10 years. In January 2001, the sales of Firestone replacement tires were down 40 percent from January 2000.[5]

The tire recall in August 2000 cost Ford $550 million and the company currently faces hundreds of lawsuits seeking cumulative damages of more than $590 million. Subsequent to the August 2000 recall, Ford announced a recall of more than one million Firestone tires that had been installed on Ford Explorers after August 2000, and in May 2001 it recalled an additional 13 million Wilderness AT tires that were original equipment on its SUVs and pickup trucks. It is estimated that Ford will spend $3 billion on replacing these tires, and Ford has indicated that it will take a charge of $2.1 billion in the second quarter of 2001. Ford officials have indicated that they expect a second quarter loss of 35 cents a share and have suspended their share repurchase program. Furthermore, the shortage of tires due to the May 2001 recall caused Ford to shut down its operations at the Ford Ranger truck plant for two weeks, and two Ford Explorer plants were idled for one week each.[6]

Automobile Design and Manufacture

The creation of a new automobile model involves many trade-offs. In attempting to respond to both consumer desires and competitive pressures, auto manufacturers often face many conflicting choices between their marketing, engineering, and manufacturing functions, and, unfortunately, safety. In designing the rugged, roomy, comfortable Explorer, Ford SUV engineers, due to previous management decisions, mounted the plush cabin on a narrow truck frame and front-end suspension system that was designed in the 1960s.

During prototype design and testing of the Explorer in the late 1980s, Ford was in the midst of responding to more than 800 lawsuits resulting from accidents involving rollovers of its Bronco II, which were eventually settled for approximately $2.4 billion. The Bronco II had a higher center of gravity and was a less aerodynamically stable vehicle with its unique "Twin I-Beam" suspension system. In spite of these problems, Ford decided to use this same suspension system on the Explorer, because it allowed Ford to manufacture its new SUV on existing assembly lines. The end result was a heavy vehicle with a high center of gravity, much of its weight above the axles, a rigid ladder frame, and extremely flexible leaf springs that when unsprung could release weight with great force—all precursors to rollover when a vehicle is driven too fast through tight turns and sudden changes of direction.[7]

Internal Ford memos and e-mails pertaining to the Explorer and Firestone Wilderness AT tire, which were made public during congressional investigations, revealed that Ford was aware, as early as 1987, that "light truck rollovers are 2 to 4 times the car rate" and that the developers of the SUV were urged to contemplate "any design actions that improve vehicle stability or help maintain the passenger safety in the vehicle." Ford engineers struggled with decisions relating to the Explorer's stability and handling, including its suspension system, weight and height, steering characteristics, and tire pressure. A 1989 internal Ford engineering report indicated that the Explorer prototype "demonstrated a rollover response . . . with a number of tire, tire pressure (and) suspension configurations," and a test report revealed that during handling maneuvers, this prototype had a greater tendency than even the Bronco II to lift its wheels off the ground while turning. In addition, although the safety record of the Bronco II was suspect, the test report noted that the Explorer had to be "at least equivalent to the Bronco II in these maneuvers to be considered acceptable for production." Still another internal Ford report included an observation that the Explorer's "relatively high engine position . . . prevents further significant improvement in the Stability Index (a measure of resistance to tipping) without extensive suspension, frame and sheet metal revisions." Ford engineers offered the following four alternatives for improving the stability of the Explorer as the 1990 production date approached: (1) widen the chassis by two inches, (2) lower the engine, (3) lower the recommended tire pressure, and (4) stiffen the springs. Ford's management chose to recommend a lower tire pressure of 26 pounds per square inch (psi) (although Bridgestone/Firestone's recommendation was 30 psi) and stiffen the springs.

By 1995, Ford had replaced the twin I-beam suspension, although they did not lower the engine or make the chassis wider. The new, lighter suspension system, however, raised, rather than lowered, the Explorer's center of gravity.

Ford chose to equip the Explorer with Firestone's Wilderness AT P235 tire, although internal Ford documents revealed that the Consumer Union (CU) tests that the Explorer underwent indicated "a high confidence of passing CU with Firestone's P225 tires and less confidence on the Firestone's P235" and that Ford's "management is aware of the potential risk with the P235 and has accepted that risk; the CU test is generally unrepresentative of the real world and I see no real risk in failing the CU test except what may result in the way of spurious litigation."[8]

Tire Design and Manufacture

The Wilderness AT tires that were mounted on the Explorer were produced by Firestone to Ford's specifications. Among the many decisions made when specifying tire characteristics is heat resistance. The heat resistance standards used at the time of the design of the Explorer to rate tires were established in 1968, nearly 20 years earlier, and were based on the ways in which motorists drove at that time. While nearly all SUV manufacturers equip these vehicles with "B" rated tires, Ford's specifications called for a lower-heat-resistant "C" rated tire. "C" rated tires must meet the standard of being able to endure two hours at 50 m.p.h. and an additional 90 minutes at speeds of up to 85 m.p.h. when the tire is inflated to the manufacturer's recommended pressure and the vehicle load is within the recommended load limit. The tire pressure recommended by Ford for the Wilderness AT was 26 psi, in spite of the fact that Firestone recommended a higher inflation pressure of 30 psi.[9]

Many manufacturers of steel-belted radial tires install a nylon layer between the steel belts and tread to decrease the steel belt's chafing on the tread rubber. This safety feature reduces the chance of tread separation in an otherwise properly constructed tire. During the investigation of the cause of the Explorer rollover accidents, tire experts testified that cost is the only reason not to install the nylon caps and it has been estimated by consumer advocates that the cost to include the nylon cap can range from pennies to as much as $1.00 per tire. The Firestone Wilderness AT tires that were on Explorers did not include this nylon safety layer.[10]

Introduced in the United States in the 1960s, steel-belted tires, which are stronger, last longer, and contribute to improved gas mileage, were considered to be a technology breakthrough in the tire industry. One of the problems, however, that tire makers have continuously attempted to overcome through changes in the way the belts are constructed and bonded is having the steel and rubber properly adhere to each other, which is somewhat

Case

akin to mixing oil and water. The fresher the rubber, the more adhesive it is, and the more adhesive the rubber, the better it adheres to the steel belts and other tire components.

Tires are highly engineered products with more than a dozen parts, such as treads and sidewalls, requiring very sophisticated equipment. To achieve the low costs demanded by automakers, tire manufacturers utilize highly automated, sprawling plants in order to obtain significant economies of scale. As a consequence, separate tire parts are often made in multiple locations throughout the plant, requiring large quantities of work-in-process inventory throughout the facility. The various parts are typically brought together and added, one by one, in the final assembly and fabrication operation, which takes place on massive tire machines. Scattered throughout the plant, inventories of sticky rubber often can pick up debris that can decrease the strength of the rubber.

Although the Firestone P235/75R-15 Wilderness AT tire is made at several Firestone plants in the United States, the highest level of tread separation complaints were for those tires made at Firestone's Decatur, Illinois, facility. During 1996, Firestone received 10 times more complaints related to tires made in Decatur than for the same size and model tire made at its other plants. Such complaints did fall by approximately 50 percent during 1997 and were much lower for tires built in Decatur during 1998 and 1999.[11]

With the exception of the Decatur plant, Firestone utilizes a slab system in which long sheets of the rubber used to coat the steel belts are extruded. The Decatur plant utilizes a process known as pelletizing, where rubber pellets are churned out and blended with a lubricant to create the rubber components. It has been reported that Firestone has discovered that rubber made by the pelletizing process was chemically different and weaker than that created by the slab system, with the lubricant apparently contributing to rubber breakdown and tread separation.

Former Firestone employees, including both production workers and tire inspectors at the Decatur plant during the period in which the allegedly flawed tires were produced, have made statements or have given testimony during litigation or government investigations that raise serious doubts about both the production and quality processes there. Among these assertions are that

- Workers punctured air bubbles that developed in the skim coat and sidewalls in some tires during production, after which, if the tire passed an air-leak test, it was returned to the production process.
- A chemical solvent, benzene, was added to old, dry rubber after it sat too long to restore its tackiness (excessive use of benzene can reduce the quality of the tire material).
- Relations between labor and management have been strained during and since a bitter 2½ year strike by the United Steelworkers of America, the union representing the tire workers.
- The ability and skills of replacement workers employed by Firestone during the strike were suspect.
- The 12-hour shifts required of workers coupled with high production quotas and the payment of an hourly rate based on meeting tire-production quotas caused lack of attention to quality.
- Tire inspectors often were required to examine 100 tires per hour and, consequently, tires often received little or no inspection.[12, 13, 14]

Case

In addition to these issues, the president of Bridgestone has acknowledged that the same quality control criteria were not applied equally to both its Bridgestone and Firestone tires. "If there was a problem with a Bridgestone tire, our technology staff in Tokyo would rush to the site" overseas to help out, he said. "But if a problem arose with a Firestone tire, they wouldn't do anything."[15]

Questions

1. In addition to the financial costs mentioned, what are some of the other costs, both internal and external to the firms, that can be associated with the poor quality of the Firestone tires and Ford Explorers?
2. Identify some of the management decisions at both Ford and Firestone that may have contributed to poor quality. What was the rationale for these decisions?
3. For both Ford and Firestone, identify the potential causes for the accidents that occurred.

Source:

This case describes an actual business situation and was prepared using information obtained from public sources. Neither Ford nor Firestone was contacted directly and asked to present their views on this matter.

Endnotes

1 Greenwald, John, "Tired of Each Other," *Time*, June 4, 2001, pp. 51–52.
2 Greenwald, John, "Tired of Each Other," *Time*, June 4, 2001, p. 51
3 Geyelin, Milo, "Theories Mount Regarding Root of Tire Defects," *The Wall Street Journal*, New York, NY, Aug. 23, 2000, p. B9.
4 Powers, Stephen, and Timothy Aeppel, "Firestone Ties Accidents To Weight of Explorer—Ford Denies That Load Increased Significantly," *Asian Wall Street Journal*, New York, NY, Dec. 23, 2000, p. 1.
5 Zaun, Todd, "Bridgestone's Net Fell 80% Last Year—Results Reflect Huge Loss at U.S. Unit After Firestone Recall—Outlook for Subsidiary's Sales and Bottom Line Remains Grim," *Asian Wall Street Journal*, New York, NY, Feb. 23, 2001, p. 4.
6 Kiley, David, "Ford Bites $3B Bullet to Replace Tires Firestone Viewed as Risk," *USA Today*, Arlington, VA, May 23, 2001, p. B1.
7 Ford, Royal, "Ford Lightens Up on Explorer for Safety's Sake," *Boston Globe*, Boston, MA,; Dec. 16, 2000, p. D1.
8 Greenwald, John, "Tired of Each Other," *Time*, June 4, 2001, p. 52.
9 Jenkins, Holman, W., Jr., "Tires and Torts: Parsing Out the Firestone Blame," *Asian Wall Street Journal*, New York, NY, May 31, 2001, p. 6.
10 Healey, James R., and Sara Nathan, "Could $1 Worth of Nylon Have Saved People's Lives? Experts: Caps on Steel Belts May Help Stop Shredded Tires," *USA Today*, Arlington, VA, Aug. 9, 2000, p. B1.
11 Eldridge, Earle, and Sara Nathan, "Data Point to Firestone Tires Made at Illinois Factory Ford Analysis Shows High Rate of Warranty Claims from Decatur Plant," *USA Today*, Arlington, VA, Aug. 14, 2000, p. B1.
12 Fogarty, Thomas, A., "Retirees Cite Production Practices Depositions in '92 Case May Shed Light on Recent Problems, but Company, Unions Dispute Claims," *USA Today*, Arlington, VA, Aug. 24, 2000, p. B3.
13 Aeppel, Timothy, "Ex-Firestone Workers to Testify in Suit—Retired Decature Employees Are Expected to Call Tire Inspection Rushed," *The Wall Street Journal*, New York, NY, Aug. 23, 2000, p. A3.
14 Healey James R., and Sara Nathan, "Could $1 Worth of Nylon Have Saved People's Lives? Experts: Caps on Steel Belts May Help Stop Shredded Tires," *USA Today*, Arlington, VA, Aug. 9, 2000, p. B1.
15 Tanikawa, Miki, "Bridgestone President Admits Tire Quality-Control Problems," *The New York Times*, New York, NY, Sept. 10, 2000, p. C12.

S6 Quality Control Tools for Improving Processes

Supplement Objectives

- Introduce the different quality control tools that are used for analyzing and improving the quality of processes.
- Describe in detail the two major approaches (that is, acceptance sampling and statistical process control) in which statistical analysis can be used to improve process quality.
- Define the two different types of errors that can occur when statistical sampling is used.
- Distinguish between attributes and variables with respect to the statistical analysis of processes.
- Discuss Taguchi methods and how they are different from traditional statistical quality control methods.
- Describe the quantitative methodology behind six sigma.

The Basic Quality Control Tools

There are a number of tools that can be used to collect, present, and analyze data about any kind of process, including service processes. Some of the tools described in this section are simple and straightforward to use; others require some understanding of statistics. Whatever tool is used, the goal in using it is to provide management with the proper information to make better decisions about how to design and improve process performance.

Within the quality literature, seven basic tools have been identified that can assist managers in improving the quality of their processes. These seven basic quality control (QC) tools are (*a*) process flowcharts (or diagrams), (*b*) bar charts and histograms, (*c*) Pareto charts, (*d*) scatterplots (or diagrams), (*e*) run (or trend) charts, (*f*) cause-and-effect (or fishbone) charts, and (*g*) statistical process control. The first six tools are presented in this section, along with checksheets, another tool that is used to collect data. Statistical process control is presented in detail later in this supplement.

Process Flowcharts (or Diagrams)

Process flow diagrams or *flowcharts* show each of the steps that are required to produce either a good or a service. As described previously in Chapter 5, tasks are typically depicted as rectangles, waits or inventories as inverted triangles, and decision points as diamonds. Arrows connecting these activities show the direction of flow in the process. In service operations, flowcharts often are referred to as "service blueprints."

The primary purpose for using flowchart analysis in Chapter 5 is to properly sequence the various tasks that are required to produce a given product or service and to identify any bottlenecks in the process that limit its overall capacity. The purpose of flowcharting, from a quality improvement perspective, is to identify those steps in the process that could be potential sources of error.

Checksheets

Most of us have collected data about some process by noting how frequently an event occurs and making a tick mark for a particular category in a *checksheet*. For example, if a company wanted to collect information about the various customer complaints it received on a product such as a vacuum cleaner, it would identify the different types of complaints and then note the frequency with which each complaint was made, as shown in Exhibit S6.1.

As another example of a checksheet, restaurant managers might want to collect information about the type of demand coming into the restaurant, in terms of group size, so they

Type of Complaint	Frequency
Cord too short	𝍸 ||||
Dirt bags hard to change	𝍸
Too heavy	𝍸 𝍸
Breaks down a lot	𝍸 ||
Accessories don't always work	|||
Other	||||

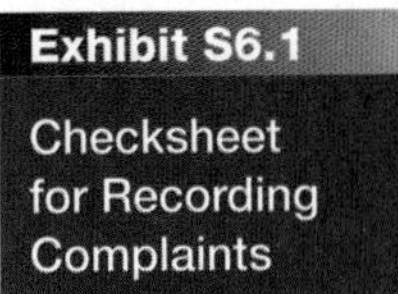

Exhibit S6.1
Checksheet for Recording Complaints

can determine how to arrange tables to meet customer demand more effectively. To collect these data, the host or hostess would use a checksheet to record the size of each group as it arrives, as shown in Exhibit S6.2.

What is most important about checksheets is that the categories not overlap and that all categories be listed; in other words, categories should be mutually exclusive and collectively exhaustive. An example of a confusing checksheet at the same restaurant would be one that, instead of listing group size, listed "couples, families, groups of friends." These categories don't capture all possibilities (business groups, for example, might not fit into any of those categories) and it is possible that the categories could overlap (families with friends). In addition, the different people collecting the data may not all make the same determination of which categories to put the same group into—and the data, when finally collected, most likely would not be very useful.

Bar Charts and Histograms

Bar charts and *histograms* visually display data variation. A bar chart is used to graph nominal data (also called "categorical" or "attribute" data), which are data that can be categorized and counted, rather than measured. For example, a manager might count the number of units produced each day on an assembly line, as shown in Exhibit S6.3.

Exhibit S6.2

Checksheet for Group Sizes in a Restaurant

Customers in Party	Count
1	||||
2	𝍸 𝍸 𝍸 𝍸 |||
3	𝍸 𝍸 ||
4	𝍸 𝍸 𝍸 𝍸 𝍸 𝍸 |
5	𝍸 𝍸 𝍸
6	𝍸 ||
>6	||

Exhibit S6.3

Bar Chart of Daily Units Produced

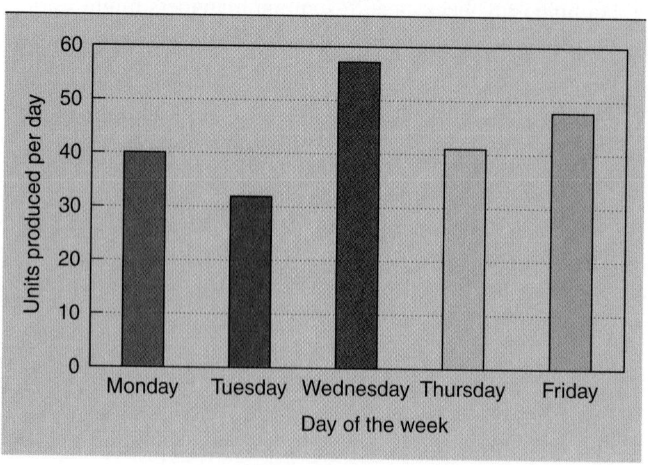

Histograms are used to display continuous data that can be measured. For example, a quality control inspector might measure the diameter of a hole on a part. Because the scale is continuous, we need to first determine how to divide it into intervals. In this case, we could use intervals of .010, .025, .050, or .100 inch, depending on how much variation there is in the diameters of the hole. If the intervals are too small, we will only have one data point in each cell; at the other extreme, if the interval is too large, we will have all the data in one cell. Histogram intervals (which also are referred to as "buckets" or "bins") must all be the same size and must not overlap. (See Exhibit S6.4.)

Pareto Charts

Pareto charts (sometimes referred to as *Pareto analysis*) are specialized bar charts. As illustrated in Exhibit S6.5, the frequency of occurrence of errors is sorted in descending order and a cumulative percent line is typically added to make it easier to determine how the errors add up. Pareto charts can help to establish priorities for action, focusing attention on those errors that occur most frequently.

Exhibit S6.5 is a Pareto chart that shows the responses to an internal hospital survey about what factors need to be changed in emergency room processes.

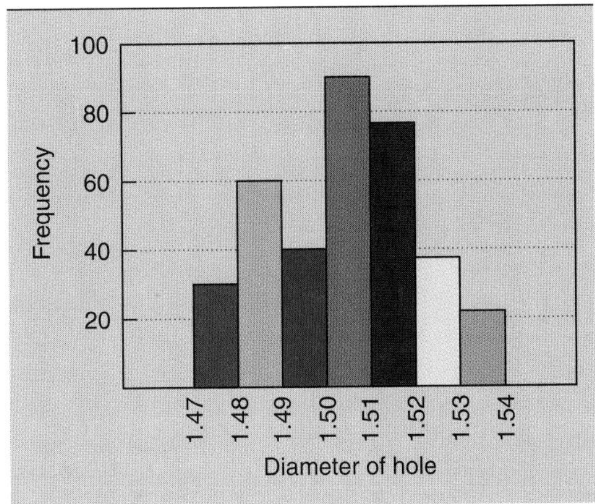

Exhibit S6.4

Histogram of Hole Diameters

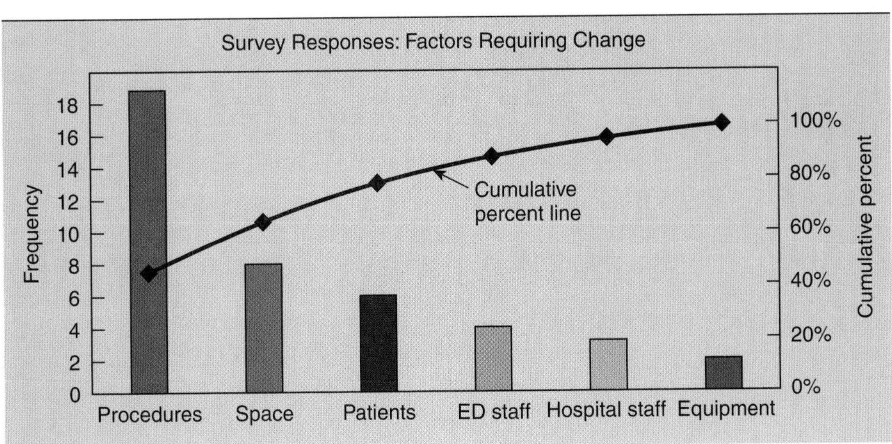

Exhibit S6.5

Pareto Chart of Factors in an Emergency Room

Operations Management in Practice

PRIORITIZING ERRORS AT FEDEX

In order to ensure the highest possible quality of delivery of its packages, FedEx measures its delivery performance every day in every facility, using a service quality index (SQI). The SQI for each location is calculated by multiplying the frequency of each of the errors that occurred in a given day by their respective weights. To illustrate how the SQI is calculated, the various errors that could occur are shown below along with their actual respective weights and a theoretical number of times each error occurred in a hypothetical region.

If the errors were unweighted, then the manager, using Pareto analysis, would assign priority to the traces, as they occurred the most often. By weighting each of the errors as shown above, the manager's first priority is to eliminate lost packages.

Type of Error	Weight	Frequency	Weighted Va
Lost package	50	1	50
Damaged package	30	1	30
Overnight wrong day	10	2	20
Other wrong day late	10	2	20
Traces	3	5	15
International priority inbound wrong day late	10	1	10
Complaint reopened	10	1	10
Late pickup stops	3	3	9
Package not cleared for international destination	3	2	6
Abandoned calls	1	4	4
Domestic right day late	1	2	2
Missing proof of delivery	1	2	2
International right day late	1	1	1
Invoice adjustment	1	1	1
		SQI for region: 180	

Source: Special thanks to Bob Wall, FedEx.

However, there are times when the frequency of occurrence by itself does not determine how important an error problem might be. For example, when making a bar chart of student complaints about a university food service, it might be known that complaints about waiting in line are twice as common as complaints about food availability, but that students consider food availability to be five times more important than waiting. The Pareto diagram can weight the factors being considered to enable managers to take action on those items that most need attention, as illustrated above in the OM in Practice box.

Scatterplots (or Diagrams)

Scatterplots show the relationship between two measured (not counted) variables. For example, in an upscale restaurant, you may want to understand the relationship between how long customers wait to have their orders taken and how satisfied they are with their service. You could measure the wait time to order in minutes and you could assess customer satisfaction with a survey, using a scale of 1 to 10. It is likely that for this restaurant, you would see a relationship resembling the one shown in Exhibit S6.6: that is, customers are less satisfied when waits are either too short or too long. If the wait is too short, customers may feel that they are being rushed because they do not have enough time to study the menu and make a decision about what they want to order; if it is too long, they may be frustrated by the slow responsiveness of the service staff.

Run (or Trend) Charts

Run charts show the behavior of some variable over time. For example, suppose a plant manager would like to keep track of the number of errors that occur each day with respect to manufacturing a given product. The manager would record the number of errors that

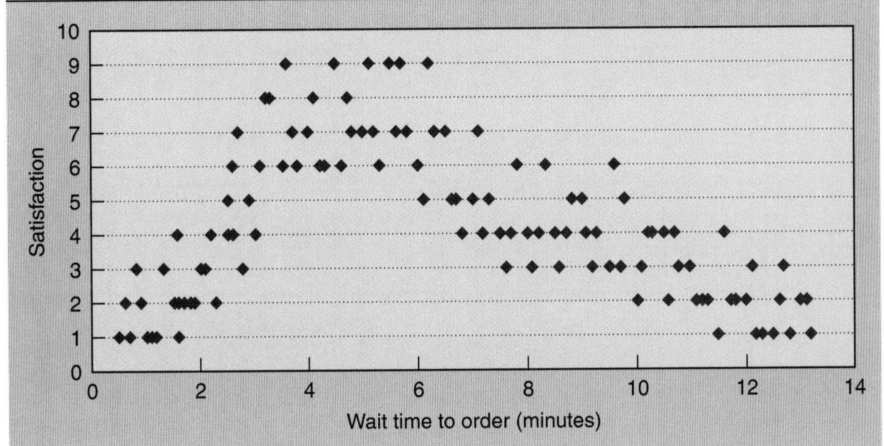

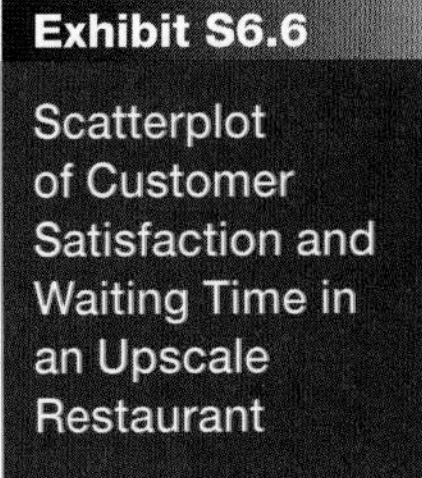
Exhibit S6.6
Scatterplot of Customer Satisfaction and Waiting Time in an Upscale Restaurant

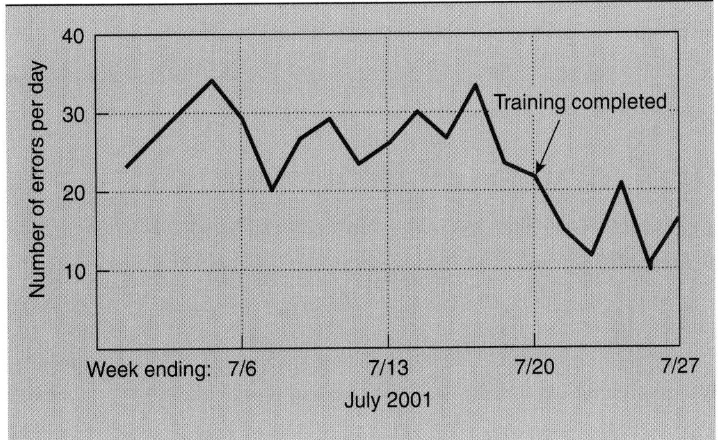

Exhibit S6.7
Run Chart of the Number of Daily Errors

occurred each day and plot them on a run chart, as shown in Exhibit S6.7. The run chart shows that after the week ending July 20, there was a significant reduction in the number of errors that occurred. (Additional investigation might reveal that the workers had completed a training course that week on how to use the new equipment that had been installed.)

Cause-and-Effect (or Fishbone) Diagrams

Cause-and-effect diagrams (also known as *fishbone diagrams* or *Ishikawa diagrams,* after their inventor) are used to identify the causes that lead to a particular outcome or effect. Major categories of the causes are first identified; then, for each cause, "why?" is asked until the root cause for that category can be identified. Exhibit S6.8 shows a cause-and-effect diagram for customer complaints in a restaurant. If customers complain about server rudeness, the cause of the rudeness must be discovered before the proper action can be taken. In this example, the servers might be rude because they are rushed, and they are rushed because they are assigned too many tables. The table assignment process should be the target of managerial action, then, rather than admonishing servers to be more polite.

Exhibit S6.8

Cause-and-Effect Diagram for Customer Complaints in a Restaurant

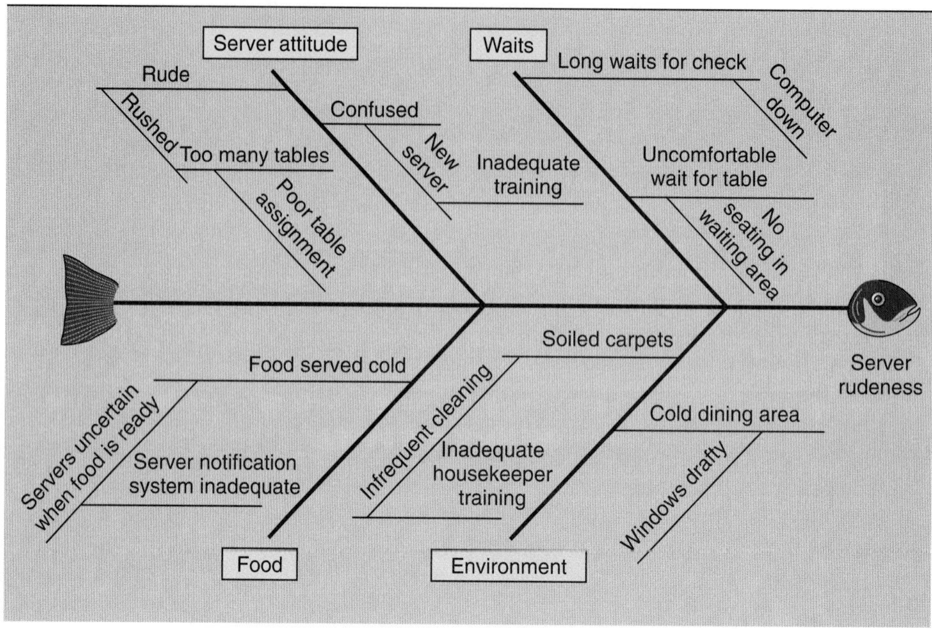

Statistical Analysis of Processes

Although developed by Walter Shewhart in the 1920s, the statistical analysis of processes was not put into widespread use until World War II, and then it was used only out of necessity. At that time, it was realized that the testing and/or inspection of a sample of parts or products (in comparison to testing/inspecting all of the parts or products) was both faster and more economical because it required significantly less labor. With a significant labor shortage during the war, manufacturers had little choice but to use statistical analysis.

Statistical analysis also is used when products are actually destroyed during the tests. For example, it would not have made sense to conduct 100 percent testing of the bombs and bullets that were manufactured during World War II. Similarly, food products cannot be 100 percent taste-tested, nor can batteries be 100 percent tested for durability. In such situations, statistical analysis must be used.

There are two broad categories of statistical tools: (*a*) acceptance sampling, which assesses the quality of the parts or products after they have been produced, and (*b*) statistical process control, which assesses whether or not an ongoing process is performing within established limits. The mathematical calculations are the same for each category, although the interpretation of results is different, as we shall see shortly.

types of data:
attribute data

Data that count items, such as the number of defective items on a sample.

variable data

Data that measure a particular product characteristic such as length or weight.

Attributes and Variables

Within each of these broad categories, statistical quality control methods can be further divided into two additional categories: the first approach uses **attribute data** (that is, data that are counted, such as the number of defective parts produced or the number of dissatisfied customers); the second approach uses **variable data** (that is, data that are measured, such as the length of a wire or the weight of a package of cereal). Each approach can be used in either acceptance sampling or statistical process control, as shown in Exhibit S6.9.

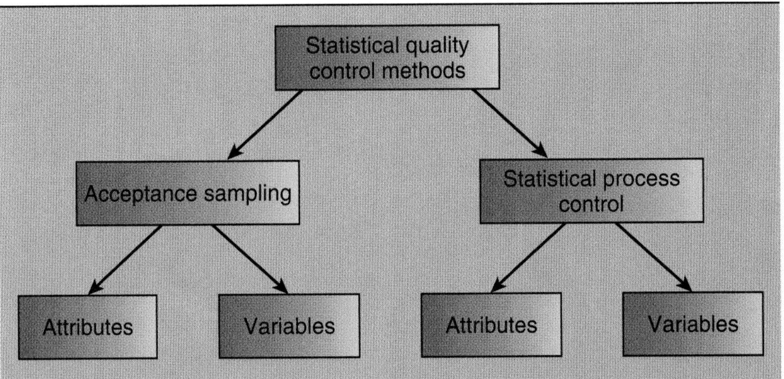

Exhibit S6.9
Statistical Quality Control Methods

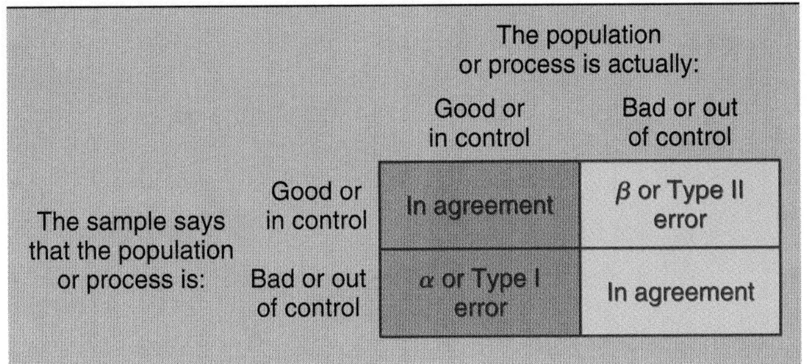

Exhibit S6.10
Types of Sampling Errors

Sampling Errors

When we use a sample from a larger population or from the output generated by a process instead of monitoring the entire population or output, there is the possibility that the sample results are not representative of the actual population or process. When this occurs, we have a sampling error. There are two types of sampling errors that can occur, as shown in Exhibit S6.10. The first occurs when the population is considered bad or the process is considered out of control, when neither is the case. This type of error is referred to as an **α error, Type I error, or producer's risk.** The second type of sampling error occurs when the population is considered good or the process is considered in control, when they really are not. This type of error is referred to as a **β error, Type II error, or consumer's risk.** Balancing the risk of occurrence between the Type I and Type II errors is a major consideration in determining the sample size and the control limits.

types of sampling errors:

α error, Type I error, or producer's risk

Occurs when a sample says parts are bad or the process is out of control when the opposite is true.

β error, Type II error, or consumer's risk

Occurs when a sample says parts are good or the process is in control when just the reverse is true.

Acceptance Sampling

Designing a Sampling Plan for Attributes

Acceptance sampling, as previously stated, is performed on goods that already exist to determine if they conform to specifications. These products may be items received from another company and evaluated by the receiving department or they may be components that have passed through a processing step and are evaluated by company personnel either in production or later in the warehousing function.

Acceptance sampling is executed through a sampling plan. In this section, we illustrate the planning procedures, with respect to attributes, for a single sampling plan—that is, a plan in which the quality is determined from the evaluation of one sample. (Other plans

At the Volkswagon factory in Brazil, inspectors do a final check of the finished vehicles.

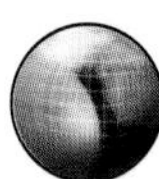

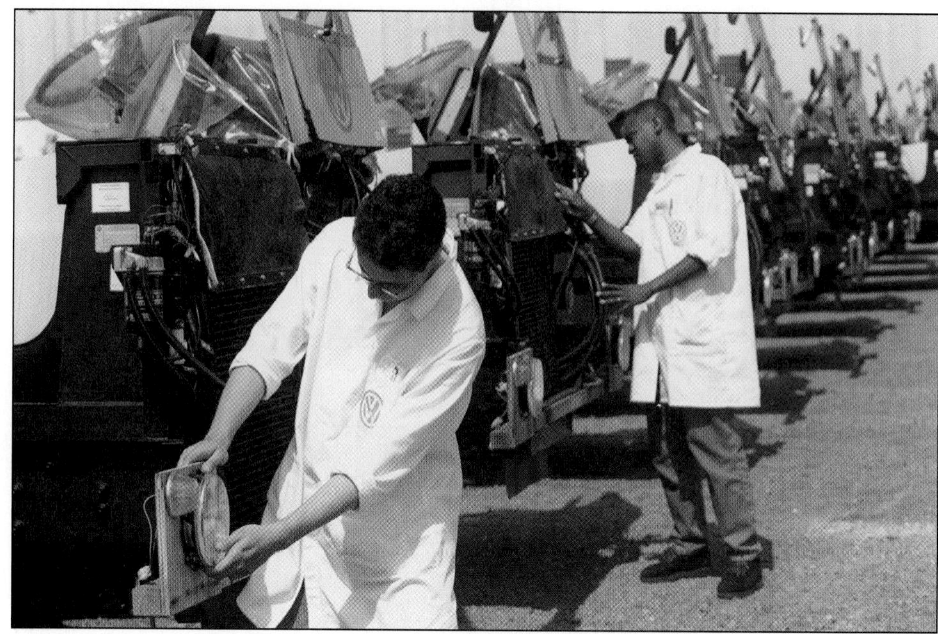

may be developed using two or more samples. See J. M. Juran and F. M. Gryna's *Quality Planning and Analysis* for a detailed discussion of these plans.)

Costs to Justify Inspection Total or 100 percent inspection is justified when the cost of a loss incurred by not inspecting is greater than the cost of inspection. For example, suppose a faulty item results in a \$10 loss. If the average percentage of defective items in a lot is 3 percent, the expected cost of faulty items is $0.03 \times \$10$, or \$0.30 each. Therefore, if the cost of inspecting each item is less than \$0.30, the economic decision is to perform 100 percent inspection. Not all defective items will be removed, however, since inspectors will pass some bad items and reject some good ones.

The purposes of a sampling plan are to test the lot to either (*a*) find its quality or (*b*) ensure that the quality is what it is supposed to be. Thus, if a quality control supervisor already knows the quality (such as the 0.03 given in the example), he or she does not sample for defects. Either all of the items must be inspected to remove the defects or none of them should be inspected, and the rejects pass into the process. The choice simply depends on economics in terms of the cost to inspect versus the cost incurred by passing a reject.

acceptable quality level (AQL)

Maximum percentage of defects that a company is willing to accept.

A single sampling plan when we are looking at attributes is defined by n and c, where n is the number of units in the sample and c is the acceptance number. The size of n may vary from one to all the items in the lot (usually denoted as N) from which it is drawn. The acceptance number c denotes the maximum number of defective items that can be found in the sample before the lot is rejected. Values for n and c are determined by the interaction of four factors (AQL, α, LTPD, and β) that quantify the objectives of the product's producer and its consumer. The objective of the producer is to ensure that the sampling plan has a low probability of rejecting good lots. Lots are defined as good if they contain no more than a specified level of defectives, termed the **acceptable quality level (AQL).**[1] The objective

[1]There is some controversy surrounding AQLs, based on the argument that specifying some acceptable percent of defectives is inconsistent with the philosophical goal of zero defects. In practice, even in the best companies, there is an acceptable quality level. The difference is that it may be stated in parts per million rather than in parts per hundred. This is the case in Motorola's six-sigma quality standard, which holds that no more than 3.4 defects per million parts are acceptable.

of the consumer is to ensure that the sampling plan has a low probability of accepting bad lots. Lots are defined as bad if the percentage of defectives is greater than a specified amount, termed *lot tolerance percent defective* (LTPD). As presented earlier, the probability associated with rejecting a good lot is denoted by the Greek letter alpha (α) and is termed the *producer's risk*. The probability associated with accepting a bad lot is denoted by the Greek letter beta (β) and is termed the *consumer's risk*. The selection of particular values for AQL, α, LTPD, and β is an economic decision based on a cost trade-off or, more typically, on company policy or contractual requirements.

There is a humorous story supposedly about Hewlett-Packard during its first dealings with Japanese vendors, who place great emphasis on high-quality production. HP had insisted on 2 percent AQL in a purchase of 100 cables. During the purchase agreement some heated discussion took place wherein the Japanese vendor did not want this AQL specification; HP insisted that they would not budge from the 2 percent AQL. The Japanese vendor finally agreed. Later, when the box arrived, there were two packages inside. One contained 100 good cables. The other package had 2 cables with a note stating: "We have sent you 100 good cables. Since you insisted on 2 percent AQL, we have enclosed 2 defective cables in this package, though we do not understand why you want them."

The following example, using an excerpt from a standard acceptance sampling table, illustrates how the four parameters—AQL, α, LTPD, and β—are used in developing a sampling plan.

Example

Values of n and c

Hi-Tech Industries manufactures Z-Band radar scanners used to detect speed traps. The printed circuit boards in the scanners are purchased from an outside vendor. The vendor produces the boards to an AQL of 2 percent defectives and is willing to run a 5 percent risk (α) of having lots of this level or fewer defectives rejected. Hi-Tech considers lots of 8 percent or more defectives (LTPD) unacceptable and wants to ensure that it will accept such poor-quality lots no more than 10 percent of the time (β). A large shipment has just been delivered. What values of n and c should be selected to determine the quality of this lot?

Solution

The parameters of the problem are AQL $= 0.02$, $\alpha = 0.05$, LTPD $= 0.08$, and $\beta = 0.10$. We can use Exhibit S6.11 to find c and n.

First divide LTPD by AQL ($0.08 \div 0.02 = 4$). Then find the ratio in column 2 that is equal to or just greater than that amount (i.e., 4). This value is 4.057, which is associated with $c = 4$.

Finally, find the value in column 3 that is in the same row as $c = 4$ and divide that quantity by AQL to obtain n ($1.970 \div 0.02 = 98.5$).

The appropriate sampling plan is $c = 4$, $n = 99$.

Exhibit S6.11

Excerpt from a Sampling Plan Table for $\alpha = 0.05$, $\beta = 0.10$

c	LTPD ÷ AQL	n · AQL	c	LTPD ÷ AQL	n · AQL
0	44.890	0.052	5	3.549	2.613
1	10.946	0.355	6	3.206	3.286
2	6.509	0.818	7	2.957	3.981
3	4.890	1.366	8	2.768	4.695
4	4.057	1.970	9	2.618	5.426

Exhibit S6.12

Operating Characteristic Curve for AQL = 0.02, $\alpha = 0.05$, LTPD = 0.08, $\beta = 0.10$

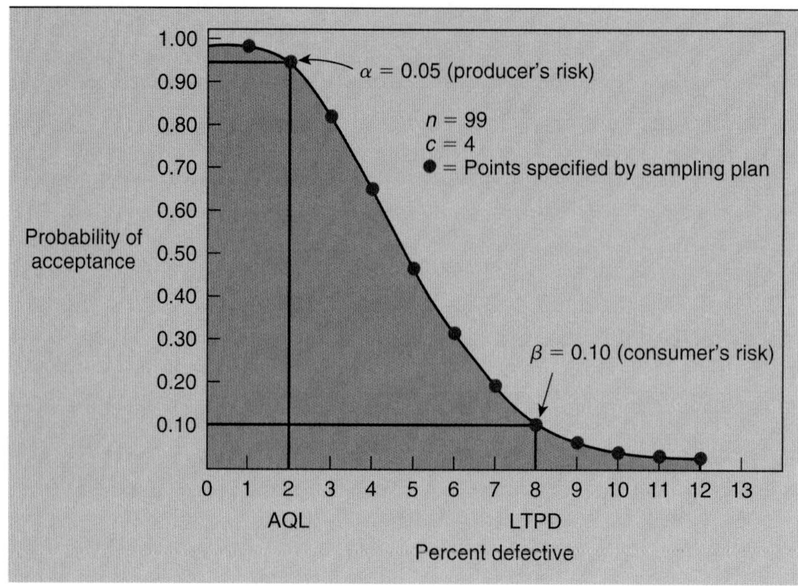

Operating Characteristic Curves

operating characteristic (OC) curves

Curves that show the probability of accepting lots that contain different percent defectives.

While a sampling plan such as the one just described meets our requirements for the extreme values of good and bad quality, we cannot readily determine how well the plan discriminates between good and bad lots at intermediate values. For this reason, sampling plans are generally displayed graphically through the use of **operating characteristic (OC) curves.** These curves, which are unique for each combination of n and c, simply illustrate the probability of accepting lots with varying percent defectives. The procedure we have followed in developing the plan, in fact, specifies two points on an OC curve: one point defined by AQL and $1 - \alpha$, and the other point defined by LTPD and β. Curves for common values of n and c can be computed or obtained from available tables.[2] (See Exhibit S6.12.)

A sampling plan discriminating perfectly between good and bad lots has an infinite slope (vertical) at the selected value of AQL. In Exhibit S6.12, percent defectives to the left of 2 percent would always be accepted and to the right, always rejected. However, such a curve is possible only with complete inspection of all units and thus is not a possibility with a true sampling plan.

An OC curve should be steep in the region of most interest (between the AQL and the LTPD), which is accomplished by varying n and c. If c remains constant, increasing the sample size n causes the OC curve to be more vertical. While holding n constant, decreasing c (the maximum number of defective units) also makes the slope more vertical, moving closer to the origin.

The size of the lot from which the sample is taken has relatively little effect on the quality of protection. Consider, for example, that samples—all of the same size of 20 units—are taken from different lots ranging from a lot size of 200 units to a lot size of infinity. If each lot is known to have 5 percent defectives, the probability of accepting the lot based on the

[2]See, for example, H. F. Dodge and H. G. Romig, *Sampling Inspection Tables—Single and Double Sampling* (New York: John Wiley & Sons, 1959), and *Military Standard Sampling Procedures and Tables for Inspection by Attributes* (MIL-STD-105D) (Washington, DC: U.S. Government Printing Office, 1983).

sample of 20 units ranges from about 0.34 to about 0.36. This means that so long as the lot size is several times the sample size, it makes little difference how large the lot is. It seems a bit difficult to accept, but statistically (on the average in the long run) whether we have a carload or box full, we'll get about the same answer. It just seems that a carload should have a larger sample size.

Designing a Sampling Plan for Variables

control limits

Points on an acceptance sampling chart that distinguish between the accept and reject region(s). Also, points on a process control chart that distinguish between a process being in and out of control.

When we use variables to determine if we should accept an entire lot, we again take a sample of the items. However, instead of counting the number of defectives in the sample, we measure the variable of interest for each item in the sample and compute the mean for the sample. We then compare the mean of the sample with **control limits** that have been previously established to determine whether or not we accept the entire lot.

There are three factors that must be taken into consideration in designing a sampling plan for an item where variables are used as the criterion for acceptance. These are: (*a*) the probability of rejecting a lot that is actually good (that is, committing an α error), (*b*) the probability of accepting a lot that is actually bad (that is, committing a β error), and (*c*) the sample size, n.

Example

ABC Electronics Company buys a 50-ohm resistor from an outside vendor. (A resistor is an electrical component used in electrical circuits to retard current. An ohm is the measure of how much a resistor retards the current.) From historical data, the standard deviation for this resistor is 3 ohms. Determine the appropriate control limits if we use a sample size of $n = 100$ and we want to be 95 percent confident that the sample results are truly representative of the total population. (In other words, the probability of committing an α error is $1 - 0.95$ or 5 percent.)

Solution

The equation for determining the control limits (CL) is

$$\text{CL} = \mu \pm z_{\alpha/2}\frac{\sigma}{\sqrt{n}} \tag{S6.1}$$

where

$\mu =$ The desired mean of the population.

$z_{\alpha/2} =$ The number of standard deviations from the mean that corresponds to the given level of α. ($\alpha/2$ indicates that this is a two-tailed test and that the α error is equally divided between the two tails of the distribution.) The value of z is obtained from the normal distribution table in Appendix B or C at the end of this book. (As noted in the table, the z-value for a two-tailed test with 95 percent confidence is 1.96.)

$\sigma =$ The value of the population's standard deviation.

Substituting, we have

$$\begin{aligned} \text{CL} &= 50 \pm 1.96\frac{(3)}{\sqrt{100}} \\ &= 50 \pm 0.588 \end{aligned}$$

The lower control limit (LCL) is therefore 49.412 and the upper control limit (UCL) is 50.588, as shown in Exhibit S6.13.

Exhibit S6.13

Establishing Control Limits for Acceptance Sampling Using Variables

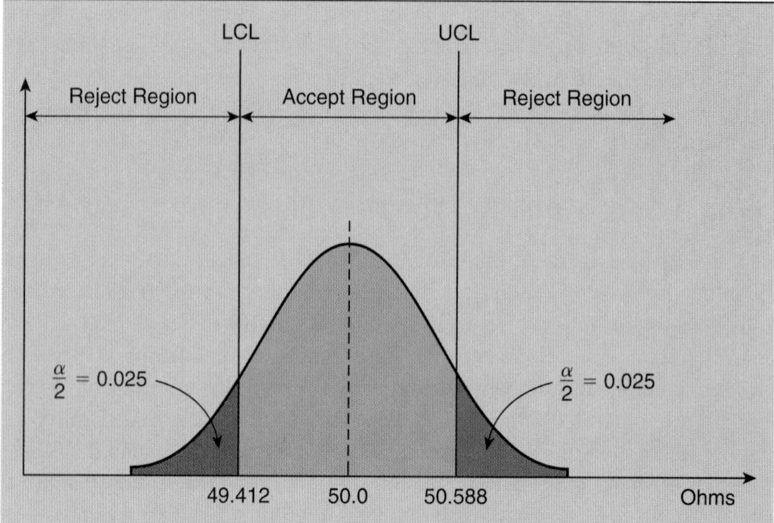

The inspection procedure for this resistor therefore is to (*a*) take a random sample of 100 resistors, (*b*) measure the number of ohms in each resistor in the sample, (*c*) compute the mean of the sample, and finally (*d*) compare the sample mean with the established control limits; in other words, if the sample mean falls within the range of 49.412–50.588, the lot is accepted; otherwise the lot is rejected.

Example

Continuing with the resistor problem, we can tolerate some variation in the number of ohms in each resistor. However, if the number of ohms falls below 49, then we would have a serious problem in our electrical circuit. What is the probability of us accepting a lot when the average resistance is 49 ohms or less?

Solution

This situation is depicted in Exhibit S6.14. It is important to note that the control limits that were previously established do not change. The probability of accepting a bad lot or committing a β error is defined by that percentage of the area under the curve with a mean of 49 that falls within the acceptance range. (Note that this is a one-tailed test because the β error occurs only in the right tail under the curve.)

The probability of committing this error is determined as follows:

$$\text{LCL} = \mu + z_\beta \frac{\sigma}{\sqrt{n}}$$

where

z_β = The number of standard deviations from the mean that corresponds to the given level of β.

Substituting, we have

$$49.412 = 49 + z_\beta \frac{(3)}{\sqrt{100}}$$

$$0.412 = (z_\beta)0.3$$

$$z_\beta = 1.373$$

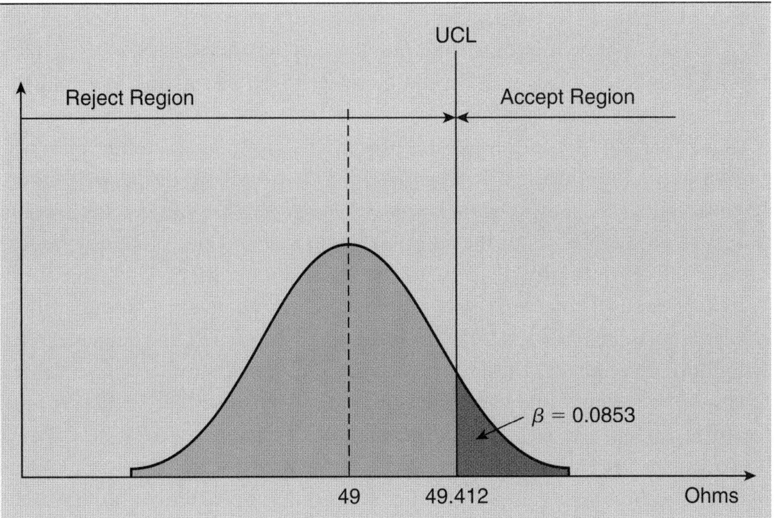

Exhibit S6.14 Determining the Probability of Committing a β Error

Again, using the normal distribution table at the end of this book, we look up the value of $z = 1.373$ and find the corresponding area under the curve of 0.0853. Thus the probability of committing a β error under these conditions is 8.53 percent.

Statistical Process Control

statistical process control (SPC) *Statistical method for determining whether a particular process is in or out of control.*

Statistical process control (SPC) is a quantitative method for monitoring a repetitive process to determine whether that process is operating properly. SPC uses process data collected in real time and compares current measures to baseline process performance measures. It then applies simple statistical techniques similar to those used in acceptance sampling to determine whether or not the process has changed. SPC allows management and workers to distinguish between random fluctuations inherent in the process and variation that might indicate that the process has changed.

At its core, SPC is about understanding the variation that occurs in a process. Every process varies in some unique way. Some processes vary a great deal; some vary only slightly. A careful analysis of the inherent variation in a given process makes it possible to compare its current performance with its expected performance, as determined by how the process has performed in the past.

As an illustration, a person uses an axe to chop logs into one-foot lengths for firewood. Over many days of chopping, he has discovered that he consistently chops the logs into lengths that can vary as much as three inches from his target length of 12 inches (in other words, the lengths he chops are 12 inches plus or minus three inches). It could be said that the expected variation—due to the random variation in his chopping process—is three inches from the target. He would expect that unless something in his chopping process changes, he would continue to chop pieces of length 12 ± 3 inches. If suddenly he was producing pieces that were shorter than nine inches and/or longer than 15 inches, he might question why his usual process has changed. He might look for nonrandom causes of variation: Is he tired or distracted? Has he changed his chopping style? Has his axe become dull? Is the wood he is currently chopping somehow different from the wood he has consistently cut within three inches of the target?

This simple example demonstrates the difference between the inherent, random variation that can be associated with a particular process and the nonrandom, or assignable, causes of variation. Assignable causes usually can be categorized as relating to either the worker, the equipment, or the materials being used.

SPC uses statistics—in particular, the power of sampling—to refine this basic understanding of variation in processes. The *central limit theorem* tells us that no matter what the actual shape of a distribution is, when samples of a given size are repeatedly drawn from that distribution and the means of the samples are calculated and plotted on a graph, these sample means will be normally distributed. If you are not convinced of this, think about a deck of cards. If each of the cards takes its face value (an ace = 1, numbered cards take their number value, a jack = 11, a queen = 12, and a king = 13), the deck represents a uniform distribution of cards: there are four of each value. The overall average value of a card in a deck would be seven. If you draw several samples of four cards each from the deck, how many of these samples will have an mean value of one? It will be a very rare sample that contains four aces. How many samples will have an mean value of 13? Again, only four kings will produce that sample mean, so that outcome will also be very rare. On the other hand, think of how many ways a sample mean of seven could be produced: four sevens, three sixes and one nine, and so on in many different combinations. If you shuffle the deck, draw a sample, calculate its mean, plot the sample mean on a graph, reshuffle the deck and begin again, you will find that your sample mean distribution will quickly take on the shape of a bell (or normal) curve, rather than the uniform flat shape of the underlying distribution of cards in the deck.

What about distributions other than the uniform? Does the central limit theorem hold true? You can do the same experiment with cards, assigning the value of four to all red cards and 10 to all black cards. The overall or grand mean of the deck is still seven, but the shape of the distribution of cards is now bimodal. Draw samples as before, calculate the mean value of each sample, plot the means on a graph, and the graph will shortly begin to look bell-shaped. Of course, the larger the sample size, the smoother the curve.

If the distribution of sample means is assumed to be normal, then we can use the well-understood properties of the normal distribution to understand variation in processes. For example, as shown in Exhibit S6.15, we know that if we have a normal distribution:

- The distribution is bilaterally symmetrical.
- 68.3 percent of the distribution lies between plus and minus one standard deviation from the mean.

Exhibit S6.15

Areas under the Normal Distribution Curve Corresponding to Different Numbers of Standard Deviations from the Mean

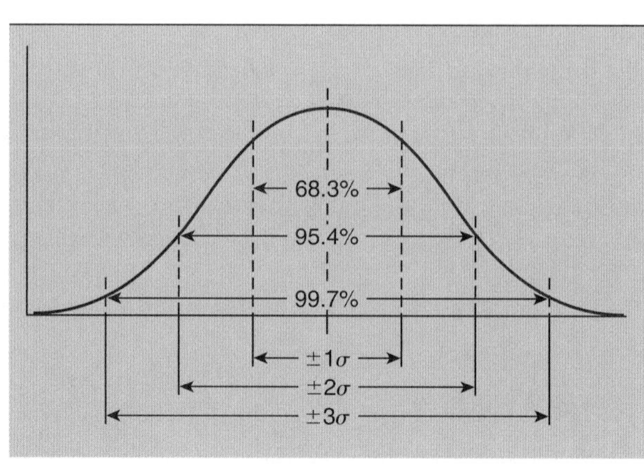

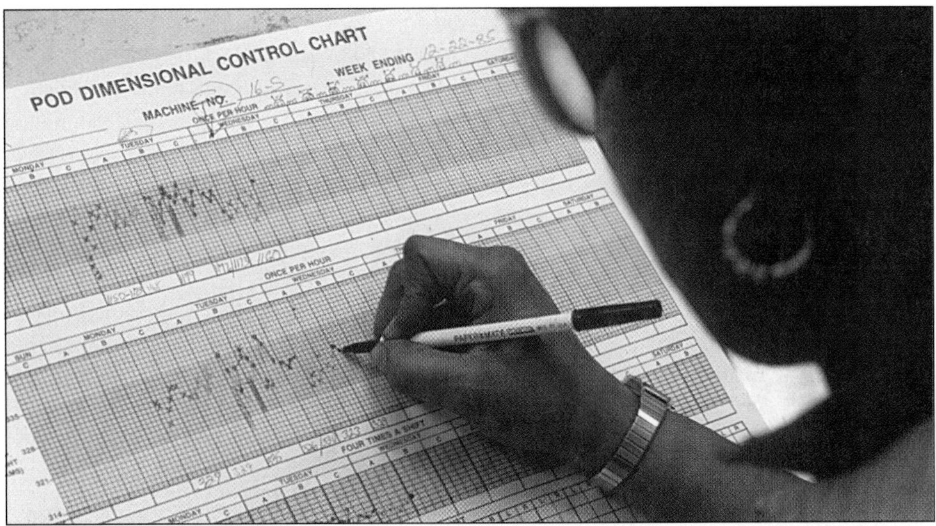

Statistical process control charts can be generated with computers, or manually, as shown. Samples are taken from the process at stated time intervals and their average parameter values are plotted on the charts. As long as these values remain within established control limits, the process is assumed to be in control. However, a value falling outside the control limits might indicate the process is no longer in control and further investigation is required.

- 95.4 percent of the distribution lies between plus and minus two standard deviations from the mean.
- 99.7 percent of the distribution lies between plus and minus three standard deviations from the mean.

If we plot the means of successive samples drawn from a process whose long-run pattern of variation is known, we can look at the pattern of the sample means and decide whether the process is behaving the way we expect it to behave, or whether it has changed.

Statistical control means that a process is exhibiting only its inherent random variation and that it is not showing any signs of "assignable" variation. Statistical control does *not* mean that a process is producing goods or services that are good or bad.

SPC Charts

SPC charts are actually a specialized category of run charts that are based on the central limit theorem. The mean value for the process is calculated (usually from past performance) and, for the sample size being used, control limits are calculated. These control limits usually are established at three standard deviations above and below the mean because plus and minus three standard deviations from the mean value encompasses 99.7 percent of the area under a normal distribution. The x-axis of the SPC chart is time; the y-axis is the variation from the mean value for the process. The center line of an attribute chart is the long-run average for that attribute, such as percent defective, and the center line of a variables chart is the mean value for the process.

For each sample, we calculate the sample mean (either the percentage of an attribute that occurs in the sample or the average measured value) and plot that point on the graph. As each sample mean is plotted, we look to see if the process is exhibiting variation that does not look random. For example, we would expect to see the points distributed around the center line in the proportion described above because of what we know about normal distributions. If we see too little or too much variation, it may indicate that there is a nonrandom factor affecting the process. If we see evidence that the points are not distributed symmetrically around the center line, it also may indicate that there is a nonrandom factor affecting the process. If we see patterns such as several points in a row going up or several points in a row going down, it again may indicate that there is a nonrandom factor affecting the process. When we look at an SPC chart, we are looking for evidence of nonrandom behavior—the process behaving in a way we would not expect it to behave, given what we know about it.

Because points on an SPC chart are plotted as the samples are drawn, the ambiguity of "too little or too much variation" or "evidence of a nonrandom pattern" has prompted the development of rules of thumb for interpreting control charts, as shown in Exhibit S6.16.

Exhibit S6.16

Control Chart Evidence for Investigation

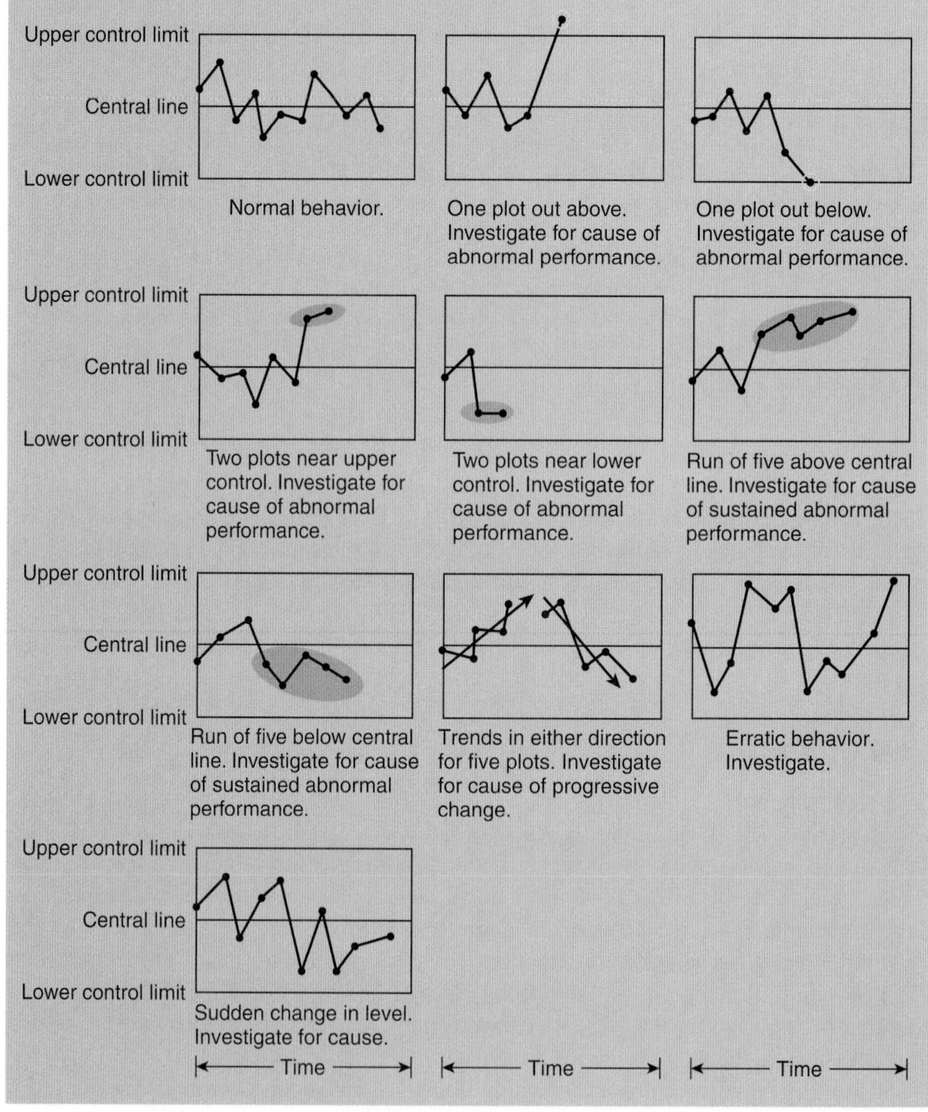

Source: Bertrand L. Hansen, *Quality Control: Theory and Applications,* © 1963, p. 65. Reprinted by permission of Pearson Education, Inc., Upper Saddle River, NJ.

These rules of thumb, or heuristics, are simply methods of standardizing the way variation in a control chart is interpreted.

A process that exhibits nonrandom variation is said to be "out of control." (Remember that "out of control" does not mean that the process is producing bad output. A process can be out of control and producing fewer defects than usual. The key is that the process is not behaving in the way it is expected to behave given what is known about the process.) When we see evidence of nonrandom variation in a process, we try to identify the factors that may have caused that variation. In other words, we look for assignable cause: changes in workers, equipment, or materials.

SPC Using Attribute Measurements

Attribute data are data that are counted, such as good or bad units produced by a machine. If we draw samples during our production run on that machine, we can count, for each sample, the number of units that are good and the number of units that are bad, based on our quality criteria. We can then compare the number of bad units in each sample to the long-run percentage of bad units for that particular machine and determine whether the process is behaving the way we expect it to behave. A process can be in control and producing bad output. For example, if the long-run percent defectives for a particular process is 20 percent, that means that 20 percent of the output is bad! The process may continue to produce the same level of defectives—in other words, be in control—but the defectives are still being produced. On the other hand, if a process usually produces 20 percent defectives and something changes so that the process now produces only 5 percent defectives, the process is out of control—but has improved! The goal is to find the cause of any nonrandom variation and either eliminate it (if it is producing more defects) or sustain it (if it has resulted in process improvement).

Calculating Control Limits The center line for an attribute chart is the long-run average for the attribute in question. For example, for a *p*-chart, or percent defective chart, the center line is $\overline{p}$ (pronounced "*p*-bar"), the long-run average percent defective.

$$\text{Center line} = \overline{p} = \text{Long-run average}$$

$$\text{Standard deviation of sample} = s_p = \sqrt{\frac{\overline{p}(1-\overline{p})}{n}}$$

Thus, we have

$$\text{CL} = \overline{p} \pm z_{\alpha/2}\sqrt{\frac{\overline{p}(1-\overline{p})}{n}} \tag{S6.2}$$

The upper control limit (UCL) and the lower control limit (LCL) are usually established at plus and minus three standard deviations from $\overline{p}$ ($z_{\alpha/2} = 3$). Thus:

$$\text{Upper control limit} = \text{UCL} = \overline{p} + 3s_p$$

$$\text{Lower control limit} = \text{LCL} = \overline{p} - 3s_p$$

If the calculated LCL is a negative number, the LCL is set equal to zero.

Sample Size in Attribute SPC The size of a sample is extremely important for successful SPC implementation. If attribute data are being collected, the sample must be large enough to be able to count the attribute. For example, if we know that a machine produces, in the long-run, 5 percent defects and we have a sample size of five, we are very unlikely to be able to answer the question: "Is the process producing defects at the rate it usually does." The usual rule of thumb for attribute SPC is that the sample should be large enough to be able to include the attribute twice, on average. So if the defect rate is 5 percent, the sample size would need to be at least 40 to expect to count two defects. Of course, since we are not looking at every unit, some samples, just by chance, will have more than two defects, while some will have fewer than two. We are looking for a pattern of defects in the samples over time that will tell us whether the process is exhibiting nonrandom variation.

Determining the Long-Run Attribute Level Because the long-run attribute percentage is critical in determining the center line and for calculating the control limits for the SPC chart, it is important to have adequate historical information about the process.

Variable Measurements Using $\overline{X}$ and R Charts

Variable data are data that are measured, such as length or weight. There are four main issues in creating a control chart that uses variable data: (*a*) the size of the sample, (*b*) the number of samples, (*c*) the frequency of the samples, and (*d*) the control limits.

Size of Samples For industrial applications in process control, it is preferable to keep the sample size small. There are two main reasons: first, the sample needs to be taken within a reasonable length of time, otherwise the process might change while the sample is being taken. Second, the larger the sample, the more it costs to take.

Sample sizes of four or five units seem to be the preferred numbers. The *means* of samples of this size have an approximately normal distribution, no matter what the distribution of the parent population looks like. Sample sizes greater than five give narrower control limits and, thus, are more sensitive. For detecting finer variations of a process, it may be necessary, in fact, to use larger sample sizes. However, when sample sizes exceed 15 or so, it would be more appropriate to use the standard deviation (σ) and $\overline{X}$ charts rather than R and $\overline{X}$ charts. One advantage of using the R charts is that the range is easier to calculate than the standard deviation.

Number of Samples Once the chart has been set up, each sample taken can be compared to the chart and a decision can be made about whether the process is acceptable. To set up the charts, however, prudence (and statistics) suggest that 25 or more samples be taken.

Frequency of Samples How often to take a sample is a trade-off between the cost of sampling (along with the cost of the unit if it is destroyed as part of the test) and the benefits of adjusting the system. Usually, it is best to start off with frequent sampling of a process and then decrease the sampling frequency as confidence in the process increases. For example, one might start with a sample of five units every half hour and end up feeling that one sample per day is adequate.

Control Limits Standard practice in statistical process control for variables is to set control limits at three standard deviations above the mean and three standard deviations below. This means that 99.7 percent of the sample means are expected to fall within these control limits (i.e., within a 99.7 percent confidence interval). Thus, if one sample mean falls outside this obviously wide band, we have strong evidence that the process is out of control.

How to Construct $\overline{X}$ and R Charts

An $\overline{X}$ chart tracks the changes in the means of the samples by plotting the means that were taken from a process. $\overline{\overline{X}}$ is the average of the means.

An R chart tracks the changes in the variability by plotting the range within each sample. The range is the difference between the highest and the lowest values in that sample. As stated earlier, R values provide an easily calculated measure of variation used like a standard deviation. $\overline{R}$ is the average of the ranges of each sample. More specifically, these terms are defined:

$$\overline{X} = \frac{\sum_{i=1}^{n} X_i}{n} \tag{S6.3}$$

where

$\overline{X}$ = Mean of the sample

i = Item number

n = Total number of items in the sample

$$\overline{\overline{X}} = \frac{\sum_{j=1}^{m} \overline{X}_j}{m} \tag{S6.4}$$

where

$\overline{\overline{X}}$ = The average of the means of the samples

j = Sample number

m = Total number of samples

$$\overline{R} = \frac{\sum_{j=1}^{m} R_j}{m} \tag{S6.5}$$

where

$\overline{R}$ = Average of the measurement differences R for all samples

R_j = Difference between the highest and lowest values in sample j

E. L. Grant and R. Leavenworth computed a table that allows us to easily compute the upper and lower control limits for both the $\overline{X}$ chart and the R chart.[3] These are defined as

Upper control limit for $\overline{X} = \overline{\overline{X}} + A_2\overline{R}$

Lower control limit for $\overline{X} = \overline{\overline{X}} - A_2\overline{R}$

Upper control limit for $R = D_4\overline{R}$

Lower control limit for $R = D_3\overline{R}$

where the values for A_2, D_3, and D_4 are obtained from Exhibit S6.17.

[3] E. L. Grant and R. Leavenworth, *Statistical Quality Control* (New York: McGraw-Hill, 1964), p. 562. Reprinted by permission.

Exhibit S6.17

Factors for Determining from $\bar{R}$ the 3-Sigma Control Limits for $\bar{X}$ and R Charts

Number of Observations in Subgroup n	Factor for $\bar{X}$ Chart A_2	Factors for R Chart: Lower Control Limit D_3	Factors for R Chart: Upper Control Limit D_4
2	1.88	0	3.27
3	1.02	0	2.57
4	0.73	0	2.28
5	0.58	0	2.11
6	0.48	0	2.00
7	0.42	0.08	1.92
8	0.37	0.14	1.86
9	0.34	0.18	1.82
10	0.31	0.22	1.78
11	0.29	0.26	1.74
12	0.27	0.28	1.72
13	0.25	0.31	1.69
14	0.24	0.33	1.67
15	0.22	0.35	1.65
16	0.21	0.36	1.64
17	0.20	0.38	1.62
18	0.19	0.39	1.61
19	0.19	0.40	1.60
20	0.18	0.41	1.59

Upper control limit for $\bar{X} = UCL_{\bar{X}} = \bar{\bar{X}} + A_2\bar{R}$ Upper control limit for $\bar{R} = UCL_R = D_4\bar{R}$

Lower control limit for $\bar{X} = LCL_{\bar{X}} = \bar{\bar{X}} - A_2\bar{R}$ Lower control limit for $\bar{R} = LCL_R = D_3\bar{R}$

Note: All factors are based on the normal distribution.

Source: E. L. Grant, *Statistical Quality Control,* 6th ed. (New York: McGraw-Hill, 1988). Reprinted by permission of McGraw-Hill, Inc.

Exhibit S6.18

Measurements in Samples of Five from a Process

Sample Number	Each Unit in Sample					Average $\bar{X}$	Range R
1	10.60	10.40	10.30	9.90	10.20	10.28	.70
2	9.98	10.25	10.05	10.23	10.33	10.17	.35
3	9.85	9.90	10.20	10.25	10.15	10.07	40
4	10.20	10.10	10.30	9.90	9.95	10.09	.40
5	10.30	10.20	10.24	10.50	10.30	10.31	.30
6	10.10	10.30	10.20	10.30	9.90	10.16	.40
7	9.98	9.90	10.20	10.40	10.10	10.12	.50
8	10.10	10.30	10.40	10.24	10.30	10.27	.30
9	10.30	10.20	10.60	10.50	10.10	10.34	.50
10	10.30	10.40	10.50	10.10	10.20	10.30	.40
11	9.90	9.50	10.20	10.30	10.35	10.05	.85
12	10.10	10.36	10.50	9.80	9.95	10.14	.70
13	10.20	10.50	10.70	10.10	9.90	10.28	.80
14	10.20	10.60	10.50	10.30	10.40	10.40	.40
15	10.54	10.30	10.40	10.55	10.00	10.36	.55
16	10.20	10.60	10.15	10.00	10.50	10.29	.60
17	10.20	10.40	10.60	10.80	10.10	10.42	.70
18	9.90	9.50	9.90	10.50	10.00	9.96	1.00
19	10.60	10.30	10.50	9.90	9.80	10.22	.80
20	10.60	10.40	10.30	10.40	10.20	10.38	.40
21	9.90	9.60	10.50	10.10	10.60	10.14	1.00
22	9.95	10.20	10.50	10.30	10.20	10.23	.55
23	10.20	9.50	9.60	9.80	10.30	9.88	.80
24	10.30	10.60	10.30	9.90	9.80	10.18	.80
25	9.90	10.30	10.60	9.90	10.10	10.16	.70
				$\bar{\bar{X}} =$		10.21	
				$\bar{R} =$			.60

Example

We would like to create an $\overline{X}$ and an R chart for a process. Exhibit S6.18 shows the measurements that were taken of all 25 samples. The last two columns show the average of the sample $\overline{X}$ and the range R.

Solution

$$\text{Upper control limit for } \overline{X} = \overline{\overline{X}} + A_2\overline{R}$$
$$= 10.21 + 0.58(0.60) = 10.56$$

$$\text{Lower control limit for } \overline{X} = \overline{\overline{X}} - A_2\overline{R}$$
$$= 10.21 - 0.58(0.60) = 9.86$$

$$\text{Upper control limit for } R = D_4\overline{R}$$
$$= 2.11(0.60) = 1.26$$

$$\text{Lower control limit for } R = D_3\overline{R}$$
$$= 0(0.60) = 0$$

Exhibit S6.19 shows the $\overline{X}$ chart and R chart with a plot of all the sample means and ranges of the samples. All the points are well within the control limits, although sample 23 is close to the $\overline{X}$ lower control limit. The $\overline{X}$ chart shows how well the process is centered about the target mean. The R chart demonstrates the degree of variability in the process.

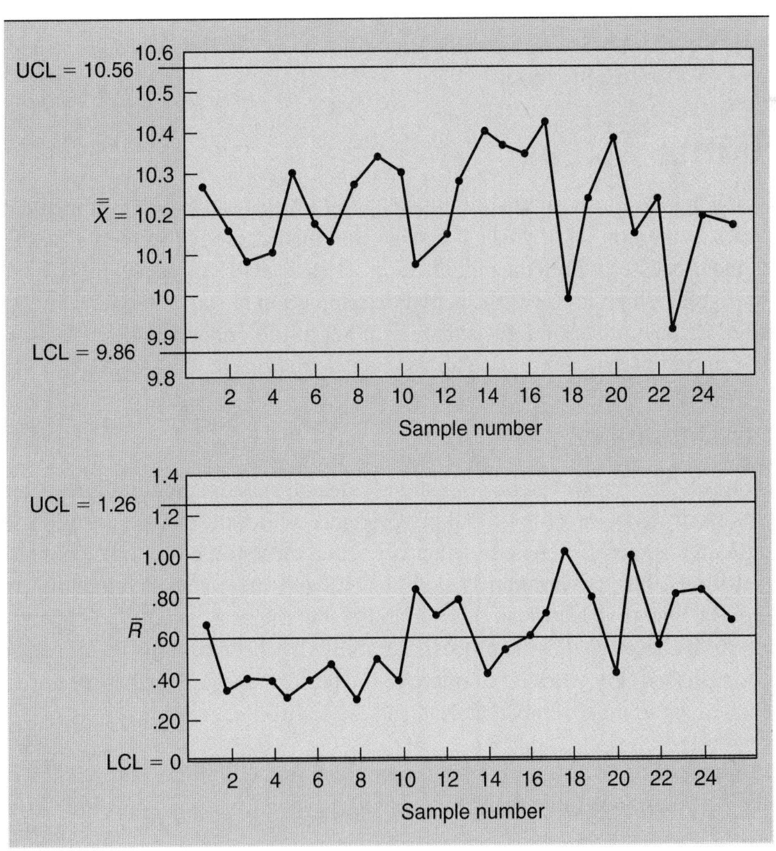

Exhibit S6.19

$\overline{X}$ Chart and R Chart

Exhibit S6.20

A Framework for Applying the Different Quality Control Tools

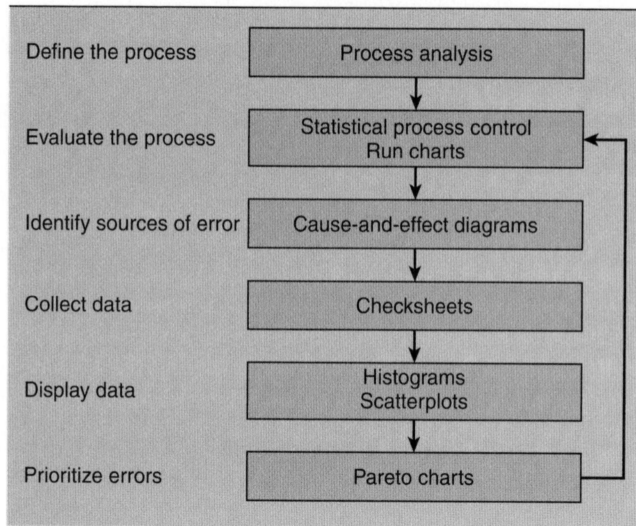

A Framework for Applying the Tools

Each of the different tools presented in this chapter provides a manager with specific information about a process. However, it is not just a matter of selecting the right tool. Equally important, the manager needs to understand how these various tools work together to improve the quality of a process.

Exhibit S6.20 provides a framework for the logical integration of these various tools. As suggested in Exhibit S6.20, these tools are used on a continuous basis in order to identify sources of error in a process.

Six Sigma

As stated in Chapter 6, six sigma, on a managerial level, is an organizationwide program that provides a common set of goals, language, and methodology for improving the overall quality of the processes within the organization. There is also a more technical, quantitative side to six sigma, which involves the actual determination of the quality level of a process, as expressed in the number of defects that occur per million opportunities. We present here a brief description of the quantitative terms and calculations that are used in six sigma.

Process Capability

Process control chart limits can be compared to design specification limits to determine if the process itself is not capable of making products within design specification (or tolerance) limits. In Exhibit S6.21A, we see a process that on average is producing items within the control limits, but its variation is such that it can't meet specifications for all items. Exhibit S6.21B shows reduction in this variability, but the process is still deficient. Finally, in Exhibit S6.21C, we see that the process variability has been brought under control. How is this accomplished? By working to improve the performance of each source of variance: workers, machine, tooling, setup, material, and the environment.

Process Capability Ratio In order for a process to be both in control and within tolerance, the part tolerance limits must be equal to or wider than the upper and lower limits

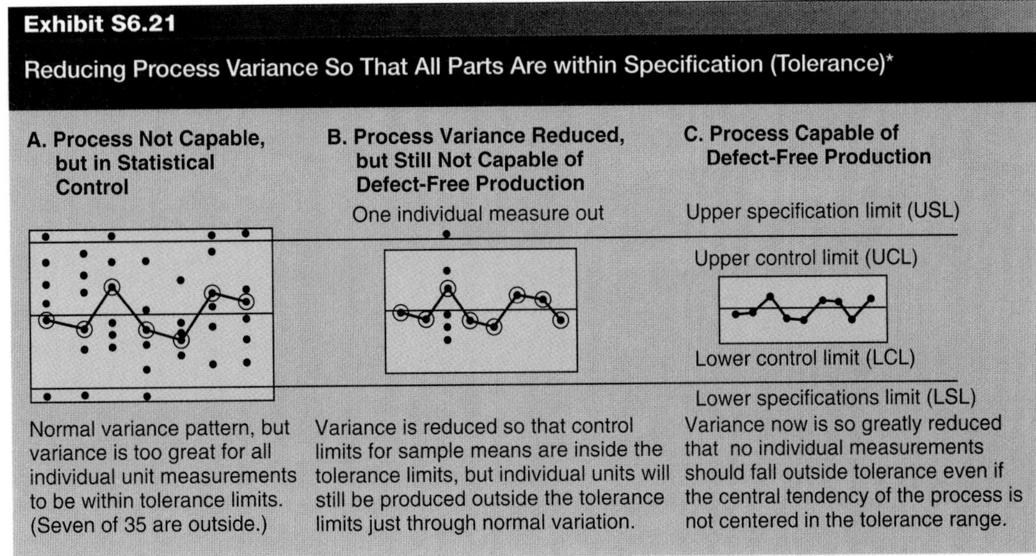

A. Process Not Capable, but in Statistical Control
B. Process Variance Reduced, but Still Not Capable of Defect-Free Production
One individual measure out
C. Process Capable of Defect-Free Production
Upper specification limit (USL)
Upper control limit (UCL)
Lower control limit (LCL)
Lower specifications limit (LSL)
Normal variance pattern, but variance is too great for all individual unit measurements to be within tolerance limits. (Seven of 35 are outside.)
Variance is reduced so that control limits for sample means are inside the tolerance limits, but individual units will still be produced outside the tolerance limits just through normal variation.
Variance now is so greatly reduced that no individual measurements should fall outside tolerance even if the central tendency of the process is not centered in the tolerance range.

Exhibit S6.21

Reducing Process Variance So That All Parts Are within Specification (Tolerance)*

*Tolerance: The range within which all individual measurements of units produced is desired to fall.
Source: Robert W. Hall, *Attaining Manufacturing Excellence: Just-in-Time Manufacturing, Total Quality, Total People Involvement* (Homewood, IL: Dow Jones–Irwin, 1987), p. 66. By permission of The McGraw-Hill Companies.

of the process control chart. Since these control limits are at plus or minus three standard deviations (3 sigma), the tolerance limits must exceed 6 sigma. A quick way of making this determination is through the use of a process capability ratio. This ratio is calculated by dividing the tolerance width by 6 sigma (the process capability), as shown in the following formula in which s, the sample standard deviation, is substituted for σ, the population standard deviation.

$$\text{Process capability ratio} = C_p = \frac{\text{Upper tolerance limit} - \text{Lower tolerance limit}}{6s} \quad \text{(S6.6)}$$

The larger the ratio, the greater the potential for producing parts within tolerance from the specified process. A ratio that is greater than 1 indicates that the tolerance limit range is wider than the actual range of measurements. If the ratio is less than 1, then some parts will be out of tolerance. The minimum capability ratio is frequently established at 1.33. Below this value, design engineers have to seek approval from manufacturing before the product can be released for production.

Capability Index (C_{pk}) The process capability ratio does not specifically indicate how well the process is performing relative to the target dimension. Thus, a second performance index, called C_{pk}, must be employed to determine whether the process mean is closer to the upper specification limit, USL, or the lower specification limit, LSL.

$$C_{pk} = \min\left[\frac{\overline{X} - \text{LSL}}{3s}, \frac{\text{USL} - \overline{X}}{3s}\right] \quad \text{(S6.7)}$$

When C_{pk} equals the capability ratio, then the process mean is centered between the two specification limits. Otherwise, the process mean is closest to the specification limit corresponding to the minimum of the two C_{pk} ratios. Consider the following example.

Example

A manufacturing process produces a certain part with a mean diameter of 2 inches and a standard deviation of 0.03 inch. The upper specification limit equals 2.05 inches, and the lower specification limit equals 1.9 inches.

Solution

From this information, a process capability ratio (C_p) and a capability index (C_{pk}) were calculated.

$$\text{Process capability ratio} = C_p = \frac{2.05 - 1.90}{6(0.03)} = 0.833$$

$$C_{pk} \text{ for LSL} = \frac{2 - 1.90}{3(0.03)} = 1.11$$

$$C_{pk} \text{ for USL} = \frac{2.05 - 2}{3(0.03)} = 0.56$$

From the process capability ratio, we can conclude that the process is not capable of producing parts within the design's specification. The C_{pk} analysis points out that the process mean is closer to the upper tolerance limit. Given this information, work can be done on the manufacturing process to increase the process capability ratio and also to center the mean between the two specification limits. This may involve, for example, a simple adjustment of a machine tool setting.

Six-Sigma Calculations

As seen in Exhibit S6.22A, the design tolerance is equal to the process variation, as defined by $\pm 3\sigma$, and the design mean equals the process mean. The process capability ratio (C_p) therefore is equal to 1. Under these conditions, we would expect the process to yield 99.74 percent good parts or, conversely, 2,700 defects per million.

With six sigma, the goal is to reduce the process variation to 50 percent of the design tolerance, as shown in Exhibit S6.22B. (Again, the design mean equals the process mean.) This results in a $C_p = 2.0$. Under these conditions, the defect rate is 2 parts per billion

Exhibit S6.22

The Goal of Six Sigma

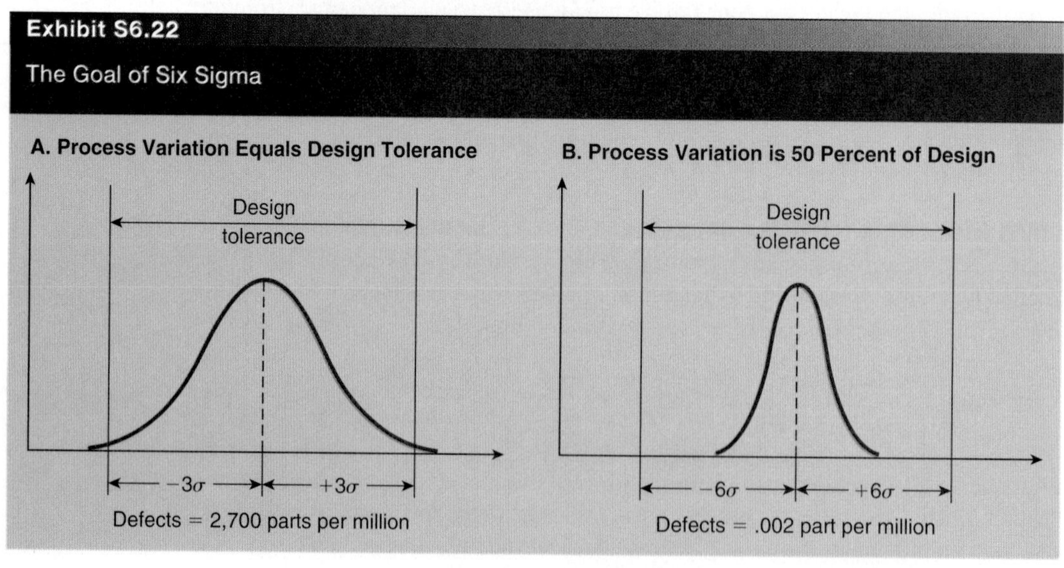

Exhibit S6.23A

Impact of 1.5σ Shift on 3σ Process

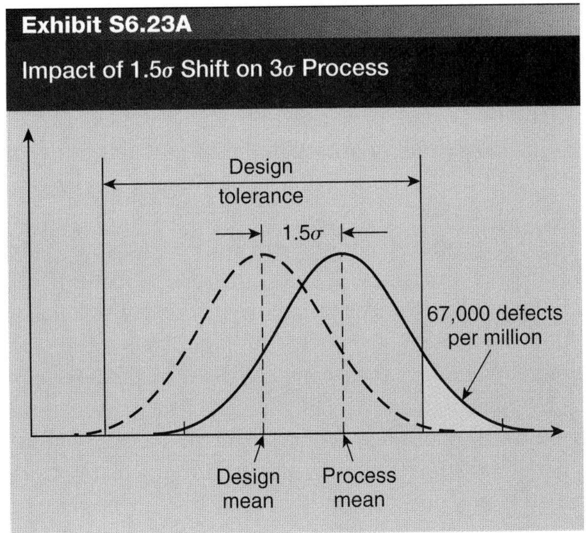

Exhibit S6.23B

Impact of 1.5σ Shift on 6σ Process

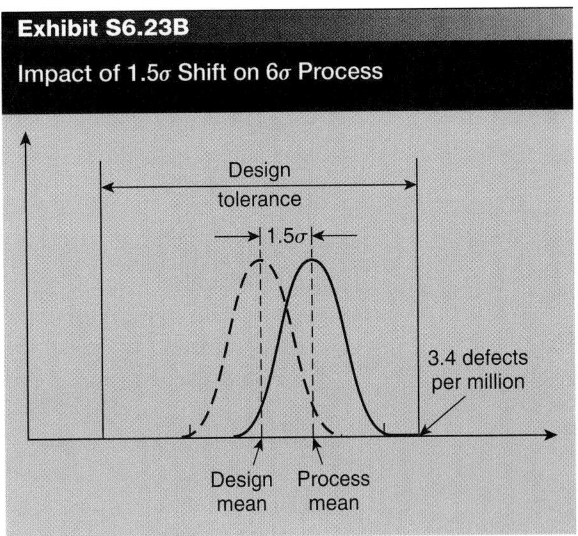

Exhibit S6.24

Defect Rates for Different Levels of Sigma (σ) Assuming a 1.5 Shift in Actual Mean from Design Mean

Sigma Level of Quality	Defects per Million
1.5σ	500,000
2.0σ	308,300
2.5σ	158,650
3.0σ	67,000
3.5σ	22,700
4.0σ	6,220
4.5σ	1,350
5.0σ	233
5.5σ	32
6.0σ	3.4

(ppb). However, to determine the number of errors associated with six sigma, we also must take into consideration the actual mean of the process relative to the design mean, which is reflected in the capability index (C_{pk}). From historical data on a wide variety of processes, the actual process means can vary as much as 1.5σ from the design mean, as shown in Exhibits S6.23A and S6.23B. This amount of variation between the two means is a major assumption in the calculation of the error rates that are presented in a six-sigma program, and which are also presented in Exhibit S6.24.

Taguchi Methods

Taguchi methods

Statistical technique for identifying the cause(s) of process variation that reduces the number of tests that are necessary.

Throughout this chapter we have discussed statistical quality control methods from the point of view of acceptance sampling and process adjustments. In what many have termed a revolution in quality thinking, Genichi Taguchi of Japan has suggested the following: Instead of constantly fiddling with production equipment to ensure consistent quality, design the product to be robust enough to achieve high quality despite fluctuations on the production line. This simple idea has been employed by such companies as Ford Motor Company, ITT, and IBM; as a result, they have saved millions of dollars in manufacturing costs.

Taguchi methods are basically statistical techniques for conducting experiments to determine the best combinations of product and process variables to make a product. *Best* means lowest cost with highest uniformity. This can be a complicated, time-consuming procedure. For example, in designing the process for a new product, one might find that a single processing step with only eight process variables (machine speed, cutting angle, and so on) could be combined in up to 5,000 different ways (which is referred to as a full factorial design). Thus, finding the combination that makes the product with the highest uniformity at the lowest cost can't be done efficiently by trial and error. Taguchi has found a way around this problem by focusing on only a fraction of the combinations that represent the overall spectrum of product/process outcomes. He developed a visual way to choose the best subset of the full number of experiments. This approach makes use of fractional factorial design, which is significantly easier for people who do not have extensive training in statistics.

Taguchi also is known for the development of the concept of a *quality loss function* (QLF) that relates the cost of quality directly to the variation in a process. Essentially, with this function Taguchi is saying that any deviation from the target quality level results in a loss to society. For example, if a defective tire goes flat, society loses the productive time of the owner who needs to either change it and/or have it repaired. If the owner doesn't change the tire, society loses the time the repair person spends on fixing the tire because he or she could have been doing work that was not repair, but instead contributed value to society (either by producing value or enjoying leisure). The following discussion from an article by Joseph Turner develops this concept in detail.

Is an Out-of-Spec Product Really Out of Spec?

Variation around Us

It is generally accepted that, as variation is reduced, quality is improved. Sometimes that knowledge is intuitive. If a train is always on time, schedules can be planned more precisely. If clothing sizes are consistent, time can be saved by ordering from a catalog. But rarely are such things thought about in terms of the value of low variability. With engineers, the knowledge is better defined. Pistons must fit cylinders, doors must fit openings, electrical components must be compatible, and boxes of cereal must have the right amount of raisins—otherwise quality will be unacceptable and customers will be dissatisfied.

However, engineers also know that it is impossible to have zero variability. For this reason, designers establish specifications that define not only the target value of something, but also acceptable limits about the target. For example, if the target value of a dimension is 10 inches, the design specifications might then be 10.00 inches $\pm$ 0.02. This would tell the manufacturing department that, while it should aim for exactly 10 inches, anything between 9.98 inches and 10.02 inches is OK.

The traditional way of interpreting such a specification is that any part that falls within the allowed range is equally good, while any part falling outside the range is totally bad. This is illustrated in Exhibit S6.25. (Note that the cost in this model is zero over the entire specification range, and then there is a quantum leap in cost once the limit is violated.)

Taguchi has pointed out that such a view is nonsense for two reasons:

1. From the customer's view, there is often practically no difference between a product just inside specifications and a product just outside. Conversely, there is a far greater difference in the quality of a product that is at the target and the quality of one that is near a limit.
2. As customers become more demanding, there is pressure to reduce variability. The underlying philosophy in Exhibit S6.26 does not recognize this pressure.

Taguchi suggests that a more correct picture of the loss is shown in Exhibit S6.26. Notice that in this graph the cost is represented by a smooth curve. There are dozens of illustrations of this notion: the meshing of gears in a transmission, the speed of photographic film, the temperature in a workplace or department store. In nearly anything that can be measured, the customer sees not a sharp line, but a gradation of acceptability. Customers see the loss function as Exhibit S6.26 rather than Exhibit S6.25.

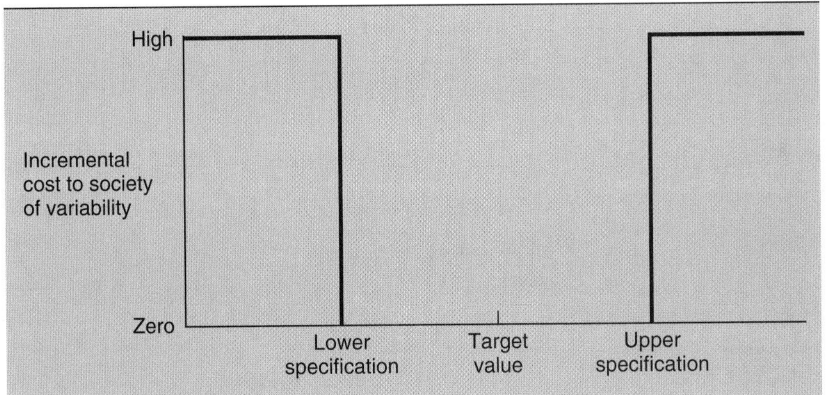

Exhibit S6.25

A Traditional View of the Cost of Variability

Source: Adapted from Joseph Turner, "Is an Out-of-Spec Product Really Out of Spec?" *Quality Progress*, December 1990, pp. 57–59.

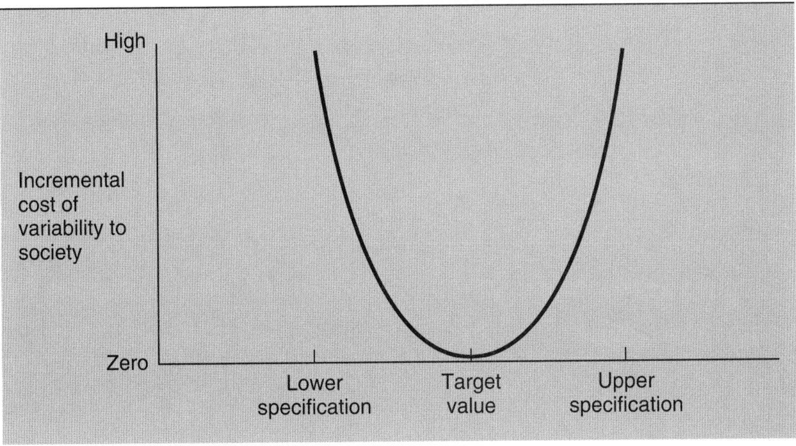

Exhibit S6.26

Taguchi's View of the Cost of Variability

What are the elements of loss to society? Internally, the more variable the manufacturing process, the more scrap generated and the more a company will have to spend on testing and inspecting for conformance. Externally, customers will find that the product does not last as long or work as well if it is not close to target. Perhaps, when used in adverse situations, the product will not perform at all, even though it meets specifications that were developed based on normal usage.[4]

Conclusion

The different quality control tools presented in this supplement provide the necessary foundation for producing high-quality goods and services. Within this group, statistical quality methods play a very significant role. Acceptance sampling provides us with a method for evaluating products after they have been made. The purpose of statistical process control is to focus on the process while the product is made.

If the inherent variation of a process is understood, managers and workers can watch the process to make sure that it is performing as expected. When the process exhibits nonrandom variation, the cause of the variation (assignable cause) needs to be sought, and eliminated (if the process has deteriorated) or continued (if the process has improved). Because variation can easily be seen on an SPC chart, managers and workers can readily identify nonrandom variation and look for its assignable causes.

[4]Joseph Turner, "Is an Out-of-Spec Product Really out of Spec?" *Quality Progress,* December 1990, pp. 57–59. Copyright © 1990, American Society for Quality. Reprinted with permission.

The introduction of quality improvement concepts such as six sigma and Taguchi methods provide us with additional ways to continuously "raise the bar" in terms of still further improving the quality of processes.

Key Formulas

Control Limits for a Variable

$$\text{CL} = \mu \pm z_{\alpha/2}\frac{\sigma}{\sqrt{n}} \qquad \text{(S6.1)}$$

Control limits for an attribute

$$\text{CL} = \overline{p} \pm z_{\alpha/2}\sqrt{\frac{\overline{p}(1-\overline{p})}{n}} \qquad \text{(S6.2)}$$

Mean of a sample

$$\overline{X} = \frac{\sum_{i=1}^{n} X_i}{n} \qquad \text{(S6.3)}$$

Average of means of all samples

$$\overline{\overline{X}} = \frac{\sum_{j=1}^{m} \overline{X}_j}{m} \qquad \text{(S6.4)}$$

Average range of all samples

$$\overline{R} = \frac{\sum_{j=1}^{m} R_j}{m} \qquad \text{(S6.5)}$$

Process capability ratio

$$C_p = \frac{\text{Upper tolerance limit} - \text{Lower tolerance limit}}{6s} \qquad \text{(S6.6)}$$

Capability index

$$C_{pk} = \min\left[\frac{\overline{X} - \text{LSL}}{3s}, \frac{\text{USL} - \overline{X}}{3s}\right] \qquad \text{(S6.7)}$$

Key Terms

acceptable quality level (AQL) p. 256
control limits p. 259
operating characteristic (OC) curves p. 258
statistical process control (SPC) p. 261
Taguchi methods p. 273
types of data:
- attribute data p. 254
- variable data p. 254

types of sampling errors:
- α error, Type I error, or producer's risk p. 255
- β error, Type II error, or consumer's risk p. 255

Review and Discussion Questions

1. Discuss the trade-off between achieving a zero AQL (acceptable quality level) and a positive AQL (e.g., an AQL of 2 percent).
2. The capability index allows for some drifting of the process mean. Discuss what this means in terms of product quality output.
3. Discuss the purposes and differences between *p*-charts and $\overline{X}$ and *R* charts.
4. In an agreement between a supplier and a customer, the supplier must ensure that all parts are within tolerance before shipment to the customer. What is the effect on the cost of quality to the customer?
5. In the situation described in Question 4, what would be the effect on the cost of quality to the supplier?
6. Discuss the logic of Taguchi methods.
7. Can you think of a way to use a deck of cards to simulate other distributions and test the central limit theorem?
8. What is the difference between a Type I error and a Type II error?
9. What is the difference between a Pareto chart and a histogram?
10. Using a checksheet, record the different colors of 40 automobiles that are in the parking lot at your school or at a shopping mall. Plot the results in a bar chart.
11. Take the results in Question 10 and plot a Pareto chart.
12. Using a checksheet, record the storage space for each of 20 document files that you and/or your classmates have for Word, Excel, and PowerPoint (or their equivalents), for a total of 60 data points. Choosing the appropriate interval, plot each of the three sets of data on a histogram. What conclusions can you draw from this histogram?

Internet Exercise

Go to the GE website (or that of any other company that has successfully implemented six sigma) and describe the role of six sigma within that organization and how it has contributed to the overall improvement of the firm.

Solved Problem

Problem 1

Completed forms from a particular department of an insurance company were sampled on a daily basis as a check against the quality of performance of that department. In order to establish a tentative norm for the department, one sample of 100 units was collected each day for 15 days, with these results:

Sample	Sample Size	Number of Forms with Errors	Sample	Sample Size	Number of Forms with Errors
1	100	4	9	100	4
2	100	3	10	100	2
3	100	5	11	100	7
4	100	0	12	100	2
5	100	2	13	100	1
6	100	8	14	100	3
7	100	1	15	100	1
8	100	3			

a. Develop a *p*-chart using a 95 percent confidence interval.

b. Plot the 15 samples collected.

c. What comments can you make about the process?

Solution

Insurance company forms.

a. $\overline{p} = \dfrac{46}{15(100)} = 0.031$

$$s_p = \sqrt{\frac{\overline{p}(1-\overline{p})}{n}} = \sqrt{\frac{0.031(1-0.031)}{100}} = \sqrt{0.0003} = .017$$

$$\text{UCL} = \overline{p} + 1.96s_p = 0.031 + 1.96(0.017) = 0.064$$

$$\text{LCL} = \overline{p} - 1.96s_p = 0.031 - 1.96(0.017) = -0.002 \text{ or zero}$$

b. The defectives are plotted here.

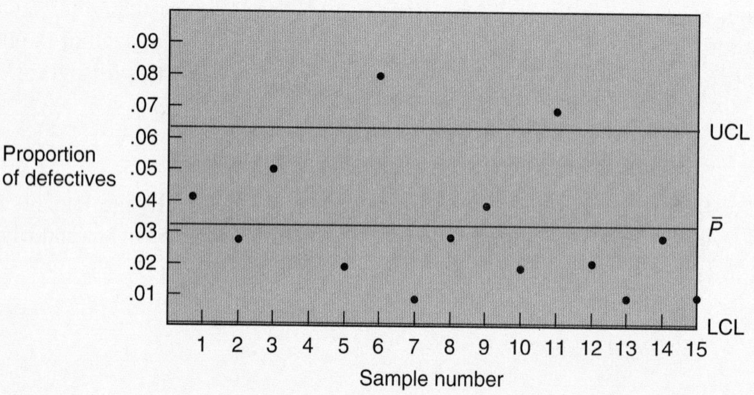

c. Of the 15 samples, 2 were out of the control limits. Since the control limits were established as 95 percent, or 1 out of 20, we would say that the process is out of control. It needs to be examined to find the cause of such widespread variation.

Problems

1. A metal fabricator produces connecting rods with an outer diameter that has a $1 \pm .01$ inch specification. A machine operator takes several sample measurements over time and determines the sample mean outer diameter to be 1.002 inches with a standard deviation of 0.003 inch.

   a. Calculate the process capability ratio and the capability index for this example.

   b. What do these figures tell you about the process?

2. Ten samples of 15 parts each were taken from an ongoing process to establish a *p*-chart for control. The samples and the number of defects in each are shown here.

Sample	n	Number of Defects in Sample
1	15	3
2	15	1
3	15	0
4	15	0
5	15	0
6	15	2
7	15	0
8	15	3
9	15	1
10	15	0

a. Develop a *p*-chart for 95 percent confidence.

b. Based on the plotted data points, what comments can you make?

3. Resistors for electronic circuits are being manufactured on a high-speed automated machine. The machine is being set up to produce a large run of resistors of 1,000 ohms each.

   To set up the machine and to create a control chart to be used throughout the run, 15 samples were taken with 4 resistors in each sample. The complete list of samples and their measured values are as follows:

Sample Number	Readings (in ohms)			
1	1010	991	985	986
2	995	996	1009	994
3	990	1003	1015	1008
4	1015	1020	1009	998
5	1013	1019	1005	993
6	994	1001	994	1005
7	989	992	982	1020
8	1001	986	996	996
9	1006	989	1005	1007
10	992	1007	1006	979
11	996	1006	997	989
12	1019	996	991	1011
13	981	991	989	1003
14	999	993	988	984
15	1013	1002	1005	992

   Develop an $\overline{X}$ chart and an *R* chart and plot the values. From the charts, what comments can you make about the process? (Use the table in Exhibit S6.17.)

4. You are the newly appointed assistant administrator at a local hospital, and your first project is to investigate the quality of the patient meals put out by the food-service department. You conducted a 10-day survey by submitting a simple questionnaire to the 400 patients with each meal, asking that they simply check off either that the meal was satisfactory or unsatisfactory. For simplicity in this problem, assume that the response was 1,000 returned questionnaires from the 1,200 meals each day. The results

ran as follows:

	Number of Unsatisfactory Meals	Sample Size
December 1	74	1,000
December 2	42	1,000
December 3	64	1,000
December 4	80	1,000
December 5	40	1,000
December 6	50	1,000
December 7	65	1,000
December 8	70	1,000
December 9	40	1,000
December 10	75	1,000
	600	10,000

a. Construct a p-chart based on the questionnaire results, using a confidence interval of 95.4 percent, which is two standard deviations.

b. What comments can you make about the results of the survey?

5. The state and local police departments are trying to analyze crime rate areas so that they can shift their patrols from decreasing crime rate areas to areas where rates are increasing. The city and county have been geographically segmented into areas containing 5,000 residences. The police recognize that all crimes and offenses are not reported; people either do not want to become involved, consider the offenses too small to report, are too embarrassed to make a police report, or do not take the time, among other reasons. Every month, because of this, the police are contacting by phone a random sample of 1,000 of the 5,000 residences in one area for data on crime (the respondents are guaranteed anonymity). The data collected for the past 12 months for one area are as follows:

Month	Crime Incidence	Sample Size	Crime Rate
January	7	1,000	0.007
February	9	1,000	0.009
March	7	1,000	0.007
April	7	1,000	0.007
May	7	1,000	0.007
June	9	1,000	0.009
July	7	1,000	0.007
August	10	1,000	0.010
September	8	1,000	0.008
October	11	1,000	0.011
November	10	1,000	0.010
December	8	1,000	0.008

Construct a p-chart for 95 percent confidence and plot each of the months. If the next three months show the number of crime incidences (out of 1,000 residences sampled) in this area as

January = 10 February = 12 March = 11

What comments can you make regarding the crime rate?

6. Some of the citizens complained to city council members that there should be equal protection under the law against the occurrence of crimes. The citizens argued that this equal protection should be interpreted as indicating that high-crime areas should have more police protection than low-crime areas. Therefore, police patrols and other methods for preventing crime (such as street lighting or cleaning up abandoned areas and buildings) should be used proportionately to crime occurrence.

   In a fashion similar to Problem 5, the city has been broken down into 20 geographical areas, each containing 5,000 residences. The 1,000 sampled from each area showed the following incidence of crime during the past month.

Area	Number of Crimes	Sample Size	Crime Rate
1	14	1,000	0.014
2	3	1,000	0.003
3	19	1,000	0.019
4	18	1,000	0.018
5	14	1,000	0.014
6	28	1,000	0.028
7	10	1,000	0.010
8	18	1,000	0.018
9	12	1,000	0.012
10	3	1,000	0.003
11	20	1,000	0.020
12	15	1,000	0.015
13	12	1,000	0.012
14	14	1,000	0.014
15	10	1,000	0.010
16	30	1,000	0.030
17	4	1,000	0.004
18	20	1,000	0.020
19	6	1,000	0.006
20	30	1,000	0.030
	300		

   Suggest a reallocation of crime protection effort, if indicated, based on a *p*-chart analysis. In order to be reasonably certain in your recommendation, select a 95 percent confidence level.

7. The Eau de Fawcett Beverage Company has developed a line of sophisticated beverages targeted for couples who both work and have no children. This segment of the consumer market is often referred to as "DINKs" (i.e., Double Income, No Kids). This new line of beverages is thus being produced under the label "Drinks for Dinks." The bottles for this product are filled on automatic equipment that has been adjusted so that the average fill per bottle is 11 ounce. Historically, it has been determined that the standard deviation of the filling equipment is 0.16 ounce. Every hour, a sample of 36 bottles is taken at random from the process, and the average volume is calculated and plotted on an $\overline{X}$ chart.

   a. Draw an $\overline{X}$ process control chart with limits of ± 3 standard deviations, correctly labeling the UCL and LCL.

   b. The average sample volumes for Monday morning were as follows:

Hour	7:00 AM	8:00 AM	9:00 AM	10:00 AM	11:00 AM
Average volume	11.09	10.95	10.82	11.06	11.23

Plot the average volume for each hour on the process control chart. Do you think that the process is in control?

8. Allison Jon, the manager of the 800-number reservation service for a nationwide chain of luxury hotels, is concerned about the productivity of her operation. Analysis of past data shows that it should take an average of five minutes to properly process a reservation and that the standard deviation is 30 seconds. Every day, Allison randomly samples how long it takes to make each of 25 reservations.
   a. Set up a process control chart with 95 percent confidence limits.
   b. If the sample results show that the average reservation time is significantly above the upper control limit, what might be some of the causes for the longer reservation times? How would you correct these problems?
   c. Should Allison have any concern if the average reservation time was significantly below the lower control limit? Why?
9. You have just returned from a trip to New York City where you stayed at a first-class hotel. After spending $250 per night for the room plus an additional $35 per night to park your car, you are very unhappy with the level of service you received during your stay at this hotel.
   a. Draw a fishbone diagram identifying the major causes for your dissatisfaction and possible secondary causes within each of these categories (do not include price).
   b. You call the hotel to voice your complaint and the manager asks you if you would be willing to collect some data for her so she can get at the root cause of the problem. You collect the following data on 100 complaints:

	Cause (Select from part *a*)	Frequency
1.	________________	16
2.	________________	11
3.	________________	27
4.	________________	42
5.	________________	4

   c. Draw a Pareto diagram for the above data, labeling the axes appropriately. How does this information assist the manager in improving the service quality of her operation?
10. You have just returned from an airline trip to California and are very unhappy with your onboard experience.
   a. Draw a fishbone diagram identifying the different possible primary causes (within each of these categories) for your dissatisfaction with your trip. Also identify several possible secondary causes.
   b. You call the airline to voice your complaint and the manager asks you if you will collect some data for him so that he can get at the root cause of the problem. You collect the following data on 100 complaints:

	Cause (Select from part *a*)	Frequency
1.	________________	6
2.	________________	22
3.	________________	14
4.	________________	43
5.	________________	10
6.	________________	5

Bibliography

Aslup, Fred, and Ricky M. Watson. *Practical Statistical Process Control: A Tool for Quality Manufacturing.* New York: Van Nostrand Reinhold, 1993.

Hradesky, John L. *Productivity and Quality Improvement: A Practical Guide to Implementing Statistical Process Control.* New York: McGraw-Hill, 1988.

Juran, J. M., and F. M. Gryna. *Quality Planning and Analysis.* 2nd ed. New York: McGraw-Hill, 1980.

Taguchi, G. *On-Line Quality Control during Production.* Tokyo: Japanese Standards Association, 1987.

Thompson, James R., and Jacek Koronacki. *Statistical Process Control for Quality Improvement.* New York: Chapman & Hall, 1993.

Turner, Joseph. "Is an Out-of-Spec Product Really Out of Spec?" *Quality Progress,* December 1990, pp. 57–59.

Wetherill, G. Barrie, and Don W. Brown. *Statistical Process Control: Theory and Practice*. New York: Chapman & Hall, 1991.

Wheeler, Donald J. *Understanding Variation: The Key to Managing Chaos*. Knoxville, TN: SPC Press, Inc., 1993.

Case

Shortening Customers' Telephone Waiting Time

This case illustrates how a bank applied some of the basic seven quality tools discussed in this supplement and storyboard concepts to improve customer service. It is the story of a QC program implemented in the main office of a large bank. An average of 500 customers call this office every day. Surveys indicated that callers tended to become irritated if the phone rang more than five times before it was answered, and often would not call the company again. In contrast, a prompt answer after just two rings reassured the customers and made them feel more comfortable doing business by phone.

Selection of a Theme

Telephone reception was chosen as a QC theme for the following reasons: (*a*) Telephone reception is the first impression a customer receives from the company; (*b*) this theme coincided with the company's telephone reception slogan, "Don't make customers wait, and avoid needless switching from extension to extension"; and (*c*) it also coincided with a companywide campaign being promoted at that time that advocated being friendly to everyone one met.

First, the staff discussed why the present method of answering calls made callers wait. Case Exhibit CS6.1 illustrates a frequent situation, where a call from customer B comes in while the operator is talking with customer A. Let's see why the customer has to wait.

At (1), the operator receives a call from the customer but, due to lack of experience, does not know where to connect the call. At (2), the receiving party cannot answer the phone quickly, perhaps because he or she is unavailable, and no one else can take the call. The result is that the operator must transfer the call to another extension while apologizing for the delay.

Cause-and-Effect Diagram and Situation Analysis

To fully understand the situation, the quality circle members decided to conduct a survey regarding callers who waited for more than five rings. Circle members itemized factors at a brainstorming discussion and arranged them in a cause-and-effect diagram. (See

Exhibit CS6.1

Why Customers Had to Wait

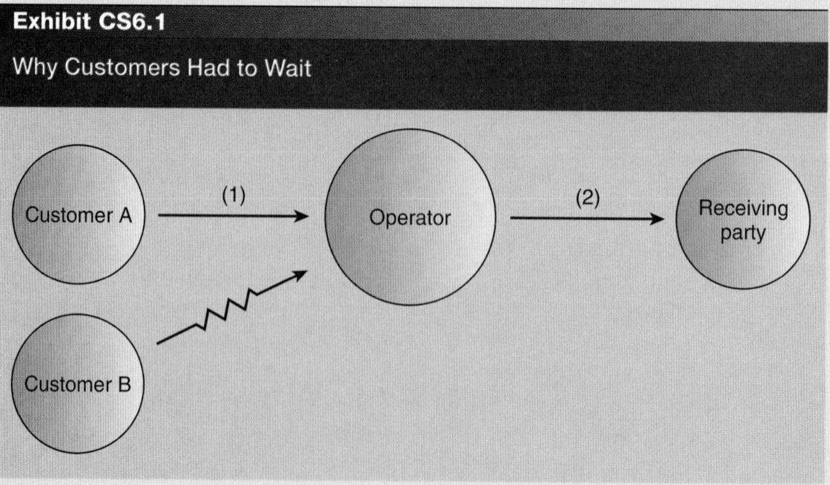

Exhibit CS6.2.) Operators then kept checksheets on several points to tally the results spanning 12 days from June 4 to 16. (See Exhibit CS6.3A.)

Results of the Checksheet Situation Analysis

The data recorded on the checksheets unexpectedly revealed that "one operator (partner out of the office)" topped the list by a big margin, occurring a total of 172 times. In this case, the operator on duty had to deal with large numbers of calls when the phones were busy. Customers who had to wait a long time averaged 29.2 daily, which accounted for 6 percent of the calls received every day. (See Exhibits CS6.3B and CS6.3C.)

Setting the Target

After an intense but productive discussion, the staff decided to set a QC program goal of reducing the number of waiting callers to zero. That is to say that all incoming calls would be handled promptly, without inconveniencing the customer.

Measures and Execution

(*a*) Taking Lunches on Three Different Shifts, Leaving at Least Two Operators on the Job at All Times

Up until this resolution was made, a two-shift lunch system had been employed, leaving only one operator on the job while the other was taking a lunch break. However, since the survey revealed that this was a major cause of customers waiting on the line, the company brought in a helper operator from the clerical section.

Exhibit CS6.2

Cause-and-Effect Diagram

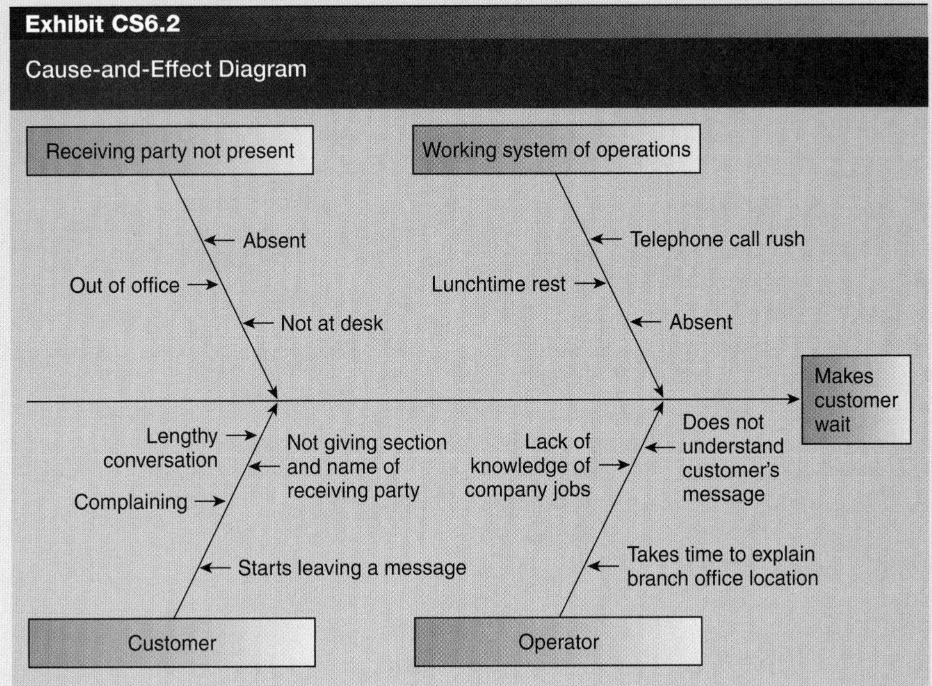

Case

(*b*) Asking All Employees to Leave Messages When Leaving Their Desks

The objective of this rule was to simplify the operator's chores when the receiving party was not at his or her desk. The new program was explained at the employees' regular morning meetings, and companywide support was requested. To help implement this practice, posters were placed around the office to publicize the new measures.

Exhibit CS6.3

Causes of Callers' Waits

A. Checksheet—Designed to Identify the Problems

Reason / Date	No one present in the section receiving the call	Receiving party not present	Only one operator (partner out of the office)	Total
June 4	\\\\	卌 \	卌 卌 \	24
June 5	卌	卌 \\\	卌 卌 \\\\	32
June 6	卌 \	\\\\	卌 卌 \\	28
June 15	卌	卌	卌 \\\	25

B. Reasons Why Callers Had to Wait

		Daily average	Total number
A	One operator (partner out of the office)	14.3	172
B	Receiving party not present	6.1	73
C	No one present in the section receiving the call	5.1	61
D	Section and name of receiving party not given	1.6	19
E	Inquiry about branch office locations	1.3	16
F	Other reasons	0.8	10
	Total	29.2	351

Period: 12 days from June 4 to 16, 1980

C. Reasons Why Callers Had to Wait (Pareto Diagram)

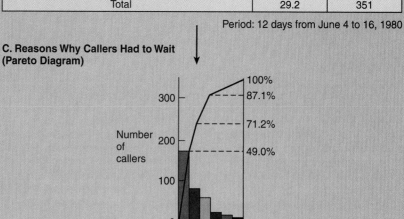

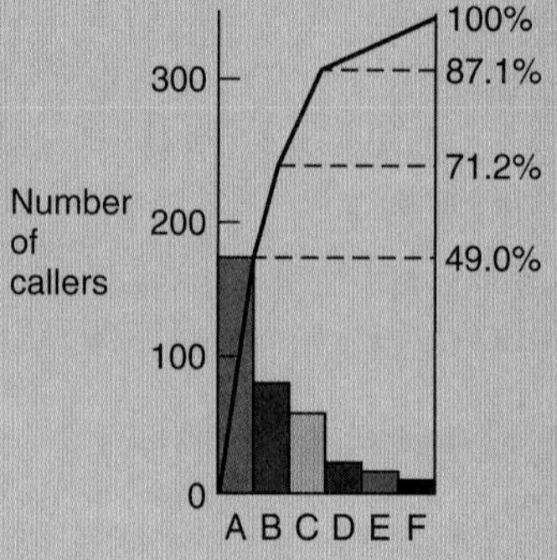

Number of callers
300
200
100
0
A B C D E F
100%
87.1%
71.2%
49.0%

(*c*) Compiling a Directory Listing the Personnel and Their Respective Jobs

The notebook was specially designed to aid the operators, who could not be expected to know the details of every employee's job or where to connect his or her incoming calls.

Confirming the Results

Although the waiting calls could not be reduced to zero, all items presented showed a marked improvement, as shown in Exhibits CS6.4A and CS6.4B. The major cause of delays, "one operator (partner out of the office)," plummeted from 172 incidents during the control period to 15 in the follow-up survey.

Source: From "The Quest for Higher Quality—the Deming Prize and Quality Control," Ricoh Company, Ltd., in Masaaki Imai, *Kaizen: The Key to Japan's Competitive Success* (New York: The McGraw-Hill Companies, 1986), pp. 54–58.

Exhibit CS6.4

Effects of QC

A. Effects of QC (Comparison Before and After QC)

		Total number		Daily average	
	Reasons why callers had to wait	**Before**	**After**	**Before**	**After**
A	One operator (partner out of the office)	172	15	14.3	1.2
B	Receiving party not present	73	17	6.1	1.4
C	No one present in the section receiving the call	61	20	5.1	1.7
D	Section and name of receiving party not given	19	4	1.6	0.3
E	Inquiry about branch office locations	16	3	1.3	0.2
F	Others	10	0	0.8	0
	Total	351	59	29.2	4.8

Period: 12 days from Aug. 17 to 30.

Problems are classified according to cause and presented in order of the amount of time consumed. They are illustrated in a bar graph. 100% indicates the total number of time-consuming calls.

B. Effects of QC (Pareto Diagram)

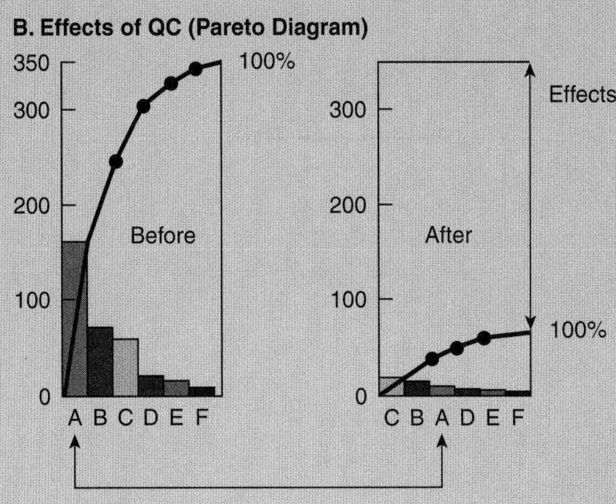

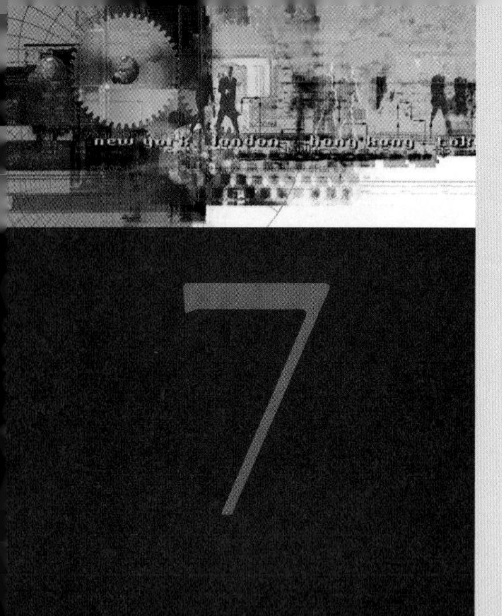

7 Facility Decisions: Location and Capacity

Chapter Objectives

- Present a framework for evaluating alternative site locations.
- Identify the various factors, both quantitative and qualitative, that should be taken into consideration when selecting a location for a manufacturing or service organization.
- Distinguish between those factors that are important for locating a manufacturing facility and those that are important for locating a service operation.
- Introduce geographic information systems (GIS) as a tool for evaluating locations.

A client of Fluor Global Location Strategies, a firm specializing in site location analysis, decided to locate its new power generation facility in Ohio because of various tax incentives and its central location within the United States. To determine specifically where in Ohio it should locate this facility, the firm provided Fluor with the following information.

- The plant had to be within 50 miles of a commercial airport.
- The manufacturing workforce of the county must be greater than 5,000.
- The facility must be within five miles of a 230-kVolt transmission line.
- The facility must be within five miles of a 12-inch or larger gas line.

To identify all of the potential areas within Ohio that met these four criteria, Fluor employed geographic information systems (GIS) software. As an example, the map shows areas within the state that met above one of the criteria—that the facility must be within fifty miles of a commercial airport. A similar map was developed for each of the other three criteria. Again, using the GIS software, Fluor overlaid the four criteria onto a single map, which identified only those areas that met all four requirements.

Source: Special thanks to Fluor Global Location Strategies.

Managerial Issues

Senior management makes a long-term commitment whenever it decides to build a manufacturing facility. Such facilities typically require a substantial investment in capital, the recovery of which takes place over a large number of years. As discussed earlier in Chapter 2, the construction of a facility involves several strategic decisions, which include (*a*) how big to make it, (*b*) when to build it, (*c*) where to build it, and (*d*) what type(s) of process(es) to install. General Motors, for example, took all of these factors into consideration when it built the Saturn plant in Spring Hill, Tennessee. Each of these decisions significantly impacts operational decisions for many years, and consequently it also can have a significant impact on the overall success of the firm.

Back-of-the-house services similarly require large capital investments. Examples of such facilities are FedEx's main distribution hub in Memphis, Tennessee, and Citicorp's credit card operations in Sioux Falls, South Dakota. On the other hand, the capital investment is usually much smaller for front-of-the-house operations that interact directly with the customer. However, the risks associated with selecting sites for front-of-the-house operations tend to be much higher, as the success of an operation at a given location is significantly affected not only by the customer demographics within its immediate area but also by the unique characteristics of the site. To illustrate the importance of selecting the right site for these types of services, there is a saying in the restaurant business that "The three most important factors for success are Location, Location and Location."

For manufacturing companies and back-of-the-house service operations, management must address many issues when adding capacity. These include: Should we close the existing facility? Can we expand the existing facility? Should the new facility have a different process from existing operations? The primary criteria in making these decisions are to minimize costs. In contrast, the decision to locate a front-of-the-house service facility is primarily driven by its revenue potential.

The globalization of business further complicates the location decision. Local customs, tax rates, tax incentives, and laws must be taken into consideration, along with infrastructure, in terms of roads, telecommunications, and supporting businesses. Ireland, for example, is attracting both manufacturing and service organizations, because of its relatively low cost and educated work force, infrastructure, and tax incentives. Another example is the creation of *maquiladora* businesses in Mexico along the U.S. border. With the establishment of the North American Free Trade Agreement (NAFTA), these firms are now able to ship products duty-free into the United States. As a result, many U.S. companies have relocated operations there due to the significantly lower labor costs in Mexico.

An incorrect site location decision is very expensive for both manufacturing and service firms. Because it is a long-term decision, management must live with the consequences of that decision for many years. Thus, a decision to build in the wrong location, at the wrong time, with the wrong capacity or the wrong process(es) can have significant negative implications on the profits of the firm. If management elects to subsequently sell off the facility as a result of recognizing a bad decision, then a substantial portion of the initial investment is frequently not recoverable because the facility is usually built for a unique purpose. Consequently, management must take a very hard look at these types of decisions.

Locating Manufacturing Facilities

The facility location decision for a manufacturing firm usually involves the location of both the manufacturing plant and the warehouse or distribution facilities. As a general rule, products that decrease in weight and volume during the manufacturing process tend to be located near the sources of raw material. An example of this would be a lumber mill that is located in a forest where the trees are being harvested. In this case, the reduction is so significant, that the mill is often moved every few years, to be closer to the trees being cut down. On the other hand, products that increase in weight and volume during the manufacturing process tend to be located near the consumers. An example of this is a soft drink bottler that is located near a major city. In both of these cases, the goal is to reduce distribution costs.

At the same time, as the world continues toward a single global economy, businesses need to take a more international perspective with respect to locating their manufacturing facilities, as seen in the OM in Practice on BSC's decision to locate in Ireland. The low labor costs provided by faraway countries often more than offset the additional transportation costs. However, there are many other factors besides costs that are involved in selecting a site. As a result, the complexity of the decision-making process increases severalfold when a firm decides to shift from a national to an international site location strategy. In weighing the advantages and disadvantages of alternative sites, the analysis therefore should include an evaluation of both qualitative and quantitative factors.[1] (One method for comparing the qualitative factors for different locations is known as **factor-rating systems,** which is presented in detail later in this chapter.)

Qualitative Factors

The qualitative factors include (*a*) local infrastructure, (*b*) worker education and skills, (*c*) product content requirements, and (*d*) political/economic stability.

Local Infrastructure The local infrastructure that is necessary to support a manufacturing operation can be divided into two broad categories: institutional and transportational. With manufacturing operations becoming more flexible and responsive to customer requirements, there is a growing dependence on local institutions or suppliers to be more flexible and responsive. In addition, the local transportation network that links the suppliers to the manufacturer must be efficient and reliable. For example, a lack of an adequate and reliable transportation infrastructure in the Former Soviet Union (FSU) or the People's Republic of China would preclude a firm that uses just-in-time (JIT) concepts from locating in these areas.

Worker Education and Skills The increased sophistication of today's manufacturing processes requires that the workforce be highly educated and equipped with a wide variety of skills. Increased emphasis on automation requires specific worker skills to operate and maintain equipment. Modern manufacturing processes like just-in-time (JIT) also require a well-educated workforce. As an illustration, the significant growth of business in Singapore in recent years can be attributed, in large part, to the investment of its government in educating and training its population.

content requirements

Requirement that a percentage of a product must be made within a country for it to be sold there.

Product Content Requirements **Content requirements** state that a minimum percentage of a product must be produced within the borders of a country in order for that product to be sold in that country. This assures jobs in the local economy while reducing the difference between imports and exports. For example, for a car to be sold in the Philippines, it must be assembled there. Consequently, each of the major car manufacturers that wants to sell cars in the Philippines has an assembly plant there even though demand for cars in that country is sufficiently small to suggest that importing them would be more economical.

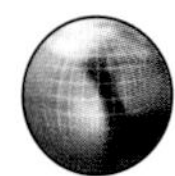

Political/Economic Stability The stability of a region refers to the number and intensity of economic and political fluctuations that might occur there. The dissolution of the

[1]Alan D. MacCormack, Laurence J. Newman III, and Donald B. Rosenfeld, "The New Dynamics of Global Manufacturing Site Location," *Sloan Management Review,* Summer 1994, pp. 69–80.

Operations Management in Practice

WHY BOSTON SCIENTIFIC LOCATED ITS PLANT IN IRELAND

Boston Scientific Corporation (BSC) is a manufacturer of disposable medical devices, with its headquarters in Natick, Massachusetts. With its strong emphasis on customer support, BSC decided to establish a physical presence that was nearer its rapidly growing European market. After analyzing several potential locations on both the continent and in the United Kingdom, BSC determined that Ireland was the most appropriate location for its operation. The reasons for selecting Ireland were many, including

- Political stability in a democratic society that was similar to that of the United States.
- Telecommunications infrastructure that was at the level of sophistication and reliability similar to that in the United States.
- Financial assistance and tax incentives provided by the Irish Development Authority (IDA) and the Irish government.
- Strong work ethic of the population, its education level, and the nearly common language.
- Ease of doing business in terms of existing support services and examples of prior successes.
- Ireland's corporate tax rate and hourly labor costs among the lowest in Europe.

As a result of its decision to locate in Ireland, BSC now has a 400,000-square-foot facility in Galway that employs nearly 2,500 people. Its experience in Ireland has been so favorable that BSC recently expanded its presence with another 200,000-square-foot facility in Cork, which employs 700.

Source: Special thanks to Doug Horka and Mike Nazzaro of Boston Scientific Corp.

Former Soviet Union provides ample evidence of the problems associated with locating a business in unstable economies.

Quantitative Factors

The quantitative factors include (*a*) labor costs, (*b*) distribution costs, (*c*) facility costs, (*d*) exchange rates, and (*e*) tax rates.

Labor Costs Labor costs can vary dramatically, depending on location. In Western Europe, the United States, and Japan, the cost of labor can exceed US$19.00 per hour in comparison to countries in Asia where the cost can be less than US$7.00 per day (see Exhibit 7.1). An important factor that must be considered is the skill requirements of the worker. Although the cost of labor in many areas is very cheap, the workers in these very same regions often lack adequate education and skills.

Distribution Costs As we become more global, distribution and transportation costs take on added importance. In addition to the cost of transportation, the time required to deliver the products also must be taken into consideration. Consequently, in many cases the low costs associated with manufacturing products in Asia are offset by the long lead times and the high cost of delivery to markets in North America and Europe.

special economic zones (SEZ)

Duty-free areas in a country established to attract foreign investment in the form of manufacturing facilities.

Facility Costs Undeveloped or third-world countries often offer incentives in the form of low-cost manufacturing facilities to attract companies. For example, within the People's Republic of China (PRC) many **special economic zones (SEZ)** have been established that are exempt from tariffs and duties—provided that the products made there are sold outside the PRC. In some countries, the local government will enter into a partnership with a firm, with the government providing the land, the building, and perhaps the training of the workforce.

Exchange Rates The volatility of the exchange rates between countries can have a significant impact on sales and profits. For example, the change in rates between the Japanese

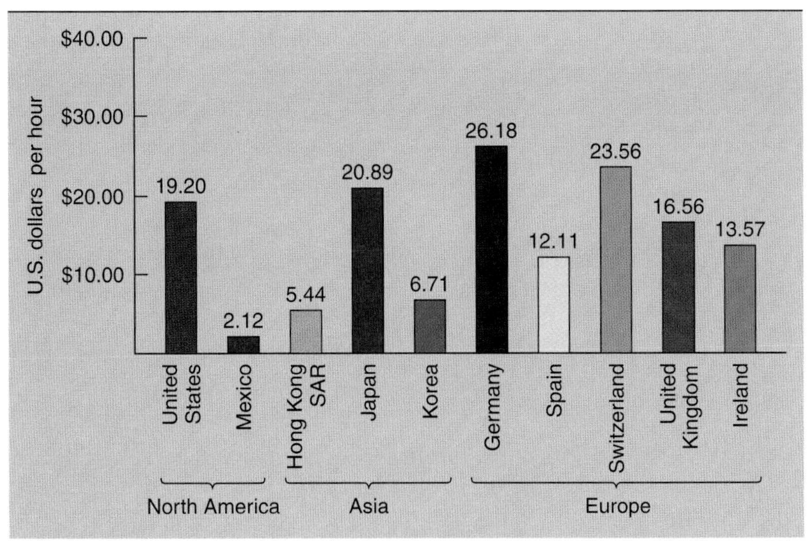

Exhibit 7.1

Comparison of 2000 Hourly Wages for Manufacturing Workers

Source: Bureau of Labor Statistics, September 7, 2000.

yen and the U.S. dollar from below 90 yen per dollar to more than 120 yen per dollar between 1996 and 1997 increased the price competitiveness of Japanese products in the United States while decreasing the ability of U.S. products to compete in Japan. A similar situation occurred in 2000–2001 with a decrease in the value of the euro from US$1.06 to less than US$0.90.

Tax Rates Tax rates can differ significantly between countries, and even within a country. For example, in the United States, some states have income and sales taxes, while others do not. Other taxes that need to be considered include property taxes and payroll taxes. In many western European countries, like France and Germany, payroll taxes can be as high as 50 percent. To attract businesses, many countries and states will offer significant tax incentives. For example, a country may exempt a firm from paying income taxes during its first five or 10 years of operation, after which normal tax rates will apply.

Locating Service Operations

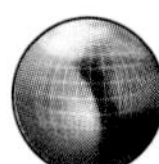

Many of the issues manufacturing companies have to address when expanding their operations internationally also must be addressed by service operations. (See the OM in Practice on Toys "Я" Us in Japan.) For example, when McDonald's opened its first restaurant in Moscow, the lack of an existing institutional infrastructure to support its operation required that it build a central commissary. This commissary prepared everything for the retail outlet, from hamburger patties to rolls and french fries. In addition, the Russian farmers had to be shown how to grow vegetables such as potatoes and lettuce that would meet McDonald's high-quality product specifications. In contrast, the opening of a McDonald's in the United States or Western Europe would only require a call to established, local suppliers.

Location Strategies

In an effort to better serve customers, service operations have adopted a variety of location strategies, depending on the particular customer requirements they are trying to address. Exhibit 7.2 presents several approaches to satisfying these customer needs.

Exhibit 7.2

Customer Requirements and Location Strategies for Service Operations

Customer Requirements	Strategy
Customers are hungry because airlines no longer serve food on short flights.	Locate "real" restaurants in airports (Legal Seafoods, Logan Airport, Boston, MA; Sam Adams Atlanta Brewhouse, Hartsfield International Airport, Atlanta, GA).
Customers want more convenient locations to save time.	Combine previously separate service operations into one location (Dunkin' Donuts in 7-Eleven; convenience stores with gas stations).
Customers are reluctant to shop frequently in large megastores because they are time consuming.	Add other services to increase convenience such as fast food and banking (McDonald's in Wal-Mart; Bank of Boston, and Barnes and Noble Bookstores at Super Stop & Shop Supermarkets).

Source: Adapted from Hal Reid, "Retailers Seek the Unique," *Business Geographics* 5, no. 2 (February 1997), pp. 32–35.

Operations Management in Practice

TOYS "Я" US IN JAPAN

On December 20, 1991, Toys "Я" Us—the world's largest toy retailer—opened its first retail store in Japan. What may now sound like an American success story in Japan traveled a difficult road for two years. The retailer had established locations in Canada, the United Kingdom, Germany, France, Singapore, Hong Kong, Malaysia, and Taiwan well before it attempted to enter the Japanese market.

In January 1990, Toys "Я" Us formally applied to open its first (large) toy store in Niigata, Japan. This caused local toy retailers to proclaim their opposition by invoking provisions contained in the Large-Scale Retail Store Act. Then they organized a lobbying group to mobilize support against the American firm. Toys "Я" Us appealed for help directly through the U.S. trade representative and other channels. Sustained American political pressure and widespread publicity finally forced MITI to confront the local lobby and limit to 18 months the application process under the restrictive retail law. It was April 1990, and Toys "Я" Us had overcome its first major hurdle.

But there was another hurdle to cross. Toys "Я" Us succeeds in large part by selling below suggested retail price. It accomplishes this mainly through exploiting economies it obtains through volume purchases. Anticipating the threat posed by that strategy to their own profit margins, Japanese toy manufacturers banded together and vowed not to sell their wares to Toys "Я" Us. But Nintendo depends heavily on Toys "Я" Us for the distribution of its products in the United States and other major markets. Nintendo's defection triggered an ultimate end to this boycott.

Private-sector countermeasures consciously adopted by numerous major Japanese corporations are replacing the falling barriers to entry of public-sector regulation.

Source: Mark Mason, "United States Direct Investment in Japan: Trends and Prospects," Copyright © 1992 by The Regents at the University of California. Reprinted from the *California Management Review,* vol. 35, no. 1. By permission of The Regents.

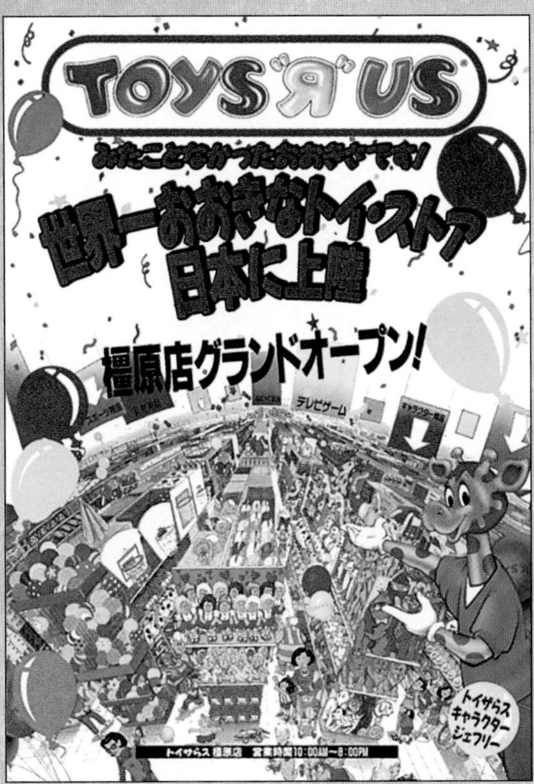

Toys "Я" Us has successfully entered the Japanese toy market through private-sector help—in this case, with the help of Nintendo.

Computer Programs for Site Selection

geographic information systems (GIS)

Computer tool that assesses alternative locations for service operations.

With the growth in **geographic information systems (GIS),** service operations are able to conduct location analysis more quickly and with greater accuracy than was previously possible. GIS allows large databases to be displayed graphically, thereby providing the service manager with a "bird's-eye view" of a particular region of interest. These regional maps can display a wide variety of demographic data, depending on the needs of the service manager. Exhibit 7.3A, for example, shows the location of housing loans for a bank, including a breakdown by income of the different areas served by the bank. Exhibit 7.3B analyzes the percentage of total sales that would be generated from different areas if a regional mall

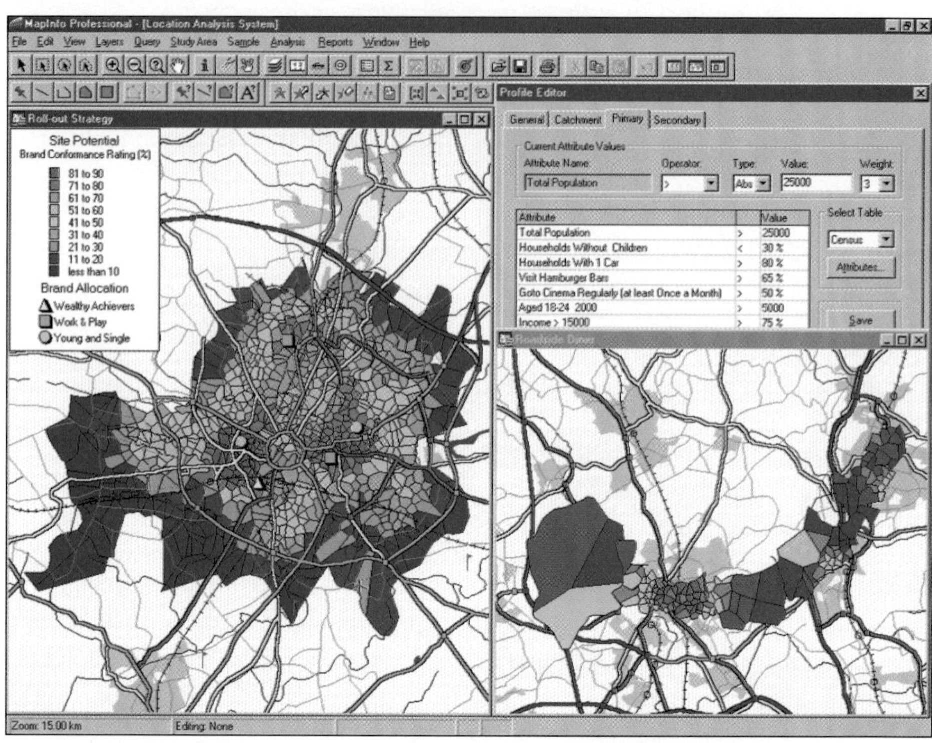

Geographic information systems (GIS), shown here from MapInfo, are used by retailers, financial services groups, insurance companies, and utilities in the site selection process. Mapping relevant information on potential sites such as demographics, customers' buying patterns, trade areas, competitors, and drive times allows this information to be seen in a single, comprehensive view for more informed and precise decision making.

were to be built. Exhibit 7.3C identifies the gap between the demand for noncritical emergency room visits and the availability of clinics and physicians to meet that demand.

In addition to GIS, there are many nongraphic computer programs available to assist the service manager in evaluating alternative site locations. Many of these models incorporate forecasting techniques such as regression analysis, which will be introduced in Chapter 9.

Types of Service Facilities

The decision where to locate a service facility is highly dependent on the specific type of service that is being provided and how it is delivered to the customer. We identify the following three types of service facilities, based upon the degree and type of contact each has with the customer:

brick-and-mortar operation

A front-of-the-house service that requires a physical structure to interact directly with the customer.

- Facilities with direct interface with the customer.
- Facilities with indirect customer contact.
- Facilities with no customer contact.

Facilities with Direct Interface with the Customer Businesses that require the actual presence of the customer as part of the service process are often referred to as **brick-and-mortar operations** because of their physical structures. Examples of these types of

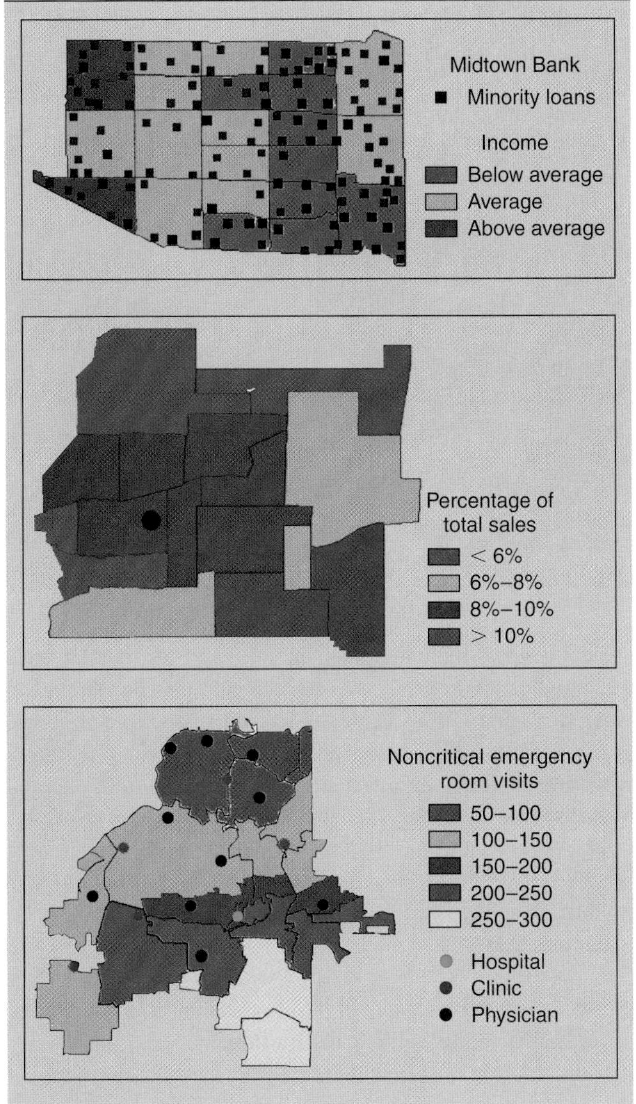

Exhibit 7.3

A. Distribution of a Bank's Housing Loans in an Area

B. Distribution of Sales for a Regional Mall by Area

C. Demand for Health care in a Region and the Services That Are Available

Source: Getting to Know Arc View GIS (Redlands, CA: Environmental Systems Research Institute, Inc., 1997). Reprinted with permission.

services include restaurants, hotels, branch offices of banks, hospitals, and traditional retail operations such as supermarkets, large department stores, and small clothing boutiques. For firms with these types of decentralized facilities, the critical success factor is the amount of sales that a given location can generate. Consequently, many multilocation services have developed sophisticated forecasting models for predicting the sales that potential new locations can generate. (Forecasting models that are used to evaluate potential new locations based on predicted sales are presented in Chapter 9.)

Facilities with Indirect Customer Contact Services such as telephone call centers and virtual firms that only link to the customer through a website do not require the customer's physical presence in order to deliver the service. Examples of the wide variety of

At a Dell call center, employees provide assistance to customers.

services that have call centers include hotels, airlines, and car rental agencies (for reservations); brokerage and financial services (for trading transactions); and mail order businesses such as L.L. Bean and Land's End (for customer orders). Call centers also provide customer service support for both services and manufacturing companies. These same services often provide a website as an alternative channel of communication with the customer. With these types of facilities, the choice of location, in terms of being near the customer, is not an issue. Consequently, the site selection process in these cases is very similar to that of back-of-the-house service operations, as discussed in the following section. In fact, both the call centers and websites are frequently located in the same facility to take advantage of economies of scale.

back-of-the-house

A service facility, or that part of the service process, that does not come in contact with the customer.

quasi-manufacturing operation

A service firm's dedicated production and distribution facility that supplies its retail operations.

Facilities with No Customer Contact Services that have no direct interaction with the customer are often referred to as **back-of-the-house** operations. Because the customer is absent from the process, these services, in many respects, tend to resemble a manufacturing operation. Services with these characteristics can be further divided into two broad categories: (*a*) the processing (sometimes) and distribution of physical goods (as illustrated by a central commissary for a restaurant chain) and (*b*) the processing and distribution of information (as illustrated by a credit card billing operation). As in selecting a manufacturing site, the location of a physical distribution center needs to consider not only the facility's operating costs but also the distribution or delivery costs, with the goal of minimizing the combined costs of both. Wal-Mart's regional distribution centers provide a good example of this type of facility.

In addition to distributing products, some of these back-of-the-house facilities also include, to some extent, manufacturing processes and are therefore often referred to as **quasi-manufacturing operations.** A central commissary for Bruegger's Bagels, where the dough is mixed and the bagels are formed (but not boiled and baked—these operations are done at the retail locations), is a good example of a quasi-manufacturing operation.

However, for those back-of-the-house services that are exclusively involved in processing information, there are only the facility operating costs to minimize, as the differences in delivery costs between alternative locations are usually nonexistent or negligible.

For example, the cost of long-distance telephone calls is the same throughout the United States, as is the cost of mail delivery. Thus, the site selection criteria for a check processing operation of a bank, or a customer billing operation for a retail chain or credit card company, will focus primarily on minimizing facility operating expenses.

As with manufacturing operations, managers need to consider both qualitative and quantitative factors in evaluating potential sites. These factors will vary in both type and relative importance, depending on the type of service facility for which the location is being evaluated. From an operational perspective, these factors are the same as those factors used in evaluating a manufacturing site. This is especially true for back-of-the-house operations. In addition, front-of-the-house operations need to consider customer-related factors that can impact sales at a location. Depending on the service, some of these factors include (*a*) average family income, (*b*) average family size, (*c*) population density, and (*d*) pedestrian and/or automobile traffic.

Methods for Evaluating Potential Locations

Both qualitative and quantitative methods are available for evaluating and comparing potential site locations. These include the factor-rating system and the center-of-gravity methods, both of which are described here in detail. In, addition, there are forecasting models that use regression analysis to predict sales for **front-of-the-house** operations. (See Chapter 9 on forecasting.) Often, a combination of these methods is used so that management can evaluate sites from several perspectives.

front-of-the-house

A service facility, or that part of the service process, that interacts directly with the customer.

Factor-Rating Systems

factor-rating systems

A qualitative approach for evaluating alternative site locations.

Factor-rating systems are probably one of the most widely used location selection techniques because they can combine very diverse issues into an easy-to-understand format. At the same time, it is important to recognize the fact that although the end result from this type of analysis is a quantitative number, factor-rating systems are used to evaluate both qualitative and quantitative factors.

Another reason that the factor-rating system approach is so popular is that it is relatively simple to use, requiring only six steps:

1. Identify the specific criteria or factors to be considered in selecting a site (see OM in Practice box on Criteria for Selecting a Location for a Back-of-the-House Service Operation).
2. Assign a weight to each factor indicating its importance relative to all of the other factors that are being considered.
3. Select a common scale for rating each factor (for example, 1–100).
4. Rate each potential location on each of the factors.
5. Multiply each factor's score by the weight assigned to that factor.
6. Sum up the weighted scores for all of the factors and select that location with the highest total score.

Example

To illustrate the factor-rating system, consider The Low-Credit Card Interest Bank, which is looking to locate its credit card operations. Two potential sites have been identified. Management has decided to use the following criteria, as suggested in the OM in Practice box, and has assigned the following weights to each of them based upon their relative importance. The two locations are then rated on each of these factors and a total score for each location is calculated.

Solution

We construct a spreadsheet as follows, and calculate the score for each of the two locations under consideration:

Factor	Weight	Rating Site A	Rating Site B	Score Site A	Score Site B
Size and education of workforce within 15 miles	20	60	75	1,200	1,500
Availability of part-time workers (students)	10	45	20	450	200
Distance to telecommunications infrastructure	25	80	90	2,000	2,250
Distance to higher-education facilities	5	50	35	250	175
Cost-of-living index	15	85	80	1,275	1,200
Cultural amenities	10	65	40	650	400
Crime statistics	15	95	90	1,425	1,350
Totals	100			7,250	7,075

Using this evaluation as a criterion, Site A, with the higher score, should be selected. As the factor-rating system is a highly qualitative technique, the use of an electronic spreadsheet, like Excel, will allow management to easily vary the factor weights to see their overall impact on the decision.

It should be noted that although the weights for the factors in this example totaled 100, this is not a requirement. What is important is that the weights assigned to each factor reflect their relative importance in selecting a site. Equally important, the scale for rating each factor, as stated earlier, should be the same. Also, in determining a rating for each factor for a specific location, the actual value assigned is not as critical as its relative value in comparison to the other sites under consideration.

Center-of-Gravity Method

center-of-gravity method

A quantitative approach for determining the optimal location for a facility based upon minimizing total distribution costs.

The evaluation of alternative regions, subregions, and communities is commonly termed *macro-analysis,* while the evaluation of specific sites in a selected community is often termed *micro-analysis*. One technique used in micro-analysis is the **center-of-gravity method.** The center-of-gravity method is a quantitative technique that can be used to determine the optimal location of a facility based upon minimizing the transportation costs between where the goods are produced and where they are sold or redistributed. A manufacturing firm might use this method to determine where to locate its factory relative to its distribution facilities. Services also would use this method. For example, Bruegger's Bagels, Bertucci's restaurants, and Au Bon Pain restaurants all have commissaries that prepare food that is then distributed to their respective retail operations. Wal-Mart's distribution centers provide an example of a service operation that delivers only manufactured goods.

The center-of-gravity method also can be used to select locations for traditional brick-and-mortar retail operations such as supermarkets, department stores, and wholesale discount operations such as Sam's Club and Costco. For these services, the location is usually dependent on the population density and the average sales per customer for the different areas to be served.

The first step in the center-of-gravity method is to locate each of the existing retail operations on an X and Y coordinate grid map. The purpose of the grid map is to establish

Operations Management in Practice

CRITERIA FOR SELECTING A LOCATION FOR A BACK-OF-THE-HOUSE SERVICE OPERATION

Fluor Global Location Strategies has identified the following general criteria for selecting a location for an office, be it for a company headquarters, an R&D facility, or a back-of-the-house operation:

- Population characteristics (size, education, diversity, etc.).
- Workforce characteristics (size, type/distribution, education, number employed, etc.).
- Availability of alternative workforces (military spouses, students, underemployed, etc.).
- Distance to commercial airports (including "direct-service" international airports).
- Distance to population centers.
- Distance to telecommunications infrastructure (COs, PoPs, fiber networks, etc.).
- Distance to higher-education facilities.
- Quality-of-life characteristics:
  - Quality-of-living index.
  - Cost-of-living index.
  - Cultural amenities.
  - Crime statistics.

Source: Special thanks to Fluor Global Location Strategies.

relative distances between the locations. Exhibit 7.4 illustrates such a grid map as part of the example presented below.

The center of gravity or the location for the supporting or distribution facility is then found by calculating the X and Y coordinates that result in minimizing the distribution costs among all facilities. To determine this location on the grid map, the following formulas are used:

$$C_x = \frac{\Sigma d_{ix} V_i}{\Sigma V_i} \tag{7.1}$$

$$C_y = \frac{\Sigma d_{iy} V_i}{\Sigma V_i} \tag{7.2}$$

where

$C_x = X$ coordinate of the center of gravity
$C_y = Y$ coordinate of the center of gravity
$d_{ix} = X$ coordinate of the ith location
$d_{iy} = Y$ coordinate of the ith location
$V_i =$ Volume of good transported to the ith location

Example

Ye Olde Bake Shoppe Company currently has four retail locations within the metropolitan area of a major city. Currently, each retail outlet makes all of its own breads and pastries from scratch (that is, prepared from basic ingredients such as flour, sugar, shortening, etc.). These locations are shown on the grid map in Exhibit 7.4. Management, to reduce costs and to ensure consistency of the firm's products among all of the locations, has decided to build a central commissary where the products will be prepared and subsequently distributed to the four retail stores. The question now is where to locate this commissary.

Exhibit 7.4

Grid Map of Ye Olde Bake Shoppe's Retail Locations

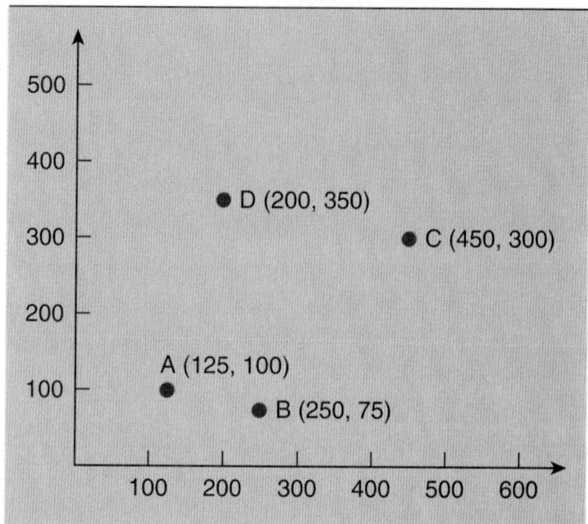

The estimated amounts of product sold weekly (in pounds) in each store along with its respective grid coordinates are provided in the table below.

Store Location	*X* Coordinate	*Y* Coordinate	Pounds of Product Sold
A	125	100	1,250
B	250	75	3,000
C	450	300	2,750
D	200	350	1,500

Solution

To determine the center of gravity, which will be the ideal location for the commissary, we set up the spreadsheet for applying Equations 7.1 and 7.2:

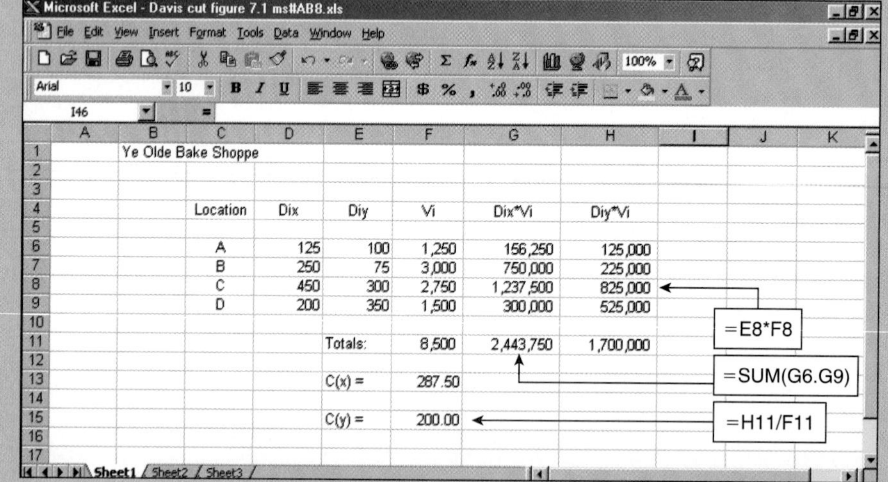

Microsoft Excel - Davis cut figure 7.1 ms#AB8.xls

	A	B	C	D	E	F	G	H
1		Ye Olde Bake Shoppe						
2								
3								
4			Location	Dix	Diy	Vi	Dix*Vi	Diy*Vi
5								
6			A	125	100	1,250	156,250	125,000
7			B	250	75	3,000	750,000	225,000
8			C	450	300	2,750	1,237,500	825,000
9			D	200	350	1,500	300,000	525,000
10								
11					Totals:	8,500	2,443,750	1,700,000
12								
13					C(x) =	287.50		
14								
15					C(y) =	200.00		

This provides management with the *X* and *Y* grid coordinates for the center of gravity, which serve as a starting point for locating the new commissary.

A Spreadsheet Approach to Locating Facilities

While the center-of-gravity method provides an optimal solution for minimizing distribution costs, the resulting solution is very often unrealistic. The location chosen by this method might be in a residential neighborhood, or may not have access to major highways, or may likely already be occupied by another business. (It does, however, provide a good starting point for searching for a location.) A more realistic approach to selecting a site, therefore, is to identify several sites that are both available and also meet the requirements of the firm. Each site is then evaluated using the same criteria as in the center-of-gravity approach, that is, to minimize the total costs of distribution. However, unlike the center-of-gravity approach which has an infinite number of solutions, this approach will be limited to a choice among the sites selected for evaluation.

Example

We use the Ye Olde Bake Shoppe chain of retail stores again to illustrate this approach and to provide a basis of comparison between the two methods. Management has identified two potential sites on which to locate the commissary. With production costs estimated to be the same at both sites, management's goal in selecting a site is to minimize distribution costs. The following information is provided on each site:

Store Location	Pounds of Product Sold	Distance to Site 1 (miles)	Distance to Site 2 (miles)
A	1,250	19.5	23.0
B	3,000	17.5	12.5
C	2,750	20.6	18.0
D	1,500	11.2	25.0

Solution

Using the same logic as in the center-of-gravity method, we set up the following spreadsheet to calculate the total distribution costs associated with each site. (For consistency with the center-of-gravity method, we define distribution costs here as total pound-miles.)

Microsoft Excel - Davis Cut figure 7.2 ms#499.xls

	A	B	C	D	E	F	G
1					Ye Olde Bake Shoppe		
2							
3		Distribution Costs for Site 1:					
4					Distance to		
5			Location	Volume (lb)	Site (miles)	lb-miles	
6				(Vi)	(Di)	(Vi x Di)	
7							
8			A	1,250	19.5	24,375	
9			B	3,000	17.5	52,500	
10			C	2,750	20.6	56,650	=D8*E8
11			D	1,500	11.2	16,800	
12							
13			Totals:		68.8	150,325	
14							
15		Distribution Costs for Site 2:					
16							=SUM(F8.F11)
17			A	1,250	23	28,750	
18			B	3,000	12.5	37,500	
19			C	2,750	18	49,500	
20			D	1,500	25	37,500	
21							
22			Totals:		78.5	153,250	

Based on the above analysis, site 1 appears to have the lower distribution cost, and therefore should be selected as the site for the new commissary.

Capacity Decisions

The capacity of the production system defines the firm's competitive boundaries. Specifically, it sets the firm's response rate to the market, its cost structure, its workforce composition, its level of technology, its management and staff support requirements, and its - general inventory strategy. If capacity is inadequate, a company may lose customers through slow service or by allowing competitors to enter the market. If capacity is excessive, a company may have to reduce its prices to stimulate demand, underutilize its workforce, carry excess inventory, or seek additional, less-profitable products to stay in business.

Factors Affecting Capacity Capacity is affected by both external and internal factors. The external factors include (*a*) government regulations (working hours, safety, pollution), (*b*) union agreements, and (*c*) supplier capabilities. The internal factors include (*a*) product and service design, (*b*) personnel and jobs (worker training, motivation, learning, job content, and methods), (*c*) plant layout and process flow, (*d*) equipment capabilities and maintenance, (*e*) materials management, (*f*) quality control systems, (*g*) product-mix decisions, and (*h*) management capabilities.

Important Capacity Concepts

In service operations we often distinguish between *maximum capacity* and *optimum capacity* because of the customer's direct interaction with the service facility. Christopher Lovelock has identified four different situations that the service manager may encounter in trying to match customer demand with the existing capacity of the operation. These situations, illustrated in Exhibit 7.5, are (*a*) demand exceeds maximum capacity causing customers to be turned away; (*b*) demand, although less than maximum capacity, exceeds optimum capacity resulting in customers who receive poor service; (*c*) demand equals optimum capacity; and (*d*) demand is less than optimum capacity, resulting in idle capacity.

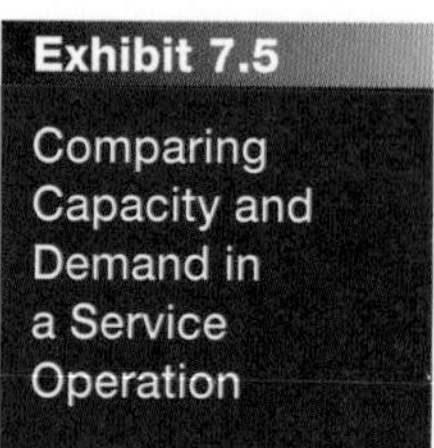

Exhibit 7.5 Comparing Capacity and Demand in a Service Operation

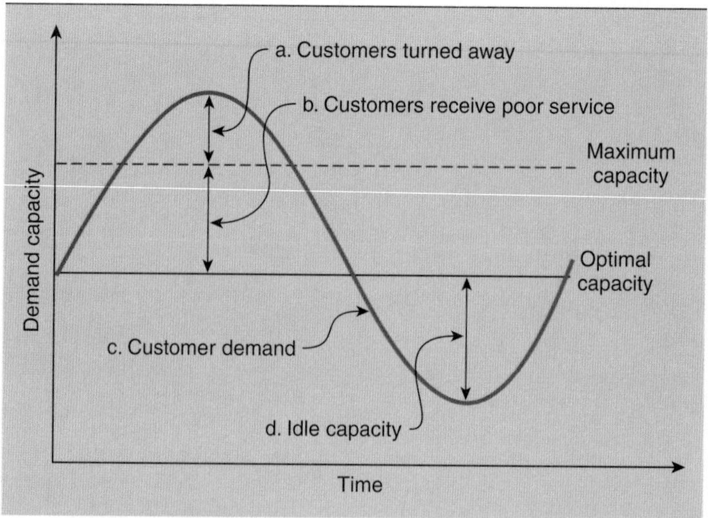

Source: Managing Services, 2/e by Lovelock, Christopher © 1992. Adapted by permission of Pearson Education, Inc., Upper Saddle River, NJ.

Best Operating Level The *best operating level* is that capacity for which the average unit cost is at a minimum. This is depicted in Exhibit 7.6. Note that as we move down the unit cost curve for each plant size, we achieve economies of scale until we reach the best operating level, and then we encounter diseconomies of scale as we exceed this point.

Economies and Diseconomies of Scale The concept of economies of scale is well known: As product volumes increase, the average cost per unit decreases. This concept can be related to a best operating level for a given plant size. As shown in Exhibit 7.6, economies of scale (as well as diseconomies of scale) are found not just between the cost curves for each plant, but within each one as well.

Exhibit 7.6 also shows the best operating levels, V_A, V_B, V_C, and V_D, for plant sizes A, B, C, and D, respectively. Economies of scale occur for several reasons. As volumes increase, fixed costs are spread out over a greater number of units, thereby reducing the amount of overhead that is allocated to each product. With large volumes, a firm also can take advantage of quantity discounts, thereby reducing material costs. Scale factors, which are associated with larger facilities, are a third source of economies of scale. For example, with processing operations such as breweries and refineries, doubling the capacity of a facility increases its costs by about 40 percent, which reflects the ratio of change in the volume in a cylinder or pipe to its outside area (in other words, to double the volume through a pipe requires about 141 percent more material for the larger pipe).

Diseconomies of scale also can occur for several reasons. When the best operating level in a plant is exceeded, additional costs are incurred. These added costs can take the form of overtime, inefficient scheduling, and machine breakdowns resulting from a lack of time to perform preventive maintenance. Diseconomies of scale also can occur with larger plants, as indicated by Plant D in Exhibit 7.6. This could be due to an inability to efficiently coordinate material flows and schedule workers. Organizational factors also can contribute to diseconomies of scale. With larger facilities, the contribution of each individual is diminished. Management and workers become more segregated and communicate less with each other. In operations that have a labor union, for example, grievances per 100 employees tend to increase in relation to the size of the plant.

Although finding the best size and operating level is illusive, managers often set policies regarding the maximum size for any one facility. As a result, the real challenge is predicting how costs will change for different output rates and facility sizes. This assessment requires careful attention to the different causes of economies of scale for each situation.

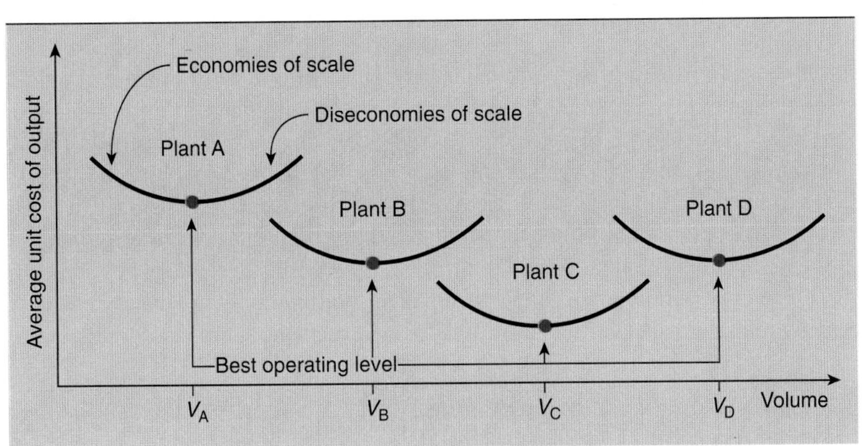

Exhibit 7.6
Economies of Scale

In the past several years, we have begun to see that diseconomies of scale come much sooner than we previously anticipated. This recognition, along with technological capability to do more in a plant, has resulted in a shift toward small facilities. The steel industry, with its declining number of large, integrated plants and its corresponding shift toward minimills, is a well-known case in point.

capacity flexibility

Ability to provide a wide range of products and volumes with short lead times.

agile manufacturing

Ability of a manufacturing process to respond quickly to changes in the marketplace.

Capacity Flexibility Having the capability to deliver what the customer wants within a relatively short lead time is how we define **capacity flexibility.** Such flexibility is achieved through flexible plants, processes, workers, and strategies that use the capacity of other organizations. **Agile manufacturing** is another term that reflects the ability of a facility to react quickly to changes in the marketplace.

Flexible plants. Perhaps the ultimate in plant flexibility is the *zero-changeover-time* plant. Using movable equipment, knockdown walls, and easily accessible and reroutable utilities, such a plant can adapt to change in real time. An analogy to a familiar service business captures the flavor quite well—a plant with equipment "that is easy to install and easy to tear down and move—like the Ringling Bros., Barnum and Bailey Circus in the old tent-circus days."[2]

Flexible processes. Flexible processes are epitomized by flexible manufacturing systems on the one hand and simple, easy-to-set-up equipment on the other. Both of these technological approaches permit rapid low-cost switching from one product line to another, enabling what is sometimes referred to as *economies of scope.* (By definition, economies of scope exist when multiple products can be produced at a lower cost in combination than they can separately.)

Flexible workers. Flexible workers have multiple skills and the ability to switch easily from one kind of task to another. They require broader training than specialized workers and need managers and staff support to facilitate quick changes in their work assignments.

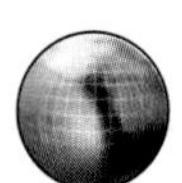

Use of external capacity. Two common strategies for creating flexibility by using the capacity of other organizations are subcontracting and sharing capacity. An example of subcontracting is Japanese banks in California subcontracting check-clearing operations to the Wells Fargo Bank of California's check clearinghouse. An example of sharing capacity is two domestic airlines flying different routes with different seasonal demands exchanging aircraft (suitably repainted) when one's routes are heavily used and the other's are not.

Capacity Balance In a perfectly balanced plant, the output of Stage 1 provides the exact input requirement for Stage 2, the output of Stage 2 provides the exact input requirement for Stage 3, and so on. In practice, however, achieving such a "perfect" design is usually both impossible and undesirable. One reason is that the best operating levels for each stage generally differ. For instance, Department 1 may operate most efficiently over a range of 90 to 110 units per month while Department 2, the next stage in the process, is most efficient at 75 to 85 units per month, and Department 3, the third stage, works best over a range of 150 to 200 units per month. Another reason is that variability in product demand and the processes themselves generally lead to imbalance except in automated production lines,

[2]See R. J. Schonberger, "The Rationalization of Production," *Proceedings of the 50th Anniversary of the Academy of Management* (Chicago: Academy of Management, 1986), pp. 64–70.

which, in essence, are just one big machine. There are various ways of dealing with imbalance. One is to add capacity to those stages that are bottlenecks. This can be done by temporary measures such as scheduling overtime, leasing equipment, or going outside the system and purchasing additional capacity through subcontracting. A second way is through the use of buffer inventories in front of the bottleneck stage to assure that it always has something to work on. A third approach involves duplicating the facilities of that department that is the cause of the bottleneck (which, in essence, eliminates the bottleneck).

Capacity Strategies

For manufacturing firms, there are three major strategies for adding capacity: proactive, neutral, and reactive. Each has its strengths and weaknesses. Which strategy to adopt is dependent, to a large extent, on the operating characteristics of the facility and the overall strategy of the firm.

Proactive With a proactive strategy, management anticipates future growth and builds the facility so that it is up and running when the demand is there, as seen in Exhibit 7.7A. With this strategy, opportunity costs resulting from lost sales due to an inability to meet demand are minimized, although the firm does have to allocate fixed costs over a relatively small volume of units during the plant's initial period of operation. This strategy is most compatible for a plant where the labor costs are a significant portion of total manufacturing costs, such as in low-volume assembly operations (e.g., footwear manufacturing).

Neutral A neutral strategy for adding capacity simply takes a middle-of-the-road approach. As seen in Exhibit 7.7B, additional capacity becomes available when demand is about 50 percent of total capacity. The issue here, as with reactive strategy, is how best to satisfy demand before the plant is up and operating.

Reactive When a reactive strategy is adopted, plant capacity is not added until all of the planned output from the facility can be sold. Thus, with this strategy, the plant is not brought on line until demand equals 100 percent of its capacity, as shown in Exhibit 7.7C. Operating costs are minimized with this approach, as the plant is producing at its desired optimal output, beginning with its first day of operation. This strategy is most conducive to process-oriented operations that have very high fixed costs, regardless of the volume produced, and low variable costs. Examples include paper mills, breweries, and refineries.

The main problem with this strategy, as with the neutral strategy, is how best to meet the unfilled demand before the plant is in operation. One approach, if the firm has other plants that produce the same product(s), is to manufacture the products temporarily (albeit inefficiently) at these other locations, utilizing additional shifts and overtime as necessary.

capacity planning

Determination of which level of capacity to operate at to meet customer demand in a cost-efficient manner.

Capacity Planning

The objective of **capacity planning** is to specify which level of capacity will meet market demands in a cost-efficient way. Capacity planning can be viewed in three time durations: long range (greater than one year), intermediate range (the next 6 to 12 months), and short range (less than six months).

Our focus in this chapter is on long-range capacity planning, where the firm makes its major investment decisions. In addition to planning large chunks of capacity (such as a new factory), typical long-range capacity planning efforts also must address the demands for individual product lines, individual plant capabilities, and allocation of production throughout

Exhibit 7.7

Strategies for Adding Capacity

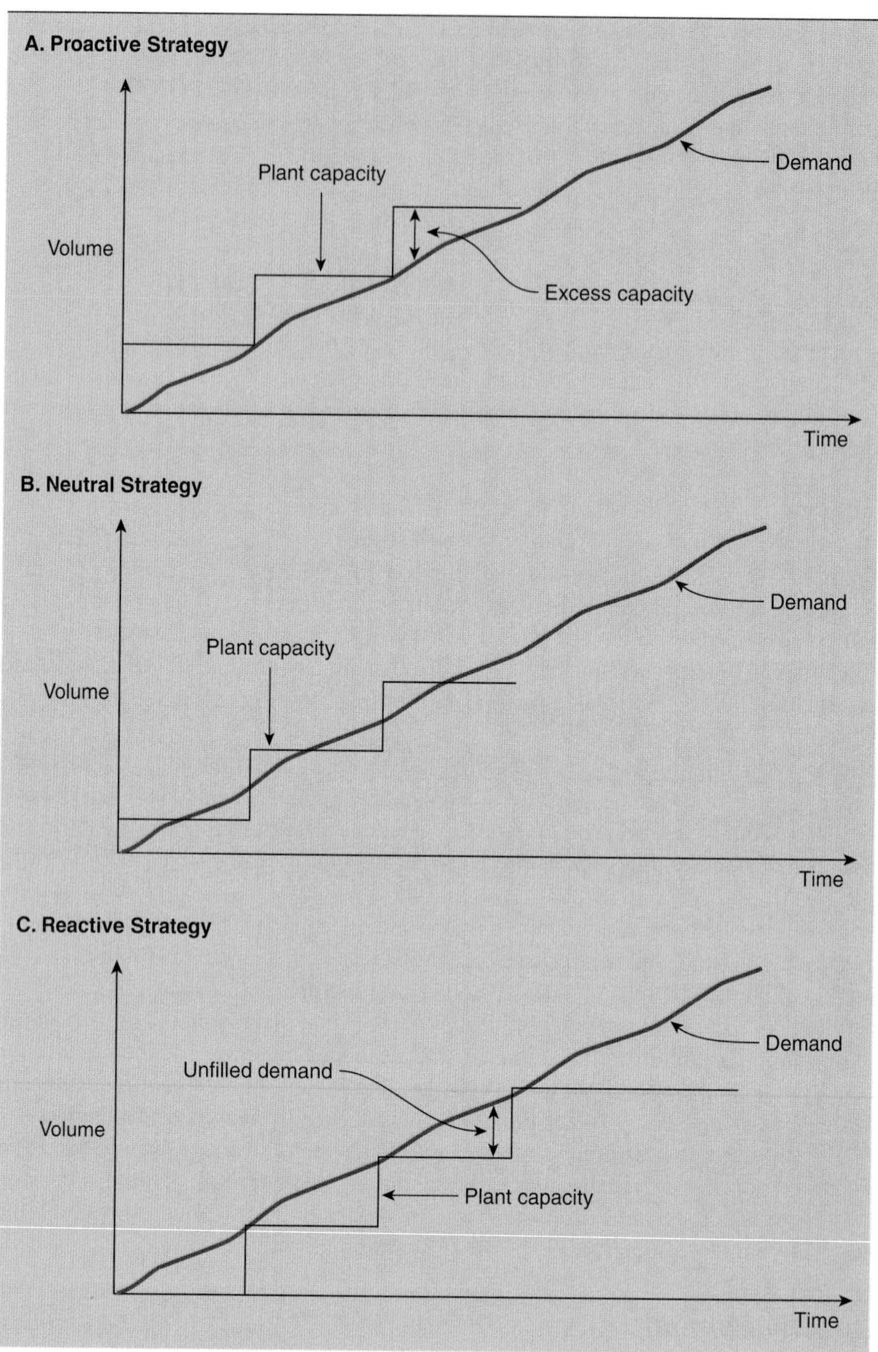

the plant network. Typically, these are carried out according to the following steps:

1. Forecast sales for each product line.
2. Forecast sales for individual products within each product line.
3. Calculate labor and equipment requirements to meet product line forecasts.
4. Project labor and equipment availabilities over the planning horizon.

Capacity Measures

As described in detail in Chapter 5, capacity is the output of a process or facility over a given time period. For a manufacturing plant, examples of capacity include: televisions per week, barrels of oil per year, and gallons of laundry detergent per month. For a service operation, capacity is usually measured over shorter time periods, because time is more critical due to the customer's interaction with the process. Examples here would include customers per hour in a restaurant, calls per hour in a call center, and guests per hour at the front desk of a hotel.

Capacity utilization, as also described in Chapter 5, defines what percentage of the available capacity is actually being used. For example, a call center might have 1,200 workstations, but, on a given day, only have 600 of them staffed with operators. In this case, the call center would be working at 600/1,200 or 50 percent capacity utilization that day.

Conclusion

The decisions where and when to locate a facility and how big to make it are critical to the success of every business, be it a manufacturing or service operation. As a result, significant analysis and planning are required to ensure that a potential location will properly support the long-term strategy and objectives of the firm. In addition, the decision where to locate a new facility is complex, involving both qualitative and quantitative factors.

Like so many topics in operations management today, location decisions and capacity planning are being significantly influenced, not only by advances in information technology, but also by the trend toward globalization. As more firms continue to focus on their core competencies, management has changed its perspective on available capacity, while at the same time becoming more dependent on its suppliers. The growth in international markets, as well as cheaper labor and other incentives offered by foreign countries, also has significantly affected decisions on where to locate new operations.

Key Terms

agile manufacturing p. 306
back-of-the-house p. 298
brick-and-mortar operation p. 296
capacity flexibility p. 306
capacity planning p. 307
center-of-gravity method p. 300
content requirements p. 291
factor-rating systems p. 299
front-of-the-house p. 299
geographic information systems (GIS) p. 295
quasi-manufacturing operation p. 298
special economic zones (SEZ) p. 293

Review and Discussion Questions

1. List some practical limits to economies of scale; that is, when should a plant stop growing in size?
2. What are some capacity balance problems faced by the following organizations or facilities?
   a. An airline terminal.
   b. A university computing center.
   c. A clothing manufacturer.
3. What are the primary capacity planning considerations for foreign companies locating their facilities in the United States?

4. What are some major capacity considerations in a hospital? How do they differ from those of a factory?
5. What are some of the location factors that a manufacturer needs to take into consideration in locating a factory in a foreign country?
6. In what respects is facility layout a marketing problem in services? Give an example of a service system layout designed to maximize the amount of time the customer is in the system.
7. Identify some of the site selection criteria that should be considered by a high-end, full-service hotel chain such as the Hilton, Hyatt, or Marriott. (By full-service we mean that the hotel has a restaurant, cocktail lounge, meeting rooms, and catering facilities to accommodate large functions such as conferences and weddings.)
8. Identify some of the site selection factors that should be considered for a budget motel that primarily provides only rooms, such as Motel 6, Days Inn, and EconoLodge.
9. What are some of the factors that should be taken into consideration when evaluating potential sites for a distribution center of quasi-manufacturing operation that directly supports retail operations?

Internet Exercise

Visit the website of an ASP (application service provider) that will give you detailed maps that include the distance and time between any two locations. What is the estimated time it takes to go from your home to your school and how many miles is it? Use the same ASP to determine how far it is from your school to the nearest McDonald's.

Solved Problems

Problem 1

Luxury Hotels, Inc., is looking to relocate its reservations call center and has identified the following factors and respective weights for evaluating each potential site:

Factor	Weight
Available workforce	30
Level of skills	15
Telecommunications infrastructure	45
Cost of labor	50
Access to major highways	25
Total	165

A consultant has identified the following three sites and has rated each of these locations on the above factors as follows:

Factor	Ratings Site A	Ratings Site B	Ratings Site C
Available workforce	65	80	90
Level of skills	50	45	75
Telecommunication infrastructure	90	70	40
Cost of labor	75	90	85
Access to major highways	80	85	55

a. Which site would you recommend for locating the call center?

b. How much does the rating for the labor cost factor have to increase for site A so that the scores for sites A and B are the same?

c. How much does the weight for the infrastructure factor have to increase before site A becomes the preferred location for the call center?

Solution

a. We set up the following spreadsheet to calculate the scores for each location:

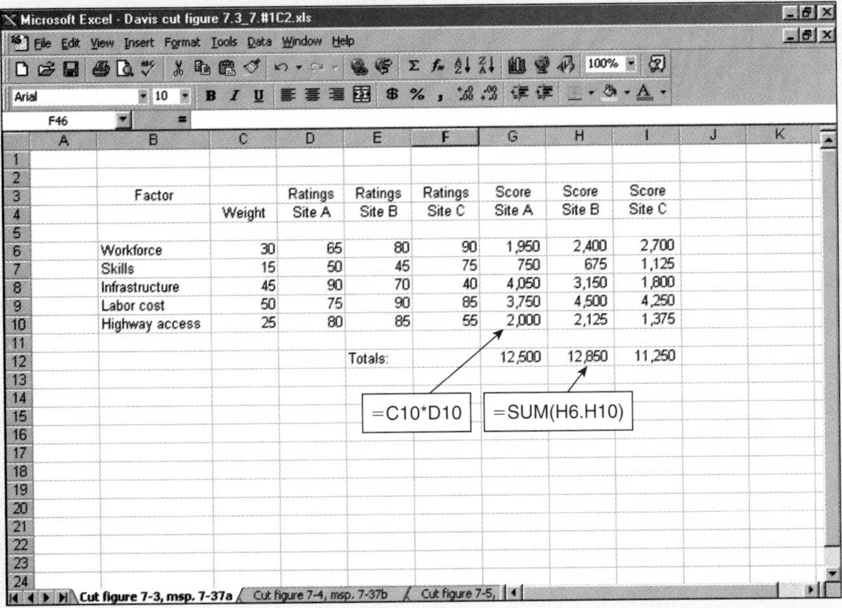

Factor	Weight	Ratings Site A	Ratings Site B	Ratings Site C	Score Site A	Score Site B	Score Site C
Workforce	30	65	80	90	1,950	2,400	2,700
Skills	15	50	45	75	750	675	1,125
Infrastructure	45	90	70	40	4,050	3,150	1,800
Labor cost	50	75	90	85	3,750	4,500	4,250
Highway access	25	80	85	55	2,000	2,125	1,375
				Totals:	12,500	12,850	11,250

Based upon this analysis, we recommend that the new call center be located at site B, which has the highest score of 12,850.

b. To determine the rating for the labor cost factor at site A that makes the scores for sites A and B identical, we again use a spreadsheet and increase the labor cost rating for site A until the scores for the two sites are the same. The desired labor cost rating for site A is 82, as illustrated in the following spreadsheet:

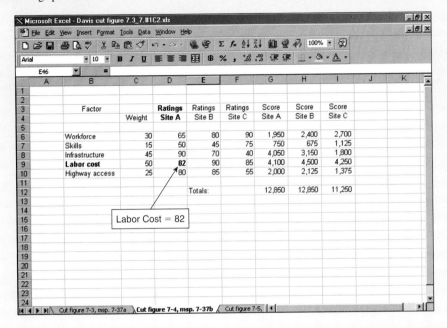

Factor	Weight	**Ratings Site A**	Ratings Site B	Ratings Site C	Score Site A	Score Site B	Score Site C
Workforce	30	65	80	90	1,950	2,400	2,700
Skills	15	50	45	75	750	675	1,125
Infrastructure	45	90	70	40	4,050	3,150	1,800
Labor cost	50	**82**	90	85	4,100	4,500	4,250
Highway access	25	80	85	55	2,000	2,125	1,375
			Totals:		12,850	12,850	11,250

Labor Cost = 82

Microsoft Excel - Davis cut figure 7.3_7.#1C2.xls — Cut figure 7-3, msp. 7-37a / Cut figure 7-4, msp. 7-37b / Cut figure 7-5, *c.* As shown in the spreadsheet below, the weight for the infrastructure has to be increased to 63 before site A becomes the preferred location.

Factor	Weight	Ratings Site A	Ratings Site B	Ratings Site C	Score Site A	Score Site B	Score Site C
Workforce	30	65	80	90	1,950	2,400	2,700
Skills	15	50	45	75	750	675	1,125
Infrastructure	**63**	90	70	40	5,670	4,410	2,520
Labor cost	50	75	90	85	3,750	4,500	4,250
Highway access	25	80	85	55	2,000	2,125	1,375
			Totals:		14,120	14,110	11,970

Infrastructure = 63

Problem 2

Personal Nursing Services (PNS) provides individualized nursing care to patients in three hospitals in the metropolitan area of a major city. For a variety of reasons, assignments often change at the last minute in terms of the number of patients to be cared for at each hospital. As a result, the nurses working for PNS report each morning to PNS's headquarters for their daily assignments. PNS then provides vans to take the nurses to their respective hospitals. The vans also pick them up at the end of the day and return the nurses to the headquarters so that they can file their reports before going home. Consequently, the vans make two round trips a day to each hospital. The location of each hospital is located on the grid map at left.

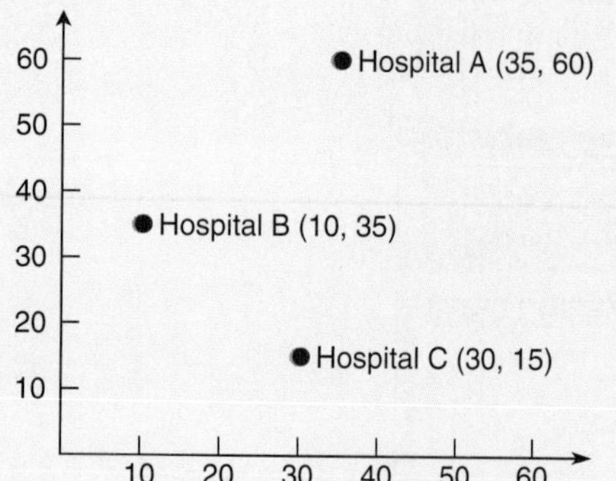

PNS has experienced rapid growth in the demand for its services and is therefore looking to move into larger facilities.

a. Using the center-of-gravity method, determine the ideal location for its new headquarters.

b. PNS has submitted a proposal to a fourth hospital that is located at coordinates $X = 20$, $Y = 5$. If it is awarded the contract for this hospital, where should its headquarters building now be located?

Solution

From looking at the grid map, we calculate the coordinates of each of three hospitals now being served as follows:

Hospital	*X* Coordinate	*Y* Coordinate
A	35	60
B	10	35
C	30	15

a. Using a spreadsheet and based upon the three hospitals that are currently under contract, we calculate the coordinates for the new headquarters as follows:

Microsoft Excel - Davis cut figures 7.6 a#C2A.xls

Row	Hospital	Dix	Diy	Vi	Dix*Vi	Diy*Vi
4	Hospital	Dix	Diy	Vi	Dix*Vi	Diy*Vi
6	A	35	60	2	70	120
7	B	10	35	2	20	70
8	C	30	15	2	60	30
10			Totals:	6	150	220
12			C(x) =	25.00		
14			C(y) =	36.67		

=E8*F8 (H8); =SUM(G6.G8) (G10); =H10/F10 (F14)

Cut figure 7-6, msp. 7-40a / Cut figure 7-7, msp. 7-40b / Sheet3

Thus, the new headquarters' location should be at coordinates $X = 25.0$, $Y = 36.7$.

b. To add the fourth hospital, we simply update the spreadsheet with the fourth hospital's coordinates and recalculate the X and Y coordinates for the new headquarters location.

Microsoft Excel - Davis cut figures 7.6 a#C2A.xls

Row	Hospital	Dix	Diy	Vi	Dix*Vi	Diy*Vi
4	Hospital	Dix	Diy	Vi	Dix*Vi	Diy*Vi
6	A	35	60	2	70	120
7	B	10	35	2	20	70
8	C	30	15	2	60	30
9	D	20	5	2	40	10
11			Totals:	8	190	230
13			C(x) =	23.75		
15			C(y) =	28.75		

=E8*F8 (H8); =SUM(G6.G9) (G11); =H11/F11 (F15)

Cut figure 7-6, msp. 7-40a / Cut figure 7-7, msp. 7-40b / Sheet3

Thus, if PNS is awarded the contract for the fourth hospital, then the ideal location for its new headquarters would be at coordinates $X = 23.8$ and $Y = 28.8$.

Problems

1. The Speedy Ambulance Service is searching for a location that will serve both as its headquarters and as a garage for its ambulances. You have been asked to chair the site selection search team. The team has identified the following factors that need to be considered in choosing a location, and also has assigned the following weights to these factors:

Factor	Weight
Proximity to hospitals	25
Population over age 65	30
Access to major highways	15
Number of nursing homes	20
Local tax incentives	10
Total	100

The search team has found three sites and has assigned the following factor ratings to each of them:

Factor	Ratings Site A	Ratings Site B	Ratings Site C
Proximity to hospitals	30	45	75
Population over age 65	60	55	35
Access to major highways	80	90	65
Number of nursing homes	45	60	55
Local tax incentives	85	70	80

a. Which site would you recommend to the search committee?

b. What is the impact on the site selection if the weight of the "access to major highways" factor is reduced to 5 and the weight of the "local tax incentives" factor is increased to 20?

2. Edtoys.com is a virtual company that offers a wide variety of educational children's toys through its website. When an order is received, it is immediately sent electronically to the manufacturer for direct shipment to the customer. With this type of structure, Edtoys.com does not have to maintain inventories of toys or become involved in their delivery. Management is therefore focusing primarily on making its website as customer friendly as possible and expanding its number of product offerings.

   Edtoys.com has seen tremendous growth in the past several years and needs to find a new and larger location for its offices. Based on conversations with several members of Edtoys.com's top management team, a consulting firm has identified the following factors that should be taken into consideration in choosing a new site for its offices, and also has assigned the following weights to each of these factors:

Factor	Weight
Proximity to business schools	20
Access to highways	20
Telecommunications infrastructure	40
Quality of life	30
Proximity to major airport	25
Total	135

The consulting firm has identified two possible locations and has assigned each of them the following factor ratings:

Factor	Rating Site A	Rating Site B
Proximity to business schools	70	55
Access to highways	40	75
Telecommunications infrastructure	75	90
Quality of life	60	85
Proximity to major airport	80	50

Which site should the consulting firm recommend to Edtoys.com?

3. Patorano's Pizza, a chain of Italian pizza restaurants, wants to expand its operations into Asia, specifically in the Peoples' Republic of China (PRC). Unfortunately, due to a lack of food purveyors and suppliers, management must build its own distribution center and commissary, where many of the foods used in the restaurant will be either partially or fully prepared. (For example, the dough for the pizza will be mixed and portioned at the commissary.) The first stage of its business plan has identified specific locations for the first three restaurants to be opened. The *X* and *Y* coordinates and estimated annual sales for each of these three locations are presented below:

Location	*X* Coordinate	*Y* Coordinate	Forecasted Sales (in yuan)
A	20	45	2,500,000
B	35	15	4,000,000
C	5	50	1,800,000

a. Draw a grid map and locate each of the planned restaurants on it.

b. Assuming that the volume of products to be shipped is directly proportional to sales, calculate the coordinates for the central commissary that will minimize distribution costs. Plot these coordinates on the grid map.

c. The second phase of the business plan calls for two more locations at the following grid locations and with estimated sales shown below:

Location	*X* Coordinate	*Y* Coordinate	Forecasted Sales (in yuan)
D	45	10	3,200,000
E	30	30	1,400,000

What is the impact of these additional restaurants on the location of the central commissary?

4. Jane's Office Supplies is a small retail chain that sells high-priced designer office supplies to senior executives. It has recently opened three locations in the metropolitan Washington, DC, area that are currently being supplied from the corporate warehouse in Dallas, Texas. The *X* and *Y* coordinates for these locations are provided in the table below along with the annual sales that each location generates. In order to reduce shipping costs, management has decided to open a distribution center in the Washington, DC, area.

Store Location	*X* Coordinate	*Y* Coordinate	Annual Sales
Downtown Washington	60	53	$745,000
Suburban Maryland	13	78	$483,000
Suburban Virginia	21	42	$612,000

a. Draw a grid map and locate each of the three stores on it.

b. Assuming that the volume of products to be shipped is directly proportional to sales in each store, calculate the coordinates for the distribution center that will minimize distribution costs. Plot these coordinates on the grid map.

5. Having determined the optimal location for its distribution facility, Jane Davajian, the president of Jane's Office Supplies, found two sites that were available. The distance each site is from each of the three retail locations is as follows:

Retail Location	Distance from Site A (miles)	Distance from Site B (miles)
Downtown Washington	17	14
Suburban Maryland	10	12
Suburban Virginia	25	18

Which location should Jane choose in order to minimize her distribution costs?

6. Gourmet Specialty Foods, an upscale grocery chain that caters to high-income families, wants to build a new supermarket that will service three affluent communities. A market research study revealed that the average weekly food purchases per family are the same for each of these three communities.

Community	Number of Families	*X* Coordinate	*Y* Coordinate
Smithtown	12,800	93	81
Jonesville	17,300	27	116
Moore City	9,500	75	34

Determine the optimal grid location for the supermarket.

7. A real estate consulting firm has found two locations that will meet Gourmet Specialties's requirements. The distance each of the locations is from the three communities is as follows:

Community	Site A (miles)	Site B (miles)
Smithtown	7.5	9.7
Jonesville	4.6	3.1
Moore City	8.0	6.2

On which site should Gourmet Specialties build its new supermarket?

8. Cool Air, a manufacturer of automotive air conditioners, currently produces its XB-300 line at three different locations, Plant A, Plant B, and Plant C. Recently, management decided to build all compressors, a major product component, in a separate dedicated facility, Plant D.

a. Using the center-of-gravity method and the information displayed in Exhibits 7.8 and 7.9, determine the best location for Plant D. Assume a linear relationship between volumes shipped and shipping costs (no premium charges).

b. Refer to the information given in Part (*a*). Suppose management decides to shift 2,000 units of production from Plant B to Plant A. Does this change the proposed location of Plant D, the compressor production facility? If so, where should Plant D be located?

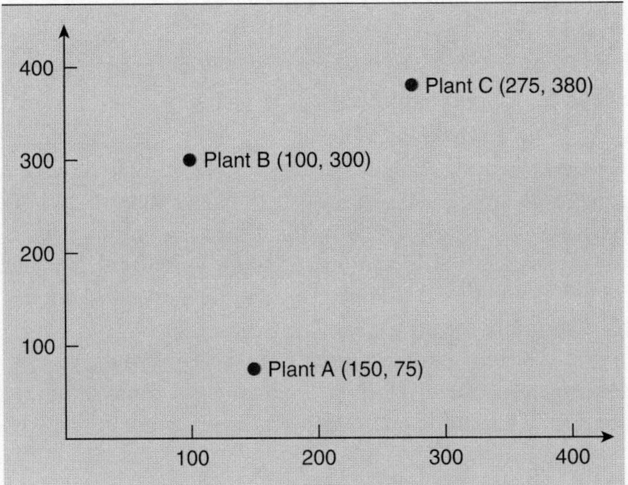

Exhibit 7.8
Plant Location Matrix

Exhibit 7.9
Quantity of Compressors Required by Each Plant

Plant	Compressors Required per Year
A	6,000
B	8,200
C	7,000

Bibliography

Blackburn, Joseph D. *Time-Based Competition: The Next Battle Ground in American Manufacturing.* Homewood, IL: Richard D. Irwin, 1991.

Exter, Thomas G. "The Next Step Is Called GIS." *American Demographics* 14, no. 5 (May 1992).

Francis, R. L.; L. F. McGinnis; and J. A. White. *Facility Layout and Location: An Analytical Approach.* 2nd ed. Englewood Cliffs, NJ: Prentice Hall, 1992.

Garrison, Sue. "After Push Came to Shove." *Business Geographics,* February 2000, p. 11.

Hayes, Robert H., and Steven C. Wheelwright. *Restoring Our Competitive Edge.* New York: John Wiley & Sons, 1984.

Joerger, Albert; Stephen D. DeGloria; and Malcolm A. Noden. "Applying Geographic Information Systems." *Cornell Hotel and Restaurant Administration Quarterly,* August 1999.

Lovelock, Christopher. "Strategies for Managing Capacity-Constrained Services." *Managing Services: Marketing, Operations Management and Human Resources.* 2nd ed. Englewood Cliffs, NJ: Prentice Hall, 1992.

MacCormack, Alan D.; Lawrence J. Newman III; and Donald B. Rosenfeld. "The New Dynamics of Global Manufacturing Site Location." *Sloan Management Review,* Summer 1994, pp. 69–80.

Manivannan, S., and Dipak Chudhuri. "Computer-Aided Facility Layout Algorithm Generates Alternatives to Increase Firm's Productivity." *Industrial Engineering,* May 1984.

Maruca, Regina F.; Raymond Burke; Sir Richard Greenbury; and Robert A. Smith, "Retailing: Confronting the Challenges That Face Brick-and-Mortar Stores." *Harvard Business Review,* July–August 1999, pp. 3–12.

Mason, Mark. "United States Direct Investment in Japan: Trends and Prospects." *California Management Review,* Fall 1992, pp. 98–115.

Moutinho, Luiz; Bruce Curry; and Fiona Davies. "Comparative Computer Approaches to Multi-Outlet Retail Site Location Decisions." *The Service Industries Journal* 13, no. 4 (October 1993), pp. 201–20.

Reid, Hal. "Retailers Seek the Unique." *Business Geographics* 5, no. 2 (February 1997), pp. 32–35.

Strazewski, Len. "Silicon Valley Holds Fertile Kids' Market." *Franchise Times,* February 1997.

Tayman, Jeff, and Louis Pol. "Retail Site Selection and Geographic Information Systems." *Journal of Applied Business Research* 11, no. 2, pp. 46–54.

Wheelwright, Steven C., ed. *Capacity Planning and Facilities Choice: Course Module.* Boston: Harvard Business School, 1979.

Case

Bruegger's Bagel Bakeries

Founded in 1983 in Burlington, Vermont, Bruegger's Bagel Bakeries is a retail bagel concept that has grown to more than 300 neighborhood bagel bakeries throughout the United States. These stores are located in major downtown areas, suburban strip shopping centers, and easy-to-drive-to, quick-service locations. In addition to bagels, the bakeries also offer a wide variety of cream cheeses, soups, coffees, and deli-style sandwiches that customers either can enjoy on the premises or take out.

Every Bruegger's bakery bakes its own bagels throughout the day, providing customers with fresh hot bagels. However, in order to ensure that only the highest quality bagels are served and that there is consistency in both the quality and size of the bagels among its many retail locations, Bruegger's initially prepares the raw bagels at central commissaries. These commissaries are responsible for mixing the dough, forming the bagels and proofing them (that is, allowing them to rise properly under a controlled temperature and humidity environment). The raw bagels are then distributed to individual locations where they are first boiled in water and then baked.

Currently, Bruegger's has more than 30 retail locations in the greater Boston area, most of them being located in downtown Boston and in the suburbs north and west of Boston. There are also four stores that are located south of Boston. The addresses for each of these bakeries and the average number of dozens of bagels that each receives daily are shown below:

Address	City/Town	Average Number of Dozens of Bagels Delivered per Day
45 Morrissey Boulevard	Dorchester, MA	180
356 Granite Avenue	East Milton, MA	135
2100 Washington St.	Hanover, MA	165
211 Lincoln St.	Hingham, MA	120

Currently these four locations are provided with bagels from a central commissary that is located in Woburn, Massachusetts, northwest of Boston. Because this commissary is reaching its maximum capacity, management has decided to locate a new commissary south of Boston to provide bagels for these four locations. (It also is expected that there will be additional future locations south of Boston that also will be served by this commissary.)

Nord Brue, founder and current CEO at Bruegger's, working with a real estate consultant in Massachusetts, has identified the following two potential locations for this commissary:

Address	City/Town
50 Derby St.	Hingham, MA
100 Independence Ave.	Quincy, MA

Questions

1. Find an ASP on the Internet that provides detailed maps that include directions with distances and times between locations. Determine the travel times and distances between the two potential commissary sites and each of the four retail locations.
2. One alternative is for Nord to subcontract out the delivery of the bagels to a local food delivery service that has quoted a delivery charge of five cents per dozen bagels per mile. Using this cost as a criterion, which site should Nord select for the commissary?
3. Another option is to use a company truck, which is available, for the deliveries. With this alternative, Nord estimates that the driver will have to make one delivery per day to each of the four locations, and that the driver and truck will cost $30.00 per hour, including the driver's benefits. Under this scenario, which commissary site should Nord select?
4. Which of these two alternative methods of delivery (that is, outsourcing or keeping it in-house) do you recommend and why?
5. What additional factors should Nord take into consideration in selecting a new commissary site south of Boston?

Source: © 2001 James Salsbury and Mark M. Davis. This case describes an actual company and its business environment, although some of the data presented here may be disguised and/or modified for proprietary reasons or to emphasize a specific teaching objective.

Case

Community Hospital

In 1983, Community Hospital, which had served the downtown area of a large West Coast city for more than 25 years, closed and then built a new hospital in a thinly populated area about 30 miles west of the city. The new hospital, also named Community Hospital, was located on a parcel of land owned by the original hospital for many years.

This new hospital, which opened October 1, 1983, is a four-story structure that includes all the latest innovations in health-care technology. The first floor houses the emergency departments; intensive care unit; operating room; radiology, laboratory, and therapy departments; pharmacy; housekeeping and maintenance facilities and supplies, as well as other supportive operations. All administrative offices, such as the business office, medical records department, special services, and so forth, are located on the second floor, as are the cafeteria and food service facilities. The two upper floors contain patient rooms divided into surgical, medical, pediatric, and obstetric units.

Community Hospital has a total capacity of 177 beds assigned as follows:

Unit	Number of Beds
Surgical	45
Medical	65
Pediatrics	35
Obstetrics	20
Intensive care	12

For the first six months of the hospital's operation, things were rather chaotic for the administrator, Sam Jones. All his time was occupied with the multitude of activities that go along with starting a new facility, such as seeing that malfunctioning equipment was repaired, arranging for new staff to be hired and trained, establishing procedures and schedules, making necessary purchasing decisions, and attending endless conferences and meetings.

All during this period, Mr. Jones had been getting some rather disturbing reports from his controller, Bob Cash, regarding Community Hospital's financial situation. But he decided that these financial matters would simply have to wait until things had settled down.

Finally, in April, Mr. Jones asked Mr. Cash to prepare a comprehensive report on the hospital's financial position and to make a presentation with his new assistant administrator, Tim Newman, who had recently received a degree in hospital administration.

In his report, Mr. Cash stated: "As you both know, we have been running at an operating cash deficit since we opened last October. We expected, of course, to be losing money at the start until we were able to establish ourselves in the community and draw in patients. We certainly were right. During our first month, we lost almost $221,000. Last month, in March, we lost $58,000.

"The reason, of course, is pretty straightforward. Our income is directly related to our patient census (i.e., patient load). On the other hand, our expenses are fixed and are running at about $235,000 a month for salaries and wages, $75,000 a month for supplies and equipment, and another $10,000 a month in interest charges. Our accumulated operating deficit for the six months we've been here totals $715,000, which we've covered with our bank line of credit. I suppose we can continue to borrow for another couple of months, but after that I don't know what we're going to do."

Mr. Jones replied, "As you said, Bob, we did expect to be losing money in the beginning, but I never expected the loss to go on for six months or to accumulate to almost three-quarters of a million dollars. Well, at least last month was a lot better than the first month. Do you have any figures showing the month-to-month trend?"

Bob Cash laid the following worksheet on the table:

COMMUNITY HOSPITAL

Six-Month Operating Statement October 1983–March 1984 (in thousands of dollars)

	1983			**1984**			
	October	**November**	**December**	**January**	**February**	**March**	**Total**
Income	$ 101	$ 163	$ 199	$ 235	$ 245	$ 262	$ 1,205
Expenses (excluding interest):							
Salaries, wages	232	233	239	235	235	235	1,410
Supplies, other	80	73	74	75	73	75	450
Total	312	306	313	310	309	310	1,860
Interest	10	10	10	10	10	10	60
Operating loss	$(221)	$(153)	($124)	($ 85)	($ 74)	($ 58)	($ 715)
Average daily census	42	68	83	98	102	109	
Occupancy	24%	38%	47%	55%	58%	62%	

Questions

1. Evaluate the situation at Community Hospital with respect to trends in daily patient census, occupancy rate, and income.
2. Has there been any change in revenue per patient-day over the six-month period (assuming a 30-day month)?
3. At what capacity level will the hospital achieve breakeven?
4. What questions might we raise about the constant level of salaries and supplies relative to past and future operations?

Source: Reprinted with permission from *Hospital Cost Containment through Operations Management,* published by the American Hospital Association. Copyright 1984.

8 Facility Decisions: Layouts

Chapter Objectives

- Introduce the different types of facility layouts that can be used in designing manufacturing and service operations.
- Present a methodology for designing a process-oriented layout.
- Introduce the concept of takt time and its relationship to the output capacity of a product-oriented layout.
- Identify the various steps and elements that are involved in balancing an assembly line.
- Discuss the current trends in facility layouts given today's shorter product life cycles and the customer's increasing desire for customized products.

TACO'S NEW FACTORY LAYOUT REDUCES INVENTORIES AND THROUGHPUT TIMES

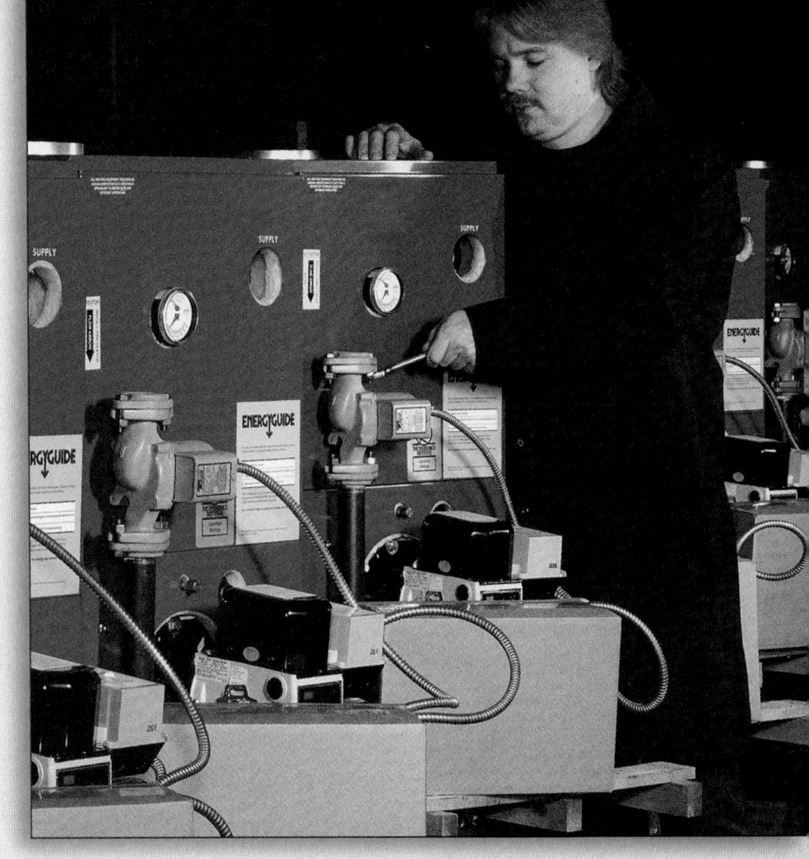

In the early 1990s, when John White Jr. became president of TACO, he found the factory floor crammed with inventories and delivery times for products taking weeks and even months. Not coincidentally, this was about the same amount of time it took for a product to make its way through the factory floor from beginning to end. The factory layout was designed according to processes, with all of the machining taking place in one area, assembly taking place in another, painting in a third area, and so forth. As a result, TACO's products spent a lot of time traveling from one work area to the next, often waiting for long periods of time before the required operation was performed. These long waits were the reasons there was so much inventory on the floor.

Taco Plant Layout

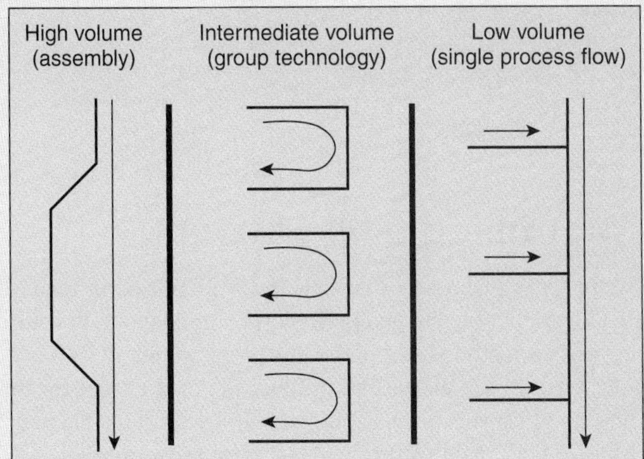

TACO is an old traditional New England manufacturer located in Cranston, Rhode Island. It has been producing circulator pumps since the early part of the 20th century when John's grandfather started the business. (Circulator pumps are used in forced hot water heating systems to move the water through the pipes.) TACO makes both residential and industrial circulator pumps. The former are made in very high volumes, whereas the latter are produced in much lower volumes, often being designed and made to order to meet the specific requirements of an individual building.

After analyzing the various products being produced, TACO redesigned its factory layout to be product-oriented rather than process-oriented. The three main bays in its factory were divided into three major product lines. One bay was devoted to the high-volume residential pump, where an assembly-line process was installed. In the middle bay, group technology cells were established, with each cell focusing on a specific family of products. In this bay, the pumps were produced in varying batch sizes of between 100 and 600 units. All of the different pieces of equipment required to make a particular family of pumps were organized in a U-shape layout in the sequential order required to make the pump, and there were several cells in the bay. Thus, a typical work cell would consist of machine tools, an assembly area, and even a small paint booth.

The third bay does all of the low-volume products, which are often the large bulky commercial units. The volumes here are very low, sometimes being as little as one or two units of a specific design. The layout in this bay uses a single-process flow approach, which in many ways resembles an assembly line. The main difference here is that the time spent at each station is very long compared to a traditional assembly line, and each station is designed so that it is very flexible in order to accommodate the wide variety of products that are made in this bay.

TACO's new product-oriented layouts have reduced the work-in-process inventories by more than 30 percent, while at the same drastically reducing the average throughput time by more than 50 percent. Products that once took weeks and even months to complete are now manufactured in days, and even hours if necessary. Another benefit of the new layouts is that TACO has been able to increase its output by more than 50 percent without requiring any additional floor space. TACO's new factory layout is one of the major reasons that it currently has a major share of the markets in which its products compete.

Source: TACO.

Types of Manufacturing Layouts

process layout

Similar operations are performed in a common or functional area, regardless of the product in which the parts are used.

product layout

Equipment/operations are located according to the progressive steps required to make the product.

There are three basic types of layouts that have been identified in manufacturing plants: (*a*) process layout, (*b*) product layout, and (*c*) fixed-position layout. In addition, there is one hybrid that is referred to as a group technology or cellular layout, which is a combination of process and product layouts. We discuss all of these in detail except for the fixed-position layout. As a starting point for this discussion, Exhibit 8.1 presents the general characteristics of a good layout for both manufacturing and service operations.

In a **process layout** (also called a *job-shop layout* or *layout by function*), similar equipment or functions are grouped together, such as in a machine shop where all the lathes are in one area and all the stamping machines are in another. A part being worked on travels from one area to the next, according to the specific sequence of operations required. This type of layout is often found in high-mix, low-volume manufacturing plants that have an intermittent process.

A **product layout** (also called a *flow-shop layout*) is one in which equipment or work processes are arranged according to the progressive steps by which the product is made. If equipment is dedicated to the continual production of a narrow product line, this is usually

Managerial Issues

Managers need to take many factors into consideration when determining which type of facility layout is most appropriate for their operations. This applies to both manufacturing and service operations alike. Product-oriented layouts like assembly lines, as we shall see, are highly efficient but tend to be very inflexible. Process-oriented layouts, on the other hand, are very flexible, in terms of the wide variety of products that can be made, but, as we saw at TACO in the opening vignette, they typically have significant work-in-process inventories and are relatively inefficient and slow.

The choice of which type of layout to adopt cannot be made lightly because it can significantly impact a company's long-term success, both in terms of product costs and its ability to compete successfully in the marketplace. In addition, the investment costs that are associated with installing a particular layout, in terms of time and money, are substantial.

The manager's goal in selecting a layout is to provide a smooth flow of material through the factory, or an uncomplicated traffic pattern for both customers and workers in a service operation. Today, there are many software packages available to assist managers in designing a layout that is both efficient and effective, as illustrated in the OM in Practice box.

Exhibit 8.1

Characteristics of a Good Layout

Manufacturing and Back-Office Service Operations	Face-to-Face Services
1. Straight-line flow pattern (or adaptation).	**1.** Easily understood service-flow pattern.
2. Backtracking kept to a minimum.	**2.** Proper waiting facilities.
3. Production time predictable.	**3.** Easy communication with customers.
4. Little interstage storage of materials.	**4.** Customer surveillance easily maintained.
5. Open plant floors so everyone can see what's going on.	**5.** Clear exit and entry points with sufficient checkout capabilities.
6. Bottleneck operations under control.	**6.** Departments and processes arranged so that customers see only what you want them to see.
7. Workstations close together.	**7.** Balance between waiting areas and service areas.
8. Minimum material movement.	**8.** Minimum walking.
9. No unnecessary rehandling of materials.	**9.** Lack of clutter.
10. Easily adjustable to changing conditions.	**10.** High sales volume per square foot of facility.

called a *production line* or *assembly line*. Examples are the manufacture of small appliances (toasters, irons, beaters), large appliances (dishwashers, refrigerators, washing machines), electronics (computers, CD players), and automobiles.

A **group technology (GT) or cellular layout** brings together dissimilar machines into work centers (or cells) to work on products that have similar shapes and processing requirements. A GT layout is similar to process layout, in that cells are designed to perform a specific set of processes, and it is similar to product layout in that the cells are dedicated to a limited range of products. Often the cell is arranged in a U-shape to allow workers to move more easily from one station to another.

group technology (G/T) or cellular layout

Groups of dissimilar machines brought together in a work cell to perform tasks on a family of products that share common attributes.

In a **fixed-position layout,** by virtue of its bulk or weight, the product remains stationary at one location. The manufacturing equipment is moved to the product rather than vice versa. Shipyards and construction sites are good examples of this format.

fixed-position layout

The product, because of its size and/or weight, remains in one location and processes are brought to it.

Manufacturing facilities may often have a combination of layout types. For example, a given floor may be laid out by process, while another floor may be laid out by product. It

Operations Management in Practice

IMPROVING A MANUFACTURING PROCESS USING PLANNING SOFTWARE

A challenge many facilities planners face today is finding a way to quickly and effectively evaluate proposed layout changes and material handling systems so that the material handling costs and distances are minimized. This challenge was addressed during a three-day, on-site software training session conducted at an appliance manufacturer. The facilities planners were learning the basics on using the FactoryFLOW software package, a computer-based, facilities planning tool developed by Cimtechnologies Corp. The training group evaluated a current layout proposal of a console assembly area to see if any improvements could be made.

The FactoryFLOW software quantitatively evaluates facility layouts and material handling systems by showing the material flow paths and costs, both in output text reports and in a graphic overlay of an AutoCAD layout drawing. FactoryFLOW evaluates the material flow and material handling costs and distances using the following input information: an AutoCAD layout drawing, part routing data (i.e., part names, from/to locations, and move quantities), and material handling system characteristics (i.e., fixed and variable costs, load/unload times, and speeds).

The facilities planners had a drawing of the area, and the industrial engineers supplied the part routing and material equipment information; therefore data entry and analysis of the current layout took about one-half of a day. Output diagrams and reports showed material handling distances of over 407 million feet per year and material handling costs of just over $900,000 per year.

The second half of the day was used to come up with alternative layouts by analyzing the output text reports and the material flow lines. One alternative was to rotate a line of 16 plastic presses 90 degrees, so they fed right into the subassembly area, and to rotate the main console assembly lines 90 degrees, so they were closer to the same area. Since the primary material handling system was an overhead conveyor, minimizing the length of the conveyor was a major concern. FactoryFLOW was used to evaluate the alternative layout, and the output reports showed the material handling costs had been reduced by over $100,000 to $792,265 per year. Also, by decreasing the material travel distance, the length of overhead conveyor needed had been reduced from 3,600 feet to just over 700 feet.

is also common to find an entire plant arranged according to general product flow (fabrication, subassembly, and final assembly), coupled with process layout within fabrication and product layout within the assembly department. Likewise, group technology is frequently found within a department that itself is located according to a plantwide process-oriented layout.

An operation's layout continually changes over time because the internal and external environments are dynamic. As demands change, so can layout. As technology changes, so can layout. In Chapter 3, we discussed a product/process matrix indicating that as products and volumes change, the most efficient layout is also likely to change. Therefore, the decision on a specific layout type may be a temporary one.

Process Layout

The most common approach for developing a process layout is to arrange departments consisting of similar or identical processes in a way that optimizes their relative placement. In many installations, optimal placement often translates into placing departments with large amounts of interdepartmental traffic adjacent to one another. The primary goal in designing a layout for a manufacturing or distribution facility is to minimize material handling costs. In a service organization, the main objective is to minimize customer and worker travel time through the process.

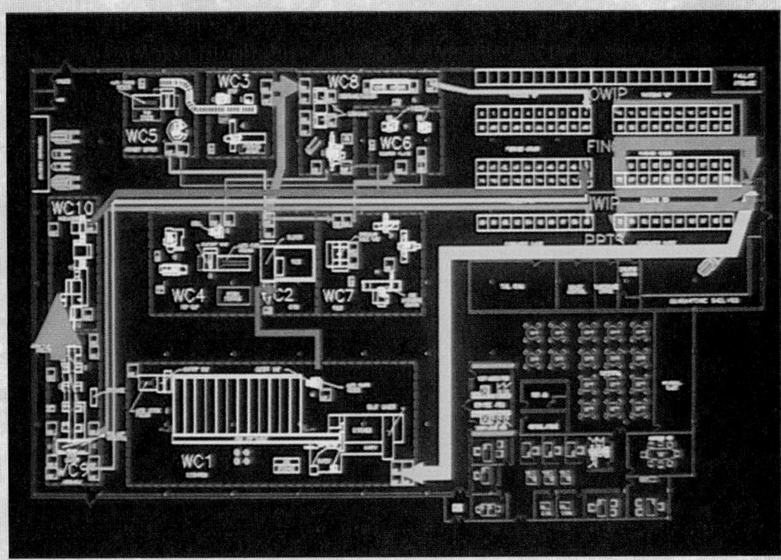

FactoryFLOW integrates material handling data and a layout drawing to compute material handling distances, costs, and equipment utilization.

The FactoryFLOW software made it possible to complete this project in a short amount of time, and the facilities planners at this company now have a tool for further evaluation of facility layouts and material handling systems.

Source: "Factory Planning Software Cimtechnologies Corp. (Ames, IA)," *Industrial Engineering,* December 1993, p. SS3.

Minimizing Interdependent Movement Costs Consider the following simple example:

Example

Suppose that we want to arrange the six departments of a toy factory to minimize the interdepartmental material handling cost. Initially, let us make the assumption that all departments have the same amount of space, say 40 feet by 40 feet, and that the building is 80 feet wide and 120 feet long (and thus compatible with the department dimensions). The first thing we would want to know is the nature of the flow between departments and the way the material is transported. If the company has another factory that makes similar products, information about flow patterns might be obtained from these records. On the other hand, if this is a new product, such information would have to come from routing sheets or from estimates by knowledgeable personnel such as process or industrial engineers. Of course these data, regardless of their source, have to be adjusted to reflect the nature of future orders over the projected life of the proposed layout.

Let us assume that this information is available. We find that all material is transported in a standard-size crate by forklift truck, one crate to a truck (which constitutes one "load"). Now suppose that transportation costs are \$1 to move a load between adjacent departments and \$1 extra for each department in between. (We assume there is two-way traffic between departments.) The expected loads between departments for the first year of operation are tabulated in Exhibit 8.2; the available plant space is depicted in Exhibit 8.3.

Solution

Given this information, our first step is to illustrate the interdepartmental flow by a model, such as Exhibit 8.4, which is Exhibit 8.2 displayed in the building layout in Exhibit 8.3. This provides the basic layout pattern, which we are trying to improve.

Exhibit 8.2 Interdepartmental Flow

	1	2	3	4	5	6
1		175	50	0	230	20
2			0	100	165	80
3				17	213	99
4					25	0
5						554
6						

Exhibit 8.3 Building Dimensions and Departments

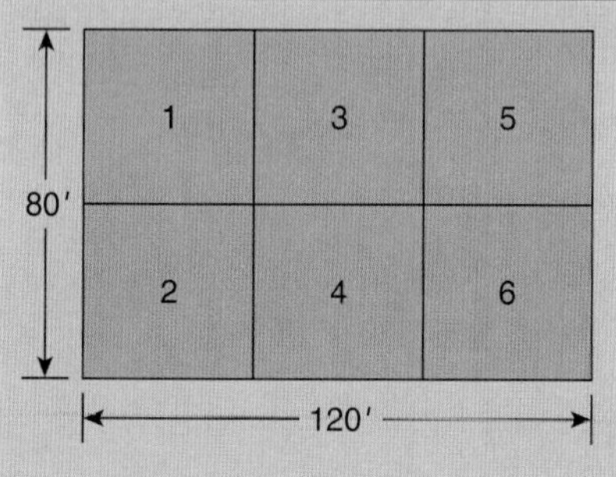

Exhibit 8.4 Interdepartmental Flow Graph with Number of Annual Movements

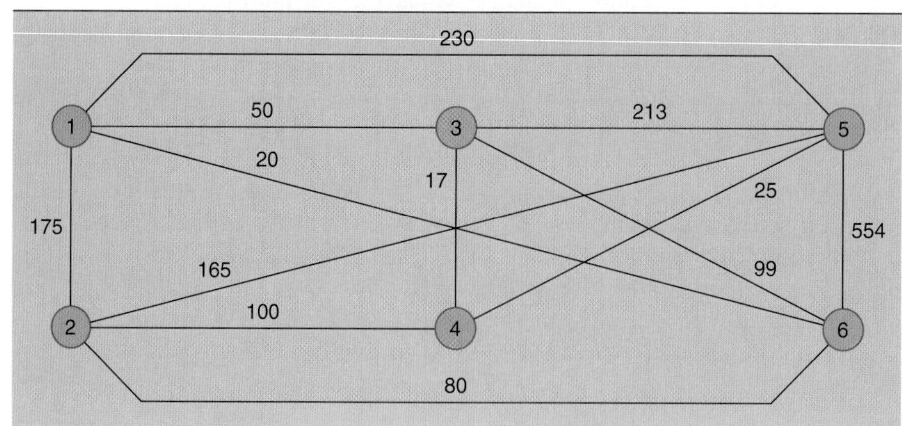

The second step is to determine the annual cost of this layout by multiplying the material handling cost per load by the number of loads moved between each department. Exhibit 8.5 presents this information, which is derived as follows: The annual material handling cost between Departments 1 and 2 is \$175 (\$1 × 175 moves), \$460 between Departments 1 and 5 (\$2 × 230 moves), and so forth. (The distances are taken from Exhibit 8.3 or 8.4, not Exhibit 8.2.)

The third step is a search for departmental changes that reduce costs. On the basis of the graph and the cost matrix, it appears desirable to place Departments 1 and 5 closer together to reduce their high move-distance costs. However, this requires shifting another department, thereby affecting other move-distance costs and the total cost of the second solution. Exhibit 8.6 shows the revised layout resulting from relocating Department 5 and an adjacent department (Department 3 is arbitrarily selected for this purpose). The revised cost matrix for the exchange, with the cost changes circled, is given in Exhibit 8.7. Note the total cost is now \$345 less than in the initial solution. While this trial-and-error approach resulted in a lower total cost in this case, even in a small problem, it is often difficult to identify the correct "obvious move" on the basis of casual inspection. The revised layout for the facility is shown in Exhibit 8.8.

Exhibit 8.5

Cost Matrix—First Solution

1	2	3	4	5	6	
	175	50	0	460	40	1
		0	100	330	160	2
			17	213	99	3
				25	0	4
					554	5
						6

Total cost: \$2,223

Exhibit 8.6

Revised Interdepartmental Flowchart*

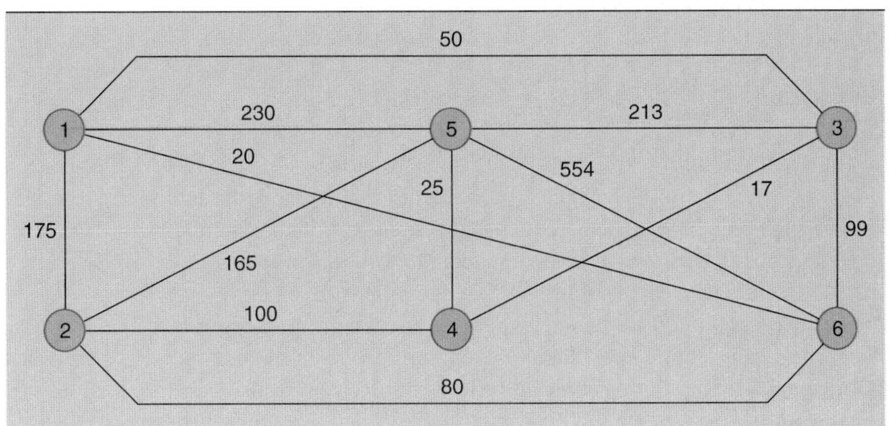

*Only interdepartmental flow with effect on cost is depicted.

Exhibit 8.7

Cost Matrix—Second Solution

	1	2	3	4	5	6	Net cost change
1		175	**100**	0	**230**	40	+50−230
2			0	100	**165**	160	−165
3				17	213	99	
4					25	0	
5						554	
6							

Total cost: $1,878 Total difference: −345

Exhibit 8.8

Revised Building Layout

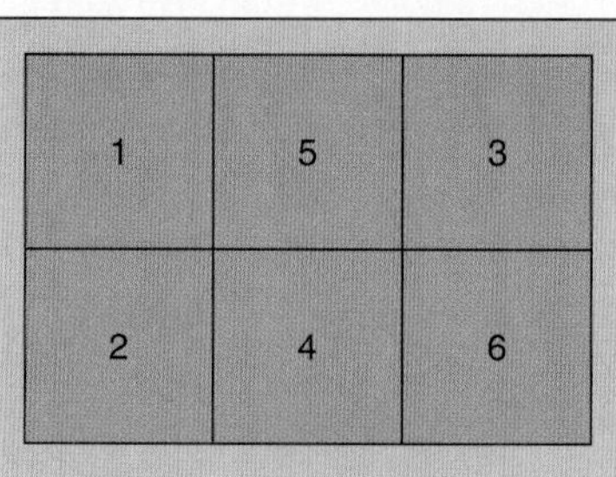

Thus far, we have shown only one exchange among a large number of potential exchanges; in fact, for a six-department problem there are 6! (or 720) possible arrangements. Therefore, the procedure we have employed would have only a remote possibility of achieving an optimal combination in a "reasonable" number of tries. Nor does our problem stop here. Other factors must be taken into consideration.

Suppose that we are able to arrive at a good trial-and-error solution solely on the basis of material handling cost. Continuing with our toy factory example, locating the sewing department next to the painting department might not only be hazardous, but also may result in defective products with lint, thread, and cloth particles drifting onto the painted items before they can dry. Thus, issues like these also must be incorporated into the final choice of layout.

Product Layout

When product demand is sufficiently high and sustainable over a long period of time, it is usually cost effective to rearrange resources from a process layout to a product layout as defined by the sequence of steps required to make the product. We often call these *assembly* lines, although the ratio of direct manual labor to machine work can vary widely. Assembly lines can vary from virtually 100 percent parts assembly by workers, to the other extreme, an *automated transfer* line, where all direct work is done by machine. In between are all types: Automobile lines have tools ranging from simple hammers and wrenches to robotic welding and painting. Assembly lines in electronics also can range widely from manual parts assembly to equipment for automatic parts insertion, automatic soldering, and automatic testing.

Assembly Lines Assembly lines are a special case of product layout. In a general sense, the term assembly line refers to a progressive assembly linked by some type of material handling device. The usual assumption is that some form of pacing is present, and the allowable processing time is equivalent for all workstations. Within this broad definition, there are important differences among line types. A few of these are material handling devices (belt or roller conveyor, overhead crane), line configuration (U-shape, straight, branching), pacing (machine, human), product mix (one product or multiple products), workstation characteristics (workers may sit, stand, walk with the line, or ride the line), and length of the line (few or many stations).

The range of products partially or completely assembled on lines includes toys, appliances, autos, garden equipment, perfumes and cosmetics, and a wide variety of electronic components. In fact, it is probably safe to say that virtually any product with multiple parts and produced in large volume uses assembly lines to some degree. Clearly, assembly lines are an important technology; to really understand their managerial requirements one must have some familiarity with how a line is balanced.

An important consideration that should not be overlooked in designing assembly lines is the human factor. Early assembly lines were machine paced; that is, they moved at a predetermined pace, regardless of whether or not the work was completed at a station. Under this structure, workers who fell behind had to rush to complete their assigned tasks, with the result often being faulty workmanship.

In recent years, worker-paced assembly lines, which were advocated initially by Japanese manufacturers, have replaced machine-paced lines in many facilities. With the worker-paced line, the operator continues to work on the product until the work assigned is satisfactorily completed. Only then is the product allowed to move on to the next station. The quality of the products made on a worker-paced line is significantly higher than that of products made on a comparable machine-paced line. When a Japanese manufacturer took over the production of televisions from a U.S. company, the number of defects dropped from 160 defects per 100 TVs to 4 defects per 100 TVs, even though the output per day and the workforce remained virtually unchanged. This dramatic increase in quality was attributed, in large part, to the installation of a worker-paced assembly line that replaced the previously existing machine-paced line.[1]

Definitions. Before we begin our analysis of assembly lines, there are two terms that need to be defined, and that are illustrated in Exhibit 8.9.

- *Product interval time.* The product interval time is the actual time between products being completed at a station. This is often referred to as *cycle time,* or more recently, **takt time** (from the Swedish word meaning "cycle or cycle time").[2] As we shall see shortly, the takt time for an assembly line determines the capacity of that line. We will use takt time to describe the product interval time in our analyses.
- *Product duration time.* The overall time it takes to complete an individual product, from start to finish, is known as the product's **throughput time,** and is also referred to as *cycle time,* especially when looking at it from the customer's perspective. Throughput time is important when you are looking at the delivery time for customized products. We will use throughput time to describe the product duration time.

takt time

The time interval between stations on an assembly line.

throughput time

The overall elapsed time from when the manufacture of a product is first begun to when that specific product is completed.

[1]Lloyd Dobyns and Frank Reuven, *If Japan Can, Why Can't We?* (New York: NBC-TV News Presentation, June 24, 1980).

[2]Robert W. Hall, "Time Prints and Takt Times," *Target: Innovation at Work* 14, no. 3 (1998), pp. 6–13.

Exhibit 8.9

Illustrating Takt Time and Throughput Time on an Assembly Line

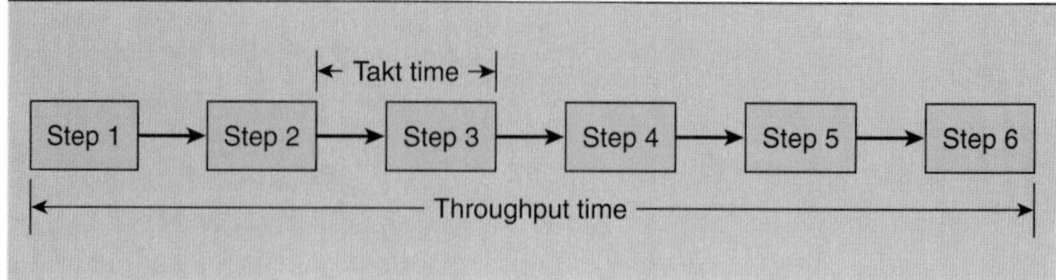

Assembly line balancing. An assembly line consists of a series of workstations, each with a uniform time interval that is referred to as a takt time (which is also the time between successive units coming off the end of the line). At each workstation, work is performed on a product by adding parts and/or by completing an assembly operation. The work performed at each station is made up of many *tasks* (also referred to as *elements,* or *work units*). Such tasks are described by motion-time analysis. Generally, they are groupings that cannot be subdivided on the assembly line without paying a high penalty in extra motions.

The total work to be performed at a workstation is equal to the sum of the tasks assigned to that workstation. The **assembly line balancing** problem is one of assigning all of the tasks required to a series of workstations so that the time required to do the work at each station does not exceed the takt time, and at the same time, the unassigned (i.e., idle) time across all workstations is minimized. An additional consideration in designing the line is to assign the tasks as equitably as possible to the stations. The problem is further complicated by the relationships among tasks imposed by product design and process technologies. This is called the precedence relationship, which specifies the order in which the tasks must be performed in the assembly process.

assembly line balancing

Assignment of tasks to workstations within a given cycle time and with minimum idle worker time.

Steps in assembly line balancing. The sequence of steps required to balance an assembly line is straightforward:

1. Specify the sequential relationship among tasks using a precedence diagram. The diagram consists of circles and arrows. Circles represent individual tasks; arrows indicate the order of task performance.
2. Determine the required takt time (T), using the following formula:

$$T = \frac{\text{Production time per day}}{\text{Output per day (in units)}}$$

3. Determine the theoretical minimum number of workstations (N_t) required to satisfy the takt time constraint, using the following formula:

$$N_t = \frac{\text{Sum of task times } (S)}{\text{Takt time } (T)}$$

4. Select a primary rule by which tasks are to be assigned to workstations, and a secondary rule to break ties.
5. Assign tasks, one at a time, to the first workstation until the sum of the task times is equal to the takt time, or no other tasks are feasible because of time or sequence restrictions. Repeat the process for Workstation 2, Workstation 3, and so on, until all tasks are assigned.
6. Evaluate the efficiency of the resulting assembly line using the following formula:

$$\text{Efficiency} = \frac{\text{Sum of task times } (S)}{\text{Actual number of workstations } (N_a) \times \text{Takt time } (T)}$$

7. If efficiency is unsatisfactory, rebalance the line using a different decision rule.

Example

A toy company produces a Model J Wagon that is to be assembled on a conveyor belt. Five hundred wagons are required per day. The company is currently operating on a one-shift, eight-hour-a-day schedule, with one hour off for lunch (i.e., net production time per day is seven hours). The assembly steps and times for the wagon are given in Exhibit 8.10. Assignment: Find the balance that minimizes the number of workstations, subject to takt time and precedence constraints.

Solution

1. Draw a precedence diagram. Exhibit 8.11 illustrates the sequential relationships identified in Exhibit 8.10. (The length of the arrows has no meaning.)
2. Takt time determination. Here we have to convert to seconds since our task times are in seconds.

$$T = \frac{\text{Production time per day}}{\text{Output per day}} = \frac{7 \text{ hrs./day} \times 60 \text{ min./hr.} \times 60 \text{ sec./min.}}{500 \text{ wagons}}$$

$$= \frac{25{,}200}{500} = 50.4 \text{ seconds}$$

3. Theoretical minimum number of workstations required (the actual number may be greater):

$$N_t = \frac{S}{T} = \frac{195 \text{ seconds}}{50.4 \text{ seconds}} = 3.86 \text{ stations} \rightarrow 4 \text{ stations}$$

(Since we cannot have a fraction of a station, we always round up to the next whole integer. For this example, the minimum number of stations is four.)

4. Select assignment rules. Research has shown that some rules are better than others for certain problem structures. In general, the strategy is to use a rule assigning tasks that either have many followers or are of long duration since they effectively limit the balance achievable. In this case, we use as our primary rule

   a. Assign tasks in order of the largest number of following tasks. Our secondary rule, to be invoked where ties exist from our primary rule, is

   b. Assign tasks in order of longest operating time.

Exhibit 8.10

Assembly Steps and Times for Model J Wagon

Task	Performance Time (in seconds)	Description	Tasks that Must Precede
A	45	Position rear axle support and hand fasten four screws to nuts	—
B	11	Insert rear axle	A
C	9	Tighten rear axle support screws to nuts	B
D	50	Position front axle assembly and hand fasten with four screws to nuts	—
E	15	Tighten front axle assembly screws	D
F	12	Position rear wheel #1 and fasten hub cap	C
G	12	Position front wheel #2 and fasten hub cap	C
H	12	Position front wheel #1 and fasten hub cap	E
I	12	Position rear wheel #2 and fasten hub cap	E
J	8	Position wagon handle shaft on front axle assembly and hand fasten bolt and nut	F, G, H, I
K	9	Tighten bolt and nut	J
	195		

Exhibit 8.11

Precedence Graph for Model J Wagon

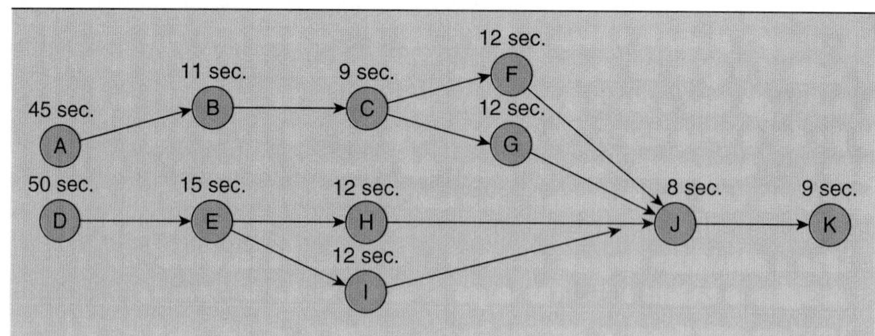

Task	Total Number of Following Tasks	Following Tasks
A	6	B, C, F, G, J, K
B or D	5	C, F, G, J, K (for B)
C or E	4	H, I, J, K (for E)
F, G, H, or I	2	J, K
J	1	K
K	0	—

5. Make task assignments to form Workstation 1, Workstation 2, and so forth, until all tasks are assigned. The actual assignment is given in Exhibit 8.12A and is shown graphically in Exhibit 8.12B.
6. Calculate the efficiency. This is shown in Exhibit 8.12C.
7. Evaluate the solution. An efficiency of 77 percent indicates an imbalance or idle time of 23 percent (1.0 – 0.77) across the entire line. From Exhibit 8.12A we can see that there are 57 total seconds of idle time, and the "choice" job is at Workstation 5.

Is a better balance possible? In this case, yes. Try balancing the line with rule *b* and breaking ties with rule *a*. (This will give you a feasible four-station balance.)

Often the longest required task time dictates the shortest possible takt time for the production line. This task time becomes the lower time bound, unless it is possible to split the task into two or more workstations.

Example

Consider the following illustration: Suppose that an assembly line contains the following task times in seconds: 40, 30, 15, 25, 20, 18, 15. The line runs for 7½ hours per day and the required output is 750 wagons per day.

Solution

The takt time required to produce 750 wagons per day is 36 seconds ([7½ × 60 minutes × 60 seconds]/750). How do we deal with the task that is 40 seconds long?

There are several ways that we may be able to accommodate the 40-second task in a line with a 36-second takt time. The possibilities include

1. *Split the task.* Can we split the task so that complete units are processed in two workstations?

Exhibit 8.12A

Balance Made According to Largest Number of Following Tasks Rule

	Task	Task Time (in seconds)	Remaining Unassigned Time (in seconds)	Feasible Remaining Tasks	Task with Most Followers	Task with Longest Operation Time
Station 1	A	45	5.4 idle	None		
Station 2	D	50	0.4 idle	None		
Station 3	B	11	39.4	C, E	C, E	E
	E	15	24.4	C, H, I	C	
	C	9	15.4	F, G, H, I	F, G, H, I	F, G, H, I
	F*	12	3.4 idle	None		
Station 4	G	12	38.4	H, I	H, I	H, I
	H*	12	26.4	I		
	I	12	14.4	J		
	J	8	6.4 idle	None		
Station 5	K	9	41.4 idle	None		

*Denotes task arbitrarily selected where there is a tie between longest operation times.

Exhibit 8.12B

Precedence Graph for Model J. Wagon

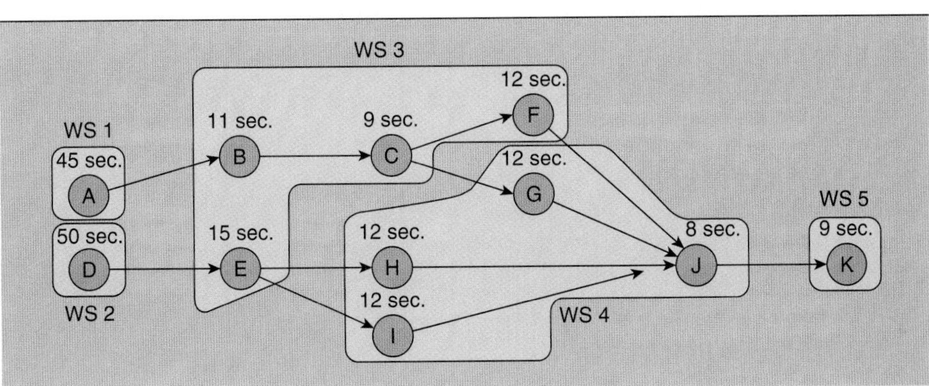

Exhibit 8.12C

Efficiency Calculation

$$\text{Efficiency} = \frac{S}{NT} = \frac{195}{(5)(50.4)} = 0.77, \text{ or } 77\%$$

2. *Duplicate the station.* By duplicating the task at two stations, the effective task time is reduced by 50 percent. If necessary, additional stations can be assigned to the same task to further lower the effective task time. Often with this approach, several tasks may be combined into one station to increase efficiency. In the example given, the first two tasks with 40 and 30 seconds each would be combined into one station, which would then be duplicated. The effective takt time for this station is then 35 seconds ([40 + 30]/2), which is below the required cycle time of 36 seconds.
3. *Share the task.* Can the task somehow be shared so an adjacent workstation does part of the work? This differs from the split task in the first option because the adjacent station acts to assist, not to do some units containing the entire task.

4. *Use a more skilled worker.* Since this task exceeds the cycle time by just 11 percent, a faster worker may be able to meet the 36-second time.
5. *Work overtime.* Producing at a rate of one unit every 40 seconds would produce 675 wagons per day, 75 short of the needed 750. The amount of overtime required to do the additional 75 wagons is 50 minutes (75 × 40 seconds/60 seconds).
6. *Redesign.* It may be possible to redesign the product to reduce the task time slightly.

Other possibilities to reduce the task time include equipment upgrading, a roaming helper to support the line, a change of materials, and multiskilled workers to operate the line as a team rather than as independent workers.

Flexible line layouts. As we saw in the preceding example, assembly line balancing frequently results in unequal workstation times. In fact, the shorter the takt time, the greater the probability of a higher percentage of imbalance in the line. Flexible line layouts such as those shown in Exhibit 8.13 are a common way of dealing with this problem. In our toy

Exhibit 8.13
Flexible Line Layouts

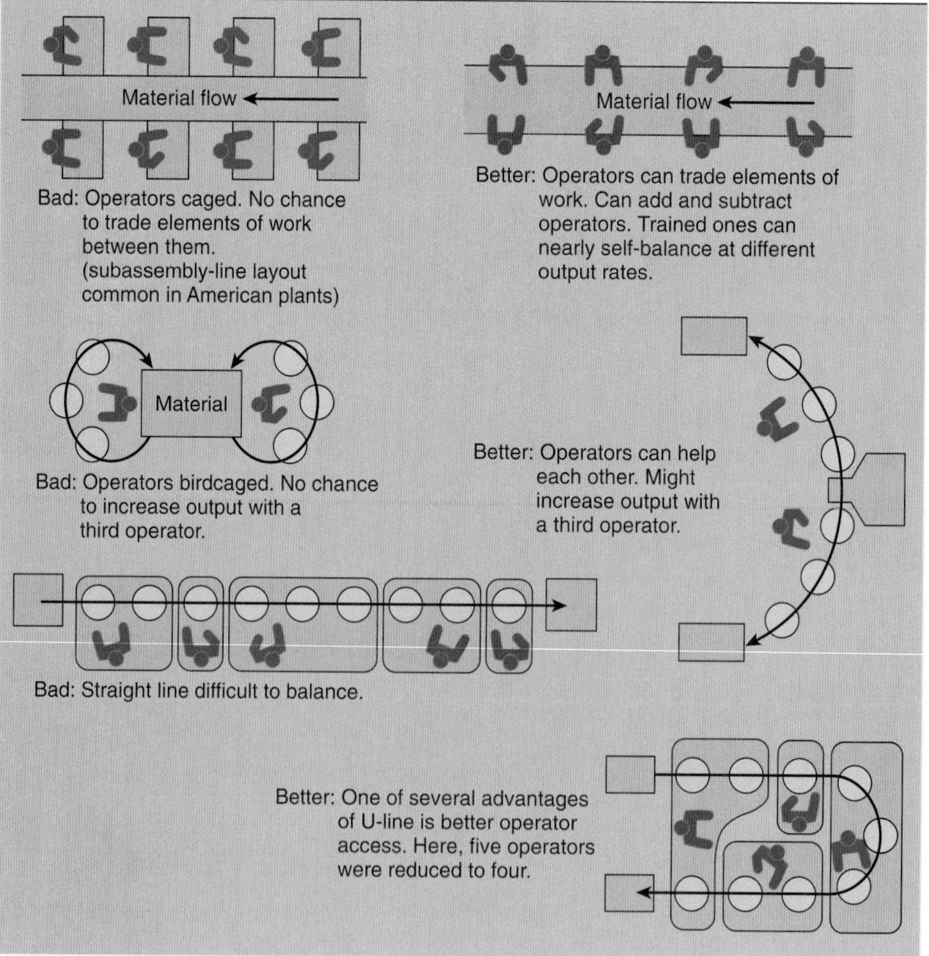

Source: Robert W. Hall, *Attaining Manufacturing Excellence* (Homewood, IL: Dow Jones-Irwin, 1987), p. 125.

company example, the U-shaped line with work sharing at the bottom of the figure could help resolve the imbalance.

Mixed-model line balancing. To meet the demand for a variety of products and to avoid building high inventories of one product model, many manufacturers often schedule several different models to be produced over a given day or week on the same line. To illustrate how this is done, suppose our toy company has a fabrication line to bore holes in its Model J Wagon frame and its Model K Wagon frame. The time required to bore the holes is different for each wagon type.

Example

Assume that the final assembly line downstream requires equal numbers of Model J and Model K wagon frames. Also assume that we want to develop a takt time for the fabrication line, which is balanced for the production of equal numbers of J and K frames. Of course, we could produce Model J frames for several days and then produce Model K frames until an equal number of frames have been produced. However, this would build up unnecessary work-in-process inventory.

If we want to reduce the amount of work-in-process inventory, we could develop a cycle mix that greatly reduces inventory buildup while keeping within the restrictions of equal numbers of J and K wagon frames.

Solution

Process times: 6 minutes per J and 4 minutes per K.

The day consists of 480 minutes (8 hours $\times$ 60 minutes).

$$6J + 4K = 480$$

Since equal numbers of J and K are to be produced (or J = K), produce 48J and 48K per day, or 6J and 6K per hour.

The following shows one balance of J and K frames.

Balanced Mixed-Model Sequence

Model sequence	JJ	KKK	JJ	JJ	KKK	Repeats
Operation time	6 6	4 4 4	6 6	6 6	4 4 4	8 times
Minitakt time	12	12	12	12	12	per day
Total takt time			60			

This line is balanced at six wagon frames of each type per hour with a minitakt time of 12 minutes.

Another balance is J K K J K J, with times of 6, 4, 4, 6, 4, 6. This balance produces three J and three K every 30 minutes with a minitakt time of 10 minutes (JK, KJ, KJ).

The simplicity of mixed-model balancing (under conditions of a level production schedule) is seen in Yasuhiro Mondon's description of Toyota Motor Corporation's operations:

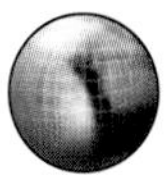

1. Final Assembly lines of Toyota are mixed product lines. The production per day is averaged by taking the number of vehicles in the monthly production schedule classified by specifications, and dividing by the number of working days.

2. In regard to the production sequence during each day, the cycle time of each different specification vehicle is calculated and in order to have all specification vehicles appear at their own cycle time, different specification vehicles are ordered to follow each other.[3]

The mixed-model line appears to be a relatively straightforward sequencing problem. This is because in our example the two models fit nicely into a common time period that also matched demand. From a mathematical standpoint, designing a mixed-model line is very difficult and no technique exists to provide the optimum assignment of tasks to workstations. This is because the mixed-model line involves multiple lot sizes, lot sequencing, setup times for each lot, differing workstation sizes along the line, and task variations. The problem is to design the assembly line and workstations and to specify exactly which tasks are to be done in each.

The objectives of a mixed-model line design are to minimize idle time and minimize the inefficiencies caused by changing from model to model. Researchers have used integer programming, branch and bound techniques, and simulation. They still are not able to find the optimal solution for a realistic sized, real-world problem.

Current Thoughts on Assembly Lines

It is true that the widespread use of assembly-line methods in manufacturing has dramatically increased output rates. Historically, the focus almost always has been on full utilization of human labor; that is, to design assembly lines minimizing human idle times. Equipment and facility utilization stood in the background as much less important. Past research tried to find optimal solutions as if the problem stood in a never-changing world.

Newer views of assembly lines take a broader perspective. Intentions are to incorporate greater flexibility in the number of products manufactured on the line, more variability in workstations (such as size, number of workers), improved reliability (through routine preventive maintenance), and high-quality output (through improved tooling and training). (See also the OM in Practice on How Ford Achieves Flexibility on the Assembly Line.)

Group Technology (Cellular) Layout

A group technology (or cellular) layout allocates dissimilar machines into cells to work on products that have similar weights, shapes, and processing requirements. Group technology (GT) layouts are now widely used in metal fabricating, computer chip manufacture, and assembly work. The overall objective is to gain the benefits of product layout in job-shop kinds of production. These benefits include

1. *Better human relations.* Cells consist of a few workers who form a small work team; a team turns out complete units of work.
2. *Improved operator expertise.* Workers see only a limited number of different parts in a finite production cycle, so repetition means quick learning.
3. *Less work-in-process inventory and material handling.* A cell combines several production stages, so fewer parts travel through the shop.
4. *Faster production setup.* Fewer jobs mean reduced tooling and hence faster tooling changes.

[3]S. Manivannan and Dipak Chudhuri, "Computer-Aided Facility Layout Algorithm Generates Alternatives to Increase Firm's Productivity," *Industrial Engineering,* May 1984, pp. 81–84.

Operations Management in Practice

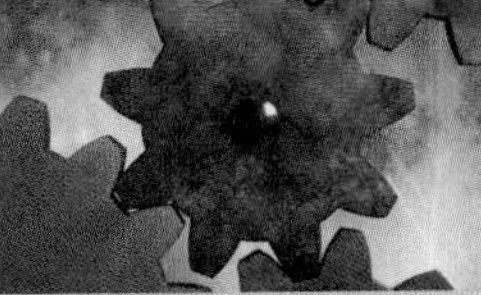

HOW FORD ACHIEVES FLEXIBILITY ON THE ASSEMBLY LINE

Ford Motor Company's assembly plant in Wixom, Michigan, provides another good example of how, with careful planning, several different products can be made on assembly lines. The Wixom plant produces the Mark VIII, the Lincoln Continental, and the Lincoln Town Car. To further complicate the situation, the Continental is a front-wheel drive vehicle on a unibody chassis, whereas the Town Car and the Mark VIII are rear-wheel drive models mounted on a standard frame chassis. The line producing the Continental and the Town Car can be balanced by having between 67 percent and 75 percent of the cars be rear-wheel drive models. Although the Mark VIII is assembled on its own line, all three models share the same paint shop. Currently, the output from the Mark VIII line is 10 cars per hour, and the Continental/Town Car line produces 42 cars per hour.

Developing a GT Layout Shifting from process layout to a GT cellular layout entails three steps:

1. Grouping parts into families that follow a common sequence of operations, which requires developing and maintaining a computerized parts classification and coding system. This is often a major expense with such systems, although many companies have developed short-cut procedures for identifying parts-families.
2. Identifying dominant flow patterns of parts-families as a basis for location or relocation of processes.
3. Physically grouping machines and processes into cells. Often some parts cannot be associated with a family and specialized machinery cannot be placed in any one cell because of its general use. These unattached parts and machinery are placed in a "remainder cell."

Facility Layouts for Services

The overall goal in designing a layout for a service facility, from an operations perspective, is to minimize travel time for workers, and, often, also for customers when they are directly involved in the process. From a marketing perspective, however, the goal is usually to maximize revenues. Frequently these two goals are in conflict with each other. It is therefore management's task to identify the trade-offs that exist in designing the layout, taking both perspectives into consideration. For example, the prescription center in a pharmacy is usually located at the rear, requiring customers to walk through the store. This encourages impulse purchases of nonprescription items, which usually have higher profit margins.

Types of Service Layouts

We use the three basic types of manufacturing facility layouts that were described earlier in this chapter as a framework for identifying the different types of layouts that exist in service operations.

Process Layout The support services for an emergency room in a hospital offer a good example of a *process layout,* with radiology, blood analysis, and the pharmacy each being located in a specific area of the hospital. Patients requiring any of these specific services therefore must go to the respective locations where these services are provided. The

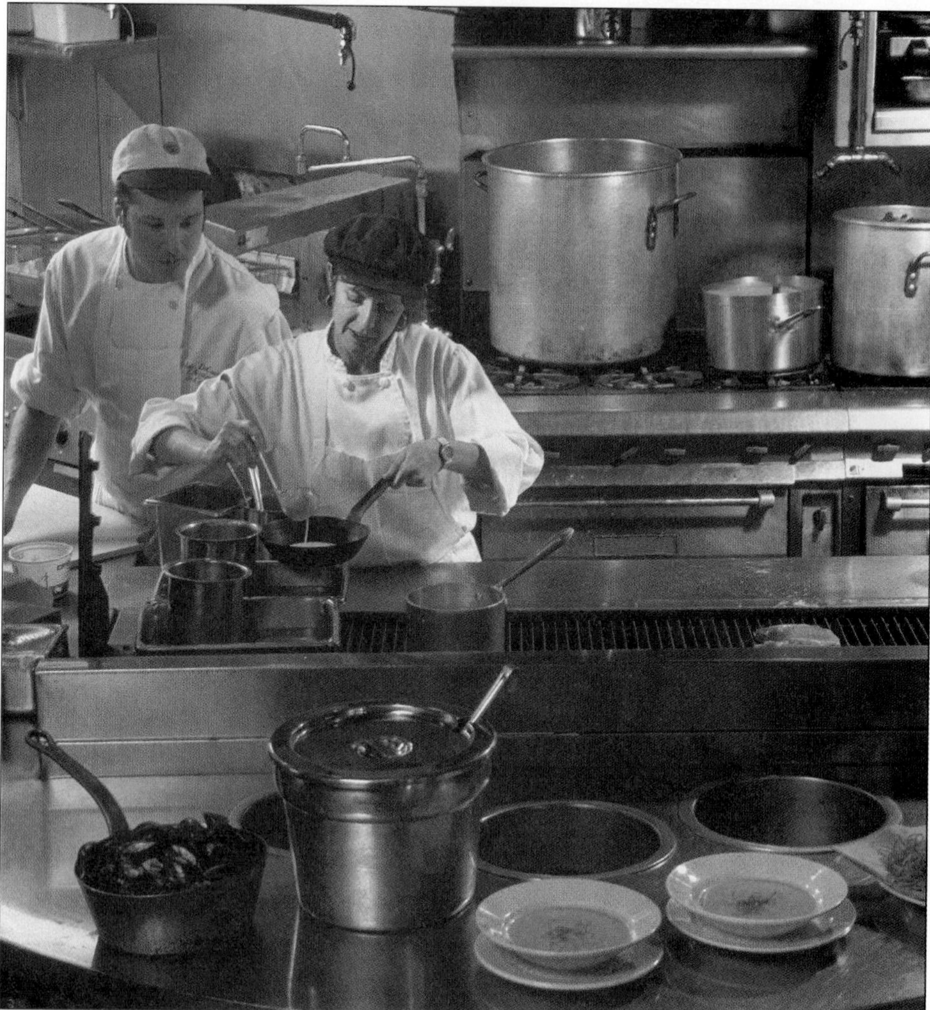

A process layout in a restaurant optimizes work processes and adds to the orderliness and efficiency of serving meals to customers.

kitchen of a large restaurant also can be viewed as a process layout. Here all of the desserts and breads are prepared in the bake shop; fruits and vegetables are peeled, sliced, and diced in the prep area; and raw meats and seafood are prepared for cooking in the butcher shop. Even the cooking line often is subdivided by type of process, with all of the frying taking place in one area, broiling and roasting in another, and sauteed dishes in a third.

Product Layout A good service example of a *product layout* is a cafeteria line where all of the various stations (for example, salads, hot and cold entrees, desserts, and beverages) are arranged in a specific order, and customers visit each station as they move through the line.

Fixed-Position Layout Examples of *fixed-position layouts* in services include (*a*) an automobile repair shop (where all of the processes such as brake repair, oil change, etc., typically take place in the same location), (*b*) an operating room in a hospital (where the patient remains in a given location on the operating table), and (*c*) a table at a restaurant where all of the different courses in a meal are brought to the customer (and in some cases even prepared at the table in front of the customer).

Layout Considerations in Services

In designing facility layouts for service operations, additional, service-unique issues need to be taken into consideration. First, the cost per square foot for retail locations is usually very expensive (in comparison to that for a manufacturing facility). Service retail operations, therefore, must design their facilities to maximize the sales generated per square foot (or square meter). To accomplish this, operations such as restaurants have reduced the percentage of area devoted to the back-of-the-house operations, like the kitchen, to allow more area for the customer in the form of additional seating. One way this is accomplished, as discussed in an earlier chapter, is through the use of a **quasi-manufacturing** facility or central commissary where food can be economically prepared in a relatively low-cost area. Another approach is taken by Benihana's of Tokyo, a chain of Japanese steak houses. There the strategy is to move the kitchen to the front of the house so customers can actually participate in the food preparation process.

Another service-unique factor that needs to be taken into consideration is the customer's presence in the transformation process. As a result, the decor package of the service operation plays an important role in determining the customer's overall satisfaction with the service encounter.

Mary Jo Bitner has introduced the expression **servicescape** to describe the physical surroundings in which the service takes place.[4] The servicescape of an operation comprises three major elements: (*a*) the ambient conditions, (*b*) the spatial layout and functionality, and (*c*) the signs, symbols, and artifacts.

servicescape

Describes the physical surroundings in a service operation that can affect a customer's perception of the service received.

Ambient Conditions These refer to the background characteristics of the operation, including noise level, lighting, and temperature. (It often is said that the prices in restaurants are inversely related to the amount of lighting—the darker the restaurant, the more expensive the food.) Hanging lights over tables, as seen in some of the better restaurants, suggests privacy; recessed lighting in ceilings, on the other hand, as seen in many fast-food operations, send different signals to the customer.

Spatial Layout and Functionality Unlike manufacturing firms where the goal in designing a layout is to minimize the cost of moving material between areas, one of the goals of a service operation is to minimize the travel time of employees, and, in some instances, customers. At the same time, the service firm is trying to maximize revenues per customer by exposing them to as many opportunities as possible to spend their money. For example, the long lines to get into the shows at Las Vegas casinos wend their way through slot machine areas so customers will play the slots while waiting. Operations such as IKEA, a chain of Swedish furniture stores, and Stu Leonard's Dairy Store in Norwalk, Connecticut, are designed so the customer, after entering the store, must go through the entire facility to exit, not unlike a maze with a single path through it.

Signs, Symbols, and Artifacts These refer to aspects of the service operation that have social significance. For example, bank buildings often include columns and stone to give the feeling of security. The offices of large law firms and consulting practices frequently are done in dark woods and thick carpets to connote success and traditional values. Waiters in tuxedos and waiters in white shirts, hats, and aprons each gives certain signals, in terms of establishing the customers' expectations of the operation.

[4]Mary Jo Bitner, "Servicescapes: The Impact of Physical Surroundings on Customers and Employees," *The Journal of Marketing,* April 1992, pp. 57–71.

Conclusion

As we saw in the opening vignette, the choice of which type of facility layout to adopt can have a significant impact on the long-term success of a firm. This decision, therefore, should not be made lightly, but only after an in-depth analysis of the operational requirements has been completed.

A major issue to be addressed in facility layout decisions in manufacturing is: How flexible should the layout be in order to adjust to future changes in product demand and product mix? Some have argued that the best strategy is to have movable equipment that can be shifted easily from place to place to reduce material flow time for near-term contracts. However, while this is appealing in general, the limitations of existing buildings and permanently anchored equipment, and the general plant disruption that is created, make this a very costly strategy.

In service systems, particularly with multi-location chains, the study of layout has become extremely important because the selected layout can be replicated at hundreds or even thousands of facilities. Indeed, a layout error in a fast-food chain has a more immediate, and generally a more far-reaching, impact on profits than a layout error in a factory.

Key Terms

assembly line balancing p. 330
fixed-position layout p. 323
group technology (G/T) or cellular layout p. 323
process layout p. 322
product layout p. 322
servicescape p. 339
takt time p. 329
throughput time p. 329

Review and Discussion Questions

1. What kind of layout is used in a health club?
2. What is the objective of assembly line balancing? How would you deal with the situation where one worker, although trying hard, is 20 percent slower than the other 10 people on a line?
3. How do you determine the idle-time percentage from a given assembly line balance?
4. What is the essential requirement for mixed-model lines to be practical?
5. Why might it be difficult to develop a group technology layout?
6. In what respects is facility layout a marketing problem in services? Give an example of a service system layout designed to maximize the amount of time the customer is in the system.
7. Visit a major hotel in your area and describe the layout of its operations.
8. Describe the layout of a branch office of a bank.
9. How might you design the layout for a walk-in clinic?
10. Visit two different supermarkets. What similarities do their layouts share in common? What differences did you notice?

Internet Exercise

Using PLANT and LAYOUT as suggested key words, search the Web to identify and describe in detail the plant layout for an individual company. As an alternative, go to the McGraw-Hill Operations Management homepage at http://www.mhhe.com/pom and take a plant tour of a company and describe the physical layout of the operation.

Solved Problems

Problem 1

A university advising office has four rooms, each dedicated to specific problems: petitions (Room A), schedule advising (Room B), grade complaints (Room C), and student counseling (Room D). The office is 80 feet long and 20 feet wide. Each room is 20 feet by 20 feet. The present location of rooms is A, B, C, D; that is, a straight line. The contact summary shows the number of contacts that each advisor in a room has with other advisors in the other rooms. Assume that all advisors are equal in this value.

Contact summary: AB = 10, AC = 20, AD = 30,
BC = 15, BD = 10, CD = 20.

a. Evaluate this layout according to one of the methods presented in this chapter.

b. Improve the layout by exchanging functions within rooms. Show your amount of improvement using the same method as in *a*.

Solution

a. Evaluate this layout according to one of the methods in the chapter.

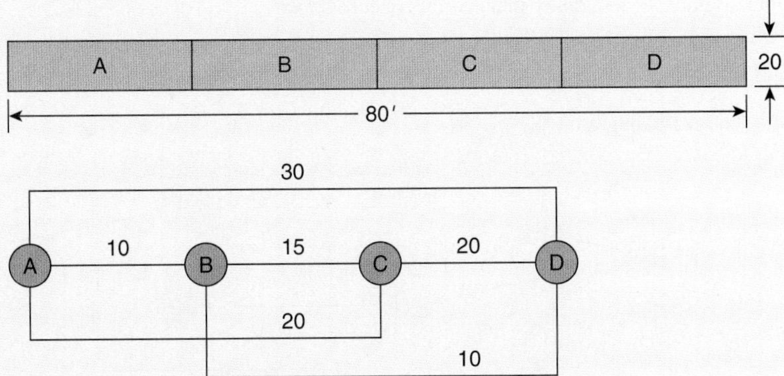

Using the material handling cost method shown in the toy company example (pages 327–330), we obtain the following costs, assuming $1 per contact between adjacent rooms and an additional $1 per contact for each room in between.

AB = 10 × 1 = 10
AC = 20 × 2 = 40
AD = 30 × 3 = 90
BC = 15 × 1 = 15
BD = 10 × 2 = 20
CD = 20 × 1 = 20
Current cost = 195

b. Improve the layout by exchanging functions within rooms. Show your amount of improvement using the same method as in *a*. A better layout would be either BCDA or ADCB.

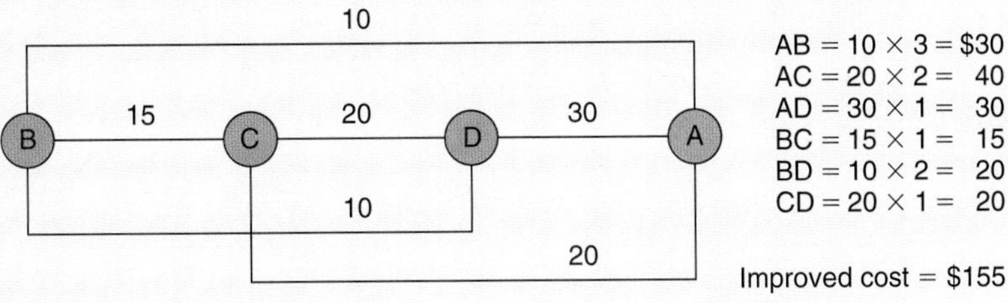

AB = 10 × 3 = $30
AC = 20 × 2 = 40
AD = 30 × 1 = 30
BC = 15 × 1 = 15
BD = 10 × 2 = 20
CD = 20 × 1 = 20

Improved cost = $155

Problem 2

The following tasks must be performed on an assembly line in the sequence and times specified.

Task	Task Time (seconds)	Tasks That Must Precede	Task	Task Time (seconds)	Tasks That Must Precede
A	50	—	E	20	C
B	40	—	F	25	D
C	20	A	G	10	E
D	45	C	H	35	B, F, G

a. Draw the schematic diagram.

b. What is the theoretical minimum number of stations required to meet a forecasted demand of 400 units per eight-hour day?

c. Use the longest-operating-time rule and balance the line in the minimum number of stations to produce 400 units per day.

d. Compute the efficiency of the line.

e. Does your solution generate any managerial concerns?

Solution

a. Draw the schematic diagram.

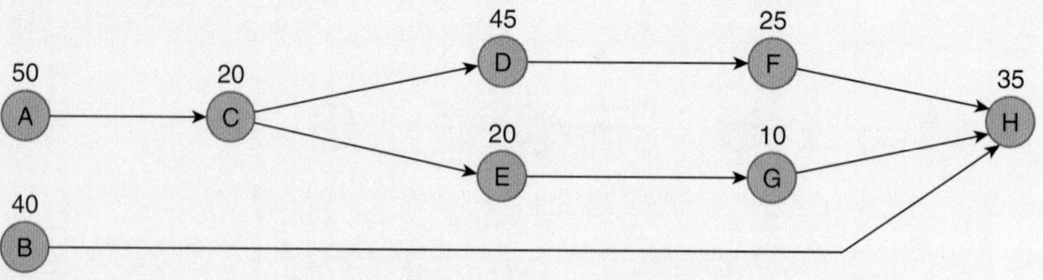

b. Theoretical minimum number of stations to meet D = 400 is

$$N_t = \frac{S}{T} = \frac{245 \text{ seconds}}{\left(\dfrac{60 \text{ seconds} \times 480 \text{ minutes}}{400 \text{ units}}\right)} = \frac{245}{72} = 3.4 \rightarrow 4 \text{ stations}$$

c. Use the longest-operating-time rule and balance the line in the minimum number of stations to produce 400 units per day.

	Task	Task Time (seconds)	Remaining Unassigned Time	Feasible Remaining Tasks
Station 1	A	50	22	C
	C	20	2	None
Station 2	D	45	27	E, F
	F	25	2	None
Station 3	B	40	32	E
	E	20	12	G
	G	10	2	None
Station 4	H	35	37	None

d. Efficiency $= \dfrac{S}{N_a \times T} = \dfrac{245}{4(72)} = 85\%$

e. Yes. Station 4 is only half as busy as the other three stations.

Problems

1. An assembly line makes two models of trucks: a Buster and a Duster. Busters take 12 minutes each and Dusters take 8 minutes each. The daily output requirement is 24 of each per day. Develop a balanced mixed-model sequence to satisfy demand.
2. The tasks and the order in which they must be performed according to their assembly requirements are shown in the following table. These are to be combined into workstations to create an assembly line.

   The assembly line operates 7½ hours per day. The output requirement is 1,000 units per day.

Task	Preceding Tasks	Time (seconds)
A	—	15
B	A	24
C	A	6
D	B	12
E	B	18
F	C	7
G	C	11
H	D	9
I	E	14
J	F, G	7
K	H, I	15
L	J, K	10

   a. What is the takt time?

   b. Balance the line based on the 1,000-unit forecast, stating which tasks would be done in each workstation.

   c. For *b* above, what is the efficiency of your assembly line?

   d. After production was started, Marketing realized that they underestimated demand and will need to increase output to 1,100 units. What action would you take? Be specific in quantitative terms, if appropriate.

3. An assembly line operates seven hours per day and produces 420 units per day. The following tasks are required with their respective performance times and preceding tasks.

Task	Time (seconds)	Preceding Tasks
A	15	None
B	15	None
C	45	A, B
D	45	C

   Compute the takt time and the theoretical minimum number of workstations, and prepare an initial line configuration. Determine the efficiency of your assembly line.

4. An initial solution has been given to the following process layout problem. Given the flows described and a transportation cost of $2.00 per unit per foot, compute the total

cost for the layout. Each location is 100 feet long and 50 feet wide as shown on the figure below. Use the centers of departments for distances and compute using rectilinear distances.

		Department			
		A	B	C	D
Department	A	0	10	25	55
	B		0	10	5
	C			0	15
	D				0

	100′	100′	100′	
50′	A	B	C	50′
			D	50′

5. An assembly line will operate eight hours per day and produce 480 units per day. The task times and precedence relationships are summarized below. Prepare an initial assembly-line configuration using the longest-operating-time rule, and determine the efficiency of your layout.

Task	Time (seconds)	Preceding Tasks
A	20	None
B	40	A
C	35	B
D	35	B
E	35	C, D

6. An assembly line is to be designed that will operate 7½ hours per day and supply a steady demand of 300 units per day. Following are the tasks and their task performance times.

Task	Preceding Tasks	Performance Time (seconds)
a	—	70
b	—	40
c	—	45
d	a	10
e	b	30
f	c	20
g	d	60
h	e	50
i	f	15
j	g	25
k	h, i	20
l	j, k	25

a. Draw the precedence diagram.

b. What is the takt time?

c. What is the theoretical minimum number of workstations?

d. Assign tasks to workstations, stating what your logic rule is.

e. What is the efficiency of your line balance?

f. Suppose demand increases by 10 percent. How would you react to this?

7. Given the following data on the task precedence relationships for an assembled product and assuming that the tasks cannot be split, what is the theoretical minimum takt time?

Task	Performance Time (minutes)	Tasks That Must Precede
A	3	—
B	6	A
C	7	A
D	5	A
E	2	A
F	4	B, C
G	5	C
H	5	D, E, F, G

a. Determine the minimum number of stations needed to meet a takt time of 10 minutes according to the "largest number of following tasks" rule.

b. Compute the efficiency of the balances achieved.

8. Simon's Mattress Factory is planning to introduce a new line of "pillow-top" mattresses. Current plans are to produce the mattresses on an assembly line. Mattresses will be built on individual platforms pulled by a chain in a track in the floor. This will allow workers to completely walk around the mattress. Tools will be suspended from the ceiling, so that there will not be a problem with tangling cords or wrapping them around the platform.

   The assembly-line process starts with the basic spring foundation and builds the mattress as it progresses down the line. There are 12 operations required, and their times and process sequence are as follows:

Operation	Time (minutes)	Tasks That Must Precede
A	1	—
B	3	A
C	4	B
D	1	B
E	5	C
F	4	D
G	1	E, F
H	2	G
I	5	G
J	3	H
K	2	I
L	3	J, K

   Tentative plans are to operate the line 7½ hours per day. Demand for the mattresses is expected to be 70 per day.

   a. Draw the schematic diagram.

   b. What is the takt time?

   c. What is the theoretical minimum number of workstations?

   d. Create a reasonably balanced assembly line.

   e. Supposing the plan was to produce these in a job shop layout. Discuss and compare the characteristics, pros, cons, and so forth of a job shop versus assembly line for this mattress production.

9. XYZ Manufacturing Company received a contract for 20,000 units of a product to be delivered in equal weekly quantities over a six-month period. XYZ works 250 days per year on a single-shift, 40-hour work week.

The table below states the tasks required and their precedence sequence and task times in seconds.

Task	Task That Must Precede	Time (seconds)
A	—	150
B	A	120
C	B	150
D	A	30
E	D	100
F	C, E	40
G	E	30
H	F, G	100

a. Develop an assembly line that meets the requirements.

b. State the takt time.

c. What is the efficiency of the line?

d. Supposing the vendor asked you to increase output by 10 percent. State specifically how you would respond to this.

10. The following tasks are to be performed on an assembly line:

Task	Time (seconds)	Tasks That Must Precede
A	20	—
B	7	A
C	20	B
D	22	B
E	15	C
F	10	D
G	16	E, F
H	8	G

The workday is 7 hours long and the demand for completed product is 750 units per day.

a. Find the takt time.

b. What is the theoretical number of workstations?

c. Draw the precedence diagram.

d. Balance the line using the longest-operating-time rule.

e. What is the efficiency of the line balanced as in *d*?

f. Suppose that demand rose from 750 per day to 800 units per day. What would you do?

g. Suppose that demand rose from 750 per day to 1,000 units per day. What would you do?

Bibliography

Choobineh, F. "A Framework for the Design of Cellular Manufacturing Systems." *International Journal of Production Research* 26, no. 7 (1988), pp. 1116–72.

Dobyns, Lloyd, and Reuven Frank. *If Japan Can, Why Can't We?* New York: NBC-TV News Presentation, June 24, 1980.

Francis, R. L.; L. F. McGinnis; and J. A. White. *Facility Layout and Location: An Analytical Approach.* 2nd ed. Englewood Cliffs, NJ: Prentice Hall, 1992.

Green, Timothy J., and Randall P. Sadowski. "A Review of Cellular Manufacturing Assumptions, Advantages and Design Techniques." *Journal of Operations Management* 4, no. 2 (February 1984), pp. 85–97.

Hall, Robert W. "Time Prints and Takt Times." *Target: Innovation at Work* 14, no. 3 (1998), pp. 6–13.

Hayes, Robert H., and Steven C. Wheelwright. *Restoring Our Competitive Edge.* New York: John Wiley & Sons, 1984.

Heskett, J. L.; W. E. Sasser Jr.; and C. W. L. Hart. *Service Breakthroughs: Changing the Rules of the Game.* New York: Free Press, 1990.

Hyer, Nancy Lea. "The Potential of Group Technology for U.S. Manufacturing." *Journal of Operations Management* 4, no. 3 (May 1984), pp. 183–202.

Manivannan, S., and Dipak Chudhuri. "Computer-Aided Facility Layout Algorithm Generates Alternatives to Increase Firm's Productivity." *Industrial Engineering,* May 1984.

Mondon, Yasuhiro. *Toyota Production System: Practical Approach to Production Management.* Atlanta, GA: Industrial Engineering and Management Press, 1983.

Schonberger, Richard J. "The Rationalization of Production." *Proceedings of the 50th Anniversary of the Academy of Management.* Chicago: Academy of Management, 1986, pp. 64–70.

Vannelli, Anthony, and K. Ravi Kumar. "A Method for Finding Minimal Bottleneck Cells for Grouping Part-Machine Families." *International Journal of Production Research* 24, no. 2 (1986), pp. 387–400.

9 Forecasting

Chapter Objectives

- Introduce the basic concepts of forecasting and its importance within an organization.
- Identify several of the more common forecasting methods and how they can improve the performance of both manufacturing and service operations.
- Provide a framework for understanding how forecasts are developed.
- Demonstrate that errors exist in all forecasts and show how to measure and assess these errors.
- Discuss some of the software programs that are available for developing forecasting models.

FORECASTING SYSTEM INCREASES SALES AND REDUCES INVENTORIES AT NABISCO

Nabisco currently produces hundreds of different cookies, crackers, and other snack foods. All of these products are produced in more than 30 company-owned and contract bakeries and shipped to over 100 distribution centers throughout the United States. With its Direct Store Delivery network, Nabisco then delivers these products directly to more than 100,000 ship-to locations, including supermarkets and other retail stores. Customer orders are usually placed with only one to two days' lead time. With such short lead times, accurately forecasting the demand for all of these products is critical. Too much of the wrong product results in excessive inventories and possible spoilage; too little results in stockouts and lost sales to competition.

Nabisco, therefore, has developed an account-based forecasting system to predict the product requirements for each of its major customers (or accounts). According to Mark Barash, manager of Sales Forecasting Systems for Nabisco's supply chain, the new forecasting system, based on the success of an initial pilot, is projected to reduce finished goods inventories 5 percent nationally. At the same time, the level of service provided to its customers has improved significantly, resulting in increased sales and profits for Nabisco. This increase in profits is attributed to the additional sales that are realized from the significant reduction in the frequency of stockouts. The cost of developing this new forecasting system was less than $200,000.

Source: Mark Barash and Donald H. Mitchell, "Account Based Forecasting at Nabisco Biscuit Company," *The Journal of Business Forecasting,* Summer 1998, pp. 3–6, and interviews with Mark Barash, manager of Sales Forecasting Systems for Nabisco Biscuit Company.

Managerial Issues

The importance of forecasting as a business tool has grown significantly in recent years, both in manufacturing and services. According to a 1998 survey conducted by the Institute of Business Forecasting, 77 percent of the firms replying said that they only began hiring full-time forecasting professionals during the previous 10 years. In fact, 62 percent indicated that they only began hiring full-time forecasting persons during the previous five years. For example, Levi Strauss has a full-time forecasting department of 30 people. Duracell, the battery manufacturer has a staff of eight full-time forecasters, as does Mary Kay Cosmetics.*

Managers now use forecasting models at all levels in their organizations, as illustrated at FedEx in the OM in Practice box. From a strategic, long-range perspective, forecasting the demand for products provides management with the ability to decide when to add capacity in the form of new manufacturing facilities; similarly, forecasting customer demand helps service managers to decide where to locate retail service outlets for maximum sales.

For manufacturing firms, forecasting demand at the tactical or intermediate level is a major input into the managerial decision-making process. For example, intermediate forecasting plays an important role in determining what portion of the workforce should be permanent and what portion should be temporary workers. Accurate forecasting is also a critical element in supply-chain management and the determination of proper inventory levels, as illustrated in the opening vignette about Nabisco.

Short-term forecasting is especially important in services, where customer demand is often unknown and ca-

Types of Forecasting

qualitative techniques

Nonquantitative forecasting techniques based upon expert opinions and intuition. Typically used when there are no data available.

time-series analysis

Analyzing data by time periods (for example, hours, days, weeks) to determine if trends or patterns occur.

causal relationship forecasting

Relating demand to an underlying factor other than time.

Forecasting techniques can be classified into three broad categories: *qualitative, time-series analysis,* and *causal relationship forecasting*.

Qualitative techniques are subjective or judgmental in nature, and are based on estimates and opinions. Such techniques are used primarily when there are no data available. **Time-series analysis,** the main focus of this chapter, is based on the idea that data describing past demand can be used to predict future demand. In other words, the time-related trends that generated demand in the past will continue to generate demand in the future. **Causal relationship forecasting,** on the other hand, assumes that demand is related to some underlying factor or factors in the environment, and that cause-and-effect relationships are at work.

Time-series analysis is typically used in short-range situations, such as forecasting worker requirements for the next week. Causal relationship forecasting is usually used for longer-term issues, such as selecting a site for a retail operation. Exhibit 9.2 briefly describes some of the different varieties of the three basic types of forecasting models. In this chapter we present the three time-series analysis methods listed in the exhibit and the first of the causal relationship forecasting techniques.

Exhibit 9.3 shows a comparison of the strengths and weaknesses of these different forecasting methods. The moving-average and exponential-smoothing methods tend to be the best and easiest techniques to use for short-term forecasting with little data required. The long-term models are more complex and require much more data. In general, the short-term models compensate for random variation and adjust for short-term changes (such as consumers' responses to a new product). Medium-term forecasts are useful for seasonal effects, and long-term models identify general trends and are especially useful in identifying major turning points. Which forecasting model or models a firm should adopt depends on several factors, including (*a*) forecasting time horizon, (*b*) data availability, (*c*) accuracy required, (*d*) size of the forecasting budget, and (*e*) availability of qualified personnel.

pacity in the form of front-line workers must be available when and where customers require it.

However, while forecasting can provide managers with future information that will allow them to run their operations more effectively and efficiently, managers also must recognize that forecasts are not perfect. Inaccuracies in forecasting occur because there are too many factors in the business environment that cannot be predicted or controlled with certainty. Rather than search for the perfect forecast, it is far more important for managers to establish the practice of continually reviewing these forecasts and to learn to live with their inaccuracies. This is not to say that we should not try to improve the forecasting model or methodology, but that we should try to find and use the best forecasting method available, *within reason*. In this respect, it is important to note that the cost of obtaining small improvements in forecasting accuracy is very high after *reasonable* forecasts have been developed, as illustrated in Exhibit 9.1.

The goal of this chapter is to present an introduction to several different forecasting techniques and models (both qualitative and quantitative) that are commonly used in business, recognizing that additional and more sophisticated forecasting techniques and models are available for people seeking more in-depth knowledge in this area. We address primarily time series techniques and causal relationships, including a discussion of the sources of errors and their measurement.

*Chaman L. Jain, "Explosion in the Forecasting Function in Corporate America," *The Journal of Business Forecasting,* Summer 1999, pp. 2, 28.

Components of Demand

In most cases, the demand for products or services can be broken down into five components: (*a*) average demand for the period, (*b*) trends, (*c*) seasonal influence, (*d*) cyclical elements, and (*e*) random variation. Exhibit 9.4 illustrates a plot of demand over a four-year period, showing the trend, cyclical, and seasonal components, and randomness (or error) around the smoothed demand curve.

Cyclical factors are more difficult to determine since either the time span or the cause of the cycle may not be known. For example, cyclical influence on demand may come from such occurrences as political elections, war, economic conditions, or sociological pressures.

Random variations are caused by chance events. Statistically, when all the known causes for demand (average, trend, seasonal, and cyclical) are subtracted from the total demand, what remains is the unexplained portion of demand. If one is unable to identify the cause of this remainder, it is assumed to be purely random chance. This unexplained portion is often referred to as the error or *noise* in the forecast.

In addition to these five components there is often autocorrelation, which denotes the persistence of occurrence. More specifically, the demand expected at any point is highly

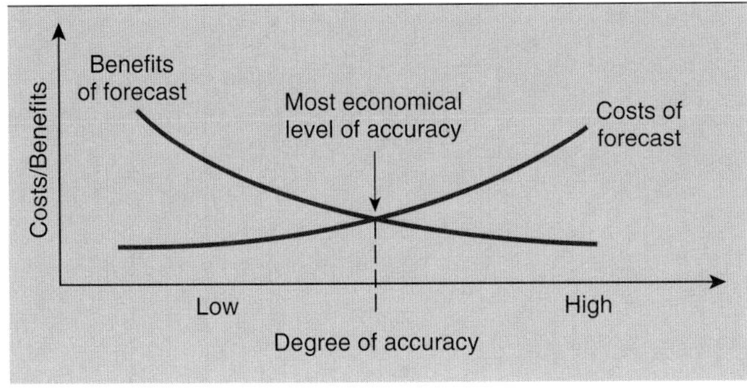

Exhibit 9.1

Comparing the Costs and Benefits of Forecasting

Exhibit 9.2

Forecasting Techniques and Common Models

I. Qualitative	***Subjective, judgmental. Based on intuition, estimates, and opinions.***
Delphi method	An interactive learning process involving a group of experts who respond to a questionnaire. A moderator compiles results and formulates a new questionnaire that is again submitted to the same group of experts.
Market research	Collects customer data in a variety of ways (surveys, interviews, etc.) to test hypotheses about the market. This information is typically used to forecast long-range and new-product sales.
Historical analogy	Ties what is being forecast to a similar product. Important in planning new products where a forecast may be derived by using the history of a similar existing product.
II. Time-Series Analysis	***Based upon the idea that the history of occurrences over time can be used to predict the future.***
Simple moving average and weighted moving average	The data points from several time periods are averaged by dividing the sum of the point values by the number of data points. These points may be weighted equally or unequally, as seen fit by experience.
Exponential smoothing	Recent data points are weighted more, with weighting declining exponentially as data become older.
Linear regression	Fits a straight line to past data generally relating the data values to time. Most common fitting technique is least squares.
Trend projections	Fits a mathematical trend line to the data points and projects it into the future.
III. Causal Relationships	***Tries to understand the system underlying and surrounding the item being forecast. For example, sales may be affected by advertising, quality, and competitors.***
Regression analysis	Similar to least squares method in time series but may contain multiple variables. Basis is that forecast is caused by the occurrence of other events or factors.
Input/output models	Focuses on sales of each industry to other firms and governments. Indicates the changes in sales that a producer industry might expect because of purchasing changes by another industry.
Leading indicators	Statistics that move in the same direction as the series being forecast but move before the series, such as an increase in the price of gasoline indicating a future drop in the sale of large cars.

Exhibit 9.3

Comparison of Forecasting Techniques

Technique	Time Horizon	Model Complexity	Data Requirements
I. Qualitative			
Delphi method	Long	High	High
II. Time Series			
Moving average	Short	Very low	Low
Exponential smoothing	Short	Low	Very low
Linear regression	Long	Medium high	High
III. Causal Relationships			
Regression analysis	Long	Fairly high	High

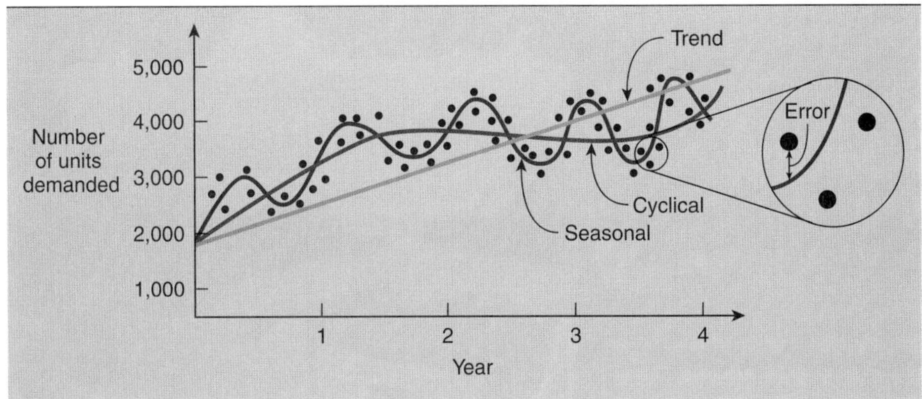

Exhibit 9.4
Historical Monthly Product Demand Consisting of a Growth Trend, Cyclical Factor, and Seasonal Demand

correlated with its own past values. For example, if demand has been high during December for the past 10 years, then one would expect high demand during December for the coming year. When demand is random, the demand from one time period to another may vary widely. Where high autocorrelation exists, the demand is not expected to change very much from one time period to the next.

Trend lines are the usual starting point in developing a forecast. These trend lines are then adjusted for seasonal effects, cyclical, and any other expected events that may influence the final forecast. Exhibit 9.5 shows four of the most common types of trends. A linear

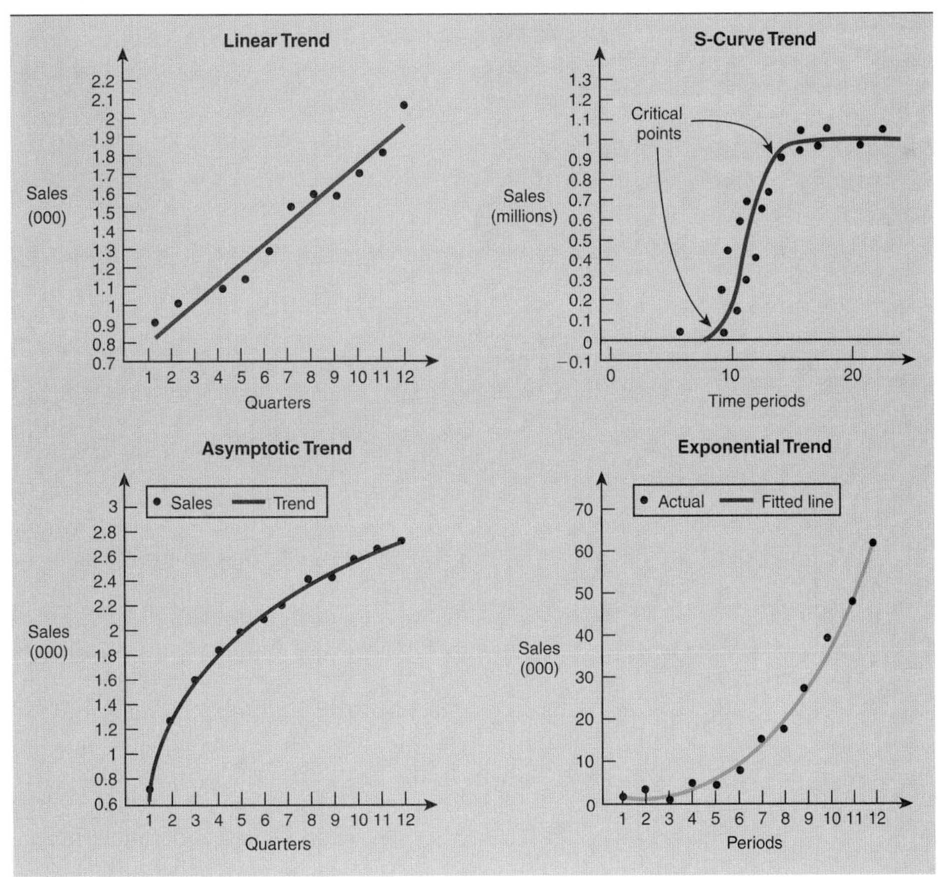

Exhibit 9.5
Common Types of Trends

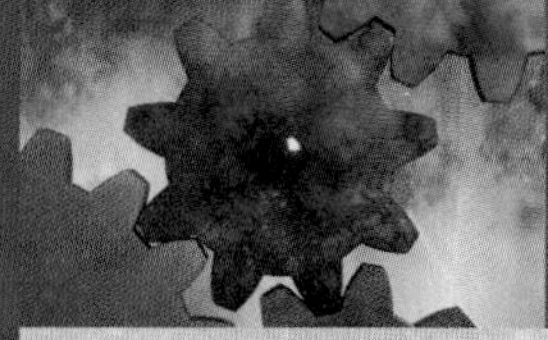

Operations Management in Practice

OUTSTANDING CUSTOMER SERVICE AT FEDEX STARTS WITH FORECASTING

FedEx is the world's largest express transportation company. To support its global transportation network, FedEx has established 51 customer service call centers throughout the world. The 16 call centers located in the United States handle about 500,000 calls a day. The service-level goal for all of its call centers is to answer 90 percent of all calls within 20 seconds or less. There are three major networks that are supported by these call centers: domestic, international, and freight.

For each network, FedEx has developed four types of forecasts, based on forecasting horizons. The strategic or long-range plan, which is revised and updated once a year, forecasts the number of incoming calls, the average handling time per call, staffing requirements, and the number of technology-handled calls (i.e., calls not requiring a customer service representative). The business plan addresses the same items as in the strategic plan but is revised on an as-needed basis, as decided by upper management. The tactical forecast provides a daily forecast of incoming calls and is done once a month. The lowest level of forecasting, the

trend obviously reflects a straight continuous relationship. An S-curve is typical of a product's growth and maturity cycle. The critical points on the S-curve are where the trend makes a transition from slow growth to fast growth and from fast to slow. An asymptotic trend starts with the highest demand growth at the beginning, which then tapers off. Such a curve could happen when a firm enters an existing market with the objective of saturating and capturing a large share of the market. An exponential curve is common in products with explosive growth, as is often experienced with new high-technology products. The exponential trend suggests that sales will continue to increase rapidly for some period of time—an assumption that may be questionable for longer time periods.

Time-Series Analysis

Time-series forecasting models attempt to predict the future based on past data. For example, sales figures collected for each of the past six weeks can be used to forecast sales for the seventh week. Quarterly sales figures collected for the past several years can be used to forecast the sales in future quarters.

We present here three types of time-series forecasting models: (*a*) simple moving average, (*b*) weighted moving average, and (*c*) exponential smoothing. In order to determine

Historical Data for FedEx Call Center

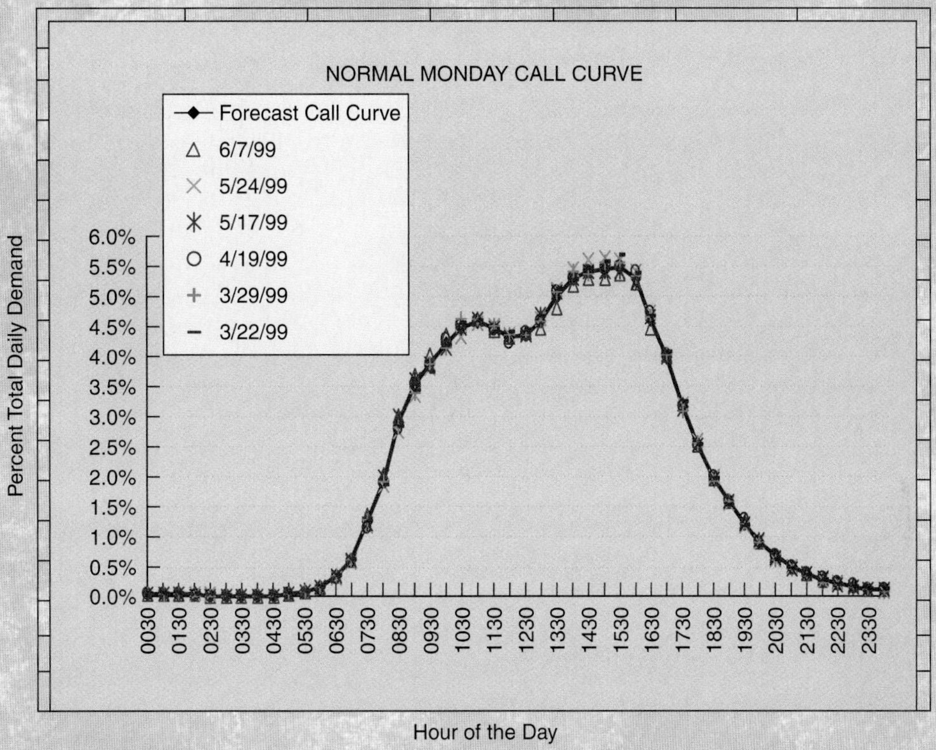

operational forecast, forecasts the number of incoming calls and average handling time in half-hour increments for each day of the week using historical data as shown. This forecast is done weekly.

Source: Weidong Xu, "Long Range Planning for Call Centers at FedEx," *The Journal of Business Forecasting,* Winter 1999–2000, pp. 6–11.

which model is most appropriate to use, the data should first be plotted on a graph. For example, if the data points appear to be relatively level, a moving average or exponential smoothing model would be appropriate; if the data points show an underlying trend, then exponential smoothing with trend adjustment would be appropriate. In addition, the errors associated with each model should be calculated and the resulting errors compared.

Simple Moving Average

If the demand for a product is neither growing nor declining rapidly, and also does not have any seasonal characteristics, a **simple moving average** can be very useful in identifying a trend within the data fluctuations. For example, if we want to forecast sales in June with a five-month moving average, we can take the average of the sales in January, February, March, April, and May. When June passes, the forecast for July would be the average of February, March, April, May, and June. The formula for a simple moving average forecast is

$$F_t = \frac{A_{t-1} + A_{t-2} + \cdots + A_{t-n}}{n} \tag{9.1}$$

simple moving average

Average over a given number of time periods that is updated by replacing the data in the oldest period with those in the most recent period.

where

$$F_t = \text{Forecasted sales in period } t$$
$$A_{t-1} = \text{Actual sales in period } t-1$$
$$n = \text{Number of periods in the average}$$

Example

Suppose we want to forecast weekly demand for a product using both a three-week and a nine-week moving average, as shown in Exhibits 9.6 and 9.7. These forecasts are computed as follows:

Solution

To illustrate, the three-week forecast for week 4 is

$$\frac{1{,}000 + 1{,}400 + 800}{3} = 1{,}067$$

and the nine-week forecast for week 10 is

$$\frac{1{,}300 + 1{,}500 + 1{,}500 + \cdots + 800}{9} = 1{,}367$$

Exhibit 9.6

Forecast Demand Based on a Three- and a Nine-Week Simple Moving Average

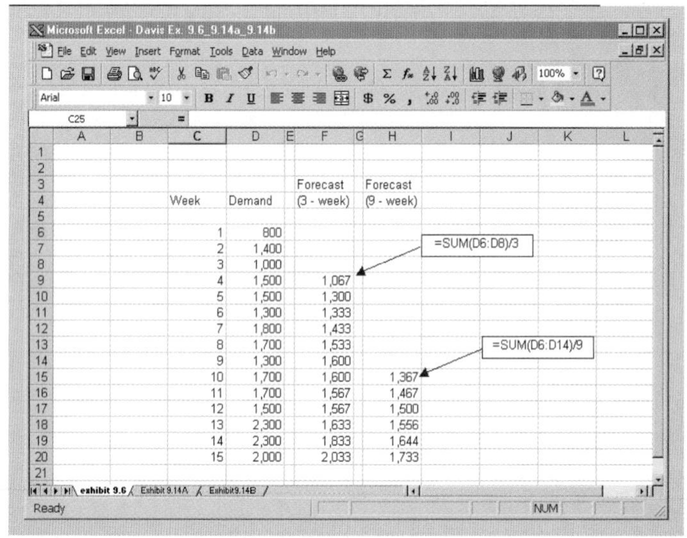

Microsoft Excel - Davis Ex. 9.6_9.14a_9.14b

Week	Demand	Forecast (3 - week)	Forecast (9 - week)
1	800		
2	1,400		
3	1,000		
4	1,500	1,067	
5	1,500	1,300	
6	1,300	1,333	
7	1,800	1,433	
8	1,700	1,533	
9	1,300	1,600	
10	1,700	1,600	1,367
11	1,700	1,567	1,467
12	1,500	1,567	1,500
13	2,300	1,633	1,556
14	2,300	1,833	1,644
15	2,000	2,033	1,733

=SUM(D6:D8)/3

=SUM(D6:D14)/9

Exhibit 9.7

Moving Average Forecast of Three- and Nine-Week Periods versus Actual Demand

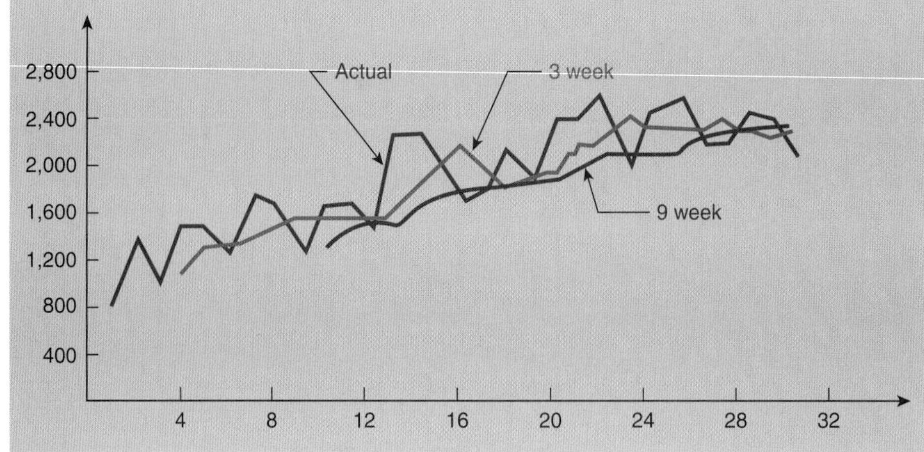

Operations Management in Practice

FORECASTING SALES AT TACO BELL REDUCES LABOR COSTS

Labor is a major cost component at Taco Bell, a large fast-food chain specializing in Mexican food, averaging 30 percent of sales. Scheduling the proper number of workers for a given time period is therefore critical in the highly competitive fast-food industry. Too many workers results in excessive costs and reduced profits. Too few workers, on the other hand, results in lost sales and/or poor service. With the demand being highly variable throughout the day (52 percent of daily sales occur between 11:00 AM and 2:00 PM), Taco Bell needs to accurately forecast sales to schedule the proper number of workers.

After evaluating several forecasting techniques, Taco Bell adopted a six-week moving average. The number of customer transactions are recorded in 15-minute time intervals for each day of the week. For example, the forecasted number of customers to be served next Friday between 10:30 AM and 10:45 AM is the six-week average of the number of customers served in that same time period for the previous six Fridays.

This forecasting model is a major element in Taco Bell's labor-management system, which is estimated to have saved Taco Bell $16.4 million in labor costs in 1996 (in comparison to the previously existing management system).

Source: Jackie Hueter and William Swart, "An Integrated Labor-Management System for Taco Bell," *Interfaces* 28, no. 1 (January–February 1998), pp. 75–91.

As noted in the above OM in Practice box, it is important to select the proper number of periods to include in the moving average. In determining the "right" number of periods to use, management must take into consideration several conflicting effects. As noted in Exhibit 9.6, the larger the number of periods included in the average, the greater the random elements are "smoothed," which may be desirable in some cases. However, if a trend exists in the data—either increasing or decreasing—the resulting moving average has the adverse affect of constantly lagging this trend. Therefore, while a smaller number of periods in the moving average produces more oscillation, the resulting forecast will more closely follow the existing trend. Conversely, the inclusion of more periods in the moving average will give a smoother forecast but at the same time it will lag the trend by a greater amount.

Exhibit 9.7 graphs the data shown in Exhibit 9.6, illustrating how the number of periods that are used in the moving average can impact the forecast. Note that the growth trend appears to level off at about the 23rd week. The three-week moving average responds better in following this change than the nine-week, although overall, the nine-week average is smoother.

The main disadvantage in calculating a moving average is that all the individual elements used in the average must be carried as data since a new forecast period involves adding the newest data and dropping the oldest data. For a three- or six-period moving average, this is not too severe; but plotting a 60-day moving average of the daily demand for each of 20,000 items in inventory would involve a significant amount of data. At the same time, today's PCs are fast and efficient at doing multiproduct moving averages for a long time period. For example, using a 60-day moving average for 20,000 products would require 61 calculations per product × 20,000 products, or 1,220,000 calculations. With today's PCs these calculations would probably take one or two seconds, at most, to complete.

weighted moving average

Simple moving average where weights are assigned to each time period in the average. The sum of all of the weights must equal one.

Weighted Moving Average

Whereas the simple moving average gives equal weight to each component of the moving-average database, a **weighted moving average** allows each element to be weighted by a factor, where the sum of all the weighting factors equals one. The formula for a weighted moving average forecast is

$$F_t = w_{t-1}A_{t-1} + w_{t-2}A_{t-2} + \cdots + w_{t-n}A_{t-n} \tag{9.2}$$

where

F_t = Forecasted sales in period t
A_{t-1} = Actual sales in period $t-1$
w_{t-1} = Weight assigned to period $t-1$
n = Number of periods in the moving average

An additional constraint when using this equation for the weighted moving average forecast is

$$\sum_{i=1}^{n} w_{t-i} = 1$$

Example

A department store may find that in a four-month period the best forecast is derived by using 40 percent of the actual sales (in units) for the most recent month, 30 percent of two months ago, 20 percent of three months ago, and 10 percent of four months ago. The actual unit sales were as follows:

Month 1	Month 2	Month 3	Month 4	Month 5
100	90	105	95	?

Solution

The forecast for month 5 therefore would be

$$\begin{aligned} F_5 &= 0.40(95) + 0.30(105) + 0.20(90) + 0.10(100) \\ &= 38.0 + 31.5 + 18.0 + 10.0 \\ &= 97.5 \text{ units} \end{aligned}$$

Suppose sales for month 5 actually turned out to be 110; then the forecast for month 6 would be

$$\begin{aligned} F_6 &= 0.40(110) + 0.30(95) + 0.20(105) + 0.10(90) \\ &= 44.0 + 28.5 + 21.0 + 9.0 \\ &= 102.5 \text{ units.} \end{aligned}$$

The weighted moving average has a definite advantage over the simple moving average because it can vary the effects between older data and more recent data. With the forecasting software that is now available, there is little computational difference between using a weighted moving average and a simple moving average. Both can be obtained in "real time." If there is a disadvantage to the weighted moving average, it is that someone must determine the weights to be used.

Exponential Smoothing

In the two previous forecasting methods that have just been presented, a major issue is the need to continually carry a large amount of historical data. Nevertheless, in many applications (perhaps even in most), the most recent data points tend to be more indicative of the future in comparison to those in the distant past. If this premise is valid—that the importance of data diminishes as the past becomes more distant—then **exponential smoothing** may be the most logical and easiest method to use.

exponential smoothing

Time-series forecasting technique that does not require large amounts of historical data.

The reason this is called "exponential smoothing" is because each increment in the past is decreased by $(1 - \alpha)$, as shown below:

	Weighting at $\alpha = 0.20$
Most recent weighting $= \alpha(1 - \alpha)^0$	0.2000
Data 1 time period older $= \alpha(1 - \alpha)^1$	0.1600
Data 2 time periods older $= \alpha(1 - \alpha)^2$	0.1280
Data 3 time periods older $= \alpha(1 - \alpha)^3$	0.1024

Therefore, the exponents 0, 1, 2, 3 … , and so on give this method its name.

Exponential smoothing is the most commonly used of all forecasting techniques. It is an integral part of virtually all computerized forecasting programs, and is widely used for ordering inventory in retail firms, wholesale companies, and other service operations.

Exponential smoothing accomplishes virtually everything that can be done with moving average forecasts, but requires significantly less data. The **exponential smoothing constant alpha (α)** is a value between 0 and 1. If the actual demand tends to be relatively stable over time, we would choose a relatively small value for α to decrease the effects of short-term or random fluctuations, which is similar to having a moving average that involves a large number of periods. If the actual demand tends to fluctuate rapidly, we would choose a relatively large value for α to keep up with these changes. This is similar to using a moving average with a small number of periods.

exponential smoothing constant alpha (α)

Value between 0 and 1 that is used in exponential smoothing to minimize the error between historical demand and respective forecasts.

The major reasons that exponential smoothing techniques have become so well accepted are

1. Exponential smoothing models are surprisingly accurate.
2. Formulating an exponential smoothing model is relatively easy.
3. The user can readily understand how the model works.
4. There is very little computation required to use the model.
5. Computer storage requirements are small because of the limited use of historical data.

In the exponential smoothing method, only three pieces of data are needed to forecast the future: the most recent forecast, the actual demand that occurred for that forecast period, and a smoothing constant alpha (α). As described above, this smoothing constant determines the level of smoothing and the speed of reaction to differences between forecasts and actual occurrences. The value for the constant is arbitrary and is determined by both the nature of the item being forecasted and the manager's sense of what constitutes a good response rate. However, error measuring techniques such as MAD (which is discussed later in this chapter) can be used to evaluate different values for α until that value is found that minimizes the historical error. For example, if a firm produced a standard item with relatively stable demand, the reaction rate to differences between actual and forecast demand would tend to be small, perhaps just a few percentage points. However, if the firm were experiencing growth, it would be desirable to have a higher reaction rate, to give greater importance to recent growth experience. The more rapid the growth, the higher the reaction rate should be. Sometimes users of the simple moving average switch to exponential smoothing but like to keep the forecasts about the same as the simple moving average. In this case, α is approximated by $2 \div (n + 1)$ where n was the number of time periods that were used in the moving average.

The equation for an exponential smoothing forecast is

$$F_t = (1 - \alpha)F_{t-1} + \alpha A_{t-1}$$

or rewritten as

$$F_t = F_{t-1} + \alpha(A_{t-1} - F_{t-1}) \tag{9.3}$$

where

F_t = Exponentially smoothed forecast for period t

F_{t-1} = Exponentially smoothed forecast made for the prior period

A_{t-1} = Actual demand in the prior period

α = Desired response rate, or smoothing constant

This equation states that the new forecast is equal to the old forecast plus a portion of the error (the difference between the previous forecast and what actually occurred).[1]

When exponential smoothing is first introduced, the initial forecast or starting point may be obtained by using a simple estimate or an average of preceding periods. If no historical forecast data are available, then the forecast for the previous period (that is, last month) is set equal to the demand for that period.

Example

To demonstrate how the exponential smoothing method works, assume that the long-run demand for a given product is relatively stable and a smoothing constant (α) of 0.05 is considered appropriate. If the exponential smoothing method were used as a continuing policy, a forecast would have been made for last month. Assume that last month's forecast (F_{t-1}) was 1,050 units, and 1,000 units were actually demanded (A_{t-1}).

Solution

The forecast for this month then would be calculated as follows:

$$\begin{aligned} F_t &= F_{t-1} + \alpha(A_{t-1} - F_{t-1}) \\ &= 1{,}050 + 0.05(1{,}000 - 1{,}050) \\ &= 1{,}050 + 0.05(-50) \\ &= 1{,}047.5 \text{ units} \end{aligned}$$

Because the smoothing coefficient is relatively small, the reaction of the new forecast to an error of 50 units is to decrease the next month's forecast by only 2.5 units.

Example

Kevin Alexander owns a small restaurant that is open seven days a week. Until just recently he forecasted the daily number of customers using his "gut feel." However, he wants to open another restaurant and recognizes the need to adopt a more formal method of forecasting that can be used in both locations. He decides to compare a three-week moving average and exponential smoothing with $\alpha = .7$ and $\alpha = .3$. The actual sales for the past three weeks are shown below, along with his forecast for last week.

[1]Some writers prefer to call F_t a smoothed average.

	Customers per Day						
Week	**Sun**	**Mon**	**Tue**	**Wed**	**Thu**	**Fri**	**Sat**
Actual:							
3 weeks ago	138	183	182	188	207	277	388
2 weeks ago	143	194	191	200	213	292	401
Last week	157	196	204	193	226	313	408
Forecast:							
Last week	155	191	192	198	204	286	396

a. Forecast sales for each day of the next week using:

- A three-week moving average
- Exponential smoothing with $\alpha = .7$
- Exponential smoothing with $\alpha = .3$

b. The actual sales for the next week are as follows:

	Customers per Day						
Week	**Sun**	**Mon**	**Tue**	**Wed**	**Thu**	**Fri**	**Sat**
Actual	160	204	197	210	215	300	421

Evaluate each of the three forecasting techniques based on the one week's data. Which technique would you recommend to Kevin?

Solution

a. The forecasts for each of the three methods are presented below.

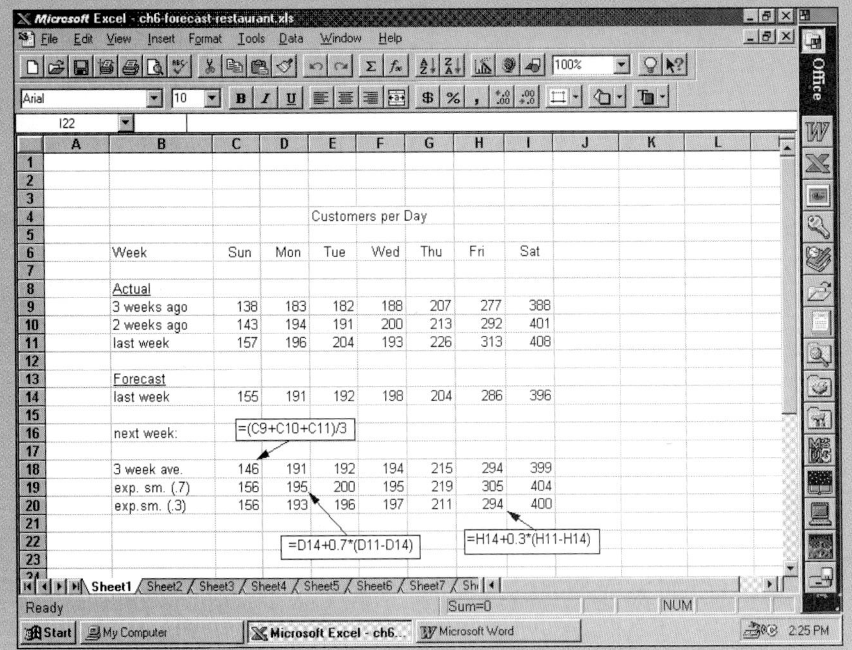

	Customers per Day						
Week	Sun	Mon	Tue	Wed	Thu	Fri	Sat
Actual							
3 weeks ago	138	183	182	188	207	277	388
2 weeks ago	143	194	191	200	213	292	401
last week	157	196	204	193	226	313	408
Forecast							
last week	155	191	192	198	204	286	396
next week:							
3 week ave.	146	191	192	194	215	294	399
exp. sm. (.7)	156	195	200	195	219	305	404
exp.sm. (.3)	156	193	196	197	211	294	400

b. Using the average mean absolute deviation (MAD) as a criterion for measuring error, a comparison of the three forecasting methods is presented below:

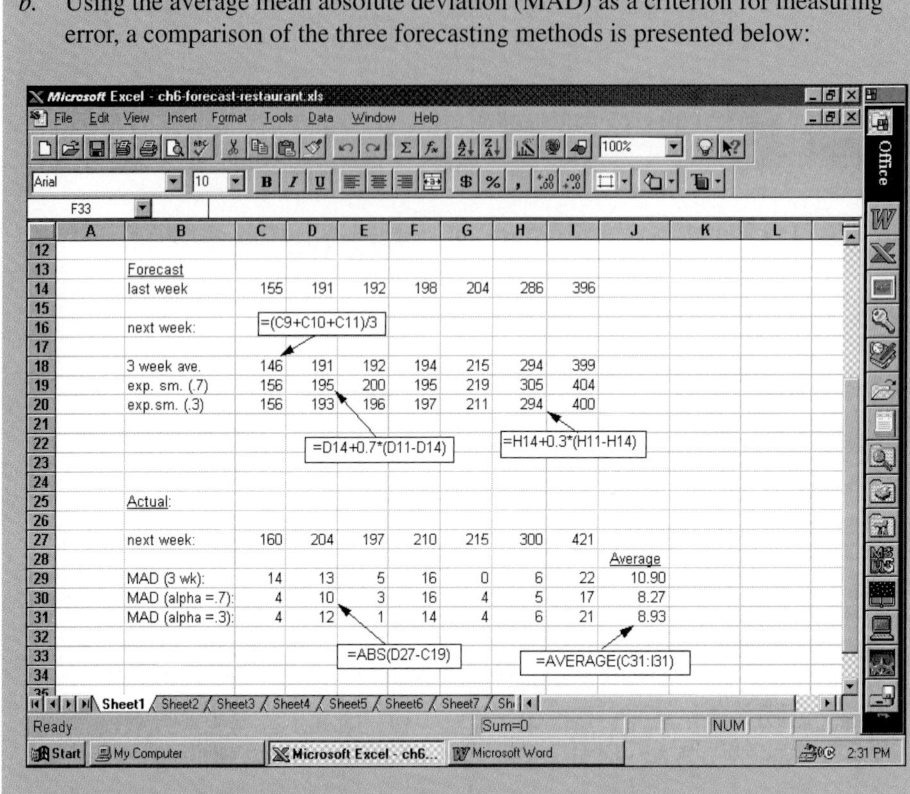

	B	C	D	E	F	G	H	I	J
13	Forecast								
14	last week	155	191	192	198	204	286	396	
16	next week:								
18	3 week ave.	146	191	192	194	215	294	399	
19	exp. sm. (.7)	156	195	200	195	219	305	404	
20	exp.sm. (.3)	156	193	196	197	211	294	400	
25	Actual:								
27	next week:	160	204	197	210	215	300	421	
28									Average
29	MAD (3 wk):	14	13	5	16	0	6	22	10.90
30	MAD (alpha =.7):	4	10	3	16	4	5	17	8.27
31	MAD (alpha =.3):	4	12	1	14	4	6	21	8.93

Based upon this analysis, Kevin should use the exponential smoothing method with $\alpha = .7$, as that method has the lowest average MAD of 8.27. (MAD, which is a measure of how much the forecasted demand differs from the actual demand, is discussed in detail later in this chapter.)

As discussed above, exponential smoothing has the shortcoming of lagging changes in demand. Exhibit 9.8 shows actual data plotted as a smooth curve to show the lagging effects of the exponential forecasts. The forecast lags the actual demand during an increase or decrease, but overshoots actual demand when a change in the direction occurs. Note that the higher the value of alpha, the more closely the forecast follows the actual. In order to more closely track actual demand, a trend factor may be added. In addition, the value of alpha can be adjusted to improve the accuracy of the forecast. This is termed *adaptive forecasting*. Both trend effects and adaptive forecasting are briefly explained in the following sections.

trend smoothing constant delta (δ)

Value between 0 and 1 that is used in exponential smoothing when there is a trend.

Trend Effects in Exponential Smoothing As stated earlier, an upward or downward trend in data collected over a sequence of time periods causes the exponential forecast to always lag behind (that is, to be above or below) the actual amount. Exponentially smoothed forecasts can be corrected somewhat by including a trend adjustment. To correct for the trend, we now need two smoothing constants. In addition to the smoothing constant α, the trend equation also requires a **trend smoothing constant delta (δ).** Like alpha, delta is limited to values between 0 and 1. The delta reduces the impact of the error that occurs

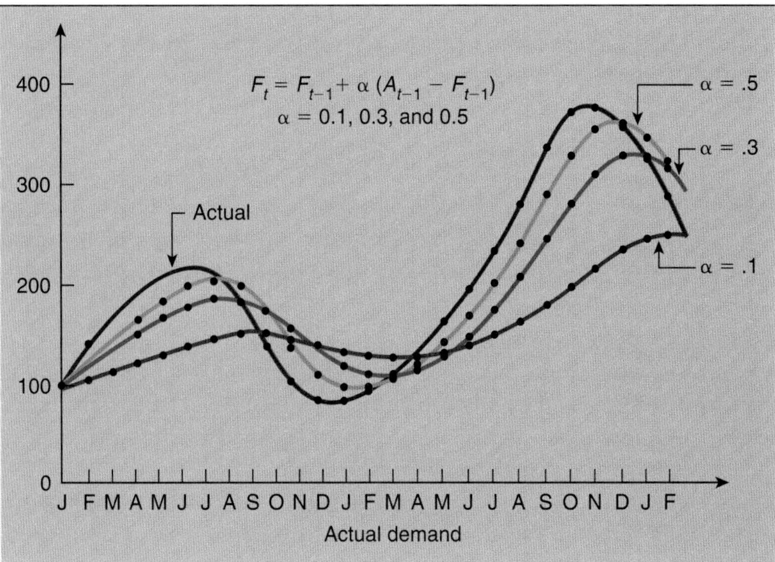

Exhibit 9.8

Exponential Forecasts versus Actual Demands for Units of a Product over Time Showing the Forecast Lag

between the actual and the forecast. If both alpha and delta are not included, the trend would overreact to errors.

To initiate the trend equation, the trend value must be entered manually. This first trend value can be an educated guess or computed from past data.

The equation to compute the forecast including trend (FIT) is

$$\text{FIT}_t = F_t + T_t \tag{9.4}$$

where

$$F_t = \text{FIT}_{t-1} + \alpha(A_{t-1} - \text{FIT}_{t-1}) \tag{9.5}$$

$$T_t = T_{t-1} + \alpha\delta(A_{t-1} - \text{FIT}_{t-1}) \tag{9.6}$$

Example

Assume an initial starting point for F_t of 100 units, a trend of 10 units, an alpha of .20, and a delta of .30. If the actual demand turned out to be 115 rather than the forecast 100, calculate the forecast for the next period.

Solution

Adding the starting forecast and the trend, we have

$$\text{FIT}_{t-1} = F_{t-1} + T_{t-1} = 100 + 10 = 110$$

The actual A_{t-1} is given as 115. Therefore,

$$\begin{aligned} F_t &= \text{FIT}_{t-1} + \alpha(A_{t-1} - \text{FIT}_{t-1}) \\ &= 110 + .2(115 - 110) = 111.0 \\ T_t &= T_{t-1} + \alpha\delta(A_{t-1} - \text{FIT}_{t-1}) \\ &= 10 + (.2)(.3)(115 - 110) = 10.3 \\ \text{FIT}_t &= F_t + T_t = 111.0 + 10.3 = 121.3 \end{aligned}$$

If, instead of 121.3, the actual turned out to be 120, the sequence would be repeated and the forecast for the next period would be

$$F_{t+1} = 121.3 + .2(120 - 121.3) = 121.04$$

$$T_{t+1} = 10.3 + (.2)(.3)(120 - 121.3) = 10.22$$

$$\text{FIT}_{t+1} = 121.04 + 10.22 = 131.26$$

Determining Alpha (α) with Adaptive Forecasting A key factor to accurate forecasting with exponential smoothing is the selection of the proper value of alpha (α). As stated previously, the value of alpha can vary between 0 and 1. If the actual demand appears to be relatively stable over time, then we would select a relatively small value for alpha, that is, a value closer to zero. On the other hand, if the actual demand tends to fluctuate rapidly, as in the case of a new product that is experiencing tremendous growth, then we would select a relatively large value of alpha that is nearer one.

Regardless of the initial value selected, α will have to be adjusted periodically to ensure that it is providing accurate forecasts. This is often referred to as *adaptive forecasting.* There are two approaches for adjusting the value of alpha. One uses various values of alpha and the other uses a tracking signal (which is discussed later in the chapter).

1. *Two or more predetermined values of alpha.* The amount of error between the forecast and the actual demand is measured. Depending on the degree of error, different values of alpha are used. For example, if the error is large, alpha is 0.8; if the error is small, alpha is 0.2.
2. *Computed values of alpha.* A tracking signal computes whether the forecast is keeping pace with genuine upward or downward changes in demand (as opposed to random changes). The tracking signal is defined here as the exponentially smoothed actual error divided by the exponentially smoothed absolute error. Alpha is set equal to this tracking signal and therefore changes from period to period within the possible range of 0 to 1.

In logic, computing alpha seems simple. In practice, however, it is quite prone to error. There are three exponential equations: one for the single exponentially smoothed forecast as done in the previous section of this chapter, one to compute an exponentially smoothed actual error, and the third to compute the exponentially smoothed absolute error. Thus, the user must keep three equations running in sequence for each period. Further, assumptions must be made during the initial time periods until the technique has had a chance to start computing values. For example, alpha must be given a value for the first two periods until actual data are available. Also, the user must select a second smoothing constant, in addition to alpha, that is used in the actual and absolute error equations. Clearly, those who use adaptive forecasting on a regular basis rely on technology for the calculations.

Forecasting Errors in Time-Series Analysis

When we use the word *error,* we are referring to the difference between the forecast value and what actually occurred. So long as the forecast value is within the confidence limits, as we discuss below in "Measurement of Error," this is not really an error. However, common usage refers to the difference as an error.

Demand is generated through the interaction of a number of factors that are either too complex to describe accurately in a model or are not readily identifiable. Therefore, all forecasts contain some degree of error. In discussing forecast errors, it is important to distinguish between *sources of error* and the *measurement of error.*

Operations Management in Practice

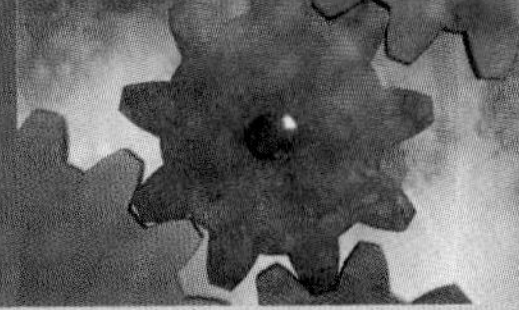

FORECASTING MODEL SAVES L.L. BEAN $300,000 IN LABOR ANNUALLY

L.L. Bean, the outdoor mail-order company located in Freeport, Maine, depends on customer telephone orders for 72 percent of its business. Scheduling telephone operators at its call centers is therefore a critical element in its success. Having too few operators results in long customer waiting times and the real possibility of losing customers to competitors. On the other hand, having too many telephone operators results in unnecessary labor costs, which impacts negatively on profits. The key to scheduling the proper number of operators to be on duty at any given time depends on the ability to accurately forecast the number and type of customer calls that will occur in a given time period. Using a time-series forecasting model developed by professors at the University of Southern Maine, L.L. Bean has been able to save approximately $300,000 annually in labor costs by scheduling their operators more efficiently. This has been done without incurring any decrease in service quality!

Source: Bruce H. Andrews and Shawn M. Cunningham, "L.L. Bean Improves Call Center Forecasting," *Interfaces* 25, no. 6 (November–December 1995), pp. 1–13.

Sources of Error

Errors can come from a variety of sources. One common source of which many forecasters are unaware is caused by the projection of past trends into the future. For example, when we talk about statistical errors in regression analysis, we are referring to the deviations of observations from our regression line. It is common to attach a confidence band to the regression line to reduce the unexplained error. However, when we subsequently use this regression line as a forecasting device by projecting it into the future, the error may not be correctly defined by the projected confidence band. This is because the confidence interval is based on past data; consequently it may or may not be totally valid for projected data points and therefore cannot be used with the same confidence. In fact, experience has shown that the actual errors tend to be greater than those predicted from forecasting models.

Errors can be classified as either bias or random. *Bias errors* occur when a consistent mistake is made, that is, the forecast is always too high or always too low. Sources of bias include (*a*) failing to include the right variables, (*b*) using the wrong relationships among variables, (*c*) employing the wrong trend line, (*d*) mistakenly shifting the seasonal demand from where it normally occurs, and (*e*) the existence of some undetected trend. *Random errors* can be defined simply as those that cannot be explained by the forecast model being used. These random errors are often referred to as "noise" in the model.

Measurement of Error

Several of the common terms used to describe the degree of error associated with forecasting are *standard error, mean squared error* (or *variance*), and *mean absolute deviation.* In addition, *tracking signals* may be used to indicate the existence of any positive or negative bias in the forecast.

Standard error is discussed in the section on linear regression later in the chapter. Since the standard error is the square root of a function, it is often more convenient to use the function itself. This is called the *mean square error,* or variance.

mean absolute deviation (MAD)

Average forecasting error based upon the absolute difference between the actual and forecast demands.

The **mean absolute deviation (MAD)** was at one time very popular but subsequently was ignored in favor of the standard deviation and standard error measures. In recent years, however, MAD has made a comeback because of its simplicity and usefulness in obtaining tracking signals. MAD is the average error in the forecasts, using absolute values. It is valuable because MAD, like the standard deviation, measures the dispersion (or variation) of observed values around some expected value.

MAD is computed using the differences between the actual demand and the forecast demand without regard to whether it is negative or positive. It therefore is equal to the sum of the absolute deviations divided by the number of data points, or, stated in equation form:

$$\text{MAD} = \frac{\sum_{t=1}^{n} |A_t - F_t|}{n} \tag{9.7}$$

where

t = Period number

A_t = Actual demand for period t

F_t = Forecast demand for period t

n = Total number of periods

$|\ |$ = A symbol used to indicate the absolute value of a number and thus disregarding positive and negative signs

When the errors that occur in the forecast are normally distributed (which is usually assumed to be the case), the mean absolute deviation relates to the standard deviation as

$$1 \text{ standard deviation} = \sqrt{\frac{\pi}{2}} \times \text{MAD, or approximately } 1.25 \text{ MAD}$$

Conversely,

$$1 \text{ MAD} \approx 0.8 \text{ standard deviation}$$

The standard deviation is the larger measure. If the MAD for a set of points was found to be 60 units, then the standard deviation would be 75 units. And, in the usual statistical manner, if control limits were set at ± 3 standard deviations (or ± 3.75 MADs), then 99.7 percent of the points would fall within these limits. (See Exhibit 9.9.)

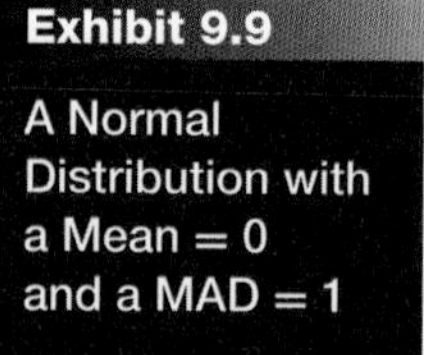

Exhibit 9.9

A Normal Distribution with a Mean = 0 and a MAD = 1

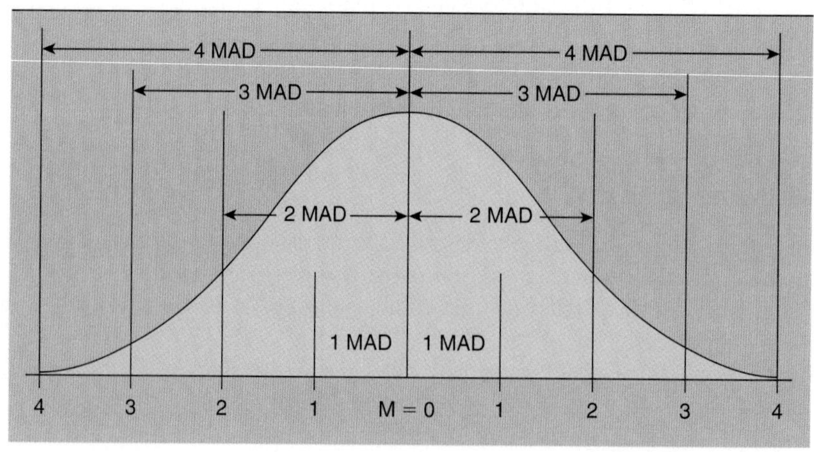

A **tracking signal** is a measurement that indicates whether the forecast average is keeping pace with any genuine upward or downward changes in demand. As used in forecasting, the tracking signal is the *number* of mean absolute deviations that the forecast value is above or below the actual occurrence. Exhibit 9.9 shows a normal distribution with a mean of zero and a MAD equal to one. Thus, if we compute a tracking signal and find it equal to −2, we can conclude that the forecast model is providing forecasts that are quite a bit above the mean of the actual occurrences.

tracking signal

Measure of error to determine if the forecast is staying within specified limits of the actual demand.

A tracking signal can be calculated using the arithmetic sum of forecast deviations divided by the mean absolute deviation, or

$$TS = \frac{RSFE}{MAD} \tag{9.8}$$

where

RSFE = Running sum of forecast errors

MAD = Mean absolute deviation

It is important to note that while the MAD, being an absolute value, is always positive, the tracking signal can take on positive and negative values.

Exhibit 9.10 illustrates the procedure for computing MAD and the tracking signal for a six-month period where the forecast had been set at a constant 1,000 and the actual demands that occurred are as shown. In this example, the forecast, on the average, was off by 66.7 units and the tracking signal was equal to 3.3 mean absolute deviations.

We can obtain a better interpretation of the MAD and tracking signal by plotting the points on a graph. While not completely legitimate from a sample size standpoint, we plotted each month in Exhibit 9.11 to show the drifting of the tracking signal. Note that it drifted from −1 MAD to +3.3 MADs. This occurred because the actual demand was greater than the forecast in four of the six periods. If the actual demand doesn't fall below the forecast to offset the continual positive RSFE, the tracking signal would continue to rise and we would conclude that the assumption that demand is 1,000 is a bad forecast. When the tracking signal exceeds a pre-established limit (for example, ±2.0 or ±3.0), the manager should consider changing the forecast model or the value of α.

Acceptable limits for the tracking signal depend on the size of the demand being forecast (high-volume or high-revenue items should be monitored frequently) and the amount

Exhibit 9.10

Computing the Mean Absolute Deviation (MAD), the Running Sum of Forecast Errors (RSFE), and the Tracking Signal from Forecast and Actual Data

Month	Demand Forecast	Actual	Deviation	RSFE	Abs Dev	Sum of Abs Dev	MAD*	$TS = \frac{RSFE^{\dagger}}{MAD}$
1	1,000	950	−50	−50	50	50	50	−1.00
2	1,000	1,070	+70	+20	70	120	60	.33
3	1,000	1,100	+100	+120	100	220	73.3	1.64
4	1,000	960	−40	+80	40	260	65	1.23
5	1,000	1,090	+90	+170	90	350	70	2.43
6	1,000	1,050	+50	+220	50	400	66.7	3.31

*Mean absolute deviation (MAD). For Month 6, MAD = 400 ÷ 6 = 66.7.

†Tracking signal = $\frac{RSFE}{MAD}$. For Month 6, $TS = \frac{RSFE}{MAD} = \frac{220}{66.7} = 3.3$ MADs.

Exhibit 9.11

A Plot of the Tracking Signals Calculated in Exhibit 9.10.

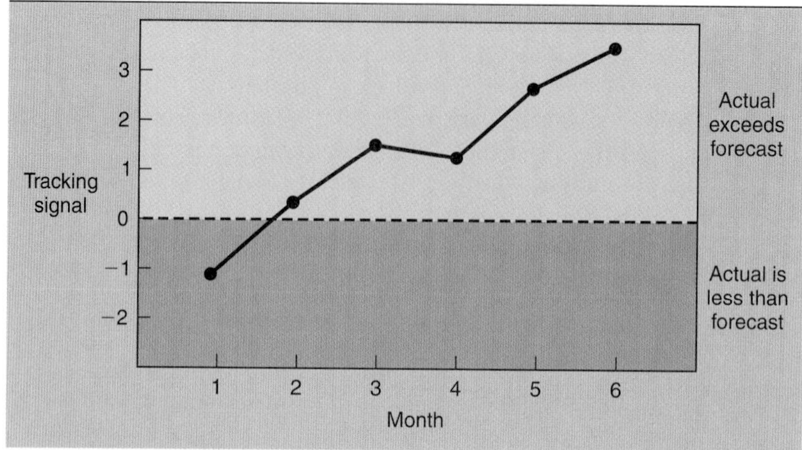

Exhibit 9.12

The Percentages of Points Included within the Control Limits for a Range of 0 to 4 MADs

Control Limits		
Number of MADS	**Related Number of Standard Deviations**	**Percentage of Points Lying within Control Limits**
=1	0.798	57.048
=2	1.596	88.946
=3	2.394	98.334
=4	3.192	99.856

of personnel time available (narrower acceptable limits cause more forecasts to be out of limits and therefore require more time to investigate). Exhibit 9.12 shows the area within the control limits for a range of zero to four MADs.

In a perfect forecasting model, the sum of the actual forecast errors would be zero; that is, the errors that result in overestimates would offset the errors that are underestimates. The tracking signal then also would be zero, indicating an unbiased model that neither leads nor lags the actual demands.

Often, MAD is used to forecast errors. It might then be desirable to make the MAD more sensitive to recent data. A useful technique to do this is to compute an exponentially smoothed MAD (often identified as MAD_t) to forecast the next period's error range. The procedure is similar to single exponential smoothing, which was presented earlier in this chapter. The value of the MAD_t forecast is to provide a range of errors; in the case of inventory control, this is useful in establishing safety stock levels. MAD_t is defined as

$$MAD_t = (1 - \alpha)MAD_{t-1} + \alpha|A_{t-1} - F_{t-1}| \tag{9.9}$$

where

MAD_t = Forecast MAD for the tth period

α = Smoothing constant (normally in the range of 0.05 to 0.20)

A_{t-1} = Actual demand in the period $t - 1$

F_{t-1} = Forecast demand for period $t - 1$

mean absolute percentage error (MAPE)

The average absolute difference between the actual and forecast demands expressed as a percentage of the actual demand.

There are occasions when it is more desirable to assess the accuracy of the forecast model in relative terms rather than in absolute terms, as presented above. When this occurs, we use the **mean absolute percentage error (MAPE)** to determine the forecasting errors as a percentage of the actual. The MAPE is calculated using the following formula:

$$\text{MAPE} = \frac{\sum_{t=1}^{n} \frac{|A_t - F_t|}{A_t}}{n} \times 100 \tag{9.10}$$

where

A_t = Actual demand

F_t = Forecasted demand

n = Number of periods in the forecast

Example

Using the data presented in Exhibit 9.10, we calculate the MAPE as follows:

Period	Forecast Demand (F_t)	Actual Demand (A_t)	Deviation ($A_t - F_t$)	Absolute Deviation $\|A_t - F_t\|$
1	1,000	950	−50	50
2	1,000	1,070	+70	70
3	1,000	1,100	+100	100
4	1,000	960	−40	40
5	1,000	1,090	+90	90
6	1,000	1,050	+50	50

Solution

$$\text{MAPE} = \frac{\sum_{t=1}^{n} \frac{|A_t - F_t|}{F_t}}{n} \times 100$$

$$\text{MAPE} = \frac{\frac{50}{950} + \frac{70}{1,070} + \frac{100}{1,100} + \frac{40}{960} + \frac{90}{1,090} + \frac{50}{1,050}}{6} \times 100$$

$$\text{MAPE} = \frac{.053 + .065 + .091 + .042 + .082 + .048}{6} \times 100$$

$$\text{MAPE} = \frac{.381}{6} \times 100 = 6.4\%$$

Linear Regression Analysis

linear regression analysis

Type of forecasting technique that assumes that the relationship between the dependent and independent variables is a straight line.

Linear regression analysis is used to define a functional relationship between two or more correlated variables. This relationship is usually developed from observed data where one or more parameters (the independent variables) are used to predict another (the dependent variable). Linear regression refers to a special class of regression where the relationship between the variables is assumed to be represented by a straight line. The equation for *simple linear regression* includes only one independent variable and takes the form

$$Y = a + bX \tag{9.11}$$

where

Y = Dependent variable we are solving for

a = Y intercept

b = Slope

X = Independent variable (in time-series analysis, X represents units of time)

This forecasting method is useful for long-term forecasting of major occurrences and aggregate planning (which is presented in Chapter 15). For example, linear regression would be very useful to forecast demands for product families. Even though demand for individual products within a family may vary widely during a time period, demand for the total product family is often surprisingly smooth.

The major restriction in using linear regression analysis is that, as the name implies, past data and future projections are assumed to fall around a straight line. While this does limit its application, sometimes, if we use a shorter period of time, linear regression analysis can still be used.

Linear regression is used for both time-series forecasting and causal relationship forecasting. When the dependent variable (which is represented on the vertical axis of a graph) changes over time (which is plotted on the horizontal axis), it is referred to as time-series analysis. If the dependent variable changes due to the change in the independent variable, then it is referred to as causal relationship forecasting (such as the number of deaths from lung cancer increasing with the number of people who smoke).

The following example illustrates time-series analysis using the least squares method for obtaining the linear regression equation that forecasts sales for future quarters.

Example

A firm's sales for a product line during the 12 quarters of the previous three years were as follows:

Quarter	Sales	Quarter	Sales
1	600	7	2,600
2	1,550	8	2,900
3	1,500	9	3,800
4	1,500	10	4,500
5	2,400	11	4,000
6	3,100	12	4,900

Solution

The firm wants to forecast each quarter of the fourth year, that is, quarters 13, 14, 15, and 16. The least squares equation for linear regression is:

$$\hat{y} = a + bX$$

where

$\hat{y}$ = Dependent variable computed by the equation (sales in this example)

y = Dependent variable data point (see below)

a = Y intercept

b = Slope of the line

X = Independent variable (time period in this example)

The least squares method is used to determine that line that *minimizes the sum of the squares of the vertical distances* between each data point (y) and its corresponding point on the line ($\hat{y}$). If a straight line is drawn through the general area of the points, the difference between the point and the line is ($y - \hat{y}$). Exhibit 9.13 shows these differences. The sum of the squares of the differences between the plotted data points and their

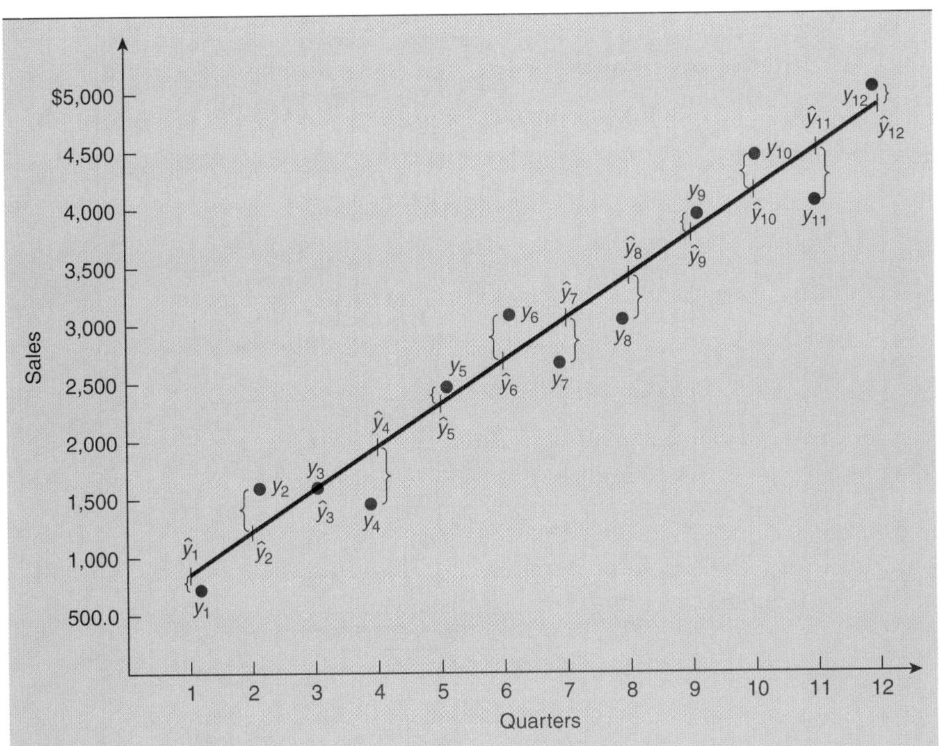

Exhibit 9.13
Least Squares Regression Line

corresponding points on the line is

$$(y_1 - \hat{y}_1)^2 + (y_2 - \hat{y}_2)^2 + \cdots + (y_{12} - \hat{y}_{12})^2$$

The best line to use is the one that minimizes this total.

In the least squares method, the equations for solving for a and b are obtained using calculus and are

$$a = \bar{Y} - b\bar{X}$$

$$b = \frac{\sum XY - n\bar{X}\bar{Y}}{\sum X^2 - n\bar{X}^2}$$

where

a = Y intercept
b = Slope of the line
$\bar{Y}$ = Arithmetic mean of all Ys
$\bar{X}$ = Arithmetic mean of all Xs
X = X value at each data point
Y = Y value at each data point
n = Number of data points
$\hat{y}_i$ = Value of the dependent variable computed with the regression equation

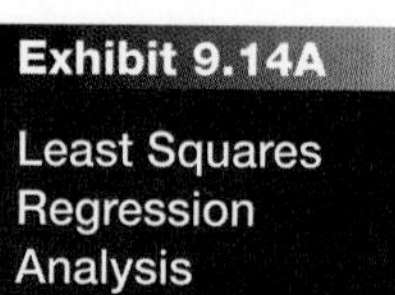

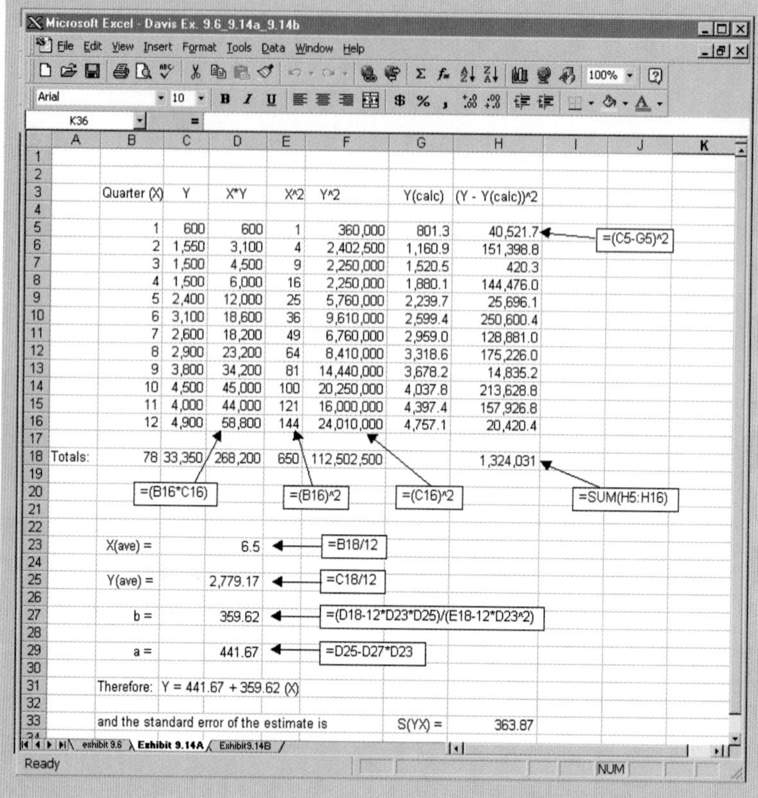

Microsoft Excel - Davis Ex. 9.6_9.14a_9.14b

Row	A	B	C	D	E	F	G	H
3		Quarter (X)	Y	X*Y	X^2	Y^2	Y(calc)	(Y - Y(calc))^2
5		1	600	600	1	360,000	801.3	40,521.7
6		2	1,550	3,100	4	2,402,500	1,160.9	151,398.8
7		3	1,500	4,500	9	2,250,000	1,520.5	420.3
8		4	1,500	6,000	16	2,250,000	1,880.1	144,476.0
9		5	2,400	12,000	25	5,760,000	2,239.7	25,696.1
10		6	3,100	18,600	36	9,610,000	2,599.4	250,600.4
11		7	2,600	18,200	49	6,760,000	2,959.0	128,881.0
12		8	2,900	23,200	64	8,410,000	3,318.6	175,226.0
13		9	3,800	34,200	81	14,440,000	3,678.2	14,835.2
14		10	4,500	45,000	100	20,250,000	4,037.8	213,628.8
15		11	4,000	44,000	121	16,000,000	4,397.4	157,926.8
16		12	4,900	58,800	144	24,010,000	4,757.1	20,420.4
18	Totals:	78	33,350	268,200	650	112,502,500		1,324,031
23		X(ave) =		6.5				
25		Y(ave) =		2,779.17				
27		b =		359.62				
29		a =		441.67				
31		Therefore: Y = 441.67 + 359.62 (X)						
33		and the standard error of the estimate is					S(YX) =	363.87

Exhibit 9.14A shows the computations that are required for the 12 data points. From these calculations, we determine that the final equation for Y has an intercept (a) of 441.6 and a slope (b) of 359.6. The slope can be interpreted to mean that for every unit change in X, Y changes by 359.6. Exhibit 9.14B shows the calculations using the Excel regression function.

Using this linear regression equation, the forecasts for periods 13 through 16 would therefore be

$$Y_{13} = 441.6 + 359.6(13) = 5,116.4$$
$$Y_{14} = 441.6 + 359.6(14) = 5,476.0$$
$$Y_{15} = 441.6 + 359.6(15) = 5,835.6$$
$$Y_{16} = 441.6 + 359.6(16) = 6,195.2$$

To calculate the regression line with the Excel regression function, use the following commands: tools → data analysis → regression.

In the table provided, input the Y-range, which in this case is C5:C16, and the X-Range, which is B5:B16. Then under "Output options" select "New worksheet." The following spreadsheet provides the same information as calculated in Exhibit 9.14A along with additional information on the regression line.

standard error of the estimate

Measure of dispersion of the data about a regression line.

A measure of how well the data fit the regression line can be determined by calculating the **standard error of the estimate** (S_{YX}). The standard error of the estimate is similar in many ways to the standard deviation (σ). Just as the standard deviation is a measure of

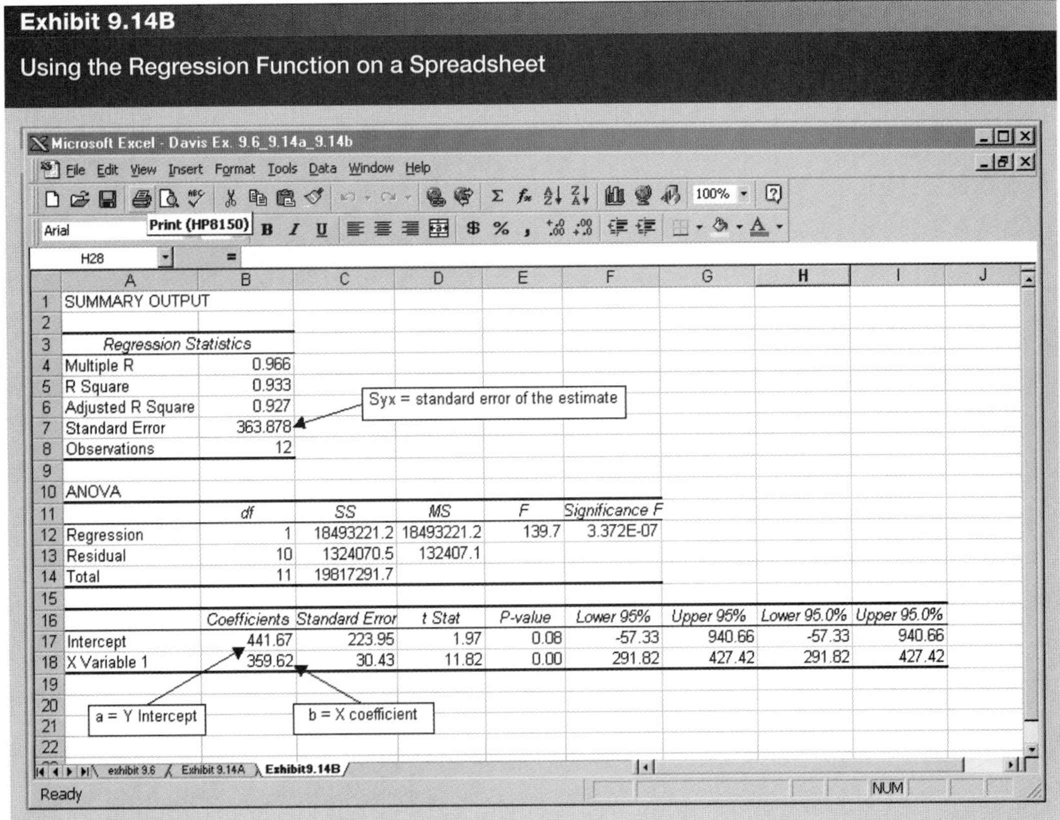

Exhibit 9.14B

Using the Regression Function on a Spreadsheet

SUMMARY OUTPUT

Regression Statistics	
Multiple R	0.966
R Square	0.933
Adjusted R Square	0.927
Standard Error	363.878
Observations	12

ANOVA

	df	*SS*	*MS*	*F*	*Significance F*
Regression	1	18493221.2	18493221.2	139.7	3.372E-07
Residual	10	1324070.5	132407.1		
Total	11	19817291.7			

	Coefficients	*Standard Error*	*t Stat*	*P-value*	*Lower 95%*	*Upper 95%*	*Lower 95.0%*	*Upper 95.0%*
Intercept	441.67	223.95	1.97	0.08	-57.33	940.66	-57.33	940.66
X Variable 1	359.62	30.43	11.82	0.00	291.82	427.42	291.82	427.42

how widely the data points are dispersed around the arithmetic mean, so does the standard error of the estimate reflect how widely the errors are dispersed around the regression line. If the error points are assumed to be normally distributed around the regression line, then, as with the standard deviation, we can conclude, for example, that 68.26 percent of the data points around the regression line fall within one standard error of the estimate.

The formula for the standard error of the estimate, or how well the line fits the data, is[2]

$$S_{YX} = \sqrt{\frac{\sum_{i=1}^{n}(y_i - \hat{y}_i)^2}{n-2}} \tag{9.12}$$

Using Equation 9.12 the standard error of the estimate in the previous example is computed from the first and last columns of Exhibit 9.14.

$$S_{YX} = \sqrt{\frac{(600 - 801.3)^2 + (1{,}550 - 1{,}160.9)^2 + (1{,}500 - 1{,}520.5)^2 + \cdots + (4{,}900 - 4{,}757.1)^2}{10}}$$

$$S_{YX} = 363.9$$

[2]An equation for the standard error that is often easier to compute is

$$S_{XY} = \sqrt{\frac{\sum Y_i^2 - a\sum Y_i - b\sum Y_i X_i}{n-2}}$$

Causal Relationship Forecasting

Any independent variable, to be of value from a forecasting perspective, must be a leading indicator. For example, if the weather service or the *Farmer's Almanac* predicts that next winter is going to have an abnormally large number of snow storms, people would probably go out and buy snow shovels and snow blowers in the fall. Thus, the weather prediction or the *Farmer's Almanac* is said to be a leading indicator of the sale of snow shovels and snow blowers. These relationships between variables can be viewed as causal relationships—the occurrence of one event causes or influences the occurrence of the other. Running out of gas while driving down a highway, however, does not provide useful data to forecast that the car will stop. The car will stop, of course, but we would like to know enough in advance in order to do something about it. A "low gas level" warning light, for example, is a good leading indicator that forecasts that the car will stop shortly.

The first step in causal relationship forecasting is to identify those occurrences that are really the causes of the change. Often leading indicators are not causal relationships but in some indirect way may suggest that some other things might happen. Other noncausal relationships just seem to exist as a coincidence. One study some years ago showed that the amount of alcohol sold in Sweden was directly proportional to teachers' salaries. Presumably this was a spurious, or noncausal, relationship.

The following problem illustrates one example of how a forecast is developed using a causal relationship.

Example

The Carpet City Store has kept records of its sales (in square yards) each year, along with the number of permits that were issued for new houses in its area. Carpet City's operations manager believes that forecasting carpet sales is possible if the number of new housing permits is known for that year.

Year	Number of Housing Permits	Sales (in sq. yds.)
1993	18	14,000
1994	15	12,000
1995	12	11,000
1996	10	8,000
1997	20	12,000
1998	28	16,000
1999	35	18,000
2000	30	19,000
2001	20	13,000

First, the data are plotted on Exhibit 9.15, with

X = Number of housing permits

Y = Sales of carpeting in square yards

Solution

Since the points appear to be in a straight line, the manager decides to use the linear relationship $Y = a + bX$. We solve this problem by using the least squares method. Solving for a and b, using the equations presented earlier in this chapter, we obtain the following forecasting equation:

$$Y = 5{,}576.0 + 387.2X$$

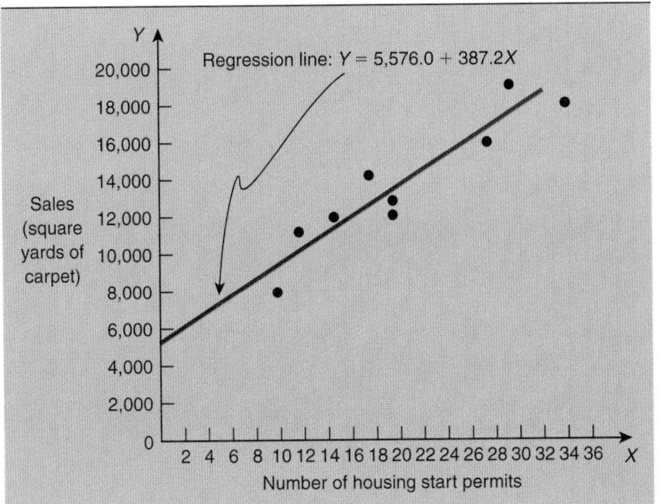

Exhibit 9.15

Causal Relationship: Sales to Housing Starts

Now, suppose that there are 25 new housing permits granted in 2002. The 2002 sales forecast would therefore be:

$$Y = 5{,}576.0 + 387.2(25) = 15{,}256.0 \text{ square yards}$$

In this problem, the lag between filing the permit with the appropriate agency and the new homeowner coming to Carpet City to buy carpet makes a causal relationship feasible for forecasting.

Reliability of the Data

With causal relationship forecasting, we are concerned with how much of the changes in the dependent variable are being "explained" by changes in the independent variable. This is measured by the variance. The greater the proportion of the variance that can be explained by the independent variable, the stronger the relationship. The **coefficient of determination (r^2)** measures the proportion of the variability in the dependent variable that can be explained by changes in the independent variable, and is calculated as follows:

coefficient of determination (r^2)

Proportion of variability in demand that can be attributed to an independent variable.

$$r^2 = \frac{\sum(y_i - \bar{Y})^2 - \sum(y_i - \hat{y}_i)^2}{\sum(y_i - \bar{Y})^2} \tag{9.13}$$

where

y_i = Actual value of Y that has been observed for a given value of X

$\bar{Y}$ = Arithmetic mean for all values of y

$\hat{y}_i$ = Value of Y corresponding to a given value of X that has been calculated from the regression equation

The relationship between these variables is shown in Exhibit 9.16. In the equation above, the first term in the numerator and the term in the denominator are the same

Exhibit 9.16

The relationship between $\bar{Y}$, y_i, and $\hat{y}_i$ in Determining r^2

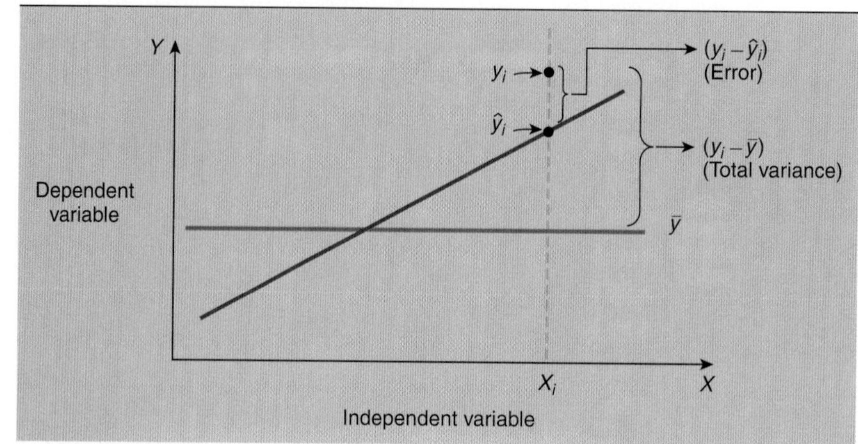

$(\sum(y_i - \bar{Y})^2)$. This term represents the total variation of the Y variable around the arithmetic mean $\bar{Y}$. The second term in the numerator represents the error or that variation in the Y variable that cannot be explained by the regression equation. Thus the numerator represents that amount of variation that can be explained by the regression equation, and the denominator represents the total variation. As stated above, the coefficient of determination therefore measures the proportion of variation in Y that can be explained by changes in X.

mean squared error (MSE)

Measure of variability in the data about a regression line.

Another measure for evaluating the reliability of a regression forecast is the **mean squared error (MSE).** Using the same notation as above, the MSE is calculated as follows:

$$\text{MSE} = \frac{\sum(y_i - \hat{y}_i)^2}{n - 2} \tag{9.14}$$

where n = the number of observations.

The following example will demonstrate the use of both of these terms.

Example

Using the data from the Carpet City Store example, we can compute the coefficient of determination (r^2) and the MSE as follows:

Year	Actual Sales (Sq. Yds)	Predicted Sales (Sq. Yds)	Total Variance	Error Variance
1993	14,000	12,546	111,111	2,114,116
1994	12,000	11,384	2,777,778	379,456
1995	11,000	10,222	7,111,111	605,284
1996	8,000	9,448	32,111,111	2,096,704
1997	12,000	13,320	2,777,778	1,742,400
1998	16,000	16,418	5,444,444	174,724
1999	18,000	19,128	18,777,778	1,272,384
2000	19,000	17,192	28,444,444	3,268,864
2001	13,000	13,320	444,444	102,400
		Totals:	98,000,000	11,756,332

Solution

$$r^2 = \frac{98{,}000{,}000 - 11{,}756{,}332}{98{,}000{,}000} = .88$$

or 88 percent of the change in carpet sales from year to year can be attributed to a change in the number of housing permits issued.

Similarly, we compute the mean squared error:

$$\text{MSE} = \frac{11{,}756{,}332}{9 - 2} = 1{,}679{,}476$$

The operations manager can use these values for r^2 and MSE to evaluate other forecasting techniques with the technique that is currently being used.

Multiple Regression Analysis

Another forecasting technique is multiple regression analysis, in which more than one independent variable is considered, together with the effects on sales of each of the items of interest. For example, in the home furnishings field, the effects of the number of marriages, housing starts, disposable income, and trend can be expressed in a multiple regression equation as

$$S = a + b_m(M) + b_h(H) + b_i(I) + b_t(T)$$

where

S = Gross sales for year
a = Base sales, a starting point from which other factors have influence
M = Marriages during the year
H = Housing starts during the year
I = Annual disposable personal income
T = Time trend (first year = 1, second = 2, third = 3, and so forth)

and b_m, b_h, b_i, and b_t represent the influence on expected sales of the number of marriages, housing starts, income, and trend, respectively.

Forecasting by multiple regression is very appropriate when a number of factors might influence a variable of interest—in this case, sales. The primary difficulty in applying multiple regression analysis is in the data gathering, and the mathematical computations. Fortunately, standard software programs for multiple regression analysis are now available for most computers, relieving the need for tedious manual calculation.

Neural Networks

neural networks

A forecasting technique simulating human learning that develops complex relationships between model inputs and outputs.

Neural networks represent a relatively new and growing area of forecasting. Unlike the more common statistical forecasting techniques such as time-series analysis and regression analysis, neural networks simulate human learning. Thus, over time and with repeated use, neural networks can develop an understanding of the complex relationships that exist between inputs into a forecasting model and the outputs. For example, in a service operation these inputs might include such factors as historic sales, weather, time of day, day of week, and month. The output would be the number of customers that are expected to arrive on a given day and in a given time period. In addition, neural networks perform computations much faster than traditional forecasting techniques. For example, the Southern Company, which is a utility company that provides electricity throughout the south, currently uses neural networks to forecast short-term power requirements a week to 10 days ahead. Previously, only midterm forecasting, that is three months ahead, was feasible with traditional forecasting techniques.[3]

The Application of Forecasting in Service Operations

Service managers are recognizing the important contribution that forecasting can make in improving both the efficiency and the level of service in a service operation. Point-of-sale (POS) equipment can now provide the service manager with historical sales data in time increments that are as small as 15 minutes. The availability of these data permits accurate forecasting of future sales in similar time increments, thereby permitting the service manager to schedule workers more efficiently. Davis and Berger[4] point out that, in addition to forecasting sales, such models also can forecast product usage, which reduces the spoilage of perishable items that have a short shelf life.

Forecasting is also an integral part of *yield management* (also known as revenue management), which is discussed in more detail in a later chapter. In brief, yield management attempts to maximize the revenues of those service operations that have high fixed costs and small variable costs. Examples of such service businesses include airlines, car rental agencies, and hotels. The goal of yield management is to maximize capacity utilization, even if it means offering large price discounts, when necessary, to fill available capacity. At the same time, the manager does not want to turn away a full-paying customer because the capacity had been previously sold to a discount customer. In order to accomplish this successfully, the manager must be able to forecast demand patterns for different market segments.

Forecasting Software Programs

There are many forecasting software programs that are now available. Some of these programs exist as library routines within a mainframe computer system while some may be incorporated or "bundled" as part of a larger program package. Still other programs can be purchased separately from software companies specializing in this area. Many of these programs are also available for PCs.

No longer does one have to be an expert in statistical forecasting techniques to use these programs, as most of them are easy to understand and user friendly. In fact, anyone with working knowledge of an electronic spreadsheet such as Lotus 1-2-3®, Quattro Pro®, SuperCalc®, or Excel® can create a forecast on a PC.

Also, a wealth of information concerning forecasting is available on the Internet. This includes reviews of different forecasting programs. George Stewart, a former editor of *Byte Magazine,* has reviewed several of these forecasting programs, including Forecast Pro for Windows, SmartForecast, Solo Statistical Software, and Autocast II. Inasmuch as this is a fast-changing area, you should conduct your own search on the Internet to obtain the latest information on forecasting programs.

---

[3]Karl Moore, Robert Burbach, and Roger Heeler, "Using Neural Networks to Analyze Qualitative Data," *Marketing Research* 7 (January 1, 1995), p. 34.

[4]Mark M. Davis and Paul D. Berger, "Sales Forecasting in a Retail Service Environment," *The Journal of Business Forecasting,* Winter 1989, pp. 8–17.

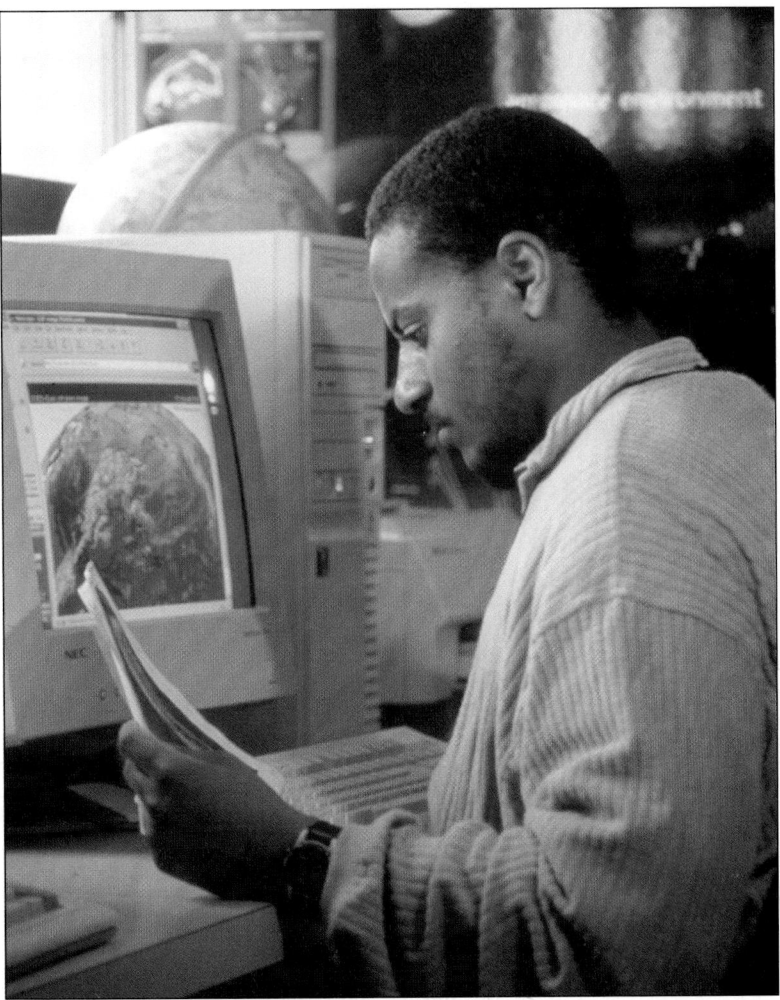

A meteorologist analyzes computer weather patterns in order to improve the accuracy of forecasting the weather.

Conclusion

Forecasting is fundamental to any operational planning effort. In the short run, a forecast is needed to predict the requirements for materials, products, services, or other resources to respond to changes in demand. Forecasts permit adjusting worker schedules and varying labor and materials. In the long run, forecasting is required as a basis for strategic changes, such as developing new markets, developing new products or services, and expanding or creating new facilities.

For long-term forecasts that lead to heavy financial commitments, great care should be taken to derive an accurate forecast. Several approaches should be used. Causal methods such as regression analysis or multiple regression analysis are beneficial as they provide a basis for discussion. Economic factors, product trends, growth factors, and competition, as well as a myriad of other possible variables, need to be considered and the forecast adjusted to reflect the influence of each.

Short- and intermediate-term forecasting, such as those required for inventory control, and labor and material scheduling, may be satisfied with simpler models, such as exponential smoothing with perhaps an adaptive feature or a seasonal index. In these applications, thousands of items are usually being forecast. The forecasting routine therefore should be simple and run quickly on a computer. The routines also should detect and respond rapidly to identifiable short-term changes in demand while at the same time ignoring the occasional spurious demands. Exponential smoothing, when monitored by management to adjust the value of alpha, is also an effective technique.

A Chinese fortune cookie once stated that "Forecasting is difficult, especially about the future." A perfect forecast is like a hole-in-one in golf: great to get but we should be satisfied just to get close to the cup—or, to push the metaphor, just to land on the green. The ideal philosophy for managers is to create the best forecast possible and then have sufficient flexibility in the system to adjust for the inevitable forecasting errors. Managers must recognize the trade-offs that exist in developing forecasting models: the greater the accuracy required, the more expensive the model. At some point, the cost of improved accuracy cannot be justified economically.

Key Formulas

Simple Moving Average Forecast

$$F_t = \frac{A_{t-1} + A_{t-2} + \cdots + A_{t-n}}{n} \tag{9.1}$$

Weighted Moving Average Forecast

$$F_t = w_{t-1}A_{t-1} + w_{t-2}A_{t-2} + \cdots + w_{t-n}A_{t-n} \tag{9.2}$$

and

$$\sum_{i=1}^{n} w_{t-i} = 1$$

Exponential Smoothing

$$F_t = F_{t-1} + \alpha(A_{t-1} - F_{t-1}) \tag{9.3}$$

Exponential Smoothing with Trend Effects

$$\text{FIT}_t = F_t + T_t \tag{9.4}$$

$$F_t = \text{FIT}_{t-1} + \alpha(A_{t-1} - \text{FIT}_{t-1}) \tag{9.5}$$

$$T_t = T_{t-1} + \alpha\delta(A_{t-1} - \text{FIT}_{t-1}) \tag{9.6}$$

Mean Absolute Deviation (MAD)

$$\text{MAD} = \frac{\sum_{t=1}^{n} |A_t - F_t|}{n} \tag{9.7}$$

Tracking Signal

$$\text{TS} = \frac{\text{RSFE}}{\text{MAD}} \tag{9.8}$$

Exponentially Smoothed MAD

$$\text{MAD}_t = (1-\alpha)\text{MAD}_{t-1} + \alpha|A_{t-1} - F_{t-1}| \tag{9.9}$$

Mean Absolute Percentage Error (MAPE)

$$\text{MAPE} = \frac{\sum_{t=1}^{n} \frac{|A_t - F_t|}{A_t}}{n} \times 100 \tag{9.10}$$

Linear Regression

$$Y = a + bX \tag{9.11}$$

Standard Error of the Estimate

$$S_{YX} = \sqrt{\frac{\sum_{i-1}^{n}(y_i - \hat{y}_i)^2}{n-2}} \tag{9.12}$$

Coefficient of Determination

$$r^2 = \frac{\sum(y_i - \bar{Y})^2 - \sum(y_i - \hat{y}_i)^2}{\sum(y_i - \bar{Y})^2} \tag{9.13}$$

Mean Squared Error

$$\text{MSE} = \frac{\sum(y_i - \hat{y}_i)^2}{n-2} \tag{9.14}$$

Key Terms

causal relationship forecasting p. 352
coefficient of determination (r^2) p. 377
exponential smoothing p. 361
exponential smoothing constant alpha (α) p. 361
linear regression analysis p. 371
mean absolute deviation (MAD) p. 368
mean absolute percentage error (MAPE) p. 370
mean squared error (MSE) p. 378
neural networks p. 379
qualitative techniques p. 352
simple moving average p. 357
standard error of the estimate p. 374
time-series analysis p. 352
tracking signal p. 369
trend smoothing constant delta (δ) p. 364
weighted moving average p. 359

Review and Discussion Questions

1. Examine Exhibit 9.3 and suggest which forecasting technique you might use for (*a*) bathing suits, (*b*) demand for new houses, (*c*) electrical power usage, (*d*) new plant expansion plans.
2. In terms of the errors, why would the operations manager wish to use the least squares method when doing simple linear regression?
3. All forecasting methods using exponential smoothing, adaptive smoothing, and exponential smoothing including trend require starting values to initialize the equations. How would you select the starting value for, say, F_{t-1}?
4. From the choice of simple moving average, weighted moving average, exponential smoothing, and simple regression analysis, which forecasting technique would you consider the most accurate? Why?
5. What is the main disadvantage of daily forecasting using regression analysis?
6. What are the main problems with using adaptive exponential smoothing in forecasting?
7. What is the purpose of a tracking signal?
8. What are the main differences between traditional forecasting techniques and neural networks?
9. Discuss the basic differences between the mean absolute deviation (MAD) and the standard error of the estimate.
10. What implications do the existence of forecast errors have for the search for ultrasophisticated statistical forecasting models such as neural networks?

Internet Exercise

The Wharton School at the University of Pennsylvania has a website devoted to forecasting at www.marketing.wharton.upenn.edu/forecast/welcome.html. Visit this website and select a firm that provides business forecasting software. Visit that firm's website and perform the following:

- Describe the company.
- Select one of its forecasting software products and describe it in detail, including costs.
- Identify specific applications for which this program would be most suitable.

Solved Problems

Problem 1

Sunrise Baking Company markets doughnuts through a chain of food stores and has been experiencing over- and underproduction because of forecasting errors. The following data are their daily demands in dozens of doughnuts for the past four weeks. The bakery is closed Saturday, so Friday's production must satisfy demand for both Saturday and Sunday.

	4 Weeks Ago	3 Weeks Ago	2 Weeks Ago	Last Week
Monday	2,200	2,400	2,300	2,400
Tuesday	2,000	2,100	2,200	2,200
Wednesday	2,300	2,400	2,300	2,500
Thursday	1,800	1,900	1,800	2,000
Friday	1,900	1,800	2,100	2,000
Saturday Sunday	2,800	2,700	3,000	2,900

Make a forecast for this week on the following basis:

a. Daily, using a simple four-week moving average.

b. Daily, using a weighted average of 0.40 for last week, 0.30 for two weeks ago, 0.20 for three weeks ago, and 0.10 for four weeks ago.

c. Sunrise is also planning its purchases of ingredients for bread production. If bread demand had been forecast for last week at 22,000 loaves and only 21,000 loaves were actually demanded, what would Sunrise's forecast be for this week using exponential smoothing with $\alpha = 0.10$?

d. Supposing, with the forecast made in (*c*), this week's demand actually turns out to be 22,500. What would the new forecast be for the next week?

Solution

a. Simple moving average, 4 weeks.

Monday $\dfrac{2{,}400 + 2{,}300 + 2{,}400 + 2{,}200}{4} = \dfrac{9{,}300}{4} = 2{,}325$ doz.

Tuesday $= \dfrac{8{,}500}{4} = 2{,}125$ doz.

Wednesday $= \dfrac{9{,}500}{4} = 2{,}375$ doz.

Thursday $= \dfrac{7{,}500}{4} = 1{,}875$ doz.

Friday $= \dfrac{7{,}800}{4} = 1{,}950$ doz.

Saturday and Sunday $= \dfrac{11{,}400}{4} = 2{,}850$ doz.

b. Weighted average with weights of .40, .30, .20, and .10.

	(.40)		(.30)		(.20)		(.10)		
Monday	960	+	690	+	480	+	220	=	2,350
Tuesday	880	+	660	+	420	+	200	=	2,160
Wednesday	1,000	+	690	+	480	+	230	=	2,400
Thursday	800	+	540	+	380	+	180	=	1,900
Friday	800	+	630	+	360	+	190	=	1,980
Saturday and Sunday	1,160	+	900	+	540	+	280	=	2,880
	5,600	+	4,110	+	2,660	+	1,300	=	13,670

c.
$$\begin{aligned} F_t &= F_{t-1} + \alpha(A_{t-1} - F_{t-1}) \\ &= 22{,}000 + 0.10(21{,}000 - 22{,}000) \\ &= 22{,}000 - 100 \\ &= 21{,}900 \text{ loaves} \end{aligned}$$

d.
$$\begin{aligned} F_{t+1} &= 21{,}900 + \alpha(22{,}500 - 21{,}900) \\ &= 21{,}900 + .10(600) \\ &= 21{,}960 \text{ loaves} \end{aligned}$$

Problem 2

A specific forecasting model was used to forecast demands for a product. The forecasts and the corresponding demands that subsequently occurred are shown below.

Month	Actual	Forecast
October	700	660
November	760	840
December	780	750
January	790	835
February	850	910
March	950	890

Use the MAD and tracking signal technique to evaluate the forecasting model.

Solution

Evaluate the forecasting model using MAD, MAPE, and tracking signal.

Month	Actual Demand	Forecast Demand	Actual Deviation	Cumulative Deviation (RSFE)	Absolute Deviation
October	700	660	40	40	40
November	760	840	−80	−40	80
December	780	750	30	−10	30
January	790	835	−45	−55	45
February	850	910	−60	−115	60
March	950	890	60	−55	60
				Total dev. =	315

$$\text{MAD} = \frac{315}{6} = 52.5$$

$$\text{MAPE} = \frac{\frac{40}{700} + \frac{80}{760} + \frac{30}{780} + \frac{45}{790} + \frac{60}{850} + \frac{60}{950}}{6} \times 100$$

$$\text{MAPE} = \frac{.058 + .105 + .038 + .057 + .070 + .063}{6} \times 100$$

$$\text{MAPE} = \frac{.39}{6} \times 100 = 6.5\%$$

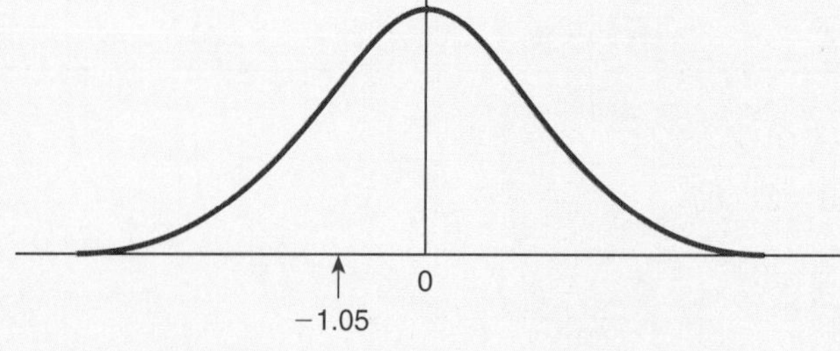

$$\text{Tracking signal} = \frac{-55}{52.5} = -1.05$$

Forecast model is well within the distribution.

Problems

1. Demand for stereo headphones and CD players for joggers has caused Nina Industries to experience a growth of almost 50 percent over the past year. The number of joggers is continuing to expand, so Nina expects demand for headsets to also expand.

   Demands for the stereo units for last year were as follows:

Month	Demand (units)	Month	Demand (units)
January	4,200	July	5,300
February	4,300	August	4,900
March	4,000	September	5,400
April	4,400	October	5,700
May	5,000	November	6,300
June	4,700	December	6,000

   a. Using least squares regression analysis, what would you estimate demand to be for each month next year? Follow the general format in Exhibit 9.14.

   b. To be reasonably confident of meeting demand, Nina decides to use three standard errors of estimate for safety. How many additional units should be held to meet this level of confidence?

2. The historical demand for a product is

Month	Demand
January	12
February	11
March	15
April	12
May	16
June	15

   a. Using a weighted moving average with weights of 0.60 for June, 0.30 for May, and 0.10 for April, find the July forecast.

   b. Using a simple three-month moving average, find the July forecast.

   c. Using single exponential smoothing with $\alpha = 0.2$ and a June forecast = 13, find the July forecast. Make whatever assumptions you wish. List these assumptions.

   d. Using simple linear regression analysis, calculate the regression equation for the preceding demand data.

   e. Using the regression equation in (*d*), calculate the forecast for July.

3. The following tabulations are actual sales of units for six months and a starting forecast in January.

	Actual	Forecast
January	100	80
February	94	
March	106	
April	80	
May	68	
June	94	

   a. Calculate the forecast for the remaining five months using simple exponential smoothing with alpha = 0.2.

   b. Calculate the MAD for the forecasts.

   c. Calculate the MAPE for the forecasts.

4. Sales data for two years is given below. The data are aggregated with two months of sales in each "period."

Period	Sales	Period	Sales
January–February	109	January–February	115
March–April	104	March–April	112
May–June	150	May–June	159
July–August	170	July–August	182
September–October	120	September–October	126
November–December	100	November–December	106

   a. Plot the data on a graph.
   b. Fit a simple linear regression model to the sales data.
   c. Using the results from part (*b*), prepare bimonthly forecasts for the next year.

5. The tracking signals that were computed using the past demand history for three different products are shown below. Each product used the same forecasting technique.

	TS 1	TS 2	TS 3
1	−2.70	1.54	0.10
2	−2.32	−0.64	0.43
3	−1.70	2.05	1.08
4	−1.1	2.58	1.74
5	−0.87	−0.95	1.94
6	−0.05	−1.23	2.24
7	0.10	0.75	2.96
8	0.40	−1.59	3.02
9	1.50	0.47	3.54
10	2.20	2.74	3.75

   Discuss the tracking signals for each product and what the implications are.

6. Prepare a forecast, using simple linear regression, for each quarter of the next year from the following past two years' quarterly sales information.

Quarter	Sales
1	160
2	195
3	150
4	140
5	215
6	240
7	205
8	190

7. Portland Machinery, Inc., manufactures computer-controlled machine tools, which sell for an average price of $500,000 each. Sales for these tools for the past two years were as follows:

Quarter	Quantity (units)	Quarter	Quantity (units)
2000		2001	
I	12	I	16
II	18	II	24
III	26	III	28
IV	16	IV	18

   Using simple linear regression analysis, prepare a sales forecast for each quarter in 2002.

8. Following are the actual tabulated demands for an item for a nine-month period, from January through September. Your supervisor wants to test two forecasting methods to see which method was better over this period.

Month	Actual
January	110
February	130
March	150
April	170
May	160
June	180
July	140
August	130
September	140

   a. Forecast April through September using a three-month simple moving average.

   b. Use simple exponential smoothing to estimate April through September. (Use $\alpha = .3$ and assume that the forecast for March was 130.)

   c. Use MAD to decide which method produced the better forecast over the six-month period.

9. A particular forecasting model was used to forecast monthly sales in a six-month period. The forecasts and the actual demands that resulted are as follows:

Month	Sales (Forecasted)	Sales (Actual)
April	250	200
May	325	250
June	400	325
July	350	300
August	375	325
September	450	400

   Calculate the tracking signal and state whether you think the model being used is giving acceptable answers. Justify your conclusion.

10. Harlen Industries has a very simple forecasting model: take the actual demand for the same month last year and divide that by the number of fractional weeks in that month, producing the average weekly demand for that month. This weekly average is used as the weekly forecast this year.

   The following eight weeks show the forecast (based on last year) and the demand that actually occurred:

Week	Forecast Demand	Actual Demand
1	140	137
2	140	133
3	140	150
4	140	160
5	140	180
6	150	170
7	150	185
8	150	205

   a. Compute the MAD and the MAPE.

   b. Using the RSFE, compute the tracking signal.

   c. Based on your answers to (*a*) and (*b*) what comments can you make about Harlen's method of forecasting?

11. The historical demand for a product is January, 80; February, 100; March, 60; April, 80; and May, 90.
    a. Using a simple four-month moving average, what is the forecast for June? If June experienced a demand of 100, what would your forecast be for July?
    b. Using exponential smoothing with $\alpha = 0.20$, if the forecast for January had been 70, compute what the exponentially smoothed forecast would have been for the remaining months through June.
    c. Using the least squares method, compute a forecast for June, July, and August.
    d. Using a weighted moving average with weights of 0.30 (May), 0.25 (April), 0.20 (March), 0.15 (February), and 0.10 (January), what is June's forecast?
12. In this problem, you are to test the validity of your forecasting model. The following are the forecasts for a model you have been using along with the actual demands that occurred:

Week	Forecast	Actual
1	800	900
2	850	1,000
3	950	1,050
4	950	900
5	1,000	900
6	975	1,100

Compute the MAD, the MAPE, and the tracking signal and draw a conclusion as to whether the forecasting model you have been using is giving reasonable results. Justify your conclusion.

13. Assume that your stock of sales merchandise is maintained based on the forecast demand. If the distributor's sales personnel call on the first day of each month, compute your forecast sales for each of the three methods requested here.

Month	Actual
June	140
July	180
August	170

    a. Using a simple three-month moving average, what is the forecast for September?
    b. Using a weighted moving average, what is the forecast for September with weights of .20, .30, and .50 for June, July, and August, respectively?
    c. Using simple exponential smoothing and assume that the forecast for June had been 130, calculate the forecasts for September with a smoothing constant alpha of .30.
14. The historical demand for a product is

Month	Demand
April	60
May	55
June	75
July	60
August	80
September	75

a. Using a simple four-month moving average, calculate a forecast for October.

b. Using simple exponential smoothing with $\alpha = 0.2$ and a September forecast $= 65$, calculate a forecast for October.

c. Using simple linear regression, calculate the trend line for the historical data. To help in your calculations, the following data are given: The X axis is April $= 1$, May $= 2$, and so on. The Y axis is demand.

$$n = 6$$

$$\sum X = 21$$

$$\sum Y = 405$$

$$\sum X^2 = 91$$

$$\sum Y^2 = 27{,}875$$

$$\sum XY = 1{,}485$$

d. Using simple linear regression, calculate a forecast for October.

15. A forecasting method you have been using to predict product demand is shown in the following table along with the actual demand that occurred.

Forecast	Actual
1,500	1,550
1,400	1,500
1,700	1,600
1,750	1,650
1,800	1,700

a. Compute the tracking signal using the MAD and running sum of forecast errors (RSFE).

b. Calculate the MAPE.

c. Comment on whether you feel the forecasting method is giving good predictions.

16. Sales during the past six months have been as follows:

January	115
February	123
March	132
April	134
May	140
June	147

a. Using a simple three-month moving average, make forecasts for April through July. What is the main weakness of using a simple moving average with data that are patterned like this?

b. Using simple exponential smoothing with $\alpha = 0.70$, if the forecast for January had been 110, compute the exponentially smoothed forecasts for each month through July. Compare the forecasts for April through July with those obtained in part (*a*). Is this method more accurate for these data? Why or why not?

c. Using the least squares method, compute the forecasts for the rest of the year. Does your regression line seem to fit the January through June data well? If so, briefly describe a pattern of data with which linear regression would not work well.

d. Calculate the MAD and the MAPE for January through June using the trend equation from (*c*).

17. Actual demand for a product for the past three months was

Three months ago	400 units
Two months ago	350 units
Last month	325 units

a. Using a simple three-month moving average, what would the forecast be for this month?

b. If 300 units actually occurred this month, what would your forecast be for the next month?

c. Using simple exponential smoothing, what would your forecast be for this month if the exponentially smoothed forecast for three months ago was 450 units and the smoothing constant was 0.20?

18. After using your forecasting model for a period of six months, you decide to test it using MAD and a tracking signal. Following are the forecasted and actual demands for the six-month period:

Period	Forecast	Actual
May	450	500
June	500	550
July	550	400
August	600	500
September	650	675
October	700	600

a. Calculate the tracking signal.

b. Decide whether your forecasting routine is acceptable.

19. Consolidated Edison Company of New York, Inc., sells electricity, gas, and steam to New York City and Westchester County. Sales revenue for the years 1989 to 1999 are shown below. Forecast the revenues for 2000 through 2003. Use your own judgment, intuition, or common sense concerning which model or method to use, as well as the period of data to include. Obtain the actual revenues for three years and evaluate your forecasting model.

Year	Revenue ($ millions)
1989	5,550
1990	5,739
1991	5,873
1992	5,933
1993	6,020
1994	6,260
1995	6,537
1996	6,960
1997	7,121
1998	7,093
1999	7,491

20. Dana and Kerry own a chain of aerobic and fitness centers for women. They recently hired a consultant to help identify which factors significantly affect the volume of sales at a location. Based on the consultant's analysis, the three most significant factors were (1) average age of adult females within a three-mile radius, (2) number of adult females living or working within a three-mile radius, and (3) average household income within a three-mile radius. Using multiple regression analysis, the consultant developed the following equation to forecast sales for a new location:

Sales = 410,411 − 4,417(average age) + 4.62(number of females) + 1.55(average income)

Dana and Kerry are currently evaluating four potential sites. The data for each of these sites follow.

Site	Average Age	Number of Females	Average Income
A	47 yrs	14,000	$77,000
B	22	21,000	49,000
C	32	9,000	54,000
D	37	16,000	83,000

Calculate the forecasted sales for each site. Which one should Dana and Kerry select for their next location if their goal is to maximize their sales?

21. Josh Francis recently has been named Director of Marketing for a consumer products company. The company has divided up the United States into different territories, with a sales manager assigned to each territory. The sales and populations for the current territories in which her firm now does business are as follows:

Territory	Population (millions)	Sales (thousands)
A	2.53	410
B	1.76	240
C	6.81	595
D	4.22	325
E	12.77	990
F	5.09	665
G	10.82	840
H	16.84	1,450
I	7.65	825
J	11.34	935
K	6.18	830

a. Using an electronic spreadsheet, calculate the least squares regression line that fits the above data.

b. What is the regression equation? What is the coefficient of determination?

c. Josh's company is planning to expand into two additional territories in the coming year. The populations of these two territories are 7.43 million and 3.87 million. What are the estimated sales that Josh can expect from these two territories?

22. Erika Bruce recently has graduated from a business school and has taken a position as the assistant manager at a small hotel with 35 rooms. One of her first assignments is to

develop a model to forecast the number of room-nights that are expected to be sold in each month in 2002. (A room-night is the sale of one room for one night.) She has collected the following historical data on how many room-nights have been sold for each month in each of the past three years.

Month	Room-Nights Sold 1999	2000	2001
January	307	275	316
February	257	209	251
March	290	304	338
April	323	312	370
May	425	469	472
June	589	548	593
July	791	734	777
August	643	658	702
September	454	420	513
October	725	690	766
November	547	493	639
December	605	584	668

a. Using exponential smoothing with an electronic spreadsheet, develop a forecast for the number of room-nights to be sold in each month of 2002. Since this is the first time Erika is doing this forecast, use $\alpha = 0.3$ and $\alpha = 0.7$ and develop two forecasts. (Assume that the forecast for each month in 1999 is equal to the actual demand.)

b. Which α would you recommend using and why?

23. A customer service call center for a major appliance manufacturer has collected the following data for the last four Mondays on incoming calls:

Time	Four Mondays Ago	Three Mondays Ago	Two Mondays Ago	Last Monday
6:00–8:00 AM	35	42	39	33
8:00–10:00 AM	66	71	78	80
10:00–Noon	90	105	112	98
Noon–2:00 PM	99	123	114	107
2:00–4:00 PM	87	101	96	94
4:00–6:00 PM	55	43	51	38
6:00–8:00 PM	25	31	34	30

a. Use exponential smoothing with $\alpha = .6$ and $\alpha = .1$ to forecast the number of calls for next Monday.

b. Using MAD as a criterion, which of the two values of α do you recommend?

c. Construct a table to calculate the average MAD for values of $\alpha = .1, .2, .3, \ldots, .9$. Which value of α do you recommend be used?

Note: This problem should be done using Excel or a comparable electronic spreadsheet. The data for this problem are in an Excel spreadsheet on the disc included with the book.

24. Chez Alex is a haute cuisine restaurant that is only open for dinner. In order to determine the proper number of waitstaff to schedule for each meal, Aspen Wang, the din-

ing room manager, needs to forecast the number of meals that will be served. To do this, she has collected the following data:

Day of the Week	Four Weeks Ago	Three Weeks Ago	Two Weeks Ago	Last Week
Sunday	56	44	63	65
Monday	87	72	79	81
Tuesday	90	93	88	95
Wednesday	101	92	107	102
Thursday	120	114	106	118
Friday	125	131	143	157
Saturday	166	152	178	179

a. Use exponential smoothing with $\alpha = .4$ and $\alpha = .8$ to forecast the number of calls for next Monday.

b. Using MAD as a criterion, which of the two values of α do you recommend?

c. Construct a table to calculate the average MAD for values of $\alpha = .1, .2, .3, \ldots, .9$. Which value of α do you recommend be used?

Note: This problem should be done using Excel or a comparable electronic spreadsheet. The data for this problem are in an Excel spreadsheet on the disc included with the book.

Bibliography

Andrews, Bruce H., and Shawn M. Cunningham. "L.L. Bean Improves Call Center Forecasting." *Interfaces* 25, no. 6 (November–December 1995), pp. 1–13.

Carlberg, Ralph. "BioComp Systems on Demand Forecasting." Biocomp Systems, Inc., Redmond, WA, 1996.

Davis, Mark M., and Paul D. Berger. "Sales Forecasting in a Retail Service Environment." *The Journal of Business Forecasting,* Winter 1989, pp. 8–17.

DeLurgio, Stephen A. *Forecasting Principals and Applications.* Burr Ridge, IL: Irwin/McGraw-Hill, 1998.

Diebold, Francis X. *Elements of Forecasting.* Cincinnati, OH: Southwestern College Publishing, 1998.

Hample, Scott. "R U Ready for AI?" *Marketing Tools,* May 1, 1996, p. 60.

Hanke, John E., and Arthur G. Reitsch. *Business Forecasting.* 6th ed. Upper Saddle River, NJ: Prentice Hall,

Hueter, Jackie, and William Swart. "An Integrated Labor-Management System for Taco Bell." *Interfaces* 28, no. 1 (January–February 1998), pp. 75–91.

Jain, Chaman L. "Explosion in the Forecasting Function in Corporate America." *The Journal of Business Forecasting,* Summer 1999, pp. 2, 28.

Makridakis, Spyros; Steven C. Wheelwright; and Rob J. Hyndman. *Forecasting: Methods and Applications.* 3rd ed. New York: John Wiley & Sons, 1998.

Moore, Karl; Robert Burbach; and Roger Heeler. "Using Neural Networks to Analyze Qualitative Data." *Marketing Research* 7 (January 1, 1995), p. 34.

Newbold, Paul, and Theodore Bos. *Introductory Business Forecasting.* Cincinnati, OH: South-Western Publishing Co., 1990.

Wilson, J. Holton, and Barry Keating. *Business Forecasting.* Burr Ridge, IL: Irwin/McGraw-Hill, 1998.

Xu, Weidong. "Long Range Planning for Call Centers at FedEx." *The Journal of Business Forecasting,* Winter 1999–2000, pp. 6–11.

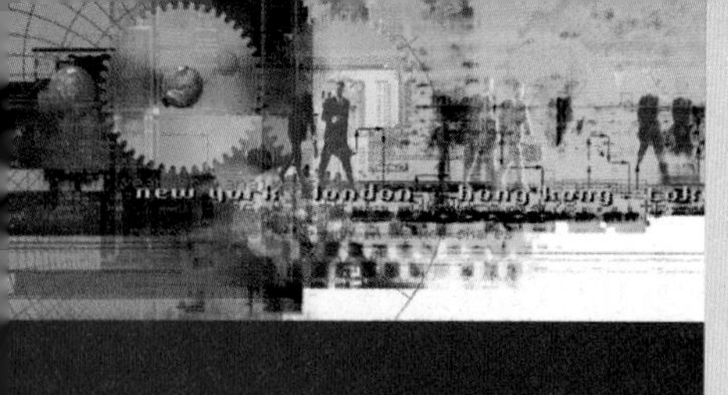

10 Human Resource Issues in Operations Management

Chapter Objectives

- Describe the changing role of the manager from one of command and control to that of being a team leader and coach, and the additional skills required.
- Identify the emerging trends that are dramatically changing the ways in which people work.
- Define the concept of employee empowerment and show how it impacts management and the organization.
- Distinguish between traditional work groups, self-managed teams, and cross-functional teams.
- Present the various ways in which technology is affecting jobs and the workplace.
- Introduce both behavioral and physical factors that should be taken into consideration when designing jobs.

AT SOUTHWEST AIRLINES, THE CUSTOMER ISN'T ALWAYS RIGHT—THE EMPLOYEE IS!

It may be hard for some people to believe, but the employees at Southwest Airlines (SWA) actually have fun at work. They hug and kiss each other as if they are part of one big happy family, which in fact they are, only in this case that "family" happens to be a corporation named Southwest Airlines. At the same time, they are a group of hard-working, dedicated professionals who are committed to providing customers with excellent service.

Herb Kelleher, Southwest Airlines' former chairman (and one of its founders), developed a corporate culture, which continues to this day, that revolves around treating people with respect. He also believed that if people enjoy what they are doing, they will tend to do a better job, including going the extra mile whenever necessary. As an example, there is a story about a frequent SWA's customer who arrived late one day and missed his flight. The Southwest Airlines' person at the ticket counter, recognizing him from his frequent flights on Southwest, offered to fly the customer to his destination in his own airplane so he could attend an important meeting. At the same time, unlike at a lot of companies, the customer is not always right at SWA, but the employee is! Customers who treat employees rudely or don't like the service that Southwest provides are asked to take their business elsewhere.

Southwest Airlines' employees are clearly its biggest asset. It spends more money to recruit and train personnel than any other airline, and its investment in them through the years has paid off many times over:

- SWA is the only U.S. airline to have made a profit every year since 1973, and its profit margins are the highest in the industry.
- In the highly competitive airline industry, SWA consistently offers the lowest fares in the markets that it serves.
- SWA has the most productive workforce in the industry with the lowest cost per passenger mile.
- SWA has the lowest employee turnover rate in the industry.
- SWA has the best performance record in the industry, based upon baggage handling, on-time arrivals, and customer complaints statistics.

Sources:

Kevin Frieberg and Jackie Frieberg, **Nuts!,** Bard Press, Austin, TX, 1996.

Jody Hoffer Gittell, "Investing in Relationships," **Harvard Business Review,** vol. 76, no. 6, June 2001, pp. 28–30.

Managerial Issues

As we have seen earlier in the book, there are many ways in which businesses compete in the marketplace, as they constantly look for new ways in which to distinguish themselves from their competition. However, as we also have seen, all too often many of these advantages are short lived, as they are readily duplicated by the competition within a short period of time.

One area, which appears to provide firms with a sustainable long-term competitive advantage, is their ability to attract, motivate, and retain highly skilled workers. Firms that are able to accomplish this successfully on a consistent long-term basis, such as General Electric under Jack Welch, Southwest Airlines under Herb Kelleher, and FedEx under Fred Smith, also have achieved enviable long-term financial success, and this is not coincidental. The management team in each of these firms knows the value and contribution of their workers, and therefore continuously invests in training, motivating, and retaining them.

The New Managerial Role

Managers in today's organizations face a rapidly changing and often unpredictable environment. Large-scale corporate restructuring and layoffs (or "downsizing") caused in part by mergers and acquisitions mean that today's managers must identify new and innovative ways to produce more with fewer workers and fewer organizational layers. Attempts to create more profitable, "lean and mean" organizations have resulted in an unexpected by-product: a sharp decline in perceptions of loyalty between the employee and the organization. In 1993, for example, 77 percent of workers surveyed said that companies were less loyal to employees than five years before. In addition, 60 percent of these workers judged that employees were less loyal to the organization.[1] As a consequence, today's managers are challenged to motivate employees who may feel less commitment to their organizations than was previously the norm.

The processes and technologies used to accomplish work also are changing, requiring managers to change with them. Total Quality Management, for example, emphasizes employee involvement. It also requires managers to assist workers in learning how to take responsibility for their work, and it requires managers to view workers from a new perspective, that of partners in the decision-making process rather than subordinates. No longer are employees expected "to leave their brains at the door" when they come to work each day. (See OM in Practice box on Employee Suggestions.) In addition, the introduction of fax machines, e-mail, the Internet, and videoconferencing have influenced the speed with which information is available and the way in which employees work together. Wal-Mart, for example, as stated earlier in this text, holds weekly employee meetings via satellite communication, thereby ensuring that everyone in the company receives the same information at the same time. Moreover, the growing use of intranets, which includes ERP systems, opens up entirely new approaches for linking organizations together that had never before been contemplated. These new technologies provide greater employee flexibility by allowing them to work from remote locations, including their homes. As a consequence, managers, in many instances, must now oversee the work of employees with whom they rarely meet face to face.

The composition of the workforce is changing as well. In the United States, for example, the number of women and minority group members entering the workforce and advancing within organizations continues to increase.

This growing diversity in the workforce, if properly managed, can improve creativity and decision making as well as make the organization more responsive to a wider variety

[1] B. B. Moskal, "Company Loyalty Dies, a Victim of Neglect," *Industry Week,* March 1, 1993.

Operations Management in Practice

EMPLOYEE SUGGESTIONS PAY OFF AT DANA CORPORATION

The Dana Corporation is a multibillion-dollar conglomerate that produces truck and car parts and components for both automobile manufacturers and the after-purchase market. Its subsidiary, Dana Commercial Credit Corp., which provides leasing and financial services, won the 1996 Malcolm Baldrige National Quality Award. The employees of Dana Corp. submitted a total of 666,120 suggestions in 1996 or 1.22 suggestions per employee per month. The result of employee input is a steady stream of improvements to the existing operation in the form of lower costs, less labor, and increased productivity, all of which directly affect the bottom line. Taking advantage of employee knowledge has become somewhat of an obsession at Dana Corp. Says CEO Woody Morcott, "It's a core part of our value system." It begins in the classroom where instructors at Dana University teach employees how to think about new ways of doing things. A major element for the success at Dana is emphasis on the fact that the workers are responsible for keeping the company competitive. Morcott admits he "stole" the idea when he visited a Japanese factory in the late 1980s. Each plant within Dana Corp. runs its own suggestion program, and it appears to be working. More than 70 percent of the suggestions submitted are adopted by the company.

Source: Adapted from Richard Teitelbaum, "How to Harness Gray Matter," *Fortune,* June 9, 1997, p. 168.

of customers. On the other hand, failure to effectively manage such a diverse workforce can lead to high turnover of valuable employees, unproductive conflicts, communication breakdowns, and expensive legal actions. For example, Southern California Edison agreed to pay $11.25 million to as many as 2,500 employees who were victims of job discrimination since 1989, and employees of Texaco filed a $520 million class-action discrimination lawsuit against the company in 1996.[2]

Expanded Managerial Skill Set All of these changes, along with other issues such as the increasing pressures generated by worldwide competition and/or the need to respond to new environmental regulations, mean that managers must now have a wider range of skills and be adept at playing a variety of organizational roles. In a study of 402 highly effective managers, Kim Whetten and David Cameron identified 10 skills that were most frequently cited as being critical to managerial effectiveness:[3]

1. Being able to communicate verbally (including the ability to listen).
2. Managing time and stress.
3. Managing individual decisions.
4. Recognizing, defining, and solving problems.
5. Motivating and influencing others.
6. Delegating.
7. Setting goals and articulating a vision.
8. Being self-aware.
9. Being able to build teams.
10. Managing conflict.

[2] *USA Today,* November 15, 1996; *Boston Globe,* November 17, 1996.

[3] Kim Whetten and David Cameron, *Developing Management Skills* (New York: Harper Collins, 1995).

At first, some of the skills may appear to be contradictory. Effective managers must have skills that foster employee participation and group work as well as skills in individual decision making and leadership. They must be visionary and, at the same time, manage day-to-day decision making. Robert Hoojberg and Robert Quinn use the term "behavioral complexity" to highlight the need for today's managers to use a variety of different, even conflicting, competencies and behaviors in an integrated way. A manager's ability to play multiple and competing roles has been related to a number of positive outcomes. These include better firm performance, higher overall managerial effectiveness as assessed by subordinates, better managerial performance, charisma, and the likelihood of making process improvements in the organization. Robert Quinn et al. depict the behavioral complexity required of managers in a model that includes eight managerial leadership roles and the core competencies required for each role. These are shown in Exhibit 10.1.

A review of these eight roles and related core competencies highlights the need for managers to work through and with other people. This, however, has a different meaning for managers today than it did in the past. The traditional managerial role was based on the following set of assumptions: (*a*) a good manager always has more technical expertise than any subordinate; (*b*) a good manager can solve all the problems; (*c*) a good manager has the

Exhibit 10.1

Eight Different Managerial Roles and Their Required Core Competencies

Type of Role	Core Competencies Required
Mentor	**1.** Understanding self and others. **2.** Communicating effectively. **3.** Developing subordinates.
Facilitator	**1.** Building teams. **2.** Using participative decision making. **3.** Managing conflict.
Monitor	**1.** Monitoring individual performance. **2.** Managing collective performance. **3.** Managing organizational performance.
Coordinator	**1.** Managing projects. **2.** Designing work. **3.** Managing across functions.
Director	**1.** Visioning, planning, and goal setting. **2.** Designing and organizing. **3.** Delegating effectively.
Producer	**1.** Working productively. **2.** Fostering a productive work environment. **3.** Managing time and stress.
Broker	**1.** Building and maintaining a power base. **2.** Negotiating agreement and commitment. **3.** Presenting ideas.
Innovator	**1.** Living with change. **2.** Thinking creatively. **3.** Creating change.

Source: R. E. Quinn, S. R. Faerman, M. P. Thompson, and M. R. McGrath, *Becoming a Master Manager: A Competency Framework* (New York: John Wiley & Sons, 1996), p. 23. Copyright © 1996 John Wiley & Sons, Inc. This material is used by permission of John Wiley & Sons, Inc.

primary (or only) responsibility for how the department works; (*d*) a good manager knows at all times exactly what is going on in the department.

In contrast, today's effective manager is rarely someone who (*a*) knows it all (and readily admits it!), (*b*) does it all alone, or (*c*) regularly instructs others in exactly what to do. Instead, a manager delegates, negotiates, communicates, develops, and is often a coach and teacher. In the emerging models of effective management, a key managerial skill is no longer "bossing" others around. "Bossing" may get the work done in the short term, but does little to develop a workforce that has either the creativity or the initiative to respond quickly to changing customer requirements, a new technology or competitor, or an unexpected obstacle. Increasingly, today's managers focus on developing employees who can manage and lead themselves to achieving the organization's goals both individually and by working in teams.

Charles Manz and Henry Sims describe managers who can lead others to lead themselves as "superleaders." A key to their managerial success is their ability to empower employees, helping them become "self-leaders." Empowered employees are highly motivated and committed to taking joint responsibility for the overall excellence of the organization. They find personal meaning in their work, know that they have the competence to perform their job well, believe that they have control over how to do their work, and understand that they have an impact on the outcomes that make a difference to the organization.

Empowerment relates directly to what research and common sense tell us about what motivates individuals to achieve peak performance. Individuals perform better when they understand the impact of their personal contribution on the success of the overall effort. They are more motivated when they can see the direct linkages between their contributions, the success of the overall effort, and the rewards they receive. They also are motivated to perform better if they know they have the requisite knowledge and skills to do the job well. And finally, individuals perform best when they have the autonomy and discretion to exercise their own best judgment about how to do the job.

The new managerial role of integrating seemingly contradictory competencies and creating empowered employees is not an easy one. It requires a manager to have not only technical and organizational skills, but also excellent people skills. An effective manager must be able to understand what it takes to effectively manage the organization's human resources.

Emerging Trends in the Workplace

There are several trends emerging today with respect to the workplace, and it is anticipated that these will continue into the foreseeable future. These trends include the external environment, from the changing demographics of the workforce to the impact of technology.

Increased Diversity in Workforce Demographics

Today's workforce is more diverse than ever before. In the United States, for example, the two-income family is almost a necessity, with the result that more women are entering the workforce. The liberal immigration policies of the United States also have contributed to this increase in diversity in the workplace. As another illustration, workers within the European Union are no longer restricted to working only in their country of origin, but instead can now seek employment in any one of the EU's member nations.

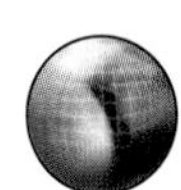

Increase in Flexible Work Hours

Many companies today offer employees flexible work schedules, which are considered a benefit. This is especially important to single parents with young children. With flexible

work hours, an employee can report to work any time between 7:00 and 9:00 AM, for example, and leave eight hours later. In Germany, flexible work hours mean that an employee can work up to 70 hours a week (without being paid overtime, and provided the work is there) during parts of the year, and take extended time off at other times. The key factor here is that the total number of hours worked over the entire year averages out to a normal week's work.

Part-Time Work and Job Sharing

A growing number of businesses offer part-time work to individuals who do not want to work on a full-time basis. (In some cases, this part-time work is dictated by the nature of the business. There are many services, for example, in which the demand for the service is limited to only a few hours a day.) One of the advantages of employing part-time workers is that payroll taxes and benefits are usually significantly less than for full-time workers. On the other hand, many firms that rely heavily on a part-time workforce will provide these employees with full benefits as an incentive for attracting them and keeping them. FedEx, for example, provides full medical and insurance benefits to all of its part-time workers even though they may work only 20 hours a week.

With job sharing, two or more individuals work together to perform the duties of a full-time position. They often will share the same office (often referred to as *hoteling*), which reduces office expense for the firm in comparison to providing each with his or her own office. Job sharing is particularly attractive to individuals with small children or who have elderly parents that need care.

Increased Use of Temporary Labor

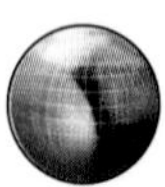

As we will see shortly, the cost of hiring and firing workers is expensive. In some countries such as Germany and France, it is almost impossible to fire an employee (although there are signs that this is changing). As a result, there has been a growing trend toward the use of temporary workers. In addition to providing the firm with the ability to quickly adjust its workforce to meet changing demand for its products, the use of a temporary workforce allows the firm to retain its full-time workers on a more permanent basis.

The Impact of Technology

Technology has impacted the workplace in many ways, from recruiting to the types of work available to how the work itself is accomplished.

Recruitment The Internet has removed many of the geographical barriers and logistics that were previously associated with recruiting. Websites such as Monster.com, HotJobs .com and JobFind.com provide electronic marketplaces that bring buyers and sellers together from literally every corner of the world. However, not only do these sites provide companies with the ability to reach a larger audience of potential employees, they also provide employees with the ability to find new job opportunities in places that were previously unknown to them.

Telecommuting The decrease in the communications cost coupled with the increase in the speed of transmission allows many businesses to employ workers that live in geographically remote locations. There were approximately 2 million telecommuters in the

United States in 1990, and this number is expected to increase to 50 million by 2030.[4] Telecommuting also has an added advantage for the company in that it doesn't have to provide the worker with office space, which can be expensive.

Increase in Training and Development Continued advances in state-of-the-art technology are requiring firms to spend more on employee training and development. No longer is this considered to be a one-shot deal, but rather it must be done on an annual basis. In 1997, for example, U.S. businesses budgeted more than $59.8 billion to provide formal training and development courses to over 49.6 million employees, or more than $1,200 per employee.[5]

In addition, the use of technology in the workplace has increasingly divided the workforce into two categories: those whose jobs require ever-increasing skills and knowledge to operate the technology-oriented equipment and those whose jobs are becoming more menial as a result of this technology. Robotics and other forms of automation, for example, will continue to replace skilled workers on many assembly lines. Unless these workers receive additional training in managing, operating, and maintaining this high-technology equipment, they will have to settle for work that has less skill requirements with correspondingly lower pay.

Increasing Emphasis on Teamwork

Nowhere is the need for effective management and the focus on employee empowerment more obvious than in the increasing use of teamwork by organizations. Although some organizations, such as Volvo and Toyota, have successfully used team models for organizing work for more than 20 years, the surge in the number of American organizations now using teams has been relatively recent. The reasons for the growing popularity in teams are many, including the fact that teams typically outperform individuals when doing tasks that require judgment, experience, and multiple skills. Companies using self-managed teams have found that they increase productivity, quality, customer satisfaction and flexibility; allow for the streamlining of functions; and produce higher worker commitment.[6]

In order to better understand the power of teams, it is important to highlight some of the differences between teams and traditional work groups. In traditional work groups, the emphasis is on sharing information and making decisions that help group members perform their functions more effectively. Work groups do not need to work collectively on tasks that require a group effort, and their members are individually accountable for their performance. Work teams, in contrast, emphasize collective performance. Work team members are both individually and mutually responsible for their contributions and performance. Work teams are characterized by a high degree of synergy. This synergy combines and improves the knowledge and skills of individual members to create products and/or decisions that are of higher quality than those made by individuals alone. Katzenbach and Smith define a team as "a small number of people with complementary skills who are committed to a common purpose, performance goals, and approach for which they hold themselves mutually accountable." They go on to say that truly high-performance teams have

---

[4]Jack M. Nilles, *Managing Telework: Strategies for Managing the Virtual Workforce* (New York: John Wiley & Sons, 1998).

[5]P. J. Guglielmino and R. G. Murdick, "Self-Directed Learning: The Quiet Revolution in Corporate Training and Development," *NSAM Advance Management Journal* 62, no. 3 (Summer 1997), p. 10.

[6]J. D. Orsburn, L. Moran, E. Musselwhite, and J. H. Zenger, *Self-Directed Work Teams: The New American Challenge* (Homewood, IL: Business One Irwin, 1990).

the added ingredient of "members who are also deeply committed to another's personal growth and success."[7]

As more organizations embrace the use of work teams, the variety of team structures and projects on which teams work continues to increase. Two types of work teams that are prevalent in today's organizations are self-managed work teams and cross-functional teams.

self-managed work teams

Autonomous teams responsible for identifying problems, implementing solutions, and measuring outcomes.

Self-Managed or Self-Directed Work Teams Unlike traditional work groups, **self-managed work teams** tend to operate very autonomously. They have responsibility not only for solving problems, but also for implementing solutions and measuring outcomes. Typically composed of 10 to 15 employees, these teams take on many of the activities and responsibilities that were formerly the duties of their supervisors. Members of a self-managed team are likely to have collective control over (*a*) work assignments for team members, (*b*) the pace at which work gets done, (*c*) assessing the quality of team and individual output, and (*d*) who joins the team. For example, self-managed teams at the General Motors plant in Fitzgerald, Georgia, which manufactures sealed, maintenance-free, automotive batteries, prepare annual material and labor budgets, evaluate group members for pay raises, and can shut down the production line to solve process and quality problems.[8]

There are, however, some unique problems with self-managed work teams, especially in service operations. For example, a guest at the front desk of a Ritz-Carlton Hotel became very upset when she was told that there was no manager for the front desk (it was a self-directed work team). To address this type of problem, each team member becomes "manager for a day" on a rotating basis to address specific guest requests "requiring a manager."

Effective self-managed teams have produced some important benefits for organizations and their employees. The greater autonomy and responsibility given to employees in self-managed teams tend to increase worker motivation and job satisfaction. Employees are empowered and can see how their efforts contribute to organizational success. This motivation and satisfaction also result in positive effects on productivity and the organization's bottom line. For example, an employee on a self-managed team at ACES, an independent electric power producer, noticed that fans similar to those used in his plant were being sold at a local discount store for one-third the cost of those bought by ACES from the original manufacturer. He took the initiative to buy the discount store's entire inventory of fans. Because of his participation in a self-managed team, he knew the cost of the ACES fans, understood the purposes for which the fans were used and how often they would need to be replaced, and felt authorized by the company to implement a solution that would save money. The self-managed teams at the General Motors Fitzgerald plant also contributed to satisfaction and productivity. The plant was able to manufacture its products at costs significantly lower than similar plants run in a more traditional, top-down management style, and its levels of employee satisfaction were among the highest throughout the entire General Motors organization.[9]

The successful implementation of self-managed teams, however, is not easy. It takes considerable time, effort, and organizational commitment. Team members must not only have technical expertise but also develop skills in problem solving, decision making, interpersonal communication, and team management. The organization must be willing to create innovative reward and incentive systems that reflect both individual and team performance.

[7]Jon R. Katzenbach and Douglas K. Smith, *The Wisdom of Teams: Creating the High Performance Organization* (Boston: Harvard Business School Press, 1993), pp. 45, 92.

[8]C. C. Manz and H. P. Sims, *Business without Bosses* (New York: John Wiley & Sons, 1995).

[9]Ibid.

Managers must learn to become facilitators and coaches of empowered, self-managed teams rather than directors and bosses of individual contributors.

Cross-Functional Work Teams **Cross-functional work teams** come together to tackle large, complex projects or solve organizational problems that cut across traditional functional lines and that, therefore, require the input and expertise from several areas within an organization. The members of a cross-functional team may come from the same organizational level but represent different departments and areas of expertise. Hallmark Cards' team reduced development of new cards and coordinated products from three years to less than a year. By using a cross-functional team to provide information from and coordinate the activities of various departments early in a project, organizations can save considerable time and money. For example, in developing the new 777 aircraft, Boeing created cross-functional teams that included designers, engineers, and maintenance and customer service personnel, as well as finance specialists and production employees. Instead of representatives from these functional areas working on the aircraft sequentially, they worked together on developing the new aircraft from the beginning of the process. Maintenance specialists were able to suggest ways to design an aircraft that would be faster to service and cheaper to operate. Production engineers helped designers develop solutions to potential production problems during the design phase. Designing these problems out rather than trying to fix them during the production phase was much less costly and time consuming.[10]

cross-functional work teams

Teams within an organization that have representatives from different areas of the firm.

As in the case of self-managed work teams, the successful implementation of cross-functional teams requires organizational commitment. The members of a cross-functional team must learn to appreciate and understand the perspectives of representatives from other parts of the organization. They also must learn to communicate their expertise and opinions in ways that representatives from other functional areas can understand. Developing an effective cross-functional team can take considerable time and effort. The organizations that have done so, however, believe that the effort pays off. For example, the cross-functional team that designed the Chrysler Neon delivered the new subcompact in 42 weeks rather than taking the several years it usually takes to design a new car.[11]

Employee Turnover

It should come as no surprise that those firms that treat their workers well have very low employee turnover as compared to the average turnover within their respective industries. Ritz-Carlton Hotels, for example, has an employee turnover rate of less than 20 percent in an industry that averages more than 100 percent annually. Similarly, Southwest Airlines' employee turnover rate of 4.5 percent is one of the lowest in the airline industry. Although all of the material presented in this chapter can impact employee turnover, we focus here on those topics that are directly related to the cost of employee turnover.

Employee Turnover Costs

The cost of employee turnover has several components, some of which are readily quantifiable, others being less easily measured. Every time an employee leaves, these costs are incurred.

---

[10]J. Main, "Betting on the 21st Century Jet," *Fortune,* April 20, 1992, pp. 102–17; D. J. Yang, "When the Going Gets Tough, Boeing Gets Touchy-Feely," *Business Week,* January 17, 1994, pp. 65–68.

[11]D. Woodruff, "Chrysler's Neon," *Business Week,* May 3, 1993, pp. 116–26.

Operations Management in Practice

RITZ-CARLTON HOTELS TREATS ITS EMPLOYEES LIKE LADIES AND GENTLEMEN

The Ritz-Carlton Hotels is the only two-time recipient of the Malcolm Baldrige National Quality Award in the service category (1992 and 1999), and attributes much of its success to its employees, most of whom come in daily contact with the hotel's guests. The motto of the Ritz-Carlton Hotel Company, as noted above, is "We are Ladies and Gentlemen Serving Ladies and Gentlemen." In order to provide outstanding service to its hotel guests, the Ritz-Carlton starts with a rigorous recruitment process that identifies those potential employees that have the personal characteristics necessary to succeed. After being selected, each new employee then goes through an in-depth orientation, followed by extensive on-the-job training and job certification. As part their orientation process, all employees receive a card with the company's credo on it and are expected to learn the credo and practice it daily. The values of the Ritz-Carlton are continuously reinforced on a daily basis through "line-ups," frequent employee recognition for extraordinary achievement, and a performance

(From NIST website, www.quality.nist.gov/.)

Loss of Knowledge When employees leave a firm, they take with them knowledge that they learned over the years. This can include knowledge of internal systems and processes, as well as knowledge of customers. Also included here is the knowledge of the organization's culture and relationships with other employees, which facilitates completing work in an efficient and effective manner.

Loss of Output When an employee leaves and the position is not filled immediately, the firm loses that worker's output while the position remains vacant. In a strong economy with low unemployment, as occurred in the United States during the late 1990s, this lag time can be considerable. For example, if a firm averages $300,000 in annual sales per employee, then a position that remains unfilled for three months costs the firm $75,000 in revenues.

Hiring Costs The cost of hiring new employees includes advertising costs, interview, and testing time. Recruitment costs also include travel expenses related to hiring. New employees are also significantly less productive during their first few months on the job. A new employee must learn the new systems and procedures, and this takes time. For example, exempt employees, on average, are only 75 percent productive during their initial six months of employment. If the average revenue per employee is $293,000 per year (revenue

THREE STEPS OF SERVICE

1
A warm and sincere greeting. Use the guest name, if and when possible

2
Anticipation and compliance with guest needs.

3
Fond farewell. Give them a warm good-bye and use their names, if and when possible.

"We Are Ladies and Gentlemen Serving Ladies and Gentlemen"

THE EMPLOYEE PROMISE

At The Ritz-Carlton, our Ladies and Gentlemen are the most important resource in our service commitment to our guests.

By applying the principles of trust, honesty, respect, integrity and commitment, we nurture and maximize talent to the benefit of each individual and the company.

The Ritz-Carlton fosters a work environment where diversity is valued, quality of life is enhanced, individual aspirations are fulfilled, and The Ritz-Carlton mystique is strengthened.

THE RITZ-CARLTON™

CREDO

The Ritz-Carlton Hotel is a place where the genuine care and comfort of our guests is our highest mission.

We pledge to provide the finest personal service and facilities for our guests who will always enjoy a warm, relaxed yet refined ambience.

The Ritz-Carlton experience enlivens the senses, instills well-being, and fulfills even the unexpressed wishes and needs of our guests.

appraisal that is based on specific expectations. To ensure that guest complaints are resolved quickly, workers are required to act at the first notice of a customer complaint, regardless of the nature of the problem. Every employee is empowered to take whatever action is necessary when a guest is dissatisfied. Consequently, much of the responsibility for ensuring high-quality guest services and accommodations rests with its employees.

Source: Adapted from "Profiles of Winners of the Malcolm Baldrige National Quality Award," www.quality.nist.gov/.

per employee being a surrogate for productivity), then revenue for six months would be 50 percent of that, or $146,500. The cost associated with an employee being non-productive in the first six months is therefore 25 percent of that, or $36,625.[12]

Termination Costs In addition to the costs associated with the exiting process, such as conducting exit interviews and changing employee personnel records and payroll status, there is also unemployment insurance. Those firms with high employee turnover tend to have higher unemployment insurance rates, particularly when workers are laid off due to a lack of work. (As noted in the opening vignette, Southwest Airlines has never had a worker layoff, even though the airline industry is very cyclical in nature.) Termination costs also can include severance pay and extended health benefits.

The Hiring Process

The first step in reducing employee turnover is to have an effective hiring process that screens out those individuals that do not have the required characteristics and skills that are

[12]J. Fitz-Enz, "It's Costly to Lose Good Employees," *Workforce,* August 1997, p. 50.

necessary for them to succeed. For example, as stated above, in the hotel industry, which is notorious for having employee turnover average more than 100 percent annually, both the Ritz-Carlton and the Four Seasons hotel chains have turnover rates that are less than 20 percent. A major factor for this low rate is the extensive hiring process that potential employees must go through before they are actually hired. This process includes in-depth interviews with several managers as well as personality and skills tests to ensure not only that they have the technical skills required, but also that they will fit in well with the cultures of these organizations.

Job Design

Central to an organization's ability to effectively manage its human resources, especially from an operations perspective, is the proper design of jobs in the organization. Without a proper job design that can support new styles of management, empowered employees, and teamwork, these innovative approaches to transform the workplace and increase organizational competitiveness are likely to fail.

In this section, we explore several issues with respect to job design and present some guidelines for carrying out the job-design function. We begin by noting some trends in job design, some of which were mentioned earlier:

worker empowerment

Providing employees with authority to make decisions pertaining to the organization.

1. *Quality as part of the worker's job.* Now often referred to as "quality at the source," improved quality is linked with the concept of **worker empowerment.** Empowerment, used in this context, refers to workers being given authority to stop a production line when there is a quality problem, or to give a customer an on-the-spot refund if service is not satisfactory.
2. *Cross-training workers to perform multiskilled jobs.* This is seen more often in the factory than in the office despite pressures on the clerical workforce as described in the next OM in Practice on The New World of Work. Indeed, bank check processing centers and the majority of high-volume clerical jobs are far more factorylike than those in many factories.

The worker here is stopping the assembly line because of a problem he sees.

Operations Management in Practice

THE NEW WORLD OF WORK

- London firms are now sending typing to Taipei. To survive, London typists must realize they are competing with Taipei typists. They must learn to "add value" (e.g., know more software programs or more languages than their Taiwanese counterparts) or else they'd better learn to love pounding the pavement.
- The FI Group, one of Britain's largest software systems houses, employs about 1,100 people, most of whom are part-time freelancers who need toil no more than 20 hours per week. More than two-thirds of the firm's work is done at home: All told, employees live in 800 sites and serve 400 clients at any time. Life at FI is captured in the November 1988 issue of *Business:* "Chris Eyles, project manager, sat down in her office in Esher, Surrey, and called up the electronic 'chit chat' mailbox . . . The printer began to churn out messages. 'Help!' said [a message] from her secretary, based a few miles away in Weybridge. Somewhere in the Esher area, a computer analyst was in trouble . . . Eyles checked the team diary and her wall plan, located the analyst and the problem, and set up a meeting at FI's work center in Horley, 25 miles away."
- So who's left to sweep the floor? A visit to a 3M facility in Austin, Texas, suggests that floor sweeping, food handling, and security guarding are fast becoming almost as sophisticated as engineering. Computer-based floor sweepers and new security systems call for a sophisticated worker in virtually every job. A new, highly automated facility belonging to the huge drug distributor Bergen Brunswig is illustrative: Most manual work is done by machine. Work teams that dot the facility are not so much in the business of "doing" (by old standards), but in the business of improving the system. They are brain-involved, improvement-project creators, not muscle-driven lump shifters. There is no room on the staff for anyone who sees himself or herself as a pair of hands, punching a time clock.

Source: Tom Peters, "Prometheus Barely Unbound," *The Executive* 4, no. 4 (November 1990), pp. 79–80, 83.

3. *Employee involvement and team approaches to designing and organizing work.* This is a central feature in Total Quality Management (TQM) and continuous improvement efforts. In fact, it is safe to say that virtually all TQM programs are team based.
4. *"Informating" ordinary workers through telecommunications network and computers, thereby expanding the nature of their work and their ability to do it.* In this context, informating is more than just automating work; it is revising the fundamental structure of work. Northeast Utilities' computer system, for example, can pinpoint a problem in a service area before the customer service representative (CSR) answers the phone. The CSR uses the computer to troubleshoot serious problems, to weigh probabilities that other customers in the area have been affected, and to dispatch repair crews before other calls are even received.
5. *Any time, any place production.* The ability to do work away from the factory or office, again due primarily to advances in information technology, is a growing trend throughout the world. (See the OM in Practice.)

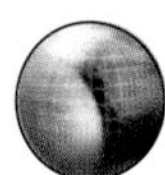

6. *Automation of heavy manual work.* Examples abound in both services (one-person trash pickup trucks) and manufacturing (robot spray painting on auto lines). These changes are driven by safety regulations as well as economics and personnel reasons. (See the OM in Practice.)
7. *Most important of all, organizational commitment to providing meaningful and rewarding jobs for all employees.*

job design

Tasks and sequences that have to be accomplished and are within an individual's job assignment.

Job design may be defined as the specification of the work activities for an individual or group within an organizational setting. Its objective is to develop work assignments that meet the requirements of the organization and the technology, and that satisfy the personal and individual requirements of the jobholder. The term *job* (in the context of nonsupervisory work) and the activities involved in it are defined as follows:

1. *Micromotion:* the smallest work activity involving such elementary movements as reaching, grasping, positioning, or releasing an object.
2. *Element:* Two or more micromotions, usually thought of as a more or less complete entity, such as picking up, transporting, and positioning an item.
3. *Task:* Two or more elements that comprise a complete activity, such as wiring a circuit board, sweeping a floor, or cutting a tree.
4. *Job:* A set of all the tasks that must be performed by a given worker. A job may consist of several tasks, such as typing, filing, and taking dictation (as in secretarial work), or it may consist of a single task, such as attaching a wheel to a car (as in automobile assembly).

Job design is a complex function because of the variety of factors that enter into arriving at the ultimate job structure. Decisions must be made about who is to perform the job, where it is to be performed, and how. And, as we can see in Exhibit 10.2, each of these factors may have additional considerations.

specialization of labor

Dividing tasks into small increments of work, resulting in efficient operations due to highly repetitive tasks.

Behavioral Considerations in Job Design

Degree of Labor Specialization **Specialization of labor** is a two-edged sword in job design. On one hand, specialization has made possible high-speed, low-cost production, and, from a materialistic standpoint, has greatly enhanced our standard of living. On the other hand, it is well known that extreme specialization, such as that encountered on traditional assembly lines in mass-production industries, often has serious adverse effects on workers, which in turn are often passed on to the production systems in the form of low-quality or defective work. In essence, the problem is to determine how much

Exhibit 10.2

Factors in Job Design

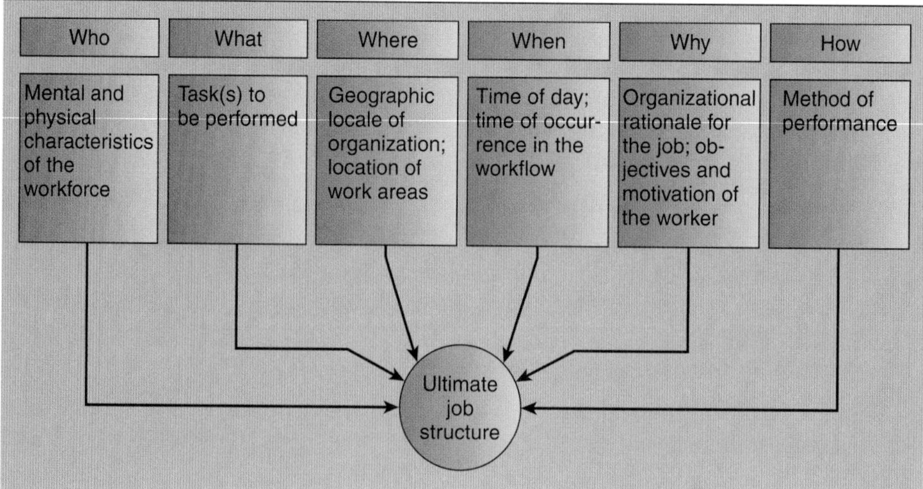

specialization is enough: At what point do the disadvantages outweigh the advantages? (See Exhibit 10.3.)

Recent research suggests that the disadvantages dominate the advantages much more than was thought in the past. However, simply stating that, for purely humanitarian reasons, specialization should be avoided is risky. The reason, of course, is that people differ in what they want from their work and what they are willing to put into it. Some workers prefer not to make decisions about their work, some like to daydream on the job, and others are simply not capable of performing highly complex work. Still, there is a good deal of worker frustration with the way many jobs are structured, leading organizations to try different approaches to job design. Two popular contemporary approaches are job enrichment and sociotechnical systems. The philosophical objective underlying these approaches is to improve the quality of work life of the employee, and so they are often applied as central features of what is termed a quality of work life (QWL) program.

job enlargement

Redesigning a job, usually by increasing the number of tasks, to make it more interesting. Also referred to as horizontal enlargement.

Job Enlargement and Job Enrichment **Job enlargement** generally entails making adjustments to a specialized job to make it more interesting to the jobholder. A job is said to be *enlarged horizontally* if the worker performs a greater number or variety of tasks, and it is said to be *enlarged vertically* if the worker is involved in planning, organizing, and inspecting his or her own work. Horizontal job enlargement is intended to counteract oversimplification and to permit the worker to perform a "whole unit of work." Vertical

Exhibit 10.3

Advantages and Disadvantages of Specialization of Labor

Advantages of Specialization	
To Management	**To Labor**
1. Rapid training of the workforce 2. Ease in recruiting new workers 3. High output due to simple and repetitive work 4. Low wages due to ease of substitutability of labor 5. Close control over workflow and workloads	1. Little or no education required to obtain work 2. Ease in learning job
Disadvantages of Specialization	
To Management	**To Labor**
1. Difficulty in controlling quality since no one person has responsibility for entire product. 2. "Hidden" costs of worker dissatisfaction, arising from *a.* Turnover *b.* Absenteeism *c.* Tardiness *d.* Grievances *e.* Intentional disruption of production process 3. Reduced likelihood of obtaining improvement in the process because of worker's limited perspective 4. Increased labor-management friction 5. Increased potential for unionization.	1. Boredom stemming from repetitive nature of work 2. Little gratification from work itself because of small contribution to each item 3. Little or no control over the work pace, leading to frustration and fatigue (in assembly-line situations) 4. Little opportunity to progress to a better job because significant learning is rarely possible on fractionated work 5. Little opportunity to show initiative through developing better methods or tools 6. Local muscular fatigue caused by use of the same muscles in performing the task 7. Little opportunity for communication with co-workers because of layout of the work area

To help prevent tendonitis and numbness, Oshkosh B'Gosh designed a pulley system allowing sewers to work with their arms at rest. In addition, jobs were enlarged through rotation to provide employees with opportunities to use various parts of the body to avoid over stressing any one area.

enlargement (traditionally termed *job enrichment*) attempts to broaden the workers' influence in the transformation process by giving them certain managerial powers over their own activities. Today, the common practice is to apply both horizontal and vertical enlargement to a given job and refer to the total approach as **job enrichment.**

job enrichment

The broadening of a worker's job description to include both a greater number of tasks and the worker's involvement in the planning and design of the work to be done.

Physical Considerations in Job Design

Beyond the behavioral components of job design, another aspect warrants consideration: the physical components. Indeed, while motivation and work-group structure strongly influence worker performance, they may be of secondary importance if the job is too demanding or is otherwise improperly designed from a physical standpoint.

Work Task Continuum One way of viewing the general nature of the physical requirements inherent in work is through the work task continuum shown in Exhibit 10.4. In this typology, *manual tasks* put stress on large muscle groups in the body and lead to overall

Exhibit 10.4

Work Task: Continuum (Human Work)

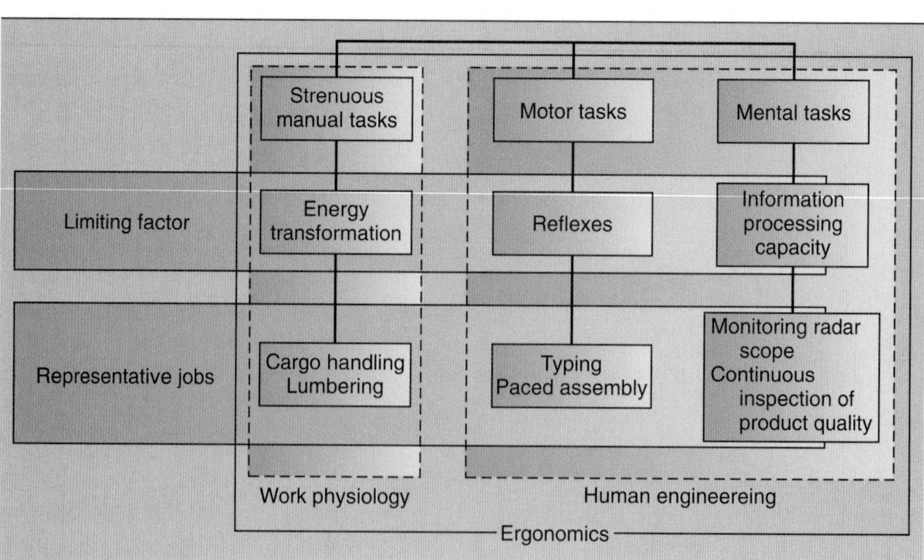

fatigue. *Motor tasks* are controlled by the central nervous system, and their measure of effectiveness is the speed and precision of movements. While these tasks lead to fatigue, the effect is localized in the smaller muscle groups, such as the fingers, hands, and arms and, hence, cannot be adequately measured by indices of *general* fatigue. *Mental tasks* involve rapid decision making based on certain types of stimuli, such as blips on a radar screen or defects in a product. Here the measure of effectiveness is generally some combination of response time and the number and types of errors.

As noted in Exhibit 10.4, motor tasks and mental tasks fall under the heading *human engineering,* while the study of the physical aspects of work in general is called *ergonomics* (from the Greek noun for "work" and the Greek verb for "to manage").

Conclusion

Today's managers face increased pressure to improve performance within their organizations. This has come about for several reasons, including the growth in international competition and the need to excel simultaneously in a wide variety of areas. In order to produce more output with a smaller workforce, managers are now turning to their employees for ideas on how to improve worker productivity and performance. Much of the improvements in this area are the result of work teams that have been rapidly forming in many of the better companies. However, changes in management style are required for the successful implementation of these teams.

The human resource issues, in terms of how we manage our workforce, and the technical issues, in terms of how we specifically design jobs, are both critical elements in the success of a company. Many management gurus today, in fact, suggest that a firm's employees are the only sustainable competitive advantage.

In the end, it takes people to run a business. Regardless of the amount of automation, adoption of the right strategy, and so forth, a company cannot function properly without highly motivated workers who have been properly trained in both interpersonal skills and the technical aspects of their respective jobs.

Key Terms

cross-functional work teams p. 405
job design p. 410
job enlargement p. 411
job enrichment p. 412
self-managed work teams p. 404
specialization of labor p. 410
worker empowerment p. 408

Review and Discussion Questions

1. Think of three examples of ways in which an organization has changed to become more competitive. What impact do you think these changes have on the employees of the organization?
2. Which of the eight managerial roles do you practice in your role as a student, . . . in activities in which you participate, . . . in your job? Which of Cameron and Whetten's 10 skills do you use in these roles?

3. What problems might arise from empowering employees? What are some of the hurdles that managers must overcome in empowering employees? What could the organization do to address these issues?
4. Would you prefer to work in a traditional work group or in a self-managed work team? Why?
5. This chapter mentioned some of benefits of and the difficulties in implementing cross-functional and self-managed work teams. What other difficulties can you predict? What other benefits do you see?
6. Is there any inconsistency when a company requires precise time standards and, at the time, encourages job enlargement?
7. The study team from one American car manufacturer observed that the Japanese used techniques such as job rotation, making workers responsible for quality control, minimal work classifications, and indirect employee participation in management. What gains can be made with this approach, in contrast to the job specialization approach? If the Japanese approach were to be adopted in a specialized job environment, what changes would have to take place for it to be successfully implemented?
8. How is Technology affecting the workplace?

Bibliography

Carlisle, Brian. "Job Design Implications for Operations Managers." *International Journal of Production and Operations Management* 3, no. 3 (1983), pp. 40–48.

Cusumano, Michael. *Japan's Software Factories: A Challenge to U.S. Management.* New York: Oxford University Press, 1991.

Fitz-Enz, J. "It's Costly to Lose Good Employees." *Workforce,* August 1997, p. 50.

Frieberg, Kevin, and Jackie Frieberg. *Nuts!* Austin, TX: Bard Press, 1996.

Gittell, Jody Hoffer. "Investing in Relationships." *Harvard Business Review,* vol. 79, no. 6, June 2001, pp. 28–30.

Guglielmino, P. J., and R. G. Murdick. "Self-Directed Learning: The Quiet Revolution in Corporate Training and Development." *NSAM Advance Management Journal* 62, no. 3 (Summer 1997), p. 10.

Hanson, Gary. "Determinants of Firm Performance: An Integration of Economic and Organizational Factors." Ph.D. dissertation, University of Michigan. Cited in David A. Cameron and Kim S. Whetten. *Developing Manager Skills.* 3rd ed. New York: Harper Collins, 1995.

Hoojberg, Robert, and Robert Quinn. "Behavioral Complexity and the Development of Effective Managers." In *Strategic Leadership: A Multiorganizational-Level Perspective,* ed. R. Phillips and J. Hunt. Westport, CT: Quorum Publishing, 1992.

Katzenbach, Jon R., and Douglas K. Smith. *The Wisdom of Teams: Creating the High Performance Organization.* Boston: Harvard Business School Press, 1993.

Konz, Stephan. *Work Design: Industrial Ergonomics.* 2nd ed. New York: John Wiley & Sons, 1983.

Lipin, Steven. "A New Vision." *The Wall Street Journal,* June 25, 1993.

Main, J. "Betting on the 21st Century Jet." *Fortune,* April 20, 1992, pp. 102–17.

Manz, Charles C., and Henry P. Sims Jr. *Business without Bosses.* New York: John Wiley & Sons, 1995.

———. "Super-Leadership: Beyond the Myth of Heroic Leadership." *Organizational Dynamics* 19, no. 4 (1991), pp. 18–35.

Mondy, R. Wayne, and Robert N. Noe. *Human Resource Management.* Upper Saddle River, NJ: Prentice Hall, 1996.

Moskal, B. B. "Company Loyalty Dies, a Victim of Neglect." *Industry Week,* March 1, 1993.

Nilles, Jack M. *Managing Telework: Strategies for Managing the Virtual Workforce.* New York: John Wiley & Sons, 1998.

Orsburn, J. D.; L. Moran; E. Mussselwhite; and J. H. Zenger. *Self-Directed Work Teams: The New American Challenge.* Homewood, IL: Business One Irwin, 1990.

Quinn, R. E.; S. R. Faerman; M. P. Thompson; and M. R. McGrath. *Becoming a Master Manager: A Competency Framework.* New York: John Wiley & Sons, 1996, p. 23.

Sasser, W. Earl, and William E. Fullmer. "Creating Personalized Service Delivery Systems." In *Service Management Effectiveness,* ed. D. Bowen, R. Chase, and T. Cummings. San Francisco: Jossey-Bass, 1990, pp. 213–33.

Scott, Gerald. "A Look at the Goings-on inside Chrysler's Plant That Builds Viper and Prowler, Tour de Force." *Chicago Tribune,* March 8, 1998.

Teitelbaum, Richard. "How to Harness Gray Matter." *Fortune,* June 9, 1997, p. 168.

Wellins, R.; W. Byham; and J. Wilson. *Empowered Teams.* San Francisco: Jossey-Bass, 1991.

Wetten, Kim, and David Cameron. *Developing Management Skills.* New York: Harper Collins, 1995.

Woodruff, D. "Chrysler's Neon." *Business Week,* May 3, 1993, pp. 116–26.

Yang, D. J. "When the Going Gets Tough, Boeing Gets Touchy-Feely." *Business Week,* January 17, 1994, pp. 65–68.

Case

AT&T Credit Corp.

Millions of clerical employees toil in the back offices of financial companies, processing applications, claims, and customer accounts on what amounts to electronic assembly lines. The jobs are dull and repetitive and efficiency gains minuscule—when they come at all.

That was the case with AT&T Credit Corp. (ATTCC) when it opened shop in 1985 as a newly created subsidiary of American Telephone & Telegraph Corp. Based in Morristown, New Jersey, ATTCC provides financing for customers who lease equipment from AT&T and other companies. A bank initially retained by ATTCC to process lease applications couldn't keep up with the volume of new business.

ATTCC President Thomas C. Wajnert saw that the fault lay in the bank's method of dividing labor into narrow tasks and organizing work by function. One department handled applications and checked the customer's credit standing, a second drew up contracts, and a third collected payments. So no one person or group had responsibility for providing full service to a customer. "The employees had no sense of how their jobs contributed to the final solution for the customer," Wajnert says.

Unexpected Bonus

Wajnert decided to hire his own employees and give them "ownership and accountability." His first concern was to increase efficiency, not to provide more rewarding jobs. But, in the end, he did both.

In 1986, ATTCC set up 11 teams of 10 to 15 newly hired workers in a high-volume division serving small businesses. The three major lease-processing functions were combined in each team. No longer were calls from customers shunted from department to department. The company also divided its national staff of field agents into seven regions and assigned two or three teams to handle business from each region. That way, the same teams always worked with the same sales staff, establishing a personal relationship with them and their customers. Above all, team members took responsibility for solving customers' problems. ATTCC's new slogan: "Whoever gets the call owns the problem."

The teams largely manage themselves. Members make most decisions on how to deal with customers, schedule their own time off, reassign work when people are absent, and interview prospective new employees. The only supervisors are seven regional managers who advise the team members, rather than give orders. The result: The teams process up to 800 lease applications a day versus 400 under the old system. Instead of taking several days to give a final yes or no, the teams do it in 24 to 48 hours. As a result, ATTCC is growing at a 40 percent to 50 percent compound annual rate, Wajnert says.

Extra Cash

The teams also have economic incentives for providing good service. A bonus plan tied to each team's costs and profits can produce extra cash. The employees, most of whom are young college graduates, can add $1,500 a year to average salaries of $28,000, and pay rises as employees learn new skills. "It's a phenomenal learning opportunity," says 24-year-old team member Michael LoCastro.

But LoCastro and others complain that promotions are rare because there are few managerial positions. And everyone comes under intense pressure from co-workers to produce more. The annual turnover rate is high: Some 20 percent of ATTCC employees either quit or transfer to other parts of AT&T. Still, the team experiment has been so successful that ATTCC is involving employees in planning to extend the concept throughout the company. "They will probably come up with as good an organizational design as management could," Wajnert says, "and it will work a lot better because the employees will take ownership for it."

Questions

1. Besides few opportunities for promotion and intense peer pressure, what other factors might contribute to the high employee turnover rate?
2. What would you do to reduce the employee turnover rate at ATTCC?

Source: John Hoerr, "The Payoff from Teamwork" *Business Week*, July 10, 1989, p. 59. © 1989 by The McGraw-Hill Companies. Reprinted by special permission.

S10 Work Performance Measurement

Supplement Objectives

- Introduce the more common types of work methods that are practiced in the workplace.
- Understand the fundamental issues involved in developing work measurements.
- Identify the basic elements associated with conducting a time study.
- Determine how to design a work sampling study and apply it to an actual operation.

Work needs to be properly designed and measured, regardless of the type of organization in which it is done, be it manufacturing or services. The proper design of work ensures that tasks are completed with a minimum of wasted effort. Proper work design, as discussed in the previous chapter, also ensures that the work is accomplished without causing injury to the employee.

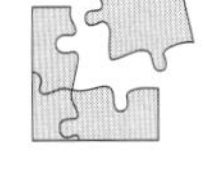

Work measurement is equally important for several reasons. First, it is used to determine the labor cost, which is usually a major component of the overall cost of producing a good or a service. Second, knowing how long it takes to complete a specific task or assignment provides management with the ability to determine the number of workers needed to meet a given level of demand. For example, the number of customer service representatives that FedEx needs at its call centers is dependent on the demand as expressed in the number of calls it receives daily and the length of time to process each call, which is referred to as the average handling time (AHT). A third reason for work measurement is to identify those workers who are meeting or exceeding standards and who should be appropriately recognized and rewarded. It also identifies those who fall below the standards and require additional training.

In the early part of this century, beginning with Frederick W. Taylor and continuing with Frank and Lillian Gilbreth, work measurements were done almost exclusively in manufacturing companies. While the specific methodology associated with work measurement has basically not changed since its inception with Taylor, the manner in which work measurements are conducted has changed significantly (see OM in Practice: Work Measurement Then and Now).

Work Methods

An integral part in the development and design of processes is the definition of the tasks that must be accomplished. But how should these tasks be done? Years ago, production workers were craftspeople who had their own (and sometimes secret) methods for doing things. However, over time products have become more complicated, as mechanization of a higher order was introduced, and output rates have increased. As a result, the responsibilities for work methods have been transferred to management. It is no longer logical or economically feasible to allow individual workers to produce the same product by different methods. Work specialization brought much of the concept of craftwork to an end, as less-skilled workers were employed to do the simpler tasks.

In some large companies, the responsibility for developing work methods is typically assigned to either a staff department designated *methods analysis* or an industrial engineering department; in small firms this activity is often performed by consulting firms that specialize in work methods design. However, as illustrated in the NUMMI example (see OM in Practice), a growing number of firms are allowing their workers to design their own jobs and also to determine how long they should take.

The principal approach to the study of work methods is the construction of charts, such as operations charts, worker-machine charts, simo (simultaneous motion) charts, and activity charts, in conjunction with time-study or standard-time data. The choice of which charting method to use depends on the activity level of the task; that is, whether the focus is on (*a*) the overall operation, (*b*) the worker at a fixed workplace, (*c*) a worker interacting with equipment, or (*d*) a worker interacting with other workers (see Exhibit S10.1).

Overall Operation

The objective in studying the overall production system is to identify non-value-added time delays, transport distances, processes, and processing time requirements, with the goal of

Operations Management in Practice

WORK MEASUREMENT THEN AND NOW

Job Design Then . . .

Frederick W. Taylor recounts his "motivation" of his trusty worker, Schmidt (in *Principles of Scientific Management,* 1910):

"Schmidt, are you a high-priced man?"

"Vell, I don't know vat you mean."

"Oh yes you do. What I want to know is whether you are a high-priced man or not. . . . What I want to find out is whether you want to earn $1.85 a day or whether you are satisfied with $1.15, just the same as all those cheap fellows are getting?"

"Vell, yes I vas a high-priced man."

"Now come over here. You see that pile of pig iron?"

"Yes."

"You see that car?"

"Yes."

"Well, if you are a high-priced man, you will load that pig iron on that car tomorrow for $1.85."

"You see that man over there? . . . Well, if you are a high-priced man, you will do exactly as this man tells you tomorrow, from morning till night. When he tells you to pick up a pig and walk, you pick it up and you walk, and when he tells you to sit down and rest, you sit down. You do that straight through the day. And what's more, no back talk."

And Now . . .

Researcher Paul S. Adler describes job design at New United Motor Manufacturing Inc.'s (NUMMI) Fremont, California, plant. NUMMI is a joint venture between General Motors and Toyota.

Team members hold the stopwatch and design their own jobs. Team members begin by timing one another, seeking the most efficient way to do each task at a sustainable pace. They pick the best performance, break it down into its component parts, and then look for ways of improving each element. The team then takes the resulting methods, compares them with those used by teams working on the other shift at the same workstation, and writes detailed specifications that become the standard work definition for everyone on both teams.

Source: Discussions with Paul S. Adler; Paul S. Adler, "Time and Motion Regained," *Harvard Business Review* 71, no. 1 (January–February 1993), pp. 97–110; and "Return of the Stopwatch," *The Economist,* January 23, 1993, p. 69.

Exhibit S10.1

Work Methods and Design Aids

Activity	Objective of Study	Study Techniques
Overall production system	Eliminate or combine steps; shorten transport distance; identify delays	Flow diagram, service blueprint, process chart
Worker at fixed workplace	Simplify method; minimize motions	Operations charts, simo charts; apply principles of motion economy
Worker interacts with equipment	Minimize idle time; find number or combination of machines to balance cost of worker and machine idle time	Activity chart, worker-machine charts
Worker interacts with other workers	Maximize productivity, minimize interference	Activity charts, gang process charts

simplifying the entire operation. The primary objective here is to eliminate any step in the process that does not add value to the product. The approach is to develop a process flowchart and then ask the following questions:

What is done? Must it be done? What would happen if it were not done?

Where is the task done? Must it be done at that location or could it be done somewhere else?

When is the task done? Is it critical that it be done then or is there flexibility in time and sequence? Could it be done in combination with some other step in the process?

How is the task done? Why is it done this way? Is there another way?

Who does the task? Can someone else do it? Should the worker be of a higher or lower skill level?

These types of questions usually help to eliminate much unnecessary work, as well as to simplify the remaining work, by combining a number of processing steps and changing the order of performance.

Use of the process chart is valuable in studying an overall operation, though care must be taken to follow the same item throughout the process. The subject may be a product being manufactured, a service being provided, or a person performing a sequence of activities. An example of a process chart (and flow diagram) for a clerical operation is shown in Exhibit S10.2. Common notation in process charting is given in Exhibit S10.3.

Worker at a Fixed Workplace

There are many jobs that require workers to remain at a specified workstation in order to complete their assigned tasks. This applies to both manufacturing and services. When the nature of the work is primarily manual (such as sorting, inspecting, making entries, or assembly operations), the focus of work design is on simplifying the work method and making the required operator motions as few and as simple as possible.

The same concepts also apply to services. For example, a customer service representative at a call center is trained to ask specific questions in a given order so that a customer's inquiry is processed as efficiently as possible. With services, however, the issue is further complicated by the presence of the customer in the process. Here efficiency cannot be achieved at the expense of angering the customer, who may perceive an efficient operator as being curt or rude.

There are two basic ways to determine the best method for performing an essentially manual task. The first is to search among the various workers performing that task and find the one who performs the job best. That person's method is then accepted as the standard, and the other workers are trained to perform it in the same way. This was basically F. W. Taylor's approach. The second method is to observe the performance of a number of workers, analyze in detail each step of their work, and pick out the superior features of each worker's performance. This results in a composite method that combines the best elements of the group studied. This was the procedure used by Frank Gilbreth, the father of motion study, to determine the "one best way" to perform a work task.

Taylor observed actual performance to find the best method; Frank Gilbreth and his wife Lillian relied on movie film. Through micromotion analysis—observing the filmed work performance frame by frame—the Gilbreths studied work very closely and defined its basic elements, which was termed **therbligs** ("Gilbreth" spelled backward, with the *t* and *h* transposed). They also used the motion model—a wire representation of the path of a motion. Their study led to the rules or principles of motion economy listed in Exhibit S10.4.

therbligs

Basic units of measurement used in micromotion analysis.

Once the various motions for performing a task have been identified, an *operations chart* is then developed, listing the individual operations and their sequence of performance. For greater detail, a *simo* (simultaneous motion) *chart* may be constructed, listing not only the operations but also the times for both left and right hands. This chart may be assembled from the data collected with a stopwatch, from analysis of a film of the operation, or from predetermined motion-time data (such as that developed by the Gilbreths and discussed later in the chapter). Many aspects of poor design become immediately obvious

Exhibit S10.2

Flow Diagram and Process Chart of an Office Procedure—Present Method*

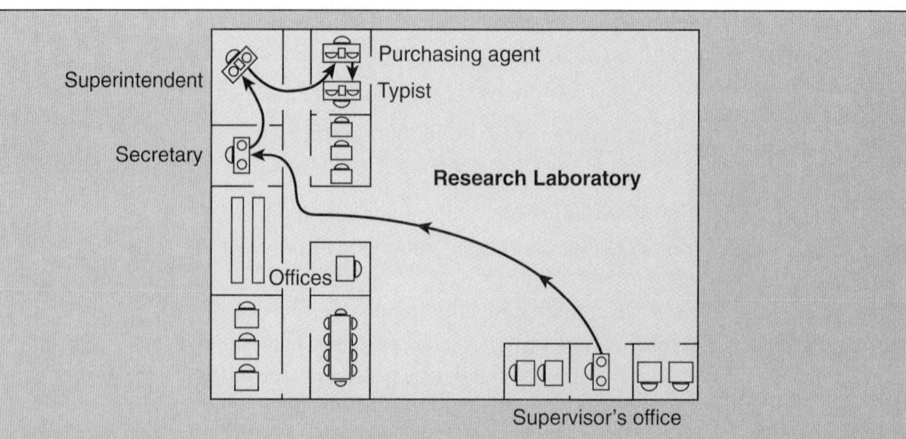

Present Method ☒ **PROCESS CHART**
Proposed Method ☐

SUBJECT CHARTED Requisition for small tools DATE ________
Chart begins at supervisor's desk and ends at CHART BY J.C.H.
typist's desk in purchasing department CHART NO. R136
DEPARTMENT Research laboratory SHEET NO. 1 OF 1

DIST. IN FEET	TIME IN MINS.	CHART SYMBOLS	PROCESS DESCRIPTION
		● ⇨ □ D ▽	Requisitions written by supervisor (one copy)
		○ ⇨ □ ◗ ▽	On supervisor's desk (awaiting messenger)
65		○ ➡ □ D ▽	By messenger to superintendent's secretary
		○ ⇨ □ ◗ ▽	On secretary's desk (awaiting typing)
		● ⇨ □ D ▽	Requisition typed (original requisition copied)
15		○ ➡ □ D ▽	By secretary to superintendent
		○ ⇨ □ ◗ ▽	On superintendent's desk (awaiting approval)
		○ ⇨ ■ D ▽	Examined and approved
		○ ⇨ □ ◗ ▽	On superintendent's desk (awaiting messenger)
20		○ ➡ □ D ▽	To purchasing department
		○ ⇨ □ ◗ ▽	On purchasing agent's desk (awaiting approval)
		○ ⇨ ■ D ▽	Examined and approved
		○ ⇨ □ ◗ ▽	On purchasing agent's desk (awaiting messenger)
5		○ ➡ □ D ▽	To typist's desk
		○ ⇨ □ ◗ ▽	On typist's desk (awaiting typing of purchase order)
		● ⇨ □ D ▽	Purchase order typed
		○ ⇨ □ ◗ ▽	On typist's desk (awaiting transfer to main office)
		○ ⇨ □ D ▽	
105		3 4 2 8	Total

*Requisition is written by supervisor, typed by secretary, approved by superintendent, and approved by purchasing agent; then a purchase order is prepared by a stenographer.

Source: Ralph M. Barnes, *Motion and Time Study,* 8th ed. (New York: John Wiley & Sons, 1980), pp. 76–79.

Exhibit S10.3

Common Notation in Process Charting

- ● *Operation.* Something is actually being done. This may be work on a product, some support activity, or anything that is directly productive in nature.
- ➡ *Transportation.* The subject of the study (product, service, or person) moves from one location to another.
- ■ *Inspection.* The subject is observed for quality and correctness.
- D *Delay.* The subject of the study must wait before starting the next step in the process.
- ▼ *Storage.* The subject is stored, such as finished products in inventory or completed papers in a file. Frequently, a distinction is made between temporary storage and permanent storage by inserting a T or P in the triangle.

Exhibit S10.4

Gilbreth's Principles of Motion Economy

Using the human body the way it works best:

1. The work should be arranged to provide a natural rhythm that can become automatic.
2. The symmetrical nature of the body should be considered:
   - *a.* The motions of the arms should be simultaneous, beginning and completing their motions at the same time.
   - *b.* Motions of the arms should be opposite and symmetrical.
3. The human body is an ultimate machine and its full capabilities should be employed:
   - *a.* Neither hand should ever be idle.
   - *b.* Work should be distributed to other parts of the body in line with their ability.
   - *c.* The safe design limits of the body should be observed.
   - *d.* The human should be employed at its highest use.
4. The arms and hands as weights are subject to the physical laws, and energy should be conserved:
   - *a.* Momentum should work for the person and not against him or her.
   - *b.* The smooth, continuous arc of the ballistic is more efficient.
   - *c.* The distance of movements should be minimized.
   - *d.* Tasks should be turned over to machines.
5. The tasks should be simplified:
   - *a.* Eye contacts should be few and grouped together.
   - *b.* Unnecessary actions, delays, and idle time should be eliminated.
   - *c.* The degree of required precision and control should be reduced.
   - *d.* The number of individual motions should be minimized along with the number of muscle groups involved.

Arranging the workplace to assist performance:

1. There should be a definite place for all tools and materials.
2. Tools, materials, and controls should be located close to the point of use.
3. Tools, materials, and controls should be located to permit the best sequence and path of motions.

Using mechanical devices to reduce human effort:

1. Vises and clamps can hold the work precisely where needed.
2. Guides can assist in positioning the work without close operator attention.
3. Controls and foot-operated devices can relieve the hands of work.
4. Mechanical devices can multiply human abilities.
5. Mechanical systems should be fitted to human use.

Source: Frank C. Barnes, "Principles of Motion Economy: Revisited, Reviewed, and Restored," *Proceedings of the Southern Management Association Annual Meeting,* Atlanta, GA, 1983, p. 298. Reprinted by permission.

Software from Deneb Robotics is designed to help companies strategically plan to meet production goals. Wearing a harness with 11 sensors, Brian Christensen of Deneb demonstrates software that helps engineers maximize efficiency on a production line by coordinating movements of humans and robots that work side by side (see the monitor).

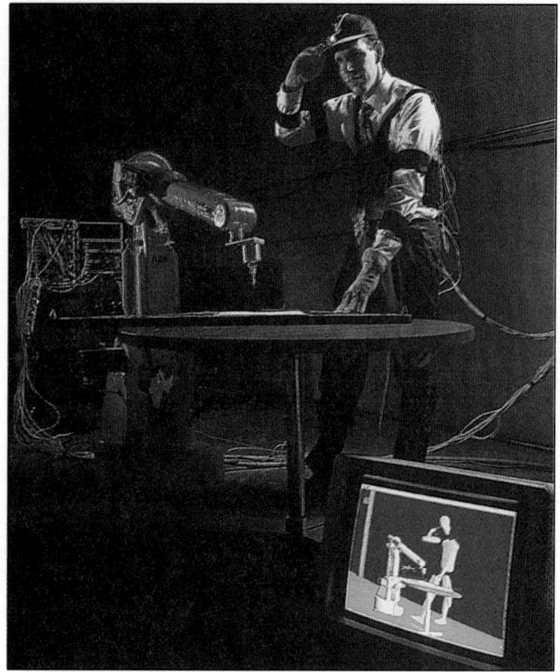

with this technique—a hand being used as a holding device (rather than a jig or fixture), an idle hand, or an exceptionally long time for positioning.

Worker Interacting with Equipment

When a person and equipment operate together to perform a given set of tasks, interest focuses on the efficient use of both the person's time and the equipment's time. When the working time of the operator is less than the equipment run time, a worker-machine chart is a useful device in analysis. If the operator can operate several pieces of equipment, the problem is to find the most economical combination of operator and equipment, such that the combined cost of the idle time of the equipment and the idle time for the worker are at a minimum.

Worker-machine charts are always drawn to scale, the scale being time as measured by length. Exhibit S10.5 gives an example of a worker-machine chart in a service setting.

With many services, however, the "machine" that the worker interacts with is often a computer, which is simultaneously providing and collecting information (as in the case of making an airline or hotel reservation). In designing these types of processes, the goal is to provide the necessary information as quickly as possible to both the worker and the customer, and also to provide a format for collecting customer data that is both accurate and fast. This is accomplished by having significantly large computer capacity, which is relatively inexpensive in comparison to the cost of the worker.

Workers Interacting with Other Workers

Increasingly, work in both manufacturing and services is being performed by teams. The degree of interaction may be as simple as one operator handing a part to another, or as complex as a cardiovascular surgical team consisting of doctors, nurses, an anesthesiologist, the

Exhibit S10.5

Worker-Machine Chart for a Gourmet Coffee Store

PERSON				MACHINE	
Customer	Time in sec.	Clerk	Time in sec.	Coffee Grinder	Time in sec.
1. Ask grocer for 1 pound of coffee (brand and grind)	5	Listen to order	5	Idle	5
2. Wait	15	Get coffee and put in machine, set grind, and start grinder	15	Idle	15
3. Wait	21	Idle while machine grinds	21	Grind coffee	21
4. Wait	12	Stop grinder, place coffee in package, and close it	12	Idle	12
5. Receive coffee from grocer, pay grocer, and receive change	17	Give coffee to customer, wait for customer to pay for coffee, receive money, and make change	17	Idle	17

Summary

	Customer	Clerk	Coffee grinder
Idle time	48 sec.	21 sec.	49 sec.
Working time	22	49	21
Total cycle time	70	70	70
Utilization in percent	Customer utilization = $\frac{22}{70} \approx 31\%$	Clerk utilization = $\frac{49}{70} = 70\%$	Machine utilization = $\frac{21}{70} = 30\%$

The customer, the clerk, and the coffee grinder (machine) are involved in this operation. It required 1 minute and 10 seconds for the customer to purchase a pound of coffee in this particular store. During this time the customer spent 22 seconds, or 31 percent of the time, giving the clerk his order, receiving the ground coffee, and paying the clerk for it. He was idle during the remaining 69 percent of the time. The clerk worked 49 seconds, or 70 percent of the time, and was idle 21 seconds, or 30 percent of the time. The coffee grinder was in operation 21 seconds, or 30 percent of the time, and was idle 70 percent of the time.

operator of the artificial heart machine, an X-ray technician, standby blood donors, and the pathologist (and perhaps a minister to pray a little).

To facilitate analysis of team efforts, an activity or a gang process chart is used to plot the activities of each individual on a time scale similar to that of the worker-machine chart. A gang process chart is usually employed to trace the interaction of a number of workers with machines of a specified operating cycle, to find the best combination of workers and machines. An activity chart is less restrictive and may be used to follow the interaction of

Exhibit S10.6

Activity Chart of Emergency Tracheotomy

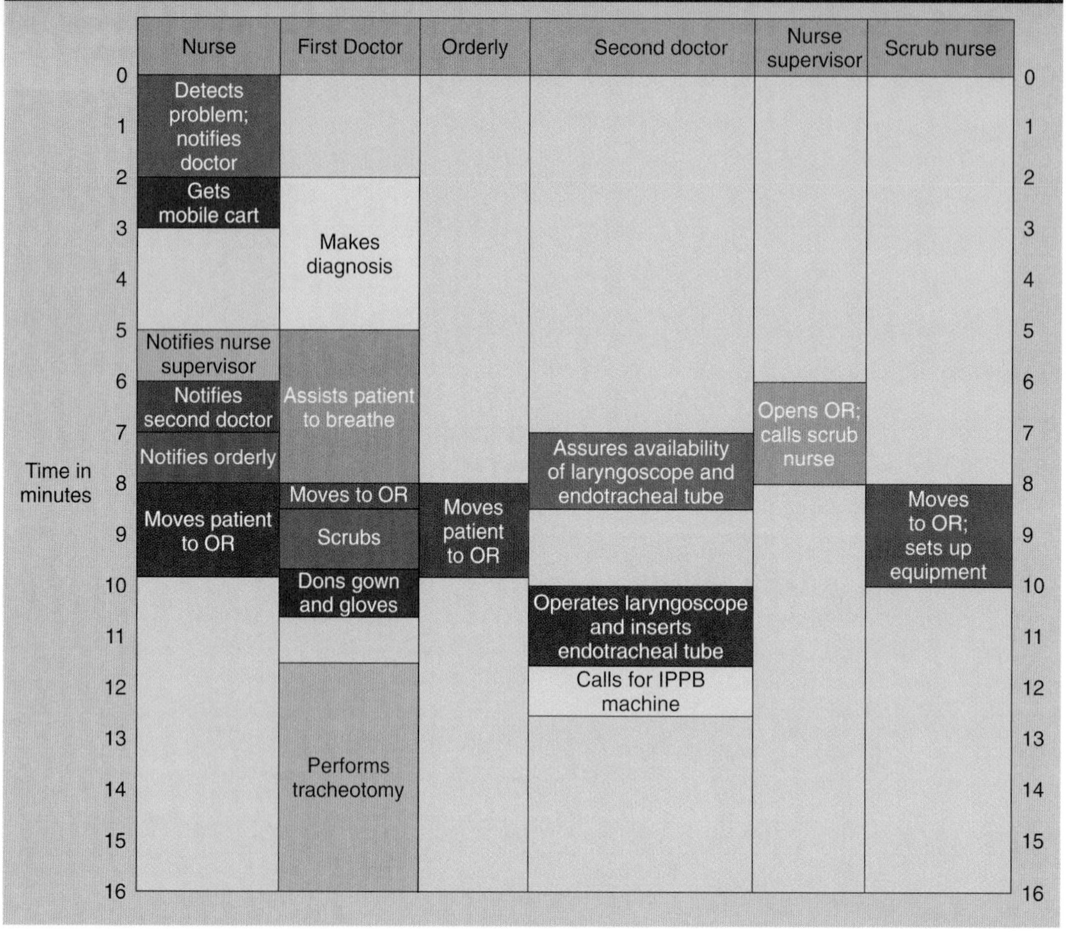

Time in minutes: 0 1 2 3 4 5 6 7 8 9 10 11 12 13 14 15 16

Nurse
Detects problem; notifies doctor
Gets mobile cart
Notifies nurse supervisor
Notifies second doctor
Notifies orderly
Moves patient to OR

First Doctor
Makes diagnosis
Assists patient to breathe
Moves to OR
Scrubs
Dons gown and gloves
Performs tracheotomy

Orderly
Moves patient to OR

Second doctor
Assures availability of laryngoscope and endotracheal tube
Operates laryngoscope and inserts endotracheal tube
Calls for IPPB machine

Nurse supervisor
Opens OR; calls scrub nurse

Scrub nurse
Moves to OR; sets up equipment

Source: Data taken from Harold E. Smalley and John Freeman, *Hospital Industrial Engineering* (New York: Reinhold, 1966), p. 409.

any group of operators, with or without equipment being involved. Such charts are often used to study and define each operator in an ongoing repetitive process, and they are extremely valuable in developing a standardized procedure for a specific task. Exhibit S10.6, for example, shows an activity chart for a hospital's emergency routine in performing a tracheotomy (an operation for opening a patient's throat surgically to allow him or her to breathe), where detailed activity analysis is of major importance because any unnecessary delay could be fatal.

Work Measurement

work measurement

Methodology used for establishing time standards.

The subject of **work measurement** for establishing time standards has been controversial since the days of Taylor. With the widespread adoption of Deming's ideas, it has become the subject of renewed criticism. (Deming argued that work standards and quotas inhibit process improvement, focusing all of the worker's efforts on speed rather than quality.)

Exhibit S10.7

Types of Work Measurement Applied to Different Tasks

Type of Work	Major Methods of Determining Task Time
Very short interval, highly repetitive	Videotape analysis
Short interval, repetitive	Stopwatch time study: predetermined motion-time data
Task in conjunction with machinery or other fixed-processing-time equipment	Elemental data
Infrequent work or work of a long cycle time	Work sampling

Nevertheless, all organizations need some form of standard time estimates for planning and budgeting, and many companies use them with success in work design, as demonstrated in the UPS case at the end of this chapter. It is therefore important to understand the basic industrial engineering methods used to set standards:

1. Time study (stopwatch and micromotion analysis).
2. Elemental standard time data.
3. Predetermined motion-time data.
4. Work sampling.

Each method has its advantages over the others and has particular areas of application. Exhibit S10.7 lists these methods and relates them to a general class of jobs.

Time Study

A **time study** is generally conducted with a stopwatch, either on the job site or by analyzing a videotape of the job. Procedurally, the job or task to be studied is separated into measurable parts or elements, and each element is timed individually. After a number of repetitions, the collected times are averaged. (The standard deviation may be computed to give a measure of variance in the performance times.) The averaged times for each element are then added together, and the result is the observed performance time for the operator. However, to make this operator's time applicable to all workers, a measure of speed, which is expressed as a *performance rating* and which reflects how hard the observed operator is working, also must be included to "normalize" the job. The application of a rating factor provides what is called *normal time.*

time study

Determination, with use of a stopwatch, of how long it takes to complete a task or set of tasks.

Example

An industrial engineer conducts a time study on an operator and determines that a specific task takes about two minutes to complete. The engineer estimates that the particular operator that she is observing is working about 20 percent faster than normal. The company has an allowance factor of 15 percent of job time for personal needs, delays, and fatigue. Calculate the standard time for this task.

Solution

$$\text{Normal time} = \text{Observed performance time per unit} \times \text{Performance rating}$$

In this example, denoting normal time by NT,

$$NT = 2(1.2) = 2.4 \text{ minutes}$$

When an operator is observed over a long period of time, the number of units produced during this time, along with the performance rating, gives the normal time as

$$NT = \frac{\text{Total time observed}}{\text{Number of units produced}} \times \text{Performance rating}$$

Standard time is derived by adding allowances to normal time. These allowances include personal needs (washroom and coffee breaks, and so forth), unavoidable work delays (equipment breakdown, lack of materials, and so forth), and worker fatigue (physical or mental). There are two equations for calculating standard time:

$$\text{Standard time} = \text{Normal Time} + (\text{Allowances} \times \text{Normal time})$$

or

$$ST = NT(1 + \text{Allowances}) \qquad \text{(S10.1)}$$

and

$$ST = \frac{NT}{1 - \text{Allowances}} \qquad \text{(S10.2)}$$

Equation S10.1 is used most often in practice. Here the allowances are stated as a percentage of the "job time." In other words, the allowance factor is added to the job time in order to obtain the standard time. However, if the allowances are stated as a percentage of the total "work time," then Equation S10.2 is the correct one to use.

In this example, the normal time to perform a task is 2.4 minutes and the allowances for personal needs, delays, and fatigue total 15 percent of the job time; then by Equation S10.1,

$$ST = 2.4(1 + 0.15) = 2.76 \text{ minutes}$$

In an eight-hour day, a worker would produce $8 \times 60/2.76 = 174$ units. This implies 174×2.4 minutes per unit (normal time) $= 417.6$ minutes working and $480 - 417.6 = 62.4$ minutes for allowances.

However, if the allowance factor is stated as a percentage of the total work time, then we would use Equation S10.2:

$$ST = \frac{2.4}{1 - 0.15} = 2.82 \text{ minutes}$$

In the same eight-hour day, using Equation S10.2, $8 \times 60/2.82$ (or 170) units are produced with 408 working minutes and 72 minutes for allowances. Depending on how the allowance factor is specified, there is a difference of four units produced and also approximately 10 minutes in the daily allowance time.

Work measurement is particularly important when workers are paid by the amount of work they actually complete, which is also referred to as *piece-rate.* Using the above example, if the hourly rate for an employee is \$12.00 per hour, then that employee, if on piece-rate, would be paid as follows:

$60/2.82 = 21.277$ pieces per hour is the standard.

\$12.00 per hour/21.277 per hour = \$0.564/piece.

Thus, a person working at 100 percent of standard would earn $12.00 per hour; a person working at 110 percent of standard would earn $13.20 per hour.

A major problem with the piece-rate system is that it tends to reward quantity at the expense of quality. As a result, firms that have adopted the piece-rate system usually will pay only for good parts that are produced.

Before a time study is conducted, each task is broken down into elements or parts. Some general rules for the break down of a task are

1. Define each work element to be short in duration but sufficiently long enough so that each can be timed with a stopwatch and the time can be written down.
2. If the operator works with equipment that runs separately—the operator performs a task and the equipment runs independently—separate the actions of the operator and that of the equipment into different elements.
3. Define any delays by the operator or equipment into separate elements.

How many observations are enough? Time study is really a sampling process; that is, we take a relatively small number of observations as being representative of many subsequent cycles to be performed by the worker. A great deal of analysis and experience indicates that the number of observations is a function of cycle length and the number of repetitions of the job over a one-year planning period.

Elemental Standard-Time Data

Elemental standard-time data are obtained from previous time studies and codified in tables in a handbook or in a computer data bank. Such data are used to develop time standards for new jobs or to make time adjustments to reflect changes in existing jobs. They are more correctly viewed as *normal-time data,* because tabled values have been modified by an average performance rating, and allowances must be added to obtain a standard time.

Calculating a **time standard** for a new job using elemental standard-time data tables entails the following steps:

time standard

Established time for completing a job, used in determining labor costs associated with making a product.

1. Break down the new job into its basic elements.
2. Match these elements to the time for similar elements in the table.
3. Adjust element times for special characteristics of the new job. (In metal cutting, for example, this is often done by a formula that modifies the time required as a function of type of metal, size of the cutting tool, depth of the cut, and so forth.)
4. Add element times together and add delay and fatigue allowances as specified by company policy for the given class of work.

The obvious benefit of elemental standard data is cost savings in that it eliminates the need for a new time study every time there is a new job. This saves staff time and avoids disruption of the workforce. The main practical requirement of the approach is that the elemental data must be kept up to date and easily accessible.

Predetermined Motion-Time Data

As with elemental standard-time data, predetermined motion-time data tables create a time standard for a job or task. There are, however, significant differences between the two approaches. Whereas the elemental standard-time data tables provide times for job-specific work elements, the predetermined motion-time data tables provide times for basic motions such as a "reach of a given length" or "the grasp of an object of a given weight." These motions, in their most basic elements, can be defined in terms of therbligs, which were described earlier in this chapter. Because they are generic in nature, predetermined motion-time data can be applied to a wide range of manual tasks. By comparison, the elemental standard-time data tables are typically specific to a given company or industry.

Work Sampling

work sampling

Technique for estimating how workers allocate their time among various activities throughout a workday.

Whereas work measurement is concerned with how long it takes to perform a specific task or activity, **work sampling** is primarily concerned with how workers spend their time among several tasks or activities. For example, we may want to know how much time workers spend on indirect activities such as material handling to determine whether or not more cost-efficient material handling equipment should be purchased. In a hotel reservation call center, we would want to know what percentage of time is actually spent on the telephone. Work sampling provides us with a method for determining the time spent on these activities, and involves observing a portion or sample of the work activity. Then, based on the findings in this sample, some statements can be made about how the employee or employees spend their time.

For example, if we were to observe a fire department rescue squad 100 random times during the day and found that it was involved in a rescue mission for 30 of the 100 times (en route, on site, or returning from a call), we would estimate that the rescue squad spends approximately 30 percent of its time directly on rescue mission calls. (The time it takes to make an observation depends on what is being observed. Often only a glance is needed to determine the activity, and the majority of studies require only several seconds' observation.)

Observing an activity even 100 times, however, may not provide the accuracy desired in the estimate. To refine this estimate, three main issues must be decided (these points are discussed later in this section, along with an example):

1. What level of statistical confidence is desired in the results?
2. How many observations are necessary?
3. Precisely when should the observations be made?

The number of observations required in a work sampling study can be fairly large, ranging from several hundred to several thousand, depending on the activity and the desired degree of accuracy. The formula for computing the required number of observations is

$$N = \frac{Z^2 p(1-p)}{E^2} \qquad \text{(S10.3)}$$

where

N = Number of observations to be made.

Z = Number of standard deviations associated with a given confidence level.

p = Estimated proportion of time that the activity being measured occurs.

E = Absolute error that is desired.

Example

For example, we want to determine what percentage of the time the front desk clerks at a hotel are idle. We want our results to be 95 percent confident within an error of 3 percent. Our initial estimate of the clerks' idle time is 20 percent.

In this example:

Z = 1.96 (corresponding to 95% confidence).

p = 0.20 (estimated percentage idle time).

E = 0.03 (absolute error).

Solution

Substituting these values into the above formula, we obtain the following:

$$N = \frac{(1.96)^2(0.2)(1-0.2)}{(0.03)^2}$$

$$N = \frac{(3.84)(0.16)}{(0.0009)}$$

$N = 682.95$ or 683 observations. (*Note:* We always round up here to ensure that we meet the minimum requirements of the study.)

Thus, with the above work sampling study, we can state that we are 95 percent confident that the true percentage of time that the clerks are idle falls within 3 percent of the study results.

However, we don't always have an initial estimate of the proportion of time spent on a given activity (in fact, that is often why we are doing the work sampling study in the first place!). In these situations, we use $p = 0.5$ which will give us a worst case scenario. (If p is equal to anything other than 0.5 we have, in effect, overestimated the sample size.)

As an illustration, suppose in the above example we don't have an initial estimate for the proportion of time the front desk clerks are idle. In this case we would use $p = 0.5$, and the calculation of the sample size would be as follows:

$$N = \frac{(1.96)^2(0.5)(1-0.5)}{(0.03)^2}$$

$$N = \frac{(3.84)(0.25)}{(0.0009)}$$

$N = 1{,}067.11$, or 1,068 observations.

The specific steps involved in conducting a work sampling study are

1. Identify the specific activity or activities that are the main purpose for the study. For example, determine the percentage of time equipment is working, idle, or under repair.
2. If it is possible, estimate the proportion of time of the activity of interest to the total time (e.g., that the equipment is working 80 percent of the time). These estimates can be made from the analyst's knowledge, past data, reliable guesses from others, or a pilot work-sampling study. If no estimate can be made, assume, as stated above, that the proportion is 0.50.
3. State the desired accuracy in the study results.
4. Determine the specific times when each observation is to be made.
5. If you are using an estimated time, recompute the required sample size at two or three intervals during the study period by using the data collected thus far. Adjust the number of observations if appropriate.

The number of observations to be taken in a work sampling study is usually divided equally over the study period. Thus, if 500 observations are to be made over a 10-day period, the observations are usually scheduled at 500/10, or 50 per day. Each day's observations are then assigned a specific time by using a random number generator. The need to divide the observations equally over the data collection period is even more important in service operations, where workers can be extremely busy during certain periods and less busy at other times.

Example

There has been a long-standing argument that a large percentage of nurses' time in a hospital is spent on non-nursing activities. This, the argument goes, creates an apparent shortage of well-trained nursing personnel, a significant waste of talent, a corresponding loss of efficiency, and increased hospital costs because nurses' wages are the highest single cost in the operation of a hospital. Further, pressure is growing for hospitals and hospital administrators to contain costs. With that in mind, let us use work sampling to test the hypothesis that a large portion of nurses' time is spent on non-nursing duties.

Assume at the outset that we have made a list of all the activities that are part of nursing and will make our observations in only two categories: nursing and non-nursing activities. (An expanded study could list all nursing activities to determine the portion of time spent in each.) Therefore, when we observe nurses during the study and find them performing one of the duties on the nursing list, we simply place a tally mark in the nursing column. If we observe a nurse doing anything besides nursing, we place a tally mark in the non-nursing column.

Solution

We now can proceed to design the work sampling study. Assume that we (or the nursing supervisor) estimate that nurses spend 60 percent of their time on nursing activities. Also assume that we would like to be 95 percent confident that the findings of our study are within the absolute error range of plus or minus 3 percent. In other words, if our study shows nurses spend 60 percent of their time on nursing duties, we are 95 percent confident that the true percentage lies between 57 and 63 percent. Using the above formula, we calculate that 1,025 observations are required for 60 percent activity time and ±3 percent error. If our study is to take place over 10 days, we start with 103 observations per day.

To determine when each day's observations are to be made, we assign specific numbers to each minute and a random number table is used to set up a schedule. If the study extends over an eight-hour shift, we can assign numbers to correspond to each consecutive minute. The list in Exhibit S10.8 shows the assignment of numbers to corresponding minutes. For simplicity, because each number corresponds to one minute, a three-number scheme is used, with the second and third numbers corresponding to the minute of the hour. A number of other schemes also would be appropriate. (If a number of studies are planned, a computer program may be used to generate a randomized schedule for the observation times.)

If we refer to a random number table and list three-digit numbers, we can assign each number to a time. The random numbers shown in Exhibit S10.9 demonstrate the procedure for seven observations.

This procedure is followed to generate 103 observation times, and the times are rearranged chronologically for ease in planning. Rearranging the times determined in Exhibit S10.9 gives the total observations per day shown in Exhibit S10.10 (for our sample of seven).

To be perfectly random in this study, we also should "randomize" the nurse we observe each time (the use of various nurses minimizes the effect of bias). In this study, our first observation is made at 7:13 AM for Nurse X. We walk into the nurse's area and check either a nursing or a non-nursing activity, depending on what we observe. Each observation need be only long enough to determine the class of activity—in most cases only a glance. At 8:04 AM we observe Nurse Y. We continue in this way to the end of the day and the 103 observations. At the end of the second day (and 206 observations), we decide to check for the adequacy of our sample size.

Exhibit S10.8

Assignment of Numbers to Corresponding Minutes

Time	Assigned Numbers
7:00–7:59 AM	100–159
8:00–8:59 AM	200–259
9:00–9:59 AM	300–359
10:00–10:59 AM	400–459
11:00–11:59 AM	500–559
12:00–12:59 PM	600–659
1:00–1:59 PM	700–759
2:00–2:59 PM	800–859

Exhibit S10.9

Determination of Observation Times

Random Number	Corresponding Time from the Preceding List
669	Nonexistent
831	2:31 PM
555	11:55 AM
470	Nonexistent
113	7:13 AM
080	Nonexistent
520	11:20 AM
204	8:04 AM
732	1:32 PM
420	10:20 AM

Exhibit S10.10

Observation Schedule

Observation	Scheduled Time	Nursing Activity (✓)	Non-Nursing Activity (✓)
1	7:13 AM		
2	8:04 AM		
3	10:20 AM		
4	11:20 AM		
5	11:55 AM		
6	1:32 PM		
7	2:31 PM		

Let's say that we made 150 observations of nurses working and 64 of them not working, which gives 70.1 percent working. Again, using the formula given above, we calculate that the required number of observations is now 895. Inasmuch as we have already taken 206 observations, we only need to take another 689 over the next eight days or 86 per day. This recalculation of the sample size should be done several times during the data collection period.

If at the end of the study we find that 66 percent of nurses' time is involved with what has been defined as nursing activities, there should be an analysis to identify the remaining 34 percent. Approximately 12 to 15 percent is justifiable for coffee breaks and personal needs, which leaves 20 to 22 percent of the time that must be justified and compared to what the industry considers ideal levels of nursing activity. To identify the non-nursing activities, a more detailed breakdown could have been originally built into the sampling plan. Otherwise, a follow-up study may be in order.

Financial Incentive Plans

The third piece of the job design equation is the paycheck. In this section we briefly review common methods for setting financial incentives.

Basic Compensation Systems

The primary forms of basic compensation are hourly pay, straight salary, piece rate, and commissions. The first two are based on time spent on the job, with individual performance ultimately rewarded by an increase in the base rate. Piece-rate plans reward on the basis of direct daily output (a worker is paid $5 a unit and if he or she produces 10 units per day, he or she earns $50). Sometimes, a guaranteed base is included in a piece-rate plan; a worker would receive this base amount regardless of output, plus his or her piece-rate bonus. (For example, the worker's hourly base pay is $8, so this coupled with $50 piece-rate earnings would give him or her $114 for an eight-hour day.) Another approach with the guaranteed base is that the worker is paid either the piece rate or the guaranteed base, whichever is higher. Commissions may be thought of as sales-based piece rates and are calculated in the same general way.

The two broad categories of financial incentive plans are individual or small group incentive plans and organizationwide plans.

Individual or Small-Group Incentive Plans

Individual and work-group plans traditionally have rewarded performance by using output (often defined by piece rates) and quality measures. Quality is accounted for by a quality adjustment factor, say percent of rework (e.g., Incentive pay = Total output × [1 − Percent deduction for rework].[1] In recent years skill development has also been rewarded. Sometimes called *pay for knowledge,* this means that a worker is compensated for learning new tasks. This is particularly important in job shops using group technology, and in banking, where supervisors' jobs require knowledge of new types of financial instruments and selling approaches.

AT&T, for example, instituted incentive programs for its managers—an Individual Incentive Award (IIA) and a Management Team Incentive Award (MTIA). The IIA provides lump-sum bonuses to outstanding performers. These outstanding performers were determined by individual performance ratings accompanied by extensive documentation. The lump-sum bonus could range between 15 and 30 percent of base pay.

MTIAs are granted to members of specific divisions or units. Appropriate division or unit goals are established at the beginning of the year. The goals include department service objectives and interdepartmental goals. A typical MTIA could call for a standard amount equivalent to 1.5 percent of wages plus overtime for the next three years based on the performance in the current year.

Organizational Plans

Profit sharing and gain sharing are the major types of organizationwide plans. *Profit sharing* is simply distributing a percentage of corporate profits across the workforce. In the United States, at least one third of all organizations have profit sharing. In Japan, most major

[1]For a complete discussion of incentive plans including quality measures, see S. Globerson and R. Parsons, "Multi-factor Incentive Systems: Current Practices," *Operations Management Review* 3, no. 2 (Winter 1985).

Operations Management in Practice

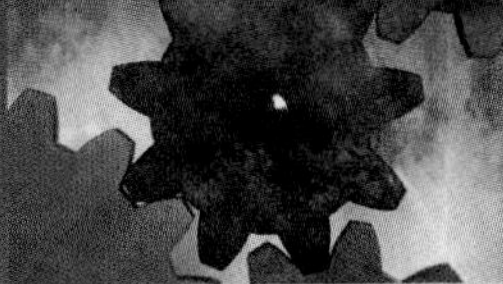

ANATOMY OF A 15-MINUTE TURNAROUND

On a recent weekday, a Southwest Airlines flight arrived at New Orleans from Houston. The scheduled arrival time was 8:00 AM, and departure for Birmingham, Alabama, was 8:15 AM. *Forbes* clocked the turnaround, half-minute by half-minute.

7:55	Ground crew chat around gate position.
8:03:30	Ground crew alerted, move to their vehicles.
8:04	Plane begins to pull into gate; crew move toward plane.
8:04:30	Plane stops; jetway telescopes out; baggage door opens.
8:06:30	Baggage unloaded; refueling and other servicing under way.
8:07	Passengers off plane.
8:08	Boarding call; baggage loading, refueling complete.
8:10	Boarding complete; most of ground crew leave.
8:15	Jetway retracts.
8:15:30	Pushback from gate.
8:18	Pushback tractor disengages; plane leaves for runway.

Source: Subrata N. Chakravarty, "Hit 'em Hardest with the Mostest" (September 16, 1991), p. 51. Reprinted by permission of FORBES Magazine © Forbes Inc., 1991.

companies give profit-based bonuses twice a year to all employees. Such bonuses may go from as high as 50 percent of salaries in good years, to nothing in bad years.

Gain sharing also involves giving organizationwide bonuses, but differs from profit sharing in two important respects: First, it typically measures controllable costs or units of output, not profits, in calculating a bonus. Second, gain sharing is always combined with a participative approach to management.

Conclusion

Most readers of this book will encounter questions of work methods and measurement in the service sector. It appears that in services, as well as in manufacturing, the new performance metric will be speed, achieved through improved work methods and teamwork. ServiceMaster, for example, has been able to dominate the institutional custodial business (hospitals, schools, and offices) by applying fast cleaning methods to such basic tasks as mopping floors and washing windows. (Rather than using cumbersome ladders to wash windows, they employ specially designed, lightweight, long-handled squeegies using easy-to-remove velcro-backed washable cleaning cloths. Between uses, the clothes are soaked in fluids developed in ServiceMaster's laboratory.) Southwest Airlines uses teamwork (involving its ground crew, baggage handlers, and flight attendants) to achieve a 15-minute turnaround of its flights. (See the OM in Practice on Anatomy of a 15-Minute Turnaround.) Interestingly enough, these examples epitomize some of the fundamental ideas that Fredrick W. Taylor introduced almost a century ago.

Key Terms

therbligs p. 421
time standard p. 429
time study p. 427
work measurement p. 426
work sampling p. 430

Review and Discussion Questions

1. Why are work measurement and time study activities still necessary today?
2. How do the latest approaches for determining time standards, as shown in the NUMMI example, fit with the concepts of worker empowerment and team work?
3. What are the major differences between work measurement and work sampling? What are the objectives in each case?
4. Is there an inconsistency when a company requires precise time standards and, at the same time, encourages job enrichment?
5. The conclusion of this chapter describes Southwest Airlines's fast flight turnarounds. What do you think has to be done inside the terminal to attain this perfomance?
6. Automated systems such as voice recognition units (VCUs) increase the efficiency of a call center, but what are the disadvantages of these systems?

Solved Problems

Problem 1

Felix Unger is a very organized person and wants to plan his day perfectly. To do this, he has his friend Oscar time his daily activities. The following are the results of Oscar timing Felix on polishing two pairs of black shoes. What is the standard time for polishing one pair? (Assume a 5 percent allowance factor for Felix to get Oscar an ashtray for his cigar. Account for noncyclically recurring elements by dividing their observed times by the total number of cycles observed.) All times shown are in minutes.

	Observed Times							
Element	**1**	**2**	**3**	**4**	**Observed Time**	$\bar{T}$	**Performance Rating**	***NT***
Get shoeshine kit	0.50						125%	
Polish each shoe	0.94	0.85	0.80	0.81			110	
Put away kit				0.75			80	

Solution

	Observed Time	$\bar{T}$	**Performance Rating**	***NT***
Get shoeshine kit	0.50	0.50/2 = 0.25	125%	0.31
Polish shoes (2 pair)	3.40	3.40/2 = 1.70	110	1.87
Put away kit	0.75	0.75/2 = 0.375	80	0.30
Normal time for one pair of shoes				2.48

Standard time for the pair = 2.48 × 1.05 = 2.61 minutes

Problem 2

A total of 15 observations have been taken on a head baker for a school district. The numerical breakdown of her activities is as follows:

Make Ready	Do	Clean Up	Idle
2	6	3	4

Based on this information, how many work sampling observations are required to determine how much of the baker's time is spent in "doing"? Assume a 5 percent desired absolute error and 95 percent confidence level.

Solution

Since 95 percent confidence is required, use $Z = 1.96$. Also,

$p =$ "Doing" $= 6/15 = 40\%$

$E = .05$ (given)

To calculate the number of observations required, we use the following formula:

$$N = \frac{Z^2 p(1-p)}{E^2} = \frac{(1.96)^2(0.4)(1-0.4)}{(0.05)^2} = 369 \text{ observations}$$

Problems

1. As a time-study analyst, you have observed that a worker has produced 40 parts in a one-hour period. From your experience, you rate the worker as performing slightly faster than 100 percent—so you estimate performance as 110 percent. The company allows 15 percent of job time for fatigue and delay.
   a. What is the normal time?
   b. What is the standard time?
   c. If a worker produces 300 units per day and has a base rate of $10.00 per hour, what would the day's wages be for this worker if the company operates on a piece-rate payment plan?
2. A time study was made of an existing job to develop new time standards. A worker was observed for a period of 45 minutes. During that period, 30 units were produced. The analyst rated the worker as performing at a 90 percent performance rate. Allowances in the firm for rest and personal time are 12 percent of job time.
   a. What is the normal time for the task?
   b. What is the standard time for the task?
   c. If the worker produced 300 units in an eight-hour day, what would the day's pay be if the basic rate was $12.00 per hour and the firm used a piece-rate payment system?
3. A time-study analysis has obtained the following performance times by observing a worker over 15 operating cycles:

Performance Number	Time (seconds)	Performance Number	Time (seconds)
1	15	9	14
2	12	10	18
3	16	11	13
4	11	12	15
5	13	13	16
6	14	14	15
7	16	15	11
8	12		

The worker was rated as performing at 115 percent. Allowances for personal time and fatigue in the company are 10 percent of job time. The base rate for the worker is $9.00 per hour and the company operates on a piece-rate payment plan.

a. What is the normal time?

b. What is the standard time?

c. If the worker produced 2,500 units in a day, what would the gross pay for the day be?

4. A work sampling study is to be conducted over the next 30 consecutive days of an activity in the city fire department. Washing trucks, which is the subject of the study, is to be observed, and it is estimated that this occurs 10 percent of the time. A 3.5 percent accuracy with 95 percent confidence is acceptable. State specifically when observations should be made on one day. Use a 10-hour day from 8:00 AM to 6:00 PM.

5. In an attempt to increase productivity and reduce costs, Rho Sigma Corporation is planning to install an incentive pay plan in its manufacturing plant.

   In developing standards for one operation, time-study analysts observed a worker for a 30-minute period. During that time the worker completed 42 parts. The analysts rated the worker as producing at 130 percent. The base wage rate of the worker is $5 per hour. The firm has established 15 percent as a fatigue and personal time allowance (as a percentage of job time).

   a. What is the normal time for the task?

   b. What is the standard time for the task?

   c. If the worker produced 500 units during an eight-hour day, what wages would the worker have earned?

6. Since new regulations will greatly change the products and services offered by savings and loan associations, time studies must be performed on tellers and other personnel to determine the number and types of personnel needed and incentive wage payment plans that might be installed.

   As an example of the studies that the various tasks will undergo, consider the following problem and come up with the appropriate answers:

   A hypothetical case was set up in which the teller (to be retitled later as an *account adviser*) was required to examine a customer's portfolio and determine whether it was more beneficial for the customer to consolidate various CDs into a single issue currently offered, or to leave the portfolio unaltered. A time study was made of the teller, with the following findings:

Time of study	90 minutes
Number of portfolios examined	10 portfolios
Performance rating	130 percent
Rest for personal time	15 percent of job time
Teller's proposed new pay rate	$12 per hour

   a. What is the normal time for the teller to do a portfolio analysis for the CDs?

   b. What is the standard time for a portfolio analysis?

   c. If the S&L decides to pay the new tellers on a "piece-rate" basis, how much would a teller earn for a day in which he or she analyzed 50 customer portfolios?

7. It is estimated that a bank teller spends about 10 percent of their time in a particular type of transaction. The bank manager would like a work-sampling study that shows, within plus or minus 3 percent, whether the clerk's time is really 10 percent (i.e., from 7 to 13 percent). The manager is well satisfied with a 95 percent confidence level.

   You estimate that, for the first "cut" at the problem, a sample size of 400 is indicated for the 10 percent activity time and ±3 percent absolute error.

   State how you would perform the work-sampling study. If the study were to be made over a five-week period with five days per week from the hours of 9:00 to 5:00, specify the exact time (in minute increments) that you would make Monday's observations.

8. The call centers of a major express delivery service receive an average of 500,000 calls a day. The average time an operator spends on the phone with a customer is 3.77 minutes, which is referred to as the average handling time (AHT). In addition, a work-sampling study revealed that the operators spend an additional 1.25 minutes per call performing other tasks related to the call, such as researching the location of a lost package.
   a. If the firm allows the operators a personal allowance factor of 15 percent of their job time, how many operators does the firm need to answer the calls for an average day?
   b. The firm has decided to institute a menu-driven call answering system, which will reduce the operator's time on the phone to 3.25 minutes, although the amount of "nontelephone time" is expected to remain the same. If the operators are paid $16.00 per hour, including fringe benefits, how much money will the new answering system save the firm on a daily basis?
9. A mail-order catalog company that specializes in high-quality outdoors clothing and accessories processes 125,000 orders a day during its peak season just before Christmas. The average time for a customer to place an order on the phone is 5.88 minutes. In addition, the customer service representative who takes the order requires an additional 2.00 minutes after completing the call to complete the necessary paperwork for the order.
   a. If the representatives are paid an average of $12.00 per hour and the firm provides them a personal allowance factor of 14 percent of total time worked, how many representatives are needed on a daily basis to take phone orders during the peak season (based upon an eight-hour work day)?
   b. Considering only the representatives' time, what is the cost to place an order?
   c. The company is currently planning to install a website that will allow customers to place orders online. If the firm receives 20 percent of its orders online, how much money will it save in labor during its three-month peak season? (Assume that the labor cost to place an order online is zero and that the peak season is 90 days long.)

Bibliography

Adler, Paul S. "Time and Motion Regained." *Harvard Business Review* 71, no. 1 (January–February 1993), pp. 97–110.

———. "The Return of the Stopwatch." *The Economist,* January 23, 1993, p. 69.

Barnes, Frank C. "Principles of Motion Economy: Revisited, Reviewed and Restored." *Proceedings of the Southern Management Association Annual Meeting,* Atlanta, GA, 1983, p. 298.

Barnes, Ralph M. *Motion and Time Study: Design and Measurement of Work.* 8th ed. New York: John Wiley & Sons, 1980.

Chakravarty, Subrata N. "Hit 'em Hardest with the Mostest." *Forbes,* September 16, 1991, p. 51.

Machalaba, Daniel. "Up to Speed: United Parcel Service Gets Deliveries Done by Driving Its Workers." *The Wall Street Journal,* April 22, 1986, p. 1.

Niebel, Benjamin W. *Motion and Time Study.* 7th ed. Homewood, IL: Richard D. Irwin, 1982.

Niles, John L. "To Increase Productivity, Audit the Old Incentive Plan." *Industrial Engineering,* January 1980, pp. 20–23.

"The Promise of Reengineering." *Fortune,* May 3, 1993, p. 96.

Smalley, Harold E., and John Freeman. *Hospital Industrial Engineering.* New York: Reinhold, 1966, p. 409.

Case

Up to Speed: United Parcel Service Gets Deliveries Done by Driving Its Workers

Grabbing a package under his arm, Joseph Polise, a driver for United Parcel Service (UPS), bounds from his brown delivery truck and toward an office building here. A few paces behind him, Marjorie Cusack, a UPS industrial engineer, clutches a digital timer.

Her eyes fixed on Mr. Polise, she counts his steps and times his contact with customers. Scribbling on a clipboard, Mrs. Cusack records every second taken up by stoplights, traffic, detours, doorbells, walkways, stairways, and coffee breaks. "If he goes to the bathroom, we time him," she says.

Such attention to detail is nothing new at UPS, the nation's largest deliverer of packages. Through meticulous human-engineering and close scrutiny of its 152,000 employees, the privately held company, which is based in Greenwich, Connecticut, has grown highly profitable despite stiff competition. In fact, UPS is one of the most efficient companies anywhere, productivity experts say.

"You never see anybody sitting on his duff at UPS," says Bernard La Londe, a transportation professor at The Ohio State University. "The only other place you see the same commitment to productivity is at Japanese companies."

Getting Up to Speed

At UPS, more than 1,000 industrial engineers use time studies to set standards for a myriad of closely supervised tasks. Drivers are instructed to walk to a customer's door at the brisk pace of three feet per second and to knock first lest seconds be lost searching for the doorbell. Supervisors then ride with the "least best drivers" until they learn to finish on time. "It's human nature to get away with as much as possible," says Michael Kamienski, a UPS district manager. "But we bring workers up to our level of acceptance. We don't go down to their level."

If UPS isn't quite a throwback to old-time work measurement, it nevertheless runs counter to the drift of many U.S. companies. To increase productivity, others are turning more often to employee-involvement techniques that stress consultation and reject the rigid monitoring of workers.

"Workers are better educated and want more to say about what happens to them," says Roger Weiss, a vice president of H. B. Maynard & Co., a consulting concern. "Time study is a dark-ages technique, and it's dehumanizing to track someone around with a stopwatch."

UPS dismisses the criticism. "We don't use the standards as hammers, but they do give accountability," says Larry P. Breakiron, the company's senior vice president for engineering. "Our ability to manage labor and hold it accountable is the key to our success."

New Competition

Those techniques are about to be tested. Long engaged in a battle for parcels with the U.S. Postal Service, UPS recently has charged into overnight delivery against Federal Express

Corporation, Purolator Courier, Airborne Freight, Emery Air Freight, and others. What's more, it now is being challenged on its own turf by Roadway Services Inc., which in the early 1990s started a parcel delivery company called Roadway Package System that is implementing management ideas of its own.

The upstart competitor boasts that its owner-operator drivers, unlike UPS's closely scrutinized, but highly paid and unionized, drivers, are motivated by the challenge of running their own business. "Our people don't drive brown trucks; they own their trucks," says Ivan Hoffman, a vice president of Roadway.

Roadway also is trying to gain the edge in productivity by eliminating people as much as possible through automation. Its package hubs use bar codes, laser scanners, computers, and special mechanical devices to sort packages, a task still handled at UPS by armies of workers. UPS calls its rival's methods unreliable, inflexible, and expensive. Those are the same epithets that Roadway hurls at UPS's human sorters.

The outcome of this budding competition interests package shippers. "UPS has taken the engineering of people as far as it can be taken," says Michael Birkholm, the director of transportation of American Greetings Corporation. "But the question is whether technologically sophisticated Roadway can dent the big brown UPS machine."

Burgeoning Competition

If the competition intensifies, productivity improvements will be at the heart of UPS's counterattack. Indeed, UPS long has used efficiency to overcome rivals. Founded in Seattle in 1907 as a messenger service, UPS over the years won parcel deliveries from department stores and captured package business once handled by the U.S. Postal Service because of its lower rates and superior service.

UPS's founder, James E. Casey, put a premium on efficiency. In the 1920s, he turned to Frank B. Gilbreth and other pioneers of time study to develop techniques to measure the time consumed each day by each UPS driver. Later, UPS engineers cut away the sides of a UPS delivery truck, or "package car" as the company calls the vehicle, to study a driver at work. Resultant changes in package loading techniques increased efficiency 30 percent.

Mr. Casey also shaped the company culture, which stresses achievement and teamwork in addition to efficiency. Copies of his tract, "Determined Men," and of "Pursuit of Excellence," a pamphlet written by one-time UPS Chairman George Smith, are handed out to the company's managers. "We still use Jim's and George's quotes in everything we do," says George Lamb Jr., a UPS director and past chairman.

Another guiding principle: a fair day's work for a fair day's pay. The company's drivers, all of them Teamsters, earn wages of $15 an hour, about $1 more than the best-paid drivers at other trucking companies earn. With overtime, many UPS drivers gross $35,000 to $40,000 a year.

In return, UPS seeks maximum output from its drivers, as is shown by the time study Mrs. Cusack is conducting. On this day in suburban Whippany, she determines time allowances for each of Polise's 120 stops while watching for inefficiency in his methods. "What are you doing, Joe?" she asks as Mr. Polise wastes precious seconds handling packages more than once. She says that a mere 30 seconds wasted at each stop can snowball into big delays by day's end.

Some UPS drivers with nicknames such as Ace, Hammer, Slick, and Rocket Shoes take pride in meeting the standards day after day. "We used to joke that a good driver could

Case

get to his stop and back to the car before the seat belt stopped swaying," Mrs. Cusack says. (UPS has since redesigned its seat belts to eliminate sway.)

But not all UPS drivers enjoy the pace. For example, Michael Kipila, a driver in East Brunswick, New Jersey, says, "They squeeze every ounce out of you. You're always in a hurry, and you can't work relaxed." Some drivers say they cut their breaks in order to finish on time.

UPS officials maintain that the company's work standards are not just a matter of increasing output, but of making the job easier. "If you do it our way, you'll be less tired at the end of the day," says a UPS spokesman.

Had Enough

The pressure causes some UPS employees—supervisors and drivers alike—to quit. Jose Vega, a former UPS supervisor, says he would ride with one New York driver, noting each time "pace too slow, customer contact too long." Vega says he tried to embarrass the driver so as to speed him up: "Are you falling asleep? Do you want a sleeping bag?" After a while, "it's like you're abusing this person," says Vega, who now drives for Roadway.

"There's a fine line between motivation and harassment, and many times UPS crosses that line," says Mario Perrucci, the secretary-treasurer of Teamsters Local 177 in Hillside, New Jersey. Mr. Perrucci has battled UPS for years over a requirement that drivers tap their horns when they approach a stop in the hopes that the customer will hurry to the door seconds sooner.

UPS's efforts to increase productivity get mixed reactions from the Teamsters union. While some local Teamsters officials such as Perrucci say that UPS is driving its workers "beyond endurance," the union's national executives are grateful that the company is successful. "I'd rather see UPS pushing the men too hard," says a Teamsters official in Washington, "than see UPS in bankruptcy court."

Many trucking companies employing Teamsters are shutting down or, like Roadway Package System, turning to nonunion workers. But UPS continues to be the largest single employer of Teamsters members, with more than 100,000 unionized workers, a 33 percent rise since 1980.

A Game of Inches

To sustain growth, UPS executives are looking for new efficiencies. For example, they are seeking to make work standards for truck mechanics more exact. And at UPS's Parsippany, New Jersey, package sorting hub, 1 of more than 100 that the company operates, officials are making the most of space by parking delivery trucks just five inches apart. But productivity has its price. New York City says that UPS drivers have received more than $1 million in unpaid parking tickets since March 1985 while making local deliveries. A company attorney says the amount is "much too high." UPS has contested the fines.

The new competition from Roadway Package System also looms large. Roadway is cutting labor expenses 20 percent to 30 percent by using independent drivers. Because Roadway drivers buy their own trucks, uniforms, and insurance, Roadway is saving money that it is using to automate package sorting. "We'll use technology to be the low-cost producer," says Bram Johnson, a Roadway vice president.

Roadway says it reduced personnel 25 percent at its five sorting hubs through automation. At its York, Pennsylvania, hub, for example, a moving belt of tilt trays following instructions from a computer drops packages down a series of chutes.

Questions

1. Describe the UPS approach to job design and work measurement.
2. What are the advantages and disadvantages of the UPS approach?
3. What would you do differently? Why?

Source: Daniel Machalaba, "Up to Speed: United Parcel Service Gets Deliveries Done by Driving Its Workers." Reprinted by permission of *The Wall Street Journal,* April 22, 1986, p. 1.

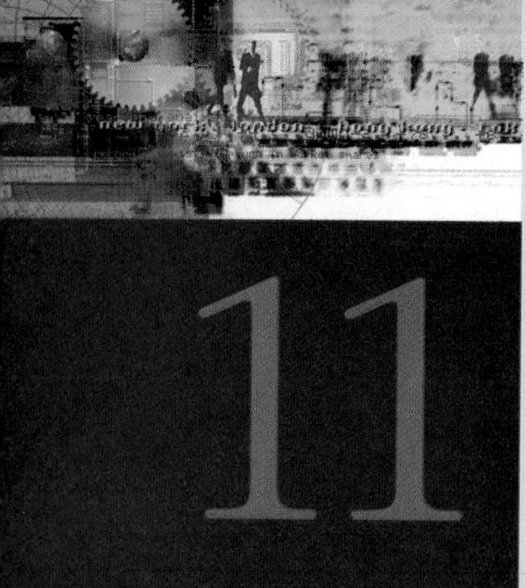

11 Waiting Line Management

Chapter Objectives

- Emphasize the importance of providing fast service as a competitive advantage to companies.
- Show the relationship between customer expectations, customer perceptions, and customer satisfaction as they pertain to waiting time.
- Identify the various factors that can affect customer satisfaction with waiting time and provide a framework for showing managers which of these factors are under their control.
- Demonstrate how service managers can design their operations and train their employees to provide faster service without incurring any additional costs.
- Illustrate how technology can assist companies in providing faster service to their customers.

You drive your car into the Hertz rental lot at the West Palm Beach, Florida, airport. As you begin to remove your luggage from the car, a service attendant greets you and asks for a copy of your rental car contract. The attendant quickly enters the contract number into a hand-held terminal, which prints a receipt before you have removed all of your luggage. Without further ado, you board the Hertz bus that takes you to your airline terminal.

At the Marriott Hotel in Newton, Massachusetts, guests who have preregistered can go directly to a self-service key rack to pick up their room keys and then can proceed directly to their rooms without the aggravation of waiting in line at the check-in desk. Guests who want to avoid the hassle of waiting in line to check out at Bally's Hotel in Las Vegas can take advantage of the express check-out feature available on the television in each room. A guest simply follows menu-driven options on the television screen. The final bill is then totaled and charged to the proper credit card. The guest simply deposits the room key in a box on the way out.

These examples illustrate a growing trend among companies in general, and service firms in particular, to provide continually faster service, and in some cases, as noted above, even totally eliminating customer waiting time.

Managerial Issues

Customer waiting lines are a fact of life that every service manager must address. Even with manufacturing companies, as technology in the form of the Internet brings customers closer to the factory, customer waiting issues take on increasing importance with respect to product delivery and subsequent customer service support. Dell computer provides a good example of this. Waiting lines occur when customers interact directly with a process. Waiting lines can take various forms: from waiting in line to be seated at a restaurant, to waiting in the checkout line at the supermarket, to waiting on the telephone to request service for a product that you purchased. Waiting also can take place on the Internet, whether it is to conduct a stock transaction, or to get your checking account balance from your bank, or to buy a book at Amazon.com.

Virtually every day we spend much of our time waiting in lines of one form or another. On our way to work in the morning, we wait in line to pay the toll on the turnpike and wait in line to park our car. If we take public transportation, we wait for the bus or the train. We wait for our coffee at our favorite morning eatery, we wait for the elevator to take us up to our office—and all of this happens before we even start work! As seen in Exhibit 11.1, we spend a good deal of our time waiting in lines.

actual waiting time

Time, as measured by a stopwatch, of how long a customer has waited prior to receiving service.

Managers need to properly manage these waiting times to ensure not only that their operations are efficient, but also that their customers are not so negatively affected by the wait that they take their future business elsewhere. To accomplish this, managers need to recognize that good waiting line management consists of two major components: the **actual waiting time** itself and the customer's **perceived waiting time.**

perceived waiting time

Amount of time customers believe they have waited prior to receiving service.

The determination of actual waiting times is presented in the supplement to this chapter, which focuses on queuing theory and mathematical waiting line models for a variety of service delivery system configurations.

Improving the level of customer satisfaction by managing the customer's perceived waiting time is the primary focus of this chapter. Understanding how customer satisfaction can be increased for a given waiting time provides service managers with an opportunity for managing their operations more effectively.

"I HAVE A BAD FEELING ABOUT THIS . . . THE HOLD MUSIC IS '100 BOTTLES OF BEER ON THE WALL.'"

Source: Reprinted courtesy of Bunny Hoest and *Parade Magazine.*

Waiting lines are usually the first encounter a customer will experience with an organization. Consequently, an unpleasant experience waiting in line often can have a negative *halo effect* on the rest of a customer's experience with a particular firm. How well managers address the waiting line issue is therefore critical to the long-term success of their firms.

The Importance of Good Service

As stated previously in Chapter 2, those companies in both manufacturing and service operations that provide outstanding service to their customers can achieve a competitive advantage in the marketplace in today's highly competitive environment. And good service begins when the customer first comes in contact with an organization and waits in some type of line or queue prior to being served. There are many factors that contribute to good service, such as the friendliness and knowledge of workers, but customers' experiences with waiting lines, which are often their initial encounter with a firm, can significantly affect their overall level of satisfaction with the organization.

Providing ever-faster service, with the ultimate goal of having zero customer waiting time, has recently received managerial attention for several reasons. First, in the more highly developed countries, where standards of living are rising, time becomes more valuable as a commodity and, consequently, customers are less willing to wait for service. As a result, customers in many cases are willing to pay a premium price to those firms that minimize their waiting time. (See OM in Practice box on Disney's Theme Parks.)

Another reason for this increased emphasis on providing fast and efficient service is the realization by organizations that how they treat their customers today significantly impacts on whether or not they will remain loyal customers tomorrow. This differs from the past, when the treatment of customers in the present was viewed to be independent of any potential future sales. This antiquated perspective has persisted because the impact of future customer behavior does not appear anywhere on the firm's financial statements.

Finally, advances in technology, especially in information technology, have provided firms with the ability to provide faster service than was previously possible. Fax machines, computers, e-mail, and satellite communications provide firms with this new capability to respond faster to the customer.

Exhibit 11.1

How People Spend Their Time

A survey of 6,000 people in the United States that tried to identify the amount of time the average American spends during a lifetime on various activities revealed the following:

Activity	Amount of Time
Sitting at stop lights	Six months
Opening junk mail	Eight months
Looking for misplaced objects	One year
Unsuccessfully returning telephone calls	Two years
Doing housework	Four years
Waiting in line	**Five years**
Eating	Six years

Source: From "Where the Time Goes," *U.S. News & World Report*, January 30, 1989, p. 81. Copyright 1989 *U.S. News and World Report*, L. P. Reprinted with permission.

Operations Management in Practice

TIME IS MONEY AT DISNEY'S THEME PARKS

Everyone goes to Disney theme parks. Everyone has to wait in lines. (Well, almost everyone.) And most people hate to wait in these lines.

Now some people have ways to avoid these lines. Disney's policy is that everyone is a VIP, but the reality is that some are more VIP than others.

For an additional cost of $50–$60 per ticket, you can buy a theme park VIP tour. This will get you special privileges such as viewing shows from preferred seating to a personal escort on and off certain attractions. This service isn't very widely known, and you almost have to jump through hoops to obtain it.

Another way to avoid waiting lines is to be a celebrity or top business executive. Disney reasons that the top executive or celebrity is an attraction in and of itself, and tries to let that celebrity enjoy his or her stay at the park as well as retaining a modicum of anonymity.

Another way to get this so-called star treatment is to work for a company that sponsors the ride. It just takes a little savvy, like having a business card from your organization, knowing how to ask the right people with the right words, and you're there! Other rides (that your company may not be affiliated with) are available simply by networking.

Yet another way of avoiding these waiting lines is to spend big bucks at the hotel. Just put down an extra $300 a night for a stay on one of the special concierge floors and your concierge may even jump through hoops to accommodate your wishes and give you special passes.

The best way to endure a theme park, unless you're exceptionally rich or a very special person? Grin and bear it, and wait in line. Who knows? You might even meet a new friend.

In providing fast service, however, the real goal of service managers should not be to ensure that customers are served within a specified time (e.g., a stated number of minutes), but rather to ensure that customers are sufficiently satisfied with the level of service provided so that they will want to return in the future.

Customer Waiting Time versus Process Efficiency: The Trade-Off in Waiting Line Management

The classical operations management model relating service and cost, illustrated in Exhibit 11.2, shows the trade-off between the cost of providing fast service and the cost of having the customer wait. This trade-off between providing high levels of customer service (i.e., fast service) and obtaining high worker productivity results from the direct interaction of the customer with the service-producing process. Although easily understood in theory, this model is not easily applied to real-world situations, due primarily to the difficulty associated with measuring the cost of having a customer wait, particularly when we are dealing with external customers (that is, customers who buy the goods and services offered by the firm). With internal customers (that is, workers within the company that require a particular service), such as a truck driver waiting for an order to deliver or a worker waiting in line to use a copy machine, the cost of waiting is much easier to measure. In these cases, the cost of waiting is the time lost by the worker while waiting in line multiplied by that worker's hourly wage. (Several examples of waiting-time costs relative to internal customers are presented in the supplement to this chapter.)

In comparing a service operation with a manufacturing firm, customers waiting for service are often viewed as being analogous to inventory in a manufacturing process. Thus, a service firm that increases its process efficiency by having customers wait for service parallels a manufacturing firm that increases its process efficiency by maintaining a work-in-process

The Internet continues to be an increasingly important tool of companies in providing fast and convenient service to customers. The ability to shop, make reservations, and get information at any time and any place without a service representative has dramatically changed how we do business.

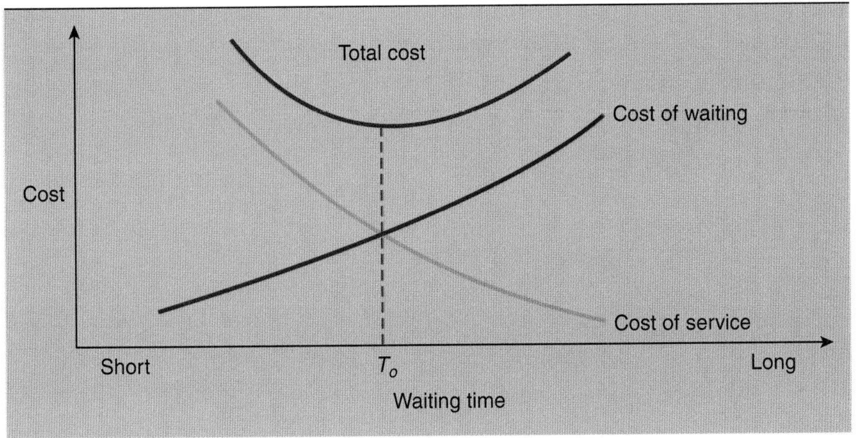

Exhibit 11.2

The Trade-Off in Waiting Line Management

inventory. In both instances, management faces a trade-off between improving process efficiency and increasing waiting time or inventory. The difference between the two, however, is that in the manufacturing facility, the parts that are waiting are inanimate objects, whereas in the service operation they are actual people in the form of customers.

An inherent assumption in the model presented in Exhibit 11.2 is that the contact workers or available service capacity remain idle when there are no customers to serve. The basis for this assumption lies in queuing theory (which is discussed in detail in the supplement to this chapter), which establishes the mathematical relationship between the number of servers or stations assigned and the average customer waiting time for a given level of demand. With this traditional approach to waiting line management, there exists an "optimal" waiting time, T_o, that minimizes the sum of the two cost components: the cost of having a customer wait and the cost of providing service. However, as presented later in this chapter, there are a variety of ways that service managers can reduce customer waiting times without increasing costs.

Defining Customer Satisfaction

The customer's direct involvement in the service delivery system suggests a need to integrate both marketing and operations perspectives into the service system's design and evaluation. A marketing-related measure of customer reaction to waiting time would more clearly indicate the true customer waiting costs instead of just the actual waiting time itself. **Customer satisfaction** appears to be the marketing measure that fulfills this need.

customer satisfaction

Measure of the customer's reaction to a specific service encounter.

Definition of Customer Satisfaction

Drawing on work done in marketing, we define customer satisfaction as being directly related to the comparison between a **customer's expectations** of a service's performance and that customer's perception of that performance. In other words, if the perceived performance meets expectations, then the customer is satisfied; if it exceeds expectations by a large amount, then the customer is highly satisfied or delighted; if the performance falls significantly short of expectations, then the customer is dissatisfied. In marketing terminology, satisfaction is said to be directly related to the **disconfirmation** (i.e., difference) between the customer's expected and perceived performance of the service.

customer's expectations

Preconceived notions of what will occur at a service operation, often influenced by prior experience, advertising, and word-of-mouth.

Customer satisfaction is a good measure of how effective the delivery system is, because it appears to provide the necessary linkage between the level of service that the company is currently providing to a customer, the customer's perception of that service, and the customer's future behavior toward the firm. Oliver suggests that customer satisfaction is part of an overall model of customer behavior that develops over time, as shown in Exhibit 11.3.

Exhibit 11.3

The Role of Satisfaction in a Customer Behavior Model

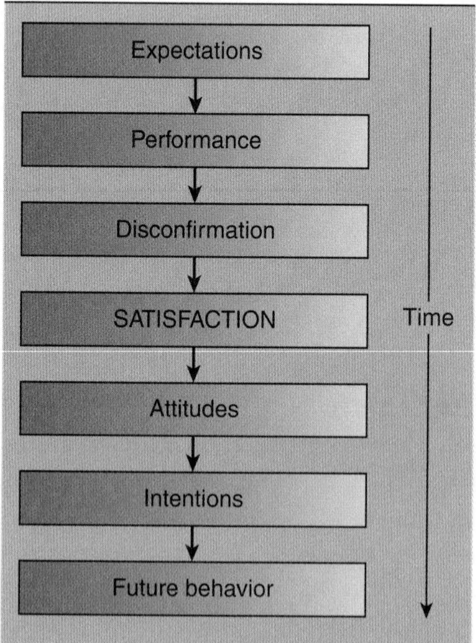

Source: Reprinted with permission from the *Journal of Marketing Research* 17 by the American Marketing Association, R. L. Oliver, "The Role of Satisfaction in a Customer Behavior Model," November 1980.

Customer Expectations

disconfirmation

Marketing measure of the difference between a customer's expectations from an operation and a customer's perception of its performance.

Customer expectations are defined as the customers' preconceived notions of what level of service they should receive from a particular service business or organization. Expectations can be derived from several sources.

One source of expectations is advertising. Many restaurants, for example, promise in their advertising that your lunch will be served in 10 minutes or less. Thus, if you have to wait longer than 10 minutes, you will be dissatisfied; if your wait is much less than 10 minutes, you will be very satisfied. Expectations also can be predicated on the customer's prior experience with the company. Additional sources of expectations include word-of-mouth and previous experiences with similar types of operations.

The overall service delivery package also influences a customer's expectations with waiting time. People tend to associate little or no waiting with upscale or higher-priced services. These types of operations, therefore, often require appointments or reservations to ensure minimal, if any, waiting. The degree of customization provided to each customer is another factor that can influence expectations. The more a service is customized, the longer a customer might expect to wait.

"IF TIME REALLY HEALS ALL WOUNDS, I SHOULD BE CURED BY NOW."

Source: Reprinted courtesy of Bunny Hoest and *Parade Magazine.*

Perceived Waiting Time

Perceived waiting time is the amount of time customers believe they have waited before receiving service. While this is directly related to the actual time a customer waits, there are often significant differences between the two. In fact, studies have shown that perceived waiting time has a greater impact in determining customer satisfaction than does actual waiting time.[1] As we will discuss later in this chapter, management can have an influence on a customer's perceived waiting time if it has an understanding of the factors that affect it.

To illustrate the difference between perceived waiting time and actual waiting time, we look at the example of a newly designed hotel that was built with insufficient elevator

[1]Mark M. Davis and Janelle Heineke, "How Disconfirmation, Perception and Actual Waiting Times Impact Customer Satisfaction," *International Journal of Service Industry Management* 9, no. 1 (1998), pp. 64–73.

capacity, especially in the morning hours when most guests were in a hurry to check out. Customer complaints about the long waits for elevators to take them to the ground floor prompted management to hire a consultant to reduce these waits. The consultant developed a scheduling algorithm for the elevators that significantly reduced the waiting times, but guest complaints still persisted. Another consultant was hired, who suggested placing full-length mirrors on both sides of the elevator doors on every floor. This was done and miraculously the complaints stopped, even though there was no further decrease in the actual waiting time. Why? Because the guests, after pushing the elevator button, now had something to occupy their time, and consequently weren't as cognizant of their wait for the elevator.[2]

Factors Affecting Customer Satisfaction with Waiting[3]

As stated previously, service managers should focus on improving the customer's level of satisfaction with waiting rather than the actual waiting time itself. Maister[4] presented an initial framework for focusing on customer satisfaction with waiting, identifying many of the factors that can affect satisfaction. To further assist the service manager, these factors can be classified into three categories: (*a*) firm-related factors, (*b*) customer-related factors, and (*c*) both firm- and customer-related factors. Service managers, in order to effectively manage the customer's waiting time, must distinguish between those factors over which they have total or at least partial control from those over which they have no control at all.

Firm-Related Factors

Factors that fall primarily within the firm's control can be grouped into four types of waits: unfair versus fair waits, uncomfortable versus comfortable waits, unexplained versus explained waits, and initial versus subsequent waits.

Unfair versus Fair Waits The successful management of the customer's perception of fairness with respect to waiting is dependent on queue design, service system design, and contact hours.

A popular approach, to ensure fairness, is to group all customers into a single queue or line. When more than one server is available, the first person in line moves to the next server that is free. This method has been adopted by many bank and airline check-in counters. Not only is the combined queue perceived as fairer, but the average wait also has been shown to be considerably shorter, even though the line itself is longer. However, managers also need to take into consideration the physical elements of the operating system. For example, the physical space required by customers and their shopping carts has precluded most supermarkets from adopting the combined queue approach.

More subtle elements of service system design, beyond the physical waiting, also can affect customer perceptions of fairness. Interruptions by telephone calls during busy periods,

---

[2]W. E. Sasser, R. P. Olsen, and D. D. Wyckoff, *Management of Service Operations: Text, Cases and Readings* (Boston: Allyn and Bacon, 1978).

[3]Adapted from Mark M. Davis and Janelle Heineke, "Understanding the Roles of the Customer and the Operation for Better Queue Management," *International Journal of Operations and Production Management* 14, no. 5 (1994), pp. 21–34.

David Maister, "The Psychology of Waiting Lines," in *The Service Encounter,* ed. J. A. Czepiel, M. R. Solomon, and C. F. Surprenant (Lexington, MA: Lexington Books, D.C. Heath & Co., 1985).

for example, give the impression (which is correct!) that the answered call is receiving priority treatment.

So that customers do not perceive unfair treatment due to their watches being off by a few minutes, the actual hours of operation that a service is open for business should exceed the posted hours. For example, if a retail operation has posted hours of 10:00 AM to 10:00 PM, then the store should be ready to receive customers and the doors unlocked at 9:50 AM, and the doors should not be closed until 10:10 PM.

Uncomfortable versus Comfortable Waits It is common sense that when one is uncomfortable, time passes more slowly. There are many ways in which service organizations can affect comfort: temperature, lighting, seating, and sound levels should all be considered. Comfort and fairness often can be combined when a "take a number" system is employed. Full-service restaurants recognize the importance of comfort by providing a lounge in which customers can wait prior to being seated. This is a good example of a win–win situation. The restaurant gains additional sales from drinks sold to waiting customers, and the customers enjoy a pleasant and comfortable environment in which to wait for their tables.

Unexplained versus Explained Waits Customer dissatisfaction with waiting increases when the waits cannot be justified or explained. For example, when airline passengers are informed that they must wait for equipment arrival, for the weather to clear, or for the wings of their plane to be de-iced, they are less likely to be dissatisfied than if no explanation is given for the delay. A word of caution, however, is necessary here. The repeated use of the same reason, no matter how valid it is, eventually will negate any benefits gained from the explanation.

Unused capacity in terms of either idle workers or idle stations is another form of unexplained waits that increases the customer's level of dissatisfaction. Although there are many justifiable reasons for apparently idle capacity (e.g., worker rest breaks, the need to complete important off-line tasks, etc.), the customer should not be expected to recognize these. Consequently, workers on rest breaks should not be within the customer's view. Thus, idle service workers and service stations should be "camouflaged" when not in use.[5]

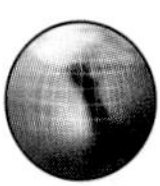

Waits of unknown duration always seem longer than waits of known duration. This relates, in part, to a customer's anxiety with waiting. Thus, it is important to provide customers with an estimate of the wait. As an example, London's subway system, often referred to as "The Tube," provides signage at every station that displays how many minutes it will be before the next train arrives. When the actual waits cannot be determined, updates or status reports at predetermined intervals can be acceptable substitutes. For example, Federal Express reports back to a customer before the close of each business day with an update on the status of the search for a lost package.

Initial versus Subsequent Waits As Maister points out, customers tend to become more dissatisfied with initial waits prior to entering a service delivery system than they are with subsequent waits after they are in the system. An example of an initial wait is the wait to place an order at a fast-food restaurant (versus the wait while the order is actually being filled). Another example is the wait while a telephone is ringing (versus the wait after the phone has been answered and you are "waiting for the next available customer service

[5]Richard B. Chase, "The Ten Commandments of Service System Management," *Interfaces* 15, no. 3 (May–June 1985).

representative"). This can be due to the fact that during the initial wait, customers see themselves as being outside the system, whereas after the initial service has been received they consider themselves to be within the system and, therefore, will be served. Thus firms should emphasize minimizing a customer's initial wait when designing the service delivery system.

Customer-Related Factors

There are some factors that affect a customer's satisfaction with waiting time that a firm cannot control. For example, how customers arrive, and the various moods they are in when they do, cannot be controlled by the firm, but an awareness of these factors and how they can contribute to dissatisfaction with waiting can help the service manager to better control those aspects of the wait that are manageable.

Solo versus Group Waits People waiting in line by themselves tend to grow more impatient with the wait in comparison to people waiting in groups. Although this is not something that can be changed by the service organization, recognition of this fact may suggest service-appropriate distractions or alternatives. Ski areas provide a good example in their lift lines, where there is usually a separate line for single skiers, and this line is typically much shorter than those for couples or larger groups. Here is another case of designing the service delivery system in such a way as to create a win–win situation. The single skier has a much shorter waiting time, and the ski area can take maximum advantage of its lift capacity during periods of peak demand by using single skiers to fill otherwise empty seats as they appear.

Waits for More Valuable versus Less Valuable Services When a product, be it a good or a service, is perceived to be of high value, customers are willing to wait longer than they would if they perceived the product to be of lower value. In other words, the perceived value of the product is large enough that customers are willing to absorb some of the cost in the form of waiting time. Firms should be forewarned, however, that in today's highly competitive environment, the ability to make customers wait extraordinarily long times will quickly result in a loss of market share to those competitors that provide the same or similar products in a shorter amount of time.

Customer Value Systems Businesses need to recognize the importance of segmenting the market by customer value systems. Customers who place a premium on obtaining fast service do not mind paying for it, and these same customers do not want to waste their time, for example, on self-service, menu-driven service systems that many companies now provide, particularly with respect to telephone inquiries. To assure consistency from a customer's perspective, the market focus on the firm therefore also must be incorporated into its operational strategy for waiting line management. The importance of doing this is recognized by Ritz-Carlton Hotels, which focuses on the top 5 percent of the hotel industry. Consequently, a real person answers the telephone when you call to make a reservation.

Customer's Current Attitude The attitudes of customers just prior to entering the service operation can have a significant impact on their level of satisfaction with the service they receive. If customers enter the service operation upset, they are more likely to be dissatisfied with their wait, regardless of its length. This type of halo effect also will impact the customers' perception of all facets of the goods and/or services that they receive.

At Disney World in Florida, customers wait to ride Big Thunder Mountain Railroad. At the Disney theme parks, long lines are managed creatively. Posted signs estimate wait times while TV monitors provide entertainment. Guests are occupied by moving under runaway railroad cars, within Space Mountain, or through theaters with movie memorabilia.

Both Firm- and Customer-Related Factors

There are some factors that relate to a customer's satisfaction with waiting that can be influenced by both the firm and the customer.

Unoccupied versus Occupied Waits As illustrated with the example of the mirrors beside the elevator doors earlier in this chapter, customers who are unoccupied tend to perceive longer waiting times than do customers who are occupied during their waits. There are many options that are available to occupy a customer's time in line: reading material, interesting displays, mirrors, and music all have been demonstrated to be useful. For example, gambling casinos do an excellent job of keeping customers occupied while they are waiting to enter their nightclubs. These waiting lines wend their way through the slot machine areas of the casino, creating another win–win situation: customers are kept occupied and slot machine revenues are increased.

Under certain circumstances, customers also can be kept busy while waiting in line doing meaningful activities that can improve the efficiency of the service. For example, customers waiting in line in a retail store can be informed, through the proper signage, of what they have to do to process a payment other than cash. Another approach to keeping customers occupied while waiting is to provide a waiting environment in which they can productively be working on their own tasks. Airport lounges with tables or private areas equipped with fax machines, PCs, and so forth, are good examples of this.

Keeping customers occupied while they are waiting also applies to telephone callers. For example, callers are prepared to wait 20 percent longer if they are entertained by music than if they are left listening to a repeated message that says, "I'm sorry, the line is busy, please hold." In addition, messages delivered during the wait that leave the customers informed and/or entertained work better than those that deliver a hard sell.[6]

[6]Richard Tomkins, "Hold on, We'll Play You a Tune," *Financial Times,* February 12, 1999, p. 28.

Anxious versus Calm Waits Customer anxiety regarding the nature of the service or the uncertainty of the wait can affect customer satisfaction. Any wait in a hospital emergency room or to hear the results from an important medical test may seem interminable, regardless of the actual length of the wait. Service organizations cannot totally eliminate the customer's anxiety associated with these types of waits, but they can, nevertheless, look critically at the nature of the service that they provide and take the necessary steps to try to reduce customer anxiety in such situations. Providing reading material that both occupies the wait and simultaneously explains the procedure to be followed can be very effective in reducing the customer's anxiety and the associated level of impatience with the wait.

A Focus on Providing Fast Service

As the OM in Practice box about MBNA clearly illustrates, leading-edge companies now focus on providing ever-better and ever-faster service to their customers. From an operations perspective, this can be accomplished in several ways, all of which center around good system design concepts.

Service System Design Concepts

front-of-the-house

Portion of the service operation that is in full sight of the customer.

back-of-the-house

Behind-the-scenes portion of the service operation which with the customer does not come into contact.

Early service system design theory advocated the splitting of the delivery system into two cores, with the goal of reducing customer contact time, thereby increasing the speed of delivery and the efficiency of the operation. With this approach, the first core, or **front-of-the-house,** interacts directly with the customer and consequently adopts a chase strategy. The second core, or **back-of-the-house,** includes all of those functions that can be accomplished without the presence of the customer, and therefore can be performed more efficiently with a level-type strategy. (Both chase and level strategies are explained in detail in Chapter 15 on "Aggregate Planning." Simply stated, a chase strategy is one in which the production in a given time period, be it a week or a month, exactly matches or "chases" the demand. This is the case with services where the delivery of the service must coincide with the customer's demand for that service. A level strategy, on the other hand, averages the demand over a specified number of periods, say four weeks or six months. This average is then the amount that is produced in each time period, thereby "leveling production," regardless of what the actual demand is in any given period.) McDonald's provides an excellent example of this split core strategy, with packaged hamburgers in the bins acting as a buffer inventory between the two stages.

However, by adopting a properly designed concept that combines the back-of-the-house operations with those in the front-of-the-house, service workers can be kept productively occupied during idle periods when there are no customers to wait on. With a well-designed facility, service workers can answer telephones or perform nontime-dependent tasks during these idle periods.

Reduced Setup Times When the back-of-the-house and the front-of-the-house are integrated, benefits also can be accrued by reducing the setup times required when a worker has to switch from one job function to another. This switching can occur frequently in a service operation whenever a customer requires service. Such reductions in setup times permit the service manager to reassign workers from time-dependent tasks, such as waiting on customers, to nontime-dependent tasks, such as cleaning and paperwork, or restocking inventories, and vice versa, without incurring any additional costs.

Operations Management in Practice

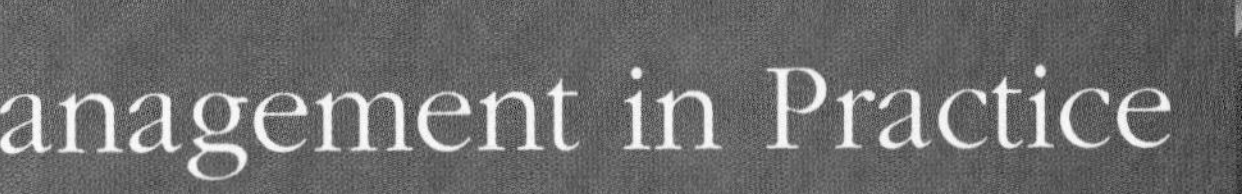

MBNA IS TRULY A SPEED FREAK

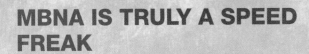

MBNA, the Wilmington, Delaware, credit card company, has developed a very loyal customer base due, in large part, to its ability to provide outstanding service. To accomplish this, MBNA has developed 15 different measures of performance, many of which pertain directly to speed. For example, customer address changes must be processed within one day; telephones must be answered within two rings; switchboard calls must be transferred to the appropriate individual within 21 seconds. State-of-the-art technology allows MBNA to monitor performance on a continuous basis. At any given moment it is possible to obtain a performance measurement that shows, for example, that employees are achieving "two-ring pick-up" 99.7 percent of the time, as shown in the picture. The current standard for the minimum level of service that is acceptable for each of the 15 performance measures is 98.5 percent, which was increased recently from 98.0 percent and is significantly up from 10 years ago when it was 90 percent.

Source: J. Martin and J. E. Davis, "Are You as Good as You Think?" *Fortune,* September 30, 1996.

Credit card issuer MBNA sets up scoreboards in its various offices to keep employees up to speed on how quickly they're serving customers.

The key to successfully adopting these concepts is that there are sufficient nontime-dependent functions available to be accomplished during the idle periods. This can be arranged, to a large extent, by carefully designing the service delivery system from the beginning.

Cross-Training of Employees An integral part of providing a fast and efficient service operation is the flexibility of the service workers, in terms of their ability to perform a variety of tasks. With broader job skills, these workers can perform additional, noncustomer-related tasks during idle periods as they occur throughout the workday. Consequently, service managers should invest resources to cross-train workers so they can perform several tasks. What is essentially being accomplished through cross-training is that the firm is inventorying worker skills, instead of inventorying customers in the form of waiting lines; in the long run, this is more profitable to the firm.

Exhibit 11.4

Why Faster Service Is Still "Optimal"

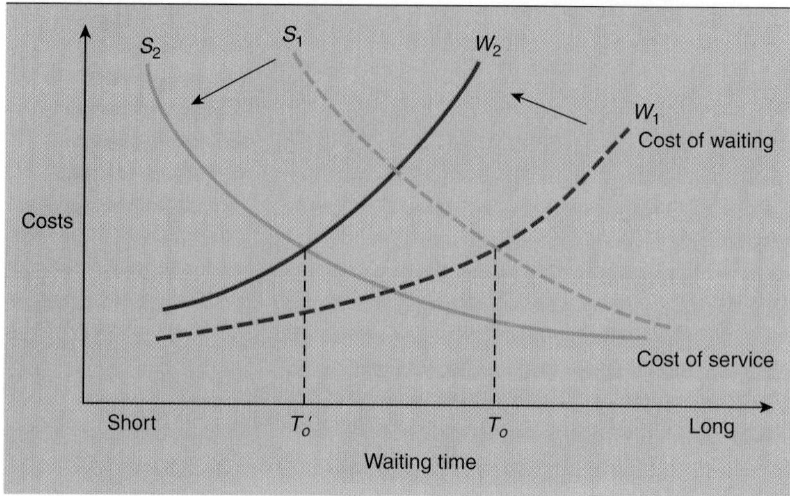

Toward Faster and More Efficient Services

As the standard of living improves, time becomes more important to individuals. As a consequence, the cost of having customers wait for service increases significantly. This is shown in Exhibit 11.4 as the cost-of-waiting line shifts from W_1 to W_2. At the same time, service managers who properly design their delivery systems and train their employees can dramatically reduce the cost of providing service without making customers wait longer. This is shown in Exhibit 11.4 in the shift of the cost-of-service line from S_1 to S_2. The result of these two trends is that there is now a new "optimal" waiting time, T_o', that minimizes total cost and, at the same time, is lower than the initial T_o. As these trends continue in the future, the "optimal" waiting time will become shorter and shorter.

How Technology Can Provide Faster Service

As shown in the beginning of this chapter, the appropriate use of technology can reduce and, in many cases, totally eliminate customer waiting time. Automated teller machines (ATMs) now provide bank customers with 7 × 24-hour service, eliminating the need for customers to wait until the bank opens in the morning. Customers with personal computers can access their accounts via the Internet at any time, day or night, and request certain transactions to take place. (See OM in Practice box on ATMs.)

Bar-code scanners at checkout counters in department stores and supermarkets reduce service processing times and also customer waiting times. Similar types of scanners are now being used on toll roads where commuters can obtain a "bar code" for their cars that is then electronically scanned each time the car passes a toll booth. On the Massachusetts Turnpike, for example, a toll booth in the Fast Lane, which uses bar-coded technology, has more than twice the capacity as a regular toll booth with a person collecting the money. (The Fast Lane toll booth processes more than 1,000 cars an hour versus 450 cars an hour for the regular toll booth.) (Currently under development for use in supermarkets are scanners that will be able to scan an entire shopping cart without having to unload it.)

Bar-code scanners are similarly used at many airports to scan tickets as passengers board airplanes. This permits passengers to board more quickly and with less waiting time. At the same time, it provides the airline with a list of those passengers who are onboard.

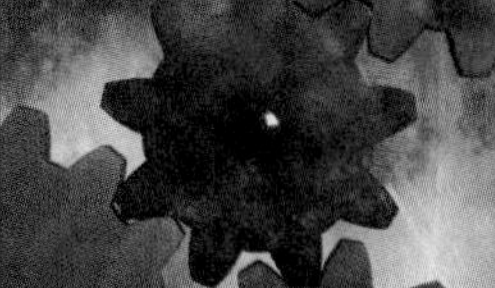

ATMS SAVE TIME BY SPROUTING WINGS

Cathay Pacific Airways now has ATMs onboard two of its 747 airplanes. These machines, supplied by Aero-Design Technology of Irvine, California, will dispense currency for bank cards as well as for all major credit cards. In addition, these ATMs will convert U.S. dollars into any one of 19 foreign currencies based on daily exchange rates that are provided by a satellite.

These airborne ATMs will eliminate the need for customers to wait in ATM lines at their own banks or at the airport. They also are attractive to security-minded passengers who are uncomfortable about using ATMs in strange airports.

Source: Dennis Blank, "ATMs at 12 o'Clock High," *Business Week,* October 13, 1997, p. 8. © 1997 by The McGraw-Hill Companies. Reprinted by special permission.

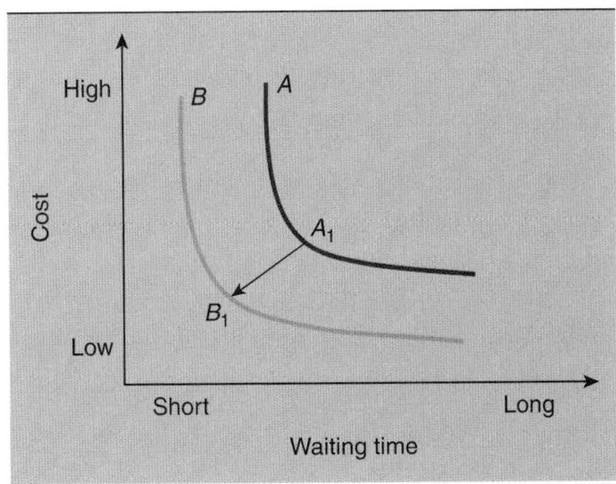

Exhibit 11.5
The Impact of Technology on Waiting Times and Costs

Menu-driven computer databases provide telephone operators with quick access to customer information, thereby allowing them to be more responsive to customer inquiries.

Technology will continue to significantly impact the speed at which service operations can respond to customers. As seen in Exhibit 11.5, technology is allowing services to operate on a superior performance curve (that is, Curve *B* instead of Curve *A*), which results in services that are both faster and more efficient. This is demonstrated in Exhibit 11.5 when a service goes from point A_1 to point B_1. In designing new service delivery systems, managers should always keep in mind the idea that no wait is better than any wait!

Conclusion

As time becomes more critical in today's fast-paced environment, those firms that can provide fast service will have a competitive advantage over those that respond more slowly to customer requirements. As we noted in Chapter 6, speed of delivery is one of the dimensions of service quality. Consequently, providing fast service also can be viewed as providing a high level of service quality, recognizing, of course, that the other service quality dimensions are also properly addressed. Today, more than ever before, service managers need to constantly seek innovative ways to provide faster and better service to customers. Advances in technology, especially information technology, can assist the service manager in accomplishing this.

In providing faster service, however, managers should not lose sight of the fact that it is the customer's perception of the wait that is critical, rather than the actual wait itself. There are many factors that can affect customer perceptions of waits, and the service manager needs to know what these factors are and which of them can be effectively managed by the firm. Such an approach will provide a proper framework for the allocation of a firm's scarce resources to ensure both faster and more efficient service.

Key Terms

actual waiting time p. 446
back-of-the-house p. 456
customer satisfaction p. 450
customer's expectations p. 450
disconfirmation p. 451
front-of-the-house p. 456
perceived waiting time p. 446

Review and Discussion Questions

1. Explain the analogy between having inventory in a manufacturing company and having customers waiting in line in a service operation.
2. What are some of the factors that you think might affect your degree of satisfaction with waiting in line in a supermarket checkout line late at night? . . . in a bank during your lunch hour? . . . at a fast-food restaurant with young children (not necessarily your own!)?
3. Calculate the opportunity cost associated with a dissatisfied customer who stops frequenting a fast-food restaurant for a year. What are your assumptions?
4. Why is it important for a service manager to be able to distinguish between the different types of factors that can affect a customer's level of satisfaction with his or her wait?
5. From your own personal experiences, cite some actual examples of both good and bad waiting line management practices.
6. For each of the different types of service operations listed below, provide specific recommendations for improving both the efficiency of the operation and the customer's level of satisfaction with the waiting time.
   - Airline check-in counter
   - Hospital emergency room
   - Department of Motor Vehicles
   - Mail-order 800 number
   - Emergency hot line
   - Upscale restaurant

Bibliography

Bearden, W. O., and J. E. Teele. "Selected Determinants of Consumer Satisfaction and Complaint Reports." *Journal of Marketing Research* 20 (February 1983).

Chase, Richard B. "The Ten Commandments of Service System Management." *Interfaces* 15, no. 3 (May–June 1985).

Churchill, G. A. Jr., and C. Surprenant. "Investigation into the Determinants of Customer Satisfaction." *Journal of Marketing Research* 19 (November 1982).

Davis, Mark M., and Janelle Heineke. "How Disconfirmation, Perception and Actual Waiting Times Impact Customer Satisfaction." *International Journal of Service Industry Management* 9, no. 1, 1998, pp. 64–73.

———. "Understanding the Roles of the Customer and the Operation for Better Queue Management." *International Journal of Operations and Production Management* 14, no. 5 (1994), pp. 21–34.

Davis, Mark M., and Michael J. Maggard. "Zero Waiting Time: A Model for Designing Fast and Efficient Service." In *Advances in Services Marketing and Management: Research and Practice* 3, ed. Teresa A. Swartz, David E. Bowen, and Stephen W. Brown. Greenwich, CT: JAI Press (June 1994), pp. 201–217.

Katz, K. L.; B. M. Larson; and R. C. Larson. "Prescription for the Waiting Time Blues: Entertain, Enlighten, and Engage." *Sloan Management Review* 32, no. 2 (Winter 1991), pp. 44–53.

Maister, David. "The Psychology of Waiting Lines." In *The Service Encounter,* ed. J. A. Czepiel, M. R. Solomon, and C. F. Surprenant. Lexington, MA: Lexington Books, D.C. Heath & Co., 1985.

Oliver, R. L. "A Cognitive Model of the Antecedents and Consequences of Satisfaction Decisions." *Journal of Marketing Research* 17 (November 1980).

Sasser, W. E.; R. P. Olsen; and D. D. Wyckoff. *Management of Service Operations: Text, Cases and Readings.* Boston: Allyn and Bacon, 1978.

Tomkins, Richard. "Hold on, We'll Play You a Tune." *Financial Times,* February 12, 1999, p. 28.

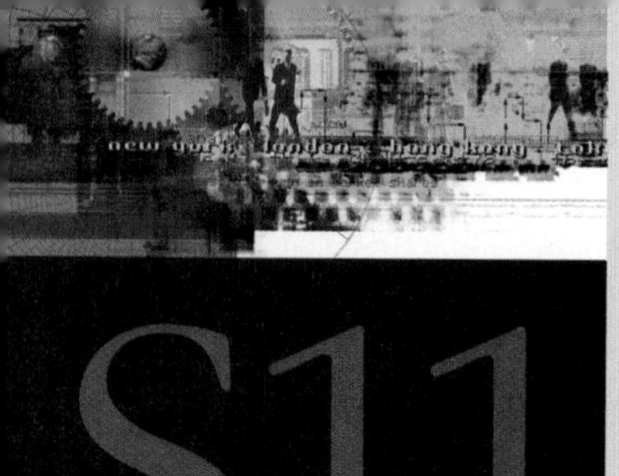

S11 Waiting Line Theory

Supplement Objectives

- Introduce the major characteristics that exist in waiting lines and describe how they can impact a customer's waiting time.
- Identify the various constraints and/or conditions that waiting line theory and its associated equations require for the results to be valid.
- Present waiting line theory in the form of a set of equations that represent various types of waiting line configurations that can be encountered.

Waiting lines form whenever an item or a person seeks a process that is fully occupied with other items or persons. In manufacturing, waiting lines occur when parts arrive at a machine and that machine is busy working on other parts. In services, waiting lines occur when customers arrive at a service facility and that facility is already engaged serving other customers. Specific examples of waiting lines in services include (*a*) waiting to check in at an airline reservations counter, (*b*) waiting on a telephone to make a hotel reservation, and (*c*) waiting to be seated in a restaurant.

The previous chapter addressed the management of the customer's satisfaction with waiting in line while here we focus on the management of the actual length of the wait, as measured in time, be it seconds, minutes or hours.

In this supplement we introduce the basic elements of waiting line problems and provide standard steady-state formulas for solving them. These formulas, developed through queuing theory, enable facility designers, managers, and planners to analyze service requirements and establish service facilities appropriate to stated conditions. Queuing theory is broad enough to cover such dissimilar delays as those encountered by customers in a shopping mall or by aircraft awaiting landing slots.

Queuing theory is used extensively in both manufacturing and service environments, and is a standard tool of operations management in areas such as service delivery system design, scheduling, and machine loading.

Waiting Line Characteristics

The waiting line (or queuing) phenomenon consists essentially of six major components: (*a*) the source population, (*b*) the way customers arrive at the service facility, (*c*) the physical line itself, (*d*) the way customers are selected from the line, (*e*) the characteristics of the service facility itself (such as how the customers flow through the system and how much time it takes to serve each customer), and (*f*) the condition of the customers when they exit the system (back to the source population or not?). These six elements, shown in Exhibit S11.1, are discussed separately in the following sections.

Population Source

Arrivals at a service system may be drawn from either a *finite* or an *infinite* population. The distinction is important because the analyses are based on different premises and require different equations for their solution.

Exhibit S11.1

Framework for Viewing Waiting Line Situations

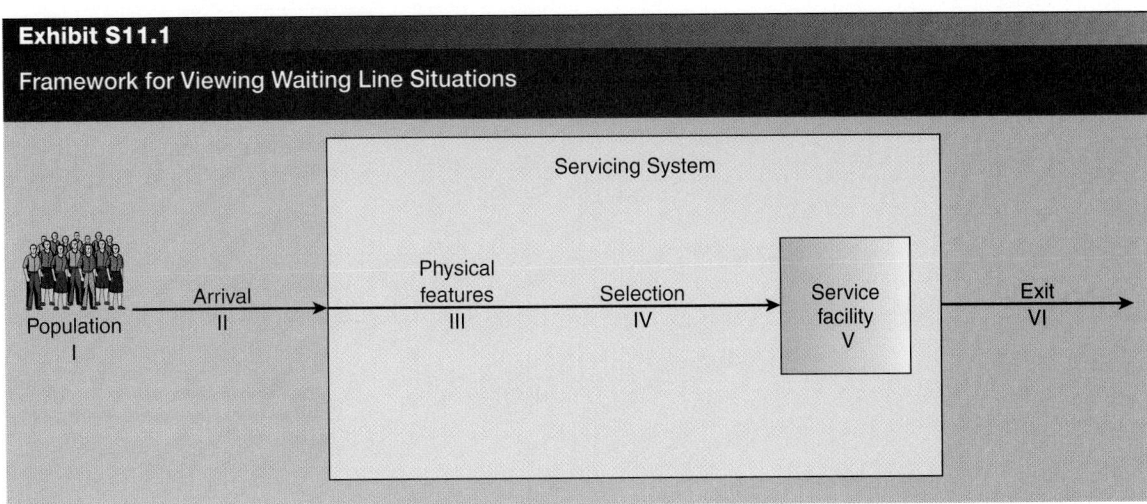

Finite Population A *finite population* refers to the limited size of the customer pool, which is the source that will use the service, and at times form a line. The reason this finite classification is important is because when a customer leaves his/her position as a member of the population of users, the size of the user group is reduced by one, which reduces the probability of a customer requiring service. Conversely, when a customer is serviced and returns to the user group, the population increases and the probability of a user requiring service also increases. This finite class of problems requires a separate set of formulas from that of the infinite population case.

Infinite Population An infinite population is one that is sufficiently large in relation to the service system that any changes in the population size caused by subtractions or additions to the population (e.g., a customer needing service or a serviced customer returning to the population) does not significantly affect the system probabilities. If, for example, there were 100 machines that were maintained by one repairperson, and one or two machines broke down and required service, the probabilities for the next breakdowns would not be very different and the assumption could be made without a great deal of error that the population, for all practical purposes, was infinite. Nor would the formulas for "infinite" queuing problems cause much error if applied to a physician who has 1,000 patients, or a department store that has 10,000 customers.

Arrival Characteristics

Another determinant in the analysis of waiting line problems is the *arrival characteristics* of the queue members. As shown in Exhibit S11.2, there are four main descriptors of arrivals: the *pattern of arrivals* (whether arrivals are controllable or uncontrollable); the *size of arrival units* (whether they arrive one at a time or in batches); the *distribution pattern* (whether the time between arrivals is constant or follows a statistical distribution such as a Poisson, exponential, or Erlang); and the *degree of patience* (whether the arrival stays in line or leaves). We describe each of these in more detail.

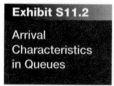

Exhibit S11.2

Arrival Characteristics in Queues

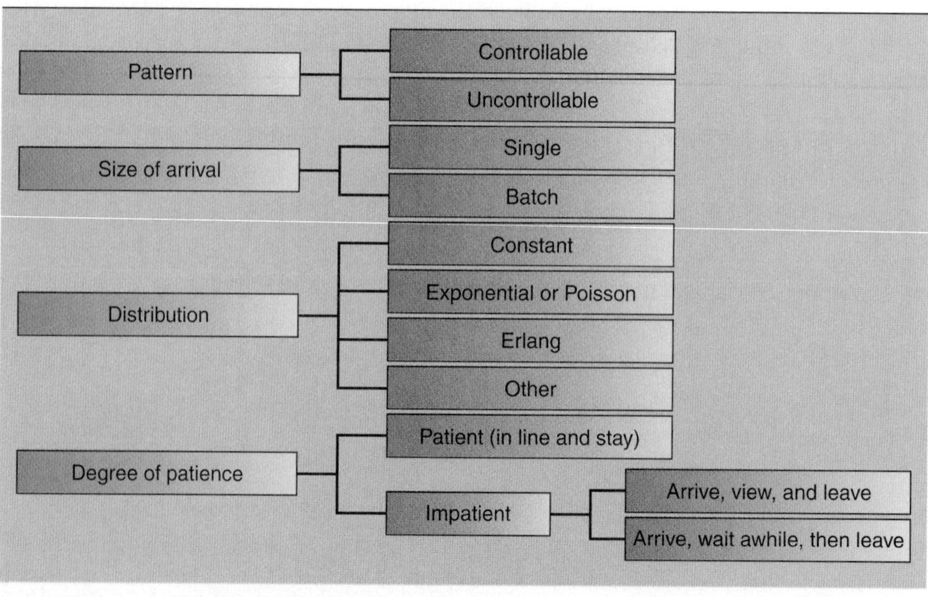

Arrival Patterns The arrivals at a system are far more *controllable* than is generally recognized. Hair saloons, as an illustration, may decrease their Saturday arrival rate (and hopefully shift it to other days of the week) by charging an extra $1 for adult haircuts or charging adult prices for children's haircuts. Department stores run sales during the off season or one-day-only sales in part for purposes of control. Airlines offer excursion and off-season rates for similar reasons. The simplest of all arrival-control devices is the posting of business hours.

Some service demands are clearly *uncontrollable,* such as emergency medical demands on a city's hospital facilities. However, even in these situations, the arrivals at emergency rooms in specific hospitals are controllable to some extent by, say, keeping ambulance drivers in the service region informed of the status of their respective host hospitals.

Size of Arrival Units A *single arrival* may be thought of as one unit (a unit is the smallest number handled). A single arrival on the floor of the New York Stock Exchange (NYSE), for example, is 100 shares of stock; a single arrival at an egg-processing plant might be a dozen eggs or a flat of two and a half dozen.

A *batch arrival* is some multiple of the unit, as a block of 1,000 shares on the NYSE, a case of eggs at the processing plant, or a party of five at a restaurant.

Distribution of Arrivals Waiting line formulas generally require an **arrival rate,** or the average number of customers or units per time period (e.g., 10 per hour). The time between arrivals is referred to as the interarrival time (such as an average of one every six minutes). A *constant* arrival distribution is periodic, with exactly the same time period between successive arrivals. In production processes, probably the only arrivals that truly approach a constant interarrival period are those that are subject to machine control. Much more common are *variable* random arrival distributions. The variable or random distribution patterns that occur most frequently in system models are described by the *negative exponential, Poisson,* or *Erlang* distributions.

arrival rate

Rate at which customers arrive into a service delivery system, usually expressed in terms of customers per hour.

Degree of Patience A *patient* arrival is one who waits as long as necessary until the service facility is ready to serve him or her. (Even if arrivals grumble and behave impatiently, the fact that they wait is sufficient to label them as patient arrivals for purposes of waiting line theory.)

There are two classes of *impatient* arrivals. Members of the first class arrive, survey both the service facility and the length of the line, and then decide to leave. Those in the second class arrive, view the situation, and join the waiting line, and then, after some period of time, depart. The behavior of the first type is termed *balking,* and the second is termed *reneging.*

Physical Features of Lines

Length In a practical sense, an infinite line is very long in terms of the capacity of the service system. Examples of *infinite potential length* are a line of vehicles backed up for miles at the tollbooths on a turnpike and customers who must form a line around the block as they wait to purchase tickets for a concert to see a popular singer.

Gas stations, loading docks, and parking lots have *limited line capacity,* which is often defined by legal restrictions or physical space characteristics. This complicates the waiting line problem not only in service system utilization and waiting line computations, but also in the shape of the actual arrival distribution as well. The arrival who is denied entry into the line because of lack of space may rejoin the population at a later time or may seek service elsewhere. Either action makes an obvious difference in the finite population case.

Exhibit S11.3

Factors in a Queuing Discipline

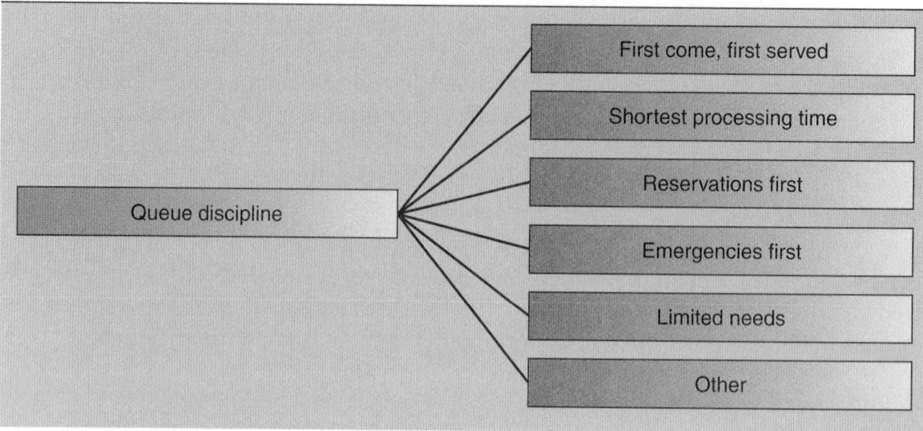

Number of Lines A *single line* or single file, of course, means that there is only one line. The term *multiple lines* refers either to the single lines that form in front of two or more servers or to single lines that converge at some central redistribution point.

Customer Selection

Queuing Discipline A queuing discipline is a priority rule, or set of rules (some of which are listed in Exhibit S11.3), for determining the order of service to customers who are waiting in line. The rules selected can have a dramatic effect on the system's overall performance. The number of customers in line, the average waiting time, the range of variability in waiting time, and the efficiency of the service facility are just a few of the factors affected by the choice of priority rules.

Probably the most common priority rule, especially in service operations, is *first come, first served* (FCFS), also known as first in, first out (FIFO). This rule states that the customers in line are served on the basis of their chronological arrival; no other characteristics have any bearing on the selection process. This is popularly accepted as the fairest rule, even though in practice, it discriminates against the customer requiring a short service time.

Reservations first, emergencies first, highest-profit customer first, largest orders first, best customers first, longest waiting time in line, and *soonest promised date* are other examples of priority rules. Each has its advantages as well as its shortcomings.

Directives such as "single transactions only" (as in a bank) or "cash only" express lanes (as in a supermarket) seem similar to priority rules, but in reality they are methodologies for structuring the line itself. Such lines are formed to serve a specific class of customers with similar characteristics. Within each line, however, priority rules still apply (as before) to the method of selecting the next customer to be served. A classic case of line structuring is the supermarket with the fast checkout line for customers with 12 items or less.

Service Facility Structure

Several types of service facility structures are presented in Exhibit S11.4, four of which are discussed in detail in the following sections. The physical flow of items or customers to be serviced may go through a single line, multiple lines, or some combination of the two. The choice of format depends partly on the volume of customers served, partly on physical constraints, and partly on the restrictions imposed by sequential requirements governing the order in which the service must be performed.

Exhibit S11.4

A Service Facility's Structure

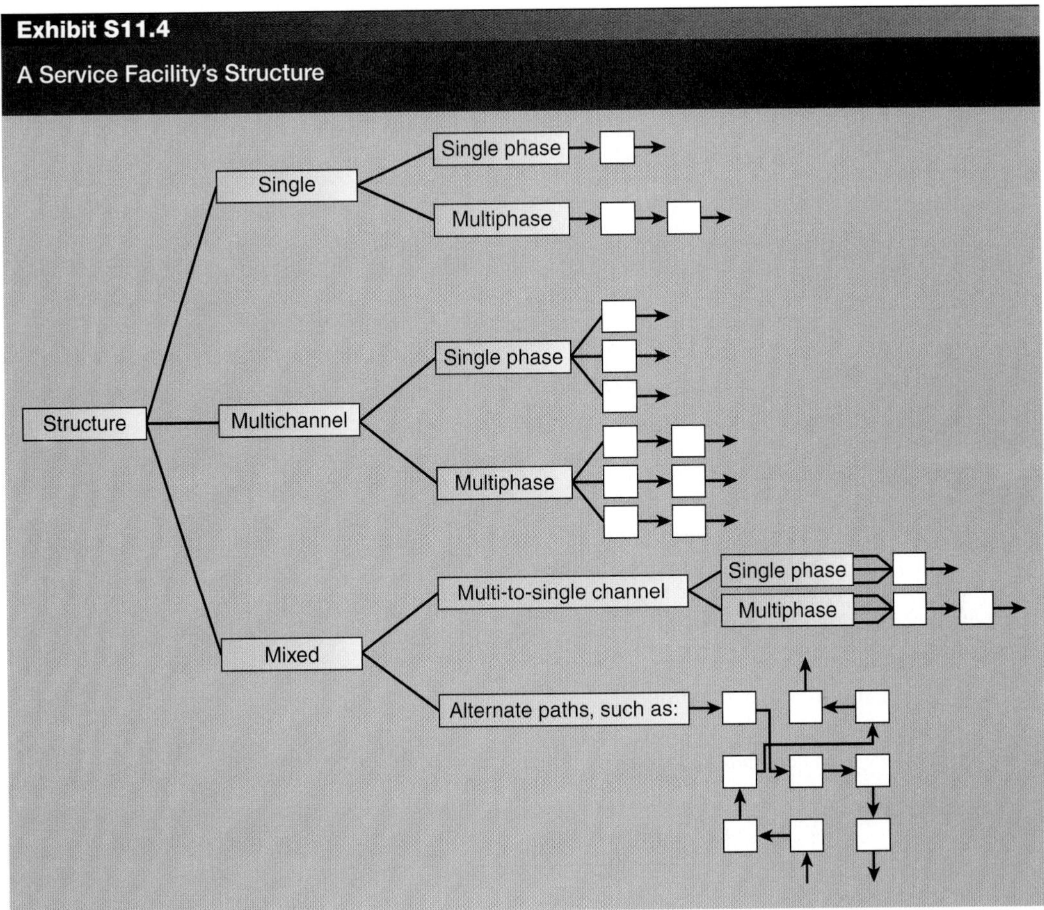

Single Channel, Single Phase This is the simplest form of waiting line structure, and straightforward formulas are available to solve the problem for standard distribution patterns of arrival and service. When the distributions are nonstandard, the problem is easily solved by computer simulation. A typical example of a single-channel, single-phase situation is the one-person barbershop.

Single Channel, Multiphase A car wash provides a good illustration for a series of services—vacuuming, wetting, washing, rinsing, drying, window cleaning, and parking—performed in a fairly uniform sequence. A critical factor in the single-channel case with service in series is the amount of buildup of items allowed in front of each service, which in turn constitutes separate waiting lines.

Because of the inherent variability in service times, the optimal situation in maximizing the use of the service station is to allow an infinite waiting line to build in front of each station. The worst situation is that in which no line is permitted and only one customer at a time is allowed. When no sublines are allowed to build up in front of each station, as in a car wash, the use of the overall service facility is governed by the probability that a long service time will be required by any one of the servers in the system. This problem is common in most product-oriented systems, such as assembly lines.

Multichannel, Single Phase Tellers' windows in banks, and checkout counters in supermarkets and high-volume department stores, exemplify this type of structure. The difficulty with this format is that the uneven service time given each customer results in unequal speed or flow among the lines. This results in some customers being served before others who arrived earlier as well as in some degree of line shifting. Varying this structure to assure the servicing of arrivals in chronological order would require forming a single line, from which, as a server becomes available, the next customer in the queue is assigned. This type of line structure is now commonly used at airport ticket counters and banks.

Multichannel, Multiphase This situation is similar to the preceding one except that two or more services are performed in sequence. The admission of patients in a hospital follows this pattern because a specific sequence of steps is usually required: initial contact at the admissions desk, filling out forms, making identification tags, obtaining a room assignment, escorting the patient to the room, and so forth. Since several servers are usually available for this procedure, more than one patient at a time may be processed.

service rate

Capacity of a service station, usually expressed in terms of customers per hour. The reciprocal of the service rate is the average time to serve a customer.

Service Rate Waiting line formulas generally define **service rate** as the capacity of the server in terms of the number of units served per time period (such as 12 customers per hour) and *not* as service time, which might average five minutes each. A *constant* service time rule states that each service takes exactly the same time. As in constant arrivals, this characteristic is generally limited to machine-controlled operations. As with arrival rates, Erlang and hyperexponential distributions represent variable service times.

A frequently used illustration of the *Erlang* distribution employs a single-channel, multiservice situation. However, the conditions that must be met for the Erlang approximation are so severe that practical application is rare.

The *exponential* distribution is frequently used to approximate the actual service distribution. This practice, however, may lead to incorrect results; few service situations are represented exactly by the exponential function since the service facility must be able to perform services much shorter than the average time of service.

Most other services also have some practical minimum time. A clerk in a checkout line may have a three-minute average service time but a one-minute minimum time. This is particularly true where another checkout aisle provides a quick service. Likewise in a hair salon, while the average service time may be 30 minutes, a person is rarely finished in less than 20 minutes or more than an hour. Hence, these and similar types of services that have strong time dependency are poorly characterized by the exponential curve.

capacity utilization

Percentage of time a service station is busy serving a customer.

Capacity Utilization The percentage of time that a service station is busy attending to the needs of a customer is referred to as the **capacity utilization** of that station. This is the percentage of time that the station is busy. The remainder of the time there are no customers to be waited on and the station is, therefore, considered to be idle. In single-channel service systems, the capacity utilization is simply the ratio of the arrival rate to the service rate. For example, if customers arrive into a system at the rate of eight per hour and the service rate is 12 customers per hour, then the capacity utilization of this service station is 8/12 or 66.7 percent. It is important to note that in determining the capacity utilization for a station, both the arrival rate and the service rate must be expressed in the same units.

Exit

Once a customer is served, two exit scenarios are possible: (*a*) the customer may return to the source population and immediately become a competing candidate for service again or (*b*) there may be a low probability of reservice. The first case can be illustrated by a machine that has been routinely repaired and returned to duty but may break down again; the second can be illustrated by a machine that has been overhauled or modified and has a low probability of reservice over the near future. We might refer to the first as the "recurring-common-cold case" and to the second as the "appendectomy-only-once case."

It should be apparent that when the population source is finite, any change in the service performed on customers who return to the population modifies the arrival rate at the service facility. This, of course, alters the characteristics of the waiting line under study and necessitates further analysis of the problem.

Waiting Line Equations

To underscore the importance and wide range of applications of waiting line analysis, we describe in this section six different waiting line systems and their characteristics (Exhibit S11.5), and present their respective steady-state equations (Exhibit S11.6). The definitions of the terms used in these equations are presented in Exhibit S11.7.

In addition to these equations, two additional formulas are important in understanding the relationships among the steady-state performance measures. First, the average total time in the system is equal to the average waiting time in the system plus the average service time, or

$$\bar{t}_s = \bar{t}_l + 1/\mu$$

In addition, the average total number of customers in the system is directly related to the total time in the system, or

$$\bar{n}_s = \lambda \bar{t}_s$$

This well-known relationship is known as Little's Law.

Exhibit S11.5

Properties of Some Specific Waiting Line Models

Model	Layout	Service Phase	Source Population	Arrival Pattern	Queue Discipline	Service Pattern	Permissible Queue Length	Typical Example
1	Single channel	Single	Infinite	Poisson	FCFS	Exponential	Unlimited	Drive-in teller at bank, one-lane toll bridge
2	Single channel	Single	Infinite	Poisson	FCFS	Constant	Unlimited	Roller coaster rides in amusement park
3	Single channel	Single	Infinite	Poisson	FCFS	Exponential	Limited	Ice cream stand, cashier in a restaurant
4	Single channel	Single	Infinite	Poisson	FCFS	Discrete distribution	Unlimited	Empirically derived distribution of flight time for a transcontinental flight
5	Single channel	Single	Infinite	Poisson	FCFS	Erlang	Unlimited	One-person barbershop
6	Multi-channel	Single	infinite	Poisson	FCFS	Exponential	Unlimited	Parts counter in auto agency, two-lane toll bridge

Exhibit S11.6

Equations for Solving Six Model Problems

Model 1

$$\bar{n}_l = \frac{\lambda^2}{\mu(\mu-\lambda)} \qquad \bar{t}_l = \frac{\lambda}{\mu(\mu-\lambda)} \qquad P_n = \left(1-\frac{\lambda}{\mu}\right)\left(\frac{\lambda}{\mu}\right)^n$$

$$\bar{n}_s = \frac{\lambda}{\mu-\lambda} \qquad \bar{t}_s = \frac{1}{\mu-\lambda} \qquad \rho = \frac{\lambda}{\mu}$$

Model 2

$$\bar{n}_l = \frac{\lambda^2}{2\mu(\mu-\lambda)} \qquad \bar{t}_l = \frac{\lambda}{2\mu(\mu-\lambda)}$$

$$\bar{n}_s = \bar{n}_l + \frac{\lambda}{\mu} \qquad \bar{t}_s = \bar{t}_l + \frac{1}{\mu}$$

Model 3

$$\bar{n}_l = \left(\frac{\lambda}{\mu}\right)^2 \left[\frac{1 - Q\left(\frac{\lambda}{\mu}\right)^{-1} + (Q-1)\left(\frac{\lambda}{\mu}\right)^{Q}}{\left(1-\frac{\lambda}{\mu}\right)\left(1-\left(\frac{\lambda}{\mu}\right)^{Q+1}\right)}\right]$$

$$\bar{n}_s = \left(\frac{\lambda}{\mu}\right) \left[\frac{1 - (Q+1)\left(\frac{\lambda}{\mu}\right)^{Q} + Q\left(\frac{\lambda}{\mu}\right)^{Q+1}}{\left(1-\frac{\lambda}{\mu}\right)\left(1-\left(\frac{\lambda}{\mu}\right)^{Q+1}\right)}\right] \qquad P_n = \left[\frac{1-\frac{\lambda}{\mu}}{1-\left(\frac{\lambda}{\mu}\right)^{Q+1}}\right]\left(\frac{\lambda}{\mu}\right)^n$$

Model 4

$$\bar{n}_l = \frac{\left(\frac{\lambda}{\mu}\right)^2 + \lambda^2\sigma^2}{2\left(1-\frac{\lambda}{\mu}\right)} \qquad \bar{t}_l = \frac{\frac{\lambda}{\mu^2} + \lambda\sigma^2}{2\left(1-\frac{\lambda}{\mu}\right)}$$

$$\bar{n}_s = \bar{n}_l + \frac{\lambda}{\mu} \qquad \bar{t}_s = \bar{t}_l + \frac{1}{\mu}$$

Model 5

$$\bar{n}_l = \frac{K+1}{2K}\cdot\frac{\lambda^2}{\mu(\mu-\lambda)} \qquad \bar{t}_l = \frac{K+1}{2K}\cdot\frac{\lambda}{\mu(\mu-\lambda)}$$

$$\bar{n}_s = \bar{n}_l + \frac{\lambda}{\mu} \qquad \bar{t}_s = \bar{t}_l + \frac{1}{\mu}$$

Model 6

$$\bar{n}_l = \frac{\lambda\mu\left(\frac{\lambda}{\mu}\right)^M}{(M-1)!(M\mu-\lambda)^2} P_0 \qquad \bar{t}_l = \frac{P_0}{\mu M M!\left(1-\frac{\lambda}{\mu M}\right)^2}\left(\frac{\lambda}{\mu}\right)^M$$

$$\bar{n}_s = \bar{n}_l + \frac{\lambda}{\mu} \qquad \bar{t}_s = \bar{t}_l + \frac{1}{\mu}$$

$$P_0 = \frac{1}{\sum_{n=0}^{M-1}\frac{\left(\frac{\lambda}{\mu}\right)^n}{n!} + \frac{\left(\frac{\lambda}{\mu}\right)^M}{M!\left(1-\frac{\lambda}{\mu M}\right)}} \qquad P_w = \left(\frac{\lambda}{\mu}\right)^M \frac{P_0}{M!\left(1-\frac{\lambda}{\mu M}\right)}$$

To illustrate how these models can be applied, we present two sample problems and their solutions for the first two models. There are more than six models, but the formulas and solutions become quite complicated and those problems are generally solved using computer simulation. Also, in using these formulas, keep in mind that they are steady-state formulas, which assume that the process under study is ongoing. Thus, they may provide inaccurate results when applied to initial operations such as the manufacture of a new product or the start of a new business day by a service firm.

Exhibit S11.7

Notations for Equations (Exhibit S11.6)

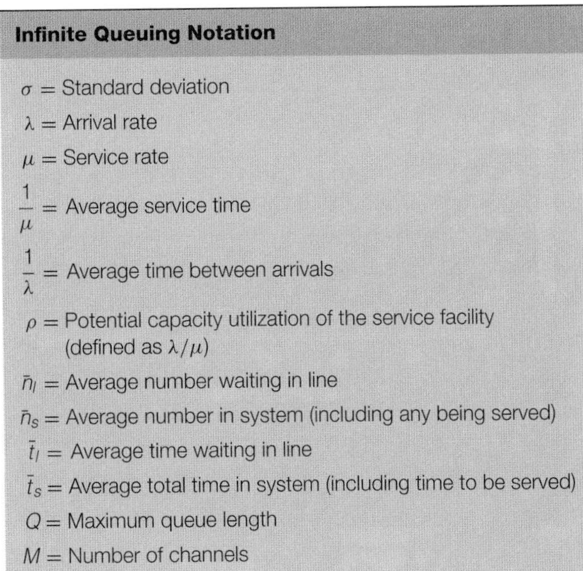

Infinite Queuing Notation

σ = Standard deviation

λ = Arrival rate

μ = Service rate

$\frac{1}{\mu}$ = Average service time

$\frac{1}{\lambda}$ = Average time between arrivals

ρ = Potential capacity utilization of the service facility (defined as λ/μ)

$\bar{n}_l$ = Average number waiting in line

$\bar{n}_s$ = Average number in system (including any being served)

$\bar{t}_l$ = Average time waiting in line

$\bar{t}_s$ = Average total time in system (including time to be served)

Q = Maximum queue length

M = Number of channels

Exhibit S11.8

Calculating the Relationship between Capacity Utilization and Waiting Time

Arrival Rate	Service Rate	Capacity Utilization	Waiting Time (hr)	Waiting Time (min)
10	60	16.67%	0.003	0.20
20	60	33.33	0.008	0.50
30	60	50.00	0.017	1.00
40	60	66.67	0.033	2.00
45	60	75.00	0.050	3.00
50	60	83.33	0.083	5.00
55	60	91.67	0.183	11.00
56	60	93.33	0.233	14.00
57	60	95.00	0.317	19.00
58	60	96.67	0.483	29.00

Capacity Utilization and Waiting Time

The capacity utilization of a service facility and the average waiting time for that facility are positively related. In other words, as capacity utilization increases, waiting time also increases. To illustrate this relationship, we use the formula for model 1 (in Exhibit S11.6) to calculate the capacity utilization and average waiting time for a single-server facility. The results are shown in the table in Exhibit S11.8 and plotted in the graph in Exhibit S11.9. As a general rule of thumb, when the capacity utilization of the service facility is greater than 75 to 85 percent, the lines become unacceptably long to the vast majority of customers.

The Trade-Off between Balking and Reneging

Service managers, in designing their facilities, also need to recognize the trade-off that exists between having a large facility where customers can wait and the customer dissatisfaction that is associated with waiting too long prior to being served. In other words, the larger the

Exhibit S11.9

The Relationship between Capacity Utilization and Waiting Time

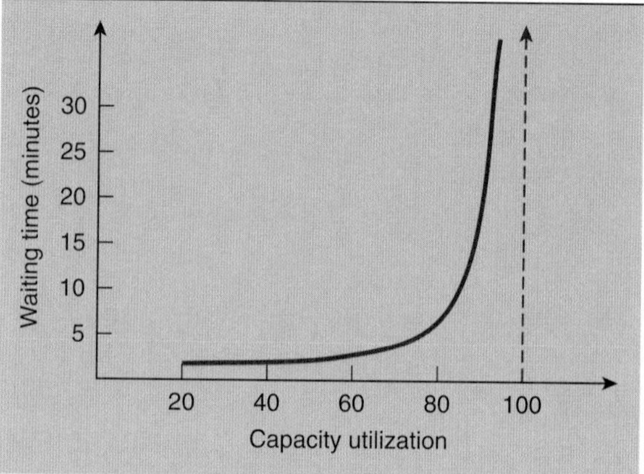

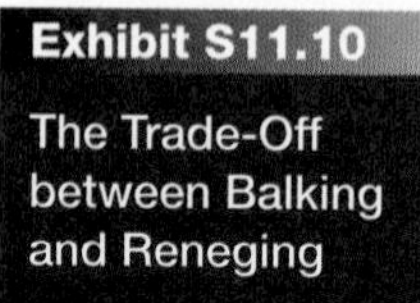

Exhibit S11.10

The Trade-Off between Balking and Reneging

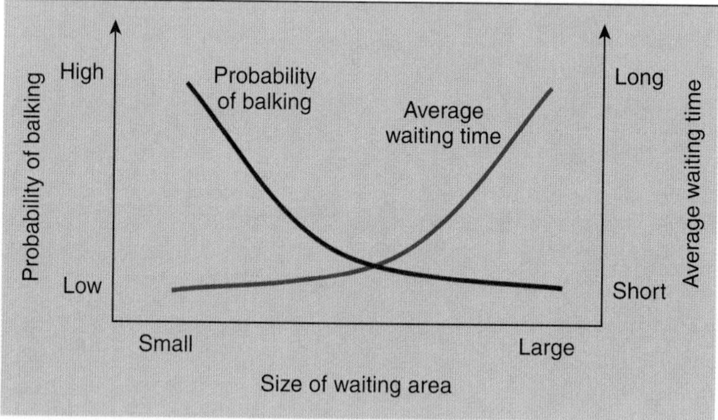

waiting area, the less likely a customer will initially balk or not enter the facility at all. At the same time, for a given number of service stations, the larger the waiting area, the longer the average waiting time for the customer. This trade-off is shown in Exhibit S11.10.

If the wait is too long so that the customer eventually reneges or leaves the line, then the customer, most likely, will be more dissatisfied than having balked or left in the first place. For example, you are likely to be very dissatisfied if you call to make an airline reservation and have to wait on the phone for such a long period of time that you eventually hang up. However, you would probably be less dissatisfied if you call to make a reservation and get a busy signal, and then call back at a later time. Similarly, you will likely be more dissatisfied if you have to wait such a long time for a table in a restaurant that you finally leave before you are seated than you would be if you found the parking lot full and decided to come back at another time.

Two Typical Waiting Line Situations

Here is a quick preview of the two problems we have used to illustrate the first two waiting line models in Exhibits S11.5 and S11.6.

Problem 1: Customers in line. A bank wants to know how many customers (or cars) are waiting for a drive-in teller, how long they have to wait, the utilization of the teller, and what the service rate would have to be so that 95 percent of the time there would not be more than three cars in the system at any one time.

Problem 2: Equipment selection. A franchisee for Robot Car Wash must decide which equipment to purchase out of a choice of three. Larger units cost more, but wash cars faster. To make the decision, costs are related to revenue.

The two problems are solved using the equations in Exhibit S11.6 with the notations defined in Exhibit S11.7.

Problem 1: Customers in Line

Example

Western National Bank wants to provide a drive-through window for its customers. Management estimates that customers will arrive in their cars at the rate of 15 per hour. The teller who will staff the window can service customers at the rate of 20 per hour.

Assuming Poisson arrivals and exponential service, find the

a. Capacity utilization of the teller.

b. Average number of cars in the waiting line.

c. Average number in the system.

d. Average waiting time in line.

e. Average waiting time in the system, including service.

Solution

a. The average capacity utilization of the teller is

$$\mu = 20 \text{ customers/hour}$$

$$\lambda = 15 \text{ customers/hour}$$

$$\rho = \frac{\lambda}{\mu} = \frac{15}{20} = 75 \text{ percent}$$

b. The average number of cars in the waiting line is

$$\bar{n}_l = \frac{\lambda^2}{\mu(\mu - \lambda)} = \frac{(15)^2}{20(20 - 15)} = 2.25 \text{ cars}$$

c. The average number in the system is

$$\bar{n}_s = \frac{\lambda}{\mu - \lambda} = \frac{15}{20 - 15} = 3 \text{ cars}$$

d. Average waiting time in line is

$$\bar{t}_l = \frac{\lambda}{\mu(\mu - \lambda)} = \frac{15}{20(20 - 15)} = 0.15 \text{ hour,} \quad \text{or 9 minutes}$$

e. Average waiting time in the system is

$$\bar{t}_s = \frac{1}{\mu - \lambda} = \frac{1}{20 - 15} = 0.2 \text{ hour,} \quad \text{or 12 minutes}$$

Example

Because of limited space and a desire to provide an acceptable level of service, the bank manager would like to ensure, with 95 percent confidence, that not more than three cars will be in the system at any one time. What is the present level of service for the three-car limit? What level of teller use must be attained and what must be the service rate of the teller to assure the 95 percent level of service?

Solution

The present level of service for three cars or less is the probability that there are 0, 1, 2, or 3 cars in the system.

From Model 1, Exhibit S11.6:

$$P_n = \left(1 - \frac{\lambda}{\mu}\right)\left(\frac{\lambda}{\mu}\right)^n$$

at $n = 0$	$P_0 = (1 - 15/20)$	$(15/20)^0 = 0.250$	
at $n = 1$	$P_1 = (1/4)$	$(15/20)^1 = 0.188$	
at $n = 2$	$P_2 = (1/4)$	$(15/20)^2 = 0.141$	
at $n = 3$	$P_3 = (1/4)$	$(15/20)^3 = 0.105$	
		0.684 or 68.4 percent	

The probability of having more than three cars in the system is 1.0 minus the probability of three cars or less (1.0 – 0.684 = 0.316 or 31.6 percent).

For a 95 percent service level to three cars or less, this states that $P_0 + P_1 + P_2 + P_3 = 95$ percent.

$$0.95 = \left(1 - \frac{\lambda}{\mu}\right)\left(\frac{\lambda}{\mu}\right)^0 + \left(1 - \frac{\lambda}{\mu}\right)\left(\frac{\lambda}{\mu}\right)^1 + \left(1 - \frac{\lambda}{\mu}\right)\left(\frac{\lambda}{\mu}\right)^2 + \left(1 - \frac{\lambda}{\mu}\right)\left(\frac{\lambda}{\mu}\right)^3$$

$$0.95 = \left(1 - \frac{\lambda}{\mu}\right)\left[1 + \frac{\lambda}{\mu} + \left(\frac{\lambda}{\mu}\right)^2 + \left(\frac{\lambda}{\mu}\right)^3\right]$$

We can solve this by trial and error for values of λ/μ. If $\lambda/\mu = 0.50$,

$$0.95 \stackrel{?}{=} 0.5(1 + 0.05 + 0.25 + 0.125)$$

$$0.95 \neq 0.9375$$

With $\lambda/\mu = 0.45$,

$$0.95 \stackrel{?}{=} (1 - 0.45)(1 + 0.45 + 0.203 + 0.091)$$

$$0.95 \neq 0.96$$

With $\lambda/\mu = 0.47$,

$$0.95 \stackrel{?}{=} (1 - 0.47)(1 + 0.47 + 0.221 + 0.104) = 0.95135$$

$$0.95 \approx 0.95135$$

Therefore, with the utilization $\rho = \lambda/\mu$ of 47 percent, the probability of three cars or less in the system is 95 percent.

To find the rate of service required to attain this 95 percent service level, we simply solve the equation $\lambda/\mu = 0.47$, where λ = number of arrivals per hour. This gives $\mu = 31.92$, or about 32 per hour.

That is, the teller must serve approximately 32 people per hour—a 60 percent increase over the original 20-per-hour capability—in order to be 95 percent confident that not more than three cars will be in the system. Perhaps service can be accelerated by modifying the method of service, adding another teller, or limiting the types of transactions available at the drive-in window. (Many banks, in fact, now limit each customer to a maximum of three transactions at the drive-in window.) Note that with the condition of 95 percent confidence that three or fewer cars will be in the system, the teller will be idle 53 percent of the time.

Problem 2: Equipment Selection

Example

The Robot Car Wash Company franchises combination gas and car wash stations throughout the United States. Robot gives a free car wash with a gasoline fill-up or, for a wash alone, charges \$5.00. Past experience shows that the number of customers that have car washes following fill-ups is about the same as for a wash alone. The average gross profit on a gasoline fill-up is about \$7.00, and the cost of the car wash to Robot is \$1.00. Robot Car Wash stations are open 14 hours a day.

Robot has three power units with drive assemblies, and a franchise must select the unit preferred. Unit I can wash cars at the rate of one every five minutes and is leased for \$120 per day. Unit II, a larger unit, can wash cars at the rate of one every four minutes but costs \$160 per day. Unit III, the largest, costs \$220 per day and can wash a car in three minutes.

The franchisee estimates that customers will not wait in line more than five minutes for a car wash. A longer time will cause Robot to lose both gasoline sales and car wash sales.

If the estimate of customer arrivals resulting in washes is 10 per hour, which wash unit should be selected?

Solution

Using Unit I, calculate the average waiting time of customers in the wash line (μ for Unit I = 12 per hour). From the Model 2 equations (Exhibit S11.6),

$$\bar{t}_l = \frac{\lambda}{2\mu(\mu - \lambda)} = \frac{10}{2(12)(12 - 10)} = 0.208 \text{ hour,} \quad \text{or } 12\tfrac{1}{2} \text{ minutes}$$

For Unit II at 15 per hour,

$$\bar{t}_l = \frac{10}{2(15)(15 - 10)} = 0.067 \text{ hour,} \quad \text{or 4 minutes}$$

If waiting time is the only criterion, Unit II should be purchased. However, before we make the final decision, we must look at the profit differential between both units.

With Unit I, some customers would balk or renege because of the 12½-minute wait. And although this greatly complicates the mathematical analysis, we can gain some estimate of lost sales with Unit I by inserting $\bar{t}_l = 5$ minutes or $\frac{1}{12}$ hour (the average length of time customers will wait) and solving for λ. This would be the effective arrival rate of customers:

$$\bar{t}_l = \frac{\lambda}{2\mu(\mu - \lambda)}$$

$$\lambda = \frac{2\bar{t}_l\mu^2}{1 + 2\bar{t}_l\mu}$$

$$\lambda = \frac{2(1/12)(12)^2}{1 + 2(1/12)(12)} = 8 \text{ per hour}$$

Therefore, since the original estimate of λ was 10 per hour, an estimated two customers per hour will be lost. Lost profit of two customers per hour × 14 hours × ½ (\$7.00 fill-up profit + \$4.00 wash profit) = \$154.00 per day.

Because the additional cost of Unit II over Unit I is only \$40 per day, the loss of \$154.00 profit obviously warrants the installation of Unit II.

The original constraint of a five-minute maximum wait is satisfied by Unit II. Therefore, Unit III is not considered unless the arrival rate is expected to increase in the future.

Computer Simulation of Waiting Lines

Some waiting line problems that seem very simple on first impression turn out to be extremely difficult or impossible to solve. Throughout this chapter we have been treating waiting line situations that are independent; that is, either the entire system consists of a single phase, or else each service that is performed in a series is independent. (This could happen if the output of one service location is allowed to build up in front of the next one so that this, in essence, becomes a calling population for the next service.) When a series of services is performed in sequence where the output rate of one becomes the input rate of the next, we can no longer use the simple formulas. This is also true for any problem where conditions do not meet the conditions of the equations, as specified in Exhibit S11.7. The analytical technique best suited for solving this type of problem is computer simulation.

Conclusion

Waiting line problems present both a challenge and a frustration to those who try to solve them. One of the main concerns in dealing with waiting line problems is what procedure or priority rule to use in selecting the next product or customer to be served.

Many queuing problems appear simple until an attempt is made to solve them. This supplement has dealt with the simpler problems. When the situation becomes more complex, such as when there are multiple phases and/or where services are performed only in a particular sequence, computer simulation is usually necessary to obtain the optimal solution.

Key Terms

arrival rate p. 465 capacity utilization p. 468 service rate p. 468

Review and Discussion Questions

1. How many waiting lines did you encounter during your last airline flight?
2. Distinguish between a *channel* and a *phase*.
3. Which assumptions are necessary to employ the formulas given for Model 1?
4. In what way might the first-come, first-served rule be unfair to the customers waiting for service in a bank or hospital?
5. Identify the various types of waiting lines you encounter in a "normal" day.
6. Compare the queuing systems of McDonald's and Wendy's.
7. Why do you think doctors' and dentists' offices usually have such long waits?

Solved Problems

Problem 1

Quick Lube, Inc., operates a fast lube and oil change garage. On a typical day, customers arrive at the rate of three per hour, and lube jobs are performed at an average rate of one every 15 minutes. The mechanics operate as a team on one car at a time.

Assuming Poisson arrivals and exponential service, determine the

a. Utilization of the lube team.

b. Average number of cars in line.

c. Average time a car waits before it is lubed.

d. Total time it takes a car to go through the system (i.e., waiting in line plus lube time).

Solution

$\lambda = 3,\ \mu = 4$

a. Utilization $(\rho) = \frac{\lambda}{\mu} = \frac{3}{4} = 75\%.$

b. $\bar{n}_l = \frac{\lambda^2}{\mu(\mu - \lambda)} = \frac{3^2}{4(4-3)} = \frac{9}{4} = 2.25$ cars in line.

c. $\bar{t}_l = \frac{\lambda}{\mu(\mu - \lambda)} = \frac{3}{4(4-3)} = \frac{3}{4} = .75$ hour $= 45$ minutes in line.

d. $\bar{t}_s = \frac{1}{\mu - \lambda} = \frac{1}{1} = 1$ hour total time in the system (waiting + lube).

Problem 2

American Vending Inc. (AVI) supplies vended food to a large university. Because students kick the machines at every opportunity out of anger and frustration, management has a constant repair problem. The machines break down on an average of three per hour, and the breakdowns are distributed in a Poisson manner. Downtime costs the company $25/hour per machine, and each maintenance worker gets $4 per hour. One worker can service machines at an average rate of five per hour, distributed exponentially; two workers, working together, can service seven per hour, distributed exponentially; and a team of three workers can do eight per hour, distributed exponentially.

What is the optimum maintenance crew size for servicing the machines?

Solution

American Vending Inc.

Case I: One worker.

$\lambda = 3/\text{hour Poisson}, \quad \mu = 5/\text{hour exponential}$

The average number of machines (either broken down or being repaired) in the system is

$$\bar{n}_s = \frac{\lambda}{\mu - \lambda} = \frac{3}{5-3} = \frac{3}{2} = 1\tfrac{1}{2} \text{ machines}$$

Downtime cost is $25 × 1.5 = $37.50 per hour; repair cost is $4.00 per hour; and total cost per hour for 1 worker is $37.50 + $4.00 = $41.50.

Downtime (1.5 × $25) =	$37.50
Labor (1 worker × $4) =	4.00
	$41.50

Case II: Two workers.

$\lambda = 3, \quad \mu = 7$

$$\bar{n}_s = \frac{\lambda}{\mu - \lambda} = \frac{3}{7-3} = 0.75 \text{ machine}$$

Downtime (0.75 × $25) =	$18.75
Labor (2 workers × $4.00) =	8.00
	$26.75

Case III: Three workers.

$$\lambda = 3, \quad \mu = 8$$

$$\bar{n}_s = \frac{\lambda}{\mu - \lambda} = \frac{3}{8 - 3} = \frac{3}{5} = 0.60 \text{ machine}$$

Downtime (0.60 × \$25)	= \$15.00
Labor (3 workers × \$4.00) =	12.00
	\$27.00

Comparing the costs for one, two, or three workers, we see that Case II with two workers is the optimal decision.

Problems

1. Burrito King is a new fast-food franchise that is opening up nationwide. Burrito King has been successful in automating burrito production for its drive-up fast-food establishments. The Burro-Master 9000 requires a constant 45 seconds to produce a burrito (with any of the standard fillings). It has been estimated that customers will arrive at the drive-up window according to a Poisson distribution at an average of 1 every 50 seconds.
   a. What is the expected average time in the system?
   b. To help determine the amount of space (in terms of number of cars) needed for the line at the drive-up window, Burrito King would like to know the average line length (in cars) and the average number of cars in the system (both in line and at the window).
2. Big Jack's drive-through hamburger service is planning to build another store at a new location and must decide how much land to lease to optimize returns. Leased space for cars will cost \$1,000 per year per space. Big Jack is aware of the highly competitive nature of the quick-service food industry and knows that if his drive-through is full, customers will go elsewhere. The location under consideration has a potential customer arrival rate of 30 per hour (Poisson). Customers' orders are filled at the rate of 40 per hour (exponential) since Big Jack prepares food ahead of time. The average profit on each arrival is \$0.60, and the store is open from noon to midnight every day. How many spaces for cars should be leased?
3. To support National Heart Week, the Heart Association plans to install a free blood pressure testing booth in El Con Mall for the week. Previous experience indicates that, on the average, 10 persons per hour request a test. Assume arrivals are Poisson from an infinite population. Blood pressure measurements can be made at a constant time of five minutes each. Assume that the queue length can be infinite with FCFS discipline.
   a. What is the average number of persons that can be expected to be in line?
   b. What is the average number of persons that can be expected to be in the system?
   c. What is the average amount of time that a person can expect to spend in line?
   d. On the average, how much time will it take to measure a person's blood pressure, including waiting time?
   e. On weekends, the arrival rate can be expected to increase to nearly 12 per hour. What effect will this have on the number in the waiting line?
4. A company has a self-service coffee station for the convenience of its workers. Arrivals at the station follow a Poisson distribution at the rate of three per minute. In serving themselves, workers take about 15 seconds, which is exponentially distributed.
   a. How many workers would you expect to see, on the average, at the coffee station?
   b. How long would you expect it to take to get a cup of coffee?

c. What percentage of time is the coffee station being used?

d. What is the probability that there would be three or more people at the station?

If an automatic coffee machine is installed that dispenses coffee at a constant time of 15 seconds, how does this change your answers to *a* and *b*?

5. Dr. L. Winston Martin is an allergist who has an excellent process in place for handling his regular patients who come in just for allergy injections. Patients arrive for an injection and fill out a name slip, which is then placed in an open slot that passes into another room staffed by one or two nurses. The specific injections for a patient are prepared and the patient is called through a speaker system into the room to receive the injection. At certain times during the day, the patient load drops and only one nurse is needed to administer the injections.

   Let's focus on the simpler case, when there is one nurse. Assume that patients arrive in a Poisson fashion and the service rate of the nurse is exponentially distributed. During this slower period, patients arrive with an interarrival time of approximately three minutes. It takes the nurse an average of two minutes to prepare the patients' serum and administer the injection.

   a. What is the average number of patients you would expect to see in Dr. Martin's facilities?

   b. How long would it take for a patient to wait, get an injection, and leave?

   c. What is the probability that there will be three or more patients on the premises?

   d. What is the utilization of the nurse?

6. The NOL Income Tax Service is analyzing its customer service operations during the month prior to the April 15 filing deadline. On the basis of past data, it has been estimated that customers arrive according to a Poisson process with an average interarrival time of 12 minutes. The time to complete a return for a customer is exponentially distributed with a mean of 10 minutes. Based on this information, answer the following questions.

   a. If you went to NOL, how much time would you allow for getting your return done?

   b. On average, how much room should be allowed for the waiting area?

   c. If the NOL service were operating 12 hours per day, how many hours on average, per day, would the office be busy?

   d. What is the probability that the system is idle?

   e. If the arrival rate remains unchanged but the average time in the system must be 45 minutes or less, what needs to be changed?

   f. A robotic replacement has been developed for preparing the new "simplified" tax forms. If the service time became a constant nine minutes, what would total time in the system become?

7. The law firm of Larry, Darryl and Darryl (L, D & D) specializes in the practice of waste disposal law and is interested in analyzing their caseload. Data were collected on the number of cases they received in a year and the times to complete each case. They consider themselves a dedicated firm and will only take on one case at a time. Calls for their services apparently follow a Poisson process with a mean of one case every 30 days. Given the fact that L, D & D are outstanding in their field, clients will wait for their turn and are served on a first-come, first-served basis. The data on the number of days to complete each case for the last 10 cases are 27, 26, 26, 25, 27, 24, 27, 23, 22, and 23.

   Determine the average time for L, D & D to complete a case, the average number of clients waiting, and the average wait for each client.

8. There is currently only one tollbooth at one of the smaller exits of a state turnpike. On average it takes about 40 seconds for the toll collector to take the money from the

driver and, if necessary, return change. Cars arrive at the tollbooth at an average rate of 70 cars per hour.

a. What is the average waiting time for a car before it pays the toll?

b. What is the capacity utilization of the toll collector?

c. The turnpike authority has decided to install another toll collection station that is equipped with an electronic scanner that will scan stickers on the windshields of cars that have signed up for this service. The scanning time is estimated to be 5 seconds, which is constant. Once the new electronic booth is installed, it is estimated that 40 percent of the cars will buy the stickers and use it. What will be the average waiting time for cars with stickers and for cars without stickers?

9. Inndependents.com is a startup dot-com company that provides a network for small independently owned inns and hotels. This network makes guest reservations and provides technical support for the managers of these properties. To begin operations, one customer service representative has been hired to answer telephone calls. (In other words, this is a one-person call center.) It is estimated that the average call will take about three minutes to answer, and that initially the demand is forecasted to be 50 calls per day over an eight-hour day.

a. What will be the average waiting time before a call is answered?

b. What is the capacity utilization of the customer service representative?

c. After one week of operation, demand is exceeding the forecast, and is now averaging 80 calls per day. To provide better service, another customer service representative is hired. In addition, the calls are segmented by guest reservations and technical support, with each representative assigned to answer only one type of call. Based upon the first week's data, 75 percent of the calls are for reservations while only 25 percent are for technical support. Additional data show that the average time to make a reservation is two minutes, while the time to answer a technical support question averages six minutes. With this additional information, determine the average waiting time for each type of call and the capacity utilization for each customer service representative.

10. An agricultural cooperative consists of a group of farmers that invest in a common business venture, which is often a processing facility for their farm products. Ocean Spray in Massachusetts (cranberries), Tillamook in Oregon (cheese), and Cabot in Vermont (cheese) are all good examples of agricultural cooperatives. As a cooperative is owned by the farmers, they share in the costs and/or profits that the cooperative generates.

A grape cooperative in California, which processes grapes for the making of wine, has one unloading dock at its facility. During the fall harvest, trucks arrive from the vineyards at an average rate of three per hour throughout the 12 hours that the facility is open every day. The growers rent these trucks with drivers at a cost of $75.00 per hour.

Joe Newpol, the manager of the processing plant is trying to decide how big a crew he should hire to unload the trucks. As a first step in determining this, he has estimated the following average times that it will take to unload a truck for different crew sizes:

Crew Size	Average Unload Time (minutes)
4	18
5	15
6	12
7	10

He is currently paying workers $16.00 per hour, which includes benefits.

Based upon this information, how big a crew size should he hire so as to minimize total costs?

11. An automotive parts distributor delivers replacement parts to gas stations and garages in its area. On average, an order consists of 18 different items. Aspen Wang, the manager of the distribution center, wants to know how many people she should assign to fill each order. The order filling times, based on the number of workers assigned to an order, are as follows:

Number of Workers	Order Filling Time
1	15
2	12
3	10
4	8

Workers are paid $12.00 per hour, including benefits. The cost of a delivery truck and driver is estimated to be $65.00 per hour.

If there is an average of 25 deliveries each day, and the facility is open 10 hours a day, how many workers should Aspen assign to fill an order to minimize total costs to the firm?

Bibliography

Bartfai, P., and J. Tomko. *Point Processes Queuing Problems.* New York: Elsevier-North Holland Publishing, 1981.

Bruell, Steven C. *Computational Algorithms for Closed Queuing Networks.* New York: Elsevier-North Holland Publishing, 1980.

Gorney, Leonard. *Queuing Theory: A Solving Approach.* Princeton, NJ: Petrocelli, 1981.

Hillier, Frederick S., et al. *Queuing Tables and Graphs.* New York: Elsevier-North Holland Publishing, 1981.

Newell, Gordon F. *Applications of Queuing Theory.* New York: Chapman and Hall, 1982.

Solomon, Susan L. *Simulation of Waiting Lines.* Englewood Cliffs, NJ: Prentice Hall, 1983.

Srivastava, H. M., and B. R. Kashyap. *Special Functions in Queuing Theory: And Related Stochastic Processes.* New York: Academic Press, 1982.

Vinrod, B., and T. Altiok. "Approximating Unreliable Queuing Networks under the Assumption of Exponentiality." *Journal of the Operational Research Society,* March 1986, pp. 309–16.

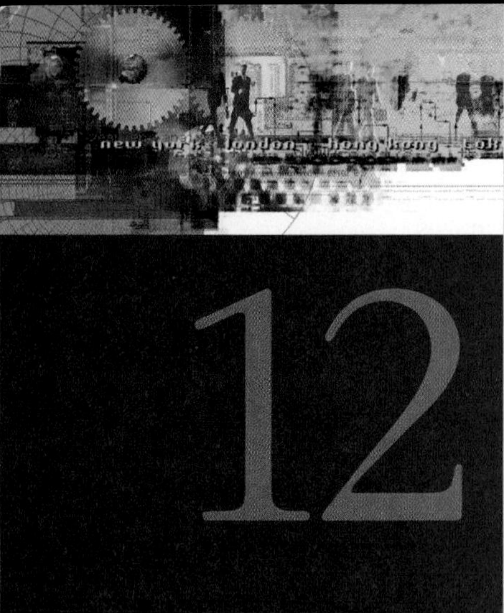

12 Scheduling

Chapter Objectives

- Provide insight into the nature of scheduling and control of intermittent production systems.
- Emphasize the prevalence of job shop environments, notably in the service sector.
- Stress the interaction and dependence of job shop planning and technology.
- Present examples showing the importance of worker scheduling in service sector job shops.
- Identify the major elements of scheduling workers in a service organization.
- Illustrate how technology can facilitate the scheduling of workers.

SCHEDULING PRIORITIES AT TAX TIME

"Every year it's the same thing. We have our corporate clients that need their tax returns completed by March 15 and our individual clients that need their personal income tax returns done by April 15, but it seems that whatever plan we have in place with respect to scheduling the work, these three months of February, March, and April are still crazy."

Ron Rice, managing partner of Weiner and Rice, a medium-sized CPA firm located in Chestnut Hill, MA, was holding his annual meeting in January with his staff of accountants to address the workload for the upcoming tax season. "What it boils down to," Ron continued, "is that we try and cram a year's worth of work into two and a half months, and that's not realistic, regardless of how many hours a week each of us works. In addition, no matter how hard we try, we always end up with some complaints from clients that we take too long to get their tax returns done."

"The issue is establishing priorities for doing the returns," chimed in Bob Mazairz, a senior accountant who had been with the firm for about five years. "We need to decide which returns we work on first, which get second priority but still get completed by the March or April deadline, and those returns that we put on extension, and which therefore don't need to be filed until August 15."

"It's not as simple as that," replied Ron, "we tell our clients that if they don't get us the information to do their returns before March 23, they may have to go on extension. However, for those we put on extension, we still need to estimate their taxes. Even then, there may be interest and penalties to pay. On the other hand, we could also get complaints from those customers that have refunds coming if we put them on extension."

"And what do we do when we get a corporate return at the last minute, and have several individual clients who have given us their tax information in early March?" added Bob, "do we delay the individual tax returns to work on the corporate return?"

"Good point," said Ron, adding "All I know is that I am tired of facing this same fiasco every year. There has to be a better way of scheduling these returns other than the one we're using, which I am not sure even I know! Anyone have any ideas on this?"

Special thanks to Ron Rice and Bob Mazairz,
Weiner and Rice, CPA, Chestnut Hill, MA

Managerial Issues

Scheduling, which is defined as the prioritizing and sequencing of work, is a critical element in both manufacturing and services. In manufacturing, scheduling is especially important in a job shop where orders or parts are typically processed in batches. Because each order requires a unique set of operations in a specified sequence, job shop scheduling can be very complicated. Consequently, management needs to look at the scheduling of both workers and equipment. To accomplish this, some type of priority system is usually used to determine the order in which jobs are to be done.

Service managers, due to the fact that labor is very often a major cost element, focus almost exclusively on scheduling workers. Worker scheduling in services can be divided into two broad categories: (a) the scheduling of back-of-the-house workers and (b) the scheduling of front-of-the-house workers. For those services that have sufficient buffer between their customers and the back-of-the-house workers, the scheduling issues are similar to those of a manufacturing operation. For both of these types of operations, managers focus on high labor productivity and/or machine capacity utilization. At the same time they need to ensure that orders are completed on time.

The scheduling of front-of-the-house service workers is complicated by the fact that these workers must interact directly with the customers. In other words, these workers have to be available when customers want the service that their company provides. As a consequence, managers face a trade-off between providing high levels of customer service, in the form of short (or even no) customer waiting times, and obtaining high worker productivity (as explained in detail in the previous chapter and its supplement). In order to obtain both high levels of worker productivity and fast customer service, service managers are increasingly turning to technology and scheduling software.

The Job Shop Defined

job shop

Organization whose layout is process-oriented (vs. product-oriented) and that produces items in batches.

A **job shop** is a functional organization whose departments or work centers are organized around particular processes that consist of specific types of equipment and/or operations, such as drilling and assembly in a factory, and scanning and printing in a computer laboratory. A good example of a job shop in a service environment is a hospital, which has designated areas for blood tests, x-rays, and radiation treatments. In all these cases, the good produced or the service provided is based upon an individual order for a specific customer.

Scheduling in a Job Shop

A schedule is a timetable for performing activities, using resources, or allocating facilities. The purpose of operations scheduling in a job shop is to disaggregate the master production schedule (MPS) into time-phased weekly, daily, and/or hourly activities—in other words, to specify in precise terms the planned workload on the production process in the very short run. Operations control focuses on job-order progress and, where necessary, expediting orders and/or adjusting system capacity to make sure that the MPS is met.

In designing a scheduling and control system, provision must be made for efficient performance of the following functions:

dispatching of orders

Releasing of orders to the factory floor.

1. Allocating orders, equipment, and personnel to work centers or other specified locations. Essentially, this is short-run capacity planning.
2. Determining the *sequence* of order performance; that is, establishing job priorities.
3. Initiating performance of the scheduled work. This is commonly termed the **dispatching of orders.**

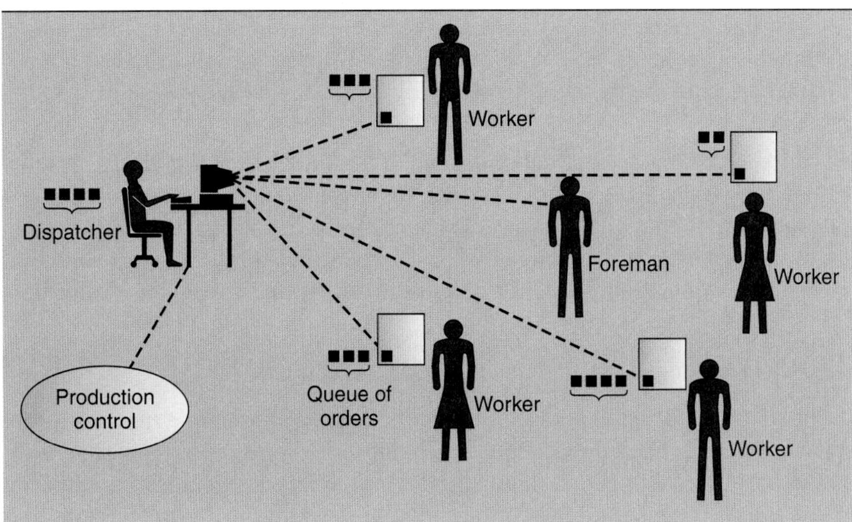

Exhibit 12.1

Typical Scheduling Process

4. Shop-floor control (or production activity control), which involves
   a. Reviewing the status and controlling the progress of orders as they are being worked on.
   b. **Expediting** late and critical orders.[1]
5. Revising the schedule to reflect recent changes in order status.
6. Assuring that quality control standards are being met.

expediting

Checking the progress of specific orders to ensure completion in a timely manner.

A simple job shop-scheduling process is shown in Exhibit 12.1. At the start of the day, the job dispatcher (in this case, a production control person assigned to this department) selects and sequences the available jobs to be run at individual workstations. The dispatcher's decisions would be based on the operations and routing requirements of each job, status of existing jobs on the machines, the queue of work before each machine, job priorities, material availability, anticipated job orders to be released later in the day, and worker and machine capabilities. To help organize the schedule, the dispatcher would draw on shop-floor information from the previous day and external information provided by central production control, process engineering, and so on. The dispatcher also would meet with the foreman or supervisor of the department to discuss the feasibility of the schedule, especially with respect to workforce considerations and identifying potential bottlenecks. Visual schedule boards provide an efficient and simple way to communicate the priority and status of work.

What makes scheduling each individual job so difficult? Consider the following factors:

- This good/service may never have been done before, so the estimates of the expected length of time for completion of the various components may be quite different from the actual time.

[1]Despite the fact that expediting is frowned on by production control specialists, it is nevertheless a reality of life. In fact, a very typical entry-level job in production control is that of expediter or "stock-chaser." In some companies a good expediter—one who can negotiate a critical job through the system or who can scrounge up materials nobody thought were available—is a prized possession.

- The sequence of operations is extremely flexible and, with a cross-trained workforce, the number of possible sequences can be huge. Trying to assess the expected results of different sequences with a goal of finding the best sequence is usually very difficult.
- For different operations, the determination of the "best" sequence may vary—for one case it may be the minimization of waste, for another it may be the minimization of idle facilities, for a third it may be the maximization of throughput, and so on. Thus, even with extensive research into the job shop scheduling problem, it is hard to find quantitative or mechanical algorithms that are always appropriate for all situations.

Elements of the Job Shop Scheduling Problem

Job shops exist everywhere and, as a result, examples are plentiful. The emergency room at a hospital may be organized by function: the examination rooms are separate from the x-ray room, which is separate from the waiting room. Depending on the needs of the patient, different jobs are performed at different physical locations within the ER, and in some cases, at locations within the hospital other than the ER. A riding academy not only boards and exercises the horses, but also provides lessons at different levels to different groups. A ski resort may similarly provide different levels of instruction for different students. The kitchen of a restaurant is also a job shop—different orders come in at different times and the different meals may be prepared by different people.

But all these examples share some common elements:

- The "jobs"—whether they are riding students at an academy or orders for dinner at a restaurant—arrive at the job shop in some pattern.
- The ability of the job shop to complete these "jobs" in a given amount of time is dependent upon the capacity or "machinery" in the shop. For example, the number of students who may take riding lessons is limited by the number of horses present at the riding academy; the number of students who enroll in a given class may be limited by the number of seats available in the classroom.
- The ability of the job shop to complete these "jobs" is also dependent on the ratio of skilled workers to "machines." A riding academy may have lots of horses, but the number of riding students is also limited by the availability of skilled instructors. The number of meals that can be prepared in a timely fashion at a restaurant can be limited by the number of chefs working that evening (in addition to the number of ovens, stoves, and other cooking equipment that are available).
- The **flow pattern** of jobs through the shop varies from job to job. At a restaurant, one order might be for a sandwich and salad while another might be for a full seven-course dinner. Consequently, the number and sequence of steps required to fill these two orders is dramatically different.

flow pattern

Routes that materials follow through a factory to make a product.

- Different jobs are often assigned different priorities. Some jobs are marked "rush" or "urgent" and may be from a preferred customer. Medical personnel at the ER in the hospital assign these priorities by performing triage so that the most serious patients are treated first.
- The criteria used to evaluate a given schedule differ from job shop to job shop. A restaurant may try to minimize the wasted food or the idle personnel.

Job Arrival Patterns Jobs often arrive in a pattern that follows a known statistical distribution (for example, the Poisson distribution is relatively common), or they may arrive in batches (also called "lot" or "bulk" arrivals), or they may arrive such that the time between arrivals is constant. Further, jobs may come with different priorities.

The "Machinery" in the Shop The scheduling problem is also dependent on the number and variety of the equipment or "machines" in the shop. Further, as these "machines" become smarter and are more capable of multitasking, the task of scheduling becomes more complicated.

machine-limited systems

Operations where the capacity of the facility is determined by number of machines.

The Ratio of Skilled Workers to Machines Job shops can be classified as either **machine-limited** or **labor-limited,** depending on whether the workers outnumber the machines or vice versa. In addition, jobs may be classified as *labor-intensive* or *machine-intensive,* depending on how much of the job may be performed using automated processes.

labor-limited systems

Operations where the capacity of the facility is determined by number of workers.

The Flow Pattern of Jobs through the Shop Exhibit 12.2 shows the various possible flows of jobs through a job shop. In some job shops, all jobs follow the same pattern; in others, the pattern is purely random. Most job shops fall somewhere in between these two extremes. Because of the apparent lack of organization, the flow of material through a job shop is often described as a *jumbled flow*.

Priority Rules for Allocating Jobs to Machines

The process of determining which job is started first on a particular machine or work center is known as sequencing or priority sequencing. **Priority rules** are the criteria by which the sequence of jobs is determined. These can be very simple, requiring only that jobs be sequenced according to one piece of data, such as processing time, due date, or order of arrival. Other rules, though equally simple, may require several pieces of information, typically to derive an index number such as in the *least slack rule* and the *critical ratio*

priority rules

Criteria for determining the sequence or priority of jobs through a facility.

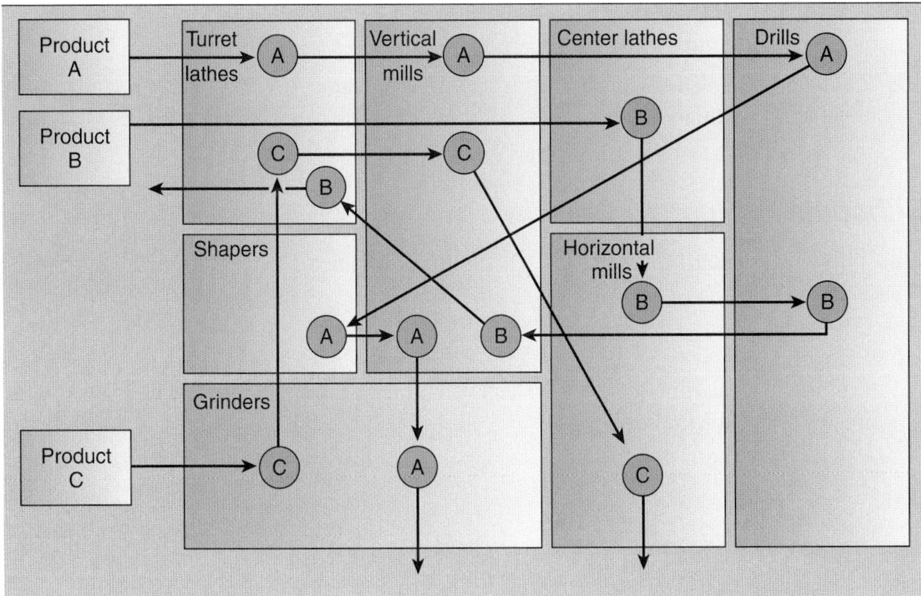

Exhibit 12.2

Material Flows through a Job Shop

rule (both defined later). Still others, such as Johnson's rule (also discussed later), apply to job scheduling on a sequence of machines and require a computational procedure to specify the order of performance. Ten of the more common priority rules for sequencing jobs are

1. *FCFS—first come, first-served.* Orders are run in the order that they arrive in the department.
2. *SPT—shortest processing time.* Run the job with the shortest completion time first, next shortest second, and so on. This is identical to SOT—shortest operating time.
3. *Due date—earliest due date first.* Run the job with the earliest due date first. DDate—when referring to the entire job; OPNDD—when referring to the next operation.
4. *Start date—due date minus normal lead time.* Run the job with the earliest start date first.
5. *STR—slack time remaining.* This is calculated as the difference between the time remaining before the due date minus the processing time remaining. Orders with the shortest STR are run first.
6. *STR/OP—Slack time remaining per operation.* Orders with shortest STR/OP are run first, calculated as follows:

$$\text{STR/OP} = \frac{\text{Time remaining before due date} - \text{Remaining processing time}}{\text{Number of remaining operations}}$$

7. *CR—critical ratio.* This is calculated as the difference between the due date and the current date divided by the work remaining. Orders with the smallest CR are run first.
8. *QR—queue ratio.* This is calculated as the slack time remaining in the schedule divided by the planned remaining queue time. Orders with the smallest QR are run first.
9. *LCFS—last-come, first-served.* This rule occurs frequently by default. As orders arrive they are placed on the top of the stack and the operator usually picks up the order on top to run first.
10. *Random order—whim.* The supervisors or the operators usually select whichever job they feel like running.[2]

Schedule Evaluation Criteria

The following standard measures of schedule performance are used to evaluate priority rules:

1. Meeting due dates of customers or downstream operations.
2. Minimizing flow time (also known as cycle time or throughput time), which is the time a job spends in the shop.

[2]This list is modified from Donald W. Fogarty, John H. Blackstone Jr., and Thomas R. Hoffmann, *Production and Inventory Management* (Cincinnati: South-Western Publishing, 1991), pp. 452–53.

3. Minimizing work in process.
4. Minimizing idle time of machines and workers.

Priority Rules and Techniques

Scheduling n Jobs on One Machine

Let us compare some of these 10 priority rules in a static scheduling situation involving four jobs on one machine. (In scheduling terminology, this class of problems is referred to as an "*n* job—one-machine problem," or simply $n/1$.) The theoretical difficulty of this type of problem increases as more machines are considered; therefore, the only restriction on *n* is that it be a specified, finite integer.

Consider the following example: Ioannis Kyriakides is the supervisor of Legal Copy-Express, which provides copy services for L.A. law firms in the downtown Los Angeles area. Five customers submitted their orders at the beginning of the week. Specific scheduling data on these orders are as follows:

Job (in order of arrival)	Processing Time (days)	Due Date (days hence)
A	3	5
B	4	6
C	2	7
D	6	9
E	1	2

All orders require the use of the only color copy machine that Legal Copy-Express has. Kyriakides therefore must decide on the processing sequence for the five orders. The evaluation criterion is to minimize flow time. Suppose that Kyriakides decides to use the FCFS rule in an attempt to make Legal Copy-Express appear fair to its customers. The FCFS rule results in the following flow times:

FCFS Schedule

Job	Processing Time (days)	Due Date (days)	Flow Time (days) Start		Job Time		Finish
A	3	5	0	+	3	=	3
B	4	6	3	+	4	=	7
C	2	7	7	+	2	=	9
D	6	9	9	+	6	=	15
E	1	2	15	+	1	=	16

Total flow time = 3 + 7 + 9 + 15 + 16 = 50 days
Mean flow time = $\frac{50}{5}$ = 10 days

Comparing the due date of each job with its flow time, we observe that only Job A will be on time. Jobs B, C, D, and E will be late by 1, 2, 6, and 14 days, respectively. On the average, a job will be late by $(0 + 1 + 2 + 6 + 14)/5 = 4.6$ days.

Let's now consider the SPT rule. Here Kyriakides gives the highest priority to the order that has the shortest processing time. The resulting flow times are

SPT Schedule

Job	Processing Time (days)	Due Date (days)	Flow Time (days)
E	1	2	$0+1=1$
C	2	7	$1+2=3$
A	3	5	$3+3=6$
B	4	6	$6+4=10$
D	6	9	$10+6=16$

Total flow time $= 1+3+6+10+16 = 36$ days
Mean flow time $= \frac{36}{5} = 7.2$ days

SPT results in lower average flow time. In addition, Jobs E and C will be ready before the due date, and Job A is late by only one day. On the average a job will be late by $(0+0+1+4+7)/5 = 2.4$ days.

If Kyriakides decides to use the DDate rule, the resulting schedule is

DDATE Schedule

Job	Processing Time (days)	Due Date (days)	Flow Time (days)
E	1	2	$0+1=1$
A	3	5	$1+3=4$
B	4	6	$4+4=8$
C	2	7	$8+2=10$
D	6	9	$10+6=16$

Total completion time $= 1+4+8+10+16 = 39$ days
Mean flow time $= 7.8$ days

In this case Jobs B, C, and D will be late. On the average, a job will be late by $(0+0+2+3+7)/5 = 2.4$ days.

In a similar manner, the flow times of the LCFS, random, and STR rules are as follows:

LCFS Schedule

Job	Processing Time (days)	Due Date (days)	Flow Time (days)
E	1	2	$0+1=1$
D	6	9	$1+6=7$
C	2	7	$7+2=9$
B	4	6	$9+4=13$
A	3	5	$13+3=16$

Total flow time $= 46$ days
Mean flow time $= 9.2$ days
Average days late/job $= 4.0$ days

Random Schedule			
Job	**Processing Time (days)**	**Due Date (days)**	**Flow Time (days)**
D	6	9	0 + 6 = 6
C	2	7	6 + 2 = 8
A	3	5	8 + 3 = 11
E	1	2	11 + 1 = 12
B	4	6	12 + 4 = 16
Total flow time = 53 days			
Mean flow time = 10.6 days			
Average days late/job = 5.4 days			

STR Schedule			
Job	**Processing Time (days)**	**Due Date (days)**	**Flow Time (days)**
E	1	2	0 + 1 = 1
A	3	5	1 + 3 = 4
B	4	6	4 + 4 = 8
D	6	9	8 + 6 = 14
C	2	7	14 + 2 = 16
Total flow time = 43 days			
Mean flow time = 8.6 days			
Average days late/job = 3.2 days			

These results are summarized below:

Scheduling Rule	Total Completion Time (days)	Average Completion Time (days)	Average Lateness (days)
FCFS	50	10.0	4.6
SPT	36	7.2	2.4
DDate	39	7.8	2.4
LCFS	46	9.2	4.0
Random	53	10.6	5.4
STR	43	8.6	3.2

For this example, the SPT is better than the rest of the scheduling rules, but is this always the case? The answer is yes. It can be shown mathematically that the SPT rule yields an optimum solution for the $n/1$ case with respect to scheduling, as well as for other evaluation criteria such as mean waiting time and mean completion time. In fact, this simple rule is so powerful that it has been termed "the most important concept in the entire subject of sequencing."[3] However, it is important to note that the SPT rule totally ignores the due dates of jobs. As a consequence, jobs with longer processing times often can be late.

[3]R. W. Conway, William L. Maxwell, and Louis W. Miller, *Theory of Scheduling* (Reading, MA: Addison-Wesley Publishing, 1967), p. 26. A classic book on the subject.

Scheduling n Jobs on Two Machines

The next step up in complexity of job shop types is the $n/2$ case, where two or more jobs must be processed on two machines in a common sequence. As in the $n/1$ case, there is an approach that leads to an optimal solution according to certain criteria. Also, as in the $n/1$ case, we assume it is a static scheduling situation. The objective of this approach, termed *Johnson's rule* or *method* (after its developer), is to minimize the flow time, from the beginning of the first job until the completion of the last. Johnson's rule consists of the following steps:

1. List the operation time for each job on both machines.
2. Select the job with the shortest operation time.
3. If the shortest time is for the first machine, do that job first; if the shortest time is for the second machine, do that job last.
4. Repeat Steps 2 and 3 for each remaining job until the schedule is complete.

Example

We can illustrate the application of Johnson's rule by scheduling four jobs through two machines:

***Step 1:* List operation times**

Job	Operation Time on Machine 1	Operation Time on Machine 2
A	3	2
B	6	8
C	5	6
D	7	4

Solution

***Steps 2 and 3:* Select shortest operation time and assign**
Job A is shortest on Machine 2 and is assigned first and performed last. (Job A is now no longer available to be scheduled.)

***Step 4:* Repeat Steps 2 and 3 until completion of schedule**
Select the shortest operation time among the remaining jobs. Job D is second shortest on Machine 2, thus it is performed second to last (remember Job A is last). Now, Jobs A and D are not available anymore for scheduling. Job C is the shortest on Machine 1 among the remaining jobs. Job C is performed first. Now, only Job B is left with the shortest operation time on Machine 1. Thus, according to Step 3, it is performed first among the remaining, or second overall (Job C was already scheduled first).

In summary, the solution sequence is C → B → D → A, and the flow time is 25 days, which is a minimum. Also minimized are total idle time and mean idle time. The final schedule appears in Exhibit 12.3.

These steps result in scheduling the jobs having the shortest time in the beginning and ending of the schedule. As a result, the amount of concurrent operating time for the two machines is maximized, thus minimizing the total operating time required to complete the jobs.

Johnson's rule has been extended to yield an optimal solution for the $n/3$ case. When flow shop scheduling problems larger than $n/3$ arise (and they generally do), analytical

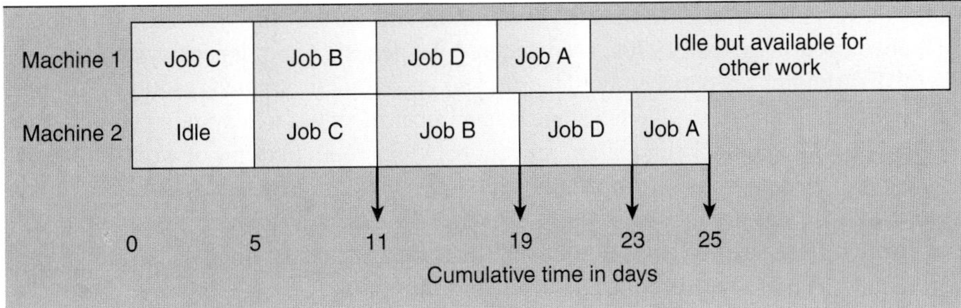

Exhibit 12.3
Optimal Schedule of Jobs Using Johnson's Rule

solution procedures leading to optimality are not available. The reason for this is that even though the jobs may arrive in static fashion at the first machine, the scheduling problem becomes dynamic, and a series of waiting lines start to form in front of machines downstream.

Scheduling n Jobs on m Machines—Complex Job Shops

Complex job shops are characterized by multiple machine centers processing a variety of different jobs arriving at the machine centers in an intermittent fashion throughout the day. If there are n jobs to be processed on m machines and all jobs are processed on all machines, then there are $(n!)^m$ alternative schedules for this job set. Because of the large number of schedules that exist for even small job shops, simulation is the only practical way to determine the relative merits of different priority rules in such situations. As in the n job on one machine case, the 10 priority rules (and more) have been compared relative to their performance on the evaluation criteria previously mentioned.

Which priority rule should be used? We believe that the needs of most manufacturers are reasonably satisfied by a relatively simple priority scheme that embodies the following principles:

1. It should be dynamic, that is, computed frequently during the course of a job to reflect changing conditions.
2. It should be based in one way or another on slack time (the difference between the work remaining to be done on a job and the time remaining to do it in).

OPT Scheduling Concepts

OPT is a software system that contains a proprietary algorithm for production scheduling. From OPT (optimized production technology) has evolved the managerial concept of theory of constraints (TOC). OPT/TOC is a production planning and control (PPC) method that attempts to optimize scheduling by maximizing the utilization of the bottlenecks in the process.

OPT
A proprietary software package for scheduling production.

Traditional production planning and control is considered today to be no more than a production tool. Integrated PPC is a concept that marries an underlying philosophy of planning with a set of tools to implement that philosophy to optimize the process.

There are three major approaches to integrated PPC: push systems, pull systems, and bottleneck systems. The forerunner to the push systems is a tool developed by Joseph Orlicky at IBM in 1974—material requirements planning (MRP). In the late 1960s, Taichi

Ohno at Toyota developed the *kanban* system, the first of the pull systems. Eli Goldratt's OPT, developed in the late 1970s, is considered the genesis of bottleneck systems.[4]

OPT distinguishes between bottlenecks and capacity constrained resources. A bottleneck applies to the case in which a stage or a number of stages in a system cannot process the good or service quickly enough to prevent backlogs (both in terms of work-in-progress and demand). A capacity-constrained resource (CCR) is a good or service necessary for the creation of the final product that is exhausted before the final product is delivered. To illustrate the difference between a bottleneck and a capacity-constrained resource, let's consider a retail laundry that specializes in cleaning shirts.

Claude's Cleaners is noted for their quality and inexpensive service, so much so that there is always a line of customers waiting for the sole clerk, Clark, to process each transaction. Unfortunately, they are not noted for speedy service; it usually takes a week just to get a shirt cleaned and pressed. Claude's has three presses, but they are used only three or four days each week because the starch for the shirts usually runs out. (In an effort to minimize costs, Claude's uses the just-in-time concept for materials management and it takes three days for the starch to be delivered after an order is placed.)

In this service process, Clark is a bottleneck. The starch is a capacity-constrained resource (CCR)—as its inventory is increased, the flow through the process component (the presses) is increased. The inventory of starch *acts* like a temporary bottleneck. The effects of CCRs typically can be reduced in the short term by relatively simple adjustments. Improvements to bottlenecks, on the other hand, are usually expensive and time consuming.

To optimize the flow through a bottleneck in the system, the bottleneck must operate continuously and at full capacity. A planning/control/communication mechanism, known as Drum-Buffer-Rope, is used to accomplish this objective. Since the bottleneck is the slowest component of the process, it sets the pace or tempo for the system—much like a drum beat sets the pace for a marching band. With the output of the process limited to the output of the bottleneck, decreases in output at the bottleneck cannot be recovered. Therefore, an inventory of goods or services, or "buffer inventory," is necessary before the bottleneck so it will always be operating at maximum capacity. To assure that the buffer is maintained at an optimal level (that is, just enough to keep the bottleneck operating), the rate at which the bottleneck is processing (the drum beat) must be communicated to the source of the goods or services that the bottleneck is processing. Since this communication is in one direction—from the bottleneck to the source of the goods or services (input)—and it pulls the input to the buffer, it is referred to as the "rope."

Returning to Claude's Cleaners, Clark is the bottleneck or drum. The buffer would be the inventory of cleaned clothing waiting for the customer. What is the rope? Is there a rope?

The quantity of goods or services sent to the buffer is called the *transfer batch.* Because the purpose of the transfer batch is to maintain the buffer at its optimal level, the quantity will be dependent on the processing rate of the bottleneck. The quantity of goods or services produced by the bottleneck's input source at one time is referred to as the *process batch.* In bottleneck systems it is critical to recognize that to optimize the entire system transfer batches and process batches may not be of the same quantity.

At Claude's Cleaners, Bettie and Bert box the shirts after they have been pressed. If we consider Bettie and Bert together as a single input source for Clark, then the process batch size from boxing to the pick-up area is two. But, since Clark can only process one transaction at a time, the transfer batch quantity is one.

[4]Daniel Sipper and Robert L. Buflin Jr., *Production: Planning, Control, and Integration* (Burr Ridge, IL: McGraw-Hill, 1998), p. 531.

With the fundamental components of a bottleneck system defined, we now can turn our attention to optimally scheduling such a system. There are five basic steps to scheduling a bottleneck system:

- Determine the bottleneck and CCRs.
- Optimize the CCRs.
- Schedule the bottleneck to its maximum.
- Schedule the process located before the bottleneck.
- Schedule the process located after the bottleneck.

There are nine basic rules that Eli Goldratt has presented for scheduling with OPT.

1. Balance the flow, not the capacity.
2. Utilization of a nonbottleneck is determined by a constraint in the system (a bottleneck).
3. Utilization and activation of an input are not the same.
4. Any loss in output at a bottleneck translates into a loss for the entire system.
5. Gains at nonbottlenecks do not translate into gains at the bottleneck or for the entire system.
6. Bottlenecks determine the throughput and inventory levels.
7. For optimization, transfer batches may not equal process batches.
8. The size of the process batches through the system should not be fixed.
9. Schedules should be established after evaluating all constraints simultaneously.

It is not uncommon to find that once a bottleneck has been scheduled that another bottleneck will appear in the process. To optimize a system it may be necessary to repeat the scheduling procedure a number of times.

OPT's basic advantage is that, by focusing on a single bottleneck resource, the problem is sufficiently simplified that it can be solved well and with intuitive support to the user. However, OPT has a number of disadvantages: "it cannot accommodate multiple and shifting bottlenecks; user interface is not strong; reactive correction to the schedule requires full rerunning; it is proprietary, so not only is the software rigid, but also simple judgmental modifications of schedules are difficult."[5]

Control in the Job Shop

Scheduling job priorities is just one aspect of **shop-floor control** (now often referred to as *production activity control*). The *American Production and Inventory Control Society (APICS) Dictionary* defines a *shop-floor control system* as

shop-floor control

Set of procedures for maintaining and communicating the status of orders and work centers.

A system for utilizing data from the shop floor as well as data processing files to maintain and communicate status information on shop orders and work centers.

The major functions of shop-floor control are

1. Assigning priority to each shop order.
2. Maintaining work-in-process (WIP) quantity information.

[5]Morton and Pentico, *Heuristic Scheduling Systems* (New York: John Wiley & Sons, 1993), p. 28.

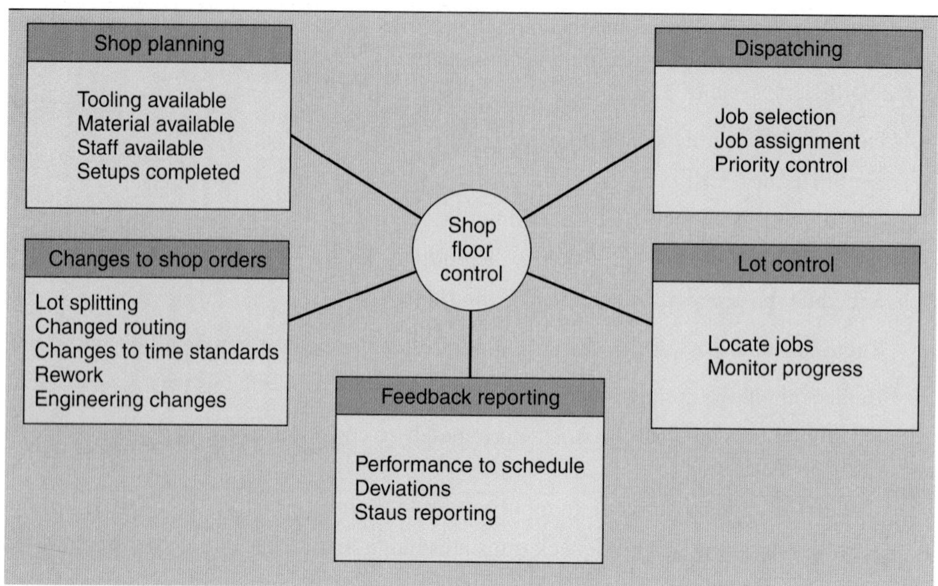

Source: "Shop Floor Control—Closing the Loop," *Inventory Management Newsletter*, August 1982. Center for Inventory Management, Stone Mountain, Georgia 30087 USA.

3. Conveying shop-order status information to the office.
4. Providing actual output data for capacity control purposes.
5. Providing quantity by location by shop order for WIP inventory and accounting purposes.
6. Providing measures of efficiency, utilization, and productivity of labor and machines.

Exhibit 12.4 illustrates more of the details related to shop-floor control.

Tools of Shop-Floor Control

There are a variety of written forms that can help the supervisor maintain control in the job shop; these are easily generated by the appropriate software and updated frequently through a normal interaction of supervisor and software.

- The *dispatch list* (usually generated on a daily basis) tells the shop foreman what jobs need to be accomplished that day, what priority each has, and how long each will take. Exhibit 12.5A presents an example of a dispatch list.
- *Exception reports* provide the supervisor with the information needed to handle special cases and problems. An example of this is the anticipated delay report shown in Exhibit 12.5B. Typically made out once or twice a week, these reports are reviewed to determine if any of the delays are serious enough to warrant revision of the master production schedule.
- The *input/output control report,* or simply the I/O report, is used by the supervisor to monitor the relationship between the workload and the capacity of each workstation. If these relationships are significantly out of balance, then the supervisor can identify where adjustments are needed. An example of such a report is shown in Exhibit 12.5C.

Exhibit 12.5

Some Basic Tools of Shop-Floor Control

A. Dispatch List

Work center 1501—Day 205

Start date	Job #	Description	Run time
201	15131	Shaft	11.4
203	15143	Stud	20.6
205	15145	Spindle	4.3
205	15712	Spindle	8.6
207	15340	Metering rod	6.5
208	15312	Shaft	4.6

B. Anticipated Delay Report

Dept. 24 April 8

Part #	Sched. date	New date	Cause of delay	Action
17125	4/10	4/15	Fixture broke	Toolroom will return on 4/15
13044	4/11	5/1	Out for plating—plater on strike	New lot started
17653	4/11	4/14	New part-holes don't align	Engineering laying out new jig

C. Input/Output Control Report (B)

Work center 0162

Week ending	5/05	5/12	5/19	5/26
Planned input	210	210	210	210
Actual input	110	150	140	130
Cumulative deviation	−100	−160	−230	−310
Planned output	210	210	210	210
Actual output	140	120	160	120
Cumulative deviation	−70	−160	−210	−300

Note: All figures are in standard hours.

- *Status reports* give the supervisor summaries on the performance of the operation, and usually include the number and percentage of jobs completed on time, the lateness of jobs not yet completed, the volume of output, and so forth. Two examples of status reports are the scrap report and the rework report.

Input/output control is a major feature of a control system. The major precept of I/O control is that the total workload accepted (the input) should never exceed the capacity to perform jobs (the output). When the input exceeds the output, then backlogs occur. This has several negative consequences: Jobs are completed late, making customers unhappy, and subsequent or related jobs incur a delay before they can be started. This delay also results in unsatisfied customers. Moreover, when jobs pile up at a work center, congestion occurs, processing becomes inefficient, and the flow of work to downstream work centers becomes sporadic. An analogy of this phenomenon to the flow of water is shown in Exhibit 12.6.

input/output control

Assuring the amount of work accepted does not exceed the capacity of the facility.

A simple but effective control device is the **Gantt chart.** It is used to help plan and track jobs, again, using software. A Gantt chart is a type of bar chart that plots tasks to be done against time. It also helps show relationships between jobs. Exhibit 12.7 shows a small Gantt chart for a job shop attempting to complete three jobs (A, B, and C). This chart

Gantt chart

Planning tool that plots activities on a time chart.

Exhibit 12.6

Shop Capacity Control Load Flow

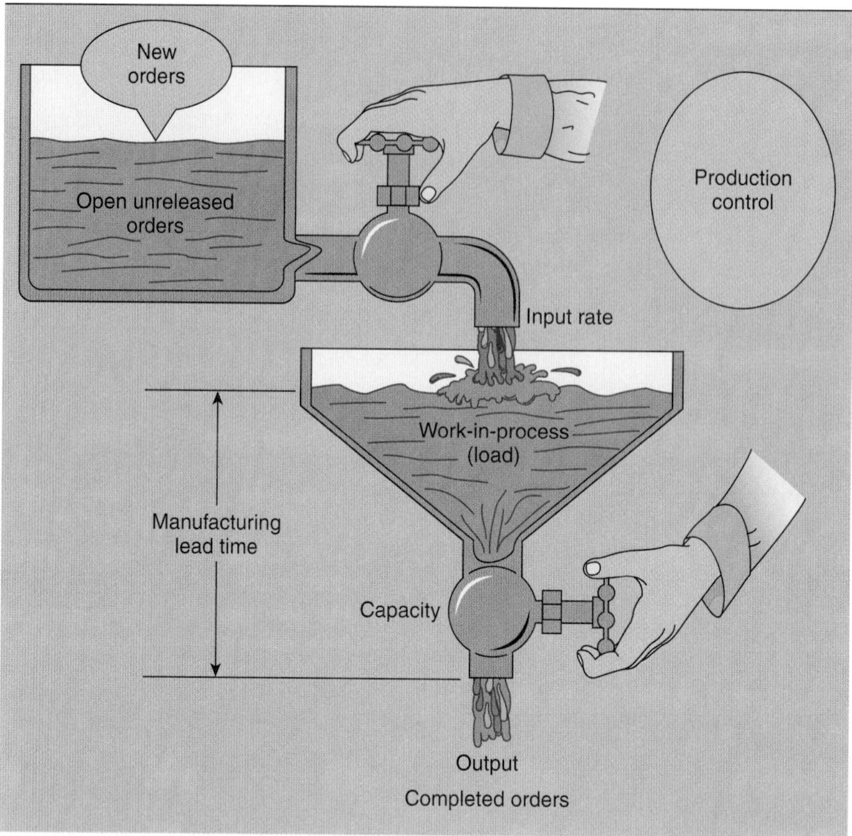

Source: American Production and Inventory Control Society, "Training Aid—Shop Floor Control," undated. Reprinted with permission.

Exhibit 12.7

Gantt Chart

Chart Review Time

Job	Monday	Tuesday	Wednesday	Thursday	Friday
A					
B					
C	Maintenance				

Gantt Chart Symbols

- Start of an activity
- End of an activity
- Schedule allowed activity time
- Actual work progress
- Time set aside for nonproduction activities; e.g., repairs, routine maintenance, material outages

Source: Professor Bob Parsons, Management Science Department, Northeastern University, Boston, MA. Used with permission.

indicates that Job A is behind schedule by about 4 hours, Job B is ahead of schedule, and Job C has been completed, but only after a delayed start for equipment maintenance. The Gantt chart shows how much ahead or behind schedule we are by comparing where we are now to where we planned to be. Other useful control devices include the PERT and CPM networks discussed in Chapter S3.

Shop-floor control systems in most modern plants are now computerized, with job status information entered directly into a computer as the job enters and leaves a work center. Some plants have gone heavily into bar coding and optical scanners to speed up the reporting process and to cut down on data-entry errors.[6] As you might guess, the key problems in shop-floor control are data inaccuracy and lack of timeliness. When these occur, the information fed back to the overall planning system is wrong and incorrect production decisions are made. Typical results are excess inventory and/or stockout problems, missed due dates, and inaccuracies in job costing.

Of course, maintaining data integrity requires that a sound data-gathering system be in place; but more important, it requires adherence to the system by everybody interacting with it. Most firms recognize this, but maintaining what is variously referred to as *shop discipline, data integrity,* or *data responsibility* is not always easy. And despite periodic drives to publicize the importance of careful shop-floor reporting by creating data-integrity task forces, inaccuracies still can creep into the system in many ways: A line worker drops a part under the workbench and pulls a replacement from stock without recording either transaction. An inventory clerk makes an error in a cycle count. A manufacturing engineer fails to note a change in the routing of a part. A department supervisor decides to work jobs in a different order than specified in the dispatch list.

Scheduling Workers in Service Operations

Why Scheduling Is Important in Services

As discussed previously, one of the main distinctions between manufacturing and service operations is the customer's direct interaction with the service delivery process. Because of this interaction, the determination of the proper number of workers to schedule at any particular time is critical to the success of every service operation. On one hand, scheduling too few workers results in unnecessarily long customer waiting times. On the other hand, scheduling too many workers results in overstaffing and the incurrence of unnecessarily high labor costs, which negatively affect profits. The service manager, consequently, needs to schedule workers in a way that effectively satisfies customer demand while minimizing unnecessary labor costs.

The cost of labor in most services is a major cost component, often running 35 percent of sales and higher. For some services, in fact, virtually all of the direct costs can be considered as labor (examples of these types of services include consulting, legal work, home care nursing, and hair salons). Thus a small but unnecessary increase in labor can have a very significant impact on a firm's profits.

A Framework for Scheduling Service Workers

Work schedules in service operations are usually developed on a weekly basis for several reasons. First, there are state and federal laws that specify the maximum number of hours and/or days an employee can work in a given week, after which overtime premiums must be paid. Second, the distinction between full-time and part-time workers is often made on the basis of the number of hours worked in a calendar week. Full-time versus part-time status often determines the benefits paid by the employer, and may be related to union

[6]Some companies also use "smartshelves"—inventory bins with weight sensors beneath each shelf. When an item is removed from inventory, a signal is sent to a central computer that notes the time, date, quantity, and location of the transaction.

Exhibit 12.8

The Required Steps in a Worker Schedule

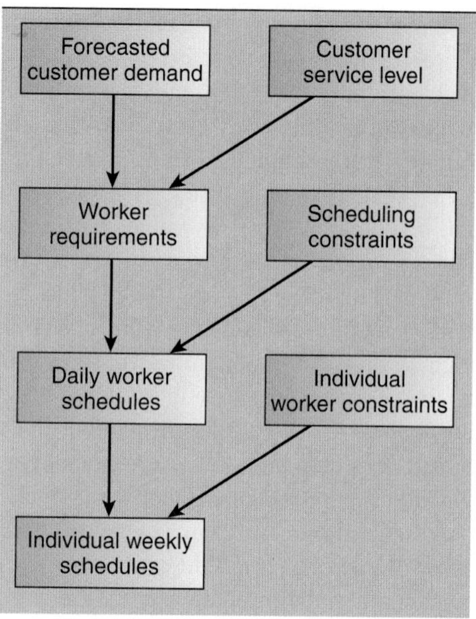

contracts that specify the minimum number of hours workers in each category may work. Finally, many workers, especially hourly workers, are paid on a weekly basis that is often mandated by local or state laws.

The procedure for developing a schedule for service workers can be divided into the following four major elements, as illustrated in Exhibit 12.8: (*a*) forecasting customer demand, (*b*) converting customer demand into worker requirements, (*c*) converting worker requirements into daily work schedules, and (*d*) converting daily work schedules into weekly work schedules.

Forecasting Demand Since the delivery of most services takes place in the presence of the customer, the customer's arrival rate directly correlates with the demand level for the service operation. For example, the customer must be present at a restaurant to partake in the meal being served; the patient must be present in the hospital to receive treatment. In addition to the customer's presence at the point of service, the potential for high variability in the pattern of customer demand makes it extremely important for service managers to efficiently schedule workers. The first step, therefore, in developing a schedule that will permit the service operation to meet customer demand is to accurately forecast that demand.

There are several patterns of demand that need to be considered: variation in demand within days (or even hours), variation across days of the week, variations within a month, and seasonal variations. Because demand is often highly variable throughout a day, forecasting within-day variation is usually done in either hour or half-hour increments. Today, with the use of computers and more sophisticated point-of-sale (POS) equipment, the ability to record customer demand in even shorter time increments is possible (for example, 15-minute time intervals).

To develop a forecast we need to collect historical data about customer demand. The actual number of customers expecting service in a given time interval (that is, half hour or hour) is the preferred data. Fortunately, there is a wide range of POS equipment available that can capture this type of data, and, in many cases, even download it onto a computer for subsequent analysis.

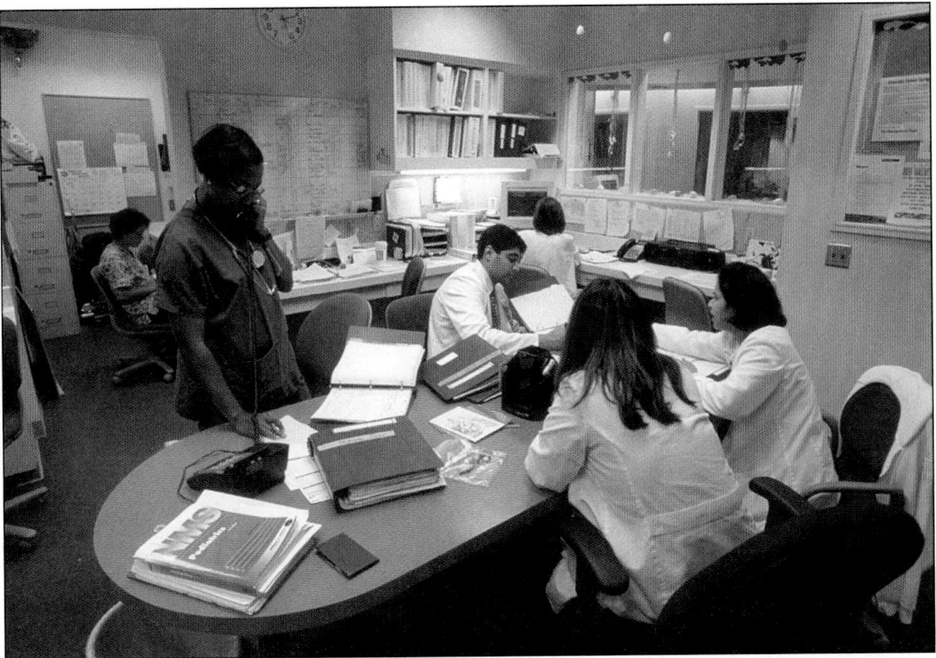

Scheduling lab tests and treatments for incoming patients requires balancing the urgency of the patient's problem with the availability of technicians and equipment.

Converting Customer Demand into Worker Requirements Worker requirements in service operations can be divided into two major categories: front-of-the-house and back-of-the-house. Front-of-the-house workers are defined as those who have direct contact with the customer. Examples would include a teller at a bank, a cashier at a discount department store, or the check-in personnel at an airline counter. Back-of-the-house workers are those workers who do not interact directly with the customers. Examples here would include a cook in a restaurant and a baggage handler for an airline. (The scheduling of back-of-the-house workers is usually very similar to scheduling workers in a manufacturing environment.)

A necessary element in the conversion of customer demand into front-of-the-house worker requirements is the establishment of a customer-service level. For example, many restaurants offer express lunches within a specified time period. Another example of a specified level of service is at Putnam Investments in Andover, Massachusetts, where Liam McMakin states that Putnam's established service level at its call centers is that "93 percent of all calls should be answered in 20 seconds or less."[7]

Knowing the average number of customers who require service in a given period of time and the average length of time it takes to provide service to each customer, a manager can determine how many workers to schedule for that time period in order to provide the desired level of service. Queuing theory, which was presented in the previous chapter, is a mathematically organized approach for establishing the relationship among the three following variables: (*a*) customer demand (for example, customers per hour); (*b*) available capacity, expressed in the number of workers on duty and the average time to service a customer; and (*c*) average customer waiting time.

To facilitate this process of converting customer demand into a specified number of workers, a service organization often will develop a labor requirements table. This table tells the manager how many workers are needed for different levels of demand. For some companies, these tables also will indicate where these workers should be assigned. With this

[7]Conversation with Liam McMakin, Vice President, Putnam Investment Services, February 15, 2002.

Exhibit 12.9

An Example of a Labor Requirements Table for a Fast-Food Operation

Sales ($)/Hour Volume Guidelines	Total No. of Workers	Specific Worker Assignments						
		Grill	Windows	Drive-Thru	Bin	Fry	Floaters*	
$120	4	1	1	1	—	—	1	(Minimum staffing level)
150	5	1	1	1	—	—	2	
180	6	2	1	1	—	—	2	
210	7	2	2	1	—	—	2	
240	8	2	2	2	1	—	1	
275	9	2	2	2	1	—	2	
310	10	3	3	2	1	—	1	
345	11	3	3	2	1	1	1	
385	12	3	3	3	1	1	1	
425	13	4	3	3	1	1	1	
475	14	4	3	3	1	1	2	
525	15	4	4	3	1	1	2	
585	16	5	4	3	1	1	2	
645	17	5	5	3	1	1	2	(Full staffing level)

*Floaters help out; they patrol the lot, lobby, and restrooms; restock; and cover on breaks.

Source: Adapted from "McDonald's," Harvard Business School Case No. 681–044, 1980.

type of table, the service manager only has to look up the forecasted demand in a given time period to determine how many workers to schedule and where they should be assigned. An example of a labor requirements table for a fast-food restaurant is shown in Exhibit 12.9.

Converting Worker Requirements into Daily Work Schedules The next step in the scheduling process is the conversion of worker requirements for each time interval into a daily work or shift schedule. The basic goal here is to schedule a sufficient number of workers in a given time period to meet the expected demand at the target service level. However, there are usually additional factors that also need to be included, such as (*a*) the minimum length of a shift that might be prescribed by a union contract (for example, when workers are called into UPS, they are guaranteed by their union contract a minimum of three hours' work), (*b*) the maximum shift length permitted by state or local labor laws, and (*c*) the company's policies about rest and meal breaks. These factors can significantly affect how efficiently the organization can meet the target service level. These minimum shift constraints often result in a worker schedule where the total number of labor hours needed to meet the minimum shift requirement(s) is greater than the actual number of labor hours required to satisfy customer demand.

In developing these schedules, many organizations use part-time rather than full-time workers to effectively meet customer-service goals while simultaneously controlling costs. Since part-time workers typically are paid less and also may be entitled to fewer (or even no) fringe benefits, the average hourly cost of the part-time worker is lower than that of the full-time worker. Part-time workers can be used to meet demand at peak periods (such as meal times in restaurants) or during periods when full-time workers would prefer not to work (such as weekends in hospitals).

Converting Daily Work Schedules into Weekly Work Schedules The conversion of daily work schedules into weekly work schedules is more complicated than simply repeating the daily schedule procedure. In developing weekly schedules, managers need to take into consideration workers' days off for illness, holidays, and vacations. They also need to factor in the additional cost of paying workers to work on holidays if services are offered on those days. Workforce scheduling in a hospital, for example, can be particularly challenging on major holidays. In addition, these weekly schedules need to be assigned to specific individuals. Therefore, inputs into this module include individual worker constraints such as days off, hours available for work, and so forth.

The Use of Technology in Scheduling

As in most facets of business, information technology has had a significant impact on the ability of the manager to schedule workers. Early computer programs for scheduling workers were often cumbersome to use and also very limited in their applications. However, the advent of faster and more powerful computers coupled with newer software programs has resulted in worker scheduling programs that are both significantly more user friendly and, at the same time, more flexible in their applications.

The use of these automated scheduling programs has several advantages. First, it significantly reduces the amount of time a manager has to devote to developing a weekly work schedule. Previously, when manually scheduling workers, it was not uncommon for a manager in a complex service environment to devote one entire eight-hour day every week to developing a worker schedule for the following week. With an automated scheduling system, managers are no longer required to commit such a large amount of time to scheduling, allowing them more time to devote to actually managing the operation. This results in a more effectively managed business.

In addition, these software programs typically contain highly sophisticated mathematical formulas designed to minimize labor hours, subject to the constraints and conditions identified earlier in this chapter (such as the minimum number of hours per shift). Worker productivity is therefore also increased. Thus, by using an automated scheduling system, a more efficient worker schedule can be generated in only a fraction of the time previously required with a manual procedure.

Many of the automated systems available today are fully integrated systems that consist of several modules. Kronos, Inc., in Waltham, Massachusetts, one of the leading producers of automated workforce scheduling systems, offers a fully integrated service worker scheduling system, as described in the accompanying OM in Practice on Automated Scheduling for Service Workers.

Examples of Scheduling in Services

As stated previously, the scheduling of service workers can be divided into two broad categories: "back-of-the-house" operations (where workers do not come into contact with customers) and "front-of-the-house" operations (where workers come into direct contact with the customers). Both types of service scheduling situations are presented here. The staffing requirements for the bank are an example of a back-of-the-house operation, while nurse staffing and scheduling are obviously a front-of-the-house operation.

Setting Staffing Levels in Banks This example illustrates how central clearinghouses and back-office operations of large banks establish staffing plans. Basically, management wants to develop a staffing plan that (*a*) requires the least number of workers to accomplish the daily workload and (*b*) minimizes the variance between actual output and planned output.

In structuring the problem, bank management defines inputs (checks, statements, investment documents, and so forth) as *products,* which are routed through different processes or *functions* (receiving, sorting, encoding, and so forth).

Operations Management in Practice

AUTOMATED SCHEDULING FOR SERVICE WORKERS

Kronos, Inc., located in Waltham, Massachusetts, provides a fully automated Workforce Management System that consists of the following three major modules: (*a*) Business Forecaster, (*b*) WorkForce Planner, and (*c*) Smart Scheduler.

The Business Forecaster module uses historical data from POS systems, traffic counters, and other sources to develop a forecast of future sales. The system is sufficiently flexible to allow the service manager to determine which variables are to be forecasted and the amount of historical data to use. The system can provide projections on a daily basis, as well as in hour, half-hour, and 15-minute intervals.

Combining the sales projections from the Business Forecaster module with previously determined staffing guidelines and constraints, the Workforce Planner module develops worker staffing requirements that will meet the forecasted demand efficiently in terms of minimizing labor costs and effectively with respect to meeting established levels of customer service. These staffing requirements can be provided in the same time intervals as the forecast.

Kronos considers Smart Scheduler to be the heart or "engine" that drives their overall system. The staffing requirements generated by the WorkForce Planner module combined with general work rules and specific constraints for individual employees are the inputs to this module. The output of the Smart Scheduler module is a detailed work schedule for the next forecast period, matching specific employees with specific shift assignments.

To solve the problem, a monthly demand forecast is first made by product for each function. This demand forecast for each product is then divided by the production rate (P/H) for those functions that the product requires. The result is the number of labor hours [H(std)] that are required to complete each function for that product. The labor hours are then converted into workers required per function. These figures are then tabled, summed, and adjusted by an absence and vacation factor to give planned hours, which are then divided by the number of hours in the workday to give us the number of workers required. This results in the daily staff hours required (see Exhibit 12.10), which becomes the basis for a departmental staffing plan that lists the workers required, workers available, variance, and managerial action in light of variance. (See Exhibit 12.11.)

In addition to their use in day-to-day planning, the hours required and the staffing plan provide information for scheduling individual workers, controlling operations, comparing capacity utilization with other branches, and starting up new branches.

Nurse Staffing and Scheduling W. Abernathy, N. Baloff, and J. Hershey state, "The key element of effective nurse staffing is a well-conceived procedure for achieving an overall balance between the size of the nursing staff and the expected patient demand."[8] Their procedure, termed *aggregate budgeting,* is based upon a variety of interrelated activities and has a short-term schedule as a primary output. A number of severe, practical problems confront hospitals in deriving an effective yet low-cost aggregate budget. These difficulties, along with possible remedies, are listed in Exhibit 12.12.

Though most hospitals still use trial-and-error methods to develop worker schedules, management scientists have applied mathematical optimizing techniques to the problem with some success.

[8]W. Abernathy, N. Baloff, and J. Hershey, "The Nurse Staffing Problem: Issues and Prospects," *Sloan Management Review* 13, no. 1 (Fall 1971), pp. 87–109.

Exhibit 12.10

Daily Staff Hours Required

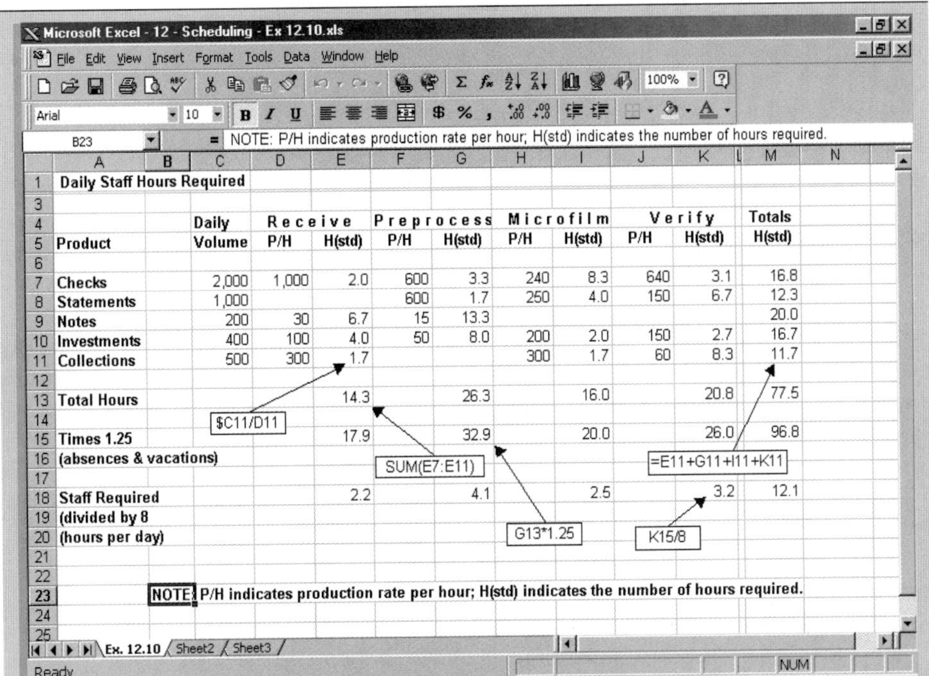

		Daily	Receive		Preprocess		Microfilm		Verify		Totals
	Product	Volume	P/H	H(std)	P/H	H(std)	P/H	H(std)	P/H	H(std)	H(std)
7	Checks	2,000	1,000	2.0	600	3.3	240	8.3	640	3.1	16.8
8	Statements	1,000			600	1.7	250	4.0	150	6.7	12.3
9	Notes	200	30	6.7	15	13.3					20.0
10	Investments	400	100	4.0	50	8.0	200	2.0	150	2.7	16.7
11	Collections	500	300	1.7			300	1.7	60	8.3	11.7
13	Total Hours			14.3		26.3		16.0		20.8	77.5
15	Times 1.25 (absences & vacations)			17.9		32.9		20.0		26.0	96.8
18	Staff Required (divided by 8 (hours per day)			2.2		4.1		2.5		3.2	12.1

Exhibit 12.11

Staffing Plan

Function	Staff Required	Staff Available	Variance (±)	Management Actions
Receive	2.3	2.0	−0.3	Use overtime
Preprocess	4.1	4.0	−0.1	Use overtime
Microfilm	2.5	3.0	+0.5	Use excess to verify
Verify	3.3	3.0	−0.3	Get 0.3 from microfilm

Exhibit 12.12

General Problems in Nurse Scheduling

Problem	Possible Solution
Accuracy of patient load forecast	Forecast frequently and rebudget monthly. Closely monitor seasonal demands, communicable diseases, and current occupancy
Forecasting nurse availability	Develop work standards for nurses for each level of possible demand (requires systematic data collection and analysis)
Complexity and time to rebudget	Use available computer programs
Flexibility in scheduling	Use variable staffing: Set regular staff levels slightly above minimum and absorb variation with broadskilled float nurses, part-time nurses, and overtime

A major problem confronting health care managers today is the changing mix of patient needs and how it affects nurse staffing requirements. With the growing trend toward more outpatient treatment, patients who are hospitalized today are typically very ill, and thus require, on average, more individual attention. Under these conditions, the demands for nursing skills actually can increase, even though the number of patients in a designated area has remained unchanged.

Because of these increased patient needs, many hospitals are adapting a worker skill mix that incorporates lower-skilled technical support personnel to assist in the delivery of patient care, with the goal of reducing their overall labor costs. This additional parameter of different worker skills has to be taken into consideration when determining personnel staffing requirements.

Scheduling Consecutive Days Off A practical problem encountered in many service organizations is setting schedules so that employees can have two consecutive days off even though the operation is open seven days a week. The importance of the problem stems from the fact that the Fair Labor Standards Act requires that overtime be paid for any hours worked (by hourly workers) in excess of 40 hours per week. Obviously, if two consecutive days off can't be scheduled each week for each employee, the likelihood of unnecessary overtime is quite high. In addition, most people probably prefer two consecutive days off per week. The following heuristic procedure was modified from that developed by James Browne and Rajen Tibrewala to deal with this problem.[9]

> *Objective.* Find the schedule that minimizes the number of five-day workers with two consecutive days off, subject to the demands of the daily staffing schedule and assuming that the workers have no preference for which days they get off.
>
> *Procedure.* Starting with the total number of workers required for each day of the week, create a schedule by adding one worker at a time. This is a two-step procedure:

Step 1 Circle the lowest pair of consecutive days off. The lowest pair is the one where the highest number in the pair is equal to or lower than the highest number in any other pair. This ensures that the days with the highest requirements are covered by staff. (Monday and Sunday may be chosen even though they are at opposite ends of the array of days.) In case of ties choose the days-off pair with the lowest requirement on an adjacent day. This day may be before or after the pair. If a tie still remains, choose the first of the available tied pairs. (Do not bother using further tie-breaking rules, such as second lowest adjacent days.)

Step 2 Subtract 1 from each of the remaining five days (i.e., the days not circled). This indicates that one less worker is required on these days, since the first worker has just been assigned to them.

Step 3 The two steps are repeated for the second worker, the third worker, and so forth, until no more workers are required to satisfy the schedule.

Example

	M	Tu	W	Th	F	S	Su
Requirement	**4**	**3**	**4**	**2**	**3**	**1**	**2**
Worker 1	4	3	4	2	3	(1)	(2)
Worker 2	3	2	3	1	(2)	(1)	2
Worker 3	2	1	2	0	2	(1)	(1)
Worker 4	1	(0)	(1)	0	1	1	1
Worker 5	0	0	1	0	0	0	0

[9]James J. Browne and Rajen K. Tibrewala, "Manpower Scheduling," *Industrial Engineering* 7, no. 8 (August 1975), pp. 22–23.

Solution

This solution consists of five workers covering 19 worker days, although slightly different assignments may be equally satisfactory.

The schedule: Worker 1 is assigned S–Su off; Worker 2, F–S off; Worker 3, S–Su off; Worker 4, Tu–W off; and Worker 5 works only on Wednesday, since there are no further requirements for the other days.

Conclusion

Job shops are prevalent throughout both the manufacturing and service sectors (see the banking and nursing examples above). Job shop scheduling has now become computer dependent and is inseparable from total manufacturing planning and control systems. In fact, the scheduling of the job shop is an integral part of this larger system.

Worker scheduling is especially important in service operations where labor is often a significant cost component. Here, too much labor negatively influences profits, but insufficient labor has a negative impact on customer service and, hence, adversely affects future sales.

Like all aspects of operations management, job shops are affected by larger trends in the global economy. Jobs shops are becoming more specialized, and the training required of the workforce is becoming increasingly sophisticated. Furthermore, the use of automated processes and technologically advanced approaches to jobs will continue to increase. The information linkages between the job shop and the rest of the firm will be accessed more frequently by all involved parties. Costs (notably energy) will continue to rise, as will competitive pressures. The customer base will be better educated, more international in scope, and more socially aware, putting greater responsibility on the job shop to be socially responsible. Natural resources will become less available, and government regulation of the use of such resources may continue to rise. In short, job shop scheduling will remain a necessary part of the operation of the firm and, for the foreseeable future, will remain a difficult task.

Key Terms

dispatching of orders p. 484
expediting p. 485
flow pattern p. 486
Gantt chart p. 497
input/output control p. 497
job shop p. 484
labor-limited systems p. 487
machine-limited systems p. 487
OPT p. 493
priority rules p. 487
shop-floor control p. 495

Review and Discussion Questions

1. Identify the characteristics of a job shop. Why are they so prevalent, especially in the service sector?
2. What practical considerations are deterrents to using the SPT rule?
3. What priority rule do you use in scheduling your study time for midterm examinations? If you have five exams to study for, how many alternative schedules exist?
4. Why is it difficult to schedule workers in a service environment?
5. In the United States, there are certain assumptions made about the customer-service priority rules used in banks, restaurants, and retail stores. If you have the opportunity,

ask an international student what rules are used in his or her country. To what factors might you attribute the differences, if any?

6. What job characteristics would lead you to schedule jobs according to "longest processing time first"?
7. In what way is the scheduling problem in the home office of a bank different from that of a branch?
8. Identify an example of a job shop where you are the scheduler/dispatcher. It might be your kitchen, your computer workstation, or something else. What priority rules would you use for this job shop, and why?
9. List some of the problems that a job shop scheduler faces when trying to estimate the personnel and machinery needed for a made-to-order job that has never been done before.
10. Assume you are the desk clerk at an upscale hotel and that you handle all registrations. You are dealing with your customers on a first-come, first-served basis when a professional football team arrives. They are playing a team from your city and will be staying at your hotel. How will you handle their registrations?
11. In many job shops, the percentage of work done by automated processes is increasing. For example, in a copy center the copy machines now collate and staple automatically. In hospitals, more and more diagnoses are made by machines with remote sensors. Discuss how the capacity of machines to "do more" impacts the role of the job shop scheduler.
12. Examples of two-dimensional Gantt charts were presented in the chapter; could a Gantt chart have three dimensions? Provide several examples.
13. What are some of the goods and services produced by a bottleneck system that you use? What characteristics do they have in common?
14. How does a bottleneck system affect the customer, the company, and the employees who work within the system?
15. In a service environment, can customer co-production be utilized to lessen the effects of a bottleneck? How?

Solved Problem

Problem 1

Joe's Auto Seat Cover and Paint Shop is bidding on a contract to do all the custom work for Smiling Ed's used car dealership. One of the main requirements in obtaining this contract is rapid delivery time, since Ed—for reasons we shall not go into here—wants the cars facelifted and back on his lot in a hurry. Ed has said that if Joe can refit and repaint five cars that Ed has just received (from an unnamed source) in 24 hours or less, the contract will be his. Following is the time (in hours) required in the refitting shop and the paint shop for each of the five cars. Assuming that cars go through the refitting operations before they are repainted, can Joe meet the time requirements and get the contract?

Car	Refitting Time (hours)	Repairing Time (hours)
A	6	3
B	0	4
C	5	2
D	8	6
E	2	1

Solution

This problem can be viewed as a two-machine flow shop and can be solved easily using "Johnson's rule."

	Original Data		Johnson's Rule	
Car	Refitting Time (hours)	Repainting Time (hours)	Order of Selection	Position in Sequence
A	6	3	4th	3rd
B	0	4	1st	1st
C	5	2	3rd	4th
D	8	6	5th	2nd
E	2	1	2nd	5th

Graph of Johnson solution (not to scale):

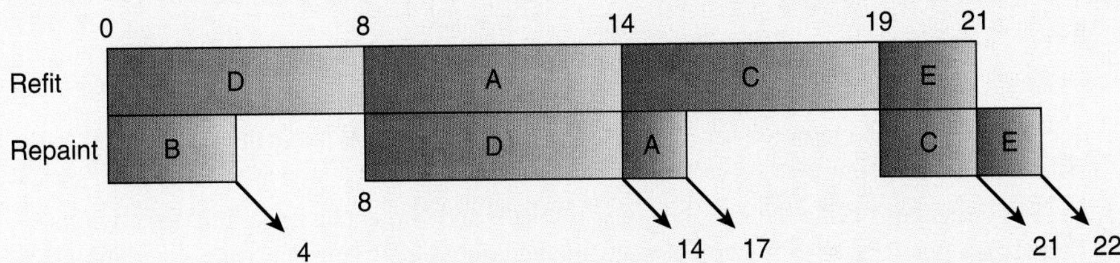

The total time for the five cars is 22 hours.

Problems

1. Joe has three cars that must be overhauled by his ace mechanic, Jim. Given the following data about the cars, use the STR/OP priority rule (least slack remaining per operation) to determine Jim's scheduling priority for each.

Car	Customer Pick-Up Time (hours hence)	Remaining Overhaul Time (hours)	Remaining Operations
A	10	4	Painting
B	17	5	Wheel alignment, painting
C	15	1	Chrome plating, painting, seat repair

2. There are seven jobs that must be processed in two operations: A and B. All seven jobs must go through A and B in that sequence—A first, then B.
   a. Determine the optimal order in which the jobs should be sequenced through the process using these times:

Job	Process A Time	Process B Time
1	9	6
2	8	5
3	7	7
4	6	3
5	1	2
6	2	6
7	4	7

b. Draw a graph similar to that for the solved problem showing the sequence of jobs.

c. What is the total completion time for all seven jobs?

3. The following list of jobs in a critical department includes estimates of their required times:

Job	Required Time (days)	Days to Delivery Promise	Slack
A	8	12	4
B	3	9	6
C	7	8	1
D	1	11	10
E	10	−10	—
F	6	10	4
G	5	−8	—
H	4	6	2

a. Use the shortest operation time rule to schedule these jobs. What is the schedule? What is the mean flow time?

b. The boss doesn't like the schedule in (*a*). Jobs E and G must be done first, for obvious reasons (they are already late). Reschedule and do the best you can while scheduling Jobs E and G first and second, respectively. What is the new schedule? What is the new mean flow time?

4. A manufacturing facility has five jobs to be scheduled into production. The following table gives the processing times plus the necessary wait times and other necessary delays for each of the jobs. Assume that today is April 3 and the jobs are due on the dates shown:

Job	Days of Actual Processing Time Required	Days of Necessary Delay Time	Total Time Required	Date Job Due
1	2	12	14	April 30
2	5	8	13	April 21
3	9	15	24	April 28
4	7	9	16	April 29
5	4	22	28	April 27

Determine *two* schedules, stating the order in which the jobs are to be done. Use the critical ratio priority rule for one. You may use any other rule for the second schedule as long as you state what it is.

5. An accounting firm, Debits R Us, would like to keep its auditing staff to a maximum of four people yet satisfy the staffing needs and the policy of two days off per week. Given the following requirements, is this possible? What should the schedule be?

Requirements (Monday through Sunday): 4, 3, 3, 2, 2, 4, 4.

6. Jobs A, B, C, D, and E must go through Processes I and II in that sequence (i.e., Process I first, then Process II).

Use Johnson's rule to determine the optimal sequence to schedule the jobs to minimize the total required time.

Job	Required Processing Time on Process I	Required Processing Time on Process II
A	4	5
B	16	14
C	8	7
D	12	11
E	3	9

7. Joe was able to land a job as production scheduler in a brand-new custom refinishing auto service shop located near the border. This system is capable of handling 10 cars per day. The sequence now is customizing first, followed by repainting.

Car	Customizing Time (hours)	Painting (hours)	Car	Customizing Time (hours)	Painting (hours)
1	3.0	1.2	6	2.1	0.8
2	2.0	0.9	7	3.2	1.4
3	2.5	1.3	8	0.6	1.8
4	0.7	0.5	9	1.1	1.5
5	1.6	1.7	10	1.8	0.7

In what sequence should Joe schedule the cars?

8. The MedSports Clinic provides specialized medical care for sports-related injuries. A patient's visit to MedSports usually involves two separate stages. First, the patient meets with the doctor to explain the nature of his or her injury, and, if necessary, to have a physical examination by the doctor. Following the visit with the doctor, a set of x-rays is taken of the injured part of the patient's body. The amount of time spent at each stage of the patient's visit can vary significantly, depending on the type of injury and whether or not this is the patient's first visit to the clinic. As MediSport has just recently opened for business, there is currently only one doctor available at any one time, and only one x-ray technician and machine. On a given day, six patients have made appointments. It is estimated that each patient requires the following times (in minutes) for each of the two stages:

	Time (minutes)	
Patient	Examination	X-Ray
A	30	15
B	45	50
C	75	35
D	20	40
E	90	25
F	60	70

a. Using Johnson's rule, determine the optimal order for scheduling these patients throughout the day.

b. If the clinic opens at 9:00 AM with the first patient, what times should each of the patients be told to come into the clinic?

9. MassBay Financial Services (MBFS) offers a wide variety of mutual funds to both corporate pension funds and individuals. Its customer service operation performs the following tasks relative to its customer accounts:

	Operations Required and Productivity (P/H)*			
Activity	**Receiving**	**Scanning**	**Processing**	**Auditing**
Change of address	125	75	100	
Change of beneficiary	125	75	50	
Transaction error	150	50	75	50
Deposit	200	100	75	150
Withdrawal	200	100	25	50

*P/H = production rate per hour.

The daily volumes for each type of transaction for the following week are estimated to be as follows:

	Day of the Week				
	Mon	**Tue**	**Wed**	**Thur**	**Fri**
Change of address	2,200	1,600	1,300	1,000	1,000
Change of beneficiary	1,000	1,200	800	600	500
Transaction error	400	300	500	400	300
Deposit	8,500	7,200	6,800	6,500	6,500
Withdrawal	3,000	3,400	4,000	3,700	4,200

Set up an Excel spreadsheet similar to that in Exhibit 12.10 and determine the number of workers needed for each function for each day of the week. (Assume that there is a 25 percent allowance factor for absences and vacations and that the normal workday is eight hours.)

10. A fast-food restaurant has forecasted hourly sales (in dollars) for next Monday to be the following:

Hour:	11:00 AM	12:00 NOON	1:00 PM	2:00 PM	3:00 PM	4:00 PM	5:00 PM	6:00 PM	7:00 PM	8:00 PM	9:00 PM	10:00 PM
Sales:	250	625	500	375	150	100	175	400	475	300	275	125

Using the staffing table shown in Exhibit 12.9, determine the number of workers required for each hour of the day. (Note: The times stated above represent the beginning of each hour in which the sales are forecasted.)

Bibliography

Abernathy, W.; N. Baloff; and J. Hershey. "The Nurse Staffing Problem: Issues and Prospects." *Sloan Management Review* 13, no. 1 (Fall 1971), pp. 87–109.

Baker, K. R. "The Effects of Input Control in a Simple Scheduling Model." *Journal of Operations Management* 4, no. 2 (February 1984), pp. 99–112.

Conway, Richard W.; William L. Maxwell; and Louis W. Miller. *Theory of Scheduling.* Reading, MA: Addison-Wesley Publishing, 1967.

Fogarty, Donald W.; John H. Blackstone Jr.; and Thomas R. Hoffmann. *Production and Inventory Management.* Cincinnati: South-Western Publishing, 1991.

Gershkoff, I. "Optimizing Flight Crew Schedules." *Interfaces* 19, no. 4 (July–August 1989), pp. 29–43.

Johnson, S. M. "Optimal Two Stage and Three Stage Production Schedules with Setup Times Included." *Naval Logistics Quarterly* 1, no. 1 (March 1954), pp. 61–68.

Moody, P. E. *Strategic Manufacturing: Dynamic New Directions for the 1990s.* Homewood, IL: Richard D. Irwin, 1990.

Morton and Pentico. *Heuristic Scheduling Systems.* New York: John Wiley & Sons, 1993, p. 28.

Richter, H. "Thirty Years of Airline Operations Research." *Interfaces* 19, no. 4 (July–August 1989), pp. 3–9.

Sipper, Daniel, and Robert L. Buflin Jr. *Production: Planning, Control, and Integration.* Burr Ridge, IL: McGraw-Hill, 1998, p. 531.

Vollman, Thomas E.; William L. Berry; and D. Clay Whybark. *Manufacturing Planning and Control.* 4th ed. Burr Ridge, IL: Irwin, 1997.

13 Supply Chain Management

Chapter Objectives

- Introduce the concept of a firm's supply chain and show how it has evolved over time to its present status.
- Identify current trends that are affecting the characteristics of a supply chain.
- Present the requirements necessary for a successful supply chain.
- Discuss the impact of technology on a firm's supply chain.
- Define in-transit inventory costs and show how they impact the purchasing decision.

SOLECTRON'S TIGHT SUPPLY CHAIN IS A KEY FACTOR IN ITS SUCCESS

Most of us have probably never heard of Solectron, but almost all of us come in contact every day with the products it makes. Solectron Corporation is one of a growing number of firms that are referred to as contract manufacturers. These firms don't manufacture products under their own brand name but, instead, produce brand name items such as printers and printer components for Hewlett Packard and computers and computer components for IBM.

Solectron's ability to play a critical role in the supply chain of these original equipment manufacturers (OEMs) is clearly demonstrated by its significant market share in a highly competitive industry. Solectron focuses on providing its outsourcing customers with significant competitive advantages in the form of access to advanced manufacturing technologies, reduced time-to-market, lower production costs, and more effective use of assets. Its continued commitment to excellence is evidenced by the fact that it is the only manufacturing firm to ever win the prestigious Malcolm Baldrige National Quality Award twice (in 1991 and again in 1997).

Solectron plays a key role in the supply chain for these OEMs by providing a seamless relationship in dealing with these firms' customers. For example, orders placed with the OEMs are usually transmitted directly to a Solectron plant to be filled. Once the product is made, it is then shipped directly to the customer with the OEM's label. From the customer's perspective, they are dealing only with the OEM.

Effective supply chain management with respect to its suppliers is also a contributing factor to Solectron's success. With 75 percent of its revenues going to purchase materials, components, and other items from its suppliers, it needs to have strong relationships with suppliers who are very reliable.

Source: Malcolm Baldrige National Quality Award—Profiles of Award Recipients. (http://www.quality.mist.gov)

Managerial Issues

In recent years, managers have continued to focus their efforts on supply chain issues for several reasons. First, in order to be more responsive to the constantly changing needs of their customers, companies are concentrating their resources on their core competencies. With this narrower focus, firms are now buying a substantially greater proportion of the goods and services that go into their products than was previously the norm. In many cases, for example, the cost of the purchased raw materials and components is 60 percent (and often higher) of the cost of goods sold. As a result there is now greater dependency on suppliers and the need to develop long-term supplier relationships. In addition, the logistical costs (that is, the transportation and distribution costs) associated with the delivery of products has continued to increase, as firms are now able to extend their supply chains to the far corners of the world.

To further complicate matters, there is increasing pressure on managers to reduce their inventories, thereby placing further dependence on their suppliers. To address the need to reduce inventories, managers have introduced such concepts as *consignment inventories* and *supplier- (or vendor-) managed inventories* (*SMI* or *VMI*), which we will discuss in this chapter.

Advances in information technology have provided managers with a wide assortment of tools that allow them to better oversee their firms' supply chains. These include electronic data interchange (EDI) and business-to-business (B2B) marketplaces. This increased emphasis on a firm's supply chain has caused a dramatic shift in the role of the purchasing function. In the past, the purchasing function was typically viewed as being primarily a transactions-oriented function. Now it is seen by many firms as playing a more strategic role in determining the overall long-term success of the firm.

Definition of Supply Chain Management

supply chain

The steps and the firms that perform these steps in the transformation of raw material into finished products bought by customers.

inbound logistics

The delivery of goods and services that are purchased from suppliers and/or their distributors.

Exhibit 13.1 shows the major elements in a firm's **supply chain,** in terms of those organizations with which it deals directly. The issues associated with the delivery of these products to the firm are referred to as **inbound logistics.** After the firm has added value by transforming the purchased goods and services, the finished products are then delivered to its customers and/or distributors. Similarly, the issues associated with the delivery of these products to the firm's customers and/or distributors are referred to as **outbound logistics.**

From a larger perspective, a supply chain can be defined as a group of organizations that perform the various processes that are required to make a finished product. Here the chain would begin with the actual raw materials and end with the finished product that is delivered to the end user or final customer. For example, if the finished product is a piece of wood furniture, then the supply chain, going backwards from the customer, would include (*a*) the retail operation where the furniture was purchased, (*b*) the shipping company that delivered it, (*c*) the furniture manufacturer, (*d*) the hardware manufacturer, and (*e*) the lumber companies that harvested the wood from the forests. If the end product is fresh fish fillets that are sold at a supermarket, then the supply chain would include (*a*) the supermarket, (*b*) the fresh fish supplier who delivered the fish, (*c*) the fish processor who filleted them, and (*d*) the fishermen who caught them.

Exhibit 13.1

A Company's Supply Chain

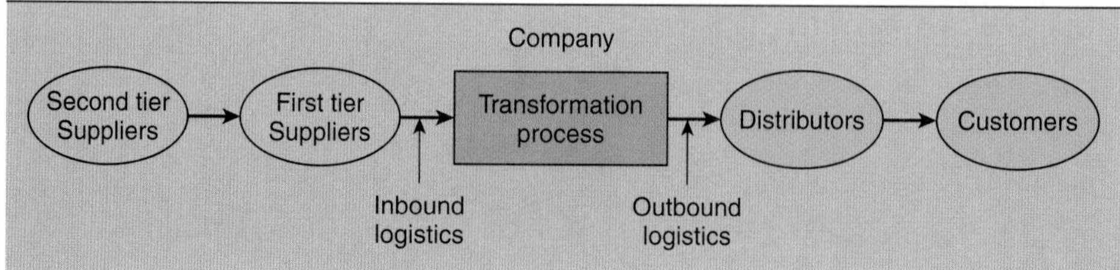

outbound logistics

The delivery of goods and services that are sold to a firm's customers and/or its distributors.

The structure of the supply chain can vary dramatically for different companies, even within the same industry. In addition, the role of an organization with respect to its span or degree of control over the supply chain can vary significantly. As an example, compare the supply chain for fish sold in a typical supermarket, described above, with that of Spenger's, a long-established fish market and seafood restaurant located in Berkeley, California. Until recently, many of the various types of fish sold in its market and restaurant were caught on its own fishing boats and processed in its own operation. (Spenger's, founded in 1890, sold the last of its fishing boats in 1994 with the retirement of its owner and now buys fish either through brokers or from fishermen who work exclusively for Spenger's.)

As an another illustration, Henry Ford, in order to support his huge River Rouge automobile plant just outside of Detroit, Michigan, invested heavily in iron ore mines, forests, coal mines, and even cargo ships that transported raw material on the Great Lakes. His goal was to gain total control over his supply chain (which, in the end, he realized was not possible). The greater the degree or span of control that a firm has with respect to its supply chain, the more vertically integrated it is said to be. In other words, Ford's operation could be described as being very vertically integrated in comparison to other automotive manufacturers who focused solely on the manufacture and assembly of the cars themselves.

Supply chain management, therefore, can be defined as the ability of a firm to work with its suppliers to provide high-quality material and components that are competitively priced. The closeness of the relationship between vendor and customer, in many respects, differentiates one type of supply chain from another. The adoption of the term *supply chain management* in lieu of materials management or purchasing reflects top management's recognition of the strategic role of suppliers in contributing to the long-term success of the firm.

The Evolution of Supply Chain Management

Supply chain management is a relatively new concept in business. Previously, management theory suggested that the overall efficiency of the technical core or production function could be significantly improved if the core could be isolated or *buffered* to the greatest extent possible from an often erratic and uncertain external environment.

In order to isolate the technical core from suppliers (and also customers), companies established significant inventories of raw material and finished goods, as shown in Exhibit 13.2A. While this approach produced highly efficient operations, it simultaneously made the core less responsive to changes in the marketplace. This inability to react quickly to changes in customer demand, preferences, and so forth was caused primarily by the significant amounts of raw material and finished goods inventories that were maintained, and that first had to be depleted before the firm could begin supplying customers with new product.

Within this type of operating environment, companies very often had an antagonistic relationship with their suppliers. Every item that was purchased had several vendors. These vendors were played off against each other in order to obtain the lowest possible price, which was the primary criterion for being awarded a contract. Suppliers, recognizing that this relationship could very likely be terminated with the next contract, invested minimal time and money to address the specific needs of individual customers. Because of this short-term perspective, very little information was shared between these firms. Under such conditions the purchasing function within a manufacturing company often reported to the operations manager, and its primary objective was to purchase raw material and components at the lowest possible cost.

Today, companies are working more closely with their suppliers so that they can be more responsive to the changing needs of their customers. In so doing, they are significantly reducing, and in some cases eliminating, these previously established buffer inventories, as

Exhibit 13.2

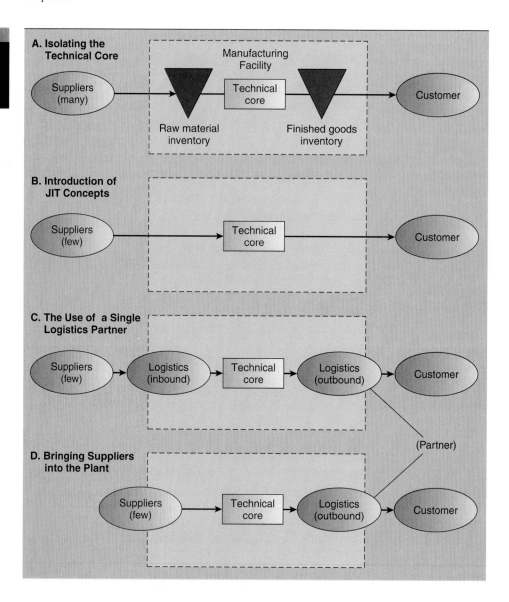

The Evolution of Supply Chain Management

shown in Exhibit 13.2B. Toyota is considered one of the early pioneers in this area with the development of the *just-in-time (JIT)* concept, which virtually eliminates all raw material and work-in-process inventories. In adopting JIT, however, companies become more dependent on their suppliers. (See related OM in Practice on Fire at Toyota's Supplier Stops Production.)

After JIT, the next stage in the supply chain management evolution was the use of a single logistics supplier to address all of the transportation and distribution functions for the firm, as shown in Exhibit 13.2C, which has led to the concept of *seamless logistics.* (Previously, firms dealt with many such transportation logistics vendors, again using cost as the primary criterion for selection.)

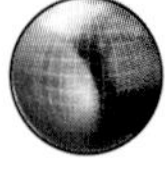

As an example, Schneider Logistics of Green Bay, Wisconsin, was named, in January 1997, the logistics provider for General Motors' Canadian parts operation. In the fall of 1996, Schneider also established a long-term relationship with Case Corp., a manufacturer of construction and agricultural equipment. Under this agreement, Schneider handles all of

Operations Management in Practice

FIRE AT TOYOTA'S SUPPLIER STOPS PRODUCTION

Aisin Seiki provides 99 percent of the brake valves that Toyota uses in the assembly of its automobiles. Because Toyota uses a just-in-time (JIT) system with its vendors, it maintains only a four-hour supply of brake valves at each of its assembly plants. Consequently, when a fire destroyed Aisin Sekei's manufacturing facility on February 1, 1997, Toyota was forced to shut down its 20 automobile plants, which were producing 14,000 cars a day.

Although many experts predicted that it would take weeks before Aisin could begin producing valves, Toyota's plants were again turning out cars five days after the fire. This was accomplished through a concerted effort of all of Toyota's suppliers who worked together around the clock to provide an interim solution.

Source: Valerie Reitman, *The Wall Street Journal,* May 8, 1997, p. A1.

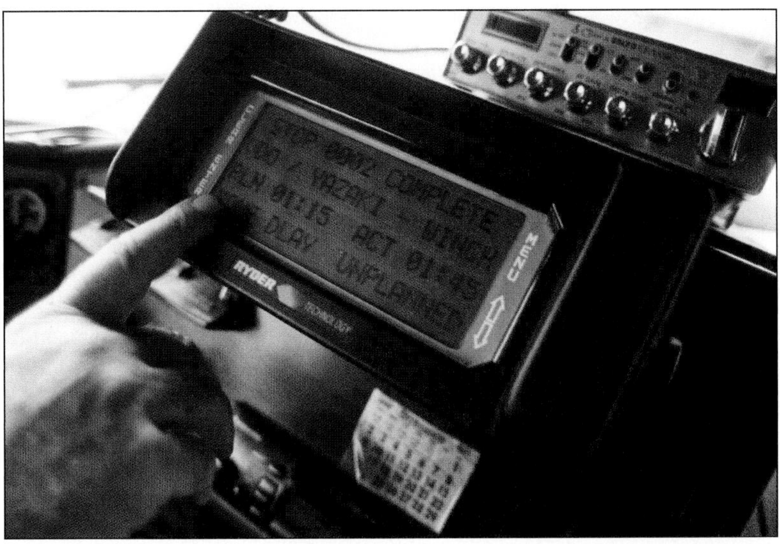

Ryder System manages Saturn's supply chain that links suppliers, factories, and dealers. Saturn turns over its parts inventory quickly—over 300 times a year—so accurate information is essential. In the photo, drivers check the on-board computer that tells them where they should go, how to get there, and how long it should take.

Case's inbound shipments of parts from nearly 2,000 suppliers worldwide, and outbound shipments of finished goods that total 40,000 pieces of equipment to some 150 countries around the world.[1]

The most recent innovation in supply chain management is the incorporation of suppliers and their workers within the same manufacturing facility. Volkswagen's new automotive assembly plant in Brazil, discussed later in this chapter, provides a good example of this innovation, which is illustrated in Exhibit 13.2D.

[1]Michael Fabey, "Time Is Money: Seamless Logistics Are in Demand," *World Trade,* July 1997, pp. 53–54.

Exhibit 13.3

The Trend toward Reducing the Number of Suppliers

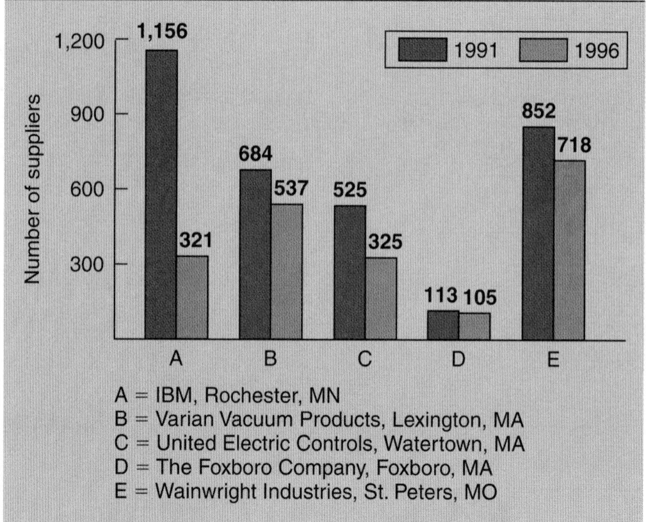

Note: IBM, Rochester, and Wainwright Industries are Malcolm Baldrige National Quality Award Winners; Varian Vacuum Products and The Foxboro Company are Massachusetts Quality Award winners; United Electric Controls is a Shingo Prize winner.

Factors Impacting the Supply Chain

Reduced Number of Suppliers

Companies, as part of their supply chain programs, have significantly reduced the number of vendors they buy from. Managers currently believe in establishing long-term relationships with a few, highly reliable vendors rather than having multiple sources for every purchased item. As seen in Exhibit 13.3, the reduction in the number of suppliers has been significant in recent years, and is even more impressive in light of the fact that most of these companies are now offering a wider variety of products to their customers.

Increase in Competition

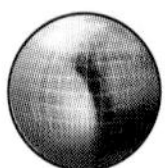

The emergence of a global economy has dramatically increased the number of competitors that offer similar products. As stated earlier, no corner of the world is immune to international competition, and this competition will only increase in intensity in the foreseeable future. As a result, supply chains will continue to grow in both directions: backwards toward suppliers in other countries and forward toward new customers in these same countries.

Shorter Product Life Cycles

Product life cycles continue to shorten as competition introduces new products at an ever-increasing rate in the hope of gaining market share and a competitive advantage. In order to respond quickly to new product introductions, a company needs to have flexible processes that can be converted easily to new product requirements. Flexibility also can be achieved by shifting more responsibility onto suppliers.

supplier-managed inventories (SMI)

Inventories in a firm's facility that are the responsibility of the supplier to maintain and replenish as necessary.

Increase in Supplier-Managed Inventories (SMI)

In order to decrease purchasing transaction costs and record-keeping costs, many firms now use a concept known as **supplier-managed inventories** (SMI) (or vendor-managed inventories (VMI)) for many of their low-cost components such as nuts, bolts, screws, and

Zara clothing store, an international retailer, sells trendy clothing for men and women. Its competitive advantage is its supply chain. Zara can design and manufacture its own clothing in less than 15 days and delivers them to its stores twice a week. All its retail stores are linked by computer to the company's headquarters in Spain where sales data and customer feedback provide real-time information for decisions on fabric, cut, and price for new garments.

other types of fasteners. This approach is sometimes referred to as the "breadman method." (The term *breadman* comes from commercial bakeries where the breadmen or salesmen determine the number of loaves of bread to deliver to each retail outlet on their routes, and who are also responsible for placing the bread on the retailer's shelves. The retail operations then receive credit for any unsold bread that is returned.)

With this approach, minimum and maximum inventory levels are established for each item. The firm's suppliers then are empowered to determine how often these items should be replenished. In addition, the suppliers have direct access to the manufacturing floor, and usually restock the items at the points where they will be used. This eliminates the need for stockrooms. With this approach, paperwork is reduced significantly because there are no purchase orders generated. The receiving function also is reduced significantly, as is the need for personnel to move the items from the stockroom onto the manufacturing floor.

Increase in Consignment Inventories

In recent years, there has been increased emphasis on the management of a firm's assets, as measured by the rate of return on assets, and the bonuses of many managers are directly related to this measure. Inasmuch as inventories are viewed as an asset on a firm's balance sheet, the less inventory that is on hand, the better the return on assets. To reduce inventories without negatively affecting operations and customer deliveries, an increasing number of companies are using **consignment inventories** wherever possible. Consignment inventories are inventories that are physically in a company's facility but are still owned by the supplier. Thus, they do not appear anywhere as an asset to the firm. Only when the components are actually used in the production of an end product does the ownership transfer to the firm, and then, it transfers almost immediately to the customer upon shipment. Consignment inventories also are used in services, where the retailer doesn't pay the manufacturer for the product until it is actually sold to the end user.

consignment inventories

Inventories that are physically present in a firm's facility but that are still owned by the supplier.

Advances in Technology

EDI (electronic data interchange)

Direct link between a manufacturer's database and that of the vendor.

Technology continues to have a significant impact on the supply chain. **EDI (electronic data interchange)** provides a direct link between a manufacturer's database and that of its vendors. In addition, the increased use of personal computers allows customers to communicate directly with their vendors' systems. For example, FedEx customers can order a pickup and track the delivery of their packages through their PCs.

Business-to-business (B2B) has been one of the fastest growing segments on the Internet. One of the reasons for its high rate of growth has been the creation of electronic or *B2B marketplaces.* B2B marketplaces are virtual markets that bring buyers and sellers together. Usually these B2B marketplaces focus on a specific industry or product category, and the items being bought and sold are typically common off-the-shelf products. Companies such as General Electric who have embraced the Internet as a purchasing tool have saved millions of dollars in the cost of their purchased goods and services.

These electronic marketplaces provide an opportunity for *reverse auctions* to take place. Reverse auctions occur when a firm requests bids for an item in an electronic marketplace, and potential suppliers keep submitting lower bids until either the bid closing deadline is reached or there is only one supplier left. As with a regular auction, the lowest bid price at any time is always available to all interested parties. The contract is then awarded to the supplier with the lowest bid. A major concern with reverse auctions is that it tends to be counterproductive, in terms of creating long term supplier relationships.

At the same time, the use of technology, in many cases, can provide suppliers with a barrier against competitors. A customer typically will establish an EDI link with only a few vendors. Potential new vendors have to demonstrate significant improvement in price and/or quality to warrant the additional costs of an added EDI link. Similarly, FedEx's customers would be reluctant to change vendors because it would require an investment in time to learn a new computer system with little or no added benefit.

In addition to EDI, a number of other systems have been developed such as quick response (QR) and efficient consumer response (ECR). In all cases these terms refer to the communication throughout a supply or distribution pipeline. This is a paperless communication between customers and vendors. For several years prior to this, there already had been some improvement in communication through the use of open computer systems using UNIX or UNIX-type software, but EDI, QR, and ECR go far beyond that.

quick response (QR) programs

Just-in-time replenishment system using bar-code scanning and EDI.

Quick response (QR) programs have grown rapidly. A survey by Deloitte & Touche showed that 68 percent of retailers either have implemented or plan to implement QR within two years.[2] Quick response is based on bar-code scanning and EDI. Its intent is to create a just-in-time replenishment system between vendors and retailers.

Virtually all medium and large retail stores use *Universal Product Code (UPC)* bar-code scanning. *Point-of-sale (POS)* scanning at the register also uses *price-look-up (PLU),* as reported by 90 percent of the respondents.

efficient consumer response (ECR)

Strategy for bringing distributors, suppliers, and grocers together using bar-code scanning and EDI.

Efficient consumer response (ECR) is a variation of QR and EDI adopted by the supermarket industry as a business strategy where distributors, suppliers, and grocers work closely together to bring products to consumers. They can use bar-code scanning and EDI. Savings come from reduced supply chain costs and reduced inventory.

A study by Kurt Salmon Associations estimated a potential savings of more than $30 billion.[3] In the dry grocery segment this could cut supply-chain inventory from 104 days to 61 days. Another study by McKinsey estimated that dry grocery consumer

---

[2]"Quick Response Grows," *Chain Store Age Executive,* May 1993, pp. 158–59.

[3]James Aaron Cooke, "The $30 Billion Promise," *Traffic Management,* December 1993, pp. 57–61.

Campbell uses a system they call Continuous Product Replenishment (CPR). At the food retailer's warehouse, Campbell product arrives from the plant to replenish inventory at the same steady rate as the consumer takes it off the shelf. CPR is driven by an electronic ordering system managed by Campbell, freeing the retailer from this task. Steady production that meets predetermined inventory levels results in cost efficiencies across the entire supply chain.

prices could be reduced an average of 10.8 percent through industrywide adoption of ECR.[4]

Without ECR, manufacturers push products on the markets by offering low prices on large quantities: A few times a year the manufacturer offers the grocer a low price on a large quantity of product. This is forward buying. The manufacturer then works with the supermarket to offer coupons and incentives to entice customers to buy the product during a promotion. Products not sold during the promotion are then stored in inventory to carry that supermarket until the next manufacturer's promotional deal.

ECR focuses on the customers to drive the system, not the manufacturers' deals. Customers pull goods through the store and through the pipeline by their purchases. This permits less inventory throughout the system.

Cooke cites a study that estimated that distributors purchase 80 percent of their merchandise during manufacturers' sales or "deals." They may buy four times per year and fill up their warehouses. Until the industry frees itself from this addiction to deal buying, all the great replenishment techniques will be worthless.[5]

Wal-Mart's Satellite Network, first installed in 1987 in Bentonville, Arkansas, provides another good example of how technology has imparted the structure of the supply chain. This network supports data, voice, and video and allows real-time sales and inventory information.

Wal-Mart's EDI, shown in the photo on the next page, installed in 1990, issues electronic purchase orders and receives electronic invoices from virtually all of Wal-Mart's vendors.

---

[4]David B. Jenkins, "Jenkins Leads EDI Effort," *Chain Store Age Executive,* March 1993, p. 147.

[5]Cooke, "$30 Billion Promise," pp. 57–61.

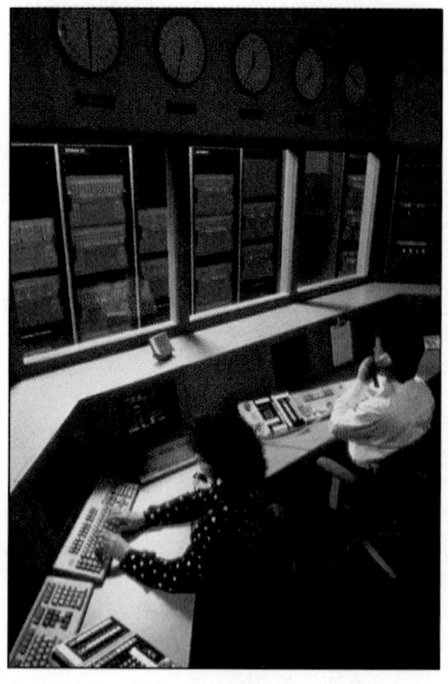

Wal-Mart's Retail Link, installed in 1991, allows vendors to directly access in real-time *point-of-sale (POS)* data. This allows vendors to create better forecasts and better inventory management. The POS data come directly from store cash registers so they reflect activity in real time. E-mail capability also is included for corresponding within the supply system concerning scheduling, payments, and so on. Retail Link also includes the spreadsheet Microsoft Excel for Windows, so that spreadsheet data can be accessed throughout the system.

Using Retail Link and point-of-sale data, arrangements have been made with some large suppliers to make their own decisions about Wal-Mart's purchases from them. They directly access point-of-sale data and create their own purchase orders. Wal-Mart is attempting to implement EDI internationally, but little progress in this area has been made so far.[6]

The ability of suppliers to access a firm's sales data significantly reduces the *bullwhip effect,* which often occurs in a supply chain when there is no sharing of information. (The bullwhip effect is when a slight change in demand by the end user causes significant fluctuations in the quantities purchased by each of the firms in the supply chain, with the fluctuations increasing the further the firm is removed from the end user.

Shared or Reduced Risk

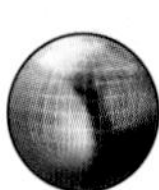

The cost of developing new products is increasing. With product life cycles becoming shorter, the risk associated with these new products also increases. To reduce their own financial exposure, many companies are requesting that vendors take on an increasing percentage of this risk. Volkswagen's new automotive plant in Brazil epitomizes this sharing of risk with vendors. (See OM in Practice box.)

Requirements for a Successful Supply Chain

Several elements are mandatory for the successful implementation of a supply chain management program. These elements often overlap and often are dependent on each other.

Trust

A primary ingredient in the establishment of a successful relationship between vendor and customer is the element of trust. Without trust, none of the other factors is possible. Trust allows vendors to participate and contribute in the new product development cycle.

Long-Term Relationships

With suppliers taking on a strategic role in a company, it is necessary to develop long-term relationships that permit the sharing of a strategic vision. The term often used in establishing these long-term relationships is *evergreen contracts,* implying they are automatically renewed as long as the vendors perform as agreed.

Information Sharing

Successful supply chain management requires the sharing of information between vendors and customers. This information can include everything from new product design specifications to capacity planning and scheduling, and even access to a customer's entire database.

---

[6]"Going beyond EDI: Wal-Mart Cited for Vendor Links," *Chain Store Age Executive,* March 1993, pp. 150–51.

Operations Management in Practice

VOLKSWAGEN BUILDS A DIFFERENT KIND OF ASSEMBLY PLANT IN BRAZIL

In November 1996, Volkswagen began operations at its new truck and bus assembly plant in Resende, Brazil. Unlike any other automotive assembly plant in the world, this facility has suppliers' personnel working side by side with VW's workers. This latest advancement in supply chain management is the concept of Jose Ignacio Lopez de Arriortua, who is in charge of purchasing for VW. As a result, only 200 out of a total workforce of 1,000 are VW employees. The remaining workers are employed by the major subcontractors such as MWM-Cummins, which produces the engines and transmissions, and Rockwell, which produces the suspension systems.

With this revolutionary approach to automotive assembly, VW hopes to increase both productivity and quality. At the same time, VW is sharing the risk of this new venture with its major suppliers, who have to shoulder a large percentage of the fixed operating costs of the plant. In exchange for this risk, these subcontractors hope to develop and maintain a long and profitable relationship with VW.

Sources: Edvaldo Pereira Lima, "VW's Revolutionary Idea," *Industry Week,* March 17, 1997, and Diana J. Schemo, "Is VW's New Plant Lean, or Just Mean?" *New York Times,* November 19, 1996.

VW's Carmaking Co-op

Like Tom Sawyer and his fence-painting project, José Ignacio López de Arriortua designed Volkswagen's new truck plant in Resende, Brazil, around work done for Volkswagen's benefit by others. Major suppliers are assigned space in the plant and supply their own workers to add components to trucks rolling down the assembly line. Volkswagen's employees, a minority in the plant, supervise the work and inspect finished trucks; only when they pass are the suppliers paid.

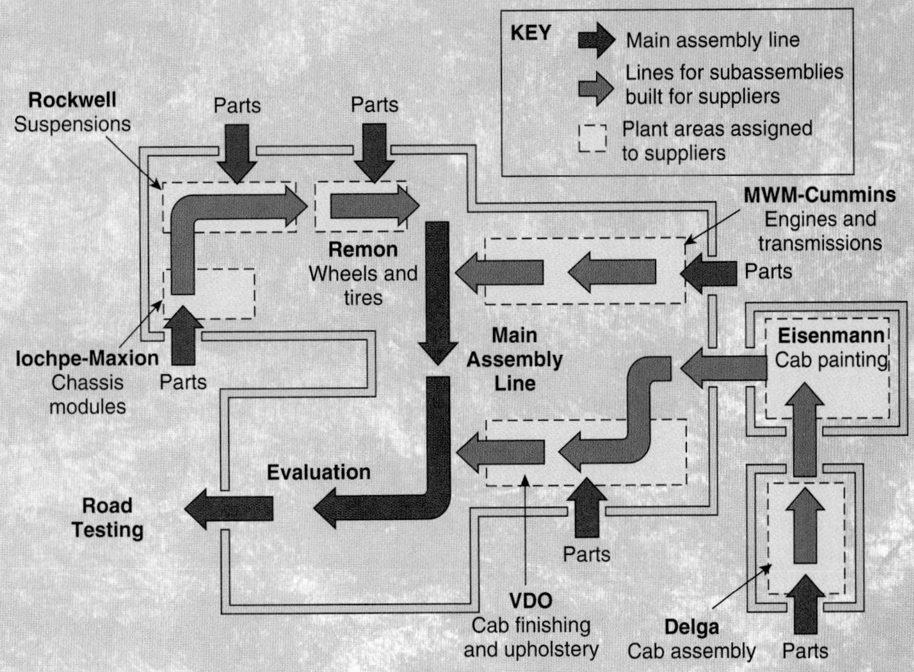

Source: Graphic from Diana J. Schemo, "Is VW's New Plant Lean, or Just Mean?" *New York Times,* November 19, 1996. Reprinted with permission.

Individual Strengths of Organizations

If a firm enters into a long-term relationship with a vendor, then it is in that firm's best interest that the vendor remain in business for a long period of time. Thus a good customer will work with a vendor to ensure that it is profitable and that it remains financially strong.

The selection of proper vendors is also important. Thus, in addition to financial strengths, each vendor should have some unique operational or engineering strengths with respect to the products it makes and delivers. This permits the firm to incorporate these strengths into its own products, which then provides an added advantage in the marketplace.

The Role of Logistics in the Supply Chain

The continued emphasis on globalization with respect to both suppliers and customers has caused the supply chain to become longer in terms of time and distance. As a consequence, the logistics associated with both the delivery of raw material and components to the company and the delivery of finished goods to its customers have taken on added importance. However, the lengthening of the supply chain runs counter to the firm's need for flexibility to provide customers with a wide variety of products that can be delivered quickly.

Companies have therefore adopted various strategies to compensate for the longer supply chain. For example, companies are locating distribution centers closer to customer markets so they can better serve these markets.

Partnering

Another approach to addressing the issue of a growing supply chain involves the establishment of a strategic alliance or partnership with a firm that specializes in transportation or logistics. For example, L.L. Bean, a well-known mail-order firm specializing in outdoor equipment and clothes, has established such a partnership with FedEx. As a result, FedEx employees, who are physically located on a full-time basis at the L.L. Bean distribution facility in Freeport, Maine, handle all of the outbound shipments to L.L. Bean's customers (including the shipment of some packages by UPS).

An alternative approach to using a logistics partner is for a firm to store finished goods at the logistics partner's hub or distribution center. Establishing an inventory at this point in the distribution channel will significantly reduce the delivery time of critical products. As an illustration, some companies that produce medical products for implants may maintain a supply of their products at FedEx's hub in Memphis, Tennessee. Requests for these products, in many cases, can be delivered the same day or, at most, the next morning, to any location in the United States. Laura Ashley, a chain of high-fashion boutiques, similarly maintains an inventory of high-usage items at FedEx's distribution center in Memphis. Such an arrangement allows retail operations to restock the following day with items that have sold out. (See OM in Practice box for another role for a logistics partner.)

in-transit inventory costs

Combination of transportation costs and carrying costs associated with delivery of products.

In-Transit Inventory Costs

The stretching of the supply chain to all corners of the globe has caused managers to take a closer look at the various costs associated with the delivery of products. These costs often are referred to as **in-transit inventory costs** and are usually associated with delivery of raw material and components that are in bound to the plant. The reason for this is that most products are sold FOB at the vendor's plant. (FOB stands for free-on-board, which is the point at which ownership and title to the goods are transferred from the supplier to the customer.)

Operations Management in Practice

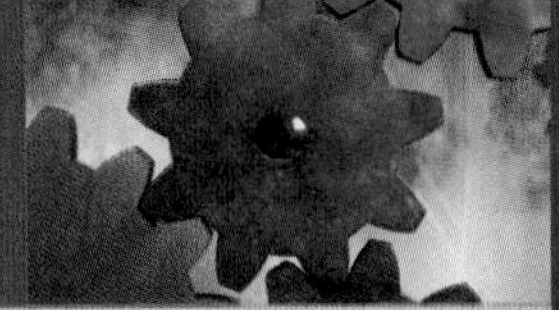

TRUCKS KEEP INVENTORIES ROLLING PAST WAREHOUSES TO PRODUCTION LINES

It seems warehouses have grown wheels.

Called "rolling inventories," trucks have become the place of choice for just-in-time stockpiles. Eighteen-wheelers pull up to factory loading docks to deliver parts that go almost immediately onto production lines, bypassing the warehouses.

"Companies now precisely plan their need of inventory so that [intermediate] warehouses aren't needed," says Don Schneider, president of trucking concern Schneider National Inc. and a member of the Chicago Federal Reserve Bank.

To be sure, just-in-time inventory methods aren't new. But as more companies come around to this approach, trucks and railcars have begun to function as warehouses for many producers—adding yet another anomaly to the economic recovery.

The construction of warehouse square footage tumbled nearly 18 percent in 1992 and 9 percent in 1993, even as the economy gained momentum and space in stores and shopping centers grew 6 percent and 12 percent, respectively.

For trucking companies, the trend means new business, but also more demanding customers. Many trucking companies say that in recent years, they've come under increasing pressure to deliver parts within a small window of time. "There are sometimes less than 10-minute lag times," says Larry Mulkey, president of Ryder Dedicated Logistics Inc., a Miami unit of transportation-services company Ryder Systems Inc.

Such use of trucks enables businesses to cut space costs, freeing up capital for investments such as equipment or new employees. "The back room decreases in size because you don't need it to store stockpiles and that means you have more floor space for selling," Mr. Mulkey says.

But a heavy reliance on trucks to keep inventories low isn't without its risks. The General Motors Corp., Toyota Motor Co. joint venture in Fremont, California, once had to shut down its production line because a just-in-time delivery truck broke down on the highway.

Ken Simonson, chief economist of the American Trucking Associations, says trucking for just-in-time orders generally works better in uncongested regions of the country.

But trucking companies have come a long way in eliminating delivery glitches. Mr. Schneider of Schneider National boasts that not one load was late because of the icy, wintry weather that hit much of the nation recently.

Technology enables trucking companies and their clients to track a load's progress from minute to minute. If a problem comes up, another truck can be dispatched immediately to pick up the load. Trucks also have become more reliable mechanically.

Source: Lucinda Harper, "Trucks Keep Inventories Rolling Past Warehouses to Production Lines," *The Wall Street Journal,* February 7, 1994, p. A7A.

In deciding which is the most economical mode of transportation to use, a manager needs to take into consideration two cost elements: the actual costs of transportation and the in-transit inventory carrying costs of product while in transit. These carrying costs consist primarily of the cost of the capital tied up when items are purchased at the vendor's plant, but are not available for use until they arrive at the firm's plant. (For a more detailed definition of the cost of capital, see Chapter 16.) Typically, the slower the mode of transportation, the lower the transportation costs, the longer the shipment time, and thus the higher the in-transit carrying cost. The trade-off between these two costs is shown in Exhibit 13.4.

The total annual costs associated with transporting products from a vendor's plant are

$$\text{Total costs} = \text{Transportation costs} + \text{In-transit inventory carrying costs} + \text{Purchase costs}$$

$$\text{TC} = DM + (X/365)iDC + DC$$

Exhibit 13.4

The Trade-Off between Transportation Costs and the Cost of Capital with Respect to the Shipment of Products

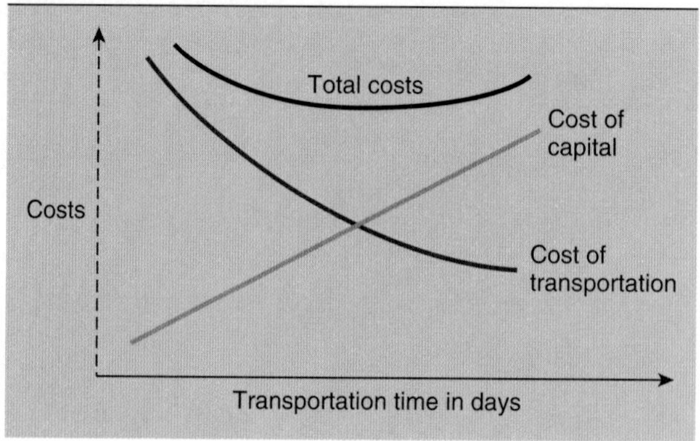

where

$D =$ Annual demand
$M =$ Transportation cost per unit
$X =$ Transportation time in days
$i =$ Annual cost of capital
$C =$ Unit cost per item

Example

A company located in Hartford, Connecticut, has agreed to purchase an item from a manufacturer in Vancouver, British Columbia, Canada. The purchasing agent in Hartford has identified two alternative methods for shipping the item: truck or cargo ship. If the item is shipped by truck, it will take 14 days at a cost of \$3 per unit to cross the continent and clear customs. A cargo ship will take 45 days through the Panama Canal, but the transportation cost will only be \$1.50 per unit. The company expects to buy 2,000 units per year at a cost of \$150 per unit. The in-transit carrying cost of inventory is estimated to be 20 percent per annum. Which mode of transportation should the purchasing agent select?

Solution

A summary of the relevant costs for each mode of transportation is as follows:

		Mode 1 (truck)	**Mode 2 (ship)**
	Number of days in-transit (*X*):	14	45
	Transportation cost per unit (*M*):	\$3.00	\$1.50
Additional data:	In-transit carrying cost (*i*):	20% per annum	
	Annual demand (*D*):	2,000 units	
	Unit cost (*C*):	\$150.00	

$$\begin{aligned}
\text{TC}_1 &= DM_1 + (X_1/365)iDC \\
\text{TC}_1 &= (2{,}000)(3.00) + (14/365)(0.20)(2{,}000)(150) \\
\text{TC}_1 &= 6{,}000 + 2{,}301.37 \\
\text{TC}_1 &= \$8{,}301.37
\end{aligned}$$

$$\begin{aligned}
\text{TC}_2 &= DM_2 + (X_2/365)iDC \\
\text{TC}_2 &= (2{,}000)(1.50) + (45/365)(0.20)(2{,}000)(150) \\
\text{TC}_2 &= 3{,}000 + 7{,}397.26 \\
\text{TC}_2 &= \$10{,}397.26
\end{aligned}$$

Based on this analysis, the more economical mode of transportation is by truck, even though the actual transportation cost per unit is twice that of sending the items by ship. Note that when evaluating alternative modes of transportation from the same vendor, the purchase cost remains the same and, for simplicity, is not included in the analysis.

Disintermediation

disintermediation

Trend to reduce many of the steps in the supply chain.

Disintermediation is a term coined by futurist Stan Davis.[7] It refers to the growing trend of companies and organizations to try to get closer to both suppliers and customers by eliminating many of the intermediate steps that currently exist in the supply chain.

For example, Wal-Mart, as part of its strategy, built large regional distribution warehouses to store items for restocking its retail operations. As a result, significant capital was tied up in both facilities and inventory. Subsequently, Wal-Mart developed the concept of *cross-docking*. By properly scheduling the arrival of vendor trucks at the receiving dock, Wal-Mart causes items to be unloaded from these trucks and immediately carried across to trucks on the shipping dock that are out-bound for its retail operations. With the introduction of cross-docking, Wal-Mart was able to increase the number of its retail outlets without increasing the number or size of its distribution facilities.

The next step in Wal-Mart's disintermediation process, as we saw earlier in this chapter, was to allow vendors direct, on-line access to their retail sales data through a satellite network. With this system, vendors now decide how much to ship to Wal-Mart. In many cases, these products are shipped directly to retail stores, bypassing the distribution centers altogether.

Another example of disintermediation is in the airline industry. Here airlines are increasing their efforts to work directly with customers rather than through travel agents in order to save commission fees. This is being accomplished through airline websites that feature on-line ticketing instructions and through the increasing use of electronic ticketing.

When disintermediation does take place, there needs to be close coordination and planning among the different firms in the supply chain that are affected.

JIT II®

JIT II®, developed in 1987 by the Bose Corp. (which produces high-end stereo equipment), is a good example of disintermediation and is now being adopted by a growing number of companies. The objective of JIT II® is for the vendor and customer to work much closer together, thereby eliminating many of the intermediate steps that now exist. To accomplish this, a vendor employee is provided with physical office space within the purchasing function of the customer. This approach eliminates the need for a buyer for the customer and a salesperson for the vendor.

This vendor representative has full access to the customer's database and therefore can translate the customer's purchase orders directly into orders for his or her company. This individual also participates in the customer's new product design process, offering suggestions for improving product performance and/or reducing costs. The two elements for successfully implementing JIT II® are (*a*) the physical presence of the vendor's representative inside the customer's manufacturing facility and, at the same time, (*b*) the ability to provide the direct data linkage between the customer's planning function and the vendor's manufacturing facility.

[7]Stanley Davis, *Future Perfect* (Reading, MA: Addison-Wesley, 1987).

Exhibit 13.5

Major SCM Software Packages

Company	Customers Include	Success Story
i2 *www.i2.com*	Dell, Nike, Southwest Airlines, Thomson Consumer Electronics	Thomson cuts its forecasting cycle from ten days to two days, and reduced inventory by 33% in its first the first 12 months.
Manugistics *www.manugistics.com*	Black & Decker, Hewlett-Packard Mitsubishi	HP slashed transportation budget by 25% cut inventory at its top three Asia-Pacific resellers by more than half within just two months.
SAP *www.sap.com*	Carlsberg, Motts Lockheed Martin	In four months Carlsberg reduced inventories by 30% and increased order accuracy by 20%.
Peoplesoft *www.peoplesoft.com*	Borden Foods, Credit Suisse First Boston, Netergy Networks	Netergy Networks integrated manufacturing and engineering processes to slash new product development time by one-third.
SynQuest *www.synquest.com*	Titleist FootJoy Worldwide, Ford, Herman Miller	Titleist cut manufacturing lead times on custom golf balls by more than half, from 12 to five days.

Source: Kayte VanScoy, "Recession-Proof Your Business," *Smart Business,* December 2001/January 2002, pp. 84–88.

The Impact of Technology

State-of-the-art software has had a significant impact on the overall management of the supply chain. These software packages, in combination with network linkages provided by the Internet, allow each of the organizations within a supply chain to share information on a real-time basis. Knowing the actual demand as it occurs allows each of the firms in the chain to operate leaner with less inventory while simultaneously providing them with the ability to respond faster to changes in the market.

Exhibit 13.5 shows some of the major SCM software packages that are available, some of their customers, and how they have impacted the supply chain.

The supply chain is also being affected by m-business. As the cost of mobile technology falls, it is becoming more economical for many firms to justify its adoption. For example, Pepsi Bottling Group's technicians previously used to phone in to find out where their next service calls were. They then faxed back billing information after the service call. Now this same information is sent directly to the technician's handheld device. By using this mobile technology, service response times have been reduced by 20 percent and the errors that occurred from using the old fax system have been eliminated.[8]

Conclusion

The importance of supply chain management continues to grow as companies become more dependent on their suppliers. The reasons for doing so include (*a*) increased emphasis on core competencies, (*b*) increased need for flexibility, and (*c*) a desire to share risk associated with new product development. As a consequence, the role of the supplier has shifted from being purely transactional, based on low cost, to being a partner that participates in strategic decisions of the firm. This dramatic shift in the role of the supplier has

[8]Heather Greene, "Winging into Wireless," *BusinessWeek e.biz,* February 18, 2002, pp. EB 8–EB 9.

caused companies to establish long-term relationships with a smaller number of suppliers than was previously the case.

Increased competition also has forced companies to look to the four corners of the globe for suppliers that can meet their needs. As a result, the logistics and associated costs of transporting goods over great distances have become major factors in vendor selection.

However, while the use of international vendors has caused the supply chain to become longer in many cases, there is a trend toward disintermediation, which eliminates many of the intermediate stages in the overall supply chain.

Key Terms

consignment inventories p. 521
disintermediation p. 529
EDI (electronic data interchange) p. 522
efficient consumer response (ECR) p. 522
inbound logistics p. 516
in-transit inventory costs p. 526
outbound logistics p. 517
quick response (QR) programs p. 522
supplier-managed inventories (SMI) p. 520
supply chain p. 516

Review and Discussion Questions

1. What are the advantages and disadvantages to a firm having a small number of suppliers?
2. Supply chain management as presented in this chapter pertains primarily to goods. What would be the different steps or elements in a supply chain for a service? Give an example.
3. How has technology impacted a firm's supply chain and the trend toward disintermediation?
4. What are the main differences between having a vendor's employees working in your manufacturing operation and you hiring your own employees to do the same work?
5. Identify all of the steps in the supply chain for a hamburger that you buy at McDonald's. How might this supply chain differ for a McDonald's located in a developing country?

Internet Exercise

Visit the website of any of the supply chain management software vendors listed in Exhibit 13.5 and describe the firm's SCM software package in terms of price, size, and capabilities.

Problems

1. An automobile company in Ohio currently purchases 100,000 tires a year from a manufacturer located 50 miles from its assembly plant. The price per tire is $40. Because of the close proximity of the two plants, the vendor delivers these tires free of charge. The purchasing agent recently has been approached by a tire manufacturer in Asia who has agreed to provide these tires for $35 each. Through inquiries, the purchasing agent has determined that it will cost an additional $4.50 per tire to ship the tires from Asia to the plant in Ohio. In addition, it will take approximately six weeks for a shipment to arrive. Currently the cost of capital for the automobile company is 20 percent per year. From which vendor should the purchasing agent buy tires?

2. A computer company in the greater Boston area currently buys electronic modules at a price of $26 per unit from a vendor located in Tijuana, Mexico. The firm's buyer is currently evaluating two alternative modes for transporting these modules. The first way is overland on a trailer truck. The cost with this method is $2.50 per module and takes approximately two weeks. The second way is to ship the modules air freight, which takes only two days to deliver at a cost of $3 per unit. Currently the computer maker is buying 25,000 modules per year. The cost of capital for the firm is estimated at 18 percent per year. Which mode of transportation do you recommend?
3. As the purchasing agent for a small company located in central France, Laurence Garreau has recently sent out a request for proposal for a small motor used in a subassembly that her firm manufactures for the automobile industry. The annual requirement for this motor is 25,000 units, and she has estimated the cost of in-transit inventory to be 25 percent per year.

   The first quotation she receives is from a company in Southeast Asia. The unit price per motor from this firm is 45 FF (French francs). In addition, the transportation cost per unit is 4 FF. The transit time from Southeast Asia, using an ocean freighter, is estimated to be 50 days in total. The second quotation she receives is from a company in Mexico that is very anxious to do business in Europe. The unit price per motor from this company is 43 FF, and the transportation cost per unit is 6,5 FF, but it will take only 10 days in total to deliver the motors because the company will be using air freight. (Note: In Europe, a comma is used instead of a decimal point to indicate less than a whole unit.)

   a. Evaluate each of these two proposals to determine which is the most economical alternative. What is your recommendation? (Be specific and show all of your calculations.)

   b. What factors, in addition to cost, need to be taken into consideration in arriving at a final decision as to which supplier to use?

Bibliography

Bowersox, Donald J., and David J. Closs. *Logistical Management: The Integrated Supply Chain Process.* New York: McGraw-Hill, 1996.

Cooke, James A. "The $30 Billion Promise." *Traffic Management,* December 1993, pp. 57–61.

Coyle, J. J.; E. J. Bardi; and C. John Langley Jr. *The Management of Business Logistics.* 6th ed. Minneapolis/St. Paul, MN: West, 1996.

Davis, Stanley M. *Future Perfect.* Reading, MA: Addison-Wesley, 1987.

Dixon, Lance E. *JIT II®.* Bose Corporation.

Fabey, Michael. "Time Is Money: Seamless Logistics Are in Demand." *World Trade,* July 1997, pp. 53–54.

"Going Beyond EDI: Wal-Mart Cited for Vendor Links." *Chain Store Age Executive,* March 1993, pp. 150–51.

Greene, Heather, "Winging into Wireless," *BusinessWeek e.biz,* February 18, 2002, pp. EB 8–EB 9.

Jenkins, David B. "Jenkins Leads EDI Effort." *Chain Store Age Executive,* March 1993, p. 147.

Leenders, Michiel R., and Harold E. Fearon. *Purchasing and Supply Management.* 11th ed. Burr Ridge, IL: Irwin/McGraw-Hill, 1997.

Lima, Edvaldo Pereira. "VW's Revolutionary Idea." *Industry Week,* March 17, 1997.

Reitman, Valerie. *The Wall Street Journal,* May 8, 1997, p. A1.

Schemo, Diana J. "Is VW's New Plant Lean, or Just Mean?" *New York Times,* November 19, 1996.

VanScoy, Kayte, "Recession-Proof Your Business," *Smart Business,* December 2001/January 2002, pp. 84–88.

Case

How a Quality Initiative Changed Whirlpool's Supply Chain

For over 30 years, Stanley Engineering Components (SEC), a division of the Stanley Works, had been manufacturing oven-door-latching mechanisms for the range-appliance industry. (The oven-door-latching mechanism locks an oven door during the self-cleaning cycle in both gas and electric ranges.) Its customers viewed SEC as a low-cost supplier of customer-designed stamped metal assemblies. In this capacity, SEC provided little input with respect to the designing, manufacturing, and marketing of their customers' end products. The largest of SEC's customers was the range-appliance division of the Whirlpool Corporation, the world's leading manufacturer and marketer of appliances. SEC has been a supplier of oven-door latches to Whirlpool for more than 20 years.

In early 1993, Whirlpool notified its existing and potential suppliers that it was instituting a new quality initiative, based on total quality management (TQM) principles, that directly affected its customer-supplier relationship. It now wanted its suppliers to be business partners, as compared to the existing customer-supplier arrangement in which price was the primary criterion for purchase. Whirlpool now asked potential suppliers to provide extra value-added services and encouraged them to (*a*) become partners who were to be experts in Whirlpool's business, (*b*) participate in customer-supplier teams, and (*c*) learn about the needs of Whirlpool's customers.

As business partners, Whirlpool wanted its suppliers to follow its strategy, which was to deliver world-class products that exceeded customer expectations. An important part of this strategy was Whirlpool's commitment to continuous quality improvement. Whirlpool was able to achieve this strategy by leveraging its suppliers' technical expertise. To accomplish this, its suppliers had to be flexible to change and proactive to the continuous quality improvement of their products. In addition, Whirlpool's suppliers had to be able to produce consistently high-quality products at low cost, while providing additional services, which included free consulting, as well as other initiatives to decrease product cost and increase product quality.

Another of Whirlpool's goals was to decrease its number of suppliers. Therefore, in addition to the oven-door-latching mechanism, Whirlpool encouraged SEC to develop a program to manufacture oven-door hinges, as this additional product was viewed as a natural extension to SEC's product line because a hinge is also a stamped metal assembly. If SEC supplied both of these products, Whirlpool could reduce its number of suppliers.

SEC had to make many changes within its organization in order to meet these new requirements. For example, SEC was now expected to initiate cost saving and quality improvement programs that extended far beyond SEC's own products. In addition, SEC had to assume significant risks. Its previous method of doing business, although far from risk free, was in a stable environment, and SEC knew what was needed to compete successfully: low-cost products. On the other hand, supplying Whirlpool under its TQM principles meant competing in a highly uncertain environment that presented a significant risk of failure. If SEC was not able to meet Whirlpool's requirements, then Whirlpool would not consider it as a potential supplier. Losing Whirlpool's business would result in a 20 percent loss in sales along with high sunk costs, which could ultimately mean business failure for SEC.

Case

As SEC considered changing its way of doing business with Whirlpool, it decided that all of its existing and future customers would also have to accept this new way of doing business, because SEC was not willing to operate two separate business structures. SEC consciously chose TQM as a competitive advantage and therefore assumed the risk of losing those customers who did not endorse TQM principles. In this respect, SEC considered Whirlpool's demands as an opportunity to force itself to change and to adopt TQM practices. SEC also realized that Whirlpool was not going to lead it through the TQM process; SEC would have to develop this on its own.

SEC also needed to change its business philosophy from being just a low-cost supplier to that of being a concerned business partner. To accomplish this, SEC began considering all aspects of the final product, not just those pertaining to the components it supplied. SEC showed its willingness to change in many ways. Perhaps the most striking example was SEC using its own personnel to co-develop a latch and a hinge with Whirlpool even though there was no guarantee that SEC would get Whirlpool's business. SEC personnel became free internal consultants to Whirlpool in order to demonstrate that they were committed to becoming a business partner.

Whirlpool expected its suppliers to provide a sustainable, competitive advantage that was consistent with its strategy, although Whirlpool did not provide any leadership to SEC. It simply imposed its demands. Developing a strategy for achieving Whirlpool's goals rested solely with the supplier. By not providing any detailed plans, Whirlpool left the strategic planning and implementation up to SEC.

Whirlpool also wanted SEC to help predict consumer preferences. It therefore sought SEC's opinions, suggestions, and solutions to problems about many aspects of its products, most of which did not relate to SEC's components. Again SEC was expected to play the role of free consultant, even before it established formal agreements with Whirlpool.

One of Whirlpool's key strategic thrusts was to "effectively manage the selected technology base that emanates from the suppliers." To meet Whirlpool's objectives, SEC had to communicate Whirlpool's needs to all of SEC's employees and suppliers. Whirlpool demanded high-quality, low-cost, timely products, and SEC had to comply with these demands. Whirlpool stated that its chosen suppliers would be the best in their class and their goals would be in line with Whirlpools' goals.

In early 1995, the buyers at Whirlpool accepted SEC's design proposals for the latch and hinge assemblies and awarded SEC the contract for these components. SEC started shipping small quantities of latches and hinges early in the spring of 1996. In mid-1996, Whirlpool awarded SEC a contract to supply smoke eliminators and venting tube assemblies. Since SEC first starting shipping components under its new supplier program, Whirlpool has awarded SEC \$5 million in additional yearly business. At the same time, others suppliers lost this \$5 million in business.

By adopting TQM, SEC became a successful competitor. Between 1993 and 1997, SEC sales to Whirlpool increased 125 percent, and its productivity increased by 76 percent. Over the same period, its sales to other customers (originally non-TQM customers) increased 25 percent. For SEC, implementing TQM, although risky and painful, was a success. SEC realized that it must solve problems immediately and provide the best possible design and quality at a competitive price. As a supplier, SEC needs to constantly initiate new technology ideas, as suppliers to organizations that use TQM principles must always be ready to change and be on the alert.

Questions

1. How did the customer-supplier relationship between SEC and Whirlpool change as a result of the TQM initiative?
2. How did Whirlpool help its suppliers to better understand Whirlpool's quality requirements? Should Whirlpool have helped more?
3. How has SEC made Whirlpool's products better?
4. What are the advantages and disadvantages when a new management initiative such as TQM is introduced into a firm's supply chain?

Source: Condensed from Christopher J. Roethlein and Paul M. Mangiameli, "The Realities of Becoming a Long-Term Supplier to a Large TQM Customer," *Interface* 29, no. 4 (1999), pp. 71–81.

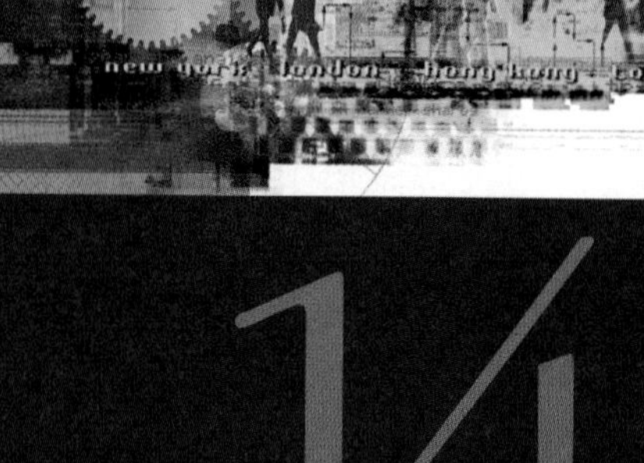

14

Just-in-Time Systems

Chapter Objectives

- Introduce the underlying concepts of just-in-time (JIT) and the Japanese approach to improving productivity.
- Identify the differences between Japanese companies and U.S. firms with respect to implementing JIT, and explore why these differences exist.
- Identify the various elements that need to be included to successfully implement JIT within an organization.
- Illustrate how many JIT concepts have been implemented in services.

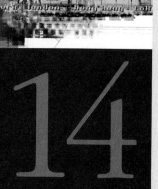

The 100 Yen Sushi House is no ordinary sushi restaurant. It is the ultimate showcase of Japanese productivity. The house features an ellipsoid-shaped serving area in the middle of the room, where three or four cooks were busily preparing sushi. Perhaps 30 stools surrounded the serving area. As we took our seats at the counters, I noticed something special. There was a conveyor belt going around the ellipsoid service area, like a toy train track. On it I saw plates of sushi. There was every kind of sushi that you can think of—from the cheapest seaweed to the more expensive raw salmon or shrimp dishes. The price was uniform, however, 100 yen per plate. On closer examination, while my eyes were racing to keep up with the speed of the traveling plates, I found that a cheap seaweed plate had four pieces, while the more expensive raw salmon dish had only two pieces.

I saw a man with eight plates all stacked up neatly. As he got up to leave, the cashier looked over and said, "800 yen, please." The cashier had no cash register; she simply counted the number of plates and then multiplied by 100 yen.

The owner's daily operation is based on a careful analysis of information. The owner has a complete summary of demand information about the different types of sushi plates, and thus knows exactly how many of each type of sushi plate he should prepare and when. Furthermore, the whole operation is based on the repetitive manufacturing principle with appropriate just-in-time and quality control systems. For example, the store has a very limited refrigerator capacity. Thus, the store uses the just-in-time inventory control system. Instead of increasing the refrigeration capacity by purchasing additional refrigeration systems, the owner has an agreement with the fish vendor to deliver fresh fish several times a day so that materials arrive just in time to be used for sushi making. The inventory cost is, therefore, minimum.

The available floor space is for workers and their necessary equipment but not for holding inventory. In the 100 Yen Sushi House, workers and their equipment are positioned so close together that sushi making is passed on hand to hand rather than as independent operations. The absence of walls of inventory allows the owner and workers to be involved in the total operation, from greeting the customer to serving what is ordered. Their tasks are tightly interrelated and everyone rushes to a problem spot to prevent the cascading effect of the problem throughout the work process.

The 100 Yen Sushi House is a labor-intensive operation, which is based mostly on simplicity and common sense rather than high technology, contrary to American perceptions. I was very impressed. As I finished my fifth plate, I saw the same octopus sushi plate going around for about the thirtieth time. Perhaps I had discovered the pitfall of the system. So I asked the owner how he takes care of the sanitary problems when a sushi plate goes around all day long, until an unfortunate customer eats it and perhaps gets food poisoning. He bowed with an apologetic smile and said, "Well, sir, we never let our sushi plates go unsold longer than about 30 minutes." Then he scratched his head and said, "Whenever one of our employees takes a break, he or she can take off unsold plates of sushi and either eat them or throw them away. We are very serious about our sushi quality."

Source: Condensed from Sang M. Lee, "Japanese Management and the 100 Yen Sushi House," *Operations Management Review* 1, no. 2 (Winter 1983), pp. 45–48.

Managerial Issues

Managers can view just-in-time from two levels. From a strategic management perspective, JIT can be used as a management change tool, similar to total quality management or six sigma, not only to reduce waste and inventories on the factory floor, but also to increase quality and operational efficiency. At the day-to-day operating level, JIT provides management with a tool for controlling the flow of materials, identifying sources of error, and minimizing inventories.

JIT concepts are applicable in virtually all types of operational environments, including manufacturing and service operations. However, managers must recognize that the successful implementation of JIT is dependent on several factors, including strong supplier relationships and the concept of production linearity. (Production linearity means that over a given period of time, a constant quantity of products is produced every day although the specific mix of the products can change within a broad range.)

JIT Logic

JIT (just-in-time)

A coordinated approach that continuously reduces inventories while also improving quality

JIT (just-in-time) is an integrated set of activities designed to achieve high-volume production using minimal inventories of raw materials, work in process, and finished goods. Parts arrive at a subsequent workstation "just in time" are completed and move through the operation quickly. Just-in-time is also based on the logic that nothing will be produced until it is needed. Exhibit 14.1 illustrates this process. Need is created by the product being pulled toward the user. When an item is sold, in theory, the market pulls a replacement from the last position in the system—final assembly in this case. This triggers an order to the factory production line where a worker then pulls another unit from an upstream station in the flow to replace the unit taken. This upstream station then pulls from the next station further upstream and so on back to the release of the raw materials and components needed to make the product. To enable this pull process to work smoothly, JIT demands high levels of quality at each stage of the process, strong vendor relations, and a fairly predictable demand for the end product.

JIT can be viewed colloquially as "big JIT" and "little JIT." Big JIT (often termed lean production[1]) is the philosophy of operations management that seeks to eliminate waste in all aspects of a firm's production activities: human relations, supplier relations, technology, and the management of materials and inventories. Little JIT focuses more narrowly on scheduling goods inventories and providing service resources where and when needed. For example, companies such as Manpower Temporary Services and Pizza Hut essentially use pull signals to fill orders for replacement workers or Sicilian pizzas, respectively. However, they do not necessarily integrate operations around other aspects of the JIT philosophy.

The Japanese Approach to Productivity[2]

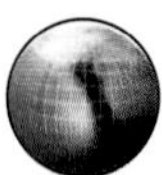

To fully appreciate the elements of Big JIT, it is useful to review the history and philosophy of its application in Japan. The ability of Japanese manufacturers to compete in high-quality, low-cost production, which was widely publicized in the 1970s and early 1980s, still holds despite their current economic problems. Indeed, the Japanese still retain the market dominance in televisions, VCRs, cameras, watches, motorcycles, and shipbuilding that they established over 20 years ago—in large part due to JIT.

[1]Paul H. Zipkin, "Does Manufacturing Need a JIT Revolution?" *Harvard Business Review,* January–February 1991, p. 41.

[2]Adapted from Kenneth A. Wantuck, "The Japanese Approach to Productivity," Southfield, MI: Bendix Corporation, 1983.

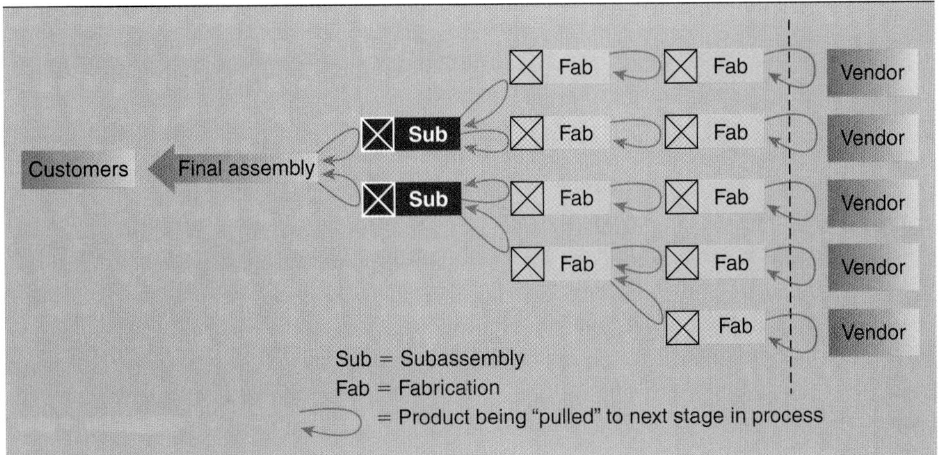

Exhibit 14.1
Pull System

Exhibit 14.2
Quasar Plant Productivity

	Under Motorola	Under Matsushita*
Direct labor employees	1,000	1,000†
Indirect employees	600	300
Total employees	1,600	1,300
Daily production	1,000	2,000
Defect rate per 100 TV sets	160	4
Annual warranty cost ($ millions)	$16	$2

*2 years later.
†Same people.

Many people believe these accomplishments are attributable to cultural differences. They envision the Japanese dedicating their lives to their companies and working long hours for substandard wages, which would be unthinkable in America. The evidence, however, is contrary to these distorted notions. Consider the following: In 1977, a Japanese company named Matsushita purchased a television plant in Chicago from a U.S. company. In the purchase contract, Matsushita agreed that all the hourly personnel would be retrained. Two years later, they still had essentially the same 1,000 hourly employees and had managed to reduce the indirect staff by 50 percent (see Exhibit 14.2). Yet, during that period, daily production had doubled. The quality, as measured by the number of defects per 100 TV sets built, improved 40-fold. Outside quality indicators also improved. Where the U.S. company (Motorola) had spent an average amount of $16 million a year on warranty costs, Matsushita's expenditures were $2 million. (That's for twice as many TV sets, so it's really a 16-to-1 ratio.) These are big differences—differences achieved here in the United States with American workers. The issue is, how do the Japanese accomplish this and what can we learn from them?

As a starting point, it's important to understand that the Japanese, as a nation, have had one fundamental economic goal since 1945: full employment through industrialization. The strategy employed to achieve this goal called for obtaining market dominance in very select product areas. They very carefully selected those industries in which they believed they could become dominant and concentrated on them, rather than diluting their efforts over a broader spectrum.

The tactics of the Japanese were threefold: (*a*) They imported their technology. (The entire Japanese semiconductor industry was built around a $25,000 purchase from Texas Instruments for the rights to the basic semiconductor process.) Instead of reinventing the wheel, they avoided major R&D expenditures and the associated risks, then negotiated license agreements to make successful, workable new products. (*b*) They concentrated their ingenuity on the factory to achieve high productivity and low unit cost. The best engineering talent available was directed to the shop floor, instead of the product design department. (*c*) Finally, they embarked on a drive to improve product quality and reliability to the highest possible levels, to give their customers product reliability that competitors were not able to supply.

The implementation of these tactics by the Japanese was governed by two fundamental concepts (most of us agree with these concepts in principle, but the difference is the degree to which the Japanese practice them):

eliminate waste

Eliminate everything not essential to production, including safety stocks, waiting times, and extra labor.

1. They are firm believers that in every way, shape, and form you must **eliminate waste.**
2. They have a great respect for people.

Elimination of Waste

When the Japanese talk about waste, the definition given by Fujio Cho, from the Toyota Motor Company, probably states it as well as anyone. He calls it "anything other than the *minimum* amount of equipment, materials, parts, and workers (working time) which are *absolutely essential* to production." That means no surplus, no safety stock. That means nothing is banked for future use. If you can't use it now, you don't make it now because that is considered waste. There are seven basic elements under this concept:

1. Focused factory networks.
2. Group technology.
3. *Jidoka*—quality at the source.
4. Just-in-time production.
5. Uniform plant loading.
6. Kanban production control system.
7. Minimized setup times.

focused factory networks

Groups of small plants, each highly specialized in products they manufacture.

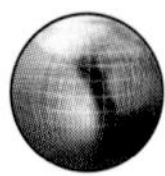

Focused Factory Networks The first element is **focused factory networks.** Instead of building a large manufacturing plant that does everything (i.e., a highly vertically integrated facility), the Japanese build small plants that are highly specialized. There are several reasons for doing this. First, it's very difficult to manage a large installation; the bigger it gets, the more bureaucratic it gets. The Japanese style of management does not lend itself to this kind of environment.

Second, when a plant is specifically designed for one purpose, it can be constructed and operated very economically. Fewer than 750 plants in Japan have as many as 1,000 or more employees. The bulk of them, some 60,000 plants, have between 30 and 1,000 workers and over 180,000 have fewer than 30 employees. When we talk about the Japanese approach to productivity and the impressive things they're doing, we're talking primarily about the middle group, in which most of their model manufacturing plants are located.

Two illustrative examples of Japanese focused factories have been cited by the Ford Motor Company: The Escort automobile needed a transaxle, which was going to require a $300 million expansion at the Ford plant in Batavia, Ohio. Ford asked the Japanese for an equivalent quotation and Tokyo–Kogyo offered to construct a brand-new plant with the same rate of output at a competitive unit price for $100 million, a one-third ratio. A second example relates to Ford's Valencia engine plant, which produces two engines per employee per day, and requires 900,000 square feet of floor space. An almost identical engine is produced by the Toyota Motor Company in Japan, where they make nine engines per employee per day in a plant that has only 300,000 square feet of space. The issue is not only productivity per person but also a much lower capital investment to achieve this manufacturing capability.

Group Technology Inside the plant the Japanese employ a technique called **group technology.** Group technology is nothing new to America; it was invented here, like so many of the techniques the Japanese successfully employ, but only relatively recently has been practiced widely in the United States. A simplified diagram of the technique is shown in Exhibit 14.3. The upper portion shows the way we operate our plants today. Most companies process a job and send it from department to department because that's the way our plants are organized (sheetmetal department, grinding department, etc.). Each machine in those departments is usually staffed by a worker who specializes in that function. Getting a job through a shop can be a long and complicated process because there's a lot of waiting time and moving time involved (usually between 90 percent and 95 percent of the total processing time).

group technology

Clustering dissimilar machines and operations in one area of the plant to manufacture one family of products.

The Japanese, on the other hand, consider all the operations required to make a part and try to group those machines together. Exhibit 14.3A depicts a typical process-oriented layout

Exhibit 14.3

Group Technology versus Departmental Specialty

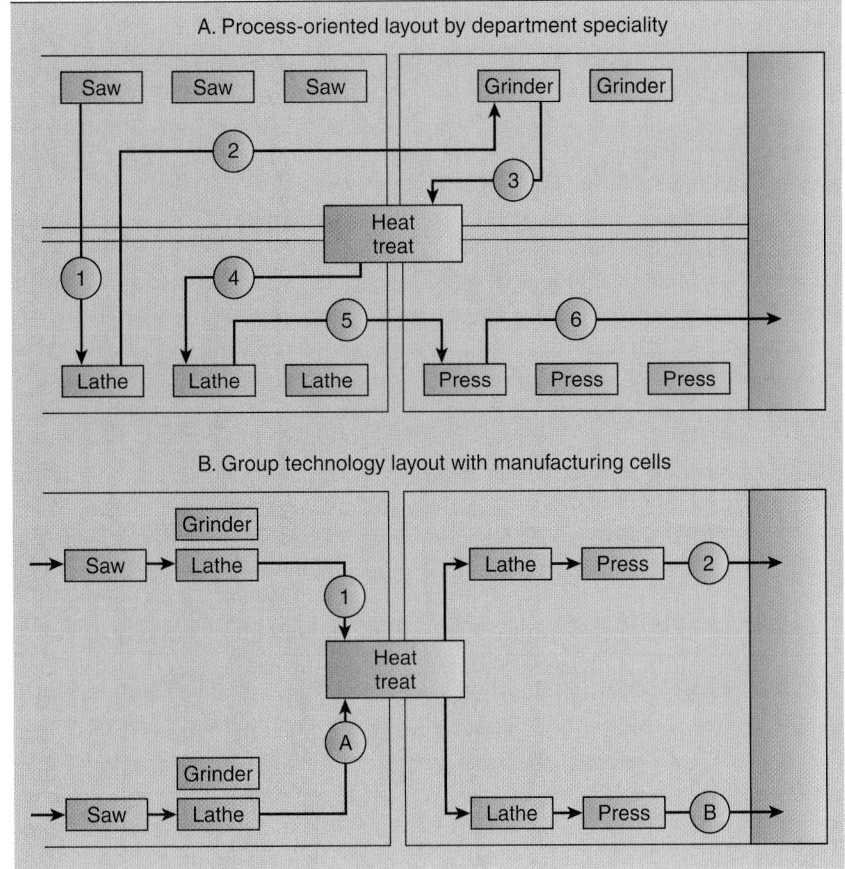

by department specialty while Exhibit 14.3B shows clusters of dissimilar machines designed to be work centers for given parts or families of parts (one cluster performs Steps 1 and 2 while the other cluster does steps A and B). One operator runs all three machines shown in the upper-left corner, increasing the utility of the individual operator and eliminating the move and queue time between operations in a given cluster. Thus, not only does productivity go up, but the work-in-process (WIP) inventory also comes down dramatically.

To achieve this, people have to be flexible; to be flexible, people must identify with their companies, have a high degree of job security, and undergo continuous training.

Jidoka

Japanese concept focusing on controlling the quality of a product at its source.

***Jidoka*—Quality at the Source** When management demonstrates a high degree of confidence in people, it is possible to implement a quality concept that the Japanese call **Jidoka.** The word means "Stop everything when something goes wrong." It can be thought of as controlling quality at the source. Instead of using inspectors to find the problems that somebody else may have created, the worker in a Japanese factory becomes his or her own inspector. This concept was developed by Taiichi Ohno, who was vice president of manufacturing for Toyota Motor Company in the early 1950s.

Ohno was convinced that one of the big problems faced by Toyota was bringing quality levels up to the necessary standards that would permit Toyota to penetrate the world automotive market. He determined that the best thing to do was to give each person only one part to work on at a time so that under no circumstances would he or she be able to bury or hide problems by working on other parts. Jidoka push buttons were installed on the assembly lines. If anything went wrong—if a worker found a defective part, if he or she could not keep up with production, if production was going too fast according to the pace that was set for the day, or if he or she found a safety hazard—that worker was obligated to push the button. When the button was pushed, a light flashed, a bell rang, and the entire assembly line came to a grinding halt. People descended on the spot where the light was flashing. It was something like a volunteer fire department: People came from the industrial engineering department, from management, from everywhere to respond to that particular alarm, and they fixed the problem on the spot.

Jidoka also encompasses automated inspection, sometimes called *autonomation.* Just like automation and robotics, the Japanese believe that wherever possible inspection should be done by a machine, because it's faster and more accurate. However, the inspection step is a part of the production process. It therefore does not involve a separate location or person to perform it, and automatically shuts off a machine when a problem arises. This prevents the mass production of defective parts.

Line shutdowns in Japan are encouraged to protect quality and because management has confidence in the individual worker. No one likes to see a line stopped, but Ohno suggests that a day without a single Jidoka drill can mean people aren't being careful enough.

Just-in-Time Production The Japanese system is based on a fundamental concept called just-in-time production. It requires the production of precisely the necessary units in the necessary quantities at the necessary time, with the objective of achieving plus or minus *zero* performance to schedule. It means that producing one extra piece is just as bad as being one piece short. In fact, anything over the minimum amount necessary is viewed as waste. This is another unique idea for American managers, since a measure of good performance in the United States has always been to meet or exceed the schedule. It is a most difficult concept for American manufacturing management to accept because it is contrary to current practice in many firms, which is to stock extra material just in case something goes wrong. Exhibit 14.4 highlights what just-in-time is, what it does, what it requires, and what it assumes.

Exhibit 14.4
Just-in-Time

What It Is	What It Does
• Management philosophy • "Pull" system through the plant	• Attacks waste (time, inventory, scrap) • Exposes problems and bottlenecks • Achieves streamlined production
What It Requires	**What It Assumes**
• Employee participation • Industrial engineering/basics • Continuing improvement • Total quality control • Small lot sizes	• Stable environment (production linearity)

Source: Adapted from Chris Gopal (of Price Waterhouse), "Notes on JIT."

The just-in-time concept applies primarily to a repetitive manufacturing process. It does not necessarily require large volumes, but typically is restricted to those operations that produce the same parts over and over again. Ideally, the finished product would be repetitive in nature. However, with customized products like Dell's PCs, the repetitive segments of the business may only appear at the component and subcomponent level. Even so, applying just-in-time concepts to a portion of the business still produces significant improvements.

Under just-in-time, the ideal lot size is *one piece*. The Japanese view the manufacturing process as a giant network of interconnected work centers, where the perfect arrangement would be to have each worker complete his or her task on a part and pass it directly to the next worker just as that person was ready for another piece. The idea is to drive all queues toward zero in order to

- Minimize inventory investment.
- Shorten production lead times.
- React faster to demand changes.
- Uncover any quality problems.

Exhibit 14.5 is an illustration that the Japanese use to depict the last idea. They look on the water level in a pond as inventory and the rocks as problems that might occur in a shop. A lot of water in the pond hides the problems. Management assumes everything is fine. Invariably, the water level drops at the worst possible time, such as during an economic downturn. Management then must address the problems without the necessary resources to solve them. The Japanese say it is better to force the water level down on purpose (especially in good times), expose the problems, and fix them now, before they cause trouble.

The zeal with which the Japanese work to reduce inventories is incredible. To begin with, inventory is viewed as a negative, not as an asset. According to Toyota, "The value of inventory is disavowed." Auto air conditioner manufacturer Nippondenso's attitude is even more severe: inventory is "the root of all evil." Almost universally, the Japanese see inventory as a deterrent to product quality. Finally, since the shop floor is programmed to have very little inventory, the slightest aberration in the process that results in extra parts is readily visible and serves as a red flag to which an immediate response is required.

Because it is impossible to have every worker in a complex manufacturing process adjacent to one another, and since the network also includes outside suppliers, the Japanese

Exhibit 14.5

Inventory Hides Problems

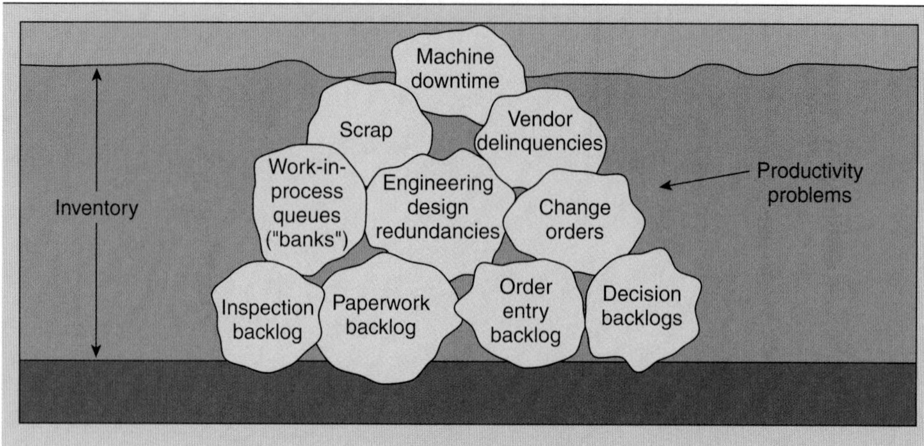

recognize that the system must allow for some transit time between centers. However, transfer quantities are kept as small as possible. Typical internal lot sizes are one tenth of a day's production, vendors deliver their products several times a day to their customers, and constant pressure is exerted to reduce the number of lots in the system.

Just-in-time production makes no allowances for contingencies. Every piece is expected to be correct when received. Every machine is expected to be available when needed to produce parts. Every delivery commitment is expected to be honored at the precise time it is scheduled. Consequently, the Japanese place heavy emphasis on quality, preventive maintenance, and mutual trust among all participants in the manufacturing enterprise. The process is given top priority and everyone conscientiously adheres to it.

Uniform Plant Loading To effectively incorporate the just-in-time production concept, it is necessary that production flow as smoothly as possible in the shop. The starting point is what the Japanese call *uniform plant loading*. Its objective is to dampen the reaction waves that normally occur in response to schedule variations. For example, when a significant change is made in final assembly, it creates changes in the requirements in the feeder operations, which are usually amplified because of lot sizing rules, setups, queues, and waiting time. By the time the impact of the change is felt at the start of the supply chain, a 10 percent change at assembly could easily translate into a 100 percent change at the beginning of the operation.

The Japanese say that the only way to eliminate that problem is to make the perturbations at the end as small as possible so that we only get ripples going through the shop, not shock waves. Japanese companies accomplish this by setting up a firm monthly production plan during which the output rate is frozen. Most U.S. manufacturers have been trying to achieve that for years, without success, because they've tried to freeze a specific, sequential configuration. The Japanese circumvent this issue by planning to build the same mix of products every day, even if the total quantities are small. For example if they're only building a hundred pieces a month, they'll build five each day. Because they expect to build some quantity of everything that's on the schedule daily, they always have a total mix that is available to respond to variations in demand.

Going even further, they'll take those five units and intermix them on the assembly line. An example of how Toyota would do this is shown in Exhibit 14.6. Let us assume that three kinds of vehicles are being made in an assembly plant: sedans, hardtops, and station wagons. The monthly rates shown are then reduced to daily quantities (presuming a 20-day

Model	Monthly Quantity	Daily Quantity	Cycle (takt) Time (minutes)
Sedan	5,000	250	2
Hardtop	2,500	125	4
Wagon	2,500	125	4
Sequence: Sedan, hardtop, sedan, wagon, sedan, hardtop, sedan, wagon, etc.			

Exhibit 14.6

Toyota Example of Mixed-Model Production Cycle in a Japanese Assembly Plant

month) of 250, 125, and 125, respectively. From this, the Japanese compute the necessary cycle times. *Cycle time* in Japan is the period of time between two identical units coming off the production line. The Japanese use this figure to adjust their resources to produce precisely the quantity that's needed—no more, no less. (This is identical to takt time, as presented in Chapter 8.)

The Japanese do not concern themselves with achieving the rated speeds of their equipment. In American shops, a given machine is rated at 1,000 pieces per hour so if we need 5,000 pieces we run it five hours to obtain this month's requirement. The Japanese produce only the needed quantity each day, as required. To them, cycle time is the driver that defines how they are to assemble their resources to meet this month's production. If the rate for next month changes, the resources are reconfigured.

Kanban Production Control System The Kanban approach calls for a control system that is simple and self-regulating and provides good management visibility. The majority of factories in Japan don't use Kanban. Kanban is a Toyota Motor Company system, not a generic Japanese one. However, many companies in both the United States and Japan use pull systems with other types of signaling devices. The shop floor/vendor release and control system is called *Kanban* (kahn-bahn), from the Japanese word meaning *card.* It is a paperless system, using dedicated containers and recycling traveling requisitions/cards. This is referred to as a **Kanban pull system,** because the authority to produce or supply comes from downstream operations. While work centers and vendors plan their work based on schedules, they execute based on Kanbans, which are completely manual.

Kanban pull system

Manual, self-regulating system for controlling the flow of material. Workers produce product only when the Kanban ahead of them is empty, thereby creating a "pull" system through the factory.

There are two types of Kanban cards. The production Kanban authorizes the manufacturing of a container of material. The withdrawal Kanban authorizes the withdrawal and movement of that container. The number of pieces in a container never varies for a given part number.

When production rates change, containers are added to or deleted from the system, according to a simple formula. The idea of safety stock is included in the basic calculation but is limited to 10 percent of a single day's demand. This gives the theoretical number of Kanban/containers required. In practice, efforts are made to reduce the number in circulation to keep inventories to a minimum.

The flow of Kanban cards between two work centers is shown in Exhibit 14.7. The machining center shown is making two parts, A and B, which are stored in standard containers next to the work center. When the assembly line starts to use Part A from a full container, a worker takes the withdrawal Kanban from the container and travels to the machining center storage area. He or she finds a container of Part A, removes the production Kanban, and replaces it with the withdrawal Kanban card, which authorizes him or her to move the container. The freed production Kanban is then placed in a rack by the machining center as a work authorization for another lot of material. Parts are manufactured in the order in which cards are placed on the rack (the Japanese call this the Kanban hanging), which makes the set of cards in the rack a priority list for scheduling work on the factory

Exhibit 14.7

Flow of Two Kanbans

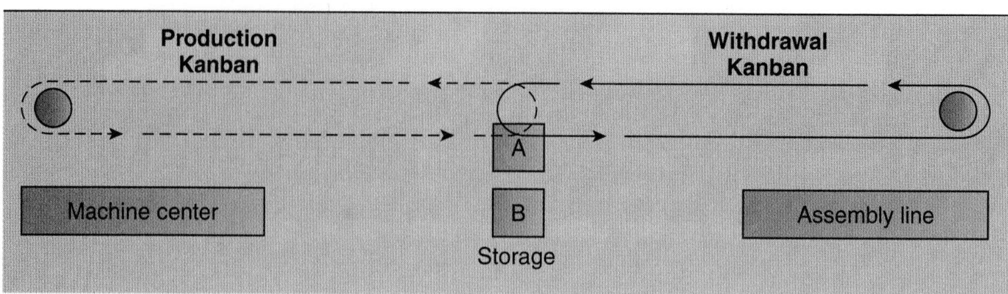

floor. Many firms use withdrawal cards only. With the simplest one-card system, the worker at the assembly line (or more likely a material handler) walks to the machine center with an empty container and a withdrawal Kanban. He or she would then place the empty container at a designated spot, attach the withdrawal card to a filled container, and carry it back to the assembly line. The worker at the machining center would know that a refill is required. This type of system is appropriate where the same part is made by the same people every day.

If it turns out that the demand for Part A is greater than planned and less than planned for Part B, the system self-regulates to these changes because there can be no more parts built than called for by the Kanban cards in circulation. Mix changes of 10 to 20 percent can be accommodated easily because the shifts are gradual and the increments are small. The ripple effect upstream is similarly dampened.

The same approach is used to authorize vendor shipments. When both the customer and the vendor are using the Kanban system, the withdrawal Kanban serves as the vendor release/shipping document while the production Kanban at the vendor's plant regulates production there.

The whole system hinges on everyone doing exactly what is authorized and following procedures explicitly. In fact, the Japanese use no production coordinators on the shop floor, relying solely on supervisors to ensure compliance. Cooperative worker attitudes are essential to its success.

Results can be impressive. Jidosha Kiki, a Bendix braking components affiliate company in Japan, installed the Kanban/just-in-time system in 1977 with the help of its customer, Toyota. Within two years they had doubled productivity, tripled inventory turnover, and substantially reduced overtime and space requirements. Jidosha Kiki stated that this was a slow and difficult learning process for its employees, even considering the Japanese culture, because all the old rules of thumb had to be tossed out the window and deep-rooted ideas had to be changed.

Minimized Setup Times The Japanese approach to productivity requires that production be run in small lots, which is impossible if machine setups take hours to accomplish. In fact, many companies in the United States use the economic order quantity (EOQ) formula to determine what quantity to make in order to absorb a long and costly setup time.

The Japanese have the same formula, but they've turned it around. Instead of accepting setup times as fixed amounts, they fixed the lot sizes (very small) and then focused on reducing setup time. Their success in this area has received widespread acclaim. Many Americans have been to Japan and witnessed a team of press operators change the dies on an 800-ton press in 10 minutes. Compare their data with those of firms in other countries, as shown in Exhibit 14.8. The Japanese aim for single-digit setup times (i.e., less than 10 minutes) for every machine in their factories. They've addressed not only big things, like presses, but small molding machines and standard machine tools as well.

Exhibit 14.8

Minimizing Setup Time—Hood and Fender Press Comparison (800-ton press)

	Toyota	USA	Sweden	Germany
Setup time	10 minutes	6 hours	4 hours	4 hours
Setups/day	3	1	—	1/2
Lot size	1 day*	10 days	1 month	—
(Measured in days of usage)				

*For low-demand items (less than 1,000 per month), as large as seven days.

Exhibit 14.9

Setup Reduction Results at JKC

	Percent of Setups in Each Time Category		
Setup Time	1976	1977	1980
>60 minutes	30%	0%	0%
31–60 minutes	19	0	0
21–30 minutes	26	10	3
11–20 minutes	20	12	7
5–10 minutes	5	20	12
100 seconds–<5 minutes	0	17	16
<100 seconds	0	41	62

Successful setup time reduction is easily achieved by a detailed analysis of the setup process. To accomplish this, the Japanese separate setup time into two segments: *internal*—that part that must be done while a machine is stopped, and *external*—that part that can be done while the machine is operating. Simple things, such as the staging of replacement dies in anticipation of a change, fall into the external category, which, on the average, represents half of the usual setup time.

Another 50 percent reduction usually can be achieved by the application of time and motion studies and practice. (It is not unusual for a Japanese setup team to spend a full Saturday practicing changeovers.) Time-saving devices like hinged bolts, roller platforms, and folding brackets for temporary die staging are commonly seen, all of which are low-cost items.

Only then is it necessary to spend larger sums of money to reduce the last 15 percent or so, on equipment such as automatic positioning of dies, rolling bolsters, and duplicate tool holders. The result is that 90 percent or *more* of the setup times can be eliminated if we have a desire to do so.

Referring again to the Jidosha Kiki Corporation (JKC), Exhibit 14.9 shows the remarkable progress the company made in just four years. These data relate to all the machines in the factory. It's interesting to note that while we are quite impressed that two-thirds of their equipment can be changed over in less than 2 minutes, the company is embarrassed that 10 percent still takes more than 10 minutes!

The savings in setup time justify an increase in the number of lots produced, with a corresponding reduction in lot sizes. This makes the use of just-in-time production principles feasible, which in turn makes the Kanban control system practical. All the pieces fit together.

respect for people

Principal of Japanese management where mutual respect is shown between management and workers.

Respect for People

The second guiding principle for the Japanese, along with elimination of waste, is **respect for people.** This principle also has seven basic elements:

1. Lifetime employment.
2. Company unions.

3. Attitude toward workers.
4. Automation/robotics.
5. Bottom-round management.
6. Subcontractor networks.
7. Quality circles.

Lifetime Employment Much has been written about the Japanese concept of lifetime employment. When Japanese workers are hired for permanent positions with a major industrial firm, they have jobs with that company for life (or until retirement age) provided they work diligently. If economic conditions deteriorate, the company attempts to maintain the payroll almost to the point of going out of business. We should understand, though, that these kinds of benefits apply only to permanent workers, who constitute about one-third of the workforce in Japan. What's important is that the concept is pervasive. When people can identify with the company as the place they're going to spend their working life, not just an interim place to get a paycheck, then they have a tendency to be more flexible and to want to do all they can do to help achieve the company's goals.

Company Unions When General Douglas MacArthur introduced the union concept to Japan during the post–World War II reconstruction period, he undoubtedly had in mind trade unions, but the Japanese didn't think that way. Japanese workers at Toyota were concerned about Toyota. They really didn't identify with the other automobile manufacturing employees in the rest of the country. They identified not with the kind of work they were doing but rather with the company for which they were working. So Toyota formed a union that included everybody who worked for Toyota, no matter what their skills were. The objective of both the union and management was to make the company as healthy as possible so there would be benefits accruing to the people in a secure and shared method. The resulting relationship was cooperative, not adversarial.

The Japanese system of compensation reinforces these goals because it is based on company performance bonuses. Everybody in a Japanese company, from the lowest employee to the highest, gets a bonus twice a year. In good times the bonus is high (up to 50 percent of their salaries), while in bad times there may be no bonus. As a result, the employees have an attitude that says, "If the company does well, I do well," which is important from the standpoint of soliciting the workers' help to improve productivity.

Attitude toward Workers The attitude of management toward the workers is also critical. The Japanese do not look at people as human machines. As a matter of fact, they believe that if a machine can do a job, then a person *shouldn't* do it because it's below his or her dignity. A corollary concept says that if workers are really important as people, you also must believe that they can do much more than you are now giving them the opportunity to do.

The Japanese say, "What workers are doing today is only tapping their capability. We must give them an opportunity to do more." Thus, a third and most significant attitude requires that the management system provides every worker with an opportunity to display his or her maximum capabilities. These concepts are practiced, not just discussed, and the Japanese spend more for employee training and education—at all levels—than any other industrial nation.

Automation/Robotics When people feel secure, identify with the company, and believe that they are being given an opportunity to fully display their talents, the introduction of automation and robotics is not considered as a staff-cutting move. The Japanese feel that this is a way to eliminate dull jobs so people can do more important things, and they have been making major capital investments in these areas. Interestingly enough, Japan has invested one-third, or 33 percent, of its gross national product in capital improvements over the last 20 years, compared to about 19 percent for the United States during the same period.

In automation, the Japanese have invested first in low-cost enhancements to existing or standard equipment, using some clever approaches. In the capital area they have been concentrating on robots. A recent survey showed that Japan had approximately five times the number of robots (some of them quite simple) as the United States.

Because the Japanese honestly believe that robots free people for more important tasks, there is little worker resistance to the robotics implementation. In fact, workers go out of their way to figure out how to eliminate their jobs, if they find them dull, because they know the company will find something better and more interesting for them to do.

Bottom-Round Management This mutual reliance between workers and management is a manifestation of the management style the Japanese call **bottom-round management.** It's also been identified as *consensus management* or *committee management.* It is an innate part of the Japanese culture because they have grown up with the concept that the importance of the group supercedes that of the individual. Consider that in Japan more than 124 million people are crowded on a tiny island group about the size of California, 80 percent of which is mountainous. In those circumstances, its citizens must have considerable respect for their neighbors, or social survival would be impossible. This cultural concept is ideal in a manufacturing environment because the process requires that people work together in a group to make a product. The individual cannot function independently, without concern for others, because he or she would only get out of synchronization with the rest of the group and disrupt the process.

bottom-round management

Mutual reliance between management and workers focusing on reaching consensus or agreement.

Bottom-round management is a slow decision-making process. In attempting to arrive at a true consensus, not a compromise, the Japanese involve all potentially interested parties, talk over a problem at great length, often interrupt the process, seek out more information, and retalk the problem until everyone finally agrees. While we have often criticized the slowness of this method, the Japanese have an interesting response.

They say, "You Americans will make an instant decision and then you'll take a very long time to implement it. The decision is made so quickly, without consulting many of the people it's going to affect, that as you try to implement it you begin to encounter all sorts of unforeseen obstacles. With our system, we take a long time to make a decision, but it only takes a short time to implement it because by the time we've finally reached a conclusion, everybody involved has had their say."

A key to bottom-round management is that decisions are made at the lowest possible level. In essence, the employees recognize a problem, work out a potential solution with their peers, and make recommendations to the next level of management. They, in turn, do the same thing and make the next recommendation up the line. And so it goes, with everyone participating in the process. As a result, top management teams in Japanese companies make very few day-to-day operating decisions, their time being almost totally devoted to strategic planning. Note, though, that the use of bottom-round management makes it extremely difficult to manage a large, complex manufacturing organization. That's another reason why the Japanese build small focused factories.

Subcontractor Networks The specialized nature of Japanese factories has fostered the development of an enormous subcontractor network; most subcontractors have fewer than 30 employees. More than 90 percent of all Japanese companies are part of the supplier network, which is many layers deep, because there is so little vertical integration in Japanese factories.

There are two kinds of suppliers: specialists in a narrow field who serve multiple customers (very much like U.S. suppliers) and captives, who usually make a small variety of parts for a single customer. The second kind is more prevalent in Japan. Sole-sourcing arrangements work in Japan because the relationships are based on a tremendous amount of mutual trust. They seek long-term partnerships between customer and supplier. Americans who do business with Japanese companies know that the very first stages of negotiation involve an elaborate ceremony of getting to know one another to determine whether there is a potential long-term relationship in the picture. Japanese businesspeople are rarely interested in a one-time buy.

Suppliers in Japan consider themselves part of their customers' families. Very often key suppliers are invited to company functions such as picnics or parties. In return, suppliers deliver high-quality parts many times per day, often directly to the customer's assembly line. There is no receiving, no incoming inspection, no paperwork, no delays. It's an almost paper-free system, all built on mutual trust.

Trust is a two-way street. Because so many of the suppliers are small and undercapitalized, Japanese customers often advance money to finance them, if necessary. Customer process engineers and quality personnel help vendors improve their manufacturing systems to meet the rigid quality and delivery standards imposed. Efforts also are made to help vendors reduce their production process costs to help ensure their profitability. When there is an economic downturn, however, the customers will perform more of the work in-house instead of buying from vendors. They do this to protect their own workforces. Vendors are small and do not have the permanent, lifetime employment guarantees that the major companies do. However, this is known in advance and suppliers consider this an acceptable risk.

quality circles

Groups of workers who meet to discuss their common area of interest and problems they are encountering.

Quality Circles Another interesting technique, with which many Americans are already familiar, is **quality circles.** The Japanese call them *small group improvement activities (SGIA).* A quality circle is a group of volunteer employees who meet once a week on a scheduled basis to discuss their function and the problems they're encountering, to try to devise solutions to those problems, and to propose those solutions to management. The group may be led by a supervisor or a production worker. It usually includes people from a given discipline or a given production area, like Assembly Line A or the machining department. It also can be multidisciplinary, consisting, for instance, of all the material handlers who deliver materials to a department and the industrial engineers who work in that department. It does have to be led, though, by someone who is trained as a group leader. The trainers are facilitators, and each one may coordinate the activities of a number of quality circles.

The quality circle really works because it's an open forum. It takes some skill to prevent it from becoming a gripe session, but that's where the trained group leaders keep the members on target. Interestingly enough, only about one-third of the proposals generated turn out to be quality related. More than half are productivity oriented. It's really amazing how many good ideas these motivated employees can contribute toward the profitability and the improved productivity of their companies. Quality circles are actually a manifestation of the consensus, bottom-round management approach but are limited to these small groups.

JIT in the United States

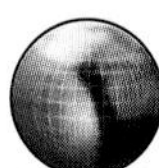

JIT evolved in Japan in great part due to the unique characteristics of that country. Japan is a very small country in area. Distances between most of the major cities are, therefore, relatively short. In addition, a large proportion of its geographic area is mountainous. Consequently, most of Japan's population lives in a relatively small area, with space at a premium.

In addition, the Japanese tend to have a strong paternalistic, family-oriented culture that extends to the relationship between large and small companies.

Consequently, the vast majority of Japanese suppliers to the major companies are usually located within a 25-mile radius of the major firms' manufacturing facilities. In addition, most of the sales of these small firms tend to be to a single large customer, thereby making these small companies highly dependent.

In contrast, the United States has a very large geographic area. Suppliers, therefore, often are located thousands of miles away from production facilities. (As companies continue to extend their supply chains globally, their suppliers will become even more remotely located.) In addition, the paternalistic relationship between large companies and small does not exist to the same extent that it does in Japan. Finally, most U.S. firms have a much wider customer base, with any one customer representing only a small percentage of its sales. For these and various other reasons, JIT is practiced differently in the United States than it is in Japan.

"JIT in the United States often stands for *J*umbo-*I*nventory-*T*ransfer," said Peter Frasso, vice president and general manager of Varian Vacuum Products in Lexington, Massachusetts, at the April 1996 Annual Meeting of the Operations Management Association in Boston, Massachusetts. In other words, there are many large companies in the United States that, instead of working with suppliers to synchronize operations, will often try to force suppliers to maintain large stocks of inventory rather than keep these inventories at their own facilities. Thus, while the large firms practice JIT within their own facilities, their suppliers deliver raw material and components from buffer inventories that are frequently located nearby. With this approach, transferring the inventory from the manufacturer to the supplier improves the performance of the large firm at the expense of the smaller supplier, which absorbs all of the risks and costs associated with these inventories. The large distances that often exist between suppliers and customers in the United States also preclude the ability to provide products in small lot sizes at short time intervals (that is, several times a day, as is often the case in Japan).

Nevertheless, other aspects or elements of JIT, such as (*a*) working with suppliers in a partnership relationship, (*b*) reducing setup times, (*c*) encouraging worker participation, and (*d*) reducing inventories and waste, are being adopted by the better companies, with recognizable benefits. A survey of U.S. manufacturers indicated that 86 percent of the respondents acknowledged some benefits from implementing JIT.[3]

Because of these differences, many U.S. companies, in addition to having a JIT system, have adopted an MRP system (as discussed later in Chapter 17) in working with their suppliers. The MRP system provides the suppliers with a forecast of the raw material and component requirements. Typically these requirements are *frozen* for the immediate future, but can change the further out the requirements are. For example, the orders placed with a supplier might be fixed for the next six weeks, but the requirements may change beyond this six-week window. This approach allows suppliers to schedule work efficiently within their own facilities. As illustrated in the OM in Practice box, Saturn provides a good example of a growing number of U.S. firms that are successfully implementing many of the concepts of JIT.

Implementing JIT Production

In this section, our objective is to explain how to accomplish JIT production. To structure our discussion we follow the steps given in Exhibit 14.10, expanding on some of the ideas

[3]Richard E. White, "An Empirical Assessment of JIT in U.S. Manufacturers," *Production and Inventory Management Journal* 34, no. 2 (1993), pp. 38–42.

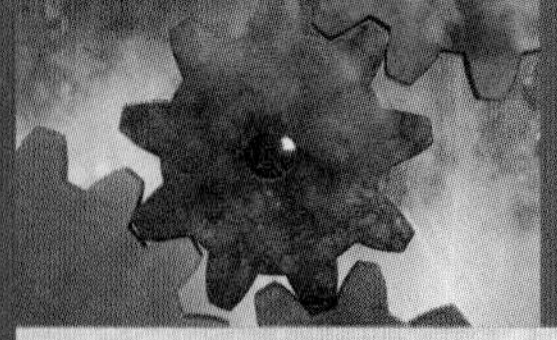

Operations Management in Practice

JIT IS INTEGRAL TO SATURN'S SUCCESS

When General Motors announced the Saturn project, its goal was very clear: to recapture the small-car market from the Japanese. To accomplish this, GM incorporated many new and innovative concepts in designing Saturn's manufacturing facility in Spring Hill, Tennessee. For example, a much higher percentage of the components are produced on-site instead of at a remote facility and transported to Spring Hill, which is the norm at other automobile assembly plants. Thus the facility includes a foundry to cast crankshafts and engine blocks, as well as huge injection molding machines to make the various plastic components.

Linking these processes together is a just-in-time (JIT) "lean" system that is the tightest JIT system in the auto industry, according to Alec Bedricky, Saturn's former VP of purchasing. There are very few buffer inventories separating the vehicle assembly line from the component manufacturing process. As an illustration, there are usually less than two-hours worth of powertrains between the engine plant and the assembly line.

Suppliers deliver their products to the plant or LOC (Local Optimization Center) 24 hours a day, and deliveries must be made within a fifteen-minute window to be considered on time. If a late delivery causes a delay in production, the supplier can be fined $500 per minute. Ryder, Saturn's logistic partner, manages the scheduling of both dock times and truck routes. Penske Corporation manages the LOC where parts are sequenced and delivered hourly to the Saturn plant. The LOC is a recent improvement that takes additional motor storage out of the plant, thereby increasing the manufacturing floor space, which allows Saturn to produce its small sport utility vehicle, the VUE, without expanding any of the manufacturing facilities.

Parts are off-loaded and delivered directly to the point of use on the assembly line. There is no receiving area and no incoming inspection of material. Production parts are delivered daily, with larger items like radiators and front-end modules delivered more frequently. For example, seats from the seating supplier are delivered in proper assembly line sequence every 30 minutes.

Sources: Adapted from Ernest Rata, "Saturn: Rising Star," *Purchasing,* September 9, 1993, pp. 44–47 and Lee Anne Carmack, Saturn Communications, 2002.

presented in the Wantuck paper (see footnote 2 earlier in the chapter) and explaining certain features that were not previously discussed. In going through these steps, we should remember that we are still talking about *repetitive* production systems—those that make the same basic product over and over again. Also keep in mind that we are talking about features of a *total system,* which means that actions taken regarding any one of these features have some impact on other features of the system. Finally, note that different companies use different terms to describe their JIT systems. IBM uses *continuous flow manufacture,* Hewlett-Packard Company uses *stockless production* at one plant and *repetitive manufacturing system* at another, while many other companies use *lean production. Synchronized material flow* is still another term used.

Exhibit 14.10

How to Accomplish Just-in-Time Production

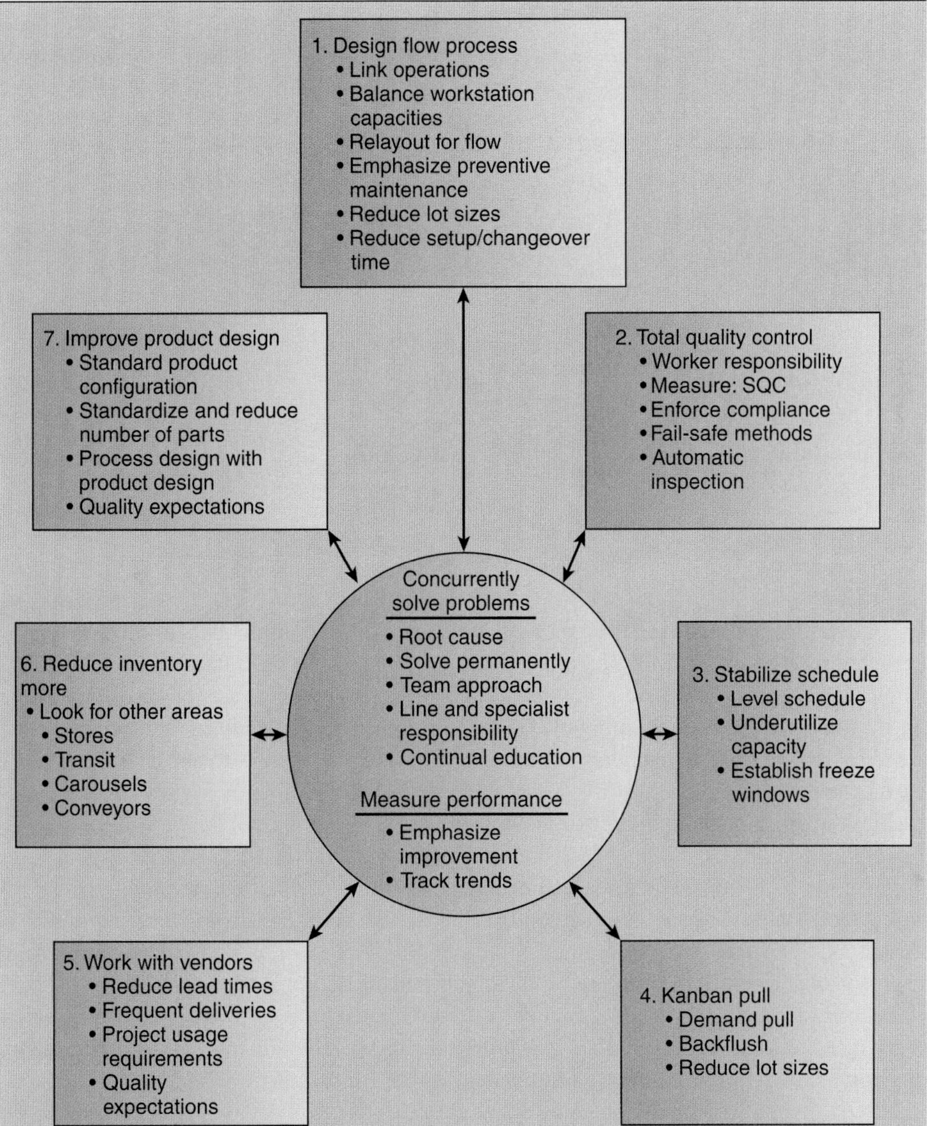

This diagram is modeled after the one used by Hewlett-Packard's Boise plant to accomplish its JIT program.

JIT Layouts/Design Flow Process

JIT requires that the plant layout be designed to ensure balanced workflow with a minimum of work in process. This means that we must view each workstation as an integral part of the overall production line, whether or not a physical line actually exists. Capacity balancing is done using the same logic as for an assembly line, and operations are linked through a pull system (described later). This also means that the system designer must have a vision of how all aspects of the internal and external logistics system are related to the layout. Consequently, the concepts of supply chain management are integrally linked to JIT.

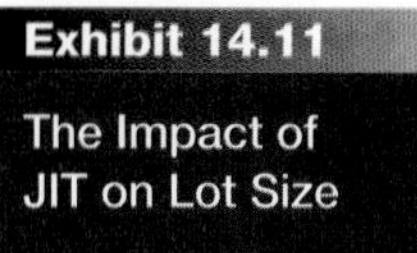
Exhibit 14.11

The Impact of JIT on Lot Size

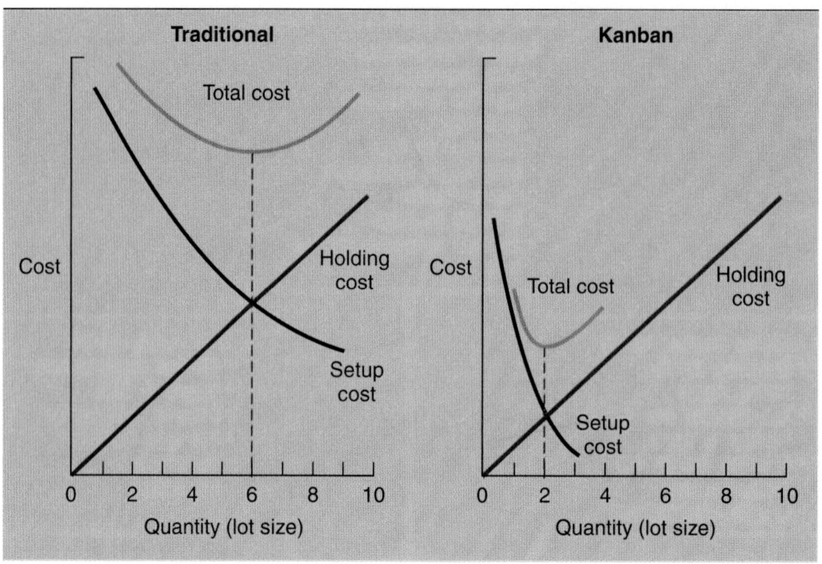

Preventive maintenance is emphasized to ensure that a continuous workflow is not interrupted by machine downtime or as a result of poor quality from malfunctioning equipment. Much of this maintenance is carried out by the operators because they are responsible for the quality of products coming off the machines, and also because of their sensitivity to the idiosyncrasies of the machines as a result of working on them day in and day out. Finally, the fact that the JIT philosophy favors many simple machines rather than a few complex ones enables the operators to handle routine maintenance activities.

Reductions in setup/changeover time and lot sizes are interrelated and are key to achieving a smooth flow (and JIT success in general). Exhibit 14.11 illustrates the fundamental relationship between lot size and setup cost. Under the traditional approach, setup cost is treated as a constant and the optimal order quantity is shown as six. Under the Kanban approach of JIT, setup cost is treated as a variable and the optimal order quantity, in this case, is reduced to two. This type of reduction can be achieved by employing setup time-saving procedures such as those described earlier in the chapter. *The ultimate goal of JIT from an inventory standpoint is to achieve an economic lot size of one.*

Even though we already have described the various types of layouts in Chapter 8, we briefly will describe a line flow operation and a job-shop layout to show how JIT can be applied.

Most people think of high-volume assembly lines when they think of JIT. This is because most of the literature and discussions on this topic have been about line layouts. However, job-shop environments, where functions are grouped together, offer perhaps the greatest benefits for JIT application.

In assembly or fabrication lines, the focus is on product flow. Volumes may be high enough or tasks simple enough or costs low enough so that the required resources (people, machines, materials, etc.) can be arranged close together in a simple flow.

The majority of manufacturing plants are process oriented, being organized by function (i.e., similar machines are grouped together). Many service facilities also are organized by function or process: hospitals, universities, department stores, and so forth. The main reason for this organization is because these machines or processes serve a variety of needs, none of which is large enough to justify a machine of its own. In this environment, the product or person requiring service must move longer distances.

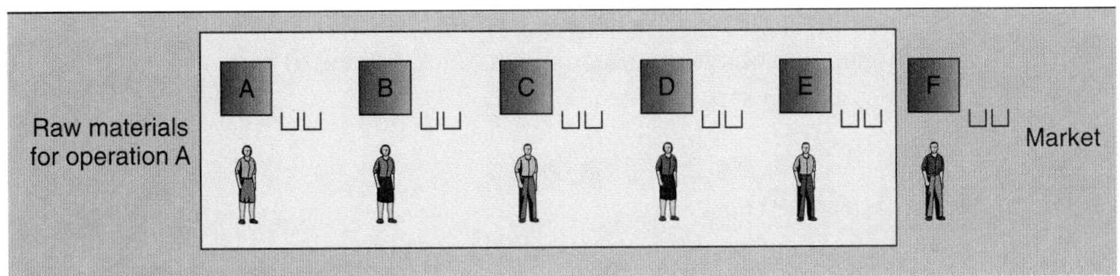

Exhibit 14.12

JIT in a Line Flow Layout

JIT in a Line Flow or Product Layout Exhibit 14.12 shows a pull system in a simple line flow. In theory, no one does any work until the product has been pulled from the end of the line. This item could have been sold or used somewhere else. To fill the void created by the pulled item, a replenishment unit is pulled from upstream. As an illustration, suppose, in Exhibit 14.12, an item of finished goods is pulled from the finished goods inventory (F). The inventory clerk then goes to processing (E) and takes replacement product to fill the void. Because operator E has an operating policy of keeping a specific number of completed units at the workstation, the operator goes upstream to process D to get replacement units, which will then be processed. This pattern is repeated to worker A, who pulls raw material from inventory or from whatever process precedes this line. In practice, however, a schedule would be created for the completion of items based on the demand, rather than using inventory clerk F to initiate the chain of events. Operating rules are straightforward: Always keep products that have been completed at your workstation. If someone takes your completed work away, go upstream and get some more to work on. Completed work stays on the "completed" side of the machine. For clarity, we haven't shown it in the exhibit, but materials and parts also may be supplied from side lines feeding each workstation as the product progresses.

JIT in a Functional or Process (Job Shop) Layout To justify considering JIT as a valid way to produce goods, the basic requirement is that there is a continual need for the product. This doesn't mean that the product has to be produced continuously in every phase of its creation. Items can be produced intermittently in batches throughout the majority of the sequence except for the final processing or final assembly, which is continuous. Consider a firm that produces several items that are in constant demand. To simplify it a bit further, assume that the demands are relatively constant throughout the entire year. Let's say that management decides to try to match the production rate with the demand rate, letting demand control production by only producing when goods are pulled from the system—that is, just-in-time.

Some of the products require a final assembly—that is, several parts and components produced in various parts of the firm are assembled together and then sold. Other parts require some types of finish machining at a work center and then are sold. In both cases, work on the products is continuous. If there is a demand pull—finished goods are pulled from the system—these steps are truly just-in-time.

The rest of the system preceding this final stage area may not be just-in-time. Consider the machine centers, paint shops, foundries, heat treating areas, and the countless other locations that these parts and components go through before they reach the final stages. Can we operate these locations in the same Kanban and container logic as we normally use for just-in-time? Yes, we can and we should.

Parts and components produced in different work centers are used in a variety of final products; therefore, these work centers should have containers of the entire variety of completed output that is designated for just-in-time production. Suppose a work center produces 10 different parts used by several products that are produced just-in-time. This work center must maintain containers of completed output of all 10 parts at the work center to be picked up by those users who need them.

Total Quality Control

JIT and total quality control have become linked in the minds of many managers—and for good reason. As stated in Chapter 6, total quality control refers to "building in" quality and *not* "inspecting it in." It also refers to all plant personnel taking responsibility for maintaining quality, not just "leaving it to the quality control department." When employees assume this responsibility, JIT is permitted to work at its optimal level, since only good products are pulled through the system. What results is having your cake and eating it too—high quality and high productivity. Exhibit 14.13 illustrates this subtle relationship.

When items are produced in small lots, such as in the Kanban system, the inspection may be reduced to just two items: the first and the last. If they are perfect, assume that those produced in between are perfect as well.

Stabilize Schedule

Efficient repetitive manufacturing requires a level schedule over a fairly long time horizon. This is sometimes referred to as production linearity. (The actual length depends on many factors, but primarily two: (*a*) whether the firm makes to order or makes to stock and (*b*) the range of product options it offers.)

Underutilization of capacity is probably the most controversial feature of JIT. Underutilized (or excess) capacity is really the cost incurred by eliminating inventories as a buffer in the system. In traditional manufacturing, safety stocks and early deliveries are used as a hedge against shortfalls in production resulting from such things as poor quality, machine

Exhibit 14.13

Relationship between JIT and Quality

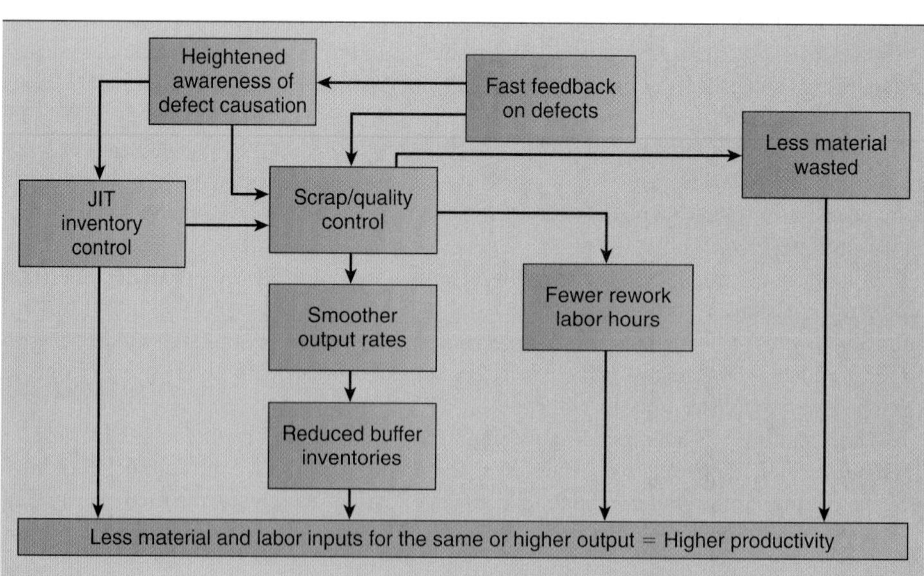

Source: Richard J. Schonberger, "Some Observations on the Advantages and Implementation Issues of Just-in-Time Production Systems," *Journal of Operations Management* 3, no. 1 (November 1982), p. 5.

failures, and unanticipated bottlenecks. Under JIT, excess labor and machine capacity provide that hedge in lieu of inventory. However, managers are now recognizing that excess capacity in the form of labor and equipment is generally far less expensive than carrying excess inventory. Moreover, excess labor can be put to work on other activities during those slow periods when it is not needed for direct production. Further, the low idle-time cost incurred by the relatively inexpensive machines favored by JIT producers makes machine utilization a secondary issue for many firms. Finally, much of the excess capacity is by design—workers are expected to have time at the end of their shifts to meet with their work groups, clean up their workstations, and ponder potential improvements.

Kanban Pull

Most people view JIT as a pull system, where the material is drawn or sent for by the users as it is needed. Production Kanbans are just one of many devices to signal the need for more parts. The signal sent is for a standard lot size conveyed in a standardized container, not just for a "bunch of parts."

Some typical Kanban-type signals used to initiate production are

"Hey Joe, make me another widget."

A flashing light over a work center, indicating the need for more parts.

A signal marker hanging on a post by the workstation(s) using the part(s). (See Exhibit 14.14.)

A pull system typically starts with the master production schedule specifying the final assembly schedule. By referring to the final assembly schedule, material schedulers and supervisors can see the days during the month when each part will be needed. They determine when to schedule supplier deliveries or internal parts manufacture by offsetting lead times from final assembly dates. The final assembly schedule therefore exerts the initial pull on the system, with Kanbans controlling the flow.

How many Kanban cards should be used? There can be a two-card system, a one-card system, or no cards at all.

Exhibit 14.14

Diagram of Outbound Stockpoint with Warning Signal Marker

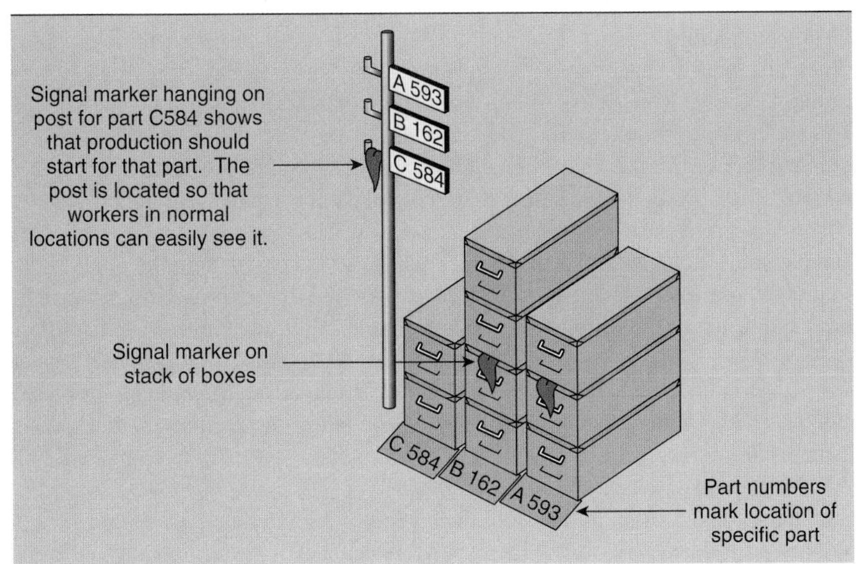
Signal marker hanging on post for part C584 shows that production should start for that part. The post is located so that workers in normal locations can easily see it.
A 593
B 162
C 584
Signal marker on stack of boxes
C 584
B 162
A 593
Part numbers mark location of specific part

Source: Robert Hall, *Zero Inventories* (Homewood, IL: Dow Jones-Irwin, 1983), p. 51.

At Bernard Welding Equipment when part bins are emptied, a Kanban card is detached from the container, transferred to the appropriate work cell, and placed on a post to indicate the bin needs to be refilled. The card contains the part number, routing quantity, and bin number.

In a system where operations are within sight of each other, no cards are needed. Workers mark a square between operations. An empty Kanban square on this factory floor visually signals the need to be filled by a disk drive unit.

This system of material control with Kanban cards replaces exactly what has been consumed and no more. The two-card system is actually one of the more complex ways of controlling this. Between two operations within sight of each other, no cards are needed at all—only a strict restriction on the inventory between. This can be done by marking a space between operations called a *Kanban square*. If any of the squares are empty, workers fill them up, but leave no extras.

A one-card system uses only the move card. Space restrictions or visible limits sufficiently restrict the quantity of each part in its location specified for pick up. If the move cards are permanently attached to the containers, the returning empty containers serve as signals to be filled up.

Replenishment signals can be sent electronically back to the supplying operation to save time. However, care needs to be observed since a large amount of the value of the Kanban system is its simplicity.

Backflush is a term used to designate how component parts are accounted for in a pull system. Rather than keeping track of each individual part on a daily basis by job, JIT systems periodically (such as once a month) develop detailed lists of all the components contained in a product and calculate how many of each part must have gone into the final product(s). This eliminates a major shop-floor data collection activity, thereby further simplifying the production management jobs. Bar-code technology allows Philips' Medical Products Group in Andover, Massachusetts, to backflush on a continuous, ongoing basis. For example, when a printed circuit board is completed with all of its components in place, that board's bar code is scanned into the system. As a result of the scanning, all of the board's components are removed from inventory while, at the same time, the completed board is placed into inventory.

Reducing lot sizes in a pull system means removing interstage inventory. This is accomplished in a variety of ways: (*a*) by better balance of operations so that only two Kanban containers are used between two workstations rather than three, (*b*) by moving workstations closer together to cut transit time, (*c*) by automating processes that have high variability, and, of course, (*d*) by just-in-time deliveries.

Work with Vendors

All the items in this category, as shown in Exhibit 14.10, except "project usage requirements," have been discussed earlier. *Project usage requirements* means that the vendors are given a long-run picture of the demands that will be placed on their production and distribution systems. This permits them to develop level production schedules. In many U.S. companies this is accomplished with MRP.

Continuous Inventory Reduction

Material transit systems, carousels, and conveyors are places where inventory is held, and thus are targets for inventory reduction efforts. Often there is heated debate when it comes to doing away with them. One reason is that such inventory locations are frequently the focus or the result of a previous inventory improvements effort that has shown good results compared to the system used before that. The people involved in such an effort are unlikely to rush to support the elimination of something that has been working.

Improve Product Design

Standard product configurations and fewer, standardized parts are important elements in good product designs for JIT. When the objective is to establish a simple routine process, anything that reduces variability in the end item or the materials that go into it is worth careful consideration.

Integrating process design with product design refers to the early involvement activities among product designers, process designers, and manufacturing personnel. Besides improving the producibility of the product, such interaction facilitates the processing of engineering changes orders (ECOs). ECOs can be extremely disruptive to the production process. They alter the specifications of the product, which in turn may call for new materials, new methods, and even new schedules. To minimize such disruptions, many JIT producers introduce their ECOs in batches, properly sequenced with the production schedule, rather than one by one, as is common in traditional manufacturing in the United States. While batching sounds obvious and simple, it requires a great deal of coordination and a willingness to delay what may be significant changes in a product design in exchange for maintaining production stability.

Concurrently Solve Problems and Measure Performance

A JIT application is not an overnight, turnkey installation. Rather, it is an evolutionary process that is continually seeking ways to improve production. Improvement is achieved by looking at problems as challenges rather than threats—problems that can be solved with common sense and detailed, rigorous analysis.

The techniques for problem solving are primarily continuous improvement methods. Effective problem solving means that the problem is solved permanently. Because JIT requires a team effort, problems are treated in a team context. Staff personnel are expected to be seen frequently on the shop floor, and in some companies are expected to arrive a half hour before production workers to ensure that everything is in order, thereby avoiding problems.

Continual education is absolutely essential if the system is to avoid stagnation. While JIT may cost little in the way of hardware, it requires the need for a substantial investment in training people at all levels of the organization to better understand what the system demands and how they fit into it.

Many performance measures emphasize the number of processes and practices changed to improve materials flow and reduce labor content, and the degree to which they do so. If the processes physically improve over time, lower costs follow. According to Hall, a department head in a Japanese JIT system is likely to be evaluated on the following factors:

1. Improvement trends, including number of improvement projects undertaken, trends in costs, and productivity.
2. Quality trends, including reduction in defect rates, improvement in process capability, and improvement in quality procedures.
3. Running to a level schedule and providing parts when others need them.
4. Trends in departmental inventory levels (e.g., speed of flow).
5. Staying within budget for expenses.
6. Developing workforce skills, versatility, participation in changes, and morale.[4]

Company Experiences with JIT

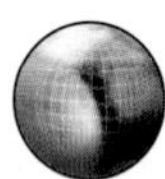

Exhibit 14.15 summarizes the experiences of five major U.S. companies that have installed JIT (and TQC, total quality control). As can be seen, the impact on these companies' performance measures is overwhelmingly positive. Similar results have been reported in European and British firms. One study of 80 plants in Europe, for example, listed the following benefits from JIT:

1. Average reduction in inventory of about 50 percent.
2. Reduction in throughput time of 50 to 70 percent.
3. Reduction in setup times of as much as 50 percent without major investment in plant and equipment.
4. Increase in productivity of between 20 and 50 percent.
5. Payback time for investment in JIT averaging less than nine months.[5]

Additional success stories abound in the production control journals. However, this does not mean that the implementation of JIT is trouble free.

JIT in Services

Service organizations and service operations within manufacturing firms present interesting opportunities for the application of JIT concepts. Despite the many differences between service and manufacturing, both share the most basic attributes of production, because they employ processes that add value to the basic inputs with the objective of creating an end product or service.

JIT focuses on processes, not products and, therefore, it can be applied to any group of processes, including manufacturing and services. The JIT goal is approached by testing

[4]Robert W. Hall, *Attaining Manufacturing Excellence* (Homewood, IL: Dow Jones-Irwin, 1987), pp. 254–55.

[5]Amrik Sohal and Keith Howard, "Trends in Materials Management," *International Journal of Production Distribution and Materials Management* 17, no. 5 (1987), pp. 3–11.

Exhibit 14.15

Summary of JIT/TQC Activities for Five U.S. Companies (® = reduced to)

Company Name (Division)	Product Category	Production Characteristics	Implementation Issues: Why Started	Implementation Issues: How Implemented	Results: Labor Productivity Improvement	Results: Setup Time (Improvement)	Results: Inventory Reductions	Results: Quality Improvements
Deere & Company	Heavy machinery Farm equipment Lawn-care equipment	Repetitive manufacturing	Survival Foreign competition	Visit to Japan Task force in plant Education Pilot projects Workflow analysis	Subassembly: 19–35% Welding: 7–38% Manufacturing cost: 10–20% Materials handling: 40%	Presses: 38–80% Drills: 24–33% Shears: 45% Grinders: 44% Average: 45%	Raw steel: 40% Purchased parts: 7% Crane shafts: 30 days® 3 days Average: 31%	Implemented process control charting in 40% of operations
Black & Decker (Consumer Power Tools)	Electrical products	Repetitive manufacturing Floor space: 385,000 sq. ft. Employees: 1,010	Large expenses in inventory carrying costs (high interest rates)	Education Balanced flow Rewrote work procedures Started to produce in weekly quantity	Assembly: 24 operators® 6 operators Support: 7® 5	Punch press: 1 hr.® 1 min. Drastic in many areas	Turns: from 16 to 30	Reduced complaints in packaging 98% 100% customer service level
Omark Industries	Forestry equipment and sporting goods	Mostly repetitive 18 plants	Corporate task force found JIT/TQC/employee involvement as reason for success	Steering committee Plant study team Presentation by corporate staff Pilot projects	Plant A: 30% Plant B: 30% Plant C: 20%	A: 165® 5 min. B: 43® 17 min. C: 360® 17 min. D: 45® 6 min.	Product A: 92% Product B: 29% Product C: 50%	Product A scrap and rework: 20% Product E customer service cost: 50%
Hewlett-Packard (Computer Systems)	Computer and test systems	Forming/assembly/testing Many options	Questioned why overseas suppliers produced quality products	TQC first Employee training/involvement Leveled schedule Process simplification	Standard hours: 87 hrs.® 39 hrs.	Not available	PC assembly inventory: $675,000 (100)® $190,000 (28)	Solder defects: 5000 PPM® 100 Scrap: $80,000/mo.® $5,000
FMC	Industrial equipment Defense Automotive Electrical	Multiple divisions with variety of products 50 manufacturing and mining operations	Survival Absence of patent protection Keen cost competition	Seminars Pilot project Pilot plants Setup time Inventory target Positive reinforcement	Direct labor productivity: 13% (Automotive service equipment division)	Defense equipment group: 60–75% Automotive/electrical: 80%	Turns: from 1.9 to 4.0 (automotive service equipment division)	Customer service from 88% to 98% Cost of quality: 3.5%® 2.1% (auto. svc. eq. div.)

Source: Adapted from Kiyoshi Suzaki, "Comparative Study of JIT/TQC Activities in Japanese and Western Companies," First World Congress of Production and Inventory Control, Vienna, Austria, 1985, pp. 63–66.

each step in the process to determine if it adds value to the product or service. If these steps do not add value, then the process is a candidate for reengineering. In this way, the process gradually and continually improves.

Both manufacturing and services can be improved with JIT because both involve processes, and JIT is essentially a process-oriented waste-elimination philosophy. The themes for JIT process improvement should therefore apply equally in a service environment.

Application of JIT to Services[6]

Duclos, Siha, and Lummus have suggested the following framework for describing the different ways in which JIT concepts have been applied to service organizations:

- Synchronization and balance of information and workflow.
- Total visibility of all components and processes.
- Continuous improvement of the process.
- Holistic approach to the elimination of waste.
- Flexibility in the use of resources.
- Respect for people.

Synchronization and Balance of Information and Workflow Because services are intangible, it is important that there be synchronization between demand and capacity. In other words, capacity must be available when the customer demands it. From a workflow balance perspective, Feather and Cross report that the application of JIT techniques identified existing bottlenecks and eliminated unnecessary inventory buffers in the processing of contracts.[7] As as result, throughput time was reduced 60 percent and the backlog in the number of contracts to be processed was reduced 80 percent.

Total Visibility of All Components and Processes A major element of JIT is that all operations that are required to complete a good or a service should be as widely visible as possible to all those involved in the process. Inasmuch as customers are usually an integral part of the service delivery process, they will often define value by what they can observe. As an example, many full-service restaurants now have open kitchens where the customers can actually see the food being prepared. The Commander's Palace in New Orleans, Louisiana, takes this one step further: customers actually have to walk through the kitchen to get to some of the dining rooms.

Continuous Improvement of the Process Another critical element in successfully implementing JIT is the recognition of the need for continuous improvement. Service operations provide significant opportunities for achieving these incremental improvements. For example, using JIT techniques, a finance company was able to improve its credit evaluation process and reduce the processing time for a loan from twelve days to four.[8]

---

[6]Adapted from L. K. Duclos, S. M. Siha, and R. R. Lummus, "JIT in Services: A Review of Current Practices and Future Directions for Research," *International Journal of Service Industry Management* 6, no. 5 (1995), pp. 36–52.

[7]J. J. Feather and K. F. Cross, "Workflow Analysis: Just-in-Time Techniques Simplify Administrative Process in Paperwork Operations," *Industrial Engineering* 20 (1988), pp. 32–40.

[8]J. Y. Lee, "JIT Works for Services Too," *CMA Magazine* 6 (1990), pp. 20–23.

Holistic Approach to the Elimination of Waste To be successful, JIT concepts must be adopted at all levels and in all functional areas within an organization. In addition, as discussed in the previous chapter, the application of JIT concepts should be expanded to include suppliers. In this respect, JIT concepts in this area have been applied successfully in the health care industry. Using JIT concepts and working closely with suppliers, hospital systems have reduced inventories at central stockrooms, with the ultimate goal of eliminating them altogether.

Flexibility in the Use of Resources Although the successful implementation of JIT requires that the level of units produced remains constant over a given period of time, the mix of those units can vary significantly. This requires a very flexible process that can accommodate a wide variety of products. Many services are highly customized, from the preparation of the food you order at a restaurant to the preparation of your tax return. Thus, a flexible process is necessary for these customized services. Wal-Mart provides a good example of process flexibility with its automated replenishment system, which can ship smaller quantities of goods to each store at frequent intervals. With this more flexible system, Wal-Mart has been able to lower the average levels of inventory at each retail store without decreasing the level of customer service that was previously provided.[9,10,11]

Respect for People Customers' direct involvement with the service delivery process most often requires them to interact directly with employees. Within services, research has shown that the way in which management treats employees highly correlates with the way in which employees treat customers.[12] Thus management must show respect for its employees if it wants them to similarly respect the needs of its customers.

Conclusion

We have presented here many of the potential benefits of just-in-time systems. At the same time, however, we need to caution that JIT applications are not universal. There are specific requirements for successful implementation and we need to be careful not to be caught up in the excitement and promises.

In 1983, Hewlett-Packard created a videotape on JIT at its Boulder, Colorado, plant. It was an excellent video and fun to watch. Its purpose was to convince viewers that a JIT pull system would produce significant benefits for most manufacturing plants. Although instructors still use this video in their classrooms, many of us caution against the message conveyed.

The video does not carry through a numerical analysis of the performance times, number of defects, work in process, and so on. This can lead to the wrong conclusions—which are that the JIT pull system was responsible for improved conditions.

---

[9]M. Ballou, "Wal-Mart Picks Progress Tools for Greater Flexibility," *Computerworld* 28, no. 9 (1994), p. 81.

[10]R. Halverson, "Logistical Supremacy Secures the Base—But Will It Translate Abroad?" *Discount Store News* 33, no. 23 (1994), pp. 107–108.

[11]G. Stalk Jr., "Competing on Capabilities: The New Rules of Corporate Strategy," *Harvard Business Review* 70, no. 2, pp. 57–69.

[12]B. Schneider and D. E. Bowen, *Winning the Service Game* (Cambridge, MA: Harvard Business School Press, 1995).

In a journal article, Jerry Bowman presented the data.[13] After analyzing the data, he commented that the most significant benefits did not result from the pull system but from reducing lot sizes. The HP video showed that the best performance occurred when items were processed using a pull system in lots of one unit. Bowman commented, "If you manufacture in lot sizes of one in a 'flow' environment, you probably couldn't tell whether you were pushing or pulling nor would it matter." Consequently, students have difficulties in distinguishing between an American automobile assembly line and a Japanese automobile assembly line.

JIT is becoming a principal manufacturing management concept and undoubtedly will continue to be so. But again, we caution you to be careful in its use.

Some of the concepts of JIT have been successfully introduced into service operations. Many of the characteristics that exist in JIT systems already are present in services, and, as a consequence, the benefits of implementing JIT in services have been readily apparent.

Key Terms

bottom-round management p. 549
eliminate waste p. 540
focused factory networks p. 540
group technology p. 541
Jidoka p. 542
JIT (just-in-time) p. 538
Kanban pull system p. 545
quality circles p. 550
respect for people p. 547

Review and Discussion Questions

1. Stopping waste is one of the most important parts of JIT. Identify some of the sources of waste and discuss how they may be eliminated.
2. Discuss JIT in a job-shop layout and in a line-flow layout.
3. Why is it important for JIT to have a stable schedule?
4. Are there any aspects of the Japanese approach that you could apply to your own current school activities? Explain.
5. Which objections might a marketing manager have against uniform plant loading?
6. What are the implications for cost accounting of JIT production?
7. Which questions would you want to ask the president of Toyota about his operations management?
8. Explain how cards are used in a Kanban system.
9. In which ways, if any, are the following systems analogous to Kanban: returning empty bottles to the supermarket and picking up filled ones; running a hot dog stand at lunchtime; withdrawing money from a checking account; collecting eggs at a chicken ranch?
10. How does the old saying, "There's no such thing as a free lunch," pertain to the Japanese elimination of inventory?
11. Explain the relationship between quality and productivity under the JIT philosophy.
12. What are the differences between implementing JIT in a manufacturing facility and implementing it in a service operation?
13. Identify some of the ways JIT can be applied to a service operation.

[13] D. Jerry Bowman, "If You Don't Understand JIT, How Can You Implement It?" *Industrial Engineering,* February 1991, pp. 38–39.

Bibliography

Ballou, M. "Wal-Mart Picks Progress Tools for Greater Flexibility." *Computerworld* 28, no. 9 (1994), p. 81.

Bowman, D. Jerry. "If You Don't Understand JIT, How Can You Implement It?" *Industrial Engineering,* February 1991, pp. 38–39.

Duclos, L. K.; S. M. Siha; and R. R. Lummus. "JIT in Services: A Review of Current Practices and Future Directions for Research." *International Journal of Service Industry Management* 6, no. 5 (1995), pp. 36–52.

Feather, J. J., and K. F. Cross. "Workflow Analysis, Just-in-Time Techniques Simplify Administrative Process in Paperwork Operations." *Industrial Engineering* 20 (1988), pp. 32–40.

Fucini, Joseph J., and Suzy Fucini. *Working for the Japanese.* New York: Free Press, 1990.

Hall, Robert. *Zero Inventories.* Homewood, IL: Dow Jones-Irwin, 1983.

———. *Attaining Manufacturing Excellence.* Homewood, IL: Dow Jones-Irwin, 1987.

Halverson, R. "Logistical Supremacy Secures the Base—But Will It Translate Abroad?" *Discount Store News* 33, no. 23 (1994), pp. 107–108.

Inman, R. Anthony, and Satish Mehra. "The Transferability of Just-in-Time Concepts to American Small Business." *Interfaces* 20, no. 2 (March–April 1990), pp. 30–37.

Klein, Janice. "A Re-examination of Autonomy in Light of New Manufacturing Practices." *Human Relations* 43 (1990).

Lee, J. Y. "JIT Works for Services Too." *CMA Magazine* 6 (1990), pp. 20–23.

Lee, Sang M. "Japanese Management and the 100 Yen Sushi House." *Operations Management Review* 1, no. 2 (Winter 1983), pp. 45–48.

Ohno, Taiichi. *Toyota Production System: Beyond Large-Scale Production.* Cambridge, MA: Productivity Press, 1988.

Ohno, Taiichi, and Setsuo Mito. *Just-in-Time for Today and Tomorrow.* Cambridge, MA: Productivity Press, 1988.

Rata, Ernest. "Saturn: Rising Star." *Purchasing,* September 9, 1993, pp. 44–47.

Schneider, B., and D. E. Bowen. *Winning the Service Game.* Cambridge, MA: Harvard Business School Press, 1995.

Schonberger, Richard J. *Japanese Productivity Techniques.* New York: Free Press, 1982.

———. *World Class Manufacturing: The Lessons of Simplicity Applied.* New York: Free Press, 1986.

———. *Building a Chain of Customers: Linking Business Functions to Create a World-Class Company.* New York: Free Press, 1989.

Shingo, Shigeo. *A Study of the Toyota Production System from an Industrial Engineering Viewpoint.* Cambridge, MA: Productivity Press, 1989.

Sohal, Amrik, and Keith Howard. "Trends in Materials Management." *International Journal of Production Distribution and Materials Management* 17, no. 5 (1987), pp. 3–41.

Stalk, G., Jr. "Competing on Capabilities: The New Rules of Corporate Strategy." *Harvard Business Review* 70, no. 2, pp. 57–69.

Suzaki, Kiyoshi. *The New Manufacturing Challenge: Techniques for Continuous Improvement.* New York: Free Press, 1987.

Wantuck, Kenneth A. "The Japanese Approach to Productivity." Southfield, MI: Bendix Corporation, 1983.

White, Richard E. "An Empirical Assessment of JIT in U.S. Manufacturers." *Production and Inventory Management Journal* 34, no. 2 (1993), pp. 38–42.

Zipkin, Paul H. "Does Manufacturing Need a JIT Revolution?" *Harvard Business Review,* January–February 1991, pp. 40–50.

Case

XYZ Products Company

XYZ Products Company is a supplier of gizmos for a large computer manufacturer located a few miles away. The company produces three different models of gizmos in production runs ranging from 100 to 300 units.

Case Exhibit I

Gizmo Production Flow

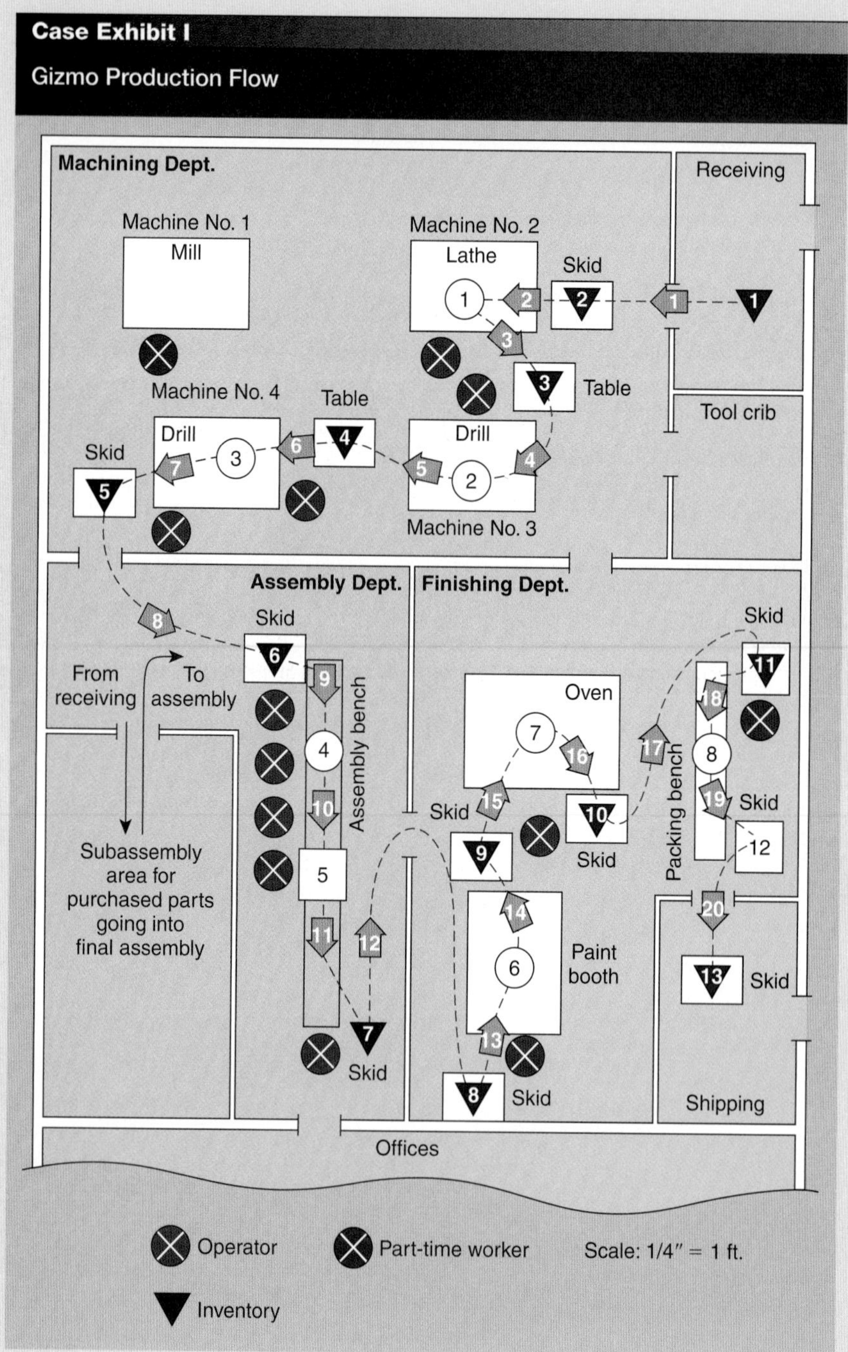

The production flow of Models X and Y is shown in Case Exhibit 1. Model Z requires milling as its first step, but otherwise follows the same flow pattern as X and Y. Skids can hold up to 20 gizmos at a time. Approximate processing times per unit by operation number and equipment setup times are shown in the following table:

	Operation Number and Name	Operation Times (minutes)	Setup Times (minutes)
—	Milling for Z	20	60
1	Lathe	50	30
2	Mod. 14 drill	15	5
3	Mod. 14 drill	40	5
4	Assembly step 1	50	
	Assembly step 2	45	
	Assembly step 3	50	
5	Inspection	30	
6	Paint	30	20
7	Oven	50	
8	Packing	5	

The demand for gizmos from the computer company ranges between 125 and 175 per month, equally divided among X, Y, and Z. Subassembly builds up inventory early in the month to make certain that a buffer stock is always available. Raw materials and purchased parts for subassemblies each constitutes 40 percent of the manufacturing cost of a gizmo. Both categories of parts are multiple sourced from about 80 vendors and are delivered at random times. (Gizmos have 40 different part numbers.)

Some other information: Scrap rates are about 10 percent each operation, inventory turns twice yearly, employees are paid on day rate, employee turnover is 25 percent per year, and net profit from operations is steady at 5 percent per year. Maintenance is performed as needed.

The manager of XYZ has been contemplating installing a new system to help control inventories and to "keep the skids filled." (It is his view that two days of work in front of a workstation motivates the worker to produce at top speed.) He also is planning to add three inspectors to clean up the quality problem. Further, he is thinking about setting up a rework line to speed up repairs. While he is pleased with the high utilization of most of his equipment and labor, he is concerned about the idle time of his milling machine. Finally, he has asked his industrial engineering department to look into high-rise shelving to store parts coming off Machine 4.

Questions

1. Which of the changes being considered by the manager of XYZ contradict the JIT philosophy?
2. Make recommendations for JIT improvements in such areas as scheduling, layout, Kanban, task groupings, and inventory. Use quantitative data as much as possible; state necessary assumptions.
3. Sketch the operation of a pull system for XYZ's current system.
4. Outline a plan for the introduction of JIT at XYZ.

15

Aggregate Planning

Chapter Objectives

- Demonstrate how aggregate planning links long-range strategic planning and short-range scheduling.
- Present alternate strategies for matching supply and demand: adjusting supply (an operations function) or adjusting demand (a marketing function).
- Introduce strategies for developing aggregate plans and ways to identify their strengths and weaknesses.
- Define marginal costs and total costs as they pertain to aggregate planning.
- Introduce the concept of yield management as a tool for matching supply and demand in service operations.

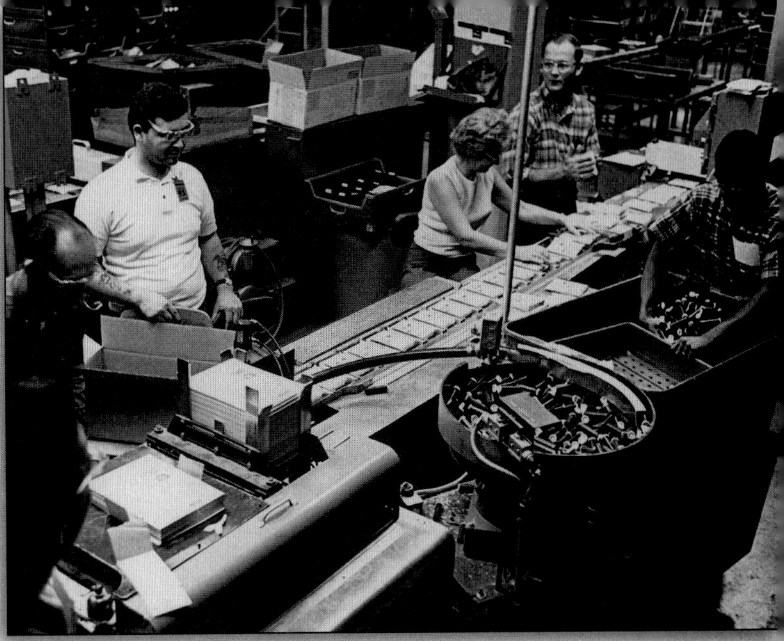

Each year, Janet Cramer, the plant manager at Polaroid's Integral Film Assembly Operation in Waltham, Massachusetts, struggles to identify the most efficient way to meet the forecasted sales for film. Janet's plant is the only film assembly operation in the United States. (There is only one other Polaroid film assembly operation in the world, located in The Netherlands.)

Historically, annual sales of Polaroid film has followed a seasonal pattern, with the maximum sales per month taking place just before Christmas time when retail operations stock their shelves in anticipation of holiday sales. There is also another peak, although somewhat smaller, in late spring and early summer, when customers purchase film for graduations, weddings, and summer vacations.

Four different types of film are assembled at the Waltham plant. The assembly of film into the cartridges for the Polaroid cameras is a highly capital intensive process with very high fixed costs and relatively low variable costs. As a result, Polaroid's operation in Waltham, which includes approximately 470 hourly employees, runs on three shifts, 24 hours a day, five days a week. In addition, the workforce primarily consists of highly skilled individuals who would be difficult to replace.

Even within this highly constrained environment, Janet has several alternatives available to her for scheduling production. The first alternative is to work overtime on Saturdays at a premium pay of 50 percent for all shifts. With this approach, inventory will be carried at an estimated cost of 20 to 25 percent per annum until the peak demand month is reached. The second alternative is to work both Saturdays and Sundays in the months just prior to the peak in order to minimize inventory carrying costs. Working on Sunday pays a premium of double time. However, with this approach there is the concern that worker fatigue (from working seven days a week) will have a negative impact on quality and productivity and, even, on employee morale.

The issues confronting Janet Cramer in selecting an aggregate planning alternative for her operation are typical of those that operations managers face when demand for their products is cyclical. There is often no one right answer, but rather a compromise that takes into consideration all of the various factors that can affect quality, productivity, cost, and employee morale.

Source: Special thanks to Janet Cramer and Laurie Mullane, Polaroid Corp.

Managerial Issues

Long-range strategic plans need to be translated into daily operational work schedules for the shop floor. To accomplish this, a series of steps, often referred to as hierarchical production planning, is required. In this process, units of production go from very broad definitions or product groups to specific items and models. For example, in the automobile industry, GM may look out five years and estimate the total number of "cars" it expects to sell. As the time horizon becomes closer, the number of cars are broken down into the number of Cadillacs, Buicks, Pontiacs, and so forth. In the short term, specific models within each car type are identified, such as the Cadillac DeVille or the Pontiac Aztek.

Aggregate planning, as an intermediate-range planning tool for management, provides the link between the long-range strategic plan and the short-range operational plan. It develops gross requirements for up to 12 to 18 months into the future, primarily for material and labor. As such, it presents a fairly broad perspective of the operation, addressing such issues as the number of workers needed in total, rather than the number of workers needed to do specific jobs.

The objective in developing an aggregate plan for a given time horizon is to match the demand for the firm's products with its ability to supply these products, and to do so at minimum cost. As part of the aggregate planning process, the operation manager identifies alternative methods for supplying the product, all of which are evaluated. Marketing management also plays a key role in this matching process, in terms of how it controls the demand for the product using such marketing tools as pricing, advertising, and promotions. Both the marketing and operations functions need to work together to develop an aggregate plan that is both effective and efficient.

Overview of Operational Planning Activities

planning activities:

long-range planning

Focuses on strategic issues relating to capacity, process selection, and plant location.

intermediate-range planning

Focuses on tactical issues pertaining to aggregate workforce and material requirements for the coming year.

short-range planning

Addresses day-to-day issues of scheduling workers on specific jobs at assigned work stations.

Every organization must plan its activities at several levels and operate these as a system. Exhibit 15.1 presents an overall view of planning and shows how aggregate production planning relates to other activities of a manufacturing firm. The time dimension is shown as long, intermediate, and short range.

Long-range planning is generally done once a year, focusing on a time horizon that is usually greater than a year. The length of the time horizon will vary from industry to industry. For those industries that require many years to plan and construct plants and facilities, and to install specific processes (e.g., refineries), the time horizon may be 5 to 10 or more years. For other industries where the ability to expand capacity is shorter (e.g., clothing manufacturing and many service industries), the time horizon may be two to five years or less.

Intermediate-range planning usually covers the period from 6 to 18 months in the future, with time increments or "buckets" that are monthly and/or quarterly. (The near-term time increments are often monthly, whereas those at the end of the time horizon tend to be quarterly, as these are usually less accurate.) Intermediate-range planning is typically reviewed and updated quarterly.

Short-range planning covers the period from one day to six months, with the time increment usually being weekly. As with long-range planning, the length of the time horizon for intermediate- and short-range planning will vary from industry to industry.

Long-Range Planning

Long-range planning begins with a statement of organizational objectives and goals for the next 2 to 10 years. *Corporate strategic planning* articulates how these objectives and goals are to be achieved in light of the company's capabilities and its economic and political environment as projected by its *business forecasting*. Elements of the strategic plan include

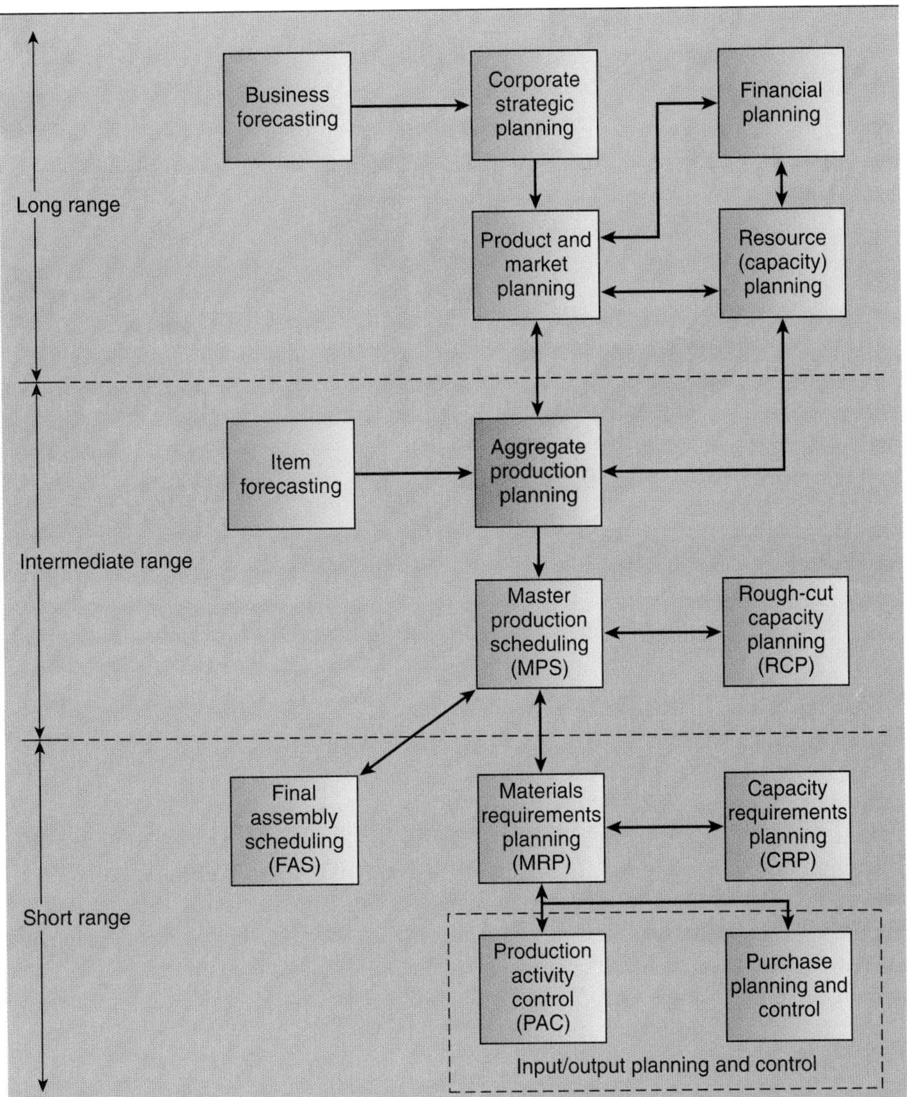

Exhibit 15.1

Overview of Manufacturing Planning Activities

product-line delineation, quality and pricing levels, and market penetration goals. *Product and market planning* translates these into individual market and product-line objectives, and includes a long-range production plan (basically a forecast of items to be manufactured for two years or more into the future). *Financial planning* analyzes the financial feasibility of these objectives relative to capital requirements and return on investment goals. *Resource planning* identifies the facilities, equipment, and personnel needed to accomplish the long-range production plan, and thus is frequently referred to as *long-run capacity planning.*

aggregate production planning

Process for determining most cost-effective way to match supply and demand over next 12–18 months.

Intermediate-Range Planning

Aggregate Production Planning As noted in Exhibit 15.1, **aggregate production planning** provides the primary link between the long-range strategic plans and the

Kawasaki Motors USA produces utility vehicles, motorcycles, all-terrain vehicles, and Jet Ski watercraft at its plant in Lincoln, Nebraska.

While the corporate plan specifies how many units to produce in each product line, the aggregate plan determines how to meet this requirement with available resources.

intermediate-range planning activities. Aggregate planning specifies monthly or quarterly output requirements by major product groups either in labor hours required or in units of production for up to 18 months into the future. Its main inputs are the product and market plans and the resource plan. Aggregate production planning seeks to find that combination of monthly or quarterly workforce levels and inventory levels that minimizes total production-related costs over the planning period while meeting the forecasted demand for product.

master production schedule

Short term schedule of specific end product requirements for the next several quarters.

rough-cut or resource capacity planning

Determination that adequate production capacity and warehousing are available to meet demand.

Item Forecasting This provides an estimate of specific products (and replacement parts), which, when integrated with the aggregate production plan, becomes the output requirement for the master production schedule (MPS). The process of monitoring and integrating this information is termed *demand management.*

Master Production Scheduling (MPS) The MPS generates the amounts and dates of specific end products. The **master production schedule** is usually fixed or "frozen" over the short run (six to eight weeks). Beyond six to eight weeks, various changes can be made, with essentially complete revisions possible after six months. As shown in Exhibit 15.1, the MPS depends on the product and market plans and resource plans outlined in the aggregate production plan.

Rough-Cut or Resource Capacity Planning This reviews the MPS to make sure that no obvious capacity constraints would require changing the schedule. **Rough-cut or Resource capacity planning** includes verifying that sufficient production and warehouse facilities, equipment, and labor are available and that key vendors have allocated adequate capacity to provide materials when needed.

Short-Range Planning

Materials Planning Also known as *materials requirements planning (MRP),* which is discussed in Chapter 17, this system takes the end product requirements from the MPS and breaks them down into their subassemblies and component parts. The materials plan specifies when production and purchase orders must be placed for each part and subassembly to complete the products on schedule.

Capacity Requirements Planning Capacity requirements planning (CRP) should really be referred to as capacity requirements *scheduling,* because it provides a detailed schedule of when each operation is to run on each work center or machine and how long it will take to process. The information it uses comes from planned (i.e., forecasted) and open (i.e., existing) orders that are generated by the materials plan. The CRP itself helps to validate the rough-cut capacity plan.

Final Assembly Scheduling This activity identifies the various operations required to put the product in its final form. It is here that customized or final features of the product are scheduled. For example, a printer manufacturer would typically specify from various options a control panel configuration at this scheduling stage.

Input/Output Planning and Control This refers to a variety of reports and procedures focusing on scheduled demands and capacity constraints derived from the materials plan.

Production Activity Control Production activity control (PAC) is a relatively new term that is used to describe scheduling and shop-floor control activities. PAC involves the scheduling and controlling of day-to-day activities on the shop floor. At this point, the master production schedule is translated into the immediate priorities of daily work schedules.

Purchase Planning and Control This activity deals with the acquisition and control of purchased items, again as specified by the materials plan. Input/output planning and control are necessary to make sure that purchasing is not only obtaining materials in time to meet the schedule, but is also aware of those orders that, for various reasons, call for rescheduling the delivery of purchased materials.

In summary, all of the planning approaches attempt to balance the capacity required with the capacity that is available, and then schedule and control production with respect to changes in the capacity balance. A good planning system is complete without being overwhelming, and has the confidence of its users up and down the organization structure.

Aggregate Production Planning

Again, aggregate production planning is concerned with setting production rates by product group or other broad categories for the intermediate term (6 to 18 months). Note again in Exhibit 15.1 that the aggregate plan precedes the master schedule. *The main purpose of the aggregate plan is to specify that combination of production rate, workforce level, and the resulting inventory on hand or backlog that both minimizes costs (efficiency) and satisfies the forecasted demand (effectiveness).* **Production rate** refers to the quantity of product

production rate

Capacity of output per unit of time (such as units per day or units per week).

workforce level

Number of workers required to provide a specified level of production.

inventory on hand

The surplus of units that results when production exceeds demand in a given time period.

backlog (or stockout)

The deficit in units that results when demand exceeds the number of units produced in a given time period.

production planning strategies:

pure strategy

Either a chase strategy when production exactly matches demand or a level strategy when production remains constant over a specified number of time periods.

mixed strategy

Combination of chase and level strategies to match supply and demand.

completed per unit of time (such as VCRs per hour or automobiles per day). **Workforce level** is the number of workers needed for production. When the number of units produced in any given period exceeds demand, the result is an **inventory on hand** of the product. When demand exceeds production, the result is a **backlog (or stockout),** which represents the shortfall. Both inventories and backlogs are carried forward to the next time period. However, there can be situations when stockouts are not carried forward because the customer decided to purchase the product elsewhere rather than wait.

The process of aggregate planning varies from company to company. In some firms, it is a formalized report containing both planning objectives and the planning premises on which it is based. In other companies, particularly smaller ones, it may be much more informal in the form of verbal communications.

The process by which the plan itself is derived also varies. One common approach is to develop it from the corporate annual plan, as was shown in Exhibit 15.1. A typical corporate plan contains a section on manufacturing that specifies how many units in each major product line need to be produced over the next 12 months to meet the sales forecast. The planner takes this information and attempts to determine how best to meet these requirements with available resources. Alternatively, some organizations combine output requirements into equivalent units and use this as the basis for aggregate planning. For example, a division of General Motors may be asked to produce a certain number of cars of all types at a particular facility. The production planner would then take the average labor hours required for all models as a basis for the overall aggregate plan. Refinements to this plan, specifically model types to be produced, would be reflected in shorter-term production plans. Another approach is to develop the aggregate plan by simulating various master production schedules and calculating corresponding capacity requirements to see if adequate labor and equipment exist at each work center. If capacity is inadequate, additional requirements for overtime, subcontracting, extra workers, and so forth are specified for each product line and combined into a rough-cut capacity plan. This plan is then modified by trial-and-error or mathematical methods to derive a final and, one hopes, lower-cost plan.

Production Planning Environment

Exhibit 15.2 illustrates the internal and external factors that make up the production planning environment. In general, the factors in the external environment are outside the production planner's direct control. In some firms, demand for the product can be managed, but even so, the production planner must live with the sales projections and orders promised by the marketing function. This leaves the internal factors as the variables that can be adjusted to arrive at a feasible production plan.

The internal factors themselves differ in their degree of control. Current physical capacity (plant and equipment) is virtually fixed in the short run and, therefore, cannot be increased; union agreements often constrain what can be done in changing the workforce; and top management may set limits on the amount of money that can be tied up in inventories. Still, there is always some flexibility in managing these factors, and production planners can implement one or a combination of the **production planning strategies** discussed here.

Production Planning Strategies

There are essentially three production planning strategies. These strategies involve tradeoffs among workforce size, work hours, inventory, and order backlogs. When there is a need to adjust the workforce on a regular basis, many firms will maintain a nucleus of full-time employees, which is then increased as required with temporary workers, who are often

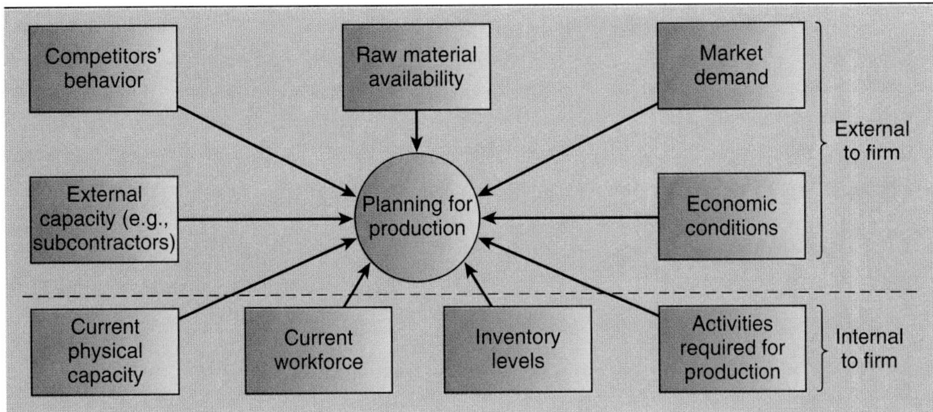

Exhibit 15.2

Required Inputs to the Production Planning System

hired through an employment agency. Those temporary workers who perform well are then hired on a full-time basis, as the need arises.

1. *Chase strategy.* Match the production rate to meet the order rate by hiring and laying off employees as the order rate varies. There are obvious motivational issues with this strategy. When order backlogs are low, employees may feel compelled to slow down out of fear of being laid off as soon as existing orders are completed.
2. *Stable workforce—variable work hours.* Vary the output by varying the number of hours worked through flexible work schedules or overtime. By varying the number of work hours, production quantities can be matched, within limits, to existing orders. This strategy provides workforce continuity and avoids many of the emotional and tangible costs of hiring and firing personnel that are associated with the chase strategy.
3. *Level strategy.* Maintain a stable workforce working at a constant output rate. Shortages and surpluses are absorbed by fluctuating inventory levels, order backlogs, and lost sales. Employees benefit from stable work hours, but inventory costs are increased. Another concern is the possibility of inventoried products becoming obsolete.

When just one of these variables is used to absorb demand fluctuations, it is termed a **pure strategy;** one or more used in combination is a **mixed strategy.** As you might suspect, mixed strategies are more widely used in industry.

Exhibit 15.3A illustrates a pure chase strategy. Here production is in lockstep with demand. In other words, the number of units required in each time interval equals the number of units that production will make. Exhibit 15.3B, on the other hand, demonstrates a pure level strategy. Here production is held constant, regardless of what the demand is. The difference between demand and production is accounted for in a "buffer" inventory of finished goods. When demand exceeds production, the difference is taken out of finished goods inventory (−I); when demand is less than production, the difference is placed back into inventory (+I). (It is assumed that when demand exceeds production in the initial cycle, as shown in Exhibit 15.3B, that there is sufficient inventory on hand at the beginning of the aggregate planning period to supply the required number of units.) When there is insufficient inventory on hand to meet demand, a backlog occurs.

Certain industries, due to their inherent operating characteristics, often favor one type of strategy over the other. For example, services tend to follow a chase strategy because the

Exhibit 15.3

Examples of Pure Chase and Pure Level Strategies

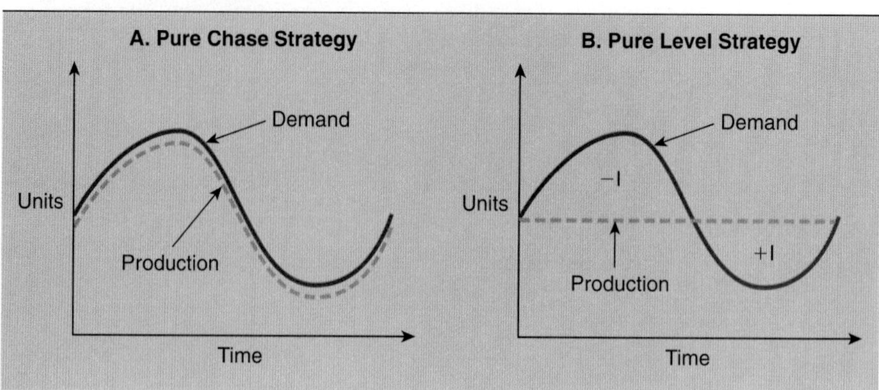

customer is involved in the service delivery process. (If your restaurant is too crowded on a Saturday night, customers will not wait until Monday morning when you have more than enough capacity available to serve them!) Process-oriented facilities, on the other hand, such as breweries and refineries, tend to follow a level strategy because the high fixed costs associated with them require that they operate at a high level of capacity utilization.

Subcontracting In addition to these strategies, managers also may choose to subcontract some portion of production. This strategy is similar to the chase strategy, but hiring and laying off are translated into subcontracting and not subcontracting. Some level of subcontracting can be desirable to accommodate demand fluctuations. However, unless the relationship with the supplier is particularly strong, a manufacturer can lose some control over schedule and quality. For this reason, extensive subcontracting may be viewed as a high-risk strategy.

Relevant Costs

There are four primary costs that are relevant to aggregate production planning. These are

1. *Basic production costs.* These are the fixed and variable costs incurred in producing a given product type in a given time period. Included are material costs, direct and indirect labor costs, and regular as well as overtime compensation.
2. *Costs associated with changes in the production rate.* Typical costs in this category are those involved in hiring, training, and laying off personnel. Additional one-time costs also might be associated with adding another shift.
3. *Inventory holding costs.* A major component is the cost of capital tied up in inventory. Other components include storage, insurance, taxes, spoilage, and obsolescence.
4. *Backlog (a stockout) costs.* Usually these costs are very difficult to measure and include costs of expediting, loss of customer goodwill, and loss of sales revenues resulting from cancelled orders because the product is not available.

(For a more detailed explanation of inventory carrying costs and backlog costs, see Chapter 16.)

Budgets To receive funding, operations managers are generally required to submit annual, and sometimes quarterly, budget requests. Aggregate planning activities are key to the success of the budgeting process. Recall that the goal of aggregate planning is to meet forecasted product demand while minimizing the total production-related costs over the planning horizon by determining the optimal combination of workforce levels and inventory levels. Thus, aggregate planning provides justification for the requested budget amount. Accurate intermediate-range planning increases both the likelihood of receiving the requested budget and operating within the limits of the budget.

In the next section, we provide examples of intermediate-range planning in both a manufacturing and a service setting. These examples illustrate the trade-offs associated with different production planning strategies.

Aggregate Planning Techniques

Companies still use simple trial-and-error charting and graphic methods to develop their aggregate plans. Computer spreadsheets and graphics packages are now available to facilitate the process. A trial-and-error approach involves costing out various production planning alternatives and selecting the one with the lowest cost. In addition to the trial-and-error method, there are more sophisticated approaches, including linear programming, the Linear Decision Rule, and various heuristic methods. Of these, only linear programming has seen broad application.

To properly develop and evaluate an aggregate plan, we need to first divide it into two stages. The first stage is the development of a feasible plan that provides the required number of products under the conditions stated. After this aggregate plan has been developed, the next step is to determine the costs associated with the plan.

Some of the costs included in an aggregate plan are presented in a form that is typically not found in the accounting records of a firm. For example, there is usually no cost of carrying inventory. Instead, the individual component costs associated with carrying inventory are listed in separate categories (e.g., the cost of storage is rent, insurance, taxes, etc.; the cost of obsolescence is reflected in higher material and labor costs, etc.).

Full Costs versus Marginal Costs

Before we can begin to solve the aggregate planning problem, we need to first recognize the difference between full costs and marginal or incremental costs. Full costs are all of the actual, out-of-pocket costs associated with a particular aggregate plan. Included in full costs are the costs of material, labor, and other direct, variable costs. Full costs are often used for developing a projected labor and material budget that will be needed to support an aggregate plan.

Marginal or incremental costs are only those unique costs that are attributable to a particular aggregate plan. With this approach, we assume that the total number of products forecasted over the time horizon need to be built, regardless of the alternative selected. The incremental costs are, therefore, only those costs that are above and beyond those required to build the product by its most economical means (which is usually on the first shift in-house). Included in marginal costs are hiring and firing costs, inventory carrying costs, and overtime and/or second- and third-shift premium costs. To demonstrate the difference, we will use both the full-cost and marginal-cost methods to solve the aggregate planning problem for the C&A Company. You will note that both methods result in selecting the same alternative plan, based on lowest cost. The different alternatives also are ranked in the same order with both methods of costing. The advantage in using the marginal-cost approach is that we do not have to include a lot of numerical figures that have no impact on the final decision.

A Simple Example of Aggregate Planning

Matt Koslow is the operations manager for the New England Shirt Company. In this capacity he is required to develop an aggregate plan for the next six months with the goal of meeting demand during this period while minimizing costs. As a first step in developing this plan, he obtained from the marketing department the following forecast for shirts:

January	February	March	April	May	June
2,400	1,200	2,800	3,600	3,200	3,600

Matt has estimated the following production data:

Inventory carrying cost	\$1.50 per shirt per month
Stockout cost	\$3.00 per shirt per month
Hiring cost	\$200 per employee
Firing cost	\$300 per employee
Labor per shirt	2 hours
Hourly wage	\$8.00 per hour
Beginning employment level	30 employees
Beginning inventory level	0 shirts
Hours per employee per day	8 hours
Work days per month	20 days

Using marginal costs, develop both a chase strategy and a level strategy to determine which is the more economical.

a. See the spreadsheet for marginal cost of chase strategy.

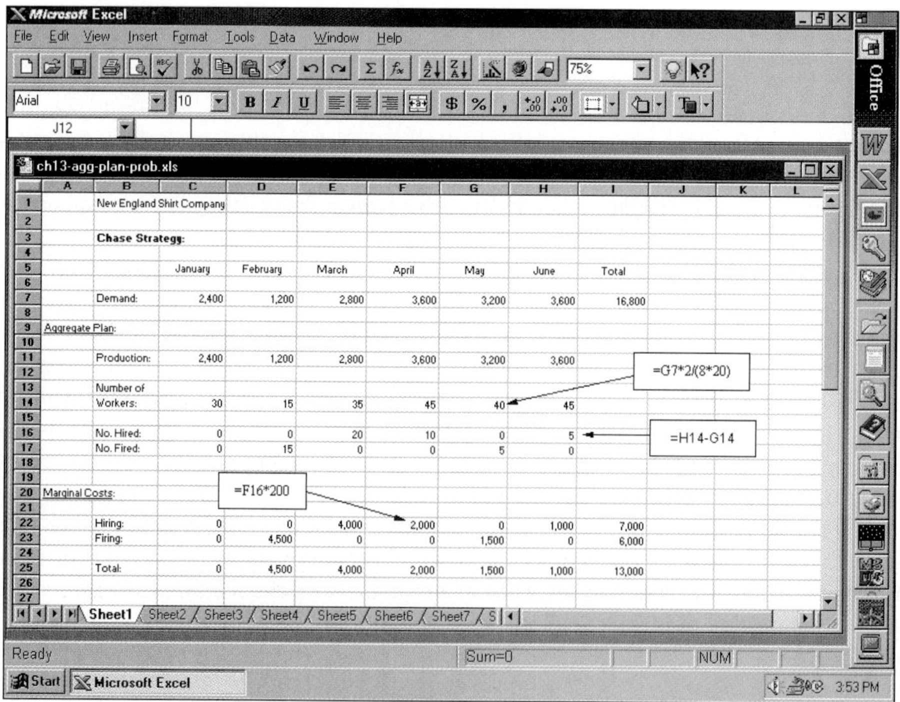

New England Shirt Company

Chase Strategy:

	January	February	March	April	May	June	Total
Demand:	2,400	1,200	2,800	3,600	3,200	3,600	16,800
Aggregate Plan:							
Production:	2,400	1,200	2,800	3,600	3,200	3,600	
Number of Workers:	30	15	35	45	40	45	
No. Hired:	0	0	20	10	0	5	
No. Fired:	0	15	0	0	5	0	
Marginal Costs:							
Hiring:	0	0	4,000	2,000	0	1,000	7,000
Firing:	0	4,500	0	0	1,500	0	6,000
Total:	0	4,500	4,000	2,000	1,500	1,000	13,000

b. See the spreadsheet for marginal cost of level strategy.

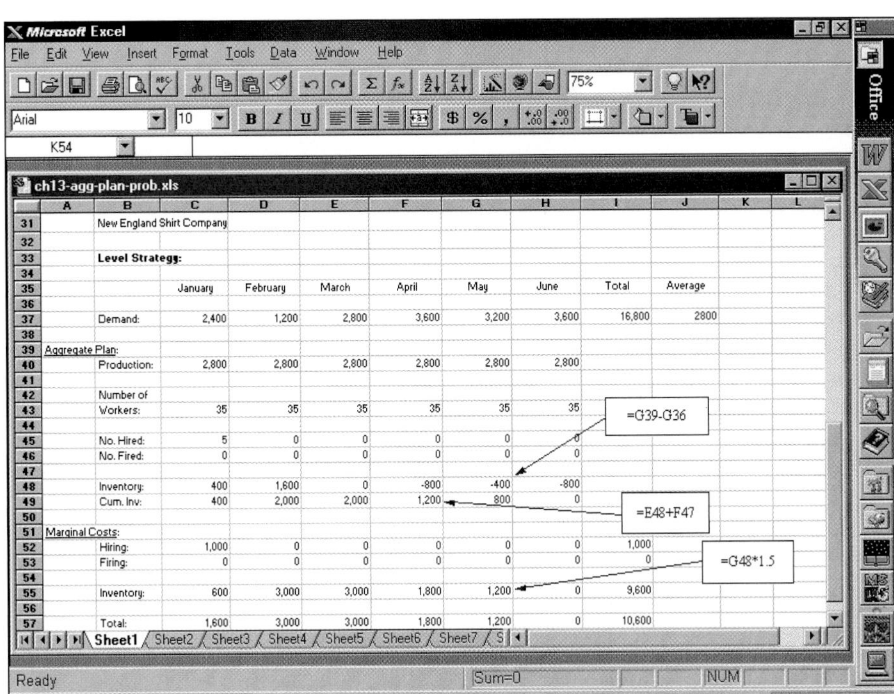

		January	February	March	April	May	June	Total	Average
	New England Shirt Company								
	Level Strategy:								
	Demand:	2,400	1,200	2,800	3,600	3,200	3,600	16,800	2800
Aggregate Plan:									
	Production:	2,800	2,800	2,800	2,800	2,800	2,800		
	Number of Workers:	35	35	35	35	35	35		
	No. Hired:	5	0	0	0	0	0		
	No. Fired:	0	0	0	0	0	0		
	Inventory:	400	1,600	0	-800	-400	-800		
	Cum. Inv:	400	2,000	2,000	1,200	800	0		
Marginal Costs:									
	Hiring:	1,000	0	0	0	0	0	1,000	
	Firing:	0	0	0	0	0	0	0	
	Inventory:	600	3,000	3,000	1,800	1,200	0	9,600	
	Total:	1,600	3,000	3,000	1,800	1,200	0	10,600	

In summary, the costs of each of the strategies are

Chase strategy	$13,000
Level strategy	$10,600

Therefore, Matt should elect to go with the level strategy.

A More In-Depth Example: The C&A Company

A firm with pronounced seasonal variation normally plans production with a 12-month time horizon in order to capture the extremes in demand during the busiest and slowest months.

Having said that, we present here an in-depth example using a six-month horizon in order more clearly to illustrate the general concepts that are involved in aggregate planning. We are given specific information about the C&A Company in Exhibit 15.4. Each alternative plan that is developed and presented is accompanied by both its full and marginal cost calculations to provide a comparison of these two approaches.

The first step in evaluating each alternative plan is to convert the demand forecast into production requirements. This is accomplished by subtracting out the amount of inventory on hand at the beginning of the forecast period. In the C&A example, the beginning inventory on hand is 400 units.

We are now ready to formulate and evaluate alternative aggregate or production plans for the C&A Company. Although one could develop a large number of alternative aggregate plans, we present four plans that we will evaluate with the objective of selecting that one with the lowest costs.

Plan 1. Produce to exact monthly production requirements using a regular eight-hour day by varying workforce size (pure chase strategy).

Exhibit 15.4

Forecasted Demand and Workdays for the C&A Company

	Jan.	Feb.	Mar.	Apr.	May	June	Total
Demand forecast (units)	2,200	1,500	1,100	900	1,100	1,600	8,400
Working days (per month)	22	19	21	21	22	20	125

	Costs
Material cost	$100/unit
Inventory holding cost	$1.50/unit-month
Stockout cost	$5/unit/month
Subcontracting cost	$125/unit
Hiring and training cost	$200/worker
Layoff cost	$250/worker
Labor required per unit	5 hours
Labor cost (first 8 hours each day)	$4/hour
Overtime cost (time and a half)	$6/hour
	Inventory
Beginning inventory	400 units
	Workforce
Number of workers currently employed	30

Plan 2. Produce to meet expected average demand over the next six months by maintaining a constant workforce. This constant number of workers is calculated by *averaging* the demand forecast over the horizon. Take the total production requirements for all six months and determine how many workers would be needed if each month's requirements were the same [(8,400 − 400) units × 5 hours per unit ÷ (125 days × 8 hours per day) = 40 workers]. Inventory is allowed to accumulate, and backlogs, when they occur, are carried forward and filled from the next month's production (pure level strategy).

Plan 3. Produce to meet the minimum expected demand (April) using a constant workforce on regular time. Subcontract to meet additional output requirements. The number of workers is calculated by identifying the minimum monthly production requirement and determining how many workers would be needed for that month [(900 units × 6 months × 5 hours per unit) ÷ (125 days × 8 hours per day) = 27 workers] and subcontracting any monthly difference between requirements and production (minimum workforce with subcontracting strategy).

Plan 4. Produce to meet expected demand for all but the first two months using a constant workforce on regular time. Use overtime to meet additional output requirements (constant workforce with overtime strategy).

The number of workers needed in this alternative is determined as follows:

$$1{,}100 + 900 + 1{,}100 + 1{,}600 = 4{,}700 \text{ units (March–June)}$$

$$4{,}700 \text{ units} \times 5 \text{ labor hours per unit} = 23{,}500 \text{ worker-hours}$$

$$23{,}500 \text{ worker-hours}/8 \text{ hours per day} = 2{,}938 \text{ worker-days}$$

$$2{,}938 \text{ worker-days}/84 \text{ days (March–June)} \cong 35 \text{ workers}$$

Having identified each of the four alternatives, the next step is to develop an aggregate plan for each alternative, showing all of the detailed calculations. These are presented in Exhibits 15.5, 15.6, 15.7, and 15.8. Once the details of each production plan have been

Exhibit 15.5

First Alternative: Pure Chase Strategy

	Jan.	Feb.	March	April	May	June	Total
Demand forecast	2,200	1,500	1,100	900	1,100	1,600	8,400
Initial inventory	400						
Production requirements	1,800	1,500	1,100	900	1,100	1,600	8,000
Aggregate plan							
Workers required	51	49	33	27	31	50	
Workers hired	21	0	0	0	4	19	
Workers fired	0	2	16	6	0	0	
Units produced	1,800	1,500	1,100	900	1,100	1,600	8,000
Costs—full							
Regular production	36,000	30,000	22,000	18,000	22,000	32,000	160,000
Material costs	180,000	150,000	110,000	90,000	110,000	160,000	800,000
Hiring costs	4,200	0	0	0	800	3,800	8,800
Firing costs	0	500	4,000	1,500	0	0	6,000
Total full costs	220,200	180,500	136,000	109,500	132,800	195,800	974,800
Costs—incremental							
Hiring costs	4,200	0	0	0	800	3,800	8,800
Firing costs	0	500	4,000	1,500	0	0	6,000
Total incremental costs	4,200	500	4,000	1,500	800	3,800	14,800

Exhibit 15.6

Second Alternative: Pure Level Strategy

	Jan.	Feb.	March	April	May	June	Total
Demand forecast	2,200	1,500	1,100	900	1,100	1,600	8,400
Initial inventory	400						
Production requirements	1,800	1,500	1,100	900	1,100	1,600	8,000
Aggregate plan							
Workers required	40	40	40	40	40	40	
Workers hired	10	0	0	0	0	0	
Workers fired	0	0	0	0	0	0	
Units produced	1,408	1,216	1,344	1,344	1,408	1,280	8,000
Monthly inventory	(392)	(284)	244	444	308	(320)	
Cumulative inventory	(392)	(676)	(432)	12	320	0	
Costs—full							
Regular production	28,160	24,320	26,880	26,880	28,160	25,600	160,000
Material costs	140,800	121,600	134,400	134,400	140,800	128,000	800,000
Hiring costs	2,000	0	0	0	0	0	2,000
Firing costs	0	0	0	0	0	0	0
Inventory carrying costs	0	0	0	18	480	0	498
Stockout costs	1,960	3,380	2,160	0	0	0	7,500
Total full costs	172,920	149,300	163,440	161,298	169,440	153,600	969,998
Costs—incremental							
Hiring costs	2,000	0	0	0	0	0	2,000
Firing costs	0	0	0	0	0	0	0
Inventory carrying costs	0	0	0	18	480	0	498
Stockout costs	1,960	3,380	2,160	0	0	0	7,500
Total incremental costs	3,960	3,380	2,160	18	480	0	9,998

Exhibit 15.7

Third Alternative: Minimum Workforce with Subcontracting Strategy

	Jan.	Feb.	March	April	May	June	Total
Demand forecast	2,200	1,500	1,100	900	1,100	1,600	8,400
Initial inventory	400						
Production requirements	1,800	1,500	1,100	900	1,100	1,600	8,000
Aggregate plan							
Workers required	27	27	27	27	27	27	
Workers hired	0	0	0	0	0	0	
Workers fired	3	0	0	0	0	0	
Units produced	950	821	907	907	950	864	5,399
Monthly inventory	0	0	0	7	0	0	
Units subcontracted	850	679	193	0	143	736	2,601
Costs—full							
Regular production	19,000	16,420	18,140	18,140	19,000	17,280	107,980
Material costs	95,000	82,100	90,700	90,700	95,000	86,400	539,900
Hiring costs	0	0	0	0	0	0	0
Firing costs	750	0	0	0	0	0	750
Inventory carrying costs	0	0	0	11	0	0	11
Subcontracting costs	106,250	84,875	24,125	0	17,875	92,000	325,125
Total full costs	221,000	183,395	132,965	108,851	131,875	195,680	973,766
Costs—incremental							
Hiring costs	0	0	0	0	0	0	0
Firing costs	750	0	0	0	0	0	750
Inventory carrying costs	0	0	0	11	0	0	11
Subcontracting costs	4,250	3,395	965	0	715	3,680	13,005
Total incremental costs	5,000	3,395	965	11	715	3,680	13,766

developed, we then can determine the costs associated with each plan. These costs (both full costs and marginal costs) also are included in their respective exhibits. A summary of these costs is presented in Exhibit 15.9, showing that the pure level strategy is the lowest cost alternative.

Aggregate Planning Applied to Services: Tucson Parks and Recreation Department

Charting and graphic techniques are also very useful for aggregate planning in service applications. The following example shows how a city's parks and recreation department could use the alternatives of full-time employees, part-time employees, and subcontracting to meet its commitment to provide service to the city.

The Tucson Parks and Recreation Department is responsible for developing and maintaining open space, all public recreational programs, adult sports leagues, golf courses, tennis courts, pools, and so forth. There are 336 full-time-equivalent employees (FTEs). Of these, 216 are full-time permanent personnel who provide the administration and year-round maintenance to all areas. The remaining 120 year-long FTE positions are part time, with about 75 percent of them being used during the summer and the remaining 25 percent being used in the fall, winter, and spring seasons. The 75 percent (or 90 FTE positions)

Exhibit 15.8

Fourth Alternative: Constant Workforce with Overtime Strategy

	Jan.	Feb.	March	April	May	June	Total
Demand forecast	2,200	1,500	1,100	900	1,100	1,600	8,400
Initial inventory	400						
Production requirements	1,800	1,500	1,100	900	1,100	1,600	8,000
Aggregate plan							
Workers required	35	35	35	35	35	35	
Workers hired	5	0	0	0	0	0	
Workers fired	0	0	0	0	0	0	
Units produced—regular	1,232	1,064	1,176	1,176	1,232	1,120	7,000
Units produced—overtime	568	436					1,004
Monthly inventory	0	0	76	276	132	(480)	
Cumulative inventory	0	0	76	352	484	4	
Costs—full							
Regular production	24,640	21,280	23,520	23,520	24,640	22,400	140,000
Overtime production	17,040	13,080	0	0	0	0	30,120
Material costs	180,000	150,000	117,600	117,600	123,200	112,000	800,400
Hiring costs	1,000	0	0	0	0	0	1,000
Firing costs	0	0	0	0	0	0	0
Inventory carrying costs	0	0	114	528	726	6	1,374
Total full costs	222,680	184,360	141,234	141,648	148,566	134,406	972,894
Costs—incremental							
Overtime production	5,680	4,360	0	0	0	0	10,040
Hiring costs	1,000	0	0	0	0	0	1,000
Firing costs	0	0	0	0	0	0	0
Inventory carrying costs			114	528	726	6	1,374
Total incremental costs	6,680	4,360	114	528	726	6	12,414

Exhibit 15.9

Summary of Costs for Alternative Aggregate Plans

Alternative	Full Costs	Marginal Costs
Pure chase	$974,800	$14,800
Pure level	$969,998	$ 9,998
Minimum workforce with subcontracting	$973,766	$13,766
Constant workforce with overtime	$972,894	$12,414

show up as approximately 800 part-time summer jobs: lifeguards, baseball umpires, and instructors in summer programs for children. The 800 part-time jobs are derived from 90 FTEs because many of these positions last only for a month or two while the FTEs are based on employment for an entire year.

Currently, the parks and recreation work that is subcontracted amounts to less than $100,000. This is for the golf and tennis pros and for grounds maintenance at the libraries and veterans cemetery.

Because of the nature of city employment, the probable bad public image, and civil service rules, the option to hire and fire full-time help daily and/or weekly to meet seasonal demand is pretty much out of the question. However, temporary part-time help is authorized and traditional. Also, it is virtually impossible to have regular (full-time) staff for all of the summer jobs. During the summer months, the approximately 800 part-time employees are staffing many programs that occur simultaneously, prohibiting level scheduling over a normal 40-hour week. Also, a wider variety of skills are required than can be expected from full-time employees (e.g., umpires; coaches; lifeguards; teachers of ceramics, guitar, karate, belly dancing, and yoga).

Under these conditions, the following three options are open to the department in its aggregate planning.

1. The present method, which is to maintain a medium-level full-time staff and schedule work during off seasons (such as rebuilding baseball fields during the winter months) and to use part-time help during peak demands.
2. Maintain a lower level of staff over the year and subcontract all additional work presently done by full-time staff (still using part-time help).
3. Maintain an administrative staff only and subcontract all work, including part-time help. (This would entail contracts to landscaping firms, pool-maintenance companies, and newly created private firms to employ and supply part-time help.)

The common unit of measure of work across all areas is full-time-equivalent jobs or employees (referred to as FTEs). For example, assume in the same week that 30 lifeguards worked 20 hours each, 40 instructors worked 15 hours each, and 35 baseball umpires worked 10 hours each. This is equivalent to $(30 \times 20) + (40 \times 15) + (35 + 10) = 1{,}550 \div 40 = 38.75$ FTE positions for that week. Although a considerable amount of workload can be shifted to the off season, most of the work must be done when required.

Full-time employees consist of three groups: (*a*) the skeleton group of key department personnel coordinating with the city, setting policy, determining budgets, measuring performance, and so forth; (*b*) the administrative group of supervisory and office personnel who are responsible for or whose jobs are directly linked to the direct-labor workers; and (*c*) the direct-labor workforce of 116 full-time positions. These workers physically maintain the department's areas of responsibility, such as cleaning up, mowing golf greens and ballfields, trimming trees, and watering grass.

Cost information needed to determine the best alternative strategy is

Full-Time Direct-Labor Employees	
Average wage rate	$8.90 per hour
Fringe benefits	17% of wage rate
Administrative costs	20% of wage rate
Part-Time Employees	
Average wage rate	$8.06 per hour
Fringe benefits	11% of wage rate
Administrative costs	25% of wage rate
Subcontracting all full-time jobs	$3.2 million
Subcontracting all part-time jobs	$3.7 million

June and July are the peak demand seasons in Tucson. Exhibit 15.10 shows the high seasonal requirements for June and July personnel. The part-time help reaches 576 full-time-equivalent positions (although in actual numbers, this is approximately 800 different employees). After a low fall and winter staffing level, the demand shown as "full-time direct"

Exhibit 15.10

Actual Demand Requirement for Full-Time Direct Employees and Full-Time-Equivalent (FTE) Part-Time Employees

	Jan.	Feb.	March	April	May	June	July	Aug.	Sept.	Oct.	Nov.	Dec.	Total
Days	22	20	21	22	21	20	21	21	21	23	18	22	252
Full-time employees	66	28	130	90	195	290	325	92	45	32	29	60	
Full-time days*	1,452	560	2,730	1,980	4,095	5,800	6,825	1,932	945	736	522	1,320	28,897
Full-time-equivalent part-time employees	41	75	72	68	72	302	576	72	0	68	84	27	
FTE days	902	1,500	1,512	1,496	1,512	6,040	12,096	1,512	0	1,564	1,512	594	30,240

Note: Some workweeks are staggered to include weekdays, but this does not affect the number of workdays per employee.

*Full-time days are derived by multiplying the number of days in each month by the number of workers.

reaches 130 in March when grounds are reseeded and fertilized and then increases to a high of 325 in July. The present method levels this uneven demand over the year to an average of 116 full-time year-round employees by early scheduling of work. As previously mentioned, no attempt is made to hire and lay off full-time workers to meet this uneven demand.

Exhibit 15.11 shows the cost calculations for all three alternatives. Exhibit 15.12 compares the total costs for each alternative. From this analysis, it appears that the department is already using the lowest-cost alternative (Alternative 1).

Yield Management

Aggregate planning in services is very different from that in manufacturing. This is due, in large part, to the fact that the capacity of service operations is often viewed as highly perishable because it cannot be saved or inventoried for future use. For example, the empty seats in a restaurant on Monday morning cannot be saved for use on Saturday night when it is very busy. Thus, services do not have the luxury to choose between chase and level strategies, as do manufacturing firms, but rather always must use the chase strategy. In other words, capacity must be available when the customer wants it.

However, even within this constraint, the service manager has considerable latitude in planning. For those services that have high fixed costs and low variable costs, it is important to maximize capacity utilization even if it means reducing prices to attract additional customers during slow periods of demand. This method, known as **yield management** or *revenue management,* attempts to simultaneously integrate demand management (by changing prices) and supply management (by controlling availability). The goal of yield management is to sell all available capacity, even at discount prices, but, at the same time, not turn away a full-paying customer because the capacity had been previously sold to a bargain hunter. Examples of industries that apply yield management concepts include airlines that offer discounts for advanced reservations and car rental agencies and hotels that offer discounts on weekends. (See OM in Practice on National Car Rental.) The concept of yield management is introduced in this chapter; the detailed mathematical theory behind yield management is explained in the next chapter. It also is mentioned in the forecasting chapter.

yield management

Concept used in certain service operations that attempts to match supply and demand.

After yield management has been applied to a service operation, the service manager would then determine the aggregate workforce requirements in a manner similar to that described previously for a manufacturing company.

Exhibit 15.11

Three Possible Plans for the Parks and Recreation Department

Alternative 1: Maintain 116 full-time regular direct workers. Schedule work during off seasons to level workload throughout the year. Continue to use 120 full-time-equivalent (FTE) part-time employees to meet high demand periods.

Costs	Days per Year (Exhibit 15.9)	Hours (employees x days x 8 hours)	Wages (full-time, $8.90; part-time, $8.06)	Fringe Benefits (full-time, 17%; part-time, 11%)	Administrative Cost (full-time, 20%; part-time, 25%)
116 full-time regular employees	252	233,856	$2,081,318	$353,824	$416,264
120 part-time employees	252	241,920	1,949,875	214,486	487,469
Total cost = $5,503,236			$4,031,193	$568,310	$903,733

Alternative 2: Maintain 50 full-time regular direct workers and the present 120 FTE part-time employees. Subcontract jobs, releasing 66 full-time regular employees. Subcontract cost, $2,200,000.

Costs	Days per Year (Exhibit 15.9)	Hours (employees x days x 8 hours)	Wages (full-time, $8.90; part-time, $8.06)	Fringe Benefits (full-time, 17%; part-time, 11%)	Administrative Cost (full-time, 20%; part-time, 25%)	Subcontract Cost
50 full-time employees	252	100,800	$ 897,120	$152,510	$179,424	
120 FTE part-time employees	252	241,920	1,949,875	214,486	487,469	$2,200,000
Subcontracting cost						
Total cost = $6,080,884			$2,846,995	$366,996	$666,893	$2,200,000

Alternative 3: Subcontract all jobs previously performed by 116 full-time regular employees. Subcontract cost, $3,200,000. Subcontract all jobs previously performed by 120 full-time-equivalent part-time employees. Subcontract cost, $3,700,000.

Cost	Subcontract Cost
0 full-time employees	
0 part-time employees	
Subcontract full-time jobs	$3,200,000
Subcontract part-time jobs	3,700,000
Total cost	$6,900,000

Operations Management in Practice

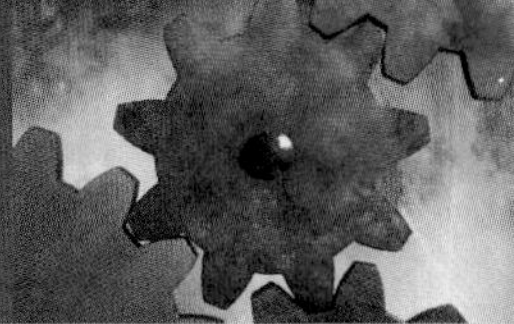

YIELD MANAGEMENT AT NATIONAL CAR RENTAL

Faced with possible liquidation in 1993 by General Motors, its parent company, National Car Rental was under significant pressure to produce both a substantial and sustainable profit. To accomplish this, management decided to adopt a comprehensive revenue management system. Instead of a constant car rental price all the time, the revenue management system demonstrated that a variable pricing policy that would fluctuate with demand would result in significantly higher profits.

The revenue management system was implemented in two phases. The first phase was introduced in July 1993, with the goal of showing immediate profits, which it did. The second phase focused on developing a state-of-the-art revenue management system for the car rental industry. This phase was successfully implemented in July 1994.

As a result of this revenue management system, profits were significantly increased, and General Motors was able to sell National Car Rental in 1995 for an amount in excess of $1 billion.

Sources: Ernest Johnson, "1994 Trophy Award: National Car Rental Systems, Inc." *Scorecard: The Revenue Management Quarterly,* First Quarter 1995; M. K. Geraghty and Ernest Johnson, "Revenue Management Saves National Car Rental," *Interfaces* 27, no. 1 (January–February 1997), pp. 107–27.

Exhibit 15.12

Comparison of Costs for All Three Alternatives

	Alternative 1: 116 Full-time Direct Labor Employees, 120 FTE Part-Time Employees	**Alternative 2: 50 Full-Time Direct Labor Employees, 120 FTE Part-Time Employees, Subcontracting**	**Alternative 3: Subcontracting Jobs Formerly Performed by 116 Direct Labor Full-time Employees and 120 FTE Part-Time Employees**
Wages	$4,031,193	$2,846,995	—
Fringe benefits	568,310	366,996	—
Administrative costs	903,733	666,893	—
Subcontracting, full-time jobs		2,200,000	$3,200,000
Subcontracting, part-time jobs			3,700,000
Total	$5,503,236	$6,080,884	$6,900,000

In order to take maximum advantage of yield management, a service should have the following characteristics: (*a*) the ability to segment its markets, (*b*) high-fixed and low-variable costs, (*c*) product perishability, and (*d*) the ability to presell capacity.[1]

Market Segmentation

A major issue in the successful implementation of yield management is the ability of the firm to segment its markets. Proper segmentation will prevent all of the firm's customers from taking advantage of price reductions when they are offered to fill available capacity.

[1]Sheryl E. Kimes, "Yield-Management: A Tool for Capacity-Constrained Service Firms," *Journal of Operations Management* 8, no. 4 (October 1989), pp. 348–63.

Market segmentation can be done in several ways. The first is to impose significant restrictions on customers who use the lower prices. For example, airlines require customers to stay over a Saturday night or to purchase their tickets from 7 to 30 days in advance to qualify for lower airfares. These very same conditions, however, prevent the business traveler, who usually travels midweek on short notice, from taking advantage of the lower fares.

Another method of segmentation is to offer lower prices on only specific days of the week or times of the day. Movie theaters offer reduced ticket prices for matinees, which senior citizens can take advantage of during weekdays. Similarly, downtown hotels typically offer discounts on weekends when business travelers are home, as an incentive for tourists.

High-Fixed and Low-Variable Costs

High-fixed and low-variable costs allow a firm to offer significant discounts while still being able to cover variable costs. When a service firm has this type of cost profile, profits are directly related to sales. In other words, the more sales generated, the more profits made.

For example, if the variable cost associated with having a hotel room cleaned is estimated at $25 (which would include the labor to clean the room and the replacement of any material that was consumed, such as soap and shampoo, as well as fresh sheets and towels), then any price that the hotel could get for the room above the $25 variable cost would be financially beneficial (as opposed to leaving the room empty for the night).

Product Perishability

The underlying reason that yield management can be applied to many types of services is the perishability of service capacity. In other words, service capacity cannot be saved for future use. (Wouldn't it be great if the airlines could save all of their empty seats during the year for use during the Thanksgiving and Christmas holiday periods!) Given that capacity in a service operation is perishable, the service manager should try and maximize capacity utilization whenever possible, even if it means offering large discounts to attract customers—provided that the discounted prices exceed the variable cost.

Presold Capacity

A final requirement for the successful implementation of yield management is that the lower-priced capacity can be sold in advance. This limits the availability of capacity to the higher-priced market segments. As an illustration, hotels usually work with conference planners several years in advance of a conference, offering a given number of rooms at the lowest room rates. Travel groups usually plan tours within a year before they need them and therefore also receive a discount. Finally, the last-minute customer, or "walk-in," will pay top dollar or the "rack rate" for a hotel room.

Conclusion

Aggregate planning provides the link between the corporate strategic and capacity plans and workforce size, inventory quantity, and production levels. It does not involve detailed planning. It is also useful to point out some practical considerations in aggregate planning.

First, demand variations are a fact of life, so the planning system must include sufficient flexibility to cope with such variations. Flexibility can be achieved by developing alternative sources of supply, cross-training workers to handle a wide variety of orders, and engaging in more frequent replanning during high-demand periods.

Second, decision rules for production planning should be adhered to once they have been selected. However, they should be carefully analyzed prior to implementation by such checks as using simulation of historical data to see what really would have happened if these rules had been in operation in the past.

Services typically require a chase strategy due to the customer's direct involvement with the service delivery system. However, services, under certain conditions, can successfully apply the concept of yield management, which simultaneously adjusts customer demand and the operation's capacity with the goal of maximizing the firm's profit.

Key Terms

aggregate production planning p. 571
backlog (or stockout) p. 574
inventory on hand p. 574
master production schedule p. 572
planning activities p. 570
intermediate-range planning p. 570
long-range planning p. 570
short-range planning p. 570
production planning strategies p. 574
mixed strategy p. 574
pure strategy p. 574
production rate p. 573
rough-cut or resource capacity planning p. 572
workforce level p. 574
yield management p. 585

Review and Discussion Questions

1. What are the basic controllable variables of a production planning problem? What are the four major costs?
2. Distinguish between pure and mixed strategies in production planning.
3. Compare the best plans in the C&A Company and the Tucson Parks and Recreation Department. What do they have in common?
4. How does forecast accuracy relate, in general, to the practical application of the aggregate planning models discussed in the chapter?
5. In which way does the time horizon chosen for an aggregate plan determine whether or not it is the best plan for the firm?
6. Under what conditions is the concept of yield management most appropriate for service operations?

Solved Problem

Problem

Jason Enterprises (JE) is producing video telephones for the home market. Quality is not quite as good as it could be at this point, but the selling price is low and Jason has the opportunity to study market response while spending more time in additional R&D work.

At this stage, however, JE needs to develop an aggregate production plan for the six months from January through June. As you can guess, you have been commissioned to create the plan. The following information is available to help you:

	Jan.	Feb.	March	April	May	June
Demand data						
Beginning inventory	200					
Forecast demand	500	600	650	800	900	800
Cost data						
Holding cost		$10/unit/month				
Stockout cost		$20/unit/month				
Subcontracting cost/unit		$100				
Hiring cost/worker		$50				
Layoff cost/worker		$100				
Labor cost/hour—straight time		$12.50				
Labor cost/hour—overtime		$18.75				
Production data						
Labor hours/unit		4				
Workdays/month		22				
Current workforce		10				

What is the cost of each of the following production strategies?

a. Chase strategy; vary workforce (assuming a starting workforce of 10).

b. Constant workforce; vary inventory and stockout only (assuming a starting workforce of 10).

c. Level workforce of 10; vary overtime only; inventory carryover permitted.

d. Level workforce of 10; vary overtime only; inventory carryover not permitted.

Solution

a. Plan 1: Chase strategy; vary workforce (assume 10 in workforce to start).

Month	(1) Production Requirement	(2) Production Hours Required (1) x 4	(3) Hours/Month per Worker 22 x 8	(4) Workers Required (2) ÷ (3)	(5) Workers Hired	(6) Workers Fired
January	300	1,200	176	7	0	3
February	600	2,400	176	14	7	0
March	650	2,600	176	15	1	0
April	800	3,200	176	18	3	0
May	900	3,600	176	20	2	0
June	800	3,200	176	18	0	2

Month	(7) Hiring Cost (5) x $50	(8) Layoff Cost (6) x $100	(9) Straight-Time Cost (2) x $12.50
January	0	$300	$ 15,000
February	350	0	30,000
March	50	0	32,500
April	150	0	40,000
May	100	0	45,000
June	0	200	40,000
	$650	$500	$202,500

Total cost for plan:

Hiring cost	$ 650
Layoff cost	500
Straight-time cost	202,500
Total	$203,650

b. Plan 2: Constant workforce; vary inventory and stockout only.

Month	(1) Cumulative Production Requirement	(2) Production Hours Available 22 x 8 x 10	(3) Units Produced (2) ÷ 4	(4) Cumulative Production
January	300	1,760	440	440
February	900	1,760	440	880
March	1,550	1,760	440	1,320
April	2,350	1,760	440	1,760
May	3,250	1,760	440	2,200
June	4,050	1,760	440	2,640

Month	(5) Units Short (1) – (4)	(6) Shortage Cost (5) x $20	(7) Units in Excess (4) – (1)	(8) Inventory Cost (7) x $10	(9) Straight-Time Cost (2) x $12.50
January	$ 0	0	140	1,400	$ 22,000
February	20	400	0	0	22,000
March	230	4,600	0	0	22,000
April	590	11,800	0	0	22,000
May	1,050	21,000	0	0	22,000
June	1,410	28,200	0	0	22,000
		$66,000		$1,400	$132,000

Total cost for plan:

Shortage cost	$ 66,000
Inventory cost	1,400
Straight-time cost	132,000
Total	$199,400

c. Plan 3: Level workforce of 10; vary overtime only; inventory carryover permitted.

Month	(1) Production Requirement	(2) Standard Time Hours Available 22 x 8 x 10	(3) Standard Time Units Produced (2) ÷ 4	(4) Overtime Required in Units (1) – (3)
January	300	1,760	440	0
February	460*	1,760	440	20
March	650	1,760	440	210
April	800	1,760	440	360
May	900	1,760	440	460
June	800	1,760	440	360
				1,410

*600 – 140 units of beginning inventory in February.

Month	(5) Overtime Required in Hours (4) x 4	(6) Overtime Cost (5) x $18.75	(7) Straight-Time Cost (2) x $12.50	(8) Excess Inventory Costs [(3) – (1)] x $10
January	0	$ 0	$ 22,000	$1,400
February	80	1,500	22,000	
March	840	15,750	22,000	
April	1,440	27,000	22,000	
May	1,840	34,500	22,000	
June	1,440	27,000	22,000	
		$105,750	$132,000	$1,400

Total cost for plan:

Straight-time cost	$132,000
Overtime cost	105,750
Inventory cost	1,400
Total	$239,150

d. Plan 4: Constant workforce of 10; vary overtime only; inventory carryover not permitted.

Month	(1) Production Requirement	(2) Standard-Time Hours Available 22 x 8 x 10	(3) Standard-Time Units Produced Min. [(2) ÷ 4; (1)]	(4) Overtime Required in Units (1) – (3)
January	300	1,760	300	0
February	600	1,760	440	160
March	650	1,760	440	210
April	800	1,760	440	360
May	900	1,760	440	460
June	800	1,760	440	360

Month	(5) Overtime Required in Hours (4) x 4	(6) Overtime Cost (5) x $18.75	(7) Standard-Time Cost (2) x $12.50	(8) Excess Inventory Costs [(3) – (1)] x $10
January	0	$ 0	$22,000	$1,400
February	640	12,000	22,000	
March	840	15,750	22,000	
April	1,440	27,000	22,000	
May	1,840	34,500	22,000	
June	1,440	27,000	22,000	
		$116,250	$132,000	$1,400

Total cost for plan:

Straight-time cost	$132,000
Overtime cost	116,250
Excess inventory cost	1,400
Total	$249,650

Problems

1. Develop a production plan and calculate the annual cost for a firm whose unit demand forecast is fall, 10,000; winter, 8,000; spring, 7,000; summer, 12,000. Inventory at the beginning of fall is 500 units. At the beginning of fall you currently have 30 workers, but you plan to hire temporary workers at the beginning of summer and lay them off at the end of summer. In addition, you have negotiated with the union an option to use the regular workforce on overtime during winter or spring if overtime is necessary to prevent stockouts at the end of those quarters. Overtime is *not* available during the fall. Relevant costs are hiring, $100 for each temp; layoff, $200 for each regular worker laid off; inventory holding, $5 per unit per quarter; back order, $10 per unit per quarter; straight time, $5 per hour; overtime, $8 per hour. Assume that worker productivity is two hours per unit, with eight hours per day and 60 days per season.
2. Develop an aggregate production plan for a four-month period: February through May. For February and March, you should produce to exactly meet the demand forecast. For April and May, you should use overtime and inventory with a stable workforce. However, government constraints put a maximum of 5,000 hours of overtime labor per month in April and May (zero overtime in February and March). If demand exceeds supply, then back orders occur. There are 100 workers on January 31. You are given the following unit demand forecast: February, 80,000; March, 64,000; April, 100,000; May, 40,000. Worker productivity is four units per hour. Assume eight hours per day, 20 days per month and zero inventory on February 1. Costs are hiring, $50 per new worker; layoff, $70 per worker laid off; inventory holding, $10 per unit per month; straight-time labor, $10 per hour; overtime, $15 per hour; back order, $20 per unit per month. Find the total cost of this plan.
3. Develop an aggregate production plan for the next year. The unit demand forecast is spring, 20,000; summer, 10,000; fall, 15,000; winter, 18,000. At the beginning of spring you have 70 workers and 1,000 units in inventory. The union contract specifies that you may lay off workers only once a year, at the beginning of summer. Also, you may hire new workers only at the end of summer to begin regular work in the fall. The number of workers laid off at the beginning of summer and the number hired at the end of summer should result in planned production levels for summer and fall that equal the demand forecasts for summer and fall respectively. If demand exceeds supply, use overtime in spring only, which means that back orders could occur in winter. You are given these costs: hiring, $100 per new worker; layoff, $200 per worker laid off; holding, $20 per unit per quarter; back order costs, $8 per unit per quarter; straight-time labor, $10 per hour; overtime, $15 per hour. Worker productivity is two hours per unit. Assume eight hours per day and 50 days per quarter. Find the total cost.
4. DAT, Inc. needs to develop an aggregate plan for its product line. Relevant data are

Production time	1 hour per unit
Average labor cost	$10 per hour
Work-week	5 days, 8 hours each day
Days per month	Assume 20 workdays per month
Beginning inventory	500 units
Safety stock	One-half of monthly forecast
Shortage cost	$20 per unit per month
Inventory carrying cost	$5 per unit per month

The forecast for January to December 1998 is

Jan.	Feb.	March	April	May	June	July	Aug.	Sept.	Oct.	Nov.	Dec.
2,500	3,000	4,000	3,500	3,500	3,000	3,000	4,000	4,000	4,000	3,000	3,000

Management prefers to keep a constant workforce and production level, absorbing variations in demand through inventory excesses and shortages. Demand that is not met is carried over to the following month.

Develop an aggregate plan that will meet the demand and other conditions of the problem. Do not try to find the optimum; just find a good solution and state the procedure you might use to test for a better solution. Make any necessary assumptions.

5. Shoney Video Concepts produces a line of CD players to be linked to personal computers for video games. CDs have much faster access time than does tape. With such a computer/CD link, the game becomes a very realistic experience. In a simple driving game where the joystick steers the vehicle, for example, rather than seeing computer graphics on the screen, the player is actually viewing a segment of a CD shot from a real moving vehicle. Depending on the action of the player (hitting a guard rail, for example) the disc moves virtually instantaneously to that segment and the player becomes part of an actual accident of real vehicles (staged, of course).

Shoney is trying to determine a production plan for the next 12 months. The main criterion for this plan is that the employment level is to be held constant over the period. Shoney is continuing in its R&D efforts to develop new applications and prefers not to cause any adverse feeling with the local workforce. For the same reasons, all employees should put in full work weeks, even if this is not the lowest-cost alternative. The number of CD players forecast for the next 12 months is

Month	Forecast Demand	Month	Forecast Demand
January	600	July	200
February	800	August	200
March	900	September	300
April	600	October	700
May	400	November	800
June	300	December	900

Manufacturing cost is $200 per player, equally divided between materials and labor. Inventory storage costs are $5 per CD player per month. A shortage results in lost sales and is estimated to cost an overall $20 per unit short. (Shortages are not carried forward since the sales are lost.)

The inventory on hand at the beginning of the planning period is 200 units. Ten labor hours are required per CD player. The workday is eight hours.

Develop an aggregate production schedule for the year using a constant workforce. For simplicity, assume 22 working days each month except July, when the plant closes down for three weeks' vacation (leaving seven working days). Make any assumptions you need.

6. The Bentley Chemical Company (BCC) is vitally concerned about generating a production schedule for their products for the coming fiscal year (July–June). The operations manager at BCC, Mr. Perspa Cassidy, has been charged with generating an

aggregate plan for this time period so that BCC can meet their demand with the minimum utilization of resources.

Mr. Cassidy first aggregates the various products that BCC sells into a single "aggregate" production unit and forecasts the demand for the following four quarters:

Quarter	Quarter #1 Jul/Aug/Sept	Quarter #2 Oct/Nov/Dec	Quarter #3 Jan/Feb/Mar	Quarter #4 Apr/May/June
Demand forecast	10,000	9,800	9,400	10,200

On March 1 (prior to quarter #1) there are 1,200 units in BCC's inventory and the forecast demand for the fourth quarter of the previous year is 9,900 units. Mr. Cassidy knows that to keep one unit in inventory for one month costs $5; further, BCC uses average inventory when computing inventory costs. The workforce on March 1 consists of 40 employees, each of whom produces exactly four (4) units in an 8-hour day. For the coming four quarters, Mr. Cassidy has determined the number of productive days for each quarter to be as follows:

Quarter	Quarter #1 Jul/Aug/Sept	Quarter #2 Oct/Nov/Dec	Quarter #3 Jan/Feb/Mar	Quarter #4 Apr/May/June
Number of productive days	56	60	61	63

Each of the regular employees is paid at the rate of $53 per day; however, overtime is available at the rate of $80 per day. BCC has a very strict quality control policy and does not allow any subcontracting. In addition, BCC wishes to maintain their reputation with their customers and has adopted a policy that *all* demand must be met on time.

Mr. Cassidy recognizes that meeting all demand can be difficult. He is faced with two limitations: (1) he is using aggregate units and (2) he has only his forecasts as a basis for his aggregate plan. However, he believes that his forecasts are quite good and decides to use his figures objectively (i.e., he decides not to keep any safety stock).

The workforce can be increased or decreased at the discretion of Mr. Cassidy, but no more than a 25 percent increase or decrease (using integer values) is allowed in any given quarter due to union regulations. Mr. Cassidy knows that should he wish to hire and/or fire, the total increase/decrease in the workforce (when using whole people) cannot exceed the 25 percent mark. Fortunately, BCC is located in an area where there is no shortage of skilled labor.

To hire a new individual and train him/her requires exactly one quarter and costs $1,200. All new employees always start on the first day of a given quarter. Hence, they cannot be considered part of the productive labor force until after their first quarter. To fire an individual costs $1,000, and when an individual is fired, he remains part of the productive workforce until the end of the quarter in which he was fired.

Mr. Cassidy believes that he has all the data he needs; hence, he starts to determine the aggregate capacity plan. He selects a strategy of trying to maintain a relatively stable workforce, while letting the inventory levels fluctuate.

a. Perform the initial calculations Mr. Cassidy would need prior to completing the grid that follows.

b. Develop an aggregate plan for Mr. Cassidy by filling in the grid.

c. What is the total cost of Mr. Cassidy's plan?

(1) Qtr.	(2) Demand	(3) Prod. Hours Req. (2) x 2	(4) Prod. Days per Qtr.	(5) Prod. Hrs. per Qtr. per Worker (4) x 8	(6) No. of Empls.	(7) Total Prod. Hrs. Avail. per Qtr. (5) x (6)	(8) Straight-Time Cost (4) x (6) x $53	(9) No. of Units Short	(10) Short Cost	(11) No. of OT Units Req.	(12) No. of OT Days Req. (11)/4
NOW	9,900	19,800	63	504	40	20,160	$133,560	0	$0	0	0
1	10,000		56						0		
2	9,800		60						0		
3	9,400		61						0		
4	10,200		63						0		

(13) Overtime Cost (12) x $80	(14) No. of Unit Sub.	(15) Sub. Cost.	(16) No. of Empls. Hired	(17) Hiring Cost (16) x $1200	(18) No. of Empls. Fired	(19) Firing Cost (18) x $1000	(20) Begin. Inv.	(21) End. Inv.	(22) Ave. Inv. $\frac{(20) + (21)}{2}$	(23) Inv. Cost (22) x $15
$0	0	$0	0	$0	0	$ 0	1,200	1,380	1,290	$19,350
							1,380			

7. Nelson's Marina on Cape Cod, as part of the service it offers to its customers, stores boats during the winter months. In addition, the marina, at the request of the customer, also will paint the hull of the boat, which must be done every year to prevent barnacles from attaching to the hull.

Dave Nelson, the owner of the marina, has received orders for the following sizes of boats to be stored and painted, and also has estimated the number of hours required to paint each size boat.

Boat Size	Number of Boats	Number of Labor Hours to Paint
Small (12'–19')	38	6
Medium (20'–34')	31	12
Large (35' and larger)	14	25

Dave currently employs one handyman during the summer months who does a wide variety of tasks. As one option, Dave can continue to employ this person during the six winter months (November–April) and have him paint the boat hulls. With this option the person would work 160 hours per month for each of the six months. Dave estimates the cost of painting the boats to be $30.00 per hour, which includes both labor and materials ($20.00 for labor and $10.00 for materials). Inasmuch as the boat owners will not pay Dave until the spring when their boats go in the water, Dave will have to borrow the money from his bank for the labor and materials at an annual rate of 18 percent, or 1.5 percent per month.

As a second alternative, Dave can let the handyman go at the end of the season and then hire the necessary number of workers to get all of the boats painted in April, just before they go into the water. At the end of the month, he would let all but the handyman go. The cost of hiring a worker for this kind of work is estimated to be $100.00 per person and the layoff cost is estimated at $75.00 per person.

A third option would be to hire less workers in April and have them all work overtime. In this case, each worker would work 60 hours a week, or 240 hours for the month. The overtime premium is 50 percent of the cost of labor, or $10.00 per hour.

Develop an aggregate plan for each of these alternatives. Which one do you recommend?

Bibliography

Geraghty, M. K., and Ernest Johnson. "Revenue Management Saves National Car Rental." *Interfaces* 27, no. 1 (January–February 1997), pp. 107–27.

Johnson, Ernest. "1994 Trophy Award: National Car Rental Systems, Inc." *Scorecard: The Revenue Management Quarterly,* First Quarter 1995.

Kimes, Sheryl E. "Yield-Management: A Tool for Capacity-Constrained Service Firms." *Journal of Operations Management* 8, no. 4 (October 1989), pp. 348–363.

Plossl, G. W. *Production and Inventory Control: Principles and Techniques*. 2nd ed. Englewood Cliffs, NJ: Prentice Hall, 1985.

Sasser, W. E.; R. P. Olsen; and D. D. Wyckoff. *Management of Service Operations*. Boston: Allyn & Bacon, 1978.

Silver, E. A., and R. Peterson. *Decision Systems for Inventory Management and Production Planning*. 2nd ed. New York: John Wiley & Sons, 1985.

Vollmann, T. E.; W. L. Berry; and D.C. Whybark. *Manufacturing Planning and Control Systems*. 3rd ed. Homewood, IL: Richard D. Irwin, 1992.

Case

XYZ Brokerage Firm

Consider the national operations group of the XYZ brokerage firm. The group, housed in an office building located in the Wall Street area, handles the transactions generated by registered representatives in more than 100 branch offices throughout the United States. As with all firms in the brokerage industry, XYZ's transactions must be settled within five trading days. This five-day period allows operations managers to smooth out the daily volume fluctuations.

Fundamental shifts in the stock market's volume and mix can occur overnight, so the operations manager must be prepared to handle extremely wide swings in volume. For example, on the strength of an international peace rumor, the number of transactions of XYZ rose from 5,600 one day to 12,200 the next.

Managers of XYZ, not unlike their counterparts in other firms, have trouble predicting volume. In fact, a random number generator can predict volume a month or even a week into the future almost as well as the managers can.

How do the operations managers in XYZ manage capacity when there are such wide swings? The answer differs according to the tasks and constraints facing each manager. Here's what two managers in the same firm might say:

Manager A: The capacity in our operation is currently 12,000 transactions per day. Of course, what we should gear up for is always a problem. For example, our volume this year ranged from 4,000 to 15,000 transactions per day. It's a good thing we have a turnover rate, because in periods of low volume it helps us reduce our personnel without the morale problems caused by layoffs. [The labor turnover rate in this department is over 100 percent per year.]

Manager B: For any valid budgeting procedure, one needs to estimate volume within 15 percent. Correlations between actual and expected volume in the brokerage industry have been so poor that I question the value of budgeting at all. I maintain our capacity at a level of 17,000 transactions per day.

Why the big difference in capacity management in the same firm? Manager A is in charge of the cashiering operation—the handling of certificates, checks, and cash. The personnel in cashiering are messengers, clerks, and supervisors. The equipment—file cabinets, vaults, calculators—is uncomplicated.

Manager B, however, is in charge of handling orders, an information-processing function. The personnel are data-entry clerks, EDP specialists, and systems analysts. The equipment is complex—computers, LANs, file servers, and communication devices that link national operations with the branches. The employees under B's control had performed their tasks manually until decreased volume and a standardization of the information needs made it worthwhile to install computers.

Because the lead times required to increase the capacity of the information-processing operations are long, however, and the incremental cost of the capacity to handle the last 5,000 transactions is low (only some extra peripheral equipment is needed), Manager B maintains the capacity to handle 17,000 transactions per day. He holds to this level even though the average number of daily transactions for any month has never been higher than 11,000 and the number of transactions for any one day has never been higher than 16,000.

Case

Because a great deal of uncertainty about the future status of the stock certificate exists, the situation is completely different in cashiering. Attempts to automate the cashiering function to the degree reached by the order-processing group have been thwarted because of the high risk of selecting a system not compatible with the future format of the stock certificate.

In other words, Manager A is tied to the chase demand strategy, and his counterpart, Manager B in the adjacent office, is locked into the level capacity strategy. However, each desires to incorporate more of the other's strategy into his own. A is developing a computerized system to handle the information-processing requirements of cashiering; B is searching for some variable costs in the order-processing operation that can be deleted in periods of low volume.

Questions

1. What appear to be the primary differences between these two departments?
2. Do these differences eliminate certain strategy choices for either manager?
3. Which factors cause the current strategy to be desirable for each manager?
4. What are the mixed or subcontracting possibilities?
5. What are the problems associated with low standardization?

Case

La Buena Compañía de España, S.A.

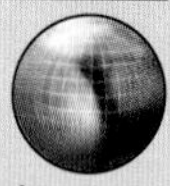

La Buena Compañía de Españia, S.A. (LBC), located just outside of Barcelona, Spain, produces kitchen tables that it sells throughout Western Europe. Sales have been increasing steadily over the past several years, due in large part to the free trade among Western European countries that has resulted from the formation of the European Union (EU).

Jordi Garolera, the operations manager at LBC, is currently developing an aggregate plan for the next six months. In order for him to be able to evaluate alternative plans, Jordi has collected the following information:

Production Data

20 workdays per month.

7.5 hours per workday.

2.5 labor-hours per table (average).

On-hand inventory: 300 tables.

Current workforce: 25 workers.

Cost Data

Hourly wages: 8 euros per hour.

Hiring costs: 200 euros per employee.

Firing costs: 700 euros per employee.

Material cost per table: 100 euros

Overtime costs: 50 percent premium.

Inventory carrying costs: 2 euros per unit per month.

Stockout costs: 10 euros per unit per month.

Jordi has just returned from a meeting with the marketing manager who provided him with a sales forecast for the next six months of 12.960 tables*, which is broken down as follows by month:

Month	Jan.	Feb.	Mar.	Apr.	May	June
Forecast (Tables)	1.740	1.740	2.460	3.240	2.220	1.860

*In Europe, decimals are separated from whole numbers by a comma, whereas thousands and millions are separated by periods, which is just the reverse of the practice in the United States. Thus US$5,000.00 in the United States would be written as US$5.000,00 in Europe.

Case

Questions

1. Using Excel or a similar spreadsheet, compare the costs of a pure chase strategy and a pure level strategy. Which type of strategy would you recommend?
2. As another alternative, Jordi was considering using a level workforce of 30 employees and working overtime to eliminate any stockouts. Evaluate this alternative and compare it to the pure strategies.
3. What alternative aggregate plans could you suggest to Jordi? What are the relative strengths and weaknesses of these plan(s)?

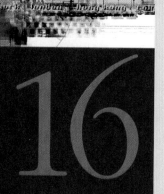

16 Inventory Systems for Independent Demand

Chapter Objectives

- Introduce the different types of inventories that can exist in an organization and provide a rationale for why companies maintain inventories.
- Identify the various costs associated with carrying and maintaining inventories.
- Define the classical inventory models and the conditions necessary for them to be applicable.
- Show how the economic order quantity is calculated for each of the different inventory models.
- Introduce the single-period inventory model and the concept of yield management with respect to service operations.
- Present some of the current inventory management trends and issues that exist in companies today.

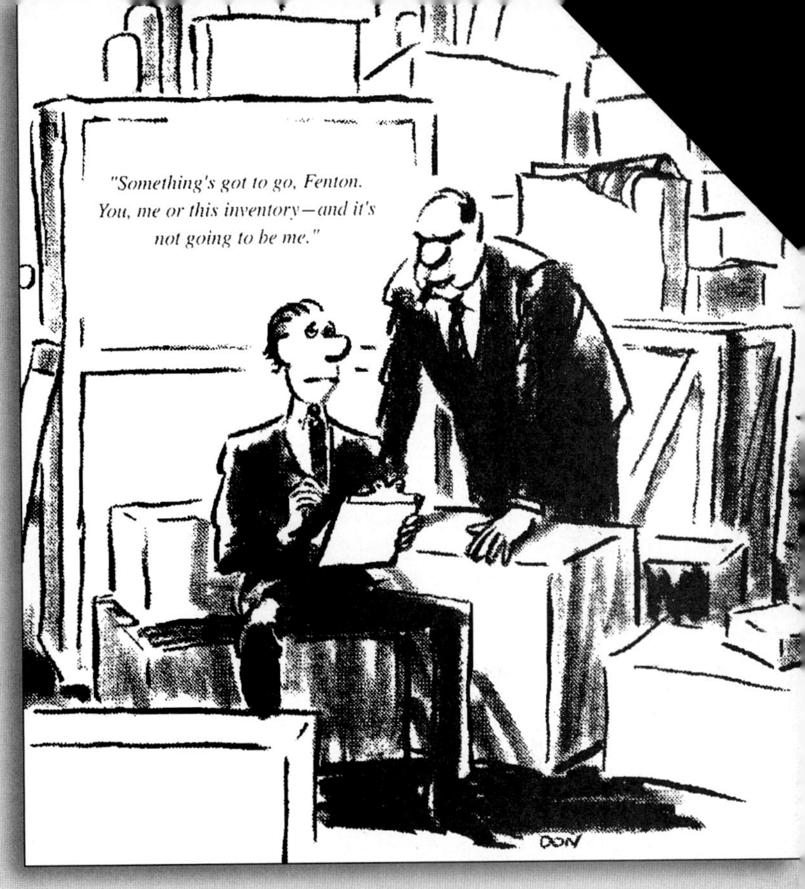

"Something's got to go, Fenton.
You, me or this inventory—and it's
not going to be me."
DON

The senior executives of Alpha Numerics were having their annual retreat to review accomplishments of the past year and to discuss major policy issues for the coming year.* As was the norm, the retreat was held at a small hotel in the mountains of eastern Pennsylvania, well removed from the company's actual manufacturing facility.

The first day's meeting had gone well, but in the early evening, after dinner, the subject of inventory control and the number of shortages that had occurred over the past year came up for discussion. The vice president of engineering suggested that, as a solution to the shortage problem, purchasing should order all of the projected material requirements at the beginning of the year.

The vice president of manufacturing was so taken back by this suggestion that, to the amazement of the others in the room, he leaped onto the conference table and shouted out, "Inventory is evil!" He turned to the president and said, "If we were to follow this suggestion, Mr. President, do you have an extra 25,000 square feet of warehouse space where we can store the material?" The president shook his head no. "And do you, Mr. Vice President of Finance, have an extra $5 million to buy all this material?" The VP of finance similarly shook his head.

"And are you, Mr. Vice President of Marketing, going to provide me with a perfect forecast of the products we expect to sell for the next year?" The VP of marketing said, "No, of course not. That would be impossible." And turning to the VP of engineering who had made the initial proposal, he said, "And you'll keep the same designs in the coming year without making any changes, won't you?" The VP of engineering said, "That would be very unrealistic." All of the individuals in the room then looked up to the VP of manufacturing still standing on the conference table and said, "We see what you mean. Inventory is indeed evil!"

*This meeting of senior corporate executives actually took place, although the name of the firm has been disguised.

Managerial Issues

nt's view towards inventory has changed significantly over the past several years. Previously, managers perceived inventory as an asset because it appears as an asset in the firm's financial reports. However, as seen in the opening vignette, this is no longer the case.

As we have seen, product life cycles are becoming ever shorter, increasing the likelihood of product obsolescence, as seen in the accompanying OM in Practice box. As we also have seen, excessive inventories on the manufacturing floor tend to conceal a wide variety of problems. Moreover, inventory storage costs are typically very expensive, averaging 30 to 35 percent annually of the value of the inventory—and in some cases they are much higher.

For all of these reasons, managers now look at inventory as a liability to the firm, something to be reduced or eliminated wherever possible, as illustrated in the GE advertisement.

Consequently, no topic in operations is more often discussed by managers or perceived to be more important by them than inventory. There is a continuous effort among managers to reduce inventories in all categories, beginning with raw materials and purchased parts, through to work-in-process, and ultimately in finished goods.

Definition of Inventory

Inventory is defined as the stock of any item or resource used in an organization. An *inventory management system* is the set of policies and controls that monitors levels of inventory and determines (*a*) what levels should be maintained, (*b*) when stock should be replenished, and (*c*) how large orders should be.

In a broader context, inventory can include inputs such as human, financial, energy, equipment, and physical items such as **raw materials;** outputs such as parts, components, and **finished goods;** and interim stages of the process, such as partially finished goods or **work-in-process (WIP).** The choice of which items to include in inventory depends on the organization. A manufacturing operation can have an inventory of personnel, machines, and working capital, as well as raw materials and finished goods. An airline can have an inventory of seats; a modern drugstore, an inventory of medicines, batteries, and toys; and an engineering firm, an inventory of engineering talent.

types of inventory:

raw material

Vendor-supplied items that have not had any labor added.

finished goods

Completed products still in the possession of the firm.

work-in-process (WIP)

Items that have been partially processed but are still incomplete.

By convention, manufacturing inventory generally refers to materials that contribute to or become part of a firm's product output. In services, inventory generally refers to the tangible goods that are sold and the supplies necessary to administer the service. Customers waiting in line at a service operation also can be viewed as inventory similar to parts waiting to be processed in a factory.

The basic purpose of inventory analysis in manufacturing and stockkeeping services is to specify (*a*) when items should be ordered and (*b*) how large the order should be. Recent trends have modified the simple questions of "when" and "how many." As we saw in an earlier chapter on supply chain management, many firms are tending to enter into longer-term relationships with vendors to supply their needs for perhaps the entire year. This changes the "when" and "how many to order" to "when" and "how many to deliver."

Reasons for Maintaining Inventory

Organizations maintain inventories for several reasons. These include

1. *To protect against uncertainty.* For purposes of inventory management, we examine uncertainty in three areas. First, there is uncertainty with respect to raw materials, which necessitates raw material inventory. Here, uncertainty pertains both to the lead time that can vary due to unexpected delays and to the amount of raw material received.

Uncertainty also occurs in the transformation process. Here work-in-process (WIP) inventories absorb the variability that exists between the stages of the process, thereby providing independence between operations and improving efficiency. In addition, this WIP inventory can be used to *decouple* the stages in a process.

Finally, uncertainty exists with respect to the demand for a firm's finished products. If the demand for a product were to be known precisely, then it could be possible to manufacture products so that demand would be exactly met. However, more often demand is not totally known, and a safety stock of finished goods inventory is therefore maintained to absorb these variations.

2. *To support a strategic plan.* As we learned in the previous chapter on aggregate planning, when a firm adopts a level strategy, an inventory of finished goods is required to buffer the cyclic demand for product from the level output generated by the transformation process. Under these circumstances, when demand exceeds production, the difference is withdrawn from inventory; when demand is less than production, the difference is placed back into inventory.
3. *To take advantage of economies of scale.* Each time we place an order or do a setup to perform an operation, we incur a fixed cost, regardless of the quantity involved. Thus, the larger the quantity ordered or produced, the lower the average total cost per unit. However, as we shall see shortly, there are trade-offs to be considered in determining the proper lot size.

   In addition, companies often offer discounts for larger-quantity orders, as an incentive to customers to buy more than they normally would. This results in accumulations of items that otherwise would not exist. Firms offer quantity discounts for several reasons, including the need to reduce excessive stockpiles and to generate positive cash flow. In addition, there are economies of scale with respect to transportation costs, especially when products are shipped in either full trailer loads or full car loads.

Inventory Costs

In making any decision with respect to inventories, the following costs should be taken into consideration:

Holding or Carrying Costs This broad category is usually subdivided into three segments: storage costs, capital costs, and obsolescence/shrinkage costs. *Storage costs* include the cost of the storage facility in the form of rent or depreciation, insurance, taxes, utilities, security, and facility personnel.

Capital costs can vary, depending on the firm's financial situation. For example, if the firm has an excess of cash, then the capital cost is the interest lost by putting the money into

Operations Management in Practice

COMPANIES WRITE OFF MILLIONS OF DOLLARS IN OBSOLETE INVENTORIES

During the economic slowdown of 2000–2001 (also referred to by some as a recession), many high-technology companies had to write off significant amounts of obsolete inventories. These inventories were the result of the inability of these firms' managers to anticipate the economic downturn and its associated decrease in sales. These excessive inventories occurred at all levels of the supply chain, including semiconductor manufacturers, electronic contract manufacturers, and PC makers. According to Steve Ward, general manager for IBM's Global sector, "Lean inventories are absolutely critical. In parts of our business, the value of components drops about 1.5 percent a month." Listed below are some of the companies and the respective amounts of inventory they wrote off.

Company	Amount of Inventory Written Off
Cisco Systems	$2.25 billion
Agere Systems	270 million
Micron Technology	260 million
Altera Corp.	115 million
Vitesse Semiconductor	50.6 million
Alliance Semiconductor	50 million
Xilinx	32 million

Source: Edward Teach, "The Great Inventory Correction," *CFO,* September 2001, pp. 58–62.

inventory instead of short-term notes. If the firm has an alternative project to invest in, then the capital cost is the opportunity cost of the anticipated return of that project. If the firm has to borrow funds to maintain an inventory, then the capital cost is the interest paid on those funds.

Obsolescence costs recognize that products tend to depreciate in value over time. This is especially true in high-technology industries where newer and better (and often cheaper) products are constantly being introduced. In this category, we also include spoilage costs associated with products that have a short shelf life, like perishable food products and some types of prescription drugs. *Shrinkage costs* track pilferage and breakage.

Setup or Ordering Costs These are fixed costs usually associated with the production of a lot internally or the placing of an order externally with a vendor. In other words, these costs are independent of the number of units that are requested. Setup costs are related to the amount of time needed to adjust the equipment to perform a specific task. This would include the alignment of special tooling such as jigs and fixtures. Order costs pertain to the costs involved in placing an order with a vendor. These may include telephone charges, a delivery fee, expediting costs, and the time required to process a purchase order.

Shortage (or Stockout) Costs When the stock of an item is depleted and a customer orders that product, then a stockout cost is incurred. This is usually the sum of the lost profit and any "ill-will" generated. There is a trade-off between carrying stock to satisfy demand and the costs resulting from stockout. This balance is sometimes difficult to obtain, since it may not be possible to accurately estimate lost profits, the effects of lost customers, or late penalties.

Purchase Costs These are the actual costs of the material purchased. Purchase costs tend to remain constant unless quantity discounts (which are discussed later in this chapter) are offered.

In addition to these traditional inventory costs, transportation costs also affect the lot size. (In determining the proper lot size, transportation costs often are included in the purchase cost of the material.)

Independent versus Dependent Demand

Briefly, the distinction between **independent** and **dependent demand** is this: With independent demand, the demands for various items are unrelated to each other and therefore the required quantities of each must be determined separately or independently. With dependent demand (which is addressed in detail in the next chapter), the requirement for any one item is a direct result of the need for some other item, usually a higher-level item of which it is a component or subassembly.

types of demand:

independent demand

Pertains to the requirements for end products.

dependent demand

Requirements for components and subassemblies that are directly dependent on the demand for the end products in which they are used.

In concept, dependent demand is a relatively straightforward computational problem. The required quantities of a dependent-demand item are simply computed, based on the number needed in each higher-level item where it is used. For example, if an automobile company plans on producing 500 automobiles per day, then obviously it will need 2,000 wheels and tires (plus spares). The number of wheels and tires needed is *dependent* on the production level for automobiles and not derived separately. The demand for automobiles, on the other hand, is *independent*—it comes from many sources external to the automobile firm and is not a part of other products and so is unrelated to the demand for other products.

To determine the quantities of independent items that must be produced, firms usually turn to their sales and market research departments. They use a variety of techniques, including customer surveys, forecasting techniques, and economic and sociological trends. Because independent demand is uncertain, extra units must be carried in inventory.

Types of Inventory Systems

An inventory system provides the organizational structure and the operating policies for maintaining and controlling the products to be stocked. The system is responsible for the ordering and the receipt of goods: timing the order placement and keeping track of what has been ordered, how much, and from whom. The system must also provide follow up to answer such questions as: Has the vendor received the order? Has it been shipped? Are the dates correct? Are the procedures established for reordering or returning undesirable merchandise?

Fixed-Order-Quantity and Fixed-Time-Period Systems

types of inventory systems:

fixed-order-quantity

System where the order quantity remains constant but the time between orders varies.

fixed-time-period

System where the time period between orders remains constant but the order quantity varies.

There are two general types of inventory systems: **fixed-order-quantity** (also called the Q-system) and **fixed-time-period** (also referred to as the P-system).

The basic distinction between the two is that the fixed-order-quantity model is "event triggered" and the fixed-time-period model is "time triggered." That is, the fixed-order-quantity model initiates an order when the event of reaching a specified reorder level occurs. This event may take place at any time, depending on the demand for the items. In contrast, the fixed-time-period model is limited to placing orders at the end of a predetermined time period; only the passage of time triggers the model. Advances in information technology, including the bar coding of products, bar code scanners, and point-of-sale (POS) computers, have greatly reduced the cost and facilitated the use of the fixed-order quantity model. As a result, there has been an increasing trend towards the fixed-order quantity model, and away from the fixed-time period model.

To use the fixed-order-quantity model, which places an order when the remaining inventory drops to a predetermined order Point, R, the inventory remaining must be continually monitored. Thus, the fixed-order-quantity model is a *perpetual* inventory system, which requires that every time a withdrawal from or an addition to inventory is made, records must be updated to ensure that the reorder point has or has not been reached. For the fixed-time-period model, inventory is counted only at the end of the review period. No counting takes place in the interim (although some firms have created variations of systems that combine features of both). Some additional differences that tend to influence the choice of systems are

- The fixed-time-period model typically has a larger average inventory since it also must protect against stockout during the review period, *T*; the fixed-quantity model has no review period.
- The fixed-time-period model is preferred when several different items are purchased from the same vendor, and there are potential economies of scale savings from ordering all these items at the same time.
- The fixed-order-quantity model is preferred for more expensive items because average inventory is lower.
- The fixed-order-quantity model is more appropriate for important items such as critical repair parts because there is closer monitoring and therefore quicker response to a potential stockout.
- The fixed-order-quantity model requires more time and resources to maintain because every addition or withdrawal is recorded.

Exhibit 16.1 illustrates the different events that occur when each of the two models is put into use and becomes an operating system. As we can see, the fixed-order-quantity

Exhibit 16.1

Comparison of Fixed-Order-Quantity and Fixed-Time-Period Reordering Inventory Systems

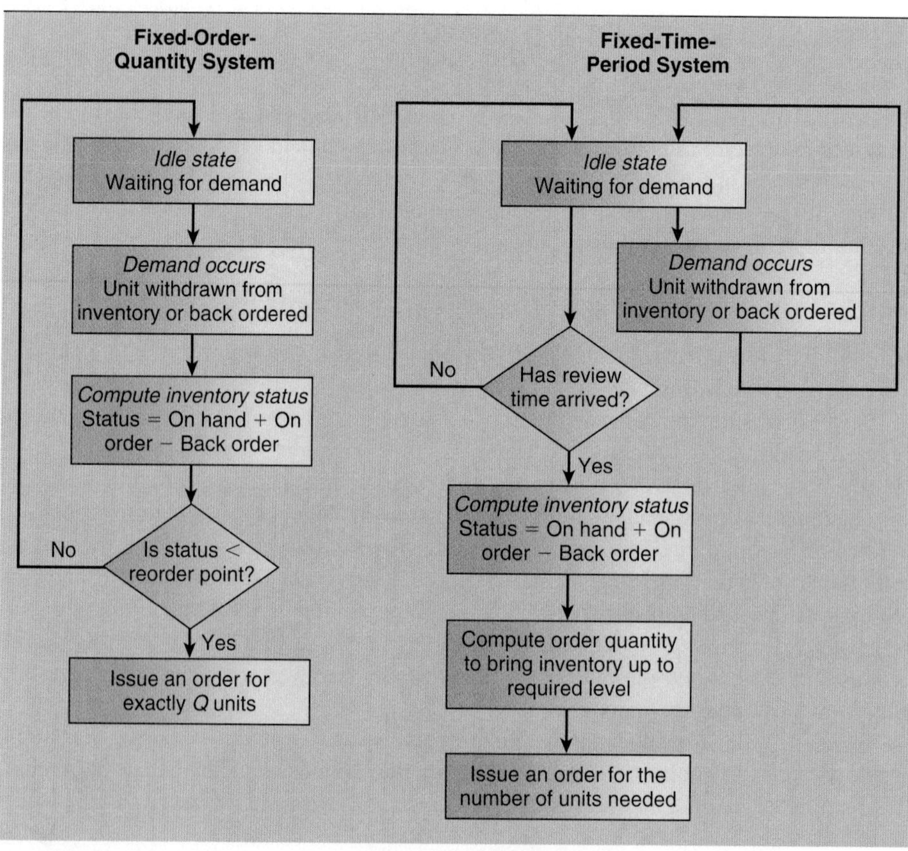

system focuses on order quantities and reorder points. Procedurally, each time a unit is taken out of stock, the withdrawal is recorded and the amount remaining in inventory is immediately compared to the reorder point. If it has dropped to this point or below, an order for Q items is placed. If it has not, the system remains in an idle state until the next withdrawal.

In the fixed-time-period system, a decision to place an order is made at a predetermined time interval (for example, each week or month), when the stock is counted or reviewed. Whether an order is actually placed depends on the inventory status at that time.

Basic Inventory Models

Basic Fixed-Order-Quantity Model

The simplest model in this category is when all aspects of the situation are known with certainty. If the annual demand for a product is 1,000 units, it is precisely 1,000—not 1,000 plus or minus 10 percent. In addition, the setup costs and holding costs are known and constant. Although the assumption of complete certainty is rarely valid, it provides a good starting point for our coverage of inventory models.

The fixed-order-quantity model attempts to determine both the specific point, R, at which an order will be placed and the size of that order, Q. The order (or reorder) point, R, is always a specified number of units actually in inventory. The solution to a fixed-order-quantity model may stipulate something like this: When the number of units of inventory on hand drops to 36, place an order for 57 more units.

Exhibit 16.2 and the discussion about deriving the optimal order quantity are based on the following assumptions of the model:

- Demand for the product is known, constant, and uniform throughout the period.
- Lead time (L), which is the time from ordering to receipt, is constant.
- Price per unit of product is constant (no quantity discounts).
- Ordering or setup costs are constant.
- All demands for the product are known with certainty; thus, there are no back orders or stockouts.
- There is no interaction with other products.

Exhibit 16.2

Basic Fixed-Order-Quantity Model

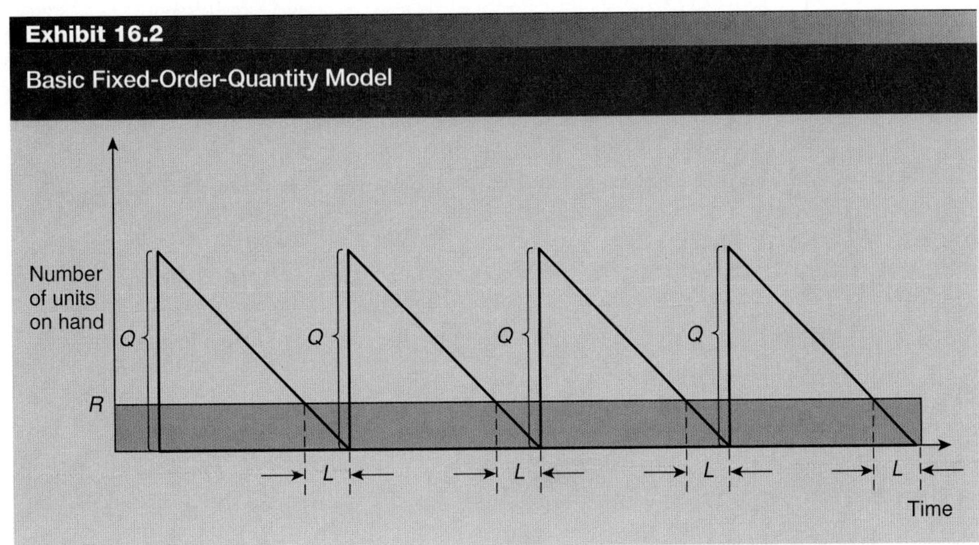

The "sawtooth effect" relating Q and R in Exhibit 16.2 shows that when inventory drops to point R, an order is placed. This order is received at the end of the lead time period L, which, as stated above, remains constant.

In constructing any inventory model, the first step is to develop a functional relationship between the variables of interest and the measure of effectiveness. In this case, since we are concerned with cost, the following equation would pertain:

$$\text{Total annual cost} = \text{Annual purchase cost} + \text{Annual ordering cost} + \text{Annual holding cost}$$

or

$$TC = DC + \frac{D}{Q}S + \frac{Q}{2}H \tag{16.1}$$

where

TC = Total annual cost
D = Annual demand in units
C = Cost per unit
Q = Quantity to be ordered (the optimum amount is termed the **economic order quantity—EOQ**)
S = Setup or ordering cost
H = Annual holding cost per unit
(*Note:* The holding cost often is defined as an annual percentage of the cost of the item. In these instances, $H = iC$, where i is the annual percentage carrying cost.)

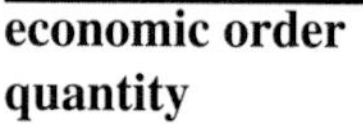

economic order quantity

Optimal quantity to order taking into consideration both the cost to carry inventory and the cost to order the item.

On the right side of the equation, DC is the annual purchase cost for the units, $(D/Q)S$ is the annual ordering cost (which is the actual number of orders placed, D/Q, times the cost of each order, S), and $(Q/2)H$ is the annual holding cost (which is the average inventory, $Q/2$, times the cost per unit for holding and storage, H). These cost relationships are shown graphically in Exhibit 16.3.

Exhibit 16.3

Annual Product Costs, Based on Size of the Order

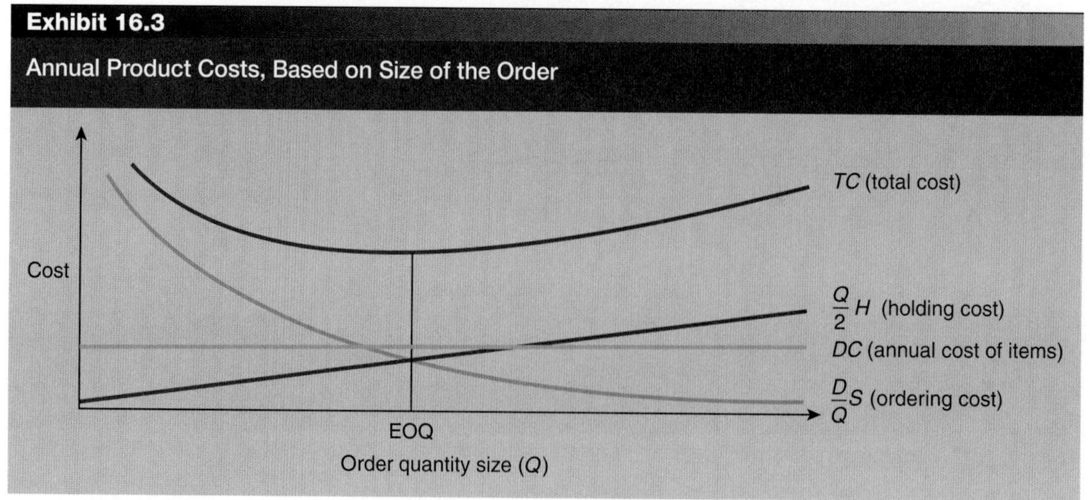

The next step is to find that order quantity, Q, for which total cost is a minimum. In Exhibit 16.3, the total cost is minimum at the point where the slope of the total cost curve is zero. Using calculus, the appropriate procedure involves taking the first derivative of total cost with respect to Q (which is the slope) and setting this equal to zero. For the basic model considered here, the calculations to obtain the economic order quantity (EOQ) would be as follows:

$$TC = DC + \frac{D}{Q}S + \frac{Q}{2}H$$

$$\text{First derivative} = \frac{dTC}{dQ} = 0 + \left(\frac{-DS}{Q^2}\right) + \frac{H}{2} = 0$$

Solving for Q gives us the economic order quantity, or EOQ,

$$\text{EOQ} = \sqrt{\frac{2DS}{H}} \tag{16.2}$$

Because this simple model assumes both constant demand and lead time, no safety stock is necessary, and the reorder point, R, is simply

$$R = \bar{d}L \tag{16.3}$$

where

R = Reorder point
$\bar{d}$ = Average demand per time period [constant]
L = Number of time periods between placing an order and its delivery [constant]

Example

Find the economic order quantity and the reorder point, given the following data:

Annual demand (D) = 1,000 units
Ordering cost (S) = \$5.00 per order
Holding cost (H) = \$1.25 per unit per year
Cost per unit (C) = \$12.50
Lead time (L) = 5 days
Average daily demand ($\bar{d}$) = 1,000/365

What quantity should be ordered, and when?

Solution

The optimal order quantity is

$$\text{EOQ} = \sqrt{\frac{2DS}{H}} = \sqrt{\frac{2(1{,}000)5}{1.25}} = \sqrt{8{,}000} = 89.4 \text{ units}$$

The reorder point is

$$R = \bar{d}L = \frac{1{,}000}{365}(5) = 13.7 \text{ units}$$

Rounding to the nearest unit, the inventory policy is as follows: When the number of units in inventory drops to 14, place an order for 89 more units.

The total annual cost will be

$$TC = DC + \frac{D}{Q}S + \frac{Q}{2}H$$

$$= 1{,}000(12.50) + \frac{1{,}000}{89}(5) + \frac{89}{2}(1.25)$$

$$= \$12{,}611.81$$

Note that in this example, the annual purchase cost of the units was not required to determine the order quantity and the reorder point. Also note that in Exhibit 16.3, the total cost curve is relatively flat around the EOQ, which is the norm, indicating that only minor increases in total cost will occur on either side of the EOQ. Thus, in the above example, we might in actuality order 90 units about once a month for the sake of simplicity and convenience without fear of incurring excessive costs.

Fixed-Order-Quantity Model with Usage

fixed-order-quantity model with usage

Considers a supplier that will provide an order quantity over a period of time rather than all at once.

The basic fixed-order-quantity model assumes that the quantity ordered is received in one lot, but frequently this is not the case. In many situations, the production of an inventory item and the usage of that item take place simultaneously (which is referred to as a **fixed-order-quantity model with usage**). This is particularly true where one part of a production system acts as a supplier to another part. For example, while aluminum extrusions are being made to fill an order for aluminum windows, the extrusions are cut and the windows assembled before the entire extrusion order is completed. Also, companies are beginning to enter into longer-term arrangements with vendors. Under such contracts, a single order or *blanket* contract may cover product or material requirements over a six-month or one-year period with the vendor making deliveries weekly or sometimes even more frequently. Often with blanket contracts, the amount to be delivered each time period will be determined at a future date. This model differs from our previous discussion of batch sizes because it includes a continual usage rate d. If we let d denote a constant demand rate (or usage rate) for an item in production and p is the production rate of the process that produces the item, we may develop the following total cost equation (obviously, the production rate must exceed the demand or usage rate; otherwise Q would be infinite, resulting in continual production):

$$TC = DC + (D/Q)S + (Q/2)H$$

However, with this model, as seen in Exhibit 16.4, Q is not the maximum inventory on hand, because we are consuming the product as it is being delivered over time. Thus, the above equation is rewritten as follows:

$$TC = DC + (D/Q)S + (I_{\max}/2)H \tag{16.4}$$

and

$$I_{\max} = (p - d)(Q/p) \tag{16.5}$$

where $(p - d)$ is the amount of inventory that accumulates each time period and (Q/p) is the number of time periods required to fill the order. Substituting, we have

$$TC = DC + \frac{D}{Q}S + \frac{(p - d)QH}{2p}$$

Exhibit 16.4

Fixed-Order-Quantity Model with Usage during Production Time

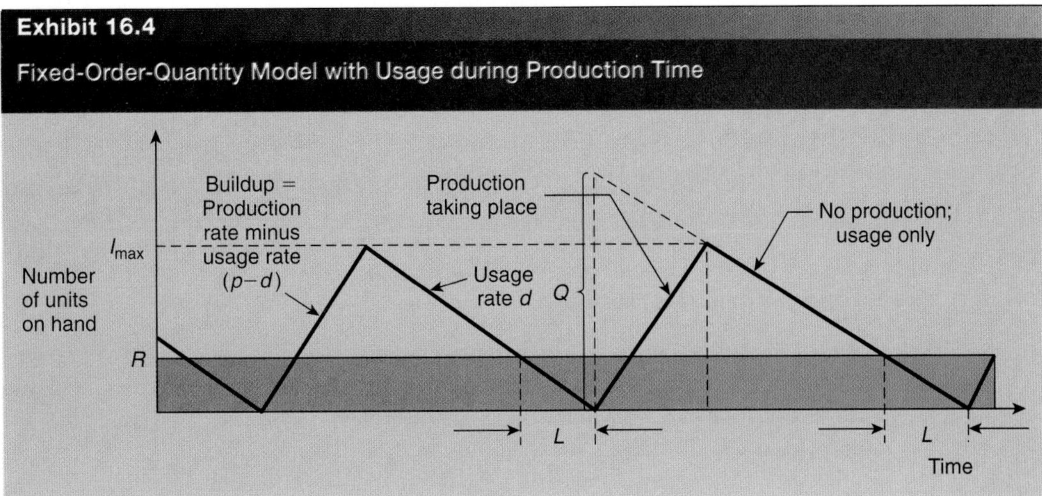

Again differentiating with respect to Q and setting the equation equal to zero, we obtain

$$\text{EOQ} = \sqrt{\frac{2DS}{H} \cdot \frac{p}{(p-d)}} \tag{16.6}$$

This model is shown in Exhibit 16.4. We can see that the maximum number of units on hand is always less than the order quantity, Q. Note in Equation 16.6, that as p becomes very large, the right-hand term $(p/(p-d))$ approaches one and we have our original EOQ formula.

Example

Product X is a standard item in a firm's inventory. Final assembly of the product is performed on an assembly line that is in operation every weekday. One of the components of product X (call it component X_1) is produced in another department. This department, when it produces X_1, does so at the rate of 100 units per day. The assembly line uses component X_1 at the rate of 40 units per day.

Given the following data, what is the optimal production lot size of component X_1? What is the reorder point?

Daily usage rate (d) = 40 units per day
Annual demand (D) = 10,000 (40 units per day × 250 working days)
Daily production (p) = 100 units per day
Cost of production setup (S) = \$50
Annual holding cost (H) = \$0.50 per unit per year
Cost of component X_1 (C) = \$7 each
Lead time (L) = 7 days

Solution

The optimal order quantity and the reorder point for component X_1 are calculated as follows:

$$\text{EOQ} = \sqrt{\frac{2DS}{H} \cdot \frac{p}{p-d}} = \sqrt{\frac{2(10{,}000)50}{0.50} \cdot \frac{100}{100-40}} = 1{,}826 \text{ units}$$

$$R = dL = 40(7) = 280 \text{ units}$$

This states that an order for 1,826 units of component X_1 should be placed when the level of inventory of X_1 stock drops to 280 units.

At 100 units per day, this run would take 18.26 days to complete and provide a 45.65-day supply for the assembly line (1,826/40). Theoretically, the producing department would be occupied with other work for the 27.39 days when component X_1 is not being produced.

Fixed-Time-Period Model

With a fixed-time-period model, inventory is counted at fixed intervals, such as every week or every month. Counting inventory and placing orders on a periodic basis are desirable for those situations when vendors make routine visits to customers and take orders for their complete line of products, or when buyers want to combine orders to save on transportation costs. Other firms operate on a fixed time period to facilitate planning their inventory count; for example, Distributor X calls every two weeks and employees therefore know that all of Distributor X's products must be counted at that time.

A convenient time interval can be chosen, or if only one item is involved it can be estimated by using the EOQ formula. Once the EOQ for the item is calculated, we can determine how many times a year we should place the order, from which we can then determine the period or interval between orders. For example, if the annual demand is 1,200 units and the EOQ is 100 units, then we know that we will place 12 orders throughout the year, and that there is a one-month interval between orders.

With a fixed-time-period model, there is usually a ceiling or *par* inventory that is established for each item. As seen in Exhibit 16.5, the difference between the par value and the quantity on hand when the count is taken is the amount ordered, which will vary from period to period, depending on the actual usage (e.g., Q_1, Q_2, and Q_3, in Exhibit 16.5). Here, negative inventory, as seen in the third cycle in Exhibit 16.5, is treated as a back order, which must be filled. Thus, in this model the time interval between orders remains fixed, but the quantity ordered varies, as compared to the fixed-order-quantity model where just the reverse is true: the order quantity remains fixed, but the time interval varies.

Exhibit 16.5

Fixed-Time-Period Inventory Model

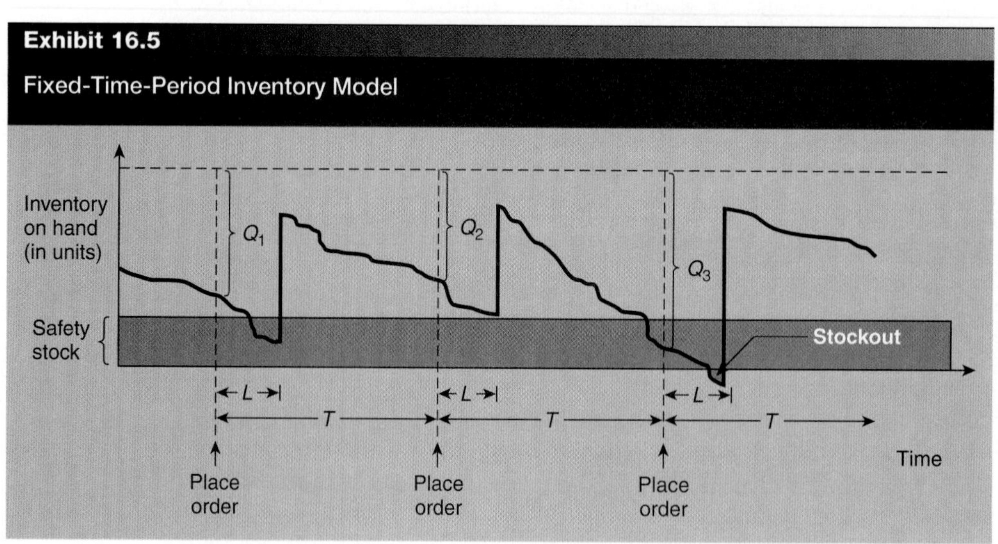

Quantity-Discount Model

quantity-discount model

Addresses price discounts associated with minimum order quantities.

The **quantity-discount model** takes into consideration the fact that the purchase cost of an item can vary with the order size. There are two types of quantity discounts: those given on an incremental basis and those given for all units. With the incremental approach, the quantity discount only applies to those units above a certain level. For example, the cost of a product is $65.00 per unit for quantities between 1 and 100 and $60.00 per unit for quantities over 100 units. We determine that we want to buy this product in quantities of 250 units at a time. With the incremental approach, we would pay $65.00 for the first 100 units and $60.00 for the remaining 150 units. With the all-units approach, which is presented here in detail, we would pay $60.00 apiece for all 250 units. Thus, the unit cost is determined by the size of the purchase order.

To determine the optimal quantity to order with this model, we first calculate the EOQ for each unit cost. (*Note:* If using H as a holding cost instead of i, then H will vary along with C.) If the resulting EOQs are all feasible, that is, the EOQs fall within their respective quantity ranges, then we select the EOQ that is associated with the lowest unit cost. However, as is more often the case, some of the EOQs may not be feasible (i.e., the quantity does not fall within the feasible unit-cost range). In these situations, we first calculate the total cost for each unit cost at the EOQ or EOQs where it is feasible. Where it is not feasible, we calculate the total cost at the minimum quantity where the respective unit cost is first applicable. These total costs are then compared and the quantity or EOQ associated with the lowest total cost is the order quantity that is selected.

Procedurally, the largest order quantity (lowest unit price) is solved first; if the resulting Q is valid or feasible, that is the answer. If not, the next largest order quantity (second lowest price) is derived. If that is feasible, the total cost of this Q is compared to the total cost of using the order quantity at the price break above, and the lowest total cost determines the optimal Q.

Example

Consider the following case, where

D = 10,000 units (annual demand)
S = $20 to place each order
i = 20 percent of cost (annual carrying costs, storage, interest, obsolescence, etc.)
C = Cost per unit:

Order Size (units)	Cost per Unit
0–499	C_1 = $5.00
500–999	C_2 = 4.50
1,000 and over	C_3 = 3.90

What quantity should be ordered?

Solution

The appropriate equations from the basic fixed-quantity model are

$$TC = DC + \frac{D}{Q}S + \frac{Q}{2}iC$$

and

$$Q = \sqrt{\frac{2DS}{iC}}$$

Exhibit 16.6

Total Cost Curves for a Quantity-Discount Model

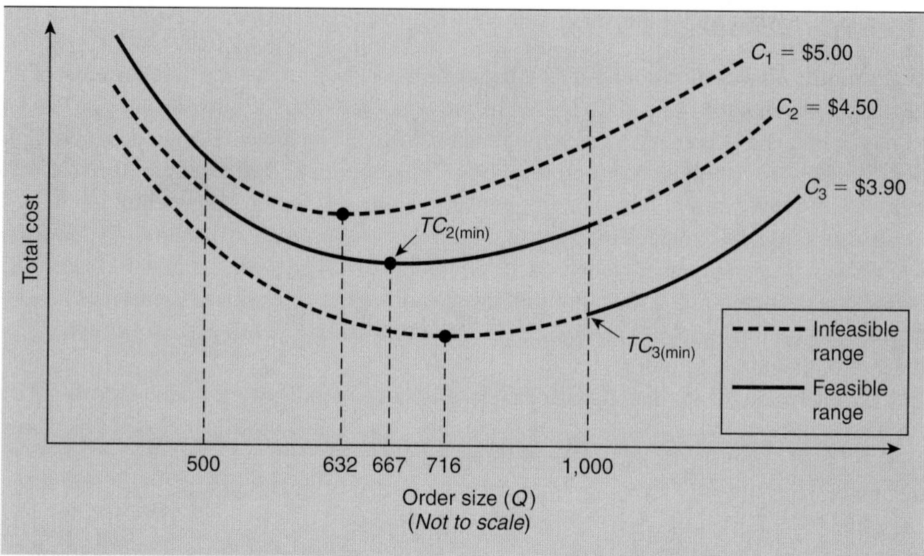

Exhibit 16.7

Total Cost Calculations in a Quantity-Discount Model

	Q = 667 where C = \$4.50	**Price Break 1,000**
Holding cost $\left(\frac{Q}{2}iC\right)$	$\frac{667}{2}(0.20)4.50 = \$300$	$\frac{1,000}{2}(0.20)3.90 = \$390$
Ordering cost $\left(\frac{D}{Q}S\right)$	$\frac{10,000(20)}{667} = \$300$	$\frac{10,000(20)}{1,000} = \$200$
Holding and ordering cost	\$600	\$590
Purchase cost (DC)	10,000(4.50)	10,000(3.90)
Total cost	$TC_{2(min)} = \$45,600$	$TC_{3(min)} = \$39,590$

Solving for the economic order size at each price, we obtain the following:

Range	**Unit Cost**	**EOQ**	**Feasible**
0–499	\$5.00	632	No
500–999	4.50	667	Yes
Over 1,000	3.90	716	No

These results are shown in Exhibit 16.6, which depicts the relationship between the total cost and the order quantity for each of the unit costs. Using the procedure described above, we now calculate the total cost for 666 units at \$4.50 per unit and 1,000 units at \$3.90 per unit. These calculations are shown in Exhibit 16.7. Comparing these two total costs, we conclude that the economic order quantity is 1,000 units.

One practical consideration in quantity-discount problems is that the cost reduction from volume purchases frequently makes it seemingly economical to order amounts larger than the EOQ. Thus, when applying the model we must be particularly careful to obtain a valid estimate of product obsolescence and warehousing costs.

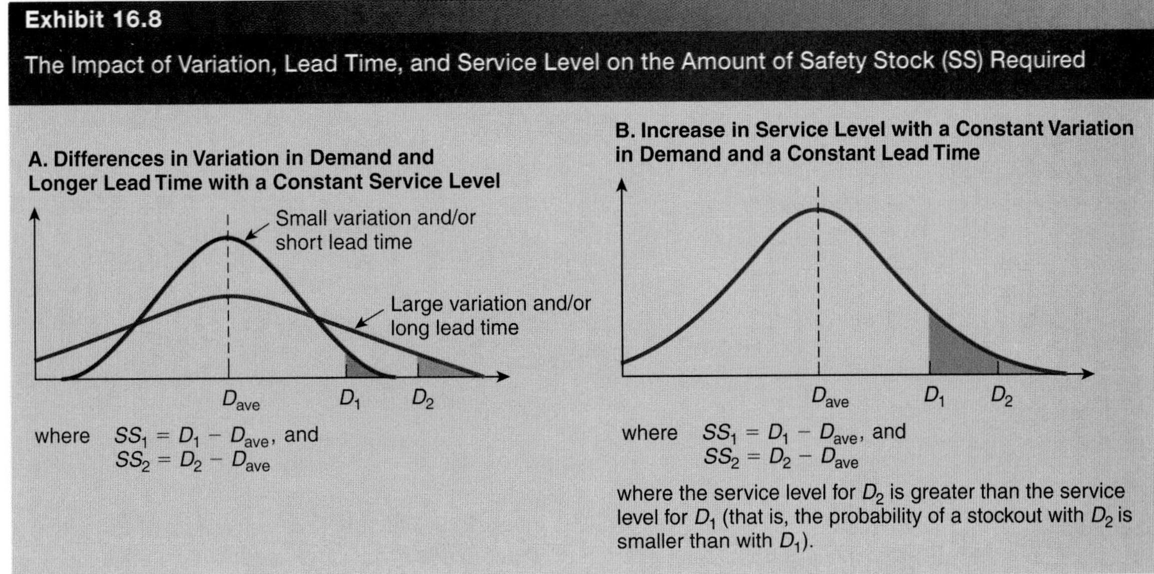
A. Differences in Variation in Demand and Longer Lead Time with a Constant Service Level
Small variation and/or short lead time
Large variation and/or long lead time
D_{ave} D_1 D_2
where $SS_1 = D_1 - D_{ave}$, and
$SS_2 = D_2 - D_{ave}$
B. Increase in Service Level with a Constant Variation in Demand and a Constant Lead Time
D_{ave} D_1 D_2
where $SS_1 = D_1 - D_{ave}$, and
$SS_2 = D_2 - D_{ave}$
where the service level for D_2 is greater than the service level for D_1 (that is, the probability of a stockout with D_2 is smaller than with D_1).

Exhibit 16.8

The Impact of Variation, Lead Time, and Service Level on the Amount of Safety Stock (SS) Required

Inventories and Service Levels

All of the inventory models presented thus far have assumed that the demand for an item is both constant and known. However, in most real-world environments, the demand for an item is not constant, but will vary from period to period (e.g., from day to day, from week to week). Consequently, in these situations it is necessary to build in a safety stock that takes into consideration this variation in demand. This safety stock is in addition to the average demand that is forecasted during the lead time.

The amount of safety stock (SS) that a firm should have for any given item is dependent on three factors: (*a*) the variation in demand, (*b*) the variability in the lead time required to replenish the item, and (*c*) the desired level of service that the company wants to provide its customers. Here, service level refers to the probability that all customer orders placed during the lead time will be filled from inventory and that customers will not have to wait because of a stockout. Thus, a 95 percent service level can be interpreted as a 95 percent probability that all customer orders placed during the lead time will be filled from on-hand inventory.

The larger the variation in demand, the larger the safety stock that is required. Similarly, the longer the lead time, the larger the safety stock that is required. A higher service level also translates into more safety stock. The impact of these three factors on the amount of safety stock that is required is shown in Exhibit 16.8.

Economic Order Quantity Models in Relation to the Real World

Recently, criticizing classical inventory models seems fashionable to some members of industry and consulting groups. Proportionately, there is much less open criticism from academia. In a manufacturing environment, the major weaknesses associated with the classical EOQ models focus on the numbers. These numbers are the values assigned to setup costs, holding costs, and demands used in the equations. These costs are often very difficult to

Exhibit 16.9

Effect of Reduced Setup Cost on Order Size and Total Cost

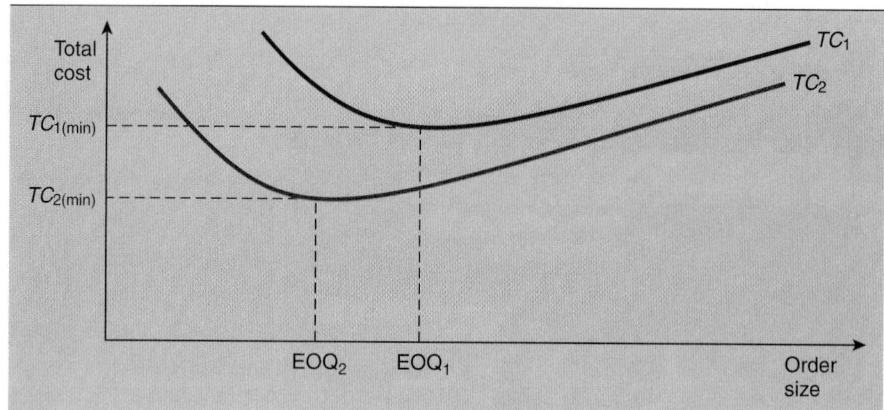

measure and, therefore, are error prone. Also, demand is rarely constant but instead is usually a fluctuating number.

Elliott Weiss states the problem nicely by explaining that many users of the equations focus on optimizing a set of numbers that often are taken as a given fact.[1] Rather, he states, we should be managing lot sizing and inventory control. The current moves toward reduced inventory costs and quantities, such as just-in-time systems, stress the importance of reducing lot sizes. The means to reducing lot sizes is to reduce setup time and cost. When smaller lots are run, holding cost is reduced. The point is to understand the logic and know where to apply it. The effect on order size resulting from reducing setup costs is shown in Exhibit 16.9. When the setup cost is reduced, the total cost curve shifts from TC_1 to TC_2. Correspondingly, the EOQ is reduced from EOQ_1 to EOQ_2 and the minimum total cost is reduced from $TC_{1_{min}}$ to $TC_{2_{min}}$.

Example

To illustrate the impact of reducing ordering or setup cost, we reduce the order cost in the example on page 611 from \$5.00 to \$1.00 and recalculate the EOQ and the total costs.

Solution

The optimal order quantity is now

$$\text{EOQ} = \frac{2DS}{H}$$

$$\text{EOQ} = \frac{2(1{,}000)(1.00)}{1.25} = 40.0 \text{ units} \quad \text{(versus 89.4 units in the original example)}$$

The total annual cost is now

$$TC = DC + \frac{D}{Q}S + \frac{Q}{2}H$$

$$TC = 1{,}000(12.50) + \frac{1{,}000}{40}(1.00) + \frac{40}{2}(1.25)$$

$$= \$12{,}550.00 \quad \text{(versus \$12,611.81 in the original example)}$$

[1]Elliot N. Weiss, "Lot Sizing Is Dead: Long Live Lot Sizing," *Production and Inventory Management Journal,* First Quarter 1990, pp. 76–78.

Perishable Inventory

While all inventories are subject to obsolescence, there are some products that are considered highly perishable in that they are only viable for a very short time period. After that period has elapsed, their value decreases significantly, and the reduced value is often only their salvage or scrap value. Examples of such products include newspapers and Christmas trees. In each case, the value of the product drops dramatically from one time period to the next. (In the case of newspapers, the time period is a day; in the case of Christmas trees, it is the month or so before Christmas.) The determination of the proper or "optimum" inventory level to establish for this group of products is often referred to as the **single-period inventory model.**

single-period inventory model

Addresses items that are highly perishable from one period to the next.

Single-Period Inventory Model

Certain characteristics are associated with products that fall into the single-period inventory model. These include (*a*) the product is only viable for sale during a single time period; (*b*) the demand for the product is highly variable, but follows a known probability distribution; and (*c*) the scrap value of the product or the value of the product after the time period has elapsed is less than the initial cost of the product.

The goal in determining the proper level of inventory for these products is to balance the gross profit generated by the sale of each unit with the cost incurred for each unit that is unsold after the time period has elapsed. Since the demand in these problems follows a probability distribution, we want to pick that level of inventory that maximizes our expected profit. When the probability distribution is discrete, we can solve the problem using an expected value matrix.

Example

Dick Moore sells Christmas trees, which he grows on his farm in upstate New York. Because bad weather and heavy snow are common in the month of December, Dick has always harvested by December 1 the trees he intends to sell in a given year. Dick has been selling trees for many years and has kept detailed records of sales in previous years. From these data, he has determined that the probability of selling various quantities of trees in a given year is as follows:

Demand (trees)	Probability
500	0.15
550	0.20
600	0.25
650	0.30
700	0.10

For the coming year, Dick will sell his trees for an average price of $25 each. His cost to grow and cut each tree is estimated to be $10. Any unsold trees at the end of the season can be sold for kindling wood at a price of $5 apiece. What is the optimal number of trees that Dick should harvest?

Solution

Using the above information, we develop the following payoff table to determine the net profit that will be generated for every combination of trees that are cut and customer demand (*Note:* profit, as defined here, also takes into account the opportunity cost associated with lost sales, which is not the strict definition by accounting standards):

Probability	0.15	0.20	0.25	0.30	0.10	
Customer Demand	500	550	600	650	700	
Number of Trees Cut						**Expected Profit**
500	7,500	6,750	6,000	5,250	4,500	$6,000
550	7,250	8,250	7,500	6,750	6,000	7,238
600	7,000	8,000	9,000	8,250	7,500	8,125
650	6,750	7,750	8,750	9,750	9,000	8,575
700	6,500	7,500	8,500	9,500	10,500	8,500

The values in the payoff table can be divided into three groups. In the first group, the number of trees cut exactly equals demand. The profit generated when this happens is

$$\text{Profit} = D(SP - C)$$

where

D = Demand

SP = Selling price per tree

C = Cost per tree

Thus, if we have a demand for 550 trees and we cut 550 trees, then the profit generated is

$$\text{Profit} = 550(25 - 10) = 550(15) = \$8,250$$

The second group consists of those combinations where demand exceeds the number of trees cut. Here we have to take into consideration the opportunity cost associated with the lost revenues resulting from unsatisfied demand. The profit generated in these cases is as follows:

$$\text{Profit} = Q(SP - C) - (D - Q)(SP - \text{C})$$

where

Q = Number of trees cut down

If we have a demand for 650 trees and we have harvested only 500 trees, then the resulting profit is

$$\begin{aligned}\text{Profit} &= 500(25 - 10) - (650 - 500)(25 - 10)\\ &= 500(15) - 150(15)\\ &= 7,500 - 2,250 = \$5,250\end{aligned}$$

The third case is when the quantity of trees we have harvested exceeds the demand. Here we have to sell off the excessive inventory at a loss. The net profit calculated is therefore as follows:

$$\text{Profit} = D(SP - \text{C}) - (Q - \text{D})(C - SV)$$

where

SV = scrap value

If we have harvested 700 trees and demand is only for 550 trees, then the profit generated is

$$\begin{aligned} \text{Profit} &= 550(25 - 10) - (700 - 550)(10 - 5) \\ &= 550(15) - (150)(5) \\ &= 8{,}250 - 750 = \$7{,}500 \end{aligned}$$

After we have determined all of the values in the payoff table, we next calculate the expected profit associated with each of the quantities of trees that we decide to harvest. This is done by multiplying the probability of each demand occurring by the profit generated by that demand. For example, if we decide to harvest 600 trees, then the expected profit from this decision is:

$$\begin{aligned} \text{Expected profit (600)} &= (0.15)(7{,}000) + (0.20)(8{,}000) + (0.25)(9{,}000) \\ &\quad + (0.30)(8{,}250) + (0.10)(7{,}500) \\ \text{EP(600)} &= 1{,}050 + 1{,}600 + 2{,}250 + 2{,}475 + 750 \\ \text{EP(600)} &= \$8{,}125 \end{aligned}$$

Finally, we select that quantity of trees to harvest that yields the maximum expected profit. In this case, Dick Moore should harvest 650 trees because the expected profit from that decision is $8,575, as shown in the table above.

Inventory Management in Services

In service operations, the "product" sold is considered highly perishable. As discussed in the previous chapter, hotel rooms that are unoccupied for one night cannot be saved for another night. Similarly, airline seats on a plane that are not used on a given date cannot be saved for use at a future time.

Yield Management or Revenue Management

Because the product sold in service operations is so perishable, the approach to managing the sale of the product is similar to that for the single-period inventory problem.

As discussed in Chapter 15, a service should have certain characteristics in order to take full advantage of yield management, including a cost structure that consists of high-fixed and low-variable costs. Examples of such services, as mentioned earlier, include airlines, hotels, and car rental companies. For these types of services, profits are directly related to sales because variable costs, as a percentage of sales, are very low. Consequently, the goal for these firms is to maximize sales or revenues by maximizing capacity utilization, even if it means selling some of the available capacity at reduced prices—as long as these prices are greater than the variable cost. For example, if the variable cost to clean and restock a hotel room with towels, soap, shampoo, and so forth is $25, then any room rate greater than $25 will contribute to profit. Thus, it would be better to let a hotel guest have the room for $50 for a night than to let the room remain empty, even if the regular or "rack" rate is $135 per night.

The challenge for managers of these types of services is to determine what percentage of available capacity to allocate to different prices. On the one hand, substantial amounts of capacity can usually be sold in advance at rates that are significantly discounted. For

Operations Management in Practice

THE APPLICATION OF YIELD MANAGEMENT AT AMERICAN AIRLINES

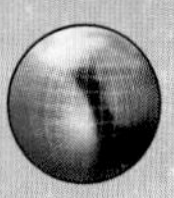

Yield management is widely used today in the airline industry to maximize revenues and profits. American Airlines was one of the first companies to use yield management to (*a*) establish prices, (*b*) determine for a given flight what percentage of capacity it should allocate to each price, and (*c*) determine the restrictions necessary to segment the markets. Listed below is a sampling of the different prices for a round-trip flight between Boston, Massachusetts, and London, England.

Fare	Season	Day of Week	Advanced Purchase (days)	Other Restrictions
$ 298	Low	Tue, Wed	0	Sat. night stay
$ 338	Low	Other Days	0	Sat. night stay
$ 548	Shoulder	Midweek	7	Sat. night stay
$ 597	Shoulder	Weekend	7	Sat. night stay
$ 824	High	Midweek	7	Sat. night stay
$ 884	High	Weekend	7	Sat. night stay
$ 2,920				Unrestricted coach
$ 7,538				Business class
$11,884				First class

Definitions:

Low season:	November 1–December 17 January 6–March 15
Shoulder season:	September 30–October 31 March 16–June 15
High season:	December 18–January 5 June 16–September 29
Midweek:	Monday–Thursday
Weekend:	Friday–Sunday

Source: Based on a telephone conversation on February 18, 2002 with "Timirra," a reservation agent with American Airlines.

example, airlines usually require a 21-day advance purchase for their super-saver fares, which offer the lowest prices; similarly, organizations holding conferences usually reserve hotel rooms years in advance of their meeting, again at substantially reduced rates.

At the same time, however, the service manager does not want to turn away a last-minute customer who usually pays the full rate because the capacity had been previously sold at a discounted rate. When this happens, opportunity costs are incurred. The methodology for determining the percentage of capacity to allocate to each market segment or price is referred to as yield management or revenue management. By using yield management, the service manager is simultaneously managing both the supply and demand for the firm's capacity. Demand is controlled by the different price structures: lower prices increase demand; higher prices decrease demand. Supply is controlled by limiting the capacity available at each of the different price structures.

As an illustration of how a service firm will use pricing to manage demand, the accompanying OM in Practice provides a sampling of the different airfares that American Airlines offers between Boston, Massachusetts, and London, England, and the restrictions associated with each airfare. It is important to note that while the level of service is significantly different for first class and business class passengers, the passengers receive the exact same level of service for all other fares. (In addition to these fares that are listed, there are frequently special fares from time to time when demand is lower than forecast.)

Example

Jacob and Evan Raser own a small hotel with 65 rooms in western Massachusetts. During the summer, there are many cultural activities going on in this region, including the Boston Symphony Orchestra at Tanglewood. The maximum room rate they charge during this time is $150 per night. However, while the hotel is usually sold out on weekends, it is never sold out during the week. From historical data, the two brothers have developed the following probability table with respect to the number of rooms occupied during a weeknight (i.e., Sunday through Thursday nights):

Number of Rooms Occupied	Probability
45	0.15
50	0.30
55	0.20
60	0.35

The variable cost to clean an occupied room is estimated to be $25. The two brothers have recently been approached by a group representing retired people who are on limited incomes. The group is doing a special promotion for their spring newsletter and want to include a hotel that would offer reduced room rates during the week if the retirees made reservations at least one month in advance. The group assures Jacob and Evan that if the rate was $95 per night, they could sell all the rooms available on a weekday night. How many rooms should Jacob and Evan allocate to this lower rate for weeknights?

Solution

As with the Christmas tree problem, we construct the following payoff table:

Probability	0.15	0.30	0.20	0.35	
Customer Demand	45	50	55	60	
Number of Rooms Available at $150					**Expected Profit**
45	7,025	6,750	6,475	6,200	$6,543.75
50	6,325	7,300	7,025	6,750	6,906.25
55	5,625	6,600	7,575	7,300	6,893.75
60	4,925	5,900	6,875	7,850	6,640.00

Similarly, as with the Christmas tree problem, the values in the payoff table can be divided into three groups. In the first group, the number of rooms that are reserved for full rate (i.e., $150/night) exactly equals demand. The profit generated when this happens is

$$\text{Profit} = D(SP - C) + (N - D)(DP - C)$$

where

D = Demand

SP = Standard room rate per night

DP = Discounted room rate per night

C = Variable cost to clean a room per night

N = Total number of rooms in the hotel

Thus, if we have a demand for 50 rooms and we allocate 50 rooms for the standard rate, then the profit generated is

$$\text{Profit} = 50(150 - 25) + (65 - 50)(95 - 25)$$
$$= 6{,}250 + 1{,}050 = \$7{,}300$$

The second group consists of those combinations where demand for the standard room rate exceeds the number of rooms allocated for this rate. Here we have to take into consideration the opportunity cost associated with the lost revenues resulting from unsatisfied demand at the standard rate, because the rooms were sold to the retirees at the discounted rate. Thus the opportunity cost is the difference between the standard rate and the discounted rate. The profit generated in these cases is as follows:

$$\text{Profit} = Q(SP - C) + (N - Q)(DP - C) - (D - Q)(SP - DP)$$

where

Q = Number of rooms allocated for the standard rate

If we have a demand for 60 rooms per night at the standard rate and we have allocated only 50 rooms, then the resulting profit is

$$\text{Profit} = 50(150 - 25) + (65 - 50)(95 - 25) - (60 - 50)(150 - 95)$$
$$= 6{,}250 + 1{,}050 - 550 = \$6{,}750$$

The third case is when the number of rooms we have allocated for the standard rate exceeds the demand. Here we have to take into account the opportunity cost of not selling the rooms earlier to the retirees. The net profit calculated is therefore as follows:

$$\text{Profit} = D(SP - C) + (N - Q)(DP - C) - (Q - D)(DP - C)$$

If we have reserved 60 rooms per night for the standard room rate and demand is only for 50 rooms, then the profit generated is

$$\text{Profit} = 50(150 - 25) + (65 - 60)(95 - 25) - (60 - 50)(95 - 25)$$
$$= 6{,}250 + 350 - 700 = \$5{,}900$$

After we have determined all of the values in the payoff table, we next have to calculate the expected profit that is associated with the number of rooms that we have reserved for the standard rate. This is calculated by multiplying the probability associated with each level of demand by the profit generated by that demand. For example, if we decide to allocate 55 rooms for the standard rate, then the expected profit from this decision is

$$\text{Expected profit } (55) = (0.15)(5{,}625) + (0.30)(6{,}600) + (0.20)(7{,}575) + (0.35)(7{,}300)$$

$$\text{EP}(55) = 843.75 + 1{,}980 + 1{,}515 + 2{,}555$$
$$= \$6{,}893.75$$

Finally, we select that amount of rooms to allocate for the standard rate that yields the maximum expected profit. In this case, Jacob and Evan should allocate 50 rooms a night during the week for the standard rate and provide the retiree group with 15 rooms a night because this decision provides the maximum expected profit of $6,906.25, as shown in the table above. Below is the Excel spreadsheet solution.

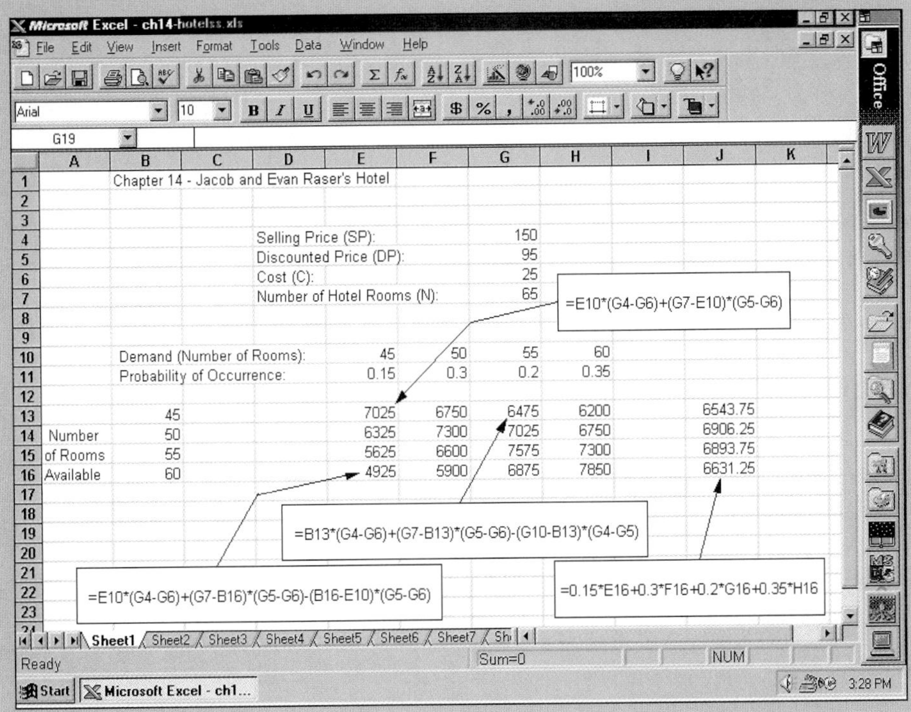

Additional Issues in Inventory Management

Determining Realistic Costs

Most inventory models give optimal solutions so long as the conditions of the system meet the constraints and/or assumptions of the model. While this is easy to state, it is difficult to implement. Obtaining actual order, setup, carrying, and shortage costs is often difficult—sometimes impossible. Part of the problem occurs because accounting data are usually averages, whereas to determine the proper lot sizes we need the marginal costs. Exhibit 16.10 compares the assumed smoothly ascending cost to the more realistic actual cost. For example, a corporate buyer is a salaried person. The marginal cost for the buyer's labor to place additional orders up to a full workload is zero. When another buyer is hired, it is a step function. (In theory, the marginal cost of the order that caused hiring the new buyer is the cost for the additional buyer.)

The same problem occurs in determining carrying costs. Warehouse costs, for example, may be close to zero if empty storage areas are available. Also, most companies only can estimate actual carrying costs, since they include obsolescence (a guess, at best), cost of capital (which depends on internal money available, alternate investment opportunities, and sources of new capital), and insurance costs (which may range from zero if current

Exhibit 16.10

Cost to Place Orders versus the Number of Orders Placed: Linear Assumption and Normal Reality

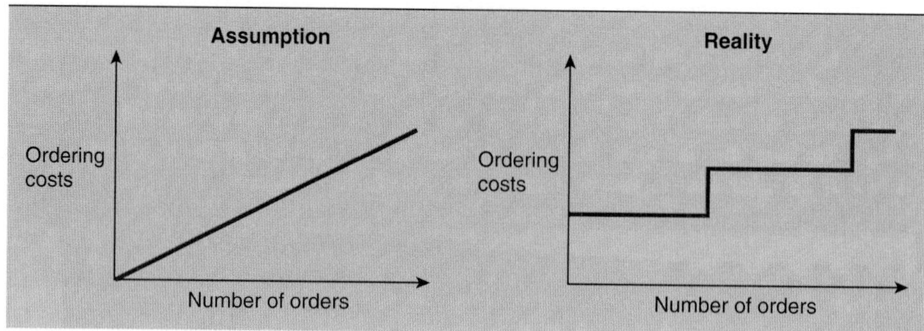

insurance premiums cover more than the assets on hand, to the cost of a new policy). It is therefore important that we take these circumstances into consideration when applying the inventory models presented in this chapter.

ABC Inventory Planning

ABC analysis

Method for grouping inventory items by dollar volume to identify those items to be monitored closely.

All inventory systems are plagued by two major problems: maintaining adequate control over each inventory item and ensuring that accurate records of stock on hand are kept. In this section, we present **ABC analysis**—an inventory system offering a control technique and inventory cycle counting that can improve record accuracy.

Maintaining inventory through counting, placing orders, receiving stock, and so on takes personnel time and costs money. When there are limits on these resources, as is most often the case, the logical move is to try to use the available resources to control inventory in the best way. In other words, focus on the most important items in inventory.

In the 18th century, Villefredo Pareto, in a study of the distribution of wealth in Milan, found that 20 percent of the people controlled 80 percent of the wealth. This logic of the few having the greatest importance and the many having little importance has been broadened to include many situations and is termed the *Pareto Principle.* This is true in our everyday lives, where most of the decisions we make are relatively unimportant but a few shape our future, and is certainly true in inventory systems, where a few items account for the bulk of our investment. (As noted earlier in Chapter 6, Pareto analysis is also used in quality management to identify the most frequent types of errors.)

Any inventory system must specify when an order is to be placed for an item and how many units to order. In most situations involving inventory control, there are so many items involved that it is not practical to model and give thorough treatment to each and every item. To get around this problem, the ABC classification scheme divides inventory items into three groupings: high dollar volume (A), moderate dollar volume (B), and low dollar volume (C). Dollar volume is a measure of importance; an item low in cost but high in volume can be more important than a high-cost item with low volume.

If the annual usage of items in inventory is listed according to dollar volume, generally the list shows that a small number of items account for a large dollar volume and that a large number of items account for a small dollar volume. Exhibitt 16.11 illustrates this relationship.

The ABC approach divides this list into three groupings by value: A items constitute roughly the top 15 percent of the items, B items the next 35 percent, and C items the last 50 percent. From observation, it appears that the list in Exhibit 16.11 may be meaningfully grouped with A including 20 percent (2 of the 10), B including 30 percent, and C including 50 percent. These points show clear delineations between sections. The result of this

Exhibit 16.11

Annual Usage of Inventory by Value

Item Number	Annual Dollar Usage	Percent of Total Value
22	$95,000	40.7%
68	75,000	32.1
27	25,000	10.7
03	15,000	6.4
82	13,000	5.6
54	7,500	3.2
36	1,500	0.6
19	800	0.4
23	425	0.2
41	225	0.1
	$233,450	100.0%

Exhibit 16.12

ABC Grouping of Inventory Items

Classification	Item Number	Annual Dollar Usage	Percent of Total Value	Percent of Total Items
A	22, 68	$170,000	72.8%	20%
B	27, 03, 82	53,000	22.7	30
C	54, 36, 19, 23, 41	10,450	4.5	50
		$233,450	100.0%	100%

segmentation is shown in Exhibit 16.12. In this example, 20 percent of the items account for 72.8 percent of the value of the inventory.

Segmentation may not always occur so neatly. The objective, though is to try to separate the important from the unimportant. Where the lines actually break depends on the particular inventory under question and on how much personnel time is available (with more time a firm could define larger A or B categories).

The purpose of classifying items into groups is to establish the appropriate degree of control for each item. On a periodic basis, for example, Class A items may be more clearly controlled with weekly ordering, B items may be ordered biweekly, and C items may be ordered monthly or bimonthly. Note that the unit cost of items is not related to their classification. An A item may have a high dollar volume through a combination of either low cost and high usage or high cost and low usage. Similarly, C items may have a low dollar volume either because of low demand or low cost. In an automobile service station, for example, gasoline would be an A item with daily tabulation, tires, batteries, oil, grease, and transmission fluid may be B items and ordered every two to four weeks; and C items would consist of valve stems, windshield wiper blades, radiator caps, hoses, fan belts, oil and gas additives, car wax, and so forth. C items may be ordered every two or three months or even be allowed to run out before reordering since the penalty for stockout is not serious.

Sometimes, an item may be critical to a system if its absence creates a sizable loss. In this case, regardless of the item's classification, sufficiently large stocks should be kept on hand to prevent runout. One way to ensure closer control is to designate this item as an A or a B item, forcing it into the category even if its dollar volume does not warrant such inclusion.

Inventory Accuracy

Every production system must have agreement, within some specified range, between what the record says is in inventory and what actually is in inventory. There are many reasons records and inventory may not agree. For example, having an open stockroom area allows items to be removed for both legitimate and unauthorized purposes. The legitimate removal may have been done in a hurry and simply not recorded. Sometimes parts are misplaced, turning up months later. Parts often are stored in several locations, but records may be lost or the location recorded incorrectly. Sometimes stock replenishment orders are recorded as received, when in fact they never were. Occasionally, a group of parts is recorded as having been removed from inventory, but the customer order is canceled and the parts are replaced in inventory without canceling the record. To keep the production system flowing smoothly without parts shortages and efficiently without excess balances, it is important that inventory records are accurate.

Current Trends in Inventory Management

As noted in the opening vignette, managers in leading-edge companies recognize that inventory really isn't an asset, but rather a liability. Consequently, the average amount of inventory that these firms have on hand relative to their annual sales has been going down in recent years, even though in many cases the number of products they make has increased.

Firms have been able to reduce their inventories for several reasons. First, companies have focused their efforts on reducing setup or order costs. The lower these costs, the smaller the economic order quantities. In addition, companies are working much closer now with their vendors. Through these relationships, product throughput times and thus lead times have been reduced significantly, again reducing the need to carry inventory. Finally, through advances in technology, many companies, like Dell Computer, are now building to order rather than to stock, thereby totally eliminating finished goods inventories.

Conclusion

This chapter introduces the two main categories of inventory demand: independent (referring to the external demand for a firm's end product) and dependent (usually referring to the demand within the firm for items created because of the demand for more complex items of which they are a part). Most industries have items in both categories. In manufacturing, for example, independent demand is common for finished products, service and repair parts, and operating supplies; and dependent demand is common for those parts and materials needed to produce the end product. In wholesale and retail sales of consumer goods, most demand is independent—each item is an end item, with the wholesaler or retailer doing no further assembly or fabrication.

We also introduce the single-period inventory model for those products that are highly perishable. We then extend this model to discuss yield management, which provides service operations with a methodology to maximize their revenues.

In this chapter we also emphasize that inventory reduction requires a knowledge of the operating system. It is not simply a case of selecting an inventory model off the shelf and plugging in some numbers. In the first place, the model might not be appropriate. In the second place, the numbers might not be relevant. It is also important to understand that inventory management is no longer a trade-off or compromise. (Very often determining order quantities is referred to as a trade-off problem; that is, trading off holding costs for setup costs. Today companies want to reduce both.)

The simple fact is that firms typically have very large investments in inventory, and the cost to carry this inventory runs from 30 to 35 percent and more of the inventory's worth annually. Therefore, a major goal of most firms today is to reduce inventory; they expect this also to lead to improved quality and performance, and to greatly reduce cost.

Key Formulas

Q model

Total annual cost for an order quantity Q, an annual demand D, a per-unit cost C, setup cost S, and an annual per-unit holding cost H.

$$TC = DC + \frac{D}{Q}S + \frac{Q}{2}H \tag{16.1}$$

Q model

Optimum or economic order quantity.

$$\text{EOQ} = \sqrt{\frac{2DS}{H}} \tag{16.2}$$

Q model

Reorder point is based upon an average demand of $\bar{d}$ units per time period (e.g., days, weeks) and lead time L (stated in the same units of time as the demand).

$$R = \bar{d}L \tag{16.3}$$

Q model with usage

Total annual cost for an order quantity Q, an annual demand D, with a maximum inventory on hand of $I_{\max}$, a per-unit cost C, setup cost S, and an annual per-unit holding cost H.

$$TC = DC + (D/Q)S + (I_{\max}/2)H \tag{16.4}$$

Q model with usage

Maximum inventory on hand for an order quantity Q, production rate of p units per time period, and usage rate of d units per time period.

$$I_{\max} = (p - d)(Q/p) \tag{16.5}$$

Q model with usage

Optimum or economic order quantity when items are produced at a rate of p units per time period and are used at a rate of d units per time period.

$$\text{EOQ} = \sqrt{\frac{2DS}{H} \cdot \frac{p}{(p - d)}} \tag{16.6}$$

Key Terms

ABC analysis p. 626
economic order quantity (EOQ) p. 610
fixed-order-quantity model with usage p. 612
quantity-discount model p. 615
single-period inventory model p. 619
types of demand p. 607
- dependent demand p. 607
- independent demand p. 607

types of inventory p. 604
- finished goods p. 604
- raw material p. 604

work-in-process (WIP) p. 604
types of inventory systems p. 607
- fixed-order-quantity model p. 607
- fixed-time-period model p. 607

Review and Discussion Questions

1. Distinguish between dependent and independent demand in a McDonald's, in an integrated manufacturer of personal copiers, and in a pharmaceutical supply house.
2. Distinguish between work-in-process inventory, safety-stock inventory, and seasonal inventory.
3. Discuss the nature of the costs that affect inventory size.
4. Under which conditions would a plant manager elect to use a fixed-order-quantity model as opposed to a fixed-time-period model? What are the disadvantages of using a fixed-time-period ordering system?
5. There is a current trend to reduce inventories. How is this being accomplished and what is the impact of lower inventories to the firm, its suppliers, and its customers?
6. Discuss the general procedure for determining the order quantity when quantity discounts are involved. Would there be any differences in the procedure if holding costs were a fixed percentage of item cost rather than a constant amount?
7. What two basic questions must be answered by an inventory-control decision rule?
8. Discuss the assumptions that are inherent in production setup cost, ordering cost, and carrying costs. How valid are they?
9. "The nice thing about inventory models is that you can pull one off the shelf and apply it so long as your cost estimates are accurate." Comment.
10. Which type of inventory system would you use in the following situations?
    a. Supplying your kitchen with fresh food.
    b. Obtaining a daily newspaper.
    c. Buying gasoline for your car.
11. Why is it desirable to classify items into groups, as the ABC classification scheme does?
12. In addition to airlines, hotels, and car rental firms, what other types of services would be appropriate for yield management?
13. Call up a hotel and ask about their room rates for weekdays, weekends, high season, and low season. Explain the logic for these prices.

Solved Problems

Problem 1

Items purchased from a vendor cost $20 each, and the forecast for next year's demand is 1,000 units. If it costs $5 every time an order is placed for more units and the carrying cost is $4 per unit per year, what quantity should be ordered each time?

a. What is the total ordering cost for a year?

b. What is the total carrying cost for a year?

Solution

The quantity to be ordered each time is

$$\text{EOQ} = \sqrt{\frac{2DS}{H}} = \sqrt{\frac{2(1{,}000)5}{4}} = 50 \text{ units}$$

a. The total ordering cost for a year is

$$\frac{D}{Q}S = \frac{1{,}000}{50}(\$5) = \$100$$

b. The carrying cost for a year is

$$\frac{Q}{2}H = \frac{50}{2}(\$4) = \$100$$

Problem 2

A department store sells (among other things) sports shirts for casual wear. Mr. Koste is in charge of the men's department, and knows that the annual demand for one of these shirts is fairly constant at 250 shirts per year. These shirts are obtained only from the manufacturer, who charges a delivery fee of \$65, regardless of the number of shirts delivered with that order. In addition, in-house costs associated with each order total \$6.

The manufacturer charges \$16.25 per shirt, but is willing to lower the price by 3 percent per shirt if the department store will order at least 2 gross (288) each time. Of course, this means that some shirts must be kept in inventory, and the holding costs have been estimated at 8.5 percent per year.

Should Mr. Koste recommend that the department store accept the offer of the quantity discount?

Solution

$$D = 250$$
$$S = 65 + 6 = \$71$$
$$H = iC$$
$$i = 0.085$$
$$C = \$16.25$$
$$Q = \sqrt{\frac{2DS}{iC}} = \sqrt{\frac{(2)(250)(71)}{(0.085)(16.25)}} \approx 160$$

As 160 < 288, compute

$$TC(160) = (16.25)(250) + \left(\frac{250}{160}\right)(71) + \left(\frac{160}{2}\right)(0.085)(16.25)$$
$$= \$4{,}283.94$$

and

$$TC(288) = [(0.97)(16.25)(250)] + \left(\frac{250}{288}\right)(71) + \left(\frac{288}{2}\right)(0.085)[(0.97)(16.25)]$$
$$= \$4{,}195.19$$

Since the total cost at 288 is lower than that at 160, accept the discount.

Problem 3

Elkin Shoes, Inc. (ESI), is a manufacturing firm that produces a variety of shoes and boots. They have recently started operation of a factory in the United States and have opened a factory outlet store adjacent to the factory. The production manager at the factory is trying to ascertain the optimal number of sheepskin boots to produce with each production run. After careful analysis, he believes that the following data are correct:

Annual demand for the boots: 12,000 pairs

Days/year the outlet store is open: 240

Daily production capacity of the factory: 200 pairs

Setup cost incurred to start boot production: $800

Annual storage cost per pair of boots: $60

What should the production manager recommend as the optimal production lot size?

Solution

D = Annual demand = 12,000

d = Daily demand = 12,000/240 = 50

p = Daily production = 200

S = Setup cost = $800

H = Holding cost = $60

$$Q = \sqrt{\frac{2DS}{H} \cdot \left(\frac{p}{p-d}\right)} = \sqrt{\frac{(2)(12000)(800)}{60} \cdot \left(\frac{200}{200-50}\right)} \approx 653$$

Problems

1. Annual demand for an item is 2,500 units. The cost to place an order is $5, and holding cost is 20 percent per annum of the cost of the item. Items have the following cost schedule:

1 to 99	$10.00 each
100 to 199	$ 9.80 each
200 and over	$ 9.60 each

   What is the economic order quantity (EOQ)?

2. Demand for an item is 1,000 units per year. Each order placed costs $10; the annual cost to carry items in inventory is $2 each.
   a. In what quantities should the item be ordered?
   b. Suppose a $100 discount on each order is given if orders are placed in quantities of 500 or more. Should orders be placed in quantities of 500, or should you stick to the decision you made in *a*?

3. Item X is a standard item stocked in a company's inventory of component parts. Each year, the firm, on a random basis, uses about 2,000 of Item X, which costs $25 each. Annual storage costs, which include insurance and cost of capital, amount to $5 per unit of average inventory. Every time an order is placed, it costs $10.
   a. Whenever Item X is ordered, what should the order size be?
   b. What is the annual cost for ordering Item X?
   c. What is the annual cost for storing Item X?

4. A particular raw material is available to a company at three different prices, depending on the size of the orders, as follows:

Less than 100 pounds	$20 per pound
100 pounds to 999 pounds	$19 per pound
1,000 pounds and more	$18 per pound

The cost to place an order is $40. Annual demand is 3,000 units. Holding (or carrying) cost is 25 percent per annum.

What is the economic order quantity to buy each time?

5. In the past, Taylor Industries has used a fixed-time inventory system that involved taking a complete inventory count of all items each month. However, increasing labor costs are forcing Taylor Industries to examine alternate ways to reduce the amount of labor involved in inventory stockrooms without increasing other costs, such as shortage costs.

The following table is a random sample of 20 of Taylor's items.

Item Number	Annual Usage	Item Number	Annual Usage
1	$ 1,500	11	$13,000
2	12,000	12	600
3	2,200	13	42,000
4	50,000	14	9,900
5	9,600	15	1,200
6	750	16	10,200
7	2,000	17	4,000
8	11,000	18	61,000
9	800	19	3,500
10	15,000	20	2,900

a. What would you recommend Taylor do to cut back its labor cost? (Illustrate using an ABC plan.)

b. Item 15 is critical to continued operations. How would you recommend it be classified?

6. Magnetron, Inc., manufactures microwave ovens for the commercial market. Currently, Magnetron is producing part 2104 in its fabrication shop for use in the adjacent unit assembly area. Next year's requirement for part 2104 is estimated at 20,000 units. Part 2104 is valued at $50 per unit, and the combined storage and handling cost is $8 per unit per year. The cost of preparing the order and making the production setup is $200. The plant operates 250 days per year. The assembly area completes 80 units per day, every working day, and the fabrication shop produces 160 units per day when it is producing part 2104.

   a. Compute the economic order quantity.

   b. How many orders will be placed each year?

   c. If part 2104 could be purchased from another firm with the same costs as described, what would the order quantity be? (The order is received all at once.)

   d. If the average lead time to order from another firm is 10 working days and a safety stock level is set at 500 units, what is the reorder point?

7. Garrett Corporation, a turbine manufacturer, operates its plants on an 18-hour day, 300 days a year. Titanium blades can be produced on its turbine blade machine number 1 (TBM1) at a rate of 500 per hour, and the average usage rate is 5,000 per day. The blades cost $15 apiece, and carrying costs are $0.10 per day per blade because of insurance, interest on investments, and space allocation. TBM1 costs $250 to set up for each run. Lead time requires production to begin after stock drops to 500 blades. What is the optimal production run for TBM1?

8. Alpha Products, Inc., is having a problem trying to control inventory. There is insufficient time to devote to all its items equally. Following is a sample of some items stocked, along with the annual usage of each item expressed in dollar volume.

Item	Annual Dollar	Item	Annual Dollar
a	$ 7,000	k	$80,000
b	1,000	l	400
c	14,000	m	1,100
d	2,000	n	30,000
e	24,000	o	1,900
f	68,000	p	800
g	17,000	q	90,000
h	900	r	12,000
i	1,700	s	3,000
j	2,300	t	32,000

Can you suggest a system for allocating inventory control time? Specify where each item from the list would be placed.

9. CU, Incorporated (CUI), produces copper contacts that it uses in switches and relays. CUI needs to determine the order quantity Q to meet the annual demand at the lowest cost.

   The price of copper depends on the quantity ordered. Following are the price-break data and other relevant data for the problem:

Price of copper	$0.82 per pound up to 2,499 pounds $0.81 per pound for orders between 2,500 and 4,999 pounds $0.80 per pound for orders greater than 5,000 pounds
Annual demand	50,000 pounds per year
Holding cost	20 percent per year
Ordering cost	$30

   Which quantity should be ordered?

10. DAT, Inc., produces digital audiotapes to be used in the consumer audio division. DAT doesn't have sufficient personnel in its inventory supply section to closely control each item stocked, so you have been asked to determine an ABC classification. The following shows a sample from the inventory records:

Item	Average Monthly Demand	Price per Unit
1	700	$6.00
2	200	4.00
3	2,000	12.00
4	1,100	20.00
5	4,000	21.00
6	100	10.00
7	3,000	2.00
8	2,500	1.00
9	500	10.00
10	1,000	2.00

    Develop an ABC classification for these 10 items.

11. Mike Coggins, owner of Bagel Maker bakery, is trying to decide how many bagels he should make each morning. He currently sells fresh bagels for $5.25 per dozen. Any bagels that are left over at the end of the day are sold the next day as "yesterday's bagels" for $3.00 per dozen. Mike estimates that the material and labor to make a

dozen bagels is $3.75. To help him decide how many bagels to make each morning, he has collected the following information based on historical data:

	Dozens of Bagels Sold						
	12	14	16	18	20	22	24
	Probability						
Weekdays (Monday–Friday)	.15	.25	.25	.20	.15	.00	.00
Weekends (Saturday–Sunday)	.05	.15	.15	.25	.20	.15	.05

a. How many dozens of bagels should Mike make weekday mornings?

b. How many dozens of bagels should Mike make on weekend mornings?

12. Sonia Groves owns a parking lot in downtown Boston with 100 spaces. She can offer an "early bird" special for $12.00 a day and she knows she can attract as many customers who work in downtown Boston as she is willing to allocate parking spaces at this low daily rate. The hourly rate that she charges is $6.00 and the average customer stays for about 3½ hours. Sonia has collected the following data on how many parking spaces a day she has had occupied at the hourly rate:

Parking spaces	65	70	75	80	85
Probability	.15	.20	.25	.30	.10

If we assume that only one hourly customer per day occupies a given parking space, how many spaces should Sonia allocate for the early bird special in order to maximize her profits?

Bibliography

Anderson, Edward J. "Testing Feasibility in a Lot Scheduling Problem." *Operations Research,* November–December 1990, pp. 1079–89.

Bernhard, Paul. "The Carrying Cost Paradox: How Do You Manage It?" *Industrial Engineering,* November 1989, pp. 40–46.

Davis, Samuel G. "Scheduling Economic Lot Size Production Runs." *Management Science,* August 1990, pp. 985–99.

Fitzsimmons, James, and Mona Fitzsimmons. *Service Management: Operations, Strategy, and Information Technology.* New York: McGraw-Hill, 1998.

Fogarty, Donald W.; John H. Blackstone; and Thomas R. Hoffmann. *Production and Inventory Management.* 2nd ed. Cincinnati, OH: South-Western Publishing, 1991.

Freeland, James R.; John P. Leschke; and Elliott N. Weiss. "Guidelines for Setup Reduction Programs to Achieve Zero Inventory." *Journal of Operations Management,* January 1990, pp. 75–80.

Harris, Ford Whitman. "How Many Parts to Make at Once." *Operations Research,* November–December 1990, pp. 947–51.

Kimes, Sheryl E. "Yield-Management: A Tool for Capacity-Constrained Service Firms." *Journal of Operations Management* 8, no. 4 (1989).

Teach, Edward. "The Great Inventory Correction." *CFO,* September 2001, pp. 58–62.

Tersine, Richard J. *Principles of Inventory and Materials Management.* 3rd ed. New York: North-Holland, 1988.

Vollmann, T. E.; W. L. Berry; and D. C. Whybark. *Manufacturing Planning and Control Systems.* 3rd ed. Homewood, IL: Richard D. Irwin, 1992.

Weiss, Elliott N. "Lot Sizing Is Dead: Long Live Lot Sizing." *Production and Inventory Management Journal,* First Quarter 1990, pp. 76–78.

Young, Jan B. *Modern Inventory Operations: Methods for Accuracy and Productivity.* New York: Van Nostrand Reinhold, 1991.

17 Inventory Systems for Dependent Demand

Chapter Objectives

- Explain the changing role of materials requirements planning (MRP) within a manufacturing organization.
- Discuss the role of MRP within an enterprise resource planning (ERP) system.
- Introduce the fundamental concepts and calculations that drive an MRP system.
- Define the various elements that make up an MRP system.
- Demonstrate how MRP-related systems are applied in service operations.
- Recognize that MRP and JIT can be used together within an organization.

Merck Frosst Canada & Co., a division of Merck and Company, produces a wide variety of high-quality pharmaceutical products. Shortly after implementing an MRP II software system, management recognized the need to focus on becoming a Class A manufacturing company in order to achieve manufacturing excellence. To accomplish this, managers began in 1998 to work closely with the Ollie Wight Company, an MRP consulting firm. As a result of this effort, Merck Frosst Canada & Co. was able to achieve Class A excellence very quickly, and with very impressive results, some of which included

- On-time delivery increased over a three-year period from 75 percent to 98 percent.
- Supplier delivery performance increased from 75 percent to 85 percent.
- Manufacturing cycle time was dramatically reduced.
- Inventories were reduced from an average of 5.3 months to 3.9 months.

Source: Provided courtesy of the Oliver Wight Companies, New London, NH.

Managerial Issues

When we are dealing with end products, such as automobiles, refrigerators, and personal computers, the inventory models presented in the previous chapter are often applicable. This is especially true when the demand for these types of products are considered to be independent and relatively constant throughout the year. However, there is another category of products: the subassemblies and components that go into these end products. For this group of products, the demand is not independent, but rather, it is dependent on the demand for the end products in which they are used. For example, the demand for automobile tires is dependent on the demand for cars. Similarly, the demand for keyboards is dependent on the demand for personal computers. In both cases, once the demand for the end product has been established, be it cars or PCs, the demand for the components used in these products can be determined easily. To address the inventory issues that are associated with these types of products, a concept known as **materials requirements planning (MRP)** is used.

MRP was originally designed as a stand-alone system that operated almost exclusively within the manufacturing or operations function of a company. Today, an MRP system is often integrated into an enterprise resource planning (ERP) system, which is typically organizationwide. In essence, as shown in the comparison between Exhibits 17.1 and 17.2, what MRP initially did for manufacturing, in terms of integrating all of the various operational elements, ERP is now doing across all of the functions within an organization.

Over the years, the role of MRP has changed significantly. Initially, MRP was used primarily for shop-floor control within the company. Today, many of the leading-edge manufacturing firms, however, use JIT for shop-floor control and utilize MRP to determine the subassembly and component requirements that are supplied by vendors, as shown in Exhibit 17.3. With continuous emphasis on reducing both inventories and lead times, the need for accurate information, in terms of the quantities of individual items required and their respective due dates, is more important today than ever before. And this type of information is readily provided with MRP.

MRP systems, in part or in whole, are used in manufacturing firms both large and small. The reason is that MRP provides a logical and readily understandable approach to the problem of determining the number of parts, components, and raw materials needed to produce each end item. MRP also provides the time schedule specifying when each of these materials, parts, and components should be ordered or produced.

The original MRP planned only materials. However, as computer power and speed increased over the past 20 or so years and applications expanded, so did the breadth of MRP. Soon it considered resources as well as materials; now MRP also stands for *manufacturing resource planning (MRP II),* which will be discussed later in this chapter.

Exhibit 17.1

The Role of MRP within the Manufacturing Function

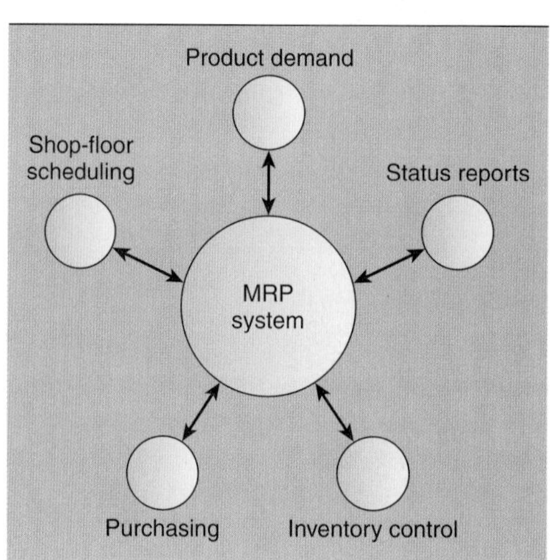

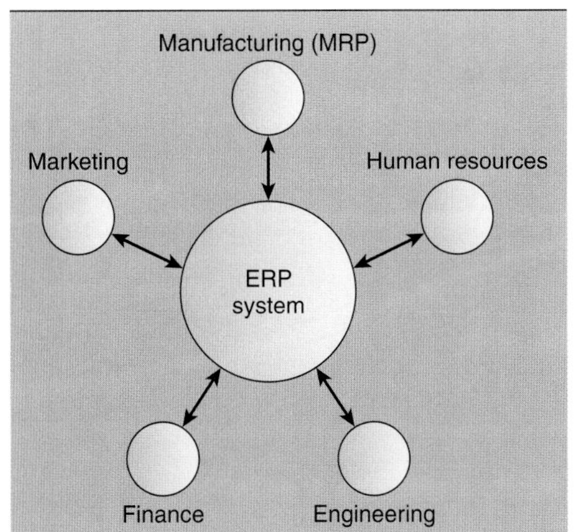

Exhibit 17.2

The Role of MRP within an ERP System

Master Production Schedule

The aggregate production plan, as presented in Chapter 15, specifies product groups. It does not specify exact items. The next level down in the planning process after the development of the aggregate plan is the master production schedule. The **master production schedule (MPS)** is the time-phased plan specifying how many and when the firm plans to build each specific end item. For example, the aggregate plan for a furniture company may specify the total volume of mattresses it plans to produce over the next month or next quarter. The MPS then goes to the next step down in the process and identifies the specific models and sizes of the mattresses. All the mattresses sold by the company would be specified by the MPS. The MPS also states period by period (which is usually weekly) how many and when each of these mattress types is needed.

master production schedule (MPS)

Production plan that specifies how many of, and when to build, each end item.

materials requirements planning (MRP)

Determines the number of subassemblies, components, and raw materials required and their build dates to complete a given number of end products by a specific date.

Still further down the disaggregation process is the MRP program, which calculates the requirements and schedules for all of the raw materials, parts, and supplies needed to make each of the different mattresses that are identified in the MPS.

Time Fences

The question of flexibility within an MPS depends on several factors, including production lead time, the commitment of parts and components to a specific end item, the relationship

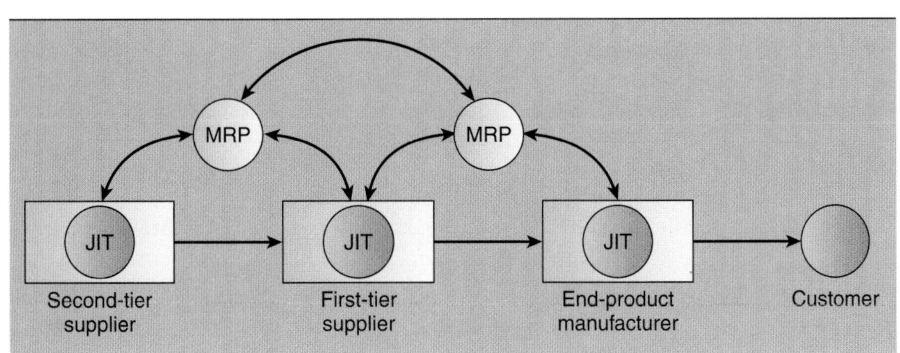

Exhibit 17.3

Integrating MRP and JIT into the Supply Chain

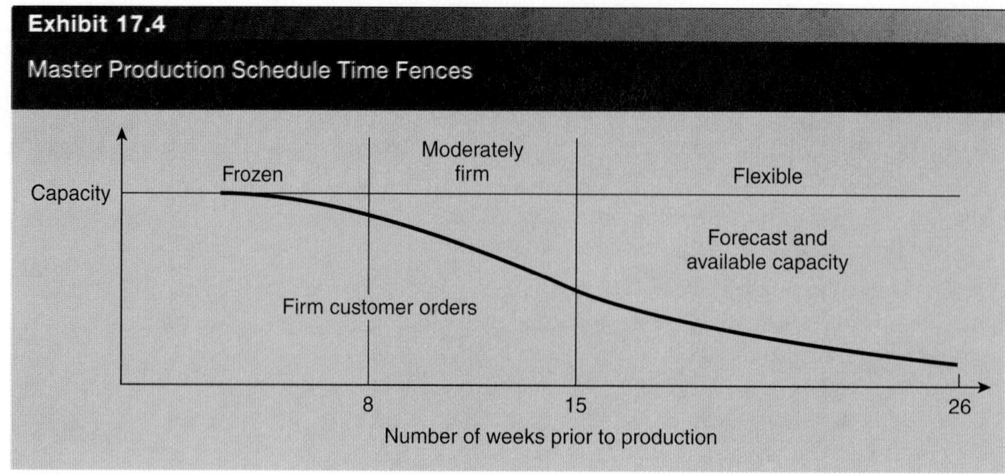

between the customer and supplier, the amount of excess capacity, and the reluctance or willingness of management to make changes.

Exhibit 17.4 shows an example of a master production schedule time fence. Management defines *time fences* as periods of time, with each period having some specified level of opportunity for the customer to make changes. (The customer may be the firm's own marketing department, which may be considering product promotions, broadening variety, etc.) Note in the exhibit that for the next eight weeks the MPS for this particular firm is frozen. Each firm has its own time fences and operating rules. Under these rules, *frozen* could be defined as anything from absolutely no changes in one firm to only the most minor of changes in another. *Moderately firm* may allow changes in specific products within a product group, so long as parts are available. *Flexible* may allow almost any variations in products, with the provision that capacity remains about the same and that there are no long lead-time items involved.

The purpose of time fences is to maintain a reasonably controlled flow through the production system. Unless some operating rules are established and adhered to, the system could be chaotic and filled with overdue orders and constant expediting.

With the trend towards reducing lead times and increasing product choices, companies are continuously trying to reduce the time period within which the MPS is frozen without wreaking havoc on the factory floor. This allows firms to react more quickly to changes in customer demand. To accomplish this, the overall quantity of products within a product group or family is typically frozen while the mix of products, within the group or family, in terms of specific models, remains flexible up until the last minute.

Materials Requirements Planning (MRP) Systems

Using an MPS that is derived from an aggregate plan, a *materials requirements planning (MRP)* system then creates the requirements and schedules for identifying the specific parts, components, and materials that are necessary to produce the end products that have been ordered. Included here are the exact numbers of each item that is needed and the dates when orders for these items should be released and be received or completed within the production cycle. Today's MRP systems use a computer program to carry out these operations. Most firms have used computerized inventory systems for years, but they were independent of the scheduling system; MRP now links these two elements together.

Materials requirements planning is not new in concept. Logic dictates that the Romans probably used it in their construction projects, the Venetians in their shipbuilding, and the Chinese in building the Great Wall. Building contractors always have been forced into planning for material to be delivered when needed and not before, because of space limitations. What is new is the larger scale and the more rapid changes that can be made through the use of computers. Now firms that produce many products involving thousands of parts and materials can take advantage of MRP.

Purposes, Objectives, and Philosophy of MRP

The main purposes of an MRP system are to control inventory levels, assign operating priorities to items, and plan capacity to load the production system. These may be briefly expanded as follows:

Inventory

Order the right part.

Order the right quantity.

Order at the right time.

Priorities

Order with the right due date.

Keep the due date valid.

Capacity

Plan for a complete load.

Plan an accurate load.

Plan for an adequate time to view future load.

The *theme* of MRP is "getting the right materials to the right place at the right time."

The *objectives* of inventory management under an MRP system are to improve customer service, minimize inventory investment, and maximize production operating efficiency.

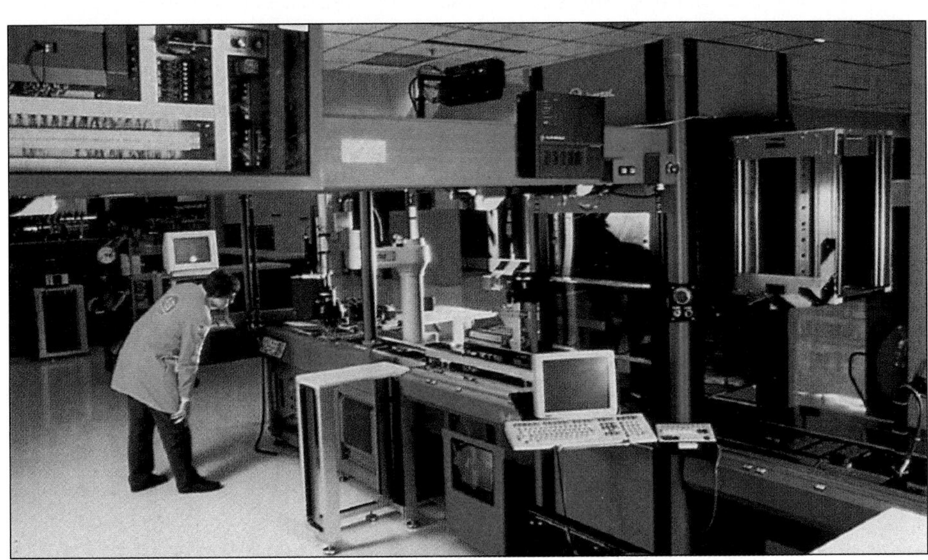

The MRP system at Allen-Bradley, a manufacturer of circuit boards, receives an order and schedules appropriate production. Board panels are automatically routed to the required process, such as this robotic cell that inserts nonstandard components.

The *philosophy* of materials requirements planning is that materials should be expedited (hurried) when their lack would delay the overall production schedule and de-expedited (delayed) when the schedule falls behind and postpones their need. Traditionally, and perhaps still typically, when an order is behind schedule, significant effort is spent trying to get it back on schedule. However, the opposite is not always true; when an order, for whatever reason, has its completion date delayed, the appropriate adjustments are not made in the schedule. This results in a one-sided effort—late orders are expedited, but early orders are not de-expedited or delayed. Aside from perhaps using scarce capacity, it is preferable not to have raw materials and work in process before they are actually needed, because inventories tie up capital, clutter up stockrooms, delay the introduction of design changes, and prevent the cancellation or delay of existing orders.

Benefits of an MRP System

Manufacturing companies with more than $10 million in annual sales are most likely to have some form of a computerized MRP system. A computerized system is necessary because of the sheer volume of materials, supplies, and components that are part of expanding product lines, and the speed that firms need to react to constant changes in the system. When firms switched from existing manual or computerized systems to an MRP system, they realized many benefits, including

- More competitive pricing.
- Lower selling price.
- Lower inventory levels.
- Improved customer service.
- Faster response to market demands.
- Increased flexibility to change the master schedule.
- Reduced setup and tear-down costs.
- Reduced idle time.

In addition, the MRP system

- Gives advanced notice so managers can see the planned schedule before the orders are actually released.
- Tells when to de-expedite as well as expedite.
- Delays or cancels orders.
- Changes order quantities.
- Advances or delays order due dates.
- Aids capacity planning.

In converting to an MRP system, many firms claimed as much as 40 percent reductions in inventory investment. (See OM in Practice Box.)

Where MRP Can Be Used

MRP is being used in a variety of industries with a job-shop environment (meaning that a number of products are made in batches using the same production equipment). The list in Exhibit 17.5 includes process industries, but note that the processes mentioned are confined

Operations Management in Practice

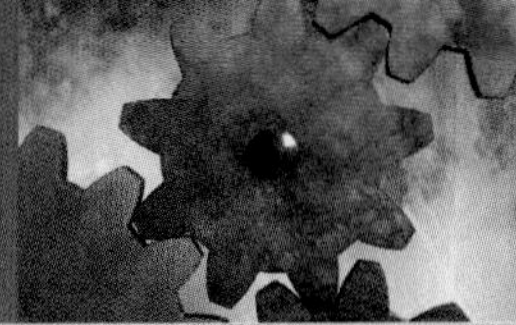

CLASS A PERFORMANCE COMPANIES REAP SIGNIFICANT BENEFITS FROM MRP

Those firms that have achieved excellence in implementing MRP are designated Class A companies. Listed below are several Class A companies and the benefits they have achieved.

Company	Product	Benefits from MRP
Allergan America Puerto Rico	Pharmaceuticals	Inventory reduced from 87 to 49 days Supplier on-time delivery up from 43 percent to 99 percent On-time customer deliveries up from 40 percent to 100 percent
The Clarkson Company Sparks, Nevada	Industrial valves	Reduced inventories 30 percent for a $500,000 savings Improved forecast accuracy to more than 90 percent Reduced lead time from 6–8 weeks to 2 weeks
Kraft Food Limited Melbourne, Australia	Foods	Inventories reduced from $9 million to $6 million On-time deliveries improved from 40 percent to 100 percent Finished goods inventories reduced by 18 percent

Source: Provided courtesy of the Oliver Wight Companies, New London, NH.

Exhibit 17.5

Industry Applications and Expected Benefits

Industry Type	Examples	Expected Benefits
Assemble-to-stock	Combines multiple component parts into a finished product, which is then stocked in inventory to satisfy customer demand. Examples: watches, tools, appliances.	High
Fabricate-to-stock	Items are manufactured by machine rather than assembled from parts. These are standard stock items carried in anticipation of customer demand. Examples: piston rings, electrical switches.	Low
Assemble-to-order	A final assembly is made from standard options that the customer chooses. Examples: trucks, generators, motors.	High
Fabricate-to-order	Items manufactured by machine to customer order. These are generally industrial orders. Examples: bearings, gears, fasteners.	Low
Manufacture-to-order	Items fabricated or assembled completely to customer specification. Examples: turbine generators, heavy machine tools.	High
Process	Industries such as foundries, rubber and plastics, specialty paper, chemicals, paint, drug, food processors.	Medium

to job runs that alternate output products and do not include continuous processes such as petroleum or steel.

As you can see in the exhibit, MRP is most valuable to companies involved in assembly operations and least valuable to those in fabrication. Another factor that affects the degree of benefit gained from an MRP system is the number of levels in the product. The greater the number of levels, the greater the benefit of MRP.

One more point to note: MRP typically does not work well in companies that produce a low number of units annually. This is especially true for companies producing complex expensive products requiring advanced research and design. Under such circumstances, experience has shown that lead times tend to be too long and too uncertain, and the product configuration too complex for MRP to handle. These types of companies need the control features that network scheduling techniques offer, and thus would be better off using project scheduling methods (covered previously in Chapter S3).

MRP System Structure

The MRP system most closely interacts with the MPS schedule, the bill of materials file, the inventory records file, and the output reports. Exhibit 17.6 shows a portion of Exhibit 15.1 in Chapter 15 with several additions. Note that capacity is not addressed here, nor are there any feedback loops to higher levels. We discuss these elements later in this chapter under MRP II and capacity requirements planning.

Each facet of Exhibit 17.6 is subsequently explained in more detail, but essentially the MRP system works as follows: Forecasted sales and firm orders for products are used to create an MPS, which states the number of items to be produced during specific time periods. A bill of materials file identifies the specific materials used to make each item and the correct quantities of each. The inventory records file contains data such as the number of units on hand and on order. These three sources—(*a*) the MPS, (*b*) the bill of materials file, and (*c*) the inventory records file—become the data sources for the MRP program, which

Exhibit 17.6

Overall View of the Inputs to a Standard Materials Requirements Planning Program and the Reports Generated by the Program

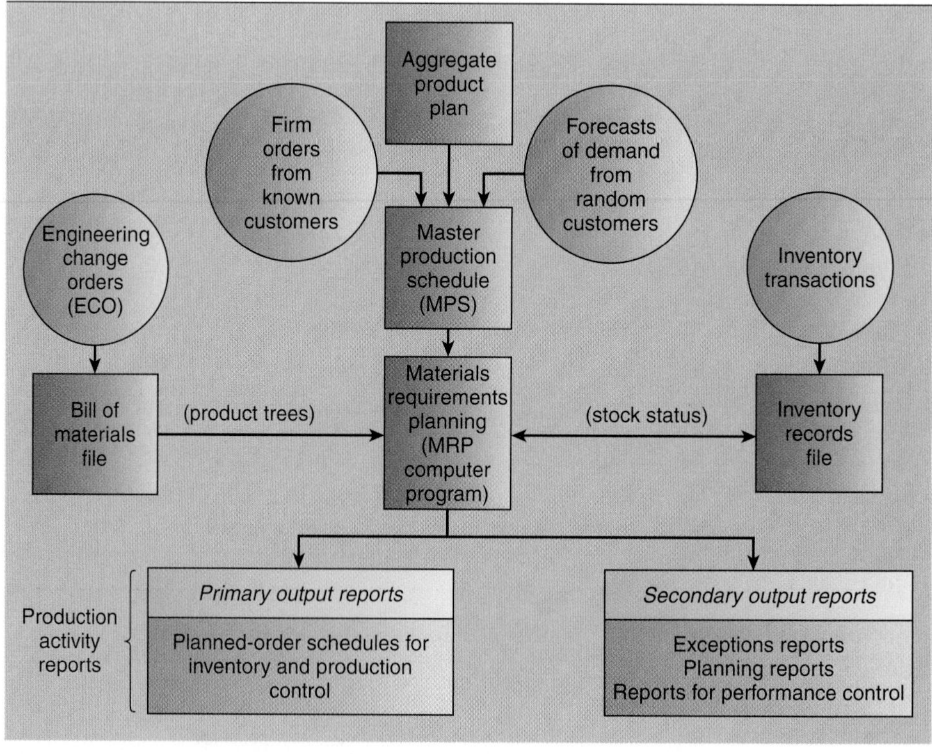

essentially expands or "explodes" the MPS into a detailed order scheduling plan for the entire production sequence.

Demand for Products

As stated earlier, the demand for end items is primarily derived from two sources: The first is known customers who have placed specific orders, such as those generated by sales personnel, or from interdependent transactions. These orders usually carry promised delivery dates. There is no forecasting involved in these orders—we simply add them up. The second source is forecasted demand. These are the normal independent-demand orders; the forecasting models presented in Chapter 9 can be used to predict the quantities. The demand from both the known customers and the forecast demand are used as inputs for developing the MPS.

Available-to-Promise When a firm manufactures products to meet a projected sales forecast, the MPS also can provide information on the quantities and dates when specific products and models will be available for delivery. The quantities and delivery dates of these products that have not been previously committed are often referred to as *available-to-promise*. As an illustration, a firm has scheduled to build 100 units of a given product during the first week of February, of which 35 are to meet specific customer orders and the remaining 65 are to meet forecasted customer orders. However, at a given point in time, for example, the third week in January, the marketing department has already taken orders for 40 of the 65 that are to be built to forecast. This leaves 25 units that are available-to-promise for delivery during that week.

Demand for Spare Parts and Supplies In addition to the demand for end products, customers also order specific parts and components as spare parts to provide for service and repair. These demands for items less complex than the end product are not usually part of the MPS; instead, they are fed directly into the MRP program at their appropriate levels. That is, they are added in as a gross requirement for that part or component.

Bill of Materials File

The **bill of materials (BOM)** file contains the complete product description, listing not only the materials, parts, and components but also the sequences in which the product is created.

bill of materials (BOM)

A list of subassemblies, components, and raw materials, and their respective quantities, required to produce specific end items.

The BOM file is often referred to as the *product structure* or *product tree file* because it shows how a product is put together. It identifies each item and the quantity used per unit of the item in which it is used. To illustrate this, consider the product tree for Product A, as shown in Exhibit 17.7. Product A consists of two units of Part B and three units of Part C. Part B consists of one unit of Part D and four units of Part E. Each Part C consists of two units of Part F, five units of Part G, and four units of Part H. In the past, BOM files often have listed subassemblies and parts as indented files. This clearly identifies each item and the manner in which it is assembled because each indentation signifies the components of the item. A comparison of the indented files in Exhibit 17.8 with the item structure in Exhibit 17.7 shows the ease of relating the two displays. From a computer standpoint, however, storing items in indented parts lists is very inefficient. To compute the amount of each item needed at the lower levels, each item would have to be expanded ("exploded") and summed. A more efficient procedure is to store parts data in a single-level explosion. That is, each item and component is listed showing only its parent and the number of units

Exhibit 17.7

Product Structure Tree for Product A

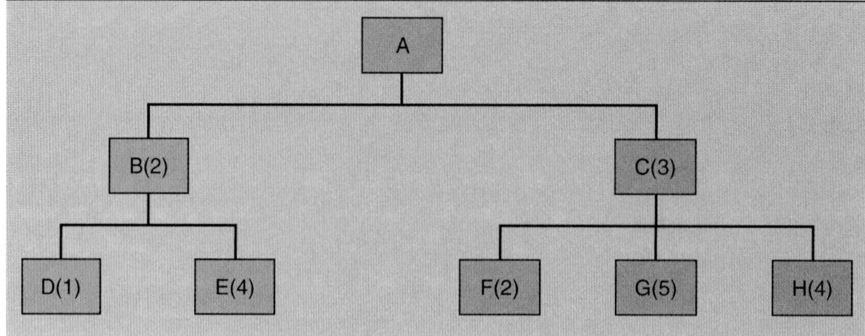

Exhibit 17.8

Subassemblies and Parts List in an Indented Format and in a Single-Level List

Subassemblies and Indented Parts List			Single-Level Subassemblies and Parts List	
A			A	
	B(2)			B(2)
		D(1)		C(3)
		E(4)	B	
	C(3)			D(1)
		F(2)		E(4)
		G(5)	C	
		H(4)		F(2)
				G(5)
				H(4)

needed per unit of its parent. This avoids duplication because it includes each assembly only once. Exhibit 17.8 shows a comparison between the single-level list and the indented list for Product A.

A data element (called a *pointer* or *locator*) also is contained in each file to identify the parent of each part and allow a retracing upward through the process.

Low-Level Coding If all identical parts occur at the same level for each end product, the total number of parts and materials needed for a product can be easily computed. However, consider Product L shown in Exhibit 17.9a. Notice that Item N in Product B, for example, occurs both as an input to L and as an input to M. Item N therefore needs to be lowered to level 2 (Exhibit 17.9b) to bring all the Ns down to their lowest common level. This is referred to as *low-level coding*. When all identical items are placed at the same level, it becomes a simple matter for the computer to scan across each level and summarize the number of units of each item required. Similarly, Items S and T are lowered to level 4.

inventory records file

Computerized record-keeping system for the inventory status of all subassemblies, components, and raw materials.

Inventory Records File

The **inventory records file** in a computerized system can be quite lengthy. Each item in inventory is carried as a separate file, and the range of details carried about an item is almost limitless. Although Exhibit 17.10 is from an earlier version of MRP, it shows the variety of information contained in the inventory records files. The MRP program accesses the *status* segment of the file according to specific time periods (called *time buckets* in MRP slang). These files are accessed as needed during the program run.

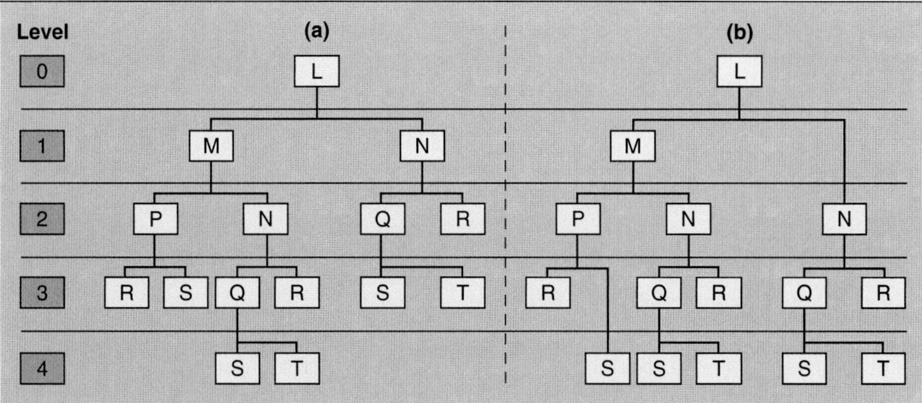

Exhibit 17.9

Product L Hierarchy in (a) Expanded to the Lowest Level of Each Item in (b)

Item master data segment	Part No.	Description	Lead time	Std. cost	Safety stock
	Order quantity	Setup	Cycle	Last year's usage	Class
	Scrap allowance	Cutting data	Pointers	Etc.	
Inventory status segment	Allocated	Control balance	Period 1 2 3 4 5 6 7 8	Totals	
	Gross requirements				
	Scheduled receipts				
	On hand				
	Planned order releases				
Subsidiary data segment	Order details				
	Pending action				
	Counters				
	Keeping track				

Exhibit 17.10

The Inventory Status Record for an Item in Inventory

The MRP program performs its analysis from the top of the product structure downward, exploding requirements level by level. There are times, however, when it is desirable to identify the parent item that caused the materials requirement. The MRP program allows the creation of a *peg record* file either separately or as part of the inventory record file. Pegging requirements allows us to retrace a materials requirement upward in the product structure through each level, identifying each parent item that created the demand.

Inventory Transactions File The inventory status file is kept up to date by posting inventory transactions as they occur. These changes are a result of stock receipts and disbursements, scrap and obsolescence losses, wrong parts, canceled orders, and so forth.

MRP Computer Program

The MRP program operates on the inventory file, the MPS, and the BOM file. It works as follows: A list of end items needed by time periods (or time "buckets") is specified by the

MPS. A description of the materials and parts needed to make each item is specified in the BOM file. The number of units of each item and material currently on hand and on order are contained in the inventory file. The MRP program "works" on the inventory file (which is segmented into time periods), while continually referring to the BOM file to compute the quantities of each item needed. The number of units of each item required is then adjusted for on-hand amounts and amounts previously ordered; the net requirements are then "offset" (set back in time) to allow for the lead time needed to obtain the material and/or to make the items.

If the MRP program being used does not consider capacity constraints, the master scheduler must manually perform some capacity balancing. Through an iterative process, the master scheduler feeds a tentative MPS into the MRP program (along with other items requiring the same resources) and the output is examined for production feasibility. The MPS is then adjusted to try to correct any imbalances, and the program is executed again. This process is repeated until the output is acceptable. Although it would seem to be a simple matter to have the computer simulate various schedules that take into consideration resource limitations, in reality it is usually a very large and very time-consuming problem.

To further complicate the problem today, there is often not one MPS but a number of them. Firms will frequently divide the scheduling work among the schedulers by assigning one master scheduler for each major product line. As a result, each master scheduler must compete for limited resources for his or her own product line. As a group, however, they are trying to balance resource usage and due dates for the production system as a whole.

Output Reports

Because the MRP program has access to the BOM file, the MPS, and the inventory records file, outputs or reports can take on an almost unlimited range of format and content. These reports are usually classified as *primary* and *secondary* output reports. (With the expansion of MRP into MRP II, many additional reports are available.)

Primary Reports Primary reports are the main or normal reports used for inventory and production control. These reports include

1. *Planned orders* to be released at a future time.
2. *Order release notices* to execute the planned orders.
3. *Changes in due dates* of open orders due to rescheduling.
4. *Cancellations or suspensions* of open orders due to cancellation or suspension of orders on the MPS.
5. *Inventory status data.*

Secondary Reports Additional reports, which are optional in an MRP program, fall into the following main categories:

1. *Planning reports* to be used, for example, in forecasting inventory and specifying requirements over some future time horizon.
2. *Performance reports* for purposes of pointing out inactive items and determining the agreement between actual and programmed item lead times and between actual and programmed quantity usage and costs.
3. *Exceptions reports* that point out serious discrepancies, such as errors, out-of-range situations, late or overdue orders, excessive scrap, or nonexistent parts.

A Simple MRP Example

To demonstrate how the various elements of an MRP system are integrated, we present a simple problem to demonstrate how quantities are calculated, lead times are offset, and order releases and receipts are established.

Bill of Materials (Product Structure Tree) File

Suppose that we want to produce Product T, which consists of two parts U, three parts V, and one part Y. Part U, in turn, is made of one part W and two parts X. Part V is made of two parts W and two parts Y. Exhibit 17.11 shows the product structure tree for Product T.

Inventory Records File

Next, we need to consider the lead times needed to obtain these items, that is, either to produce the parts internally or to obtain them from an outside vendor. Assume that the lead times to make the parts and their respective on-hand inventories and scheduled receipts are as follows:

Part	Lead Time (weeks)	On-Hand Inventory	Scheduled Receipts*
T	1	25	—
U	2	5	5
V	2	15	—
W	3	30	—
X	2	20	—
Y	1	10	—

*Subassemblies or parts that have been previously ordered but are not scheduled for delivery until a future date (week three for subassembly U in this example).

Running the MRP Program

If we know when Product T is required, we can create a time schedule chart specifying when all the material necessary to build T must be ordered and received to meet this requirement. Using a lot-for-lot ordering policy, Exhibit 17.12 shows which items are needed and when. We thus have created a materials requirements plan based on the demand for Product T and the knowledge of how T is made, current inventories on hand, and the time needed to obtain each part.

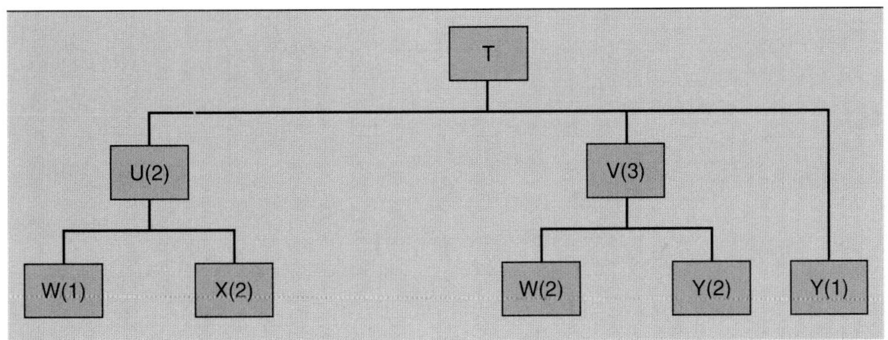

Exhibit 17.11 Product Structure Tree for Product T

Exhibit 17.12

Materials Requirements Plan for Completing 100 units of Product T in Period 8

Part No. T	1	2	3	4	5	6	7	8	9
Gross requirements								100	
Scheduled receipts									
On-hand inventory: 25								25	
Net requirements								75	
Planned order releases							75		

Part No. U	1	2	3	4	5	6	7	8	9
Gross requirements							150		
Scheduled receipts			5				5		
On-hand inventory: 5							5		
Net requirements							140		
Planned order releases					140				

Part No. V	1	2	3	4	5	6	7	8	9
Gross requirements							225		
Scheduled receipts									
On-hand inventory: 15							15		
Net requirements							210		
Planned order releases					210				

Part No. W	1	2	3	4	5	6	7	8	9
Gross requirements					560				
Scheduled receipts									
On-hand inventory: 30					30				
Net requirements					530				
Planned order releases		530							

Part No. X	1	2	3	4	5	6	7	8	9
Gross requirements					280				
Scheduled receipts									
On-hand inventory: 20					20				
Net requirements					260				
Planned order releases			260						

Part No. Y	1	2	3	4	5	6	7	8	9
Gross requirements					420		75		
Scheduled receipts									
On-hand inventory: 10					10				
Net requirements					410		75		
Planned order releases				410		75			

From this simple illustration, it should be obvious that manually developing a materials requirements plan for thousands or even hundreds of items would be impractical—a great deal of computation is needed, and a tremendous amount of data must be available about the inventory status (number of units on hand, on order, and so forth) and about the product structure (how the product is made and how many units of each material are required). A computer is an integral part of every MRP system. However, our emphasis in this chapter is on understanding the general structure of the system and on the supporting computer files that are required because the underlying logic of the program is essentially the same as that for our simple example.

Generally, the MPS, which is the primary driver of the MRP system, deals with finished products or end items. If the end item is quite large and/or quite expensive, the MPS, however, may schedule major subassemblies or components instead.

All production systems have limited capacity and limited resources. This presents a challenge for the master scheduler. Exhibit 17.13 shows the environment in which the master scheduler works. While the aggregate plan provides the general range of operation, the master scheduler must massage the aggregate plan into an MPS that specifies exactly what is to be produced. These decisions are made while responding to pressures from various functional areas.

To determine an acceptable schedule that is feasible for the shop, trial master production schedules are run through the MRP program in an iterative process. The resulting planned order releases (the detailed production schedules) are reviewed to ensure that resources are available and the completion times are reasonable. What may appear to be a feasible MPS may, in fact, require excessive resources when the resource requirements for the materials, parts, and components for the lower levels are determined. If this occurs (which is usually the case), the MPS is then adjusted to reflect these limitations and the MRP program is run again. To ensure good master scheduling, the master scheduler (i.e., the human being) must

- Include all demands from product sales, warehouse replenishment, spares, and interplant requirements.
- Never lose sight of the aggregate plan.
- Be involved with customer order promising.

Exhibit 17.13

The Environment of the Master Scheduler

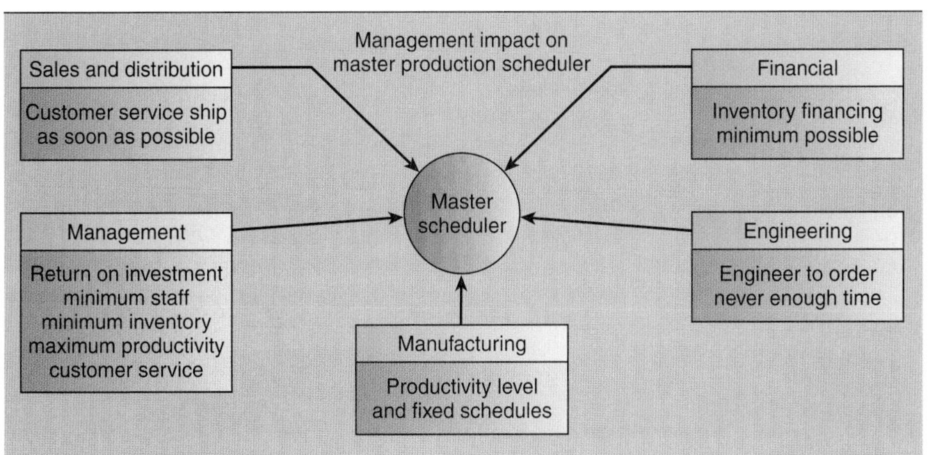

Source: Romeyn C. Everdell and Woodrow W. Chamberlain, "Master Scheduling in a Multi-Plant Environment," *Proceedings of the American Production and Inventory Control Society* (1980), p. 421. Reprinted with permission.

Exhibit 17.14

The Aggregate Plan and the Master Production Schedule for Mattresses

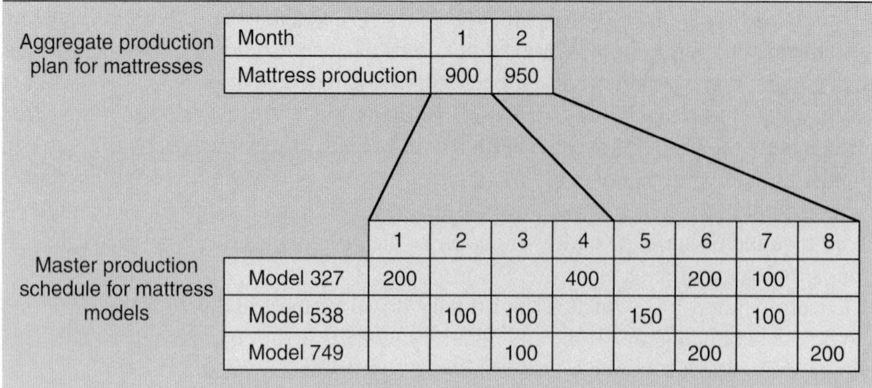

Aggregate production plan for mattresses
Month 1 2
Mattress production 900 950
1 2 3 4 5 6 7 8
Master production schedule for mattress models
Model 327 200 400 200 100
Model 538 100 100 150 100
Model 749 100 200 200

- Be visible to all levels of management.
- Objectively trade off manufacturing, marketing, and engineering conflicts.
- Identify and communicate all problems.

Exhibit 17.14 illustrates the relationship between an aggregate plan and its master production schedule. The upper portion of the exhibit shows an aggregate plan for the total number of mattresses planned per month for a furniture manufacturer, without regard to mattress type. The lower portion of the exhibit shows an MPS specifying the exact type of mattress and the quantity planned for production by week. The next level down (not shown) would be the MRP program that develops detailed schedules showing when cotton batting, springs, and hardwood are needed to make the mattresses.

Capacity Requirements Planning (CRP)

In the previous sections of this chapter that focused on the MPS and running the MRP program, we mentioned that production capacity is usually some finite amount and obviously has limits. We also cited the interaction between the scheduler and rerunning the MRP program to obtain feasible schedules in light of this limited capacity. In this section we explicitly point out how capacity is computed and what the usual procedure is for addressing capacity constraints.

Computing Work Center Load

Each work center is generally a functionally defined center where jobs routed to it require the same type of work, on the same type of equipment. From the work center view, if there is adequate capacity, the problem is one of priorities: which job to do first. If there is insufficient capacity, however, the problem must be resolved by the master scheduler.

Exhibit 17.15 shows a work center that has various jobs assigned to it. Note that the capacity per week was computed at the bottom of the exhibit at 161.5 hours. The jobs scheduled for the three weeks result in two weeks with undercapacity and one week requiring overcapacity.

Exhibit 17.15 uses the terms *utilization* and *efficiency*. Both of these terms have been defined and used in a variety of ways, some conflicting. In this exhibit, *utilization* refers to the actual time that the machines are used. *Efficiency* refers to how well the machine is performing while it is being used. Efficiency is usually defined as a comparison of actual performance to a defined standard output or an engineering design rate. For instance, a

Exhibit 17.15

Workload for Work Center A

Week	Job No.	Units	Setup Time	Run Time per Unit	Total Job Time	Total for Week
10	145	100	3.5	0.23	26.5	
	167	160	2.4	0.26	44.0	
	158	70	1.2	0.13	10.3	
	193	300	6.0	0.17	57.0	137.8
11	132	80	5.0	0.36	33.8	
	126	150	3.0	0.22	36.0	
	180	180	2.5	0.30	56.5	
	178	120	4.0	0.50	64.0	190.3
12	147	90	3.0	0.18	19.2	
	156	200	3.5	0.14	31.5	
	198	250	1.5	0.16	41.5	
	172	100	2.0	0.12	14.0	
	139	120	2.2	0.17	22.6	128.8

Computing Work Center Capacity

The available capacity in standard hours is 161.5 hours per five-day week, calculated as (2 machines) (2 shifts) (10 hours/shift) (85% machine utilization) (95% efficiency).

Exhibit 17.16

Scheduled Workload for Work Center A

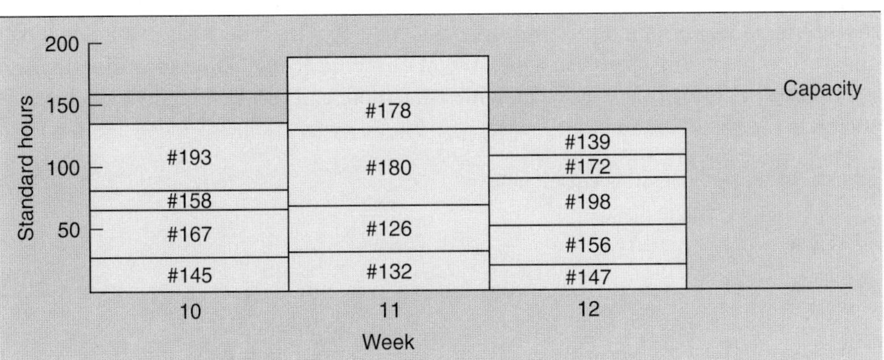

machine used for six hours of an eight-hour shift was utilized $\frac{6}{8}$ or 75 percent. If the standard output for that machine is established at 200 parts per hour and an average of 250 parts per hour were actually produced, then the efficiency of that machine is 125 percent. Note that in these definitions efficiency can be more than 100 percent, but utilization can never exceed 100 percent.

Exhibit 17.16 shows a loading representation of Work Center A for the three weeks. The scheduled work exceeds capacity for Week 11. There are several options available:

1. Work overtime.
2. Select an alternate work center that could perform the task.
3. Subcontract to an outside shop.
4. Try to schedule part of the work of Week 11 earlier into Week 10, and delay part of the work into Week 12.
5. Renegotiate the due date and reschedule.

An MRP program with a capacity requirements planning module allows rescheduling to try to level capacity. Two techniques used are backward scheduling and forward scheduling—the fourth option on the preceding list. The objective of the master scheduler is to try to level out the load in Exhibit 17.16 so that the requirements for the work center remain within the available capacity.

Manufacturing Resource Planning (MRP II)

Earlier in this chapter, our discussion of MRP focused only on the *materials* requirements that resulted from an explosion of the master schedule. We did not include the needs of all the other types of resources, such as staffing, facilities, and tools. In addition, while we discussed *capacity requirements planning,* we did this somewhat externally to the MRP system. In this section we discuss the logic of more advanced versions of MRP that include a wider range of resources and outputs.

MRP II

An expansion of the materials requirements planning program to include other portions of the production system was natural and to be expected. One of the first to be included was the purchasing function. At the same time, there was a more detailed inclusion of the production system itself—on the shop floor, in dispatching, and in the detailed scheduling control. MRP already had included work center capacity limitations, so it was obvious the name *materials requirements planning* no longer adequately described the expanded system. Someone (probably MRP pioneer Ollie Wight) introduced the name **manufacturing resource planning (MRP II)** to reflect the idea that more and more of the firm was becoming involved in the program. To quote Wight,

manufacturing resource planning (MRP II)

Advanced MRP system that takes into consideration the equipment capacities and other resources that are associated with a manufacturing facility.

> The fundamental manufacturing equation is:
> What are we going to make?
> What does it take to make it?
> What do we have?
> What do we have to get?[1]

The initial intent for MRP II was to plan and monitor all the resources of a manufacturing firm—manufacturing, marketing, finance, and engineering—through a closed-loop system generating financial figures. The second important intent of the MRP II concept was that it simulate the manufacturing system. It is generally conceived now as being a total, companywide system that allows everyone (buyers, marketing staff, production, accounting) to work with the same game plan and use the same numbers and is capable of simulation to plan and test alternative strategies. (See the OM in Practice on Furniture Manufacturer Uses MRP II to Cut Delivery Time.)

Sales and Operations Planning[2]

Sales and operations planning (S&OP) is an extension of MRP II that goes outside of the manufacturing function, aligning customer demand with both in-house and supplier

[1] Oliver Wight, *The Executive's Guide to Successful MRP II* (Williston, VT: Oliver Wight Limited Publications, 1982), pp. 6, 17.

[2] Adapted from George Palmatier, "Sales and Operations Planning—An Executive Level Synopsis" (New London, NH: The Oliver Wight Companies).

Operations Management in Practice

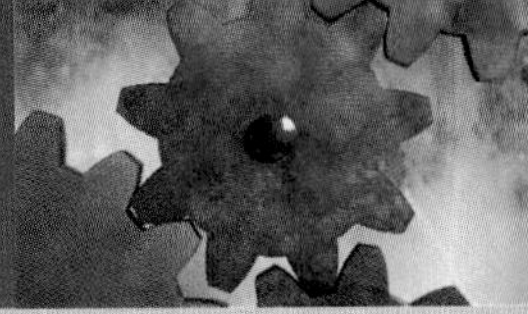

FURNITURE MANUFACTURER USES MRP II TO CUT DELIVERY TIME

In 1988, Harpers, Inc., an office furniture manufacturer located in California, was experiencing sustained growth in sales, but profits continued to fall. To reverse the downward trend in profits, management determined that it would have to reduce manufacturing costs by 15 percent, reduce product delivery times from six weeks (which was the industry standard) to three weeks, and reduce the new product time-to-market from three years to six months.

At the same time, Harpers recognized the need to focus its efforts on one segment of the office furniture market, which was "custom furniture solutions." To accomplish all of this, Harper needed a flexible manufacturing system that would allow customers to change the features of any furniture configuration.

The heart of its manufacturing system was centered around an MRP II system that would "integrate our engineering, marketing, manufacturing, and accounting efforts, and simultaneously engineer and deliver those custom products," said Joe Wisniewski, executive vice president and general manager at Harpers.

The system was installed and running by 1990, and by the end of 1991, 20 percent of the company's furniture was shipping within two weeks, with the remaining orders shipping in four weeks.

Source: Adapted from Robert M. Knight, "Furniture Maker Uses MRP II to Cut Lead Time," *Computerworld*, June 8, 1992, p. 80.

resources. The S&OP review process is typically performed on a monthly basis, with a rolling planning horizon of 18 to 24 months. The outputs of the S&OP process include (*a*) revised sales plan, (*b*) production plan, (*c*) inventory levels, and (*d*) customer lead times or backlogs.

A key goal of the S&OP process is to balance the firm's resources with customer demand, which frequently involves the decoupling of demand from supply. As we learned in the chapter on aggregate planning, a firm can manufacture products in different volumes and time periods than that requested by the customer in order to maximize the overall efficiency of the process. Therefore, in decoupling supply from demand, some of the decisions to be made include (*a*) producing to order or to inventory, (*b*) adjusting customer lead times or backlogs, and (*c*) changing capacity, such as working overtime or adding another shift.

MRP in Services

In general, MRP systems have not made significant inroads in service operations. This is due, in part, to the belief that MRP is strictly a manufacturing tool. However, modified versions of MRP are used in service operations where an actual product is manufactured as part of the service delivery process. Examples of these quasi-manufacturing services, as stated in an earlier chapter, include restaurants and bakeries where food is prepared on-site. In these types of service operations, the inventory management system usually consists of one or more point-of-sale (POS) terminals (or cash registers) that are connected to a central computer. This computer can be located either on-site at the retail operation or at a remote regional or headquarters location.

The POS terminals are designed for *single-item pricing,* where the cashier simply pushes a single key on the terminal that represents a specific item on the menu. The computer system then automatically posts the price of that item. At the same time, within the central computer system, is the bill-of-materials (or recipe) for the item that has just been sold. All of the ingredients that go into that item are subtracted out from the inventory records file. The computer inventory files are then compared against the actual physical inventories on a periodic basis. Typically these systems have reorder points built into them that will automatically signal when a specific item is running low.

Some of these service operations also use this modified MRP system to order raw ingredients to meet future sales, in a manner similar to that of an MRP system in a manufacturing environment. First, a forecast of end items to be sold is generated (for example, hamburgers). The forecasted demand for these items is then "exploded" against the bills of materials (or recipes) for the end items to determine the gross requirements. Finally these requirements are compared to on-hand inventories to determine the actual amounts of raw ingredients to be ordered and the delivery dates for when they are needed.

Lot Sizing in MRP Systems

The determination of lot sizes in an MRP system is a complicated and difficult problem. Lot sizes are the part quantities issued in the planned order receipt and planned order release sections of an MRP schedule. For parts produced in house, lot sizes are the production quantities or batch sizes. For purchased parts, these are the quantities ordered from the supplier. Lot sizes generally meet part requirements for one or more periods.

Most lot-sizing techniques deal with how to balance the setup or order costs and holding costs associated with meeting the net requirements generated by the MRP planning process. Many MRP systems have options for computing lot sizes based on some of the more commonly used techniques. It should be obvious, though, that the use of lot-sizing techniques increases the complexity in generating MRP schedules. When fully exploded, the numbers of parts scheduled can be enormous.

There are four lot-sizing techniques that are commonly used with MRP systems: (*a*) lot-for-lot (L4L), (*b*) economic order quantity (EOQ), (*c*) least total cost (LTC), and (*d*) least unit cost (LUC).

Lot-for-lot (L4L) is the most common technique; it

- Sets planned orders to exactly match the net requirements.
- Produces exactly what is needed each period with none carried over into future periods.
- Minimizes carrying cost.
- Does not take into account setup costs or capacity limitations.

Exhibit 17.17 illustrates the lot-for-lot method, with the production lot sizes in each period equalling the net requirements in each respective period.

Exhibit 17.17

Lot-for-Lot Method of Determining Production Quantities

Period	1	2	3	4	5	6
Net Requirements	50	60	70	60	95	75
Production Quantity	50	60	70	60	95	75

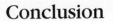

Conclusion

Since the 1970s, MRP has grown from its initial purpose of determining simple time schedules, to its present role that ties together all major functions of an organization. During its growth and its application, MRP's disadvantages as a scheduling mechanism have been well recognized. This is largely due to the fact that MRP tries to do too much in light of the dynamic, often jumpy environment in which it is trying to operate.

However, MRP is recognized for its excellent databases and linkages within the firm. MRP also does a good job generating master schedules. Many firms in repetitive manufacturing are installing JIT systems that are linked with their MRP systems. JIT takes the master production schedule as its pulling force but does not use MRP's generated schedule. Results indicate that this combined approach is working very well.

MRP's service applications have not fared as well, although they are making inroads in various forms in quasi-manufacturing service operations such as restaurants and bakeries. The MRP approach would appear to be valuable in producing services since service scheduling consists of identifying the final service and then tracing back to the resources needed, such as equipment, space, and personnel. Consider, for example, a hospital operating room planning an open-heart surgery. The master schedule can establish a time for the surgery (or surgeries, if several are scheduled). The BOM could specify all required equipment and personnel—MDs, nurses, anesthesiologist, operating room, heart/lung machine, defibrillator, and so forth. The inventory status file would show the availability of the resources and commit them to the project. The MRP program then could produce a schedule showing when various parts of the operation are to be started, expected completion times, required materials, and so forth. Checking this schedule would allow "capacity planning" in answering such questions as "Are all the materials and personnel available?" and "Does the system produce a feasible schedule?"

We still believe that MRP systems eventually will find their way into a greater variety of service applications. One reason for the delay is that even service managers who are aware of it believe that MRP is just a manufacturing tool. Also, service managers tend to be people-oriented and skeptical of tools from outside their industry.

Key Terms

bill of materials (BOM) p. 645

inventory records file p. 646

manufacturing resource planning (MRP II) p. 654

master production schedule (MPS) p. 638

materials requirements planning (MRP) p. 639

Review and Discussion Questions

1. Because MRP appears so reasonable, discuss reasons why it did not become popular until recently.
2. Discuss the meaning of MRP terms such as *planned order releases* and *scheduled order receipts.*
3. Most practitioners currently update MRP weekly or biweekly. Would it be more valuable if it were updated daily? Discuss.
4. What is the role of safety stock in an MRP system?
5. Contrast the significance of the term *lead time* in the traditional EOQ context and in an MRP system.

6. Discuss the importance of the MPS in an MRP system.
7. "MRP just prepares shopping lists—it doesn't do the shopping or cook the dinner." Comment.
8. What are the sources of demand in an MRP system? Are these dependent or independent, and how are they used as inputs to the system?
9. State the types of data that would be carried in the bill of materials file and the inventory record file.
10. How does MRP II differ from MRP?
11. Why isn't MRP more widespread in services?
12. MRP often is referred to as a "push" system, whereas JIT often is said to be a "pull" system. Comment.
13. How does MRP relate to an ERP system?

Solved Problems

Problem 1

Product X is made of two units of Y and three of Z. Y is made of one unit of A and two units of B. Z is made of two units of A and four units of C.

Lead time for X is one week; Y, two weeks; Z, three weeks; A, two weeks; B, one week; and C, three weeks. The beginning inventory for each item is zero.

a. Draw the product structure tree.

b. If 100 units of X are needed in week 10, develop a planning schedule showing when each item should be ordered and in what quantity.

Solution

a.

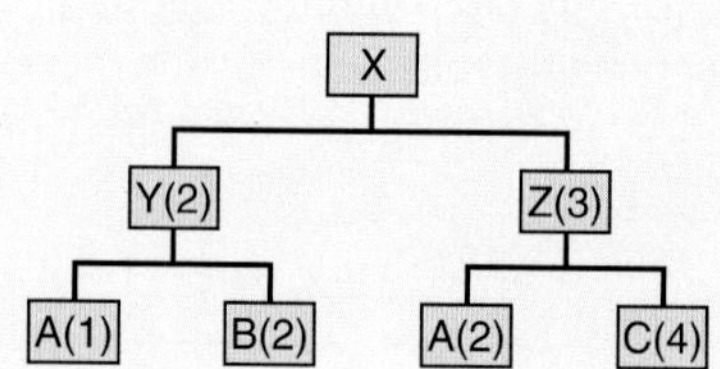

b.

		3	4	5	6	7	8	9	10
X	LT = 1							100	100
Y	LT = 2					200		200	
Z	LT = 3				300			300	
A	LT = 2		600	200	600	200			
B	LT = 1				400	400			
C	LT = 3	1200			1200				

Problem 2

Product M is made of two units of N and three of P. N is made of two units of R and four units of S. R is made of one unit of S and three units of T. P is made of two units of T and four units of U.

a. Show the product structure tree.

b. If 100 Ms are required, how many units of each component are needed?

c. Show both a single-level bill of material and an indented bill of material.

Solution

a.

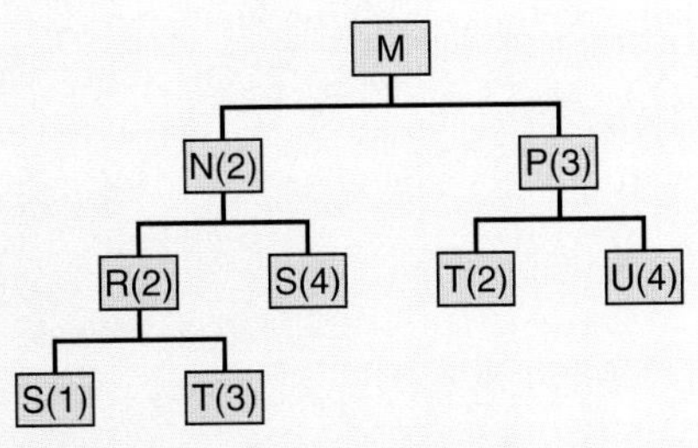

b. $M = 100$ $\quad S = 800 + 400 = 1{,}200$

$N = 200$ $\quad T = 600 + 1{,}200 = 1{,}800$

$P = 300$ $\quad U = 1{,}200$

$R = 400$

c.

Single-level BOM

Parent	Components
M	N
	P
N	R
	S
R	S
	T
P	T
	U

Indented BOM

M			
	N		
		R	
			S
			T
		S	
	P		
		T	
		U	

Problems

1. In the following MRP planning schedule for Item J, indicate the correct net requirements, planned order receipts, and planned order releases to meet the gross requirements. Lead time is one week.

	Week Number					
Item J	0	1	2	3	4	5
Gross requirements			75		50	70
On-hand inventory: 40						
Net requirements						
Planned order receipt						
Planned order releases						

2. Assume that Product Z is made of two units of A and four units of B. A is made of three units of C and four of D. D is made of two units of E.

   The lead time for purchase or fabrication of each unit to final assembly: Z takes two weeks; A, B, C, and D take one week each; and E takes three weeks.

Fifty units are required in Period 10. (Assume that there is currently no inventory on hand of any of these items.)

a. Draw a product structure tree.

b. Using a lot-for-lot ordering policy develop an MRP planning schedule showing gross and net requirements and order release and order receipt dates.

Note: For Problems 3 through 6, to simplify data handling to include the receipt of orders that have actually been placed in previous periods, the six-level scheme shown below can be used. (There are a number of different techniques used in practice, but the important issue is to keep track of what is on hand, what is expected to arrive, what is needed, and what size orders should be placed.) One way to calculate the numbers is as follows:

	Week								
Gross requirements									
Scheduled receipts									
On-hand inventory:									
Net requirements									
Planned order receipt									
Planned order release									

3. One unit of A is made of three units of B, one unit of C, and two units of D. B is composed of two units of E and one unit of D. C is made of one unit of B and two units of E. E is made of one unit of F.

   Items B, C, E, and F have one-week lead times; A and D have lead times of two weeks.

   Assume that lot-for-lot (L4L) lot sizing is used for items A, B, and F; lots of size 50, 50, and 200 are used for items C, D, and E, respectively. Items C, E, and F have on-hand (beginning) inventories of 10, 50, and 150, respectively; all other items have zero beginning inventory. We are scheduled to receive 10 units of A in week 5, 50 units of E in Week 4, and also 50 units of F in Week 4. There are no other scheduled receipts. If 30 units of A are required in Week 8, use the low-level-coded product structure tree to find the necessary planned order releases for all components.

4. One unit of A is made of two units of B, three units of C, and two units of D. B is composed of one unit of E and two units of F. C is made of two units of F and one unit of D. E is made of two units of D. Items A, C, D, and F have one-week lead times; B and E have lead times of two weeks. Lot-for-lot (L4L) lot sizing is used for items A, B, C, and D; lots of size 50 and 180 are used for items E and F, respectively. Item C has an on-hand (beginning) inventory of 15; D has an on-hand inventory of 50; all other items have zero beginning inventory. We are scheduled to receive 20 units of item E in week 4; there are no other scheduled receipts.

   Construct simple and low-level-coded product structure trees and indented and summarized bills of materials.

   If 20 units of A are required in Week 8, use the low-level-coded product structure tree to find the necessary planned order releases for all components. (See note prior to Problem 3.)

5. One unit of A is made of one unit of B and one unit of C. B is made of four units of C and one unit each of E and F. C is made of two units of D and one unit of E. E is made of three units of F. Item C has a lead time of one week; items A, B, E, and F have two-week lead times; and item D has a lead time of three weeks. Lot-for-lot (L4L) lot sizing

is used for items A, D, and E; lots of size 50, 100, and 50 are used for items B, C, and F, respectively. Items A, C, D, and E have on-hand (beginning) inventories of 20, 50, 100, and 10, respectively; all other items have zero beginning inventory. We are scheduled to receive 10 units of A in week 5, 100 units of C in Week 6, and 100 units of D in Week 4; there are no other scheduled receipts. If 50 units of A are required in Week 10, use the low-level-coded product structure tree to find the necessary planned order releases for all components. (See note prior to Problem 3.)

6. One unit of A is made of two units of B and one unit of C. B is made of three units of D and one unit of F. C is composed of three units of B, one unit of D, and four units of E. D is made of one unit of E. Item C has a lead time of one week; items A, B, E, and F have two-week lead times; and item D has a lead time of 3 weeks. Lot-for-lot (L4L) lot sizing is used for items C, E, and F; lots of size 20, 40, and 160 are used for items A, B, and D, respectively. Items A, B, D, and E have on-hand (beginning) inventories of 5, 10, 100, and 100, respectively; all other items have zero beginning inventories. We are scheduled to receive 10 units of A in Week 3, 20 units of B in Week 7, 60 units of E in Week 2, and 40 units of F in Week 5; there are no other scheduled receipts. If 20 units of A are required in Week 10, use the low-level-coded product structure tree to find the necessary planned order releases for all components. (See note prior to Problem 3.)

7. (This problem is intended as a very simple exercise to go from the aggregate plan to the master schedule to the MRP.) Gigamemory Storage Devices, Inc., produces CD-ROMs (Read Only Memory) and WORMs (Write Once Read Many) for the computer market. Aggregate demand for the WORMs for the next two quarters are 2,100 units and 2,700 units. Assume that the demand is distributed evenly for each month of the quarter.

   There are two models of the WORM: an internal model and an external model. The drive assemblies in both are the same but the electronics and housing are different. Demand is higher for the external model and currently is 70 percent of the aggregate demand.

   The bill of materials and the lead times follow. One drive assembly and one electronic and housing unit go into each WORM.

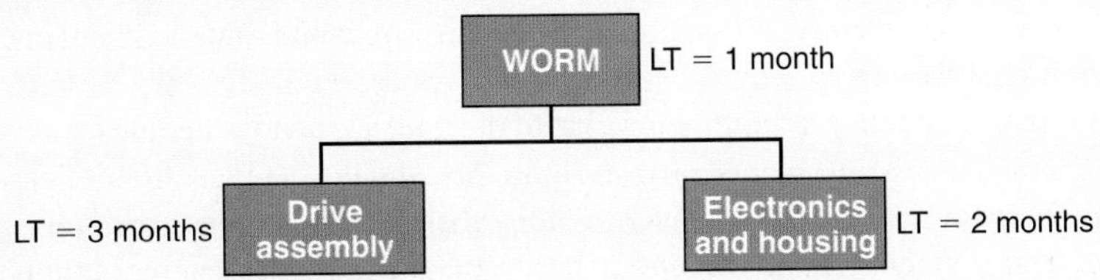

   The MRP system is run monthly. Currently, 200 external WORMs and 100 internal WORMs are in stock. Also in stock are 250 drive assemblies, 50 internal electronic and housing units, and 125 external electronic and housing units.

   Problem: Show the aggregate plan, the master production schedule, and the full MRP with the gross and net requirements and planned order releases. (Assume a lot-for-lot ordering policy.)

8. Product A is an end item and is made from two units of B and four of C. B is made of three units of D and two of E. C is made of two units of F and two of E.

   A has a lead time of one week. B, C, and E have lead times of two weeks, and D and F have lead times of three weeks. Currently, there are no units of inventory on hand.

   a. Draw the product structure tree.

   b. If 100 units of A are required in Week 10, develop the MRP planning schedule, specifying when items are to be ordered and received. (Assume a lot-for-lot ordering policy.)

9. Product A consists of two units of subassembly B, three units of C, and one unit of D. B is composed of four units of E and three units of F. C is made of two units of H and three units of D. H is made of five units of E and two units of G.
   a. Construct a simple product structure tree.
   b. Construct a product structure tree using low-level coding.
   c. Construct an indented bill of materials.
   d. To produce 100 units of A, determine the numbers of units of B, C, D, E, F, G, and H are required. (Assume a lot-for-lot ordering policy.)
10. Audio Products, Inc., produces two AM/FM cassette players for automobiles. Both radio/cassette units are identical, but the mounting hardware and finish trim differ. The standard model fits intermediate- and full-size cars, and the sports model fits small sports cars.

    Audio Products handles its production in the following way. The chassis (radio/cassette unit) is assembled in Mexico and has a manufacturing lead time of two weeks. The mounting hardware is purchased from a sheet steel company and has a three-week lead time. The finish trim is purchased from a Taiwan electronics company with offices in Los Angeles as prepackaged units consisting of knobs and various trim pieces. Trim packages have a two-week lead time. Final assembly time may be disregarded, since adding the trim package and mounting are performed by the customer.

    Audio Products supplies wholesalers and retailers, who place specific orders for both models up to eight weeks in advance. These orders, together with enough additional units to satisfy the small number of individual sales, are summarized in the following demand schedule:

	Week							
	1	2	3	4	5	6	7	8
Standard model				300				400
Sports model					200			100

    There are currently 50 radio/cassette units on hand but no trim packages or mounting hardware.

    Prepare a material requirements plan to meet the demand schedule exactly. Specify the gross and net requirements, on-hand amounts, and the planned order releases and receipts for each period for the cassette/radio chassis, the standard trim and sports car model trim, and the standard mounting hardware and the sports car mounting hardware.
11. Brown and Brown Electronics manufactures a line of digital audiotape players. While there are differences among the various products, there are a number of common parts within each player. The product structure, showing the number of each item required, lead times, and the current inventory on hand for the parts and components, follows:

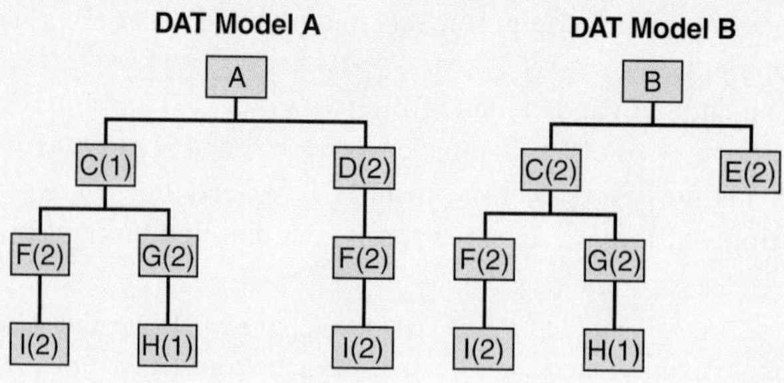

	Number Currently in Stock	Lead Time (weeks)
DAT Model A	30	1
DAT Model B	50	2
Subassembly C	75	1
Subassembly D	80	2
Subassembly E	100	1
Part F	150	1
Part G	40	1
Raw material H	200	2
Raw material I	300	2

Brown and Brown created a forecast that it plans to use as its master production schedule, producing exactly to schedule. Part of the MPS shows a demand for 700 units of Model A and 1,200 units of Model B in Week 10.

Develop an MRP schedule to meet that demand.

Bibliography

Biggs, Joseph R., and Ellen J. Long. "Gaining the Competitive Edge with MRP/MRP II." *Management Accounting,* May 1988, pp. 27–32.

Flapper, S. D. P.; G. J. Miltenburg; and J. Wijngaard. "Embedding JIT into MRP." *International Journal of Production Research* 29, no. 2 (1991), pp. 329–41.

Goodrich, Thomas. "JIT & MRP Can Work Together." *Automation,* April 1989, pp. 46–47.

Knight, Robert M. "Furniture Maker Uses MRP II to Cut Lead Time." *Computerworld,* June 8, 1992, p. 80.

Orlicky, Joseph. *Materials Requirements Planning*. New York: McGraw-Hill, 1975. (This is the classic book on MRP.)

Production and Inventory Management Journal and *APICS: The Performance Advantage*. Practitioner journals with numerous articles on MRP and MRP II. Many of these cite the difficulties and experiences of practitioners.

Sipper, Daniel, and Robert Bulfin. *Production Planning, Control and Integration*. New York: McGraw-Hill, 1997.

Staiti, Chris. "Customers Drive New Manufacturing Software." *Datamation,* November 15, 1993, p. 72.

Turbide, David A. *MRP+: The Adaptation, Enhancement and Application of MRP II*. New York: Industrial Press, 1993, p. 11.

Vollmann, Thomas E.; William L. Berry; and D. Clay Whybark. *Manufacturing Planning and Control Systems*. 4th ed. Burr Ridge, IL: Irwin, 1997.

Case

Nichols Company

This particular December day seemed bleak to Joe Williams, president of Nichols Company (NCO). He sat in his office watching the dying embers of his fireplace, hoping to clear his mind. Suddenly there came a tapping by someone gently rapping, rapping at his office door. "Another headache," he muttered, "tapping at my office door. Only that and nothing more."*

The intruder was Barney Thompson, director of marketing. "A major account has just canceled a large purchase of A units because we are back ordered on tubing. This can't continue. My sales force is out beating the bushes for customers and our production manager can't provide the product."

For the past several months, operations at NCO have been unsteady. Inventory levels have been too high, while at the same time there have been stockouts. This resulted in many late deliveries, complaints, and cancellations. To compound the problem, overtime was excessive.

History

Nichols Company was started by Joe Williams and Peter Schaap, both with MBAs from the University of Arizona. Much has happened since Williams and Schaap formed the company. Schaap has left the company and is working in real estate development in Queensland, Australia. Under the direction of Williams, NCO has diversified to include a number of other products.

NCO currently has 355 full-time employees directly involved in manufacturing its three primary products, A, B, and C. Final assembly takes place in a converted warehouse adjacent to NCO's main plant.

The Meeting

Williams called a meeting the next day to get input into the problems facing NCO and to lay the groundwork for some solutions. Attending the meeting, besides himself and Barney Thompson, were Phil Bright of production and inventory control, Trevor Hansen of purchasing, and Steve Clark of accounting.

The meeting lasted all morning. Participation was vocal and intense.

Bright said, "The forecasts that marketing sends us are always way off. We are constantly having to expedite one product or another to meet current demand. This runs up our overtime."

Thompson said, "Production tries to run too lean. We need a larger inventory of finished goods. If I had the merchandise, my salespeople could sell 20 percent more product."

Clark said, "No way! Our inventory is already uncomfortably high. We can't afford the holding costs, not to mention how fast technology changes around here causing even more inventory, much of it obsolete."

Bright said, "The only way I can meet our stringent cost requirements is to buy in volume."

At the end of the meeting, Williams had lots of input but no specific plan. What do you think he should do?

Use Case Exhibits 1–4 showing relevant data to answer the specific questions at the end of the case.

*With apologies to E.A.P.

Case Exhibit 1

Bills of Materials for Products A, B, and C

Product A			Product B			Product C		
.A			.B			.C		
	.D(4)			.F(2)			.G(2)	
		.I(3)		.G(3)				.I(2)
	.E(1)				.I(2)		.H(1)	
	.F(4)							

Case Exhibit 2

Work Center Routings for Products and Components

Item	Work Center Number	Standard Time (hours per unit)
Product A	1	0.20
	4	0.10
Product B	2	0.30
	4	0.08
Product C	3	0.10
	4	0.05
Component D	1	0.15
	4	0.10
Component E	2	0.15
	4	0.05
Component F	2	0.15
	3	0.20
Component G	1	0.30
	2	0.10
Component H	1	0.05
	3	0.10

Case Exhibit 3

Inventory Levels and Lead Times for Each Item on the Bill of Material at the Beginning of Week 1

Product/Component	On Hand (units)	Lead Time (weeks)
Product A	100	1
Product B	200	1
Product C	175	1
Component D	200	1
Component E	195	1
Component F	120	1
Component G	200	1
Component H	200	1
1 (raw material)	300	1

Case

Case Exhibit 4

Forecasted Demand for Weeks 4–27

Week	Product A	Product B	Product C
1			
2			
3			
4	1,500	2,200	1,200
5	1,700	2,100	1,400
6	1,150	1,900	1,000
7	1,100	1,800	1,500
8	1,000	1,800	1,400
9	1,100	1,600	1,100
10	1,400	1,600	1,800
11	1,400	1,700	1,700
12	1,700	1,700	1,300
13	1,700	1,700	1,700
14	1,800	1,700	1,700
15	1,900	1,900	1,500
16	2,200	2,300	2,300
17	2,000	2,300	2,300
18	1,700	2,100	2,000
19	1,600	1,900	1,700
20	1,400	1,800	1,800
21	1,100	1,800	2,200
22	1,000	1,900	1,900
23	1,400	1,700	2,400
24	1,400	1,700	2,400
25	1,500	1,700	2,600
26	1,600	1,800	2,400
27	1,500	1,900	2,500

Questions Use Excel (or another spreadsheet if you prefer) to solve the Nichols Company case.

Simplifying assumption: To get the program started, some time is needed at the beginning because MRP backloads the system. For simplicity, assume that the forecasts (and therefore demands) are zero for Periods 1 through 3. Also assume that the starting inventory specified in Case Exhibit 3 is available from Week 1. For the master production schedule, use only the end Items A, B, and C.

To modify production quantities, adjust only Products A, B, and C. Do not adjust the quantities of D, E, F, G, H, and I. These should be linked so that changes in A, B, and C automatically adjust them.

1. Disregarding machine-center limitations, develop an MRP schedule and also capacity profiles for the four machine centers.
2. Work center capacities and costs follow. Repeat Question 1 creating a *feasible* schedule (within the capacities of the machine centers) and compute the relevant costs. Do this by adjusting the MPS only. Try to minimize the total cost of operation for the 27 weeks.

	Capacity	Cost
Work center 1	6,000 hours available	$20 per hour
Work center 2	4,500 hours available	$25 per hour
Work center 3	2,400 hours available	$35 per hour
Work center 4	1,200 hours available	$65 per hour
Inventory carrying cost		
End items A, B, and C	$2.00 per unit	
Components D, E, F, G, and H	$1.50 per unit	
Raw material I	$1.00 per unit	
Back-order cost		
End items A, B, and C	$20 per unit per week	
Components D, E, F, G, and H	$14 per unit per week	
Raw material I	$ 8 per unit per week	

3. Suppose end items had to be ordered in multiples of 100 units, components in multiples of 500 units, and raw materials in multiples of 1,000 units. How would this change your schedule?

Appendixes

Appendix A: Interest Tables for Financial Analysis

Table 1

Compound Sum of $1

Year	1%	2%	3%	4%	5%	6%	7%
1	1.010	1.020	1.030	1.040	1.050	1.060	1.070
2	1.020	1.040	1.061	1.082	1.102	1.124	1.145
3	1.030	1.061	1.093	1.125	1.158	1.191	1.225
4	1.041	1.082	1.126	1.170	1.216	1.262	1.311
5	1.051	1.104	1.159	1.217	1.276	1.338	1.403
6	1.062	1.126	1.194	1.265	1.340	1.419	1.501
7	1.072	1.149	1.230	1.316	1.407	1.504	1.606
8	1.083	1.172	1.267	1.369	1.477	1.594	1.718
9	1.094	1.195	1.305	1.423	1.551	1.689	1.838
10	1.105	1.219	1.344	1.480	1.629	1.791	1.967
11	1.116	1.243	1.384	1.539	1.710	1.898	2.105
12	1.127	1.268	1.426	1.601	1.796	2.012	2.252
13	1.138	1.294	1.469	1.665	1.886	2.133	2.410
14	1.149	1.319	1.513	1.732	1.980	2.261	2.579
15	1.161	1.346	1.558	1.801	2.079	2.397	2.759
16	1.173	1.373	1.605	1.873	2.183	2.540	2.952
17	1.184	1.400	1.653	1.948	2.292	2.693	3.159
18	1.196	1.428	1.702	2.026	2.407	2.854	3.380
19	1.208	1.457	1.754	2.107	2.527	3.026	3.617
20	1.220	1.486	1.806	2.191	2.653	3.207	3.870
25	1.282	1.641	2.094	2.666	3.386	4.292	5.427
30	1.348	1.811	2.427	3.243	4.322	5.743	7.612

Year	8%	9%	10%	12%	14%	15%	16%
1	1.080	1.090	1.100	1.120	1.140	1.150	1.160
2	1.166	1.188	1.210	1.254	1.300	1.322	1.346
3	1.260	1.295	1.331	1.405	1.482	1.521	1.561
4	1.360	1.412	1.464	1.574	1.689	1.749	1.811
5	1.469	1.539	1.611	1.762	1.925	2.011	2.100
6	1.587	1.677	1.772	1.974	2.195	2.313	2.436
7	1.714	1.828	1.949	2.211	2.502	2.660	2.826
8	1.851	1.993	2.144	2.476	2.853	3.059	3.278
9	1.999	2.172	2.358	2.773	3.252	3.518	3.803
10	2.159	2.367	2.594	3.106	3.707	4.046	4.411
11	2.332	2.580	2.853	3.479	4.226	4.652	5.117
12	2.518	2.813	3.138	3.896	4.818	5.350	5.936
13	2.720	3.066	3.452	4.363	5.492	6.153	6.886
14	2.937	3.342	3.797	4.887	6.261	7.076	7.988
15	3.172	3.642	4.177	5.474	7.138	8.137	9.266
16	3.426	3.970	4.595	6.130	8.137	9.358	10.748
17	3.700	4.328	5.054	6.866	9.276	10.761	12.468
18	3.996	4.717	5.560	7.690	10.575	12.375	14.463
19	4.316	5.142	6.116	8.613	12.056	14.232	16.777
20	4.661	5.604	6.728	9.646	13.743	16.367	19.461
25	6.848	8.623	10.835	17.000	26.462	32.919	40.874
30	10.063	13.268	17.449	29.960	50.950	66.212	85.850

Table 1

(Concluded)

Year	18%	20%	24%	28%	32%	36%
1	1.180	1.200	1.240	1.280	1.320	1.360
2	1.392	1.440	1.538	1.638	1.742	1.850
3	1.643	1.728	1.907	2.067	2.300	2.515
4	1.939	2.074	2.364	2.684	3.036	3.421
5	2.288	2.488	2.932	3.436	4.007	4.653
6	2.700	2.986	3.635	4.398	5.290	6.328
7	3.185	3.583	4.508	5.629	6.983	8.605
8	3.759	4.300	5.590	7.206	9.217	11.703
9	4.435	5.160	6.931	9.223	12.166	15.917
10	5.234	6.192	8.594	11.806	16.060	21.647
11	6.176	7.430	10.657	15.112	21.199	29.439
12	7.288	8.916	13.215	19.343	27.983	40.037
13	8.599	10.699	16.386	24.759	36.937	54.451
14	10.147	12.839	20.319	31.691	48.757	74.053
15	11.974	15.407	25.196	40.565	64.359	100.712
16	14.129	18.488	31.243	51.923	84.954	136.97
17	16.672	22.186	38.741	66.461	112.14	186.28
18	19.673	26.623	48.039	85.071	148.02	253.34
19	23.214	31.948	59.568	108.89	195.39	344.54
20	27.393	38.338	73.864	139.38	257.92	468.57
25	62.669	95.396	216.542	478.90	1033.6	2180.1
30	143.371	237.376	634.820	1645.5	4142.1	10143.

Year	40%	50%	60%	70%	80%	90%
1	1.400	1.500	1.600	1.700	1.800	1.900
2	1.960	2.250	2.560	2.890	3.240	3.610
3	2.744	3.375	4.096	4.913	5.832	6.859
4	3.842	5.062	6.544	8.352	10.498	13.032
5	5.378	7.594	10.486	14.199	18.896	24.761
6	7.530	11.391	16.777	24.138	34.012	47.046
7	10.541	17.086	26.844	41.034	61.222	89.387
8	14.758	25.629	42.950	69.758	110.200	169.836
9	20.661	38.443	68.720	118.588	198.359	322.688
10	28.925	57.665	109.951	201.599	357.047	613.107
11	40.496	86.498	175.922	342.719	642.684	1164.902
12	56.694	129.746	281.475	582.622	1156.831	2213.314
13	79.372	194.619	450.360	990.457	2082.295	4205.297
14	111.120	291.929	720.576	1683.777	3748.131	7990.065
15	155.568	437.894	1152.921	2862.421	6746.636	15181.122
16	217.795	656.84	1844.7	4866.1	12144.	28844.0
17	304.914	985.26	2951.5	8272.4	21859.	54804.0
18	426.879	1477.9	4722.4	14063.0	39346.	104130.0
19	597.630	2216.8	7555.8	23907.0	70824.	197840.0
20	836.683	3325.3	12089.0	40642.0	127480.	375900.0
25	4499.880	25251.	126760.0	577060.0	2408900.	9307600.0
30	24201.432	191750.	1329200.	8193500.0	45517000.	230470000.0

Table 2

Sum of an Annuity of $1 for *N* Years

Year	1%	2%	3%	4%	5%	6%
1	1.000	1.000	1.000	1.000	1.000	1.000
2	2.010	2.020	2.030	2.040	2.050	2.060
3	2.030	3.060	3.091	3.122	3.152	3.184
4	4.060	4.122	4.184	4.246	4.310	4.375
5	5.101	5.204	5.309	5.416	5.526	5.637
6	6.152	6.308	6.468	6.633	6.802	6.975
7	7.214	7.434	7.662	7.898	8.142	8.394
8	8.286	8.583	8.892	9.214	9.549	9.897
9	9.369	9.755	10.159	10.583	11.027	11.491
10	10.462	10.950	11.464	12.006	12.578	13.181
11	11.567	12.169	12.808	13.486	14.207	14.972
12	12.683	13.412	14.192	15.026	15.917	16.870
13	13.809	14.680	15.618	16.627	17.713	18.882
14	14.947	15.974	17.086	18.292	19.599	21.051
15	16.097	17.293	18.599	20.024	21.579	23.276
16	17.258	18.639	20.157	21.825	23.657	25.673
17	18.430	20.012	21.762	23.698	25.840	28.213
18	19.615	21.412	23.414	25.645	28.132	30.906
19	20.811	22.841	25.117	27.671	30.539	33.760
20	22.019	24.297	26.870	29.778	33.066	36.786
25	28.243	32.030	36.459	41.646	47.727	54.865
30	34.785	40.568	47.575	56.085	66.439	79.058

Year	7%	8%	9%	10%	12%	14%
1	1.000	1.000	1.000	1.000	1.000	1.000
2	2.070	2.080	2.090	2.100	2.120	2.140
3	3.215	3.246	3.278	3.310	3.374	3.440
4	4.440	4.506	4.573	4.641	4.770	4.921
5	5.751	5.867	5.985	6.105	6.353	6.610
6	7.153	7.336	7.523	7.716	8.115	8.536
7	8.654	8.923	9.200	9.487	10.089	10.730
8	10.260	10.637	11.028	11.436	12.300	13.233
9	11.978	12.488	13.021	13.579	14.776	16.085
10	13.816	14.487	15.193	15.937	17.549	19.337
11	15.784	16.645	17.560	18.531	20.655	23.044
12	17.888	18.977	20.141	21.384	24.133	27.271
13	20.141	21.495	22.953	24.523	28.029	32.089
14	22.550	24.215	26.019	27.975	32.393	37.581
15	25.129	27.152	29.361	31.772	37.280	43.842
16	27.888	30.324	33.003	35.950	42.753	50.980
17	30.840	33.750	36.974	40.545	48.884	59.118
18	33.999	37.450	41.301	45.599	55.750	68.394
19	37.379	41.446	46.018	51.159	63.440	78.969
20	40.995	45.762	51.160	57.275	72.052	91.025
25	63.249	73.106	84.701	93.347	133.334	181.871
30	94.461	113.283	136.308	164.494	241.333	356.787

Table 2
(Concluded)

Year	16%	18%	20%	24%	28%	32%
1	1.000	1.000	1.000	1.000	1.000	1.000
2	2.160	2.180	2.200	2.240	2.280	2.320
3	3.506	3.572	3.640	3.778	3.918	4.062
4	5.066	5.215	5.368	5.684	6.016	6.362
5	6.877	7.154	7.442	8.048	8.700	9.398
6	8.977	9.442	9.930	10.980	12.136	13.406
7	11.414	12.142	12.916	14.615	16.534	18.696
8	14.240	15.327	16.499	19.123	22.163	25.678
9	17.518	19.086	20.799	24.712	29.369	34.895
10	21.321	23.521	25.959	31.643	38.592	47.062
11	25.733	28.755	32.150	40.238	50.399	63.122
12	30.850	34.931	39.580	50.985	65.510	84.320
13	36.786	42.219	48.497	64.110	84.853	112.303
14	43.672	50.818	59.196	80.496	109.612	149.240
15	51.660	60.965	72.035	100.815	141.303	197.997
16	60.925	72.939	87.442	126.011	181.87	262.36
17	71.673	87.068	105.931	157.253	233.79	347.31
18	84.141	103.740	128.117	195.994	300.25	459.45
19	98.603	123.414	154.740	244.033	385.32	607.47
20	115.380	146.628	186.688	303.601	494.21	802.86
25	249.214	342.603	471.981	898.092	1706.8	3226.8
30	530.312	790.948	1181.882	2640.916	5873.2	12941.0

Year	36%	40%	50%	60%	70%	80%
1	1.000	1.000	1.000	1.000	1.000	1.000
2	2.360	2.400	2.500	2.600	2.700	2.800
3	4.210	4.360	4.750	5.160	5.590	6.040
4	6.725	7.104	8.125	9.256	10.503	11.872
5	10.146	10.846	13.188	15.810	18.855	22.370
6	14.799	16.324	20.781	26.295	33.054	41.265
7	21.126	23.853	32.172	43.073	57.191	75.278
8	29.732	34.395	49.258	69.916	98.225	136.500
9	41.435	49.153	74.887	112.866	167.983	246.699
10	57.352	69.814	113.330	181.585	286.570	445.058
11	78.998	98.739	170.995	291.536	488.170	802.105
12	108.437	139.235	257.493	467.458	830.888	1444.788
13	148.475	195.929	387.239	748.933	1413.510	2601.619
14	202.926	275.300	581.859	1199.293	2403.968	4683.914
15	276.979	386.420	873.788	1919.869	4087.745	8432.045
16	377.69	541.99	1311.7	3072.8	6950.2	15179.0
17	514.66	759.78	1968.5	4917.5	11816.0	27323.0
18	700.94	1064.7	2953.8	7868.9	20089.0	49182.0
19	954.28	1491.6	4431.7	12591.0	34152.0	88528.0
20	1298.8	2089.2	6648.5	20147.0	58059.0	159350.0
25	6053.0	11247.0	50500.0	211270.0	824370.0	3011100.0
30	28172.0	60501.0	383500.0	2215400.0	11705000.0	56896000.0

Table 3

Present Value of $1

Year	1%	2%	3%	4%	5%	6%	7%	8%	9%	10%	12%	14%	15%
1	.990	.980	.971	.962	.952	.943	.935	.926	.917	.909	.893	.877	.870
2	.980	.961	.943	.925	.907	.890	.873	.857	.842	.826	.797	.769	.756
3	.971	.942	.915	.889	.864	.840	.816	.794	.772	.751	.712	.675	.658
4	.961	.924	.889	.855	.823	.792	.763	.735	.708	.683	.636	.592	.572
5	.951	.906	.863	.822	.784	.747	.713	.681	.650	.621	.567	.519	.497
6	.942	.888	.838	.790	.746	.705	.666	.630	.596	.564	.507	.456	.432
7	.933	.871	.813	.760	.711	.665	.623	.583	.547	.513	.452	.400	.376
8	.923	.853	.789	.731	.677	.627	.582	.540	.502	.467	.404	.351	.327
9	.914	.837	.766	.703	.645	.592	.544	.500	.460	.424	.361	.308	.284
10	.905	.820	.744	.676	.614	.558	.508	.463	.422	.386	.322	.270	.247
11	.896	.804	.722	.650	.585	.527	.475	.429	.388	.350	.287	.237	.215
12	.887	.788	.701	.625	.557	.497	.444	.397	.356	.319	.257	.208	.187
13	.879	.773	.681	.601	.530	.469	.415	.368	.326	.290	.229	.182	.163
14	.870	.758	.661	.577	.505	.442	.388	.340	.299	.263	.205	.160	.141
15	.861	.743	.642	.555	.481	.417	.362	.315	.275	.239	.183	.140	.123
16	.853	.728	.623	.534	.458	.394	.339	.292	.252	.218	.163	.123	.107
17	.844	.714	.605	.513	.436	.371	.317	.270	.231	.198	.146	.108	.093
18	.836	.700	.587	.494	.416	.350	.296	.250	.212	.180	.130	.095	.081
19	.828	.686	.570	.475	.396	.331	.276	.232	.194	.164	.116	.083	.070
20	.820	.673	.554	.456	.377	.312	.258	.215	.178	.149	.104	.073	.061
25	.780	.610	.478	.375	.295	.233	.184	.146	.116	.092	.059	.038	.030
30	.742	.552	.412	.308	.231	.174	.131	.099	.075	.057	.033	.020	.015
Year	**16%**	**18%**	**20%**	**24%**	**28%**	**32%**	**36%**	**40%**	**50%**	**60%**	**70%**	**80%**	**90%**
1	.862	.847	.833	.806	.781	.758	.735	.714	.667	.625	.588	.556	.526
2	.743	.718	.694	.650	.610	.574	.541	.510	.444	.391	.346	.309	.277
3	.641	.609	.579	.524	.477	.435	.398	.364	.296	.244	.204	.171	.146
4	.552	.516	.482	.423	.373	.329	.292	.260	.198	.153	.120	.095	.077
5	.476	.437	.402	.341	.291	.250	.215	.186	.132	.095	.070	.053	.040
6	.410	.370	.335	.275	.227	.189	.158	.133	.088	.060	.041	.029	.021
7	.354	.314	.279	.222	.178	.143	.116	.095	.059	.037	.024	.016	.011
8	.305	.266	.233	.179	.139	.108	.085	.068	.039	.023	.014	.009	.006
9	.263	.226	.194	.144	.108	.082	.063	.048	.026	.015	.008	.005	.003
10	.227	.191	.162	.116	.085	.062	.046	.035	.017	.009	.005	.003	.002
11	.195	.162	.135	.094	.066	.047	.034	.025	.012	.006	.003	.002	.001
12	.168	.137	.112	.076	.052	.036	.025	.018	.008	.004	.002	.001	.001
13	.145	.116	.093	.061	.040	.027	.018	.013	.005	.002	.001	.001	.000
14	.125	.099	.078	.049	.032	.021	.014	.009	.003	.001	.001	.000	.000
15	.108	.084	.065	.040	.025	.016	.010	.006	.002	.001	.000	.000	.000
16	.093	.071	.054	.032	.019	.012	.007	.005	.002	.001	.000	.000	
17	.080	.060	.045	.026	.015	.009	.005	.003	.001	.000	.000		
18	.069	.051	.038	.021	.012	.007	.004	.002	.001	.000	.000		
19	.060	.043	.031	.017	.009	.005	.003	.002	.000	.000			
20	.051	.037	.026	.014	.007	.004	.002	.001	.000	.000			
25	.024	.016	.010	.005	.002	.001	.000	.000					
30	.012	.007	.004	.002	.001	.000	.000						

Table 4

Present Value of an Annuity of $1

Year	1%	2%	3%	4%	5%	6%	7%	8%	9%	10%
1	0.990	0.980	0.971	0.962	0.952	0.943	0.935	0.926	0.917	0.909
2	1.970	1.942	1.913	1.886	1.859	1.833	1.808	1.783	1.759	1.736
3	2.941	2.884	2.829	2.775	2.723	2.673	2.624	2.577	2.531	2.487
4	3.902	3.808	3.717	3.630	3.546	3.465	3.387	3.312	3.240	3.170
5	4.853	4.713	4.580	4.452	4.329	4.212	4.100	3.993	3.890	3.791
6	5.795	5.601	5.417	5.242	5.076	4.917	4.766	4.623	4.486	4.355
7	6.728	6.472	6.230	6.002	5.786	5.582	5.389	5.206	5.033	4.868
8	7.652	7.325	7.020	6.733	6.463	6.210	6.971	5.747	5.535	5.335
9	8.566	8.162	7.786	7.435	7.108	6.802	6.515	6.247	5.985	5.759
10	9.471	8.983	8.530	8.111	7.722	7.360	7.024	6.710	6.418	6.145
11	10.368	9.787	9.253	8.760	8.306	7.887	7.449	7.139	6.805	6.495
12	11.255	10.575	9.954	9.385	8.863	8.384	7.943	7.536	7.161	6.814
13	12.134	11.348	10.635	9.986	9.394	8.853	8.358	7.904	7.487	7.103
14	13.004	12.106	11.296	10.563	9.899	9.295	8.745	8.244	7.786	7.367
15	13.865	12.849	11.938	11.118	10.380	9.712	9.108	8.559	8.060	7.606
16	14.718	13.578	12.561	11.652	10.838	10.106	9.447	8.851	8.312	7.824
17	15.562	14.292	13.166	12.166	11.274	10.477	9.763	9.122	8.544	8.022
18	16.398	14.992	13.754	12.659	11.690	10.828	10.059	9.372	8.756	8.201
19	17.226	15.678	14.324	13.134	12.085	11.158	10.336	9.604	8.950	8.365
20	18.046	16.351	14.877	13.590	12.462	11.470	10.594	9.818	9.128	8.514
25	22.023	19.523	17.413	15.622	14.094	12.783	11.654	10.675	9.823	9.077
30	25.808	22.397	19.600	17.292	15.373	13.765	12.409	11.258	10.274	9.427

Year	12%	14%	16%	18%	20%	24%	28%	32%	36%
1	0.893	0.877	0.862	0.847	0.833	0.806	0.781	0.758	0.735
2	1.690	1.647	1.605	1.566	1.528	1.457	1.392	1.332	1.276
3	2.402	2.322	2.246	2.174	2.106	1.981	1.868	1.766	1.674
4	3.037	2.914	2.798	2.690	2.589	2.404	2.241	2.096	1.966
5	3.605	3.433	3.274	3.127	2.991	2.745	2.532	2.345	2.181
6	4.111	3.889	3.685	3.498	3.326	3.020	2.759	2.534	2.339
7	4.564	4.288	4.039	3.812	3.605	3.242	2.937	2.678	2.455
8	4.968	4.639	4.344	4.078	3.837	3.421	3.076	2.786	2.540
9	5.328	4.946	4.607	4.303	4.031	3.566	3.184	2.868	2.603
10	5.650	5.216	4.833	4.494	4.193	3.682	3.269	2.930	2.650
11	5.988	5.453	5.029	4.656	4.327	3.776	3.335	2.978	2.683
12	6.194	5.660	5.197	4.793	4.439	3.851	3.387	3.013	2.708
13	6.424	5.842	5.342	4.910	4.533	3.912	3.427	3.040	2.727
14	6.628	6.002	5.468	5.008	4.611	3.962	3.459	3.061	2.740
15	6.811	6.142	5.575	5.092	4.675	4.001	3.483	3.076	2.750
16	6.974	6.265	5.669	5.162	4.730	4.033	3.503	3.088	2.758
17	7.120	6.373	5.749	5.222	4.775	4.059	3.518	3.097	2.763
18	7.250	6.467	5.818	5.273	4.812	4.080	3.529	3.104	2.767
19	7.366	6.550	5.877	5.316	4.844	4.097	3.539	3.109	2.770
20	7.469	6.623	5.929	5.353	4.870	4.110	3.546	3.113	2.772
25	7.843	6.873	6.097	5.467	4.948	4.147	3.564	3.122	2.776
30	8.055	7.003	6.177	5.517	4.979	4.160	3.569	3.124	2.778

Appendix B: Areas of the Standard Normal Distribution

z	.00	.01	.02	.03	.04	.05	.06	.07	.08	.09
0.0	.0000	.0040	.0080	.0120	.0160	.0199	.0239	.0279	.0319	.0359
0.1	.0398	.0438	.0478	.0517	.0557	.0596	.0636	.0675	.0714	.0753
0.2	.0793	.0832	.0871	.0910	.0948	.0987	.1026	.1064	.1103	.1141
0.3	.1179	.1217	.1255	.1293	.1331	.1368	.1406	.1443	.1480	.1517
0.4	.1554	.1591	.1628	.1664	.1700	.1736	.1772	.1808	.1844	.1879
0.5	.1915	.1950	.1985	.2019	.2054	.2088	.2123	.2157	.2190	.2224
0.6	.2257	.2291	.2324	.2357	.2389	.2422	.2454	.2486	.2517	.2549
0.7	.2580	.2611	.2642	.2673	.2703	.2734	.2764	.2794	.2823	.2852
0.8	.2881	.2910	.2939	.2967	.2995	.3023	.3051	.3078	.3106	.3133
0.9	.3159	.3186	.3212	.3238	.3264	.3289	.3315	.3340	.3365	.3389
1.0	.3413	.3438	.3461	.3485	.3508	.3531	.3554	.3577	.3599	.3621
1.1	.3643	.3665	.3686	.3708	.3729	.3749	.3770	.3790	.3810	.3830
1.2	.3849	.3869	.3888	.3907	.3925	.3944	.3962	.3980	.3997	.4015
1.3	.4032	.4049	.4066	.4082	.4099	.4115	.4131	.4147	.4162	.4177
1.4	.4192	.4207	.4222	.4236	.4251	.4265	.4279	.4292	.4306	.4319
1.5	.4332	.4345	.4357	.4370	.4382	.4394	.4406	.4418	.4429	.4441
1.6	.4452	.4463	.4474	.4484	.4495	.4505	.4515	.4525	.4535	.4545
1.7	.4554	.4564	.4573	.4582	.4591	.4599	.4608	.4616	.4625	.4633
1.8	.4641	.4649	.4656	.4664	.4671	.4678	.4686	.4693	.4699	.4706
1.9	.4713	.4719	.4726	.4732	.4738	.4744	.4750	.4756	.4761	.4767
2.0	.4772	.4778	.4783	.4788	.4793	.4798	.4803	.4808	.4812	.4817
2.1	.4821	.4826	.4830	.4834	.4838	.4842	.4846	.4850	.4854	.4857
2.2	.4861	.4864	.4868	.4871	.4875	.4878	.4881	.4884	.4887	.4890
2.3	.4893	.4896	.4898	.4901	.4904	.4906	.4909	.4911	.4913	.4916
2.4	.4918	.4920	.4922	.4925	.4927	.4929	.4931	.4932	.4934	.4936
2.5	.4938	.4940	.4941	.4943	.4945	.4946	.4948	.4949	.4951	.4952
2.6	.4953	.4955	.4956	.4957	.4959	.4960	.4961	.4962	.4963	.4964
2.7	.4965	.4966	.4967	.4968	.4969	.4970	.4971	.4972	.4973	.4974
2.8	.4974	.4975	.4976	.4977	.4977	.4978	.4979	.4979	.4980	.4981
2.9	.4981	.4982	.4982	.4983	.4984	.4984	.4985	.4985	.4986	.4986
3.0	.4987	.4987	.4987	.4988	.4988	.4989	.4989	.4989	.4990	.4990

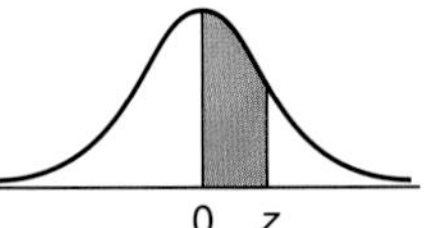

An entry in the table represents the proportion under the shaded curve that is between $z = 0$ and a positive value of z. Areas for negative values of z are obtained by symmetry.

Source: Paul G. Hoel, *Elementary Statistics* (New York: John Wiley & Sons, 1960), p. 240.

Appendix C: Areas of the Cumulative Standard Normal Distribution

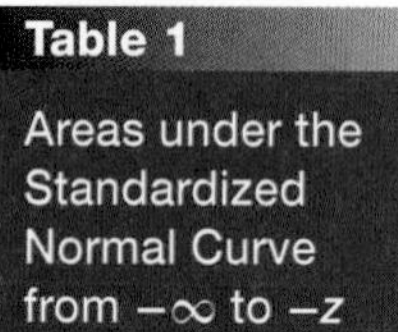

Table 1

Areas under the Standardized Normal Curve from $-\infty$ to $-z$

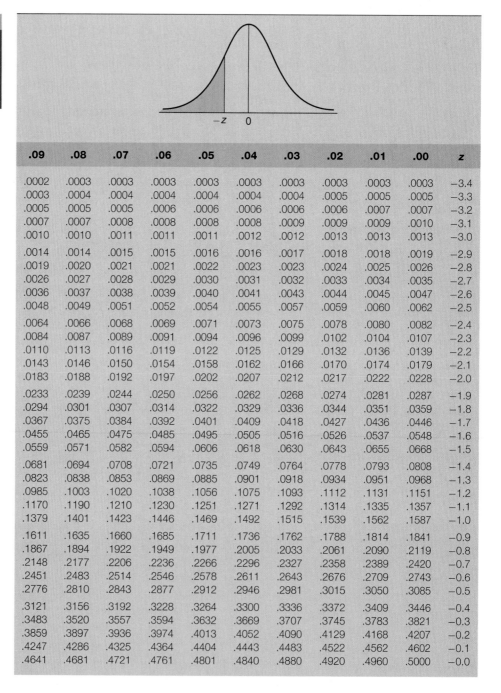

.09	.08	.07	.06	.05	.04	.03	.02	.01	.00	z
.0002	.0003	.0003	.0003	.0003	.0003	.0003	.0003	.0003	.0003	−3.4
.0003	.0004	.0004	.0004	.0004	.0004	.0004	.0005	.0005	.0005	−3.3
.0005	.0005	.0005	.0006	.0006	.0006	.0006	.0006	.0007	.0007	−3.2
.0007	.0007	.0008	.0008	.0008	.0008	.0009	.0009	.0009	.0010	−3.1
.0010	.0010	.0011	.0011	.0011	.0012	.0012	.0013	.0013	.0013	−3.0
.0014	.0014	.0015	.0015	.0016	.0016	.0017	.0018	.0018	.0019	−2.9
.0019	.0020	.0021	.0021	.0022	.0023	.0023	.0024	.0025	.0026	−2.8
.0026	.0027	.0028	.0029	.0030	.0031	.0032	.0033	.0034	.0035	−2.7
.0036	.0037	.0038	.0039	.0040	.0041	.0043	.0044	.0045	.0047	−2.6
.0048	.0049	.0051	.0052	.0054	.0055	.0057	.0059	.0060	.0062	−2.5
.0064	.0066	.0068	.0069	.0071	.0073	.0075	.0078	.0080	.0082	−2.4
.0084	.0087	.0089	.0091	.0094	.0096	.0099	.0102	.0104	.0107	−2.3
.0110	.0113	.0116	.0119	.0122	.0125	.0129	.0132	.0136	.0139	−2.2
.0143	.0146	.0150	.0154	.0158	.0162	.0166	.0170	.0174	.0179	−2.1
.0183	.0188	.0192	.0197	.0202	.0207	.0212	.0217	.0222	.0228	−2.0
.0233	.0239	.0244	.0250	.0256	.0262	.0268	.0274	.0281	.0287	−1.9
.0294	.0301	.0307	.0314	.0322	.0329	.0336	.0344	.0351	.0359	−1.8
.0367	.0375	.0384	.0392	.0401	.0409	.0418	.0427	.0436	.0446	−1.7
.0455	.0465	.0475	.0485	.0495	.0505	.0516	.0526	.0537	.0548	−1.6
.0559	.0571	.0582	.0594	.0606	.0618	.0630	.0643	.0655	.0668	−1.5
.0681	.0694	.0708	.0721	.0735	.0749	.0764	.0778	.0793	.0808	−1.4
.0823	.0838	.0853	.0869	.0885	.0901	.0918	.0934	.0951	.0968	−1.3
.0985	.1003	.1020	.1038	.1056	.1075	.1093	.1112	.1131	.1151	−1.2
.1170	.1190	.1210	.1230	.1251	.1271	.1292	.1314	.1335	.1357	−1.1
.1379	.1401	.1423	.1446	.1469	.1492	.1515	.1539	.1562	.1587	−1.0
.1611	.1635	.1660	.1685	.1711	.1736	.1762	.1788	.1814	.1841	−0.9
.1867	.1894	.1922	.1949	.1977	.2005	.2033	.2061	.2090	.2119	−0.8
.2148	.2177	.2206	.2236	.2266	.2296	.2327	.2358	.2389	.2420	−0.7
.2451	.2483	.2514	.2546	.2578	.2611	.2643	.2676	.2709	.2743	−0.6
.2776	.2810	.2843	.2877	.2912	.2946	.2981	.3015	.3050	.3085	−0.5
.3121	.3156	.3192	.3228	.3264	.3300	.3336	.3372	.3409	.3446	−0.4
.3483	.3520	.3557	.3594	.3632	.3669	.3707	.3745	.3783	.3821	−0.3
.3859	.3897	.3936	.3974	.4013	.4052	.4090	.4129	.4168	.4207	−0.2
.4247	.4286	.4325	.4364	.4404	.4443	.4483	.4522	.4562	.4602	−0.1
.4641	.4681	.4721	.4761	.4801	.4840	.4880	.4920	.4960	.5000	−0.0

Table 2

Areas under the Standardized Normal Curve from $-\infty$ to $+z$

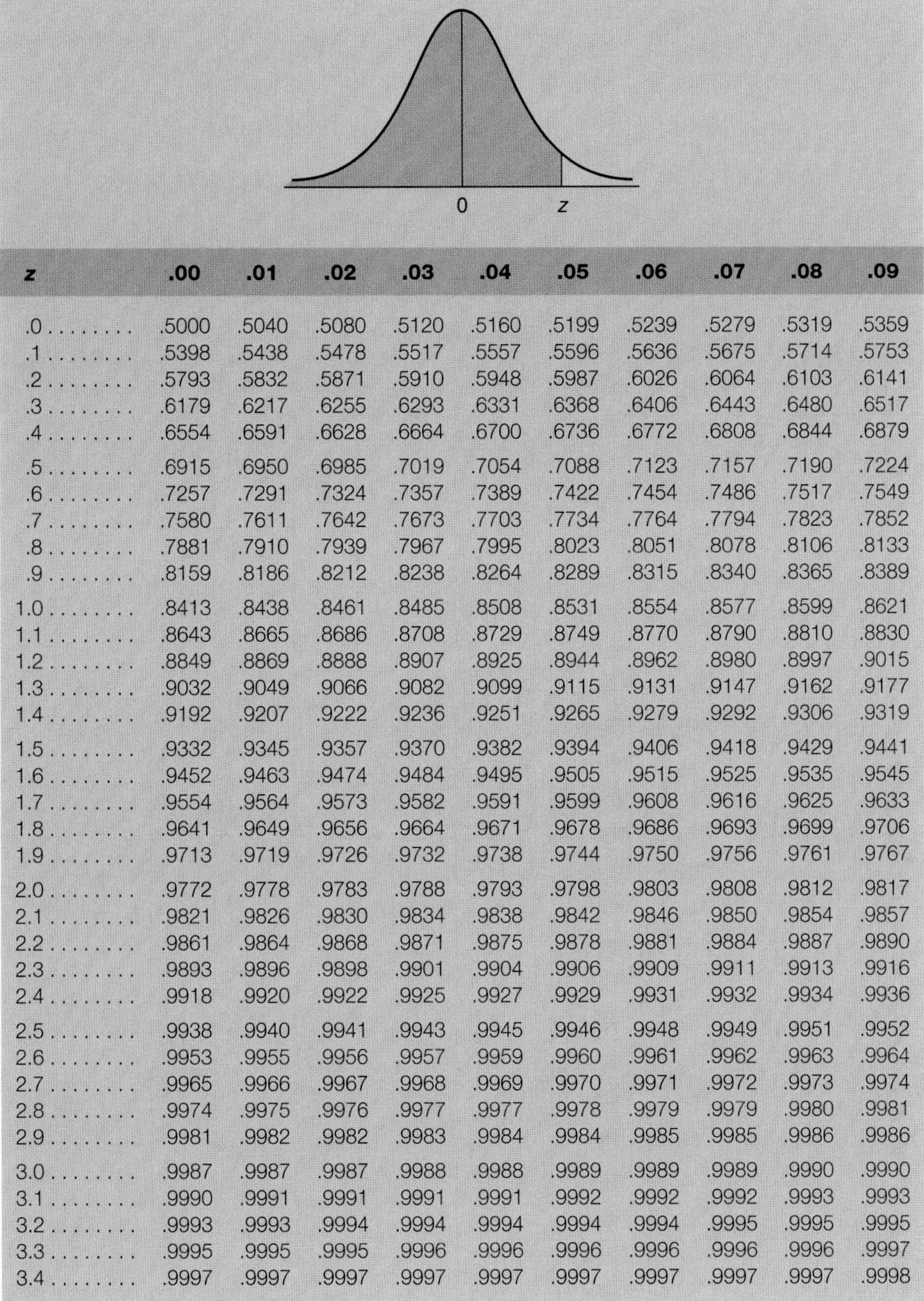

z	.00	.01	.02	.03	.04	.05	.06	.07	.08	.09
.0	.5000	.5040	.5080	.5120	.5160	.5199	.5239	.5279	.5319	.5359
.1	.5398	.5438	.5478	.5517	.5557	.5596	.5636	.5675	.5714	.5753
.2	.5793	.5832	.5871	.5910	.5948	.5987	.6026	.6064	.6103	.6141
.3	.6179	.6217	.6255	.6293	.6331	.6368	.6406	.6443	.6480	.6517
.4	.6554	.6591	.6628	.6664	.6700	.6736	.6772	.6808	.6844	.6879
.5	.6915	.6950	.6985	.7019	.7054	.7088	.7123	.7157	.7190	.7224
.6	.7257	.7291	.7324	.7357	.7389	.7422	.7454	.7486	.7517	.7549
.7	.7580	.7611	.7642	.7673	.7703	.7734	.7764	.7794	.7823	.7852
.8	.7881	.7910	.7939	.7967	.7995	.8023	.8051	.8078	.8106	.8133
.9	.8159	.8186	.8212	.8238	.8264	.8289	.8315	.8340	.8365	.8389
1.0	.8413	.8438	.8461	.8485	.8508	.8531	.8554	.8577	.8599	.8621
1.1	.8643	.8665	.8686	.8708	.8729	.8749	.8770	.8790	.8810	.8830
1.2	.8849	.8869	.8888	.8907	.8925	.8944	.8962	.8980	.8997	.9015
1.3	.9032	.9049	.9066	.9082	.9099	.9115	.9131	.9147	.9162	.9177
1.4	.9192	.9207	.9222	.9236	.9251	.9265	.9279	.9292	.9306	.9319
1.5	.9332	.9345	.9357	.9370	.9382	.9394	.9406	.9418	.9429	.9441
1.6	.9452	.9463	.9474	.9484	.9495	.9505	.9515	.9525	.9535	.9545
1.7	.9554	.9564	.9573	.9582	.9591	.9599	.9608	.9616	.9625	.9633
1.8	.9641	.9649	.9656	.9664	.9671	.9678	.9686	.9693	.9699	.9706
1.9	.9713	.9719	.9726	.9732	.9738	.9744	.9750	.9756	.9761	.9767
2.0	.9772	.9778	.9783	.9788	.9793	.9798	.9803	.9808	.9812	.9817
2.1	.9821	.9826	.9830	.9834	.9838	.9842	.9846	.9850	.9854	.9857
2.2	.9861	.9864	.9868	.9871	.9875	.9878	.9881	.9884	.9887	.9890
2.3	.9893	.9896	.9898	.9901	.9904	.9906	.9909	.9911	.9913	.9916
2.4	.9918	.9920	.9922	.9925	.9927	.9929	.9931	.9932	.9934	.9936
2.5	.9938	.9940	.9941	.9943	.9945	.9946	.9948	.9949	.9951	.9952
2.6	.9953	.9955	.9956	.9957	.9959	.9960	.9961	.9962	.9963	.9964
2.7	.9965	.9966	.9967	.9968	.9969	.9970	.9971	.9972	.9973	.9974
2.8	.9974	.9975	.9976	.9977	.9977	.9978	.9979	.9979	.9980	.9981
2.9	.9981	.9982	.9982	.9983	.9984	.9984	.9985	.9985	.9986	.9986
3.0	.9987	.9987	.9987	.9988	.9988	.9989	.9989	.9989	.9990	.9990
3.1	.9990	.9991	.9991	.9991	.9991	.9992	.9992	.9992	.9993	.9993
3.2	.9993	.9993	.9994	.9994	.9994	.9994	.9994	.9995	.9995	.9995
3.3	.9995	.9995	.9995	.9996	.9996	.9996	.9996	.9996	.9996	.9997
3.4	.9997	.9997	.9997	.9997	.9997	.9997	.9997	.9997	.9997	.9998

Appendix D: Answers to Selected Problems

Supplement 3

1. *b.* A–C–D–E–G.

   c. 26 weeks.

   d. 6 weeks (15 − 9).

8. *a.* Critical path is A–C–D–F–G.

   b.

Day	Cost	Activity
First	$1,000	A
Second	1,200	C
Third	1,500	D (or F)
Fourth	1,500	F (or D)
	$5,200	

Supplement 5

2. *a.*

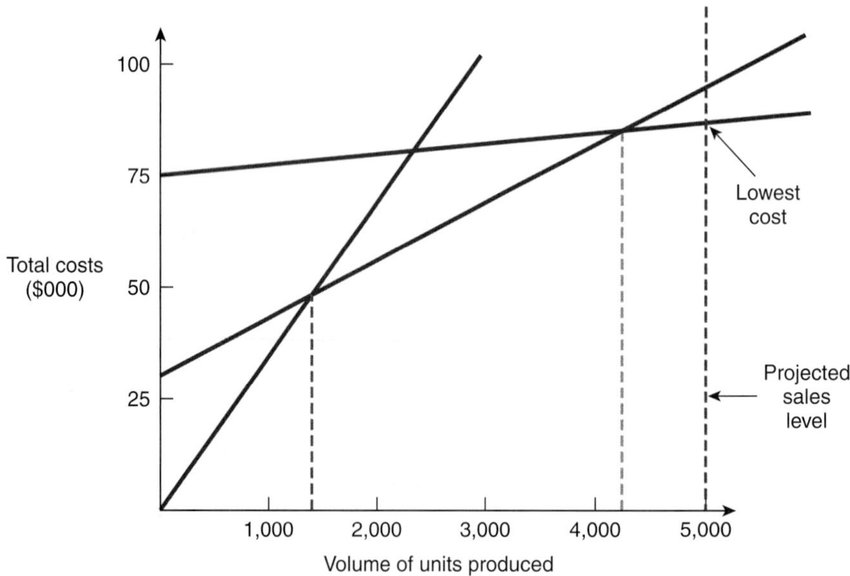

   b. Break-even between Alternatives 1 and 2:

$$32x = 30{,}000 + 12x$$
$$20x = 30{,}000$$
$$x = 1{,}500 \text{ units}$$

   Break-even between Alternatives 2 and 3:

$$30{,}000 + 12x = 75{,}000 + 2x$$
$$10x = 45{,}000$$
$$x = 4{,}500 \text{ units}$$

   c. Based on lowest total costs, the company should choose Alternative 3, which is to invest the $75,000 in fixed costs and use unskilled labor.

7. The straight-line depreciation method yields a 15.9 percent return. The sum-of-the-years' digits yields a 17.1 percent return. Thus, neither method of depreciation will provide the minimum 20 percent return.

Supplement 6

1. *a.* $C_{pk} = .889$.

   b. $C_{pk} = 1.11$.

   The process is capable but needs to adjust mean downward to achieve 100 percent perfect quality.

2. *a.* $p = .067$.
   UCL = .194.
   LCL = 0.

   b. Stop the process. There is wide variation and two are out of limits.

Chapter 8

1. Output/day: 24B + 24D.
   Process times: 12 min./B and 8 min./D.
   BB/DDD BB BB/DDD repetitively.

2. *a.* 27 seconds.

   b. 7 stations.

   c. 78.3 percent.

   d. Reduce cycle time to 25 seconds and work 8½ minutes overtime.

4. $44,500.

Chapter 9

2. *a.* 15.

   b. 14.3.

   c. 13.4.

   d. $Y = a + bX = 10.8 + .77X$.

   e. $Y = 10.8 + .77(7) = 16.2$.

9. MAD = 58.3
   TS = −6
   Model is poor at giving a good forecast.

Supplement 10

1. *a.* 1.65 minutes.

   b. 1.90 (minutes rounded).

   c. $94.86.

5. *a.* $NT = .9286$ minute/part.

   b. $ST = 1.0679$ minute/part.

   c. Daily output = 449.50.
   Day's wages = $44.49.

Supplement 11

1. $\bar{t}_s = 4.125$ minutes.
   $\bar{n}_j = 4.05$ cars.
   $\bar{n}_s = 4.95$ cars.

2. *4 spaces:* Stand busy 67.2 percent
   5 spaces: Stand busy 69.6 percent
   6 spaces: Stand busy 71.15 percent
   7 spaces: Stand busy 72.22 percent
   8 spaces: Net loss = $160;
   7 spaces should be leased.

Chapter 12

1.

Car	Priority
C	First
A	Tie for second
B	Tie for second

6. Johnson's method: E, A, B, D, C.

Chapter 13

1.

Transportation Costs	Carrying Costs
TC = $450,000.00	$80,547.95
= $530,547.95	
Cost per tire: $5.305479	
Total cost: $40.30548	

Continue buying from current supplier at $40.00 per tire delivered.

Chapter 15

1. Total cost = $413,600.

4. Ending inventory = safety stock.
   Inventory cost includes forecast and safety stock.
   Shortage cost is only based on the forecast.
   Total cost = $413,750.

Chapter 16

1. TC = $24,254.50.
   Q at 200 is the optimum order size.

4. TC = $56,370.
   1,000 at a time.

5. *a.* A (4, 13, 18), B (2, 5, 8, 10, 11, 14, 16), C (remainder).

   b. Classify as A.

Chapter 17

2.

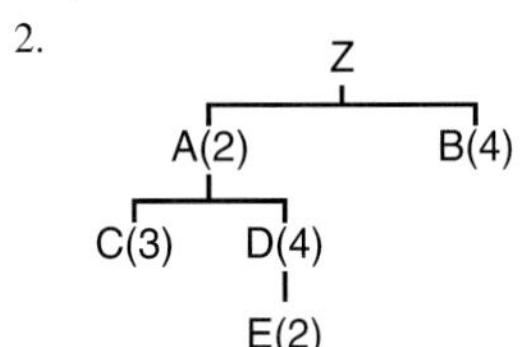

9. *c.* .A
   .B(2)
   .E(4)
   .F(3)
   .C(3)
   .D(3)
   .H(2)
   .E(5)
   .G(2)
   .D(1)

   d.

Level 0	100 units of A
Level 1	200 units of B
	300 units of C
Level 2	600 units of F
	600 units of H
	1000 units of D
Level 3	3800 units of E
	1200 units of G

Photo Credits

Chapter 1

Courtesy of Avid; Courtesy of Amazon.com; © Sergio Dorantes/CORBIS; Ford-Werke AG, Koeln; From the collection of Henry Ford Museum and Greenfield Collection

Chapter 2

Courtesy Dell Corporation; Corbis Stock Market/Ed Bock; Louis Psihoyos, Matrix International, Inc.

Chapter 3

Courtesy of Gillette; Courtesy Toyota Motor Sales U.S.A., Inc.; Courtesy AMPREX Corporation; David Young Wolf/Photo Edit; Courtesy Miller Brewing Company; Courtesy Kawasaki Motors Manufacturing Corporation, U.S.A.

Supplement 3

Courtesy of Hewlett-Packard Company

Chapter 4

Courtesy of Avis; Courtesy of Magnus and Company; Courtesy of LandsEnd.com; Courtesy of BMWUsa.com; Courtesy EMC Corporation

Chapter 5

Richard Lord/The Image Words; J. Greenberg/The Image Works; Courtesy of John Deere

Chapter 6

Courtesy of Sunny Fresh Food and Monticello Times; Dwayne Newton/Photo Edit; Courtesy of the National Institute of Standards and Technology, Office of Quality Programs, Gaithersburg, Maryland 20899. Photograph by Steuben

Supplement 6

John Maier, Jr./The Image Works; © Richard Pasley

Chapter 7

Courtesy Toys R Us, Inc.; Courtesy of Map Info Corporation; Courtesy of Dell Corporation

Chapter 8

Courtesy Cimtechnologies Corporation; Kay Chernush/The Image Bank/Getty Images

Chapter 9

Photo provided courtesy of Nabisco; Federal Express; © Dwayne Newton/Photo Edit

Chapter 10

AP/Wide World Photo/Southwest Airlines; Courtesy of NIST; Courtesy of Ritz-Carlton Hotel Company; MANUFACTURING ENGINEERING MAGAZINE, Society of Manufacturing Engineers. Photo courtesy of Mid-West Conveyer Co., Kansas City, Kansas; © Chris Corsmeier

Supplement 10

© 2002 Bob Sacha. All Rights Reserved

Chapter 11

Courtesy of Hertz; Courtesy of Travelocity.com; Jeff Goldberg/PhotoEdit; Steve Rubin/The Image Works

Chapter 12

© Richard Pasley; © Spencer Grant/Photo Edit

Chapter 13

Courtesy of Solectron Corporation, Bob Day Photographer; © 2002 Jessica Wecker; F. Hoffman/The Image Works; Courtesy of Campbell's Soup Company; Courtesy of Campbell's Soup Company; Courtesy of Campbell's Soup Company; Michael Abramson

Chapter 14

Greg Davis/Image Works; Saturn Communications, Spring Hill Manufacturing Complex, 2001; Courtesy Bernard Welding Equipment Company; Courtesy Bernard Welding Equipment Company

Chapter 15

Courtesy of Polaroid; Courtesy Kawasaki Motors Manufacturing Corporation, U.S.A.; Courtesy Kawasaki Motors Manufacturing Corporation, U.S.A.

Chapter 16

© 1995 GE Information Services, Inc.

Chapter 17

Courtesy Merck Forest Canada; Courtesy of Allen-Bradley, a Rockwell Interactive Company

Name Index

I

J

K

L

M

N

O

P

Q

R

S

T

U

V

W

X

Y

Z

Subject Index

A

B

D

G

H

I

J

K

N

O

Q

R

S

T

U

V

W

X

Y

Z